Sex, Gender, and Sexuality

Sex, Gender, and Sexuality
The New Basics

An Anthology

THIRD EDITION

Abby L. Ferber
University of Colorado Colorado Springs

Kimberly Holcomb
University of Colorado Colorado Springs

Tre Wentling
Syracuse University

New York   Oxford
OXFORD UNIVERSITY PRESS

Oxford University Press is a department of the University of Oxford.
It furthers the University's objective of excellence in research, scholarship,
and education by publishing worldwide. Oxford is a registered trade mark
of Oxford University Press in the UK and certain other countries.

Published in the United States of America by Oxford University Press
198 Madison Avenue, New York, NY 10016, United States of America.

© 2017, 2013, 2009 by Oxford University Press

Library of Congress Cataloging-in-Publication Data

CIP data is on file at the Library of Congress
ISBN number: 978-0-19-027864-9

9 8 7 6 5 4 3

Printed by Webcom Inc., Canada

Dedication

"There are stars whose radiance is visible on earth though they
have long been extinct.
There are people whose brilliance continues to light the world
even though they are no longer among the living.
These lights are particularly bright when the night is dark.
They light the way for humankind."
—Hannah Senesh

Rest in Power:
Papi Edwards, 20 years old
Lamia Beard, 30 years old
Ty Underwood, 24 years old
Yazmin Vash Payne, 33 years old
Taja Gabrielle DeJesus, 36 years old
BriGolec, 22 years old
Keyshia Blige, 33 years old
London Chanel, 21 years old
Mercedes Williamson, 17 years old
Jasmine Collins, 32 years old
Ashton O'Hara, 25 years old
India Clarke, 25 years old
K.L. Haggard, 66 years old
Shade Schuler, 22 years old
Amber Monroe, 20 years old
Kandis Capri, 35 years old
Elisha Walker, 20 years old
Tamara Dominguez, 36 years old
Kiesha Jenkins, 22 years old
Zella Ziona, 21 years old

and too many more trans* women of color whose names we don't know.
#SayHerName

Contents

* An asterisk indicates new to the third edition.

Acknowledgments

We were both thrilled and absolutely humbled when our amazing editor at Oxford University Press, Sherith Pankratz, asked us to compile a third edition of *Sex, Gender, and Sexuality*. This many years into the journey of this text, it is incredible to know students and scholars are still finding it useful and pertinent to the ever-growing fields of gender and sexuality and intersectional theory. To that end, we committed right away with this edition to maintaining the theoretical "core" of the book with important canonical texts and sought once again to add cutting-edge narratives and other pieces commensurate with new developments in the field. We also once again added more specific sections without necessarily increasing the length of the text to augment the content of prior editions and to make the text more classroom-friendly. As always, we tried to offer a compilation of quality intersectional works with a queer and forward-thinking bent. We believe we have compiled the best and most utilitarian edition of *Sex, Gender, and Sexuality* yet. We hope you agree.

We wish to thank Sherith Pankratz, as well as Meredith Keffer, our Oxford editors who tirelessly and swiftly answered all manner of questions for this edition. Your unending commitment to this text is truly humbling. We were also blessed with a group of thorough and generous reviewers for the second edition, without whom the third edition would not be what it is. We sincerely thank:

Traci B. Abbott, Bentley University
Elizabeth Boskey, Boston University
Mary C. Burke, University of Vermont
Kelly Dagan, Illinois College
Kathleen J. Fitzgerald, Loyola University of New Orleans

Julianne Guillard, University of Richmond
Laurie Shrage, Florida International University
Three anonymous reviewers

Finally, our unending gratitude goes to the faculty, students, and activists who continue to grapple with and advance the fields of gender and sexuality and intersectional theory and who challenge us to do the same. We hope this text continues to be a tool in the good fight.

New to the Third Edition

- Reorganization of sections
  - New discussion questions included with new chapters
  - Removed 19 chapters and added 26 new ones
  - Chapters highlighting positive social change integrated into each section
  - Personal narratives integrated throughout the book, rather than segregated in one section
  - Increased number of chapters addressing heterosexuality, religion, class, disability, and aging
  - Added new chapters about bisexuality, asexuality, and polyamory
  - Added chapters examining technology and social media, as well as the socialization of youth
  - A new final section looks toward the future and encourages students to imagine new possibilities
  - Updated and expanded Key Terms

Introduction

Before you read any further, we are going to engage in a very brief activity: take a moment to think about the key concepts examined by this text: sex, gender, and sexuality. How would you define each of these terms? Take out a piece of paper and jot down your own definitions for each term before we continue.

If you are anything like our students, this exercise may have been more difficult than you first imagined. Though we are bombarded with images regarding sex, gender, and sexuality every day and tend to use these terms all the time, many of us operate with different understandings of just what, exactly, they refer to. We assume these concepts are a matter of common sense, so much so that we rarely stop to think about what they really mean. Yet as these readings will clearly demonstrate, the meanings of these terms are constantly shifting and far from clear-cut.

Each semester we ask our students to complete this very exercise, and each semester we receive a wide array of definitions. For *sex*, students often reference biology, the body, genitals, hormones, chromosomes, and so on. *Gender* often evokes a similar roster, with a few more references to "culture" and/or "socialization," "man" and "woman," and, more recently, "transgender" and "cisgender" (if any of these terms are new to you, please check the Key Terms). Definitions of *sexuality* often refer to desire, sexual acts with persons of the same or opposite sex, masculinity/femininity, and/or identity markers like "gay," "lesbian," "bisexual," "heterosexual," and so on.

We can draw a number of conclusions from this exercise. First, while we use these terms all the time, we are clearly not in unison when it comes to what they actually mean. There is much confusion and overlap in our understanding of these concepts, such that we often use them interchangeably. So don't be discouraged if these terms confuse you. Keep in mind that there has been little agreement on their meanings even among researchers and scholars who study these subjects, and the definitions change as swiftly as new discoveries are made and new theories advanced. Indeed, we hope that the chapters in this volume will lead you to question the terms even further. The answer may not lie in finding clear-cut definitions but in thinking about why we construct these classifications in the first place, how they operate, what social purposes they serve, and why they have become so important to us. In fact, instead of providing simple answers, our goal is to complicate readers' understandings of these terms even further.

To that end, another important fact to remember as you move through the readings is that theories involving sex, gender, and sexuality vary not only from individual to individual but trans-historically and cross-culturally as well, making uniformity impossible. Today many of our nonacademic contemporary discussions involve words like *opposite sex* and often imply astronomical differences between males and females. Books like John Gray's *Men Are from Mars, Women Are From Venus* have been best-sellers, and news articles, blogs, and magazines are always eager to publish headlines promising to reveal "real" sex differences. However, this was certainly not always the case. The ancient Greek philosopher Aristotle theorized that men and women were essentially the same and that females actually *were* males who failed to fully form in the womb because of a lack of properly heated sperm at the time of conception. In fact, many theories of biological sameness flourished in antiquity and battled for scientific proof. One such theory argued that the vagina was a sort of inside-out penis, while another suggested that the uterus was a penis that had not yet dropped outside the body. Ironically, both theories of difference and sameness viewed women as inferior.

Sexuality in ancient Greece was also conceptualized in vastly dissimilar terms than we see today. Sexual relationships between men and women, men and men, and women and women were all common, and one's sexual or affectional desire was not a marker for social classification, stigma, or identity; however, there were strict norms governing who played what role in sexual acts. Still, ancient knowledge and attitudes toward sex and sexuality were quite different from our contemporary adherence to the heterosexual–homosexual binary, wherein the former is prized and naturalized and the latter is often seen as abnormal, ungodly, and even at times pathological. This dichotomy is so pervasive today in popular culture and discourse regarding sex and sexuality that it is seen as a timeless and innate, biological fate. Yet, in fact, the words *homosexual* and *heterosexual* were coined scarcely more than 100 years ago and were first used discursively to posit a procreative sex imperative. That is, heterosexuality was "natural" because of its procreative potential and homosexuality—its requisite opposite—was "unnatural" for its lack of the same. Sigmund Freud further reinforced this idea when he claimed that exclusive heterosexuality was the ultimate sign of sexual maturation and homosexuality a sign of neurosis or stunted development.

Fast-forward to contemporary times, and you can see quite easily how and why sexual and gender identities have become such a central form of hierarchization in our society. Indeed, the array of theories and conceptualizations involving sex and sexuality (and their social implications) from antiquity to the present make clear the ways in which our understandings of these concepts are socially constructed and change over time. Thus it is important to study the history of theories involving sex and sexuality, because doing so allows us to expose the illusion that these categories are ageless and unchanging and rooted in biology, rather than in relations of power. Ignoring this history keeps us from looking critically at the social effects of our sex, gender, and sexual categorizations and the harm, violence, and emotional pain they facilitate.

Outdated theories like essentialism and biological determinism are swiftly being replaced by more applicable social constructionist models for understanding sex, gender, and sexuality. Whereas essentialists posit a basic model that assumes one's gender will automatically reflect one's anatomical sex and that heterosexuality will naturally result, social constructionists provide theoretical insights that help us to understand the far more complex reality of our lived experiences. According to these theories, our ideas of gender, sexuality, and even anatomical sex are not static and immutable but instead are socially constructed. We learn, internalize, and practice gender prescriptions to the point that they *seem* natural or inborn, but in fact they are not. Many of the chapters in this volume advance a range of social constructionist perspectives, look at the wide variety of lived, embodied experience, and examine some of the historical and contemporary debates in conceptualizing sex, gender, and sexuality.

Many of our common-sense assumptions about race, gender, and sexuality are embedded in what we call an *"essentialist"* approach. *Essentialism* assumes that social identities such as gender, sex, race, ability, and so on are inherent and unchanging. They are frequently seen as intrinsic to bodies themselves and biologically determined. Cultural essentialisms, on the other hand, posit differences and traits as inherently rooted in a specific culture and as impervious to change. These differences are believed to be innate and unchanging and are seen as more significant than environmental factors in explaining differences among people. Essentialism, however, is not supported by the research. For example, while our common-sense assumptions may tell us that race is rooted in biology, almost all biologists today reject such notions.

Instead, most contemporary theories of social differences fall under the broad umbrella of *"social constructionism."* Social constructionist approaches have been embraced in a wide array of disciplines, including philosophy, sociology, literature, psychology, and anthropology. Social constructionist approaches emphasize the role of human interaction and culture in shaping classifications of difference and producing inequality.

Unfortunately, essentialist approaches are still sedimented in our culture. After all, identities like race and sex seem purely biological and visible, don't they? We can clearly see that there are differences among us in terms of skin color, and isn't the first thing the doctor pronounces upon the birth of a baby either "It's a boy!" or "It's a girl!"? Movies, television, and music continue to reinforce essentialist assumptions, reaffirming their status as "common sense" and making it difficult for people to grasp the social constructionist approach at first. While there is a wide range of social constructionist approaches, and ongoing debates among scholars that might be grouped together as social constructionists, they provide a shared critique of essentialism that apply to our understanding of sex, gender, and sexuality, especially as we explore them in this text:

1. There is no strictly biological basis for these categories of identity.
2. Each of these categories varies tremendously across cultures and globally.
3. Each of these categories varies historically.
4. The meaning of these categories is shaped by institutions, local contexts, and culture.
5. Specific sex, gender, and sexual identities also vary and are currently proliferating shifting, and fluid.

We often tend to reduce problems to a nature versus nurture perspective; however, the world is not that clear-cut. The social constructionist perspective is often assumed to be a purely "nurture" account, as opposed to an essentialist "nature" perspective. However, few constructionist perspectives ignore biology and nature completely. Instead, nature and culture are seen as interconnected and inseparable. After all, we have no access to the biological realm except through the realm of culture and society. Additionally, scholars of human development have provided significant evidence that human bodies and minds develop in constant interaction with their social contexts.

Because the basic classifications and definitions of sex, gender, and sexuality are constructed by our culture, they change frequently and cannot be pinned down. Historically, and still today, people use the terms in different ways.

In the early stages of second-wave feminism, *sex* was seen in essentialist terms and gender assumed to loosely follow. *Gender* was embraced to refer to behaviors, roles, and personality traits, conceptualized as the product of socialization processes, which were juxtaposed with the notion of a biologically sexed body. Linda Nicholson suggests that from this perspective, sexed bodies are analogous to a coat rack, upon which different cultures throw different articles of clothing (the various "pieces" of gender). While gender is defined as a cross-cultural variable according to this view, the biological coat rack is taken as an unchanging, universal, and given foundation. In other words, this perspective moved one step away from essentialism by positing a socially constructed notion of gender that was assumed to follow from one's essential sex but was more flexible and open to change.

This perspective was soon challenged. Even though *gender* was defined as a social construct, it ended up reifying both gender and sexuality in essentialist terms, because gender was assumed to follow from, and correspond to, one's given sex. For example, a biological male was assumed to adopt the social gender roles constructed for men and assumed to desire women. Thus sexuality and gender were still seen as following directly from biological sex categories.

Over the past few decades, scholars and activists have argued that not only gender, but sex itself, is socially constructed. Bodies themselves are embedded in webs of culture and open to social interpretation. This perspective does not ignore the body; instead, the body itself becomes a social variable, which can no longer ground claims about gender. For example, in his study *Making Sex: Body and Gender from the Greeks to Freud*, Thomas Laqueur has demonstrated that Western conceptions of human sexual anatomy and sexual difference have changed drastically throughout history. There is no direct access to the body, then, outside of cultural contexts.

Other critiques have reconceptualized gender as performative and argued that it is through the performance of gender that sex itself is made real (Butler 1990, Zimmerman and West 1987). These theorists reverse the typical trajectory and argue that gender precedes sex. Yet other critiques have brought race, class, and other forms of inequality into the picture. Essentialist notions of sex, gender, and sexuality have all assumed that there is some common essence among those in each category that in reality reflects only the experiences of the most privileged. Women of color have charged that this basis for commonality assumes a white, heterosexual, upper-middle-class ideal. This perspective, in fact, ignores within-group differences. For example, social movements based on gender or race throughout US history have often been divisive in demanding that their constituents prioritize only one aspect of their identity. The suffrage movement was divided by race, as women of color were sacrificed by some segments in order to appeal to whites in the South and advance suffrage for white women. Women of color were asked to leave issues of race aside and focus only on the "woman question." The civil rights and second-wave women's movements repeated this pattern, again expecting women of color to focus only on race, or gender, and largely excluded lesbian, gay, bisexual, transgender, and intersex issues and concerns. Intersectional theories have challenged this impossible expectation, highlighting the ways in which race, gender, sexuality, and other categories of identity are inextricably connected. Legal scholar Kimberle Crenshaw is credited with coining the term *"intersectionality,"* and her analyses demonstrate the need for an intersectional perspective to address major social problems. She and the African American Policy Forum argue that

> "Intersectionality is a concept that enables us to recognize the fact that perceived group membership can make people vulnerable to various forms of bias, yet because we are simultaneously members of many groups, our complex identities can shape the specific way we each experience that bias." For example, men and women can often experience racism differently, just as women of different races can experience sexism differently, and so on. (African American Policy Forum, 2013)

These discussions are not merely academic. Notions of sex, gender, and sexuality remain at the fore of political, religious, and social debate in the United States. Just open a newspaper or flip on the television and it will become clear that we are presently in the throes of a major shift. The chapters throughout this volume document the tremendous change that has been accomplished, as well as the challenges we still face.

Knowledge is essential to creating change. Our goal in this book is to introduce readers to the wide range of exciting contemporary research on sex, gender, and sexuality, with particular emphasis on their intersections. Examining these works provides a new way of thinking about sex, gender, and sexuality and considers the ways in which they are inextricably linked and mutually constitutive. Conceptualizing and studying these terms together allows us to ask ourselves important questions: Would we need categories of gender today if we did not feel compelled to define ourselves as heterosexual or homosexual? Beyond this, an intersectional approach allows us to consider other social factors, such as race/ethnicity, class, age, and ability, as they relate to and shape people's experiences of sex, gender, and sexuality. In our daily lives, our experiences and opportunities are shaped by the combination of all these systems of inequality. We are never simply our gender or simply our race. It is time that our theories better grasp the complexity of our individual daily experiences. As with the definitions themselves, there is no universal with regard to these concepts. They are as multifarious as the people who experience them.

Today is an exciting moment to be studying sex, gender, and sexuality. It is our hope that you will find the following readings engaging, challenging, and exciting and that they will help you to glean a greater understanding of contemporary debates and issues surrounding sex, gender, and sexuality, as well as provide you with the tools and insights to reexamine your own life experience and identity. As you read, consider the ways in which the chapters relate to and complement one another and, most important, how the concepts of sex, gender, and sexuality are interrelated. Some of these readings may be challenging or make you feel uncomfortable, but as we always tell our students, that is a sure sign that you are learning and pushing the boundaries of what you already knew and took for granted.

REFERENCES

African American Policy Forum. (2013). Accessed July 27, 2016 at: http://www
.aapf.org/2013/2013/01/intersectionality
Butler, Judith. (1990). Gender Trouble: Feminism and the Subversion of Identity. NY:
Routledge.
West, C., & Zimmerman, D. H. (1987). Doing gender. *Gender & Society, 1*(2),
125–151.

Key Terms

The following definitions provide merely a starting point for readers to interrogate as language is, and especially identity categories are, embedded in state and political histories, medical and scientific discourse, and social movements. Identity terms are often advanced as tools of liberation and for community building, but they always exclude and constrict. Many of these terms and definitions will and should change over time as social actors construct new identities, demand recognition, improve theories, and provide new knowledge(s).

Ableism A system of oppression that privileges (temporarily) able-bodied people over disabled people through everyday practices, attitudes, assumptions, behaviors, and institutional rules; encompasses prejudice, stereotyping, and discrimination.

Ageism A system of oppression that privileges some people over others based on age through everyday practices, attitudes, assumptions, behaviors, and institutional rules; encompasses prejudice, stereotyping, and discrimination.

Androgen Insensitivity Syndrome (AIS) A medical condition in which bodies do not respond to androgen, which is described as a "male" hormone. For more information regarding AIS, visit Intersex Society of North America (www .isna.org).

Androgynous (1) A self-ascribed state of embodiment among individuals rejecting the binary structure of woman and man; similar to gender queer and neutrois. (2) Also used as an adjective to describe others.

Androphilia A controversial and hotly debated term that describes sexual desire and attraction to masculinity or men without relation to the object's sex category. It is controversial because of its history in sexologist literature and diagnoses, as well as its relation to "autogynephilia."

Anti-Semitism A system of oppression that privileges non-Jewish persons through everyday practices, attitudes, assumptions, behaviors, and institutional rules; it encompasses prejudice, stereotyping, and discrimination.

Asexual A self-ascribed state of being among individuals not interested in sexual expression or practice.

BDSM An abbreviation for bondage–discipline (or domination)–sadomasochism, which broadly encompasses consensual role play and performance acts of domination and submission related to sexual desire, fantasy, and gratification.

Bisexual A self-ascribed state of embodiment among people who desire emotional, physical, and/or sexual relations with persons of both sexes and genders.

Bullying Any type of repeated verbal harassment, physical assault, intimidation, or coercion that targets a person based on perceived and/or real social statuses.

Chromosomes DNA that socially is defined to categorically represent females as XX, males as XY, and intersex as a myriad of possibilities.

Cisgender Latin prefix *cis* means "same"; refers to people who embody the gender associated with their birth-assigned sex.

Classism A system of oppression that privileges some people over others based on socioeconomic status through everyday practices, attitudes, assumptions, behaviors, and institutional rules; it encompasses prejudice, stereotyping, and discrimination.

Coming Out (1) A continual and selective narrative speech act among individuals who choose to publicly affirm their state of embodiment, which may also reject assumed heterosexual and/or gender identities. (2) Also used by individuals who choose to publicly reject assumptions about their person (i.e., race membership, religious membership, etc.). (3) Allies may also come out to publicly announce their commitments.

Congenital Adrenal Hyperplasia (CAH) A medical condition in which the adrenal glands release cortisol into the bloodstream, which results in higher levels of hormones and can lead to a "masculinization" of developing XX fetus' genitalia. For more information regarding the most common form of intersex conditions, visit Intersex Society of North America (www.isna.org).

Cross-Dresser (CD) A self-ascribed state of embodiment among individuals who wear clothing and accessories associated with a different gender and may be inspired for both sexual and nonsexual reasons. Although antiquated and stigmatized, cross-dresser is sometimes synonymous with "transvestite."

Deep Stealth Mostly associated with transgender or transsexual individuals who have chosen to keep their sexed and gendered history private from everyone, including an intimate partner.

Diagnostic and Statistical Manual of Mental Disorders (DSM) A text developed and maintained by the American Psychiatric Association that establishes the classification standards of mental disorders and psychiatric illnesses.

Discourse Typically refers to a formal or academic speech or written work on a particular topic (i.e., "Feminist discourse relies heavily upon sociological and intersectional theories").

Discrimination The unequal allocation of valued goods and resources based on one's social position and group membership, which includes limiting the access of some groups to full benefits, privileges, and rights.

Disorders of Sex Development (DSD) An emergent medical term that describes congenital conditions in which chromosomal, gonadal, or anatomic sex development is "atypical" from that of "standard" female and male. Some medical clinicians prefer DSD rather than "intersex" because of their shared DSD definition.

Domestic Violence (Intimate Partner Violence) Various forms of violence within partner and familial relationships, ranging from emotional (intimidation, isolation, threats) to physical, financial, and sexual abuse.

Drag Artists People who perform entertaining acts by wearing clothing and accessories associated with the different sex and gender of the performer.

Drag King A self-ascribed state of embodiment among female-bodied people who dress and perform as men, at times in a subversive way to expose some expressions of masculinity.

Drag Queen A self-ascribed state of embodiment among males who dress and perform as women.

Dyke (1) A self-ascribed identity term among female-bodied people who desire emotional, physical, and/or sexual relations with women. (2) May also be used as an epithet.

Electrolysis (Electro) A process that uses an electric current to remove facial and other body hair, eliminating the need to shave.

Endocrinologist (Endo) A medical doctor specializing in the endocrine system (i.e., hormones).

Essentialism A theoretical perspective that naturalizes differences between social groups (such as gender differences, racial differences, etc.), often positing their origins in biology (i.e., genes, chromosomes, DNA, etc.).

Estrogen Hormone most often associated with females; however, estrogen is present in all bodies.

Ethnicity A socially constructed category based on characteristics such as national origin or heritage, geography, language, customs, or cultural practices (i.e., Italian, Puerto Rican, Cuban, Kurdish, Serbian, etc.).

Ethnocentrism The practice of judging another culture using the standards of one's own culture.

Eugenics A set of beliefs or practices that aims to improve the human race by methodically "weeding out" particular traits seen as undesirable, usually through systematic genocide and/or sterilization. The American eugenics movement was founded by biological determinist Francis Galton in the late nineteenth century, from whom many Nazi leaders eventually took their ideas and practices. Though some eugenic practices remain in effect the world over (selective female fetal abortion, sterilization of oppressed communities, etc.), the theory is generally considered obsolete given the atrocities committed in its name.

Female to Male (FtM/F2M) (1) A self-ascribed state of embodiment among individuals labeled female at birth who identify as men and/or present in a masculine expression. (2) Also used as an adjective to describe a transition process.

Feminism A wide range of theoretical and political perspectives that value women and their experiences. Feminism is committed to activism, social change, and equality.

Gay (1) A self-ascribed state of embodiment among men who desire emotional, physical, and/or sexual relations with men. (2) Also used to refer to all gay men and lesbians. (3) Commonly used to describe something as stupid or dumb.

Gender Socially constructed categories that divide bodies into a binary system of women and men. Recently, new gender identities such as transgender, androgynous, and genderqueer categories have been embraced and advanced.

Gender-Bender A person who chooses to cross or violate the gender roles and/or expressions that are associated with his or her socially assigned sex category.

Gendercide The systematic extermination of a particular gender. Most often refers to girls and women (usually in cultures with laws or customs that see girls/women as a liability; selective-sex abortion of female fetuses, etc.); however, it may also refer to boys/men and gender-nonconforming people.

Gender Dysphoria The controversial *DSM* term used to describe some individuals seeking transition-related medical technologies.

Gender Identity Disorder (GID) A controversial *DSM* diagnosis that practitioners use to describe individuals who express and identify with a gender embodiment not associated with their birth-assigned sex.

Gender Ideology A set of ever-changing culturally and historically specific meanings that shape the social expectations for bodies, behaviors, emotions, and family and work roles, based on gender classifications.

Gender Image/Display The presentation of oneself through social interaction using culturally appropriate gender symbols and markers.

Genderqueer A self-ascribed state of embodiment among individuals who reject the binary gender structure of woman and man; similar to androgynous and neutrois.

Gender Reassignment Surgery (GRS) Various types of surgical procedures that some transgender individuals undergo to medically and physically align their bodies with their gender identity.

Hate Crime Crimes that are motivated by bias and hate against an individual based on perceived or actual social status membership (i.e., race, ethnicity, gender, sexuality, ability, religion, etc.).

Hegemonic Dominant beliefs or ideals that are taken for granted and thus, "naturalized" in a culture at any given time.

Hermaphrodite An antiquated and stigmatizing scientific term that was used to describe individuals with varying and/or multiple sex characteristics (i.e., chromosomes, genitalia, reproductive organs, hormones, etc.) that challenge sex determinations of "female" or "male." An emergent medical literature describes sex development processes that are different from "standard" female or male as Disorders of Sex Development (DSD).

Heteronormativity A system that institutionalizes heterosexuality as the standard for legitimate and expected social and sexual relations (Ingraham).

Heterosexism A system of oppression that privileges heterosexual people through everyday practices, attitudes, behaviors, and institutional rules through the promotion of heterosexuality as natural and normal.

Heterosexual (1) A self-ascribed state of embodiment among individuals who desire emotional, physical, and/or sexual relations with people of their opposite sex and gender. (2) Also used as an adjective to describe others.

Homophobia The fear, hatred, or disapproval of and discrimination against lesbian, gay, and bisexual people.

Homosexual (1) A self-ascribed state of embodiment among individuals who desire emotional, physical, and/or sexual relations with people of the same sex and/or gender. Some consider this an antiquated term linked to a medicalized history of stigma and shame.

Hormone Replacement Therapy (HRT) A medical process sometimes prescribed for or requested by women in menopause and transgender persons.

Homonormativity The incorporation or assimilation of heterosexual culture/ideals into homosexual culture. Homonormative theories question a queer politics that does not problematize heterosexual and binary gender ideals and also address racial, class, and other relative privileges within queer communities.

Ideology A belief system that shapes interpretations, makes sense of the world, and guides actions and behaviors. Ideologies often provide justification for inequality and oppression.

Intersectionality or Intersectional Theory The study of overlapping and/or intersecting identities or oppressive institutions (sexism, heterosexism, racism, ableism, etc.). This approach acknowledges that privilege and oppression are interconnected and cannot be examined separately. Attributed first to theorist Kimberlé Crenshaw.

Intersex (Intersexual) A broad term that describes individuals medically labeled outside of "typical" or "standard" sex categories (i.e., female or male). There are many causes and varieties of intersex expression. For more information, visit Intersex Society of North America (www.isna.org).

Kink Typically refers to what may be considered unusual, taboo, or unconventional sexual practices such as fetish play, bondage, domination, submission, sado-masochism, or role play.

Klinefelter Syndrome A medical condition in which male bodies inherit an extra X chromosome. For more information regarding Klinefelter Syndrome, visit Intersex Society of North America (www.isna.org).

Lesbian A self-ascribed state of embodiment among women who desire emotional, physical, and/or sexual relations with women.

Male to Female (MtF/M2F) (1) A self-ascribed state of embodiment among individuals labeled male at birth who identify as women and/or in a feminine expression. (2) Also used as an adjective to describe a transition process.

Matriarchy A system of inequality that privileges women and girls over men and boys.

Misogyny The hatred of women.

Neutrois A new term of self-description embraced by individuals who reject the binary structure of woman and man; similar to androgynous and genderqueer.

Non-op A popular colloquialism used in transgender communities to describe a transgender person's current embodiment and/or decision to not undergo surgical transition.

Oppression The systematic denial of access to cultural and institutional resources based on perceived or actual social status membership (i.e., race, ethnicity, gender, sexuality, ability, religion, etc.).

Outted A nonconsensual public speech act or written announcement concerning an individual's identity or status that he or she wants to keep private (i.e., sexual identity, gender history, rape survivor, living with AIDS, etc.).

Pansexual A self-ascribed state of embodiment among individuals who recognize multiple sexes and genders and desire emotional, physical, and/or sexual relations with individuals, regardless of sex membership or gender embodiment.

Passing A process whereby individuals are perceived in ways that affords keeping private an identity or status (i.e., sexual identity, gender history, rape survivor, living with AIDS, etc.).

Patriarchy A dynamic system of power and inequality that privileges men and boys over women and girls in social interactions and institutions.

Polyamory The state or practice of being sexually and/or romantically involved with more than one person at a time.

Post-op A popular colloquialism used in transgender communities to describe a transgender person's current embodiment after surgical procedures to medically or physically transition.

Pre-op A popular colloquialism used in transgender communities to describe a transgender person's current embodiment prior to undergoing elective surgical procedures to transition (assumes decision has already been made).

Privilege The systematic access to valued cultural and institutional resources that are denied to others based on social status membership (i.e., race, ethnicity, gender, sexuality, ability, religion, etc.).

Queer Historically and still a controversial term that (1) is a self-ascribed state of embodiment among individuals who reject and live outside of heteronormative structures; (2) a broad umbrella term used in place of the "LGBT" acronym.

Race Socially constructed categories that group people together based on physical features, such as phenotypic expression, skin tone, and hair textures, as well as on social, cultural, and economic characteristics.

Racism A system of oppression that privileges people over others based on constructed racial classifications. Racism privileges those with greater social power and oppresses others through everyday practices, attitudes, assumptions, behaviors, and institutional rules and structures.

Rape Any forced sexual act.

Secondary Sex Characteristics Biological attributes that most often, but not always, emerge during puberty and have social meaning related to gender and sexuality.

Sex Socially constructed categories based on culturally accepted biological attributes. In Western culture, females and males are categorized on the basis of chromosomes, genitalia, reproductive organs, and hormones.

Sexism A system of oppression that privileges men over women through everyday practices, attitudes, assumptions, behaviors, and institutional rules and structures.

Sex Reassignment Surgery (SRS) Various types of surgical procedures that some transgender individuals undergo to medically and physically align their bodies with their identity.

Sexual Harassment Unwelcome sexual advances or attention, including environments that foster unsafe conditions and/or discomfort based on sexual threat or innuendo.

Sexuality A broad term that encompasses a range of concepts, ideologies, identities, behaviors, and expressions related to sexual personhood and desire.

Sexual Identity (1) Sexual desire, attraction, and practice based on sexual object choice; similar to sexual orientation. (2) Category that encompasses identity terms including lesbian, gay, bisexual, pansexual, queer, or asexual.

Social Institution An organized system that has a set of rules and relationships that govern social interactions and activities in which people participate to meet basic needs.

Sexual Orientation A self-ascribed state of embodiment that describes sexual desires and practices; also implies an essential, unchanging orientation.

Significant Other (SO) A popular colloquialism used by queer and allied communities to refer to an intimate partner.

Social Constructionism A theoretical approach that emphasizes the role of social interaction and culture in meaning-making practices including those that shape social statuses (i.e., race, ethnicity, gender, sexuality, ability, religion, etc.) and produce inequality.

Social Stratification A system by which individuals are divided into social positions that are ranked hierarchically and tied to institutional inequality.

Stealth A popular colloquialism used in transgender communities to describe individuals who have chosen to keep private various identities or statuses.

Testosterone Hormone most often associated with masculinity; however, testosterone is present in all bodies.

Transgender (TG) (1) An umbrella term that includes individuals who change, cross, and/or go beyond or through the culturally defined binary gender categories (woman/man). (2) A self-ascribed state of embodiment.

Transition A process of social and/or medical gender transition.

Transman A self-ascribed state of embodiment among female-bodied people who identify as men and/or masculine.

Transphobia/Transphobic A system of oppression that privileges nontransgender or cisgender people through everyday practices, attitudes, assumptions, behaviors, and institutional rules; encompasses prejudice, stereotyping, and discrimination.

Transsexual (TS) Rooted in the medical and sexological development of "trans" knowledge that regards people who desire to live differently than their assigned sex at birth. Historically, this term has implied medical (i.e., surgical and hormonal) transition.

Tranny/Trannie (1) A self-ascribed state of embodiment among some transgender people. (2) Extremely contextual and depends on the user's intentions and tone; may be offensive and considered an epithet.

Transvestite An antiquated medicalized term that describes individuals who cross-dress for sexual and/or nonsexual reasons.

Transwoman A self-ascribed embodiment among male-bodied people who identify as women and/or feminine.

Turner Syndrome A medical condition in which bodies do not have a second X chromosome. For more information regarding Turner Syndrome, visit Intersex Society of North America (www.isna.org).

REFERENCES

Intersex Society of North America. www.isna.org
Johnson, Allan G. 2006. *Privilege, Power and Difference*, 2nd ed. Boston: McGraw-Hill.
Lober, Judith, and Lisa Jean Moore. 2006. *Gendered Bodies: Feminist Perspectives*. London: Roxbury.
Transsexual Road Map Glossary. 2006. http://www.tsroadmap.com/index.html
Yoder, Janice D. 2007. *Women & Gender: Making a Difference*, 3rd ed. Cornwall-on-Hudson, NY: Sloan Educational.

Sex, Gender, and Sexuality

SECTION ONE

Theoretical Foundations

The theoretical developments of the past 40 years have provided a rich literature to guide our understanding of the myriad ways in which the categories and identities of sex, gender, and sexuality are interdependent. The chapters included in Section One each represent contemporary contributions to rethinking our conceptualizations of sex, gender, and sexuality and the tangled relationships among them. We have opted not to include the seminal works of theorists such as Michel Foucault, Steven Seidman, Adrienne Rich, Audre Lorde, Rosemarie Garland-Thompson, Judith Butler, Eve Kosfsky Sedgewick, and the many, many others deserving of our attention. Instead, we have selected a sample of more recent theoretical contributions that have built on and are advancing, challenging, and nuancing the foundational contributions of these earlier theorists, whose works have made these more recent contributions possible.

Biologist Ann Fausto-Sterling has been a strong voice in debates over classifications of sex, gender, and sexuality. While this piece may be the one exception to the aforementioned caveats, it is important because it provides an example of biological, scientific contributions that refute many of our closely held assumptions. She argues that whether and how a culture creates categories of sex or sexuality are social decisions. As a scientist, she examines the physical, material world, but she argues that our understanding of this is always within the context of a specific culture, shaped by our language, values, politics, and needs.

Bethany Coston and Michael Kimmel narrow in on the construction of gender, and masculinity in particular, to demonstrate the varieties and hierarchy of masculinities. They bring in an intersectional approach to examine the ways in which other identities shape experiences of masculinity, complicating the simple binary that assumes masculinity similarly privileges all men.

Leila Rupp shifts our attention away from US hegemonic structures to examine those of other cultures, at various historical junctures. In highlighting the tremendous cross-cultural variation in how sexuality is constructed and understood, she questions the limits of any one language or theory for exploring other times and places.

Chrys Ingraham examines the important supposition that heterosexuality is an institution. Her work exemplifies the ways in which various feminist scholars have made a critique of heterosexuality central to their analyses of gender hierarchy and inequality. Further, her work encourages us to examine the ways in which gender and heterosexuality are normalized in the minutiae of our daily existence. Her chapter explores weddings as one site where heteronormativity is naturalized. Readers should also consider the many other sites where heteronormativity is normalized (e.g., in the greeting-card industry, Disney films, and the world of Barbie, My Little Pony, and other children's toys and books).

Kristen Schilt and Laurel Westbrook further the analysis of heteronormativity and the relationship between assigned sex, gender, and sexuality. They focus on interactions between "gender normals" (also referred to as cisgender) and transgender people, analyzing the shifting criteria for gender in disparate contexts and focusing on how the performance of gender (which is assumed to reflect one's assigned sex) is dissimilar in sexualized and social situations, where the consequences also vary.

Robert McRuer extends from the concept of heteronormativity and compulsory heterosexuality to argue that our experiences and identities are also performed in the context of a compulsory able-bodiedness. He further critiques the notion of "normalcy," examines the intertwined performance of heterosexual and able-bodied identity, and invokes queer theory in his analysis of how definitions of normalcy operate to exclude, devalue, and harm transgressors. McRuer makes an important contribution to our theoretical foundation, providing insight into both queer theory and intersectionality.

Adam Isaiah Green examines the key theoretical contributions of Michel Foucault, whose work has had a tremendous influence on the early development of contemporary theories of sexuality, and demonstrates its continuing roles in engaging scholars today. Green introduces us to Foucault's concept of "disciplinary power" and examines the possibilities of both normalization as well as empowerment and the expansion of sexual identities that it opens up.

Jane Ward further complicates and nuances our understanding of the relationship between sex, gender, and sexuality and the various ways in which sexual identity, performance, and desire are intertwined and carried out in ways that do not match normative assumptions. She explores practices, usually labeled as gay sexual behavior, engaged in by college men who identify as straight. These practices have been explored by other scholars, in other contexts, yet are rarely spoken about outside of academic research. Her chapter presents many questions that we will continue to encounter throughout this book: the fluidity of sex, gender, and sexual identities; the performative nature of these identities; the importance of culture and context; the complexity of dynamics too often assumed to be common sense; the operation of power, privilege, and oppression; and more.

Each of these perspectives contributes to advancing our theoretical knowledge about sex, gender, and sexuality and the multifarious, complex ways they are interconnected and mutually constitutive. While reading the following chapters, think about how they relate to each other. Where do you see these authors building upon the work of the others? Do any contain inherent critiques or contradictions of other chapters? Which of these perspectives is most compelling? Which help you to reflect on and better understand your own life experience? Which do you find most surprising? And how does this section expand (or even explode) your understanding of sex, gender, and sexuality?

1 • *Anne Fausto-Sterling*

DUELING DUALISMS

DISCUSSION QUESTIONS

1. Why does Fausto-Sterling argue that imposing categories of sex and gender are socially, not scientifically, driven?
2. How do contemporary categories of sexual identity complicate our understanding of historical findings of same-sex sexual behavior?
3. Why does the sex/gender dualism limit feminist analysis, according to Fausto-Sterling?
4. What limitations are there in using developmental systems theory?

MALE OR FEMALE?

In the rush and excitement of leaving for the 1988 Olympics, Maria Patiño, Spain's top woman hurdler, forgot the requisite doctor's certificate stating, for the benefit of Olympic officials, what seemed patently obvious to anyone who looked at her: she was female. But the International Olympic Committee (IOC) had anticipated the possibility that some competitors would forget their certificates of femininity. Patiño had only to report to the "femininity control head office," scrape some cells off the side of her cheek, and all would be in order—or so she thought.

A few hours after the cheek scraping she got a call. Something was wrong. She went for a second examination, but the doctors were mum. Then, as she rode to the Olympic stadium to start her first race, track officials broke the news: she had failed the sex test. She may have looked like a woman, had a woman's strength, and never had reason to suspect that she wasn't a woman, but the examinations revealed that Patiño's cells sported a Y chromosome, and that her

labia hid testes within. Furthermore, she had neither ovaries nor a uterus. According to the IOC's definition, Patiño was not a woman. She was barred from competing on Spain's Olympic team.

Spanish athletic officials told Patiño to fake an injury and withdraw without publicizing the embarrassing facts. When she refused, the European press heard about it and the secret was out. Within months after returning to Spain, Patiño's life fell apart. Spanish officials stripped her of past titles and barred her from further competition. Her boyfriend deserted her. She was evicted from the national athletic residence, her scholarship was revoked, and suddenly she had to struggle to make a living. The national press had a field day at her expense. As she later said, "I was erased from the map, as if I had never existed. I gave twelve years to sports."

Down but not out, Patiño spent thousands of dollars consulting doctors about her situation. They explained that she had been born with a condition called *androgen insensitivity.* This meant that, although she had a Y chromosome and her testes made plenty

---

Anne Fausto-Sterling, "Dueling Dualisms" from *Sexing the Body: Gender Politics and the Construction of Sexuality.* 2000. Reprinted by permission of Perseus Books Group.

of testosterone, her cells couldn't detect this masculinizing hormone. As a result, her body had never developed male characteristics. But at puberty her testes produced estrogen (as do the testes of all men), which, because of her body's inability to respond to its testosterone, caused her breasts to grow, her waist to narrow, and her hips to widen. Despite a Y chromosome and testes, she had grown up as a female and developed a female form.

Patiño resolved to fight the IOC ruling. "I knew I was a woman," she insisted to one reporter, "in the eyes of medicine, God and most of all, in my own eyes." She enlisted the help of Alison Carlson, a former Stanford University tennis player and biologist opposed to sex testing, and together they began to build a case. Patiño underwent examinations in which doctors "checked out her pelvic structures and shoulders to decide if she was feminine enough to compete." After two and a half years the International Amateur Athletic Federation (IAAF) reinstated her, and by 1992 Patiño had rejoined the Spanish Olympic squad, going down in history as the first woman ever to challenge sex testing for female athletes. Despite the IAAF's flexibility, however, the IOC has remained adamant: even if looking for a Y chromosome wasn't the most scientific approach to sex testing, testing *must* be done.

The members of the International Olympic Committee remain convinced that a more scientifically advanced method of testing will be able to reveal the true sex of each athlete. But why is the IOC so worried about sex testing? In part, IOC rules reflect cold war political anxieties: during the 1968 Olympics, for instance, the IOC instituted "scientific" sex testing in response to rumors that some Eastern European competitors were trying to win glory for the Communist cause by cheating—having men masquerade as women to gain unfair advantage. The only known case of a man infiltrating women's competition occurred back in 1936 when Hermann Ratjen, a member of the Nazi Youth, entered the women's high-jump competition as "Dora." His maleness didn't translate into much of an advantage: he made it to the finals, but came in fourth, behind three women.

Although the IOC didn't require modern chromosome screening in the interest of international politics until 1968, it had long policed the sex of Olympic competitors in an effort to mollify those who feared that women's participation in sports threatened to turn them into manly creatures. In 1912, Pierre de Coubertin, founder of the modern Olympics (from which women were originally banned), argued that "women's sports are all against the law of nature." If women were *by nature* not athletic competitors, then what was one to make of the sportswomen who pushed their way onto the Olympic scene? Olympic officials rushed to certify the femininity of the women they let through the door, because the very act of competing seemed to imply that they could not be true women. In the context of gender politics, employing sex police made a great deal of sense.

SEX OR GENDER?

Until 1968 female Olympic competitors were often asked to parade naked in front of a board of examiners. Breasts and a vagina were all one needed to certify one's femininity. But many women complained that this procedure was degrading. Partly because such complaints mounted, the IOC decided to make use of the modern "scientific" chromosome test. The problem, though, is that this test, and the more sophisticated polymerase chain reaction to detect small regions of DNA associated with testes development that the IOC uses today, cannot do the work the IOC wants it to do. A body's sex is simply too complex. There is no either/or. Rather, there are shades of difference.... One of the major claims I make in this book is that labeling someone a man or a woman is a social decision. We may use scientific knowledge to help us make the decision, but only our beliefs about gender—not science—can define our sex. Furthermore, our beliefs about gender affect what kinds of knowledge scientists produce about sex in the first place.

Over the last few decades, the relation between *social expression* of masculinity and femininity and their *physical underpinnings* has been hotly debated in scientific and social arenas. In 1972 the sexologists John Money and Anke Ehrhardt popularized the idea that sex and gender are separate categories.

Sex, they argued, refers to physical attributes and is anatomically and physiologically determined. *Gender* they saw as a psychological transformation of the self—the internal conviction that one is either male or female (gender identity) and the behavioral expressions of that conviction.

Meanwhile, the second-wave feminists of the 1970s also argued that sex is distinct from gender—that social institutions, themselves designed to perpetuate gender inequality, produce most of the differences between men and women. Feminists argued that although men's and women's bodies serve different reproductive functions, few other sex differences come with the territory, unchangeable by life's vicissitudes. If girls couldn't learn math as easily as boys, the problem wasn't built into their brains. The difficulty resulted from gender norms—different expectations and opportunities for boys and girls. Having a penis rather than a vagina is a sex difference. Boys performing better than girls on math exams is a gender difference. Presumably, the latter could be changed even if the former could not.

Money, Ehrhardt, and feminists set the terms so that *sex* represented the body's anatomy and physiological workings and *gender* represented social forces that molded behavior. Feminists did not question the realm of physical sex; it was the psychological and cultural meanings of these differences—gender—that was at issue. But feminist definitions of sex and gender left open the possibility that male/female differences in cognitive function and behavior could *result* from sex differences, and thus, in some circles, the matter of sex versus gender became a debate about how "hardwired" intelligence and a variety of behaviors are in the brain, while in others there seemed no choice but to ignore many of the findings of contemporary neurobiology.

In ceding the territory of physical sex, feminists left themselves open to renewed attack on the grounds of biological difference. Indeed, feminism has encountered massive resistance from the domains of biology, medicine, and significant components of social science. Despite many positive social changes, the 1970s optimism that women would achieve full economic and social equality once gender inequity was addressed in the social sphere has faded in the face of a seemingly recalcitrant inequality. All of which has prompted feminist scholars, on the one hand, to question the notion of sex itself, while on the other to deepen their inquiry into what we might mean by words such as *gender, culture,* and *experience.* The anthropologist Henrietta A. Moore, for example, argues against reducing accounts of gender, culture, and experience to their "linguistic and cognitive elements." In this book . . . I argue, as does Moore, that "what is at issue is the embodied nature of identities and experience. Experience . . . is not individual and fixed, but irredeemably social and processual."

Our bodies are too complex to provide clear-cut answers about sexual difference. The more we look for a simple physical basis for "sex," the more it becomes clear that "sex" is not a pure physical category. What bodily signals and functions we define as male or female come already entangled in our ideas about gender. Consider the problem facing the International Olympic Committee. Committee members want to decide definitively who is male and who is female. But how? If Pierre de Coubertin were still around, the answer would be simple: anybody who desired to compete could not, by definition, be a female. But those days are past. Could the IOC use muscle strength as some measure of sex? In some cases. But the strengths of men and women, especially highly trained athletes, overlap. (Remember that three women beat Hermann Ratjen's high jump.) And although Maria Patiño fit a common-sense definition of femininity in terms of looks and strength, she also had testes and a Y chromosome. But why should these be the deciding factors?

The IOC may use chromosome or DNA tests or inspection of the breasts and genitals to ascertain the sex of a competitor, but doctors faced with uncertainty about a child's sex use different criteria. They focus primarily on reproductive abilities (in the case of a potential girl) or penis size (in the case of a prospective boy). If a child is born with two X chromosomes, oviducts, ovaries, and a uterus on the inside, but a penis and scrotum on the outside, for instance, is the child a boy or a girl? Most doctors declare the child a girl, despite the penis, because of her potential to give birth, and intervene using surgery and hormones to carry out the decision. Choosing which criteria to use in determining sex, and choosing to make the determination at all, are social decisions for which scientists can offer no absolute guidelines.

REAL OR CONSTRUCTED?

I enter the debates about sex and gender as a biologist and a social activist. Daily, my life weaves in and out of a web of conflict over the politics of sexuality and the making and using of knowledge about the biology of human behavior. The central tenet of this book is that truths about human sexuality created by scholars in general and by biologists in particular are one component of political, social, and moral struggles about our cultures and economies. At the same time, components of our political, social, and moral struggles become, quite literally, embodied, incorporated into our very physiological being. My intent is to show how these mutually dependent claims work, in part by addressing such issues as how—through their daily lives, experiments, and medical practices—scientists create truths about sexuality; how our bodies incorporate and confirm these truths; and how these truths, sculpted by the social milieu in which biologists practice their trade, in turn refashion our cultural environment.

My take on the problem is idiosyncratic, and for good reason. Intellectually, I inhabit three seemingly incompatible worlds. In my home department I interact with molecular biologists, scientists who examine living beings from the perspective of the molecules from which they are built. They describe a microscopic world in which cause and effect remain mostly inside a single cell. Molecular biologists rarely think about interacting organs within an individual body, and even less often about how a body bounded by skin interacts with the world on the other side of the skin. Their vision of what makes an organism tick is decidedly bottom up, small to large, inside to outside.

I also interact with a virtual community—a group of scholars drawn together by a common interest in sexuality—and connected by something called a listserve. On a listserve, one can pose questions, think out loud, comment on relevant news items, argue about theories of human sexuality, and report the latest research findings. The comments are read by a group of people hooked together via electronic mail. My listserve (which I call "Loveweb") consists of a diverse group of scholars—psychologists, animal behaviorists, hormone biologists, sociologists, anthropologists, and philosophers. Although many points of view coexist in this group, the vocal majority favor body-based, biological explanations of human sexual behavior. Loveweb members have technical names for preferences they believe to be immutable. In addition to homosexual, heterosexual, and bisexual, for example, they speak of *hebephilia* (attracted primarily to pubescent girls), *ephebephilia* (aroused by young males in their late teens or early twenties), *pedophilia* (aroused by children), *gynephilia* (aroused by adult women), and *androphilia* (attracted to adult men). Many Loveweb members believe that we acquire our sexual essence before birth and that it unfolds as we grow and develop.

Unlike molecular biologists and Loveweb members, feminist theorists view the body not as essence, but as a bare scaffolding on which discourse and performance build a completely acculturated being. Feminist theorists write persuasively and often imaginatively about the processes by which culture molds and effectively creates the body. Furthermore, they have an eye on politics (writ large), which neither molecular biologists nor Loveweb participants have. Most feminist scholars concern themselves with real-world power relationships. They have often come to their theoretical work because they want to understand (and change) social, political, and economic inequality. Unlike the inhabitants of my other two worlds, feminist theorists reject what Donna Haraway, a leading feminist theoretician, calls "the God-trick"—producing knowledge from above, from a place that denies the individual scholar's location in a real and troubled world. Instead, they understand that all scholarship adds threads to a web that positions racialized bodies, sexes, genders, and preferences in relationship to one another. New or differently spun threads change our relationships, change how we are in the world.

Traveling among these varied intellectual worlds produces more than a little discomfort. When I lurk on Loveweb, I put up with gratuitous feminist-bashing aimed at some mythic feminist who derides biology and seems to have a patently stupid view of how the world works. When I attend feminist conferences, people howl in disbelief at the ideas debated on Loveweb. And the molecular biologists don't think much of either of the other worlds. The questions asked by feminists and Loveweb participants seem too complicated; studying sex in bacteria or yeast is the only way to go.

To my molecular biology, Loveweb, and feminist colleagues, then, I say the following: as a biologist, I believe in the material world. As a scientist, I believe in building specific knowledge by conducting experiments. But as a feminist Witness (in the Quaker sense of the word) and in recent years as a historian, I also believe that what we call "facts" about the living world are not universal truths. Rather, as Haraway writes, they "are rooted in specific histories, practices, languages and peoples." Ever since the field of biology emerged in the United States and Europe at the start of the nineteenth century, it has been bound up in debates over sexual, racial, and national politics. And as our social viewpoints have shifted, so has the science of the body.

Many historians mark the seventeenth and eighteenth centuries as periods of great change in our concepts of sex and sexuality. During this period a notion of legal equality replaced the feudal exercise of arbitrary and violent power given by divine right. As the historian Michel Foucault saw it, society still required some form of discipline. A growing capitalism needed new methods to control the "insertion of bodies into the machinery of production and the adjustment of the phenomena of population to economic processes." Foucault divided this power over living bodies (*bio-power*) into two forms. The first centered on the individual body. The role of many science professionals (including the so-called

human sciences—psychology, sociology, and economics) became to optimize and standardize the body's function. In Europe and North America, Foucault's standardized body has, traditionally, been male and Caucasian. And although this book focuses on gender, I regularly discuss the ways in which the ideas of both race and gender emerge from underlying assumptions about the body's physical nature. Understanding how race and gender work—together and independently—helps us learn more about how the social becomes embodied.

Foucault's second form of bio-power—"*a biopolitics of the population*"—emerged during the early nineteenth century as pioneer social scientists began to develop the survey and statistical methods needed to supervise and manage "births and mortality, the level of health, life expectancy and longevity." For Foucault, "discipline" had a double meaning. On the one hand, it implied a form of control or punishment; on the other, it referred to an academic body of knowledge—the discipline of history or biology. The disciplinary knowledge developed in the fields of embryology, endocrinology, surgery, psychology, and biochemistry have encouraged physicians to attempt to control the very gender of the body—including "its capacities, gestures, movements, location and behaviors."

By helping the normal take precedence over the natural, physicians have also contributed to populational biopolitics. We have become, Foucault writes, "a society of normalization." One important mid-twentieth-century sexologist went so far as to name the male and female models in his anatomy text Norma and Normman [*sic*]. Today we see the notion of pathology applied in many settings—from the sick, diseased, or different body, to the single-parent family in the urban ghetto. But imposing a gender norm is socially, not scientifically, driven. The lack of research into the normal distributions of genital anatomy, as well as many surgeons' lack of interest in using such data when they do exist..., clearly illustrate this claim. From the viewpoint of medical practitioners, progress in the handling of intersexuality involves maintaining the normal. Accordingly, there *ought* to be only two boxes: male and female. The knowledge developed by the medical disciplines empowers doctors to maintain a mythology of the normal by changing the intersexual body to fit, as nearly as possible, into one or the other cubbyhole.

One person's medical progress, however, can be another's discipline and control. Intersexuals such as Maria Patiño have unruly—even heretical—bodies. They do not fall naturally into a binary classification; only a surgical shoehorn can put them there. But why should we care if a "woman" (defined as having breasts, a vagina, uterus, ovaries, and menstruation) has a "clitoris" large enough to penetrate the vagina of another woman? Why should we care if there are individuals whose "natural biological equipment" enables them to have sex "naturally" with both men and women? Why must we amputate or surgically hide that "offending shaft" found on an especially large clitoris? The answer: to maintain gender divisions, we must control those bodies that are so unruly as to blur the borders. Since intersexuals quite literally embody both sexes, they weaken claims about sexual difference.

This book reflects a shifting politics of science and of the body. I am deeply committed to the ideas of the modern movements of gay and women's liberation, which argue that the way we traditionally conceptualize gender and sexual identity narrows life's possibilities while perpetuating gender inequality. In order to shift the politics of the body, one must change the politics of science itself. Feminists (and others) who study how scientists create empirical knowledge have begun to reconceptualize the very nature of the scientific process. As with other social arenas, such scholars understand practical, empirical knowledge to be imbued with the social and political issues of its time. I stand at the intersection of these several traditions. On the one hand, scientific and popular debates about intersexuals and homosexuals—bodies that defy the norms of our two-sex system—are deeply intertwined. On the other, beneath the debates about what these bodies mean and how to treat them lie struggles over the meaning of objectivity and the timeless nature of scientific knowledge.

Perhaps nowhere are these struggles more visible than in the biological accounts of what we would today call sexual orientation or sexual preference.

Consider, for instance, a television newsmagazine segment about married women who "discovered," often in their forties, that they were lesbian. The show framed the discussion around the idea that a woman who has sex with men must be heterosexual, while a woman who falls in love with another woman must be lesbian. On this show there seemed to be only these two possibilities. Even though the women interviewed had had active and satisfying sex lives with their husbands and produced and raised families, they knew that they must "be" lesbian the minute they found themselves attracted to a woman. Furthermore, they felt it likely that they must always have been lesbian without knowing it.

The show portrayed sexual identity as a fundamental reality: a woman is either inherently heterosexual or inherently lesbian. And the act of coming out as a lesbian can negate an entire lifetime of heterosexual activity! Put this way, the show's depiction of sexuality sounds absurdly oversimplified. And yet, it reflects some of our most deeply held beliefs—so deeply held, in fact, that a great deal of scientific research (on animals as well as humans) is designed around this dichotomous formulation....

Many scholars mark the start of modern scientific studies of human homosexuality with the work of Alfred C. Kinsey and colleagues, first published in 1948. Their surveys of sexual behavior in men and women provided modern sex researchers with a set of categories useful for measuring and analyzing sexual behaviors. For both men and women, they used a rating scale of 0 to 6, with 0 being 100 percent heterosexual, 6 being 100 percent homosexual. (An eighth category—"X"—was for individuals who experienced no erotic attractions or activities.) Although they designed a scale with discrete categories, Kinsey and co-workers stressed that "the reality includes individuals of every intermediate type, lying in a continuum between the two extremes and between each and every category on the scale."

The Kinsey studies offered new categories defined in terms of sexual arousal—especially orgasm—rather than allowing terms such as *affection, marriage,* or *relationship* to contribute to definitions of human sexuality. Sexuality remained an individual characteristic, not something produced within relationships in particular social settings. Exemplifying my claim that with the very act of measuring, scientists can change the social reality they set out to quantify, I note that today Kinsey's categories have taken on a life of their own. Not only do sophisticated gays and lesbians occasionally refer to themselves by a Kinsey number (such as in a personal ad that might begin "tall, muscular Kinsey 6 seeks..."), but many scientific studies use the Kinsey scale to define their study population.

Although many social scientists understand the inadequacy of using the single word *homosexual* to describe same-sex desire, identity, and practice, the linear Kinsey scale still reigns supreme in scholarly work. In studies that search for genetic links to homosexuality, for example, the middle of the Kinsey scale disappears; researchers seek to compare the extreme ends of the spectrum in hopes of maximizing the chance that they will find something of interest. Multidimensional models of homosexuality exist. Fritz Klein, for example, created a grid with seven variables (sexual attraction, sexual behavior, sexual fantasies, emotional preference, social preference, self-identification, hetero/homo lifestyle) superimposed on a time scale (past, present, future). Nevertheless, one research team, reporting on 144 studies of sexual orientation published in the *Journal of Homosexuality* from 1974 to 1993, found that only 10 percent of these studies used a multidimensional scale to assess homosexuality. About 13 percent used a single scale, usually some version of the Kinsey numbers, while the rest used self-identification (33 percent), sexual preference (4 percent), behavior (9 percent), or, most shockingly for an academic publication, never clearly described their methods (31 percent).

Just as these examples from contemporary sociology show that the categories used to define, measure, and analyze human sexual behavior change with time, so too has a recent explosion of scholarship on the social history of human sexuality shown that the social organization and expression of human sexuality are neither timeless nor universal. Historians are just beginning to pry loose information from the historical record, and any new overviews written are sure to differ. . . .

As historians gather information, they also argue about the nature of history itself. The historian David Halperin writes: "The real issue confronting any cultural historian of antiquity, and any critic of contemporary culture, is...how to recover the terms in which the experiences of individuals belonging to past societies were actually constituted." The feminist historian Joan Scott makes a similar argument, suggesting that historians must not assume that the term *experience* contains a self-evident meaning. Instead, they must try to understand the workings of the complex and changing processes "by which identities are ascribed, resisted, or embraced and 'to note' which processes themselves are unremarked and indeed achieve their effect because they are not noticed."

For example, in her book *The Woman Beneath the Skin,* the historian of science Barbara Duden describes coming upon an eight-volume medical text. Written in the eighteenth century by a practicing physician, the books describe over 1,800 cases involving diseases of women. Duden found herself unable to use twentieth-century medical terms to reconstruct what illnesses these women had. Instead she noticed "bits and pieces of medical theories that would have been circulating, combined with elements from popular culture; self-evident bodily perceptions appear alongside things that struck [her] as utterly improbable." Duden describes her intellectual anguish as she became more and more determined to understand these eighteenth-century German female bodies on their own terms:

> To gain access to the inner, invisible bodily existence of these ailing women, I had to venture across the boundary that separates...the inner body beneath the skin, from the world around it...the body and its environment have been consigned to opposing realms: on the one side are the body, nature, and biology, stable and unchanging phenomena; on the other side are the social environment and history, realms of constant change. With the drawing of this boundary the body was expelled from history.

In contrast to Duden's anguish, many historians of sexuality have leaped enthusiastically into their new field, debating with one another as they dug into their freshly discovered resources. They delighted in shocking the reader with sentences such as: "The year 1992 marked the 100th anniversary of heterosexuality in America" and "From 1700–1900 the citizens of London made a transition from three sexes to four genders." What do historians mean by such statements? Their essential point is that for as far back as one can gather historical evidence (from primitive artwork to the written word), humans have engaged in a variety of sexual practices, but that this sexual activity is bound to historical contexts. That is, sexual practices and societal understandings of them vary not only across cultures but over time as well.

The social scientist Mary McIntosh's 1968 article, "The Homosexual Role," provided the touchstone that pushed scholars to consider sexuality as a historical phenomenon. Most Westerners, she pointed out, assumed that people's sexuality could be classified two or three ways: homosexual, heterosexual, and bisexual. McIntosh argued that this perspective wasn't very informative. A static view of homosexuality as a timeless, physical trait, for instance, didn't tell us much about why different cultures defined homosexuality differently, or why homosexuality seemed more acceptable in certain times and places than in others. An important corollary to McIntosh's insistence on a history of homosexuality is that heterosexuality, and indeed all forms of human sexuality, have a history.

Many scholars embraced McIntosh's challenge to give human sexual expression a past. But disagreement about the implications of this past abounds. The authors of books such as *Gay American History* and *Surpassing the Love of Men* eagerly searched the past for role models that could offer psychological affirmation to members of the nascent gay liberation movement. Just as with the initial impulses of the women's movement to find heroines worthy of emulation, early "gay" histories looked to the past in order to make a case for social change in the present. Homosexuality, they argued, has always been with us; we should finally bring it into the cultural mainstream.

The initial euphoria induced by these scholars' discovery of a gay past was soon complicated by heated debates about the meanings and functions of history. Were our contemporary categories of sexuality inappropriate for analyzing different times and places? If gay people, in the present-day sense, had always existed, did that mean that the condition is inherited in some portion of the population? Could the fact that historians found evidence of homosexuality in whatever era they studied be seen as evidence that homosexuality is a biologically determined trait? Or could history only show us how cultures organize sexual expression differently in particular times and places? Some found the latter possibility liberating. They maintained that behaviors that might seem to be constant actually had totally different meanings in different times and places. Could the apparent fact that in ancient Greece, love between older and younger men was an expected component of the development of free male citizens mean that biology had nothing to do with human sexual expression? If history helped prove that sexuality was a social construction, it could also show how we had arrived at our present arrangements and, most important, offer insights into how to achieve the social and political change for which the gay liberation movement was battling.

Many historians believe that our modern concepts of sex and desire first made their appearance in the nineteenth century. Some point symbolically to the year 1869, when a German legal reformer seeking to change antisodomy laws first publicly used the word *homosexuality*. Merely coining a new term did not magically create twentieth-century categories of sexuality, but the moment does seem to mark the beginning of their gradual emergence. It was during those years that physicians began to publish case reports of homosexuality—the first in 1869 in a German publication specializing in psychiatric and nervous illness. As the scientific literature grew, specialists emerged to collect and systematize the narratives. The now-classic works of Krafft-Ebing and Havelock Ellis completed the transfer of homosexual behaviors from publicly accessible activities to ones managed at least in part by medicine.

The emerging definitions of homo- and heterosexuality were built on a two-sex model of masculinity and femininity. The Victorians, for example, contrasted the sexually aggressive male with the sexually indifferent female. But this created a mystery. If only men felt active desire, how could two women develop a mutual sexual interest? The answer: one of the women had to be an *invert,* someone with markedly masculine attributes. This same logic applied to male homosexuals, who were seen as more effeminate than heterosexual men. [T]hese concepts linger in late-twentieth-century studies of homosexual behaviors in rodents. A lesbian rat is she who mounts; a gay male rat is he who responds to being mounted.

In ancient Greece, males who engaged in same-sex acts changed, as they aged, from feminine to masculine roles. In contrast, by the early part of the twentieth century, someone engaging in homosexual acts *was,* like the married lesbians on the TV news show, a homosexual, a person constitutionally disposed to homosexuality. Historians attribute the emergence of this new homosexual body to widespread social, demographic, and economic changes occurring in the nineteenth century. In America, many men and eventually some women who had in previous generations remained on the family farm found urban spaces in which to gather. Away from the family's eyes, they were freer to pursue their sexual interests. Men seeking same-sex interactions gathered in bars or in particular outdoor spots; as their presence became more obvious, so too did attempts to control their behavior. In response to police and moral reformers, self-consciousness about their sexual behaviors emerged—a budding sense of identity.

This forming identity contributed to its own medical rendering. Men (and later women) who identified themselves as homosexual now sought medical help and understanding. And as medical reports proliferated, homosexuals used them to paint their own self-descriptions. "By helping to give large numbers of people an identity and a name, medicine also helped to shape these people's experience and change their behavior, creating not just a new disease, but a new species of person, 'the modern homosexual.'"

Homosexuality may have been born in 1869, but the modern heterosexual required another decade of gestation. In Germany in 1880 the word *heterosexual* made its public debut in a work defending homosexuality. In 1892, heterosexuality crossed the ocean to America, where, after some period of debate, a consensus developed among medical men that "heterosexual referred to a normal 'other-sex' Eros. [The doctors] proclaimed a new heterosexual separatism—an erotic apartheid that forcefully segregated the sex normals from the sex perverts."

Through the 1930s the concept of heterosexuality fought its way into the public consciousness, and by World War II, heterosexuality seemed a permanent feature of the sexual landscape. Now, the concept has come under heavy fire. Feminists daily challenge the two-sex model, while a strongly self-identified gay and lesbian community demands the right to be thoroughly normal. Transsexuals, transgendered people, and a blossoming organization of intersexuals all have formed social movements to include diverse sexual beings under the umbrella of normality.

The historians whose work I've just recounted emphasize discontinuity. They believe that looking "for general laws about sexuality and its historical evolution will be defeated by the sheer variety of past thought and behavior." But some disagree. The historian John Boswell, for instance, applies Kinsey's classification scheme to ancient Greece. How the Greeks interpreted the *molle* (feminine man) or the *tribade* (masculine woman), in Boswell's view, did not necessarily matter. The existence of these two categories, which Boswell might consider to be Kinsey 6s, shows that homosexual bodies or essences have existed across the centuries. Boswell acknowledges that humans organized and interpreted sexual behaviors differently in different historical eras. But he suggests that a similar range of bodies predisposed to particular sexual activities existed then and now. "Constructions and context shape the articulation of sexuality," he insists, "but they do not efface recognition of erotic preference as a potential category." Boswell regards sexuality as "real" rather than "socially constructed." While Halperin sees desire as a product of cultural norms, Boswell implies we are quite possibly born with particular sexual inclinations wired into our bodies. Growth, development, and the acquisition of culture show us how to express our inborn desires, he argues, but do not wholly create them.

Scholars have yet to resolve the debate about the implications of a history of sexuality. The historian Robert Nye compares historians to anthropologists. Both groups catalogue "curious habits and beliefs" and try, Nye writes, "to find in them some common pattern of resemblance." But what we conclude about people's past experiences depends to a large extent on how much we believe that our categories of analysis transcend time and place. Suppose for a minute that we had a few time-traveling clones—genetically identical humans living in ancient Greece, in seventeenth-century Europe, and in the contemporary United States. Boswell would say that if a particular clone was homosexual in ancient Greece, he would also be homosexual in the seventeenth century or today. The fact that gender structures differ in different times and places might shape the invert's defiance, but would not create it. Halperin, however, would argue that there is no guarantee that the modern clone of an ancient Greek heterosexual would also be heterosexual. . . . The identical body might express different forms of desire in different eras.

There is no way to decide whose interpretation is right. Despite surface similarities, we cannot know whether yesterday's *tribade* is today's butch or whether the middle-aged Greek male lover is today's pedophile.

NATURE OR NURTURE?

While historians have looked to the past for evidence of whether human sexuality is inborn or socially constructed, anthropologists have pursued the same questions in their studies of sexual behaviors, roles, and expressions found in contemporary cultures around the globe. Those examining data from a wide variety of non-Western cultures have discerned two general patterns. Some cultures, like our own, define a permanent role for those who

engage in same-sex coupling—"institutionalized homosexuality," in Mary McIntosh's terminology.

In contrast are those societies in which all adolescent boys, as part of an expected growth process, engage in genital acts with older men. These associations may be brief and highly ritualized or may last for several years. Here oral-genital contact between two males does not signify a permanent condition or special category of being. What defines sexual expression in such cultures is not so much the sex of one's partner as the age and status of the person with whom one couples.

Anthropologists study vastly differing peoples and cultures with two goals in mind. First, they want to understand human variation—the diverse ways in which human beings organize society in order to eat and reproduce. Second, many anthropologists look for human universals. Like historians, anthropologists are divided about what information drawn from any one culture can tell them about another, or whether underlying differences in the expression of sexuality matter more or less than apparent commonalities. In the midst of such disagreements, anthropological data are, nevertheless, often deployed in arguments about the nature of human sexual behavior.

The anthropologist Carol Vance writes that the field of anthropology today reflects two contradictory strains of thought. The first she refers to as the "cultural influences model of sexuality," which, even as it emphasizes the importance of culture and learning in the molding of sexual behavior, nevertheless assumes "the bedrock of sexuality . . . to be universal and biologically determined; in the literature it appears as the 'sex drive' or 'impulse.'" The second approach, Vance says, is to interpret sexuality entirely in terms of social construction. A moderate social constructionist might argue that the same physical act can carry different social meanings in different cultures, while a more radical constructionist might argue that "sexual desire is itself constructed by culture and history from the energies and capacities of the body."

Some social constructionists are interested in uncovering cross-cultural similarities. For instance, the anthropologist Gil Herdt, a moderate constructionist, catalogs four primary cultural approaches to the organization of human sexuality. *Age-structured homosexuality,* such as that found in ancient Greece, also appears in some modern cultures in which adolescent boys go through a developmental period in which they are isolated with older males and perform fellatio on a regular basis. Such acts are understood to be part of the normal process of becoming an adult heterosexual. In *gender-reversed homosexuality,* "same-sex activity involves a reversal of normative sex-role comportment: males dress and act as females, and females dress and behave as males." Herdt used the concept of *role-specialized homosexuality* for cultures that sanction same-sex activity only for people who play a particular social role, such as a shaman. Role-specialized homosexuality contrasts sharply with our own cultural creation: *the modern gay movement.* To declare oneself "gay" in the United States is to adopt an identity and to join a social and sometimes political movement.

Many scholars embraced Herdt's work for providing new ways to think about the status of homosexuality in Europe and America. But although he has provided useful new typologies for the cross-cultural study of sexuality, others argue that Herdt carries with him assumptions that reflect his own culture. The anthropologist Deborah Elliston, for instance, believes that using the term *homosexuality* to describe practices of semen exchange in Melanesian societies "imputes a Western model of sexuality...that relies on Western ideas about gender, erotics and personhood, and that ultimately obscures the meanings that hold for these practices in Melanesia." Elliston complains that Herdt's concept of age-structured sexuality obscures the composition of the category "sexual," and that it is precisely this category that requires clarification to begin with.

When they turn their attention more generally to the relationships between gender and systems of social power, anthropologists face the same sorts of intellectual difficulties when studying "third" genders in other cultures. During the 1970s European and North American feminist activists hoped that anthropologists could provide empirical data to support their political arguments for gender equality. If,

somewhere in the world, egalitarian societies existed, wouldn't that imply that our own social structures were not inevitable? Alternatively, what if women in every culture known to humankind had a subordinate status? Didn't such cross-cultural similarity mean, as more than one writer suggested, that women's secondary standing must be biologically ordained?

When feminist anthropologists traveled around the world in search of cultures sporting the banner of equity, they did not return with happy tidings. Most thought, as the feminist anthropologist Sherry Ortner writes, "that men were in some way or other 'the first sex.'" But critiques of these early cross-cultural analyses mounted, and in the 1990s some prominent feminist anthropologists reassessed the issue. The same problem encountered with collecting information by survey emerges in cross-cultural comparisons of social structures. Simply put, anthropologists must invent categories into which they can sort collected information. Inevitably, some of the invented categories involve the anthropologists' own unquestioned axioms of life, what some scholars call "incorrigible propositions." The idea that there are only two sexes is an incorrigible proposition, and so too is the idea that anthropologists would know sexual equality when they saw it.

Ortner thinks that argument about the universality of sexual inequality has continued for more than two decades because anthropologists assumed that each society would be internally consistent, an expectation she now believes to be unreasonable: "no society or culture is totally consistent. Every society/culture has some axes of male prestige and some of female, some of gender equality, and some (sometimes many) axes of prestige that have nothing to do with gender. The problem in the past has been that all of us...were trying to pigeonhole each case." Now she argues instead that "the most interesting thing about any given case is precisely the multiplicity of logics operating, of discourses being spoken, of practices of prestige and power in play." If one attends to the dynamics, the contradictions, and minor themes, Ortner believes, it becomes possible to see both the currently dominant system *and* the potential for minor themes to become major ones.

But feminists, too, have incorrigible propositions, and a central one has been that all cultures, as the Nigerian anthropologist Oyeronke Oyewumi writes, "organize their social world through a perception of human bodies" as male or female. In taking European and North American feminists to task over this proposition, Oyewumi shows how the imposition of a system of gender—in this case, through colonialism followed by scholarly imperialism—can alter our understandings of ethnic and racial difference. In her own detailed analysis of Yoruba culture, Oyewumi finds that relative age is a far more significant social organizer. Yoruba pronouns, for example, do not indicate sex, but rather who is older or younger than the speaker. What they think about how the world works shapes the knowledge that scholars produce about the world. That knowledge, in turn, affects the world at work.

If Yoruba intellectuals had constructed the original scholarship on Yoruba-land, Oyewumi thinks that "seniority would have been privileged over gender." Seeing Yoruba society through the lens of seniority rather than that of gender would have two important effects. First, if Euro-American scholars learned about Nigeria from Yoruba anthropologists, our own belief systems about the universality of gender might change. Eventually, such knowledge might alter our own gender constructs. Second, the articulation of a seniority-based vision of social organization among the Yoruba would, presumably, reinforce such social structures. Oyewumi finds, however, that African scholarship often imports European gender categories. And "by writing about any society through a gendered perspective, scholars necessarily write gender into that society.... Thus scholarship is implicated in the process of gender-formation."

Thus historians and anthropologists disagree about how to interpret human sexuality across cultures and history. Philosophers even dispute the validity of the words *homosexual* and *heterosexual*—the very terms of the argument. But wherever they fall along the social constructionist spectrum, most argue from the assumption that there is a fundamental split between nature and culture, between "real bodies" and their cultural interpretations. I take seriously the ideas of Foucault, Haraway, Scott, and others that our bodily experiences are brought into being by our development in particular cultures and historical periods. But especially as a biologist, I want to make the argument more specific. As we grow and develop, we literally, not just "discursively" (that is, through language and cultural practices), construct our bodies, incorporating experience into our very flesh. To understand this claim, we must erode the distinctions between the physical and the social body.

DUALISMS DENIED

"A devil, a born devil, on whose nature nurture can never stick." So Shakespeare's Prospero denounces Caliban in *The Tempest*. Clearly, questions of nature and nurture have troubled European culture for some time. Euro-American ways of understanding how the world works depend heavily on the use of dualisms— pairs of opposing concepts, objects, or belief systems. This book focuses especially on three of these: sex/gender, nature/nurture, and real/constructed. We usually employ dualisms in some form of hierarchical argument. Prospero complains that nature controls Caliban's behavior and that his, Prospero's, "pains humanely taken" (to civilize Caliban) are to no avail. Human nurture cannot conquer the devil's nature. In the chapters that follow we will encounter relentless intellectual struggle over which element in any particular pair of dualisms should (or is believed to) dominate. But in virtually all cases, I argue that intellectual questions cannot be resolved nor social progress made by reverting to Prospero's complaint. Instead, as I consider discrete moments in the creation of biological knowledge about human sexuality, I look to cut through the Gordian knot of dualistic thought. I propose to modify Halperin's *bon mot* that "sexuality is not a somatic fact, it is a cultural effect," arguing instead that sexuality *is* a somatic fact *created by* a cultural effect.

Why worry about using dualisms to parse the world? I agree with the philosopher Val Plumwood, who argues that their use makes invisible the inter-dependencies of each pair. This relationship enables sets of pairs to map onto each other. Consider an extract of Plumwood's list:

Reason	Nature
Male	Female
Mind	Body
Master	Slave
Freedom	Necessity (nature)
Human	Nature (nonhuman)
Civilized	Primitive
Production	Reproduction
Self	Other

In everyday use, the sets of associations on each side of the list often run together. "Culture," Plumwood writes, accumulates these dualisms as a store of weapons "which can be mined, refined and rede-ployed. Old oppressions stored as dualisms facilitate and break the path for new ones." For this reason, even though my focus is on gender, I do not hesitate to point out occasions in which the constructs and ideology of race intersect with those of gender.

Ultimately, the sex/gender dualism limits femi-nist analysis. The term *gender,* placed in a dichotomy, necessarily excludes biology. As the feminist theo-rist Elizabeth Wilson writes: "Feminist critiques of the stomach or hormonal structure...have been rendered unthinkable."... Such critiques remain unthinkable because of the real/constructed divide (sometimes formulated as a division between nature and culture), in which many map the knowledge of the real onto the domain of science (equating the constructed with the cultural). Dichotomous for-mulations from feminists and nonfeminists alike conspire to make a sociocultural analysis of the body seem impossible.

Some feminist theorists, especially during the last decade, have tried—with varying degrees of success—to create a nondualistic account of the body. Judith Butler, for example, tries to reclaim the material body for feminist thought. Why, she wonders, has the idea of materiality come to signify that which is irreducible, that which can support construction but cannot itself be constructed? We have, Butler says (and I agree), to talk about the material body. There *are* hormones, genes, prostates, uteri, and other body parts and physiologies that we use to differentiate male from female, that become part of the ground from which varieties of sexual experience and desire emerge. Furthermore, variations in each of these aspects of physiology profoundly affect an individ-ual's experience of gender and sexuality. But every time we try to return to the body as something that exists prior to socialization, prior to discourse about male and female, Butler writes, "we discover that matter is fully sedimented with discourses on sex and sexuality that prefigure and constrain the uses to which that term can be put."

Western notions of matter and bodily material-ity, Butler argues, have been constructed through a "gendered matrix." That classical philosophers associated femininity with materiality can be seen in the origins of the word itself. "Matter" derived from *mater* and *matrix,* referring to the womb and problems of reproduction. In both Greek and Latin, according to Butler, matter was not understood to be a blank slate awaiting the application of external meaning. "The matrix is a...formative principle which inaugurates and informs a development of some organism or object...for Aristotle, 'matter is potentiality, form actuality.'...In reproduction women are said to contribute the matter, men the form." As Butler notes, the title of her book, *Bodies That Matter,* is a well-thought-out pun. To be mate-rial is to speak about the process of materializa-tion. And if viewpoints about sex and sexuality are already embedded in our philosophical concepts of how matter forms into bodies, the matter of bod-ies cannot form a neutral, pre-existing ground from which to understand the origins of sexual difference.

Since matter already contains notions of gender and sexuality, it cannot be a neutral recourse on which to build "scientific" or "objective" theories of sexual development and differentiation. At the same time, we have to acknowledge and use aspects of materiality "that pertain to the body." "The domains of biology, anatomy, physiology, hormonal and chemical composition, illness, age, weight, metabolism, life and death" cannot "be denied." The critical theorist Bernice Hausman concretizes this point in her discussion of surgical technologies available for creating male-to-female versus female-to-male transsexual bodies. "The differences," she writes, "between vagina and penis are not merely ideological. Any attempt to engage and decode the semiotics of sex...must acknowledge that these physiological signifiers have functions in the real that will escape...their function in the symbolic system."

To talk about human sexuality requires a notion of the material. Yet the idea of the material comes to us already tainted, containing within it pre-existing ideas about sexual difference. Butler suggests that we look at the body as a system that simultaneously produces and is produced by social meanings, just as any biological organism always results from the combined and simultaneous actions of nature and nurture.

Unlike Butler, the feminist philosopher Elizabeth Grosz allows some biological processes a status that pre-exists their meaning. She believes that biological instincts or drives provide a kind of raw material for the development of sexuality. But raw materials are never enough. They must be provided with a set of meanings, "a network of desires" that organize the meanings and consciousness of the child's bodily functions. This claim becomes clear if one follows the stories of so-called wild children raised without human constraints or the inculcation of meaning. Such children acquire neither language nor sexual drive. While their bodies provided the raw materials, without a human social setting the clay could not be molded into recognizable psychic form. Without human sociality, human sexuality cannot develop. Grosz tries to understand how human sociality and meaning that clearly originate outside the body end up incorporated into its physiological demeanor and both unconscious and conscious behaviors.

Some concrete examples will help illustrate. A tiny gray-haired woman, well into her ninth decade, peers into the mirror at her wrinkled face. "Who *is*

that woman?" she wonders. Her mind's image of her body does not synchronize with the mirror's reflection. Her daughter, now in her mid-fifties, tries to remember that unless she thinks about using her leg muscles instead of her knee joint, going up and down the stairs will be painful. (Eventually she will acquire a new kinesic habit and dispense with conscious thought about the matter.) Both women are readjusting the visual and kinesic components of their body image, formed on the basis of past information, but always a bit out of date with the current physical body. How do such readjustments occur, and how do our earliest body images form in the first place? Here we need the concept of the psyche, a place where two-way translations between the mind and the body take place—a United Nations, as it were, of bodies and experiences.

In *Volatile Bodies,* Elizabeth Grosz considers how the body and the mind come into being together. To facilitate her project, she invokes the image of a Möbius strip as a metaphor for the psyche. The Möbius strip is a topological puzzle..., a flat ribbon twisted once and then attached end to end to form a circular twisted surface. One can trace the surface, for example, by imagining an ant walking along it. At the beginning of the circular journey, the ant is clearly on the outside. But as it traverses the twisted ribbon, without ever lifting its legs from the plane, it ends up on the inside surface. Grosz proposes that we think of the body—the brain, muscles, sex organs, hormones, and more—as composing the inside of the Möbius strip. Culture and experience would constitute the outside surface. But, as the image suggests, the inside and outside are continuous and one can move from one to the other without ever lifting one's feet off the ground.

As Grosz recounts, psychoanalysts and phenomenologists describe the body in terms of feelings. The mind translates physiology into an interior sense of self. Oral sexuality, for example, is a physical feeling that a child and later an adult translates into psychosexual meaning. This translation takes place on the inside of the Möbius surface. But as one traces the surface toward the outside, one begins to speak in terms of connections to other bodies and objects—things that are clearly not-self. Grosz writes, "Instead of describing the oral drive in terms of what it feels like...orality can be understood in terms of what it does: creating linkages. The child's lips, for example, form connections...with the breast or bottle, possibly accompanied by the hand in conjunction with an ear, each system in perpetual motion and in mutual interrelation."

Continuing with the Möbius analogy, Grosz envisions that bodies create psyches by using the libido as a marker pen to trace a path from biological processes to an interior structure of desire. It falls to a different arena of scholarship to study the "outside" of the strip, a more obviously social surface marked by "pedagogical, juridical, medical, and economic texts, laws, and practices" in order to "carve out a social subject...capable of labor, or production and manipulation, a subject capable of acting as a subject." Thus Grosz also rejects a nature versus nurture model of human development. While acknowledging that we do not understand the range and limits of the body's pliability, she insists that we cannot merely "subtract the environment, culture, history" and end up with "nature or biology."

BEYOND DUALISMS

Grosz postulates innate drives that become organized by physical experience into somatic feelings, which translate into what we call emotions. Taking the innate at face value, however, still leaves us with an unexplained residue of nature. Humans are biological and thus in some sense natural beings *and* social and in some sense artificial—or, if you will, constructed entities. Can we devise a way of seeing ourselves, as we develop from fertilization to old age, as simultaneously natural and unnatural? During the past decade an exciting vision has emerged that I have loosely grouped under the rubric of developmental systems theory, or DST. What do we gain by choosing DST as an analytic framework?

Developmental systems theorists deny that there are fundamentally two kinds of processes: one guided by genes, hormones, and brain cells (that is, nature), the other by the environment, experience, learning, or inchoate social forces (that is, nurture). The pioneer systems theorist, philosopher Susan Oyama promises that DST: "gives more clarity, more coherence, more consistency and a different way to interpret data; in addition it offers the means for synthesizing the concepts and methods...of groups that have been working at cross-purposes, or at least talking past each other for decades." Nevertheless, developmental systems theory is no magic bullet. Many will resist its insights because, as Oyama explains, "it gives less...guidance on fundamental truth" and "fewer conclusions about what is inherently desirable, healthy, natural or inevitable."

How, specifically, can DST help us break away from dualistic thought processes? Consider an example described by systems theorist Peter Taylor, a goat born with no front legs. During its lifetime it managed to hop around on its hind limbs. An anatomist who studied the goat after it died found that it had an S-shaped spine (as do humans), "thickened bones, modified muscle insertions, and other correlates of moving on two legs." This (and every goat's) skeletal system developed as part of its manner of walking. Neither its genes nor its environment determined its anatomy. Only the ensemble had such power. Many developmental physiologists recognize this principle. As one biologist writes, "enstructuring occurs during the enactment of individual life histories."

A few years ago, when the neuroscientist Simon LeVay reported that the brain structures of gay and heterosexual men differed (and that this mirrored a more general sex difference between straight men and women), he became the center of a firestorm. Although an instant hero among many gay males, he was at odds with a rather mixed group. On the one hand, feminists such as myself disliked his unquestioning use of gender dichotomies, which have in the past never worked to further equality for women. On the other, members of the Christian right hated his work because they believe that homosexuality is a sin that individuals can choose to reject. LeVay's, and later geneticist Dean Hamer's, work suggested to them that homosexuality was inborn or innate. The language of the public debate soon became polarized. Each side contrasted words such as *genetic, biological, inborn, innate,* and *unchanging* with *environmental, acquired, constructed,* and *choice.*

The ease with which such debates evoke the nature/nurture divide is a consequence of the poverty of a nonsystems approach. Politically, the nature/nurture framework holds enormous dangers. Although some hope that a belief in the nature side of things will lead to greater tolerance, past history suggests that the opposite is also possible. Even the scientific architects of the nature argument recognize the dangers. In an extraordinary passage in the pages of *Science,* Dean Hamer and his collaborators indicated their concern: "It would be fundamentally unethical to use such information to try to assess or alter a person's current or future sexual orientation. Rather, scientists, educators, policy-makers and the public should work together to ensure that such research is used to benefit all members of society."

The feminist psychologist and critical theorist Elisabeth Wilson uses the hubbub over LeVay's work to make some important points about systems theory. Many feminist, queer, and critical theorists work by deliberately displacing biology, hence opening the body to social and cultural shaping. This, however, is the wrong move to make. Wilson writes: "What may be politically and critically contentious in LeVay's hypothesis is not the conjunction neurology-sexuality per se, but the particular manner in which such a conjunction is enacted." An effective political response, she continues, doesn't have to separate the study of sexuality from the neurosciences. Instead, Wilson, who wants us to develop a theory of mind and body—an account of psyche that joins libido to body—suggests that feminists incorporate into their worldview an account of how the brain works that is, broadly speaking, called connectionism.

The old-fashioned approach to understanding the brain was anatomical. Function could be located in particular parts of the brain. Ultimately function and anatomy were one. This idea underlies the corpus callosum debate, ... for example, as well as the uproar over LeVay's work. Many scientists believe that a structural difference represents the brain location for measured behavioral differences. In contrast, connectionist models argue that function emerges from the complexity and strength of many neural connections acting at once. The system has some important characteristics: the responses are often nonlinear, the networks can be "trained" to respond in particular ways, the nature of the response is not easily predictable, and information is not located anywhere—rather, it is the net result of the many different connections and their differing strengths.

The tenets of some connectionist theory provide interesting starting points for understanding human sexual development. Because connectionist networks, for example, are usually nonlinear, small changes can produce large effects. One implication for studying sexuality: we could easily be looking in the wrong places and on the wrong scale for aspects of the environment that shape human development. Furthermore, a single behavior may have many underlying causes, events that happen at different times in development. I suspect that our labels of homosexual, heterosexual, bisexual, and transgender are really not good categories at all, and are best understood only in terms of unique developmental events affecting particular individuals. Thus, I agree with those connectionists who argue that "the developmental process itself lies at the heart of knowledge acquisition. Development is a process of emergence."

In most public and most scientific discussions, sex and nature are thought to be real, while gender and culture are seen as constructed. But these are false dichotomies. I start ... with the most visible, exterior markers of gender—the genitalia—to illustrate how sex is, literally, constructed. Surgeons remove parts and use plastic to create "appropriate" genitalia for people born with body parts that are not easily identifiable as male or female. Physicians believe that their expertise enables them to "hear" nature telling them the truth about what sex such patients ought to be. Alas, their truths come from the social arena and are reinforced, in part, by the medical tradition of rendering intersexual births invisible.

Our bodies, as well as the world we live in, are certainly made of materials. And we often use scientific investigation to understand the nature of those materials. But such scientific investigation involves a process of knowledge construction. I illustrate this in some detail in chapter 5, which moves us into the body's interior—the less visible anatomy of the brain. Here I focus on a single scientific controversy: Do men and women have differently shaped corpus callosums (a specific region of the brain)? In this chapter, I show how scientists construct arguments by choosing particular experimental approaches and tools. The entire shape of the debate is socially constrained, and the particular tools chosen to conduct the controversy (for example, a particular form of statistical analysis or using brains from cadavers rather than Magnetic Resonance Image brain scans) have their own historical and technical limitations.

Under appropriate circumstances, however, even the corpus callosum is visible to the naked eye. What happens, then, when we delve even more deeply—into the body's invisible chemistry? In chapters 6 and 7, I show how in the period from 1900 to 1940 scientists carved up nature in a particular fashion, creating the category of sex hormones. The hormones themselves became markers of sexual difference. Now, the finding of a sex hormone or its receptor in any part of the body (for example, on bone cells) renders that previously gender-neutral body part sexual. But if one looks, as I do, historically, one can see that steroid hormones need not have been divided into sex and nonsex categories. They could, for example, have been considered to be growth hormones affecting a wide swath of tissues, including reproductive organs.

Scientists now agree about the chemical structure of the steroid molecules they labeled as sex hormones, even though they are not visible to the naked eye. In chapter 8, I focus in part on how scientists used the newly minted concept of the sex hormone to deepen understanding of genital development in rodents, and in part on their application of knowledge about sex hormones to something even less tangible than body chemistry: sex-related behavior. But, to paraphrase the Bard, the course of true science never did run smooth. Experiments and models depicting the role of hormones in the development of sexual behaviors on rodents formed an eerie parallel with cultural debates about the roles and abilities of men and women. It seems hard to avoid the view that our very real, scientific understandings of hormones, brain development, and sexual behavior are, nevertheless, constructed in and bear the marks of specific historical and social contexts.

This book, then, examines the construction of sexuality, starting with structures visible on the body's exterior surface and ending with behaviors and motivations—that is, with activities and forces that are patently invisible—inferred only from their outcome, but presumed to be located deep within the body's interior. But behaviors are generally social activities, expressed in interaction with distinctly separate objects and beings. Thus, as we move from genitalia on the outside to the invisible psyche, we find ourselves suddenly walking along the surface of a Möbius strip back toward, and beyond, the body's exterior. In the book's final chapter, I outline research approaches that can potentially show us how we move from outside to inside and back out again, without ever lifting our feet from the strip's surface.

2 • *Bethany M. Coston and Michael Kimmel*

SEEING PRIVILEGE WHERE IT ISN'T: MARGINALIZED MASCULINITIES AND THE INTERSECTIONALITY OF PRIVILEGE

DISCUSSION QUESTIONS

1. Why do Coston and Kimmel critique the many monolithic analyses of privilege? What are the limitations of such an approach?
2. What are the consequences of generic explanations of masculine privilege? Who is made visible and who is made invisible?
3. Identify another example where one specific form of privilege may be threatened or mediated by someone's other social identities (or identity).
4. What do you see as the most significant contribution of this chapter?

Systems of privilege exist worldwide, in varying forms and contexts, and while this examination of privilege focuses on only one specific instance (the United States), the theorizing of said privilege is intended to be universal. This is because no matter the context, the idea that "privilege is invisible to those who have it" has become a touchstone epigram for work on the "super-ordinate"—in this case, White people, men, heterosexuals, and the middle class (Privilege: A reader, 2010). When one is privileged by class, or race or gender or sexuality, one rarely sees exactly how the dynamics of privilege work. Thus, efforts to make privilege visible, such as McIntosh's (1988) "invisible knapsack" and the "Male Privilege

Checklist" or the "heterosexual questionnaire" have become staples in college classes.

Yet unlike McIntosh's autobiographical work, some overly-simple pedagogical tools like the "heterosexual questionnaire" or "Male Privilege Checklist" posit a universal and dichotomous understanding of privilege: one either has it or one does not. It's as if all heterosexuals are white; all "males" are straight. The notion of intersectionality complicates this binary understanding. Occasionally, a document breaks through those tight containers, such as Woods' (2010) "Black Male Privilege Checklist," but such examples are rare.

We propose to investigate sites of inequality within an overall structure of privilege. Specifically,

Coston, Bethany M. and Kimmel, Michael. "Seeing Privilege Where It Isn't: Marginalized Masculinities and the Intersectionality of Privilege." *Journal of Social Issues*, Vol. 68, No. 1 (2012): 97–111. Reprinted by permission John Wiley & Sons.

we look at three groups of men—disabled men, gay men, and working class men—to explore the dynamics of having privilege in one sphere but being unprivileged in another arena. What does it mean to be privileged by gender and simultaneously marginalized by class, sexuality, or bodily status?

This is especially important, we argue, because, for men, the dynamics of removing privilege involve assumptions of emasculation—exclusion from that category that would confer privilege. Gender is the mechanism by which the marginalized are marginalized. That is, gay, working class, or disabled men are seen as "not-men" in the popular discourse of their marginalization. It is their masculinity—the site of privilege—that is specifically targeted as the grounds for exclusion from privilege. Thus, though men, they often see themselves as reaping few, if any, of the benefits of their privileged status as men (Pratto & Stewart, 2012).

Of course, they do reap those benefits. But often, such benefits are less visible, since marginalized men are less likely to see a reduced masculinity dividend as much compensation for their marginalization. This essay will explore these complex dynamics by focusing on three groups of marginalized men: working class, disabled, and gay men.

DOING GENDER AND THE MATRIX OF OPPRESSION

. . .

The idealized notion of masculinity operates as both an ideology and a set of normative constraints. It offers a set of traits, attitudes and behaviors (the "male role") as well as organizing institutional relationships among groups of women and men. Gender operates at the level of interaction (one can be said to "do" gender through interaction) as well as an identity (one can be said to "have" gender, as in the sum total of socialized attitudes and traits). Gender can also be observed within the institutionally organized sets of practices at the macro level—states, markets, and the like all express and reproduce gender

arrangements. One of the more popular ways to see gender is as an accomplishment; an everyday, interactional activity that reinforces itself via our activities and relationships. "Doing gender involves a complex of socially guided perceptual, interactional, and micropolitical activities that cast particular pursuits as expressions of masculine and feminine 'natures'" (West & Zimmerman, 1987).

These "natures," or social *norms* for a particular gender, are largely internalized by the men and women who live in a society, consciously and otherwise. In other words, these social norms become personal identities. Moreover, it is through the intimate and intricate process of daily interaction with others that we fully achieve our gender, and are seen as valid and appropriate gendered beings. For men, masculinity often includes preoccupation with proving gender to others. Indeed, "In presenting ourselves as a gendered person, we are making ourselves accountable—we are purposefully acting in such a way as to be able to be recognized as gendered" (West & Fenstermaker, 1995).

Society is full of men who have embraced traditional gender ideologies—even those who might otherwise be marginalized. While the men we discuss below may operate within oppression in one aspect of their lives, they have access to alternate sites of privilege via the rest of their demographics (e.g., race, physical ability, sexual orientation, gender, sex, age, social class, religion). A working class man, for example, may also be White and have access to white privilege and male privilege. What is interesting is how these men choose to navigate and access their privilege within the confines of a particular social role that limits, devalues, and often stigmatizes them as not-men.

. . . At the same time, marginalization also frames power and privilege from an interesting vantage point; it offers a seemingly existential choice: to overconform to the dominant view of masculinity as a way to stake a claim to it or to resist the hegemonic and develop a masculinity of resistance.

. . .

DYNAMICS OF MARGINALIZATION AND STIGMA

Marginalization is both gendered and dynamic. How do marginalized men respond to the problematization of their masculinity as they are marginalized by class, sexuality or disability status? Goffman's (1963) understanding of stigma may be of use to explicate this dynamic. Stigma is a stain, a mark, and "spoiled identity," Goffman writes, an attribute that changes you "from a whole and usual person to a tainted and discounted one." People with stigmatized attributes are constantly practicing various strategies to ensure minimal damage. Since being stigmatized will "spoil" your identity, you are likely to attempt to alleviate it.

Goffman identified three strategies to neutralize stigma and revive a spoiled identity. He listed them in order of increased social power—the more power you have, the more you can try and redefine the situation (these terms reflect the era in which he was writing, since he obviously uses the Civil Rights Movement as the reference). They are:

1. *Minstrelization*: If you're virtually alone and have very little power, you can over-conform to the stereotypes that others have about you. To act like a minstrel, Goffman says, is to *exaggerate* the differences between the stigmatized and the dominant group. Thus, for example, did African Americans over-act as happy-go-lucky entertainers when they had no other recourse? Contemporary examples might be women who act "ultra-feminine"—helpless and dependent—in potentially harassing situations, or gay men who really "camp it up" like Carson Kressley on "Queer Eye for the Straight Guy." Minstrels exaggerate difference in the face of those with more power; when they are with other stigmatized people, they may laugh about the fact that the powerful "actually think we're like this!" That's often the only sort of power that they feel they have.

2. *Normification*: If you have even a small amount of power, you might try to minimize the differences between the stigmatized groups. "Look," you'll

say, "we're the same as you are, so there is no difference to discriminate against us." Normification is the strategy that the stigmatized use to enter institutions formerly closed to them, like when women entered the military or when Black people ran for public office. Normification is the process that gays and lesbians refer to when they argue for same-sex marriage, or that women use when they say they want to be engineers or physicists. Normification involves exaggerating the similarities and downplaying the differences.

3. *Militant Chauvinism*: When your group's level of power and organization is highest, you may decide to again <u>maximize</u> differences with the dominant group. But militant chauvinists don't just say "we're different," they say "we're also better." For example, there are groups of African-Americans ("Afrocentrists" or some of the Nation of Islam) who proclaim Black superiority. Some feminist women proclaim that women's ways are better than the dominant "male" way. These trends try to turn the tables on the dominant group. (Warning: Do not attempt this if you are the only member of your group in a confrontation with members of the dominant group.)

These three responses depend on the size and strength of the stigmatized group. If you're alone, minstrelizing may be a life-saving technique. If there are many of you and you are strong, you might try and militantly turn the tables. However, we might see these three strategic responses to stigma through a somewhat different lens. The over-conformity of normification accepts the criteria that the dominant group uses to maintain its power; normifiers simply want to be included. By contrast, both minstrelizers and militant chauvinists resist their marginalization by rejecting the criteria by which they are marginalized.

We realize that it might also seem to be arguable in the exact opposite frame—that, for example, normifiers may be seen to be resisting their own marginalization, while minstrelizers and militant chauvinists accept their marginalization and over-conform to those stereotypic characterizations that the dominant culture may hold about them. However, we argue that resistance comes in the posture towards those criteria themselves: normifiers accept the criteria and make efforts to demonstrate their legitimate claim for inclusion. Minstrelizers and militant chauvinists turn the criteria on their head, play with them paradoxically, and suggest that the dominant culture is impoverished for being unable to express those traits.

. . .

DISABLED MEN

Discrimination against men with disabilities is pervasive in American society, and issues of power, dominance, and hegemonic masculinity are the basis. Over time, hegemonic masculinity has grown to encompass all aspects of social and cultural power, and the discrimination that arises from this can have an alarmingly negative affect on a man and his identity. Disabled men do not meet the unquestioned and idealized standards of appearance, behavior, and emotion for men. The values of capitalist societies based on male dominance are dedicated to warrior values, and a frantic able-bodiedness represented through aggressive sports and risk-taking activities, which do not make room for those with disabilities.

For example, one man interviewed by Robertson (2011) tells the story of his confrontations with those who discriminate against him. Frank says,

> If somebody doesn't want to speak to me 'cause I'm in a chair, or they shout at me 'cause I'm in a chair, I wanna know why, why they feel they have to shout. I'm not deaf you know. If they did it once and I told them and they didn't do it again, that'd be fair enough. But if they keep doing it then that would annoy me and if they didn't know that I could stand up then I'd put me brakes on and I'd stand up and I'd tell them face-to-face. If they won't listen, then I'll intimidate them, so they will listen, because it's important. (p. 12)

Scholars seem to agree that terms such as "disability" and "impairment" refer to limitations in function resulting from physiological, psychological and anatomical dysfunction of bodies (including minds), causing restrictions in a person's ability to perform culturally defined normal human activities (World Health Organization). Normal life activities are defined as walking, talking, using any of the senses, working, and/or caring for oneself.

Men with physical disabilities have to find ways to express themselves within the role of "disabled." Emotional expression is not compatible with the aforementioned traits because it signifies vulnerability; in this way, men, especially disabled men, must avoid emotional expression. If they fail in stoicism, discrimination in the form of pejorative words ("cripple," "wimp," "retard") are sometimes used to suppress or condemn the outward expressions of vulnerability.

But, men with disabilities don't need verbal reminders of their "not-men" status. Even without words, their social position, their lack of power over themselves (let alone others), leads them to understand more fully their lacking masculinity. One man, Vernon, detailed these feelings specifically,

> Yeah, 'cause though you know you're still a man, I've ended up in a chair, and I don't feel like a red-blooded man. I don't feel I can handle 10 pints and get a woman and just do the business with them and forget it, like most young people do. You feel compromised and still sort of feeling like 'will I be able to satisfy my partner.' Not just sexually, other ways, like DIY, jobs round the house and all sorts. (Robertson, 2011, pp. 8–9)

It seems that in the presence of their disability, these men are often left with three coping strategies: they can reformulate their ideas of masculinity (minstrelize); rely on and promote certain hegemonic ideals of masculinity (normify); or reject the mass societal norms and deny the norms' importance, creating another set of standards for themselves (militant chauvinism) (Gerschick & Miller, 1995).

. . .

Indeed, some men find that hypermasculinity is the best strategy. Wedgwood (2011) interviewed disabled men and Carlos was certainly one who appreciated gender conformity:

> The thrill you get out of doing it because I'm an adrenaline junkie! [laughs]. Contact for me, gets your

adrenaline going, gets your blood going and it's a rush . . . if I have a really hard match and I'm getting bruised and getting smashed in there and I'm still trying to go for the ball and I keep getting hit—that's what I love about contact sports—I keep getting hit and everything and still getting up. (p. 14)

Scott Hogsett, a Wheelchair Rugby player, detailed this feeling as well in the movie "Murderball" when he discussed some people's perceptions that their Special Olympics sport wasn't difficult or a "real" sport. He said, "We're not going for a hug. We're going for a fucking gold medal."

However, as Erving Goffman (1963) writes, "The stigmatized individual tends to hold the same beliefs about identity that we do . . . His deepest feelings about what he is may be his sense of being a "normal person," a human being like anyone else" (p. 116). Failing to maintain the hegemonic norms for masculinity has a direct, sometimes negative psychological effect. People tend to judge themselves and measure their worth based upon an intersubjective, sometimes impossible reality. . . . Identity, self-worth, and confidence depend on whether or not he accepts, conforms to, or relies on the social norms.

. . .

The desire to maintain a disabled man's masculinity does not just stem from within that man, however. The model of rehabilitation of people with disabilities, the medical model of disability, has a male body and male sexuality in mind. "Rehabilitation programs seek to cultivate 'competitive attitudes' and address 'concerns about male sexuality'" (Jeffreys, 2008). They are about "enabling men to aspire to dominant notions of masculinity" (Begum, 1992).

Robert David Hall is an actor on the hit American television show *CSI* (Crime Scene Investigation) and walks on two artificial legs due to having both of his legs amputated in 1978 after an 18-wheeler crushed his car. His character is not defined by his disability. "I used to hate the word 'disability'," he said. "But I've come to embrace the fact that I'm one of more than 58 million Americans with some kind of physical or learning disability" (p. 1). "After the accident, I realized I had more strength than I knew,"

Hall says. "I was forced to face up to reality, but facing such a reality helped me face any fears I had of taking risks" (Skrhak, 2008).

In today's world, men with disabilities fight an uphill battle against hegemonic masculinity—their position in the social order—and its many enforcers. Men with disabilities seem to scream, "I AM A STILL A MAN!" They try to make up for their shortcoming by overexaggerating the masculine qualities they still have, and society accommodates this via their support of disabled men's sexual rights and the sexist nature of medical rehabilitation programs and standards.

Gay Men

Male homosexuality has long been associated with effeminacy (i.e. not being a real man) throughout the history of Western societies; the English language is fraught with examples equating men's sexual desire for other men with femininity: molly and nancy-boy in 18th-century England, buttercup, pansy, and she-man of early 20th-century America, and the present-day sissy, fairy, queen, and faggot (Chauncey, 1994; Edwards, 1994; Pronger, 1990). Moreover, the pathologization of male homosexuality in the early 20th century led to a rhetoric of de-masculinization. By the 1970s, a number of psychiatric theorists referred to male homosexuality as "impaired masculine self-image" (Bieber, 1965), "a flight from masculinity" (Kardiner, 1963), "a search for masculinity" (Socarides, 1968), and "masculine failure" (Ovesey & Person, 1973).

Today in the United States, gay men continue to be marginalized by gender—that is, their masculinity is seen as problematic. In a survey of over 3,000 American adults (Levitt & Klassen, 1976), 69% believed homosexuals acted like the opposite sex, and that homosexual men were suitable only to the "unmasculine" careers of artist, beautician, and florist, but not the "masculine" careers of judges, doctors, and ministers. Recent studies have found similar results, despite the changing nature of gay rights in America (Blashill & Powlishta, 2009; Wright & Canetto, 2009; Wylie, Corliss, Boulanger, Prokop, & Austin, 2010).

The popular belief that gay men are not real men is established by the links among sexism (the systematic devaluation of women and "the feminine"), homophobia (the deep-seated cultural discomfort and hatred felt towards same-sex sexuality); and compulsory heterosexuality. Since heterosexuality is integral to the way a society is organized, it becomes a naturalized, "learned" behavior. When a man decides he is gay (if this "deciding" even occurs), he is rejecting the *compulsion* toward a heterosexual lifestyle and orientation (Rich, 1980).

More than this, though, compulsory heterosexuality is a mandate; society demands heterosexuality; our informal and formal policies and laws all reflect this (Fingerhut, Riggle, & Rostosky, 2011). And, in response, men find that one of the key ways to prove masculinity is to demonstrate sexual prowess. Thus, a normifying process can be discerned among gay men of the pre-HIV, post-Stonewall era.

The ideological turn in the 1970s made by gay men, away from camp and drag, and toward a more hypermasculine affective style, dominated mainstream gay male culture through the 1980s. Hypermasculine men began to emerge in many major Western cities in the 1970s (Badinter, 1992; Levine, 1992; Messner, 1997). "Like the less visible queer movement of the early 1900s, the hypermasculine appearance and sensibility announced a new masculine gay identity to replace the "limp-wristed swish" stereotype of the previous eras" (Taywaditep, 2001).

Levine's classic ethnography of clone culture makes clear that, among gay men, hypermasculine display—clothing, affective styles, fashion, and, above all, sexual promiscuity—consisted of a large promissory note to the larger culture—a culture that was both heterosexist and sexist in its anti-gay sentiments (Levine, 1995). "We are real men!" that note read. "We not only perform masculinity successfully, but we embrace the criteria that denote and confer masculinity. And so we want you, the larger dominant culture, to confer masculinity on us."

. . .

In the wake of the liberation movement, gay men seemed to rely on similar coping strategies as the disabled men detailed earlier: they reformulated their ideas of masculinity; relied on and promoted certain hegemonic ideals of masculinity; or rejected the mass

societal norms and deny the norms' importance, creating another set of standards for themselves (Gerschick & Miller, 1995). Such a move also opened up an oppositional culture within the gay community—a culture of resistance to masculinist overconformity. It consisted in reclaiming the nelly queen, the camp and drag affective styles that the mainstream had discarded.

Sociologist Tim Edwards detailed this type of rejection and reliance: on one hand, there are the *effeminists* who express gender nonconformity and/or seek to denounce traditional masculinity because of their personal style or a commitment to feminism—in other words, they reject mass social norms and deny their importance or very foundation; on the other hand, there are the *masculinists* who are proponents of gay male "machismo" and seek to challenge the long-held effeminate stereotype of gay men—they rely heavily on the hegemonic ideals.

This reliance is, interestingly, the main site of access to privilege for these gay men. Gay men's misogyny in humor and argot, as well as some politico-ideological departures from feminism, have been well documented (Goodwin, 1989). As noted by Astrachan (1993), though it would seem beneficial for gay men and women to unite under their common experiences within the oppressive gender system, some gay men oppress and dominate women by "searching for people they can define as inferior—and finding women. A gay man told me, 'We want to be the equals of straight men, and if that means screwing women—figuratively—we'll do it.'"

The gay men who conform to hegemonic norms, secure their position in the power hierarchy by adopting the heterosexual masculine role and subordinating both women and effeminate gay men. Having noted that hypermasculine gay men have been accused of being "collaborators with patriarchy," Messner (1997) pointed out the prominence of hegemonic masculinity in gay culture: "it appears that the dominant tendency in gay culture eventually became an attempt to claim, eroticize, and display the dominant symbols of hegemonic masculinity" (p. 83).

Historically, camp and drag were associated with minstrelizers, those who exaggeratedly expressed stereotypic constructions of homosexual masculinity.

The 1950s hairdresser, interior decorator and florist of classic cultural stereotype were embraced as lifestyle choices, if not yet a political position. Minstrelizers embraced the stereotypes; their effeminacy asked the question: "who wants to be butch all the time anyway? It's too much work."

On the other hand, there was a group of effeminists who were explicitly political. As a political movement, effeminism emerged in the first years of the modern post-Stonewall Gay Liberation movement, but unlike it's normifying brethren, effeminists explicitly and politically rejected mainstream heterosexual masculinity. Largely associated with the work of Steve Dansky, effeminists published a magazine, *Double F*, and three men issued "The Effeminist Manifesto" (Dansky, Knoebel, & Pitchford, 1977).

The effeminists pointed to the possibilities for a liberated masculinity offered by feminism. Effeminism, they argued, is a positive political position, aligning anti-sexist gay men with women, instead of claiming male privilege by asserting their difference from women. Since, as Dansky et al. (1977) argued, male supremacy is the root of all other oppressions, the only politically defensible position was to renounce manhood itself, to refuse privilege. Dansky and his effeminist colleagues were as critical of mainstream gay male culture (and the denigration of effeminacy by the normifiers) as by the hegemomnic dominant culture.

. . .

Working-Class Men

Working class men are, perhaps, an interesting reference group when compared to disabled men and gay men. The way(s) in which they are discriminated against or stigmatized seem very different. These men, in fact, are often seen as incredibly masculine; strong, stoic, hard-workers, there is something particularly masculine about what they have to do day-in and day-out. Indeed, the masculine virtues of the working class are celebrated as the physical embodiment of what all men should embrace (Gagnon & Simon, 1973; Sanders & Mahalingam, 2012).

Working-class White males may work in a system of male privilege, but they are not the main beneficiaries; they are in fact expendable. The working class is set apart from the middle and upper classes in that the working class is defined by jobs that require less formal education, sometimes (not always) less skill, and often low pay. For men, these jobs often include manual labor such as construction, automotive work, or factory work. The jobs these men hold are typically men-dominant.

If the stereotypic construction of masculinity among the working class celebrates their physical virtues, it also problematizes their masculinity by imagining them as dumb brutes. Working class men are the male equivalent of the "dumb blonde"—endowed with physical virtues, but problematized by intellectual shortcomings. Minstrelizing might be the sort of self-effacing comments such as "I'm just a working stiff." It can be a minstrelizing strategy of low-level resistance because these behaviors actually let the working class man off the hook when it comes to accountability or responsibility. He exempts himself from scrutiny because he clearly isn't capable of such deep analytic thought.

. . .

Here is a sociological example of minstrelizing. In their classic work, *The Hidden Injuries of Class,* Sennett and Cobb (1993) document a difference between working class and middle class men as they view the relationships between fathers and sons. Middle class men see themselves as role models, Sennett and Cobb found. They want their sons to grow up to be "just like me." Such a posture requires a certain accountability and probity on the part of the middle-class father. Being a role model is a responsibility.

However, by contrast, the working class fathers saw themselves as negative role models.

"If you grow up to be like me," they said, "I'll feel like a failure." "Don't make the same mistakes I made." Or, as one of the essay's authors own father used to say all the time: "If a son does not surpass his father then both are failures." Such sentiments remove responsibility and actually place the onus for acting responsibly on the son, not the father. It's too late for me, but not for thee. Thus, working class men, by conforming to the dumb brute stereotype, offer a modest resistance to the dominant mode of masculinity as upwardly mobile striver. Giving up can also imply not actually giving in.

Of course, there are elements of militant chauvinism in the proclamation of those stereotypes as well. For men in these positions, sexism and patriarchy are key features of their masculine dominance. When the work force is decidedly all or mostly male, relationships are often "built through a decidedly male idiom of physical jousting, sexual boasting, sports talk, and shared sexual activities" (Freeman, 1993). Here, what is key for men is how they can effectively "compensate" for being underlings in the eyes of the managers that rule over them and the families they go home to. Using physical endurance and tolerance of discomfort, required by their manual labor, they signify a truer masculinity than even their office-working bosses can embody. They somehow signify a truer masculinity than their effeminate, "yes-men," paper-pushing managers can lay claim to (Collinson, 1992).

Moreover, those in the working, or blue-collar class, form a network of relationships with other blue-collar workers that serves to support them and give them a sense of status and worth, regardless of actual status or worth in the outside world (Cohen & Hodges, 1963). In fact, because those in the working class cannot normally exercise a great amount of power in their jobs or in many other formal relationships, they tend to do so in their relationships with other working class members. "To a greater extent than other classes, [the lower—lower class] will tend to measure status by power, and to validate his own claim to status, where he feels entitled to it, by asserting a claim to power" (Cohen & Hodges, 1963).

However, for those who want to minimize the apparent differences between them and the more dominant masculine ideal, a site of normification could be the focus on all men's general relationship to women and the family. Those involved in the union movement, for example, stake claims to manhood and masculinity by organizing around the principal of men as breadwinners. The basic job that all "real men" should share is to provide for their wives and children. This would explain the initial opposition to women's entry into the workplace, and also now the opposition to gay men's and lesbian women's entrance. There is a type of White, male, working-class solidarity vis-à-vis privilege that these men have constructed and maintained, that promotes and perpetuates racism, sexism, and homophobia—the nexus of beliefs that all men are supposed to value (Embrick, Walther, & Wickens, 2007).

This power in the workplace translates directly to the home, as well. In the absence of legitimated hierarchical benefits and status, working class husbands and partners are more likely to "produce hypermasculinity by relying on blatant, brutal, and relentless power strategies in their marriages, including spousal abuse" (Pyke, 1996). However, violence can also extend outside the home. As Pyke (1996) points out, "The hypermasculinity found in certain lower-status male locales, such as on shop floors, in pool halls, motorcycle clubs, and urban gangs, can be understood as both a response to ascendant masculinity and its unintentional booster." Willis (1977) details how working class boys refuse to submit to the "upper-class" imperatives of social mobility, knowledge and skill acquisition; instead choosing to reproduce themselves as working class, despite the social and financial consequences. These students become agentic, rebellious even; but in doing so also become "uneducated" workers of manual labor.

CONCLUSION

Privilege is not monolithic; it is unevenly distributed and it exists worldwide in varying forms and contexts. Among members of one privileged class, other mechanisms of marginalization may mute or reduce privilege based on another status. Thus, a White gay man might receive race and gender privilege, but will be marginalized by sexuality. In this paper, we described these processes for three groups of men in the United States—men with disabilities, gay men, and working class men—who see their gender privilege reduced and their masculinity questioned, not confirmed, through their other marginalized status. We described strategies these men might use to restore, retrieve, or resist that loss. Using Goffman's discussion of stigma, we described three patterns of response. It is through these strategies—minsterlization, normification, and militant chauvinism—that a person's attempt to access privilege can be viewed, and, we argue, that we can better see the standards, ideals, and norms by which any society measures a man and his masculinity, and the benefits or consequences of his adherence or deviance.

REFERENCES

Astrachan, A. (1993). Dividing lines: Experiencing race, class, and gender In the United States. In M. S. Kimmel & M. A. Messner (Eds.), *Men's lives* (pp. 63–73). New York, NY: Macmillan.

Badinter, E. (1992). *XY. De l'Identite Masculine.* Paris: Odile.

Begum, N. (1992). Disabled women and the feminist agenda. *Feminist Review, 40,* 70–84.

Bieber, I. (1965). Clinical aspects of male homosexuality. In J. Marmor (Ed.), *Sexual inversion: The multiple roots of homosexuality* (pp. 248–267). New York, NY: Basic Books.

Blashill, A. J., & Powlishta, K. K. (2009). The impact of sexual orientation and gender role on evaluations of men. *Psychology of Men & Masculinity, 10*(2), 160. doi: 10.1037/a0014583

Cheng, C. (2008). Marginalized masculinities and hegemonic masculinity: An introduction. *The Journal of Men's Studies, 7*(3), 295–315.

Cohen, A. K., & Hodges Jr., H. M. (1963). Characteristics of the lower-blue-collar-class. *Social Problems, 10*(4), 303–334.

Collinson, D. (1992). Managing the shopfloor: Subjectivity, masculinity, and workplace culture. New York, NY: Walter de Gruyter.

Connell, R. W. (1995). *Masculinities.* Berkeley: University of California Press.

Dansky, S., Knoebel, J., & Pitchford, K. (1977). The effeminist manifesto. In J. Snodgrass (Ed.), *A book of readings: For men against sexism* (pp. 116–120). Albion, CA: Times Change Press.

Earle, S. (2001). Disability, facilitated sex and the role of the nurse. *Journal of Advanced Nursing, 36*(3), 433–440. doi: 10.1046/j.1365-2648.2001.01991.x.

Edwards, T. (1994). Erotics & politics: Gay male sexuality, masculinity, and feminism. New York, NY: Routledge.

Embrick, D. G., Walther, C. S., & Wickens, C. M. (2007). Working class masculinity: Keeping gay men and lesbians out of the workplace. *Sex roles, 56*(11), 757–766.

Fingerhut, A. W., Riggle, E. D. B., & Rostosky, S. S. (2011). Same-sex marriage: The social and psychological implications of policy and debates. *Journal of Social Issues, 67*(2), 225–241.

Freeman, J. B. (1993). Hardhats: Construction workers, manliness, and the 1970 pro-war demonstrations. *Journal of Social History, 26*(4), 725–744. Retrieved from http://www.jstor.org.libproxy.cc.stonybrook.edu/stable/pdfplus/3788778.pdf.

Gagnon, J. H., & Simon, W. (1973). *Sexual conduct: The social origins of human sexuality.* Chicago, IL: Aldine.

Gerschick, T. J., & Miller, A. S. (1995). Coming to terms: Masculinity and physical disability. In D. Sabo & D. F. Gordon (Eds.), *Men's health and illness: Gender, power, and the body, Research on men and masculinities series* (Vol. 8, pp. 183–204). Thousand Oaks, CA: Sage Publications.

Goffman, E. (1963). *Stigma.* Engelwood Cliffs: Prentice-Hall.

Goodwin, J. P. (1989). More man than you'll ever be: Gay folklore and acculturation in middle America. Indiana: Indiana University Press.

Jeffreys, S. (2008). Disability and the male sex right. *Women's Studies International Forum, 31*(5), 327–335. doi: 10.1016/j.wsif.2008.08.001.

Kardiner, A. (1963). The flight from masculinity. In H. M. Ruisenbeck (Ed.), *The problem of homosexuality in modern society* (pp. 17–39). New York, NY: Dutton.

Lehne, G. K. (1989). Homophobia among men: Supporting and defining the male role. In M. Kimmel & M. Messner (Eds.), *Men's lives* (pp. 416–429). New York, NY: Macmillan.

Levine, M. (1992). The status of gay men in the workplace. In M. Kimmel & M. Messner (Eds.), *Men's Lives.* Boston: Allyn and Bacon.

Levine, M. (1995). *Gay Macho.* New York: New York University Press.

Levitt, E. E., & Klassen, A. D. (1976). Public attitudes toward homosexuality. *Journal of Homosexuality, 1*(1), 29–43. doi: 10.1300/J082v01n01_03.

McIntosh, P. (1988). White privilege and male privilege: A personal account of coming to see correspondences through work in women's studies. Working Paper no. 189. Wellesley, MA: Wellesley College Center for Research on Women.

Messner, M. A. (1997). Politics of masculinities: Men in movements. New York, NY: Sage.

Mitchell, R. W., & Ellis, A. L. (2011). In the eye of the beholder: Knowledge that a man is gay promotes American college students' attributions of cross-gender characteristics. *Sexuality & Culture, 15*(1), 80–100.

Ovesey, L., & Person, E. (1973). Gender identity and sexual psychopathology in men: A psychodynamic analysis of homosexuality, transsexualism, and transvestism. *Journal of the American Academy of Psychoanalysis and Dynamic Psychiatry, 1*(1), 53–72.

Pratto, F., & Stewart, A. L. (2012). Group Dominance and the Half-Blindness of Privilege. *Journal of Social Issues, 68*(1), 28–45. doi: 10.1111/j.1540-4560.2011.01734.x.

Pronger, B. (1990). Gay jocks: A phenomenology of gay men in athletics. *Sport, men, and the gender order: Critical feminist perspectives,* 141–152.

Pyke, K. D. (1996). Class-based masculinities: The interdependence of gender, class, and interpersonal power. *Gender and Society, 10*(5), 527–549.

Rich, A. (1980). Compulsory heterosexuality and lesbian existence. *Signs, 5*(4), 631–660.

Sanders, M. R., & Mahalingam, R. (2012). Under the radar: The role of invisible discourse in understanding class-based privilege. *Journal of Social Issues, 68*(1), 112–127. doi: 10.1111/j.1540-4560.2011.01739.x.

Schwartz, L. (2008). *For one night only.* Melbourne: The Age.

Sennett, R., & Cobb, J. (1993). *The hidden injuries of class.* New York, NY: WW Norton.

Skrhak, K. S. (2008). CSI's Robert David Hall is still standing. *Success Magazine.* Retrieved from http://www.successmagazine.com/csi-robert-david-hall-is-still-standing/PARAMS/article/1134/channel/22 retrieved on October 11, 2011.

Socarides, C. W. (1968). A provisional theory of aetiology in male homosexuality—a case of preoedipal origin. *International Journal of Psycho-Analysis, 49,* 27–37.

Stoltenberg, J. (1989). *Refusing to be a man.* Portland, OR: Breitenbush Books.

Taywaditep, K. J. (2001). Marginalization among the marginalized: gay men's anti-effeminacy attitudes. *Journal of Homosexuality, 42*(1), 1–28.

West, C., & Fenstermaker, S. (1995). Doing difference. *Gender & Society, 9*(1), 8–37.

West, C., & Zimmerman, D. (1987). Doing gender. *Gender and Society, 1*(2), 125–151.

Willis, P. E. (1977). Learning to labor: How working class kids get working class jobs. New York, NY: Columbia University Press.

Woods, J. (2010). The black male privileges checklist. In M. Kimmel & A. L. Ferber (Eds.), *Privilege: A Reader,* (2nd ed., pp. 27–37). Boulder, CO: Westview Press.

Wright, S. L., & Canetto, S. (2009). Stereotypes of older lesbians and gay men. *Educational Gerontology, 35*(5), 424–452. doi: 10.1080/03601270802505640.

Wylie, S. A., Corliss, H. L., Boulanger. V., Prokop. L. A., & Austin, S. B. (2010). Socially assigned gender nonconformity: A brief measure for use in surveillance and investigation of health disparities. *Sex roles,* 1–13.

3 • *Leila J. Rupp*

TOWARD A GLOBAL HISTORY OF SAME-SEX SEXUALITY

DISCUSSION QUESTIONS

1. Why is it so difficult to identify a term such as "gay" or "same-sex sexuality" that can be employed in historical and anthropological research?
2. Identify some of the factors that have been most salient in other times and places in structuring sexual relationships and desires.

Originally published as the article "Toward a Global History of Same-Sex Sexuality," by Leila Rupp, from *Journal of the History of Sexuality,* Volume 10, Issue 2, pp. 287–302. Copyright © by the University of Texas Press. All rights reserved. Used by permission.

3. Rupp poses the provocative question: "How can we know for sure what is a sexual act?" Does your answer to this question change after reading this chapter?
4. How does even a cursory review of the construction of sexuality in various different cultures throughout history help us to better understand our own?

The blossoming of research on a wide range of manifestations of same-sex sexuality calls for an attempt at global thinking. Although my own work is rooted in U.S. and European history, I would like to make use of the work of scholars focusing on different parts of the world to reflect on what patterns might emerge. I take up this task from the perspective of one firmly committed to a social constructionist perspective on sexuality. Thus, I recognize that making transhistorical comparisons can be a risky business. Nevertheless, I think we can learn something by thinking about same-sex sexuality from a global viewpoint.

I favor the term "same-sex sexuality" as one that gets beyond the use of terms such as "queer," "gay," "lesbian," or "homosexual." Yet I would like to proceed by looking at manifestations of what we call "same-sex sexuality" in different times and places both to explore global patterns and to consider how those patterns make the two parts of the term "same-sex sexuality" problematic. That is, sometimes such manifestations cannot really be considered "same-sex," and sometimes they should not really be labeled "sexuality." These complications suggest that even the attempt to avoid assumptions about the meanings of desires, acts, and relationships by using a term such as "same-sex sexuality" may inadvertently lump together phenomena that are quite different. This is the difficulty of thinking about a global history of same-sex sexuality.

There are various ways that sexual acts involving two genitally alike bodies may in fact not be best conceptualized as "same-sex." In some cases, what is more important than genital similarity is the fact of some kind of difference: age difference, class difference, gender difference. As numerous scholars have pointed out, across time and space those differences

have in more cases than not structured what we call same-sex acts in ways that are far more important to the people involved and to the societies in which they lived than the mere fact of the touching of similar bodies.[1] (My favorite way to explain this to my students is through the story of my colleague's five-year-old son, who was one day playing with the family dog and a girl from his school. The girl said, "I love Lily [the dog] so much I wish I could marry her. But I can't because she's a girl." My colleague's son, viewing the relevant categories in a different way, responded, "That's not the reason you can't marry Lily. You can't marry Lily because she's a dog!") Looking at the whole question of sameness and difference from an entirely different angle, Jens Rydström's work on homosexuality and bestiality in rural Sweden reminds us that these two categories of deviant acts were not conceptually distinct in the past.[2] Thus, the lines between same-sex and different-species acts were not clearly drawn.

To start, probably the most familiar example is from ancient Athenian society where age difference between older and younger men determined the ways they engaged in sex acts, and such relationships had educative functions that were as much the point as the sex. Furthermore (although this is a bit controversial), the lack of an age or other differential was considered deviant, while same-sex and different-age (or different-status) relationships were not. Adult male citizens of Athens could penetrate social inferiors, including women, boys, foreigners, and slaves.[3] The privilege of elite men to penetrate anyone other than their equals lingered on into early modern Europe. "Missing my whore, I bugger my page," wrote the Earl of Rochester in Restoration England.[4] Were such men "bisexual," or was the whole notion of sexual object choice irrelevant? Was this "same-sex

sex"? Or are such relations or acts best described as "different-status sex"?

We find examples of age differences structuring sexual acts in other parts of the world as well. In seventeenth-century Japan, men expected to desire sexual relations with both women and boys.[5] Two different words described love of women and love of boys. Styles of dress and distinct haircuts differentiated youths from men, thus creating visible categories of difference based on age. When a youth became a man, ceremonially donning the proper garment and having his forelocks shaved, he would cease his role as the anally penetrated partner and take on the adult male penetrator role in a new relationship.

Yet age itself could become a socially constructed category. That is, although it was a violation of the norms, men might keep the boy role well past youth. In *The Great Mirror of Male Love*, a collection of short stories published in Japan in 1687, "Two Old Cherry Trees Still in Bloom" tells of two samurai lovers in their sixties who had first met when one was sixteen and the other nineteen. "Han'emon still thought of Mondo as a boy of sixteen. Though his hair was thinning and had turned completely white, Mondo sprinkled it with 'Blossom Dew' hair oil and bound it up in a double-folded topknot anyway.... There was no sign that he had ever shaved his temples; he still had the rounded hairline he was born with."[6] John Boswell, who vehemently denied that age difference structured male same-sex relations in ancient Athens and the Roman Empire, suggests that the term "boy" might simply mean "beautiful man" or one who was beloved.[7] Boswell took this to signify that age difference was irrelevant, but it is also possible that this means, as in Japan, that age difference was crucial but that the concept of age might be only loosely tied, or not tied at all, to the number of years a person had lived.

In some societies, transgenerational same-sex relations are thoroughly institutionalized. We know the most about a number of cultures in New Guinea in which boys cannot grow into men without incorporating the semen of older men into their bodies, either through oral sex, anal sex, or simply smearing

it on the skin.[8] Such "boy-inseminating rituals" transmit life-giving semen, which produces masculinity and a warrior personality. What is critical here is that all boys take part in the ritual, and once they become men (sometimes through marriage, sometimes through fathering a child), they take on the adult role. Different cultures prescribe different lengths of time for such same-sex relations, different rules for which men should penetrate which boys (sometimes a mother's brother, sometimes a sister's husband), and different ways to transmit the semen.

Note that almost all of the information we have about age-differentiated relationships is about men. . . . Perhaps . . . comparable is a ritual among the Baruya in Melanesia in which lactating mothers nourish young girls who are not their own daughters by offering a breast, believing that breast milk is produced from men's semen and thus essential to womanhood.[9] A young girl at the breast, however, is reminiscent of motherhood, while a boy enclosing a penis has nothing to do with traditional men's roles. A more convincing, if still very sketchy, example can be found in Big Nambas society in the New Hebrides, where higher-ranking women took younger girls as sexual partners.[10]

The point here, of course, is that our construction of these interactions as same-sex may be totally foreign to the people involved. That is even more true for transgenderal relations, which can be found in a variety of cultures throughout history and around the globe. For a number of reasons—spiritual, political, economic, social, cultural—individuals take on (or are forced to take on) the social role, dress, and other markers of the (here our language fails us) "other" sex. Sexual relations may then occur between biological males of female gender and biological males of male gender, or biological females of male gender and biological females of female gender. (Here again, our language describes just two genders where other cultures may see three or more.) Such "gender-transformed relationships" can be found in many parts of the world.

We know the most about transgenderal relations among North American native peoples. The term "berdache," a derogatory French word bestowed by the horrified European invaders, emphasized the sexual aspects of the role, but in fact the spiritual characteristics of what some scholars now call the "two-spirit person" were sometimes more important.[11] The male transgendered role could be found in over a hundred American Indian tribes, the female in about thirty.[12] Among the Mohave Indians in the western United States, both male (*alyha*) and female (*hwame*) two-spirit roles existed. A two-spirit male would take a female name, engage in female occupations, and even enact menstruation and childbirth. "Manly-hearted women" would take on male characteristics and have children with their wives through adoption. Men—women sought orgasm through anal sex, while women-men engaged in tribadism or genital rubbing, with the two-spirit on top.[13]

Third-gender roles also existed in a number of Polynesian societies. From the late eighteenth century, European explorers and missionaries commented on men dressed as women who were sexually involved with men in Tahiti. *Mahus*, as they are known, according to an English missionary, "chose this vile way of life when young; putting on the dress of a woman they follow the same employments, are under the same prohibitions with respect to food, etc., and seek the courtship of men as women do, nay are more jealous of the men who cohabit with them, and always refuse to sleep with women."[14] More recently, *mahus* tend to be effeminate and interested in women's household tasks but do not dress entirely as women. They seek oral sex with men, who may ridicule them in public but also seek them out for fellatio.

Other examples of transgenderal relations involve transformation of the body in some way. The *hijras* of India are defined by their sexual impotence with women.[15] Some are born hermaphrodites, but others simply lack desire for women and as a result undergo the surgical removal of their male genitals. They wear women's clothes and hairstyles, imitate women's walk and talk, and prefer male sexual partners. But they also exaggerate femininity and exhibit an aggressive sexuality that is unlike that of Indian women. They also have religious and ceremonial functions, performing at marriages and the birth of male children and serving as servants of Matar, the Mother goddess, at her temples. This is not to say that this is a high-status role in Indian society, for the *hijras* are much despised.

Not all cases of transgenderal relations have spiritual or religious origins or implications. The *travestis* of Brazil are transgendered prostitutes who, beginning at a young age, take female names and wear women's clothes as a result of their desire to attract men.[16] Although they do not, like the *hijras*, remove their genitals, they do take female hormones and inject silicone in order to enlarge their buttocks, thighs, and breasts. They work as prostitutes, attracting men who define themselves as resolutely heterosexual.

In the case of women who passed as men in early modern Europe, the motivation may have been a desire for occupational or literal mobility, although this is undoubtedly something we will never know for sure.[17] Women who dressed in men's clothing in order to join the army or take a man's job had to impersonate men in all ways, including in their relations with women. When discovered, punishment could be swift and severe for the usurpation of male privilege, particularly if it involved the use of what were called "material instruments" to "counterfeit the office of a husband," as a 1566 case put it.[18] In Germany in the early eighteenth century, a woman named Catharine Margaretha Linck dressed as a man, served in the army, and, after discharge, worked as a cotton dyer. She married a woman who, following a quarrel, confessed to her mother that her husband was not what he seemed. When the outraged mother took Linck to court and produced what another trial transcript in a similar case described as "the illicit inventions she used to supplement the shortcomings of her sex," Linck was sentenced to death for her crimes.[19] Were women who risked death looking only for better job prospects, or were these gender-crossers what we would today consider transgendered?

The connection between women's cross-dressing and same-sex desire becomes tighter over time.

Lisa Duggan, in her analysis of the case of Alice Mitchell, a nineteen-year-old Memphis woman who murdered the girl she loved when their plans to elope came to naught, ties together the threads of romantic friendship, gender transgression, and the emerging definitions of lesbianism.[20] Jennifer Robertson's pathbreaking work on cross-dressing women in the Japanese Takarazuka Revue, founded in 1913, does much the same thing in a very different context. Exploring a rash of lesbian double suicides in Japan in the 1930s, Robertson details the erotics of fandom inspired by the Revue.[21] Like Duggan and Robertson, Lucy Chesser, in her dissertation on cross-dressing in Australia, shows the development over time of the idea that cross-dressing had something to do with same-sex desire.[22]

The point of all these examples is, once again, that sexual relations between two genitally alike (or originally alike) bodies are in many cases better defined as different-gender than same-sex relations. This seems clear in the case of two-spirit people or the *hijras* or *travestis*, but as the spectrum of transgendered relations moves from those who alter their bodies to those who simply take on some characteristics traditionally associated with the other/another gender, the lines get blurry. What about the "mollies" of eighteenth-century London? Like men in subcultures in other large European cities, including Paris and Amsterdam, "mollies" were effeminate men who frequented taverns, parks, and public latrines; sought out male sexual partners; and shared a style of feminine dress and behavior.[23] An agent of the English Societies for the Reformation of Manners entered a London club in 1714 and found men "calling one another my dear, hugging and kissing, tickling and feeling each other, as if they were a mixture of wanton males and females; and assuming effeminate voices, female airs."[24] What about the "roaring girls" of London or the "randy women" of Amsterdam, cross-dressed but not entirely? Mary Frith, known by her pseudonym, Moll Cutpurse, the model for a number of early-seventeenth-century English accounts, struck one observer as "both man and woman."[25] Examples of gender-differentiated

pairings—the *bichas* (faggots) and *bofes* (real men) of Brazil, the *jotas* (homosexuals) and *mayates* (men who have sex with *jotas*) of Mexico City, the butches and fems of 1950s American bar culture, the "mine wives" and "husbands" of South Africa—can be found in many parts of the world, and how much they are perceived within their own cultures as different-gender and how much as same-sex is a tricky question.[26]

In the narrowest sense, then, "same-sex sexuality" may best refer to modern Western notions of relations between individuals undifferentiated by gender, age, class, or any other factors—in other words, those (or some of those) who adopt a "gay" or "lesbian" identity. That is an irony of a term designed to do just the opposite.

The second part of my critique of the term "same-sex sexuality" is already implicit here. That is, how do we determine what is "sexuality" and what is something else in these different interactions? Scholars have argued that "sexuality" itself is a relatively modern concept, that, for example, acts of fellatio or anal penetration in ancient Athens were expressions of power, acts of domination and submission, not "sexuality."[27] In the case of the Sambia boys in New Guinea who ingest semen through acts of fellatio on older men, we can ask, "Is that a sexual act? Or akin to taking vitamins?" Is it significant that the boys swallow the semen directly from a penis rather than from a bowl with a spoon?[28]

How can we know for sure what is a sexual act? There are really two questions here. How do we think about acts—such as fellatio, cunnilingus, anal penetration—that seem clearly sexual yet may have other meanings? What do we make of acts—such as kissing, hugging, cuddling—that may or may not be considered "sex"? These questions in turn raise a third: Are certain acts associated with specific forms of relationships?

We have already considered the possibility that fellatio and a girl's mouth on the breast of a woman not her mother may be about a kind of spiritual nutrition rather than sexuality; and even that a whole range of acts might be the assertion of elite male privilege, a sign of power. Some scholars argue that particular acts—especially anal penetration—carry meanings that are far more about power than sex and did so even before the advent of the concept "sexuality." Richard Trexler, for example, interprets the cross-gender male role in the Americas at the time of conquest as just another form of a long-lasting practice of men dominating other men by raping them, either literally or symbolically.[29] Eva Keuls, in her study of sexual politics in ancient Athens, argues that anal intercourse was an "initiatory rite of submission to the desires of the established class," an assertion of superiority rather than a source of pleasure. Agreeing with Trexler, Keuls asserts that "anal sex is charged with aggression and domination: The submitting partner is in a helpless position, penetration can be painful, and opportunity for the gratification of the passive participant is limited."[30] If these are accurate conclusions (and I know that a chorus of voices will be raised to shout that they are not!), can we think of such interactions as "same-sex sexuality" at all, or are they, rather, "same-sex domination"?

What about societies that make room for loving relations that seem sexual to outsiders but not to the participants? In Basotho society in contemporary Lesotho, girls and women exchange long kisses, putting their tongues in each others' mouths; they fondle each other and endeavor to lengthen the labia minora; they rub their bodies together and engage in cunnilingus without defining any of this as sexual. They fall in love and form marriage-like unions. In this context sex requires a penis and marriage means sex with a man, so there is no such concept as lesbian sex or lesbian relationships.[31] Are these sexual acts? . . .

Although I am bold enough to dare to address a global history of same-sex sexuality, I am not foolish enough to pretend to have answers to all of these questions. As the Euramerican nature of most of the evidence I use to consider the nature of sexual acts makes plain, we (or, certainly, I) do not know enough about such questions in other parts of the world to say anything even suggestive. But I do think these are good questions for future research.

NOTES

1. Stephen O. Murray, "Homosexual Categorization in Cross-Cultural Perspective," in *Latin American Male Homosexualities*, ed. Stephen O. Murray (Albuquerque: University of New Mexico Press, 1995), 3–32, cites a number of schemes for the social structuring of homosexuality and adopts that of Barry Adam, "Age, Structure, and Sexuality," *Journal of Homosexuality* 11 (1986): 19–33. This includes age-structured, gender-defined, profession-defined, and egalitarian. In Murray's most recent book, *Homosexualities* (Chicago: University of Chicago Press, 2000), he includes "profession-defined" under "gender-defined." John Howard, in his comment on the paper I delivered at Oslo, added race and ethnicity to this list, citing Nayan Shah's work on Indian and Chinese men arrested in British Columbia for their sexual relations with Anglo-Canadian men, along with his own work on African American and white same-sex interactions in the U.S. South. See Nayan Shah, "The Race of Sodomy: Asian Men, White Boys, and the Policing of Sex in North America" (paper presented at the Organization of American Historians conference, St. Louis, April 2000); John Howard, *Men Like That: A Southern Queer History* (Chicago: University of Chicago Press, 1999).

2. Jens Rydström, "Beasts and Beauties: Bestiality and Male Homosexuality in Rural Sweden, 1880–1950" (paper presented at the 19th International Congress of Historical Sciences, Oslo, Norway, August 2000).

3. The classic work is K. J. Dover, *Greek Homosexuality* (New York: Vintage, 1978). More recent studies include Eva C. Keuls, *The Reign of the Phallus: Sexual Politics in Ancient Athens* (New York: Harper and Row, 1985); David Halperin, *One Hundred Years of Homosexuality and Other Essays on Greek Love* (New York: Routledge, 1990); Eva Cantarella, *Bisexuality in the Ancient World* (New Haven, CT: Yale University Press, 1992); and Wayne R. Dynes and Stephen Donaldson, eds., *Homosexuality in the Ancient World* (New York: Garland, 1992). See also Craig A. Williams, *Roman Homosexuality: Ideologies of Masculinity in Classical Antiquity* (New York: Oxford University Press, 1999). John Boswell, "Revolutions, Universals, and Sexual Categories," in *Hidden From History: Reclaiming the Gay and Lesbian Past*, ed. Martin Bauml Duberman, Martha Vicinus, and George Chauncey, Jr. (New York: New American Library, 1989), 17–36, disputes the notion that an age or status difference was essential to same-sex relations in Athenian society, and, more recently, Murray, in

Homosexualities, has argued that undifferentiated (what he calls "egalitarian") relationships between men existed in ancient Greece and Rome (as well as in other premodern places) and that age difference did not always determine sexual role.

4. Quoted in James M. Saslow, "Homosexuality in the Renaissance: Behavior, Identity, and Artistic Expression," in *Hidden From History*, 90–105, quotation on 92. See Alan Bray, *Homosexuality in Renaissance England* (New York: Columbia University Press, 1982); Michael Rocke, *Forbidden Friendships: Homosexuality and Male Culture in Renaissance Florence* (New York: Oxford University Press, 1996); Louise Fradenburg and Carla Freccero, eds., *Premodern Sexualities* (New York: Routledge, 1996); Carolyn Dinshaw, *Getting Medieval: Sexualities and Communities, Pre- and Postmodern* (Durham, NC: Duke University Press, 1999); James M. Saslow, *Pictures and Passions: A History of Homosexuality in the Visual Arts* (New York: Viking, 1999); Glenn Burger and Steven F. Kruger, eds., *Queering the Middle Ages* (Minneapolis: University of Minnesota Press, 2001).

5. Paul Gordon Schalow, ed., *The Great Mirror of Male Love* (Stanford, CA: Stanford University Press, 1990); Stephen O. Murray, "Male Homosexuality in Japan before the Meiji Restoration," in *Oceanic Homosexualities*, ed. Stephen O. Murray (New York: Garland, 1992), 363–70; Gary P. Leupp, *Male Colors: The Construction of Homosexuality in Tokugawa Japan* (Berkeley: University of California Press, 1995).

6. Quoted in Paul Gordon Schalow, "Male Love in Early Modern Japan: A Literary Depiction of the 'Youth,'" in *Hidden from History*, 118–28, quotation on 126.

7. John Boswell, *Christianity, Social Tolerance, and Homosexuality* (Chicago: University of Chicago Press, 1980), 28–30.

8. David F. Greenberg, *The Construction of Homosexuality* (Chicago: University of Chicago Press, 1988), 26–40; Gilbert Herdt, *Same Sex, Different Cultures* (Boulder, CO: Westview Press, 1997), 64–88; Murray, *Oceanic Homosexualities*.

9. Greenberg, *Construction of Homosexuality*, 29.

10. Herdt, *Same-Sex, Different Cultures*, 86.

11. Herdt, *Same-Sex, Different Cultures*, 90–102; Walter L. Williams, *The Spirit and the Flesh: Sexual Diversity in American Indian Culture* (Boston: Beacon Press, 1986); Sue-Ellen Jacobs, Wesley Thomas, and Sabine Lang, eds., *Two-Spirit People: Native American Gender Identity, Sexuality, and Spirituality* (Urbana: University of Illinois Press, 1997). There is disagreement about the status of transgendered individuals in the Americas. For a contrary view to those cited above, see Richard C.

Trexler, *Sex and Conquest: Gendered Violence, Political Order, and the European Conquest of the Americas* (Ithaca, NY: Cornell University Press, 1995).

12. Herdt, *Same Sex, Different Cultures*, 91.

13. Herdt, *Same Sex, Different Cultures*, 92–94.

14. Quoted in Greenberg, *Construction of Homosexuality*, 58. See also Raleigh Watts, "The Polynesian Mahu," in Murray, *Oceanic Homosexualities*, 171–84.

15. Serena Nanda, "Hijras: An Alternative Sex and Gender Role in India," in *Third Sex, Third Gender: Beyond Sexual Dimorphism in Culture and History*, ed. Gilbert Herdt (New York: Zone Books, 1996), 373–417.

16. Don Kulick, *Travesti: Sex, Gender and Culture among Brazilian Transgendered Prostitutes* (Chicago: University of Chicago Press, 1998).

17. Rudolf M. Dekker and Lotte C. van de Pol, *The Tradition of Female Transvestism in Early Modern Europe* (London: Macmillan Press, 1989).

18. Quoted in Lillian Faderman, *Surpassing the Love of Men* (New York: William Morrow, 1981), 51.

19. Faderman, *Surpassing the Love of Men*, 51–52.

20. Lisa Duggan, *Sapphic Slashers: Sex, Violence, and American Modernity* (Durham, NC: Duke University Press, 2001).

21. Jennifer Robertson, *Takarazuka: Sexual Politics and Popular Culture in Modern Japan* (Berkeley: University of California Press, 1998); Jennifer Robertson, "Dying to Tell: Sexuality and Suicide in Imperial Japan," *Signs: Journal of Women in Culture and Society* 25: 1–36 (1999).

22. Lucy Sarah Chesser, "'Parting with My Sex for a Season': Cross-Dressing, Inversion and Sexuality in Australian Cultural Life, 1850–1920," (Ph.D. diss., La Trobe University, 2001). See also Lucy Chesser, "'A Woman Who Married Three Wives': Management of Disruptive Knowledge in the 1879 Australian Case of Edward De Lacy Evans," *Journal of Women's History* 9:53–77 (winter 1998).

23. Rictor Norton, *Mother Clap's Molly House: The Gay Subculture in England 1700–1830* (London: GMP Publishers, 1992); Michael Rey, "Parisian Homosexuals Create a Lifestyle, 1700–1750: The Police Archives," *Eighteenth-Century Life* 9, new series 3: 179–91 (1985); Jeffrey Merrick, "Sodomitical Scandals and Subcultures in the 1720s," *Men and Masculinities* 1:365–84 (April 1999); Arend H. Huussen, Jr., "Sodomy in the Dutch Republic during the Eighteenth Century," *Unauthorized Sexual Behavior during the Enlightenment*, ed. Robert P. Maccubbin (Williamsburg, VA: College of William and Mary Press, 1985), 169–78.

24. Randolph Trumbach, "The Birth of the Queen: Sodomy and the Emergence of Gender Equality in Modern Culture, 1660–1750," in *Hidden from History*,

129–40, quotation on 137. See also Randolph Trumbach, *Sex and the Gender Revolution: Heterosexuality and the Third Gender in Enlightenment London* (Chicago: University of Chicago Press, 1998).

25. Quoted in Faderman, *Surpassing the Love of Men*, 57. "Randy women" is a rough translation of *lollepotten*, a term analyzed by Myriam Everard in "Ziel en zinnen: Over liefde en lust tussen vrouwen in de tweede helft van de achttiende eeuw" (Ph.D. diss., Rijksuniversiteit Leiden, 1994).

26. See James N. Green, *Beyond Carnival: Male Homosexuality in Twentieth-Century Brazil* (Chicago: University of Chicago Press, 1999); Annick Prieur, *Mema's House, Mexico City: On Transvestites, Queens, and Machos* (Chicago: University of Chicago Press, 1998); Elizabeth Lapovsky Kennedy and Madeline D. Davis, *Boots of Leather, Slippers of Gold: The History of a Lesbian Community* (New York: Routledge, 1993); Stephen O. Murray and Will Roscoe, eds., *Boy-Wives and Female Husbands: Studies of African Homosexualities* (New York: St. Martin's, 1998).

27. David M. Halperin, "Sex before Sexuality: Pederasty, Politics, and Power in Classical Athens," in *Hidden from History*, 37–53.

28. This is a point made by Carole S. Vance, "Social Construction Theory: Problems in the History of Sexuality," in *Which Homosexuality?*, ed. Dennis Altman et al. (Amsterdam: Dekker/Schorer, 1989), 13–34. Vance credits a student with the incisive question about the bowl and spoon. On a Sambia man who sought out fellatio with initiates, see Gilbert H. Herdt, "Semen Depletion and the Sense of Maleness," in Murray, *Oceanic Homosexualities*, 33–68.

29. Trexler, *Sex and Conquest*.

30. Keuls, *The Reign of the Phallus*, 276.

31. Kendall, "'When a Woman Loves a Woman' in Lesotho: Love, Sex, and the (Western) Construction of Homophobia," in Murray and Roscoe, *Boy-Wives and Female Husbands*, 223–41.

4 • *Chrys Ingraham*

HETEROSEXUALITY
It's Just Not Natural!

DISCUSSION QUESTIONS

1. How do *you* define heterosexuality? Why does Ingraham argue that it is a *social institution*? What are the implications of seeing heterosexuality as an institution?
2. Why did second-wave feminists link heterosexuality to women's oppression?
3. How does the heterosexual imaginary normalize heterosexuality?
4. Ingraham examines weddings as one site where the heterosexual imaginary is pervasive and obscures the various relations of power at work. What are some other locations we might examine?

Chrys Ingraham, "Heterosexuality: It's Just Not Natural!" from Handbook of Lesbian and Gay Studies, 2002. Reprinted by permission of Sage Publications Ltd.

Since I began teaching courses on gender and sexuality in the early 1980s, I've struggled with debates that claim that heterosexuality is both 'natural and normal'. As a sociologist, I frequently find such positions lacking in that they fail to attend to the social conditions upon which most things depend. In other words, the question is not whether (hetero)sexuality is natural. *All* aspects of our social world—natural or otherwise—are given meaning. The real issue is, how we give meaning to heterosexuality and what interests are served by these meanings? . . .

Historically, we have witnessed the scientific establishment determine which phenomena can be considered normal and natural only to turn around years later and say they were wrong or that their judgement was premature. Consider the instance of women's entry into higher education. At a time when white middle-class women entering higher education was frowned upon, nineteenth-century scientists discovered that women's reproductive organs would be harmed if they were exposed to a college education. And, in an historical moment when the notion of former slaves being equal to whites was not a popular notion, it was scientists who claimed that people of African descent had smaller brains than those of European lineage. In each case, scientists succumbed to the political interests of their time in formulating and interpreting research on such topics. As social conditions shifted, so too did scientific discovery. In each instance, scientists eventually overturned their previous findings in the face of overwhelming evidence to the contrary. . . .

Typically studied as a form of sexuality, heterosexuality is, in reality, a highly regulated, ritualized, and organized set of practices, e.g. weddings or proms. Sociologically, then, heterosexuality as an established order made up of rule-bound and standardized behavior patterns qualifies as an institution. Moreover, heterosexuality as an arrangement involving large numbers of people whose behavior is guided by norms and rules is also a *social* institution.

Heterosexuality is much more than a biological given or whether or not someone is attracted to someone of another sex. Rules on everything from who pays for the date or the wedding rehearsal dinner to who leads while dancing, drives the car, cooks dinner or initiates sex, all serve to regulate heterosexual practice. What circulates as a given in western societies is, in fact, a highly structured arrangement. As is the case with most institutions, people who participate in these practices must be *socialized* to do so. In other words, women were not born with a wedding gown gene or neo-natal craving for a diamond engagement ring! They were taught to want these things. Women didn't enter the world with a desire to practice something called dating or a desire to play with a 'My Size Bride Barbie', they were rewarded for desiring these things. Likewise, men did not exit the womb knowing they would one day buy a date a corsage or spend two months' income to buy an engagement ring. These are all products that have been sold to consumers interested in taking part in a culturally established ritual that works to organize and institutionalize heterosexuality and reward those who participate.

HETERONORMATIVITY

In the 1970s as second wave feminists attempted to theorize and understand the source of women's oppression, the notion of heterosexuality as normative emerged. In one of the earliest examples of this effort, The Purple September Staff, a Dutch group, published an article entitled 'The normative status of heterosexuality' (1975). They maintain that heterosexuality is really a normalized power arrangement that limits options and privileges men over women and reinforces and naturalizes male dominance. . . .

> Heterosexuality—as an ideology and as an institution— upholds all those aspects of female oppression . . . For example, heterosexuality is basic to our oppression in the workplace. When we look at how women are defined and exploited as secondary, marginal workers, we recognize that this definition assumes that all women are tied to men . . . It is obvious that heterosexuality upholds the home, housework, the family as both a personal and economic unit. (Bunch, 1975: 34)

In this excerpt from Charlotte Bunch, the link between heterosexuality and systems of oppression is elaborated.

While many of these arguments were made by heterosexually-identified feminists, some of the more famous works were produced by lesbian feminists, making a link to the interests of both feminism and lesbian and gay rights. Adrienne Rich's essay 'compulsory heterosexuality and lesbian existence' (1980), a frequently reprinted classic, confronts the institution of heterosexuality head on, asserting that heterosexuality is neither natural nor inevitable but is instead a compulsory, contrived, constructed and taken-for-granted institution which serves the interests of male dominance.

> Historians need to ask at every point how heterosexuality as institution has been organized and maintained through the female wage scale, the enforcement of middle-class women's leisure, the glamorization of so-called sexual liberation, the withholding of education from women, the imagery of high art and popular culture, the mystification of the personal sphere, and much else. We need an economics which comprehends the institution of heterosexuality, with its doubled workload for women and its sexual divisions of labor, as the most idealized of economic relations. (ibid.: 27)

Understanding heterosexuality as compulsory and as a standardized institution with processes and effects is what makes Rich's contribution to these debates pivotal.

Monique Wittig's 'The category of sex' (1976), takes the argument to a different level, declaring heterosexuality a political regime. The category of sex, she argues, is the political category that founds society as heterosexual:

> As such it does not concern being but relationships...The category of sex is the one that rules as natural the relation that is at the base of (heterosexual) society and through which half of the population, women, are heterosexualized...and submitted to a heterosexual economy...The category of sex is the product of a heterosexual society in which men appropriate for themselves the reproduction and production of women and also their physical persons by means of a contract called the marriage contract. (Wittig, 1992: 7)

This regime depends upon the belief that women are sexual beings, unable to escape or live outside of male rule.

These positions signal a paradigm shift in how heterosexuality is understood, challenging the very centrality of institutionalized heterosexuality and beginning the work of offering a systematic analysis of heterosexuality. When queer theory emerged in the 1990s, these critical analyses of heterosexuality were revisited and reinvigorated (e.g. Butler, 1990; de Lauretis, 1987; Fuss, 1991; Hennessy, 1995; Ingraham, 1994; Jackson, 1996; Sedgwick, 1990; Seidman, 1991, 1992, 1995; Warner, 1993; Wittig, 1992). In his anthology *Fear of a Queer Planet*, Michael Warner rearticulated these debates through his creation of the concept of 'heteronormativity'. According to Warner:

> So much privilege lies in heterosexual culture's exclusive ability to interpret itself as society. Het culture thinks of itself as the elemental form of human association, as the very model of intergender relations, as the indivisible basis of all community, and as the means of reproduction without which society wouldn't exist...Western political thought has taken the heterosexual couple to represent the principle of social union itself. (1993: xxi)

In this same passage Warner relates his notion of heteronormativity to Wittig's idea of the social contract. For Wittig the social contract is heterosexuality. 'To live in society is to live in heterosexuality...Heterosexuality is always there within all mental categories' (1992: 40). Like whiteness in a white supremacist society, heterosexuality is not only socially produced as dominant but is also taken-for-granted and universalizing.

Steven Seidman in his introduction to the groundbreaking work *Queer Theory/Sociology* (1996) assesses the role of queer theorists in developing a new critical view of normative heterosexuality. Given the history of sociology as a 'de-naturalizing force', he argues that it is time for queer sociologists to denaturalize heterosexuality as a 'social and political organizing principle'. Seidman asserts that the contribution of queer sociology is to analyse normative heterosexuality for the ways it conceals from view particular social processes and inequalities.

Drawing on these early arguments heteronormativity can be defined as the view that institutionalized heterosexuality constitutes the standard for legitimate and expected social and sexual relations. Heteronormativity insures that the organization of heterosexuality in everything from gender to weddings to marital status is held up as both a model and as 'normal'. Consider, for instance, the ways many surveys or intake questionnaires ask respondents to check off their marital status as either married, divorced, separated, widowed, single, or, in some cases, never married. Not only are these categories presented as significant indices of social identity, they are offered as the only options, implying that the organization of identity in relation to marriage is universal and not in need of explanation. Questions concerning marital status appear on most surveys *regardless of relevance*. The heteronormative assumption of this practice is rarely, if ever, called into question and when it is, the response is generally dismissive. (Try putting down 'not applicable' the next time you fill out one of these forms in a doctor's office!)

Or try to imagine entering a committed relationship without benefit of legalized marriage. We find it difficult to think that we can share commitment with someone without a state-sponsored license. People will frequently comment that someone is afraid to 'make a commitment' if they choose not to get married even when they have been in a relationship with someone for years! Our ability to imagine possibilities or to understand what counts as commitment is itself impaired by heteronormative assumptions. We even find ourselves challenged to consider how to marry without an elaborate white wedding. Gays and lesbians have participated in long-term committed relationships for years yet find themselves desiring state sanctioning of their union in order to feel legitimate. Heteronormativity works in all of these instances to naturalize the institution of heterosexuality while rendering real people's relationships and commitments irrelevant and illegitimate....

To expand the analytical reach of the concept of heteronormativity, it is important to examine how heterosexuality is constructed as normative. A concept that is useful for examining the naturalization of heterosexual relations is 'the heterosexual imaginary'.[1] The 'imaginary' is that illusory relationship we can have to our real conditions of existence. It is that moment when we romanticize things or refuse to see something that makes us uncomfortable. Applied to the study of heterosexuality it is that way of thinking that conceals the operation of heterosexuality in structuring gender (across race, class, and sexuality) and closes off any critical analysis of heterosexuality as an organizing institution. It is a belief system that relies on romantic and sacred notions in order to create and maintain the illusion of well-being. At the same time this romantic view prevents us from seeing how institutionalized heterosexuality actually works to organize gender while preserving racial, class, and sexual hierarchies as well. The effect of this illusory depiction of reality is that heterosexuality is taken for granted and unquestioned while gender is understood as something people are socialized into or learn. By leaving heterosexuality unexamined as an institution we do not explore how it is learned, what it keeps in place, and the interests it serves in the way it is practiced. Through the use of the heterosexual imaginary, we hold up the institution of heterosexuality as timeless, devoid of historical variation, and as 'just the way it is' while creating social practices that reinforce the illusion that as long as this is 'the way it is' all will be right in the world. Romancing heterosexuality—creating an illusory heterosexuality—is central to the heterosexual imaginary.

Frequently, discussions about the legalization of gay marriage depend on this illusion. Gays and lesbians are seeking equal access to economic resources such as benefits and see marriage as the site for gaining equity with heterosexuals. The central problem with this position is that it constructs the debates in terms of coupling. All those who do not couple for whatever reason are left out of the discussion. Consider some of the other consequences of participating in the heterosexual imaginary, of perpetuating the notion that heterosexuality is naturally a site for tranquility and safety. This standpoint keeps us from seeing and dealing with issues of marital rape, domestic violence, pay inequities, racism, gay bashing, and sexual harassment. Instead, institutionalized heterosexuality organizes those behaviors we ascribe to men and women—gender—while keeping in place or producing a history of contradictory and unequal social relations. The production of a division of labor that results in unpaid domestic work, inequalities of pay and opportunity, or the privileging of married couples in the dissemination of insurance benefits are examples of this. The heterosexual imaginary naturalizes the regulation of sexuality through the institution of marriage and state domestic relations laws. These laws, among others, set the terms for taxation, health care, and housing benefits on the basis of marital status. Laws and public- and private-sector policies use marriage as the primary requirement for social and economic benefits and access rather than distributing resources on some other basis such as citizenship or ability to breathe, for example. The distribution of economic resources on the basis of marital status remains an exclusionary arrangement even if the law permits gays and lesbians to participate. The heterosexual imaginary works here as well by allowing the illusion of well-being to reside in the privilege heterosexual couples enjoy while keeping others from equal access—quite a contradiction in a democratic social order.

WEDDINGS

. . . To study weddings using this theory of heterosexuality is to investigate the ways various practices, arrangements, relations, and rituals work to standardize and conceal the operation of this institution. It means to ask how practices such as weddings become naturalized and prevent us from seeing what is at stake, what is kept in place, and what consequences are produced. To employ this approach is to seek out those instances when the illusion of tranquility is created and at what cost. Weddings, like many other rituals of heterosexual celebration such as anniversaries, showers, and Valentine's Day become synonymous with heterosexuality and provide illusions of

reality which conceal the operation of heterosexuality both historically and materially. When used in professional settings, for example, weddings work as a form of ideological control to signal membership in relations of ruling as well as to signify that the couple is normal, moral, productive, family-centered, upstanding citizens and, most importantly, appropriately gendered. . . .

To study weddings means to interrupt the ways the heterosexual imaginary naturalizes heterosexuality and prevents us from seeing how its organization depends on the production of the belief or ideology that heterosexuality is normative and the same for everyone—that the fairy tale romance is universal. It is this assumption that allows for the development and growth of a $32 billion per year wedding industry. This multi-billion dollar industry includes the sale of a diverse range of products, many of which are produced outside of the USA—wedding gowns, diamonds, honeymoon travel and apparel, and household equipment. Also included in the market are invitations, flowers, receptions, photos, gifts, home furnishings, wedding cakes, catering, alcohol, paper products, calligraphy, jewelry, party supplies, hair styling, make-up, manicures, music, books, and wedding accessories, e.g., ring pillows, silver, chauffeurs and limousines. In the name of normative heterosexuality and its ideology of romance the presence and size of the sometimes corrupt wedding industry escape us.

While newlyweds make up only 2.6 per cent of all American households, they account for 75 per cent of all the fine china, 29 per cent of the tableware, and 21 per cent of the jewelry and watches sold in the USA every year. Even insurers have entered the primary wedding market by offering coverage 'if wedding bells don't ring' to cover the cost of any monies already spent on the wedding preparation. Fireman's Fund Insurance Company offers 'Weddingsurance' for wedding catastrophes such as flood or fire but not for 'change of heart' (Haggerty, 1993). In fact, attach the words wedding or bridal to nearly any item and its price goes up. With June as the leading wedding month followed by August and July, summer becomes a wedding marketer's dream. According to industry estimates, the average wedding in the USA costs $19,104. Considered in relation to what Americans earn, the cost of the average wedding represents 51 per cent of the mean earning of a white family of four and 89 per cent of the median earnings for black families. The fact that 63.7 per cent of Americans earn less than $25,000 per year (US Bureau of the Census, 1997) means the average cost of a wedding approximates a year's earnings for many Americans. . . .

Probably the most significant wedding purchase is the wedding gown. Industry analysts have noted that most brides would do without many things to plan a wedding and stay within budget, but they would not scrimp when it comes to the purchase of the wedding gown. With the US national average expenditure at $823 for the gown and $199 for the veil, the bride's apparel becomes the centerpiece of the white wedding. Most of us have heard the various phrases associated with the bride and her gown, the symbolic significance attached to how she looks and how beautiful her gown is. The marketing of everything from weddings to gowns to children's toys to popular wedding films to Disney is laced with messages about fairy tales and princesses, the fantasy rewards that work to naturalize weddings and heterosexuality. Even couture fashion shows of world-class designers traditionally feature wedding gowns as their grand finale.

One particularly troubling practice widely engaged in by gown sellers is the removal of designer labels and prices from dresses. In many surveys, from *Modern Bride* to Dawn Currie's interview study (1993), brides indicate that they rely upon bridal magazines to give them ideas about what type of gown to choose. They take the ad for the gown they like best to area stores and attempt to try on and purchase that particular dress. What they encounter is a system of deception widely practiced by many bridal shops. First, sellers remove the labels. Brides ask for a Vera Wang or an Alfred Angelo or a Jessica McClintock and are told to get the number off the gown and the clerk will check their book and see which designer it is. The bride has no way of knowing if she actually has the brand she seeks. As I toured various shops and saw how widespread this

practice was, I asked store owners why they removed the labels from the dresses. Without exception they told me that it was to maintain the integrity of their business and to prevent women from comparison shopping. The truth is, this practice is *illegal* and provides shop owners with a great deal of flexibility in preserving their customer base and profit margin. In addition to this federal consumer protection law there are many states which provide similar protections. All in all, bridal gown stores have little to fear: This law is not enforced. And, perhaps more importantly, the romance with the white wedding gown distracts the soon-to-be brides from becoming suspicious of store practices.

If you look at the portion of tags gown-sellers leave in the dresses you will see that most are sewn outside the USA in countries such as Guatemala, Mexico, Taiwan, and China. Nearly 80 per cent of all wedding gowns are produced outside the USA in subcontracted factories where labor standards are nowhere near US standards and no independent unions or regulators keep watch.

The recruitment by US companies to contract offshore labor benefits manufacturers on many levels: cheap labor, low overhead, fewer regulations, and higher profits. And with the proliferation of free trade agreements such as the North Atlantic Free Trade Agreement (NAFTA) and the General Agreement on Tariffs and Trade (GATT), labor and environmental abuses abound. In a survey conducted by UNITE in April 1997 of three factories in Guatemala, it was discovered that one American manufacturer's gowns were being made by 13 year olds in factories with widespread violations of their country's child labor laws, wage and hour laws, and under life-threatening safety conditions. At two of the firms, 14 and 15 year olds worked as long as 10 hours a day earning $20.80 a week.

Another area of the wedding industry dominated by messages about romance is the marketing of diamonds. As part of the fantasy of the ever-romantic marriage proposal, the diamond ring takes center stage. In fact, for 70 per cent of all US brides and 75 per cent of first-time brides, the first purchase for the impending wedding is the diamond engagement ring. The central marketing strategy of the world's largest diamond mining organization, DeBeers, is to convince consumers that 'diamonds are forever'. Once you accept this slogan, you also believe that you are making a life-long investment, not just purchasing a bauble for your bride! In fact, DeBeers spends about $57 million each year in this advertising campaign and has 'committed to spending a large part of [their] budget—some $200 million this year—on the promotion of diamond jewelry around the world' (Oppenheimer, 1998: 8). DeBeers and its advertisers have developed a new 'shadow' campaign to sell to consumers the advice that the 'appropriate' diamond engagement ring should cost at least 'two months' salary' for the groom (*Jewelers*, 1996). This advertising strategy signals to newlyweds, grooms in particular, that anything less is not acceptable. In effect, the diamond industry has made use of heteronormativity and the heterosexual imaginary and has convinced us that purchasing a diamond engagement ring is no longer a want but is 'natural', and therefore, a must. Not surprisingly, according to wedding industry estimates, this message is reaching its target. The average annual expenditure for engagement rings is $3000 (*Modern Bride*, 1996). If that constitutes the equivalent of two months' salary, the groom is expected to earn an annual salary of approximately $26,000 per year, the income bracket many of these ads target. What gets naturalized here is not just heterosexuality and romance but also weddings and commodity consumption....

The contemporary white wedding under transnational capitalism is, in effect, a mass-marketed, homogeneous, assembly-line production with little resemblance to the utopian vision many participants hold. The engine driving the wedding market has mostly to do with the romancing of heterosexuality in the interests of capitalism. The social relations at stake—love, community, commitment, and family—become alienated from the production of the wedding spectacle while practices reinforcing heteronormativity prevail.

The heterosexual imaginary circulating throughout the wedding industry masks the ways it secures racial, class, and sexual hierarchies. For instance, in nearly all of the examples offered above, the wedding industry depends upon the availability of cheap labor from developing nations with majority populations made up of people of color. The wealth garnered by white transnational corporations both relies on racial hierarchies, exploiting people and resources of communities of color (Africa, China, Haiti, Mexico, South Asia), and perpetuates them in the marketing of the wedding industry....

CONCLUSION

Heterosexuality is just not natural! It is socially organized and controlled. To understand how we give meaning to one of our major institutions is to participate as a critical consumer and citizen actively engaged in the production of culture and the social order. Heteronormativity—those practices that construct heterosexuality as the standard for legitimate and expected social and sexual relations—has enormous consequences for all members of a democratic social order, particularly in relation to the distribution of human and economic resources that affect the daily lives of millions of people. When the expectation is that all are equal under the law and that all citizens in a democracy can participate fully in the ruling of that society, rendering one form of sociosexual relations as dominant by constructing it as 'natural' is both contradictory and violent. In other words, the heterosexuality we learn to think of as 'natural' is anything but.

NOTE

1. See 'The heterosexual imaginary: feminist sociology and theories of gender', *Sociological Theory*, 12: 203–19. 2 July 1994 for further elaboration of this concept.

REFERENCES

Adams, Mary Louise (1997) *The Trouble with Normal: Postwar Youth and the Making of Heterosexuality*. Toronto: University of Toronto Press.

Best, Amy (2000) *Prom Night: Youth, Schools, and Popular Culture*. New York: Routledge.

Bunch, Charlotte (1975) 'Not for lesbians only', *Quest: A Feminist Quarterly*, (Fall).

Butler, Judith (1990) *Gender Trouble*. New York: Routledge.

Currie, D. (1993) 'Here comes the bride': The making of a 'modern traditional' wedding in western culture', *Journal of Comparative Family Studies*, 24 (3): 403–21.

de Lauretis, Teresa (1987) 'Queer theory: lesbian and gay sexualities', *Differences*, 3: iii–xviii.

Field, Nicola (1995) *Over the Rainbow: Money, Class and Homophobia*. London: Pluto Press.

Fuss, Diana (1991) *Inside/Out*. New York: Routledge.

Graff, E. J. (1999) *What is Marriage for?: The Strange Social History of our Most Intimate Institution*. Boston: Beacon Press.

Harman, Moses (1901) *Institutional Marriage*. Chicago: Lucifer.

Helms, Jesse (1996) 'The defense of marriage act'. *Senate Congressional Quarterly* September 9.C. 1996 Senate proceedings. *Congressional Record*, September 9.

Hennessy, Rosemary (1995) 'Incorporating queer theory on the left', Antonio Callari, Stephen Cullenberg, and Carole Beweiner (eds.), *Marxism in the Postmodern Age*. New York: Guilford.

Heywood, Ezra (1876) *Cupid's Yokes*. Princeton, NJ: Co-operative Publishing Company.

Ingraham, Chrys (1994) 'The heterosexual imaginary: feminist sociology and theories of gender', *Sociological Theory*, 12, 2 (July): 203–19.

Ingraham, Chrys (1999) *White Weddings: Romancing Heterosexuality in Popular Culture*. New York: Routledge.

Jackson, Stevi (1996) 'Heterosexuality and feminist theory', in Diane Richardson (ed.), *Theorising Heterosexuality*. Buckingham: Open University Press.

Jackson, Stevi (1999) *Heterosexuality in Question*. London: Sage Publications.

Jewelers Circular-Keystone (1996) 'Diamond sales hit record', New York: Chilton.

Katz, Jonathan Ned (1995) *The Invention of Heterosexuality*. New York: Plume.

Maynard, Mary and Purvis, June (eds) (1995) *(Hetero)sexual Politics*. London: Taylor & Francis.

Modern Bride (1996) 'The bridal market retail spending study: $35 billion market for the 90's', New York: Primedia.

Oppenheimer, Nicholas (1998) 'Chairman's statement', *Annual Report*. De Beers.

Rich, Adrienne (1980) 'Compulsory heterosexuality and lesbian existence', *Signs*, 5 (Summer): 631–60.

Richardson, Diane (ed.) (1996) *Theorising Heterosexuality*. Buckingham: Open University Press.

Sears, Hal D. (1977) *The Sex Radicals: Free Love in High Victorian America*. Lawrence: Regents Press of Kansas.

Sedgwick, Eve (1990) *Epistemology of the Closet*. Berkeley, CA: University of California Press.

Seidman, Steven (1991) *Romantic Longings*. New York: Routledge.

Seidman, Steven (1992) *Embattled Eros*. New York: Routledge.

Seidman, Steven (1993) 'Identity and politics in a postmodern gay culture: some conceptual and historical notes', in M. Warner (ed.), *Fear of a Queer Planet*. Minneapolis: University of Minnesota Press.

Seidman, Steven (1996) *Queer Theory/Sociology*. Cambridge, MA: Blackwell.

US Bureau of the Census (1997) *Statistical Abstracts of the U.S.* Washington DC: Government Printing Office.

Wilkinson, Sue and Kitzinger, Celia (eds) (1993) *Heterosexuality: A Feminism and Psychology Reader*. London: Sage Publications.

Wittig, Monique (1992) *The Straight Mind and Other Essays*. Boston: Beacon Press.

5 • *Kristen Schilt and Laurel Westbrook*

DOING GENDER, DOING HETERONORMATIVITY

"Gender Normals," Transgender People, and the Social Maintenance of Heterosexuality

DISCUSSION QUESTIONS

1. What does it mean to "do gender" and to "do heteronormativity"? Identify some of the different ways you "do gender" in different contexts or in different stages over your life course.
2. What makes the gender performance of transgender people riskier and more threatening in specific arenas?
3. In addition to the contexts discussed by Schilt and Westbrook, can you identify other situations where transgender people might face greater risks?
4. What does the significance of genitalia tell us about the normative story of the relationship between sex, gender, and sexuality (which we refer to as *essentialism* in the Introduction to the book)?

In "Feminism, Marxism, Method and the State," Catherine MacKinnon (1982, 533) argued that "sexuality is the linchpin of gender inequality." This argument echoed earlier conceptualizations of heterosexuality as a compulsory, institutionalized system that supports gender inequality (Rich 1980). Despite these important insights, however, theorizing heterosexuality did not become central to feminist sociology (Ingraham 1994). Rather, it was queer theory that picked up the theoretical mantle, turning the gaze onto how the "heterosexual matrix" (Butler 1989) maintains inequality between men and women (see Seidman 1995). Shifting the object of analysis from the margins (women, homosexuals) to the center (men, heterosexuals) allowed for the theorization of heteronormativity—the suite of cultural, legal, and institutional practices that maintain normative assumptions that there are two and only two genders, that gender reflects biological sex, and that only sexual attraction between these "opposite" genders is natural or acceptable (Kitzinger 2005). Heterosexuality plays a central role in "maintaining the gender hierarchy that subordinates women to men" (Cameron and Kulick 2003, 45). Yet the relationship between heterosexuality and gender oppression remains undertheorized in social science research.

Schilt, Kristen and Westbrook, Laurel. "Doing Gender, Doing Heteronormativity: "Gender Normals," Transgender People, and the Social Maintenance of Heterosexuality." *Gender and Society*, Vol. 23, No. 4 (Aug 2009): 440–464. Sage Publications, Inc.

In this article, we bring attention to the everyday workings of heteronormativity by examining potential challenges to this "sex/gender/sexuality system" (Seidman 1995): people who live their lives in a social gender that is not the gender they were assigned at birth. People who make these social transitions—often termed "transgender" people—disrupt cultural expectations that gender identity is an immutable derivation of biology (Garfinkel 1967; Kessler and McKenna 1978). In social situations, transgender people—as all people—have "cultural genitalia" that derive from their gender presentation (Kessler and McKenna 1978). Yet in sexual and sexualized situations—interactional contexts that allow for the performance of both gender and heterosexuality—male-bodied women and female-bodied men present a challenge to heteronormativity. . . .

Taking methodological insights from queer theory, we consider how cisgender men and women[1]—whom Garfinkel (1967) terms "gender normals"—react to transgender people. This focus inverts the typical model of using transgender people (the margins) to illuminate the workings of everybody else (the center) (see Garfinkel 1967; Kessler and McKenna 1978; West and Zimmerman 1987). We draw on two case studies: an ethnographic study of transmen who socially transition from female to male (FtM) in the workplace and a textual analysis of media narratives about the killings predominantly of transwomen who socially transition from male to female (MtF). Attention to how gender normals react to the discovery of what they perceive as a mismatch between gender identity and biological sex in these public and private relationships reveals the interactional precariousness of the seemingly natural heterosexual gender system. We argue that these responses demonstrate that the processes of "doing gender" (West and Zimmerman 1987) are difficult to separate from the maintenance of heteronormativity. Our case studies show that doing gender in a way that does not reflect biological sex can be perceived as a threat to heterosexuality. Cisgender men and women attempt to repair these potential ruptures through the deployment of normatively gendered tactics that reify gender and sexual difference.

These tactics simultaneously negate the authenticity of transmen and transwomen's gender and sexual identities and reaffirm the heteronormative assumption that only "opposite sex" attraction between two differently sexed and gendered bodies is normal, natural, and desirable.

LITERATURE REVIEW

The persistence of gender inequality is well documented within sociology. Behind this reproduction of inequality are cultural schemas about the naturalness of a binary gender system in which there are two, and only two, genders that derive from biology (chromosomes and genitalia) (West and Zimmerman 1987). . . . The gender order is hierarchical, which means there is consistently a higher value on masculinity than on femininity (Connell 1987; Schippers 2007).

Ethnomethodological theories of gender (see Garfinkel 1967; Kessler and McKenna 1978; West and Zimmerman 1987) argue that an empirical focus on social interactions makes the mechanisms that maintain this gender system visible, as "social interactions can reflect and reiterate the gender inequality characteristic of society more generally" (Fenstermaker, West, and Zimmerman 2002, 28). This theoretical body of work examines what has come to be termed "doing gender" (West and Zimmerman 1987)—the interactional process of crafting gender identities that are then presumed to reflect and naturally derive from biology. As masculinity and femininity are not fixed properties of male and female bodies, the meanings and expectations for being men and women differ both historically and across interactional settings. Normative expectations for men and women maintain gender inequality, as strictures of masculinity push men to "do dominance" and strictures of femininity push women to "do submission" (West and Zimmerman 1987). . . .

Fully illuminating the mechanisms that uphold gender inequality, however, requires a more thorough analysis of the interplay between gender and sexuality—what some feminists have termed the connection between patriarchy and compulsory heterosexuality (Rich 1980)—than is offered in these theories. Heterosexuality—like masculinity and femininity—is taken for granted as a natural occurrence derived from biological sex. . . . The hierarchical gender system that privileges masculinity also privileges heterosexuality. Its maintenance rests on the cultural devaluation of femininity and homosexuality. . . .

Heterosexuality requires a binary sex system, as it is predicated on the seemingly natural attraction between two types of bodies defined as opposites. The taken-for-granted expectation that heterosexuality and gender identity follow from genitalia produces heteronormativity—even though in most social interactions genitals are not actually visible. . . . Transgender people—people who live with a social gender identity that differs from the gender they were assigned at birth—can successfully do masculinity or femininity without having the genitalia that are presumed to follow from their outward appearance.

. . . Sexual encounters, however, can disrupt the taken-for-granted assumptions that people who look like women have vaginas and people who look like men have penises. In these situations, gender normals, particularly men, can have strong, even violent reactions. A question arises: Is the reaction related to (trans)gender or (hetero)sexuality? Framed as a (trans)gender issue, this violence operates as a disciplinary force on bodies that transgress the seemingly natural gender binary. Yet (hetero)sexuality is also an important factor as "the heterosexual framework that centers upon the model of penis-vagina penetration undoubtedly informs the genital division of male and female" (Bettcher 2007, 56). Transgender people have their claim to their gender category of choice challenged in these situations on the basis of genitalia, which in turn calls the heterosexuality of cisgender people they have been sexual with into question. . . .

METHODS

The first case study examined reactions to open workplace transitions—situations in which transgender people announce their intention to undergo a gender transition and remain in the same job. Between 2003 and 2007, Schilt conducted in-depth interviews with 54 transmen in Southern California and Central Texas. Generating a random sample of transmen is not possible, as there is not an even dispersal of transmen by state or transgender-specific neighborhoods from which to sample. Respondents were recruited from transgender activist groups, listservs, support groups, and personal contacts. After the interview, each respondent was asked if he felt comfortable recommending any coworkers for an interview about their experience of the workplace transition. Fourteen coworkers (10 women and four men) of eight transmen in professional and blue-collar jobs were interviewed.

There were few demographic differences between transmen from the two regions. Thirty-five of these men had openly transitioned at one point in their lives, 19 in California and 16 in Texas. The majority were white (86 percent), with relatively equal numbers of queer, bisexual, and gay men and heterosexual men. The average age of California respondents was higher than that of the Texas respondents (35 vs. 25). California transmen also had a wider range of years of transition—from the mid-1980s to the mid-2000s—while all of the transmen interviewed in Texas openly transitioned in the early to mid-2000s. In both states, most transmen transitioned in professional occupations or in service industry/retail occupations (72 percent), with a minority transitioning in blue-collar occupations and "women's professions."

In the second case study, Westbrook systematically collected all the available nonfiction texts produced by the mainstream news media in the United States between 1990 and 2005 about the murders of people described as doing gender so as to possibly be seen as a gender other than the one they were assigned at birth. Texts included those identifying a murder victim as wearing clothing, jewelry, and/or makeup associated with a gender other than the one they were labeled at birth; naming a murder victim as *transsexual, transgender,* a *cross-dresser,* or a *transvestite*; and/or describing the victim of fatal violence as *a man in a dress, a man posing as a woman, passed as a man, a woman posing as a man, female impersonator,* or *a woman who is really a man.* For this article, we will refer to this group of people using the term "transgender."

In total, Westbrook collected and analyzed 7,183 individual news stories about 232 homicides. Most texts came from searches of the databases Lexis Nexis and Access World News and included print newspaper articles and news magazine articles produced for a general audience. To gather these texts, Westbrook compiled a list of names of people identified as transgender murder victims by transgender activists and then searched for articles about these victims. She then assembled a list of names and terms used to describe victims in these news stories, such as "posed as a woman," and performed a new search using those terms. This process was repeated a number of times. The extensiveness of the search makes these texts a census of all available stories, not just a sample, and all cases identified by transgender activists were written about at least once in the mainstream press.

Westbrook analyzed texts using the qualitative data analysis software Atlas.ti. Coding focused on how each news story explained the act of violence being reported, with explanations conceptualized as "frames"—ways that people make sense of the world by highlighting certain aspects of an event while ignoring others (Benford and Snow 2000; Goffman 1986). News media framings of this violence were analyzed not in an attempt to access what "really happened" in these interactions but as reflections of dominant explanations of why such violence may occur. The mainstream news media both reflect and shape dominant belief systems (Ferree et al. 2002; Gamson et al. 1992); as such, attention to media framings of violence against transgender people provides useful insight into the sex/gender/sexuality system.

Although journalists framed the violence in many ways, more often than not they described the violence as a response to actual or perceived deception of the perpetrator by the transgender person. Westbrook coded stories as using this deception framing if they explicitly claimed that the perpetrator felt deceived and, as a result, killed the victim. Stories that described the killing as resulting from anger at a

"discovery" that the victim was really a man, really a woman, or transgender were also included under the code "deception frame." In examining these stories, Westbrook also attended to the genders of the victim(s) and perpetrator(s) and the context in which the crime occurred, including the relationship between the victim and perpetrator and location of the crime. Other variables of interest, such as race and class of those involved, were rarely mentioned in news stories and so were not part of the analysis.

There are some potential limitations to this comparative model. The first lies in the populations we compare. While transmen and transwomen are lumped together as "transgender" in many situations, their experiences do not mirror one another. Still, we find these comparisons to be fruitful for our analyses for several reasons. First, while the selection of transmen in the first case study was purposive, the focus on transwomen in the second case study was not. The lack of any documented incidents involving heterosexual cisgender women killing transmen suggests that the tactics used to police gender and sexual transgressions are themselves gendered—a point we develop in our analysis. Second, this comparison reveals how responses to transmen and transwomen vary across public and private sexualized/sexual relationships. This comparison illuminates how criteria for membership in gender categories differ in sexual, as compared to non-sexual, situations.

DOING GENDER AND HETERONORMATIVITY IN PUBLIC RELATIONSHIPS

Open workplace transitions—situations in which a transgender employee informs her employers that she intends to begin living and working as a man—present an interesting empirical setting for examining how gender and heteronormativity "work" in public relationships. Reactions to this announcement could play out in multiple ways. Transmen could be fired for making a stigmatized identity public, thus neutralizing this potential challenge to the binary gender order. They could experience no change to their workplace experiences. Or they could be repatriated as men by being expected to follow the men's dress and behavioral codes and being moved into new jobs or positions that employers see as better suited to masculine abilities and interests.

The experiences of transmen in both Texas and California are largely consistent: They are incorporated into men's jobs and men's workplace cultures. These incorporations are not seamless, however. When transmen's (hetero)sexuality is raised at work, heterosexual men often encourage an open display of shared sexual desire for women—emphasizing their new sameness with transmen. Heterosexual women, in contrast, police the boundaries of who can be counted as a man—negating their new "oppositeness" with transmen. In sexualized situations, transmen's masculinity is simultaneously reinforced—as men frame them as heterosexual men—and challenged—as women position them as homosexual women.

REAFFIRMING "NATURAL" GENDER DIFFERENCE

Employers and coworkers find new ways to do gender "naturally" by incorporating transmen into the workplace as one of the guys. On an organizational level, some employers rehire transmen as men, institutionally sanctioning their transition into a man's career track. . . . Employers also issue top-down dictates that give transmen access to men's restrooms and lockers and ask coworkers to change names and pronouns with their transgender colleague. These employer responses show how gender boundaries can shift—former women can be accepted as men—without a change in structural gender relations or organizational policies.

When transmen receive top-down support for their workplace transitions, men and women coworkers often show their adherence to these dictates by enlisting transmen into masculine "gender rituals" (Goffman 1977). For the first few weeks of Jake's transition, heterosexual men colleagues began signaling in an obvious way that they were treating him like a guy:

A lot of my male colleagues started kind of like slapping me on the back [laughs]. But I think it was with

more force than they probably slapped each other on the back. . . . And it was not that I had gained access to "male privilege" but they were trying to affirm to me that they saw me as a male. . . . That was the way they were going to be supportive of me as a guy, or something of the sort [laughs].

The awkwardness of these backslaps illustrates his colleagues' own hyperawareness of trying to do gender with someone who is becoming a man. Jake felt normalized by this incorporation and made frequent references to himself as a *trans*man to disrupt his colleagues' attempts to naturalize his transition.

Women also engage transmen in heterosocial gender rituals, such as doing heavy lifting around the office. The change is so rapid that many transmen are, at first, not sure how to make sense of these new expectations. Kelly, who transitioned in a semiprofessional job, notes,

Before [transition] no one asked me to do anything really and then [after], this one teacher, she's like, "Can you hang this up? Can you move this for me?" . . . Like if anything needed to be done in this room, it was me. Like she was just, "Male? Okay you do it." That took some adjusting. I thought she was picking on me.

. . . This enlistment into heterosocial gender rituals suggests that while open transitions might make gender trouble for coworkers who struggle with how they should treat their transgender colleague, this disruption does not make them reconsider the naturalness of the gender binary. Treating transmen as men gives them their "rightful" place in the dichotomy—and allows schemas about men and women's natural differences to go unchanged.

Interviews with coworkers illuminate how they grapple with this potential breach to their ideas about gender. Heterosexual men emphasized that if they were not discussing the transition in an interview, it would not cross their minds. They position this transition from female to male as "natural" for a masculine woman. One man in a blue-collar job says,

I chuckle to myself every now and then, how just natural it seems. [It] took a while for the pronouns to catch on but now it just comes out naturally. It just seems like a natural fit. It just seems like my inclination or my intuition at the beginning was correct; it just seemed, like, natural that she should go through with something like this because she was gonna be more comfortable as a man than as a woman.

Another man says he was unsurprised about the transition because his colleague "was an unattractive woman." As many transmen move from being masculine (e.g., gender-nonconforming) women to gender-conforming men, their decisions to transition can be seen as a natural fit for someone who was viewed as doing femininity unsuccessfully. Many transmen also move from being gender nonconforming women who are assumed to be lesbians to gender-conforming men who are assumed to be heterosexual—a move that coworkers can justify as confirmation of the naturalness and desirability of a heteronormative gender system.

Women coworkers express more hesitation about seeing transmen as men. Several women discuss their concern about what they perceive as a mismatch between their colleague's gender presentation—male—and his biological sex—female. One woman who works with a transman in a female-dominated job says,

> It's a hard thing for me [to say I see him as a man]. . . . On some levels yes, but in other ways, no. If I think about it, I start thinking about his body. I feel that his body would be different than any man that I would know. . . . When I think a lot about it, I definitely think about his body and what's happened to it. I wouldn't think of him as I would another male friend.

Another woman in a blue collar job makes a similar comment, saying,

> I can't say yes [I see him as a man] but I can't really say no. The appearance has changed. You know . . . he always looked like a guy . . . dressed like a guy . . . and what's changed is that his hair is cut short. But I can't really say I accept him as a guy.

These comments demonstrate the power of gender attributions as, on one hand, these women see their colleagues as men because they look like men. However, when they think too much about their bodies—what they see as an authentic and unchangeable sexed reality—they are hesitant to include them in the category of man.

Yet, showing the power of institutionally supported public relationships, many coworkers will validate transmen's new social identities as men regardless of their personal acceptance of this identity—in effect "passing" as supportive colleagues. While sociologists have positioned transgender people as gender overachievers who attempt to be 120 percent male or female (see Garfinkel 1967), coworkers' adherence to these gender rituals suggests that in these public interactions, gender normals may have more anxiety about how gender *should* be done than the person who is transitioning. Whether or not this adherence reflects authentic support for transmen *as men,* it maintains the idea of natural gender differences that create "opposite" personality types with different abilities and interests.

GENDERED RESPONSES TO HETEROSEXUALITY

The incorporation of transmen as one of the guys at work is not seamless. . . . While the workplace often is framed as nonsexual, interactions can become sexualized, as in sex talk and sexual banter; and/or sexual, in ways both consensual and nonconsensual (Williams, Giuffre, and Dellinger 1999). Heterosexual women's perception of a mismatch between their colleague's biological sex and gender identity comes to the forefront in (hetero)sexualized interactions. Women can accept transmen as men when doing masculine roles at work—heavy lifting, killing spiders—but not in sexualized relationships with female-bodied people. Illustrating this, Preston remembers telling a woman coworker that he had a new girlfriend. He was shocked when she yelled across the room, "How do you have sex if you don't have a dick?" Her comment shows that in his coworker's mind, Preston does not have the essential signifier of manhood and therefore cannot *really* have penis-vagina intercourse—the hallmark of heterosexuality.

In sexualized situations, some women frame transmen as deceptive—tricking women into seemingly heterosexual relationships without the necessary biological marker of manhood. At a volunteer organization Peter participated in for many years, before and after his transition, he developed a flirtatious relationship with a woman volunteer. He says, "We were flirting a bit and someone noticed. She pulled me aside and said, 'Does she know about you? I am concerned she doesn't know about you. What is going on between you two? This is totally inappropriate.'" Having known his co-volunteers for several years, he was surprised to realize they saw him as suspicious and threatening. Chris encountered a similar experience in his first job as a man. Hired as a man, he planned not to come out as transgender at work. However, his transition became public knowledge when a high school colleague recognized him. While she originally agreed not to tell anyone, she changed her mind. He says, "So basically for the first time in my life—I was nineteen—I had girls *like* like me, you know. And I think what happened was [this former classmate] was thinking, 'Oh that's sick, I better warn them.'" . . . His experience shows how women's acceptance of transmen's gender can be negated in sexualized interactions. In these situations, women regender transmen as biological females passing as men in an attempt to trick women into homosexuality.

Conversely, rather than policing transmen's heterosexuality, heterosexual men encourage it by engaging them in sex talk about women. Kelly notes,

> I definitely notice that the guys . . . they will say stuff to me that I know they wouldn't have said before [when I was working as a female]. . . . One guy, recently we were talking and he was talking about his girlfriend and he's like, "I go home and work it [have sex] for exercise."

He adds that this same coworker went out of his way to avoid him before his transition. The coworker later told Kelly that he was uncomfortable with gays and lesbians. This disclosure reflects heteronormativity, as becoming a presumably heterosexual man can be viewed more positively than being a lesbian. While some transmen personally identify as gay or queer men, heteronormativity ensures that their co-workers imagine they are transitioning to become heterosexual men. These responses show that when

an open transition has employer support, heterosexual men are willing in many cases to relate to transmen they see as heterosexual on the basis of shared sexual desire for women. . . .

As heteronormativity requires men to ignore other men's bodies, heterosexual men do masculinity, and simultaneously uphold their heterosexuality, by ignoring the bodily details of transmen's transitions. Cisgender men are hesitant to admit any interest in genital surgery. Those who did ask questions about genital surgery in their interview qualified that this interest was purely "scientific," rather than prurient. Ignoring genitalia gives transmen a "sameness" with heterosexual men at work. This sameness allows cisgender men to enlist transmen into discussions of heterosexuality that never go beyond the theoretical. Heterosexual women, in contrast, now have an "oppositeness" with transmen, making them and other women at work part of a potential dating pool. . . .

These experiences illustrate that while both cisgender men and women treat transmen as socially male in nonsexualized public interactions, there are gender differences in responses to sexualized public interactions. In these situations, men gender transmen as heterosexually male on the basis of gender presentation, while women gender them as homosexually female on the basis of biological sex. . . . This difference suggests that cisgender people react more strongly toward transgender people who become the "opposite gender" but are presumed to still be the "same sex," as they—and their entire gender—now run the risk of unwittingly engaging in homosexuality. Yet the public context of these relationships still mediates the methods used to enforce heteronormativity. As the next section shows, in private, sexual relationships, men show more extreme reactions.

DOING GENDER AND HETERONORMATIVITY IN PRIVATE RELATIONSHIPS

Examining media accounts of killings of transgender people provides important insight into the beliefs that maintain gender inequality and heteronormativity.

Journalists frame a minority of the murders of trans-people in the United States between 1990 and 2005 as caused by reasons wholly, or mostly, unrelated to their membership in the group "transgender." These sorts of cases—the result of personal conflict, random violence, or membership in categories such as "woman" or "person of color"—account for about 33 percent of transgender homicides in which reporters provide a cause for the violence. Journalists attribute the other 67 percent to reasons more closely related to being transgender. Articles describe homophobia or trans-phobia as the primary cause of violence in only 6 percent of the total cases, while in the majority of cases, 56 percent, journalists depict violence as resulting from private, sexual interactions in which the perpetrator feels "tricked" into homosexuality by "gender deceivers." An additional 5 percent depict the murder as resulting from cisgender men defending themselves from unwanted sexual advances.

As with reactions to public, sexualized relationships, the response patterns in these private, sexual interactions are gendered. Almost ninety-five percent of reported cases involve a cisgender man murdering a trans-woman, while no articles describe a cisgender woman killing a transman.[2] The gendered pattern of violence represented in mainstream news stories echoes, although significantly exceeds, that for all reported homicides in the United States, as 65.3 percent involve a male offender and male victim and 2.4 percent of cases are females killing females (Bureau of Justice Statistics 2007). . . .

GENDER AND HETEROSEXUALITY IN PRIVATE

Most of the transgender homicides covered in the mainstream news media occur in what can be understood as private relationships, such as those between lovers, family members, friends, acquaintances, and strangers met on the street or in bars; or outside the realm of socially authorized public relationships, such as people engaged in illegal activities like prostitution and drug dealing. Of the 136 cases in which journalists identify the relationship between the perpetrator and victim, only one is said to be a relationship between coworkers, and it occurs far outside the

realm of legally sanctioned working relationships—an MtF prostitute portrayed as killing her transsexual madam in an argument over money (Grace 2003). . . .

Almost two-thirds of the reported fatal violence in these private interactions transpired within sexual relationships of short duration, such as the victim and perpetrator engaging in a physical sexual encounter for the first time, or the perpetrator or victim propositioning the other for a sexual relationship (either with or without the exchange of money). Many articles describe the perpetrators and victims as strangers or very recent acquaintances. In these narratives, cisgender men approach or are approached by a woman for sex and the pair immediately go to a place where they can engage in such an encounter. Upon becoming sexual, the cisgender man discovers the transwoman's penis and reacts with physical violence. Articles explain the resulting violence as caused by the perpetrators feeling deceived by the transwomen about their "true gender" and "tricked" into a homosexual encounter.

News articles described the murder of Chrissey Johnson (nee Marvin Johnson) in such a way:

Man Charged in Death of Transvestite

A Baltimore man has been arrested for killing a 29-year-old man whom he had brought home believing the victim was a woman. The police said that Allen E. Horton, 22, went into a rage Saturday night when he discovered Marvin Johnson, who was dressed as a woman, was really a man, a police spokesman said yesterday. (*Washington Times* 1993)

News coverage frames fatal sexual encounters between cisgender men and transwomen sex workers similarly, as this description of the murder of Jesse Santiago (nee Jesus) shows:

Man Kills Transvestite, Then Himself, Police Say

A bizarre case of mistaken sexual identity ended in the fatal screwdriver stabbing of a transvestite Bronx prostitute and the suicide of his killer early yesterday, police said. It began late Friday night when 47-year-old Augustin Rosado propositioned what he believed was a female prostitute in the University Heights section. The two headed to Rosado's fourth-floor furnished room in a transient hotel on Cresten Avenue, police said. Once inside, Rosado discovered the prostitute was a male transvestite and flew into a rage, stabbing the unidentified 30-year-old man repeatedly with a screwdriver and hitting him with a metal pipe, police said. . . . A detective working on the case said it is nearly impossible to tell on sight which prostitutes plying their trade in the area are men and which are women. "Some of these transvestites look sexier than some women," he said. "I could see how someone could be surprised." (Jamieson 1992)

The "deception" in these frames is a dual one; articles portray victims as lying both about their gender and about their sexual orientation. Showing how the sexual context of the relationship matters, reporters never use the deception frame for cases in which there has been no sexual interaction between the transgender person and a cisgender person. This lack of the deception frame in these nonsexual situations highlights the salience of genitalia as the key determiner of gender and sexual identity in sexual situations.

Gender "Deception" and the Precariousness of (Male) Heterosexuality

Accusations of false doings of gender in sexual interactions dominate the news coverage of the murder of transwomen by cisgender men through phrases such as "secret," "lied," "tricked," "misled," "avoid detection," "posed as a woman," "true gender," "really a woman," "true identity," "double life," "fooled," "deceit," "pretended," "masquerade," and "gender secret." One typical news story opened,

Gregory Johnson's friends and a cousin think they know why someone shot the 17-year-old boy and his 18-year-old friend, and then left their bodies to burn beyond recognition inside a blazing SUV. Rage. Johnson, they say, was a sweet and funny young man who liked to dress as a woman, fooling his dates. They suspect one of them became enraged upon learning the truth and killed Johnson and his female friend. (Horne and Spalding 2003)

. . . To utilize gender deception as the explanation for violence requires an underlying conception of a true gender that the victim intentionally did not display to the perpetrator. Indeed, the phrase "true gender" is often used in these articles, and the idea of a truth of gender is constructed using other terms; for example, reporters often say that victims had a "gender secret" and were "actually" or "really" another gender. "True gender" in these stories functions both as a synonym for "sex" as well as a reference to the ways that journalists and perpetrators feel that the victims *should* have been doing gender. . . . Descriptions of the murder of MtF Gwen Araujo, who had not had genital surgery, illustrate this point, as journalists regularly defined her "true gender" as male.

Passion Blamed for Teen's Slaying: Client's Discovery of Victim's True Gender Led to Chaos, Attorney for One Murder Suspect Says

A defense attorney for one of three men charged with killing a transgender teen described his client Thursday as a quiet, even-tempered man caught up by ungovernable passions the night he discovered he had unwittingly had sex with a man. "What followed was absolute pandemonium and chaos," said attorney Michael Thorman, who described the killing as "classic manslaughter," not murder. . . . The four men met Araujo, whom they knew as "Lida," in the summer of 2002. Merel and Magidson, according to Nabors, had sex with Araujo, but became suspicious about the teen's gender after comparing notes. On Oct. 3, 2002, the men confronted Araujo at Merel's house in Newark, a San Francisco suburb, and demanded: "Are you a woman or a man?" Another woman at the house found out the truth by grabbing Araujo's genitals. Uproar ensued. The 17-year-old Araujo was punched, choked, hit with a skillet, kneed in the face, tied up and strangled. Araujo was buried in a remote area near Lake Tahoe; about two weeks later Nabors led police to the victim's body. (Associated Press 2004)

. . .

We can see the importance of the shape of genitals, rather than transgender status, in determining "true gender" by comparing journalists' explanations of murders of transwomen who have and have not had genital surgery. Between 1990 and 2005, the mainstream news reported on the murder of six transwomen who had had genital surgery. None of them were said to have been killed because they "deceived" their sexual partner about their "true gender." Journalists do not use the deception frame to explain the murder of postoperative transwomen, as they possess the "correct" biological credentials to do gender as women in sexual interactions. . . .

In many of these murder cases, journalists and perpetrators portray transwomen as deceptive gay men, seeking to trick innocent heterosexual men into homosexuality. This "trick" carries a heavy social weight through what we term the "one-act rule of homosexuality." Similar to the idea that anyone with one drop of black blood is black (Davis 1991), both straight and gay people often believe that engaging in sexual encounters with people of the same sex demonstrates an innate, previously hidden, homosexuality, no matter what sexual identity one may personally avow (Ward 2006). In interviews and court testimony, the accused killers of Gwen Araujo articulate a belief that for a man to have sex with a person who has male-shaped genitals makes him homosexual, even if he were unaware of those genitals at the time. Mainstream news stories describe one of the convicted killers as starting to cry and repeating "I can't be gay" over and over again when the group of men "discovered" that Gwen Araujo had testicles. The punishment for attempting to "trick" someone into homosexuality is death—the only way to literally destroy the evidence of the violation of the one-act rule. Because the "true gender" for sexual encounters is determined by genital shape, self-identity is not sufficient for deciding either gender or sexuality. Thus, heterosexual men are constantly at risk of losing their claim to heterosexual status—just as transwomen are at risk for losing their claim to their chosen gender identity—because both gender and sexuality are produced in interaction. Individuals alone cannot determine their gender or sexuality and must, instead, prove them through fulfilling the appropriate criteria, including having the "right" genitals and never desiring someone with the "wrong" genitals.

The belief that gender deception in a sexual relationship would result in fatal violence is so culturally resonant that, even in cases where there is evidence that the perpetrator knew the victim was transgender prior to the sexual act, many people involved in the case, including journalists and police officers, still use the deception frame.[3] In one such case, that of the murder of Chanelle Pickett (nee Roman Pickett) by William Palmer in 1995, Palmer claimed that he only discovered that Pickett had male genitals once they were engaged in sex. Countering this, a few news articles include quotes from friends of Pickett's who said that Palmer was a regular at transgender hangouts and intentionally pursued transwomen who had not had genital surgeries. Despite these claims, journalists usually explain the murder as resulting from the discovery of Pickett's gender. During the trial, both framings of the violence were told, and the jury found the deception narrative more convincing, convicting Palmer of only assault and battery and sentencing him to two years in jail. Following the logics of heteronormativity and gender inequality, people often ignore counterevidence in these cases and accept the violence as justified.

In mainstream news media portrayals, when faced with the discovery of the transgender status of a sexual partner, men and women respond differently. We cannot account for this gap by only attending to questions of gender. Instead, we must look to the intersections of gender and sexuality. When heterosexual cisgender men and women discover that their sexual partner is transgender, this new information could challenge their claims to heterosexuality, as well as to their gender category of choice. As we saw with the cases of cisgender men, their masculinity is challenged as they feel "raped" and feminized through their connection to homosexuality. To repair this breach, they respond with violence—a masculine-coded act. Because of the interconnectedness of gender and sexuality, cisgender men reclaim their heterosexuality by emphasizing their masculinity. . . .

But while cisgender men can repair the sexuality breach by emphasizing masculinity through violence, cisgender women cannot use the same tactic.

To do violence and, thus, do masculinity would further destabilize women's claims to both femininity and heterosexuality. Given that masculine behavior in women is associated with lesbianism, cisgender women who wish to emphasize heterosexuality must respond differently—either ending the relationship or accepting their partner in one way or another. This gender difference can be seen clearly in portrayals of the life of Brandon Teena. Before he was killed by two men enraged by his sexual encounters with the local women, he had several heterosexually identified cisgender women partners "discover" his "true gender," but not one responded with fatal violence. Thus, men, not women, can use violence to repair the breach in gender and the challenge to their sexuality caused by the discovery of transgender status in private, casual sexual relationships. The extremity of men's responses shows the depth of the threat of transgender bodies to heteronormativity within sexual situations and the need to neutralize that threat through hypergendered reactions.

CONCLUSION

This article examines how responses by gender normals to transmen and transwomen demonstrate the ways gender and (hetero)sexuality are interrelated. The sex/gender/sexuality system rests on the belief that there are two, and only two, opposite sexes, determined by biology and signaled primarily by the shape of genitals. The idea of sexual difference naturalizes sexual interactions between "opposite" bodies; within this logic it seems . . . sex/gender/sexuality system rests on the belief that gendered behavior, (hetero)-sexual identity, and social roles flow naturally from biological sex, creating attraction between two opposite personalities. This belief maintains gender inequality, as "opposites"—bodies, genders, sexes—cannot be expected to fulfill the same social roles and, so, cannot receive the same resources.

. . . Much of the literature on violence against transpeople points to gender norm transgression as the cause of violence and assumes that all transgender people are at risk for the same type of violence across social situations. Our two studies complicate this explanation. In public interactions not coded as sexual, self-identity and gender presentation can be sufficient to place someone in his or her gender category of choice—particularly in situations where this new identity is supported by people in authority positions. This adherence reflects the accountability to situational norms in public interactions (Goffman 1966). Highlighting the importance of these public norms, when open workplace transitions do not receive top-down support, cisgender men and women are more likely to express resistance to their transgender colleague (Schilt 2009)—even when they have worked unproblematically for many years with their transgender colleague prior to his or her transition. This resistance is heightened when public interactions become sexualized. In these situations, responses that police heterosexuality are, in themselves, gendered: cisgender women regulate transmen's sexualized behaviors through talk and gossip, whereas cisgender men police transwomen through aggressive verbal harassment (Schilt 2009; Schilt and Connell 2007).

Examining gender normals' reactions to private, sexual interactions with transmen and transwomen presents something of a paradox, however. The majority of cases in the textual analysis present cisgender men murdering transwomen after learning that their sexual partner is transgender. Yet although surely interactions occur in which cisgender women "discover" that the transmen with whom they have been sexually intimate were assigned female at birth, there were no reported cases of cisgender women reacting violently to such a discovery. The gender gap in use of violence to repair the breach in gender and (hetero)sexuality occurs because violence can be used to claim masculine, but not feminine, heterosexuality. Although the one-act rule of homosexuality may well apply equally to men and women, a woman cannot undo the violation by responding with violence.

The extremity of the violence cisgender men use to punish transwomen in private, sexual situations highlights gender inequality in the forms of the cultural devaluation of femininity, homosexuality, and, particularly, males choosing to take on characteristics coded as feminine. . . . Similarly, the intense harassment of transwomen by cisgender men in the workplace derives from the valuation of masculinity over femininity. Whereas transmen may face less censure because they are adopting the socially respected traits of masculinity, transwomen are understood as committing the double sin of both abandoning masculinity and choosing femininity.

These gender differences further suggest the importance of the context of interactions (nonsexual/sexualized/sexual; public/private). Sexual and nonsexual situations require different degrees of "oppositeness." Heterosexual interactions entail both opposite genitals as well as opposite gendered behavior. By contrast, nonsexual heterosocial interactions only require opposite gendered behavior, so self-identity can be accepted without biological credentials. . . . As the criteria for gender membership are different in social versus (hetero)sexual circumstances; only in sexual situations is there a requirement that gender (self-presentation) equals sex (genitals). Accepting transgender people's self-identity in nonsexual situations does not threaten cisgender people's claims to heterosexual status. Men can be *homosocial* with other men, including those who lack the biological credentials for maleness, without being *homosexual*. In sexualized circumstances, however, heterosexuality is threatened by the one-act rule of homosexuality. Cisgender men stand to lose not just their sexual identity but also their standing as "real" men.

. . .

Examining the reactions of cisgender people to transgender people helps to illuminate the mechanisms that uphold the heteronormative sex/gender/sexuality system and illustrates the lengths to which gender normals will go to maintain a gender/sexual order that occurs "naturally." However, it would be a mistake to assume cisgender sexual desire for transgender bodies "must be paid for in blood," as Halberstam (2005) has argued. Some cisgender people—men, women, gay, straight, bisexual, pansexual—seek sexual and romantic partnerships with people they know to be transgender. Under a heteronormative system, this open desire for transgender bodies typically is framed as pathological or fetishistic

(Serano 2009). Future research should examine the purposeful sexual and romantic relationships between cisgender and transgender people outside of this pathological frame, as these relationships have the potential to create (hetero)sexual trouble within a heteronormative gender system.

AUTHORS' NOTE

We are extremely grateful to Beth Schneider, Jane Ward, Dana Britton, and the anonymous reviewers at *Gender & Society* for the detailed and thoughtful feedback that they provided on earlier versions of this article. In addition, we wish to thank Wendy Brown, Karl Bryant, Richard Juang, Dawne Moon, Charis Thompson, Barrie Thorne, Aliya Saperstein, and Mel Stanfill for comments on previous versions of this work. Portions of this research have been supported by funding from the Regents of the University of California.

NOTES

1. *Cis* is the Latin prefix for "on the same side." It compliments *trans,* the prefix for "across" or "over." "Cisgender" replaces the terms "nontransgender" or "bio man/bio woman" to refer to individuals who have a match between the gender they were assigned at birth, their bodies, and their personal identity.

2. Of the reported murders in which both the gender of the victim and perpetrator were known, 94.9 percent (149 of 157 cases) were instances of cisgender men killing transwomen. The remaining cases included three in which a cisgender woman killed a transwoman (1.91 percent), two in which a transwoman killed another transwoman (1.27 percent), and three in which one or more cisgender men killed a transman (1.91 percent).

3. Perpetrators may claim deception, even when none occurred, to try to reduce both legal and social castigation. As desire for opposite gender transgender bodies is culturally understood as *homosexual* desire, following the belief that genitalia determine gender in sexual interactions, perpetrators may claim they were deceived to try to cleanse themselves of the stigma from the one-act rule of homosexuality. They may also make such a claim to attempt to reduce criminal charges from homicide to manslaughter.

REFERENCES

Associated Press. 2004. Passion blamed for teen's slaying: client's discovery of victim's true gender led to chaos, attorney for one murder suspect says. *Los Angeles Times,* 16 April.

Benford, Robert, and David Snow. 2000. Framing processes and social movements: An overview and assessment. *Annual Review of Sociology* 26:611–39.

Bettcher, Talia. 2007. Evil deceivers and make believers: On transphobic violence and the politics of illusion. *Hypatia* 22:45–62.

Bureau of Justice Statistics. 2007. Homicide trends in the U.S.: Trends by gender. http://www.ojp.usdoj.gov/bjs/homicide/gender.htm (accessed 7 March, 2009).

Butler, Judith. 1989. *Gender trouble: Feminism and the subversion of identity.* New York: Routledge.

Cameron, Deborah, and Don Kulick. 2003. *Language and sexuality.* Cambridge: Cambridge University Press.

Connell, R. W. 1987. *Gender & power.* Berkeley: University of California Press.

Davis, Floyd James. 1991. *Who is Black? One nation's definition.* University Park: Pennsylvania State University Press.

Fenstermaker, Sarah, Candace West, and Don Zimmerman. 2002. Gender inequality: New conceptual terrain. In *Doing gender, doing difference,* edited by Sarah Fenstermaker and Candace West, 25–40. New York: Routledge.

Ferree, Myra Marx, William Anthony Gamson, Jurgen Gerhards, and Dieter Rucht. 2002. *Shaping abortion discourse: Democracy and the public sphere in Germany and the United States.* Cambridge: Cambridge University Press.

Franklin, Karen. 2000. Antigay behaviors among young adults: Prevalence, patterns and motivators in a noncriminal population. *Journal of Interpersonal Violence* 15:339–62.

Gamson, William A., David Croteau, William Hoynes, and Theodore Sasson. 1992. Media images and the social construction of reality. *Annual Review of Sociology* 18:373–93.

Garfinkel, Harold. 1967. *Studies in ethnomethodology.* Englewood Cliffs, NJ: Prentice Hall.

Goffman, Erving. 1966. *Behavior in public places: On the social organization of groups.* New York: Free Press.

———. 1977. The arrangement between the sexes. *Theory & Society* 4 (3): 301–31.

———. 1986. *Frame analysis: An essay on the organization of experience.* Boston: Northeastern University Press.

Grace, Melissa. 2003. Nabbed in tricky transsexual slay. *Daily News* (New York), 21 May.

Halberstam, Judith. 2005. *In a queer time and place: Transgender bodies, sub-cultural lives.* New York: New York University Press.

Hennen, Peter. 2008. *Faeries, bears, and leathermen: Men in community queering the masculine.* Chicago: University of Chicago Press.

Horne, Terry, and Tom Spalding. 2003. Dating habits may have led to teen's death. *Indianapolis Star,* 26 July.

Ingraham, Chrys. 1994. The heterosexual imaginary: Feminist sociology and theories of gender. *Sociological Theory* 12:203–19.

Jamieson, Wendell. 1992. Man kills transvestite, then himself, police say. *Newsday* (Melville, NY), 9 February.

Kessler, Suzanne, and Wendy McKenna. 1978. *Gender: An ethnomethodological approach.* Chicago: University of Chicago Press.

Kitzinger, Celia. 2005. Heteronormativity in action: Reproducing the heterosexual nuclear family in after-hours medical calls. *Social Problems* 52 (4): 477–98.

MacKinnon, Catherine. 1982. Feminism, Marxism, method and the state: An agenda for theory. *Signs: Journal of Women in Culture and Society* 7 (13): 515–44.

Pascoe, C. J. 2007. *Dude, you're a fag: Masculinity and sexuality in high school.* Berkeley: University of California Press.

Rich, Adrienne. 1980. Compulsory heterosexuality and lesbian existence. *Signs: Journal of Women in Culture and Society* 5 (4): 631–60.

Schilt, Kristen. 2009. (Trans)gender at work: The persistence of gender inequality. Manuscript.

Schilt, Kristen, and Catherine Connell. 2007. Do workplace gender transitions make gender trouble? *Gender, Work and Organization* 14 (6): 596–618.

Schippers, Mimi. 2007. Recovering the feminine other: Masculinity, femininity, and gender hegemony. *Theory & Society* 36 (1): 85–102.

Seidman, Steven. 1995. Deconstructing queer theory or the under-theorization of the social and the ethical. In *Social postmodernism: Beyond identity politics,* edited by Linda Nicholson and Steven Seidman. Cambridge: Cambridge University Press.

Serano, Julia. 2009. Why feminists should be concerned with the impending revisions of the DSM. http://www.feministing.com/archives/015254.html (accessed 6 May, 2009).

Ward, Jane. 2006. Straight dude seeks same: Mapping the relationship between sexual identities, practices, and cultures. In *Sex matters: The sexuality and society reader,*

2nd ed., edited by Mindy Stombler. Needham Heights, Massachusetts: Allyn & Bacon.

Washington Times. 1993. Man charged in death of transvestite. 4 January.

West, Candace, and Don Zimmerman. 1987. Doing gender. *Gender & Society* 1 (2): 125–51.

Williams, Christine, Patti Giuffre, and Kirsten Dellinger. 1999. Sexuality in the workplace. *Annual Review of Sociology* 25:73–93.

Wolf, Leslie. 1998. Man to stand trial in stabbing death of female impersonator. *San Diego Union-Tribune,* 21 October.

6 • *Robert McRuer*

COMPULSORY ABLE-BODIEDNESS AND QUEER/DISABLED EXISTENCE

DISCUSSION QUESTIONS

1. What justifications does McRuer provide for linking heterosexual and able-bodied "normalcy" theoretically?
2. How does McRuer utilize and expand on the seminal work of Judith Butler?
3. Why does the author ultimately argue for the intensifying of the "crisis" threatening compulsory able-bodied/queer existence?

CONTEXTUALIZING DISABILITY

In her famous critique of compulsory heterosexuality Adrienne Rich opens with the suggestion that lesbian existence has often been "simply rendered invisible" (178), but the bulk of her analysis belies that rendering. In fact, throughout "Compulsory Heterosexuality and Lesbian Existence," one of Rich's points seems to be that compulsory heterosexuality depends as much on the ways in which lesbian identities are made visible (or, we might say, comprehensible) as on the ways in which they are made invisible or incomprehensible. She writes:

Any theory of cultural/political creation that treats lesbian existence as a marginal or less "natural" phenomenon, as mere "sexual preference," or as the mirror image of either heterosexual or male homosexual relations is profoundly weakened thereby, whatever its other contributions. Feminist theory can no longer afford merely to voice a toleration of "lesbianism" as an "alternative life-style," or make token allusion to lesbians. A feminist critique of compulsory heterosexual orientation for women is long overdue. (178)

The critique that Rich calls for proceeds not through a simple recognition or even valuation of "lesbian existence" but rather through an interrogation of how the system of compulsory heterosexuality utilizes that existence. Indeed, I would extract from her suspicion of mere "toleration" confirmation for the idea that one of the ways in which heterosexuality is currently constituted or founded, established as the foundational sexual identity for women, is precisely through the deployment of lesbian existence as always and everywhere supplementary—the margin to heterosexuality's center, the mere reflection of (straight and gay) patriarchal realities. Compulsory heterosexuality's casting of some identities as alternatives ironically buttresses the ideological notion that dominant identities are not really alternatives but rather the natural order of things.[1]

More than twenty years after it was initially published, Rich's critique of compulsory heterosexuality is indispensable, the criticisms of her ahistorical notion of a "lesbian continuum" notwithstanding.[2] Despite its continued relevance, however, the realm of compulsory heterosexuality might seem to be an unlikely place to begin contextualizing disability.[3] I want to challenge that by considering what might be gained by understanding "compulsory heterosexuality" as a key concept in disability studies. Through a reading of compulsory heterosexuality, I want to put forward a theory of what I call compulsory able-bodiedness. The Latin root for *contextualize* denotes the act of weaving together, interweaving, joining together, or composing. This chapter thus contextualizes disability in the root sense of the word, because I argue that the system of compulsory able-bodiedness that produces disability is thoroughly interwoven with the system of compulsory heterosexuality that produces queerness, that—in fact—compulsory heterosexuality is contingent on compulsory able-bodiedness and vice versa. And, although I reiterate it in my conclusion, I want to make it clear at the outset that this particular contextualizing of disability is offered as part of a much larger and collective project of unraveling and decomposing both systems.[4]

The idea of imbricated systems is, of course, not new—Rich's own analysis repeatedly stresses the imbrication of compulsory heterosexuality and patriarchy. I would argue, however, as others have, that feminist and queer theories (and cultural theories generally) are not yet accustomed to figuring ability/disability into the equation, and thus this theory of compulsory able-bodiedness is offered as a preliminary contribution to that much-needed conversation.[5]

ABLE-BODIED HETEROSEXUALITY

In his introduction to *Keywords: A Vocabulary of Culture and Society,* Raymond Williams describes his project as

> the record of an inquiry into a *vocabulary*: a shared body of words and meanings in our most general discussions, in English, of the practices and institutions which we group as *culture* and *society.* Every word which I have included has at some time, in the course of some argument, virtually forced itself on my attention because the problems of its meaning seemed to me inextricably bound up with the problems it was being used to discuss. (15)

Although Williams is not particularly concerned in *Keywords* with feminism or gay and lesbian liberation, the processes he describes should be recognizable to feminists and queer theorists, as well as to scholars and activists in other contemporary movements, such as African American studies or critical race theory. As these movements have developed, increasing numbers of words have indeed forced themselves on our attention, so that an inquiry into not just the marginalized identity but also the dominant identity has become necessary. The problem of the meaning of masculinity (or even maleness), of whiteness, or of heterosexuality has increasingly been understood as inextricably bound up with the problems the term is being used to discuss.

One need go no further than the *Oxford English Dictionary* to locate problems with the meaning of heterosexuality. In 1971 the *OED Supplement* defined *heterosexual* as "pertaining to or characterized by the normal relations of the sexes; opp. to *homosexual*." At this point, of course, a few decades of critical work by feminists and queer theorists have made it possible to acknowledge quite readily that heterosexual and homosexual are in fact not equal and opposite identities. Rather, the ongoing subordination of homosexuality (and bisexuality) to heterosexuality allows for heterosexuality to be institutionalized as "the normal relations of the sexes," while the institutionalization of heterosexuality as the "normal relations of the sexes" allows for homosexuality (and bisexuality) to be subordinated. And, as queer theory continues to demonstrate, it is precisely the introduction of normalcy into the system that introduces compulsion: "Nearly everyone," Michael Warner writes in *The Trouble with Normal: Sex, Politics, and the Ethics of Queer Life,* "wants to be normal. And who can blame them, if the alternative is being abnormal, or deviant, or not being one of the rest of us? Put in those terms, there doesn't seem to be a choice at all. Especially in America where [being] normal probably outranks all other social aspirations" (53). Compulsion is here produced and covered over, with the appearance of choice (sexual preference) mystifying a system in which there actually is no choice.

A critique of normalcy has similarly been central to the disability rights movement and to disability studies, with—for example—Lennard Davis's overview and critique of the historical emergence of normalcy or Rosemarie Garland-Thomson's introduction of the concept of the "normate" (Davis, 23–49; Thomson, 8–9). Such scholarly and activist work positions us to locate the problems of able-bodied identity, to see the problem of the meaning of able-bodiedness as bound up with the problems it is being used to discuss. Arguably, able-bodied identity is at this juncture even more naturalized than heterosexual identity. At the very least, many people not sympathetic to queer theory will concede that ways of being heterosexual are culturally produced and culturally variable, even if and even as they understood heterosexual identity itself to be entirely natural. The same cannot be said, on the whole, for able-bodied identity. An extreme example that nonetheless encapsulates currently hegemonic thought on ability and disability is a notorious *Salon* article by

Norah Vincent attacking disability studies that appeared online in the summer of 1999. Vincent writes, "It's hard to deny that something called normalcy exists. The human body is a machine, after all—one that has evolved functional parts: lungs for breathing, legs for walking, eyes for seeing, ears for hearing, a tongue for speaking and most crucially for all the academics concerned, a brain for thinking. This is science, not culture."[6] In a nutshell, you either have an able body, or you don't.

Yet the desire for definitional clarity might unleash more problems than it contains; if it's hard to deny that something called normalcy exists, it's even harder to pinpoint what that something is. The *OED* defines *able-bodied* redundantly and negatively as "having an able body, i.e. one free from physical disability, and capable of the physical exertions required of it; in bodily health; robust." *Able-bodiedness,* in turn, is defined vaguely as "soundness of health; ability to work; robustness." The parallel structure of the definitions of *ability* and *sexuality* is quite striking: first, to be able-bodied is to be "free from physical disability," just as to be heterosexual is to be "the opposite of homosexual." Second, even though the language of "the normal relations" expected of human beings is not present in the definition of *able-bodied,* the sense of "normal relations" is, especially with the emphasis on work: being able-bodied means being capable of the normal physical exertions required in a particular system of labor. It is here, in fact, that both able-bodied identity and the *Oxford English Dictionary* betray their origins in the nineteenth century and the rise of industrial capitalism. It is here as well that we can begin to understand the compulsory nature of able-bodiedness: in the emergent industrial capitalist system, free to sell one's labor but not free to do anything else effectively meant free to have an able body but not particularly free to have anything else.

Like compulsory heterosexuality, then, compulsory able-bodiedness functions by covering over, with the appearance of choice, a system in which there actually is no choice. I would not locate this compulsion, moreover, solely in the past, with the rise of industrial capitalism. Just as the origins of heterosexual/homosexual identity are now obscured for most people so that compulsory heterosexuality functions as a disciplinary formation seemingly emanating from everywhere and nowhere, so too are the origins of able-bodied/disabled identity obscured, allowing what Susan Wendell calls "the disciplines of normality" (87) to cohere in a system of compulsory able-bodiedness that similarly emanates from everywhere and nowhere. Able-bodied dilutions and misunderstandings of the minority thesis put forward in the disability rights movement and disability studies have even, in some ways, strengthened the system: the dutiful (or docile) able-bodied subject now recognizes that some groups of people have chosen to adjust to or even take pride in their "condition," but that recognition, and the tolerance that undergirds it, covers over the compulsory nature of the able-bodied subject's own identity.[7]

Michael Bérubé's memoir about his son Jamie, who has Down syndrome, helps exemplify some of the ideological demands currently sustaining compulsory able-bodiedness. Bérubé writes of how he "sometimes feel[s] cornered by talking about Jamie's intelligence, as if the burden of proof is on me, official spokesman on his behalf." The subtext of these encounters always seems to be the same: *In the end, aren't you disappointed to have a retarded child? [. . .] Do we really have to give this person our full attention?"* (180). Bérubé's excavation of this subtext pinpoints an important common experience that links all people with disabilities under a system of compulsory able-bodiedness—the experience of the able-bodied need for an agreed-on common ground. I can imagine that answers might be incredibly varied to similar questions—"In the end, wouldn't you rather be hearing?" and "In the end, wouldn't you rather not be HIV positive?" would seem, after all, to be very different questions, the first (with its thinly veiled desire for Deafness not to exist) more obviously genocidal than the second. But they are not really different questions, in that their constant repetition (or their presence as ongoing subtexts) reveals more about the able-bodied culture doing the asking than about the bodies being interrogated. The culture asking such questions assumes in advance that we all agree: able-bodied identities and able-bodied perspectives are preferable and what we

all, collectively, are aiming for. A system of compulsory able-bodiedness repeatedly demands that people with disabilities embody for others an affirmative answer to the unspoken question: Yes, but in the end, wouldn't you rather be more like me?

It is with this repetition that we can begin to locate both the ways in which compulsory able-bodiedness and compulsory heterosexuality are interwoven and the ways in which they might be contested. In queer theory, Judith Butler is most famous for identifying the repetitions required to maintain heterosexual hegemony:

> The "reality" of heterosexual identities is performatively constituted through an imitation that sets itself up as the origin and the ground of all imitations. In other words, heterosexuality is always in the process of imitating and approximating its own phantasmatic idealization of itself—*and failing.* Precisely because it is bound to fail, and yet endeavors to succeed, the project of heterosexual identity is propelled into an endless repetition of itself. ("Imitation," 21)

If anything, the emphasis on identities that are constituted through repetitive performances is even more central to compulsory able-bodiedness—think, after all, of how many institutions in our culture are showcases for able-bodied performance. Moreover, as with heterosexuality, this repetition is bound to fail, as the ideal able-bodied identity can never, once and for all, be achieved. Able-bodied identity and heterosexual identity are linked in their mutual impossibility and in their mutual incomprehensibility—they are incomprehensible in that each is an identity that is simultaneously the ground on which all identities supposedly rest and an impressive achievement that is always deferred and thus never really guaranteed. Hence Butler's queer theories of gender performativity could be easily extended to disability studies, as this slightly paraphrased excerpt from *Gender Trouble* might suggest (I substitute, by bracketing, terms having to do literally with embodiment for Butler's terms of gender and sexuality):

> [Able-bodiedness] offers normative . . . positions that are intrinsically impossible to embody, and the persistent

failure to identify fully and without incoherence with these positions reveals [able-bodiedness] itself not only as a compulsory law, but as an inevitable comedy. Indeed, I would offer this insight into [able-bodied identity] as both a compulsory system and an intrinsic comedy, a constant parody of itself, as an alternative [disabled] perspective. (122)

In short, Butler's theory of gender trouble might be resignified in the context of queer/disability studies to highlight what we could call "ability trouble"—meaning not the so-called problem of disability but the inevitable impossibility, even as it is made compulsory, of an able-bodied identity.

QUEER/DISABLED EXISTENCE

The cultural management of the endemic crises surrounding the performance of heterosexual and able-bodied identity effects a panicked consolidation of hegemonic identities. The most successful heterosexual subject is the one whose sexuality is not compromised by disability (metaphorized as queerness); the most successful able-bodied subject is the one whose ability is not compromised by queerness (metaphorized as disability). This consolidation occurs through complex processes of conflation and stereotype: people with disabilities are often understood as somehow queer (as paradoxical stereotypes of the asexual or oversexual person with disabilities would suggest), while queers are often understood as somehow disabled (as ongoing medicalization of identity, similar to what people with disabilities more generally encounter, would suggest). Once these conflations are available in the popular imagination, queer/disabled figures can be tolerated and, in fact, utilized in order to maintain the fiction that able-bodied heterosexuality is not in crisis. As lesbian existence is deployed, in Rich's analysis, to reflect back heterosexual and patriarchal "realities," queer/disabled existence can be deployed to buttress compulsory able-bodiedness. Since queerness and disability both have the potential to disrupt the performance of able-bodied heterosexuality, both must be safely contained—embodied—in such figures.

. . .

CRITICALLY QUEER, SEVERELY DISABLED

The crisis surrounding heterosexual identity and able-bodied identity does not automatically lead to their undoing. . . . Neither gender trouble nor ability trouble is sufficient in and of itself to unravel compulsory heterosexuality or compulsory able-bodiedness. Butler acknowledges this problem: "This failure to approximate the norm [. . .] is not the same as the subversion of the norm. There is no promise that subversion will follow from the reiteration of constitutive norms; there is no guarantee that exposing the naturalized status of heterosexuality will lead to its subversion" ("Critically Queer," 22; qtd. in Warner, "Normal and Normaller" 168–169, n. 87). For Warner, this acknowledgment in Butler locates a potential gap in her theory, "let us say, between virtually queer and critically queer" (Warner, "Normal and Normaller," 168–169, n. 87). In contrast to a virtually queer identity, which would be experienced by anyone who failed to perform heterosexuality without contradiction and incoherence (i.e., everyone), a critically queer perspective could presumably mobilize the inevitable failure to approximate the norm, collectively "working the weakness in the norm," to use Butler's phrase ("Critically Queer," 26).[8]

A similar gap could be located if we appropriate Butler's theories for disability studies. Everyone is virtually disabled, both in the sense that able-bodied norms are "intrinsically impossible to embody" fully, and in the sense that able-bodied status is always temporary, disability being the one identity category that all people will embody if they live long enough. What we might call a critically disabled position, however, would differ from such a virtually disabled position; it would call attention to the ways in which the disability rights movement and disability studies have resisted the demands of compulsory able-bodiedness and have demanded access to a newly imagined and newly configured public sphere where full participation is not contingent on an able body.

We might, in fact, extend the concept and see such a perspective not as critically disabled but rather as severely disabled, with *severe* performing work similar to the critically queer work of *fabulous*. Tony Kushner writes:

> *Fabulous* became a popular word in the queer community—well, it was never *un*popular, but for a while it became a battle cry of a new queer politics, carnival and camp, aggressively fruity, celebratory and tough like a streetwise drag queen: "FAAAAABU-LOUS!" [. . .] *Fabulous* is one of those words that provide[s] a measure of the degree to which a person or event manifests a particular, usually oppressed, subculture's most distinctive, invigorating features. (vii)

Severe, though less common than *fabulous,* has a similar queer history: a severe critique is a fierce critique, a defiant critique, one that thoroughly and carefully reads a situation—and I mean reading in the street sense of loudly calling out the inadequacies of a given situation, person, text, or ideology. "Severely disabled," according to such a queer conception, would reverse the able-bodied understanding of severely disabled bodies as the most marginalized, the most excluded from a privileged and always elusive normalcy, and would instead suggest that it is precisely those bodies that are best positioned to refuse "mere toleration" and to call out the inadequacies of compulsory able-bodiedness. Whether it is the "army of one-breasted women" Audre Lorde imagines descending on the Capitol; the Rolling Quads, whose resistance sparked the independent living movement in Berkeley, California; Deaf students shutting down Gallaudet University in the Deaf President Now action; or ACT UP storming the National Institutes of Health or the Food and Drug Administration, severely disabled/critically queer bodies have already generated ability trouble that remaps the public sphere and reimagines and reshapes the limited forms of embodiment and desire proffered by the systems that would contain us all.[9]

Compulsory heterosexuality is intertwined with compulsory able-bodiedness; both systems work to (re)produce the able body and heterosexuality. But precisely because these systems depend on a queer/disabled existence that can never quite be contained, able-bodied heterosexuality's hegemony is always in danger of being disrupted. I draw attention to

critically queer, severely disabled possibilities to further an incorporation of the two fields, queer theory and disability studies, in the hope that such a collaboration (which in some cases is already occurring, even when it is not acknowledged or explicitly named as such) will exacerbate, in more productive ways, the crisis of authority that currently besets heterosexual/able-bodied norms. Instead of invoking the crisis in order to resolve it (as in a film like *As Good As It Gets*), I would argue that a queer/disability studies (in productive conversations with disabled/queer movements outside the academy) can continuously invoke, in order to further the crisis, the inadequate resolutions that compulsory heterosexuality and compulsory able-bodiedness offer us. And in contrast to an able-bodied culture that holds out the promise of a substantive (but paradoxically always elusive) ideal, a queer/disabled perspective would resist delimiting the kinds of bodies and abilities that are acceptable or that will bring about change. Ideally, a queer/disability studies—like the term *queer* itself—might function "oppositionally and relationally but not necessarily substantively, not as a positivity but as a positionality, not as a thing, but as a resistance to the norm" (Halperin, 66). Of course, in calling for a queer/disability studies without a necessary substance, I hope it is clear that I do not mean to deny the materiality of queer/disabled bodies, as it is precisely those material bodies that have populated the movements and brought about the changes detailed above. Rather, I mean to argue that critical queerness and severe disability are about collectively transforming (in ways that cannot necessarily be predicted in advance) the substantive uses to which queer/disabled existence has been put by a system of compulsory able-bodiedness, about insisting that such a system is never as good as it gets, and about imagining bodies and desires otherwise.

NOTES

1. In 1976, the Brussels Tribunal on Crimes against Women identified "compulsory heterosexuality" as one such crime (Katz, 26). A year earlier, in her important

article "The Traffic in Women: Notes on the 'Political Economy' of Sex," Gayle Rubin examined the ways in which "obligatory heterosexuality" and "compulsory heterosexuality" function in what she theorized as a larger sex/gender system (179, 198; cited in Katz, 132). Rich's 1980 article, which has been widely cited and reproduced since its initial publication, was one of the most extensive analyses of compulsory heterosexuality in feminism. I agree with Jonathan Ned Katz's insistence that the concept is redundant because "any society split between heterosexual and homosexual is compulsory" (164), but I also acknowledge the historical and critical usefulness of the phrase. It is easier to understand the ways in which a society split between heterosexual and homosexual is compulsory precisely because of feminist deployments of the redundancy of compulsory heterosexuality. I would also suggest that popular queer theorizing outside of the academy (from drag performances to activist street theater) has often employed redundancy performatively to make a critical point.

2. In an effort to forge a political connection between all women, Rich uses the terms "lesbian" and "lesbian continuum" to describe a vast array of sexual and affectional connections throughout history, many of which emerge from historical and cultural conditions quite different from those that have made possible the identity of lesbian (192–199). Moreover, by using "lesbian continuum" to affirm the connection between lesbian and heterosexual women, Rich effaces the cultural and sexual specificity of contemporary lesbian existence.

3. The incorporation of queer theory and disability studies that I argue for here is still in its infancy. It is in cultural activism and cultural theory about AIDS (such as John Nguyet Erni's *Unstable Frontiers* or Cindy Patton's *Fatal Advice*) that a collaboration between queer theory and disability studies is already proceeding and has been for some time, even though it is not yet acknowledged or explicitly named as such. Michael Davidson's "Strange Blood: Hemophobia and the Unexplored Boundaries of Queer Nation" is one of the finest analyses to date of the connections between disability studies and queer theory.

4. The collective projects that I refer to are, of course, the projects of gay liberation and queer studies in the academy and the disability rights movement and disability studies in the academy. This chapter is part of my own contribution to these projects and is part of my longer work in progress, titled *Crip Theory: Cultural Signs of Queerness and Disability*.

5. David Mitchell and Sharon Snyder are in line with many scholars working in disability studies when they point out the "ominous silence in the humanities" on the subject of disability (1). See, for other examples, Simi Linton's discussion of the "divided curriculum" (71–116), and assertions by Rosemarie Garland-Thomson and by Lennard Davis about the necessity of examining disability alongside other categories of difference such as race, class, gender, and sexuality (Garland-Thomson, 5; Davis, xi).

6. Disability studies is not the only field Vincent has attacked in the mainstream media; see her article "The Future of Queer: Wedded to Orthodoxy," which mocks academic queer theory. Neither being disabled nor being gay or lesbian in and of itself guarantees the critical consciousness generated in the disability rights or queer movements, or in queer theory or disability studies: Vincent herself is a lesbian journalist, but her writing clearly supports both able-bodied and heterosexual norms. Instead of a stigmaphilic response to queer/disabled existence, finding "a commonality with those who suffer from stigma, and in this alternative realm [learning] to value the very things the rest of the world despises" (Warner, *Trouble,* 43), Vincent reproduces the dominant culture's stigmaphobic response. See Warner's discussion of Erving Goffman's concepts of stigmaphobe and stigmaphile (41–45).

7. Michel Foucault's discussion of "docile bodies" and his theories of disciplinary practices are in the background of much of my analysis here (135–169).

8. See my discussion of Butler, Gloria Anzaldua, and critical queerness in *The Queer Renaissance: Contemporary American Literature and the Reinvention of Lesbian and Gay Identities* (149–153).

9. On the history of the AIDS Coalition to Unleash Power (ACT UP), see Douglas Crimp and Adam Rolston's *AIDS Demo-Graphics*. Lorde recounts her experiences with breast cancer and imagines a movement of one-breasted women in *The Cancer Journals*. Joseph P. Shapiro recounts both the history of the Rolling Quads and the Independent Living Movement and the Deaf President Now action in *No Pity: People with Disabilities Forging a New Civil Rights Movement* (41–58; 74–85). Deaf activists have insisted for some time that deafness should not be understood as a disability and that people living with deafness, instead, should be seen as having a distinct language and culture. As the disability rights movement has matured, however, some Deaf activists and scholars in Deaf studies have rethought this position and have

claimed disability (that is, disability revalued by a disability rights movement and disability studies) in an attempt to affirm a coalition with other people with disabilities. It is precisely such a reclaiming of disability that I want to stress here with my emphasis on severe disability.

WORKS CITED

As Good As It Gets. Dir. James L. Brooks. Perf. Jack Nicholson, Helen Hunt, and Greg Kinnear. TriStar, 1997.

Berube, Michael. *Life As We Know It: A Father, a Family, and an Exceptional Child.* New York: Vintage-Random House, 1996.

Butler, Judith. "Critically Queer." *GLQ: A Journal of Lesbian and Gay Studies* 1.1 (1993): 17–32.

———. *Gender Trouble: Feminism and the Subversion of Identity.* New York: Routledge, 1990.

———. "Imitation and Gender Insubordination." In *Inside/Out: Lesbian Theories, Gay Theories,* edited by Diana Fuss, (13–31). New York: Routledge, 1991.

Crimp, Douglas, and Adam Rolston. *AIDS DemoGraphics.* Seattle: Bay Press, 1990.

Davidson, Michael. "Strange Blood: Hemophobia and the Unexplored Boundaries of Queer Nation." In *Beyond the Binary: Reconstructing Cultural Identity in a Multicultural Context,* edited by Timothy Powell (39–60). New Brunswick: Rutgers UP, 1999.

Davis, Lennard J. *Enforcing Normalcy: Disability, Deafness, and the Body.* London: Verso, 1995.

Erni, John Nguyet. *Unstable Frontiers: Technomedicine and the Cultural Politics of "Curing" AIDS.* Minneapolis: U of Minnesota P, 1994.

In the Gloaming. Dir. Christopher Reeve. Perf. Glenn Close, Robert Sean Leonard, and David Strathairn. HBO, 1997.

Foucault, Michel. *Discipline and Punish: The Birth of the Prison.* Translated by Alan Sheridan. New York: Vintage-Random House, 1977.

Garland-Thomson, Rosemarie. *Extraordinary Bodies: Figuring Physical Disability in American Culture and Literature.* New York: Columbia UP, 1997.

Katz, Jonathan Ned. *The Invention of Heterosexuality.* New York: Dutton, 1995.

Kushner, Tony. "Foreword: Notes Toward a Theater of the Fabulous." In *Staging Lives: An Anthology of Contemporary Gay Theater,* edited by John M. Clum, vii–ix. Boulder: Westview Press, 1996.

Linton, Simi. *Claiming Disability: Knowledge and Identity.* New York: NYU Press, 1998.

Lorde, Audre. *The Cancer Journals.* San Francisco: Aunt Lute Books, 1980.

McRuer, Robert. "As Good As It Gets: Queer Theory and Critical Disability." *GLQ: A Journal of Lesbian and Gay Studies* 9.1–2 (2003): 79–105.

———. *Crip Theory: Cultural Signs of Queerness and Disability.* New York: NYU Press, 2006.

———. *The Queer Renaissance: Contemporary American Literature and the Reinvention of Lesbian and Gay Identities.* New York: NYU Press, 1997.

Mitchell, David T., and Sharon L. Snyder. "Introduction: Disability Studies and the Double Bind of Representation." In *The Body and Physical Difference: Discourses of Disability,* edited by Mitchell and Snyder, 1–31. Ann Arbor: U of Michigan P, 1997.

Norden, Martin F. *The Cinema of Isolation: A History of Physical Disability in the Movies.* New Brunswick: Rutgers UP, 1994.

Patton, Cindy. *Fatal Advice: How Safe-Sex Education Went Wrong.* Durham: Duke UP, 1997.

Rich, Adrienne. "Compulsory Heterosexuality and Lesbian Existence." In *Powers of Desire: The Politics of Sexuality,* edited by Ann Snitow, Christine Stansell, and Sharon Thompson, 177–205. New York: Monthly Review Press, 1983.

Rubin, Gayle. "The Traffic in Women: Notes on the 'Political Economy' of Sex." In *Toward an Anthropology of Women,* edited by Rayna R. Reiter, 157–210. New York: Monthly Review Press, 1975.

Shapiro, Joseph P. *No Pity: People with Disabilities Forging a New Civil Rights Movement.* New York: Times Books-Random House, 1993.

Vincent, Norah. "Enabling Disabled Scholarship." *Salon.* Aug. 18, 1999. Available at http://www.salon.com/books/it/1999/08/18/disability

———. "The Future of Queer: Wedded to Orthodoxy." *The Village Voice* 22 Feb. 2000: 16.

Warner, Michael. "Normal and Normaller: Beyond Gay Marriage." *GLQ: A Journal of Lesbian and Gay Studies* 5.2 (1999): 119–171.

———. *The Trouble with Normal: Sex, Politics, and the Ethics of Queer Life.* New York: The Free Press, 1999.

Watney, Simon. *Policing Desire: Pornography, AIDS, and the Media.* 2nd ed. Minneapolis: U of Minnesota P, 1989.

Wendell, Susan. *The Rejected Body: Feminist Philosophical Reflections on Disability.* New York: Routledge, 1996.

Williams, Raymond. *Keywords: A Vocabulary of Culture and Society.* Rev. ed. New York: Oxford UP, 1983.

7 • *Adam Isaiah Green*

REMEMBERING FOUCAULT: QUEER THEORY AND DISCIPLINARY POWER

DISCUSSION QUESTIONS

1. What are some of Foucault's foundational insights that continue to engage sexuality scholars?
2. What contribution does Green make to expanding Foucault's analysis of discourse in new directions? Do you agree with his argument? Why or why not?
3. What role have gender and sexual discourses played in your own conception of your gender and sexual identities? Provide at least three very concrete examples.
4. What is "power" according to Foucault and Green? How does this differ from more common understandings of power?

INTRODUCTION

Contemporary students of gender and sexuality, particularly those trained from a humanities or queer theoretical perspective, could be forgiven for leaving the classroom with the sentiment that social categories are a highly problematic evil requiring the tools of deconstruction and the mentorship of the resident PhD to exorcise. Indeed, some of the most popular post-structural feminist and queer theoretical approaches are founded on the axiom that modern discourses of gender and sexual orientation constitute subjectivities in a process of domination and social control (Butler, 1993, 2004; Eng et al., 2005; Fuss, 1991; Warner, 1993; Wilchins, 2004). And with good reason. Whereas Weber conceived of power as the ability to realize

one's will in the face of resistance from another (Weber, 1978), Foucault (1977, 1980), in the early and middle part of his career, observed a form of modern power found in the capacity of discourse to constitute identities, desires and practices (Frank, 1998). Held by no one but inherent in all relations, this modern form of power—*disciplinary power*—transforms 'docile bodies' into disciplined subjects, including subjects of the state (the good citizen, the welfare mother), subjects of medicine and psychiatry (the female, the homosexual, the HIV infected), and subjects of empire (the racialized Other), among others. From this theoretical starting point, a now rich queer theoretical literature puts disciplinary power in high relief, 'denaturalizing' the discursively constituted post-structural 'subject' (Dunn, 1997; Green, 2007; Jagose, 1996) while promoting

Green, Adam Isaiah. "Remembering Foucault: Queer Theory and Disciplinary Power." *Sexualities*, Vol. 13, No. 3 (2010): 316–337. Reprinted by permission of SAGE Publications.

a politics of transgression . . . (Butler, 1993; Green, 2002; Stein and Plummer, 1996).

In the present article I draw on the sexual and gendered self in the sociological literature to offer an alternative reading of disciplinary power that finds its roots in and extends Foucault's own reflections on the matter of subjectivity and discourse. My discussion takes two directions. First, I review cases from the literature whereby sexual and gender discourses—such as the categories of sexual orientation and transgender—appear to *expand* upon, rather than narrow and set in stone, the possibilities of the self. In these cases, the subjects of discourse are exposed to empowering content that opens up new pathways for self-development and life satisfaction that were previously unimaginable or unforeseeable. Ironically, despite the foundational anti-identity position that defines a queer theoretical epistemology (Seidman, 1993; Stein and Plummer, 1996), queer theory itself may work precisely in this fashion, providing a new identity category (Green, 2007) and a corresponding set of critical practices for anchoring a 'queer' self emancipated from an otherwise determined field of normalization. More than simply an instance of 'reverse discourse' (Foucault, 1980), these cases call into question the degree to which disciplinary power works only in the service of domination and social control. . . .

Second, following Giddens (1992), I argue that late modernity provides the historical conditions under which some individuals gain reflexive distance from their subject positions in a manner obscured by the standard queer theoretical account. In this context and for these individuals, the multiplicity of available discourses and their often contradictory content may resemble more a menu of sensitizing *self-schemas* than a regime of social control. . . . In short, I argue that sexual and gender discourses can function as *both* building blocks of subjectification and pliable identity schemas that offer a terrain of expanded opportunities for self-development. . . . This argument, too, is not inconsistent with Foucault's analysis of power and subjectivity but, on the contrary, is embedded within all three volumes of *The History of Sexuality,* most especially his late work on the care of the self (Foucault, 1980, 1985, 1986).

. . .

DISCIPLINARY POWER AND THE MODERN SELF: A GLANCE AT THE LITERATURE

THE DISCIPLINARY SOCIETY

Perhaps no one has had as central a role in the formulation of the concept of disciplinary power than Foucault, who both founded the concept and applied it across a wide range of social and historical cases. It was Foucault (1977) who argued that, much like the moulding of the 18th-century male body into the punishing, machine-like European soldier, modern citizens, too, are objects of transformation and discipline. Under the sway of the reigning ideas of a given knowledge producer—be it the state, the prison or the mental hospital—modern individuals are members of the 'disciplinary society' within which identities are constituted in a process of discursive subjectification. Here, subjectification—or, the making of subjects and subjectivities—occurs not through physical coercion, but through 'disciplinary coercion' (Foucault, 1977: 138), whereby individual 'bodies'—from thoughts to the corpus—are meticulously produced in a variety of 'projects of docility' (1977: 136). These projects are enacted in the form of institutional practices, but they are first and foremost guided by the modern quest for the 'truth' of the self. As such, actors cultivate the bodies and identities of a given social classification in the name of self-knowledge, to become agents of their own construction and regulation—that is, their own subjectification. These classifications are not merely empty taxonomic signifiers but, rather, are filled with content that establish the basis of identity and social intelligibility (Butler, 1993). This is the poststructural making of the subject whereby an actor's subjugation is accomplished through his or her own 'will to knowledge.' . . . With regard to modern sexuality, Foucault's concept of disciplinary power is most fully realized.[1] Here, sexuality is less something discovered than something cultivated and implanted—an effect of various institutionalized practices and expert discourses producing the 19th-century hysterical female body (Bartky, 1988; Beechy and Donald, 1985; Foucault, 1980); the dangerous sexuality of children (Edelman, 2004; Foucault,

1980); the homosexual 'personage' (Foucault, 1980; Katz, 2007), among many other 'perverse' (i.e. non-reproductive) sexualities and identities. In these instances, disciplinary power is not a coercive restraint or 'negative', as is the case of the traditional, Weberian concept of sovereign power, but is instead 'positive' insofar as it is productive of identity, subjectivity, and practice.

Nevertheless, if the post-structural formulation of power is 'positive' because it is productive, it at the same time regards power as 'negative' in the normative sense. That is, disciplinary power works to produce bodies, practices and subjectivities that, while not reducible to a particular political domain, nevertheless, bear the imprint of a given interest and logic—including patriarchy (Butler, 1993; Currie, 1999; Haraway, 1991; McNay, 1995; Miller, 1993; Smith Rosenberg, 1989), the consolidation of the 19th- and 20th-century western middle class (Chauncey, 1994; Foucault, 1980), neo-liberalism (Bratich et al., 2000; Ferguson, 2005) and colonialism (McClintock, 1995; Stoller, 1995), among others. . . . Put more broadly, classifications of sex, sexual orientation and race fix bodies, subjectivities and identities in socially constructed categories, which, in turn, form the basis of stratification, social regulation and control. Hence Butler issues the quintessential post-structural rejection of social categories: 'I'm permanently troubled by identity categories, consider them to be invariable stumbling-blocks and understand them, even promote them, as sites of necessary trouble' (Butler, 1991; 14). Similarly, Eng et al. (2005), writing on the contemporary objectives of queer theory, confirm: '[I]t is crucial to insist yet again on the capacity of queer studies to mobilize a broad social critique of race, gender, class, nationality, and religion, as well as sexuality' (2005: 4).

While rejecting a project of liberation grounded in the simplistic premise of freedom from power, these formulations nevertheless regard discourse as a problem to be overcome. . . .

POWER, GENDER, AND SEXUAL ORIENTATION

With regard to gender and sexual orientation, queer theory and post-structural feminist approaches analyse these as effects of disciplinary power whereby the state, medicine and eventually the lay public take hold of an infinite human potentiality and transform it into fixed binary oppositions—homosexuality and heterosexuality, woman and man (Wilchins, 2004). More specifically, with regard to sexual orientation, queer theory adopts a Foucaultian historical perspective whereby the categories 'heterosexual' and 'homosexual' are said to be the invention of 'expert' knowledges disseminated through medical texts, psychiatric conferences, the practice of medicine and psychiatry, the law, the education system and the popular imaginary (Chauncey, 1994; Valocchi, 1999). Subsequently, individuals internalize these categories and organize their identities, practices and politics around the category itself. Thenceforth, what was construed as nothing more than a set of (sinful) sexual acts prior to the 19th century, became a primary source of identity after it. . . . Once sexual orientation established a foothold in social relations, individuals were then compelled to comply with the norms of heterosexuality and homosexuality in order to obtain social intelligibility. . . .

DISCIPLINARY POWER AND THE SEXUAL AND GENDERED SELF

Despite the enormous influence of post-structural theory in the study of gender and sexuality (Epstein, 1996; Seidman, 1996; Valocchi, 2005), there is a domain of empirical research within which the effects of disciplinary power are less clear. In fact, as I show later, in certain social and historical contexts, classifications related to gender and sexual orientation carry content tied as much to an *expansion* of the horizons of what is imaginable for the self (Adam, 2000) as to subordination and social control. . . . Put another way, discursive power has the potential to work in an emancipatory process that promotes new pathways for self-development and life satisfaction that were previously unimaginable. . . .

For instance, in regard to sexual orientation, work by Adam (2000) and Bereket and Adam (2006) make this point strikingly clear. Among a sample of men who reported having sex with men (MSM), Adam (2000) found marked differences in the ways they self-identified, including appropriation of the labels 'not gay,' 'bisexual' and 'gay'. Differences in self-categorization were associated with distinctions in how these groups of men conceived their intimate lives. Those men who self-identified as 'gay' articulated a broader repertoire of ideas about intimate relationships between men than those who self-identified in the other two categories. That is, while the 'not gay'- and 'bisexual'-identified men typically spoke of intimate relations between men in terms of sexual acts alone, 'gay'-identified men articulated not only the sexual dimensions of their sexual identification but, more, the emotional and romantic elements that can develop between homosexual men. In this regard, gay discourses provided a broader repertoire of possibilities of intimate life in a same-sex dyad, including those found in books and through conversations with other gay-identified men. Perhaps most importantly, against an otherwise heteronormative discursive monopoly on intimate life, gay discourse offered alternative possibilities for same-sex relationships and the gay self that made the men who appropriated the discourse receptive to a broader array of experiences and possibilities. . . .

In a related vein, perhaps nowhere in the arena of gender and sexuality is the impact of identity discourse on experience and the self more clear than in the emergence of transgender identities in the past 30 years. In this period, multiple discourses of gender identity, including an ever-broadening array of gender identity classifications, have provided a set of options for gender identity and embodiment heretofore unseen in the modern West. While other societies have recognized that human beings need not present as one of two, 'opposing' genders, but may occupy, in fact, a *third* gender—such as the berdache of Native American societies (Whitehead, 1993) or the Hijras of India (Nanda, 1990)—the same insight has been slow to gain traction in North America. In the USA and Canada, for instance, sex and gender have been conceptually aligned such that one's gender is assumed to follow "naturally" from one's birth sex (Kessler and McKenna, 1978; West and

Zimmerman, 1987). Consequently, deviation from this binary sex-gender system has been the occasion for widespread stigmatization and medicalization (Cromwell, 1999; Scott-Dixon, 2006). However, over the last 30 years, a transgender movement has gained increasing momentum, broadening the possibilities of gender identification far beyond the traditional binary sex-gender system. Fostered, in part, by transgender organizing in the 1990s, including coalitions of cross dressers, transsexuals and the intersexed (Meyerowitz, 2002), trans organizations, trans subcultures and their academic counterparts have produced a body of discourse around sex and gender for which 'transition' to either one sex or the other is eroding in importance (Hansbury, 2005). In its place, the category 'transgender' reconceives the basic elements of gender—sex assignment, gender identity and gender role—and promotes a much wider range of identifications and embodiments.

Hansbury's (2005) analysis of 'transmasculinity' makes this point eminently clear. Transmasculinity is a broad identity category that defines a person, usually born female, for whom masculine identification is more salient than female identification, but for whom the binary classifications of 'man/woman' do not suffice. In other words, transmasculine individuals traverse a wide spectrum of self-reflexive identifications and embodiments that favour but do not reduce to male/masculinity. In Hansbury's words:

> The real difference among the various identities are based less on how many testosterone injections one has had or which surgeries one has opted to undergo, and more on how each person interprets his or her identity—how she or he perceives himself or herself and how he or she wishes to be perceived by others. Someone may identify as a Transsexual Man yet still maintain his breasts and forgo testosterone. Another may choose to undergo a mastectomy, take low dosage testosterone, and identify as a Passing Woman. (2005: 245)

Organized in this manner, the category 'transmasculine' expands both what is imaginable and what is possible for those exposed to the discourse. . . .

The array of labels used within the transmasculine spectrum are many and attest to the infinitude of the community . . . Arranged here in an unscientific, somewhat linear fashion, from (perhaps) the more male-identified to the more nonbinary, these labels include, but are not limited to, Man, MTM, FTM, Transsexual Man, Man of Transsexual Experience, New Man, Transman, Transfag, Transqueer, Gender-Queer, Guy, Boi, Trans-Butch, Tomboy, Boy-Chick, Gender Outlaw, Drag King, Passing Woman, Bearded Female, Two-Spirit, Ungendered, Gender Trash, Questioning, Just Curious. (Hansbury, 2005: 245)

In total, the transmasculine category does not dissolve gender as a foundational axis for human subjectivity, any more than the category 'gay' dissolves sexual orientation. Nevertheless, in certain historical contexts, these classifications and their content do less to ensnare individuals in broader regimes of social control than provide an ideational foundation upon which to expand the range of who and what one may be beyond the dominant field of discourse. . . .

Ironically, despite the axiomatic repudiation of identity at the heart of queer theory, the category 'queer' in queer discourse and critical practice may work in precisely the same fashion. While queer theory was never intended to produce a new identity or a 'fixed referent' (Eng et al., 2005), the term 'queer' nevertheless denotes a subject position outside of normalization and the traditional configurations of gender and sexuality (Epstein, 1996; Gamson, 2000; Green, 2002). . . .

DISCIPLINARY POWER AND THE SELF IN LATE MODERNITY

If sexual and gender discourses—including those attached to the categories of 'gay,' 'transmasculine' and 'queer'—can serve to expand the possibilities of self in a way that promotes a process of self-fashioning, so too, the profusion of competing and sometimes contradictory identity discourses characteristic of the late modern period may introduce a degree of self reflexivity and identity negotiation in a manner not captured by the post-structural turn. I do not intend

here to suggest that late modernity is an era free from the imperative of identity (nay, far from it), nor the domain of self-determining agents but, rather, that identity itself is an epochal project subject to a unique degree of self-scrutiny and transformation (Giddens, 1992; Hall, 1996). Under these conditions, disciplinary power and the 'project of docility' it animates are perhaps more complex, more mediated, and much less clear in their effects than suggested by popular post-structural scholarship.

. . .

CONCLUSION: THE PROBLEM OF DISCIPLINARY POWER

To the extent that, as Berger and Luckmann observe, human beings have 'underdeveloped instincts' (1966: 48), the absence of which necessitates a symbolic system for survival, post-structuralists are right to emphasize the significance of disciplinary power in shaping the self. Indeed, even as discourse and identity categories are not of the natural world, they nonetheless come to constitute 'the natural' for human beings (Connell, 1995). What is less clear, however, is the extent to which disciplinary power has the kind of effects that are central to the post-structural analysis of social classifications. The question is important because it bears on how we theorize the self, its relationship to knowledge and the institutional order, and the conditions under which self-development (within system constraints) may be more or less possible.

. . .

Notably, a more complex rendering of disciplinary power is not antithetical to Foucault's framework but, rather, recalls lines of theoretical development indigenous to his analysis. Beyond the mere possibility of reverse discourse, disciplinary power was seen by Foucault to be the source of expanded pleasure and desire, too. With regard to the relationship of power and sexuality, for instance, Foucault writes:

The power which thus took charge of sexuality set about contacting bodies, caressing them with its eyes, intensifying areas, electrifying surfaces, dramatizing troubled moments. It wrapped the sexual body in its embrace. There was undoubtedly an increase in effectiveness and an extension of the domain controlled; but also a sensualization of power and a gain of pleasure (1980: 44).

In fact, Foucault framed the very 'problem' of disciplinary power as one characterized by a 'regime of power-knowledge-pleasure' (1980: 11).

> Why has sexuality been so widely discussed, and what has been said about it? What were the effects of power generated by what was said? What are the links between these discourses, these effects of power, and the pleasures that were invested by them? . . . The object, in short, is to define the regime of power-knowledge-pleasure that sustains the discourse on human sexuality in our part of the world. (1980: 11) . . .

While the late modern self is ripe for subjectification, disciplinary power does not work in the same ways and for the same people across time, space and society. These distinct possibilities call out for a historical and sociological analysis of the variable effects of disciplinary power, and the conditions that make these effects more or less likely.

That said, the conditions that underpin the effects of disciplinary power are unlikely to subscribe in any simple or clear way to existing theories around social structure and power within sociology. For instance, while class may in some instances shape the conditions under which one has more or less choice in appropriating a given discourse, it would be a mistake to assume that economic necessity is related in any linear way to subjectification, as if the poor were always and in all cases more susceptible to discursive power than the well off. As an example, it is now widely agreed that sexological discourse of the 19th and early 20th centuries affected the middle classes first and foremost in the western world, decades *before* the working classes, and in a manner commensurate with the particular problems of an embattled middle class (D'Emilio, 1993; Foucault, 1980; Greenberg, 1988). . . .

Ultimately, whether and to what extent disciplinary power serves as a point of departure for the elaboration of self or, rather, a moment of social control, is not fully knowable in the abstract. But this is precisely the point. Rather, in each instance, the analyst must contextualize disciplinary power in light of the content of these discourses and the structural conditions within which individuals live. To be sure, identity categories are unlikely to be equally tractable across time and space, and processes of subjectification and, perhaps, negotiation, will always emerge within the constraints of particular social histories. This means, ultimately, that disciplinary power is a historical and sociological phenomenon that will require greater care in identifying the social conditions that give rise to modern subjects and selves.

NOTE

1. There is some disagreement about the extent to which Foucault's conception of the disciplinary society was indigenous to his work or an artefact of migration across the Atlantic to North America. For instance, see Didier Eribon (1994) on this point.

REFERENCES

Adam, Barry (1987) *The Rise of a Gay and Lesbian Movement.* Boston, MA: Twayne.

Adam, Barry (2000) 'Love and Sex in Constructing Identity Among Men Who Have Sex with Men', *International Journal of Sexuality and Gender Studies* 5(4); 325–39.

Almaguer, Thomas (1993) 'Chicano Men: A Cartography of Homosexual Identity and Behavior', in Henry Abelove, Maichele Aina Barale and David M. Halperin (eds) *The Lesbian and Gay Studies Reader,* pp. 255–73. New York: Routledge.

Altman, Dennis (1973) *Homosexual Oppression and Liberation.* New York: Outerbridge & Dienstfrey.

Armstrong, Elizabeth (2002) *Forging Gay Identities: Organizing Sexuality in San Francisco, 1950–1994.* Chicago, IL: University of Chicago Press.

Bartky, S.L. (1988) 'Foucault, Femininity and the Modernization of Patriarchal Power', in I. Diamond and L. Quinby (eds) *Feminism and Foucault: Reflections on Resistance,* pp. 61–86. Boston, MA: Northeastern University Press.

Beechy, V. and Donald, J. (1985) *Subjectivity and Social Relations.* Milton Keynes: Open University Press.

Bereket, Tarik and Adam, Barry (2006) 'The Emergence of Gay Identities in Contemporary Turkey', *Sexualities* 9(2): 131–51.

Bereket, Tarik and Adam, Barry (2008) 'Navigating Islam and Same-Sex Liaisons Among Men in Turkey', *Journal of Homosexuality* 55(2): 204–22.

Berger, P. and Luckmann, T. (1966) *The Social Construction of Reality: A Treatise in the Sociology of Knowledge.* New York: Penguin.

Bratich, J., Packer, J. and McCarthy, C. (2000) *Foucault, Cultural Studies and Governmentality.* Albany; State University of New York Press.

Butler, Judith (1991) 'Imitation and Gender Insubordination', in Diana Fuss (ed.) *Inside/Out: Lesbian Theories, Gay Theories,* pp. 13–31. New York: Routledge.

Butler, Judith (1993) *Bodies That Matter: On the Discursive Limits of 'Sex'.* New York: Routledge.

Butler, Judith (2004) *Undoing Gender.* New York: Routledge.

Carrillo, Hector (2002) *The Night is Young: Sexuality in Mexico in the Times of AIDS.* Chicago, IL: University of Chicago Press.

Chauncey, George (1994) *Gay New York: Gender, Urban Culture, and the Making of the Gay Male World 1890– 1940.* Chicago, IL: University of Chicago Press.

Connell, R.W. (1995) *Masculinities.* Cambridge: Polity Press.

Cromwell, Jason (1999) *Transmen and FTMs: Identities, Bodies, Genders and Sexualities.* Urbana: University of Illinois Press.

Currie, D. (1999) *Girl Talk: Adolescents Magazines and Their Readers.* Toronto: University of Toronto Press.

D'Emilio, John (1993) 'Capitalism and Gay Identity', in H. Abelove, M. Barale and D. Halperin (eds) *The Lesbian and Gay Studies Reader,* pp 467–78. New York and London: Routledge.

Dunn, R.G. (1997) 'Self, identity, and difference: Mead and the Post-structuralists', *Sociological Quarterly* 38(4): 687–705.

Edelman, Lee (2004) *No Future: Queer Theory and The Death Drive.* Durham, NC: Duke University Press.

Eng, D.L., Halberstam, J. and Muñoz, J.E. (2005) 'Introduction: What's Queer about Queer Studies Now?' *Social Text* 84–85: 1–17.

Epstein, Steven (1996) 'A Queer Encounter: Sociology and the Study of Sexuality', in S. Seidman (ed.) *Queer Theory/Sociology,* pp. 145–67. Cambridge, MA: Blackwell.

Eribon, Didier (1994) *Michel Foucault* (trans. Besty Wing). Cambridge, MA: Harvard University Press.

Ferguson, Rodnick (2005) 'Introduction: What's Queer about Queer Studies Now?' special issue (eds D.L. Eng, J. Halberstam and J.E. Muñoz), *Social Text* 23(3–4) 84–5: 1–17.

Frank, Arthur (1998) 'Stories of Illness as Care of the Self: A Foucauldian Dialogue', *Health* 2(3): 328–48.

Foucault, Michel (1977) *Discipline and Punish: The Birth of the Prison.* New York: Vintage.

Foucault, Michel (1980) *The History of Sexuality: An Introduction.* New York: Vintage.

Foucault, Michel (1985) *The History of Sexuality Volume II: The Use of Pleasure,* New York: Vintage.

Foucault, Michel (1986) *The History of Sexuality Volume III: The Care of the Self.* New York: Vintage.

Fuss, D. (1991) 'Inside/Out', in D. Fuss (ed.) *Inside/Out. Lesbian Theories, Gay Theories,* pp. 1–10. New York and London: Routledge.

Gamson, Josh (1996) 'Must Identity Movements Self-Destruct?: A Queer Dilemma', in Seidman, Steven (ed.) *Queer Theory/Sociology,* pp. 399–420. New York: Blackwell.

Gamson, Josh (2000) 'Sexualities, Queer Theory, and Qualitative Research', in N. Denzin and Y. Lincoln (eds) *Handbook of Qualitative Research* (2nd edn), pp. 347–65. Thousand Oaks, CA and London: SAGE.

Giddens, Anthony (1992) *The Transformation of Intimacy: Sexuality, Love, and Eroticism in Modern Societies.* Stanford, CA: University of Stanford Press.

Green, Adam Isaiah (2002) 'Gay But Not Queer: Toward a Post-Queer Sexuality Studies', *Theory and Society* 31(4): 521–45.

Green, Adam Isaiah (2007) 'Queer Theory and Sociology: Locating the Subject and the Self in Sexuality Studies', *Sociological Theory* 25(1): 26–45.

Greenberg, David (1988) *The Construction of Homosexuality.* Chicago, IL: University of Chicago Press.

Hall, Stuart (1996) 'Who Needs Identity?' in Stuart Hall and Paul du Gay (eds) *Questions of Cultural Identity,* pp. 1–17. London: SAGE.

Halperin, David (1995) *Saint Foucault. Towards a Gay Hagiography.* New York and Oxford: Oxford University Press.

Halperin, David (2002) *How to Do the History of Homosexuality.* Chicago, IL and London: University of Chicago Press.

Hansbury, Grifin (2005) 'The Middle Men: An Introduction to the Transmasculine Identities', *Studies in Gender and Sexuality* 6E(3): 241–64.

Haraway, Donna J. (1991) *Simians, Cyborgs and Women: The Reinvention of Nature.* New York: Routledge.

Held, David (1986) *Models of Democracy*. Cambridge: Polity Press.

Katz, Jonathan Ned (2007) *The Invention of Heterosexuality*. Chicago, IL; University of Chicago Press.

Kessler, S. and McKenna, W. (1978) *Gender: An Ethomethodological Approach*. Chicago, IL: University of Chicago Press.

Jagose, A. (1996) *Queer Theory: An Introduction*. New York: New York University Press.

Levine, Martin (1998) *Gay Macho: The Life and Death of the Homosexual Clone*. New York: New York University Press.

McClintock, Anne (1995) *Imperial Leather: Race, Gender, and Sexuality in the Colonial Context*. New York: Routledge.

McIntosh, M. (1968) 'The Homosexual Role', in S. Seidman (ed.) *Queer Theory, Sociology*, pp. 33–40. Cambridge, MA: Blackwell.

McNay, Lois (1992) *Foucault and Feminism: Power, Gender and the Self*. New York: Polity Press.

McNay, Lois (1995) *Foucault and Feminism*. Boston, MA: Northeastern University Press.

Meyerowitz, Joanne (2002) *How Sex Changed: A History of Transsexuality in the United States*. Cambridge, MA: Harvard University Press.

Miller, L. (1993) 'Claims-Making from the Underside: Marginalization and Social Problems Analysis', in J.A. Holstein and G. Miller (eds) *Reconsidering Social Constructionism: Debates in Social Problems Theory*, pp. 349–76. New York: Aldine de Gruyter.

Murray, Stephen O. (1996) *American Gay*. Chicago, IL: University of Chicago Press.

Murray, Stephen O. (2000) *Homosexualities*. Chicago, IL: University of Chicago. Press.

Nanda, Serena (1990) *Neither Man Nor Woman: The Hijras of India*. Belmont, CA: Wadsworth Publishing Company.

Riley, Denise (1988) *'Am I That Name?' Feminism and the Category of Women in History*. London: Macmillan.

Rose, Nikolas (1996) *Inventing Our Selves*. Cambridge: Cambridge University Press.

Rose, Nikolas and Miller, Peter (1992) 'Political Power Beyond the State: Problematics of Government', *British Journal of Sociology*. 43(2): 173–205.

Rupp, Leila and Taylor, Verta (2004) *Drag Queens at the 801 Cabaret*. Chicago, IL: University of Chicago Press.

Scott-Dixon, Krista (2006) 'Trans/Forming Feminisms', in Krista Scott-Dixon (ed.) *Trans/Forming Feminisms: Trans-Feminist Voices Speak Out*, pp. 11–33. Toronto: Sumach Press.

Sedgwick, Eve Kosofsky (1990) *Epistemology of the Closet*. Berkeley: University of California Press.

Seidman, Stephen. (1993) 'Identity and Politics in a "Postmodern" Gay Culture: Some Historical and Conceptual Notes', in M. Warner (ed.) *Fear of a Queer Planet. Queer Politics and Social Theory*, pp. 105–42. Minnesota, MN: University of Minnesota Press.

Seidman, Stephen (1996) 'Introduction', in S. Seidman (ed.) *Queer Theory, Sociology*, pp. 1–29. Cambridge, MA: Blackwell.

Smith Rosenberg, Carroll (1989) 'The Body Politic', in Elizabeth Week (ed.) *Coming to Terms: Feminism, Theory Politics*, pp. 101–26. New York and London: Routledge.

Stein, A. and Plummer, K. (1996) '"I Can't Even Think Straight"; "Queer" Theory and the Missing Sexual Revolution in Sociology', in S. Seidman (ed.) *Queer Theory, Sociology*, pp. 129–44. Cambridge, MA: Blackwell.

Stevenson, Deborah (2002) 'Women, Sport and Globalization: Competing Discourses of Sexuality and Nation', *Journal of Sport & Social Issues* 26(2): 209–25.

Stoller, Ann Laura (1995) *Race and the Education of Desire: Foucault's History of Sexuality and the Colonial Order of Things*. London: Duke University Press.

Valocchi, Steve (1999) 'The Class-Inflected Nature of Gay Identity', *Social Problems* 46(2): 207–24.

Valocchi, Stephen (2005) 'Not Yet Queer Enough: The Lessons of Queer Theory for the Sociology of Gender and Sexuality', *Gender & Society* 19(6): 750–70.

Villarejo, Amy (2005) 'Tarrying with the Normative: Queer Theory and Black History', *Social Text* 23(3–4) 84–85: 69–84.

Warner, M. (1993) 'Introduction', in M. Warner (ed.) *Fear of a Queer Planet. Queer Politics and Social Theory*, pp. viii–xxxi. Minneapolis: University of Minnesota Press.

Weber, Max (1978) *Economy and Society: An Outline of Interpretive Sociology*. Berkeley: University of California Press.

West, C. and Zimmerman, D. (1987) 'Doing Gender', *Gender and Society* 1(2): 125–51.

Whitehead, Evelyn (1993) 'The Bow and the Burden Strap: A New Look at Institutionalized Homosexuality in Native North America', in H. Abelove, M. Barale and D. Halperin (eds), *The Lesbian and Gay Studies Reader*. New York and London: Routledge.

Wilchins, Riki (2004) *Queer Theory, Gender Theory. An Instant Primer*. Los Angeles, CA: Alyson Books.

8 • *Jane Ward*

NOWHERE WITHOUT IT
The Homosexual Ingredient in the Making of Straight White Men

DISCUSSION QUESTIONS

1. Do you find the specific cases Ward describes in her chapter surprising? Why or why not?
2. What insights does sexual activity between self-identified straight men provide us for advancing our understanding the construction of both masculinity and heterosexuality?
3. Based on Ward's analysis, can you identify other contexts where homosexual activity among heterosexual men might be most likely to take place?
4. Do you think similar activities occur among women? Why or why not?

About fifteen years ago, in the late 1990s, I was a young dyke who would occasionally date boring straight men, especially after a difficult queer breakup. I am not proud of this time in my life, but it is where this story begins. On one such date, one of these men sheepishly agreed to tell me some of the details of his experience in a fraternity at a Southern California university he had attended a few years prior. Looking for something—*anything*—to shift our conversation to my newfound queer feminist rage, I probed him for the most damning information about fraternity life at his notorious party school. I waited to hear contemptible stories of violations committed against drunken young women. I imagined that what he would tell me would offend my feminist sensibilities, that I would get angry, and that this would push me to stop seeing him and get back into the more personally meaningful and high-stakes terrain

of queer life. I do not doubt that he had tales of women and Rohypnol to tell, but when asked for the most confidential details about fraternity life, his response surprised me. He offered instead a story about a fairly elaborate hazing ritual called the "elephant walk," in which young men inserted their fingers into each other's anuses. Participants in the elephant walk were required to strip naked and stand in a circular formation, with one thumb in their mouth and the other in the anus of the young, typically white, man in front of them. Like circus elephants connected by tail and trunk, and ogled by human spectators, they walked slowly in a circle, linked thumb to anus, while older members of the fraternity watched and cheered.

At first I was a bit shocked, but then his story prompted me to recall another experience, one of watching a video in a senior seminar on Sexual

---

Ward, Jane. "Nowhere Without It: The Homosexual Ingredient in the Making of Straight White Men." Pp. 1–50. *Not Gay: Sex Between Straight White Men.* New York: NYU Press.

Politics that I took while I, too, was an undergraduate in college. There were nine students in our course, and our final project was to produce a multimedia presentation that would creatively explore the complexities of "postmodern sexuality." My presentation—basically a fanatical ode to Madonna—did not receive a warm reception from the graduate student teaching the seminar, but all of us *were* impressed by an ethnographic film submitted by the only male student in the course. The video, a compilation of chaotic footage he had shot exclusively inside the bedrooms and bathroom of his fraternity house, showed nude white boys laughing and holding down other white boys whom they mounted and "pretended" to fuck on top of a bunk bed. I recall the small frat-house bedroom packed wall to wall with shirtless young white men wearing baseball caps, screaming hysterically, playfully pushing and punching their way through the crowd of bodies to obtain a better view of the "unfortunate" boys underneath the pile of their naked fraternity brothers. The boys on top were laughing and calling those underneath lugs: the boys on the bottom were laughing, too, and calling the aggressors fags as they struggled to switch the scenario and get on top. None of these boys seemed like fags to me. The student who shot and edited the video, himself a member of this fraternity, had remarkably little to say about the meaning of these images. "We're just fucking around. It's a frat thing. . . . It's hard to explain," he told us.

As a young feminist, I was repelled by the hetero-masculine culture of abjection and aggression in which these encounters were embedded, and I believed that this way of relating to sexuality was not unrelated to homophobia and misogyny. Both of these men—the date who reported to me about the elephant walk and my classmate who had filmed his fraternity brothers engaged in "pretend" sex—seemed to take for granted that these were scenes of power and humiliation, not sex. These encounters can be read as humiliating or disgusting precisely because they involve normal, heterosexual young men behaving like fags, or being subjected, ostensibly against their will, to homosexual contact. And yet, despite the homophobia of the participants, I

was also captivated and excited by the existence of this kind of contact between straight men. The budding queer critic (and pervert) in me was impressed by the imagination required to manufacture these scenarios, the complex rules that structured them, and the performative and ritualistic way that straight men touched one another's bodies or ordered others to do so.

I also sensed that the men involved believed they were doing something *productive*—something fundamentally *heterosexual, masculine,* and *white*—as they fingered each other's anuses. Consider, for instance, this quotation from a currently popular website by and for young men in fraternities (also known as "bros"), which explains the purpose of the elephant walk as follows:

> The rule of thumb is the heavier the hazing, the stronger the bros [brothers]. By doing things like forcing your pledges/rooks to eat human shit or do an elephant walk you are basically saying, "Hey, by learning what your fellow bros' shit tastes like you will be better bros," and I have to say—I really respect that. . . . War builds amazing bonds. Hazing is basically war, only instead of freedom the end goal is getting hammered constantly with bros who are cool as shit and banging hot slam pieces [women]. It's still up in the air which goal is more important, but one thing is for sure, bros would be nowhere without hazing.[1]

Is it possible that straight white men would really be nowhere without the opportunity for intimate contact with one another's anuses? Before I answer that question, I will say that what *is* clear is that when young white men grope one another, they believe they are getting work done. They are, as the straight dude quoted above suggests, engaged in something urgent and powerful—a form of bonding comparable to what soldiers experience during times of war, and a kind of relief and triumph comparable to freedom.

To the extent that sexual contact between straight white men is ever acknowledged, the cultural narratives that circulate around these practices typically suggest that they are *not gay* in their identitarian consequences, but are instead about building heterosexual men, strengthening hetero-masculine bonds, and strengthening the bonds of white manhood in particular. . . .

Why focus on white men? All heterosexual practices—indeed, all sexual practices—are embedded within gendered and racialized circuits of meaning. For instance, as Chrys Ingraham demonstrates in the book *White Weddings,* the whiteness of weddings is not simply a matter of white bridal gowns, but a description of the white women who appear disproportionately in bridal magazines, the whiteness of Mattel's bridal-themed Barbies, and the racial hierarchy of the wedding industry itself. Idealized white femininity is central to the construction of weddings as special and perfect, and the wedding industry in turn reinforces the normalcy and legitimacy of whiteness. Similarly, this book attends to what whiteness *does* for white heterosexual men as they come into homosexual contact, and what homosexual contact does for white hetero-masculinity. While much attention has been paid to the ways that race and culture crosscut the sex practices of men of color, including and especially straight men of color who have sex with men "on the down low," the links between whiteness and male sexual fluidity are mostly unacknowledged. Most accounts of the down low suggest that straight-identified men of color who have sex with men are doing so because they are actually gay, but cannot come out due to elevated levels of homophobia in their ethnoracial communities. I'll return to this story later, but for now I raise it to point out that, in contrast, the links between whiteness and white male sexual fluidity have been largely ignored, as if white men's sex practices have nothing to do with their racial and cultural location. By focusing on straight white men, I want to think about the ways that whiteness and masculinity—as a particular nexus of power—enable certain kinds of sexual contact, sexual mobility, and sexual border crossing that are not possible, or at least don't carry the same cultural meanings, when enacted by men of color.

. . .

Research psychologists have long been concerned with the reasons that straight men engage in homosexual sex. The sheer number of terms invented by U.S. psychologists in the 1950s to describe such practices—"deprivational homosexuality," "facultative homosexuality," "functional homosexuality," "situational homosexuality," "opportunistic homosexuality," and so forth[2]—provides a window into the amount of effort researchers have expended to distinguish "false" homosexualities from their authentic, or truly gay, counterparts. A considerable body of twentieth-century psychological research on sex between straight men suggests that this sex most often results from desperate circumstances, such as in situations of heterosexual deprivation that occur in prisons and the military. According to this logic, a man with a heterosexual constitution may engage in homosexual sex acts (and presumably, vice versa), but if his homosexual encounters are *situational* (i.e., occurring only in prison, or while at sea, in military barracks, and so forth), these encounters are a blip on the otherwise static sexual radar screen. They signal nothing particularly meaningful about his sexuality.

Still today, the dominant mode of thinking within the disciplines of psychology and sexology—and arguably within the broader culture—is that the sexual content of male heterosexuality is fundamentally different from that of male homosexuality. When heterosexual men *do* engage in homosexual sex, and if they are not immediately presumed to be in the closet, these practices are treated as momentary aberrations, and a good deal of work goes into explaining why they occurred and why they are misrepresentative of, or discordant with, the true sexual orientation of participants.

. . .

FLUID SUBJECTS: THE GENERATION, GENDER, AND RACE OF SEXUAL FLUIDITY

"SHIT HAPPENS": THE HETEROFLEXIBLE YOUTH GENERATION

Regardless of how often the elephant walk or similar encounters actually occur in fraternities or elsewhere,[3] they are part of an increasingly familiar narrative about the sexual fluidity of a new generation of young heterosexuals. Consider, for instance, the most popular definition of "heteroflexible" that appears on the now iconic, youth-driven website urbandictionary.com: "I'm straight, but shit happens." This definition has received over 11,000 votes of approval by users of urbandictionary. While fraternity members who engage in the elephant walk, for instance, probably do not identify as "heteroflexible"—this *identity,* as distinct from the practice, is reportedly more popular with young women—the term certainly captures the driving logic behind the elephant walk. The very concept of heteroflexibility, as defined on urbandictionary.com and elsewhere, communicates three popular notions about human sexuality, notions that form the theoretical basis now used to explain a broad range of homosexual encounters experienced by heterosexuals, including those of recent interest to the corporate media, such as "the phenomenon of straight girls kissing":

1. Sexual *behaviors* are often random, accidental, and meaningless ("shit" can and does "happen").
2. But, regardless of a person's sexual *behavior,* it is possible to be certain about one's fundamental sexual *constitution* ("I'm straight"), which is increasingly believed to be hardwired or biologically determined, a fact I will soon address.
3. And, *individuals are not to be blamed* for sexual behaviors that are in conflict with their sexual constitution, especially when various circumstances demand, or at least encourage, flexibility. (Consider, for instance, the sentence offered on urbandictionary.com to illustrate how one would use the term "heteroflexible" in speech: "Dude, it's not my fault. I was drunk and it was fun. What can I say? I'm heteroflexible.")

A fourth "fact" about heteroflexibility, according to some sociologists,[4] is that it is a *new* phenomenon. That heterosexuals engage in homosexual sex is nothing new, they argue. But what *is* ostensibly new is the openness with which young people, especially girls who kiss girls, are approaching their sexual fluidity; in fact, they are so open about it that they have given it a name, an identity—heteroflexible—something heretofore unheard of. In fact, the existence of heterosexuals who cross the border into homosexual terrain is consistently viewed as a signal of the arrival of a

new and surprising sexual order, one ushered in by young people with their new-fangled ideas about sex. For instance, sociologist Laurie Essig, blogging for Salon.com, describes her irritated reaction after first being introduced to the term "heteroflexible," a reaction she explains primarily through the lens of a generational divide between her students and herself:

> There is nothing like teaching college students to make a person feel hopelessly out-of-date. . . . What I'm talking about here is "heteroflexibility." If you don't know what that is, it's time to admit that you're as out of it as I am. Heteroflexibility is the newest permutation of sexual identity. . . . [It] means that the person has or intends to have a primarily heterosexual lifestyle, with a primary sexual and emotional attachment to someone of the opposite sex. But that person remains open to sexual encounters and even relationships with persons of the same sex. It is a rejection of bisexuality since the inevitable question that comes up in bisexuality is one of preference, and the preference of the heteroflexible is quite clear. Heteroflexible, I am told, is a lighthearted attempt to stick with heterosexual identification while still "getting in on the fun of homosexual pleasures." . . . My reaction was predictable. . . . How could these kids go and invent yet another identity when "we" solved that problem for them in the 1980s and '90s? The word they were looking for was "queer" or even "bisexual," damnit. I was angry that they would throw out the politics and the struggles of naming that had come before them. . . . And then my middle-aged rage mellowed enough to see the true genius behind this new term. Heteroflexibility—not homosexuality or bisexuality—would bring about an end to the hegemony of heterosexuality. . . . The opposite of heteroflexible is heterorigid. Imagine saying to anyone that you're heterorigid. Sounds awful, right?[5]

Essig's characterization of heteroflexibility as "the newest permutation of sexual identity" mirrors most commentary on the topic. *TIME* reporter Jeffrey Kluger describes girl—girl heteroflexibility as a youth-driven trend, one facilitated by alcohol, girls' need for attention, and occasionally "genuine experimentation."[6] Kluger draws heavily on the work of feminist scholars Leila Rupp and Verta Taylor, who offer a more nuanced analysis, yet one still largely focused on youth and the characterization of hetero-flexibility as a new behavior. In their view, college-aged women "are engaging in new kinds of sexual behaviors," namely "using the heterosexual hookup culture [of college] to experiment with or engage in same-sex sexual interactions." They explain that "what young women call 'heteroflexibility' allows for behavior outside one's claimed sexual identity, although the lines between lesbian and non-lesbian women, whether heterosexual or bisexual, remain firmly in place."[7]

. . .

THE GENDER OF SEXUAL FLUIDITY

Commentary on heteroflexibility suggests that sexual fluidity is not only a youth trend, but a female one as well. Feminist sociologists point out that girls and women are given more room to explore gender and sexuality than boys, and are also influenced by a culture that both celebrates the sexual fluidity of female celebrities (Madonna, Britney Spears, Lady Gaga) and depicts lesbianism as an effective means of seducing men. Conversely, boys and men suffer greater gender regulation, have fewer models of male sexual fluidity, and are presumably unrewarded by women for any sexual fluidity they may express. As Rupp and Taylor explain, "men do not, at least in contemporary American culture, experience the same kind of fluidity. Although they may identify as straight *and* have sex with other men, they certainly don't make out at parties for the pleasure of women."[8]

Examinations of heteroflexibility also inevitably turn to the research findings of psychologists and human development scholars who believe that men's sexual desire is less flexible than women's for a variety of evolutionary reasons. Lisa Diamond, author of *Sexual Fluidity: Understanding Women's Love and Desire,* argues that women's sexual desires are more variable than men's, and that sexual variability, in general, is both hormonal and situational. In Diamond's view, female arousal is more easily triggered by situational factors and more linked to romantic love than men's. This, she argues, is an outcome of the fact that women's

hormonal cycles produce a relatively limited window of "proceptive" desire—the kind of intense, visceral, reproduction-oriented,[9] and lust-driven desire that emerges without any particular stimuli—as compared to men's presumably near-constant experience of this state. In contrast with men, women spend more time experiencing "receptive arousal," or sexual responsiveness to nonhormonal, social cues (e.g., watching a romantic movie, developing a strong emotional bond with someone, and so on). In this view, women have a biological leg up, so to speak, when it comes to sexual fluidity. If one accepts the premise of this research—women have more fluid sexual desires than men for reasons that are governed by hormonal cycles and generally beyond our control—it stands to reason that to find "heteroflexibility," we should look to (young) women.

Setting aside the feminist objections one might have to this characterization of women's sexuality, one thing is clear: the now common perception that women are more sexually receptive and flexible, and that men by contrast are more sexually rigid, has rendered men's sexual fluidity largely invisible. Straight men *do* make out at parties for the pleasure of women and engage in virtually the same teasing/kissing/sex-for-show behaviors that straight young women do, though research demonstrating this has received relatively little attention. Sociologist Eric Anderson's research on young men and sports is a goldmine of information about straight male college athletes kissing, taking "body shots" off of one another, and "jacking each other off" during three-some's with girls and male teammates.[10] In ways that are virtually indistinguishable from scenarios in which straight girls kiss or have sex for the pleasure of male spectators,[11] the straight college football players interviewed by Anderson describe a host of situations in which they have sexual contact with one another in order to please a female sex partner. One reported:

> "I'm not attracted to them [men]. It's just that there has to be something worth [it] like, this one girl said she'd fuck us if we both made out. So the ends justified the means. We call it a good cause. There has to be a good cause."[12]

Another explained:

> "There has got to be a reward. If I have to kiss another guy in order to fuck a chick, then yeah it's worth it. . . . Well, for the most part it would be about getting it on with her, but like we might do some stuff together too. It depends on what she wants."[13]

In a different study Anderson conducted,[14] this one in the United Kingdom, he found that of the 145 male students he interviewed, 89 percent had kissed another male on the lips, and 37 percent had engaged in extended kissing with another man. In both cases, participants conceptualized kissing men as "a means of expressing platonic affection among heterosexual friends." Here, men explain their same-sex contact in terms nearly identical to the familiar and century-old narrative about "romantic friendships" among women. Taking Anderson's research alongside research on "straight girls kissing," we discover that heterosexuals, both men and women, conceptualize kissing and other forms of sexual contact in a variety of ways, including as an extension of heterosexual friendship or as a means of heterosexual seduction.

Some accounts of straight men's sex with men suggest that terms like "heteroflexible" might already be outdated, especially to the extent that being heteroflexible has been misinterpreted as a euphemism for bisexuality. In a 2010 article for the *Good Men Project,* developmental psychologist Ritch Savin-Williams describes his interviews with "securely" heterosexual young men who report that they occasionally experience attraction to other men. Savin-Williams explains that many of these men, such as a research participant named Dillon, are uncertain about how to characterize their "potential" for attraction to men:

> Though [Dillon] wants to "fuck lots of girls" before graduation, he's not entirely heterosexual. "I'm not sure there's a name for what I am," he says. . . . By his own admission, Dillon says he resides in the "Sexual Netherlands" (his words), a place that exists between heterosexuality and bisexuality. In previous generations, such individuals might have been described as "straight but not narrow," "bending a little," and

"heteroflexible." Dillon is part of a growing trend of young men who are secure in their heterosexuality and yet remain aware of their potential to experience far more—sexual attractions, sexual interactions, crushes, and, occasionally romantic relationships with other guys.[15]

Savin-Williams reports that 3 to 4 percent of male teenagers in the United States and Canada describe themselves as "mostly heterosexual" or "predominantly heterosexual," even when given the choice to select the terms "heterosexual" or "bisexual." These percentages increase among college-aged men, which, as Savin-Williams points out, suggests there are more young men who feel they are "mostly straight" than who say they are bisexual or gay. Other studies have yielded similar findings,[16] demonstrating that a good number of straight-identified men feel at least somewhat open to the possibility of a sexual interaction with another man and do not view this possibility as a challenge to their heterosexuality. While such reports are often imagined to be surprising, the same accounts of young straight women's occasional desire for sex with women rarely produce the same puzzlement. . . .

Though homosexual contact is a feature of straight men's private lives and friendships, it also takes ritualized forms in the institutional environments in which straight men come into contact with one another's bodies. Avowedly heterosexual institutions, like the United States military, are sites in which sexual encounters between heterosexual men are integrated into the culture and practice of the institution. In his book *Sailors and Sexual Identity,* based on interviews with U.S. sailors and marines, Steven Zeeland explains that the boundaries between homosexual and heterosexual, sexual and nonsexual, are kept intentionally blurry in the military. Zeeland describes a range of intimate and sexual behaviors that are part of standard military practice and "known to the Joint Chiefs of Staff to be a natural part of military life." These are conveniently ambiguous in their meaning:

> Navy initiation rituals involving cross-dressing, spanking, simulated oral and anal sex, simulated ejaculation,

nipple piercing, and anal penetration with objects and fingers might be [perceived as] homosexual. An officer's love for his men might be homosexual. The intimate buddy relationships that form in barracks, aboard ship, and most especially in combat—often described as being a love greater than between a man and a woman—might be homosexual—whether or not penetration and ejaculation ever occur. The U.S. military does not want these things called homosexual. To maintain the illusion that these aspects of military life are heterosexually pure it is necessary to maintain the illusion that there is no homosexuality in the military.[17]

Zeeland points not only to the ubiquity and normalization of homosexual contact in the U.S. military, but also to the military's investment in conceptualizing homosexual contact as "heterosexually pure" in its meaning and motivation.

. . . I take the position that indeed we *should* view straight men's homosexual contact as primarily heterosexual in meaning. The problem, however, is that this perspective has been used as a way to elide the complexity of straight-identified men's sexuality. All too often a "boys will be boys" analysis of straight men's homosexual activity functions more to obscure rather than to illuminate the implications of these behaviors for our thinking about heterosexuality, and the sexual binary more broadly. We can and should be giving far greater attention to the ways that the construction of heterosexuality so thoroughly allows for, and in fact, requires, a remarkable amount of homosexual contact. . . .

Findings such as Anderson's, Savin-William's, and Zeeland's are hard to accept as they run so deeply counter to conventional wisdom about the rigidity of men's sexuality. Surely these are just exceptional cases, or only the behavior of men who are actually gay or bisexual, or who find themselves in the most extreme of circumstances? To break through this tendency to exceptionalize male sexuality, we need only look to research on *female* sexual fluidity as our guide. For instance, Lisa Diamond opens her aforementioned book *Sexual Fluidity* with the examples of actresses Anne Heche, Julie Cypher, and Cynthia Nixon, all of whom left their heterosexual lives and began lesbian relationships and, in Heche and Cypher's case, later returned to heterosexual relationships. Diamond argues that these women are not "confused"; instead, their cases illuminate the fact that fluidity is a core feature of female sexual orientation. . . .

There is no doubt that straight men's sexuality is structured differently from straight women's, but not with regard to their capacity for homosexual sex, desire, and even relationships. While attractive white heterosexual women like Nixon, Cypher, and Heche are forgiven, if not celebrated, for their forays into same-sex coupling, men are offered a different, far more limited set of possibilities. Perhaps Nixon's, Cypher's, and Heche's male counterparts are men like evangelical megachurch leader Ted Haggard, former Senator Larry Craig, and former Representative Bob Allen. Ted Haggard, a white male in his early sixties, had a three-year sexual relationship with a male massage therapist; he also identifies as heterosexual and has long been married to a woman. Haggard now reports that his homosexual desires have completely disappeared as a result of effective Christian counseling. Larry Craig and Bob Allen are also both heterosexual-identified, white married men. Both were also arrested in 2007 for homosexual prostitution in public restrooms. Both remain married to their wives.

What are the differences between the women whom Diamond offers up as examples of female sexual fluidity and men like Haggard, Craig, and Allen? For one, these women pursued long-term, romantic, loving, presumably monogamous, public relationships with other women, while the men's sexual relationships with men involved sex for money and were kept hidden from wives and the public. Nixon, Cypher, and Heche are all proponents of gay rights and have expressed no shame about or disidentification from their same-sex relationships. Haggard, Craig, and Allen are committed to their heterosexual marriages, are vocal opponents of gay rights, and wish for the public to view their homosexual behaviors as temporary and unfortunate symptoms of stress, addiction, trauma, and/or loss of faith. Surely, in light of these differences, we would be more inclined to view women like Nixon, Cypher, and Heche as the *real* bi- or homosexuals, while men like Haggard, Craig, and Allen are simply acting from a place of situational need or occasional curiosity. But this is the opposite of the way that commentators have interpreted such cases. Cypher and Heche have received a warm reception upon their return to heterosexual partnerships, their relationships with women imagined as an unusual but ultimately harmless detour in their otherwise heterosexual lives (Heche has since been cast in heterosexual roles, for instance). On the other hand, gays and straights alike have proclaimed Haggard, Craig, and Allen to be closeted gay men, religious or political hypocrites, and cowards who have duped their pitiable wives and children. Commentators seem unconcerned with how these men actually want to live their lives—in heterosexual marriages, in heterosexual communities, and invested in heteronormativity. Haggard, in particular, was thoroughly ridiculed by the American public for sexual hypocrisy, even as his explanation for his behavior was thoroughly consistent with the Christian logic that he, like all of us, is vulnerable to occasional sins of the flesh (a logic that allowed his followers back in Colorado Springs to forgive him).

This is all to say that when straight-identified women have sex with women, the broader culture waits in anticipation for them to return to what is likely their natural, heterosexual state; when straight-identified men have sex with men, the culture waits in anticipation for them to admit that they are gay. Though it may at first appear that women are offered a more nuanced, complex sexuality, it is perhaps more accurate to suggest that women are granted a longer suspension of judgment before their same-sex encounters and even their same-sex relationships are presumed to signal true lesbian subjectivity (and not a hetero-erotic "bicuriosity"). Men, conversely, must manage their sexual fluidity within the context of a culture that they know will immediately equate male homosexual behavior with gay subjectivity. It should come as little surprise to us, then, that for the most part, straight men's homosexual behaviors are marked by shame, secrecy, homophobia, and disavowal of queerness. In other words, the fact that the

homosexual behaviors of heterosexual men and women take very different cultural forms is important and needs investigation, but it is hardly evidence that male sexuality is less fluid or receptive to cultural stimuli than women's.[18]

The evidence of men's sexual flexibility (and *all* people's sexual flexibility) surrounds us, so this raises the question: Why this investment in telling a different story about women's sexuality than we do about men's? My purpose is not to dispute the notion that women are more sexually fluid than men, so I won't belabor this point. However, the persistent refusal to recognize male sexual fluidity is important here to the extent that it is the primary reason I have chosen to focus my analysis on men. Over the past few years, students and some colleagues have reacted to early iterations with outright denial. Many state that they simply cannot believe that straight men behave in such ways. Others can only assume that, whether I am aware of it or not, what I am truly studying is the experience of being in the closet. Heterosexual women, I have come to find out, are among the most fervent deniers of male sexual fluidity. Many are only able to conclude that men who have had homosexual sex, even if only once, must be gay and closeted. And yet, they do not come to this same conclusion about straight women, for whom they imagine that circumstances mean everything, and "playing around" with other women ultimately means little. It is not a stretch to imagine that this view of women is the enduring legacy of the Victorian belief that what women do together sexually is simply not real sex, but a precursor to, or substitute for, heterosexual intercourse.[19] In light of these notions about the inherent fluidity and rigidity of female and male sexuality respectively, my goal in focusing on men is not to highlight male sexuality per se, but to add men and masculinity to our understanding of the permeability of heterosexuality.

THE RACE OF SEXUAL FLUIDITY

This is also limited to an analysis of *white* men. While some might wonder why straight white men would deserve any more attention than they already receive, my hope is to make a compelling case that investigating white male heterosexuality deepens our understanding of the racial construction of sexuality, particularly the ways that whiteness continues to function—even in an allegedly "post-racial" era—as a stand-in for normal sexuality. Straight white men, as I will show, can draw on the resources of white privilege—an "invisible package of unearned assets"[20]—to circumvent homophobic stigma and assign heterosexual meaning to homosexual activity. Among the many privileges of whiteness, the power to both normalize and exceptionalize one's behavior, including one's "discordant" sex practices, is central.[21] But as white supremacy and privilege "smooth over" any imagined inconsistencies in the sexual behavior of whites, especially white men, the sexual fluidity of men of color quickly falls subject to heightened surveillance and misrepresentation. Illustrating this, the last two decades have been marked by a media-fueled panic about the sexual fluidity of men of color, particularly black men.

Indeed, to the extent that the media has acknowledged that straight-identified men have sex with men, it has focused disproportionately on men of color "on the down low." Like heteroflexible college women who have been the subject of media fascination—and who, significantly, are almost always white in these accounts—black and Latino men on the down low (DL) are reported to "live heterosexual lives": we are often told that they have wives or girlfriends; that they are invested in heterosexual culture and appearances; and that they don't identify as gay or bisexual. Though there are some parallels between this construction and the story of (white) girls "hooking up" with girls, men of color on the DL are not granted the sexual fluidity and complexity attributed to young white women. Instead, as C. Riley Snorton illuminates in the incisive book *Nobody Is Supposed to Know*, "the 'down low' has been one in myriad discursive practices that link black sexuality to duplicity," thereby airing white "anxieties about the possibilities of refusing to comply with sexual identifications, of resisting being gay."[22] In media coverage of the down low, black men have been repeatedly depicted as closeted and as fundamentally dishonest about their real

lives and desires. Black men on the down low and Latino "men-who-have-sex-with-men" (an epidemiological category, typically abbreviated as MSMs) have been central figures in both scholarly and popular discussions regarding internalized homophobia, sexual repression, extreme religiosity, HIV/AIDS, the betrayal of unsuspecting wives and girlfriends, and the failure to come out of the closet.[23] To make sense of their sexual practices, analyses of men of color who have sex with men have drawn heavily on theories of the closet and its racialized underpinnings.[24] Black men on the DL, in particular, have been described as "a new subculture of gay men" for whom "masculinity . . . is so intertwined with hyper-heterosexuality [that it] renders an openly gay identity impossible."[25] Similarly, Latino MSMs are implicitly characterized as closeted gay or bisexual men for whom cultural barriers, rigid cultural ideas about gender, and strong ties to family and religion prevent public identification as gay or bisexual.[26]

In contrast with the media's sensationalized and panic-inducing representation of a dangerous black male sexual underworld, scholars working in black queer studies have described the discursive construction of the DL as the latest example of the hyper-surveillance of black men's sex practices. According to Jeffrey McCune, whites have long viewed black male sexuality as a spectacle, leaving black men with no closet to hide in, and hence nowhere from which to "come out." In contrast with the dominant white view of the DL as a tragic and dangerous consequence of black homophobia, McCune views the DL as a subversive practice of black sexual world-making, one that both adheres to the black politics of sexual discretion while also refusing to conform to the mainstream/white lesbian and gay movement's emphasis on sexual labeling and "coming out." The embrace of heteronormative hip-hop, masculine cool, sexual discretion, and other features of black heterosexual culture is not so much a denial of queer desire, argues McCune, but a mode of connecting with a broader black culture. He explains that when men on the DL go to black queer clubs, "they have arrived in a queer space that welcomes them, but does not require them to become official members. . . . The discursive demand that one must be 'out' to participate in gay activities ignores that all gay activity does not take place in actual public domain: neither does individual participation always guarantee membership."[27] C. Riley Snorton concurs that while the down low is ostensibly a secret practice, the media's fascination with it serves to expose the racist conditions of hypervisibility in which black sexuality takes form.[28] Drawing on Eve Sedgwick's conceptualization of the "glass closet," a form of visible concealment maintained through silence, Snorton points to volumes of troubling media commentary on the down low, reading these texts not as accurate accounts of a hidden sex practice, but as examples of the regulation and exposure of black sexuality more generally.

These critiques of the media's framing of the DL illuminate the racialized and gendered conditions of visibility and invisibility that shape how we understand the sexual fluidity of people of color and whites, women and men. Bringing together these critical analyses of DL discourse with feminist critiques of the objectification of women's bodies, we can begin to see why and how straight white men's sexual practices are those that are truly invisible and unmarked, while men of color and women are subject to narratives that reinforce their already subordinate position within hierarchies of normal sexuality. For women, the hetero-patriarchal view that female sexuality is naturally receptive and flexible, more subdued or controllable than men's hydraulic sexuality, and a commodity to be exchanged among men is a perfect set-up to interpret "straight girls kissing girls" as a titillating spectacle of special interest to straight men and a nonthreatening extension of women's innate sensuality. For black men, the long-standing construction of black male sexuality as predatory and violent and of black culture as beholden to traditional gender and sexual formations is the context in which the homosexual contact of not-gay black men is offered up as a matter of considerable risk and urgency, a black secret—and in many accounts, a black *lie*—in need of exposure and management.[29] Women of color arguably sit at the intersection of these forces, often scrutinized, pathologized, and criminalized for any sexual practice that extends

beyond dominant constructions of normative female sexuality.

The story is different for straight white men. When straight white men have sex with men, they are either presumed gay or their behavior is dismissed as inconsequential and nonsexual. Rarely, if ever, are their sexual practices racialized, or attributed to particular ethnoracial sexual norms within white culture. Blacks, Latinos, Muslims, and other non-white and non-Christian "cultures" become the repository for cultural difference, sexual repression, homophobia, and hyper-religiosity, thereby masking the normative white Christian secularism that fuels white male homophobia and undergirds dominant U.S. discourse about the relationship between sexuality and subjectivity.[30] In contrast with this narrative about the rationality of whiteness (and maleness), I will show that white male privilege, rituals, anxieties, and delusions are central to the operation of homosexuality within straight white men's lives. While straight white men not only draw on many of the same logics used by women to account for their homosexual experiences (such as the football players in Anderson's study who engage in sex acts with men in order to seduce women), they also leverage white masculinity to assist in the preservation or recuperation of heterosexuality in the context of sex with men. This is a set of uniquely white hetero-masculine logics—namely, that sex with men is often necessary, patriotic, character-building, masculinity-enhancing, and paradoxically, a means of inoculating oneself against authentic gayness—forms the subjects of the chapters to follow.

The late sociologist Ruth Frankenberg explained that one of the truisms about whiteness is that it is an invisible or unmarked category, an empty container that white people themselves cannot describe. And yet, Frankenberg also asserted, the notion that whiteness is unmarked is also a white delusion, as whiteness has a clear history and set of forms, both past and present, and is certainly not unmarked in the eyes of people of color. "Whiteness" first emerged as a Western European colonial project, a self-made category used to justify the colonization of "Others"—people of African, Native American, Latin American, and Asian descent. Colonization was not only a process of violent occupation and theft of culture, land, and resources, but also a process whereby self-proclaimed white colonizers named themselves, named the Other, and then became "apparently invisible."[31] For Frankenberg, whiteness in the contemporary United States is "a place of advantage and privilege intersected by other social categories (gender, class, sexuality, & ability); a position, an attitude or outlook from which to see 'selves' and others; a complex spectrum of cultural practices that are either seen as 'normative' or rational and not racial; and a culture whose character and identity have been shaped by history (e.g., colonialism)."[32] Drawing on Frankenberg's definition of whiteness, this attends to the ways that whiteness intersects with masculinity and sexuality, shaping the relationship between men's homosexual sex and their sense of "self," their status as "normal," and their position within structural hierarchies. In making whiteness a central unit of analysis, along with masculinity and heteronormativity, my aim is to build on a growing body of work that racializes whiteness and unmasks its delusions.

In sum, the pairing of homosexual sex with heterosexual life is not a new phenomenon; nor is it limited to young people, women, or Black, Latino, or other men of color. And yet, despite a good amount of evidence suggesting that homosexual contact is part of the basic fabric of human sexuality, and central even to the social organization of heterosexuality, it is of course difficult to chart homosexuality's presence within cultural formations—like that of straight white American masculinity—that have defined themselves, in large part, by homosexuality's absence. Hence, we must attend to the apparent paradox that homosexual encounters are both everywhere and nowhere within the lives and culture of straight white men. Doing so requires some attention to the cultural construction of the heterosexual/homosexual binary itself, the subject to which I now turn.

WHAT IS HETEROSEXUALITY?

When I think about the mood and flavor of straight men's sex with men, I am reminded of the kind of sexual games my friends and I played as young girls (starting around seven or eight years old), before any of us knew what sex would later be. In the absence of a coherent and normative conceptualization of sex, we cobbled together the gendered and sexual tropes familiar to us as kids. We crafted highly detailed narratives about ourselves (we were beautiful fairies, rebellious teenagers, wealthy movie stars, doctors and patients) and our circumstances (the various events that presumably resulted in the *need*—whether we liked it or not—to reveal/touch/kiss certain body parts). We knew we were playing. We invented scenes. They had to be negotiated. There were rules. People were bossy. Body parts were gross. But we touched each other anyway.

Homosexual encounters between adult heterosexuals constitute a unique erotic domain that is characterized by many of the features of childhood sexuality. This is not because it is a "childish" act for adult heterosexuals to have sex with one another, or because straight men in fraternities (or military barracks, prisons, and so forth) are less evolved or self-aware than men in other contexts, or for any other reasons that might stem from such a simplistic and moralizing reading of sexuality. Instead, it is because homosexual sex enacted by heterosexuals— like sex between children—occupies a liminal space within sexual relations, one that sits outside of the heterosexual/homosexual binary and is sometimes barely perceptible as sex. Like childhood sex, it goes by many other names: "experimentation," "accident," "friendship," "joke," "game," and so on. Participants must painstakingly avoid being mistaken as sincere homosexuals by demonstrating that the sexual encounter is something other than sex, and in many cases, they do this by agreeing that the encounter was *compelled* by others (such as older fraternity brothers) or by circumstances that left them little choice (such as the apparently quite dire need to obtain access to a particular fraternity).

. . .

Part of what is said to distinguish heteroflexibility from gayness is that it involves engaging in same-sex sexuality while distancing oneself from the lesbian and gay movement, or, in Essig's words, "throw[ing] out the politics and the struggles" associated with same-sex desire. But this characterization could use a bit more nuance, as many sexually fluid straight people *do* identify as allies to the LGBT movement, or even loosely as "queer." This is not to mention that many self-identified gay men and lesbians couldn't be less political about their sexuality, or more invested in assimilation and respectability. While some degree of insistence that one is "not gay" is generally part and parcel of heteroflexibility, a more significant distinction is that people who identify as heterosexual, unlike gay men and lesbians, are generally content with *straight culture,* or heteronormativity; they enjoy heterosexual sex, but more importantly for the purposes of this book, they enjoy heterosexual culture. Simply put, being sexually "normal" suits them. It feels good; it feels like home.

Unfortunately, the domain of culture is generally lost in popular discourses about sexual desire, which focus largely on whether homosexual activity is either "chosen" or "biological." This entire framing is far too simplistic. People certainly have tendencies toward particular objects of desire, including bodies defined in their time and place as "the same" or "the opposite" from their own. And yet, for the vast majority of us, these tendencies—whatever they may be—are shaped and experienced under the constraints of heteronormativity, or within cultures strongly invested in opposite-sex coupling. The amount of psychic and cultural labor expended to produce and enforce heterosexual identification and procreative sexuality suggests that heterosexuality, as we now know it, is hardly an automatic human effect. It is for this reason that scholars of heterosexuality have described it as a psychic and social accomplishment, an institution, and a cultural formation.[33]

Of course the traditional view of sexuality is that heterosexuality is nature's design, the driving force behind human reproduction and the gendered division of labor that keeps societies running (i.e., the unpaid care work done by women to sustain children and male laborers). In the last several decades, this view has been slightly revised to account for the existence of the homosexual, who is now typically understood to result from a harmless hormonal or genetic aberration in nature's plan.

But from a queer perspective, sexual desire is not determined by bio-evolutionary processes, but is instead fluid and culturally contingent. As first elaborated by Freud in *Three Essays on the Theory of Sexuality,* nature may provide human infants with sexual desire, but this desire takes form as a polymorphous capacity to experience pleasure in response to a broad range of stimuli, including an array of one's own bodily functions as well as various modes of contact with objects, animals, and humans of all types. It is only through disciplined conformity to societal norms, typically directed by parents, that young children's sexual impulses are redirected toward a sanctioned, and most often singular, object of desire (most often, a person of the "opposite" sex). Hence, from both psychoanalytic and social constructionist perspectives, the hetero/homo binary is not the essential order of things, but the product of cultural norms and political-economic imperatives.

And yet, sexual binaries often *feel* natural because they are internalized in early childhood, resulting in strong sexual (and gender) identifications. But central to the larger project at hand is the question of what happens to all of those polymorphous desires once they are repressed in the service of conformity to prevailing sexual norms. For Freud, the process of sublimating these desires in order to achieve heterosexuality and normative gender is not an easy one; instead it is tenuous, labored, and requires the disavowal and loss of original homosexual attachments. Moreover, this loss cannot be recognized or grieved, as doing so would expose the fragility and constructedness of heterosexuality. As the philosopher Judith Butler has argued, this bind produces a unique form of melancholy, a kind of repressed sadness that is generated as heteromasculinity comes into being through the disavowed and unmourned loss of homosexual possibilities.[34]

. . .

This way of understanding the formation of sexuality helps to explain the apparent paradox that homosexuality is a constitutive feature of hetero-masculinity. Because homosexual attachments are always present within the psychic structure of heterosexuality, boys and men, rather than mourning "the homosexuality that could not be," arguably work out this loss via ongoing acts of homophobic repudiation, wherein they locate "the homosexual" outside of themselves and go to great and performative lengths to reject people and things associated with it. As I will soon make clear, this rejection of homosexual subjectivity sometimes occurs within and alongside straight men's sexual activity with men. As long as these activities are recast as nonsexual and the dividing line between gay and straight subjectivity is secured, homosexual contact can function as a powerful means of asserting heterosexual authenticity, or a "not gay" constitution.

. . .

Many social scientists have attempted to elaborate the difference between sexual orientation (most often defined as the quantity and duration of one's same-sex or other-sex desires, often believed to be hardwired), sexual identity (how one identifies oneself—as straight, lesbian, gay, bisexual, etc.), and actual sexual behavior. I take the less popular position that the question of "sexual orientation"—as it is conventionally understood—is not a very interesting one. I am not concerned with whether the men I describe in this book are "really" straight or gay, and I am not arguing that they (or that all men) are really homosexual or bisexual in their orientation. Instead, what I am arguing is that homosexual sex plays a remarkably central role in the institutions and rituals that produce heterosexual subjectivity, as well as in the broader culture's imagination of what it means for "boys to be boys." To my mind, the nearly obsessive focus on whether individual people are born gay or straight functions as a bizarre distraction from the greater cultural significance of homosexuality, both historically and at present.

I conceptualize straightness and queerness primarily as cultural domains. I recognize that people have real bodies and real sexual responses to other bodies, but I also contend that bodies do not respond only to the "raw facts" of other people's genitals or other sexed body parts. Instead, our bodies desire other bodies and particular sex acts *in their social context*; we desire what those body parts *represent*. We desire particular bodies and particular sex acts and particular erotic scenes and cultural spheres in large part because they have significant cultural and erotically charged

meanings. As Judith Butler's work has made clear, sexual desire itself operates under the conditions of a heterosexual matrix, in which sex (femaleness and maleness), gender (femininity and masculinity), and heterosexual desire are imagined and required to follow logically from one another. Bodies that fall outside this matrix are rendered abject and unintelligible. That our desires are subject to these enduring cultural prescriptions does not make them any less embodied, but it does indicate that our bodies respond to a social field already characterized by narrow gender and sexual binaries to which much cultural significance has been assigned. In other words, to call oneself "gay" or "straight" is to take on the cultural baggage associated with these categories, and whether or not this baggage is appealing is a separate matter altogether from the appeal of homosexual or heterosexual sex.

Whether a man thinks of himself and his homosexual behavior as "gay" or "straight" makes all the difference with regard to how he will make sexual contact with men: how he will set the scene, the narratives he will use to describe what is happening and why, the time and place the sex occurs, and whether it will be possible to imagine that the sex was never actually "sexual" at all. Let me be more concrete. Some men like to have sex with men in backrooms of gay bars after dancing to techno music; others like to have sex with men while watching straight porn and talking about "banging bitches." Some women like to have sex with women in the woods at feminist music festivals or while cohabitating in the suburbs; others, as sociologist Laura Hamilton's research explores, like to "hook up" with women on couches at fraternity parties in front of cheering male spectators.[35] These temporal, spatial, and cultural factors are not inconsequential; they are precisely what make sex "hot" for participants, *and* they are the details that people take as evidence of their heterosexual and homosexual orientations. It is for this reason that I conceptualize heterosexual subjectivity as constituted not by a lack of homosexual sex or desire, but by an enduring investment in heteronormativity, or in the forces that construct heterosexuality as natural, normal, and right and that disavow association with abnormal, or queer, sexual expressions. This investment in hetero-normativity is itself a *bodily desire*; in fact, I believe it is *the* embodied heterosexual desire, more powerful than, say, a woman's yearning for male torsos or penises or a man's longing for vaginas or breasts. It is the desire to be sexually unmarked and normatively gendered. It is the desire not simply for heterosexual sex and partnership, but for all of its concomitant cultural rewards. It is a desire that people may well feel within their genitals. In sum, this chapter works from the premise that heterosexuality is, in part, a fetishization of the normal.[36]

There is no doubt that many, and perhaps most, gay and lesbian people also want to be "normal." But even those who might wish for complete homonormative[37] assimilation (with regard to their political, employment, or economic standing) often find themselves unable or unwilling to achieve gender normativity or to conform to heteronormative dictates for appropriate sexuality. In other words, they find themselves generally not "at home" within, and sometimes repelled by, heterosexual ways of life. Conversely, the straight men who are the subjects find heteronormativity attractive and compelling. They desire it; they are aroused by it. It calls to them; it feels like home. In this way, I do not discount the possibility of a mind/body connection or of the interplay between nature and nurture in shaping our desire. Instead I want to suggest that what we are desiring may not be body parts or people who fall within particular sex and gender categories, but the far broader experiences of sexual and gender normalcy and difference. Some of us, for understandable reasons, are very invested in sexual and gender normalcy; others, for less well-known reasons (which need hardly be innate), desire rebellion, difference, or outsiderness—a desire that may have been present for as long as we can remember. Some of us—who typically go by the names "gay," "lesbian," "bisexual," or "queer"—want our same-sex desires to be taken seriously, viewed as meaningful and sometimes political features of our lives. Others—who typically go by the names "heterosexual" or "straight"—want our same-sex attractions and encounters to be viewed in opposite terms, as accidental, temporary, meaningless, and decidedly apolitical.

. . .

THE BIRTH OF THE CONGENITAL HETEROSEXUAL

Another key piece of the story about heterosexuality is that straightness always takes form in relation to its Other—or to queerness—with the latter serving as the former's mirror and foil. To the extent that straight people think about what it means to be heterosexual, and to be part of a heterosexual culture with particular norms and practices, they often do so by imagining themselves through the eyes of queers. As Jonathan Ned Katz explains in *The Invention of Heterosexuality,* the budding visibility of gay culture in the 1960s produced what we might call a "heterosexual looking-glass self," in which the more visible gay men and lesbians became, the more possible it became for heterosexuals to compare themselves to their "homosexual" counterparts. Katz cites, for example, a 1963 *New York Times* article in which a heterosexual reporter attempts to describe gay subculture for the paper's presumably heterosexual readership, and in so doing, speculates that homosexuals "probably derive secret amusement" from coopting innocent heterosexual words (like the word "gay" itself). According to Katz, "the image of two gay people laughing together secretly over the unknowing language of straights marks the emergence in *The New York Times* of heterosexuals as a majority newly nervous about the critical gaze of The Homo-Other."[38]

Today, over fifty years after the publication of this article, the relationship between straight culture and gay culture is more interconnected than ever, especially as the latter—in the form of queer style, queer music, queer imagery, queer political discourse—has demonstrated its appeal and profitability within mainstream culture. The influence of mediated, mainstream gay culture on straight people's lives has consequences not only for how straight people consume or fashion themselves, but also for how they have sex. Many commentators believe that the increasing visibility and acceptance of gay and lesbian people has given heterosexuals permission to explore same-sex desire without fear of devastating stigma. And yet, if heterosexuals' erotic possibilities are broadened by a gay rights movement that celebrates the fluidity of sexual *behavior,* what about the effect of the movement's stance on the immutability of sexual *orientation?* The percentage of Americans who believe in the biological foundations of sexual orientation has steadily increased over the last four decades, from 13 percent in 1977, to 31 percent in 1998, to 52 percent in 2010.[39] Many gay-friendly heterosexuals have been taught, primarily by proponents of gay rights, that gay people—and, by extension, straight people—have a fundamental sexual constitution, one already determined by nature. If sexual orientation cannot be changed, acceptance of gay people becomes the compassionate heterosexual's best option.

Scientific efforts to prove that sexual orientation is innate are not new; they are rooted in nineteenth- and early twentieth-century sexology. In fact, research aimed at identifying body parts that might hold the tell-tale signs of homosexuality—from bad blood, beady eyes, and angular facial features, to finger length and brain structure—have persisted since the very advent of heterosexual and homosexual categories in the nineteenth century.[40] Nonetheless, it is only in the last two decades that the notion that homosexuals are "born this way" has gained widespread public acceptance in the United States, including (and especially) among lesbians and gay men. Though numerous feminist and queer scholars have been critical of biological determinism and the concomitant depoliticization of queer difference, little attention has been paid to the effects of the "biological turn" on *heterosexuality.* How has over forty years of a visible lesbian and gay identity movement—increasingly articulated in sociobiological terms[41]—influenced the way that heterosexuals understand *their* sexuality?

According to Lisa Diamond, proponents of the argument that sexual orientation is hardwired have steered clear of the subject of sexual fluidity, fearing that fluidity might appear to suggest that sexual orientation can be chosen or learned. In response to the question "does fluidity mean that sexual orientation is a matter of choice?," Diamond offers some apparently reassuring words: "No. Even when women undergo significant shifts in their patterns of erotic response, they typically report that such changes are unexpected and beyond their control. In some cases, they actively resist these changes, to no avail."[42] Diamond's defense of sexual fluidity as consistent with immutability represents what is soon likely to become the prevailing sexual logic of our time. Diamond, like other sexologists and psychologists, believes that people are born with a core sexual orientation that remains the same regardless of periodic and/or situational attractions and desires that fall outside of its boundaries. Sexual fluidity is not a challenge to the fixity of sexual orientation; in many ways, the opposite is true. When we know we are born straight or gay, this knowledge enables us to experiment, to stray, to act out, and to let "shit happen" without fear that we have somehow hidden or misrecognized or damaged our true sexual constitution. More importantly, knowing that our sexual orientation was present at birth allows us to make sense of our discordant behaviors as exceptional, not bound to the same identitarian consequences experienced by true homosexuals (or heterosexuals).

Returning, then, to the question about the consequences of the biological turn for heterosexuals, we see that like the homosexual-at-birth, the heterosexual-at-birth can do nothing to change his or her innate sexual constitution. Compassionate heterosexuals accept this biological imperative as it reportedly determines the sexual subjectivities of their gay friends, and now, too, they accept the way it determines their own. No amount of homosexual sex or desire can change nature's heterosexual design. If one knows one is not born gay, then one's homosexual desires and behaviors simply cannot be gay, regardless of their content or frequency. So accepted now is the idea of sexual hardwiring—and so central now is this idea to most thinking about "heteroflexibility," "situational homosexuality," and all other homosexual behaviors of heterosexuals—that it is no longer possible to investigate straight men's sex with men (or straight women's sex with women) without starting from this foundation.

To be very clear, I agree with the contention that when straight-identified people participate in homosexual behavior, they are still best understood as straight. . . . What I take issue with here, however, is the need to explain the sexual desires we experience and the sexual cultures we inhabit as forces purely outside of our control and buried within our bodies. This explanation leaves little room to consider the ways that sexual desires are culturally embedded and performative, or the ways our desires direct us not simply towards bodies with particular "parts," but towards the complete cultural experience that those bodies represent and make possible. The biological hypothesis treats heteronormativity, for instance, as an unfortunate byproduct of a neutral, clinically descriptive sexual orientation called "heterosexuality." In contrast, from a more critical and queer perspective, attraction to the culture and privileges of heteronormativity is inseparable from the sensation of "straightness." It is in this way that the original construction of heterosexuality, or its historical *invention* to use Jonathan Ned Katz's term, provides a crucial backdrop for this project, and an essential counterpoint to the now nearly hegemonic narrative about the congenital nature of sexual orientation. . . .

HETERONORMATIVE VIOLENCE AND THE DEMAND FOR SINCERE QUEERS

I find sexual practices interesting in their own right, but I come not simply out of interest in the details of the sex that straight people are having. In this project, as elsewhere, any investment is in the work of resisting heteronormativity, particularly the violent ways that state and cultural institutions punish gender and sexual non-normativity. On its surface, the sexual fluidity of heterosexuals—especially when represented by young women playfully kissing one another at parties—appears to have little to do with heteronormative violence. If anything, it appears to be a progressive development, one marked by the expansion of acceptable ways to be heterosexual men and women.

And yet, when straight men have sex with men, it is frequently—though certainly not always—bound up with violence. The line between straight men having sex with men and "actual" homosexuality is under constant scrutiny, and for straight men, violence

is a key element that imbues homosexuality with heterosexual meaning, or untangles hetero-erotic forms of homosexuality from the affective, political, and romantic associations with gay and lesbian life. Sometimes this violence takes the form of humiliation or physical force enacted by one straight man as he makes sexual contact with another; in other cases, it may take the form of two men fantasizing about sexual violence against women. In many cases, violence is a central part of the work of refraining homosexual sex as an act that men do to build one another's strength, or to build what I call "anal resilience," thereby inoculating one another against what they imagine are the sincere expressions of gay selfhood.

. . .

In attending to the mutual construction of heterosexuality and queerness, my analysis pushes back against the notion of an essential sexual binary in which heterosexuality and homosexuality are oppositional sexual orientations determined by nature. And yet, my arguments also rest on the premise that straightness and queerness are distinct cultural domains that differently conceptualize homosexual encounters—a premise that may appear to reinforce a hetero/homo binary. To argue, as I do, that straightness relates to homosexual sex in unique ways raises the question: "Unique from what?" The answer is complex because the subject positions and sexual and political orientations that fall under the banner of "straightness" and "gayness" are themselves complex and multiple. Many queer scholars have noted that the radical queer relationship to homosexual sex departs from the mainstream gay relationship to homosexual sex, with the former ironically sharing in common some of the insincerity and "meaninglessness" I have attributed to most straight engagements with homosexual sex, and the latter sharing in common with straightness the claim to "being normal." Heterosexuals who have disinvested in sexual normalcy—through engagement with kink, non-monogamy, and other marginalized sex practices—are queered via these practices, and hence, differently arranged vis-à-vis homosexuality. In sum, the relation between straightness and queerness is more a complex network than a linear dualism.

. . .

NOTES

1. See #53 from "The Complete List" of things bros like on broslikethissite.com, July 23, 2009, http://www .broslikethissite.com/2009/07/53-hazing.html.

2. For a brief review of this literature, see John F. DeCecco and David A. Parker's *Sex, Cells, and Same Sex Desire: The Biology of Sexual Preference* (New York: Routledge, 1995), 12–13. See also Jeffrey Escoffier, "Gay for Pay: Straight Men and the Making of Gay Pornography," *Qualitative Sociology* 26, no. 4 (2003): 531–555, for a genealogy of the term "situational homosexuality."

3. In one documented case in 1999, the University of Vermont hockey team was disbanded by the university for requiring new recruits to "parade in an elephant walk." See CBS News, "College Hazing under Fire," 2000. http://www.cbsnews.com/2100–201_162–179106.html.

4. Laurie Essig, "Heteroflexibility," Salon.com, November 15, 2000, http://www.salon.com/2000/11/15/heteroflexibility/; Leila Rupp and Verta Taylor. "Straight Girls Kissing," *Contexts* 9, no. 3 (Summer 2010): 28–32.

5. Essig, "Heteroflexibility."

6. Jeffrey Kluger, "Girls Kissing Girls: Explaining the Trend," TIME.com, September 15, 2010, http:// healthland.time.com/2010/09/15/girls-kissing-girls-what-up-with-that/.

7. Rupp and Taylor, "Straight Girls Kissing," 28–32.

8. Ibid.

9. In Lisa Diamond's *Sexual Fluidity: Understanding Women's Love and Desire* (Cambridge: Harvard University Press, 2008), she argues that the evolutionary function of proceptive desire is reproduction, and therefore our ancestors' proceptive desires were likely to be heterosexual in orientation while their receptive desires had no gender orientation. In this quite heteronormative model, occasional same-sex arousability—greater in women than in men—is part of the human condition, while more fixed homosexual "orientations" stem from a later "alteration in the intrinsic gender coding of proceptive desire" (210–211).

10. Eric Anderson, "Being Masculine Is Not about Who You Sleep With …: Heterosexual Athletes Contesting Masculinity and the One-Time Rule of Homosexuality," *Sex Roles: A Journal of Research* 58, no. 1–2 (2008): 104–115.

11. See Laura Hamilton, "Trading on Heterosexuality: College Women's Gender Strategies and Homophobia," *Gender & Society* 21 no. 2 (2007): 145–172, for an empirical account of this practice.

12. Anderson, "Being Masculine," 109.

13. Ibid.

14. Eric Anderson, "I Kiss Them Because I Love Them: The Emergence of Heterosexual Men Kissing in British Institutes of Education," *Archives of Sexual Behavior* 41, no. 2 (2012): 421–430.

15. Ritch Savin Williams and Kenneth Cohen, "Mostly Straight, Most of the Time," Good Men Project.com, November 3, 2010, http://goodmenproject.com/featured-content/mostly-striaght/?utm_content=bufferfdb4f&utm_medium=social&utm_source=facebook.com&utm_campaign=buffer.

16. See, for instance, Michael Bartos. John McLeod, and Phil Nott, *Meanings of Sex Between Men* (Canberra: Australian Government Publishing Service, 1993): and Amanda Lynn Hoffman. "I'm Gay, For Jamie': Heterosexual/Straight-Identified Men Express Desire to Have Sex with Men" (M.A. thesis, San Francisco State University, 2010). Thank you to David Halperin for pointing me in the direction of this research.

17. Steven Zeeland, *Sailors and Sexuality Identity: Crossing the Line between "Straight" and "Gay" in the U.S. Navy* (New York: Harrington Park Press, 1995), 5.

18. Lest we imagine that young straight women's sexual contact with women always takes romantic, seductive, and noncoercive forms that differ fundamentally from those of straight men, we need only look to cases of sorority hazing rituals. In one reported hazing exercise, young women were required to take off their bras and have their breasts ranked by their "sisters": in another, a young women was required to either take a hit of cocaine or penetrate herself with a dildo in front of her sisters. See "Sorority Hazing Increasingly Violet, Disturbing," ABC News, February 17, 2010, http://abcnews.go.com/Health/Wellness/sorority-hazing-increasingly-violent-disturbing-college-campus/story?id=9798604&page=2.

19. Lilian Faderman, *Odd Girls and Twilight Lovers: A History of Lesbian Life in America* (New York: Columbia University Press, 1991).

20. Peggy McIntosh, "White Privilege and Male Privilege: A Personal Account of Coming to See Correspondences through Work in Women's Studies," in Richard Delgado and Jean Stefancic, eds., *Critical White Studies: Looking behind the Mirror* (Philadelphia: Temple University Press, 1997), 291.

21. See Aida Hurtado, *The Color of Privilege: Three Blasphemies on Race and Feminism* (Ann Arbor: University of Michigan Press, 1997), for a rich account of the processes by which dominant groups preserve their unmarked, normative status.

22. C. Riley Snorton, *Nobody Is Supposed to Know: Black Sexuality on the Down Low* (Minneapolis: University of Minnesota Press, 2014), 3, 25.

23. See Keith Boykin, *Beyond the Down Low: Sex, Lies, and Denial in Black America* (New York: Carroll & Graf, 2005): Patricia Hill Collins, *Black Sexual Politics: African Americans, Gender, and the New Racism* (New York: Routledge, 2005): J. L. King. *On the Down Low: A Journey Into the Lives of "Straight" Black Men Who Sleep with Men* (New York: Harmony, 2004).

24. Boykin, *Beyond the Down Low: Collins, Black Sexual Politics*; King. *On the Down Low.*

25. Collins, *Black Sexual Politics*, 207.

26. Rafael Diaz, *Latino Gay Men and HIV: Culture, Sexuality, and Risk Behavior* (New York, Routledge, 1997).

27. Jeffrey Q. McCune, "'Out' in the Club: The Down Low, Hip-Hop, and the Atchitexture of Black Masculinity," *Text and Performance Quarterly* 28, no. 3. (2008): 298–314. Thanks to Mark Broomfield for drawing my attention to McCune's dazzling analysis.

28. Snorton, *Nobody Is Supposed to Know.*

29. Boykin, *Beyond the Down Low*; see also M. Alferdo González, "Latinos On Da Down Low: The Limitations of Sexual Identity in Public Health," *Latino Studies* 5 no. 1 (2007): 25–52.

30. See Janet Jakobsen and Ann Pellegrini's introduction to *Secularisms* (Durham, NC: Duke University Press, 2008), in which they argue that despite rising claims to secular university in the United States, U.S. secularism remains deeply tied to white Protestantism.

31. Ruth Frankenberg "Mirage of an Unmarked Whiteness," in Birgit Brander Rasmussen et al., eds., *The Making and Unmaking of Whiteness* (Durham, NC: Duke University Press, 2001), 75.

32. Ibid., 76–77.

33. Judith Butler, *Gender Trouble: Feminism and the Subversion of Identity* (New York: Routledge, 1990); Jonathan Ned Katz. *The Invention of Heterosexuality* (New York: Plume, 1996); James Dean *Straights: Heterosexuality in Post-Closeted Culture* (New York: New York University Press, 2014): Chrys Ingraham,

Thinking Straight: The Power, Promise and Paradox of Heterosexuality (New York: Routledge, 2004).

34. Judith Butler. *The Psychic Life of Power: Theories of Subjection* (Palo Alto, CA: Stanford University Press, 1997).

35. Hamilton, "Trading on Heterosexuality."

36. Thank you to Margaux Cowden and the students at Williams College for helping me articulate this point in such succinct terms.

37. Building on Michael Warner's term "heteronormativity," which refers to all of the ways that heterosexuality is taken for granted in both cultural and institutional life, historian Lisa Duggan coined the term "homonormativity" (see *The Twilight of Equality* [New York: Beacon Press, 2004]) to draw attention to what is now taken for granted about gay identity and culture—namely, that what lesbians and gay men want most is access to mainstream institutions (like marriage and the military) and a private, respectable, domestic existence.

38. Katz, *Invention of Heterosexuality*, 108.

39. F. Newport, "Americans Remain More Likely to Believe Sexual Orientation Due to Environment, Not Genetics," *Gallop Poll Monthly*, July 25, 1998, 14–16: L. Marvin Overby, "Etiology and Attitudes: Beliefs about the Origins of Homosexuality and Their Implications for Public Policy," *Journal of Homosexuality* 61, no. 4 (2014): 568–587.

40. DeCecco and Parker, *Sex, Cells, and Same Sex Desire*; Rainer Herra "On the History of Biological Theories of Homosexuality," cited in ibid.

41. The sociobiological premise is exemplified in pro-gay discourse by the now well-worn refrain: "No one would *choose* a life of homophobic discrimination; hence, homosexuality is biological in origin; and hence, you must accept me because I cannot change." Consider, for also, the rapid speed at which Lady Gaga's 2011 hit song "Born This Way" became America's new gay anthem.

42. Diamond, *Sexual Fluidity*, 198.

SECTION TWO

Identity

As Section One demonstrated, discussions of sex, gender, and sexuality are often limited to heteronormative constructions that assume a natural binary between female and male sex categories. These heteronormative assumptions manifest in socially acceptable gender and sexual identities, behaviors, and practices. Additionally, discussions typically reify white, able-bodied, middle-class ideologies by leaving these social statuses unmarked. Section Two of the volume intervenes in these discussions to expand questions associated with identity as these carefully selected articles offer intimate insights of empowerment, recognition, resistance, trauma, desire, action, community, solidarity, and hope. Some chapters represent empirical research while others are first-person accounts. Ultimately, this section of the book may inspire readers to reflect on their own personal identities and narratives of resistance, trauma, empowerment, struggle, and pride.

Martin Rochlin begins with a simple, rhetorical questionnaire designed to discursively shed light on the multiple privileges held by heterosexual people. Related to heterosexual privileges, Nicholas Solebello and Sinikka Elliott interview 23 fathers regarding their own taken-for-granted discussions about sexual identity and sexual practices with their kids. The authors expose paradoxes and tensions in the fathers' hopes and desires regarding their children's sexuality and sexual practices. Many of the fathers' concerns, of course, are embedded in heteronormativity and the stigma related to sexualities and sexual practices on the margins of normative society. Andrew Matzner interrogates normative society by demanding attention to settler colonialism and resistance to Western cultural demands. Matzner introduces readers to *mahu* identity, practice, and tradition.

In the next chapter, Shiri Eisner offers a definition of bisexuality that she posits is like an umbrella, expanding the sole focus on sexuality and simultaneously challenging dominant understandings that rely on a binary. Eisner, self-identified as a feminist bisexual and genderqueer activist, writer, and researcher, reads bisexual stereotypes three different ways to challenge readers' epistemological understanding of bisexuality. Authors Karli June Cernakowski and Megan Milks introduce readers to the idea of asexuality as an identity and a social movement, paying particular attention to the relation of asexuality to both feminist and queer theory. Ultimately, they hope to invite dedicated study and dialogue about asexuality within the interdisciplinary study of human sexuality. Focused on the UK, Elizabeth McDermott demands attention to the intersection between sexuality and class among lesbian and gay youth using Pierre Bourdieu's concepts of habitus and cultural capital. McDermott argues that researchers must take these concepts into consideration as they both influence the educational trajectories of young lesbian, gay, bisexual, and transgender people.

Activist poet Eli Clare gently, but painfully, makes clear the entanglements of multiple systems of oppression. Clare's maneuvering in/between and beyond rural/urban, heteronormative/queer, home/exile, bourgeoisie/proletariat, freak/normal, and so many more artificial binaries gives readers the chance to ask the question: Why do we demand that people neatly fit? Ahoo Tabatabai asks a different question in her chapter: How does identity, especially as it shifts, shape belonging and community? Based on semistructured interviews, Tabatabai exposes the borders and boundaries, as well as strategic identity management practices, among women who had previously identified as lesbian but have since shifted to a different identity. In the next chapter, Margaret Cruikshank asks important questions about how aging shapes identity and how identity shapes aging. Perhaps thinking about Bourdieu's concept of habitus may be useful after reading Cruikshank's article since our bodies are so integral to our identities and experience of age. Finally, Sonya Bolus offers her deeply intimate narrative of crossing multiple borders as her partner gender-transitions.

We hope that the chapters in this section help move the dominant discourse beyond narrow confines of traditional discussions and research about sex, gender, sexuality, identity, behavior, and practice. We encourage readers to raise new questions about how we think about identity and sexual practices. What sort of language exists to make sense of contemporary identities and behaviors? Which experiences are central but excluded from theoretical frameworks? As these chapters demonstrate, lived experience is often more complex, varied, and fluid than our theoretical frameworks reflect, and as researchers we must be accountable to exclusionary research questions and limited theoretical frameworks. As readers continue to make their way through this volume, we want them to consider which theories best help them to grasp and comprehend lived experiences.

9 • *Martin Rochlin*

HETEROSEXISM IN RESEARCH
The Heterosexual Questionnaire

DISCUSSION QUESTION

1. What are your first reactions upon reading this questionnaire?

Purpose: The purpose of this exercise is to examine the manner in which the use of heterosexual norms may bias the study of gay men's and lesbians' lives.

Instructions: Heterosexism is a form of bias in which heterosexual norms are used in studies of homosexual relationships. Gay men and lesbians are seen as deviating from a heterosexual norm, and this often leads to marginalization and pathologizing of their behavior.

Read the questionnaire below with this definition in mind. Then respond to the questions that follow.

. . .

1. What do you think caused your heterosexuality?
2. When and how did you first decide you were a heterosexual?
3. Is it possible that your heterosexuality is just a phase you may grow out of?
4. Is it possible that your heterosexuality stems from a neurotic fear of others of the same sex?
5. If you have never slept with a person of the same sex, is it possible that all you need is a good gay lover?
6. Do your parents know that you are straight? Do your friends and/or roommate(s) know? How did they react?
7. Why do you insist on flaunting your heterosexuality? Can't you just be who you are and keep it quiet?
8. Why do heterosexuals place so much emphasis on sex?
9. Why do heterosexuals feel compelled to seduce others into their lifestyle?
10. A disproportionate majority of child molesters are heterosexual. Do you consider it safe to expose children to heterosexual teachers?
11. Just what do men and women *do* in bed together? How can they truly know how to please each other, being so anatomically different?
12. With all the societal support marriage receives, the divorce rate is spiraling. Why are there so few stable relationships among heterosexuals?
13. Statistics show that lesbians have the lowest incidence of sexually transmitted diseases. Is it really safe for a woman to maintain a heterosexual lifestyle and run the risk of disease and pregnancy?
14. How can you become a whole person if you limit yourself to compulsive, exclusive heterosexuality?

Martin Rochlin, *The Heterosexual Questionnaire* from *Changing Men: New Directions in Research on Men and Masculinity*, edited by Michael S. Kimmel. Copyright © 1987 by Sage Publications. Reprinted with permission by the publisher.

15. Considering the menace of overpopulation, how could the human race survive if everyone were heterosexual?
16. Could you trust a heterosexual therapist to be objective? Don't you feel s/he might be inclined to influence you in the direction of her/his own leanings?

17. There seems to be very few happy heterosexuals. Techniques have been developed that might enable you to change if you really want to. Have you considered trying aversion therapy?
18. Would you want your child to be heterosexual, knowing the problems that s/he would face?

10 • *Nicholas Solebello and Sinikka Elliott*

"WE WANT THEM TO BE AS HETEROSEXUAL AS POSSIBLE"

Fathers Talk about Their Teen Children's Sexuality

DISCUSSION QUESTIONS

1. Do the fathers in this interview group believe heterosexuality is natural and inevitable, or do they view heterosexuality as a social construct?
2. What role does gender play in the way fathers talk about, and interact with, their child regarding sexuality? How does the gender of their child shape discussion about their child's sexual identity?
3. What are some of the paradoxes and tensions in the fathers' desires and accounts about their child's sexuality? How are these gendered, either in ideology, discourse, or based on child's gender?

Gender and sexuality are intricately intertwined: Individuals may assess others' sexual identities based on their gender performances and police gender interactionally through the use of sexual epithets such as *slut* and *fag*. Girls and women in high school and college often report monitoring their sexual behavior in an effort to avoid the label *slut* (Hamilton and Armstrong 2009; Schalet 2010; Tanenbaum 1999), and some teen boys use the term *fag* to police one another for perceived signs of weakness, emotion, or effeminacy—things coded gay and feminine (Pascoe 2007). Along with schools and peers, studies show parents actively strive to shape their young children's gender and sexual identities (Kane 2006; Martin

Solebello, Nicholas and Sinikka Elliott. 2011. "We Want Them to Be As Heterosexual As Possible: Fathers Talk about Their Teen Children's Sexuality." *Gender & Society*, 25(3): 293–315.

2009). The links between gender and sexuality may be particularly salient as young people move through the middle and high school years, however. How do parents make sense of and try to direct their older children's gender and sexuality? We address part of this question by examining how fathers think about and talk to their teen sons and daughters about dating, sexuality, and sexual orientation.

. . .

FAMILY SEXUAL COMMUNICATION

We take an expansive view of family sexual communication as including not only the more structured conversations fathers may have with their children around puberty, dating, and sexuality but also more casual conversations about sexual images on television or the Internet, for example. Studies suggest that for many reasons (such as a sense of discomfort and/or desire to focus on the moral aspects of sex), parents' lessons to their children about sexuality tend to be vague and general, providing little factual information (Angera, Brookins-Fisher, and Inungu 2008; Byers, Sears, and Weaver 2008). However, despite a number of factors shaping parent–child communication about sex—including the extent of parents' sexual knowledge and education, comfort levels of the parent and child, and the gender/age of the child (see review in Byers, Sears, and Weaver 2008)—many parents do try to provide some form of sex education to their children. In general, parents are more likely to talk with children who share their biological sex (i.e., mothers–daughters, fathers–sons) because they feel better equipped to answer these children's questions (Kirkman, Rosenthal, and Feldman 2002; McHale, Crouter, and Whiteman 2003; Walker 2001). Nevertheless, regardless of whether the child is a boy or a girl, the responsibility of providing sex education falls on mothers most often (see review in Martin 2009). Mothers report a great deal of discomfort and difficulty around these conversations (Jaccard, Dittus, and Gordon 2000; Walker 2001), although some research finds that African American and Latina mothers indicate more discomfort and less communication than white mothers when discussing sex with their children (Meneses 2004; Somers and Vollmar 2006). Yet other studies find that African American adolescents report more communication from their mothers than other adolescents (e.g., Epstein and Ward 2008).

Parents' lessons to their teenagers about sex and sexuality tend to be restrictive, focusing on the dangerous and/or damaging consequences of relationships and sexual activity (Elliott 2010; Moore and Rosenthal 2006; Schalet 2000, 2010). Parents often base these restrictions on assumptions of their own teen children's sexual innocence while at the same time characterizing other teens as sexually deviant and dangerous (Elliott 2010; Moore and Rosenthal 2006). For example, immigrant parents may enforce restraints on their children's, especially daughters', sexual behavior in an attempt to protect them not only from the consequences of sex but also from their Western, "promiscuous" peers (Espiritu 2001; Gonzalez-Lopez 2004). White, middle-class, American parents "dramatize" their children's sexuality and base their lessons, especially to their daughters, on a heterosexual "battle of the sexes" (Schalet 2000). These lessons reinforce a "boys against the girls" attitude (Martin 1996, 126) and stereotypical notions of sexually passive girls and sex-driven boys (Hamilton and Armstrong 2009).

. . .

GENDER, SEXUALITY, AND HETERONORMATIVITY

. . .

Research examining parents' gender and sexual lessons to their children emphasizes the prominent role heteronormativity plays in these lessons (Kane 2006; Martin 2009; Nolin and Petersen 1992). For instance, in her study of mothers of three- to six-year-olds, Martin (2009) finds most mothers assume their children are heterosexual. However, some mothers (particularly those who hold conservative religious beliefs) express concern about their sons' non-normative gender behavior, worrying that it implies a possible future homosexual identity. These mothers actively seek to teach their children that homosexuality is wrong and in this way preemptively steer their children toward heterosexuality. Yet a majority of the mothers Martin (2009) surveyed report never thinking or worrying about their children's sexual identities because of the heteronormative ways both they and their children talk about love and relationships and because "they [find] 'evidence' of heterosexuality in [their] children's cross-gender behavior" (Martin 2009, 197).

Even so, parents do not take their children's gender or sexual identities for granted. Instead, they actively work to try to ensure that their children, especially sons, enact gender normatively and feel accountable when they do not (Martin 2009; McGuffey 2005; White 1994). In her study of heterosexual parents of gay children, Fields (2001) finds that parents often blame themselves for their children's homosexuality. Similarly, some fathers of sexually abused sons encourage their sons to engage in girl watching and roughhousing with them in an effort to guide them toward heterosexuality and "'fix' what had happened" (McGuffey 2005, 637). Kane (2006, 150) finds parents of preschool-aged children feel accountable for "doing gender both for and with their children." Kane's research also demonstrates the importance of heterosexuality to parents of young children and the links between gender and heteronormativity—heterosexual fathers, in particular, express concern that their sons' gender nonconformity might be an indication of homosexuality. Kane speculates that parents may worry about both sons' *and* daughters' gender nonconformity in their teen years, a period characterized by heightened gender differentiation in schools (Pascoe 2007) and increased adult concerns about girls' sexuality (Martin 1996; Schalet 2010; Tolman 1994).

In this article, we consider how heterosexual fathers think about their teen children's sexuality and how gender and heteronormativity shape their understandings. Our analyses reveal that fathers participate very little in their sons' or daughters' sex education. However, they want their children—particularly their sons—to be heterosexual. Fathers care a great deal about their sons being heterosexual and attempt to craft masculine and heterosexual identities for

them. In contrast, some fathers of daughters accept and even encourage their daughters to be lesbians but "deny women [their own] sexuality" (Rich 1980, 638) by simultaneously minimizing and infantilizing their sexuality. Thus, although fathers may accept lesbian daughters more readily than gay sons, fathers of both sons and daughters construct and reinforce male sexual privilege and heterosexuality's status as the "natural" and "right" form of sexuality.

METHOD

The data and analyses offered here are based on interviews with 23 fathers of at least one teenage child between the age of 13 and 19. We recruited study participants through their children's schools (5), through on-street solicitation at various local businesses (14), and through referrals (4). The second author conducted pilot interviews in 2006–7. These initial interviews helped us refine our interview protocol and identify research areas to explore further in subsequent interviews (Charmaz 2006). We completed the bulk of the interviews between the fall of 2008 and the summer of 2009 in an urban area in the Southeast. The first author (a white man who is a graduate student) conducted 15 of the interviews (mainly with fathers of sons), while the second author (a white woman assistant professor) completed the other eight (mainly with fathers of daughters). We thought fathers might be more willing to talk openly if interviewed by someone who matched the sex of their child, especially fathers of daughters. However, some fathers had both a son and daughter, and at other times we could not match the interviewer with the sex of the child. Yet when we compared the transcripts we detected no major differences in how the fathers responded to the questions based on the sex of the interviewer.

The interviews, which lasted on average an hour, occurred in the participant's or interviewer's place of employment, the participant's home, or local restaurants. All of the fathers participated voluntarily without promise of incentive, and we assured everyone that their identities and responses would remain confidential. We digitally recorded the interviews with participants' permission and transcribed them, assigning all fathers pseudonyms. Of the fathers, 19 identified as white, while four identified as African American. All identified as heterosexual. The average age of the fathers was 50. Most of the fathers lived with a spouse (20; 17 with their teenage children's biological mothers), and in most instances these were dual-income households (15). Of the fathers, 19 had graduated from college or had a graduate degree, but the fathers' occupations were quite diverse—ranging from a maintenance worker and a school teacher to a veterinarian and a CEO of a nonprofit organization. Table 10.1 provides more detailed information about the fathers.

We began this project with a general interest in fathers' experiences raising teenagers and a specific focus on issues around puberty, dating, and sexuality. Initially, we told fathers we wanted to hear about their "experiences," broadly defined, raising teens. We provided more details in follow-up correspondence, informing fathers that the interview would focus specifically on issues pertinent to raising teenagers, such as puberty, dating, and sex. Each semistructured interview started with general questions asking fathers to describe their teenagers and daily family life.[1] From there, topics ranged from their experiences with their children's pubertal changes, to issues and advice about teen dating, to questions that

TABLE 10.1. Demographic Characteristics of Sample

Pseudonym	Age	Self-Reported Race	Occupation	Teenage Children
Adam	43	African American	Asst, director of state agency	Daughter (18)
Bernie	39	African American	Customer service rep.	Daughter (13), sons (16, 17)
Bob	47	White	Sales manager	Daughter (15)
Brendon	74	African American	Retired	Son (19)
Brett	48	White	Professor	Daughter (14), son (15)
Charles	50	White	Engineer	Daughter (14)
Chris	56	White	Minister	Sons (14, 17)
Frank	53	White	Consultant	Daughters (16, 19)
Garth	57	White	Engineer	Sons (13, 18)
Greg	43	White	Teacher	Daughters (15, 18)
Harley	45	White	Unemployed	Daughter (18), son (15)
Jimmy	51	White	Veterinarian	Son (14)
Joe	50	White	CEO of a nonprofit org.	Daughter (16)
Kirk	45	White	Auditor	Son (15)
Leonard	58	White	Unemployed	Son (17)
Linus	48	White	Sales engineer	Daughter (19), sons (14, 17)
Patrick	43	White	Consultant	Son (13)
Paul	62	White	Therapist	Son (17)
Ron	50	White	Mechanic	Daughter (17), son (15)
Scott	34	White	Engineer	Son (14)
Tony	47	White	Programmer	Daughters (13, 17)
Vinnie	55	White	Construction superintendent	Son (15)
Will	44	African American	Maintenance worker	Sons (14, 17)

addressed the extent and content of conversations about sexual issues. We also asked fathers if they had talked with their child or children in general about sexual orientation—about being gay, straight, or bisexual. If, in response to this question, a father was not forthcoming about his feelings about his teen child's or children's sexual identity, we followed up with, "Have you ever wondered about your [son's/daughter's] sexual orientation?" and "How would you feel if your [son/daughter] told you [he/she] was gay?" We made no mention of sexual orientation before this question, although by previously mentioning sex as a topic, some fathers may have anticipated talking about sexual orientation. However, the questions clearly surprised some fathers possibly because they thought they had already established their teens as heterosexual and/or because their heteronormative assumptions precluded thinking about the possibility that their children might be gay.

. . .

FATHERS' ACCOUNTS OF FAMILY SEXUAL COMMUNICATION

Although many fathers mentioned talking briefly over the years about issues related to puberty, dating, and sex with their children, when we asked about the details of these conversations, they often could not remember. For instance, Brett stated, "I haven't really sat down and talked to him about 'Here's what to expect. Here's what's going to happen to you.'" Indeed, of the 23 fathers, 16 made it clear that they have had very few explicit discussions about sexual issues with their children, presuming they get this information from other sources. Garth's response was typical: "Apparently he's got sex education from the schools, friends, wherever. . . . I figured I learned about it, all kids learn about it. . . . [W]e haven't had those conversations." Instead of long, detailed, or regular conversations, most fathers indicated engaging in spot checks—episodic teaching moments with their children around sexual issues. While this lack of involvement echoes previous research (e.g., Kirkman, Rosenthal, and Feldman 2001), it may

also reflect our sample of mostly white, educated, and middle-class fathers. Some studies suggest less educated fathers and fathers from other racial/ethnic groups communicate more often with their children (Gonzalez-Lopez 2004; Lehr et al. 2005). Nevertheless, despite their apparent marginal involvement in family sexual communication, the fathers still had quite a bit to say about their children's sexuality, especially in response to questions about dating and sexual orientation.

"CHIP OFF THE OLD BLOCK": FATHERS AND SONS

Most of the fathers described discussing sexual orientation either explicitly or implicitly with their sons. Until we prompted them with a specific question about sexual identity, however, the fathers did not directly mention their sons' sexual orientation or made comments suggesting their teen sons are heterosexual. Some fathers, for example, said they knew their sons were entering puberty when they began to show an interest in girls. Garth finished up his response to one of the first questions, "How would you describe your 18-year-old son?" by concluding, "He just seems to be a regular kid. He does have an interest in girls. He's had girlfriends." Garth sees his son's interest in girls (and its implied heterosexuality) as a natural extension of growing up. Similarly, even though his two sons have not shown an interest in dating, Will said, "I'm still on red alert. Because all it takes is a Sally or Jane to come over the right way . . . ," suggesting Will assumes his sons are on the brink of establishing heterosexual identities.

We eventually asked fathers whether they had spoken with their children about sexual orientation. In response, many explicitly said it is very important that their sons be heterosexual. When asked if he had ever talked with his two sons about sexual orientation, Bernie exclaimed, "Oh yeah. Definitely. Yeah, we want them to be as heterosexual as possible." Other fathers similarly described how disappointing and/or difficult it would be to have a gay son. Some fathers, however, particularly those who identified as politically liberal, expressed a begrudging acceptance of homosexuality. These comments often resembled "semantic moves" (Bonilla-Silva and Forman 2000): discursive maneuvers to avoid sounding homophobic. Jimmy said,

> Yeah, I'd be OK. I mean I can't honestly say that would be my preference, but I would live with that . . . he's my kid. I'm not going to banish him because of his sexual orientation . . . but you know I can't honestly say that'd be [on] my top list of things that I would prefer but . . . *Why? Does that prevent him from something?* No. Well, in some portions of society there still is some stigma associated with it.

Ultimately Jimmy diverted attention away from his own personal misgivings about homosexuality and instead established that his concern stems from unease over the prejudice his son might encounter if he was gay. To be sure, gay teens may encounter intolerance and gay bashing, especially if they are gender nonconforming (Kimmel 2004; Pascoe 2007); yet by preferring that his son is heterosexual, Jimmy reproduces the views of the "portions of society" that worry him.

Beyond caring a great deal about their sons' attainment of heterosexuality, the fathers also indicated a sense of accountability for cultivating heterosexual identities for their sons (Kane 2006). Indeed, underlying many fathers' accounts of their sons' sexuality was a notion that heterosexuality is not a given; it has to be taught. Responding to a question about how he would feel if his son or daughter was gay, Brett answered, "I don't think it would make any difference if it was my daughter but with a son . . . I think I would feel like I had failed in coaching in some way . . . that I didn't coach, advise, [or] lead in a way to help clarify some of those thoughts." Here Brett made a distinction between the importance of his son's versus his daughter's heterosexuality (an issue addressed in the next section) and explicitly articulated how important it is for him to be active in coaching his son toward heterosexuality. Thus, while heterosexuality remains normative and taken for granted in U.S. culture (Martin 2009; Wolkomir 2009), it does not seem guaranteed, at least not for boys.

Fathers like Brett see themselves as pivotal in directing their sons' future sexual preferences. This fits with much of the literature on the fragile and contested status of masculinity. Men must perform and prove their masculinity, and men accomplish and "do" masculine identities in large part by establishing themselves as heterosexual (Connell 2005; Kimmel 2004; Pascoe 2007; Schrock and Schwalbe 2009). By repudiating femininity and homosexuality and enacting heterosexual desire, men construct themselves as masculine and heterosexual, but this status remains precarious and men must constantly reassert it (Pascoe 2007). Heterosexuality is thus intrinsically woven into the idealized presentation of a masculine identity.

There is a fundamental paradox in these fathers' views, however. Although they stressed their desire for, and role in crafting, heterosexual sons, many said they hope their sons stay away from heterosexual relationships. Similar to the findings of other studies of American parents (e.g., Schalet 2000), fathers often presented their sons' teenage years as fraught with the potential for negative consequences from heterosexual sex and relationships. As Kirk succinctly put it: "That's all we try to explain: Every decision that you make has a consequence." Fathers said they are especially concerned about the consequences of teen sex (like STDs and pregnancies), and some described discouraging dating. Linus put it this way: "[We] encourage them to hang out in groups, you know. There's no sense at this point of pairing off in couples." Other fathers emphasized their sons' sexual vulnerability. Chris said, "We have told him a little bit about 'Be careful of aggressive girls who may want to have sex with you.' . . . We have warned him about that area." In her study of parents of teens, Elliott (2010) finds that parents equate teen sexual activity with deviance and negative consequences and construct their own children as sexually innocent while at the same time describing their children's peers as hypersexual. These fathers' attitudes and recommendations about dating may thus serve to solidify perceptions of their sons as "good" boys who avoid sexual activity.

The few fathers who allow and encourage their sons to date said they view their sons' past and current relationships with girls as evidence of heterosexuality. Paul expressed this:

There were moments when I wondered if he was going to be gay . . . . and if I had my choice I wish that he wouldn't be, but if he was I knew that my wife and I would both be fine with it. . . . And then just watching for clues you know? Is he more interested in men than women? And then he started to move very clearly into the female direction so there was a sense of OK! [Paul does a fist pump in the air.] Chip off the old block.

Paul (like Garth) assumes his son's interest in girls means he is heterosexual. Paul's comment also illustrates that his son's presentation of heterosexuality is wrapped up in his own. This is perhaps all the more significant considering Paul identified as politically liberal and was one of only four fathers who said he would be "fine" if his son was gay. However, the qualification "if I had my choice" casts doubt on Paul's acceptance level—suggesting again that liberal fathers may semantically position themselves in a positive light while still affirming heterosexuality as the "better," more desirable option (Valocchi 2005).

Fathers who do not allow their sons to date or whose sons show no interest in dating said they look for evidence elsewhere to establish their sons as heterosexual. After being asked how he would feel if his son was gay, Vinnie, a father of a 15-year-old son who plays football, said he would be "shocked" because his son "is very much a male's male." Like the mothers in Martin's (2009) study, Vinnie assumes his son is heterosexual because he presumably engages in normatively masculine pursuits and "acts" masculine. He firmly established a link between his son's masculine gender display and a heterosexual identity by describing his son as a "man's man," a phrase that implies the ability to attract, and be attracted to, women. Harley, who lives apart from his son and daughter, also linked his son's gender display to sexuality. He explained that he used to worry about his son's sexuality "because being small and somewhat timid . . . when he was younger—and like I said, his

stepfather was not very masculine—I worried about the softness and just hoping and praying that he's straight [laughs]." Harley said he recently laid his fears to rest when his ex-wife demanded that he punish their son for trying to download heterosexual pornography. He described what happened the next time his son came to visit:

And then, you know, I've got—not adult magazines—but FHM [For Him Magazine] and car magazines that have girls in them and I leave them lying around because . . . well you know they're fully covered. But my son had a little more curiosity. . . . I didn't discipline him when he came to spend time with me, I left more of them out!

Clearly, Harley views his son's recent interest in pornography as evidence of an interest in girls (i.e., heterosexuality) and as something he should cultivate further. Harley's actions seem designed to both craft heterosexuality for his son and model his own heteromasculinity by bonding with his son through the objectification of women. Several other fathers also indicated catching their sons downloading or viewing pornography and expressed tacit permission for this. Indeed, scholars observe that girl watching is a central way boys and men confirm masculinity within homosocial groups (e.g., Pascoe 2007; Quinn 2002). Harley also stated he did not want to reprimand his son for something he sees as "natural curiosity," implying an interest in pornography is a normal sign of growing up. Yet some fathers did express concern about the consequences of their sons' pornography use and said they attempt to curtail their access. According to Jimmy, "[The age of 14 is] too young to be looking at hardcore porn. . . . I think it sets unrealistic expectations." Despite their reservations, however, these fathers also interpreted their sons' interest in pornography as a rite of passage and a telltale sign of heterosexuality.

Only one father we interviewed spoke of having a son who is interested in gay pornography. Though Scott explained that when he was young he learned about sex by watching heterosexual pornography, he expressed discomfort with his own son's interest in pornographic images of men having sex with other men. Scott heterosexualized his son's use of gay pornography, however, by stating that he does not think his son is excited by this kind of pornography but rather watches it because he is worried about the size of his penis and wants to see how he measures up. Illustrating the power of compulsory heterosexuality (Rich 1980), Scott simultaneously imposes and manages heterosexuality for his son, defining his consumption of gay pornography as educational—not unlike Scott's own use of pornography as a teenager.

Fathers whose sons had not yet dated seemed especially intent on modeling heterosexuality. Will, whose sons show no interest in dating, said he points out "pretty girls" to his sons: "I just point them out. Like a flower. 'Say wow, son, come on now. Let's tell the truth. You don't think Janet Jackson or Halle Berry is. . . .' So I let them understand, to not think it's strange if this appetite tries to get into you." Through encouraging his sons to participate in girl watching with him, Will normalizes and promotes heterosexuality—providing examples of women his sons should naturally desire and modeling his own heterosexual desire. Other fathers want their sons to wait to date until they are older and said they use their own life examples to reinforce this message. Bernie, who said he wants his teenage sons to be as heterosexual as possible, tells them,

> "I wouldn't even look at dating seriously right now. I wouldn't even get involved right now." I tell [them] about my experiences when I went to college . . . playing basketball, you start getting the attention of women and then you start going out and hanging out and the next thing you know, you're failing out.

Kirk, who described his 15-year-old son as "shy" and "a late bloomer," said, "I basically tell him the truth that, you know, I had sex with people prior to marriage . . . [but] that's something that probably he should not do." Yet, like Will's encouragement, these stories also establish the fathers' relational and sexual competence and presumably model these things for their sons.

An interesting tension emerges in the fathers' accounts: Even while hoping for and encouraging heterosexuality in their sons, fathers base their lessons on a battle of the sexes paradigm that puts heterosexual relationships in an unfavorable light and suggests fathers do not view their sons as fully agentic, desiring sexual actors. Similar to the findings of previous research (Elliott 2010; Moore and Rosenthal 2006), these fathers presented their sons as innocent while casting their peers as sexually predatory. However, fathers still look for "evidence" of heterosexuality. For fathers whose sons date girls, this seems obvious. Fathers who discourage dating, or whose sons show no interest in dating girls, see their role in crafting heterosexuality for their sons as *especially* important or rely on other evidence that establishes their sons as heterosexual.

"PROTECT YOURSELF, GUARD YOURSELF, GUARD YOUR HEART": FATHERS AND DAUGHTERS

Although many of the fathers indicated being only marginally involved in conveying sexual information to their children, fathers of daughters overwhelmingly informed us that mothers handle these conversations. Bob said, "I think it would have been embarrassing for me to say something. . . . I don't know it that well what all you go through. So the mother had the conversations with her. I felt that she . . . has the experience and she seemed to be comfortable with it. . . ." Other fathers conveyed similar levels of discomfort with their teen daughter's pubertal changes and sexuality. Greg explained that his 15-year-old stepdaughter's appreciation for her breasts bothers him:

> She's . . . very vain. She's aware that she has breasts. She's very happy with her breasts. She annoys us with them. She likes to talk about them. . . . [And] you'll come in the room and you'll go, "Honey, let go of your boobs!" . . . I mean she's not fondling herself, she's just holding them. . . . She's very proud of her breasts.

In line with social discourse and sex education curricula that elide and evade girls' sexual desire (Fields 2008; Fine 1988; Garcia 2009; Tolman 1994), by defining his stepdaughter as vain Greg seemingly ignored any pleasure she might derive from touching herself intimately and in fact made a point to convey to the interviewer that she was not "fondling herself." Instead, he externalized her self-touching in terms of pride in her breast size (and presumably attractiveness)—an explanation that may reconcile his daughter's actions with normative conceptions of femininity and stands in contrast to fathers' attempts to cultivate heterosexual desire in their sons.

Instead of talking about female sexuality during the infrequent conversations they have with their daughters, fathers said they focus on providing a male perspective on sex. Greg described his conversations with his daughters this way:

> With my girls, what I've said was, "What are the guys thinking? You know how I know that? 'Cause I'm a guy. That's what we think, you know. And [other guys] weren't any different. So I'm just asking you to protect yourself, guard yourself, guard your heart."

Adam—a father of four daughters—echoed Greg:

> I tried to give them a boy's perspective on how they look at young girls at that age. . . . [I told them,] "Here's what I did when I was 14 and 15 and I'm certain that little boys haven't changed. Here's what guys think and here's what they do and if you let them do this then they'll take advantage of you."

Overall, fathers stressed their daughters' sexual vulnerability and the need to protect their virtue. Charles said he tells his daughter, "'Okay, honey, right now you have something that's valuable. Right? You have your sex. And the guys, they want it.'"

These descriptions appear to serve three purposes: First, they establish the fathers' own identities as normatively masculine and heterosexual. Second, they cast their daughters as heterosexual insofar as they assume their daughters need protection from heterosexual encounters with boys and define their daughters' sexuality as passive, vulnerable, and in need of saving—things stereotypically associated with female heterosexuality. Third, they reinforce the gender binary—demarcating "proper" performances of masculinity and femininity in hetero-relationships. To be sure, the myriad potentially negative consequences of sexual activity for girls in a sexist society (Hamilton and Armstrong 2009) shape these fathers' responses; but fathers did not link girls' sexual vulnerability to

sexism, and their descriptions may reify girls' victim status. Indeed, Frank seemed ambivalent about his use of the discourse of sexually driven boys: "We've talked generally about sex and what boys want. Boys have an interest in, you know, sex and sexual conquests perhaps. I don't know, it wasn't quite that barbaric."

Although fathers described their lessons to their daughters using a heterosexual framework, they did not explicitly mention their daughters' sexual identity until prompted. Once asked, many fathers of daughters said they would accept, and two implied they encourage, homosexuality for their daughters. Charles responded to a question about sexual orientation by saying, "Well, no we've talked about that. In fact, I've told her, 'If you want to bring girls home, it's okay with me.'" Similarly, Joe described joking with his daughter about her best friend:

> We also kid my daughter all the time about her close relationship with her friend that she plays hockey with. They are very close, very friendly, and very affectionate to one another, and so we joke with them about which one's wearing the dress and which one's wearing the suit at the wedding. . . . And if it did turn out that she was gay, I don't think it would surprise me and it wouldn't really matter.

Of course, we do not know how Charles's and Joe's daughters respond to their comments. For instance, Joe's jokes could be seen as supportive or policing of his daughter's (already) gender-transgressive involvement in hockey.[2] Yet we note these comments largely because none of the fathers treated their sons' sexuality as a laughing matter.

Fathers less open than Charles and Joe to the idea that their daughters might be gay nevertheless did not express overwhelming disappointment about this possibility. However, these fathers often qualified their support with statements that called the legitimacy of teen lesbianism into question. Frank said he does not care whether or not his 16-year-old daughter is gay. Throughout the interview, however, he often returned to the following:

> My daughter claims that a couple of her friends are lesbians. Maybe they are, maybe they aren't. I don't

know. . . . Perhaps they are. . . . I'm indifferent about that but what I am concerned about is that it's kind of stylized, a little bit fake, probably not real, and that the kids do it to get attention.

Frank questioned the validity of his daughter's friends' lesbianism and heterosexualized it by echoing the notion that "women's sexuality is a direct consequence of men's desire," which helps render lesbian identities invisible (Hamilton 2007, 168). Indeed, he undermined his earlier supportive statements about his daughter's potential homosexuality later in his interview by stating he hopes his daughter would have some "substantive thought" before claiming to be gay. Like some of the more liberal fathers of sons, Frank used semantic moves to avoid sounding overtly homophobic. He projected an air of ambivalent acceptance of his daughter's friends' lesbianism but then rejected the legitimacy of homosexuality. Other fathers of daughters referred to homosexuality as a "lifestyle" that teenagers are too young to understand and participate in; yet no father suggested that a teen's heterosexual identity might be just a phase or something that requires serious consideration. Instead, like fathers of sons, these men positioned heterosexuality as the "natural or right" form of sexuality and "homosexuality as its binary opposite" (Valocchi 2005, 756).

Some fathers also suggested that their apparent acceptance of a lesbian identity for their daughters stems from their concerns about teen heterosexual relationships. These fathers (like the fathers of sons) did not paint a positive picture of heterosexual relationships. Joe, the father who teases his daughter about marrying her best friend, ended his discussion of whether his daughter might be lesbian by saying, "It really doesn't matter if she is from the standpoint of my [advice]—'boys are mean, throw rocks at them'—she'll buy right into that. I'd feel a little safer to say that sort of jokingly." Similar to other fathers who provided their daughters with the "male perspective," Joe presented an essentialized view of boys centered on a fully realized version of masculinity steeped in heterosexual conquest. This version stands in stark contrast to fathers' depictions of their sons' sexual identities as vulnerable and in need of crafting. By viewing their daughters' sexuality through a heterosexual lens, these fathers do not seem to connect girls' same-sex activity to a fully realized homosexual identity (Hamilton 2007; Rupp and Taylor 2010). Their professed acceptance of lesbianism may thus stem from their belief that it is a phase or a fad some girls go through before permanently establishing heterosexual identities. Given that parents talk more often with children who share their biological sex (Kirkman, Rosenthal, and Feldman 2002; McHale, Crouter, and Whiteman 2003; Walker 2001), fathers may also base their seeming acceptance on a sense that their daughters' sexual orientation does not reflect their own.

DISCUSSION

The fathers in this study represent a select group: All volunteered to be interviewed about their experiences raising teenagers, thereby expressing an interest in and concern about the task of parenting. Yet consistently, many of the fathers described their role in family sexual communication as virtually nonexistent. This is not to say fathers think their children do not need this information—all of the fathers said their children should learn about puberty, relationships, and sex. Rather, most fathers we interviewed do not see it as their job to provide this information. Despite their reported noninvolvement, these heterosexual fathers' accounts shed light on fathers' feelings about their teen children's gender and sexual identities. They also elucidate the operations of heteronormativity. Our analyses reveal that while most of these fathers posit heterosexuality as either the preferable or more authentic sexual identity for their children, they do not simply assume their children are straight: Many actively promote heterosexuality for their sons and sexual passivity (associated with normative female heterosexuality) for their daughters. Thus, while fathers may treat sons and daughters differently, their expectations for "proper" behavior reinforce gender binaries and marginalize alternative sexual identities, potentially adding to the challenges and conflicts

LGBT and heterosexual youth face when navigating sexuality at school and at home (Fields 2008; Garcia 2009; Pascoe 2007; Schalet 2010).

Examining fathers' descriptions of their conversations about sexuality with their teen children contributes to the literature that frames gender and sexuality as a set of social practices rather than immutable traits (Connell 2005; Pascoe 2007; Schrock and Schwalbe 2009). The fathers see their sons' sexuality as something that must be coached and modeled (Kane 2006; McGuffey 2005) and engage in various strategies to craft masculine and heterosexual identities. Fathers' desire for heterosexuality seems to come from a sense that their sons' sexuality reflects their own, but they may also recognize that male dominance rests on heterosexuality and homophobia. A careful reading of the fathers' accounts suggests they have gained certain privileges and status through their enactments of heterosexuality—privileges they may both consciously and unconsciously wish for their sons.

The fathers of daughters did not articulate a sense of accountability for their daughters' sexual orientation, but they strongly expressed accountability for protecting their daughters from boys and sexual harm. Although fathers of sons also emphasized the risks of sex and said they warn their sons about "aggressive girls," fathers of daughters overwhelmingly said their conversations with their daughters focus on how girls must guard themselves from the hazards of relationships with boys and sexual intercourse. Yet fathers of daughters appeared somewhat more accepting of the possibility that their daughters are lesbian. Most fathers nevertheless qualified their acceptance with comments that called teen lesbianism into question. In doing so, they drew on the increasingly widespread notion that girls perform lesbian desire to attract boys (Hamilton 2007; Rupp and Taylor 2010). The belief that girls "might be the losers in both [heterosexual sex] and relationships" (Hamilton and Armstrong 2009, 591) also shapes fathers' tepid acceptance of homosexuality for their daughters. Fathers overwhelmingly constructed their daughters' sexuality as passive and imperiled, and no father described his daughter as a sexually desiring

subject. Perhaps this narrative is impossible given that fathers see their role in relation to their daughters' sexuality as defender and protector.

Taken together, fathers' constructions of their teen children's sexualities reflect the current state of gender and sexual hierarchies: Masculinity remains dominant and privileged, but that dominance relies on heterosexuality. With femininity subordinate and devalued, girls and women have more leeway for varied gender and sexual expression, as long as they do not challenge heterosexual male privilege. Yet despite tending to prefer heterosexuality for their children, overall fathers characterized teen heterosexual relationships quite negatively. There was no "idealization of heterosexual romance" (Rich 1980, 638–39) in these fathers' narratives. Instead, fathers described their teen children as vulnerable and potential victims in heterosexual relationships and said they encourage them to wait until they are older to date or get serious.

This negative characterization of teen heterosexuality sets up an interesting tension for fathers who nonetheless want their sons to be heterosexual. Fathers whose sons do not date girls see their own role in crafting heterosexuality for their sons as particularly important. They also described using various indicators, such as a normatively masculine gender display or an interest in pornography, as evidence that their sons are heterosexual. Much pornography is highly degrading to women, misogynistic, and racist, however, potentially giving those who consume it distorted perceptions of heterosexual sex and relationships (Dines 2010). Thus, fathers' tacit permission of their sons' consumption of pornography may bolster the gender (and racial) order. Future research should examine other ways parents find "evidence" of heterosexuality in their children as well as their consequences.

. . .

NOTES

1. Interview guides were semistructured to help ensure both researchers covered similar material during the interviews.
2. We thank an anonymous reviewer for this helpful observation.

REFERENCES

Angera, J., J. Brookins-Fisher, and J. Inungu. 2008. An investigation of parent/child communication about sexuality. *American Journal of Sexuality Education* 3:165–81.

Bonilla-Silva, E., and T. A. Forman. 2000. "I am not a racist but . . .": Mapping white college students' racial ideology in the USA. *Discourse Society* 11:50–85.

Byers, S., H. Sears, and A. Weaver. 2008. Parents' reports of sexual communication with children in kindergarten to grade 8. *Journal of Marriage and Family* 70:86–96.

Cabrera, N., C. Tamis-LeMonda, R. Bradley, S. Hofferth, and M. Lamb. 2000. Fatherhood in the twenty-first century. *Child Development* 71:127–36.

Charmaz, K. 2006. *Constructing grounded theory: A practical guide through qualitative analysis.* Thousand Oaks, CA: Sage.

Connell, R. W. 2005. *Masculinities.* Berkeley: University of California Press

Dines, G. 2010. *Pornland: How porn has hijacked our sexuality.* Boston: Beacon.

Elliott, S. 2010. Parents' constructions of teen sexuality: Sex panics, contradictory discourses, and social inequality. *Symbolic Interaction* 33:191–212.

Epstein, M., and L. M. Ward. 2008. "Always use protection": Communication boys receive about sex from parents, peers, and the media. *Journal of Youth and Adolescence* 37:113–26.

Espiritu, Y. L. 2001. "We don't sleep around like white girls do": Family, culture and gender in Filipina American lives. *Signs* 26:415–40.

Fields, J. 2001. Normal queers: Straight parents respond to their children's "coming out." *Symbolic Interaction* 24:165–87.

Fields, J. 2008. *Risky lessons: Sex education and social inequality.* New Brunswick, NJ: Rutgers University Press.

Fine, M. 1988. Sexuality, schooling and adolescent females: The missing discourse of desire. *Harvard Educational Review* 58:29–53.

Garcia, L. 2009. "Now why do you want to know about that?" Heteronormativity, sexism, and racism in the sexual (mis)education of Latina youth. *Gender & Society* 23:520–41.

Gonzalez-Lopez, G. 2004. Fathering Latina sexualities: Mexican men and the virginity of their daughters. *Journal of Marriage and Family* 66:1118–30.

Hamilton, L. 2007. Trading on heterosexuality: College women's gender strategies and homophobia. *Gender & Society* 21:145–72.

Hamilton, L., and E. A. Armstrong. 2009. Gendered sexuality in young adulthood: Double binds and flawed options. *Gender & Society* 23:589–616.

Ingraham, C. 1994. The heterosexual imaginary: Feminist sociology and theories of gender. *Sociological Theory* 12:203–19.

Jaccard, J., P. Dittus, and V. Gordon. 2000. Parent-teen communication about premarital sex: Factors associated with the extent of communication. *Journal of Adolescent Research* 15:187–208.

Kane, E. 2006. "No way my boys are going to be like that!" Parents' responses to children's gender nonconformity. *Gender & Society* 20:149–76.

Kimmel, M. S. 2004. Masculinity as homophobia: Fear, shame, and silence in the construction of gender identity. In *Race, class and gender in the United States: An integrated study,* edited by P. S. Rothenberg. New York: Worth.

Kirkman, M., D. Rosenthal, and S. Feldman. 2001. Freeing up the subject: Tension between traditional masculinity and involved fatherhood through communication about sexuality with adolescents. *Culture, Health, & Sexuality* 3:391–411.

Kirkman, M., D. Rosenthal, and S. Feldman. 2002. Talking to a tiger: Fathers reveal their difficulties in communicating about sexuality with adolescents. *New Directions for Child and Adolescent Development* 97:57–74.

Lehr, S., A. Demi, C. Dilorio, and J. Facteau. 2005. Predictors of father–son communication about sexuality. *Journal of Sex Research* 42:119–29.

Martin, K. 1996. *Puberty, sexuality, and the self: Boys and girls at adolescence.* New York: Routledge.

Martin, K. 2009. Normalizing heterosexuality: Mothers' assumptions, talk, and strategies with young children. *American Sociological Review* 74:190–207.

McGuffey, C. S. 2005. Engendering trauma: Race, class, and gender reaffirmation after child sexual abuse. *Gender & Society* 19:621–43.

McHale, S., A. Crouter, and S. Whiteman. 2003. The family contexts of gender development in childhood adolescence. *Social Development* 12:125–48.

Meneses, L. 2004. Ethnic differences in mother-daughter communication about sex. *Journal of Adolescent Health* 34:154.

Moore, S., and D. Rosenthal. 2006. *Sexuality in adolescence: Current trends.* New York: Routledge.

Nolin, M. J., and K. K. Petersen. 1992. Gender differences in parent–child communication about sexuality: An exploratory study. *Journal of Adolescent Research* 7:59–79.

Pascoe, C. J. 2007. *Dude, you're a fag: Masculinity and sexuality in high school.* Berkeley: University of California Press.

Quinn, B. A. 2002. Sexual harassment and masculinity: The power and meaning of "girl watching." *Gender & Society* 16:386–402.

Rich, A. 1980. Compulsory heterosexuality and lesbian existence. *Signs* 5:631–60.

Robb, M. 2004. Exploring fatherhood: Masculinity and intersubjectivity in the research process. *Journal of Social Work Practice* 18:395–406.

Rupp, L. J., and V. Taylor. 2010. Straight girls kissing. *Contexts* 9:28–32.

Schalet, A. 2000. Raging hormones, regulated love: Adolescent sexuality and the constitution of the modern individual in the United States and the Netherlands. *Body & Society* 6:75–105.

Schalet, A. 2010. Sexual subjectivity revisited: The significance of relationships in Dutch and American girls' experiences of sexuality. *Gender & Society* 24:304–29.

Schrock, D., and M. Schwalbe. 2009. Men, masculinity, and manhood acts. *Annual Review of Sociology* 35:277–95.

Somers, C. L., and W. L. Vollmar. 2006. Parent-adolescent relationships and adolescent sexuality: Closeness, communication, and comfort among diverse U.S. adolescent samples. *Social Behavior and Personality* 34:451–60.

Tanenbaum, L. 1999. *Slut! Growing up female with a bad reputation.* New York: Seven Stories Press.

Tolman, D. 1994. Doing desire: Adolescent girls' struggles for/with sexuality. *Gender & Society* 8:324–42.

Valocchi, S. 2005. Not yet queer enough: The lessons of queer theory for the sociology of gender and sexuality. *Gender & Society* 19:750–70.

Walker, J. L. 2001. A qualitative study of parents' experiences of providing sex education for their children: The implications for health education. *Health Education Journal* 60:132–46.

White, N. 1994. About fathers: Masculinity and the social construction of fatherhood. *Journal of Sociology* 30:119–31.

Wolkomir, M, 2009. Making heteronormative reconciliations: The story of romantic love, sexuality, and gender in mixed-orientation marriages. *Gender & Society* 23:494–519.

11 • *Andrew Matzner*

'O AU NO KEIA
Voices from Hawai'i's Mahu and Transgender Communities

DISCUSSION QUESTIONS

1. How did Western colonization impact mahu culture, ritualism, and practice?
2. How does space and place (i.e., rural vs. city) influence mahu expressions according to the author?
3. Is being mahu the same as being gay or lesbian or transgender? Why or why not?

Andrew Matzner, "Kaua'i Iki" from 'O Au no Keia: Voices from Hawai'i's Mahu and Transgender Communities. Reprinted with permission of the author.

I was brought up in Kaua'i in a household where it was OK to be *mahu,* unlike a lot of people I know who were ostracized and kicked out of the house; I was loved within my own household. My mom and dad raised me as a *mahu.* I still did all of the tasks a boy would do, but I also did the tasks the girls would do. I was taught everything. Of course, just because my immediate family accepted me didn't mean that my other relatives were as accepting. My cousins used to make fun of me and call me "Diana." My given name is Dana, which was already *fish.* For some reason my mom had given me a name which could go either way, so it was lovely....

We lived in the countryside, in the center of a small plantation town. We ran the theater, which was right in front of our house. On my mother's side, her father was pure Filipino and her mother was pure Hawaiian. My mother's side has ten children; they were primarily farmers and fishermen. My grandfather worked on the sugar cane plantation and while he was doing that, my grandmother and the kids worked on the taro farm. We had a large taro farm which all of the *mo'opuna* took care of, and during my mom's time they also cared for that. But my mom actually went on and attained a college degree at Kaua'i Community College. She was a registered nurse. I believe that she's the only one in her family that attained a college degree. I was proud of my mother. She went to work and went to school, did all of her homework and actually raised all of us. But we were also raised by our grandparents, which is Hawaiian style. So while mom and dad were working, we were taken care of by our grandparents.

My father is Filipino-Spanish-Chinese. My father's side were laborers, too—sugar cane workers. My father was one of twelve brothers and sisters. When they were young, their mother would take them to help the father work in the fields. During my grandparents' days, they got paid a dollar a day....

My parents were very non-judgmental. They always accepted people as they were. We always had *mahus* at our house. My parents were like foster parents to many other children. When we were growing up, all the unwanted children ended up at our house. My parents took them in, even though we didn't

have any legal rights or foster-home papers. They'd say, "Your mother no like you? Then get all your crap together—you're living here with us." We already had eight kids, but my parents took these other kids in, too. We never asked for money. My parents just gave the kids the love that they needed. I'm sure their parents loved them, but any kid that needed a place to go had a place to go....

Our house was located right in the middle of town. Right in front of us was the movie theater. It was very quaint, and old-fashioned style. The theater was destroyed in 1982, after hurricane Eva. The town we lived in had a strong community association. During the holidays they always had programs for the kids, treats at Christmas, Easter Egg hunts, Halloween treats, all that kind of stuff, but the proceeds from the theater went to fund all of those things. We actually ran the films and picked up and dropped off the films, rewound the films, cleaned the theater, and even ran the concession stand sometimes. We did all that. It was community. A lot of the community people would come out and help. When we had the theater cleaning, for instance, they would open up the whole theater during the daytime, and people would come with their water hoses and brooms and mops, and sweep up the whole thing. I think about two hundred people could fit in the theater.

Next to the theater was Kunamoto Stores, something like Arakawa's used to be, a plantation store where you could buy everything—clothes, shoes, fresh meat, bread, everything that you needed to survive. You could charge it on your account. Everybody had a *bango* number. Ours was 2567, and you could go there and charge whatever. Occasionally I would go to the store and charge what I wanted to eat. [laughs] It was real nice....

Our town was all dirt roads. The only paved road was the one fronting the theater and store. Also the main road in front of the town, along the beach. Those were the only paved roads at that time, so everything else was all dirt roads....

About 1970 they cut the tree down and paved the road where my house was, but not the other dirt roads. Today, it's completely torn down and taken away—all the old houses, the mango trees.... The town was known for mango. There was a general store, the Filipino social hall, and a post office down the road. The whole life of the town was in the center. Our house was centrally located. None of these places exist today—they were all bulldozed around 1980. That whole way of life was erased.

. . . From a young age, I was my grandmother's *puna hele*—her favorite. She used to call me "Glamour Boy." When relatives came in from off-island, she would introduce me and say, "This is my Glamour Boy." But I don't think I got special treatment because I was *mahu*. I was special, but everybody was special, too. However, I did feel a closer affinity to my grandmother simply because she never gave me lickins. I was raised before all this child abuse stuff—I got lickins! Everybody got lickins in those days. You act up, you act silly, you bad-mouth somebody—you're gonna get lickins. And like I said, oftentimes I was just caught in the cross-fire—guilt by association.

My family knew I was *mahu*. They didn't see anything wrong with it. They didn't make a big issue of it. It was just natural. I had a very natural upbringing. I was loved no matter what. But I was *mahu*. I was *mahu* as *mahu* could be. And the thing is, my grandmother and my mom's brother were the only ones who never spanked me. They recognized how I was and loved me for that. My grandmother would always talk to me each morning, to all of us, whoever was around. She would tell us different things. From her we learned the facts of life, about having sex, who you're having sex with, when you're having sex, when not to have sex. My grandmother taught us about that kind of stuff. Because when we were young, we had sex. I had sex with girls and boys. Because everybody wanted to have sex. And I was just there. [laughs] When you're young you don't really think about it in an intimate way. You just go for the experience.

But as far as being *mahu* and being treated or raised in a special way, I really wasn't. My grandmother would sit me down and tell me stories about this and stories about that, or take me to different places around the island. I thought that everything

she told me and the places she showed me, I thought that everybody else knew these things, this family folklore. But it wasn't until her death that I realized that no one else had been told or shown these things. So then I began to think, "Why did she tell *me* these stories? I don't want to be responsible!" Because with the stories comes responsibility.

For example, she gave me the responsibility of caring for the graves of our ancestors. We have many in the mountains which are difficult to find. If you don't know they are there, you won't know. And we have ancestors buried in caves along areas that are populated now, but where the caves are still protected. If people ever want to develop certain areas, I'll have to say, "You cannot, because my ancestors are buried there!" So one of the things I was charged with was to care for our dead, our ancestors' bones. It's an important responsibility. And for some reason or other my grandmother, who had been their caretaker, had entrusted that to me.

Throughout my years, starting from childhood, I was also raised by my mom's brother. He was the oldest male child in my mother's family. He was a marine. There were times that my uncle would show up, pick me up and not come back for a few days. My mom would be hysterical—"Where the hell were you?!" And he would say, "I took him up into the mountains." Or, "I took him down to the beach." My mom would be all worried—"He doesn't know anything about the mountains." And my uncle would say, "Well, that's why I'm taking him." Throughout my childhood it was always like that. Even more so during my high school years. When I had come back to Kaua'i for high school after going to school here on O'ahu, I was a dropout for a while. During that time, when I wasn't in school, my uncle said, "Hey—if you're not going to be in school, come to my house." So I would hitchhike to the other end of the island, all the way to Hanalei. . . .

My uncle took care of me and raised me in the mountains. I lived with him in the mountains of the Na Pali Coast, from Hanalei Valley all the way in. He taught me how to run, fish, jump and hunt. Survival skills are what he gave me. He would always brief me before an activity. "We're going to go here and there. These are the things we're going to see. These are things we're going to do. This is what I want you to do. This is what I don't want you to do." Whatever my uncle said, I followed to the T. If he told me to climb that mountain, I would climb the mountain like a goat. If he told me dive into the sea, I would dive into the sea. Whatever he told me to do. Whether it was climb that tree, build a house. Anything I had to do, I did for my uncle, to make him happy. Not just to make him happy. It was also survival.

We would often go and stay in the mountain without any supplies. We were lucky if we had a small zip-lock bag of rice or salt. Or maybe a bag of *poi*. The deal was always that if we don't catch anything then we won't eat anything. We'll just have salt and *poi* to eat. But it never worked out like that; we always had something to eat. The way my uncle worked was, we would go down to the beach and he would throw his net no more than three times, and whatever fish we caught—and we always caught, *always*—I'd clean. On the way home he'd give all the fish away, except for what we needed for the day. I mean, the people we met were so lucky because they got free fish! The first time I saw him do that I said, "Uncle, you're giving away all our fish!" He replied, "Don't worry." Because when we got home we still had our fish for dinner. The next day we went back to the sea and the same thing happened.

By the time I was in my high school years and I had dropped out of school, that was when he was able to show me and tell me more, give me more. Because I was getting to be a young adult already, going through all those changes. Everybody was looking at me, *"Oh, mahu."* But it didn't bother my uncle one bit.

In fact, the whole time my uncle knew I was *mahu*. People had the nerve to ask him in front of me, "How come you're taking him with you—he's *mahu*." My uncle would turn to them and say, "He's the only one in the family who can handle all of the things that have to be done." That's why my uncle took me with him. I was the only one in the family

who was taken with him to those places. No one else. Not any of my brothers, who today are excellent fishermen and hunters. Not any of my other cousins. No one.

My uncle was also one of the family's caretakers of our ancestors. That's why I was taken to learn about that and learn to fend for myself in the wild. He felt that no matter how I was, it was important that I knew how to survive. It was the same thing with my grandmother—how to survive, how to protect myself from any kind of evil that might be following me. Because we believe in the Hawaiian ways, which are very mysterious in a lot of ways. We do certain things to counteract those events we believe are the cause of some kind of illness or whatever. We were raised with all the *kahuna* beliefs, steeped in them. . . .

. . . My family never made a big issue about me being *mahu*. I just was. There were no ifs, ands or buts about it. I lived like any regular child. The people who surrounded me never gave a damn I was a *mahu*. . . .

All the *mahus* who came to my house were loved and accepted by all of us. The queens would love to come and visit with my family because my family didn't care. You know how it is when you go into a room and people start whispering, "Oh, there's a *mahu* over there." They're pointing or making snide remarks under their breath. We never had that. That only happened when we went beyond the Waimea Bridge, for instance. Or when I came to Honolulu. My whole life I knew how I was and it didn't seem like a problem. It was only when I came out here to Honolulu that it became a big problem. I felt people here made a big problem out of nothing. I remember thinking, "This is nothing—why are you guys acting so stupid? This is nothing."

I was raised as a Christian and I went to Catholic school as a child. I remember reading in Leviticus about all the things you're not allowed to do and thinking, "I'm doing that, so I must be evil." But as I grew older my understanding changed. Because what did Jesus come for? He came to give us one more commandment: to love one another as you love yourself. So as a child, when I read that I said to myself, "That's why Jesus came. So that everybody can know the extra commandment, know how to pray to the Lord and know that we have to love each other the way we love ourselves. The first time he never told us that. He said to honor your mother and father, don't steal, don't covet this, don't covet that. But he forgot to tell us to love one another. That's why Jesus Christ had to come back—to remind us."

People use the word of God for their own good and to blaspheme everybody else. But I believe the word of God is a positive thing that you cannot use or manipulate. Today I don't consider myself a Christian, but I have ideals and beliefs which are the same as Christianity because they stem from a long time ago. Those are the ancient beliefs I have. I just freak out sometimes when I see religious leaders who blaspheme anybody who's gay or this or that. They keep quoting the Old Testament and don't mention that when God's son was on earth, he said to love everybody.

By the time I was around ten years old I knew that I would never fit the norm—I knew that I didn't like sleeping with girls and that I would never get married. I had slept with girls and didn't like it. Actually, by the time I was five years old I completely knew. I was attracted to boys from the time I was small. My neighbors were beautiful boys and were attracted to me for some reason, not the girls. [laughs] What could I do? We were attracted to each other. How I felt inside, though...I felt like everybody else. It's just that I had feelings for the same sex. When you're in love or you feel *aloha* for somebody, you just feel that. Maybe people looked at me like I was different, but I didn't feel different inside, and I was never made to feel different. Although I was different I felt like anybody else. I never had to hide anything....

I think the first time my being *mahu* really became an issue was when I was in intermediate school. I had come to Honolulu for boarding and went to Kamehameha Schools [which are funded specifically for the education of Hawaiian children]. On one occasion when my mother was visiting, some counselors pulled my mother to the side and said, "Oh, we think your son has tendencies...He might be gay or *mahu*." My mother turned to them and said, "So what of it?" They were shocked at her answer. They thought she was going to be concerned. In fact, they had wanted to send me for psychiatric treatment in the seventh grade because they felt it was a problem...that I was going to be a problem. In my mother's mind there was no problem. Later she told me what the counselors had said. But she didn't care. For her my being *mahu* was totally natural....

...Around 1973, '74 the Glades [a well-known nightclub in Honolulu] was still going, and I used to go down there. I was about twelve, thirteen, fourteen then. I would head downtown because everybody was heading there. After living in Honolulu as a boarder, I started to get a little bit braver. I used to run away from school. On the weekends I'd check myself out of the dorms, saying I was going to a relative's, but I wouldn't go. Instead I'd just go around, cruise, meet friends. Oftentimes I would sneak in and out of the dormitory without them knowing.

Later on, after the Glades had shut down, I ended up working for the owner of the Glades. I worked for her and lived with the costume designer of the Glades. After I graduated I worked for her. The Glades was the hottest club in Hawai'i at one time. The best shows were found at the Glades. Today, female impersonation here in O'ahu, at Fusions [nightclub]—everything stems from the Glades. Any drag show in Hawai'i stems from the Glades. You have to compare it with the Glades days. Those days were fabulous, fun days, because downtown was fabulous, so alive and full of color. Unlike today—when you go downtown at night it's just full of drug addicts. During that time it was full of color because of all the queens on the street. Hairdos, clothing . . . As a child, I was very intrigued by what they did. Being already acclimated to show business and performing, I enjoyed glamorous things—after all, "Glamour Boy" was my nickname from my grandmother. So I enjoyed what Honolulu had to offer. I loved the country, too, but I did enjoy Honolulu, seeing all these people on the streets. Of course, other activities were going on which I wasn't oblivious to, like prostitution. . . .

It was a rough time, because in Honolulu if people found out you were *mahu,* they would really let you have it. When I came here it was the first time I had ever heard the words "fag" and "faggot" being used to refer to me. I was like, "What?! You're calling me a fag—what the hell is that?" I had never known about that word until I came to Honolulu, and then I found out that fag meant *mahu.* I had never been called that before. But I didn't give a damn. I was raised with the kind of attitude that if somebody is going to come to hurt you, then you know how to take care of yourself. Teasing words— those are nothing. When they come at you and are ready to hurt you, then you know how to protect yourself. So that was my safeguard—I always knew how to protect myself. If anybody was going to come and try to hurt me, I was going to stop them from doing that before they got there. Because I was raised by a marine; I learned how to hunt, fish, kill, jump—so you're not going to do anything to me! I wasn't afraid of people. I was nonconfrontational at the same time. But just because I was nonconfrontational doesn't mean I was afraid. I just didn't waste my time.

There was another culture shock I experienced when I came to Honolulu. On Kaua'i I had been accustomed to greeting each and every person I saw. It's because we were raised with the trail mentality. If you meet someone on the trail, you always say hello. So when I came to Honolulu I was walking down the sidewalk and saying hello to everybody I saw. And people were looking at me like I was crazy. So I had culture shock when I first came to Honolulu. But being called faggot. . .It hurt sometimes. It does. But the thing is, I had been so conditioned to not let words like that bother me, that it really didn't. But I have to admit that sometimes I wanted to just slap people or punch someone in the mouth for being so small-minded. . . .

Today I'm a college graduate. A four year graduate from the University of Hawai'i in Hawaiian

Studies. Art and music were my concentration. I originally started off in college going for an early education degree, and I'm two credits short of graduating from that. But I changed my major to a Bachelor of Fine Arts. I decided I would do the dance and theater thing. Then I thought, "I don't need a degree in dancing. Let me change again." So I changed to Hawaiian Studies, which was an easy road for me because I had been brought up with all of that stuff. So after twelve years of being in the university system I got my BA in 1992. I was very happy; somebody like me actually made it through a four year college. . . .

Hula and dance took me all over the world. Had it not been for another queen I knew, a family member whose name was Tiane Clifford, it wouldn't have happened. I was in a *hula* competition in Las Vegas that year, I think it was 1987, and I hadn't seen her for a long, long time. When I went out for that *hula* competition, she was there also, and she invited me to her room. When I came in I saw it was full of beautiful clothing and beautiful jewelry, and all her implements and prizes and trophies. . .there was all this stuff surrounding her. She was lying in her bed and she said to me, "*Ti,* you see that thing over there hanging? Beautiful, isn't it? You want it? You should do *hula.* All of these things—they're all from *hula.* I go here, there, here, there, and all around the world teaching this and teaching that—*all through hula.*"

So she encouraged me. She said, "If you want to travel the world, if you want to have these beautiful things, do the *hula.*" That's when it clicked in my mind because I actually had somebody now who was giving me a focus and a direction to go in. That summer, a month later, she came home to Kaua'i, and brought me my first *ipuheke*—my first gourd drum. I composed my first chant on the day she gave it to me. And from that day on, I have only moved forward in the *hula.* I attribute all of my successes to her—she's like my spiritual guide, my *aumakua,* in the *hula.* I feel she is always with me.

She guided me back to my grand-aunt, for instance, who was a *kumu hula,* and I went to live with her. Both Tiane and my grand-aunt were the ones who insured that I would be doing *hula* for the rest of my life. Because they gave me the direction. They said, "You're going this way. Don't turn back for anything. Look ahead and just move forward.". . .

. . . When I think about *mahus* and think back to my time as a child growing up in Hawaiian culture and learning the *hula*, we were always told that Laka, the goddess of the *hula*, was the god of the *hula*. The god or goddess of the *hula* was in male and female form. We were always told that. They never told us that Laka was *mahu*. They said that Laka had a male and female form in one. We never questioned. All our lives we were taught that Laka was male and female. Then when I got older I realized that must have meant that *Laka was mahu.* That was my introduction to Laka and how something in Hawaiian culture was *mahu*, and that was Laka. A god, goddess of the *hula* is like this.

I also heard stories of chiefs who slept with *aikane*. We were taught about our culture and they said that each of the chiefs had *aikane*. What is *aikane*? "*Ai kane*" means "to eat men" or "to have sexual relations." And each chief had an *aikane*—a man that they ate! I kept wondering what was going on. Later I found out that every chief always had a male lover. We were told that this was because women were believed to be *haumia*, or unclean. A man or a chief who slept with a woman of lower rank than him would lose *mana*. But if he slept with another man he wouldn't be affected. That's why, according to my *kupunas*, the chiefs had these male lovers. They were there to be with the chiefs as a friend and companion. In their time it was an accepted practice and actually bisexuality seemed the norm for most people in old Hawai'i. That's the way I look at it.

The place of *mahu*. . . You can read about *mahu* in certain books. But actually it's kind of unclear about *mahu* in the old days. But in certain stories and books you can read about them. . . . Like in this Hula Perspective book, this one anthropologist who went to the area where I live on Kaua'i wrote of seeing a "hermaphrodite"—that's the word she used—teaching the *hula*. That particular hermaphrodite was named Ho'okano and came from where we lived. And

according to what the old people tell me, that's what the *mahus* did. They were the keepers of the culture, they did the *hula*, and Laka herself was male/female, which is *mahu*.

In fact, we were told that all people are androgynous. All humans are born androgynous and as they grow up, a person's male or female side becomes stronger. But for *mahu*, both sides are strong. That's why when I think about *mahus*, I think of strong people. I think of soft people. I think of sweet, beautiful people. Stern people. But they're not weaklings. All the *mahus* from my family are strong—they can do everything. They can do everything that a male can do and everything that a female can do.

Oftentimes the line between male and female in ancient Hawai'i was very clear cut. But when you had certain ceremonies that required a male and a female. . . It was like in Elizabethan England in the old days, when males played the parts of the females in the dramas. That's what *mahus* did. They played the female roles in the dramas of ancient times and danced as females in the temples where only males could go. That's what my *kupunas* always told me: the *mahu* danced the parts of Pele and Haumeia and all of these goddesses to induce the goddesses' help and to appease the goddesses. Because the women could not go in certain temples. So *mahus* could play the role of the woman in these places because they were still male. Other people might not agree, but this is what my *kupunas* told me. My source of this information is my *kupunas*, who actually lived through and experienced those things.

If you go into Mo'oku'auhau genealogies, you'll come across people who are *mahu*. But being *mahu* didn't mean that they couldn't have sex with the opposite sex. Because they did. From what I've studied, it seemed that bisexualism was the norm. Hawaiians loved whomever loved them. They didn't have animosity towards any particular sex. If they felt *aloha* for somebody then they loved them. It carries on even today. You'd be surprised—even the most butchiest-looking guys still love queens. I don't know why, but it's a part of the culture which still carries over today. Our role was to satisfy and please the chiefs. And that's how I feel. Even today I feel that's our role.

As far as *mahus* in the culture, I don't associate with being gay. I associate with being *mahu*. For me, the difference between being gay and *mahu* is that there is a place for me in my culture, in my society. There was a role which we once played and still play. So I believe in my culture; I'm an accepted and integral part of my culture. That's why I don't feel anything. Because I know I'm an integral part of my culture. It's necessary for me to be here. Whereas if you're gay, you're not part of society. You're not with the norm. You're an outcast, a "faggot." So I don't like to be labeled "gay." I'd rather be called *mahu* straight to my face. Being called gay is degrading to me. Because I've been called *mahu* my whole life. I don't feel part of the group which is labeled "gay" because culturally that group is not accepted. It's not loved—they are outcasts.

I think some of the *mahus* today still carry on their traditional roles, like in *hula*. A lot of *mahus* today are prominent in *hula*. A lot of them are prominent athletes as well. You'd be surprised. A lot of people don't think *mahus* are strong, but they were strong in the old days and they're still strong today. Some *mahus* that I know are the strongest in their family! They still maintain the strength and ability to do anything. They're working in all kinds of fields today. For instance, they're healers; I know a lot of *mahus* who are doing *lomilomi* massage.

When you talk about today, because we live in Western society, all the norms of that society have been imposed on us. A lot of the old thinking and old ways have gotten shoved under the rug. Because of the new thinking, *mahu* began to alienate themselves and were alienated by the rest of society. That's why you get the gay and the straight today. We never had that in the olden days. We never had gay and straight. Everybody was bisexual, or more open. That's the difference today—because of assimilation into Western culture and Christianity, less *mahus* are willing to or want to show their true colors. They're finding it confusing and difficult to act out their role in society today. So they become drag queens, or go into prostitution—they go into all of those things

that are stereotyped for *mahus*. And those are only stereotypes because *mahus* have much more to offer society as a whole. To bring beauty and sunshine and warmth and color and *culture* to the world. It all stems from that Western concept and the Christianity concept. That's the sad part to me, because when you talk about *mahus* and Hawaiian society, they were an integral part of the society. But in today's society they are considered a *detriment*.

Even in *hula* . . . I've held the title of Queen of Hula for a year, which is a contest for *mahus* in *hula*. It's overwhelming for people to accept that a *mahu* can be skillful in dancing. And for women to accept it . . . If a *mahu* walks into a crowd and she looks better than all the ladies there, they hate it. They are upset that a *mahu* can look better than them. Or you go to an area with all these guys, and one *mahu* can lift more than all those guys, a *mahu* can shoot a pig, clean it, cook it and all of that, and they cannot. So although I'm kind of assimilated into Western culture, I will remain a remnant of my culture forever. That's my role. I am *mahu*. I will do all the things that are culturally appropriate for me. And I don't feel any pain.

I choose to live as a woman today. I'm not sure if in ancient times all *mahus* did that. I'm sure they didn't. Because diversity is what made the culture thrive. I give the fullest to my culture when I can be myself by acting out the roles I am supposed to. For example, naming children. Doing all of the different things which traditionally were—and still are—for *mahu* to do. People come to me and ask me to name their children. That's what I'm here for, that's my role. I don't have any other purpose other than to act out my role. And if it's my role to be *mahu,* then it's my role. I accept it graciously. It's not an easy role to play. It's even more difficult because of Westernization and Christianity. It's harder to be in that role and feel comfortable. But I do it. A lot of people don't feel comfortable. They have a lot of fear. They're afraid of things like gay-bashing.

Nowadays it takes a lot of courage for *mahu* to be transgender. Walking down the street, knowing you've got something hanging between your legs. But you look like this. I keep telling people: "I can't change the way that I look. This is only my physical shell; I cannot change that. I have to live with the body that I have." I'm one of those who hasn't had any surgicals done—no implants, no hormones, no nothing.

I have a husband, the man I live with. I don't consider my husband gay. Society might, but I don't. I have three children. They are his natural children. I have raised them for ten years. I'm acting out and living in the role of a woman. I'm not their mother, but I'm their guide. I have guided them all these years. It's been a very difficult role for me to live in today. Not just for me, but for my children because they are subject to the whole gamut of emotions which I go through or I might have felt before because. . .you know how people are in society—we might be out together and people will give looks or snide remarks and the kids will pick it up. Or even now as they're getting older, they know what gay is, they've learned about that kind of stuff, and that it's *bad*. It's made out to be *evil*. It's made out to be such a horrible thing that for my kids—growing up and knowing that I'm like this, and that their father is sleeping with me—it's difficult. But I always have to remind them, "Who's buying your food? Who's loving you? Who's taking care of you? It's us. Those other people on the outside aren't doing anything for you. I'm doing my best for you." I try to assure them because a lot of times they feel bad.

The way I was brought up, when kids had things like events and games, we'd all go and give moral support. Whereas in this situation, I want to give moral support, but sometimes my giving moral support will actually inhibit or hurt my children's performance by making them feel ashamed. So I have to give in and say, "OK, I won't go to that, then." Which is sad. To me it's sad, sad, sad. It breaks my heart not to be able to give one of my children moral support because it might make him feel funny around his friends. It's not an easy situation. I don't know of many queens or *mahus* around today who are in the kind of situation I am in. . .Most of the *mahus* I know are young and single and doing their own thing. But I have a stable family life, I have children to worry about. It's very different for me. I have people I have

to worry about twenty-four hours a day. When you're a transgendered person it's something, I tell you!. . .

Actually, I have been more fortunate than a lot of people, beyond my wildest dreams, to have left Hawai'i and traveled. I've gone all over Asia, all over the South Pacific, and all over the United States, including Alaska, as a performer. I've also worked in museums as a conservator of items, of objects. I have training in that kind of specialized work. I'm not working in that field now, but I feel one day it will come into play, because that's another role of *mahus*: to maintain and nurture the culture and art of our people, of the Polynesian people. To *maintain* and to continue the cultural side of our people because if *mahus* don't do that. . .I guess we've got a lot of other people doing that as well, but the role of *mahus* is, to me, to maintain the art and culture connection in Hawai'i, so people from elsewhere can learn and be nurtured by that and be able to grow from our experience here in our homeland. Because when you look at Hawai'i as a whole and Hawai'i as a place, we Hawaiians don't own Hawai'i. We are just a part of this land that you see which is so beautiful. We are the ones that make the land come to life. We give it life. . .the flowers blossom and grow because of us. If we don't continue to practice our culture, as fragmented as it might be, then we will not have a culture to look back on.

I believe the reason we have this wonderful culture today is because of *mahus*. *Mahus* have been the ones in the forefront, standing up when nobody else was standing up, leading and fighting. I'm an activist [for Hawaiian sovereignty], too, so I've been on countless marches and demonstrations, both big and small. I've been at demonstrations where there were only five of us. But I'm yelling like five hundred. I'm not afraid. I don't care what anybody says. If I feel there's injustice, then there's injustice. I can play the games they want me to. I can do it the American way—I can go down to the legislature, I can do all of that crap, I can lobby, I can do all that stuff. But I choose to live in my culture. I choose to do culturally related activities.

I worked as a *hula* dancer in the tourist industry for years and years and years. I worked as a performer, a singer, dancer—I did it all. I was a fire-knife dancer,

WHAT IS BISEXUALITY? • 117

you name it. All the experiences I've had . . . I've stood on the Great Wall of China. I've been everywhere. So I always ask the queens today, "Why don't you come to *hula?* Because *hula* will fill your mind, fill your soul, your spirit. And if travel is in your blood, that's what it's going to do—it's going to take you around the world, like it's taken me. It's going to take you to places that you never imagined existed. To the places in your dreams." That's how I try to encourage my students. Be in *hula,* and you're going to travel. You're

going to learn. The gay community, the *mahu* community in Hawai'i is so small. And I am known for being in *hula,* I'm known for cultural things. I'm known not just in the *mahu* community, but also in the community at large, in the *hula* community. They know I'm *mahu;* I *want* them to know I'm *mahu.* I am *mahu,* and I am proud. What are you going to do? I cannot help how I look. I'm only enhancing what the Lord has given me. What the gods have given me, I just work with.

---

12 • *Shiri Eisner*

WHAT IS BISEXUALITY?

DISCUSSION QUESTIONS

1. How does Eisner approach defining bisexuality, and what are some of her concerns about bisexual definitions?
2. What is the use-value of *bisexuality* as an umbrella term? Why is it important to think about bisexuality as a political project?
3. What did you learn from reading the stereotypes about bisexuality from three different perspectives: hegemonic society, the bisexual movement, and radical bisexual political thought?

. . .

SOME HISTORY

Bisexuality, as a term and as a concept, was born around the end of the nineteenth and beginning of the twentieth century, a time when minority-world men

(mostly Europeans) first started their all-encompassing project of categorizing (and pathologizing) the world around them—and specifically, where it came to bodies, sexualities, and desire. Researchers such as Richard von Krafft-Ebing, Henry Havelock Ellis, and Magnus Hirschfeld considered bisexuality either a physical or a psychological condition, having traits of what was once thought of as "both sexes."

Eisner, Shiri. 2013. *Bi: Notes for a Bisexual Revolution.* Berkeley, CA: Seal Press. Reprinted by permission of the author.

At the time, one of the popular theories about sexuality was that of *inversion*. According to inversion theory, gay men and lesbians were "inverts"—people who were physically male or female, but internally the "opposite sex." Same-gender desire was explained as latent heterosexuality: gays and lesbians were really just heterosexual people born in the wrong bodies. Inversion theory understood sex, gender, and desire as one and the same, imagining homosexuality and transgender as expressions of one another, and creating the still-standing myth that gay men are necessarily "internally feminine," that lesbians are necessarily "internally masculine," and that transgender people are actually "gay men" (when applied to trans women) or "lesbian" (when applied to trans men).

According to this theory, "bisexuality" was used to describe what we now call *intersexuality* (formerly *hermaphroditism,* meaning bodies with nonbinary genitals and other sexual traits). Bisexual desire was called *psychosexual hermaphroditism,* linking the concepts of bisexuality as both a physical state and desire. Bisexual people were seen as psychologically intersex, bringing the logic of inversion (latent heterosexual attraction) into the field of bisexual desire. In other words, a bi person's "male" part desires women, whereas her "female" part desires men.

You might notice that this theory is at once incredibly gender-binary *and* androgynous. Despite its *binarism* and heterosexism, I like the way that this theory connects bisexuality to intersexuality and opens a sort of "third space" for bodies, genders, and desires. In minority-world societies, both intersex bodies and bisexual identities are perceived as an aberration. They are perceived as needing immediate "correction" to fit the binary standards of society: intersex babies are treated as a medical emergency and undergo imposed sex-reassignment surgeries, often immediately after birth and without consent. In a similar, though certainly less violent and more symbolic way, bisexual identity is often treated as a sexual emergency: bisexual individuals face strong resistance and social pressure to immediately change our sexual identity into something else (often *anything* else, just as long as we don't use the "B-word").

Freud was one of the first minority-world thinkers to use the word *bisexuality* in order to describe desire (instead of a physical or psychological state). The way Freud described it, bisexuality (also named "polymorphous perversity") was the ground from which ("normal") heterosexuality and ("pathological") homosexuality developed. Very few remember to mention bisexuality as the basis for Freud's oedipal theory: According to Freud, the (male) child is born bisexual, desiring both his mother and his father, overcoming and repressing his bisexual desire through the oedipal process. Success in this process would leave the child heterosexual (read: "healthy"), while failure would make the child homosexual (read: "sick"). Bisexuality, in itself, ceases to be an option for the child, and is relegated to a "primitive" psychological past.[1] In Freud's theory, then, bisexuality can't be thought of as a sexual orientation (such as hetero- or homosexuality), but only the repressed basis for the development of other sexualities.

As a result of this, Freud's theory is responsible for several of the popular beliefs generally associated with bisexuality in minority world societies:

- Everyone is "actually bisexual" or "born bisexual."
- No one is, in fact, bisexual.
(These first two are different sides of the same coin.)
- Bisexuality is a passing phase.
- Bisexuality is an unfinished process.
- Bisexuality is immature.

(Note, by the way, that I don't necessarily agree or disagree with the three latter meanings, and I intentionally refrained from calling them *myths*. In fact, I think many of these so-called myths can be very helpful in building radical bisexual political thought—more on that later.)

The first important minority-world researcher to have treated bisexuality as an existing sexuality, and as a viable option, was Alfred Kinsey in his landmark research *Sexual Behavior in the Human Male,* first published in 1948. Kinsey, bisexual himself, famously wrote:

> "Males do not represent two discrete populations, heterosexual and homosexual. The world is not to be

divided into sheep and goats. Not all things are black, nor all things white. It is a fundamental of taxonomy that nature rarely deals with discrete categories. Only the human mind invents categories and tries to force facts into separated pigeon-holes."

Kinsey was also responsible for creating the now-famous Kinsey Scale, categorizing different degrees of homosexuality and heterosexuality, using numbers from zero (exclusively heterosexual) to six (exclusively homosexual). On Kinsey's scale, the "true bisexual" was imagined to be a three, equally attracted to both males and females (other sexes and genders were not regarded). In this way, Kinsey is responsible for the popular concept that we all experience desire on a sliding scale, adding to the Freudian-based myth that very few people are actually *monosexual* (a homophobic notion that disrespects monosexualities and erases unique bisexual identity and experience).

You will notice that so far, the only people who talked about bisexuality in minority-world cultures were the white *cisgender* of the medical and psychological institutions and schools. This means that the people who controlled the definition, concept, and *discourse* about bisexuality were people representing the system, medicalizing and often pathologizing our desires and ways of life. By this, of course, I don't mean to insinuate that these people didn't make important contributions to our understanding of sexuality in general, and bisexuality in particular, or that their importance is to be dismissed. I also do not mean to insinuate that they meant to harm bisexual people or operated maliciously. What I do mean is to highlight that, much like many other LGBT and queer identities, bisexuality, too, was first invented and scrutinized by *hegemonic* powers under the mass project of categorizing and then pathologizing various human experiences and behaviors, only later to be reclaimed by the bisexual movement. Bisexual people themselves served as research objects, the ground upon which to base theories about bisexuality and, indeed, about the entire continuum of bodies, gender, and desire. This means that bisexual people served as the "raw material" for theories that

they could not control. Researchers gained their prestigious reputations and *symbolic capital* on the backs of bisexual research subjects, their lives and experiences, while distributing none of their gains—symbolic or material—back to the community. This problem is shared by many marginalized groups (including LGBTs, women, intersex people, racialized people, disabled people, and many, many more), and is indeed widespread to this day in many ways.

However, it's also worth noting that in many ways, this categorization and *pathologization* of bisexuality was one of the things that eventually gave rise to the creation of a bisexual movement. To adapt from French philosopher Michel Foucault: After the medical institution's project of categorization, "the [bisexual] was now a species." Before this bout of sexuality research, what we now call bisexuality was a series of sexual acts, which in and of themselves had nothing to do with a bisexual person or her self-identity. Medical and psychological research first created the category of bisexuality (while also controlling its contents and definitions). From the moment that bisexuality became a category, it also became adoptable as a personal identity, a mark for a type of person rather than a series of isolated acts. What remained, then, for the bisexual movement, was to reclaim bisexuality—as a term, an identity, and a concept—back into the hands of bisexual people, in a way that would benefit bisexual populations and give something back to them.

It is somewhat surprising, then, that a minority-world bisexual movement took until the 1970s—and then again until the 1990s—to do that very thing. Very little research is available regarding the lives of bisexuals in those intermediate years, but from what can be gleaned, it seems as though many bisexuals in the 1950s and 1960s were part of gay or lesbian communities, as well as taking part in the very first gay rights organizations in the United States ("homophile" organizations, as they were called). Despite the fact that bisexuality was even then considered a subset of homosexuality (a biphobic notion that erases the uniqueness and specificity of bisexuality), bisexuals still suffered from biphobic treatment within gay and lesbian communities.[2] However, it seems as though LGBT communities, as a whole, were at such risk and were so intent on survival that there was little freedom for anyone to speak about or create different identities or spaces. Although biphobia had been present even then, only once the gay movement (and later the lesbian movement) gained enough ground was there enough breathing room to found a separate bisexual movement. (Interestingly, this process was shared, in many ways, by the transgender movement, which came out as a movement of its own at around the same time as the bisexual movement.)

In the 1970s, and again in the 1990s,[3] the bisexual movement reclaimed bisexuality both as an identity and as a subject for research and political thought, in what appeared—and to this day appears—to be a mass project for proving the existence, validity, and the normativity of bisexuality (all problematic concepts that I criticize below). This movement normally defined bisexuality as attraction to "both men and women" (following the medical institution), with variations as to what kinds of attraction might constitute bisexuality (emotional, sexual, behavioral, etc.). Between the 1990s and the 2000s, bisexuality's definition gradually changed in order to accommodate nonbinary gender identities that found themselves erased from the language of desire. Today most bisexual movements use the expanded definitions of bisexuality: attraction to people of more than one sex or gender; attraction to people of genders similar to our own, and to people of genders different from our own; or attraction to people of multiple genders.

However, timelines are limited. They create the illusion that time, movements, and definitions and their development move forward on a straight line. Do not be fooled by this: There is no one definition to bisexuality, and all the definitions I mentioned above (including the medical ones) are still used in some form. This chapter, then, will be an attempt to explore some of the meanings of bisexuality that are often invoked in minority-world culture.

DEFINING BISEXUALITY

In this part, I'll try to define bisexuality as a contemporary identity, diverging from traditional medical definitions and instead seeking new ways of observing it. Bisexuality isn't only a form of desire but also a carrier of multiple meanings (a concept that I will go deeper into later). Bisexuality can be defined and politicized on all or any of three axes that I will describe: desire, community, and politics.

It's important to mention that, though I suggest definitions for bisexual identity, I won't be trying to define bisexuality for everyone, rather describing the way that I see it and why I connect to it, hoping that it resonates with you. However, if you identify as bisexual, the only person who can define what your bisexual identity means is you.

It's also important to note that this section is about definitions that I *like*, which means it does not include binary definitions of bisexuality, despite their (unfortunate) popularity.

DESIRE

The first type of meaning I'd like to give bisexuality is that of desire. I'd like to examine two definitions of this type, and extend their political and personal implications: *more than one* and *same and different.* The first definition is wide and enabling, giving us tools to think of bisexuality as a continuum. The second definition brings hierarchical differences to the forefront and enables us to address power relations in our intimate relationships as well as our communities.

More Than One

My favorite definition for bisexuality so far is the one popularized by (the wonderful) bisexual activist Robyn Ochs. Ochs says, "I call myself bisexual because I acknowledge that I have in myself the potential to be attracted—romantically and/or sexually—to people of more than one sex, and/or gender, not necessarily at the same time, not necessarily in the same way, and not necessarily to the same degree."

This is by far the broadest and most enabling definition of bisexuality that I've found to date. Its strength is in the way it enables anyone who wants to identify as bisexual to do so. (In other words, it reassures people.) In a world in which bisexuality is usually very narrowly defined, many people who experience bisexual desire, and want to identify as bi, often feel afraid to start (or keep) identifying as such, as they feel as though they "don't qualify." The role that an enabling definition for bisexuality can fulfill to counter these feelings of internalized biphobia is invaluable—and I feel that Ochs's definition does just that. It reassures people that they are "allowed" to identify as bisexual if they wish to do so.

Though this definition is already quite popular, having been in use for many years, it still remains innovative and challenging in several ways: First, it challenges the gender binary system, pointing out that bisexual desire can work toward any number of genders beyond one. This gives space for people to identify as bisexual even when they are attracted to more than the mythological "both genders," as well as removing the **cissexist** emphasis on partners' genitals for determining bisexuality. Second, by specifying that bisexual desire can be either romantic, sexual, or both, this definition assures people who only feel one of those things, without the others, that they are not lacking in anything for their bisexual identity. Third, this definition's acknowledgment that attraction to more than one sex or gender doesn't necessarily happen at the same time opens up space to consider lifelong stories and narratives.[4] Through this, people who experience shifts in their desire over time are again given space to identify as bisexual. Lastly, acknowledging that bisexual desire does not necessarily happen in the same way or to the same degree reassures people that they do not necessarily need to desire (or have experience with) every gender on their palate equally in order to "qualify" as bisexual. This enables the option to identify as bisexual for people who prefer one gender over others, who have had more experience with one gender than with others, or who have felt differently about their desires toward each gender that they like.

. . .

Same and Different

This definition was popularized around 2009 by *The Bisexual Index* website and by the blog *Bi Furious!* It relies on the "classical" definition of bisexuality as a "combination" or "unification" of homosexuality and heterosexuality. If homosexuality is understood to mean "attraction to people of genders similar to one's own" and heterosexuality is understood to mean "attraction to people of genders different from one's own," then bisexuality can just as well mean attraction to people of genders similar to and different from one's own.

What I love about this definition is how it invokes the topic of gender, but without limiting its options—pertaining to two categories, but leaving their contents open. As an inherent effect, this definition gently questions people about their own gender identities and how their own gender is related to their desires toward others. In other words, it manifests difference.

This definition opens up significant questions about things that many people regard as obvious nonissues: How do I define gender? What is my gender identity? What are the genders that are different from mine? How would I define similarity in terms of gender? How would I define difference? Which differences do I eroticize, and how? Which similarities? Do I eroticize mixed gender traits when they exist in one person, or am I more attracted to clear differentiation? How does my gender influence my desire and my relationships? How do they interact? How do my desire and my relationships influence my gender identity?

The answers to these questions are never trivial, and whichever conclusions one might end up with, their importance is in the questioning of gender identities, gender binaries, and gender-based interactions. In fact, many people might, through these questions, think about things they'd never thought of before, find angles through which they'd never examined themselves. These questions might enable us to examine the social context for our personal interactions, as well as provide tools for more specific descriptions of our experiences of bisexuality.

This definition also identifies hierarchies. In a society that is *patriarchal* and cissexist, gender differences always carry the baggage of hierarchy with them. Male or masculine-spectrum people occupy a higher place in the social order than female and feminine-spectrum people. Cisgender people likewise occupy a higher hierarchical place than transgender and *genderqueer* people. Even cisgender femininities and masculinities are different from culture to culture, and white (cis)gender expression is considered superior to any other. Think, for example, about the differences—and the differences in perception—between white, black, Latino, Jewish, Middle Eastern, and Asian masculinities (to name just a few). Each carries its own weight, each is perceived differently, yet it's clear that the only type of masculinity that is wholly validated in white/minority-world society is the white kind (and the same, of course, goes for femininity). In addition, these hierarchies don't only apply outside in the public sphere; they exist in our homes, in our relationships, and in every aspect of our personal lives, creating power imbalances within our intimate relations. Recognizing difference in gender (in all its multiplicity and complexity) might also inform us about the hierarchies at work in our intimate interactions, and encourage us to work at deconstructing them.

Recognizing gender hierarchies, in turn, might help us also identify other kinds of hierarchies that might be present in our relationships and influence them: race, class, ability, age, education, sexuality (straight/queer, monosexual/bisexual, etc.), and many more. Indeed, these factors might also function as components of sexual desire of the kind questioned earlier. Recognizing each of these things and attempting to deconstruct the power relations that go along with them might also serve as a tool for revolutionary bisexual relationships, changing and reconstructing what it means to be in intimate interactions with each other.

. . .

COMMUNITY

This type of definition looks at bisexuality as a community identity. It marks an identification with bisexual communities and movements, in addition to—or separately from—bisexual desire.

"You Can Stand Under My Umbrella"

Recently the word *bisexual* has been assigned a new use with increasing popularity: that of an umbrella term for multiple bi-spectrum identities, those that involve attraction to people of more than one sex and/or gender. . . . Some bisexual-spectrum identities are:

Bisexual: as defined earlier and throughout this chapter.

Pansexual/omnisexual: people who are attracted (sexually, romantically, and/or otherwise) to people of all genders and sexes, or to multiple genders and sexes, or regardless of sex and gender, and who identify as pan/omni. Pansexuality and omnisexuality differ from each other by their Greek and Latin roots (*pan* meaning *all* in Greek, and *omni* the same in Latin).

Polysexual: people who are attracted (sexually, romantically, and/or otherwise) to people of many genders and sexes (but not all), and who identify as poly.

Queer: a nonspecific identity that describes anyone diverging from heterosexuality, monogamy, and vanilla (non-kink) sexuality. In a bi-spectrum context, it's used to denote attraction to people of more than one, or of many, gender(s).

Fluid: describes attraction that changes or might change over time (toward people of various genders).

Homoflexible/Lesbiflexible: people who are usually attracted to people of genders similar to their own, but might occasionally be attracted to people of genders different from their own.

Heteroflexible: people who are usually attracted to people of genders different from their own, but might occasionally be attracted to people of genders similar to their own.

Bi-curious: people who are usually heterosexual, lesbian, or gay, and who are curious about experimenting with people of genders different from their usual preference.

Other bi-spectrum identities: include biromantic, panromantic, bisensual, pansensual, bidyke, byke, bisexual-lesbian, ambisextrous, anthrosexual, multisexual, gender-blind, pomosexual, and many more. Where appropriate, it might also include *questioning* and *unlabeled*.

It's important to note that though some people might feel uncomfortable identifying with the word *bisexuality,* even through its umbrella use, many others often do consider themselves part of the bisexual community/movement and thus identify under the broad term. It is with respect to these people that I offer the usage of the umbrella term. I include under it only those people who want to be included under it. However, as an alternative term for inclusion of those who feel uncomfortable with the bisexual umbrella, Julia Serano (in her blog post "Bisexuality and Binaries Revisited") has suggested the acronym "BMNOPPQ", "where B = bisexual, M = multisexual, N = no label, O = omnisexual, P = pansexual, P = polysexual, and Q = experientially bisexual folks who primarily identify as queer (arranged alphabetically)."

Notwithstanding, I also mean this as a suggestion for solidarity between the various groups under the bi umbrella. This would allow us to examine the enormous common ground that we all share by virtue of our attraction to people of more than one gender. . . .

The idea of bisexuality as an umbrella term emphasizes one of the greatest meanings often associated with bisexuality: that of multiplicity. Whereas bisexuality as *desire* as well as a cultural idea might invoke a multiplicity of attractions, objects choices, and sexual or romantic partners, the idea of bisexuality as an *umbrella term* can emphasize a multiplicity of identities, forms of desire, lived experiences, and politics. What it means is that an umbrella definition of bisexuality might give us more space for what I enjoy thinking about as the three Ds: difference, diversity, and deviation.

What it means is that bisexuality under this definition enables us to resist a single standard. To be different from each other as well as from the norm, to be diverse and diversify ourselves, to deviate from paths we've been pushed into by society and by oppression. It means that bisexual communities and movements can resist standardization imposed upon us by straight society, gay communities, or even the mainstream bisexual movement itself. Our communities can refuse to toe the lines, to police or impose order upon bisexual people or anyone at all. It means

no one gets thrown overboard, rather that our differences can serve as a source of power.

. . .

Difference, diversity, and deviation are not only sexual, however. They mean recognizing and drawing strength from the fact that along with cisgender, monogamous, vanilla, HIV-, nondisabled, white, middle class citizens of the country and community, the bisexual community is also shared by transgender and genderqueer people; nonmonogamous, *polyamorous,* slutty or promiscuous people; sex workers; BDSM practitioners; drug users; HIV+ people, disabled, chronically ill and mentally disabled people; working class people, migrants, illegal immigrants, refugees, racialized people, and many, many more. This does not mean that we should encourage or glamorize social oppression or unsafe behaviors. It means that our political struggle needs to reflect the interests of everyone, address everyone's needs, and endeavor to attain resources for and empower people of all groups—not just the ones who fit a certain palatable standard.

This also does not mean creating a new "inverted" standard for people in bisexual communities; nor does it mean erasing differences or ignoring them. It means that each identity and group within the community is uniquely celebrated, accepted, and empowered, no matter who they are. It means every different perspective is listened to and honored. It means acknowledging hierarchies and making sure that every group gets its voice and that no one group takes up space, resources, or attention at the expense of any other. It means dismantling the single standard currently operating, breaking it into a million little pieces and giving solidarity to each and every piece. This usually entails specifically working from the bottom, to empower the groups that are the most marginalized, both within the community and in general.

. . .

POLITICS, OR: THE TRUE MEANING OF BI

Bisexuality is much more than just an identity. Like with every concept in society, bisexuality carries many associations and connotations—not only about itself, but also about the world in general. As opposed to the popular belief I mentioned in the beginning, not only is bisexuality worth talking about, but it offers us a very rich array of connotations and knowledge, with enormous political and activist potential. These meanings that accompany bisexuality are independent of bisexual identity and are not linked to any specific bisexual person. Rather, these ideas and connotations are a result (or a reading, if you will) of the way that bisexuality is, and was, imagined in culture. These ideas are reflected in the arts, literature, media, history, and any other record of society in which the concept of bisexuality is invoked.

In academic language, this way of looking at things is called *epistemology*. The questions that bisexual epistemology asks are:

[What are] the ways in which [bisexual] meanings accrue; . . . and what strategies can be used to effect a more useful or enabling range of meanings?—Bi Academic Intervention

How [does] bisexuality [generate] or [how] is [it] given meaning in particular contexts[?]—Clare Hemmings

[W]hat other functions does bisexuality perform in discourses on sexuality? When does it get invoked, and how? When and why does it disappear, and with what effects? What other issues seem to attach to it; what questions does it perennially raise?—Stacey Young

Looking at bisexuality as an identity to be reinforced and nothing more is politically limiting, leaving us with only one concept and one purpose on our hands. The straightforward idea that bisexuality is a valid and normal (though erased and silenced) sexual orientation very easily leads us to the idea that all we need to do is validate bisexuality, validate bisexual people, validate bisexual identity, validate bisexual community . . . These are all true things—but this is where this approach ends.

. . . I want to take an epistemological approach to bisexual politics, to examine how bisexuality is thought of or imagined and contemplate why. By connecting these things to a political agenda, I hope to expand the ideology, options, and scope of the bisexual movement as a whole. It needs to be noted that this is not done in vain, nor simply as an intellectual game: Connecting between different struggles is one of the cornerstones to radical political thinking. To acknowledge that all forms of oppression are interrelated is to acknowledge that we all have a stake in each other's liberation, that none of us is free until everyone is free.

. . .

More than anything, stereotypes are the immediate meanings attached to bisexuality and bisexual people. When people think about bisexuality, stereotypes are what they think about—this is what they "know." These stereotypes comprise a body of (imagined) knowledge about bisexual people, about the meaning of bisexuality, and of the way it works. A reading of biphobic stereotypes can be enlightening for our understanding of the social and cultural meanings given to bisexuality. Afterward we could proceed to ask: How can we, as bisexuals, use these meanings to our benefit?

SOME HEGEMONIC THOUGHT

Here is a basic list of commonly cited stereotypes about bisexuality. If you've traveled through a patch of life carrying a bisexual identity, there's a pretty good chance you'd find these familiar:

Bisexuality Doesn't Exist

Perhaps the most popular belief about bisexuality. According to this stereotype, there is no such thing as bisexuality—and people who do claim to be bisexual are simply wrong or misguided. Needless to say, this notion both feeds and is fed by bisexual erasure. It creates the impression that bisexuality doesn't appear in popular culture (or indeed anywhere) because it really doesn't exist. This also causes people to ignore (erase) bisexuality where it does appear for that very same reason. (What you know is what you see.)

Bisexuals Are Confused, Indecisive, or Just Going Through a Phase

A "natural" extension of the first one, this stereotype explains how it happens that some people actually do identify as bisexual—they simply have it all wrong. This stereotype also invokes the idea of alternating between partners of different genders, meaning: a perceived failure of consistency. If a "true choice" can only be defined as a single gender preference, then structurally, bisexuality is impossible by definition.

Bisexuals are Slutty, Promiscuous, and Inherently Unfaithful

If a single gender preference is the only choice imaginable, then anything exceeding that number would automatically be perceived as excess. The idea of excessive sexuality then naturally leads to a notion of promiscuity. According to this stereotype, by virtue of having more than one gender preference, bisexuals are indiscriminate about their choice of partners and are therefore slutty or promiscuous. The idea of inherent unfaithfulness comes from the widely held belief that bisexuals are incapable of being satisfied with only one partner (since, evidently, they can't be satisfied with only one gender).

Bisexuals Are Carriers or Vectors of HIV and Other STIs

Relying on the previous stereotype, bisexuals are often thought to be more likely than monosexual people to carry and spread HIV and other STIs. Often combined together, this stereotype and the previous one both imagine bisexuals—bisexual men in particular—as people who engage in indiscriminate sex with multiple partners, collecting various STIs as they go along and spreading them on as they go. This stereotype, of course, leans heavily upon the assumption that having sex is infectious in and of itself, conveniently dismissing information about safer sex practices as well as other, nonsexual ways of contracting these diseases.

Another component of this stereotype is *ableism*, as it is heavily charged with negative views toward disabled and chronically ill people. It draws on severe social stigma working against people with HIV,

AIDS, and other STIs, as well as the notion that STIs are in fact a punishment for promiscuity or for certain sexual practices.

Bisexuals are Actually Gay or Actually Straight

This stereotype draws upon the second cluster of stereotypes listed above, according to which bisexuals are confused—that we are actually anything other than bisexual. In hegemonic discourse, this "anything" is usually imagined as the narrow option of either gay or straight. Interestingly, for bisexual women the presumption is that we're really straight, while bisexual men are often presumed to be really gay. This suggests a presumption that everyone is really into men—a *phallocentric* notion testifying to this stereotype's basic reliance on sexism.

Bisexuals Can Choose to Be Gay or Straight

This stereotype envisions bisexuals as people who can choose between gay or straight identities and lifestyles. The stereotype couples bisexuality together with an idea of "privilege," and in this way is used to decrease the legitimacy of unique bisexual identity as well as politics. It disqualifies bisexuals from participating in gay movements by implying that bisexuals will always leave their gay or lesbian partners for an "opposite sex" relationship. (Relationships with nonbinary-gender people never seem to be part of this popular imagination.)

All of these stereotypes are personalized, relating to particular people (who identify as bisexual), and are taken literally and at face value. They imagine bisexual people—and bisexuality itself—as inauthentic, unstable, predatory, infectious, and dangerous. Implicitly, these stereotypes also entail a demand for normalcy because they present bisexuality as a deviation from the norm, and therefore inherently perverse.

In light of that, it is odd to see that the mainstream bisexual movement's rebuttals, or, more popularly, "myth busting," generally remain within this literal and personalized framework. In addition to being personalized and literal, they also hearken to the demand for normalcy presented therein.

"BUT THAT'S NOT TRUE!"

In the overwhelming majority of cases, the bisexual movement's rebuttals have been based on a single-value reading and denial of these stereotypes, using a "that's not true!" formula for any such stereotype (or: "that's not *necessarily* true" for those who consider themselves more progressively minded). Lists of such stereotypes, coupled with rebuttals/denials, abound both on the Internet and in the bisexual activist field. In addition, they have become characteristic of bisexual political discourse in many other contexts as well.

Here is my list again, this time with rebuttals (or "myth busting" replies) typical to the bisexual movement (and including one or two grains of salt):

Bisexuality Doesn't Exist

Yes, it does! Many studies and statistics exist that attest to the existence of bisexuality. I'm bisexual myself, and I'm not imaginary, right? Also, there's a whole bisexual movement for people who feel or identify as such. Bisexual people definitely exist; so no more denial.

Bisexuals Are Confused, Indecisive, or Just Going Through a Phase

No, we're not! We know who we are and have decided that we are bisexual. Many bisexuals have identified as such for many, many years and couldn't possibly be accused of being unstable or going through a phase. In addition, research says that many bisexuals have gone through phases of identifying as gay or lesbian—however, gay and lesbian people aren't accused of going through a phase. Plus, research says that if you change your sexual identity, most chances are that you'll be changing it from monosexual to bisexual, not the other way around. So really, bisexuality isn't a phase at all. It's just as stable as any other sexual identity.

Bisexuals Are Slutty, Promiscuous, or Inherently Unfaithful

No, we're not! We are perfectly capable of being monogamous, and we are just as likely to cheat on our partners as anyone else. Many bisexual people have succeeded in maintaining happy, long-term, exclusive relationships for years. Just because we like more than one gender doesn't mean we have sex indiscriminately. I mean, seriously, we have taste too! (Oh, and some of us might be polyamorous or enjoy sex with multiple partners, but that means nothing about the rest of us!)

Bisexuals Are Carriers or Vectors of HIV and Other STIs

No, we're not! What gives people HIV and other STIs is sexual behavior, not sexual identity. People get infected with HIV through unsafe sex, needle sharing, and infected blood transfusions. Being bisexual doesn't make you infected or infectious.

Bisexuals Are Actually Gay or Actually Straight

No, we're not! We really are bisexual and are truly attracted to people of more than one gender. Even if some of us have a preference for one gender over others, that still doesn't make us any less bisexual. It's enough to have any portion of attraction to more than one gender to qualify. Also, don't be tempted to think that we're just closeted and cowardly or just experimenting: We're out and proud!

Bisexuals Can Choose to Be Gay or Straight

No, we can't! You can't choose to be gay, right? So how can you choose to be bisexual? Bi people can't choose who to fall in love with or who to be attracted to. Yes, we can choose with whom we have relationships, but giving up on one part of our sexuality is just as painful as being in the closet. Gays and lesbians can choose a heterosexual lifestyle just as well, yet bisexuals are the only ones who get scapegoated for it.

. . .

No Myths, No Busting

"I want to have adventures and take enormous
risks and be everything they say we are."

—Dorothy Allison, lesbian activist

Taken from an epistemological perspective, these stereotypes should not be taken literally at all, but rather read as metaphors about the subversive potential of bisexuality. What I mean is that bisexuality as an idea is something that society finds threatening to its normal order. This has nothing to do with bisexual individuals. I certainly do not mean to suggest that being bisexual is subversive or radical in and of itself (if only it were). Being politically subversive or radical takes a lot of work, thought, and effort, which a simple identity label is insufficient to achieve. I also do not mean to set a whole new standard for bisexual behavior that might alienate large portions of the bisexual community. And I do not mean to imply that the stereotypes are correct as far as the personal behavior of bisexual people goes. What I do mean to do is to examine why society places bisexuality on the side of anxiety, threat, and subversion. And how can we use these very things to disrupt social order and create social change?

In so doing, what I'm attempting to do is step away from the binary discourse of Yes versus No, True versus False, or Good versus Bad, and open a third, radical choice of transgression, subversion, and multiplicity. Such a move, in my opinion, is also bisexual in character, marking a resistance to binaries, a collapse of boundaries, and a subversion of order. (You'll see what I mean in just a bit.)

So here is a third reading of the same stereotypes— this time, trying to understand why they're there and what we can do with them:

Bisexuality Doesn't Exist

This is by far the simplest: Society routinely tries to deny subversive ideas out of existence. Bisexuality is charged with meanings that attest to society's various anxieties. The attempt to eliminate bisexuality's existence is an attempt to eliminate the subversive potential that it holds. Simply put, if society gets so hysterical around a certain idea that it tries to eradicate its existence in any way possible, it affirms that this idea is perceived as threatening. Bisexuality has a lot of revolutionary potential. Society recognizes this. It's time for us to start as well.

Bisexuals Are Confused, Indecisive, or Just Going Through a Phase

Confusion, indecision, and phases indicate a state of instability, fluidity, and process. Confusion points to instability as well as doubt, marking bisexuality as a vantage point for questioning, as well as marking a radical potential for change. Bisexuality can be thought of as a destabilizing agent of social change, promoting doubt in anything, starting with our own sexual identities, going through the structure of sex, gender, and sexuality; heteropatriarchy, and racism; and ending with such oppressive structures as the state, law, order, war, and capitalism.

The indecision, that is, fluidity associated with bisexuality can be used as a refusal to conduct ourselves through society's narrow constrictions. It is a refusal and deconstruction of any socially dictated boundaries at all. This marks a collapse of both binaries and boundaries, and a collapse of separation and isolation (embedded in us by both capitalist culture and internalized biphobia). It gives us the opportunity to call for difference, solidarity, and connection. It also comprises a powerful tool for looking into hierarchical social structures (which so often come in the form of binaries) and opposing them from a uniquely bisexual standpoint.

The idea of a phase associated with bisexuality implies the option of process, allowing us to think about sexuality not as a fixed, unmoving, complete thing, but rather as an open-ended, complex, multiple, and continual process of learning, feeling, and experiencing. It allows us the opportunity to learn attention and sensitivity, to ourselves as well as others—and not only on a personal level, but also a political one: sensitivity to oppression and encouragement of processes, which facilitate change.

Bisexuals Are Slutty, Promiscuous, or Inherently Unfaithful

This marks minority-world society's fear of sexuality. Bisexuality is here being *hypersexualized* under the presumption that sex is bad, that wanting too much of it is bad, that wanting any of it is bad, that wanting people of more than one gender is bad, and that wanting more than one person is bad. The concept of infidelity or unfaithfulness might help us think about monogamy as one of society's oppressive structures. Monogamy has been used historically and currently as a capitalist and patriarchal tool for controlling women, and for keeping all people in small, docile units where they are isolated and unable to connect and organize (especially in minority-world cultures). This keeps resistance to a bare minimum. In a society based on sexual fear and a *culture of rape,* the sexualization of bisexuality can open a window to a different kind of sexual culture, encouraging sexual independence, exploration, and enjoyment of our bodies, our sexualities, our various genders, and our sexual interactions. It can subvert and transgress boundaries of identity, body, sexuality, and gender. It can give us a vantage point of opposing patriarchy and heterosexism, and to creating a sexually radical culture.

In addition and on the other hand, it can allow us to look into the ways in which sexuality is imposed on us, without consent and to the satisfaction of others. It can allow us to examine—and oppose—rape culture, sexual harassment, and asexuality-phobia, pointing out the ways that sexuality is imposed on all of us.

The idea that bisexuals are indiscriminate about their choice of partners also echoes society's anxiety about subversion of cissexist norms. It is often said that "a bisexual is the kind of person who can reach down someone's pants and be happy with whatever they find." This emphasizes the fact that we can never actually know what's "down" anyone's "pants." This marks bisexuals as "accomplices" to transgender and genderqueer people, and it connects bisexuality and transgender as two intertwining ideas, both of which deviate society's rules about normative gender and its enforcement.

The idea of unfaithfulness also brings into light the metaphor of the bisexual as traitor (one of my personal favorites). The dictionary defines treason as "a betrayal of trust," or as "an attempt to overthrow the government . . . or to kill . . . the sovereign," a definition that betrays, if you will, bisexuality's function as an agitator. We can think about bisexuality as betrayal of the trust imposed on us by power structures, as well as embodying an attempt to overthrow or "kill" hegemonic order. We can then use this as a gateway to betraying monogamy, patriarchy, governments, countries, and wars, betraying the "LGBT" (meaning, the *GGGG*) movement, for promoting the assimilation of our communities and cooperating with oppressive structures. We can be traitors to anything that confines us, and to anything that stands in our way: all power structures, all oppression.

Bisexuals Are Carriers or Vectors of HIV and Other STIs

Taken metaphorically, AIDS is always imagined as the "queer disease," being both a "punishment" for being queer and the embodiment of the straight population's fear of being "infected" by queerness. Bisexual men are always imagined as contagious agents of disease, having unprotected bisex only to return home and infect their innocent, straight wives and children. In this way, bisexuality destabilizes the clear-cut border between gay and straight, symbolizing anxiety of the invasion of queerness into straight populations. We can envision bisexuality as the carrier of queerness into the straight population, having the potential to infect—that is, disrupt and queer up—*heteronormative* structures.

Taken from another angle, this image of bisexuality also destabilizes the border between sickness and health, calling society's ableism into question and marking disabled and chronically ill bodies as yet another site of transgression and resistance.

Bisexuals Are Actually Gay or Actually Straight

This stereotype can be thought of as yet another way of trying to redraw the borders threatened with transgression, and once again deny bisexuality out of existence. However, more central to this one is the presumption I mentioned in the first part, that bisexual women are actually straight, while bisexual men are actually gay. The idea presented here is that of the immaculate phallus, suggesting that phallic adoration is the one true thing uniting all bisexual people. It projects society's own phallocentrism onto the idea of bisexuality. This permits us to critically reflect this phallocentrism back into society, exposing the underlying system of sexism and *misogyny* as we do so. It might also help us explore alternative ways of relating to the penis itself, as well as to masculinity, subverting sexist connotations of the penis as an all-powerful, all-forceful, all-domineering, hypersexualized, and *hypermasculinized* phallus. Instead, we can reconstruct the male body and masculinity and create new visions of subversive and feminist masculinities.[5]

Bisexuals Can Choose to Be Gay or Straight

The idea that bisexuals can choose their sexuality stems from a standpoint that sees choice as negative or as a mark of illegitimacy. In a movement where the dominant discourse relies on lack of choice as its political path to equal rights, this lack of choice (the "born this way" argument) becomes a "tool" for attaining legitimacy and acceptance by society.

The way this argument usually goes is: "We were born this way; we can't help it; if we could choose then we would never have chosen to be gay. Now give us rights because we can't change." Internalized homophobia aside, this argument marks immutability—that is, "nature"—as authentic and therefore legitimate, while marking choice—that is, "culture"—as inauthentic and illegitimate. Bisexuality's place as an

"unnatural" choice is a point of strength in my opinion, opening a space for bisexuality to challenge notions of authenticity, legitimacy, and normalcy (as the "natural" is also always imagined as "normal"). We can also think about a challenge to the very concept of nature and the politics of the "natural," as well as human exploitation of "nature" (in symbolic and material ways). Bisexuality can offer an alternative politics of inauthenticity, the unnatural, the illegitimate, and the chosen: the rejection of nature, natural categories, human exploitation of nature, and the politics of the natural. Promoting a politics of the inventable, the unimaginable, the possible, and the impossible: everything we can be and everything we can't.

What this reading offers, I hope, is a new way of reading and creating bisexual politics. The political weight that society places on bisexuality (as seen through bisexual stereotypes) can be levered by us and used as a force. . . .

NOTES

1. "Primitive" is a word used in psychoanalysis to describe early developmental stages, though it also certainly draws its sources from colonialist discourses.
2. For (unchecked) descriptions of biphobia in pre-Stonewall lesbian communities, see: Davis, Madeline and Elizabeth Kennedy. *Boots of Leather, Slippers of Gold: The History of a Lesbian Community.* Penguin (Non-Classics), 1994.
3. In the 1980s the bisexual community, along with all the other LGBT communities, was mainly busy dealing with AIDS.
4. For more about the idea of bisexual temporality, see: Ku, Chung-Hao. (See Further Reading List).
5. Note that not all bodies with penises are male, and that not all male people have penises.

13 • *Karli June Cerankowski and Megan Milks*

NEW ORIENTATIONS: ASEXUALITY AND ITS IMPLICATIONS FOR THEORY AND PRACTICE

DISCUSSION QUESTIONS

1. When and where did you first hear the term *asexuality*? What do you think is the significance of this initial context compared to what information this article presents?
2. How do the medical and psychological discourses understand asexuality, and how is this different from the authors' conception? Why is it important to attend to the epistemology of asexuality?
3. What do the authors think that both feminist and queer theory can offer asexuality and the asexual movement and vice versa? Why do you think the relations between asexuality and feminism as well as asexual and queer communities are important to understand?

Feminist studies, women's studies, gender studies, sexuality studies, gay and lesbian studies, queer studies, transgender studies . . . asexuality studies? Although asexuality may not necessarily belong to its own field of study (yet), and may not make an easy fit with any preexisting field of study, the emergence and proliferation of the asexual community pose interesting questions at the intersections of these fields that interrogate and analyze gender and sexuality. As we know, these fields are neither independent of one another nor are they easily conflated; and they are ever shifting, revising, expanding, subdividing, and branching off. Where, then, might we place the study of a "new," or at least newly enunciated, sexuality? How do we begin to analyze and contextualize a sexuality that by its very definition undermines perhaps the most fundamental assumption about human sexuality: that all people experience, or *should* experience, sexual desire?

These questions are not readily answerable, especially in this brief dispatch; for now we are compelled simply to pose them in an effort to open up a ripe new space for inquiry. Indeed, asexuality has won little attention in any of the fields listed previously or in academic fields generally. The discourse of asexuality has been primarily concentrated in the social sciences, despite its clear connections with theories of gender and sexuality. In this article, we are particularly interested

Cerankowski, Karli June and Megan Milks. 2010. "New Orientations: Asexuality and Its Implications for Theory and Practice." *Feminist Studies* 36(3): 650–64. Reprinted by permission of *Feminist Studies*.

in pushing beyond scientific analysis, as young schol-ars like ourselves are beginning to theorize asexuality in relation to sexuality studies, feminist studies, and queer studies—all interdisciplinary fields that span not only the sciences and social sciences but also the humanities. Recognizing that asexuality has a mean-ing both plural and mutable, we believe it necessary to expand and complicate the scant amount of scientific research on the topic. In that vein, we would like to consider asexuality as it relates to identity, orientation, and the politics of an asexual movement, which has given a name and a new understanding to what has commonly been viewed as dysfunctional or repressed sexuality. As we trace the possibilities for the future study of asexuality, we would like to begin by intro-ducing our readers to asexuality in general—its defi-nition, community formation, and politics. Then, we briefly survey the literature on asexuality before turn-ing to a few of the many implications, questions, and possibilities the study of asexuality poses for feminist and queer studies.

INTRODUCING THE ASEXUAL COMMUNITY

"Asexual: a person who does not experience sexual attraction." This definition is provided on the home page of the Asexual Visibility and Education Net-work (AVEN), a Web community where members from around the world communicate with each other via Web forums, often using these communication networks to arrange in-person meetings for social or political action.[1] It is around this definition that the asexual community has organized, but that is not to say that it is a homogeneous group of people, nor even that all asexual individuals agree with this defi-nition. As mentioned, members of AVEN are located around the world, coming from different back-grounds; identifying with various genders, races, and classes; forming different types of relationships; and even variously identifying as romantic and aromantic, monogamous and polyamorous, gay, straight, bisexual, and lesbian. This variation is unsurprising given the community's large and growing membership. Since its founding in 2001, the online community has amassed just over 19,000 users worldwide, with the most signifi-cant growth occurring between 2006 and 2008 when membership more than doubled from the near 6,000 users accounted for in January 2006. AVEN founder David Jay states that when he adds that number to the sum of members using the forums in languages other than English (these forums can be linked from the AVEN site), he accounts for nearly 30,000 members worldwide.[2] Although, as with most online communi-ties, it is difficult to know how many registered mem-bers are unique users, and in this case, it is difficult to know if these unique users identify as asexual, we sug-gest that the increasing numbers of registered AVEN users indicate that the community of self-identified asexuals and their allies is indeed growing.

. . .

LOCATING ASEXUALITY IN ACADEMIC DISCOURSE

The modest attention human asexuality has received has come mainly from medical and psychological discourse, which has acknowledged asexuality only relatively recently, and then solely in pathologizing terms. In the 1980 third edition of *Diagnostic and Statistical Manual of Mental Disorders* (*DSM-III*), the American Psychiatric Association added the diagnos-tic category "inhibited sexual desire," later renamed Hypoactive Sexual Desire Disorder (HSDD) in the *DSM-IV* (1994) and defined as "persistently or recur-rently deficient (or absent) sexual fantasies and desire for sexual activity."[3] Although there are cases in which these diagnoses must be taken seriously, cases that demand psychiatric or medical attention, the presumption that all cases of disinterest in sex are pathological is what has contributed to the pejorative flavor of the word "asexual," a view that the growing asexual community has been working with some success to change. In fact, the group has put together a small taskforce to "create a new definition (of HSDD) that's more friendly to asexual people," which they hope to include in the newest edition of the *DSM*.[4] We would like to emphasize this point: there is a marked difference between those who experience a decrease in sex drive or lack of sexual desire and are distressed by this and those who do not experience sexual desire and are not distressed by this supposed "lack." We are interested in the latter group here and in locating asexuality as a viable sexual and social identity.

The project of separating asexuality from presumptive pathology has been taken up in a handful of social sciences studies published in the past six years. Two studies by Anthony F. Bogaert, who works in social psychology, are groundbreaking in this respect. In his 2004 article based on preexisting questionnaire data, Bogaert suggests that approximately 1 percent of the population is asexual; this is the first known empirical study of asexuality. Later he asks in a conceptual article, published in 2006, whether asexuality, here defined as "a lack of any sexual attraction," should be viewed as a unique sexual orientation and argues that indeed it should. Bogaert's two articles have accomplished much in distancing asexuality from pathology. His work has since been expanded by psychologists Nicole Prause and Cynthia A. Graham, whose 2007 study is the first (that we have come across) to analyze responses produced by individuals who self-identify as asexual. In 2008, Kristin S. Scherrer, working within sociology, furthers Prause and Graham's study with one that also uses responses from asexual-identified individuals in an attempt to more fully understand the identity-based (as opposed to behavioral and desire-based) aspects of asexuality.[5]

In addition to these short studies, we note one book-length exploration of asexual relationships, published in 1993, that focuses specifically within the lesbian community. *Boston Marriages: Romantic but Asexual Relationships among Contemporary Lesbians* is a collection of theoretical articles and personal stories edited and compiled by psychologist Esther D. Rothblum and psychotherapist Kathleen A. Brehony. Describing their research process, they suggest that thinking through asexual relationships forced them to confront their own biases about sex and intimacy: they write that they "hope that readers will be challenged to reconsider the very basis of what constitutes a lesbian relationship."[6] Indeed, the selections in the book open up interesting possibilities for rethinking intimacy in relationships, and although the focus is on lesbian relationships, such a project resonates across many populations and communities.

. . .

AN EMERGENT FIELD

. . . We hope to begin an ongoing conversation about asexuality and the asexual movement within the discourses of feminist and queer theory.

These interdisciplinary fields seem to be ever in flux, constantly interrogated by new identity categories. As an example, we might look back to how Gayle Rubin in 1984 first raised the question of whether feminism, as a "theory of gender oppression," could adequately theorize sex and sexuality in all their complexities. With foresight for the development of the field of sexuality studies (and later queer studies), in her landmark essay, "Thinking Sex: Notes for a Radical Theory of the Politics of Sexuality," Rubin suggests that "in the long run, feminism's critique of gender hierarchy must be incorporated into a radical theory of sex, and the critique of sexual oppression should enrich feminism. But an autonomous theory and politics specific to sexuality must be developed." Rubin believes that the study of sexuality is indeed an important component of feminist thought, but she also suggests the need for a new field of inquiry that would continue to enrich the feminist conversation. Similarly, we might consider the more recent development of the field of transgender studies. In the introduction to the voluminous *Transgender Studies Reader*, Susan Stryker describes how transgender studies developed at the nexus of feminism and queer studies: "Neither feminism nor queer studies, at whose intersection transgender studies first emerged in the academy, were quite up to the task of making sense of the lived complexity of contemporary gender at the close of the last century." She goes on to describe how "transgender studies emerged in the 1990s not just in conjunction with certain intellectual trends within feminism and queer theory, but also in response to broader historical circumstances." Here Stryker is pointing to the historical and contextual necessity for the emergence of the field of transgender studies, not entirely separate from, but indeed very much informed by, feminist and queer studies. Similarly, we suggest that the current historical situation demands a concentrated study of asexuality, which is most appropriately begun at the crossroads of feminist and queer studies, as asexuality challenges many existing assumptions about gender and sexuality.[7]

ASEXUAL FEMINISMS, FEMINIST ASEXUALITIES

In thinking about relationships and connections between asexuality and feminist studies, perhaps the key question to address is how the recognition of asexuality as an identity meets and potentially challenges feminist conceptions of sex and female sexuality. Although asexuality compels us to reconsider multiple approaches to the feminist project of liberating female sexuality, it is perhaps especially conversant with radical feminism, pro-sex feminism, and the oppositional discourse that characterizes both.

. . .

The emergence of the asexual movement compels us to reconsider the ways in which female sexuality was and still is framed by the rhetoric of liberation in the feminist movement. The crucial problem of the discourse surrounding the anti-porn/pro-sex debates is that it situates female sexuality as either empowered or repressed: the attendant assumption is that anti- or asexuality is inherently repressive or dysfunctional. The asexual movement challenges that assumption, working to distance asexuality from pathology and in so doing challenging many of the basic tenets of pro-sex feminism—most obviously its privileging of transgressive female sexualities that are always already defined against repressive or "anti-sex" sexualities.

Even as the asexual movement boldly challenges sex-positive feminism's view of asexuality as repressive, however, it is not necessarily more easily aligned with radical feminism. Although radical feminists did produce a few concepts of feminist asexuality, it is unclear

how the asexual movement might reckon with their politicization of asexuality as a way out of phallocentric sexuality. Thus far, asexual individuals have not politicized their (a)sexual practices in the same way that radical feminists such as Andrea Dworkin have.

So what might feminist theorists do with asexuality, and what might asexuals do with feminist theory? Although the distancing of asexuality from pathology retains political primacy for an intersection of asexuality and feminist theory, at least with respect to the asexual movement's goals of visibility and education, we want to also identify two impulses that we can see as potential approaches to a feminism that acknowledges asexuality. The first impulse is to look at asexuality as a way to critique the liberatory rhetoric by which sex is still to a large extent framed within feminism. The second impulse is to theorize modes of asexuality that are or can be feminist, likely beginning by extending the work of radical feminists.

One approach to thinking through asexuality from a feminist perspective is to consider how asexuality might critique the rhetoric of liberation in which sex is still steeped within feminism. The asexual movement's politicization of sex is at this point very basic, its nominal goal being visibility and education, with no gestures toward explicitly challenging norms. That is, asexuality thus far is not politicized in the same way that female sexuality has been. (Of course, this does not mean that the asexual movement is not heading in that direction.) Whether female sexuality is conceived of from a radical feminist or from a pro-sex perspective, both are too steeped in the rhetoric of liberation to make sense in a way that can be inclusive of asexual persons who are simply uninterested in having sex and who may not be actively or explicitly engaged in radical politics.

. . .

A second approach to thinking through asexuality from a feminist perspective might attempt to theorize asexuality as feminist. In doing so, we would do well to begin with theories of feminist asexuality and anti-sexuality that emerged from radical feminism. Dworkin, for instance, in *Intercourse,* holds up Joan of Arc as an example of someone who has, exercising feminist agency, dropped out of phallocentric sex.[8] In the early fifteenth century, Dworkin argues, Joan of Arc's anti-sexuality indicated freedom from the inferiority of a female subjectivity. Dworkin's use of the word "virginity" to describe Joan of Arc's sexuality is perhaps problematic when linked with theories of asexuality; however, Dworkin's virginity is understood not as pureness or innocence (a sexist and repressive configuration) but as resistance to sexism and misogyny (a feminist configuration).

Can Joan of Arc be considered asexual? The question takes us back to the definition of asexuality. It seems clear that AVEN's "official" formulation of asexuality as not a choice, but a biologically determined orientation (a definition that itself opens up the larger ongoing nature/nurture debate in studies of human sexuality), does not easily map on to a theory of asexuality as a chosen, feminist mode of resistance. In fact, AVEN repeatedly opposes asexuality to celibacy, in its literature, in the General FAQ, and on the AVENwiki. For example, in an informational brochure, AVEN claims, "Celibacy is a choice to abstain from sexual activity. Asexuality is not a choice, but rather a sexual orientation describing people who do not experience sexual attraction. While most asexual people do not form sexual relationships, some asexuals participate in sexual behavior for the pleasure of others."[9] This not only raises questions about choice versus fixed identity but also forces us to question to what extent the practice of or abstention from sex acts matters to the definition of asexuality.

Importantly, that definition is not fixed; nor is it agreed upon by self-identified asexuals. AVEN's AVENwiki contains several pages devoted to competing formulations of asexual identity. We do not have the space to detail them here, but one seems especially of note: the Collective Identity model. This model constructs asexuality as a collective identification: someone who has no sex drive but does not see herself as asexual is not asexual; but someone who does experience a sex drive but sees herself as asexual is asexual. In theorizing feminist asexuality, then, we might look to this model, which proposes that those who describe themselves as asexual have *"chosen* to actively disidentify with sexuality" (our emphasis).[10]

This model, which seemingly contradicts AVEN's more widely held essentialist formulation, is perhaps the most likely model to dialogue with radical feminism. A feminist mode of asexuality, accordingly, might consider as asexual someone who is not intrinsically/biologically asexual (i.e., lacking a sexual drive) but who is sexually inactive, whether short-term or long-term, not through a religious or spiritual vow of celibacy but through feminist agency.

. . . The emergence of the asexual movement compels us to revisit feminist theories of sex and sexuality in ways that will likely complicate the politics of both the asexual and feminist movements. The asexual movement encourages the feminist movement to think further about how to theorize a feminist asexuality that cannot be dismissed as conservative, repressive, or anti-sexual. On the other side of things, revisiting feminist theories of sexual practice and sexuality may complicate AVEN's definition of "asexual" and bring more attention to the various ways of being asexual that already exist within the community. Further, in light of the important developments of feminist theorists of color, and with a nod toward queer scholarship, we are compelled to question the isolation of sexuality as a solitary category of analysis to allow for the possibility of shifting meanings of asexuality across different racial, ethnic, cultural, and class contexts.

IS ASEXUALITY QUEER?

In the General FAQ on the AVEN Web site, this question is framed as such: "I think asexuality is inherently queer. Do you agree?" The response to this question provides a perfect example of the palpable ambivalence between queerness and asexuality: "This has been the subject of much debate and discussion. On the one hand 'queer' is 'anything that differs from the norm,' especially the norm of sexuality, and there are asexual people who consider the relationships they form to be completely unconventional and therefore queer. Other asexuals consider their relationships to be entirely conventional and do not identify as queer in any way."[11] This response hinges upon the definition of "queer" as nonnormative, and such a definition comes up against the ongoing conflicts and questions within queer studies: how do we define "queer" and can anyone be queer? Such questions are specifically linked to the focus on sex as part of the definition of queerness. There is an ongoing worry among queer theorists and activists that "queer" is becoming a blanket term for, as the AVEN definition suggests, any variation from the norm. In such a universalizing move, as Leo Bersani has argued, "queer" desexualizes the gay and lesbian movement. Building from Michael Warner's suggestion in his introduction to *Fear of a Queer Planet: Queer Politics and Social Theory* that queer struggles are able to challenge social institutions, Bersani suggests that such a challenge is impossible "unless we define how the sexual specificity of being queer (a specificity perhaps common to the myriad ways of being queer and the myriad conditions in which one is queer) gives queers a special aptitude for making that challenge." Although Bersani often returns to "an erotic desire for the same" as the definitive way of being queer, we think a more generous reading is possible, wherein asexuality is one of Bersani's sexually specific "myriad ways of being queer."[12] By its very definition, asexuality brings a focus to the presence or absence of sexual desire as a way to queer the normative conceptions about how sex is practiced and how relationships are (or are not) formed around that practice.

. . . How might asexuality fit into a community where sexual culture is at the center? Paradoxical as it may seem, is it possible that not desiring sex can be part of that radical sexual culture? In short, does the asexual person threaten to remove sex from politics all over again, or does she or he challenge the ways we think about sex and desire even within queer communities?

We would of course argue for the latter, as we suggest that asexuality as a practice and a politics radically challenges the prevailing sex-normative culture. If the asexual community is indeed a part of a radical sexual political movement, we believe that it is critical to continue the conversation about whether queer communities can provide at least a coalition site for community building and social activism, even while challenging queer conceptions of sex and relationships. In other words, does the asexual movement as a visible political entity require that the queer movement rethink its equivalence of radical sex with radical politics or, even more, its definition of what constitutes radical sex? Within this discussion of queerness, the questions of oppression and marginalization also arise. The reality is that asexuality is often pathologized and medicalized and also that asexual people are often told that they are inchoate, that they haven't yet fully developed and experienced their sexuality, or they are interrogated about past trauma and sexual abuse. Similarly, asexual individuals experience the alienation that comes from lacking sexual desire in a world that presumes sexual desire and that attaches great power to sexuality. How does this experience compare with that of queers living in a heterosexist world? The parallels to the historical treatment of homosexuality and other queer modes of being should be clear, but is that overlap enough to ally asexual persons with those who practice queer sex?

. . .

CONCLUSION

Admittedly, we more so raise questions here than provide answers. In doing so, we hope to open up a new field of interrogation in the study of human sexuality. It is with an affinity to our own academic interests, and with attention to the interests of the readers of *Feminist Studies,* that we have focused our dialogue primarily on feminist and queer theories. Although we do not suggest that asexuality is decidedly feminist or queer, we do think that the study of asexuality informs, and is fruitfully informed by, both feminist and queer studies. Additionally, we realize that we have only touched on a miniscule sample of feminist and queer writing and readily acknowledge the much larger realm of dialogic possibility that we cannot give mention to here.

We would like to end by noting the exciting work that is being produced in conversation with and beyond not only the sciences but also these two concentrations. Within the (relatively) newly emergent field of disability studies, Eunjung Kim is working to raise critical awareness of the "cultural representations of asexual individuals with disabilities and their relationship with the totalizing perception of asexuality of disabled people." She argues that "perceived asexuality is constructed by social desexualization that denies the diverse sexual and asexual embodiments of disabled people."[13] Additionally, one of us, Cerankowski, is working not only within queer studies but also within performance studies to theorize what visibility means to asexual politics and how asexuality is performed in media appearances, in public spectacles, such as the aforementioned Pride parade, and in everyday life. The other of us, Milks, is examining how the emergence of asexuality may reconfigure the rhetoric of contemporary queer and sex-positive feminism, specifically with regard to the anti-porn/pro-sex debates it has grown out of. . . .

NOTES

1. AVEN, "Asexual Visibility and Education Network," www.asexuality.org.

2. David Jay, e-mail message to Cerankowski, 14 Aug. 2009.

3. *Diagnostic and Statistical Manual of Mental Disorders*, 4th ed. (Washington, D.C.: American Psychiatric Association, 1994), 539.

4. David Jay and Andrew H., "DSM Fireside Chat," www.youtube.com/watch?v=4z3u0DyUe6U.

5. Anthony F. Bogaert, "Asexuality: Prevalence and Associated Factors in a National Probability Sample," *The Journal of Sex Research* 41, no. 3 (2004): 279–87; Anthony F. Bogaert, "Toward a Conceptual Understanding of Asexuality," *Review of General Psychology* 10, no. 3 (2006): 243; Nicole Prause and Cynthia A. Graham, "Asexuality: Classification and Characterization," *Archives of Sexual Behavior* 36, no. 3 (2007): 341–56; Kristin S. Scherrer, "Coming to an Asexual Identity: Negotiating Identity, Negotiating Desire," *Sexualities* 11, no. 5 (2008): 621–40.

6. Esther D. Rothblum and Kathleen A. Brehony, "Introduction: Why Focus on Romantic but Asexual Relationships among Lesbians?" in *Boston Marriages: Romantic but Asexual Relationships among Contemporary Lesbians*, ed. Esther D. Rothblum and Kathleen A. Brehony (Amherst: University of Massachusetts Press, 1993), 12.

7. Gayle Rubin, "Thinking Sex: Notes for a Radical Theory of the Politics of Sexuality," in *Pleasure and Danger: Exploring Female Sexuality*, ed. Carole S. Vance (Boston: Routledge & Kegan Paul, 1984), 307, 309; Susan Stryker, "(De)subjugated Knowledges: An Introduction to Transgender Studies," in *Transgender Studies Reader*, ed. Susan Stryker and Stephen Whittle (New York: Routledge, 2006), 7, 8.

8. Andrea Dworkin, "Virginity," in her *Intercourse* (New York: Basic Books, 2006), 103–51.

9. AVEN, "Asexuality: Not Everyone Is Interested in Sex" (unpublished document circulated in San Francisco, 2008).

10. AVEN, "Collective Identity Model," www.asexuality.org/wiki/index.php?title=Collective_identity_model.

11. AVEN, "General FAQ," www.asexuality.org/home/general.html.

12. Leo Bersani, *Homos* (Cambridge: Harvard University Press, 1995), 72–73. Michael Warner, introduction to *Fear of a Queer Planet: Queer Politics and Social Theory*, ed. Michael Warner (Minneapolis: University of Minnesota Press, 1993), vii–xxxi.

13. Eunjung Kim, e-mail message to Cerankowski, 5 Aug. 2009.

THE WORLD SOME HAVE WON: SEXUALITY, CLASS AND INEQUALITY

DISCUSSION QUESTIONS

1. According to McDermott, why did the study of social class disappear within queer theory, and why does Bourdieu's conceptualization of social class offer promise to queer theory?
2. How does access to gay consumer culture and the gay community shape one's habitus—that is, one's sense of identity and belonging? What are the types of resources needed to transform one's habitus, positively?
3. In what ways might differing degrees of cultural capital influence decisions to attend college? How does cultural capital affect your own sense of identity and belonging at college/university?

INTRODUCTION

There is concrete evidence of the widening acceptance of sexual diversity within contemporary western societies (Plummer, 2008; Weeks, 2007). Richardson suggests that we are, in fact, "witnessing a certain disruption and destabilization of heterosexuality" (2000: 3). There is no doubt that, over the last half century, there have been significant transformations in the possibilities for lesbian, gay, bisexual and transgender (LGBT) people to live confident, affirmed, open lives. Many of the gains have been as a result of the lesbian and gay movement's campaigns to challenge negative understandings of homosexuality and demands for the same rights and legitimations as heterosexual people. In the UK, new legislation has enshrined in law same-sex partnerships (Civil Partnership Act 2004) and provided protection against discrimination

and homophobia (e.g. Equality Employment Regulations [2003], Equality Act Regulations [2007], Criminal Justice and Immigration Bill [2008]). This liberalization is further embedded by sexual orientation being included, for the first time, within the equality remit of the public body responsible for equality, the Equality and Human Rights Commission (EHRC, 2007).

. . .

It is reasonable to speculate that LGBT people are likely to experience this social transformation differently depending on class resources (and gender, ethnicity, age and geography and so on). However, academic discourses contributing to the liberalization taking place in our intimate and sexual life have tended to neglect the implications of social class. The aim of this article is to argue that class resources and advantages are likely to be crucial to negotiating and

McDermott, Elizabeth. 2011. "The World Some Have Won: Sexuality, Class and Inequality." *Sexualities* 14(1): 63–78. Reprinted by permission of SAGE Publications.

claiming, within this new liberal framework, equal lives. Furthermore, it is necessary to find ways to research at the intersection of sexuality and social class, and I suggest that Bourdieu's (1984) concepts habitus, capital and field may offer a potential theoretical framework for empirical study. As an example, I draw on the accounts of LGBT young people participating in two studies, to explore how sexual identity intersects with social class in post-compulsory schooling choices. The intention is to begin to unearth the hidden processes involved in the reproduction of inequalities at the intersection of sexuality and class.

. . .

THE RETREAT AND RE-EMERGENCE OF CLASS

The retreat from social class within the academy in the early 1980s is well documented (Crompton, 1998; Skeggs, 1997). Class was seen to be an outdated analytical concept that failed to capture the complexities of the social world. Specifically, poststructuralist, postmodern theorists claimed that class was developed for explaining 'modern' societies. Contemporary societies have irrevocably changed and, therefore, class was perceived to no longer have meaning in the analysis of social life (Clark and Lipset, 1991; Gorz, 1982). More recently, social class has reemerged as a subject of interest across a number of disciplines, for example, in feminist theory, psychology, geography, history and sociology (see for example Bondi, 1998; Devine, 1997; Finch, 1993; Lawler, 2000; Reay, 1998; 2008; Savage, 2000; Skeggs, 1997; 2004a; Walkerdine and Lucey, 1989). These authors suggest that social class has not disappeared but is being reconfigured and known through other categorizations and across a range of sites (Lawler, 2004; Skeggs, 2004a). Scholars have reasserted the centrality of class to partly explain the growing chasm between the rich and the poor in the global economy, and demonstrate the ways in which class is produced in and through the economy, state, family, school, individual and linked to gender, race and sexuality (albeit this is explored less often).

However, the resurgence of interest in class has been less obvious in specific academic arenas that concentrate on sexuality such as feminism, sociology, lesbian and gay studies, and queer theory.

'QUEER TURN'

While there has been a proliferation of literature that attempts to deconstruct taken-for-granted categories of gender and sexuality (Plummer, 2008), it is much rarer for these investigations to attempt to gain a view of the connections with other social stratifications (the interconnection between 'race' and sexuality is explored more often than class). Plummer (2008: 18) states "despite all the talk about 'intersectionality,' we really do not hear much about class these days." This is partly due to the discrediting of Marxism as a narrow reductive class analysis in which sexuality was made irrelevant, which opened a theoretical gap that was filled by a postmodern queer emphasis upon identity as a cultural and discursive construction rather than a social one (Hennessy, 2000). Queer theory has come to dominate thinking on sexual and gender identities and elides much feminist and sociological work on sexualities that preceded the 'queer turn' (Jackson, 1999).

Queer theory, with an account of sexual/gender identity as performative (Butler, 1990), and the conceptualization of the social as a matter of representation, discourse or symbolic, means there is a limited engagement with the material conditions of sexuality. The resulting theory, divorced from wider politics, empirical research and connections with grass roots activism, frequently leaves undisturbed the analysis of the politics and practices of the state, capital and family in producing and reproducing structured gendered and sexual relations (Edwards, 1998; Hennessy, 1995). Some critics claim that queer theories and cultural analyses of sexual identity overlook the significance of class inequalities because they work with Foucault's notion of power as highly dispersed (Hennessy, 1995). It is an account of power as working on and through individuals, and constitutive rather than repressive, which is unhelpful for the analysis of social inequalities (Jackson, 2006; McNay, 1992). This is because for Foucault, power does not have a subject (it is discursive) and does not operate to further the interests of particular groups or individuals. Without an understanding that power is aggregated in institutions and distributed disproportionately amongst individuals, there is no means of analysing the power relations involved in systematic structural inequalities such as those related to social class (Jackson, 1999).

. . .

QUEERING BOURDIEU

Bourdieu theorizes social class as a social practice, not as a category or as a lifestyle, or even a set of dispositions but as an activity in which categorization, structures, dispositions and agency combine. He attempts to overcome the dualism between what individuals do as social actors and the determinative social structures operating on and through individuals, using the concepts of habitus, capital (economic, cultural, social and symbolic) and field (Bourdieu, 1984). Feminists have begun to adapt Bourdieu's theories (see Adkins and Skeggs, 2004) and I want to consider here this work in relation to Bourdieu's concept of habitus (Lawler, 2004; Reay, 1998). I have found this concept useful for overcoming binaries such as structure/agency, recognition/redistribution, culture/material; and as a conceptual mechanism for keeping multiple social identities, experiences and categories (class and sexuality) 'in the body.' As Lawler (2004: 113) suggests about habitus:

> It is an important means through which 'large scale' social inequalities (such as class and gender) are made real, and are also made to inhere within the person, so that it is the persons themselves who can be judged and found wanting, and persons themselves who can be made to bear the 'hidden injuries' of inequality.

Habitus is Bourdieu's way of conceiving the embodiment of social structures and history in individuals, it is a "socialized subjectivity" (Bourdieu and Wacquant, 1992: 126). Habitus concerns a set of lasting dispositions, created and reformulated within the individual, which reflect their position in social space (relating to the distribution of an individual's capital). It is important to note that habitus is not determining but generative, in that it influences how an individual perceives the world and acts. Human behaviour is not mechanical obedience but "the habitus as the feel for the game is the social game embodied and turned into second nature" (Bourdieu, 1990: 63).

Despite the divergences between Bourdieu's and queer perspectives, there are some productive convergences. Both sets of theories argue that the social world is organized along binaries, and suggest that these dichotomies are embodied by individuals. Bourdieu's incorporation of the social into the body has similarities to feminist/queer work of gender and sexual identity as individually embodied (Fraser, 1999). However, there is a tension between Bourdieu's notion of habitus as complicit with the dominant symbolic order and queer theory's view of the unstable nature of sexual identities. Bourdieu's (1991) version of symbolic power relies on the supposition that the habitus of dominated groups veils the conditions of their subordination through a process of misrecognition. A central component of this theory is the unconsciousness of habitus: an unconscious complicity between habitus and the field which does not allow for resistance to the symbolic order. Skeggs (2004b) argues that for the women in her research, gender was not prereflexive, unconscious and based on misrecognition but that gender was a classed experience of which the women were very aware and critical; they were resisting the dominant values.

To have an 'othered' sexual identity, is to overcome the fundamental gender binary, argued by feminist/queer theorists and Bourdieu as the earliest and most powerful and durable aspects of socialization/habitus. The recognition of not 'being like other girls/boys or women/men' requires a conscious acknowledgement of 'inappropriate' erotic feelings, desires or acts. This raises questions about the relationship of consciousness and habitus, and reflexivity and identity. In contrast to Bourdieu, queer theories of identity transformation tend to emphasize the rational, conscious, strategic processes of the self, which overlooks the unconscious and durable parts of identity. McNay warns against the inclination of postmodern theories of identity to "elide symbolic detraditionalization with social detraditionalization" (1999: 106). She argues that some theories exaggerate the reflexive opportunities for the transformation of identities in late capitalist society.

In my view, the concept of habitus allows for a more entrenched account of embodied experiences that might avoid an overemphasis on the processes of reflexivity in identity construction. Although Bourdieu (1984) maintains that habitus is durable, he does not rule out strategic choice and conscious deliberation. He argues that habitus can be transformed, within definite boundaries, by the effect of a social trajectory or controlled through socio-analysis and this enables the individual to understand some of his or her dispositions. . . .

For people experiencing same-sex desire, it is the concrete social tensions inherent in the conflict of having same-sex erotic feelings which provides the potential battleground for reflexivity and, possibly, gives rise to the questioning of the conventional heteronormative binary. I have tentatively attempted to bring together Bourdieu's concepts, particularly habitus, and queer theory to develop a theoretical framework for the empirical study of the intersections of sexuality and social class. After a brief methodology section, the remainder of the article presents, using this framework, an analysis of data from two studies, which centres on young LGBT people's post-compulsory schooling choices.

METHODOLOGY

Study 1 aimed to investigate the effects of sexual identity and social class on psycho-social health and was based on semi-structured interviews with 24 women who self-identified, for example, as butch, dyke, lesbian and gay (n = 24. See McDermott, 2003, 2010). The participants all lived in the north west of England and were aged between 21 and 56 years old. The sample was generated through informal lesbian networks using purposeful theoretic snowball sampling (Weston, 1991) from a diverse range of starting points. The participants self-defined as white (17), black or mixed race (5) and Jewish (2). Of the participants, 15 lived in cities; the other nine lived in small

towns or villages. The women were from three broad class backgrounds/trajectories: working class (10), middle class (7) and university educated women from a working-class background (7).

Study 2, called the "On The Edge Project," explored through 13 interviews and 11 focus groups the relationship between sexual and gender identity and self-destructive behaviours (e.g. suicide, self-harm, risky behaviour) in young people (aged 16–25) in north-west England and south Wales (n = 69. See McDermott et al., 2008). The findings presented here draw on a subset of data consisting of interviews with specifically lesbian, gay, bisexual and transgender young people (n = 7). The LGBT participants were all white and recruited via LGBT support groups in both rural and urban locations. The young people may have been referred to a support group through professional networks (social services, education, health) or found the group themselves via the internet, leaflets or word of mouth. Both Study 1 and Study 2 operated under clear ethical research guidelines and were reviewed by university ethics committees.

OPERATIONALIZING SOCIAL CLASS AND SEXUAL IDENTITY

In both studies, sexual and gender identifications were defined by the participants; these included, for example, lesbian, gay, bisexual, transgender, dyke, butch, and queer. Due to word restrictions, LGBT is used as shorthand when discussing the participants in general but individuals will be referred to by their specified sexual and/or gender identity. Social class was attributed to participants using occupation and education. In Study 1, participants were categorized as "middle class" if they were university educated, professionally employed and one of their parents was the same. Women who had no higher education, were non-professionally employed and whose parents were the same were categorized as "working class." Women who were university educated and whose parents had no higher education and non-professional jobs were categorized as "working-class educated." In Study 2, the information on social class was limited to the participants' occupation and education and classifications were made using the National Statistics Socio-Economic classification (NS-SEC).

. . .

LGBT YOUNG PEOPLE'S POST-COMPULSORY SCHOOLING CHOICES

Schools are an intensive environment for young people in terms of their sexuality, and research consistently demonstrates that they function as deeply gendered and heterosexual regimes of domination and subordination (Mac an Ghaill, 1994; Nayak and Kehily, 2008). Epstein et al.'s work on the reproduction of heterosexuality in schools argues that there is a silence about different sexualities and "normative heterosexuality is promoted, sustained and made to appear totally natural" (p. 2). They state that the reproduction of heterosexuality requires a

> tremendous amount of work that children and young people, regardless of their own sexual identifications, must do in dealing with, resisting, coming to terms with, negotiating or adopting normative versions of heterosexuality. It does not matter who you are, or who you wish to be, you will have to be/come that person within the frame of the heterosexual matrix. (Epstein et al., 2003: 145)

Research has also revealed that social class is implicated in the ways in which young LGBT people negotiate the normative boundaries of heterosexuality. Taylor's (2007: 85) study shows the "double depreciation via class and sexuality" that the working-class lesbians in her study faced when trying to deal with and resist the low expectations of compulsory schooling. She suggests the "dual force of class and sexuality" accounts for their exit from schooling at an early age (Taylor, 2006: 450).

Similarly, the accounts from participants in my two studies indicate that social class and sexual identity were important to the ways the young LGBT people were able to negotiate their post-compulsory education pathways. It was the mid to late teens (14–18) when

sexual and gendered emotions and desires that are 'at odds' with heterosexuality emerged, usually with some degree of confusion and/or fear. At a key point in their educational trajectories, when they were taking GCSEs (General Certificate of Secondary Education) and A levels (Advanced Level General Certificate of Education) or applying to university, they had to contend with some high octane feelings and uncertainties regarding their sexual identity. The disruption of the heterosexual habitus can be psychologically and socially demanding. As Angela (21, gay, white, working class [Study 1]) described when she first began to experience same-sex desire, "I didn't know where I was, what I was doing, or what I was" (Study 1).

The young LGBT people in the studies from working-class backgrounds were more likely to leave school aged 16–17 than their counterparts from middle-class families. For example, Stacey was 22 when I interviewed her, she had left school at 17 because she was able to gain employment. She had wanted to continue with her qualifications but her family's dire financial situation, her mother's ill health, and the fear of unemployment (she lived in an area of few employment opportunities) influenced her decision to leave school. She explains her thoughts when she was offered employment in a school:

> So I just thought I may as well get a job, when this come up, something that I love doing . . . working with the kids and all that so I took it . . . I was just made up like, getting myself, it felt boss because I was bringing me own money in, as well as giving me mum money like as rent, cos it would help her you see, whereas [brother & sister], I always say they couldn't give two shits, they do but, not the way I am with me mum, like if me mum said have you got any money? They'd say no, whereas I'd go out and find it for her, and make sure she's got it. (Stacey, gay, white, working class [Study 1])

Stacey's emotional, material and financial concerns influenced her educational choices. She had lived close to the poverty line most of her life and her interview is saturated with the struggle of necessity, the worry and tension of ensuring her mother is supported. She was not passive but her experience of necessity and poverty shapes the meaning of education and work. Stacey's decision not to continue her education and to enter the labour force is what Bourdieu (1984: 379) would describe as "the choice of the necessary."

In addition to the importance of securing permanent, well-paid (relatively) work to her family's financial circumstances, Stacey is managing an emerging young gay adult identity. Employment is a source of independence and self-esteem ('it felt boss'), securing her status as an adult but it also facilitates the construction of her gay identity by providing the resources for the consumption of gay bars and clubs. In the next extract, she describes the importance of the gay scene to the construction of her sexual identity:

> It was frustrating like at first because I was shit scared when I first went out but er, I felt like there was loads of pressure, say like holding someone's hand or something because it was all new to us at the time, so I was worried what others would think, we were all in the same boat really, everybody was the same, it was alright, everybody made you feel welcome, cos we were all on the same wave length weren't we? (Stacey, 22, gay, white, working class [Study 1])

Stacey was able to use gay consumerist leisure space to find a way to legitimate herself, to give herself value and position herself with a positive sexual identity. She was resisting the dominant symbolic order of heteronormativity, and disrupting the deeply embodied gender binary—the heterosexual habitus. This would constitute, in Bourdieu's terms, a "time of crisis" when the "routine adjustment of subjective and objective structures is brutally disrupted" (Bourdieu and Wacquant, 1992: 131); as Stacey describes, she was "shit scared." But this work of transforming the habitus requires resources—psychological, social, cultural and economic. For Stacey, employment enabled her to financially support her family and provide the economic resources necessary to access gay consumerist leisure spaces and contest the dominant heteronormative symbolism to construct a positive gay identity.

In contrast, the incentives to stay at school for Stacey do not "make sense." Habitus mediates our interaction with the social world, it is a kind of practical sense for what needs to be done in any given situation. The combination of limited economic, symbolic and

cultural capital in the education field, and a habitus disposed to survival but disrupted through same-sex desire means Stacey perceives the "practical sense" of paid work, not further investment in schooling.

The intersection of class and sexuality in young people's educational trajectories are evident in Angela's account, who had aspirations, along with her family, to attend university to train as a teacher. When I interviewed her, aged 21, she was working in a gay bar and planning to apply to the police force. Despite showing considerable determination and aspiration, and having support from her close family, she found it difficult to navigate a range of issues relating to her sexual identity and class, to achieve her aim. The first stumbling block was her A levels (qualifications necessary for university entry) which were complicated by her gay relationship break-up and tensions with her family because of her sexuality. She explains the effects this had on her study:

> . . . this is when [girlfriend] finished with me, when I was doing me A levels, so I can honestly remember sitting in the . . . class with [teacher] teaching us, and just not taking in anything she was saying, I was sitting in a world of me own . . . (Angela, 21, gay, white, working class [Study 1])

Conducting a covert same-sex relationship in school, experiencing hostility from her parents and receiving little support when her relationship failed proved too much to cope with and Angela failed her A levels. However, three years later, with an A level and HND (Higher National Diploma), she gained a place at a new university in her home city. She decided not to take up the offer:

> I had a place with [New University] for September just started, er, but in the meanwhile I changed my mind and wanted to be a police officer cos I couldn't be bothered to go through another three years of study and also student loans, financially, so, also paying for me course, cos I had to pay for my HND as well, that was like two grand, well it's £1025 a year isn't it?

Angela had shown great resilience and resolve to achieve a place at university, despite leaving home because of her sexuality, and working while studying. The financial burden of higher education fees and loans are enough, after huge effort, to "persuade" her to seek a debt-free career in the police force. In Bourdieu's (1984) schema, cultural capital is key to the processes of schooling and a child's educational career and class trajectory. Cultural capital is primarily transmitted through the family and it is middle-class cultural capital that is legitimated to be translated into educational profits. We can understand cultural capital as degrees of confidence and entitlement, educational knowledge and information. The differing access to cultural capital is key in the reproduction of class inequalities in education (Luttrell, 1997; Reay, 1998). Angela's family, despite fully supporting her attempts to attend university, had neither enough economic capital nor the 'right' cultural capital to facilitate easily her higher education intentions. In addition, Angela's turmoil was related to a transformation of habitus in terms of class mobility and sexual identity. She was contesting both the dominant heteronormative symbolic order and disrupting class educational expectations regarding higher education. The combination of both requires a tremendous amount of effort and resilience, and in the end, she practically reasoned that a career without debt made more sense.

In comparison to Angela and Stacey's experiences, the accounts of LGBT young people from middle-class backgrounds suggested that the pathway to university is a way of constructing their sexual identity in a liberal safe environment.

> I decided before I went to uni I was going to be quite open about it for the first time and to just see what I felt like just to be this person without any kind of past to him. And no one from my school was coming here so it was a completely fresh start, which was so nice. (Andrew, 19, middle class, bisexual, white [Study 2])

> I mean a lot of people just see it as an escape when they go to university they can actually be themselves. (Rosie, 19, middle class, lesbian, white [Study 2])

As Andrew's extract suggests, he decided *before* he went to university he was going to be open about his sexual identity. Research has shown that for some young LGBT people university can be a way to explore the sexual and gendered self away from the family 'gaze' (Epstein et al., 2003). The LGBT young

people from middle-class backgrounds in the studies expected to go to university. As Reay (2008) argues drawing on Bourdieu, the dominant middle-class educational experience is "like a fish in water," a seamless transfer from school to university. This educational trajectory is expected by the young person, their family, school and social networks. They have a habitus, with a "self assured relation to the world" (Bourdieu, 1984: 54), with a sense of entitlement, confidence and self-worth which comes from privilege, status and success. Rather than transforming their classed habitus, as Angela tried, the middle class LGBT young people were replicating the dominant middle-class habitus (Reay, 1998). The middle-class LGBT students' assumption that they will inevitably attend university, suggests they were able to anticipate and plan for university as a safe space in which to 'come out.' This 'coming out' strategy is one that relied on class resources and is less likely to cause disruption to both their family's expectations and the young person's education trajectory. This does not mean that class advantages eradicated the emotional and psychological work required for contesting the heteronormative dominant order; for example, Andrew described later in his interview his homophobic experiences at university and the difficulties this presented. What I am suggesting is that it is the interconnection between the positionings of class and sexuality that complicate both the accumulation and deployment of capitals, and the contesting of the heterosexual habitus.

The data also indicate that the *choice* of university was influenced by concerns regarding the participants' sexual and gender identities, and social class priorities. In the following extracts, Rosie and Joanne explain how they identified a suitable university:

> Yes there are certain things about university which just kind of show that, I mean the fact that they have a women's officer . . . I mean I actually looked into this kind of thing anyway. (Rosie, 19, lesbian, white, middle class [Study 2])

> I looked at Leeds, no where like, apart from Brighton, that was the furthest one, that had a good gay scene, the reason I didn't go further away, the reason I chose [*New University*] was er, I was comfy here, I was

settled here, I knew where the clubs were here . . . plus I'd just started going out with a girl . . . and to be close to me mum. (Joanne, 21, gay, white, working class educated [Study 1])

For Rosie, her choice of university was influenced by traditional middle-class concerns regarding the ranking of the university (not a 'new' university), the course she wanted to study but also locating a university which had visible indicators that they were liberal spaces for LGBT students. Rosie's research showed her chosen university had a Student Union Women's Officer (who aims to ensure gender equality) and was in a city with a 'mix' of people. Rosie is demonstrating here the middle-class self which is produced through choice and self-management (Skeggs, 2004a). She has a practical sense that the 'game' in this instance is the hetero-gendered relations of the higher-education market, and Rosie understood that the rules are heterosexual. Her class position also means that she had the right capitals and a habitus with a sense of entitlement and confidence; she expects to exert choice and control over her life.

In contrast, Joanne is from a working-class background and her university choice is also influenced by her class and sexuality. Her selection is based on differing access to economic, cultural and social capital in conjunction with a transforming habitus—through class mobility and same-sex desire. These narratives/experiences resonate with research that suggests that working-class young people's higher education choices are influenced by restraints in economic capital, and social capital. For example, Reay et al. (2001) found a 'localism' in working-class students' choice of university and Henderson et al. (2007) document the ways that ties to families and communities can influence educational pathways. Joanne's university choice is also shaped by financial restrictions and important relationships (with her mother and new girlfriend) but in addition, a changing classed and heterosexualized habitus. Her relationships and known safe gay spaces are important because, in some senses, they provide a secure way in which the disrupted heterosexual habitus can be

realigned; in other words, 'gay' subjective dispositions can align with objective conditions through safe relationships and spaces. This has a powerful 'pulling' effect and contributes to Joanne's decision to attend a university in her home city.

While more working-class students are entering university than in the past, they attend different universities to [sic] the middle classes. The old elite universities are overwhelmingly white and middle class (Reay, 2008). Rosie and Joanne both need to ensure their choice of university is low risk for 'different' sexualities (similar to ethnic minority students choosing universities where they felt safe (Reay et al., 2001) but they draw upon different class expectations and resources to achieve a safe university education. The data from the LGBT young people in my studies suggest all students have the disadvantage of negotiating their sexual and gendered identities but class resources mediated the degree to which post-compulsory schooling trajectories were likely to be disrupted and opportunities restricted.

CONCLUSION

Drawing on two qualitative studies, I have focused on young LGBT people's education as an example of the complex and 'hidden' ways class privilege and disadvantage may conflate or compound sexual or gender inequalities and difficulties. I have argued that the middle-class young LGBT people had the 'right' capitals, and a habitus with a "self assured relation to the world" (Bourdieu, 1984: 54) despite the uncertainties regarding their sexual or gender identity. As a consequence, their post-compulsory schooling choices and opportunities were less likely to be curtailed. Research has demonstrated the considerable effort required by working-class students to reach higher education (Henderson et al., 2007; Reay et al., 2001). The LGBT students from less affluent backgrounds had fewer of the legitimated capitals and a more tenuous and apprehensive investment in education, the extra pressure of a transforming heterosexual and classed habitus often disrupted their choices and narrowed their opportunities.

Evidence from these young LGBT people's educational experiences indicates we need to take seriously the inequalities and injustices arising from the intersection of class and sexuality. The marginalization of social class from sexualities research raises epistemological questions about whose experiences are being used to generalize understandings of sexual and intimate life. Theoretically, there is much more work to be done in developing ways to frame empirical studies of the intersection of sexuality and social class. I have suggested that combining Bourdieu's concepts with aspects of queer theory may overcome the material/cultural binary, which has proven problematic to the development of intersectional studies of class and sexuality. This theoretical framework is by no means ideal, but I have found it has enabled an analysis of the interconnection between the positionings of class and sexuality which goes beyond binaries such as structure/agency, recognition/redistribution and culture/material. It provides a framework where it is possible to keep multiple social identities, experiences and categories (class and sexuality) 'in the body.' Crucially, it has helped to unveil the concealed and complex processes involved in the production and re-production of inequality and disadvantage at the intersection of sexuality and class, which operate at an individual, subjective, embodied, structural and material level.

Young LGBT people's educational trajectories are one of the key mechanisms for securing the social, cultural and economic resources that are necessary for negotiating and claiming, within the new liberal framework, equal lives. If we are to ensure the transformations of sexual and intimate life for all, we must work to understand the ways in which class and sexuality interact to position *some* unequally and unjustly. Otherwise, the danger is that the world will only be 'won' by the socially privileged.

REFERENCES

Adkins L and Skeggs B (eds) (2004) *Feminism After Bourdieu*. Oxford: Blackwell.

Binnie J (1995) Trading places: Consumption, sexuality and the production of queer space. In: Bell D and Valentine G (eds) *Mapping Desire*. London: Routledge, 182–199.

Bondi L (1998) Gender, class and urban spaces: Public and private space in contemporary urban landscapes. *Urban Geography* 19(2): 160–185.

Bourdieu P (1984) *Distinction*. London: Routledge and Kegan Paul.

Bourdieu P (1990) *In Other Words: Essays Towards a Reflexive Sociology*. Cambridge: Polity Press.

Bourdieu P (1991) *Language and Symbolic Power*. Cambridge: Polity Press.

Bourdieu P and Wacquant LJD (1992) *An Invitation to Reflexive Sociology*. Cambridge: Polity Press.

Butler J (1990) *Gender Trouble: Feminism and the Subversion of Identity*. New York: Routledge.

Clark TN and Lipset SM (1991) Are social classes dying? *International Sociology* 6(4): 397–410.

Clarke D (1991) Commodity lesbianism. *Camera Obscura* 25/26: 181–201.

Crompton R (1998) *Class and Stratification: An Introduction to Current Debates*. Cambridge: Polity Press.

Devine F (1997) *Social Class in America and Britain*. Edinburgh: Edinburgh University Press.

Edwards T (1998) Queer fears against the cultural turn. *Sexualities* 1(4): 471–484.

EHRC (2007) Equality and Human Right Commission. URL (retrieved 4 July 2009): http://www .equalityhumanrights.com.

Epstein D, O'Flynn S and Telford D (2003) *Silenced Sexualities in Schools and Universities*. Stoke on Trent: Trentham.

Finch L (1993) *The Classing Gaze: Sexuality, Class and Surveillance*. London: Allen & Unwin.

Fraser M (1999) Classing queer. *Theory, Culture and Society* 16(2): 107–131.

Gluckman A and Reed B (eds) (1997) *Homoeconomics: Capitalism, Community and Lesbian and Gay Life*. London: Routledge.

Gorz A (1982) *Farewell to the Working Class*. London: Pluto, trans. Michael Sonenscher.

Henderson S, Holland J, McGrellis S, Sharpe S and Thomson R (2007) *Inventing Adulthoods: A Biographical Approach to Youth Transitions*. London: SAGE.

Hennessy R (1995) Queer visibility in commodity culture. In: Nicholson L and Seidman S (eds) *Social Postmodernism*. Cambridge: Cambridge University Press, 142–183.

Hennessy R (2000) *Profit and Pleasure: Sexual Identities in Late Capitalism*. London: Routledge.

Hennessy R (2006) The value of a second skin. In: Richardson D, McLaughlin J and Casey ME (eds)

Intersections Between Feminist and Queer Theory. Basingstoke: Palgrave Macmillan, 116–135.

Jackson S (1999) Feminist sociology and sociological feminism: Recovering the social in feminist thought. *Sociological Research Online* 4(3). URL (retrieved 3 November 2010): http://www.socresonline.org.uk/4/3/jackson.html.

Jackson S (2006) Gender, sexuality and heterosexuality: The complexity (and limits) of heteronormativity. *Feminist Theory* 7(1): 105–121.

Johnson P (2008) Rude boys: The homosexual eroticization of class. *Sociology* 42(1): 65–82.

Lawler S (2000) *Mothering the Self.* London: Routledge.

Lawler S (2004) Rules of engagement: Habitus, power and resistance. In: Adkins L and Skeggs B (eds) *Feminism after Bourdieu.* Oxford: Blackwell, 110–128.

Luttrell W (1997) *SchoolSmart and Motherwise: Working Class Women's Identity and Schooling.* London: Routledge.

Mac an Ghaill M (1994) *The Making of Men: Masculinities, Sexualities and Schooling.* Buckingham: Open University Press.

Mason J (1996) *Qualitative Researching.* London: SAGE.

McDermott E (2003) *Hidden Injuries, Happy Lives: The Influence of Lesbian Identity and Social Class on Wellbeing.* Lancaster University, Unpublished PhD thesis.

McDermott E (2004) Telling lesbian stories: Interviewing and the class dynamics of talk. *Women's Studies International Forum* 27(3): 177–187.

McDermott E (2006) Surviving in dangerous places: Lesbian identity performances in the workplace, social class and psychological health. *Feminism and Psychology* 16(2): 193–211.

McDermott E (2010) 'I wanted to be totally true to myself': Class, reflexivity and the making of the sexual self. In: Taylor Y (ed.) *Classed Intersections: Spaces, Selves, Knowledges.* Aldermaston: Ashgate, 199–216.

McDermott E, Roen K and Scourfield J (2008) Avoiding shame: Young LGBT people, homophobia and self-destructive behaviours. *Culture, Health & Sexuality* 10(8): 815–829.

McLaughlin J (2006) The return of the material: Cycles of theoretical fashion in Lesbian, Gay and Queer studies. In: Richardson D, McLaughlin J and Casey ME (eds) *Intersections Between Feminist and Queer Theory.* Basinstoke: Palgrave Macmillan, 59–77.

McNay L (1992) *Foucault and Feminism.* Cambridge: Polity.

McNay L (1999) Gender, habitus and the field: Pierre Bourdieu and the limits of reflexivity. *Theory, Culture and Society* 16(1): 95–117.

Nayak A and Kehily MJ (2008) *Gender, Youth and Culture: Young Masculinities and Femininities.* Basingstoke: Palgrave Macmillan.

Plummer K (1995) *Telling Sexual Stories.* London: Routledge.

Plummer K (2008) Studying sexualities for a better world? Ten years of *Sexualities. Sexualities* 11(1–2): 7–22.

Reay D (1998) *Class Work.* London: UCL Press.

Reay D (2008) Class out of place: The white middle classes and intersectionalities of class and 'race' in urban state schooling in England. In: Weis L (ed.) *The Way Class Works: Readings on School, Family, and the Economy.* New York: Routledge, 87–99.

Reay D, Davies J, David M and Ball S (2001) Choices of degree or degrees of choice? Class, race and the higher education choice process. *Sociology* 35(4): 855–874.

Richardson D (2000) *Rethinking Sexuality.* London: SAGE.

Savage M (2000) *Class Analysis and Social Transformation.* Buckingham: Open University Press.

Skeggs B (1997) *Formations of Class and Gender.* London: SAGE.

Skeggs B (2004a) *Class, Self, Culture.* London: Routledge.

Skeggs B (2004b) Context and background: Pierre Bourdieu's analysis of class, gender and sexuality. In: Adkins L and Skeggs B (eds) *Feminism After Bourdieu.* Oxford: Blackwell, 19–34.

Taylor Y (2006) Intersections of class and sexuality in the classroom. *Gender and Education* 18(4): 447–452.

Taylor Y (2007) *Working-Class Lesbian Life: Classed Outsiders.* Basingstoke: Palgrave Macmillan.

Taylor Y (2009) Complexities and complications: Intersections of class and sexuality. *Journal of Lesbian Studies* 13(2): 189–203.

Walkerdine V and Lucey H (1989) *Democracy in the Kitchen: Regulating Mothers and Socialising Daughters.* London: Virago.

Weeks J (2007) *The World We Have Won.* London: Routledge.

Weeks J, Heaphy B and Donovan C (2001) *Same Sex Intimacies: Families of Choice and Other Life Experiments.* London: Routledge.

Weston K (1991) *Families We Choose: Lesbians, Gays and Kinship.* New York: Columbia University Press.

15 • *Eli Clare*

NAMING AND LOSING HOME

DISCUSSION QUESTIONS

1. Identify the many systems of oppression Clare lives in/between.
2. What relationships between anonymity and safety, isolation and violence, and home and community are examined in this chapter?
3. Why is the loss of "home" and the experience of "exile" about class? How does the "upward scramble" relate to this loss and exile?
4. Why and how is "queer identity" and "queer culture" an urban—not rural—specificity and possibility?

NAMING

Handicapped

A disabled person sits on the street, begging for her next meal. This is how we survived in Europe and the United States as cities grew big and the economy moved from a land base to an industrial base. We were beggars, caps in hand. This is how some of us still survive. Seattle, 1989: a white man sits on the sidewalk, leaning against an iron fence. He smells of whiskey and urine, his body wrapped in torn cloth. His legs are toothpick-thin, knees bent inward. Beside him leans a set of crutches. A Styrofoam cup, half full of coins, sits on the sidewalk in front of him. Puget Sound stretches out behind him, water sparkling in the sun. Tourists bustle by. He strains his head up, trying to catch their eyes. Cap in hand. *Handicapped.*[1]

Disabled

The car stalled in the left lane of traffic is disabled. Or alternatively, the broad stairs curving into a public building disable the man in a wheelchair. That word used as a noun (the *disabled* or people with *disabilities*), an adjective (*disabled* people), a verb (the accident *disabled* her): in all its forms it means "unable," but where does our inability lie? Are our bodies like stalled cars? Or does disability live in the social and physical environment, in the stairs that have no accompanying ramp? I think about language. I often call nondisabled people able-bodied, or, when I'm feeling confrontational, *temporarily* able-bodied. But if I call myself disabled in order to describe how the ableist world treats me as a person with cerebral palsy, then shouldn't I call nondisabled people *enabled*? That word locates the condition of being nondisabled, not in the nondisabled body, but in the world's reaction to that body. This is not a semantic game.

Cripple

The woman who walks with a limp, the kid who uses braces, the man with gnarly hands hear the word *cripple* every day in a hostile nondisabled world.

At the same time, we in the disability rights movement create crip culture, tell crip jokes, identify a sensibility we call crip humor. Nancy Mairs writes:

> I am a cripple. I choose this word to name me.... People—crippled or not—wince at the word *cripple*, as they do not at *handicapped* or *disabled*. Perhaps I want them to wince. I want them to see me as a tough customer, one to whom the fates/gods/viruses have not been kind, but who can face the brutal truth of her existence squarely. As a cripple, I swagger.[2]

Gimp

Slang meaning "to limp." *Gimp* comes from the word *gammy*, which hobos in the 18th century used among themselves to describe dangerous or unwelcoming places. Hobo to hobo, passing on the road: "Don't go there. It's gammy." Insider language, hobo solidarity. And now a few centuries later, one disabled person greets another, "Hey, gimp. How ya doin?" Insider language, gimp solidarity.

Retard

I learned early that words can bruise a body. I have been called *retard* too many times, that word sliding off the tongues of doctors, classmates, neighbors, teachers, well-meaning strangers on the street. In the years before my speech became understandable, I was universally assumed to be "mentally retarded." When I started school, the teachers wanted me in the "special education" program. My parents insisted I be given yet another set of diagnostic tests, including an IQ test, and I—being a white kid who lived in a house full of books, ideas, and grammar-school English, being a disabled kid who had finally learned how to talk—scored well. They let me join the "regular" first grade. I worked overtime to prove those test results right. Still I was *retard, monkey, defect* on the playground, in the streets, those words hurled at my body, accompanied by rocks and rubber erasers. Even at home, I heard their echoes. My father told me more than once to stop walking like a *monkey*. My mother often talked about my birth *defect*. Words

bruise a body more easily than rocks and rubber erasers.

Differently Abled, Physically Challenged

Nondisabled people, wanting to cushion us from the cruelty of language, invented these euphemisms. In explaining her choice of the word *cripple*, Nancy Mairs writes:

> *Differently abled*...partakes of the same semantic hopefulness that transformed countries from *undeveloped* to *underdeveloped*, then to *less developed*, and finally *developing* nations. People have continued to starve in those countries during the shift. Some realities do not obey the dictates of language.[3]

Differently abled is simply easier to say, easier to think about than *disabled* or *handicapped* or *crippled*.

Freak

I hold fast to my dictionary, but the definitions slip and slide, tell half stories. I have to stop here. *Freak* forces me to think about naming.

Handicapped, Disabled, Cripple, Gimp, Retard, Differently Abled

I understand my relationship to each of these words. I scoff at *handicapped*, a word I grew up believing my parents had invented specifically to describe me, my parents who were deeply ashamed of my cerebral palsy and desperately wanted to find a cure. I use the word *disabled* as an adjective to name what this ableist world does to us crips and gimps. *Cripple* makes me flinch; it too often accompanied the sticks and stones on my grade school playground, but I love crip humor, the audacity of turning *cripple* into a word of pride. *Gimp* sings a friendly song, full of irony and understanding. *Retard* on the other hand draws blood every time, a sharp, sharp knife. In the world as it should be, maybe disabled people would be *differently abled*: a world where Braille and audiorecorded editions of books and magazines were a matter of course, and hearing people signed ASL; a world where schools were fully integrated, health care, free and unrationed; a world where universal access meant exactly that; a world where disabled people were not locked up at home or in nursing homes, relegated to sheltered employment and paid sweatshop wages. But, in the world as it is, *differently abled, physically challenged* tell a wishful lie.

Handicapped, Disabled, Cripple, Gimp, Retard, Differently Abled, Freak

I need to stop here. *Freak* I don't understand. It unsettles me. I don't quite like it, can't imagine using it as some politicized disabled people do. Yet I want *freak* to be as easy as the words *queer* and *cripple*.

Queer, like *cripple*, is an ironic and serious word I use to describe myself and others in my communities. *Queer* speaks volumes about who I am, my life as a dyke, my relationship to the dominant culture. Because of when I came out—more than a decade after the Stonewall Rebellion—and where—into a highly politicized urban dyke community—*queer* has always been easy for me. I adore its defiant external edge, its comfortable internal truth. *Queer* belongs to me. So does *cripple* for many of the same reasons. *Queer* and *cripple* are cousins: words to shock, words to infuse with pride and self-love, words to resist internalized hatred, words to help forge a politics. They have been gladly chosen—*queer* by many gay/lesbian/bi/trans people, *cripple*, or *crip*, by many disabled people.

Freak is another story. Unlike *queer* and *crip*, it has not been widely embraced in my communities.[4] For me *freak* has a hurtful, scary edge; it takes *queer* and *cripple* one step too far; it doesn't feel good or liberating.

This profusion of words and their various relationships to marginalized people and politicized communities fascinates me. Which words get embraced, which don't, and why? *Queer* but not *pervert. Cripple*, and sometimes *freak*, but not *retard*. Like most of the ugly and demeaning words used to batter and bait marginalized peoples—racist, sexist, classist, ableist, homophobic slurs—*pervert* and *retard* nearly burst with hurt and bitterness, anger and

reminders of self-hatred.[5] I doubt the l/g/b/t community and the disability community respectively will ever claim those words as our own. In contrast *crip, queer,* and *freak* have come to sit on a cusp. For some of us, they carry too much grief. For others, they can be chosen with glee and pride. *Queer* and *crip* are mine but not *freak*, and I want to know why. What is it about that word? What bitterness, what pain, does it hold that *cripple*, with its connotations of pitiful, broken bodies, and *queer*, with its sweeping definitions of normality and abnormality, do not? . . .

LOSING HOME

I must find the words to speak of losing home. Then I never want to utter them again. They throb like an abscessed tooth, simply hurt too much. *Homesick* is a platitude. I need to grab at seemingly unrelated words. *Queer. Exile. Class.* I reach for my red and gold *American Heritage Dictionary* but restrain myself. I know the definitions. I need to enter the maze created by dyke identity, class location, and rural roots.

Let me start with *queer*, the easiest point of entry. In its largest sense, queer has always been where I belong. A girl child not convinced of her girlness. A backwoods hick in the city. A dyke in a straight world. A gimp in an ableist world. The eldest child of a poor father and a working-class mother, both teachers who tried to pull themselves up by their own bootstraps, using luck and white-skin privilege.

In its narrower sense, queer has been home since I became conscious of being a dyke. At age 17, I left the backwoods of Oregon with a high school diploma and a scholarship to college, grateful not to have a baby or a husband. A year later, after months of soul-searching, I finally realized that I was a dyke and had been for years. Since then, I have lived among dykes and created chosen families and homes, not rooted in geography, but in shared passion, imagination, and values. Our collective dyke household in Oakland with its vegetable garden in the front yard and chicken coop in the back. The women's circle on the Great Peace March from Los Angeles to Washington, D.C. The Women's Encampment for a Future of Peace and Justice in upstate New York. Queer potlucks in Ann Arbor, where I now live. Whether I've been walking across the country for peace or just hanging out listening to lesbian gossip, learning to cook tofu, or using red-handled bolt cutters to cut fence at the Army Depot, being a dyke in dyke community is as close as I've ever felt to belonging. And still I feel queer.

Exile

If *queer* is the easiest, then *exile* is the hardest. I lie when I write that home is being a dyke in dyke community. Rather, home is particular wild and ragged beaches, specific kinds of trees and berry brambles, the exact meander of the river I grew up near, the familiar sounds and sights of a dying logging and fishing town. Exile is the hardest because I have irrevocably lost that place as actual home....

...Let me take you to my maternal grandfather's funeral. At the service I sat with family, my sister to the right, my great aunt Esther to the left, my aunt Margaret in front of us, her lover of many years to her right. Barb is an African-American dyke, unmistakable whether or not she's in heels and a skirt. I am quite sure my aunt has never introduced Barb to Uncle John or Aunt Esther, Uncle Henry or Aunt Lillian as her partner, lover, or girlfriend. Yet Barb is unquestionably family, sitting with my grandfather's immediate relatives near the coffin, openly comforting my aunt. My grandfather was a mechanic in Detroit; his surviving brothers and sisters are Lutheran corn farmers from southern Illinois. Most of them never graduated from high school, still speak German at home, and have voted Republican all their lives. From the perspective of many middle- and upper-class urban folks, they are simple rednecks, clods, hillbillies. Working-class writer and activist Elliott maps out three definitions of the word *redneck*. Its denotation: "A member of the white rural laboring class...."[6] Its connotation: "A person who advocates a provincial, conservative, often bigoted sociopolitical attitude characteristic of a redneck...."[7] And lastly its usage by progressives, including many queers: "1. Any person who is racist,

violent, uneducated and stupid (as if they are the same thing), woman-hating, gay-bashing, Christian fundamentalist, etc. 2. Used as a synonym for every type of oppressive belief except classism."[8] Many urban queer folks would take one look at my great aunts and uncles and cast them as over-the-top rednecks and homophobes.

Yet in this extended working-class family, unspoken lesbianism balanced against tacit acceptance means that Barb is family, that Aunt Margaret and she are treated as a couple, and that the overt racism Barb would otherwise experience from these people is muffled. Not ideal, but better than frigid denial, better than polite manners and backhanded snubs, better than middle-class "don't ask, don't tell," which would carefully place Barb into the category marked "friend" and have her sit many pews away from immediate family at her lover's father's funeral.

At the same time, it is a balance easily broken. In Port Orford I would never walk down Main Street holding hands with a woman lover. That simple act would be too much. It is also a balance most readily achieved among family or folks who have known each other for decades. If I moved back and lived down the road from a dyke—closeted or not—who hadn't grown up in Port Orford, whose biological family didn't live in town, who was an "outsider," I would worry about her safety.

It isn't that outside the bounds of this fragile balance these rural white people are any more homophobic than the average urban person. Rather the difference lies in urban anonymity. In Ann Arbor if a group of frat boys yells, "Hey, lezzie!" at me or the man sitting next to me on the bus whispers "queer" and spits at me, I'll defend myself in whatever ways necessary, knowing chances are good that I'll never see these men again, or if I do, they won't remember me. On the other hand, in Port Orford if someone harassed me—the balance somehow broken, some invisible line overstepped, drunken bravado overcoming tacit acceptance—I would know him, maybe work with his wife at the cannery, see his kids playing up the river at Butler Bar, encounter him often enough in the grocery store and post office. He would likewise know where I lived, with whom I lived, what car I drove, and where I worked. This lack of anonymity is a simple fact of rural life, one that I often miss in the city, but in the face of bigotry and violence, anonymity provides a certain level of protection.

If I moved back to Port Orford, the daily realities of isolation would compete with my concerns about safety. Living across the street from the chainsaw shop, I would have to drive an hour to spend an evening at a dyke potluck, three hours to hang out at a women's bookstore or see the latest queer movie, seven hours to go to a *g/l/b/t* pride march. I don't believe I could live easily and happily that isolated from queer community, nor could I live comfortably while always monitoring the balance, measuring the invisible lines that define safety. My loss of home is about being queer.

Let me return now to *exile*. It is a big word, a hard word. It implies not only loss, but a sense of allegiance and connection—however ambivalent—to the place left behind, an attitude of mourning rather than of good riddance. It also carries with it the sense of being pushed out, compelled to leave. Yes, my loss of home is about being queer, but is it *exile?* To answer that, I need to say another thing about anonymity, isolation, and safety, a messier thing.

Throughout my childhood and young adulthood, my father, along with a number of other adults, severely sexually and physically abused me, tying me up, using fire and knives and brute force on my body. My father, who taught for 30 years at the local high school. My father, whom everyone in town knew and respected, even if they thought he was quirky, odd, prone to forgetfulness and unpredictable anger. He no longer lives there, although some of the other adults who abused me still do. In the years since leaving Port Orford, I have been able to shake my perpetrators' power away from me, spending long periods of time uncovering the memories and working through persistent body-deep terror, grief, and confusion. I've done this work in community, supported by many friends, a few good professionals, and a political framework that places the violence I experienced into a larger context. For much of that time, I could not have returned to Port Orford and been physically safe. I lived a kind of exile, knowing

I needed the anonymity of a small city halfway across the country to protect me, a city where no one knew my father, where not a single person had participated either tangentially or centrally in my abuse. Today my safety depends less on anonymity and more on an internal set of resources. Even so, I don't know how I would deal, if I moved back, with seeing a small handful of my perpetrators on a regular basis, being known as Bob's kid everywhere I went. Simply put, my desire for community, for physical safety, for emotional well-being and psychological comfort compelled me to leave. Being a queer is one piece of this loss, this exile; abuse is another.

And class is a third. If *queer* is the easiest and *exile* the hardest, then *class* is the most confusing. The economics in Port Orford are simple: jobs are scarce. The life of a Pacific Northwest fishing and logging town depends on the existence of salmon and trees. When the summer salmon runs dwindle and all the old growth trees are cut, jobs vanish into thin air. It is rumored that fishermen now pay their boat mortgages by running drugs—ferrying marijuana, crack, and cocaine from the freighters many miles out at sea back to the cannery where they are then picked up and driven inland. Loggers pay their bills by brush cutting—gathering various kinds of ferns to sell by the pound to florists—and collecting welfare. What remains is the meager four-month-a-year tourist season and a handful of minimum-wage jobs—pumping gas, cashiering, flipping burgers. The lucky few work for the public school district or own land on which they run milk cows and sheep. In short, if I moved back, I probably wouldn't find work. Not only are jobs scarce, but my CP makes job-hunting even harder. Some jobs, like cashiering or flipping burgers, I simply can't do; I don't have enough manual dexterity. Other jobs, like clerical work that requires a lot of typing, I can do but more slowly than many people. Still other jobs I can do well, but potential employers are reluctant to hire me, confusing disability with inability. And if, miraculously, I did find work, the paycheck probably wouldn't stretch around food, gas, and rent.

To leap from economic realities to class issues in Port Orford holds no challenge. The people who live in dying rural towns and work minimum- or sub-minimum-wage jobs—not temporarily but day after day for their whole working lives—are working-class and poor people. There are some middle-class people who live in Port Orford: the back-to-the-land artists who grow marijuana for money (or did until the federal crackdown more than a decade ago), the young teachers whose first jobs out of college bring them to Pacific High School, the retirees who have settled near Port Orford, lured to Oregon by cheap land. But these people don't stay long. The artists bum out. The young teachers find better jobs in other, more prosperous towns. The retirees grow older and find they need more services than are available in Curry County. The people who stay are poor and working-class. I left because I didn't want to marry and couldn't cashier at Sentry's Market. I left because I hoped to have money above and beyond the dollars spent on rent and food to buy books and music. I left because I didn't want to be poor and feared I would be if I stayed. I will never move back for the same reasons. My loss of home, my exile, is about class.

Leaving is a complicated thing. I left with a high school diploma and a scholarship to college, grateful to be leaving, but this is only half the truth. The other half is that everyone around me—my parents, teachers, classmates and friends, the women who cashiered at Sentry's Market, the men who drove logging trucks—assumed I would leave, go to college, and become "successful." No one expected me to marry a week after graduation and move up the road from my parents, to die in a drunk-driving car accident or a high-speed game of chase down Highway 101, to have a baby and drop out of school at 15. A high school diploma and a college scholarship were givens in my life.

This is all about class location, which is where class gets confusing. In Port Orford, my family and I were relatively well off: we always had enough to eat; my father was securely employed at the high school; my mother bragged that she had the only Ph.D. in town. We eventually built a big house of our own. Books filled my childhood. We borrowed them by the arm-load from the public library; we bought them by mail-order from book clubs; we cherished trips to the one bookstore in Coos Bay, a town of 10,000 an hour's drive away. We always had health care. I grew up among people for whom none of these things were givens. On the other hand, we wore hand-me-downs and home-made clothes, for years rented tiny two-bedroom houses, owned one beat-up car, and balanced dental bills against new school shoes. I didn't know that in a middle-class town or neighborhood these things would have marked my family and me as something other than well-off.

Who left and who stayed measured in pan the class differences at Pacific High School. My best friend from sixth to twelfth grade was poor. She and I spent high school together in college-prep classes, poring over pre-calculus problems and biology experiments. We both wanted to go to college, to leave rural Oregon, and yet in our senior year as I filled out college applications, Judy made plans to marry her boyfriend of four years. I know now that her decision arose out of financial desperation—her father had just died, and her family was falling deeper into poverty—but at the time, I thought Judy was copping out. I walked away, glad to be leaving Port Orford behind me. Or so I thought.

Only later did I understand what I lost by leaving. Loss of a daily sustaining connection to a landscape that I still carry with me as home. Loss of a rural, white, working-class culture that values neighbors rather than anonymity, that is both tremendously bigoted—particularly racist—and accepting of local eccentricity, that believes in self-sufficiency and depends on family—big extended families not necessarily created in the mold of the Christian right. Loss of a certain pace of life, a certain easy trust. I didn't know when I left at 17 that I would miss the old cars rusting in every third front yard. Miss the friendly chatting in the grocery store, the bank, the post office. Miss being able to hitchhike home, safe because I knew everyone driving by....

My siblings and I inherited this halfway successful scramble. Our grandparents and great uncles and aunts were farmers, gravediggers, janitors, mechanics; our parents, teachers; and we were to be professors, lawyers, or doctors. As I try to sort the complexity out, I have to ask, does this upward scramble really work: this endless leaving of home, of deeply embodied culture and community, in search of a mirage called the "American Dream"? Instead of professor, lawyer, or doctor, my brother is a high school teacher, my sister, a low-level administrator, and I, a bookkeeper. Did my parents become middle class in their scramble? Did my siblings and I?

The answers are not that important except for the betrayal that can creep up behind us, make home under our skins. If we leave, never come back, somehow finding ourselves in the middle class, will we forget—or worse, start mocking—the men who can't read, the women who can make a bag of potatoes and five pounds of Velveeta last nearly forever? Will we train the accents out of our voices so far that we'll wake up one day and not recognize ourselves? And what about the people we leave behind? The last time I saw Judy, her two sons playing hide-and-go-seek nearby, we could find nothing to say to each other, that woman who had been my best—and sometimes only—friend for so many years. How do we deal with the loss? For decades my mother missed living in a big, industrial, working-class city; my father would drive every day to the ocean just to see a long, flat horizon like the one he left behind in North Dakota. My brother has returned to rural Oregon, my sister dreams of leaving Seattle for some small town in the North Cascades, and I entertain fantasies of a rural queer community. Is the upward scramble worth the loss? This question leads me back to being queer, to another, similar question: is queer identity worth the loss?

Queer identity, at least as I know it, is largely urban. The happening places, events, dialogues, the strong communities, the journals, magazines, bookstores, queer organizing, and queer activism are all city-based. Of course rural lesbian, gay, bi, and trans communities exist, but the people and institutions defining queer identity and culture are urban.

For me, coming into my queer identity and untangling my class location have both been rooted in urban life. In moving to an urban, private, liberal arts college, I found what I needed to come out as a dyke: the anonymity of a city, the support of lesbian-feminist

activists, and access to queer culture. In that same move, I also found myself living among middle-class people for the first time. Because in Port Orford my family had always defined itself as middle-class—and in truth we were well-educated people who lived somewhere between the working-class loggers and the middle-class retirees—I believed the class differences I felt in my bones amounted to my being a country bumpkin. I assumed my lack of familiarity with trust funds, new cars, designer clothes, trips to Paris, and credit cards was the same as my lack of familiarity with city buses, skyscrapers, one-way streets, stop lights, and house keys.

Even now after a decade of urban living, the two are hard to separate. I am remembering the first time I went to OutWrite, a national queer writer's conference. From the moment I walked into the posh Boston hotel where the conference was being held, I gawked, staring unbelievingly at the chandeliers, shiny gold railings, ornate doors, in the same way I used to gawk at twenty-story buildings. Saturday night before the big dance party, to which I couldn't afford to go, I had dinner with an acquaintance and a group of her friends, all white, lesbian writers from New York City. We ate at the hotel restaurant, where I spent too much money on not enough food, served by brown-skinned men who were courteous in spite of our ever-changing party and ever-changing food orders. Jo and her friends were all going to the party after dinner and were dressed accordingly, in black plastic mini-skirts and diamond earrings, three-piece suits and gold cufflinks, hair carefully molded and shaved in all the right places. In my blue jeans and faded chamois shirt, I felt conspicuous and embarrassed.

At some point the conversation turned to gossip about queer writers not at the conference. Cathy, an editor for a well-known lesbian press, started in on one of "her" writers, a novelist from rural Oregon. Having heard me talk earlier about growing up there, Cathy turned to me and asked, "When Laura asks me to send stuff to her P.O. box because during the winter rains the mail carrier might not be able to navigate the dirt road to her mailbox, is she serious?" I wanted to laugh, to have some clever retort to slide off my tongue. Instead, I politely explained about dirt roads and months of rain. What this New York femme didn't know about rural living didn't offend me; rather it was the complete urban bias of the evening that did. Was I uncomfortable, feeling conspicuous and embarrassed, because of class or because of urban/rural differences? I can't separate the two....

Just how urban is the most visible of queer identities, how middle class, how consumer-oriented? I am remembering Stonewall 25, media shorthand for New York City's celebration of the 25th anniversary of the Stonewall Rebellion. If one were to believe the mainstream media and much of the queer media, it was a defining event of queer identity in the '90s. I didn't go. I can't tolerate New York City: its noise, crowds, grime, heat, concrete, and traffic. I inherited my father's rural fear of cities as big and tall as New York. I've gone to queer pride marches for the last 15 years, but Stonewall 25 was different, a commercial extravaganza of huge proportions. From the reports I heard, the tickets for many of the events cost outrageous amounts of money. Who could afford the benefit dance at $150, the concert at $50, the t-shirt at $25? I know that at the 1993 March on Washington trinkets and souvenirs flourished. Not only could one buy 14 different kinds of t-shirts but also coffee mugs, plastic flags, freedom rings, and posters. I can only assume this proliferation was even more astonishing at Stonewall 25. And sliding-scale prices? They're evidently a thing of the past. Stonewall 25 strikes me not so much as a celebration of a powerful and life-changing uprising of queer people, led by transgendered people of color, by drag queens and butch dykes, fed up with the cops, but as a middle- and upper-class urban party that opened its doors only to those who could afford it.

Why does the money that creates Stonewall 25 and events like it rarely find its way to working-class and poor queers? Why does the money stay urban? What about AIDS prevention programs, l/g/b/t youth services, hate-crime monitoring, queer theater in the mountains of rural Oregon, the cornfields of rural Nebraska, the lowlands of rural South Carolina? Have we collectively turned our backs on the small towns in Oregon that one by one are passing local anti-gay ordinances? Are we in effect abandoning

them to the Oregon Citizens Alliance, the Christian right coalition which spearheaded the outrageously homophobic Proposition 9 in 1992 and which, after losing that vote, has directed its attention toward local initiatives? Will we remember and support Brenda and Wanda Hansen of Camp Sister Spirit, white, rural, working-class lesbians who are building and maintaining lesbian and feminist space in rural Mississippi, when the homophobic violence they face—dead dogs in their mailbox, gunfire at night—no longer makes the headlines?...

My leaving gave me a dyke community but didn't change my class location. Before I left, I was a rural, mixed-class, queer child in a straight, rural, working-class town. Afterwards, I was an urban-transplanted, mixed-class, dyke activist in an urban, mostly middle-class, queer community. Occasionally I simply feel as if I've traded one displacement for another and lost home to boot. Most of the time, however, I know that living openly in relative safety as a queer among queers; living thousands of miles away from the people who raped and tortured me as a child; living in a place where finding work is possible; living with easy access to books and music, movies, and concerts, when I can afford them—this is lifeblood for me. But I hate the cost, hate the kind of exile I feel....

...My displacement, my exile, is twined with problems highlighted in the intersection of queer identity, working-class and poor identity, and rural identity, problems that demand not a personal retreat, but long-lasting, systemic changes. The exclusivity of queer community shaped by urban, middle-class assumptions. Economic injustice in the backwoods. The abandonment of rural working-class culture. The pairing of rural people with conservative, oppressive values. The forced choice between rural roots and urban queer life. These problems are the connective tissue that brings the words *queer, class,* and *exile* together. Rather than a relocation back to the Oregon mountains, I want a redistribution of economic resources so that wherever we live—in the backwoods, the suburbs, or the city—there is enough to eat, warm, dry houses for everyone, true universal access to health care and education. I want queer activists to struggle against homophobic violence in rural areas with the same kind of tenacity and creativity we bring to the struggle in urban areas. I want rural queers, working-class queers, poor queers to be leaders in our communities, to shape the ways we will celebrate the 50th anniversary of Stonewall. I want each of us to be able to bring our queerness home.

NOTES

1. The word *handicap* means to compensate each participant in a contest differently in order to equalize the chances of winning and derives from a lottery game called "hand in cap," in which players held forfeits in a cap. In spite of this derivation, the word play "cap in hand" resonates ironically with the ways in which disabled people have survived as beggars.

2. Mairs, Nancy, *Plaintext* (Tucson: University of Arizona Press, 1986), p. 9.
3. Mairs, p. 10.
4. *Freak* actually is used by a number of marginalized peoples: hippies, drug users, and l/g/b/t people, as well as disabled people.
5. *Pervert* is sometimes used by queer people in leather and s/m communities who feel marginalized within the larger queer culture. The point here isn't that *pervert* and *retard* are never spoken with affection or pride but that they haven't been embraced and used to construct both individual and communal identities.
6. Elliott, "Whenever I Tell You the Language We Use Is a Class Issue, You Nod Your Head in Agreement—And Then You Open Your Mouth," in *Out of the Class Closet: Lesbians Speak*, Penelope, Julia, ed. (Freedom, California: The Crossing Press, 1994), p. 277.
7. Elliott, p. 278.
8. Elliott, p. 280.

16 • *Ahoo Tabatabai*

PROTECTING THE LESBIAN BORDER: THE TENSION BETWEEN INDIVIDUAL AND COMMUNAL AUTHENTICITY

DISCUSSION QUESTIONS

1. How do the concepts of "border" and "boundary" inform sexual identifications/labels among the women participants, as well as their community membership?
2. In what ways do the women participants resist being perceived as "not straight," and why is this important?
3. How does public space become an important site of identification and authentic membership for the women participants?

Ahoo Tabatabai, "Protecting the Lesbian Border: The Tension Between Individual and Communal Authenticity." *Sexualities* 13(5):563–581. Reprinted by permission of SAGE Publications, Inc.

The stories of lesbians who begin relationships with men inform us not only about the complex ways in which sexuality is lived but also about how individuals account for potential changes in their identities, how they navigate issues of belonging and the embodiment of desire, and how they connect identity and community. Their negotiations with notions of authenticity and belonging can inform how such matters are engaged in a variety of other scenarios. I begin here with the story of Jennifer, a woman who, after many years of living as a lesbian, became involved with a man.

Jennifer, a 39-years-old white professional, came out as a lesbian in her early 20s. She was politically active and involved in AIDS prevention work. She recalls that her parents were at first taken aback but then settled into acceptance of her identity, going as far as becoming active in Parents, Families, and Friends of Lesbians and Gays (PFLAG), a support organization for friends and family members of gay and lesbian individuals. In her late 20s, while on a trip away from home, Jennifer met Tom. It was a friend who pointed out that Jennifer might be attracted to Tom. "I was embarrassed," she says "that I hadn't noticed." Of the moment she noticed her attraction to Tom, Jennifer says she was "kind of horrified because that meant that everything was going to be different." At first, she tried to hide her involvement.

> I kept it a secret for a good while...[but once] it became clear that this is not going to go away, and he was not going to somehow miraculously become a woman, and that I had to really stop being closeted, I started telling people.

Jennifer eventually married Tom, something about which she still expresses mixed emotions. She explains feeling "absolutely horrible about it. . . . I often lie to people and say that we did not." She does not refer to Tom as her husband, preferring instead the term "partner." They have two children together. Today, Jennifer refrains from using the word lesbian to define herself.

> The label of lesbian was tremendously important. I identified as a radical lesbian, feminist and as a dyke

and all of those terms were absolutely empowering and my complete identity. They were powerful, powerful important words in my life and there's nothing that remotely compares to that now. And lesbian also still counts as that core of my identity, so it feels kinda dishonest also to identify as anything else. Those terms still feel like important terms for me, but I don't use those terms because I think it's politically very damaging for the lesbian community.

She continues.

> I absolutely feel like I have lost my, I can't think of how to say it, I think I lost my right to claim my identity and the terms that feel right for me for defining my identity.

For Jennifer, the change to a partner of a different gender brings about a change in identity, not an identity that she considers her "core," but the identity with which she publicly affiliates.

COMMUNITIES

Many authors have discussed the fact that sexual identities are socially constructed (Esterberg, 1997; Gagnon and Simon, 1973; Garber, 1995; Green, 2002; Kitzinger and Wilkinson, 1995; McIntosh, 1968; Plummer, 1995; Rust, 2000, 1993; Stein, 1993; Weeks, 1985). Identities have shifting meanings that are dependent on the social context in which they exist. But despite their shifting meanings, identities continue to inform notions of belonging and community. Identities serve as anchors to the self and as entry points into particular communities.

The definition of a lesbian community and what it means to belong to such a community is contested (Esterberg, 1997). But what remains true is that the lesbian community is a powerful concept in the lives of American lesbians (Esterberg, 1997; Inness, 1997; Rothblum, 2008). Kitzinger and Wilkinson (1995) show that for many women, being a part of the lesbian community is a significant part of living as a lesbian. Many stage models of gay and lesbian identity development put community integration as the final and most positive indicator of a healthy identity (Floyd and

Stein, 2002). As Shugar notes, lesbian communities are important sites of security, safety and political activism. Community is central to identity and in turn, identity is central to the "production, maintenance, and continuation of lesbian communities" (Shugar, 1999: 13). Heterosexual women, on the other hand, tend to not accord as much importance to a community based on sexual identity (Rothblum, 2008).

Although community has been a central tenet of the lesbian identity, the idea of membership in such communities is itself contested. Much of the debate about who belongs in the lesbian community and who does not has centered on bisexual women. Some have questioned whether bisexual women, because of their presumed attraction to and involvement with men, can be considered members of a lesbian community. Involvement with men has emerged as a central criterion for exclusion from lesbian communities (Jeffreys, 1999, 1994; MacKinnon, 1982; Walters, 1996).

Some lesbians do end up having sexual relationships with men on a short-term, or long-term basis. Other lesbians do not. The difference between lesbians and heterosexual women may be "one of degree rather than kind" (Diamond, 2005: 119), but previous research shows that the border between the two groups is heavily policed not only by group members but also scholars who study sexual communities.

The desire on the part of academics to organize lesbians into groups based on their involvement with men is an example of the way the boundary between "real" lesbian and others is maintained. Diamond (2005) classifies women who do not engage in relationships with men as "stable lesbians" and the women who do as "fluid lesbians." . . .

This boundary keeping is visible even in the very limited media representations of lesbians who are involved with men. An example includes the character of Tina on the Showtime mini-series *The L-Word*. Of course, it is not surprising that there would be a need to police the boundaries of a community that is stigmatized (Plummer, 1982). Nevertheless, this border, or boundary, although socially constructed, is very much real. There may be little difference between the experiences of lesbians who do and do not get involved with men. But this "border" is socially important.

Labels matter to people. They create communities (Esterberg, 1997; Green, 2002; Phelan, 1994).

This study examines how women who experience a change to a partner of a different gender, use categories of gender, sexual identity, and sexual orientation to make sense of this shift both to themselves and to others. In examining these categories, the study contributes to the area of research concerned with the way sexual identity categories, although socially constructed and at times fluid, are shaped and become powerful forces in shaping people's lives and their communities (Green, 2002; Esterberg, 1997; Phelan, 1994). More specifically, I examine the women's narratives of change in partners. Since narrative analysis gives prominence to human agency, it is well suited for studies of identity (Riessman, 1993). . . .

For lesbian women who have begun relationships with men, few scripts are readily available. There is no readily available way of being a lesbian who is now partnered with a man, partially because the women are no longer part of a "community of discourse" (Swidler, 2001) that gives them resources and allows them the opportunity to articulate identities. There are no stories readily available of lesbians dating men. The exception to this is a handful of Hollywood representations like the character of Tina on the Showtime miniseries *The L-Word*, the 1997 film *Chasing Amy*, and a brief mention in the 1994 film *Go Fish*.

When I tell people what my research is about, most venture the guess that women who were once partnered with women and are now with men think of themselves as bisexual. But this is not how the women thought of themselves; in fact, most emphatically rejected the label of bisexual. In other words, although the label of bisexual is one that many would associate with these women, and although bisexuality provides a ready-made alternative identity, the women in this study do not feel at home under the banner of bisexuality. It becomes clear that the women consider the common perceptions of bisexuality to be a hindrance to their ability to fully embrace the label. Among the stereotypes associated with bisexuality, one that is most difficult to surmount is that of non-monogamy. Bisexuals are assumed to be non-monogamous (Garber, 1995; Rust,

2000). The women themselves bring up this matter time and again. Non-monogamy implies a desire to or a propensity to be involved with more than one partner at one time. The combination of bisexuality and non-monogamy implies switching to partners of different genders, or going "back and forth" between the two genders. The trouble for the women in this study is that they wish to guard against this notion of "back and forth." They want to embody something more stable. In order not to be mistaken for someone who would go "back and forth," the women painstakingly express their commitment to their male partners. A legitimate claim to their identities, the women believe, is grounded in stability. They see themselves as authentic when they can also present their identity as stable. The label of bisexual does not offer them authenticity in this way because it lacks that element of stability. The women make attempts to uncouple stability and authenticity but nevertheless fall back on notions of stability to make their claim to authenticity. They claim to be the "same person" as they were when involved with women, and they claim to be attracted to the "same qualities" in men and in women. The label of bisexual is thus rejected. The notion of a stable self is maintained.

Interestingly, the identity of "straight" or heterosexual is one that is also actively rejected by the majority of women in the study, but for different reasons. Being straight implies a lot of things that the women do not wish to take part in, such as being traditionally feminine and sexually submissive. Being perceived as "not straight" is both a goal and an ongoing task. Despite their efforts, the women are often read as straight, or as they themselves indicate, they are not read as "anything at all." The women acknowledge that when they are assumed to be straight, in fact, it is because their sexuality goes under the radar, so to speak. And so, during any given interaction, the women have a choice to make. They can let assumptions stand, and not challenge the fact that they are perceived as straight. They do this on occasion. Or, they have to work not to appear straight. The desire not to appear straight requires a particular set of negotiations. It requires the women to make choices about disclosure and requires them to challenge,

sometimes verbally, unspoken assumptions. This proves to be difficult or nearly impossible at times.

. . . This research shows that there are limitations to what identity can be embraced. Self-identified lesbian women who begin relationships with men are not free to embrace any label that they feel reflects their identities, as Jennifer's story shows. Instead, in the process of settling on an identity after their involvement with men, these women not only negotiate what feels authentic to them, but also consider their obligations towards their previous lesbian communities, communities to which they no longer belong. The fluidity in the identities is balanced by their commitment to real communities.

When individuals move out of a community, as opposed to into one, the notion of authenticity is made more complex. In the case of a woman who once identified as lesbian and now is partnered with a man, there may be many different authenticities, in relation to families or in-laws, other lesbians, or ex-partners (Vannini, 2007). This does not imply that the notion of an authentic self is any less important than it was before. What is different in the case of the women in this study is that they have many sources of authentification (Gubrium and Holstein, 2009). The women show a concern for what might be considered localized authenticity or multiple authenticities.

INVESTMENT IN IDENTITY

According to Stein (1997), lesbians who get involved with men are dissatisfied with their lesbian identity and, by extension, with the lesbian community. In fact, according to Stein, the lesbians who do partner with men are different from those who do not. These women, ex-lesbians as Stein calls them, are motivated by a sense of pursuit for their real identity. They get involved with men and cease to be lesbians and thus settle into an identity that feels more authentic to them. No doubt this is true for some people, but recent research shows that women who relinquish lesbian and bisexual identities do not differ significantly from women who do not in terms of their sexual milestones of first same-sex attraction, conduct, questioning, and most importantly identifi-cation (Diamond, 2003; Peplau and Garnet, 2000; Rothblum, 2000; Rust, 2000).

For lesbians who become involved with men, no-tions of community and belonging are deeply tied into the process of self-identification. Esterberg (1997) finds that for lesbians who become involved with men, involvement in the lesbian community, which she translates into a political commitment to lesbian rights, can affect what identity is settled into after involvement with men. She examines the stories of two women who left relationships with women to begin relationships with men. One woman, Cheryl, chose to label herself bisexual after partnering with a man and the other, Sally, chose to maintain her les-bian label. Esterberg explains this difference in terms of involvement in a lesbian community. Involvement in the lesbian community made the lesbian identity more salient for Sally and so she felt more connected to the label of lesbian and sought to preserve it de-spite her marriage to a man. Cheryl, on the other hand, having been less politically involved, chose to re-label herself. According to Esterberg, the process of re-labeling was not straining for Cheryl because bisexuality was not a source of political identity and community belonging for her. . . .

Commitment and salience are partially conse-quences of relationships in which the individual is invested. If an identity is implicated in many com-mitments, if many relationships are based on it, the identity is more likely to be salient. A salient iden-tity is less likely to change. Thus, relationships have a role in maintaining identities. This would lead one to believe, as Esterberg has shown, that the women in this study would try any means necessary to keep their lesbian labels, especially if they, like Jennifer, are deeply involved in a lesbian community. How-ever, this is not what I found.

DATA COLLECTION AND METHOD

I collected data through semi-structured interviews with 32 women who had at some point in their lives self-identified as lesbian, bisexual or queer but who

were subsequently involved with men. This article concerns itself with the 14 women out of the initial 32 who specifically identified as lesbian prior to their involvement with men, as opposed to bisexual or queer. The women ranged in age from 20 to 43. At the time of the interview, four women had begun relationships with women once again. Of the 14 self-identified lesbian women, 9 women identified as white and/or Caucasian, 2 identified as African American, one identified as Iranian, one identified as Chinese and another identified as "other." The women all lived or had ties to the same mid-size Midwestern city in the USA. The group consisted of a mix of students and professionals. All women either had or were working toward a university degree (BA, MA, Ph.D.), except for one woman who ended her formal education after high school.

As Esterberg (1997) notes, the meaning of sexual identities depends on the social and historical con-text in which they are produced. Being a lesbian, bi-sexual or queer woman in the USA is different than being lesbian, bisexual or queer elsewhere in the world. And even in the context of the USA, being in the part of the country known as the Midwest may give identities a different character than being in larger coastal cities such as New York and San Fran-cisco, which are known for their large and visible LGBTQ populations. This fact certainly contributes to the limitations of this study. But a preliminary study such as this can and should lead to further re-search that examines the impact that regionality can have on these particular identity processes. A second limitation of the study is the overrepresentation of professionals and students, although this group rep-resents racial and ethnic diversity, which is generally lacking in LGBTQ research. People occupy intersec-tions of identities and since sociocultural factors, such as race, ethnicity, and class, affect sexual identi-ties; they have to be accounted for in research (Garnets, 2002). . . .

As Gagnon (2004: 127) states "Conducting re-search on this movement from same to other-gender erotic preference is very difficult in that the persons involved may be treated as socially dead by the gay and lesbian communities." The methods for participant recruitment were sensitive to this issue and I made attempts to seek out as many diverse women as possible. The women with whom I spoke are those who do not mind "being found" and thus this makes them particular kinds of individuals. This is, of course, a symptom of doing research in a homophobic society. I have attempted to recruit participants through gay and lesbian organizations as well as social-networking websites that do not necessarily cater to LGBTQ persons. This was done in hopes of capturing anyone who, since the move to a male partner, has abandoned their lesbian, bisexual or queer label. Through my own personal contacts, I was able to include the accounts of two women who had previously identified as lesbian but who now identify as heterosexual and seek to keep their previous identity "private." . . .

SYMBOLIC AND PHYSICAL PROTECTIONISM

Of the 14 women who previously self-identified as lesbian, none sought to retain the label of lesbian after their involvement with men. The women in this study showed a great deal of protectionism towards the lesbian label. By distancing themselves from lesbian spaces, both physical and symbolic, they sought to preserve the authenticity of those spaces. In some cases the distancing was not one of their choosing, but in most cases it was.

This protectionism toward "lesbianism" manifested itself in two different ways. First, women exhibited a great sense of preservation towards the label of lesbian. They sought to keep the label untainted by removing themselves from under its umbrella, as in the case of Jennifer, although they still felt that the label captures something about their true identity. Second, they physically sought to preserve lesbian public spaces either by not occupying them anymore or at the very least, not occupying them with their male partners. In the following sections, I outline the ways in which this sense of protectionism manifests itself in the process of

(1) self-labeling or symbolic protectionism, and (2) navigating public spaces or physical protectionism. I then show how investment in identity coupled with notions of fluidity create a boundaried fluidity in which the women find spaces to define who they are.

SELF-LABELING

The process of choosing an identity label is by no means uncomplicated. None of the women with whom I spoke had an essentialist notion of what it means to be lesbian. They acknowledged variability in the lesbian experience. Despite this fact, the women, through their own experiences, sought to make room for an authentic lesbian experience that they no longer took part in. What exactly counted as an authentic lesbian experience, of course, varied from woman to woman, and sometimes varied within the same interview. Although the women were quick to explain that they knew of many lesbians who in the past had been or were currently in a relationship with a man, none of the women with whom I spoke currently identified as lesbian. I asked the women to explain this choice. If there is so much variety in the lesbian experience, why not continue to use the label?

Karen, a 29-year-old white professional, who had previously identified as lesbian-queer, explains why she no longer identified as lesbian.

'Cause I'm a word-fiend, I like definitions to actually mean something and what I hate about labels for myself is also what I love about words, that they mean something and so, if I say tree you might picture a palm tree and somebody else may picture an oak tree and that's fine, just like when I say lesbian you might picture lipstick and curly hair and I might picture flannel or whatever and that's fine but, like we would all agree that a tree is a plant and it has roots, they go down in the ground, it takes up water, chlorophyll, whatever some kind of leaves or pine needles, brown and green, and so there's a general framework that everybody understands and I think it makes the word tree very powerful because it's universal, it's understood. There's variations on it but we know what it means, and what I would love about more flexible labels and just having a jillion labels for people's sexuality is also what I would hate if it happened to the rest of my words, like I want them to be kinda boxed in just a little bit so that there's a universal understanding.

Despite the fact that she mentions that many different types of "trees" exist, Karen considers her choice to be with a man as a difference of kind and not of degree, a universally understood difference. Although she refrains from completely framing her argument in essentialist terms, by arguing that sexuality is innate, Karen nevertheless creates space for a discussion of a "real" lesbian experience. Just where that threshold of difference resides is unclear, or perhaps differs from woman to woman. The implication of Karen's reasoning for no longer considering herself a lesbian is that including her experience in the definition would make the definition itself meaningless. It would, in short, take power away from the word lesbian and this is clearly something that Karen does not wish to take part in. The fact that she offers no universally accepted definition of lesbian seems not to be of concern. Heather, a 41-year-old white student, makes a point similar to Karen.

> I called myself lesbian for a while when I was, when I started dating my [male] partner. But I feel like that's not, I feel like I'm taking away somehow, from women who are exclusively with women, if I use the word lesbian.

As Heather's statement hints, the process of choosing a label is not an individually isolated process. Her assumption that she is "taking away somehow" outlines her feelings that her choice to keep the label does injury to women who do not have relationships with men. It seems that her very existence as a lesbian with a male partner is a threat to the legitimacy of a community that she cares greatly about. As a way to reconcile that, Heather, like Jennifer and Karen, gives up a label that she otherwise would want to use in order to preserve the authenticity of the community in which she used to belong.

Why would these women's choice to keep the label have any implication for anyone other than themselves? This is precisely because of the central role that the community plays in defining a lesbian identity. While involved with women, many of these women, like many other LGBTQ women have been bombarded by messages that their attraction and involvement with other women is a phase, or is otherwise not to be taken seriously. As Diamond (2009: 52) notes, there is an "assumption among scientists and laypeople alike that authentic sexual orientation develops early and is consistent through one's life." What is authentic is what is stable. "So the familiar battlegrounds are drawn: fixed ¼ biological ¼ deserving of acceptance and protection, whereas variable ¼ chosen ¼ fair game for stigma and discrimination" (Diamond, 2009: 246).

Amy, a white 36-year-old student, recalls:

> I sometimes felt a sort of eye rolling, like it was some sort of phase for me or something, or a novelty of some kind.

Meg, a 30-year-old white student, recalls her discomfort with the assumption.

> I think they feel, and not just like my parents, my extended family my grandma, grandpa, like we're talking and I'll be like "we're not in a monogamous relationship and I may still sleep with women" just because I want them to realize that this wasn't a phase and whatever.

The idea that their attraction to women can be read by others as having been a phase is a constant backdrop to the women's personal narratives. So they find themselves in a difficult place. On one hand, they need to make it clear that their attraction to women and the identities that they embraced previously were authentic, and not an experimental phase. They seek to make their previous choices authentic by confirming that they still find themselves attracted to other women. But they can only take this point so far. They refrain from continuing to identify as lesbian, in order to not fall into the stereotype that as Jennifer states: "All lesbians need is to meet the right man." Emily, a 32-year-old white student, explains the situation as follows:

> Part of my fear is that I think that, you know, to the ears of someone who doesn't understand what it means to be gay, I think that unfortunately that my experience makes the case that it's a choice and I know that, I think that, I know that's not true for so many people that I love. It's not, you know, so I do feel guilt about that.... I think my guilt is that it sounds like I make the case for choice, which I think is a very unhelpful, not even, it's a harmful experience to talk about to the biased ear, to the ear that wants to already reject and hate.

The women's experience, as they explain, can too easily serve as an example of "choice." The lesbian community as they understand it, is built around notions of essentialism, or being born a lesbian. The women fear that their experience will harm...the lesbian community. The women's choice of identity after involvement with men is not about settling on a label that feels right to them alone. Their choice is also motivated by the consequences of their choice for the lesbian community.

Jennifer remembers some direct feedback from friends.

> A couple of people specifically said I can't believe that you would do this, you know, this is exactly the stereotype that people have about gay people and specifically about lesbians and now you've proven them right and why not just not date this guy because it's really really bad.

Now involved with men, these women's fear is that they will further serve as an example of the perceived impermanence and the inauthentic nature of a lesbian identity. These women have to come to terms with exactly the idea that lesbians really just haven't found the right man. On the matter of becoming an example of choice, Jennifer explains:

> I think it's too damaging. It fits into the stereotypes and I think does a lot of damage to the lesbian, gay, bisexual and transgendered queer movement too, there's so much of the civil rights activism that rests on, and I think inappropriately so, but that rests on we're born gay, we can't help it and my story flies in the face of that

and I think would be used as an example by people in the ex-gay movement and in the, you know, people that want to change people's sexual orientation, who say that it's a choice, you can just choose something else, that I would be more fodder for that crap and I don't want to be that. So, in many ways, I think it's oppressive heterosexual society, you know, I talk about how I lost friends like that's, and I did, but I think I lost friends because of heterosexist oppression not because my friends were bad people although I'm pissed it wasn't, they weren't wrong about what image that creates.

When navigating the events following their partnership with men, these women are constantly working against the backdrop of their lesbian experiences having been a choice, and thus inauthentic. Their sense of personal authenticity is in conflict with a community's authenticity. On one hand, they work to explain that their involvement with women was not a phase. On the other hand, they work to not make the case for choice. This is an extremely difficult balance to maintain. In addition to maintaining this balance, the women distance themselves from the community, despite sometimes feeling profound loss. Karen, a 29-year-old white professional, puts it simply:

> I think the biggest hesitance is about like going back into the closet or whatever, you know, you've set up your community and then how does this affect the rest of your community.

Explaining her sense of loss, Tina, a 38-year-old white professional, states:

> You know, I love watching *The L-Word* and sometimes I feel like this isn't really your show anymore. You're not a lesbian anymore. I used to get *Curve Magazine* and I, you know, like you're not really a lesbian anymore so, I do, I feel like I kinda lost, part, being part of the club or whatever. And I feel like I lost that sense of solidarity.

Tina expresses her sense of loss but is inadvertently implying that there is an authentic lesbian whom she no longer embodies. By placing *Curve Magazine* and *The L-Word* together and placing herself out, Tina is drawing a circle around what she considers to be "real" lesbian. She herself serves as an example of what is not real; and through that process of exclusion, she inadvertently solidifies the notion of a real lesbian.

PUBLIC SPACES

Not only do some women relinquish the label of lesbian, but their desire to maintain an authentic lesbian community extends to avoiding lesbian public spaces, or at least, avoiding such places when in the company of their male partners. Riley, a 24-year-old white student, explains this in terms of respect for a space that is made for a particular purpose. She says:

> I wouldn't enjoy them if I was with a man but also that I would feel, like honestly, being disrespectful, and I know that, you know, in theory that's ridiculous, but you know, I'm slightly sort of keeping it that way by respecting those kind of boundaries but there's something I kinda like about things being separate. I think it's important to have spaces that are not necessarily explicitly exclusive but that especially for, for the lack of a better word, minority groups, incredibly important, you know, and also I love feeling like there's almost this like social service quality to my social behavior... there is something that's like, this isn't accessible for everyone.

Riley feels that bringing a man into a space that is considered lesbian would be disrespectful. She does what she considers "social service" by helping to maintain the integrity of the lesbian space.

Celia, a 33-year-old white student, echoes these sentiments:

> I'm always concerned too, I want to remain respectful, like I won't be really affectionate with my husband in a gay bar. I do try to, you know, be respectful. And I don't go overboard, like I don't make sure that everybody knows he's my husband but at the same time, I don't deny that he's my husband. But, I'm conscious of that balance.

Celia wants to be respectful of the queer space she occupies. Somehow being affectionate with her husband is a sign of disrespect. One could assume that, according to Celia, it is not the affection that is disrespectful but the heteronormativity it signals. The relationship is a symbol of the structurally privileged social position of heterosexuality.

I ask Meg, a 30-year-old white student, about her experience of being in a gay bar with her husband. In this context, gay bar is used as a descriptor for a space that caters to lesbian women. She explains:

> I think certainly, I felt uncomfortable dancing with him and being straight in a gay bar. But still if I were not with him I probably wouldn't have an issue with dancing with him in a gay bar, if he wasn't my partner.

The issue that Meg highlights is interesting. It is not the presence of a man in a gay bar that is of concern. Meg explains that she would dance with men at gay bars. The issue is bringing her heterosexual relationship into a gay bar, the same sentiment echoed by Celia. All three women show great reverence for a space that they consider serving a particular purpose, that of letting those who occupy it interact outside of the heterosexual gaze. The women perform the same level of policing of public spaces as they do of symbolic spaces. They physically refrain from coming into lesbian public spaces, thus protecting those spaces. They symbolically avoid such identity spaces, by refraining from identifying as lesbian.

As some authors have noted, the legitimacy accorded to heterosexuality is not just a by-product of individual interactions (Jackson, 2006). Heteronormativity and heterosexuality are not synonymous (Berlant and Warner, 2000; Ward and Schneider, 2009; Schlichter, 2004). The term heteronormativity captures the "taken-for-granted and simultaneously compulsory character of institutionalized heterosexuality" (Nielson et al., 2000: 284). Despite this difference, the women in this study see their individual relationships and interactions as symbols of the legitimacy of heterosexuality and its privileged position with regards to other forms of sexuality....

CONCLUSION

Some sociologists argue that in a postmodern era there is more fluidity in all identities. Gergen (2000) for example argues that today, individuals experience self-multiplication, or the capacity to be present in many places at once. This diversification makes identity commitment nearly impossible. Individuals are no longer bound to particular locales, as they were in modern times, that is they are in the presence of a variety of "going concerns" or identity resources (Holstein and Gubrium, 2000). Gergen argues that this lack of commitment allows for fluidity in many identities and that the traditional goal of a stable self (self as object) has been replaced with a fluid self (self as process). The self, as Gergen argues, is in jeopardy (2000: 6). Although he does not specifically theorize about sexuality, one could assume that the same mechanism would be at play in navigating postmodern sexual identities. One could assume that individuals are no longer bound by any social structures and that they are free to define themselves, however temporarily in whatever way they wish. But the idea that we live in a time where anything goes in terms of identity is not supported by these accounts. Plummer (2003) notes that not everyone's life is marked by the lack of commitment that Gergen sees as possible. He argues that many individuals are still bound by very traditional understandings of sexuality with strict guidelines about appropriate behavior. In the case of the majority of the women in this study, that is not entirely true either. The women in this study occupy the uncharted territory between these two identity extremes; they are neither liberated by fluidity nor confined by tradition. They do not necessarily hold an essentialist notion of lesbianism but they do have a commitment to the lesbian community. These women themselves draw and redraw boundaries around their communities. Plummer is correct in stating that it is perhaps premature to assume that in the current social arrangement, sexual identities are fluid beyond any concrete boundaries. But it is not that these women have somehow accepted an essentialist notion of sexuality. They are aware that no real definition of lesbian exists. But they also know, based on first hand experience that a real lesbian community does exist. Although they can no longer actively participate in the social aspects of that community, they still have a

hand in shaping it. They see this "shaping" as part of their responsibility. The last thing that these women desire is to have their experiences used as a platform to erode the sense of authenticity of the community that they cherish.

REFERENCES

Baudrillard J (1995) The Gulf War Did Not Take Place. Bloomington: Indiana University Press.
Berlant L and Warner M (2000) Sex in public. In: Berlant L (ed.) Intimacy. Chicago, IL: University of Chicago Press, 311–360.
Burke PJ (1991) Identity processes and social stress. American Sociological Review 56(3): 836–849.
Burke PJ (2006) Identity change. Social Psychology Quarterly 69(1): 81–96.
Callero PL (1985) Role-identity salience. Social Psychology Quarterly 48(3): 203–214.
Denzin NK (1991) Images of Postmodern Society: Social Theory and Contemporary Cinema. Newbury Park, CA: SAGE.
Diamond LM (2003) Was it a phase? Young women's relinquishment of lesbian/bisexual identities over a 5-year period. Journal of Personality and Social Psychology 84(2): 352–364.
Diamond LM (2005) A new view of lesbian subtypes: Stable versus fluid identity trajectories over an 8-year period. Psychology of Women Quarterly 29(2): 119–128.
Diamond LM (2009) Sexual Fluidity: Understanding Women's Love and Desire. Cambridge, MA: Harvard University Press.
Esterberg KG (1997) Lesbian and Bisexual Identities: Constructing Communities, Constructing Selves. Philadelphia, PA: Temple University Press.
Floyd F and Stein TS (2002) Sexual orientation identity formation among gay, lesbian, and bisexual youths: Multiple patterns of milestone experiences. Journal of Research on Adolescence 12(2): 167–191.
Gagnon JH (2004) An Interpretation of Desire. Chicago, IL and London: University of Chicago Press.
Gagnon JH and Simon W (1973) Sexual Conduct: The Social Sources of Human Sexuality. Chicago, IL: Aldine.
Garber M (1995) Vice Versa: Bisexuality and The Eroticism of Everyday Life. Simon & Schuster: New York.
Garnets LD (2002) Sexual orientations in perspective. Cultural Diversity and Ethnic Minority Psychology 8(2): 115–129.

Gergen KJ (2000) The Saturated Self: Dilemmas of Identity in Contemporary Life. New York: Basic Books.

Green AI (2002) Gay but not queer: Toward a post-queer study of sexuality. Theory and Society 31(4): 521–545.

Gubrium JF and Holstein JA (2009) Analyzing Narrative Reality. London: SAGE Publications.

Holstein JA and Gubrium JF (2000) The Self We Live By: Narrative Identity in a Postmodern World. New York, NY: Oxford University Press.

Inness SA (1997) The Lesbian Menace: Ideology, Identity, and the Representation of Lesbian Life. Amherst: University of Massachusetts Press.

Jackson S (2006) Gender, sexuality and heterosexuality: The complexity (and limits) of heteronormativity. Feminist Theory 7(1): 102–121.

Jeffreys S (1994) The queer disappearance of lesbians. Women's Studies International Forum 17(5): 459–472.

Jeffreys S (1999) Bisexual politics: A superior form of feminism? Women's Studies International Forum 22(3): 273–285.

Kitzinger C and Wilkinson S (1995) Transitions from heterosexuality to lesbianism: The discursive production of lesbian identities. Developmental Psychology 31(1): 95–104.

MacKinnon C (1982) Feminism, Marxism, method and the state: An agenda for theory. Signs 7(3): 515–544.

McIntosh M (1968) The homosexual role. Social Problems 17(2): 262–270.

Nielson JM, Walden G and Kunkel CA (2000) Gendered heteronormativity empirical illustrations in everyday life. Sociological Quarterly 41(2): 283–296.

Peplau LA and Garnets LD (2000) A new paradigm for understanding women's sexuality and sexual orientation. Journal of Social Issues 56(2): 329–350.

Phelan S (1994) Getting Specific: Postmodern Lesbian Politics. Minneapolis: University of Minnesota Press.

Plummer K (1982) Symbolic interactionism and sexual conduct: An emergent perspective. In: Brake M (ed.) Human Sexual Relations: Towards a Redefinition of Sexual Politics. New York: Pantheon, 223–241.

Plummer K (1995) Telling Sexual Stories: Power, Change and Social Worlds. London and New York: Routledge.

Plummer K (2003) Queers, bodies and postmodern sexualities: A note on revisiting the 'sexual' in symbolic interactionism. Qualitative Sociology 26(4): 515–530.

Ponse B (1978) Identities in the Lesbian World: The Social Construction of Self. Westport CT: Greenwood Press.

Riessman CK (1993) Narrative Analysis. London: SAGE.

Rothblum E (2000) Sexual orientation and sex in women's lives: Conceptual and methodological issues. Journal of Social Issues 56(2): 193–204.

Rothblum E (2008) Finding a large and thriving lesbian and bisexual community: The costs and benefits of caring. Gay and Lesbian Issues and Psychology Review 4(2): 69–79.

Rust P (1993) Coming out in the age of social constructionism. Gender and Society 7(1): 50–77.

Rust P (2000) Bisexuality: A contemporary paradox for women. Journal of Social Issues 56(2): 205–221.

Schlichter A (2004) Queer at last? Straight intellectuals and the desire for transgression. GLQ 10(4): 543–564.

Shugar DR (1999) To(o) queer or not? Journal of Lesbian Studies 3(3): 11–20.

Stein A (ed.) (1993) Sisters, Sexperts, Queers: Beyond the Lesbian Nation. New York: Penguin.

Stein A (1997) Sex and Sensibility: Stories of a Lesbian Generation. Berkeley, Los Angeles, London: University of California Press.

Stryker S and Burke PJ (2000) The past, present and future of an identity theory. Social Psychology Quarterly 63(4): 284–297.

Stryker S and Serpe RT (1994) Salience and psychological centrality: equivalent, overlapping, or complementary concepts? Social Psychology Quarterly 57(1): 16–35.

Swidler A (2001) Talk of Love: How Culture Matters. Chicago, IL and London: University of Chicago Press.

Vannini PA (2007) The changing meanings of authenticity: An interpretive biography of professors' work experiences. Studies in Symbolic Interaction 29: 63–90.

Walters SD (1996) From here to queer: Radical feminism, postmodernism, and the lesbian menace (or why can't a woman be more like a fag?) Signs 21(4): 830–869.

Ward J and Schneider B (2009) The research of heteronormativity: An introduction. Gender and Society 23(4): 433–439.

Weeks J (1985) Sexuality and its Discontents: Meanings, Myths and Modern Sexualities. New York: Routledge.

17 • *Margaret Cruikshank*

AGING AND IDENTITY POLITICS

DISCUSSION QUESTIONS

1. In Cruikshank's own telling, how does the naming of identity become both imperative to individuals and yet dangerously limiting to a group defined by that same identity?
2. What does "old" conjure up for you, and what significance does the concept of "old" have in sexuality studies? What arguments might you make that "old" must remain a (fixed) category?
3. How does Cruikshank resist the notion of "old" and the entrapment of "the old"? How do aging people in your life practice similar types of resistance?

Recently I was lying on the living room floor of a friend doing a few stretches when her seven-year-old daughter said, matter-of-factly and with no trace of derision, "You have to do that because you are old." Later Lauren may see other facets of me to comment on, but her observation reminded me that although I am ready to claim "older" as appropriate, to others I will simply seem "old." When the doctor greets me with a hearty, "And how are you today, young lady?" he not only calls attention to my age but offers fake flattery as well. Maggie Kuhn told off President Gerald R. Ford when he made this blunder; I am not as bold.

No one surprised me by calling me "woman" or "lesbian," those identities seemingly more fundamental than "old." Thinking about the succession of these identities—first "woman," then "lesbian," and now "old," I wonder about their interconnections and limits. Will critical gerontology unravel the last identity?

"Woman" as a category usefully served feminists as a fixed identity and rallying cry; indeed, the feminist movement was more commonly called the "women's" movement. The popular line "I am woman, hear me roar," sung enthusiastically, made "woman" into "Woman." This universalizing name was challenged by women of color who worked on feminist issues in the 1970's, most dramatically by the publication in 1981 of *This Bridge Called My Back: Writings by Radical Women of Color,* edited by Gloria Anzaldua and Cherrie Moraga. White readers were shocked into recognition that feminists could be racist. No one sang, "I am a White Middle-Class Woman, Hear Me Roar." *This Bridge Called My Back* proved so influential that the National Women's Studies Association honored the anthology at its 2007 conference.

When "woman" became "women," other differences were more readily acknowledged—of class, education, work history, location—and "woman" could no longer designate a fixed identity. By the 1990's, feminists declared that gender was not a free-standing category but rather embedded with ethnicity and class. Even now, the impact of age upon these other identities is not well understood. In the realm of statistics, nonetheless, "woman" usefully denotes shared characteristics, such as lower pay than men's,

Margaret Cruikshank. 2008. "Aging and Identity Politics." *Journal of Aging Studies* 22:147–151.

expectations of child care and elder care, and biological likenesses.

Moving to San Francisco in 1977 to be part of gay/lesbian liberation and women's liberation was a major change in my life. For the first time, I fit in completely. I had been a clumsy adolescent, a sickly graduate student, a lapsed Catholic in a Benedictine research center, a closeted lesbian English professor at a small Protestant college in Iowa, and (still closeted) a director of a fledgling women's studies program in Minnesota.

. . .

For many like me, identities were hard won through women's liberation and gay liberation, and in both cases, prejudice and discrimination heightened our sense of identification with our movement. Many of us became writers because we now had material to write about, and we now had an audience. Without the social context of greater visibility for lesbians, we would not have been able to publish work on topics that led us to self-understanding. My collection of autobiographical essays, *The Lesbian Path* (1980; 1985) illustrated the belief of the time that lesbianism was a core identity, fundamental to who we were. We certainly did not expect that to change. In fact, in *The Lesbian Path* and *The Coming Out Stories* (1980), edited by Julia Stanley and Susan Wolfe, the tone of some writers suggested an awakening comparable to religious conversion: "I once was lost and now am found." Queer theorists would later find this sort of proclamation distastefully retrograde. They could not comprehend the dangers of coming out in the 1970's and the absolute need for a fixed identity.[1]

Queer theory emphasizes sex rather than gender. Affirmation of the worth of gay, lesbian, bisexual and transgendered people is central to gay/lesbian studies, whereas queer theory's aim is to de-center heterosexuality. Another difference is that the claims of queer theory are extremely bold. Gay studies announced that the curriculum would be enriched by the inclusion of our issues and our scholarship, but queer theorists such as Eve Sedgwick believe that Western culture cannot be understood without their perspectives.

What queer theorists overlook in assessing lesbian/gay identities, however, is the power of *naming*. The act of claiming a stigmatized identity in the company of thousands of others empowered people accustomed

to being dismissed as sick or sinful or as less worthy than heterosexuals. Queer theory forgets recent history. At the same time, its spirited challenges both to heterosexist bias and identity politics have enlivened the humanities and to a lesser extent the social sciences. On the other hand, lesbian identity can be erased under the "queer" rubric.

. . .

The identity "gay" is also complicated, for example, because by the 1990's that identity had morphed into gay, lesbian, bisexual, and transgender—as fluid a category as one could imagine. In the early 1980's, City College of San Francisco began a course in "gay literature" that soon changed its name to the more inclusive "gay and lesbian literature" when I began to teach it. Now courses and programs across the United States label themselves LGBT or GLBT, and the great differences among these courses suggest that the once definitive identity "gay" may be losing its former salience. Bisexual and transgender activists have a much higher profile than in the 1970's, and the notion that identify [sic] is fluid rather than fixed prevails. Nonetheless, "gay" remains a fixed marker for the right-wing preachers who fulminate against it. Since "gay" is an identity they would choose to obliterate, they think they know its signifiers. When Vice-President Dick Cheney's daughter Mary and her female partner had a son, Samuel David Cheney, his arrival no doubt blurred the focus of James Dobson's Focus on the Family, an anti-gay, right-wing religious group. When two women have a baby, presumably by alternative insemination, lesbian identity cannot easily be reduced to sexual behavior.

In the early 1990's, my LGBT courses at City College of San Francisco assumed both the existence of a movement and the fixed nature of gay identity. Even before I encountered queer theory, though, I wondered if sexual identity would continue to be as central to self-definition as ethnicity, class, and sex. Thirty years from now, I asked students, will being gay be as important as being Jewish, black, or female? For the present, we concluded that gay men and lesbians would retain a keen sense of their social difference. In my LGBT Aging class, I pointed out to students that people who are both old and gay share identities that others have wanted to cure.

Even though two sharply defined identities, age and sexual orientation, brought us together, we acknowledged that neither this convergence of identities nor any other could fully account for our unique individual histories.

. . .

Given the trend away from identity politics in sexuality studies, it seems curious that the identity "old" has not undergone similar transformation in age studies. The social construction of aging is widely acknowledged, but the expansive and revisionist thought on "woman" and "gay" finds few parallels with "old" as an identity.

Elderly people dislike all the negative connotations of "old," but gerontologists and service providers have a vested interest in maintaining a fixed identity of "old." Their professional lives require the category. That helps to explain why "old" has not undergone the mutations of "woman" and "gay." If "old" were fluid, changing, and indeterminate, it would be hard to tell who "they" are. In her account of participating in the film "Strangers in Good Company," Mary Meigs writes that the subjects thought of themselves as "semi old," until the director's request for a nude swimming scene proved that they were really *old* (cited in Chivers, 92).

One difference between "old" and the other identities is that it covers only part of a life, although the same is true for some gay men, lesbians, bisexuals, and transgendered people. Moreover, "old" calls up a more specific body image than "black," "woman" or "gay." A gay identity is self-consciously chosen, unlike "old." The group Old Lesbians Organizing for Change proudly declares both identities, however, offering a current example of identity politics.

. . .

I have several reservations about embracing "old" as an identity, however. Since chronological age is over-emphasized in American culture for biomedical/pharmaceutical profit and to reinforce the conservative ideology that creates fear of an aging population, feminists who take on age as a primary identity may unwittingly align with forces they elsewhere oppose. Both they and the "anti-aging" marketers want "old" to carry heavy loads of meaning. Only the latter, of course, sell shame.

Another difficulty is that a primary identity of "old" sharply separates one group of citizens from another and reinforces the dualism young/old. The fear of an aging population depends partly on the perception that "the old" are a monolithic group. Furthermore, the category "old" reflects essentialism. While proclaiming "old" as an identity confronts prejudice, it also gives to chronological age meanings that it cannot bear, the claim of special worth, for example. It may be true in some cases that being over sixty-five or seventy confers special insight or awareness, but the identity "old," covering everyone from 65–100, cannot guarantee this benefit.

Those who take on the identity "old" rightly reject assumptions about aging that limit women, that their lives will be mostly about decline and loss of function, that physical appearance matters greatly, or that loss of dignity accompanies passage into late life. I can imagine situations in which calling myself "old" will be both bracingly assertive and a tactic for puncturing someone's prejudice, but I do not think that claiming this identity by itself challenges ageism. Instead, I anticipate that my identity as old will be interwoven with other identities. I may even evolve into an amiable atheist. After all, as Barbara Macdonald observed twenty-five years ago, a woman in her sixties is still in process. If I reach "deep old age," I may become one-who-needs-care, an identity that may overshadow other identities. Perhaps I resist "old" because no matter how positive its meanings in critical gerontology and feminist gerontology, in popular usage "old" has negative connotations.

Resistance to "old" as a category does not mean denial of aging, but "how does age resistance differ from age denial"? (Twigg, 63). With the former, I deliberately step out of the box provided for me by deeply-ingrained cultural messages. In denial, on the other hand, I claim to be ageless or exceptional. The noxious and now popular "anti-aging" paradigm not only encourages denial but assumes loss, universality, and disease simultaneously. And many will agree with Nora Ephron in *I Feel Bad About my Neck* that no matter how many upbeat books are written about aging, it is still better to be young. Ephron finds one big advantage to her sixties, however: she needn't shave her legs as often.

Another difference among the identities is that the women's movement and gay rights movement are inherently political, whereas American elders mobilize politically on occasion, when their welfare is at stake, but otherwise tend to vote their social class interests, rather than as an elder bloc. When Bush urged "privatization" of Social Security in 2005, for example, elderly people strongly resisted introducing risk into a supposedly "secure" system and lobbied against it.

Many years ago, I remember concluding as I read Sharon Kaufman's book *The Ageless Self* that her subjects did not wish to identify as "old" because of low consciousness or worse, internalized ageism. Now that I am older, I think the reason people over sixty-five or seventy resist the category is that it is ill-fitting. They know that many characteristics describe them, of which chronological age is only one. They observe middle-aged people who are falling apart and octogenarians who are robust. Elders delude themselves, however, if they claim to be only as old as they feel; assuredly they are as old as their internal organs. At sixty-eight, I regard "old" as ill-fitting for myself, but I am well aware that as long as others see me as old, I cannot simply shrug off the label. It has some meaning, even if provisional and ironic.

Whatever their personal feelings about "old," elderly people live in a society in which "old" is in fact an all-encompassing identity. They may reject the designation, but others provide it for them, and "old" covers them like a blanket. Yet, just as women and gay people differ greatly in social class, education, income, political affiliation, and health status, so too do people over sixty-five. These numerous, strong differences, if focused upon, may reduce "old" to a fairly unimportant identity marker.

What cultural shift might eliminate "young lady" as a popular tag for old women in public places? During a conversation I had at a retirement home in Orono, several women expressed resentment at being patronized in this way, while one woman declared that she liked it very much. I did not think to ask the old men in the group whether they risk being addressed as "young man" when they step outside their community.

When I consider identity politics through slogans and rally chants—"Black is Beautiful," "Gay is Good," "Three, Five, Seven, Nine: Lesbians are Mighty Fine," "Older is bolder," I pause at "old." What if "old" is a fictive category, a convenient illusion far more relevant to the not-old than to those whose chronological age is thought to mean a great deal? What if the country of the old has no borders?

How invigorating to discover that in 1915 the anthropologist Elsie Clews Parsons argued in *Social Freedom* that we fear "those who are unclassified or unclassifiable [and] social categories take on a life of their own." The following year she elaborated by stating that social categories are "an unparalleled means of gratifying the will to power. The classified individual may be held in subjection in ways the unclassified escapes" (Deacon, 1997:128). Personality would substitute for some more fixed identity. The relevance of these ideas to aging is obvious: classifying a group as "old" subordinates them to those unmarked by classification. Parsons envisioned a future in which categories were contested (as we say today), in which "differences in others will no longer be recognized as troublesome or fearful . . . Nor will presumptions of superiority or inferiority attach to differences *per se*" (Deacon, 1997:129–130).

Certainly with aging, the binary old/young holds within itself a presumption of superiority for "young." When part of usual aging, loss becomes the whole; not only does a presumption of inferiority occur, but possibilities of growth, renewal, change, repair and healing are overlooked. However, a recent experience showed me that loss may co-exist with vitality. I spent time with a woman who relies on a walker. Her energy and force of personality de-emphasized loss so thoroughly that her walker signified change or adaptation rather than loss. She drove her Prius across roadless land as if it were a Jeep. "Not what the Japanese had in mind for this car," she joked. A critical gerontologist would observe that Maureen's class privilege facilitates the process of integrating loss with other strands of aging. Parsons would see Maureen as an example of personality resisting classification.

Another example is Ruth Ellis, a Black woman who owned a printing business in Detroit [*sic*] and died in 2000 at the age of 101. Her life is recounted in the film "Living with Pride: Ruth Ellis at 100." In her nineties, Ruth befriended a group of white lesbians who treasured her stories about her own lesbian history.[2] The film shows Ruth jogging around the gym of her old high school, very slowly and with small steps, a triumphant grin on her face. Ruth ran errands for her neighbors; her survivorhood was not only about herself but about connections to others.

Jogging centenarians make impressive survivors, but stories of less robust women, including those who use a wheelchair or who contend with problems such as hearing loss, macular degeneration, and arthritis, are needed to balance the picture of personalities resisting classification. If I become too stiff to walk and too bent to sit at a computer, I probably won't describe myself as "aged by culture." Social construction carries us just so far. On the other hand, if I do last until infirm, the ways I interpret my infirmities and the ways others regard me will inevitably be determined by culture.

I take heart from this observation by Janet R. Jakobsen: "Queer was supposed to name a space of difference that didn't just produce a new identity—homosexuals who are different from heterosexuals, gays who are different from straights—but might also allow us to remain in the space of difference itself, without being trapped in identity" (2003:81). What could this mean for critical gerontology?

We could elucidate the ways in which "the old" are trapped in that identity. I have suggested a few here. Acting on their own behalf, people who have survived to late life can resist assignment to a narrow space and thereby express their sense of difference on their own terms. Age denial is fruitless; resistance to a proffered identity may be physically and psychologically healthy. In the space of difference, late life might be seen as inherently worthy, not requiring qualifiers like "positive" or "successful" to render it desirable.

. . .

Age studies lead me to ask when my chronological age matters, when it does not, and whose interest is served when age becomes my identifying marker. As an old lesbian, I (usually) have more in common with heterosexual women my age than with my gay male contemporaries. I imagine my various identities as a mobile, with distinct parts in harmony and balance. I am a white, middle-class native Midwesterner, a lover of beaches and trails, who enjoys the privileges of an academic life, though as a lowly adjunct professor. I am incipiently old, resisting the category even as I note bodily changes that mean my days of scrambling over rocks may soon be over.

"Woman" remains my core identity, however. I am ruefully essentialist in the end. And in the space of gender difference, I feel good about my neck.

NOTES

1. I elaborate this point in "Through the Looking Glass: A '70s Lesbian Feminist on Queer Theory." *Twenty-First Century Lesbian Studies.* Edited by Noreen Gifney and Katherine O'Donnell (New York: Haworth: 2007). See also Linda Garber, "Where in the World are the Lesbians?" *Journal of the History of Sexuality* 14, Nos. 1/2 (2005): 28–50.
2. *Living with Pride: Ruth Ellis at 100* is directed by Yvonne Welbon. Ruth's House, a home for Detroit lesbian and gay teens whose families have rejected them, is named for her.

REFERENCES

Abod, J. (2006). Look us in the eye. The old women's project. Long Beach: Profile Productions.

Chivers, S. (2003). *From old woman to older women.* Contemporary culture and women's narratives. Columbus: Ohio State University Press.

Cruikshank, M. (1978). Thomas Babington Macaulay. Boston: G.K. Hall.

Cruikshank, M. (1985). *The lesbian path,* rev. ed. San Francisco: Grey Fox Press.

Deacon, D. (1997). *Elsie Clews Parsons: Inventing modern life.* Chicago: University of Chicago Press.

Ephron, N. (2006). *I feel bad about my neck. And other thoughts on being a woman.* New York: Knopf.

Kaufman, S. (1986). *The ageless self: Sources of meaning in late life.* Madison: University of Wisconsin Press.

Jakobsen, J. R. (2003). Queers are Jews, aren't they? In D. Boyarin, D. Itzkovitz, & A. Pellegrini (Eds.), *Queer theory and the Jewish question.* New York: Columbia University Press.

Morell, C. (2003). Empowerment theory and long-living women: A feminist and disability perspective. *Journal of Human Behavior in the Social Environment, 7* (Nos. 3–4), 225–236.

Sedgwick, E. K. (1990). *The epistemology of the closet.* Berkeley: University of California Press.

Stanley, J. P. & Wolfe, S. J. (Eds.). (1980). *The coming out stories.* Watertown: Persephone Press.

Twigg, J. (2004). The body, gender, and age: Feminist insights in social gerontology. *Journal of Aging Studies, 18*(No.l), 59–73.

18 • *Sonya Bolus*

LOVING OUTSIDE SIMPLE LINES

DISCUSSION QUESTIONS

1. In general, how might a person's development, growth, and/or experience of major life changes affect their intimate partner(s)?
2. More specifically, how might a person's decision to gender transition, both socially and medically, affect their intimate partner(s)?
3. Imagine yourself in a relationship with someone who decided to gender transition. How might you respond to their decisions? What particular challenges would be most difficult for you?

Leaning over you in bed, I run my hand across your shirted torso, caressing breast and muscle, smoothing abdomen and flank. My touch on your female body does not emasculate you. You are not a woman to me. You are butch. My fingers tell you I understand.

My stone butch; I am prepared for you to pull away every time I reach for you. I don't understand the strange sense that guides my approach to you, but it is innate, instinctive, natural.

You gaze at me with trust and wonder that you can let me touch you so freely. I tell you I could make love to you for hours. I, young and novice femme, could make love to you, skilled and knowing butch, for hours. And you, tough from years of living as you do, lie quiet beneath my touch.

Sometimes I have to trick you. We pretend you are fucking me, so you don't have to think about what I am doing to you. I make my body available to you as a distraction.

Sometimes I use words: "Let me suck your dick." Whether I go down on a dildo or a cunt, I am sucking your dick. I see it. I feel it. I know it. We both believe in this absolutely, and there is a shift from role play into another kind of reality.

Always, I give you my body, completely. I luxuriate in how well you know my needs, how well you match me and capture every strength and grace I hold within. I give over to you, and you take me to total release, drive me to sexual madness, then bring me back to safety in your embrace.

Without knowing that anyone like you existed, I searched for you. And now that I've found you, I feel such relief to know that you are real. Now I want to know the wealth of your mind, body, and soul, the hell of being you in this world, and the joy that also comes from living outside simple lines.

You ask me to marry you. "Yes" is my answer. And I say yes to life. I say yes with my eyes wide open. You will be my husband, for you are butch, and I can call you no other way. You will be my husband because you are worthy of that title, far more than any man I have known. You'll not own me, but I'll be your wife. I am already your femme and your girl, and I feel my own strength and power as never before. I marry you, and it is more than words or

Sonya Bolus, "Loving Outside Simple Lines" from Genderqueer: *Voice from Beyond the Sexual Binary*, edited by J. Nestle, C. Howell, and R. Wilchins. 2002. Permission granted by Joan Nestle.

license or tax break, more than a church wedding or a white dress/tuxedo affair, more than a political statement, commitment ceremony, holy union. Marriage with you is life. You extend your hand to me. I step into your world and unite you to mine.

Comes the day you tell me you want your breasts removed. Top surgery. Chest reconstruction. I am oddly not surprised. I think I always knew we would do this together someday. And somewhere in me, though you have not said it aloud, I know this is the first step of a profound transition.

I love you. So I go with you to the computer, and we look up different transgender Web sites (places I have already been because I knew that someday you would want this information). We read about procedures and options. We have an animated and revelatory conversation. But inside me, a deep, overwhelming panic begins to build.

I want to scream, "I love you...as you are!" My desire for you is not confused. I'm a femme who loves butches, who knows butches. I understand your body. Why can't that be enough?

Ever since I met you, I have struggled to reconcile your breasts with your masculine face, your cunt with your masculine presentation, your body with your masculine soul. I have wanted to "figure you out," using an intellect fettered by narrow expectations, so implicit in my culture that even I have rarely, if ever, questioned them.

You, simply by existing, question all gender assumptions. Gradually I have learned not to try to understand you with my intellect but instead to trust my heart, so clear in its acceptance and love for you.

Yet now, I fear, I want you to agree with me: "Perhaps if you had been recognized, accepted and validated as you are, maybe now you would not want to alter your body." Please, my eyes beg. I want there to be an easier way. I want that you should not need to do this. I want even the possibility that there might have been a chance for you not to need to do this.

You patiently shake your head. "The world is only part of this," you tell me. "The rest of it is inside me."

And my heart knows better. I know you better. You were transgendered before socialization tried to force you to choose "one or the other."

"Are you a boy or a girl?" has been ringing in your ears from earliest memory.

"What do you think?" you flip to them now, tired of explaining. Confusion turns in their eyes. What they say is: freak. What they do is: turn away. Stare. Laugh. Spit. Kill. Beat the spirit from your heart.

You fight them. Survival. Best defense is Get Them First. Show your menace; you are not to be toyed with. "Dangerous" is the message in your eyes, clothes, walk. The razor edge walks with you. You anticipate attack or threat at every turn, exchange, and glance. You talk through. Survival. And "tough" encases your heart.

End of the day and your voice is cold. Your eyes, too old for your years. Tears backed up, held in at what cost? I draw you into the circle of my arms and feel your tension ease. You breathe, and I know you are quietly bringing yourself to me. You can hardly believe you can let it all down, that you can let the tears fall. You can. I know your strength; you have nothing to prove to me. Every part of you that they hate and fear gives me delight. In loving you, I am assured of my own normality.

It is this I fear losing.

The next morning I am driving to work. As I hand my $2 to the toll collector at the bridge, I try to calm myself. "Whatever happens, she will still be my Mary," I whisper again and again, like a mantra. But then I realize you will not be Mary anymore; you will have a new name. And as if that were not enough, you will not even be "she."

We are in uncharted territory.

One night, several weeks later, I awaken to see you sleeping next to me. Your breasts—dusky in the half-light—are spilling onto the bed. Your breasts, which I never touch without knowing a part of you shrinks from my hand. Beautiful, womanly breasts.

Suddenly I can't lie beside you another moment. Tears from nowhere stream hot down my cheeks. In the bathroom I leave the light off, sit on the edge of the bathtub, double over in the moonlight. I rock against my confusion.

Anger. How dare you throw my universe into disarray! Just when I think I finally know myself! When I think I know you!

Fear. This is too much to ask of me! I can't bear this weight. It is impossible. I feel insane!

Betrayal. Who are you? Are you a butch only because there was no other choice! Am I really a lesbian? What does this mean? How can I be a femme if you are a man?

I want to scream at you. Hate you. Instead I stifle my crying in a towel until at last the tears come silent, flow gently. In the morning you find me curled on the couch in the living room. You hold me. Your eyes are so sad. You tell me how sorry you are.

For what? For being true to yourself? I don't want you to apologize for this. I don't know what I want!

I let you hold me, and it does feel better. But I berate myself for being so angry. For hurting you. I wish I could just get to the other side without going through the pain.

Every day I feel different: I drift in and out of anger and pride, excitement and fear. I grapple with monumental theories and insignificant—but suddenly important—consequences of your transition.

My greatest fear is of how this might affect my own sense of self. "Just don't ask me to be straight," I tell you. "It took me too much pain and time and struggle to come out queer, lesbian, and femme-proud. I can't go back." But you never step on or dictate my identity, and for this I am grateful beyond words.

Instead you inspire me to look with courage at my self-definitions. I see how they are true to me. I also see how they sometimes limit me. Though they have often given me security and a means to self-awareness, I notice parts of myself I have suppressed: the attraction I once felt for men, the desire I feel now for other femmes, the need to examine my own "othergenderedness."

Some days I feel very alone in the world, like the biggest "freak among the freaks," and I turn old internalized hatred upon myself. Other days I feel like part of an ancient, unspoken tradition, as one who is particularly "wired" to partner a transperson. I feel almost sacred.

Months pass quickly. Every time you bleed, you feel a little more insane, and I feel less able to be

your safe harbor. We go to meetings, get to know other transmen and their lovers and wives. We search the Internet for surgeons. We figure out which credit cards can hold the weight of this surgery. Time eases pain, it is true. I love your breasts, but now I release this part of you so beautiful and mysterious to me.

I am changing. Part of me begins to address this surgery with a note of erotic anticipation. I notice that much of my desire is linked to the disparity between your gender expression and your body. When you bind your breasts, pack a dick, when you wear a suit and tie, T-shirt and boxers, when you shift before my eyes from woman into man, I am aroused, excited beyond belief.

I relish the way you construct your gender despite the dictates this world links to your body, which further manifests your particular gender.

Christmas week we travel from San Francisco to Maryland for your surgery. We make love in the cheap motel room near the surgeon's office. I want to touch you, but you tell me you just can't. I could cry.

Later I ask if I can kiss your breasts goodbye. You grant me this, though I know what an effort it is. But I have to ask for this; I'll never have another chance. I kiss your nipples as tenderly as if they were made of snow. I let my tears fall onto your soft skin. I know I will always remember how your nipples quietly harden, even under such a gentle touch.

The next day we go to the clinic. You leave me in the hallway as you make your way to the operating room, looking back to mouth, "I love you." Your eyes are wide in fright, but you are smiling.

Then you are gone. I spend four hours waiting.

There is a strip mall next door. In the coffee shop, I write in my journal. In the drugstore, I buy you a card and makeshift bandages. I try to be objective about whether sanitary pads or diapers will be more comfortable and absorbent against your wounds. The lady at the checkout counter asks me how I'm spending my holidays. I tell her, "Quietly."

After three hours, I come back to the waiting room. It is a cosmetic surgery office, so a little like a hotel lobby, underheated and expensively decorated, with candy in little dishes, emerald-green plush chairs, and upscale fashion magazines artfully displayed against the wall.

A young woman comes in, frantic to get a pimple "zapped" before she sees her family over the holidays. An older woman comes in with her daughter for a follow-up visit to a face-lift. She is wearing a scarf and dark glasses. The nurse examines her bruises right out in the waiting room.

And you are in the operating room having your body and your gender legally altered. I feel like laughing, but I know it makes me sound like a lunatic.

After a lifetime of waiting, I am finally called to the recovery room. You are woozy and weak but smile at me when I take your hand. I remember why I am willing to nurse you through this and anything.

Over the course of the next several months we embark upon a journey filled with dramatic peaks and valleys. You start testosterone treatments and your very thinking is changed, along with your body. Most profound is the change in your sexuality. You are more driven, yet more open and vulnerable. You want me like men have wanted me. Sometimes I am so frightened; it is only your love that makes sex possible.

And yet, if anything, you are more sensual to me now. On you, "more masculine" seems like "more butch." I never thought it possible that you could be more butch.

You strut more. Sometimes I find you looking at yourself in the mirror, curious and even delighted. I never saw you take such an interest in your body before. You let me touch you more.

There is a giddy feeling to our lives. Clothes shopping, making love, just being together in this journey is funny, surreal, and filled with a strange, joyful expectation.

And there are stray moments when I stop in my tracks, suddenly realizing my own transition, how I have also changed. How I am changing even now.

On one such day I make a word for myself: *transensual*. And in naming myself, I feel substantial—connected. I am reminded of when I discovered the word *lesbian* and later *femme*. These words name me and help create me at once. My self has reached for these identifiers, found them and filled them out. Now I make them unique to me. Transensual femme lesbian.

I often bless this path you have taken, for your own sake and for mine; it has propelled me into my own journey, and I have found a part of me which needed to emerge. I see people, the world, differently. I am different.

I am trans-formed.

When you came out over 30 years ago, a young butch in the Chicago bars before the lesbian-feminist movement swept you up in its passion, did you ever long for this second chance?

When you burned your last bra and wore your last dress, did you ever think your path would lead you to this future?

When you swore to yourself as a child that you would somehow find a way to put your elbow in your ear if it would change you into a boy, did you ever think your wish would come true?

You are a boy now. And you are a transgendered butch with a 50-year history. Your politics and passion, your anger and hurt, your emotional capacity and human consciousness—these can never be erased. When I move against you, when I hold you to my breast, when I take you in my mouth, I take in your whole self. You feel my soul and I respond to you, as a femme, as a lesbian, as a transensual woman . . . as myself.

Tonight I wake up to see you lying next to me, your chest softly rising and falling with each breath. I hardly notice the scars, you are so beautiful. Sleep well, my butch, my boy, my man. I will be here when you wake.

SECTION THREE

Whose Body Is This?
Bodies as Battlegrounds

Section Three explores actual bodies as battlegrounds for conflicting discourses. Institutions, cultures, and discourses actually touch our bodies, wrap their tentacles around us, and discipline and control different bodies in varying ways that reinforce normative constructions of sex, gender, and sexuality and reproduce and extend systems of oppression. Yet bodies are not simply docile; they also resist.

This section takes its title from Jacob Hale's chapter, "Whose Body Is This Anyway?" In this very short personal narrative, he reveals the many institutional, cultural, and interactional attempts to literally mold his physical body into specific forms. For some going under the surgeon's knife is normative; for others it is mutilation. Just what our bodies should look like is subject to intense scrutiny. While certain bodies are defined as needing fixing, Hale's chapter also raises questions that have implications for many other forms of body modification, including the now-normalized forms of cosmetic surgery that continue to proliferate and promise to mold "ideal" body parts.

Jennifer Finley Boylan also provides a short but powerful statement. She extends our understanding of intersectionality, privilege, and oppression. She reveals that even among those oppressed and marginalized, their experiences are not the same based on their other intersecting identities. While transgender people face frightening rates of hate crime and murder, transgender people of color (women in particular) are especially targeted. Boylan reminds us to consider our own experiences through an intersectional lens.

The next chapter, by Gabrielle Lucero, examines sexual violence within one specific context: the military. Sexual assault in the military has become increasingly visible in recent years and finally acknowledged by some leaders as a very real problem. Besides helping us to understand the extent of this problem, and the potential solutions that have been implemented, at a broader level this chapter demonstrates the important role of context. While approximately one in five women and one in 70 men experience rape in their lifetime, context plays an important role in influencing rates of violence, reporting, and prosecution. Further, different solutions are needed in different settings. Thus the epidemic of sexual assault on college campuses requires different responses and preventive measures than those that may work in the military.

The following chapters continue to address the significance of context and place, while raising new insights. Andrea Smith's chapter expands our examination of violence against women, asking us to contemplate a subject addressed, in one way or another, by many of the authors in this volume: Whose lives are valued? She explores the many ways in which Native women and their bodies have and continue to be abused and manipulated and yet continue to remain invisible even in movements for social justice. How do our definitions of sex, gender, and sexuality construct certain bodies as valuable and others as disposable? Who has the power to construct or contest these assumptions?

Kate Harding continues with these themes and explores the body as battleground metaphor that resonates throughout this section. Her story viscerally exposes the traumas created by structural violence against women who are labeled fat. The daily embodied experience of people whose bodies transgress the normative are constantly engaged in resisting the ways in which others define them, simply in order to survive.

Kamala Kempadoo contributes a global perspective, examining the way in which the sex trade largely depends on the exploitation of women of color. This chapter examines the many global projects that have contributed to and benefitted from sex trafficking, scrutinizing historical US military practice, economic restructuring led by the International Monetary Fund, development projects, the growth of the tourism industry, global capitalist profits, and more. In this context, trafficked bodies are valuable as commodities while simultaneously disposable. Importantly, Kempadoo emphasizes the importance of global power dynamics on local contexts.

The remaining two chapters in this section all take this question of whose bodies matter, and why, in a different direction. They each examine the politics of reproduction. How do laws, policies, medical institutions, and even social movements determine who can or should reproduce? Whose babies are valued, and whose are defined as disposable? Loretta Ross provides us with the historical context to understand the reproductive priorities and needs of African American women. In contrast to the traditional feminist pro-choice framework, she demonstrates that, for women of color, the right to choose to *have* children is also a priority. Highlighting the exclusive power of the language of choice, she advances a "reproductive justice" framework.

The chapter by Alison Piepmeier extends the reproductive justice framework to include the needs of women with disabilities. People with disabilities are often assumed to be nonsexual, sterilized without their consent, assumed incapable of parenting, and more. Women pregnant with a fetus that will have disabilities are frequently pressured to abort, defining people with disabilities as disposable. The reproductive justice framework, first introduced by the Sister-Song Women of Color Reproductive Justice Collective in 2003, argues for the "the right to have children, not have children, and to parent the children we have in safe and healthy environments. Reproductive Justice addresses the social reality of inequality, specifically, the inequality of opportunities that we have to control our reproductive destiny."

19 • *C. Jacob Hale*

WHOSE BODY IS THIS ANYWAY?

DISCUSSION QUESTIONS

1. What social systems or institutions regulate Hale's personal experience of embodiment and identity?
2. How might identity politics play a role in finding support for transition-related decisions among trans people?
3. Why do you think there is such an emphasis placed on genitalia in our society as essential markers of "real" maleness or femaleness?

There was the doctor who told me that if I wanted testosterone, I should be looking for a surgeon to cut on my genitals.

There was the passport agency official who told me that if I want an M on my passport, I should have already had a surgeon cut on my genitals.

There was the human relations employee who told me that if I wanted a faculty ID card with a current picture and a name matching the one on my driver's license, I should have already had a surgeon cut on my genitals.

There are FTMs who tell me that if I want to go to their meetings, if I am a real/true/genuine transsexual, if I am one of them, I should be looking for a surgeon to cut on my genitals.

There are FTMs who tell me that if I want to be one of them, I should be delighted and congratulatory when one of them finds a surgeon to cut on his genitals.

There are FTMs who tell me that if I want to be one of them, I should be filled with pity or disdain when another FTM finds a surgeon to cut on his genitals.

There are FTMs who tell me that I should want to look at the results when one of them has had a surgeon cut on his genitals.

There was the psychiatrist who told me that if I want to have sex, I should get a surgeon to cut on my genitals first.

There was the nontransexual butch leatherman who told me that if I want to suck his cock, I should have plans to find a surgeon to cut on my genitals.

There was the MTF who shoved her tits in my face and told me that I should give her a call after I had gotten a surgeon to cut on my genitals because I'm just so cute.

There is Donald Laub, who says that if I am to have sex that isn't lesbian sex, I should have him cut on my genitals—but only if I quit my job first.

There are the leathermen of Hellfire who say that if I want to be one of them, I must have had a surgeon cut on my genitals because Inferno is for people without vaginas.

There is David Gilbert, who says that if he cuts on my genitals, he will remove my vagina no matter what I want because otherwise he would be making a chick with a dick, and no one wants that.

There was the nontransexual gay man who told a group of FTMs how glad he is that not all of us have surgeons cut on our genitals because he likes fucking our hot sexy wetness.

There was the nontransexual bi-guy who told a group of FTMs how glad he is that not all of us have surgeons cut on our genitals because we are the best of both worlds—male psyches in female bodies.

There are MTFs who tell me that if I am really transexual, I should define myself according to whether or not I have, or intend to have, a surgeon cut on my genitals. "Pre-op or post-op or non-op?"

Which op?

There was the social service agency director who shook my hand—the first FTM hand he had knowingly shaken—after a political meeting and asked if I'd had a surgeon cut on my genitals.

There are people in the audiences at the academic trans theory talks I give who don't ask about the content of my work but do ask about whether or not I've had a surgeon cut on my genitals.

There are shrinks who tell me that if I want testosterone, I should get myself diagnosed with a mental disorder and seek a surgeon to cut on my genitals when the shrinks tell me I am ready to have a surgeon cut on my genitals.

There are all those nontransexuals who tell me that if I get some surgeon to cut on my genitals, I will be mutilating myself or sinning or making myself into a monster or a freak.

There is Sheila Jeffreys who says that Janice Raymond didn't go far enough and that surgeons should be prohibited from cutting on transexuals' genitals because it is mutilation.

There are all those transexuals who tell me that if I want to have a surgeon cut on my genitals, I must believe myself to be mentally disordered or disabled or suffering from a birth defect.

There are some nontransgendered academic theorists who tell me that if I am a transexual rather than a cross-dresser or a transvestite or a butch lesbian, this must mean I want a surgeon to cut on my genitals. And they tell me that if I get a surgeon to cut on my genitals, this will show my internalized misogyny or my internalized homophobia or my lack of agency or my complicity with the medical regime, consumer capitalism, or the bipolar gender system.

There are all those transexuals who tell me that if I get a surgeon to cut on my genitals, I will no longer be a transexual but a complete man who blends into society, pays his taxes, and lives a normal life.

I'm tired of listening to other people talking about whether or not I should have a surgeon cut on my genitals. And I'm also tired of people talking about whether or not my trans sisters should have some surgeon cut on their genitals. Whose genitals are these anyway?

20 • *Jennifer Finney Boylan*

TRANS DEATHS, WHITE PRIVILEGE

DISCUSSION QUESTIONS

1. What do you see as the most powerful insights of this chapter?
2. How does Boylan contribute to our understanding of both privilege and intersectionality?
3. Among the transgender population, transgender women of color are the most frequent victims of hate crime and murder. Why do you think this is?

It was snowing in Maine on Jan. 9. I'd been to the dentist's the day before. The staff there were pleasant enough when I changed genders 12 years ago. "We'll just change your forms," the receptionist had said, cheerfully. "It's no problem."

That day, Papi Edwards, 20, a transgender woman of color, was shot to death outside a hotel in Louisville, Ky.

If you'd told me in 2000, as a transgender woman just coming out, that I was a person of privilege, I'd have angrily lectured you about exactly how heavy the burden I'd been carrying was. It had nearly done me in: the shame, the secrecy, the loneliness. It had not yet occurred to me that other burdens, carried by other women, could be weightier.

On Jan. 17, I moved into a new apartment on 106th and West End in Manhattan, in anticipation of the spring semester at Barnard College, where I teach English. My son Zach came down with me, helping to carry my luggage. He was heading back to college the next day. We had lunch at an Ethiopian restaurant called Awash, on Amsterdam. I pointed out the window at the building across the street, where I'd lived with the screenwriter Charlie Kaufman in the early 1980s. I wasn't out as transgender then; I couldn't imagine it. Yet here I was, 30 years later, a Barnard professor, having lunch with my son, who is a drama major at Vassar.

Lamia Beard, a 30-year-old black trans woman, was shot that day in Norfolk, Va. It was the weekend before the Martin Luther King Jr. federal holiday.

Feminist scholars write of the concept of "intersectionality"—the way people who occupy multiple oppressed identities can be understood only in terms of their sum, rather than as a set of independent experiences. As two trans women, Ms. Beard and I had some common experiences. But the differences between us have to be understood not only in terms of race but also in the way the oppressions generated by race and gender are bound together.

It snowed hard on Jan. 26. The subways closed that night. The day before I'd gone to services at Riverside Church. Sitting in the pews, staring at stained glass, I'd felt the power of God shining on me like a bright light.

Jennifer Finney Boylan. 2015. "Trans Deaths, White Privilege." *New York Times*, ICM Partners. Used by permission. All rights reserved.

Later, I talked to a friend about the thing I'd felt. My friend, an astrophysicist at Columbia, is a trans woman, too. We are both white.

They found Ty Underwood's body in her car that day. She was a black trans woman, a nursing assistant who lived in Tyler, Tex.

Like a lot of white people, a lot of the time I'm not aware of having "white privilege." In a similar way, I can tell you that I wasn't aware of having "male privilege," either, in the years before transition. It's something you come to understand only when it's gone, like the first time I walked down an empty street alone after midnight as a woman, and heard a man's heavy footsteps behind me.

On January 31, my wife came down from Maine. We went to see the movie "Selma" at the AMC theater on West 84th Street. There, we saw the actor playing Dr. King say, "It is unacceptable that they use their power to keep us voiceless."

Firefighters found Yazmin Vash Payne that day in an apartment in Los Angeles. She'd died of multiple stab wounds, reportedly the third trans woman killed in Los Angeles in four months.

On Feb. 1, I spent the day grading papers. That morning I worshiped at Riverside again. Sitting there listening to the carillon, I remembered the words my mother used to say: Love will prevail.

Around the time I was at Riverside, Taja Gabrielle DeJesus was found dead in a stairwell in San Francisco. She'd been stabbed. A trans woman of color in her 30s, she was a member of Bayview Church. Her mother described her as "beautiful inside and out."

The 2012 National Transgender Discrimination Survey reported that trans people faced pervasive bias in housing and employment and suffered from higher rates of suicide. In almost every area, black trans people reported that they were doing worse than white trans people.

On Feb. 11, I appeared on MSNBC with the anchor Thomas Roberts and the actress Judith Light, who stars in the Amazon series "Transparent," about a family with a transgender parent. We talked about the progress being made on transgender issues. But the progress isn't equal for everyone.

Penny Proud, a 21-year-old trans woman of color, was shot to death the day before, in New Orleans.

On Feb. 16 Barnard—an all-women's college—had a community forum for students, alumni, faculty and staff members to talk about the issue of admitting transgender women. I spoke at the event, and told everyone to open their hearts.

Kristina Gomez Reinwald, also known as Kristina Grant Infiniti, was found dead the day before in Miami. She was a transgender Latina in her mid-40s. A Miami TV station reported that, since there were no signs of forced entry in her home, she may have known her killer—a person whose heart, one might guess, had not been opened.

I talked to Caitlyn Jenner by phone for the first time on May 18. She struck me as a kind soul, from a very different world than my own, but determined to do good. "We don't want people dying over this issue," she told me.

Londyn Chanel, a 21-year-old black trans woman, was found dead in North Philadelphia that day of stab wounds. One of her friends told a local station, "She had a heart of gold."

On May 30, I was in San Francisco for a meeting of the board of GLAAD, the L.G.B.T. advocacy group.

Mercedes Williamson, a 17-year-old trans woman, reportedly disappeared that same day in Rocky Creek, Ala. Her body was found a few days later, in a field behind the house of the alleged murderer's father.

On July 21, my wife and I were in a Los Angeles restaurant with the transgender minister Allyson Robinson. "God knows us," she told me, "before we know ourselves."

India Clarke, a 25-year-old trans woman of color, was found beaten to death in Tampa that day. A local station referred to her as a "man dressed as a woman." Her father said: "The Lord made us this way. It's a shame that we could lose the life because of who we are."

Two days later, I spent an evening on the set of the Amazon series "Transparent" on the Paramount lot. My son, who knows all about having a transgender parent, is working on the show as a production assistant.

K. C. Haggard was killed that day, in Fresno, stabbed by someone passing in a car.

On Aug. 8, I went to dinner at the Village Inn in Belgrade Lakes, Me. The inn is across the lake from our house. My wife and I traveled there by boat.

Amber Monroe, 20, a trans woman of color, was killed in Detroit that day. Someone shot her as she was getting out of a car near Palmer Park.

In the last three weeks, news reports have come out about the deaths of at least five more trans or gender-nonconforming people including Shade Schuler, in Dallas; Kandis Capri, in Phoenix; Ashton O'Hara, in Detroit; *Elisha Walker, near Smithfield, N.C.; and Tamara Dominguez, in Kansas City, Mo.*

My mother told me that love would prevail, and for me it has, as it often does for people of privilege in this country, people who can find themselves insulated from injustice by dint of race or class or education or accident of birth.

For many trans women, though, especially those of color, something other than love prevails: loss. Did their lives matter any less than mine?

21 • *Gabrielle Lucero*

MILITARY SEXUAL ASSAULT: REPORTING AND RAPE CULTURE

DISCUSSION QUESTIONS

1. Why are reported sexual assaults in the military so much lower than the actual number of assaults?
2. What are some of the fears of reporting identified in this chapter? What are some specific fears held by people outside of the military context?
3. What is a "rape culture"? Identify specific examples that contribute to creating rape culture, other than those discussed in the chapter.
4. Do you see the continuation and specific examples of the myths about rape and sexual assault identified in the chapter in the world around you?
5. Why does Lucero argue that changing policy and implementing new programs is not enough to create significant change?

Lucero, Gabrielle. 2015. "Military Sexual Assault: Reporting and Rape Culture." *Sanford Journal of Public Policy*, 6(1): 1–32. Used by permission of the author.

This paper analyzes the low rates of reporting among victims of sexual assault within the military. While a Pentagon survey found that 26,000 respondents cited instances of unwanted sexual contact, only 3,374 cases were reported. Overall, victims that are unwilling to report cite fears of retaliation, of losing one's career, of the justice system, and of a military culture that is intertwined with rape culture. In response to the national attention regarding the issue of military sexual assault and victims' recent outcries, Congress and the military have created a number of new reforms and programs, including the National Defense Authorization Act for Fiscal Year 2014, the Safe Helpline, and the Special Victims Counsel Program. The success of these programs can be attributed to their focus on advocating for victims and incorporating training from survivor advocacy groups. While there has been progress in supporting victims, this analysis finds that the programs' continued success and improvement rely heavily on military leadership due to the hierarchical influence of commanders within the military.

INTRODUCTION

Current media attention has shined a spotlight on the problem of sexual assault within the military, placing the issue on the political agenda. While this spotlight produces a strong impetus for change, change will be difficult without understanding a key problem within the framework of military sexual assault: lack of reporting. If addressed, there can be a great impact on getting victims the support they need and furthering methods of prevention. Victim rates of reporting to police and to confidential services are very low. This paper addresses victims' own claims of why they do not report. It also outlines the structures and attitudes that victims name as those that perpetuate a culture of normalized sexual assault. This paper explores victims' fears of consequences from reporting and some of the recent programs created to address those fears.

THE NUMBERS

. . . As is the case with sexual assault throughout the United States, there are both female and male victims of sexual assault within the military. While females do commit sexual assault, males are overwhelmingly the perpetrators[1] (Department of Defense 2013, v. I). The military has large numbers of both female and male victims. For example, the Department of Veterans Affairs identified almost 50,000 male veterans that screened positive for military sexual trauma (Ellison 2011). It especially affects women, though, who are proportionally victimized at a higher rate than men in the military[2] (Department of Defense 2013, v. I). Women in the military are more likely to be sexually assaulted by other military personnel than killed in combat (Ellison 2011).

. . .

REPORTING

There is a clear discrepancy between the number of assaults occurring and the number being reported. . . .

Within the military, there are two reporting options available to victims: restricted and unrestricted. Restricted reporting is a means of reporting to confidential personnel within the military, including healthcare personnel, a Sexual Assault Response Coordinator (SARC), and a Victim Advocate (VA) (Military Reporting 2014). When a victim chooses a restricted report, only the previously listed personnel may be notified, the chain of command of the victim will not be told, and no investigation will take place (ibid.). It allows victims to receive medical treatment and other sexual assault response services. Unrestricted reporting allows for the victim to receive the same medical and sexual assault response services; however an official investigation will also take place, which includes informing the commander of the victim, legal personnel, and the military investigative agency (ibid.). Based on SAPRO's [Sexual Assault Prevention and Response Office] report, however, both forms of reporting are not often utilized. There were 26,000 incidents and only 3,374 reports, including both restricted and unrestricted types (Department of Defense 2013, v. I).

The main question, then, becomes, "Why do victims not report?" Because of the media furor surrounding military sexual assault, that question is being asked of victims now more than ever. The overwhelming answer from victims has been fear: fear of retaliation, fear of losing one's career, and fear of military culture. Before delving into the fears victims face within the military through support systems, the justice system, and their general professional environment, it is important to first understand the concept of rape culture.

RAPE CULTURE

"Rape culture," a term coined by feminists in the 1970s, is not unique to the military. It is a culture that permeates throughout the United States in civilian and military life (Wolf 2013). It is the idea that institutions, media, and popular culture normalize and excuse sexual violence by "encouraging male aggression," using "victim-blaming," and "tasking victims with the burden of rape prevention" (McEwan 2009). It causes misconceptions about why rape occurs and who gets raped. Feminist Naomi Wolf explains how rape culture causes people to believe rape occurs in two ways, ". . . an isolated, mysterious event, caused by some individual man's sudden psychopathology, or it is 'explained' by some seductive transgression by the victim" (2013). As Wolf demonstrates, misconceptions about rape create a culture in which sexual assault is defined in two ways. The first is where the perpetrator is a clear criminal—a deranged stranger who hides in the bushes. In this idea, the victim is seen only as pure, nonsexual, and a woman. The second cultural perpetuation is where the victim is the wrongdoer. Her actions, dress, intoxication level, sexuality, etc. are questioned and thus rather than being the perpetrator's fault, the rape is the result of the victim's "bad" decisions.

These misconceptions stem from a general culture in the U.S. that encourages men to be aggressive and constantly want sex, whereas women are supposed to protect their bodies and not want sex. These ideas are specific to rape culture because the same reactions are not given to victims of other crimes. Rape culture is not defined solely through an objectification of women, but rather encompasses misconceptions about the crime itself, victim blaming, and the confluence of sex and power. Rape culture has permeated throughout society so much that when questioned, perpetrators of rape admit to engaging in forced sex and "almost none considered it to be a crime" (Kamenetz 2014). Facing relatively low chances of negative consequences, shame, accusation, and punishment, these men were products of a culture that taught them misconceptions about what rape looks like and that victims can be blamed. The reality of rape, however, is very different. Statistics show that both in the civilian world and within the military, sexual assault happens to both men and women. The assault is usually committed by someone they know, often in their own home, and often the perpetrators are repeat offenders (Statistics 2009).

Since the 1970s, academic research on rape has argued that sexual violence is not about sexual gratification, but about power and control (Brownmiller 1975). Sexual assault is used as a means of intimidation and control over the victim. For example, the majority of perpetrators of male on male sexual assault are heterosexual, and use sexual assault to "put people in their place" (Ellison 2011).

Victims of sexual assault are already subjected to a state of intimidation and violence and have felt a loss of control caused by the assault. On top of those effects, victims must also face rape culture that normalizes sexual assault and blames those victims for their own assault. Again, this rape culture persists throughout the civilian world, and the military is no exception. Sexual assault leaves victims in fear, and rape culture further perpetuates those fears and prevents them from reporting their assault. It is necessary to address sexual assault throughout the country, but the military has a unique structure that requires attention as to why victims of military sexual assault are not reporting.

VICTIMS' FEARS

When victims' fears cause them not to report, they face further consequences that threaten their emotional and physical well beings. Known effects of sexual assault include post-traumatic stress disorder, substance abuse, self-harm/self-injury, depression, eating disorders, sleep disorders, and flashbacks (Effects 2014). Without reporting, victims do not have access to the support services that help them deal with these effects; trauma causes them further emotional and physical harm, and often negatively impacts their careers within the military. Even when some victims do report, support systems within the military sometimes do not protect them from the negative effects of sexual assault. Former Marine corporal Sarah Albertson reported that a superior officer had raped her. She stated, "I was told I needed to suck it up until the end of the investigation and I was told to respect the rank he deserves" (Isikoff 2011). Because of the assault, she gained 30 pounds and suffered from depression. Her weight gain caused her to be put on a weight-loss training program, which was run by her assaulter, which allowed him further control over her because "[h]e was in charge of judging my body" (ibid.). Many victims thus feel that they lack a support system when they report. This is often compounded by having to continue to work with their assaulter, especially if the assaulter is in a position of power over the victim.

Another fear commonly expressed by victims is the possible inability to progress professionally within the military. Former Army sergeant Myla Haider claims, "I've never met one victim who was able to report the crime and still retain their military career" (Lawrence & Peñaloza 2013). The negative effects of sexual assault previously mentioned often interfere with the victims' ability to function within the military and causes them to eventually leave the service. Victims also claim that reporting has caused their colleagues and superiors to question their judgment and effectiveness, which again lessens their ability to advance within the military (ibid.). Haider became an agent in the Army's Criminal Investigation Command (CID). She explains that CID and the

military has a culture of doubting victims' claims of sexual assault, which not only led to her story being questioned, but also caused her colleagues and superiors to question her credibility to testify as a CID agent in other rape cases (ibid.). Haider states, "[B]y making that choice, my reporting of it took over my life, ruined my career, and wound up, ultimately, getting me kicked out of the Army" (ibid.).

The fear of losing one's career in the military also stems from the possibility of retaliation. Among the victims who reported their assaults in 2012, 62 percent were met with retaliation for reporting, and 43 percent heard about negative experiences of other victims who had reported (Schwellenbach 2013). Of the 67 percent of victims who did not report their assaults, 47 percent said they did not because of fear of retaliation (Department of Defense 2013, v. I). This retaliation came in many forms: 3 percent experienced professional retaliation, 31 percent experienced social retaliation, 2 percent experienced administrative action, and 26 percent experienced a combination of professional retaliation, social retaliation, administrative action, and/or punishment (ibid.). One example is Marine Private Stephanie Schroeder, who not only had to work with her rapist for a year after her attack but saw her rank and pay reduced, and also was discharged for a "personality disorder" (Gupta 2012). She explains, "If you want to keep your career you don't say anything. . . . You just deal with it" (ibid.). Another veteran, Diana, comments on her decision to not make an unrestricted report, "Maybe if I was not in a combat zone and maybe if I didn't see a future in the military, and if I didn't fear retribution. If I didn't fear gossip and rumors or the fact that the trial would be lengthy and the punishment wouldn't fit the crime because it never does" (McCrummen 2014).

Diana's comment also leads into the final fear felt by victims: a lack of faith in the justice system. Victims fear that the justice system leads to inaction, which aligns with the effects of rape culture. There is a strong fear that the justice system will not punish perpetrators nor protect victims; 50 percent of victims that did not report believed nothing would be done with their report (Department of Defense 2013,

v. I). Victims fear that the chain of command will not go forward with the case or that even if there is a conviction, it will be overturned (ibid.). A chief prosecutor for the Air Force, Col. Don Christensen, stated, "Commanders would much rather believe they have a woman who's lying and crying rape than that there's a sex offender in their midst" (Draper 2014).

Victims also cite how the justice system permits commanders, military police, and their peers to blame them for their assaults, a common aspect of rape culture. Victim Rebekhah Havrilla explains, "Initially, I chose not to do a report of any kind because I had no faith in my chain of command, as my first sergeant previously had sexual harassment accusations against him, and the unit climate was extremely sexist and hostile in nature towards women" (Fantz & Levs 2013). Victim Brian Lewis adds, "The culture of victim blaming and retaliation while failing to punish the perpetrator must end" (ibid.). Victims learn about these experiences of other victims and decide not to report because they do not want to go through the same ordeal. They feel that the justice system not only blames them for their own assaults, but also re-traumatizes them (ibid.). One victim, Kris, was told that she "needed to keep her 'emotions in check'" after reporting her rape. This caused the prosecutor working on her case to note, "When the commander is so obviously supporting the accused over the victim, it sends a clear message that it's OK not to believe her and to shun her. And so why would a woman come forward, knowing what Kris had gone through?" (Draper 2014).

Another example of the justice system's use of victim blaming can be found in a Naval Academy case in which a Navy football player was found not guilty of sexually assaulting a female midshipman. In the Article 32 hearing, the victim was asked intense and blaming questions that "legal experts say frighten many victims from coming forward" (Steinhauer 2013). The victim was asked whether or not she wore a bra or underwear to the party, whether she "felt like a ho" afterward, and how widely she opens her mouth during oral sex (ibid.). These questions are reminiscent of those often cited by sexual assault advocates as victim blaming questions, like

questioning what someone was wearing, his/her past sexual history, and what actions they had taken to "cause the assault" (Rape Culture 2014).

RESPONDING TO THE PROBLEM

Military victims of sexual assault have laid out the fears that prevent them from reporting their assaults, and in recent years the military has responded with a variety of reforms and programs. The majority of these programs as well as the Pentagon reports and prevention education literature dispersed to military personnel are provided through SAPRO. Three reforms and programs of note will be addressed: the National Defense Authorization Act for Fiscal Year 2014, the Safe Helpline, and the Special Victims Counsel Program.

The recent Defense Authorization Act for Fiscal Year 2014 saw the most sexual assault reforms included in one bill, with 19 reforms. Some of the major reforms include: prohibiting the military from recruiting a person convicted of a sex offense, the creation of Special Victims Units within the Military Police, commanders are no longer able to overturn jury convictions, dishonorable discharge is now mandated for anyone convicted of sexual assault, retaliation against victims who report a sexual assault has been criminalized, and the statute of limitations in rape and sexual assault cases has been eliminated (Pentagon 2014). These reforms strive to place more faith in the justice system while also aiming to stem an environment that perpetuates rape culture.

An important program is the Safe Helpline. In 2011, the Department of Defense partnered with The Rape, Abuse and Incest National Network to create a hotline specifically for victims of sexual assault within the military (About 2014). The Safe Helpline provides victims the ability to call, chat online, or receive text messages with referrals (ibid.). It offers information about reporting, support, and recovery, as well as provides referrals (ibid.). . . .

Another strong program that provides support for victims is the Special Victims Counsel (SVC). Originally an Air Force program created in early 2013, Secretary of Defense Chuck Hagel mandated all branches to implement the SVC program (Clark 2014). SVC are military lawyers trained to act as advocates for victims of sexual assault (Biesecker & Dalesio 2014). While they help with legal advocacy, their main mission is to protect the victims by advocating for their needs (ibid.). . . .

STRENGTHENING THE RESPONSE

While these strong reforms and programs have been making a positive impact on the experiences of sexual assault victims, they still find problems of rape culture within the military that need to be addressed. While programs and reforms might be strong on paper, their actual effectiveness will depend on the leadership within the military and the culture that persists. While many military leaders such as Secretary Hagel and General Odierno have come out in strong support for victims and call for changes in the military, other members of leadership demonstrate a lack of attention or care for the issue. In the past year there have been some examples of this attitude. Through a rescreening of military personnel in sensitive positions of trust ordered by Secretary Hagel, the Army disqualified 588 soldiers as sexual assault counselors, recruiters, and drill sergeants for offenses ranging from reckless driving to sexual assault (Brook & Gillibrand 2014). The Army's top prosecutor for sexual assault cases was suspended after being accused of sexually assaulting a lawyer working for him while at a sexual assault legal conference (Carroll & Vandiver 2014). The former head of the Air Force Sexual Assault Prevention and Response Office faced allegations of sexual battery in 2013 (ibid.). An Army sergeant at Fort Hood, who was the coordinator of the post's sexual assault harassment prevention program, faces 21 charges in a prostitution ring case (Paresh 2014). Reforms and programs to prevent and respond to sexual assault can only be as effective as the leadership that runs them and the culture that surrounds the issue of sexual assault. When some leadership not only treat sexual assault casually but also sometimes commit the crime, victims will continue to not report.

SVC also reports pushback from commanders and prosecutors, claiming that they have been excluded from hearings and denied access to crucial information (Clark 2014). Others have also reported being threatened with retaliation when they challenge higher-ranking officers (Biesecker & Dalesio 2014). Rape culture that permeates through leadership and through the ranks within the military must be reduced and eventually eliminated in order for victims to truly feel comfortable reporting. SVC have acknowledged that much of their success stems from the program's partnership with survivor advocacy groups within the civilian world. The training that helps them to fully understand rape culture and advocate for their victims is boosted by the involvement of organizations whose sole purposes are to do just that. . . .

CONCLUSION

The military is not excluded from cultural norms and beliefs that persist within the civilian world, and those norms include rape culture. In the past year, victims have strongly expressed their concerns with the way the military handles sexual assaults. Their fears have been enumerated, and programs and reforms have been and must continue to respond to these fears. Though usually muted through violence and control, military sexual assault victims' voices now have a platform through which victims can confront rape culture. Military leadership must continue to heed these voices and use their own to truly create a zero tolerance policy for sexual assault. The military must verify that their leadership is taking the crime seriously and responding to victims in a way that does not blame them and does not fall into the misconceptions created by rape culture. . . .

NOTES

1. For example, in 2012 90 percent of alleged perpetrators of sexual assault in the military were male (Miller & Rosenthal 2013).
2. Veterans' organizations like the Service Women's Action Network and individual veterans confronted the

military's rape culture in 2011 when four previous service members filed a lawsuit claiming that the Pentagon failed to act on reported sexual assaults and "turned a blind eye" (Isikoff 2011).

REFERENCES

About Department of Defense (DoD) Safe Helpline. (2014). *Department of Defense.* Retrieved from https://safehelplinc.org/about-dod-safe-helpline

Biesecker, M. & Dalesio, E. (2014). New Corps of Military Lawyers Helping Sexual Assault Victims. *Huffington Post.* Retrieved from http://www.huffingtonpost.com/2014/03/30/military-lawyers- sexual-assault_n_5059582.html

Brook, T. (2014). Gillibrand Demands More Details on Reassigned Soldiers. *USA Today.* Retrieved from http://www.usatoday.com/story/nation/2014/04/16/gillibrand-army-military-sexual-assault/7776509/

Brook, T. (2014). Military Hotline Aids Sexual Assault Victims. *USA Today.* Retrieved from http://www.usatoday.com/story/news/nation/2014/04/16/military-sexual-assault-safehelp-claire-mccaskil-kirsten-gillibrand/7751143/

Brownmiller, S. (1975). *Against Our Will: Men, Women and Rape.* New York: Ballantine Books.

Carroll, C. & Vandiver, J. (2014). Army's Top Sex Assault Prosecutor Suspended After Assault Allegations. *Stars and Stripes.* Retrieved from http://www.stripes.com/army-s-top-sex-assault-prosecutor-suspended-after-assault-allegation-1.271461

Clark, M. (2014). New Military Program to Protect Victims Sees Early Success. *MSNBC.* Retrieved from http://www.msnbc.com/msnbc/military-sex-assault-svc-program

Department of Defense Sexual Assault Prevention and Response Office. (2013). *Department of Defense Annual Report on Sexual Assault in the Military: Fiscal Year 2012 Volume I.* Retrieved from http://www.sapr.mil/public/does/reports/FY12_DoD_SAPRO_Annual_Report_on_Sexual_Assault-VOLUME_ONE.pdf

Department of Defense Sexual Assault Prevention and Response Office. (2013). *Department of Defense Annual Report on Sexual Assault in the Military; Fiscal Year 2012 Volume II.* Retrieved from http://www.sapr.mil/public/does/reports/FY12_DoD_SAPRO_Annual_Report_on_Sexual_Assault-VOLUME_TWO.pdf

Draper, R. (2014). The Military's Rough Justice on Sexual Assault. *The New York Times.* Retrieved from http://www.nytimes.com/2014/11/30/magazine/the-militarys-rough-justice-on-sexual-assault.html

Effects of Sexual Assault. (2014). *Rape, Abuse and Incest National Network.* Retrieved from http://www.rainn.org/statistics

Ellison, J. (2011). The Military's Secret Shame. *Newsweek.* Retrieved from http://www.newsweek.com/militarys-secret-shame-66459

Fantz, A. & Levs, J. (2013). Military Rape Victims: Stop Blaming Us. *CNN.* Retrieved from http://www.cnn.com/2013/03/13/us/military-sexual-assault/

Gupta, S. (2012). Stephanie Schroeder's Military Sex Assault Claim Leads to Psych Discharge. *KSDK.* Retrieved from http://archive.ksdk.com/news/world/article/317006/28/Military-sex-assault-claim-leads-to-psych-discharge

Isikoff, M. (2011). Lawsuit Claims Pentagon Turned Blind Eye to Military Rape Victims. *NBC News.* Retrieved from http://www.nbcnews.com/id/41598622/ns/us_news-life/t/lawsuit-claims-pentagon-turned-blind-eye-military-rape-victims/

Kamenetz, A. (2014). The History of Campus Sexual Assault. *National Public Radio.* Retrieved from http://www.npr.org/blogs/ed/2014/11/30/366348383/the-history-of-campus-sexual-assault

Lawrence, Q. & Peñaloza, M. (2013). Sexual Violence Victims Say Military Justice System Is 'Broken.' *National Public Radio.* Retrieved from http://www.npr.org/2013/03/21/174840895/sexual-violence-victims-say-military-justice-system-is-broken

McCrummen, S. (2014, April 12). The Choice. *The Washington Post.* Retrieved from http://www.washingtonpost.com/sf/national/2014/04/12/the-choice/

McEwan, M. (2009). Rape Culture 101. *Shakesville.* Retrieved from http://www.shakesville.com/2009/10/rape-culture-101.html

Military Reporting Options FAQ. (2014). *DOD Safe Helpline.* Retrieved from https://safehelpline.org/reporting-options.cfm

Miller, K. & Rosenthal, L. (2013). 5 Myths About Military Sexual Assault. *American Progress.* Retrieved from https://www.americanprogress.org/issues/military/news/2013/06/06/65602/5-myths-about-military-sexual-assault/

Paresh, D. (2014). Soldier Coordinating Sex Assault Program Charged in Prostitution Case. *Stars and Stripes.* Retrieved from http://www.stripes.com/news/soldier-coordinating-sex-assault-program-charged-in-prostitution-case-1.271942

Pentagon Updates McCaskill on Sexual Assault Reform. (2014). *ABC KSPR.* Retrieved from http://www.kspr.com/news/local/pentagon-updates-mccaskill-sexual-assault-reform/21051620_25320534

Rape Culture. (2014). *Marshall University Women's Center.* Retrieved from http://www.marshall.edu/weenter/sexual-assault/rape-culture/

Scarborough, R. (2014). Doubts on Military's Sex Assault Stats as Number Far Exceed Those for the U.S. *The Washington Times.* Retrieved from http://www.washingtontimes.com/news/2014/apr/6/doubts-on-militarys-sex-assault-stats-as-numbers-f/

Schwellenbach, N. (2013). Fear of Reprisal: The Quiet Accomplice in the Military's Sexual-Assault Epidemic. *TIME.* Retrieved from http://nation.time.com/2013/05/09/fear-of-reprisal-the-quiet-accomplice-in-the-militarys-sexual-assault-epidemic/

Statistics. (2014). *Rape. Abuse and Incest National Network.* Retrieved from http://www.rainn.org/statistics

Steinhauer, J. (2013). Navy Hearing in Rape Case Raises Alarm. *The New York Times.* Retrieved from http://www.nytimes.com/2013/09/21/us/intrusive-grilling-in-rape-case-raises-alarm-on-military-hearings.html?pagewanted-all

Wolf, N. (2013). The US Military's Rape Culture. *Project Syndicate.* Retrieved from http://www.project-syndicate.org/commentary/the-us-military-s-rape-culture-by-naomi-wolf

22 • *Andrea Smith*

RAPE AND THE WAR AGAINST NATIVE WOMEN

DISCUSSION QUESTIONS

1. How much of the history Smith provides was new to you? Why do you think issues such as forced sterilization and medical experimentation are often not included in history classes or other courses? Should all students learn this history?

2. Does the Ivory soap advertisement surprise you? Do you think our culture continues to equate cleanliness with whiteness? Consider phrases like "forces of darkness" and "she was shown the light." Do you think these phrases reinforce notions of white cleanliness, purity, and superiority? Can you think of other similar phrases?

3. What does the author mean when she says Indian people "learn to internalize self-hatred"? Do you think this is a common occurrence among oppressed groups?

4. The author asserts that white feminists have failed to call attention to the rapes and murders of indigenous people in Guatemala, despite being outraged at similar events in Bosnia. Why do you think this elision has occurred?

"Rape and the War against Native Women" by Andrea Smith as found on pages 63–76 in *Reading Native American Women*. 2004 edited by Harvey Ines Vila.

In Indian Country, there is a growing "wellness" movement, largely spearheaded by women, that stresses healing from personal and historic abuse, both on the individual and the community level. This wellness movement is based on the fact that Native peoples' history of colonization has been marked on our bodies. In order to heal from personal abuse, such as sexual abuse, we must also heal from the historic abuse of every massacre, every broken treaty, that our people have suffered. As Cecelia Fire Thunder states:

> We also have to recognize and understand that we carry the pain of our grandmothers, mothers, and the generation that came before us. We carry in our heart the pain of all our ancestors and we carry in our hearts the unresolved grief [and] the loss of our way of life. . . . There is no way we can move forward and be stronger nations without recognizing the trauma and pain that took place within our nations, our families, and within ourselves.[1]

One of the barriers, however, to healing from violence in Native communities is the reluctance to openly address violence against Native women. Native women who are survivors of violence often find themselves caught between the tendency within Native communities to remain silent about sexual and domestic violence in order to maintain a united front against racism and colonialism and the insistence on the part of the white-dominated antiviolence movement that survivors cannot heal from violence unless they leave their communities. The reason Native women are constantly marginalized in male-dominated discourses about racism and colonialism and in white-dominated discourses about sexism is the inability of both discourses to address the inextricable relationship between gender violence and colonialism. That is, the issue is not simply that violence against women happens during colonization but that the colonial process is itself structured by sexual violence. It is not possible for Native nations to decolonize themselves until they address gender violence because it is through this kind of violence that colonization has been successful. It is partly because the history of colonization of Native people is

interrelated with colonizers' assaults upon Indian bodies. It is through the constant assaults upon our bodily integrity that colonizers have attempted to eradicate our sense of Indian identity.

As a multitude of scholars such as Robert Allen Warrior, Albert Cave, H. C. Porter, and others have demonstrated, Christian colonizers[2] often envisioned Native peoples as Canaanites, worthy of mass destruction as they went about the task of creating a "New Israel."[3] What makes Canaanites supposedly worthy of destruction in the biblical narrative and Indian peoples supposedly worthy of destruction in the eyes of their colonizers is that they both personify sexual sin. In the Bible, Canaanites commit acts of sexual perversion in Sodom (Gen. 19:1–29), are the descendants of the unsavory relations between Lot and his daughters (Gen. 19:30–38), are the descendants of the sexually perverse Ham (Gen. 9:22–27), and prostitute themselves in service of their gods (Gen. 28:21–22; Deut. 28:18; 1 Kings 14:24; 2 Kings 23:7; Hos. 4:13; Amos 2:7).

Similarly, Native peoples, in the eyes of the colonizers, are marked by their sexual perversity.[4] Alexander Whitaker, a minister in Virginia, wrote in 1613, "They live naked in bodie, as if their shame of their sinne deserved no covering: Their names are as naked as their bodie: They esteem it a virtue to lie, deceive and steale as their master the divell teacheth them."[5] Furthermore, according to Bernardino de Minaya, "Their [the Indians'] marriages are not a sacrament but a sacrilege. They are idolatrous, libidinous, and commit sodomy. Their chief desire is to eat, drink, worship heathen idols, and commit bestial obscenities."[6]

Because they personify sexual sin, Indian bodies are inherently "dirty." As white Californians described in the 1860s, Native people were "the dirtiest lot of human beings on earth."[7] They wore "filthy rags, with their persons unwashed, hair uncombed and swarming with vermin."[8] The following 1885 Procter & Gamble ad for Ivory Soap also illustrates this equation between Indian bodies and dirt.

We were once factious, fierce and wild,
  In peaceful arts unreconciled,

Our blankets smeared with grease and stains
From buffalo meat and settlers' veins.
Through summer's dust and heat content,
From moon to moon unwashed we went,
But IVORY SOAP came like a ray
Of light across our darkened way
And now we're civil, kind and good
And keep the laws as people should,
We wear our linen, lawn and lace
As well as folks with paler face
And now I take, where'er we go,
This cake of IVORY SOAP to show
What civilized my squaw and me
And made us clean and fair to see.[9]

Because Indian bodies are "dirty," they are considered sexually violable and "rapable." That is, in patriarchal thinking, only a body that is "pure" can be violated. The rape of bodies that are considered inherently impure or dirty simply does not count. For instance, prostitutes have almost an impossible time being believed if they are raped because the dominant society considers the prostitute's body undeserving of integrity and violable at all times. Similarly, the history of mutilation of Indian bodies, both living and dead, makes it clear to Indian people that they are not entitled to bodily integrity. Andrew Jackson, for instance, ordered the mutilation of approximately 800 Muscogee Indian corpses, cutting off their noses and slicing long strips of flesh from their bodies to make bridle reins.[10] Tecumseh's skin was flayed and made into razor straps.[11] A soldier cut off the testicles of White Antelope to make a tobacco pouch.[12] Colonel John Chivington led an attack against the Cheyenne and Arapahoe in which nearly all the victims were scalped; their fingers, arms, and ears were amputated to obtain jewelry; and their private parts were cut out to be exhibited before the public in Denver.[13]

In the history of massacres against Indian people, colonizers attempted not only to defeat Indian people but also to eradicate their very identity and humanity. They attempted to transform Indian people from human beings into tobacco pouches, bridle reins, or souvenirs—an object for the consumption of white people. This history reflects a disrespect not only for Native people's bodies but also for the integrity of all creation, the two being integrally related. That is, Native people were viewed as rapable because they resemble animals rather than humans. Unlike Native people, who do not view the bodies of animals as rapable either, colonizers often senselessly annihilated both animals and Indian people in order to establish their common identity as expendable. During the Washita massacre, for example, Captain Frederick W. Benteen reported that Colonel Custer "exhibits his close sharpshooting and terrifies the crowd of frightened, captured squaws and papooses by dropping the straggling ponies in death near them.... Not even do the poor dogs of the Indians escape his eye and aim, as they drop dead or limp howling away."[14] Whereas Native people view animals as created beings deserving of bodily integrity, Bernard Sheehan notes that Europeans at that time often viewed animals as guises for Satan.[15] As one Humboldt County newspaper stated in 1853, "We can never rest in security until the redskins are treated like the other wild beasts of the forest."[16] Of course, if whites had treated Native people with the same respect that Native people have traditionally treated animals, Native people would not have suffered genocide. Thus, ironically, while Native people often view their identities as inseparable from the rest of creation, and hence the rest of creation deserves their respect, colonizers also viewed Indian identity as inseparably linked to that of animal and plant life, and hence deserving of destruction and mutilation.

Today, this mentality continues in new forms. One example is the controversial 1992 hepatitis B trial vaccine program conducted among Alaska Native children. In this experiment, almost all Alaska Native children were given experimental vaccines without their consent. Dr. William Jordan of the U.S. Department of Health has noted that virtually all field trials for new vaccines in the United States are first tested on indigenous people in Alaska, and most of the vaccines do absolutely nothing to prevent disease.[17] As Mary Ann Mills and Bernadine Atcheson (Traditional Dena'ina) point out, this constant influx of vaccines into Native communities is a constant assault on their immune systems. They are particularly concerned about this hepatitis B vaccine because they contend it might have been tainted with HIV. They note that even Merck Sharp & Dohme seems to acknowledge that the vaccine contained the virus when it states in the *Physicians' Desk Reference* (PDR) that "clinical trials of HEPTAVAX-B provide no evidence to suggest transmission of ... AIDS by this vaccine, even when the vaccine has been used routinely in infants in Alaska."[18] According to Mills and Atcheson, alarming cases of AIDS soon broke out after these experiments, mostly among women and children, and now some villages are going to lose one-third of their population to AIDS.[19]

The equation between indigenous people and laboratory animals is evident in the minds of medical colonizers. The PDR manual notes that Merck Sharp & Dohme experimented both on "chimpanzees and ... Alaska Native children."[20] Mills and Atcheson question why these drugs are being tested on Native people *or* chimpanzees when Alaska Native people did not have a high rate of hepatitis B to begin with.[21] Furthermore, they question the precepts of Western medicine, which senselessly dissects, vivisects, and experiments on both animals and human beings when, as they argue, much healthier preventative and holistic indigenous forms of medicine are available. This Western medical model has not raised the life expectancy of indigenous people past the age of forty-seven. States Mills, "Today we rely on our elders and our traditional healers. We have asked them if they were ever as sick as their grandchildren or great-grandchildren are today. Their reply was no; they are much healthier than their children are today."[22]

Through this colonization and abuse of their bodies, Indian people learn to internalize self-hatred. Body image is integrally related to self-esteem.[23] When one's body is not respected, one begins to hate oneself. Thus, it is not a surprise that Indian people who have survived sexual abuse say they do not want to be Indian. Anne, a Native boarding school student, reflects on this process:

You better not touch yourself....If I looked at somebody...lust, sex, and I got scared of those sexual feelings. And I did not know how to handle them....What really confused me was if intercourse was sin, why are people born?...It took me a really long time to get over the fact that...I've sinned: I had a child.[24]

As her words indicate, when the bodies of Indian people are inherently sinful and dirty, it becomes a sin just to be Indian. Each instance of abuse we suffer is just another reminder that, as Chrystos articulates, "If you don't make something pretty / they can hang on their walls or wear around their necks / you might as well be dead."[25]

While the bodies of both Indian men and women have been marked by abuse, Inés Hernández-Avila (Nez Perce) notes that the bodies of Native women have been particularly targeted for abuse because of their capacity to give birth. "It is because of a Native American woman's sex that she is hunted down and slaughtered, in fact, singled out, because she has the potential through childbirth to assure the continuance of the people."[26] David Stannard points out that control over women's reproductive abilities and destruction of women and children are essential in destroying a people. If the women of a nation are not disproportionately killed, then that nation's population will not be severely affected. He says that Native women and children were targeted for wholesale killing in order to destroy the Indian nations. This is why colonizers such as Andrew Jackson recommended that troops systematically kill Indian women and children after massacres in order to complete extermination.[27] Similarly, Methodist minister Colonel John Chivington's policy was to "kill and scalp all little and big" because "nits make lice."[28]

Because Native women had the power to maintain Indian nations in the face of genocide, they were dangerous to the colonial world order. Also, because Indian nations were for the most part not patriarchal and afforded women great esteem, Indian women represented a threat to colonial patriarchy as they belied the notion that patriarchy is somehow inevitable. Consequently, colonizers expressed constant outrage that Native women were not tied to monogamous marriages and held "the marriage ceremony in utter disregard,"[29] were free to express their sexuality, had "no respect for...virginity,"[30] and loved themselves. They did not see themselves as "fallen" women as they should have. Their sexual power was threatening to white men; consequently, they sought to control it.

> When I was in the boat I captured a beautiful Carib woman....I conceived desire to take pleasure....I took a rope and thrashed her well, for which she raised such unheard screams that you would not have believed your ears. Finally we came to an agreement in such a manner that I can tell you that she seemed to have been brought up in a school of harlots.[31]

> Two of the best looking of the squaws were lying in such a position, and from the appearance of the genital organs and of their wounds, there can be no doubt that they were first ravished and then shot dead. Nearly all of the dead were mutilated.[32]

> One woman, big with child, rushed into the church, clasping the altar and crying for mercy for herself and unborn babe. She was followed, and fell pierced with a dozen lances....The child was torn alive from the yet palpitating body of its mother, first plunged into the holy water to be baptized, and immediately its brains were dashed out against a wall.[33]

> The Christians attacked them with buffets and beatings....Then they behaved with such temerity and shamelessness that the most powerful ruler of the island had to see his own wife raped by a Christian officer.[34]

> I heard one man say that he had cut a woman's private parts out, and had them for exhibition on a stick. I heard another man say that he had cut the fingers off of an Indian, to get the rings off his hand. I also heard of numerous instances in which men had cut out the private parts of females, and stretched them over their saddle-bows and some of them over their hats.[35]

American Horse said of the massacre at Wounded Knee:

> The fact of the killing of the women, and more especially the killing of the young boys and girls who are to make up the future strength of the Indian people, is the saddest part of the whole affair and we feel it very sorely.[36]

Ironically, while enslaving women's bodies, colonizers argued that they were actually somehow freeing Native women from the "oppression" they supposedly faced in Native nations. Thomas Jefferson argued that Native women "are submitted to unjust drudgery. This I believe is the case with every barbarous people....It is civilization alone which replaces women in the enjoyment of their equality."[37] The *Mariposa Gazette* similarly noted that when Indian women were safely under the control of white men, they "are neat, and tidy, and industrious, and soon learn to discharge domestic duties properly and creditably."[38] In 1862, a Native man in Conrow Valley was killed and scalped, his head twisted off, with his killers saying, "You will not kill any more women and children."[39] Apparently, Native women can only be free while under the dominion of white men, and both Native and white women need to be protected from Indian men rather than from white men.

While the era of Indian massacres in their more explicit form is over in North America, in Latin America, the wholesale rape and mutilation of indigenous women's bodies continues. During the 1982 massacre of Mayan people in Rio Negro (Guatemala), 177 women and children were killed; the young women were raped in front of their mothers, and the mothers were killed in front of their children. The younger children were then tied at the ankles and dashed against the rocks until their skulls were broken. This massacre was funded by the U.S. government.[40] While many white feminists are correctly outraged by the rapes in Bosnia, organizing to hold a war crimes tribunal against the Serbs, one wonders why the mass rapes in Guatemala or elsewhere against indigenous people in Latin America has not sparked the same outrage. In fact, feminist legal scholar Catherine MacKinnon argues that in Bosnia "the world has *never* seen sex used this consciously, this cynically, this elaborately, this openly, this systematically...as a means of destroying a whole people."[41] She seems to forget that she lives on this land only because millions of Native people were raped, sexually mutilated, and murdered. Is perhaps mass rape against European women genocide while mass rape against indigenous women is business as usual? In even the white feminist imagination, are Native women's bodies more rapable than white women's bodies?

In North America, while there does not seem to be the same wholesale massacres of Indian people as in Latin America, colonizers will revert back to old habits in times of aggravated conflict. In 1976, Anna Mae Aquash (Micmac), who had been fighting U.S. policies against Native people as a member of the American Indian Movement (AIM), was found dead—apparently raped. Her killer was never brought to justice, but it is believed that she was killed either by the FBI or as a result of being badjacketed by the FBI as an informant. After her death, the FBI cut off her hands. Later, when the FBI pressured Myrtle Poor Bear into testifying against political prisoner Leonard Peltier, they threatened that she would end up just like Anna Mae if she did not comply.[42] In the 1980s when I served as a nonviolent witness for the Chippewa spearfishers, who were being harassed by white racist mobs, one white harasser carried a sign saying "Save a fish; spear a pregnant squaw."[43] Even after 500 years, in the eyes of the colonizers, Native women's bodies are still rapable. During the 1990 Mohawk crisis in Oka, a white mob surrounded the ambulance of a Native woman who was attempting to leave the Mohawk reservation because she was hemorrhaging after having given birth. She was forced to "spread her legs" to prove she had given birth. The police at the scene refused to intervene. An Indian man was arrested for "wearing a disguise" (he was wearing jeans), and he was brutally beaten, his testicles crushed. Two women from Chicago WARN (Women of All Red Nations, the organization I belong to) went to Oka to videotape the crisis. They were arrested and held in custody for eleven hours without being charged and were told they could not go to the bathroom unless the male police officers could watch. The place they were held was covered with pornographic magazines.[44]

This colonial desire to subjugate Indian women's bodies was quite apparent when, in 1982, Stuart Kasten marketed a new video game, "Custer's Revenge," in which players get points each time they, in the form of Custer, rape an Indian woman. The

slogan of the game is "When you score, you score." He describes the game as "a fun sequence where the woman is enjoying a sexual act willingly." According to the promotional material,

> You are General Custer. Your dander's up, your pistol's wavin'. You've hog-tied a ravishing Indian maiden and have a chance to rewrite history and even up an old score. Now, the Indian maiden's hands may be tied, but she's not about to take it lying down, by George! Help is on the way. If you're to get revenge you'll have to rise to the challenge, dodge a tribe of flying arrows and protect your flanks against some downright mean and prickly cactus. But if you can stand pat and last past the strings and arrows—You can stand last. Remember? Revenge is sweet.[45]

Just as historically white colonizers who raped Indian women claimed that the real rapist was the Indian man, today white men who rape and murder Indian women often make this same claim. In Minneapolis, a white man, Jesse Coulter, raped, murdered, and mutilated several Indian women. He claimed to be Indian, adopting the name Jesse Sittingcrow and emblazoning an AIM tattoo on his arm.[46] This is not to suggest that Indian men do not rape now. After years of colonialism and boarding school experience, violence has also been internalized within Indian communities. However, this view of the Indian man as the "true" rapist obscures who has the real power in this racist and patriarchal society.

Also, just as colonizers in the past targeted Native women for destruction because of their ability to give birth, colonizers today continue their attacks on the reproductive capabilities of Native women. Dr. Connie Uri, a Cherokee/Choctaw doctor, first uncovered sterilization abuses of Native women when a Native woman requested from her a "womb transplant." Dr. Uri discovered that this woman had undergone a hysterectomy for sterilization purposes but was told the procedure was reversible. The doctor began investigating sterilization abuses, which led Senator James Abourezk to request a study on IHS (Indian Health Services) sterilization policies. The General Accounting Office released a study in November 1976 indicating that Native women were being sterilized without informed consent. Dr. Uri conducted further investigations, leading her to estimate that 25 percent of all Native women of childbearing age had been sterilized without their informed consent, with sterilization rates as high as 80 percent on some reservations.[47]

While sterilization abuse has been curbed somewhat with the institution of informed consent policies, it has reappeared in the form of dangerous contraceptives such as Norplant and Depo-Provera.[48] These are both extremely risky forms of long-acting hormonal contraceptives that have been pushed on Indian women. Depo-Provera, a known carcinogen that has been condemned as an inappropriate form of birth control by several national women's health organizations,[49] was routinely administered to Indian women through IHS before it was approved by the FDA in 1992.[50] There are no studies on the long-term effects of Norplant, and the side effects (constant bleeding—sometimes for over ninety days—tumors, kidney problems, strokes, heart attacks, sterility) are so extreme that approximately 30 percent of women on Norplant want the device taken out in the first year, with the majority requesting it be removed within two years, even though it is supposed to remain implanted in a woman's arm for five years.[51] To date, more than 2,300 women suffering from 125 side effects related to Norplant have joined a class action suit against Wyeth Pharmaceuticals, the manufacturer of the product.[52] The Native American Women's Health Education Resource Center conducted a survey of IHS policies regarding Norplant and Depo-Provera and found that Native women were not given adequate counseling about the side effects and contraindications.[53]

Native women (as well as other women of color) are seen by colonizers as wombs gone amok who threaten the racist world order. In 1979, it was discovered that seven in ten U.S. hospitals that performed voluntary sterilizations for Medicaid recipients violated the 1974 DHEW guidelines by disregarding sterilization consent procedures and by sterilizing women through "elective" hysterectomies.[54] One recently declassified federal document, National Security Study Memorandum 200, revealed that even in 1976 the U.S. government regarded the growth of the nonwhite population as a threat to national security.[55] As one doctor stated in *Contemporary Ob/Gyn*:

> People pollute, and too many people crowded too close together cause many of our social and economic problems. These in turn are aggravated by involuntary and irresponsible parenthood. . . . We also have obligations to the society of which we are part. The welfare mess, as it has been called, cries out for solutions, one of which is fertility control.[56]

Consequently, Native women and women of color, because of their ability to reproduce, are "overpopulating the world" and pose "the single greatest threat to the health of the planet."[57] Consequently, Native women and women of color deserve no bodily integrity—any form of dangerous contraception is appropriate for them so long as it stops them from reproducing.[58]

Finally, completing the destruction of a people involves destroying the integrity of their culture and spirituality, which forms the matrix of Native women's resistance to sexual colonization. Native counselors generally agree that a strong cultural and spiritual identity is essential if Native people are to heal from abuse. This is because a Native woman's return to wellness entails healing from not only any personal abuse she has suffered but also from the patterned history of abuse against her family, her nation, and the environment in which she lives.[59] Because Indian spiritual traditions are holistic, they are able to restore survivors of abuse to the community, to restore their bodies to wholeness. That is why the most effective programs for healing revolve around reviving indigenous spiritual traditions.

In the colonial discourse, however, Native spiritual traditions become yet another site for the commodification of Indian women's bodies. As part of the genocidal process, Indian cultures no longer offer the means of restoring wholeness but become objects of consumerism for the dominant culture. Haunani-Kay Trask, Native Hawaiian activist, describes this process as "cultural prostitution."

> "Prostitution" in this context refers to the entire institution which defines a woman (and by extension the

"female") as an object of degraded and victimized sexual value for use and exchange through the medium of money....My purpose is not to exact detail or fashion a model but to convey the utter degradation of our culture and our people under corporate tourism by employing "prostitution" as an analytical category....

The point, of course, is that everything in Hawai'i can be yours, that is, you the tourist, the non-native, the visitor. The place, the people, the culture, even our identity as a "Native" people is for sale. Thus, Hawai'i, like a lovely woman, is there for the taking.[60]

Thus, this "New Age" appropriation of Indian spirituality represents yet another form of sexual abuse for Indian women, hindering its ability to help women heal from abuse. Columnist Andy Rooney exemplifies this dominant ideology when he argues that Native spiritual traditions involve "ritualistic dances with strong sexual overtones [that are] demeaning to Indian women and degrading to Indian children."[61] Along similar lines, Mark and Dan Jury produced a film called *Dances Sacred and Profane,* which advertised that it "climaxes with the first-ever filming of the Indian Sundance ceremony."[62] This so-called ceremony consisted of a white man, hanging from meat hooks from a tree, praying to the "Great White Spirit" and was then followed by C. C. Sadist, a group that performs sadomasochistic acts for entertainment. Similarly, "plastic medicine men" are often notorious for sexually abusing their clients in fake Indian ceremonies. Jeffrey Wall was recently sentenced for sexually abusing three girls while claiming this abuse was part of American Indian spiritual rituals that he was conducting as a supposed Indian medicine man.[63] David "Two Wolves" Smith and Alan "Spotted Wolfe" Champney were also charged for sexually abusing girls during supposed "cleansing" ceremonies.[64] That so many people do not question that sexual fondling would be part of Indian ceremonies, to the point where legitimate spiritual leaders are forced to issue statements such as "No ceremony requires anyone to be naked or fondled during the ceremony,"[65] signifies the extent to which the colonial discourse attempts to shift the meaning

of Indian spirituality from something healing to something abusive.

Nevertheless, as mentioned earlier, Native women resist these attacks upon their bodies and souls and the sexually abusive representations of their cultures through the promotion of wellness. The University of Oklahoma sponsors two national wellness and women conferences each year, which more than 2,000 Indian women attend (it also sponsors smaller gatherings for Native men). These conferences help women begin their healing journeys from various forms of abuse and teach them to become enablers for community healing. The Indigenous Women's Network also sponsors gatherings that tie together the healing of individuals and communities from the trauma of this nation's history. At the 1994 conference, each of the four days had a different focus: individual healing, family healing, community healing, and political struggles in North America and the world.

I belonged to a wellness and women circle where Native women share their stories and learn from each other as they travel on the road toward wellness. At one circle, where we discussed the effect of hormonal contraceptives on our bodies, women talked about the devastating effects these hormones were having on their bodies, but the response of their medical providers was simply to give them more hormones. We began to see that we do not need to rely on the "experts" who have their own agendas; we need to trust our bodies, which colonizers have attempted to alienate from us. Our colonizers have attempted to destroy our sense of identity by teaching us self-hatred and self-alienation. But through such wellness movements, we learn to reconnect, to heal from historical and personal abuse, and to reclaim our power to resist colonization.

NOTES

1. Cecelia Fire Thunder, "We Are Breaking a Cycle," *Indigenous Woman* II (1995): 3.
2. I shall not discuss how Jewish traditions have interpreted the Canaanite narratives, nor whether there even was a wholesale conquest of the Canaanites, which many scholars doubt. I am describing how the

Christian appropriation of Canaanite narratives has impacted Native people; I make no claims either for or against Jewish colonialism.

3. Albert Cave, "Canaanites in a Promised Land," *American Indian Quarterly* (Fall 1988): 277–97; H. C. Porter, *The Inconstant Savage* (London: Gerald Duckworth, 1979), pp. 91–115; Ronald Sanders, *Lost Tribes and Promised Lands* (Boston: Little, Brown, 1978), pp. 46, 181, 292; Djelal Kadir, *Columbus and the Ends of the Earth* (Berkeley: University of California Press, 1992), p. 129.

4. Richard Hill, "Savage Splendor: Sex, Lies and Stereotypes," *Turtle Quarterly* (Spring/Summer 1991): 19.

5. Robert Berkoher, *The White Man's Indian* (New York: Vintage, 1978), p. 19.

6. David Stannard, *American Holocaust* (Oxford: Oxford University Press, 1992), p. 211.

7. Charles Loring Brace (1869), quoted in James Rawls, *Indians of California: The Changing Image* (Norman: University of Oklahoma, 1984), p. 195.

8. Hinton Rowan Helper (1855), quoted in Rawls, *Indians of California,* p. 195.

9. Andre Lopez, *Pagans in Our Midst* (Mohawk Nation: Akwesasne Notes), p. 119. It should be noted, as Paula Gunn Allen points out, that Native people in fact bathed much more frequently than did Europeans; see Paula Gunn Allen, *The Sacred Hoop* (Boston: Beacon, 1986), p. 217.

10. Stannard, *American Holocaust,* p. 121.

11. William James, *A Full and Correct Account of the Military Occurrences of the Late War between Great Britain and the United States of America* (London: printed by the author, 1818), Vol. 1, pp. 293–96, in *Who's the Savage?* ed. David Wrone and Russet Nelson (Malabar: Robert Krieger, 1982), p. 82.

12. U.S. Congress. Senate, Special Committee Appointed under Joint Resolution of March 3, 1865. *Condition of the Indian Tribes,* 39th Congress, Second Session, Senate Report 156, Washington, DC, 1867, pp. 95–96, quoted in *Who's the Savage?* p. 113.

13. John Terrell, *Land Grab* (New York: Dial Press, 1972), p. 13.

14. Terrell, *Land Grab,* p. 12.

15. Bernard Sheehan, *Savagism and Civility* (Cambridge: Cambridge University Press, 1980).

16. Rawls, *Indians of California,* p. 200.

17. Traditional Dena'ina, *Summary Packet on Hepatitis B Vaccinations* (Sterling, AK, November 9, 1992).

18. *Physicians' Desk Reference* (PDR) (Oradell, NJ: Medical Economics, 1991), pp. 1292–93.

19. Traditional Dena'ina, *Hepatitis B.*

20. PDR, pp. 1292–93.

21. Traditional Dena'ina, *Hepatitis B.*

22. Mary Ann Mills (speech delivered at a WARN Forum, Chicago, IL, September 1993).

23. For further discussion on the relationship between bodily abuse and self-esteem, see Ellen Bass and Laura Davis, *The Courage to Heal* (New York: Harper and Row, 1988), pp. 207–222, and Bonnie Burstow, *Radical Feminist Therapy* (London: Sage, 1992), pp. 187–234.

24. Celia Haig-Brown, *Resistance and Renewal* (Vancouver: Tilacum, 1988), p. 108.

25. Chrystos, "The Old Indian Granny," in *Fugitive Colors* (Cleveland: Cleveland State University Press, 1995), p. 41.

26. Inés Hernández-Avila, "In Praise of Insubordination, or What Makes a Good Woman Go Bad?" in *Transforming a Rape Culture,* ed. Emilie Buchwald, Pamela R. Fletcher, and Martha Roth (Minneapolis: Milkweed, 1993), p. 386.

27. Stannard, *American Holocaust,* p. 121.

28. Stannard, *American Holocaust,* p. 131.

29. *Cattaraugus Republican,* II February 1897, in Lopez, *Pagans in Our Midst,* p. 9.

30. Dominican monk Thomas Ortiz, quoted in Kirkpatrick Sale, *The Conquest of Paradise* (New York: Penguin, 1990), p. 201.

31. From Cuneo, an Italian nobleman, quoted in Sale, *Conquest of Paradise,* p. 140.

32. U.S. Commissioner of Indian Affairs, *Annual Report for 1871* (Washington, DC: Government Printing Office, 1871), pp. 487–88, cited in *Who's the Savage?* p. 123.

33. Le Roy R. Hafen, ed. *Ruxton of the Rockies* (Norman: University of Oklahoma Press, 1950), pp. 46–149, cited in *Who's the Savage,* p. 97.

34. Bartolome de Las Casas, *The Devastation of the Indies,* trans. Herma Briffault (Baltimore: Johns Hopkins University Press, 1992), p. 33.

35. Lieutenant James D. Cannon, quoted in "Report of the Secretary of War," 39th Congress, Second Session, Senate Executive Document 26, Washington, DC, 1867, printed in *The Sand Creek Massacre: A Documentary History* (New York: Sol Lewis, 1973), pp. 129–30.

36. James Mooney, "The Ghost Dance Religion and the Sioux Outbreak of 1890." In *Fourteenth Annual Report of the United States Bureau of Ethnology* (Washington, DC: U.S. Government Printing Office, 1896). p. 885, quoted in Stannard, *American Holocaust,* p. 127.

37. Roy Harvey Pearce, *Savagism and Civilization* (Baltimore: Johns Hopkins University Press, 1965), p. 93.

38. Robert Heizer, ed., *The Destruction of California Indians* (Lincoln: University of Nebraska Press, 1993), p. 284.

39. Rawls, *Indians in California*, p. 182.
40. Information gathered by the Guatemalan Forensic Anthropology team and posted by Stefan Schmitt, online at garnet.aces.fsu.edu/~sss4407/RioNeg.htm.
41. Catherine MacKinnon, "Turning Rape into Pornography: Postmodern Genocide," *Ms. Magazine* 4, no. 1: 27 (emphasis mine).
42. Johanna Brand, *The Life and Death of Anna Mae Aquash* (Toronto: Lorimer), pp. 28, 140.
43. "Up Front," *Perspectives: The Civil Rights Quarterly* 14, no. 3 (Fall 1982).
44. Personal conversations with author (Summer 1990).
45. Promotional material from Public Relations: Mahoney/Wasserman & Associates, Los Angeles, CA, n.d.
46. Mark Brunswick and Paul Klauda, "Possible Suspect in Serial Killings Jailed in N. Mexico," *Minneapolis Star and Tribune*, 28 May 1987, IA.
47. See "The Threat of Life," *WARN Report*, pp. 13–16 (available through WARN, 4511 N. Hermitage, Chicago, IL 60640); Brint Dillingham, "Indian Women and IHS Sterilization Practices," *American Indian Journal* (January 1977): 27–28; Brint Dillingham, "Sterilization of Native Americans," *American Indian Journal* (July 1977): 16–19; Pat Bellanger, "Native American Women, Forced Sterilization, and the Family," in *Every Woman Has a Story*, ed. Gaya Wadnizak Ellis (Minneapolis: Midwest Villages & Voices, 1982), pp. 30–35; "Oklahoma: Sterilization of Native Women Charged to I.H.S." *Akwesasne Notes* (Mid Winter, 1989): 30.
48. For a description of the hazards of Depo-Provera, see Stephen Minkin, "Depo-Provera: A Critical Analysis," Institute for Food and Development Policy, San Francisco. He concludes that "the continued use of Depo-Provera for birth control is unjustified and unethical." For more information on the effects of Norplant, see *Womanist Health Newsletter*, Issue on Norplant, available through Women's Health Education Project, 3435 N. Sheffield, #205, Chicago, IL 60660.
49. For a statement on Depo-Provera from the National Black Women's Health Project, National Latina Health Organization, Native American Women's Health Education Resource Center, National Women's Health Network, and Women's Economic Agenda Project, contact NAWHERC, PO Box 572, Lake Andes, SD 57356–0572.
50. "Taking the Shot," series of articles from *Arizona Republic* (November 1986).
51. Debra Hanania-Freeman, "Norplant: Freedom of Choice or a Plan for Genocide?" *EIR* 14 (May 1993): 20.
52. Kathleen Plant, "Mandatory Norplant Is Not the Answer," *Chicago Sun-Times*, 2 November 1994, p. 46.
53. "A Study of the Use of Depo-Provera and Norplant by the Indian Health Services" from Native American Women's Health Education Resource Center, South Dakota, 1993.
54. "Survey Finds Seven in 10 Hospitals Violate DHEW Guidelines on Informed Consent for Sterilization," *Family Planning Perspectives* II, no. 6 (Nov/Dec 1979): 366; Claudia Dreifus, "Sterilizing the Poor," *Seizing Our Bodies*, ed. and intro. by Claudia Dreifus (New York: Vintage Books, 1977), pp. 105–20.
55. Debra Hanania-Freeman, "Norplant," p. 20.
56. *Akwesasne Notes*, p. II.
57. Population Institute, *Annual Report*, 1991. See also Zero Population Growth, fundraising appeal, undated; "Population Stabilization: The Real Solution," pamphlet from the Los Angeles chapter of the Sierra Club—Population Committee; and Population Institute fund-raising appeal, which states that the population growth is the root cause of poverty, hunger, and environmental destruction.
58. For a more detailed discussion of the population control movement and its impact on communities of color, see Andy Smith, "Women of Color and Reproductive Choice: Combating the Population Paradigm," *Journal of Feminist Studies in Religion* (Spring 1996).
59. Justine Smith (Cherokee), personal conversation, 17 February 1994.
60. Haunani-Kay Trask, *From a Native Daughter: Colonialism & Sovereignty in Hawai'i* (Maine: Common Courage Press, 1993), pp. 185–94.
61. Andy Rooney, "Indians Have Worse Problems," *Chicago Tribune*, 4 March 1992.
62. Jim Lockhart, "AIM Protests Film's Spiritual Misrepresentation," *News from Indian Country* (Late September 1994): 10.
63. "Shaman Sentenced for Sex Abuse," *News from Indian Country* (Mid June 1996): 2A.
64. David Melmer, "Sexual Assault," *Indian Country Today* 15 (30 April–7 May 1996): 1.
65. Michael Pace, in David Melmer, "Sexual Assault," *Indian Country Today* 15 (30 April–7 May 1996): 1.

23 • *Kate Harding*

HOW DO YOU FUCK A FAT WOMAN?

DISCUSSION QUESTIONS

1. What forms of violence manifest against women who are socially constructed as "fat" in Harding's account?
2. What roles do "cognitive dissonance" and "body image" play in shaping notions of sexual identity, desirability, attraction, and love?
3. How do constant messages of diet fads, gym memberships, and body-mass-index measures, among other things, frame notions of "chubby," "fat," and "obese" as an individual problem as opposed to a structural system that constructs beauty and body ideals?

THAT'S AN ACTUAL COMMENT left on the blog of a friend of mine, in response to a post she wrote about being raped and nearly killed. Every feminist blogger with more than four readers has dealt with comments along these lines. There are certain people who feel it's their sacred duty to inform us, again and again, that *rape is a compliment.* (Or, more precisely, "Rape is a compliment, you stupid whore.") Rape is not a violent crime meant to control and dehumanize the victim, see; it's evidence that you were just so ding-dang attractive to some perfectly average guy, he couldn't stop himself from fucking you, against your will, right then and there! He thought you were pretty! Why are you so upset?

All in a day's work for a feminist blogger, sadly—and when you're a *fat* feminist blogger, it comes with a special bonus message: No one *but* a rapist would ever, ever want you. In this iteration of the "rape is a compliment" construct, our hypothetical rapist is no longer a perfectly average guy—because perfectly average guys aren't driven to sexual incontinence by fat chicks. I mean, *duh.* No, the guy who would rape a fat chick is not only paying her a compliment, but doing her an enormous *favor.* He's a fucking philanthropist, out there busting his ass to save fat girls everywhere from vaginal atrophy.

You fat whores would be lucky to even get raped by someone. I hope you whiny cunts find your way on top of a pinball machine in the near future.

Whoever raped you could have just waited at the exit of a bar at 3 am and gotten it consensually without the beached whale–like "struggle" you probably gave.

Kate Harding, "How Do You Fuck a Fat Woman?" from Yes Means Yes: Visions of Female Sexual Power and a World Without Rape, edited by Jaclyn Friedman and Jessica Valenti. Copyright © 2008 by Seal Press. Reprinted with the permission of Seal Press, a member of Perseus Book Group.

If any man would want to rape your gigantic ass, I'd be shocked.

It's tempting to dismiss the lowlife assholes who leave comments like that on feminist blogs as . . . well, lowlife assholes. As in, people beneath not only our contempt but also our notice. Problem is, these comments show up frequently enough that they're clearly not just the isolated thoughts of a few vicious, delusional wackjobs. They're part of a larger cultural narrative about female attractiveness in general, and fat women's sexuality in particular.

It starts here: Women's first—if not only—job is to be attractive to men. Never mind straight women who have other priorities or queer women who don't *want* men. If you were born with a vagina, your primary obligation from the onset of adolescence and well into adulthood will be to make yourself pretty for heterosexual men's pleasure. Not even just the ones you'd actually want to have a conversation with, let alone sex with—*all* of them.

So if you were born with a vagina *and* genes that predispose you to fatness, then you've got a real problem. You've already failed—fat is repulsive! Sure, there are men out there who particularly dig fat women, and plenty of other men who would be hot for the *right* fat woman if she came along. But those men, the culture helpfully explains, are outliers. Freaks. Even if you chanced upon one—which you could go a whole lifetime without doing, so exquisitely rare are they!—who would want to be with a man who's so broken, he finds fat women attractive? Besides which, as we've discussed, your job as a woman is to be attractive not only to the men who will love you and treat you well, but to *all* heterosexual men. And if you're fat? Well, as the kids on the Internet say, epic fail.

I'm against rape. Unless it's obese women. How else are they going to get sweet, sweet cock?

People really say this shit.

Whether they really *believe* it is almost immaterial. The purpose of comments like these isn't to argue sincerely that rapists are doing a favor to fat chicks; it's to wound the fat woman or women at whom they're directed, as deeply as possible. And it works, to the extent that it does (which depends on the person and

the day), because too many of us fully believe the underlying premise on which that twisted leap of logic is based: *No one wants to fuck a fatty.*

When I was in college—long before I discovered, let alone joined, the fat acceptance movement—I had a months-long non-relationship with this dude whose girlfriend was studying abroad for the year. We started out as Just Friends, then moved on to Friends Who Give Each Other Backrubs, and then to Friends Who Give Each Other Half-Naked Backrubs, Like, Three Times Daily. As you do in college.

One afternoon, I was lying on my stomach on a dorm bed, shirt and bra on the floor next to me, while this dude straddled my ass. He was giving me a backrub that, as usual, involved his sliding his fingers under my waistband and kneading handfuls of side-boob as if he just didn't *notice* it wasn't back fat. Sarah McLachlan's *Fumbling Towards Ecstasy* was on the stereo (appropriately enough), a cheap vanilla votive candle was burning, and I was trying to regulate my breathing so he wouldn't notice me pretty much panting. Because, after all, we were *just friends.* He had a girlfriend, even if she was on the other side of the world. This backrub thing was just . . . I don't know, a hobby?

And then, out of nowhere, he says, "Hey, I kind of feel like making out."

Now, I wanted to make out with this dude more than anything in the world just then—I'd wanted it more than anything in the world for *months.* And he'd totally just opened the door! Finally!

So here's what I said: *"What?"*

I'm slick like that.

And here's what he said: "Oh—oh, nothing. I didn't say anything. Forget it."

And with that, I immediately convinced myself he *hadn't* just expressed interest in making out with me, for the very same reason I'd asked him to repeat himself instead of throwing him on his back and kissing him in the first place: *I didn't believe it was possible.*

Let's review. This guy was coming to my room every day, more than once, to doff substantial amounts of clothing and touch me a whole lot. On top of that, we were both nineteen. *And I didn't believe he was attracted to me.*

It sounds absurd to me now, but back then, it somehow made all the sense in the world. I was a fat girl! Nobody wants to have sex with a fat girl!

Compounding the absurdity of it all, I was just barely *chubby* back then, but of course body image doesn't necessarily have jack shit to do with reality. My closest female friends were positively waifish, both naturally thin and not yet settled into their adult bodies. The guys I was attracted to—including this one—dated only skinny girls, at least on the record. And the guy in question had, in fact, mentioned on more than one occasion that it would be cool if I worked out more, while straddling my ass and groping side-boob. He'd made it perfectly clear that he did *not* find me especially attractive— certainly nowhere near as attractive as his girlfriend— while rubbing his hands all over my bare skin.

I didn't know what "cognitive dissonance" meant back then. I knew only this: I was fat. And that meant he *couldn't* want me. Sex was a nonissue because I was a nonsexual being—never mind what I felt, thought, or did on my own time. The important thing wasn't my *actual* sexuality, or even how this particular dude perceived me; the important thing was how *all* heterosexual men perceived me. Remember?

And the culture never failed to remind me how I was perceived, via women's magazines offering a new way to lose weight and "look good naked" every goddamned month; cheery radio jingles for fitness centers about destroying your "flubbery, rubbery gut"; Courteney Cox Arquette dancing in a fat suit on *Friends*, between ads for weight-loss programs; low-cal, low-fat menus with cutesy names like the Guiltless Grill in restaurants; sidelong glances in the dining hall; size 4 friends who were dieting; and—just in case all that was too subtle—the NO FAT CHICKS bumper stickers, the "How do you fuck a fat woman?" jokes, the fatcalls on the street. Women with bodies like mine were unwantable, unlovable, and *definitely* unfuckable. I was utterly, unwaveringly convinced of this.

So I really believed that dude and I were just, you know, backrub buddies. It was strictly platonic—even

if I have never in thirty-three years had another platonic relationship in which a friend and I would greet each other by ripping our shirts off and getting into bed.

I have a dozen more stories like that. Add in my friends' stories, and I've got a book. *The Ones That Got Away: Fat Women on Their Own Goddamned Romantic Cluelessness*, something like that. In our thirties, with most of us partnered off, we can laugh about it—but in our teens and twenties, the pain of rejection was fierce, and we truly had no idea that probably half the time, that rejection wasn't even coming from outside us. We rejected *ourselves* as potential dates or partners or fuck buddies before anyone else got the chance.

Worse yet, some of us assumed our manifest unfuckability meant that virtually any male attention was a thing to be treasured. While I don't know any women who have bought into the "rape is a compliment" theory, I certainly know some who believed abusive boyfriends when they said, "You can't leave, because no one but me would want your fat ass." I know several who have had multiple semi-anonymous one-night stands, not because that's what floats their boats but because they were so happy to find men— any men, just about—who expressed sexual interest in their bodies. There's a reason why so many TV shows, movies, and rude jokes represent fat women as pathetically grateful to get laid; some (though nowhere near all) of us *are* grateful, because after years of being told you're too physically repulsive to earn positive male attention, yeah, it's actually kind of nice to be noticed. And from there, it's a frighteningly short leap to "You'd be lucky to be raped." Even if you never officially make that leap—and I really, really hope there aren't women out there who would— you're still essentially believing that you have no agency in your own sexual experiences. Your desires aren't important, because they can never be fulfilled anyway—you aren't pretty enough to call the shots. The best you can hope for is that some man's desire for sex will lead him to you, somewhere, some night.

Of all the maddening side effects of our narrow cultural beauty standard, I think the worst might be the way it warps our understanding of attraction. The reality is, attraction is unpredictable and subjective—even people who are widely believed to meet the standard do not actually, magically become Objectively Attractive. I fall right in line with millions of heterosexual women when it comes to daydreaming about George Clooney, but Brad Pitt does absolutely nothing for me. I think Kate Winslet is breathtaking, but my boyfriend thinks she's *meh*. Ain't no such thing as a person who's categorically hot in the opinion of every single person who sees them.

But that's exactly what we're trained to believe: "Hot" is an objective assessment, based on a collection of easily identifiable characteristics. Thin is hot. White is hot. Able-bodied and quasi-athletic is hot. Blond is hot. Clear skin is hot. Big boobs (so long as there's no corresponding big ass) are hot. Little waists are hot. Miniskirts and high heels and smoky eyes are hot. There's a proven formula, and if you follow it, you will be hot.

Of course, very few people can follow that formula to the letter, and some of us—fat women, nonwhite women—physically disabled women, flat-chested, apple-shaped, acne-prone women—basically have no fucking prayer. That doesn't stop purveyors of the beauty standard from encouraging us to keep trying, though—with enough hard work and money spent, we can all at least move closer to the ideal. Sure, women of color can't be expected to surmount that whole white-skin requirement (sorry, gals—better luck next millennium!), but they can torture their hair with chemicals and get surgery on those pesky non-European features if they're really committed. There's something for everyone in this game!

And for fat women, the solution is actually quite simple, they tell us: You can diet. You can work out as much and eat as little as it takes until you look like your naturally thin friend who loves fast food and despises the gym. Never mind that studies have shown over 90 percent of dieters gain all the weight back within five years.[1] Never mind that twin studies show weight and body shape are nearly as inheritable as height.[2] And definitely never mind that your one friend can maintain this shape without ever consuming a leafy green vegetable or darkening the door of a gym, and another friend can maintain it while eating satisfying meals and working out for half an hour, three times a week, but for you to maintain it requires restricting your calories to below the World Health Organization's threshold for starvation and spending way more time exercising than you do hanging out with friends and family. The unfairness of that is irrelevant. You just have to *want it* badly enough.

And you must want it that badly, because fat is Not Hot. To anyone, ever.

How else are you going to get sweet, sweet cock?

It's really tempting to simply declare that fat women oppress ourselves, demean ourselves, cut off our own romantic opportunities—and the obvious solution is to knock it the fuck off. It's tempting to say that because, you know, it's kind of true. But it's ultimately a counterproductive and nasty bit of victim blaming. When you're a fat woman in this culture, *everyone*—from journalists you'll never meet to your own mother, sister, and best friend—works together to constantly reinforce the message that you are not good enough to be fucked, let alone loved. *You'd be so pretty if you just lost weight. You'd feel so much better about yourself if you just lost weight. You'd have boys beating down your door if you just lost weight.*

You'd be lucky to be raped, you fat cunt.

That's just the way it is, baby. Fat chicks are gross. Accept it.

Refusing to accept it is hard fucking work. And being tasked with doing that is, frankly, every bit as unfair as being tasked with keeping "excess" weight off a naturally fat body. We shouldn't have to devote so much mental energy to the exhausting work of *not hating ourselves*. Believing that we can be desirable, that we deserve to be loved, that that guy over there really *is* flirting should not be a goddamned daily struggle. It should not feel like rolling a boulder up a hill.

But it does. So the question is, which boulder are you going to choose to roll? The "must lose weight" boulder or the "fuck you, I will boldly, defiantly accept the body I've got and *live in it*" boulder? It's backbreaking and frequently demoralizing work either way. But only one way can lead to real sexual power, to real ownership of your body, to real strength and confidence.

Imagine for a minute a world in which fat women don't automatically disqualify themselves from the dating game. A world in which fat women don't believe there's anything intrinsically unattractive about their bodies. A world in which fat women hear that men want only thin women and laugh our asses off, because that is not remotely our experience—our experience is one of loving and fucking and navigating a big damn world in our big damn bodies with grace and optimism and power.

Now try to imagine some halfwit dickhead telling you a rapist would be doing you a favor, in that world. Imagine a man poking you in the stomach and telling you you need to work out more, moments after he comes inside you. Imagine a man going on daytime TV to announce to the world that he's thinking of getting a divorce because his wife is thirty pounds heavier than she was the day they were married. Imagine a man telling you that you can't leave him, because no one else will ever want your disgusting fat ass.

None of it makes a lick of sense in that world, does it?

It doesn't in this one, either.

Imagine if more of us could believe that.

---

24 • *Kamala Kempadoo*

WOMEN OF COLOR AND THE GLOBAL SEX TRADE
Transnational Feminist Perspectives

DISCUSSION QUESTIONS

1. How does the global sex trade support "development" in "underdeveloped" nations?
2. How have feminist approaches to prostitution changed over time?
3. What unique insights does Kempadoo's intersectional, transnational, postcolonial feminist approach offer that are distinct from the other analyses she reviews?
4. Why does Kempadoo argue that concepts and theories of prostitution and the sex trade need to be more fluid and local?

Kamala Kempadoo, "Women of Color and the Global Sex Trade: Transnational Feminist Perspectives." Meridians: Feminism, Race, Transnationalism 1(2):28–51. Reprinted by permission of the author.

The global sex trade has received increasing attention since the mid-1990s from a variety of researchers, activists, organizations, law and policy makers, and international agencies, particularly under the rubrics of "trafficking" and "sexual slavery." The assumption commonly underpinning the widespread interest it has aroused is that the sex trade is premised upon a universal principle of male violence to women. Indeed, even though several feminists and scholars, including this author, have argued for more complex and nuanced approaches, we are often asked to participate in discussions on the subject in the context of conferences and public events that concentrate on violence to women. Similarly, among nongovernmental organizations and increasingly in the mainstream media, the global sex trade is more often than not portrayed through this one dimension, with the women involved represented as "victims" of male sexual violence.

In this article, I expand the argument that the global sex trade cannot be simply reduced to one monolithic explanation of violence to women. Research and theorizing require a framework that embraces the realities, contradictions, and intersections of various global relations of power. To illustrate this point, I draw on recent feminist studies showing that colonialisms, recolonizations, and cultural imperialisms, as well as specific local cultural histories and traditions that shape the sexual agency of women are important for any account of global manifestations of sex work. The goal is to articulate a framework that will allow us to explore and theorize differences and commonalities in meanings and experiences in the sex trade. Here, I focus particularly on experiences of, and definitions by, women of color,[1] tracing the contours of what may be named a "transnational feminist" framework for studies of prostitution and sex work. While this article may offer to some readers new insights and arguments, it does not represent a new study. Rather it aims to bring together and further circulate ideas and knowledge produced by and about women of color in the global sex trade and to make explicit the framework that underpins this current trend of feminist theorizing.[2]

REPRESENTATIONS OF WOMEN OF COLOR IN THE GLOBAL SEX TRADE

In the late 1980s, when I first started investigating the global sex trade, I was struck by the apparent over-representation of women of color in sex industries in western Europe. Living in Amsterdam—in the midst of the red-light district—I could not help but notice the preponderance of Thai, Dominican, Colombian, and Ghanaian women in sex work in clubs, behind windows, or in massage parlors. This concentration of non-Dutch and non-European women in the district was simultaneously a focus of attention for a Dutch prostitution research organization (Brussa 1989). The research indicated that around 60 percent of the population working in red-light districts in Amsterdam and other large Dutch cities were foreign/migrant/Third World women. My initial work built upon some of the insights from this research as well as from my own observations in the red-light district, exploring the mechanisms that drew women from Latin America and the Caribbean into the Dutch sex industry and forcing an engagement with the interplay of global relations of power around gender, race, nationality, and the economy (Kempadoo 1994, 1996, 1998).

While the situation in the Netherlands has drastically changed "color" since the late 1980s due to a movement of Eastern European and Russian women into Western European sex industries after the collapse of the Soviet Union, it appears that the concentration of women of Asian, African, Caribbean, and Latin American descent in the global sex trade is a continuing, if not escalating, trend as we enter a new century. This claim is difficult to substantiate with figures, given that sex work occurs for the most part underground and in informal sectors, and is invisible in most accounts of women's work, commercial activities, and economic and labor force reports. It is also complicated by the fact that sex work is commonly a highly stigmatized activity; the women who provide the sexual services and labor are the subjects of discriminatory, often criminalizing, policies, laws, and ideologies. Nevertheless, three features of the global sex trade combine to illuminate the overrepresentation of women of color.

In the first place, prostitution around military bases has been well documented in "Other" (that is, non-Western/non-European) countries, most notably in Asia and the Pacific. In India, Hawaii, Vietnam, the Philippines, Japan, and Korea, the operation of foreign—colonial, imperial, or Allied—troops at various times in history has produced particular forms of prostitution where the military, often in collusion with the local state or government, tolerated, regulated, or encouraged the provision of sexual services by local women to the troops (Pivar 1981; Enloe 1989; Sturdevant and Stoltzfus 1992; Bailey and Farber 1992; Moon 1997; Lim 1998). In the Caribbean militarized prostitution has also been noted in various social studies as well as in calypsos and other cultural productions in places such as Trinidad, Curacao, Belize, Puerto Rico, and Cuba (Del Omo 1979; Kane 1993; Kempadoo 1996; Martis 1999; Findlay 1999; T. Hall 1994). Here too, Brown and Black women provided sexual labor and services, whether they were "native" to the specific countries or worked as migrants. Militarized prostitution in the Caribbean, while scantily researched, continues through U.S. military activities in the region in the late twentieth century, Martis notes:

> In 1996 St. Maarten became the homeport for an U.S. Navy ship that docks at the port every three months and stays for about a week. The crew of this ship consists of between 4,000 and 5,000 men (and some women). It is accepted and expected that the sailors need entertainment and release of their physical needs, and the brothels and bars overflow with customers. The demand for sex workers is so great that more women are flown in during the week the ship stays in port. The Commissioner of Tourism calculates that the navy personnel spend around U.S. $1,000,000 on each visit. (1999, 209)

The stationing of UN peacekeeping troops in Haiti during the 1990s also raised questions about a renewed arena for prostitution activities, and HIV/

AIDS specialists and health agencies have flagged militarized prostitution as an increasing area for concern.[3] Furthermore, while only a few studies have addressed militarized prostitution in African countries in the past, the recent deployment of UN peacekeeping troops in Congo and Sierra Leone has led to a concern in UN circles about the transmission of HIV/AIDS via visits to brothels and other prostitution activities.[4] Irrespective of the tasks assigned overseas military troops, sexual access to local women (of color) remains important.

Sex with local women has a longstanding history for armed forces. Not only has access to women's sexuality and regular sexual intercourse been considered within dominant discourse integral to the making of men under heteropatriarchy, but the specific construction of militarized masculinity demands heterosexual sex on a regular basis. That a large number of women upon whose bodies and labor such constructions of masculinity depend are of nations, "races," and ethnicities other than those of the men is a contemporary reality that cannot be neglected or ignored.

Second, in the context of discussions of "trafficking" of women for sex work, domestic service, marriage, sweatshop labor, farming, and other un- or semi-skilled work, Third World women appear as the most frequent "victims." While estimates of the number of trafficked persons vary from anywhere between one to four million per year, the predominant focus has been on the trade of young women that takes place from Nepal to India, from Sri Lanka and Bangladesh to Saudi Arabia, from the Philippines to Italy, Thailand to the Netherlands, or from the Dominican Republic to Spain for work in sex industries and domestic service. The UN estimated in 1999 that of the approximately 700,000 women and girls trafficked into Western Europe, the Middle East, Japan, Australia, and North America, 75 percent were drawn from countries in Latin America, Africa, South Asia, and Southeast Asia (*Gender Matters* 1999).

A 1999 CIA report indicated that around 50,000 women per year were brought into the U.S. for work in sex industries, domestic labor, and sweatshops. At least twenty-six American cities have been reported to employ trafficked female labor, with the primary "sending" countries identified as Thailand, Vietnam, China, Mexico, Russia, and the Czech Republic, followed by the Philippines, Korea, Malaysia, Nigeria, Latvia, Hungary, Poland, Brazil, and Honduras (O'Neill 1999). Reports on trafficking to Canada also signal that the concern revolves around women from Asia and Latin America, as well as Eastern Europe (*National Post* 17 May 2000). In England, where the trafficking of Filipinas and Thai women is not unknown, the case of the fifty-eight Chinese men and women who were found dead in a container on arrival at Dover in June 2000 spurred further probes into both the trafficking and smuggling of Asians into Britain. In other Western European countries, Eastern Europeans and Russians are thought to be cornering the sex work market, but Italy's pronounced concern is about migrant women trafficked from Africa, while the Spanish government similarly has called for a crack down on the traffic of persons from sub-Saharan Africa (*Guardian Weekly* 31 August 2000).

The representation of women from Third World or postcolonial countries as "trafficked victims" combines with descriptions of conditions of excessive force and violence. Debt-bondage, where sums of up to $20,000 are loaned to families and paid back by women and girls through work in underground or informal sectors; indentureship, where women are forced into prostitution, domestic work, or sweatshops and are required to pay the trafficker for travel and documents[5]; and slavery-like conditions, where women are locked into rooms or a building, chained up, or otherwise held against their will, forced to have sex both with clients and their "protectors" and traffickers, are raped and abused by their "managers," and are starved or are not allowed freedom of movement, are most commonly linked with Third World and non-western women's experiences in the global sex trade. The dominant image in the West of the trafficked, victimized sex worker is of a young Brown, Asian, or Black woman, an image refracted through mainstream television programs and newspaper reports, as well as in some feminist writings and in international debates on trafficking.[6]

Third, "sex tourism" takes place for the most part in "exotic" (i.e., "Third World") countries, where Western European, Japanese, and North American men (primarily) buy sex in various ways from women, men, boys, and girls who, in turn, are "encouraged" by local governments to bring in foreign exchange and to sustain the image of their country as an appealing vacation destination. In the 1960s tourism was promoted by the United Nations as a way for the "developing world" to participate in the global capitalist economy and since then has been heavily promoted and adopted as a development strategy for and by national governments of "poor countries" around the world. Studies of tourism in various parts of Asia, for example, have documented how governments have not simply embraced tourism but have deliberately relied upon longstanding racist stereotypes of Asian women as exotic and erotic to attract tourists. It is through the reliance on the sexuality and sexual labor of Asian women that sex tourism has become vital to the national economies (Truong 1990; Lim 1998).

With the economic restructuring that many former Third World countries have been forced to accept under International Monetary Fund (IMF) and World Bank dictates—so-called structural adjustment programs that rest upon neoliberal free-market policies—tourism has received an even greater boost, as these countries can no longer depend upon their participation in the global markets on the basis of agricultural production or the exploitation of other resources. Sex tourism, a service that caters to the new leisure demands by citizens of the wealthy, as well as to more traditional types of travelers, such as businessmen, has for some countries become an integral part of the tourism industry that sustains the nation (see also Bishop and Robinson 1998, and Kempadoo 1999).[7]

The global sex trade leans heavily on the bodies of women of color. Sex work of Brown and Black women is drawn upon as a way to "develop" "underdeveloped" regions of the world, either by attracting foreign exchange or as an export commodity servicing industries abroad. Remittances from migrant women to their families and home communities also are fast becoming a staple of small national economies. Bodies of women of color are employed to sustain underground sex industries such as massage parlors and exotic dance clubs in "over-developed" countries, to boost militarized masculinity, to secure profits for multinational elites and corporations that govern tourism industries, as well as to keep local economies and underdeveloped nations afloat.

The flip side of this development is that sex work has become so embedded in social relations that it is often seen as one of the few options for women of postcolonial societies to keep their heads above water in a world where the highly unequal distribution of wealth and power on an international scale, as well as the agencies and classes that defend this inequality, induce poor people and nations to seek alternative, sometimes underground, strategies for survival. For many Black and Brown women, and increasingly for more young men of color, sex work is more lucrative than Free Trade Zone work, domestic service, export processing, farm work, or other hard manual labor (Cabezas 1999; Mayorga and Velasquez 1999). Sex with an "exotic" is desired and valued among many tourists, and exoticized subjects devise strategies to benefit from this situation to the best of their ability. Their sexual labor is often a supplement to meager wages or incomes from other sources of work, or can provide the sole financial contribution to the household....

FEMINIST THEORIZING

If we take into account the apparent importance of women of color's sexual labor in the maintenance of the contemporary global sex trade as well as to the survival of whole communities and families in developing countries, where does this place feminist theories of prostitution? Can we ignore the evidence, and continue to adhere to twentieth-century ideas about the universality of prostitution as violence to women, or can we begin to entertain the idea that, in the twenty-first century, in a world steeped in global restructuring, postmodern and postcolonial conditions "social relations, subjects, and subjectivities are

undergoing profound changes" and that "concepts and categories of prostitution and prostitute are not static" but also are subject to change? (Marchand et al. 1998, 959, 963)....

Feminist accounts of prostitution have barely scratched the surface here. Too often we still rely heavily on older feminist formulations. In the 1970s, prostitution, along with marriage and the family, was defined by Western feminism as an expression of patriarchy and violence to women, illustrating the way in which female sexuality and the female body were controlled, subordinated, and exploited by male and masculine interests. Kathleen Barry made popular the term "sexual slavery" to refer to some of the conditions that women faced under patriarchy, asserting that sex constituted the primary basis for power and authority in society (1984, 194). The concepts of sex and gender were given primacy in this analysis of prostitution, and the cause for prostitution defined as universal in nature....

Since the 1980s sex work has been made synonymous with sexual slavery by various women's organizations in various parts of the world. The notion of sexual slavery has been widely used in relation to "comfort women" who were "drafted" from Korea, China, Taiwan, Indonesia, Thailand, the Philippines and Japan to sexually service Japan's Imperial Army during the 1930s and 1940s, and to agitate for compensation for these abused and exploited women (Hicks 1994; Howard 1995; Bang-Soon Yoon 1997; Henson 1999). The international circulation of ideas about prostitution and other forms of sex work exclusively in terms of "violence to women" or "sexual slavery" has also more generally informed the contemporary discourse of international human rights agencies....

While these definitions of the sex trade have been contested by other African and Asian women and sex workers in these locations,[8] they are nevertheless often assumed to represent the condition for all women in the sex trade....

It is critical to keep in mind that the reduction of prostitution to masculine violence and sexual slavery also has been viewed by other feminists as inadequate to capture the various histories, oppressions, and experiences of women of color. In Japan, against the dominant feminist trend, Sisterhood—a group of feminist intellectuals and lawyers—has argued the necessity of defining prostitution as labor. Masumi Yoneda states:

It is all the more necessary to recognize prostitution as work and improve working conditions for these women. Isn't it our job to secure a liveable environment where they won't be exploited illegally, to create a situation where they can network among themselves, and where they can voice their demands, and to help them build up the power to get out of prostitution when they want to? They are not going to accept us as long as we work on the premise that they are victims who are forced into prostitution, something that humans shouldn't practice, that our mission is to protect and rehabilitate them, that we should abolish prostitution from the face of the earth! That's simply a nuisance to them. If I were a prostitute I would say to hell with the do-gooders. The situation won't go away by telling them that they were forced into it and that they are victims. (Group Sisterhood 1998, 94)

Others have pointed out that legacies of racism, colonialism, and imperialism have produced conditions and situations for women that are experienced, and can be read, in quite different ways. This needs to be taken into consideration when theorizing prostitution. Ofreneo and Ofreneo, for example, insist that "Imperialism, militarism and racism provided the 'geopolitical-economic' context of military prostitution and sex tourism" in the Philippines (1998, 104). . . . In this framework sexual labor/sex work is viewed as having been, and continuing to be, performed and organized in a variety of ways, with no universal expression or meaning.

. . . In other words it would seem erroneous, if not socially irresponsible, to ignore these national and geo-political contexts, as well as specific histories and experiences, when talking about women in the global sex trade. Reducing sex work to a violence inflicted upon women due to notions of a universality of patriarchy and masculinist ideologies and structures, or through the privileging of gender as the primary factor in shaping social relations, dismisses the great variety of historical and socio-economic conditions, as well as cultural histories, that produce sexual relations and desire.

Challenges to the prevalent reductionistic discourse on prostitution parallel those that took place over feminist conceptualizations of "the family" and "the household" during the 1980s. At that time the dominant Euro-American definition of the family, domestic work and the household as exclusive sites of oppression for women were opposed by Black and anti-imperialist feminists and redefined to encompass different women's histories and legacies of and resistance to slavery, colonialism, and racism. As Hazel Carby so poignantly stated in her article "White Women Listen!" in 1982:

We would not want to deny that the family can be a source of oppression for us but we also wish to examine how the black family has functioned as a prime source of resistance to oppression. We need to recognize that during slavery, periods of colonialism and under the present authoritarian state [Britain in the 1980s], the black family has been a site of political and cultural resistance to racism.

The meaning of the family to Black women in light of a history of racialized and colonial oppression needed special attention and could not simply be covered by a blanket definition that had emerged from a white, Euro-American middle class experience.

Similarly, Angela Davis addressed the relationship between domestic work and Black struggles against racism. She argued that it was

precisely through performing the drudgery which has long been a central expression of the socially conditioned inferiority of women [domestic labor] the Black woman in chains could help to lay the foundations for some degree of autonomy both for herself and her men. Even as she was suffering under her unique oppression as female, she was thrust into the center of the slave community. She was, therefore, essential to the survival of the community. (1982, 17)

Examinations of particular colonial, imperial, and neocolonial histories in the construction of prostitution and of the "erotic–exotic" woman of color are needed for feminist frameworks that purport to study, analyze, and produce knowledge about sex work and the global sex trade, for without taking these relations of power and dominance into account, commonalities and differences in social histories, lives, and experiences of women around the world are erased, and various complicities and contestations ignored....

The notion of Black women as "breeders" on plantations during slavery throughout the Americas has not gone unnoticed in feminist historiography. Abraham-van der Mark notes about the Jewish male elite in nineteenth-century Curaçao in the Dutch Caribbean, that "concubinage gave them the benefits of a category of children which, if necessary, provided labor but could not make any legal demands and were excluded from inheritance" (1973, 46). In other instances in the Caribbean, Black slave women were put to work as prostitutes by the owner or plantation manager during slumps in the plantation economy and when extra cash was needed for the plantation household (Beckles 1989). In these and other studies a continuous theme is the unconditional sexual access that white men had to Black and Brown women's bodies and the force and coercion that was involved....

The positioning of Asian, African, Caribbean, and Latin American women as sexual objects, and the obfuscations of their agency, in particular relations of power and domination, have not ground to a halt but rather can be seen to extend into the twenty-first century in both theory and practice. Women of color remain in various ways racialized as highly sexual by nature, and positioned as "ideal" for sex work. They continue to be overrepresented globally in "body-work"—as sexual, domestic, and un- or semi-skilled manual workers—and are underrepresented in intellectual activities in which social theory is produced. The agency of Brown and Black women in prostitution has been avoided or overlooked and the perspectives arising from these experiences marginalized in dominant theoretical discourse on the global sex trade and prostitution. Our insights, knowledges, and understandings of sex work have been largely obscured or dominated by white radical feminist, neo-Marxist, or Western socialist feminist inspired analyses that have been either incapable or unwilling to address the complexities of the lives of women of color. Third World, transnational, or post-colonial feminisms have offered possibilities for theorizing prostitution within the matrix of gendered, racialized, sexualized, and international relations of power, as well as from the experiences and perspectives of women of color in prostitution (Mohanty 1991; Grewal and Kaplan 1994; Alexander 1997), yet it is remarkable that to date, very little has been explicitly advanced as a transnational or postcolonial feminist approach to the subject of prostitution....

Various inroads are being made on this front, such as in the analyses of Amalia Cabezas, Rama Kapur, Siobhan Brooks, Joan Phillips, Jacqueline Sanchez Taylor, and Jenn Guitart, who extend the tentative steps made earlier in this direction by Truong (1990), Moon (1997), Lim (1998), and this author.[9]...

A transnational feminist theory and politics on prostitution and other forms of sex work also includes a rethinking of practical strategies and programs to address the specific situations for women of color in the global sex trade. The radical feminist strategy to seek the abolition of prostitution can seem to many to be worthwhile, yet has its limitations. Based on a universalistic construction of prostitution, it does not allow space for addressing the multiple ways the sex trade is constituted and the myriad arrangements for the involvement of women's sexual agency. Paralleling the call for the abolition of marriage as an institution of male power and violence to women, it tends to ignore the strategies that women have undertaken to reform or transform social institutions and relations of power, instead demanding a single, monolithic strategy for change. Those who start from a "victim approach" to prostitution often advocate prosecuting men who participate in the sex trade as pimps, clients, traffickers, or brothel owners, proposing laws that criminalize working women in the belief that they can rehabilitate men who use prostitutes and can "rescue" or "save" women in a missionary fashion.

Little is advanced from this perspective that allows for the empowerment of women who strategically use their sexual labor to secure a place in the modern world, or for the recognition of sex workers' rights. Therefore, while we cannot lose sight of the vicious realities that many women of color face in the global sex trade, it is imperative that we build strategies that start from a recognition that sex work is an integral part of the global economy and is deeply embedded in, and cannot easily be disassembled from, many women's everyday lives, strategies, and identities. By embracing an abolitionist position on the subject, we will certainly ignore the different meanings and daily realities, constraints, and possibilities that sex work affords women in the global economy.

Moreover, in building an appropriate strategy, we need to recognize that oppression in the sex trade is not always experienced and defined as the sex act itself, but rather that it is the conditions that sex workers must endure that often are defined as the problem. Recent research in the Caribbean, for example, found that the problems identified by women in the sex trade emanated from the criminal status of sex work in many of the Caribbean countries that encouraged police harassment and abuse, and from lack of legal access to workers' rights, health care, social security benefits, pensions, appropriate childcare, and so forth (see Mellon 1999). Criminalization and stigmatization of sex workers ensured poor working conditions and sustained notions of prostitutes as disposable people....

These experiences of women of color in the sex trade—their perspectives, visions and dreams—need to be listened to carefully by feminists of color. Rather than simply remaining silent and thus complicit with rendering them as victims or as oversexualized racialized subjects, we could, from our academic and other non-sex work locations, collaborate with sex workers to struggle for everyday changes and transformations in the sex trade and for policies and practices that would strengthen them as autonomous, knowing subjects. We could also acknowledge their efforts as part of the contemporary transnational women's movement. Legacies of Black radical feminism and Third World feminism position

us well to listen to our "subaltern" or marginalized sisters and to avoid reproducing the hierarchies, privileges and priorities that characterize much of postmodern academic feminism. It is certainly possible, then, for us to reflect on sex worker demands as part of our feminist theorizing, and to collaboratively build strategies for change.

Feminists of color around the world need also to be more vigilant and attentive to the ways the global economy is pushing increasingly larger numbers of people into marginality and informal sector work, recognizing that to thwart the growth of the sex trade requires a much larger reorganization of the global economy. Without real economic alternatives for women and young men today, attempts to halt or change exploitative situations for women will remain a futile exercise. The 1999/2000 proposals and bills brought before the U.S. Senate and House regarding trafficking richly illustrate this problem. While the 1999 CIA research indicates that the current "epidemic" of trafficking is directly related to the diminishing resources for poor people in developing countries and to the greed of large transnational corporations, the proposals focus on punishing individual traffickers and the local governments of sending countries. They do not address structural global inequalities of wealth and power, the demand being made by industries and corporations in the North for cheap labor, or the fact that unless something else is made available, families will continue to rely on prostitution as an income generator....

Finally, this transnational feminist politics of articulation on sex work examines and contests the ways in which the transnational middle classes and elites—both men and women—construct racialized sexualized ideologies and practices that lock women and men of color into the positions and roles of sexual servants. It examines how some notions of obtaining gender equity among women and feminists in postindustrial world centers also can be highly oppressive to poor women of color, and it interrogates more fully the implications of the emergence onto the global scene of such phenomena as the Western European or North American female sex tourist. It follows a strategy that allows women to probe histories of racialization in the formation of identities, desire, and knowledge and to take responsibility for our varying contemporary positions in international relations of power and privilege. Most important, it asks how feminists can relate to and communicate with sex workers of color to build a sustainable future. A transnational feminism that relinquishes colonizing narratives about prostitution and the global sex trade, draws from women of color's experiences and perspectives in sex work, and builds global alliances, could be a useful theory and practice for many women around the world.

NOTES

1. The term "women of color" is used in this article interchangeably with "Brown and Black," "Third World," "African, Asian, Latin American, and Caribbean," or "Thai, Dominican, Nepalese, Ghanaian, Colombian" women, and could easily be replaced by the notion of "postcolonial women." I am acutely aware, however, that these categories, while speaking to the historical and shared experiences of, and struggles against, colonialism, neocolonialism, Western imperialism, masculine domination, and racialized/ethnicized oppression, may collapse differences between women, may not relate to the self-identification or political identity in particular societies, or could make some nationalities invisible. However, I use them to highlight the significance of the racialization of the global sex trade.

2. I would like to thank an anonymous reviewer for helpful feedback and comments on earlier drafts of this article and for bringing to my attention that the emphasis on "women of color" may lead to an undertheorizing and strategizing around the roles of white Eastern European and Russian women and "non-U.S., non-European and/or nonwhite men's roles as customers" in the sex trade. This is certainly not my intention, although I am aware that any emphasis on the subjectivity and agency of any single category of people (sex workers, white women, Black men, pink-collar workers, poor women, etc.) can implicitly lead to the invisibility of larger relations of power and to the elision of other subjectivities and actors. However, it would take another article to do full justice to these other dimensions of the sex trade.

I have also chosen to retain my focus on "sex workers of color" in this article in light of a new trend in the media and international discussions, where concern with white Eastern and Russian women in prostitution has begun to eclipse the centrality of "Third World women" in the global sex trade. Furthermore, I can only hope that readers will grasp that while sex tourism, militarized prostitution, and trafficking are premised for a large part on international, racialized, gendered relations between postindustrial and postcolonial societies, the involvement of Sri Lankan women in the contemporary Middle East, Nepali women in India, Brazilian women in Suriname, or Korean and Chinese women serving men in the Imperial Japanese army in the 1940s also poses questions about the significance of cultural/racial/ethnic difference between client and sex worker in constructions of prostitution.

3. According to Dr. Julio Javier Espinola, former PanAmerican Health Organization (PAHO) consultant to Haiti, during a meeting in April 2000.

4. UN press release reported in the *Washington Post* 17 March 2000.

5. Transportation and trafficking fees vary but prices of around $10,000 are common. A Reuters report on 3 July 2000 on trafficking notes "the price for Chinese passage to the United States has risen to about $50,000 a person from $30,000 a few years ago"—one of the highest fees in the world.

6. See Kempadoo and Doezema (1998), and Doezema 1998 and forthcoming for various critiques of this neo-colonial image of Third World women.

7. While the majority of sex tourists appear to be men, women sex tourists are also becoming more common and have been the subject of recent investigations in Asia and the Caribbean. See, for example, O'Connell Davidson and Sanchez Taylor (1999), Dahles (1998), and Albuquerque (1998).

8. See Kempadoo and Doezema (1998), where sex work is defined as "work" or labor by various individuals and by women's and sex workers' organizations in India, Malaysia, Japan, Thailand, South Africa, Ghana, Senegal, Brazil, the Dominican Republic, Mexico, Ecuador, Suriname, and so forth. These definitions and understandings of sex work are perhaps as widely spread as the "prostitution-as-violence to women" approach in these parts of the world.

9. Some of this work is yet to be published, but I refer here to the Ph.D. dissertation by Amalia Cabezas (1999) on sex work in the Dominican Republic; the presentation by Ratna Kapur at the Fifth LatCrit

conference, Breckenridge 5–7 May, 2000 about sex work, the law, and desire in the Indian context; an interview with Angela Davis by Siobhan Brooks (1999) about Black American women's sexuality and prostitution; Joan Phillip's doctoral study on Black male sex workers in Barbados that builds upon her earlier research on this subject; studies by Jacqueline Sanchez Taylor on female sex tourism in the Caribbean; and Jean Guitart's research on sex work in Cuba.

REFERENCES

Abraham-van de Mark, E. E. 1973. *Yu'i Mama: Enkele Facetten van Gexinsstructuur op Curacao.* Assen: Van Gorcum.

Albuquerque, Klaas de. 1998. "Sex, Beach Boys, and Female Tourists in the Caribbean." *Sexuality and Culture* 2: 87–112.

Alexander, M. Jacqui. 1997. Erotic Autonomy as a Politics of Decolonization: An Anatomy of Feminist and State Practice. In *Feminist Genealogies, Colonial Legacies, Democratic Futures,* edited by M. Jacqui Alexander and Chandra Talpade Mohanty. New York: Routledge: 63–100.

Bailey, Beth and David Farber. 1992. "Hotel Street: Prostitution and the Politics of War." *Radical History Review*: 54–77.

Bang-Soon Yoon. 1997. "Sexism, Racism and Militarism: Imperial Japan's Sexual Slavery Case." Paper presented at the First North Texas UN Conference on Women, University of Texas-Dallas, 25 October.

Barry, Kathleen. 1984. *Female Sexual Slavery.* New York: New York University Press.

Beckles, Hilary. 1989. *Natural Rebels: A Social History of Enslaved Black Woman in Barbados.* London: Zed.

Bishop, Ryan and Lillian S. Robinson. 1998. *Night Market: Sexual Cultures and the Thai Economic Miracle.* New York: Routledge.

Brooks, Siobhan. 1999. "Sex Work and Feminism: Building Alliances through a Dialogue between Siobhan Brooks and Professor Angela Davis." *Hastings Women's Law Journal* 10 (Winter): 181–87.

Cabezas, Amalia Lucía. 1999. *Pleasure and Its Pain: Sex Tourism in Sosúa, the Dominican Republic.* Ph.D. diss. University of California.

Carby, Hazel. 1982. White Women Listen! Black Feminism and the Boundaries of Sisterhood. In *The Empire Strikes Back: Race and Racism in '70s Britain,* edited by the Centre for Contemporary Cultural Studies, London: Hutchinson.

Dahles, Heidi. 1998. Of Birds and Fish: Street Guides, Tourists, and Sexual Encounters in Yogyakarta, Indonesia. In *Sex Tourism and Prostitution: Aspects of Leisure, Recreation, and Work,* edited by Martin Oppermann. New York: Cognizant Communication Corporation: 60–70.

Davis, Angela. 1982. *Women, Race and Class.* New York: Vintage.

Del Omo, Rosa. 1979. "The Cuban Revolution and the Struggle Against Prostitution." *Crime and Social Justice* 12: 34–40.

Doezema, Jo. 1998. "Loose Women or Lost Women? The Re-emergence of the Myth of 'White Slavery' in Contemporary Discourses of 'Trafficking' in Women." MA Thesis, University of Sussex.

Enloe, Cynthia. 1989. *Bananas, Beaches and Bases: Making Feminist Sense of International Politics.* Berkeley: University of California Press.

Findlay, Eileen J. Suárez. 1999. *Imposing Decency: The Politics of Sexuality and Race in Puerto Rico, 1870–1920.* Durham: Duke University Press.

Gender Matters. 1999. USAID Office of Women in Development, GenderReach Project, Issue. 1, February.

Group Sisterhood. 1998. "Prostitution, Stigma, and the Law in Japan: A Feminist Roundtable Discussion." In Kempadoo and Doezema 1998: 87–98.

Hall, Tony. 1994. "Jean and Dinah . . . Who Have Been Locked Away in the World Famous Calypso Since 1956 Speak Their Minds Publicly." Lord Street Theatre Company, Trinidad and Tobago.

Henson, Maria, Rosa. 1999. *Comfort Woman: A Filipina's Story of Prostitution and Slavery Under the Japanese Military.* Boulder: Rowman and Littlefield.

Hicks, George. 1994. *The Comfort Women.* New York: W.W. Norton.

Howard, Keith. 1995. *True Stories of the Korean Comfort Women.* Testimonies Compiled by the Korean Council for Women Drafted for Military Sexual Slavery by Japan and the Research Association on the Women Drafted for Military Sexual Slavery in Japan. London: Cassell.

Kane, Stephanie C. 1993. "Prostitution and the Military: Planning AIDS Intervention in Belize." *Social Science and Medicine* 36: 965–79.

Kempadoo, Kamala. 1994. *Exotic Colonies: Caribbean Women in the Dutch Sex Trade.* Ph.D. Diss. University of Colorado.

———. 1996. "Prostitution, Marginality, and Empowerment: Caribbean Women in the Sex Trade." *Beyond Law* 5.14: 69–84.

———. 1998. "Globalizing Sex Workers' Rights."
In Kempadoo and Doezema 1998: 2–28.

——— ed. 1999. *Sun, Sex and Gold: Tourism and Sex Work in the Caribbean*. Lanham, MD: Rowman and Littlefield.

Kempadoo, Kamala and Jo Doezema, eds. 1998. *Global Sex Workers: Rights, Resistance, and Redefinition*. New York: Routledge.

Lim, Lin Lean, ed. 1998. *The Sex Sector: The Economic and Social Bases of Prostitution in Southeast Asia*. Geneva: International Labour Office.

Marchand, Marianne H., Julian Reid and Boukje Berents. 1998. "Migration, (Im)mobility and Modernity: Toward a Feminist Understanding of the 'Global' Prostitution Scene in Amsterdam." *Millennium* 27.4: 955–83.

Martis, Jacqueline. 1999. "Tourism and the Sex Trade in St. Marten and Curacao." In Kempadoo 1999: 201–15.

Mayorga, Laura and Pilar Velasquez. 1999. "Bleak Pasts, Bleak Futures: Life Paths of Thirteen Young Prostitutes in Cartagena, Colombia." In Kempadoo 1999: 157–82.

Mellon, Cynthia. 1999. "A Human Rights Perspective on the Sex Trade in the Caribbean and Beyond." In Kempadoo 1999: 309–22.

Mohanty, Chandra Talpade. 1991. Cartographies of Struggle: Third World Women and the Politics of Feminism. In *Third World Women and the Politics of Feminism*, edited by Chandra T. Mohanty, Ann Russo, and Lourdes Torres. Indiana University Press: 1–50.

Moon, Katharine. 1997. *Sex Among Allies: Military Prostitution in U.S.-Korea Relations*. New York: Columbia University Press.

O'Connell Davidson, Julia and Jacqueline Sanchez Taylor. 1999. "Fantasy Islands: Exploring the Demand for Sex Tourism." In Kempadoo 1999: 37–54.

O'Neill, Amy. 1999. *International Trafficking in Women to the United States: A Contemporary Manifestation of Slavery and Organized Crime*. U.S. Center for the Study of Intelligence.

Ofreneo, Rene E. and Rosalinda Pineda Ofreneo. 1998. Prostitution in the Philipines. In *The Sex Sector: The Economic and Social Bases of Prostitution in Southeast Asia*, edited by Lin Lean Lim. Geneva: International Labour Office: 100–30.

Pivar, David J. 1981. "The Military, Prostitution and Colonial Peoples: India and the Phillipines, 1885–1917." *Journal of Sex Research* 17.3: 256–67.

Sturdevant, Saundra Pollock and Brenda Stoltzfus. 1992. *Let the Good Times Roll: Prostitution and the U.S. Military in Asia*. New York: New Press.

Truong, Than-Dam. 1990. *Sex, Money and Morality: The Political Economy of Prostitution and Tourism in South East Asia*. London: Zed.

25 • *Loretta J. Ross*

AFRICAN-AMERICAN WOMEN AND ABORTION

DISCUSSION QUESTIONS

1. How has the abortion rights/reproductive choice movement failed to represent the lived experiences of African-American women?
2. What are some of the most significant historical factors that have shaped African American women's specific understanding of their reproductive needs?
3. How have African American women worked to meet and advocate for their needs?
4. What is "reproductive justice," and how does it expand our understanding of reproductive rights and politics?

Only justice can stop a curse.

—Alice Walker

This essay reviews the activism of African-American women in the abortion rights movement, highlighting the past fifty years.[1] Many observers mistakenly view African-American women's struggle for abortion rights and reproductive freedom in the 1990s as reflecting a relatively recent commitment. More accurately, this activism should be placed in the context of our historical struggle against racism, sexism, and poverty.

The fact is, when methods of fertility control have been available and accessible, African-American women have advocated for and used these strategies even more frequently than their white counterparts.[2] For example, when family planning was first institutionalized in Louisiana in 1965, Black women were six times more likely than white women to sign up for contraception.[3]

But when contraceptives were unavailable and abortion was illegal, septic abortions were a primary killer of African-American women. One study estimated that 80 percent of deaths caused by illegal abortions in New York in the 1960s involved Black and Puerto Rican women.[4] In Georgia between 1965 and 1967 the Black maternal death rate due to illegal abortion was fourteen times that of white women.[5]

. . .

Ross, Loretta. "African-American Women and Abortion." Reprinted with permission of the author.

When we demand control over our own bodies, we must not depend solely on our history of slavery, our African traditions, or even on a colorized white feminist analysis. We need to support abortion rights from an analysis that is built from a strong and shared understanding of how the forces of racism, sexism, homophobia, and economic oppression affect our lives. . . .

What we need is a new feminist theory of reproductive freedom for Black women. We have a strong understanding of the role that race, class, and gender have played in our lives—our triple-oppression theories. But despite our history of activism, many Black women still do not see abortion rights as a stepping-stone to freedom because abortion rights do not automatically end the oppression of Black women. On the other hand, these rights do allow some control over our biology, freeing us from unwanted pregnancies, and they are fundamental to bodily and political self-determination. To ask whether African-American women favor or oppose abortion may currently be fashionable and an opportunity for manipulative politicians. But the answer is obviously yes: we obtain 24 percent of the abortions in the United States, more than 500,000 annually.[6] The question is not *if* we support abortion, but how, and when, and why. Our circumstances have dictated our choices. Neither persuasive analysis nor ideology influenced African-American women to support abortion and birth control. We did so because we needed to. Necessity was the midwife to our politics.

Regrettably, African-American women have been reluctant to analyze our history regarding abortion and to speak out collectively and publicly in support of abortion rights. To do so in the 1960s and 1970s seemed to support arguments of Black genocide, a charge that was not unreasonable in view of a multitude of attacks on African Americans. To speak out also risked highlighting abortion over other aspects of our struggle to achieve reproductive freedom. These struggles involve our experiences of pregnancy, infant mortality, sterilization abuse, welfare abuse, and sexuality in general. Even since legalization, the word *abortion* has remained one of the most emotionally charged words within

the African-American community, bringing forth twin fears of genocide and suicide. In some circles, we still refer to it as the "A" word!

To compound the problem, Black women are ambivalent about the mainstream pro-choice movement. While a 1991 poll by the National Council of Negro Women and the Communications Consortium revealed that 83 percent of African Americans support abortion and birth control, little of that support translates into membership in predominantly white pro-choice organizations.[7] The pro-choice movement, as a subset of the larger women's movement, has not been able to attract significant numbers of Black women into its ranks, even though many special projects targeting women of color proliferated in the 1980s.[8] At the same time, the anti-abortion movement became adept at manipulating Black fears about genocide to silence the voices of Black women who believe in reproductive freedom. Anti-abortion proponents have made frightening inroads into Black churches, which often find it difficult to openly discuss issues of Black sexuality including abortion, AIDS, homosexuality, premarital sex, and teen sexuality. A generation ago, Black ministers were at the forefront of the struggle for reproductive freedom. Today, the silence of our churches—the moral cornerstones of our community—is a reflection of the church's disconnection from the real history of African-American women.

It is up to Black women living in these difficult times to define abortion rights for ourselves. By exploring the nature of our silence, we can connect ourselves to our foremothers who were activists for reproductive freedom. As Black feminist bell hooks says, "Moving from silence into speech is a revolutionary gesture."[9] Our "revolutionary gesture" means finding our voices and rediscovering our history. We must document our own stories and give ourselves permission to speak proudly about the experiences of "ordinary" Black women whose "unexceptional" actions enabled us and the race to survive. We must dispel the myths surrounding our fertility and activism by developing our own critical analysis of abortion and birth control that does more than simply appropriate someone else's dogma. . . .

HISTORICAL CONTEXT: SLAVERY, EARLY BLACK FEMINISM, AND FERTILITY CONTROL ACTIVISM

Before the Civil War, almost 20 percent of the total United States population consisted of African-American slaves.[10] Plantation owners tried to keep knowledge of birth control and abortion away from both slaves and white women to maintain the system of white supremacy used to justify slavery and to increase their investments in human chattel.[11] In addition to the rape of slave women by slave masters to increase the number of children, breeding techniques included giving pregnant slave women lighter workloads and more rations to increase their willingness to have children. Punitive measures were also used: infertile women were treated "like barren sows and . . . passed from one unsuspecting buyer to the next."[12]

African Americans covertly used contraceptives and abortions to resist slavery. Often they employed African folk knowledge to do so. In the context of slavery, abortion and infanticide expressed a woman's desperate determination to resist the oppressive conditions of slavery.[13] As Angela Davis points out, when Black women resorted to abortion, the stories they told were not so much about the desire to be free of pregnancy, but rather about the miserable social conditions that dissuaded them from bringing new lives into the world.[14]

Throughout the nineteenth century, white southerners repeatedly expressed their racist nightmares about a huge Black population increase. In fact, the Black population of the South was growing much more slowly than the white population. In 1870 there were 5 million Blacks in the South, and in 1910 there were 8.7 million, whereas there were 8.6 million whites in 1870 and 20.5 million in 1910.[15]

By the early 1900s Black women were making significant gains in controlling their fertility by marrying late and having few children.[16] In this era the Black women's club movement, the organized voice of African-American women during the late nineteenth and early twentieth centuries, directly addressed issues of Black women's sexuality[17] and sought to "confront and redefine morality and assess its relationship to 'true womanhood.'"[18] Stereotypes about Black women's sexuality and alleged immorality prompted many African-American women to "make the virtues as well as the wants of the colored women known to the American people . . . to put a new social value on themselves."[19] The main organization for Black women's clubs, the National Association of Colored Women, had between 150,000 and 200,000 members, mainly middle-class women, in forty-one states in the mid-1920s.[20] The club movement was integral to the networks that shared contraceptive information and supported "voluntary motherhood."[21]

In 1894 *The Women's Era,* an African-American women's journal edited by Josephine St. Pierre Ruffin, declared that "not all women are intended for mothers. Some of us have not the temperament for family life."[22] Club members and others supported this perspective, and many responded to advertisements in Black newspapers in the early twentieth century for a medicated douche product called Puf, which was reported to "end your calendar worries."

THE BIRTH CONTROL CAMPAIGN, 1915–1950

Today it is commonplace to link the emergence of the birth control movement in the early twentieth century to the coercion of African-American women by a population control establishment anxious to limit Black fertility. While the population control establishment may have had its agenda, African Americans were willingly involved in the national birth control debate for their own reasons. African-American women were sensitive to the intersection of race, gender, and class issues that affected their drive for equality in early-twentieth-century American society. According to historian Jessie Rodrique, grassroots African Americans were "active and effective participants in the establishment of local [family planning] clinics . . . and despite cooperation with white birth control groups, Blacks maintained a degree of independence" that allowed the development of an African-American analysis of family planning and the role it played in racial progress.[23]

African-American women saw themselves not as breeders or matriarchs but as builders and nurturers of a race, a nation. . . .

In this spirit, the Black women's club movement supported the establishment of family-planning clinics in Black communities. . . .

The *Baltimore Afro-American* wrote that pencils, nails, and hat pins were instruments commonly used for self-induced abortions, and that abortions among Black women were deliberate, not the spontaneous result of poor health or sexually transmitted diseases. Statistics on abortions among African-American women are scarce, but 28 percent of Black women surveyed by an African-American doctor in Nashville in 1940 said they had had at least one abortion.[24]

REACTION

The opposition to fertility control for women in the 1920s came primarily from the Catholic Church, from white conservatives who feared the availability of birth control for white women, and from Black nationalist leaders like Marcus Garvey, who believed in increasing the African population in response to racial oppression. President Theodore Roosevelt condemned the tendency toward smaller family sizes among white women as race suicide. He denounced family planning as "criminal against the race."[25]

As racism, lynchings, and poverty took their heavy toll on African Americans in the early twentieth century, fears of depopulation arose within a rising Black nationalist movement. These fears produced a pronatalist shift in the views of African Americans. The change from relative indifference about population size to using population growth as a form of political currency presaged the inevitable conflict between those who believed in the right of Black women to exercise bodily self-determination and those who stressed the African-American community's need to foster political and economic self-determination.

In the United States, eugenics proponents believed that the future of native-born whites in America was threatened by the increasing population of people of color and whites who were not of Nordic-Teutonic descent. The eugenics movement not only affected the thinking in social Darwinist scientific circles, but it also grew to affect public policy, receiving the endorsement of President Calvin Coolidge, who said in 1924, "America must be kept American. Biological laws show . . . that Nordics deteriorate when mixed with other races."[26]

Unlike Malthus, the neo-Malthusians of the eugenics movement believed in contraception, at least for those they deemed inferior. To promote the reproduction of self-defined "racially superior" people, eugenics proponents argued for both "positive" methods, such as tax incentives and education for the desirable types, and "negative" methods, such as sterilization, involuntary confinement, and immigration restrictions for the undesirables.[27] The United States became the first nation in the world to permit mass sterilization as part of an effort to "purify the race." By the mid-1930s about 20,000 Americans had been sterilized against their will, and twenty-one states had passed eugenics laws.

Among supporters of eugenics were not only the rabid haters in the Ku Klux Klan but also respectable mainstream white Americans who were troubled by the effects of urbanization, industrialization, and immigration. During this same period, thousands of Blacks fled the Jim Crow South and migrated to the North. These fast-paced demographic changes alarmed many nativist whites, who questioned birth control for themselves but approved it as a way to contain people of color and immigrants.

When the movement for birth control began, organizers like Margaret Sanger believed that fertility control was linked to upward social mobility for all women, regardless of race or immigrant status. Because the medical establishment largely opposed birth control, Sanger initially emphasized woman-controlled methods that did not depend on medical assistance. Her arguments persuaded middle-class women, both Black and white, to use birth control when available.[28]

Sanger's immediate effect on African-American women was to help transform their covert support for and use of family planning into the visible public support of activists in the Club Movement. But African-American women envisioned an even more pointed concept of reproductive justice: the freedom to have, or not to have, children.

The early feminism of the birth control movement, which promoted equality and reproductive rights for all women regardless of race or economic status, collapsed under the weight of support offered by the growing number of nativist whites. Under the influence of eugenicists, Sanger changed her approach, as did other feminists. In 1919 her American Birth Control League began to rely heavily for legitimacy on medical doctors and the growing eugenics movement.[29] The eugenics movement provided scientific and authoritative language that legitimated women's right to contraception.[30] This co-optation of the birth control movement produced racist depopulation policies and doctor-controlled birth control technology.[31]

. . .

It is extremely likely that the racism of the birth control organizers, coupled with the genocidal assumptions of eugenics supporters, increased Black distrust of the public health system and has fueled Black opposition to family planning up to the present time. By 1949 approximately 2.5 million African-American women were organized in social and political clubs and organizations.[32] Many of them supported birth control and abortion, but at the same time they offered a strong critique of the eugenicists. A clear sense of dual or "paired" values emerged among African-American women: they wanted individual control over their bodies, but at the same time they resisted government and private depopulation policies that blurred the distinction between incentives and coercion.

POST–WORLD WAR II ACCESS

The birth control clinics established by Sanger and others met only a fraction of the demand for contraceptive services. The methods of birth control most commonly available to Black women in the 1950s included abstinence or infrequency of coitus, the withdrawal method, spermicidal douching, condoms, diaphragms, and the rhythm method. Of course when these methods failed (and they frequently did), Black women relied on underground abortion.

. . .

Ebony's readers had reason to be concerned because a disproportionate number of Black women died abortion-related deaths in Detroit, for example, from 1950 to 1965, revealed that of the 138 fatalities from septic abortions, all involved poor women, most of them Black.[33]

Long after the "granny" midwives in other ethnic groups had been replaced by medically based hospital practices, there were still hundreds of Black lay midwives practicing in the Deep South, who provided most of the abortion and contraceptive services for southern Black women.[34] According to Linda Janet Holmes, some of these women had midwifery lineages that extended as far back as slavery. Although these services [were] technically illegal, the women developed informal networks of communication that furtively shared contraceptive and abortion information.

Abortion was every bit as illegal in the 1950s as it had been in the 1920s, but until the years after World War II the crime of abortion had a protected status because law enforcement authorities often tolerated the practice as long as no one died.[35] After World War II, however, the medical profession and the legal authorities stepped up their campaign to eliminate underground practitioners who provided illegal abortions. Black women who provided underground abortions were harassed and prosecuted more frequently than their white counterparts, especially white men.[36]

. . .

POPULATION POLICIES FOR THE AFRICAN-AMERICAN COMMUNITY

In the mid-1950s population "time-bomb" theories offered an updated approach to eugenics. These still fashionable theories suggested that population growth in the Third World threatened the ability of the United States to govern world affairs. Brochures published by groups like the Draper Fund and the Population Council showed "hordes of Black and brown faces spilling over a tiny earth."[37] By the early 1960s the United States government began supporting population control policies overseas, and linked foreign aid to anti-natalist depopulation programs. Many U.S. politicians argued by analogy that urban whites in America needed to be protected from the "explosiveness" of overpopulated Black ghettos.

. . .

Generally speaking, family planning associated with racism was most frequently supported; associated with sexism, this support evaporated. This fissure among white conservatives about women's reproductive rights is still apparent today.

. . .

During this period African-American women were not blind to the irony of a government plan to make contraceptives free and extremely accessible to Black communities that lacked basic health care. They criticized linking the alleged population problem with women's personal decisions to control their fertility. The only population problem, according to many African-American women, was that some people had problems with some segment of the population. There was much in the debate on population pressures that was reminiscent of the eugenicists. Those who blamed every social issue—riots, pollution, hunger, high taxes, ghettos, crime, and poor health—directly on the population growth of people of color ignored the maldistribution of land and wealth and racist and sexist discrimination in the job market.[38]

Because of the unavailability of contraceptives and abortions, many desperate African-American women chose sterilization as their only hope for avoiding unwanted pregnancies. Birth control by hysterectomy was widely available, and some Black women adapted themselves to the limited choices that existed. Yet African-American women warily watched state legislative proposals to sterilize poor women who had too many "illegitimate" children. None of these proposals succeeded, largely because of the militancy of women activists like Fannie Lou Hamer, who said that "six out of every ten Negro

women were . . . sterilized for no reason at all. Often the women were not told that they had been sterilized until they were released from the hospital."[39] A national fertility study conducted by Princeton University found that 20 percent of all married African-American women had been sterilized by 1970.[40]

Despite the ways that racist politics cut across the bodily integrity of African-American women in the 1960s and 1970s, many women continued to sustain informal networks that spread the news about the availability of services. They became activists in support of birth control, for better health care, for abortion rights, and against sterilization abuse and population control, linking these issues to the project of improving the overall health status of the African-American community.

THE FEMINIST UNDERGROUND RAILROAD

Before abortion was legalized nationally in 1973, countless women perilously attempted self-abortion, and dangerous practitioners flourished because there were no safety standards without legalization. Despite the dangers, it is estimated that 200,000 to 1,000,000 illegal abortions occurred annually in the late 1960s.[41]

During the last decade of the illegal era, a few organizations operated an "underground railroad," referring women to illegal practitioners.[42] Underground abortions were facilitated by church and community-based referral services and cooperative doctors' networks in the 1960s. . . .

To address the problems associated with the lack of safe and affordable abortions, a group of women in Chicago began to provide abortions in 1969 through an illegal, floating underground network called Jane, officially known as the Abortion Counseling Service of Women's Liberation. Deliberately patterned after the Underground Railroad that freed slaves, the group provided over 11,000 safe abortions between 1969 and 1973.[43] While abortions from other illegal practitioners cost between $600 and $1,000, the women in Jane learned how to do abortions themselves and lowered the cost to an average of $40.[44]

During its last year of operation, more than half of the collective's clients were women of color, most of whom were poor and Black.[45]

Although the members of the collective were predominantly white, there were a few Black women who provided services, according to Jane member Laura Kaplan. Because the group's clients were increasingly African American, the collective felt an urgency to seek out Black women to join the collective. They did not feel that turning to the militant Black organizations was an option, since most radical Black groups believed that abortion was genocide. Black male spokespersons viewed women's liberation as a threat to Black solidarity and claimed that abortion was a weapon against their community.[46]

One of the earliest African American members of Jane was Lois Smith,[47] who has described her experiences as an abortion provider:

I discovered Jane when I escorted a girlfriend to get an abortion. You have to understand that the main problem was the secrecy; you couldn't tell people what you were doing. When I arrived at the facility, I saw that the clients were predominantly Black, but all the workers were white. Even while I waited for my friend, I began counseling the women, telling them they would be all right.

When I joined the collective, our primary problem was the illegality of what we were doing. This produced extreme secrecy and paranoia, but in a sense, it helped us bond as a group. It wasn't a Black or a white thing, but women's need. The only alienation I experienced was caused by the secrecy, but our family and friends supported us. Sometimes we even used their houses, but we couldn't tell anyone outside of our circle. The Black women were most supportive by keeping silent and taking risks. Fears of police arrests were real. Women had to endure many risks to give our number to a friend, but the networking was steady in the Black women's community.

But abortion was not openly discussed in the Black community because other survival issues were key. Women had been surviving for years using abortion as necessary. But the illegality of the procedure made women feel marginalized and terrified. They had heard so many horror stories about back-alley abortionists that they were often afraid when they came to us. They couldn't tell their doctors or nurses or their husbands. They got support from each other. It was very consistent how sisters supported each other.

The Black women who worked at Jane didn't come in as a group. Mostly we were involved one at a time, so we could never develop a critical mass, or even three to four of us, to get together to talk about what we were doing. But we didn't look on it as a Black or white women's issue; women needed termination of pregnancies, and there was unity created by women who were desperate.[48]

BLACK OPPOSITION TO REPRODUCTIVE RIGHTS

In the 1960s and 1970s, visible Black male political support for abortion rights was limited. As Angela Davis concluded, this was "a period in which one of the unfortunate hallmarks of some nationalist groups was their determination to push women into the background. The brothers opposing us leaned heavily on the male supremacist trends which were winding their way through the movement."[49] Some Black male scholars of the period echoed the genocidal arguments previously used, but infused their analyses with new elements of sexism and anti-Semitism. . . .

The Black Power conference held in Newark in 1967, organized by Amiri Baraka (LeRoi Jones), passed an anti-birth control resolution. Two years later, the May 1969 issue of *The Liberator* warned, "For us to speak in favor of birth control for Afro-Americans would be comparable to speaking in favor of genocide."[50] Four years later, Congress appeared to confirm their suspicions: testimony before the U.S. Senate revealed that at least two thousand involuntary sterilizations had been performed with OEO funds during the 1972–73 fiscal year.[51]

The Black Panther Party was the only nationalist group to support free abortions and contraceptives on demand, although not without considerable controversy within its ranks.[52] "Half of the women in the Party used birth control, and we supported it because of our free health care program. We understood the conditions of the Black community," remembers Nkenge Toure, a former member. . . .

BLACK WOMEN RESPOND

The assault on birth control and abortion came from both the left and the right. White conservatives saw family planning as an assault on traditional values of motherhood, while some Blacks saw it as a race- and class-directed eugenics program. That such disparate forces aligned themselves against African-American women demonstrated that both white bigots and Black sexists could find common cause in the assertion of male authority over women's decisions regarding reproduction.

In contrast, many African-American women exerted a dynamic and aggressive influence on the family-planning movement. . . . These activists were articulate and well organized and constituted the largest single bloc of support for family planning. . . . African-American women fully understood the racist impulse that located Planned Parenthood clinics in poor Black neighborhoods but not in poor white neighborhoods. Still, they perceived the free services to be in their own best interests. Quoting from DuBois, they declared, "We're not interested in the quantity of our race. We're interested in the quality of it."[53]

. . .

In this period, in diverse places and in different ways, African-American women took leadership roles in promoting African-American women's rights to control their own bodies. Dr. Dorothy Brown, one of the first Black female general surgeons in the South, graduated from Meharry Medical College in 1948 and, while in the Tennessee state legislature, became one of the first state legislators to introduce a bill to legalize abortion in 1967.[54] Her bill, which would have legalized abortion for victims of rape and incest, fell only two votes short of passing. . . .

A distinct Black feminist consciousness began consistently to counter the reactionary opponents to family planning. . . .

. . . This combined support for fertility control and opposition to population control, a unique voice within the women's movement at the time, did much to inform both the feminist and the civil rights movements in later decades. African-American women rejected the single-issue focus of the women's movement on abortion, which excluded other issues of reproductive freedom. They also opposed the myopic focus on race of the male-dominated civil rights movement, which ignored concerns of gender justice. Activist women also learned a valuable lesson about sexist backlash that equated Black male domination with African-American progress.

REPRODUCTIVE RIGHTS LEADERSHIP AFTER *ROE V. WADE*

. . .

It is important to highlight the connection between the anti-violence and the reproductive rights movements because many of the newer activists in the abortion rights movement in the mid-1970s actually came from the movement to end violence against women. They, like myself, worked at rape crisis centers or battered women's shelters. Significantly, few of the early activists came directly out of the civil rights movement without passing through some feminist crucible that heightened their awareness of gender inequalities.

Unfortunately, the early feminists in NBFO report that frictions within the group split them apart. Fortunately, the ideas they promoted remain our legacy.

Some Boston-based activists in NBFO, including noted author Barbara Smith, formed the Combahee River Collective in 1975, named after a Harriet Tubman guerrilla action in 1863 that freed more than 750 slaves and is the only military campaign in American history planned and led by a woman.[55] This collective issued a Black feminist manifesto in 1976 that became a rallying cry for Black feminists, combining for the first time a comprehensive critique of racism, sexism, poverty, and heterosexism for Black women activists seeking ideological cohesion. Collective members worked for abortion rights and against sterilization abuse and presented many workshops in communities and on college campuses on Black feminism, reaching hundreds of young Black women.

. . .

When the Hyde Amendment, which eliminated subsidies for poor women's abortions, was upheld by the Supreme Court, a number of Black women joined or started reproductive rights organizations, such as the multiracial Committee for Abortion Rights and Against Sterilization Abuse (CARASA). Brenda Joyner assessed the post-Hyde situation this way: "The government will not pay for a $200 or $300 abortion procedure for a poor woman on Medicaid. But it will pay for a $2,000 to $3,000 sterilization procedure for that same poor woman."[56]

. . .

It had begun to seem to [former congresswoman Shirley Chisholm] that the question was not whether the law should allow abortions. Experience shows that pregnant women who feel they have compelling reasons for not having a baby, or another baby, will break the law and, even worse, risk injury and death if they must get one. Abortions will not be stopped . . . The question becomes simply that of what kind of abortions society wants women to have—clean, competent ones performed by licensed physicians or septic, dangerous ones done by incompetent practitioners.[57]

Most prominently, Faye Wattleton, a former nurse-midwife at Harlem Hospital, became the first African-American president of Planned Parenthood Federation of America in 1978. Wattleton was motivated, she said, because of her memories of the "desperation and suffering that resulted from unintended pregnancy and illegal, unsafe abortions."[58] Between 1978 and 1992, Wattleton made a tremendous impact on the visibility of African-American women in the reproductive freedom movement.

. . .

The fact is, many African-American women did not join mainstream pro-choice organizations, despite the visible Black leadership. In 1981 Gloria Joseph and Jill Lewis wrote, "The negative feelings expressed by Black women in 1969 about the women's movement are virtually unchanged today. Most Black women still feel a sense of distrust: they believe that the White women in the movement are largely middle-class and exhibit racist mentalities, and they are convinced that the concerns of the movement are not relevant to their material conditions."[59]

. . .

AFRICAN-AMERICAN WOMEN MOBILIZE

Several key events increased African-American women's visibility in the abortion rights movement in the late 1970s and 1980s. Among these were the United Nations' Decade for Women, the formation of several new Black women's organizations, the fight for the Civil Rights Restoration Act of 1988, and the *Webster* Supreme Court decision in 1989.

. . .

The racial insensitivity white women displayed in the 1980s as they pursued influence within the Democratic Party was extremely unfortunate, as it coincided with the Black women's public visibility within the feminist movement. Black women felt the same sense of betrayal that club women of the 1890s did when they were refused membership in white women's organizations, and that anti-lynching crusaders like Ida B. Wells felt when they looked in vain for support from white feminists of that era.

The National Political Congress of Black Women, with Donna Brazile as its first executive director, brought grassroots women into contact with elected officials from both the Republican and Democratic parties and issued one of the first statements by African-American women in support of abortion rights in 1986. The statement was supported by hundreds of women throughout local and national political activities and was key to the development of the African American Women for Reproductive Freedom coalition in 1989.

NOW'S WOMEN OF COLOR PROGRAM

The National Organization for Women created a Women of Color Program in 1985 to mobilize support for its planned "March for Women's Lives" in April 1986. I was the first director of this program, from 1985 to 1989. My daunting task was to attract the endorsement of organization of women of color for the first national march dedicated to abortion rights.

NOW did not enjoy a good reputation among most women of color, despite the fact that a Black woman, Pauli Murray, a lawyer and later an Episcopalian priest, had co-authored NOW's first statement of purpose in 1966 and had articulated a vision for African-American women that included working for reproductive freedom. Aileen Hernandez, a commissioner for the Equal Employment Opportunity Commission and a union organizer with the International Ladies' Garment Workers' Union, became NOW's second national (and first Black) president in 1971. Along with other early Black NOW activists, such as Addie Wyatt and Flo Kennedy, she insisted that NOW add other issues affecting African-American women to its agenda.[60] NOW, Hernandez asserted, "cannot afford the luxury of a single-issue focus—even when that issue was as important as the ERA."[61] Hernandez resigned from NOW in 1979 after sponsoring a resolution saying that Black women should not join the organization until it had confronted its own racism. California state senator Diane Watson concurred: "If they [NOW] don't really go after a mixed group of women, we should not support such an organization, and we should dramatize our non-support."[62]

NOW's negligence regarding racism dissuaded many Black women from affiliating. Only seven organizations of women of color had endorsed NOW's Equal Rights Amendment (ERA) march in 1978, and little changed over time. In some cases, relations got much worse between Black women and NOW, over such issues as which candidate to support at the 1984 Democratic National Convention.

In 1986 Black women were skeptical about joining a march for abortion rights sponsored by what was perceived as a white women's organization. For one thing, though abortion had shaped the personal experiences of many of these women, it was not part of their lives as political activists. Although all the leaders of Black women's organizations I contacted privately supported abortion rights, many perceived the issue as marginal, too controversial, or too "white" for their ready endorsement. Only a few, like Byllye

Avery, Shirley Chisholm, and Dorothy Height, spoke out publicly in support of the march. Many of the others, as Angela Davis has observed, were uncomfortable about subtleties that seemed to escape popular discussion of abortion among white women—for example, "the distinction between *abortion rights* and the general advocacy of *abortions*. The [abortion rights] campaign often failed to provide a voice for women who wanted the right to legal abortions while deploring the social conditions that prohibited them from bearing more children."[63] Because the abortion rights movement focused on legality and public advocacy, it failed to touch the lives of many women for whom access—simply having a clinic to go to and the means to pay for service—was the only understanding of abortion they felt they needed. The same class and race issues that segregated the women's movement in the 1890s hampered our collaboration in the 1980s.

By 1987 NOW was responding more clearly to the voices of women of color; it sponsored the First National Conference on Women of Color and Reproductive Rights in Washington, D.C., which attracted over 400 women of color, two-thirds of whom were African American. No national organization of women of color working on reproductive rights existed at the time, and this conference was significant because it was the first conference in history that brought women from the feminist, civil rights, and Black nationalist movements together to promote reproductive freedom.

Although the April 1986 abortion rights march was endorsed by 107 organizations of women of color, three years later, when NOW held its second abortion rights march, more than 2,000 women came together, to form the largest delegation ever of women of color marching to support abortion rights. The National Black Women's Health Project sent thirteen busloads of people to the 1989 march, becoming the largest single delegation of African-American women.[64]

This time, prominent civil rights leaders also affirmed their support for abortion rights. In January 1989 a statement denouncing Operation Rescue's attempts to shut down abortion clinics was signed by thirty-four leaders, including Maxine Waters, Andrew Young, Rosa Parks, John Lewis, Barbara Jordan,

William Gray, Cardiss Collins, Leah Wise, Julian Bond, Louis Stokes, John Jacob, and Roger Wilkins.[65] Jesse Jackson, who spoke at the abortion marches in 1986 and 1989, recruited other Black male leaders to the cause. Joseph Lowery, head of the Southern Christian Leadership Conference, made his first appearance at an abortion rights demonstration in 1989.[66]

Teen Pregnancy and Other Programs

During the 1980s, many black feminists were involved in activities related to reproductive health, particularly teen pregnancy programs, which received significant funding in the Reagan/Bush years, and which sometimes demanded silence on the abortion issue in exchange for federal funding.

The National Council of Negro Women, Delta Sigma Theta, the Urban Coalition, and the Coalition of 100 Black Women all mounted teen pregnancy projects, as did civil rights organizations such as the National Urban League, the Southern Christian Leadership Conference, and the NAACP. All attempted to respond to charges in the media that Black teen pregnancy rates were out of control. A 1986 CBS special report, for example, on the "vanishing" Black family attributed teen pregnancy to the so-called moral degeneracy of the Black family. In a report that refuted this racist and sexist premise, the Alan Guttmacher Institute examined interstate and racial differences in teen pregnancy rates. Research sponsored by the institute found that although one of every four Black children is born to a teenage mother, states with higher percentages of poor people and people living in urban areas—whatever their race—have significantly higher teen pregnancy and birthrates.[67] Poverty, not race, the institute explained, was the major factor in teen pregnancy.

Black women involved in social work founded programs to combat infant mortality, a problem closely associated with poverty and teen pregnancy. As an indicator of Black progress, or lack thereof, infant mortality and teen pregnancy programs received relatively strong support from the government, particularly when compared with the attack on abortion and contraceptive programs for African

Americans, manifested by the passage of the 1977 Hyde Amendment, the 1980 Mexico City policy (which prohibited funding for abortions overseas), and the 1989 "gag rule."[68]

By the mid-1980s, in response to the Reagan administration's various attacks on reproductive rights, and as an outgrowth of increased organizing by women of color after the Decade for Women, African-American and other women of color were beginning to voice strong support for reproductive rights. At this time, Eleanor Holmes Norton declared, "We ought to be out there explaining that we stand at the head of the line on the issue of reproductive rights. We are, after all, the first and foremost affected."[69]

African American Women for Reproductive Freedom

In the late 1980s many Black women determined to focus on mainstream civil rights organizations. A series of legislative fights pitted abortion rights against civil rights when opponents of both tried to divide and weaken the civil rights coalitions. The effort to pass the Civil Rights Restoration Act of 1988–a bill intended to close several loopholes in the law regarding civil rights coverage—was a case in point. Opponents added several anti-abortion amendments to the bill. In a compromise (mostly between Black and white men), the bill was passed with the anti-abortion amendments, weakening the alliance between the women's and the civil rights movements. This divide-and-conquer strategy would likely have failed if Black feminists had had a role in the debate, because we bridge both worlds. Our absence allowed men to trade away abortion rights and offered an alarming glimpse into the future—if we are silent.

At the time, most civil rights groups believed they had other priorities: AIDS, drug wars, teen pregnancy, attacks on affirmative action, crime—and simply did not recognize the accumulating threats on *Roe v. Wade* that alarmed Black women. But the Supreme Court's *Webster* decision changed all that. "Now we have to mobilize," declared Faye Wattleton.[70]

Following the *Webster* decision, which opened the door for more restrictive state regulation of abortion,

African-American women responded with furious organizing. In fact, the *Webster* decision created its own form of political backlash as the "carts full of mail" and "streets full of demonstrators" that Supreme Court justice Antonin Scalia predicted indeed materialized.

In August 1989 Donna Brazile and I organized a telephone conference among twelve leaders of Black women's organizations to discuss creating a national response to the *Webster* decision. This group became the coalition of African American Women for Reproductive Freedom (also called African American Women for Reproductive Choice in some newspaper accounts).

These powerful and highly visible women decided to issue a statement that would "give permission" for African-American women to talk publicly about abortion. This was a critical decision because most of the leaders of major Black women's organizations had not yet publicly affirmed their support for abortion, although several had endorsed marches and other campaigns by mainstream pro-choice organizations—a situation that underwrote the silence of Black women around the country.

The public statement affirming abortion rights, written by Marcia Gillespie of *Ms.* magazine, became a brochure titled "We Remember: African American Women for Reproductive Freedom." Emily Tynes, former press secretary of NARAL and a sophisticated media consultant, organized a press conference the day before the opening of the 1989 Congressional Black Caucus national conference at which Faye Wattleton became the first reproductive rights activist to receive the CBC's national leadership award. Featured at the press conference were Dorothy Height (National Council of Negro Women), Faye Wattleton (Planned Parenthood), Congresswoman Cardiss Collins, Byllye Avery (National Black Women's Health Project), Beverly Smith (Delta Sigma Theta), Janet Ballard (Alpha Kappa Alpha), Jewell McCabe (Coalition of 100 Black Women), Pat Tyson (Religious Coalition for Abortion Rights), and Shirley Chisholm (National Political Congress of Black Women). These women spoke forcefully about the need to maintain Operation Push and Jacqui Gates

of the National Association of Negro Business and Professional Women's Clubs sent messages as well. Such broad support from Black women's organizations, church groups, sororities, and political leaders was unprecedented in the history of our movement.

Two thousand copies of the brochure were initially printed, but we underestimated the huge demand. The strategy awoke what one reporter called "the sleeping giant of the pro-choice movement."[71] By the end of an eighteen-month campaign, over 250,000 copies of the brochure had been distributed in response to requests from African-American women from around the country.

The brochure campaign was extremely effective because it linked the collective powerlessness Black people felt about the slavery experience to the callous assault on abortion rights in the 1980s. The public statement did, in fact, give everyday Black women "permission" to bring abortion out of the closets of our lives. The brochure read in part:

> Choice is the essence of freedom . . . we have known how painful it is to be without choice in this land . . . Now once again somebody is trying to say that we can't handle the freedom of choice . . . [that] African American women can't think for themselves . . . that we must have babies whether we choose to or not . . . We understand why African Americans seek safe legal abortion now. It's . . . a matter of survival.[72]

A year later, in June 1990, African American Women for Reproductive Freedom joined the National Black Women's Health Project in sponsoring the first-ever national conference on Black women and Reproductive Rights at Spelman College, which was also supported by the National Council of Negro Women, the Coalition of 100 Black Women, Delta Sigma Theta, Operation Push, The National Urban Coalition, and the National Association of Negro Business and Professional Women's Clubs. The strategy of the conference was to mobilize Black women in as many ways and organizations as possible. Over the next two years, most of these groups sponsored their first-ever conferences on reproductive rights for Black women. "We Remember!" became a rallying cry for our movement as Black women demanded the right to speak for themselves in the abortion debate.

ADDITIONAL ACTIONS FOR REPRODUCTIVE FREEDOM

In 1988 the Center for Women's Development at Medgar Evers College in New York sponsored its first conference on Black women and reproductive rights. The center's work to date had focused on the rights of single Black mothers, and the expansion into reproductive rights activism was a significant shift—the result of the center's Black "nationalist feminist" politics and its leadership role in the Black nationalist movement.

Black students on college campuses also became involved in the movement; for example, students at Spelman published a statement in defense of abortion rights in the student newspaper late in 1989. Black students at Yale and Howard also organized reproductive rights events in the late 1980s. This infusion of young people into the reproductive rights movement is perhaps the best achievement of our activism—the true legacy for the future.

Black women who worked within the pro-choice mainstream created partnerships with Black women's organizations, bringing financial resources together with the militancy of the African-American women. For example, NOW, NARAL, and Planned Parenthood funded the "We Remember" brochures while agreeing to respect the organizational autonomy of African-American women.

In 1988 the Reagan administration began to push regulations limiting the right of women to receive information about abortion from federally funded family-planning clinics. The proposed "gag rule" deeply offended African-American women, who viewed the regulations as encroachments on free speech and on the patient-doctor relationships. Most seriously, the proposal threatened the health needs of poor women, for whom abortion can be a necessity. In response, Sherrilyn Ifill and Charlotte Rutherford of the American Civil Liberties Union (ACLU) and the NAACP Legal Defense and Education Fund,

respectively, organized an amicus brief that was submitted to the Supreme Court on behalf of women of color. More than one hundred organizations of women of color became signatories to the first abortion rights brief in history submitted by African-American and other women of color to the Supreme Court.[73]

Earlier, the Women of Color Partnership Program of the Religious Coalition for Abortion Rights, established in the mid-1980s, had begun organizing pro-choice women of color in churches. Its first director was an African-American woman, Judy Logan-White. Working with NOW's Women of Color Program, regional conferences were organized in Washington, D.C., Oakland, Philadelphia, and Atlanta between 1986 and 1992. Other conferences sponsored by RCAR were held in Hartford, Connecticut; Sioux Falls, South Dakota; and Raleigh, North Carolina. In collaboration with the ACLU Reproductive Freedom Project under Lynn Paltrow and the NOW Women of Color Program, in 1989 the Partnership Program sponsored "In Defense of *Roe*," a national conference in Washington, D.C. for women of color.

In July 1994 Black women attending a national pro-choice conference in Chicago decided to launch another highly visible campaign for abortion rights because the Clinton administration was in the process of designing a health care reform proposal that many Black women feared would deemphasize abortion rights. Under the leadership of "Able" Mable Thomas, the group called itself Women of African Descent for Reproductive Justice (the Reproductive Justice Coalition, for short). Fast-paced organizing brought together more than 800 Black abortion rights supporters, who raised more than $21,000 in two weeks to purchase a full-page signature ad in *The Washington Post* on August 16, 1994. The ad sent a clear message to members of Congress that the various health care reform proposals must address concerns of Black women, including abortion, universal coverage, equal access to health care services, and protection from discrimination.

This remarkable series of events, compressed into a relatively brief period, marked the first time many

African-American activists had ever publicly defended abortion rights and demonstrated a new awareness among African-American women who mobilized support for an expanded reproductive freedom agenda. They had an impact on both the Black community and the women's movement. By now, prominent Black male writers, such as Manning Marable, openly challenged sexist views on reproductive rights. Marable insisted: "We must fight for women's rights to control their own bodies and not submit to the demagogies of the rabid right who would return us to back alley abortionists, to those who would destroy young women's lives. Those who oppose the woman's right to choose express so much love for the rights of the fetus, yet too frequently express contempt for child nutrition programs, child care, and education after the child has come into the world."[74]

. . .

By the mid-1990s African-American and other women of color have forced the abortion rights movement to become a broader struggle for reproductive freedom. I do not believe it is an overstatement to say that the activism of Black women and other women of color expanded the focus of the abortion rights movements in the 1990s. This activism influenced several pro-choice organizations to change their names and priorities: the National Abortion Rights Action League was renamed the National Abortion and Reproductive Rights Action League in 1994; the Religious Coalition for Abortion Rights became the Religious Coalition for Reproductive Choice that same year. NOW added welfare rights as one of its top priorities in 1993. This broadening of the agenda of organizations that were primarily seen as narrowly focused was due, in large part, to the demands of women of color for a more inclusive and relevant reproductive rights movement.

This transformation in the politics of the pro-choice movement required an assessment of the interrelatedness of race, gender, and class issues and how they affected different groups of women. Despite our biological similarities, different groups of women cope with vastly different social realities. Black women have placed reproductive health issues

in a historical context that makes the reproductive freedom movement relevant to the ongoing struggle against racism and poverty. Today, more Black women publicly support abortion and birth control than ever before; more are working with predominantly white women's organizations than before; and, in many ways, the ideological gaps between Black and white feminists have diminished as the reproductive freedom movement seeks to make services available and accessible to all women.

Abortion rights has moved from the margin to the center of the dialogue about Black feminist activism. The leadership of the 1960s was finally matched by a constituency in the 1990s that supported full reproductive rights for Black women. In a sense, the deferred dreams of our foremothers of the 1920s were finally affirmed when Black women declared, "We Remember!"

CONCLUSION: IN PURSUIT OF PERFECT CHOICE

As we plan our activist future, we must clearly envision what we want to create for ourselves, so that we end up where we want to be. We must wrestle with concepts like "perfect choice," the opposite of the very imperfect choices we presently have. (I first heard this sentiment expressed by Naima Major at the National Black Women's Health Project in 1989, when I was its program director; it seemed to capture our aspirations so accurately.) We demand perfect choice: the right to have the resources to make the reproductive choices that make sense.

Perfect choice must involve access not only to abortion services but also to prenatal care, quality sex education, contraceptives, maternal infant and child health services, housing, and reform of the health care delivery system. As Gloria Joseph has said, "Given these realities of health care seen by Black people, White women must understand why Black women do not devote their full energies to the abortion issue. The emphasis has to be on total health care."[75]

. . .

NOTES

1. Linda Gordon, in her critically acclaimed book *Woman's Body, Woman's Right* (New York: Penguin, rev. ed., 1990), separates the reproductive freedom movement into distinct historical phases, evolving from "voluntary motherhood" to "birth control" to "family planning" to "reproductive freedom." Each of these phrases has historical antecedents and associations, but for the purpose of this essay I will use them rather interchangeably.

2. Martha C. Ward, *Poor Women, Powerful Men: America's Great Experiment in Family Planning* (Boulder: Westview Press, 1986), 18.

3. Ibid., 55.

4. Robert Stapes, *The Black Women in America* (Chicago: Nelson Hall, 1974), 146.

5. Melanie Tervalon, "Black Women's Reproductive Rights," in *Women's Health: Readings on Social, Economic and Political Issues,* ed. Nancy Worcester and Marianne H. Whatley (Dubuque, Iowa: Kendall/Hunt, 1988), 136.

6. Stanley K. Henshaw, Lisa M. Koonin, and Jack S. Smith, "Characteristics of U.S. Women Having Abortions," *Family Planning Perspectives* 23 (March/April 1991): 75–81.

7. National Council of Negro Women and Communications Consortium Media Center, "Women of Color Reproductive Health Poll," August 30, 1991.

8. Hull et al., *But Some of Us Are Brave,* xx.

9. bell hooks, *Talking Back* (Boston: South End Press, 1989), 6.

10. Thomas B. Littlewood, *The Politics of Population Control* (Notre Dame, Ind.: University of Notre Dame Press, 1977), 18.

11. Patricia Hill Collins, *Black Feminist Thought: Knowledge, Consciousness and the Politics of Empowerment* (New York: Routledge, 1991), 50; Deborah Gray White, *"Ar'n't I a Woman?": Female Slaves in the Plantation South* (New York: Norton, 1985), 98.

12. D. White, *"Ar'n't I a Woman?"* 101.

13. Elizabeth Fox-Genovese, *Within the Plantation Household: Black and White Women in the Old South* Chapel Hill: University of North Carolina Press, 1988), 324.

14. Angela Davis, "Racism, Birth Control, and Reproductive Rights," in Fried, ed., *From Abortion,* 17.

15. Gordon, *Woman's Body,* 151.

16. Paula Giddings, *When and Where I Enter: The Impact of Black Women on Race and Sex in America* (New York: William Morrow, 1984), 137.

17. Guy-Sheftall, *Words of Fire,* 6.

18. Giddings, *When and Where I Enter,* 85.

19. Gerda Lerner, ed., *Black Women in White America* (New York: Vintage, 1972), 576.

20. Nancy F. Cott, *The Grounding of Modern Feminism* (New Haven: Yale University Press, 1987), 92–93.

21. Gordon, *Women's Body,* xix.

22. Giddings, *When and Where I Enter,* 108.

23. Many thanks are due Jessie Rodrique, the first scholar I encountered who was doing serious research on the birth control activism of Black women. It was her work that encouraged me to investigate and expand on this history to include abortion rights history and to connect it with modern-day activism. As a measure of the sensitivity of her work, most of the Black women who read her research did not realize she was white until she confessed it on the last page. The familiar racial biases and assumptions that frequently mar white women's writings on Black women were totally absent from her work, a tribute to her feminist consciousness and feminist ethics. See Jessie M. Rodrique, "The Black Community and the Birth Control Movement," in *Unequal Sisters: A Multicultural Reader in U.S. Women's History,* ed. Ellen Carol Dubois and Vicki L. Ruiz (New York: Routledge, 1990), 335, 333.

24. Ibid.

25. Gordon, *Woman's Body,* 133.

26. Alan L. Stoskopf, "Confronting the Forgotten History of the American Eugenics Movement," *Facing History and Ourselves News,* 1995, 7.

27. Petchesky, *Abortion and Woman's Choice,* 86.

28. Ward, *Poor Women,* 8.

29. Cott, *Grounding of Modern Feminism,* 91.

30. Carole R. McCann, *Birth Control Politics in the United States, 1916–1945* (Ithaca, N.Y.: Cornell University Press, 1944), 100.

31. Betsy Hartmann, *Reproductive Rights and Wrongs: The Global Politics of Population Control and Contraceptive Choice* (New York: Harper & Row, 1987), 97.

32. Claudia Jones, "An End to the Neglect of the Problems of the Negro Woman!" in Guy-Sheftall, *Words of Fire,* 113.

33. Rickie Solinger, *The Abortionist: A Woman Against the Law* (New York: Free Press, 1994), 36.

34. Linda Janet Holmes, "Thank You Jesus to Myself: The Life of a Traditional Black Midwife," in *The Black Women's Health Book: Speaking for Ourselves,* ed. Evelyn C. White (Seattle: Seal Press, 1990), 98.

35. Solinger, *The Abortionist,* 5.

36. Ibid., 15.

37. Petchesky, *Abortion and Woman's Choice,* 118.

38. Corea, *Hidden Malpractice,* 144.

39. Littlewood, *Population Control*, 80.
40. Davis, "Racism, Birth Control," 23.
41. Ibid., 12.
42. Ward, *Poor Women*, 58.
43. Jane, "Just Call Jane," in Fried, *From Abortion*, 93.
44. Ibid., 95.
45. Kaplan, *Story of Jane*, 267.
46. Ibid., 175.
47. Not her real name. Ms. Smith requested anonymity.
48. Author's interview, January 17, 1996.
49. Giddings, *When and Where I Enter*, 318.
50. Giddings, *When and Where I Enter*, 318.
51. Ward, *Poor Women*, 95.
52. Ibid., 92.
53. Ward, *Poor Women*, 93.
54. Author's interview with Dr. Brown, January 12, 1992.
55. The Combahee River Collective, "A Black Feminist Statement," in *This Bridge Called My Back: Writings by Radical Women of Color*, ed. Cherrie Moraga and Gloria Anzaldua (Watertown, Mass.: Persephone Press, 1981), 211.
56. Ninia Baehr, *Abortion without Apology: A Radical History for the 1990s* (Boston: South End Press, 1990), 56.
57. Chisholm, *Unbought and Unbossed*, 113–22.
58. Planned Parenthood Federation of America, biographical sketch of Faye Wattleton, president, March 1989.
59. Gloria I. Joseph and Jill Lewis, *Common Differences: Conflicts in Black and White Feminist Perspectives* (New York: Anchor Books, 1981), 276.
60. Giddings, *When and Where I Enter*, 300–311.
61. Ibid., 346.
62. Ibid., 347.
63. Davis, "Racism, Birth Control," 205–206.
64. Judy D. Simmons, "Abortion: A Matter of Choice," in Evelyn C. White, *Black Women's Health Book*, 120.
65. Statement on "Operation Rescue" by National Civil Rights Leaders, January 22, 1989.
66. Sam Fulwood III, "Black Women Reluctant to Join Pro-Choice Forces," *Los Angeles Times*, November 27, 1989, 18.
67. Faye Wattleton, "Teenage Pregnancy: A Case for National Action," in Evelyn C. White, *Black Women's Health Book*, 108–9.
68. Infant mortality programs received special attention because Black infants in America die at twice the rate of white infants in the first year of life. This Black/white infant mortality gap has always existed, and since the 1920s, has actually widened. While the African-American infant mortality rate declined throughout the 1970s, the rate subsequently leveled off and then rose in the 1980s, a trend that can be attributed in part to cuts in federal programs. See Virginia David Floyd, "Too Soon, Too Small, Too Sick: Black Infant Mortality," in *Health Issues in the Black Community*, ed. Ronald L. Braithwaite and Sandra E. Taylor (San Francisco: Jossey-Bass, 1992), 165.
69. Chiquita G. Smith, "A Congresswoman's Call to Action," in *Common Ground, Different Planes*, ed. Religious Coalition for Abortion Rights (Washington, D.C., 1992), 1.
70. Paul Ruffins, "Blacks Backing Pro-Choice Add a Compelling Voice," *Los Angeles Times*, September 17, 1989, 2.
71. Ibid., 1.
72. African American women for Reproductive Freedom, brochure, September 1989.
73. Loretta Ross, Sherrilyn Ifill, and Sabrae Jenkins, "Emergency Memorandum to Women of Color," in Fried, *From Abortion*, 147.
74. Manning Marable, "Black America: Multicultural Democracy in the Age of Clarence Thomas and David Duke, and the Los Angeles Uprisings," in *Open Fire*, ed. Greg Ruggiero and Stuart Ashulka (New York: New Press, 1993), 256.
75. Joseph and Lewis, *Common Differences*, 40.

26 • *Alison Piepmeier*

THE INADEQUACY OF "CHOICE": DISABILITY AND WHAT'S WRONG WITH FEMINIST FRAMINGS OF REPRODUCTION

DISCUSSION QUESTIONS

1. What new perspectives does Piepmeier introduce that expand our comprehension of the limitations of the abortion rights/reproductive choice framework?
2. What are the common pressures and assumptions about disability faced by pregnant women with the knowledge or strong likelihood that they will produce a child with disabilities?
3. What do these views reveal about how our society views and values people with disabilities?
4. Why is it important to listen to the voices and experiences of parents with disabled children?

When I was intentionally pregnant, I experienced a complex reproductive decision: whether to undergo prenatal testing. Our cultural expectation is that pregnant women have prenatal testing performed so that they can make the choice to terminate pregnancies with "defects." Down syndrome is a condition for which much prenatal screening and testing are done, and up to 90 percent of fetuses identified as having Down syndrome are terminated. I didn't want to be faced with that choice, and so I did not have an amniocentesis. I am now the happy parent of a daughter with Down syndrome.

I shared this experience in a March 2012 article on the *Motherlode* blog on *The New York Times*

website. *The New York Times* is aimed at a thoughtful audience, many of whom identify as liberal. Given this readership, it wasn't surprising that many of the more than 170 online comments made about the article accepted abortion as an available option. What did surprise me is the eugenicist use to which many of these readers would put abortion. They offered the choice of abortion as a way to avoid what they saw as an unacceptable situation, having a child with a disability. Here are several of the comments:

A condition that brings with it guaranteed cognitive disabilities is not something I'm willing to inflict on another human being, much less my own beloved child.

Piepmeier, Alison. 2013. "The Inadequacy of "Choice": Disability and What's Wrong with Feminist Framings of Reproduction." *Feminist Studies* 39(1): 159–186. Reprinted by permission of *Feminist Studies*.

Knowingly giving birth to a special needs child is a crime against the child.

I resent having to pay for children who are going to be a huge drain on society, financially and resource wise, if the parents knew in advance that they were going to have a special needs child.

I was raised to believe that knowingly giving birth to a severely disabled or mentally retarded baby was a sin—a really terrible sin—because it harmed not just the baby (who would never have a normal life) but also the family (including siblings who would be pressed into caring for an aging disabled brother or sister, no longer "cute" in their 50s) and society (stuck with enormous bills for a lifetime). I still feel that way. Hopefully in time, that 92% [of fetuses with Down syndrome that are terminated] will become 100%.[1]

The comments as a whole were quite diverse, but these comments here were not rare. They are examples of the ignorant, troubling, and offensive narratives that surround reproduction, disability, and parenting in our culture. For instance, readers described giving birth to a person with a disability as an act of "harm" or cruelty, even as a "crime"— deeply stereotypical framings that individuals with disabilities might well dispute. People with disabilities were being defined principally as "a huge drain on society." The term "normal life" was used as though it were an unambiguous goal, without acknowledging the extent to which "normal life" here is a narrowly imagined construct that does not embrace the diversity of human existence. The final comment here concludes with the clearly eugenicist hope that 100 percent of fetuses with Down syndrome will be terminated. The world, presumably, is a better place if people with Down syndrome or intellectual disabilities aren't in it.

. . . The fact is, most feminist conversations haven't gone beyond the level of this online commentary. This isn't simply an observation about feminist understandings of disability; it's about feminist framings of reproduction. The narrative of "choice" that surrounds and defines US reproductive rights discourse is simply inadequate. During my pregnancy,

when my partner and I were deciding whether to have an amniocentesis and, presumably, an abortion if the fetus had Down syndrome, I discovered that feminist texts had little to offer me. My story isn't one that many feminists are talking about—or if they are talking about it, it is in ways that I found troubling rather than helpful. Feminist writing offers a number of reductive and stereotypical narratives about reproduction and disability. These problematic narratives are particularly visible in (rare) feminist discussions of prenatal testing and abortion. These discussions are often built around stereotypes— stereotypes of people with disabilities, of parenting people who have disabilities, and of what "choice" means and how it functions.

These feminist conversations about disability and abortion are indicative of broader problems within feminist discussions of reproduction. Reproduction should not be defined by "choice," a concept that is individualized and ignores the broader societal contexts that shape reproduction, parenting, and our understanding of children. For feminist scholars to address reproduction in a meaningful way, they must become resistant to stereotyping narratives that perpetuate oppression and instead listen to a different set of narratives, those told by pregnant women and by parents who exist at complex intersections. We need scholarly and activist feminist conversations about reproduction that embrace, rather than fear, the complexity of reproductive decision making.

This project emerged in part from my desire to hear the stories of other individuals' decision-making processes. I've conducted a series of interviews with parents of children with Down syndrome and with pregnant women. What I've learned from these conversations is that the process of reproductive decision making is far more complex than mainstream feminist narratives suggest. Prenatal testing and selective abortion were the starting point for my conversations, but this isn't an argument exclusively about prenatal testing, or about Down syndrome or disability. The narratives emerging from decisions about prenatal testing and whether or not to terminate a fetus can serve as case studies for ways that feminist discourse around reproduction needs to change. This essay will present both activist and scholarly feminist conversations around disability as examples of inadequate feminist discourse. I will then look to parents' narratives as a site for the complexity that feminists need to engage with. Finally, I'll turn to reproductive justice framings that allow for far more complex understandings.

FEMINIST NARRATIVES

The gap between reproductive rights and disability rights has been problematic for some time. As early as 1984, Marsha Saxton was articulating her ideology as a feminist who supports reproductive rights and also "question[s] the practice of systematically ending the life of a fetus *because it is disabled*."[2] In 1998 she more thoroughly articulated the divide involving reproduction: "The reproductive rights movement emphasizes the right to have an abortion; the disability rights movement, the right *not to have to have* an abortion. . . . We must actively pursue close connections between reproductive rights groups and disabled women's groups with the long-range goal of uniting our communities."[3]

In 2007 and 2008, Generations Ahead convened a series of meetings in which disability rights and reproductive rights and justice advocates gathered.[4] These meetings were necessary because, as Sujatha Jesudason noted, "The disability rights and reproductive rights communities have often been at odds." Because reproductive rights are continually under threat, "some reproductive rights advocates . . . strategically argued for the need for abortion in the cases of rape, incest and disability as a way to undermine their opposition and win undecided voters to their side."[5] By rhetorically equating disability to rape and incest, reproductive rights advocates participate in the dehumanization of people with disabilities, presenting disability not only as inhuman but as an act of terrorism. This equivalence between disability and rape is damaging, and it highlights the ways that feminist strategies are

distorting and stereotyping an important public conversation about reproduction.

. . .

PARENTAL STORIES

In summer 2011, I began interviewing parents of children with Down syndrome, having conversations with them about their pregnancies, their prenatal testing, and their parenthood. These were semi-structured qualitative interviews, each lasting between one and three hours. These interviews were intended to be "conversations with a purpose": I am interested in these individuals' narratives of their reproductive decision making.[6] Although I went into every interview with a list of questions, I discovered that I only had to ask one: "Did you have prenatal testing when you were pregnant?" Almost every conversation has taken off from that single question and has needed very little encouragement from me.

. . . The vast majority of the people I interviewed were white, although I sought out women of color and talked with four African American women.[7] Virtually all the people I spoke with were middle class, and class strikes me as a particularly significant variable here: these were people with access to prenatal medical care and access to second trimester abortion services, even if those services would mean they had to leave the state.

The narratives these parents and potential parents shared did not fit within any of the reductive models our culture offers; indeed, there's no way to make sense of these stories within the framework of the familiar narratives about reproduction and disability because these stories are neither about choice nor tragedy. They do more than challenge our cultural stereotypes and misunderstandings of Down syndrome; they challenge our conventional feminist understanding of reproductive decision making. Parents talked with me about how their experiences exceeded standard cultural frameworks, as several of the mothers were supportive of abortion and yet did not terminate their pregnancies. They grappled with the distinction between a "fetus" and a "child," a distinction that they found unclear and shifting. They addressed the fact that the pregnant woman was the decision maker, and they experienced this as isolating rather than empowering. Ultimately, the interviews highlighted the inadequacy of the narrative of "choice."

A familiar cultural narrative is that people who don't terminate pregnancies when fetal disability is identified are people who are opposed to abortion for ideological or religious reasons.[8] My interviews challenge that explanation. Some of the women I interviewed chose not to have testing because of their religious beliefs. They believed that the reason to test for anomalies is because you might choose to terminate, and because they had religious objections to termination, they did no screening. Other women made the same set of decisions without religious foundations. One woman I interviewed identified very strongly as religious but did have an initial screening performed. When the screening reported that she had a higher-than-average possibility of having a child with Down syndrome, she decided to do no more testing. Many other women I interviewed characterized themselves as "pro-choice," but their narratives demonstrate that the concept of "choice" is far too limited a term to explain their experiences. Tricia expressed a sentiment I heard repeatedly: "I'm pro-choice, but it's awfully complex when it's close to home."[9] At least three of the women I interviewed had had abortions in the past, but in the case of the pregnancies with fetuses identified as having Down syndrome, they did not terminate.

Elizabeth had had an abortion in college and felt devastated by the decision. She wasn't opposed to abortion (indeed, she was an activist for women's rights in many areas, starting in college and continuing into adulthood), but she said, "After that time, I knew I would never have another abortion if I became pregnant unplanned. I would find a way to manage whatever the situation." In discussing her pregnancy with her daughter who had Down syndrome, she said,

> With Rachel . . . she was so wanted by me. I planned her and did everything I could to get pregnant short of *begging* Dan for another child. The heart defect and

then the Down syndrome were overwhelming pieces of news, and sometimes during the pregnancy I wondered if the baby might die before birth and all would be better for her. I attached these feelings to the heart defect (not Down syndrome) because we were unsure of the severity and how she would manage once born. I was so scared she would die shortly after birth. Never once considered terminating after we got the Down syndrome news.

Elizabeth's story reveals her complex mixed feelings; on the one hand she thought that the prenatal death of the fetus "would be better for her," but then Elizabeth was "so scared [the baby] would die shortly after birth." She was certain that she wouldn't terminate the pregnancy, but she wasn't certain what would be the best decision for the child.

Others grappled with the possibility of abortion more directly. Leanne had had two abortions earlier in her life, when she wasn't ready to be a parent. When she was pregnant with her second child, amniocentesis revealed that this fetus had Down syndrome, and she explained,

> I was just kind of shell-shocked. I really actually went through the process of deciding whether or not to go through with [an abortion] or not. I had another ultrasound, and I was almost sure I couldn't do it. That I couldn't go down the path of terminating. So, I would set up little things for myself. I would have an ultrasound where they're really going to look at the heart. If anything was wrong, I wasn't going to go through with [the pregnancy] because it wasn't worth it for the child. When really, they could have surgery, you know. So, I said that that will make my decision, because I didn't really want to make that decision myself. I wanted something to determine it for me. If the heart's okay . . . then the heart was okay.

INTERVIEWER: Was that a relief, or like, "Damn it, decision still not made"?

LEANNE: Yeah, it was kind of like that.

For Leanne, the diagnosis of Down syndrome and the decision of whether to continue with the pregnancy were somewhat traumatic experiences. She wasn't opposed to abortion in general terms, and she didn't perceive her earlier abortions as devastating, as Elizabeth did. For this particular pregnancy, however, there was no easy decision. Leanne's thought process mirrors some of the comments from the *Motherlode* piece; she was evaluating her decision making by considering what would be "worth it for the child," an impossible line of questioning. Even four years later, discussing this with me, Leanne was quite emotional. She is delighted by her daughter. Her emotion wasn't grief at having a child with Down syndrome; it was sadness at remembering how painful the decision-making process was. Note that Leanne was grappling with a familiar, limited narrative, trying to use it to help her make sense of a complex situation.

As Leanne's story shows, the notion of "choice" doesn't always apply to the experiences pregnant women have. Leanne "didn't really want to make that decision myself," so she looked for reasons to terminate: "If anything was wrong, I wasn't going to go through with it." She was searching for a way out of "choice"—for validation or for some kind of assistance. Another woman I interviewed, Diane, also resisted the framework of individual choices. Like Leanne, although to an even more dramatic extreme, Diane wasn't sure what to do, and she wanted external guidance. As she progressed in her pregnancy, she discovered that she kept moving the line to determine whether or not she would have an abortion.

Diane became pregnant unexpectedly. Before the testing even began, Diane and her partner weren't sure that they wanted to continue with the pregnancy.

> I was already kind of in a situation where we were trying to decide—because it was such an unplanned thing and my boyfriend and I weren't together very long—whether he and I were even going to keep the baby regardless of what the testing told us. So we're still kind of, "Do we even want to have the baby at all, regardless of whether it's Down syndrome, special needs, or whatever?"

The prenatal testing became a way for her to try to gather information to make a decision about whether or not to have an abortion. She initially thought that if the fetus had a disability, she'd terminate. When Down syndrome was identified, she decided that Down syndrome was acceptable, but if the fetus had anything else, she'd terminate. Then when a significant heart condition was diagnosed, she decided that as long as the child could have a meaningful life, she would continue, but if the child's life was in danger, she'd terminate. When testing revealed that the child's life was in danger, she discovered that she still wasn't ready to terminate.

Part of the uncertainty was that there was no clear line between this entity being a fetus-which-isn't-yet-a-person and being a child.

> We got to the point of the amnio. We had already named him, I had already seen him a couple of times, and you know, he was my son. And regardless of whatever issues he had, he was still my child, and I was going to go through with it. And if that meant, you know, a long, hard road for me, then that's what it was going to have to be. But I still got thinking in my head, *just Down syndrome*. When we get to something else, that's like hitting another brick wall and I had to start all over again.

Here Diane reports knowing that this was her son, her child, a person who already had a name. She felt ready for whatever challenges his life might pose for her. She didn't frame her experience using an easy binary of "tragedy" versus "bliss"; instead, she identified parenthood as "a long, hard road." And yet even in that space of having identified the fetus as a person, Diane still wasn't certain that she would or should continue the pregnancy. It was never intuitively obvious to her, since each new diagnosis required "start[ing] all over again." Diane explained of the heart diagnosis, "His heart defect made things more complicated, more and more complicated—as if it could get any more complicated."

Not knowing, not being able to decide, seemed to characterize much of Diane's experience of being pregnant with Chase. . . .

In our conversation, Diane revealed the complexity of this sort of thought process. There were no easy narrative frameworks for explaining her experience. A feminist assertion of Diane's right to make a "choice" doesn't help her figure out what "choice" means in her individual context. She knew that she had a "choice," but she wanted something more: guidance, information, real options, meaningful support. One helpful circumstance was her relationship with her boyfriend's father and stepmother, who was pregnant at the same time. Their support and sympathy for her challenging situation—their offer of food as well as their offer of in-utero comparisons—made the process easier for her.

The difficulty with choice might be related to another pattern that emerged in these conversations: for most of my interviewees, the decision of whether to terminate was made by the woman. This is, of course, legally appropriate, but it spoke to a pressure that the women felt they had to bear alone. Several women said that they and their partners had different opinions about abortion. While Diane was trying to decide what to do, her partner was scheduling an abortion. Diane explained, "I think that's really where he thought we were going to go, and I wasn't saying no at that point. I was just saying, 'I don't know, I don't know, I don't know.'" The difference of opinion between the potential father and mother was very clear to many of the women with whom I spoke. A woman who was pregnant at the time of our interview had an older child with Down syndrome, and she had just recently had an amniocentesis for this second pregnancy. She was discussing whether she would terminate if the results showed that the fetus had Down syndrome, and she knew that she would be alone in her decision because her husband had a very different opinion.

INTERVIEWER: So, did this really feel to you like your decision?

JULIA: Yes, which made it so much harder because I knew he would never do it.

INTERVIEWER: He would never terminate the pregnancy?

JULIA: No.

Many of the women were very aware of the decision making being their obligation. For instance, Leanne disagreed when her husband Stefan said they'd made the decision together. She reminded him that after the amniocentesis he began identifying the fetus as a child, and he agreed.

Another woman had an amniocentesis, but she realized that by the time the test results returned, she wouldn't terminate in any case. She explained that she went into the testing without a clear agenda, because "this was the next thing to do, whatever." She then felt certain she would terminate if the results showed a fetus with a disability. When the results returned, her pregnancy was at eighteen weeks, she and her husband knew the fetus's gender, and her feelings had changed: she didn't want to terminate. She said that she thought she could approach the issue "rationally," but then realized, "No. No way." Her husband was much more open to the question of terminating, but she wasn't at all.

Pregnant women can feel pressure from partners and family members who don't want an abortion and those who do. Many women expressed surprise at the extent to which they felt, if not pressure to terminate, an openness to termination from people who they had understood to be explicitly opposed to abortion. For instance, Leanne's parents said they would support her whatever she decided, and she seemed to feel this as a slap in the face.

LEANNE: I thought, excuse me? I just didn't expect that from my parents. My mother's a solid Christian, and my dad's a retired pastor.

INTERVIEWER: So you felt like they were saying that if you decide to terminate, that it's okay?

LEANNE: Yeah. Maybe even more for my mother.

By articulating that the decision was all hers, one that they would support, Leanne felt that her parents were giving her the message that she should terminate, thus adding to her feeling of isolation. At this moment she was eager for a different kind of support, a family community that would help her navigate having a child with a disability.

An emphasis on individual choice is pervasive in much feminist writing about reproductive rights, but these interviews demonstrate that individual rights and responsibilities don't solve all problems or even explain them. These women didn't discuss the individualized decision-making process as empowering, with meaningful options available to them. Instead, they felt frightened and pressured, as if those around them had unpredictable agendas that had to be negotiated and manipulated.

These stories illustrate the complexities that can characterize reproductive experiences, complexities that need to appear in feminist discussions of reproduction. Women who are supportive of reproductive rights, even those who have had abortions, may still decide to have a child with Down syndrome. These narratives suggest that "choice" needs to stop being used as a universal, easy answer, because reproductive decision making is messy, sometimes painful, and often involves negotiations, which the term "choice" doesn't suggest. "Choice," as used in feminist rhetoric, generally refers to the availability of abortion, but this wasn't the focus for these parents and potential parents. While resting on an individual woman, reproductive decision making often demands support from family, community, and medical services. Certainly these narratives are partly about our cultural understanding of disability, but these mothers' stories do more than challenge our cultural stereotypes and misunderstandings of Down syndrome; they challenge our feminist understanding of reproductive rights.

This is where a reproductive justice approach offers more useful tools. Mainstream reproductive rights conversations are politically strategic; they are defensive and "safe." Reproductive justice offers a different model, one that "emphasize[s] the relationship of reproductive rights to human rights and economic justice."[10] There are no pat slogans that oversimplify difficult decisions. Reproductive justice makes room for messier questions and concerns. It emphasizes social justice, which removes this decision from an individualized space and makes it part of a broader set of community priorities.

REPRODUCTIVE JUSTICE

Reproductive justice is a scholarly and activist framework that expands conversations around a host of questions relating to reproduction. Rather than framing the central issue as "choice," which is unrealistically and unproductively individualized, reproductive justice demands that we recognize how social context shapes reproduction and how community opens and closes particular possibilities. Reproductive justice demands that we understand how stigmas and stereotypes are created and perpetuated, so that we can recognize how these narratives play a role in reproductive decision making. It demands attention to "a much wider set of concerns. Access to resources and services, economic rights, freedom from violence, and safe and healthy communities are all integral to [this] expanded vision."[11] Perhaps more to the point of this article, it acknowledges the complexity of reproduction.

Reproductive rights discourse generally addresses the legal right to have an abortion, and this tends to be a framework that's individualized. Of course, legally it's a very important right for an individual woman to decide about her own reproduction.[12] But this is a limited model. My interviews have revealed that parents and potential parents may resist this individualized expectation. They recognize that decision making happens in an intimate as well as a societal context. They want a *we* framework, not an *I* framework, and they resist the simplistic notion of "choice" because they recognize that they are making a decision that's far more complex than the rhetoric of "choice" suggests.

Reproductive justice asks scholars to view reproduction as something that extends far beyond the individual. Legal scholar Dorothy Roberts makes this point clearly.

> Reproductive liberty must encompass more than the protection of an individual woman's choice to end her pregnancy. It must encompass the full range of procreative activities, including the ability to bear a child, and it must acknowledge that we make reproductive decisions within a social context, including inequalities of wealth and power. *Reproductive freedom is a matter of social justice,* not individual choice.[13]

Roberts's emphasis on social justice is similar to Rothman's argument that the social system "fails to take collective responsibility for the needs of its members, and leaves individual women to make impossible choices. We are spared collective responsibility, because we individualize the problem. We make it the woman's own. She 'chooses,' and so we owe her nothing. Whatever the cost, she has chosen, and now it is her problem, not ours."[14] Both scholars, like many others in this vein, identify reproductive decision making as extending beyond simple, individual choice.[15] Reproductive justice scholarship also stresses the importance of the community for reproductive decision making.[16] . . .

My conversations with potential parents and parents demonstrated again and again how inadequate "choice" was as a way to describe their experiences. These people were in a sense having to pretend to be individuals, making individual choices, but they were—as Roberts says—operating "within a social context." This social context is multilayered, from the intimate to the institutional, which Roberts describes as "including inequalities of wealth and power." That social context plays a large role in dictating the value of the fetus, the rational decision, the right thing to do. It generates stigma and stereotypes that have effects not only on individual beliefs but on educational and financial support. Mapping this larger social context is part of the work that feminist disability studies scholars are doing. . . .

There are also more intimate social contexts in which parents and potential parents are operating, and these intimate contexts were part of every interview I conducted: parents and potential parents were eager for community. One part of this community is a family that often has multiple opinions, a family that may have a large part to play in the life the child lives. Most interviewees shared stories of their families' responses and how important they were. They also discussed the broader community responses, from their friends and coworkers to the people they encounter daily. . . .

. . . No parent is actually an *I*—we are always a *we.* Some find this objectionable: a reader of the *Motherlode* blog argued, "I resent having to pay for children who are going to be a huge drain on society." Some resent the *we,* the fact that they're part of a

community helping to support people with disabilities. And yet parenting a child always requires a community. Kimala Price explains that the reproductive justice movement's "three core values" are "the right to have an abortion, the right to have children, and the right to parent those children."[17] Price argues that if we really want women to have control over their reproduction, that doesn't merely mean that they are able to choose not to be pregnant. It also means that they are able to choose to have children *and* parent children—a very meaningful aspect of the narrative for the parents I interviewed and an aspect of the narrative that many feminist scholars of reproductive rights have overlooked. Perhaps even more pointedly, Generations Ahead, echoing several reproductive justice advocates from the global South, calls for "a framing away from the right not to have children to a right to have children, and a framing away from creating a self-sufficient, productive individual to re-shaping society to provide for the needs of all people, regardless of gender, race, ability, sexual orientation, citizenship status and class."[18] The need for community support may be more visible when parenting a child with a disability, but dependence is part of the human condition, as Garland-Thompson has noted.[19] . . .

NOTES

1. Comments to Alison Piepmeier, "Choosing to Have a Child with Down Syndrome," *Motherlode* (blog), *The New York Times,* March 2, 2012, http://parenting.blogs.nytimes.com/2012/03/02/choosing-to-have-a-child-with-down-syndrome.

2. Marsha Saxton, "Born and Unborn: The Implications of Reproductive Technologies for People with Disabilities," in *Test-Tube Women: What Future for Motherhood?* ed. Rita Arditti, Renate Duelli Klein, and Shelley Minden (London: Pandora Press, 1984), 302, italics in original.

3. Marsha Saxton, "Disability Rights and Selective Abortion," in Abortion Wars: A Half Century of Struggle, 1950–2000, ed. Rickie Solinger (Berkeley: University of California Press, 1998), 375, 389, italics in original.

4. According to its mission statement, "Generations Ahead was the only organization in the United States

that worked with a diverse spectrum of social justice stakeholders—including reproductive health, rights and justice, racial justice, LGBTQ, and disability and human rights organizations—on the social and ethical implications of genetic technologies." It closed in January 2012.

5. Sujatha Jesudason, "Executive Summary," for Generations Ahead, Bridging the Divide: Disability Rights and Reproductive Justice Advocates Discussing Genetic Technologies (Generations Ahead Report, 2008), 1, 4, http://www.generationsahead.org/files-for-download/articles/GenAheadReport_BridgingThe Divide.pdf.

6. B. L. Berg, Qualitative Research Methods for the Social Sciences, 4th ed. (Boston: Allyn & Bacon, 2007), 89. Anthropologists Rayna Rapp and Faye Ginsburg offer an excellent explanation of the work that I hope these parent narratives do: "The cultural activity of rewriting life stories and kinship narratives around the fact of disability . . . enables families to comprehend (in both senses) this anomalous experience, not only because of the capacity of stories to make meaning but because of their dialogical relationship with larger social arenas. In other words, the way that family members articulate changing experiences and awareness of disability in the domain of kinship not only provides a model for the body politic as a whole but also helps to constitute a broader understanding of citizenship in which disability rights are understood as civil rights." Rayna Rapp and Faye Ginsburg, "Enabling Disability: Rewriting Kinship, Reimagining Citizenship," in Going Public: Feminism and the Shifting Boundaries of the Private Sphere, ed. Joan W. Scott and Debra Keates (Urbana: University of Illinois Press, 2004), 189.

7. I identified some women of color through online communities of bloggers who are parents of children with Down syndrome. Others came to me via a graduate student, Michael Owens, who spent two semesters doing independent studies about people of color who are parents of children with disabilities. He let parents know about my research, and several were willing to talk with me. All of the women of color with whom I spoke said that the other parents of children with Down syndrome with whom they interact are white.

8. As Sujatha Jesudason and Julia Epstein note, "feminist disability advocates end up feeling shut out of reproductive rights conversations because they assume their pro-choice counterparts believe any questioning of pregnancy termination to be anti-choice." Sujatha Jesudason and Julia Epstein, "Disability and Justice in Abortion Debates," Center for Women Policy Studies, in Reproductive Laws for the 21st Century Papers, no. 2 (February 2012), http://www.centerwomenpolicy.org/news/newsletter/documents/REPRO_Disabilityand JusticeinAbortionDebates_JesudasonandEpstein.pdf. Alison Kafer makes a similar observation in Feminist, Queer, Crip (Bloomington: Indiana University Press, 2013), 163.

9. Some names of the people I interviewed have been changed, based on their preferences. The names of all the children have been changed.

10. Jael Silliman, Marlene Gerber Fried, Loretta Ross, and Elena R. Gutierrez, Undivided Rights: Women of Color Organize for Reproductive Justice (Cambridge, MA: South End Press, 2004), 4.

11. Ibid.

12. I align my political views with those of Kafer: "Abortion for any reason and under any circumstance must then be accompanied by accessible and affordable prenatal care for all women, as well as reliable and affordable child care, access to social services, and the kind of information about and supports for disability mandated in the Kennedy Brownback Act." Kafer, Feminist, Queer, Crip, 167.

13. Dorothy Roberts, Killing the Black Body: Race, Reproduction, and the Meaning of Liberty (New York: Pantheon Books, 1997), 6, italics in original. Reproductive justice was a term that emerged after her book was published, so she uses the terms "reproductive liberty" and "reproductive freedom."

14. Barbara Katz Rothman, The Tentative Pregnancy: How Amniocentesis Changes the Experience of Motherhood (New York: W. W. Norton, 1993), 189.

15. For instance, well-respected abortion scholar Rickie Solinger argues, "I am convinced that choice is a remarkably unstable, undependable foundation for guaranteeing women's control over their own bodies, their reproductive lives, their motherhood, and ultimately their status as full citizens." Rickie Solinger, Beggars and Choosers: How the Politics of Choice Shapes Adoption, Abortion, and Welfare in the United States (New York: Hill and Wang, 2001), 7. In January 2013, Planned Parenthood gave up the "pro-choice" label to characterize their work.

16. Kafer explains, "Both reproductive justice activists and disability rights activists interrogate the rhetoric of choice found in reproductive rights movements. The language of choice fails to account for the ableist context in which women make decisions about pregnancy, abortion, and reproduction in general."

Kafer, Feminist, Queer, Crip, 162. Andrea Smith critiques the "pro-life versus pro-choice advocates who make their overall political goal either the criminalization or decriminalization of abortion," noting that reproduction depends not only on individuals but also on communities. Andrea Smith, "Beyond Pro-Choice Versus Pro-Life: Women of Color and Reproductive Justice," NWSA Journal 17, no. 1 (2005): 120. Jesudason argues that advocates must "recognize the relationship of individual lives to larger social, political, and economic factors, and the intersectional and contextual nature of individual and family decision making. They appreciate that the difficult decisions that women and people with disabilities make must be understood in terms of structural and pervasive inequality, mistreatment, and bias." Generations Ahead, Bridging the Divide, 5

17. Kimala Price, "What Is Reproductive Justice? How Women of Color Activists Are Redefining the Pro-Choice Paradigm," Meridians: Feminism, Race, Transnationalism 10, no. 2 (2010): 43.

18. Generations Ahead, Bridging the Divide, 116.

19. "Our bodies need care; we need assistance to live; we are fragile, limited, and pliable in the face of life itself. Disability is thus inherent in our being: What we call disability is perhaps the essential characteristic of being human." Rosemarie Garland-Thomson, "The Case for Conserving Disability," Bioethical Inquiry 9, no. 3 (September 2012): 342.

SECTION FOUR

Constructing Knowledge

In Section Four we examine the importance of power and context and the many attendant factors that shape our understandings of sex, gender, and sexuality. These chapters examine politics and power in different social settings and institutional locations. Sex, gender, and sexuality are constructed differently across time and place. Section Four asks: What factors shape the specific forms those constructions take? It is not just random but rather specific economic, social, and cultural interests and relations of power that produce those varied incarnations. In order to understand what form these constructs take, and why, we must ask critical questions about how they are defined, maintained, and reinforced and to whose benefit.

The chapters in this section begin to answer these questions by examining specific institutional contexts. They highlight the ways in which we perform gender differently according to diverse contexts. They also point to various factors that shape those performances, including organizational practices and structural forces that contribute to defining our identities, practices, and desires. Throughout, we see how both the social constructions and lived realities of sex, gender, and sexuality are intertwined and mutually constitutive.

The first few chapters in this section examine multiple aspects of science, medicine, and technology. For instance, Emily Martin discusses the ways in which many authors of scientific textbooks have described male and female reproductive functions in terms of stereotypical male/female gender roles. Descriptions of "valiant" sperm and "passive" eggs demonstrate the extent to which our notions of gender are ingrained, so much so that they become apparent even in the way we personify and describe biological *activity*. Likewise, Siobhan Somerville examines scientific-medical constructions focused on racial and homosexual bodies and their intersecting origins, while Preves troubles the medical/hormonal/surgical treatment of intersexed children. Tre Wentling takes up the phenomenon of medicalization from other angles, examining the power of the medical establishment to define what is or is not a "disorder" with regard to gender and sexuality. He focuses on the effects that the inclusion of "gender dysphoria" in the *Diagnostic and Statistical Manual of Mental Disorders* ultimately have on transgender persons. While specific discourses have evolved, their consequences are similarly problematic and demonstrate the productive exercise of institutional power.

Elisabeth Sheff and Corie Hammers examine the social stakes related to participating in sexual practices considered to be taboo, as well as the effect that social researchers have on shaping the image of so-called perverse sexual sub-cultures. Based on their own research and a meta-analysis of 36 studies, the authors illustrate how race and class shape not only the membership of kink and polyamorous communities but also the very research samples who create the knowledge about kinky and poly subcultures, which tend to be overwhelmingly white and of high socioeconomic status. To end Section Four, Nadine Naber explores the complex emotional terrain negotiated by those straddling cultural borders. She shares the narrative of a second-generation, Arab American woman, living in a post-9/11 San Francisco, California.

The chapters in this section teach us to investigate the reproduction and enforcement of sex, gender, and sexual identities and challenge the inequality all around us every day. They make visible the structural and cultural mechanisms that constantly work to make sex, gender, and sexuality invisible and seemingly natural.

27 • *Emily Martin*

THE EGG AND THE SPERM

How Science Has Constructed a Romance Based on Stereotypical Male–Female Roles

DISCUSSION QUESTIONS

1. The author notes that the wording in many scientific textbooks "stresses the fragility and dependency of the egg." How does this correspond with our ideas of femaleness/femininity in humans?
2. Can you think of other instances in the field of science (or other disciplines) in which concepts seem to be "gendered" to fit our ideas of male/female and/or masculine/feminine?
3. How do these "gendered" depictions of ova and sperm correspond to our ideas of male–female roles in heterosexual intercourse? How do they reinforce heterosexuality as an institution?

The theory of the human body is always a part of a world-picture....

The theory of the human body is always a part of a *fantasy.*

—James Hillman, *The Myth of Analysis*[1]

As an anthropologist, I am intrigued by the possibility that culture shapes how biological scientists describe what they discover about the natural world. If this were so, we would be learning about more than the natural world in high school biology class; we would be learning about cultural beliefs and practices as if they were part of nature. In the course of my research I realized that the picture of egg and sperm drawn in popular as well as scientific accounts of reproductive biology relies on stereotypes central to our cultural definitions of male and female. The stereotypes imply not only that female biological processes are less worthy than their male counterparts but also that women are less worthy than men. Part of my goal in writing this article is to shine a bright light on the gender stereotypes hidden within the scientific language of biology. Exposed in such a light, I hope they will lose much of their power to harm us.

Emily Martin, "The Egg and the Sperm: How Science Has Constructed a Romance Based on Stereotypical Male-Female Roles" from *Signs: Journal of Women and Culture and Society* 16(1991): 485–501. Reprinted by permission of University of Chicago Press.

EGG AND SPERM: A SCIENTIFIC FAIRY TALE

At a fundamental level, all major scientific textbooks depict male and female reproductive organs as systems for the production of valuable substances, such as eggs and sperm.[2] In the case of women, the monthly cycle is described as being designed to produce eggs and prepare a suitable place for them to be fertilized and grown—all to the end of making babies. But the enthusiasm ends there. By extolling the female cycle as a productive enterprise, menstruation must necessarily be viewed as a failure. Medical texts describe menstruation as the "debris" of the uterine lining, the result of necrosis, or death of tissue. The descriptions imply that a system has gone awry, making products of no use, not to specification, unsalable, wasted, scrap. An illustration in a widely used medical text shows menstruation as a chaotic disintegration of form, complementing the many texts that describe it as "ceasing," "dying," "losing," "denuding," "expelling."[3]

Male reproductive physiology is evaluated quite differently. One of the texts that sees menstruation as failed production employs a sort of breathless prose when it describes the maturation of sperm: "The mechanisms which guide the remarkable cellular transformation from spermatid to mature sperm remain uncertain. . . . Perhaps the most amazing characteristic of spermatogenesis is its sheer magnitude: the normal human male may manufacture several hundred million sperm per day."[4] In the classic text *Medical Physiology,* edited by Vernon Mountcastle, the male/female, productive/destructive comparison is more explicit: "Whereas the female *sheds* only a single gamete each month, the seminiferous tubules *produce* hundreds of millions of sperm each day" (emphasis mine).[5] The female author of another text marvels at the length of the microscopic seminiferous tubules, which, if uncoiled and placed end to end, "would span almost one-third of a mile!" She writes, "In an adult male these structures produce millions of sperm cells each day." Later she asks, "How is this feat accomplished?"[6] None of these texts expresses such intense enthusiasm for any female processes. It is surely no accident that the "remarkable" process of making sperm involves precisely what, in the medical view, menstruation does not: production of something deemed valuable.[7]

One could argue that menstruation and spermatogenesis are not analogous processes and, therefore, should not be expected to elicit the same kind of response. The proper female analogy to spermatogenesis, biologically, is ovulation. Yet ovulation does not merit enthusiasm in these texts either. Textbook descriptions stress that all of the ovarian follicles containing ova are already present at birth. Far from being *produced,* as sperm are, they merely sit on the shelf, slowly degenerating and aging like overstocked inventory: "At birth, normal human ovaries contain an estimated one million follicles [each], and no new ones appear after birth. Thus, in marked contrast to the male, the newborn female already has all the germ cells she will ever have. Only a few, perhaps 400, are destined to reach full maturity during her active productive life. All the others degenerate at some point in their development so that few, if any, remain by the time she reaches menopause at approximately 50 years of age."[8] Note the "marked contrast" that this description sets up between male and female: the male, who continuously produces fresh germ cells, and the female, who has stockpiled germ cells by birth and is faced with their degeneration.

Nor are the female organs spared such vivid descriptions. One scientist writes in a newspaper article that a woman's ovaries become old and worn out from ripening eggs every month, even though the woman herself is still relatively young: "When you look through a laparoscope . . . at an ovary that has been through hundreds of cycles, even in a superbly healthy American female, you see a scarred, battered organ."[9]

To avoid the negative connotations that some people associate with the female reproductive system, scientists could begin to describe male and female processes as homologous. They might credit females with "producing" mature ova one at a time, as they're needed each month, and describe males as having to face problems of degenerating germ cells. This degeneration would occur throughout life among spermatogonia, the undifferentiated germ cells in the testes that are the long-lived, dormant precursors of sperm.

But the texts have an almost dogged insistence on casting female processes in a negative light. The texts celebrate sperm production because it is continuous from puberty to senescence, while they portray egg production as inferior because it is finished at birth. This makes the female seem unproductive, but some texts will also insist that it is she who is wasteful.[10] In a section heading for *Molecular Biology of the Cell,* a best-selling text, we are told that "oogenesis is wasteful." The text goes on to emphasize that of the seven million oogonia, or egg germ cells, in the female embryo, most degenerate in the ovary. Of those that do go on to become oocytes, or eggs, many also degenerate, so that at birth only two million eggs remain in the ovaries. Degeneration continues throughout a woman's life: by puberty 300,000 eggs remain, and only a few are present by menopause. "During the 40 or so years of a woman's reproductive life, only 400 to 500 eggs will have been released," the authors write. "All the rest will have degenerated. It is still a mystery why so many eggs are formed only to die in the ovaries."[11]

The real mystery is why the male's vast production of sperm is not seen as wasteful.[12] Assuming that a man "produces" 100 million (10^8) sperm per day (a conservative estimate) during an average reproductive life of sixty years, he would produce well over two trillion sperm in his lifetime. Assuming that a woman "ripens" one egg per lunar month, or thirteen per year, over the course of her forty-year reproductive life, she would total five hundred eggs in her lifetime. But the word "waste" implies an excess, too much produced. Assuming two or three offspring, for every baby a woman produces, she wastes only around two hundred eggs. For every baby a man produces, he wastes more than one trillion (10^{12}) sperm.

How is it that positive images are denied to the bodies of women? A look at language—in this case, scientific language—provides the first clue. Take the egg and the sperm.[13] It is remarkable how "femininely" the egg behaves and how "masculinely" the sperm.[14] The egg is seen as large and passive.[15] It does not *move* or journey, but passively "is transported," "is swept,"[16] or even "drifts"[17] along the fallopian tube. In utter contrast, sperm are small, "streamlined,"[18]

and invariably active. They "deliver" their genes to the egg, "activate the developmental program of the egg,"[19] and have a "velocity" that is often remarked upon.[20] Their tails are "strong" and efficiently powered.[21] Together with the forces of ejaculation, they can "propel the semen into the deepest recesses of the vagina."[22] For this they need "energy," "fuel,"[23] so that with a "whiplashlike motion and strong lurches"[24] they can "burrow through the egg coat"[25] and "penetrate" it.[26]

At its extreme, the age-old relationship of the egg and the sperm takes on a royal or religious patina. The egg coat, its protective barrier, is sometimes called its "vestments," a term usually reserved for sacred, religious dress. The egg is said to have a "corona,"[27] a crown, and to be accompanied by "attendant cells."[28] It is holy, set apart and above, the queen to the sperm's king. The egg is also passive, which means it must depend on sperm for rescue. Gerald Schatten and Helen Schatten liken the egg's role to that of Sleeping Beauty: "a dormant bride awaiting her mate's magic kiss, which instills the spirit that brings her to life."[29] Sperm, by contrast, have a "mission,"[30] which is to "move through the female genital tract in quest of the ovum."[31] One popular account has it that the sperm carry out a "perilous journey" into the "warm darkness," where some fall away "exhausted." "Survivors" "assault" the egg, the successful candidates "surrounding the prize."[32] Part of the urgency of this journey, in more scientific terms, is that "once released from the supportive environment of the ovary, an egg will die within hours unless rescued by a sperm."[33] The wording stresses the fragility and dependency of the egg, even though the same text acknowledges elsewhere that sperm also live for only a few hours.[34]

In 1948, in a book remarkable for its early insights into these matters, Ruth Herschberger argued that female reproductive organs are seen as biologically interdependent, while male organs are viewed as autonomous, operating independently and in isolation:

> At present the functional is stressed only in connection
> with women: it is in them that ovaries, tubes, uterus,

and vagina have endless interdependence. In the male, reproduction would seem to involve "organs" only.

Yet the sperm, just as much as the egg, is dependent on a great many related processes. There are secretions which mitigate the urine in the urethra before ejaculation, to protect the sperm. There is the reflex shutting off of the bladder connection, the provision of prostatic secretions, and various types of muscular propulsion. The sperm is no more independent of its milieu than the egg, and yet from a wish that it were, biologists have lent their support to the notion that the human female, beginning with the egg, is congenitally more dependent than the male.[35]

Bringing out another aspect of the sperm's autonomy, an article in the journal *Cell* has the sperm making an "existential decision" to penetrate the egg: "Sperm are cells with a limited behavioral repertoire, one that is directed toward fertilizing eggs. To execute the decision to abandon the haploid state, sperm swim to an egg and there acquire the ability to effect membrane fusion."[36] Is this a corporate manager's version of the sperm's activities—"executing decisions" while fraught with dismay over difficult options that bring with them very high risk?

There is another way that sperm, despite their small size, can be made to loom in importance over the egg. In a collection of scientific papers, an electron micrograph of an enormous egg and tiny sperm is titled "A Portrait of the Sperm."[37] This is a little like showing a photo of a dog and calling it a picture of the fleas. Granted, microscopic sperm are harder to photograph than eggs, which are just large enough to see with the naked eye. But surely the use of the term "portrait," a word associated with the powerful and wealthy, is significant. Eggs have only micrographs or pictures, not portraits.

One depiction of sperm as weak and timid, instead of strong and powerful—the only such representation in western civilization, so far as I know—occurs in Woody Allen's movie *Everything You Always Wanted To Know About Sex**But Were Afraid to Ask*. Allen, playing the part of an apprehensive sperm inside a man's testicles, is scared of the man's approaching orgasm. He is reluctant to launch himself into the

darkness, afraid of contraceptive devices, afraid of winding up on the ceiling if the man masturbates.

The more common picture—egg as damsel in distress, shielded only by her sacred garments; sperm as heroic warrior to the rescue—cannot be proved to be dictated by the biology of these events. While the "facts" of biology may not *always* be constructed in cultural terms, I would argue that in this case they are. The degree of metaphorical content in these descriptions, the extent to which differences between egg and sperm are emphasized, and the parallels between cultural stereotypes of male and female behavior and the character of egg and sperm all point to this conclusion.

NEW RESEARCH, OLD IMAGERY

As new understandings of egg and sperm emerge, textbook gender imagery is being revised. But the new research, far from escaping the stereotypical representations of egg and sperm, simply replicates elements of textbook gender imagery in a different form. The persistence of this imagery calls to mind what Ludwik Fleck termed "the self-contained" nature of scientific thought. As he described it, "the interaction between what is already known, what remains to be learned, and those who are to apprehend it, go to ensure harmony within the system. But at the same time they also preserve the harmony of illusions, which is quite secure within the confines of a given thought style."[38] We need to understand the way in which the cultural content in scientific descriptions changes as biological discoveries unfold, and whether that cultural content is solidly entrenched or easily changed.

In all of the texts quoted above, sperm are described as penetrating the egg, and specific substances on a sperm's head are described as binding to the egg. Recently, this description of events was rewritten in a biophysics lab at Johns Hopkins University—transforming the egg from the passive to the active party.[39]

Prior to this research, it was thought that the zona, the inner vestments of the egg, formed an impenetrable barrier. Sperm overcame the barrier by mechanically burrowing through, thrashing their tails and slowly working their way along. Later research showed that the sperm released digestive enzymes that chemically broke down the zona; thus, scientists presumed that the sperm used mechanical *and* chemical means to get through to the egg.

In this recent investigation, the researchers began to ask questions about the mechanical force of the sperm's tail. (The lab's goal was to develop a contraceptive that worked topically on sperm.) They discovered, to their great surprise, that the forward thrust of sperm is extremely weak, which contradicts the assumption that sperm are forceful penetrators.[40] Rather than thrusting forward, the sperm's head was now seen to move mostly back and forth. The sideways motion of the sperm's tail makes the head move sideways with a force that is ten times stronger than its forward movement. So even if the overall force of the sperm were strong enough to mechanically break the zona, most of its force would be directed sideways rather than forward. In fact, its strongest tendency, by tenfold, is to escape by attempting to pry itself off the egg. Sperm, then, must be exceptionally efficient at *escaping* from any cell surface they contact. And the surface of the egg must be designed to trap the sperm and prevent their escape. Otherwise, few if any sperm would reach the egg.

The researchers at Johns Hopkins concluded that the sperm and egg stick together because of adhesive molecules on the surfaces of each. The egg traps the sperm and adheres to it so tightly that the sperm's head is forced to lie flat against the surface of the zona, a little bit, they told me, "like Br'er Rabbit getting more and more stuck to tar baby the more he wriggles." The trapped sperm continues to wiggle ineffectually side to side. The mechanical force of its tail is so weak that a sperm cannot break even one chemical bond. This is where the digestive enzymes released by the sperm come in. If they start to soften the zona just at the tip of the sperm and the sides remain stuck, then the weak, flailing sperm can get oriented in the right direction and make it through the zona—provided that its bonds to the zona dissolve as it moves in.

Although this new version of the saga of the egg and the sperm broke through cultural expectations, the researchers who made the discovery continued to write papers and abstracts as if the sperm were the active party who attacks, binds, penetrates, and enters the egg. The only difference was that sperm were now seen as performing these actions weakly.[41] Not until August 1987, more than three years after the findings described above, did these researchers reconceptualize the process to give the egg a more active role. They began to describe the zona as an aggressive sperm catcher, covered with adhesive molecules that can capture a sperm with a single bond and clasp it to the zona's surface.[42] In the words of their published account: "The innermost vestment, the *zona pellucida,* is a glycoprotein shell, which captures and tethers the sperm before they penetrate it.... The sperm is captured at the initial contact between the sperm tip and the *zona*.... Since the thrust [of the sperm] is much smaller than the force needed to break a single affinity bond, the first bond made upon the tip-first meeting of the sperm and *zona* can result in the capture of the sperm."[43]

Experiments in another lab reveal similar patterns of data interpretation. Gerald Schatten and Helen Schatten set out to show that, contrary to conventional wisdom, the "egg is not merely a large, yolk-filled sphere into which the sperm burrows to endow new life. Rather, recent research suggests the almost heretical view that sperm and egg are mutually active partners."[44] This sounds like a departure from the stereotypical textbook view, but further reading reveals Schatten and Schatten's conformity to the aggressive-sperm metaphor. They describe how "the sperm and egg first touch when, from the tip of the sperm's triangular head, a long, thin filament shoots out and harpoons the egg." Then we learn that "remarkably, the harpoon is not so much fired as assembled at great speed, molecule by molecule, from a pool of protein stored in a specialized region called the aerosome. The filament may grow as much as twenty times longer than the sperm head itself before its tip reaches the egg and sticks."[45] Why not call this "making a bridge" or "throwing out a line" rather than firing a harpoon? Harpoons pierce prey and injure or kill them, while this filament only sticks. And why not focus, as the Hopkins lab did, on the stickiness of the egg, rather than the stickiness of the sperm?[46] Later in the article, the Schattens replicate the common view of the sperm's perilous journey into the warm darkness of the vagina, this time for the purpose of explaining its journey into the egg itself: "[The sperm] still has an arduous journey ahead. It must penetrate farther into the egg's huge sphere of cytoplasm and somehow locate the nucleus, so that the two cells' chromosomes can fuse. The sperm dives down into the cytoplasm, its tail beating. But it is soon interrupted by the sudden and swift migration of the egg nucleus, which rushes toward the sperm with a velocity triple that of the movement of chromosomes during cell division, crossing the entire egg in about a minute."[47]

Like Schatten and Schatten and the biophysicists at Johns Hopkins, another researcher has recently made discoveries that seem to point to a more interactive view of the relationship of egg and sperm. This work, which Paul Wassarman conducted on the sperm and eggs of mice, focuses on identifying the specific molecules in the egg coat (the zona pellucida) that are involved in egg–sperm interaction. At first glance, his descriptions seem to fit the model of an egalitarian relationship. Male and female gametes "recognize one another," and "interactions…take place between sperm and egg."[48] But the article in *Scientific American* in which those descriptions appear begins with a vignette that presages the dominant motif of their presentation: "It has been more than a century since Hermann Fol, a Swiss zoologist, peered into his microscope and became the first person to see a sperm penetrate an egg, fertilize it and form the first cell of a new embryo."[49] This portrayal of the sperm as the active party—the one that *penetrates* and *fertilizes* the egg and *produces* the embryo—is not cited as an example of an earlier, now outmoded view. In fact, the author reiterates the point later in the article: "Many sperm can bind to and penetrate the zona pellucida, or outer coat, of an unfertilized mouse egg, but only one sperm will eventually fuse with the thin plasma membrane surrounding the egg proper (*inner sphere*), fertilizing the egg and giving rise to a new embryo."[50]

The imagery of sperm as aggressor is particularly startling in this case: the main discovery being reported is isolation of a particular molecule *on the egg coat* that plays an important role in fertilization! Wassarman's choice of language sustains the picture. He calls the molecule that has been isolated, ZP3, a "sperm receptor." By allocating the passive, waiting role to the egg, Wassarman can continue to describe the sperm as the actor, the one that makes it all happen: "The basic process begins when many sperm first attach loosely and then bind tenaciously to receptors on the surface of the egg's thick outer coat, the zona pellucida. Each sperm, which has a large number of egg-binding proteins on its surface, binds to many sperm receptors on the egg. More specifically, a site on each of the egg-binding proteins fits a complementary site on a sperm receptor, much as a key fits a lock."[51] With the sperm designated as the "key" and the egg the "lock," it is obvious which one acts and which one is acted upon. Could this imagery not be reversed, letting the sperm (the lock) wait until the egg produces the key? Or could we speak of two halves of a locket matching, and regard the matching itself as the action that initiates the fertilization?

NOTES

1. James Hillman, *The Myth of Analysis* (Evanston, Ill.: Northwestern University Press, 1972), 220.
2. The textbooks I consulted are the main ones used in classes for undergraduate premedical students or medical students (or those held on reserve in the library for these classes) during the past few years at Johns Hopkins University. These texts are widely used at other universities in the country as well.
3. Arthur C. Guyton, *Physiology of the Human Body,* 6th ed. (Philadelphia: Saunders College Publishing, 1984), 624.
4. Arthur J. Vander, James H. Sherman, and Dorothy S. Luciano, *Human Physiology: The Mechanisms of Body Function,* 3d ed. (New York: McGraw-Hill, 1980). 483–84.
5. Vernon B. Mountcastle, ed., *Medical Physiology,* 14th ed. (London: Mosby, 1980), 2: 1624.
6. Eldra Pearl Solomon, *Human Anatomy and Physiology* (New York: CBS College Publishing, 1983), 678.

7. For elaboration, see Emily Martin, *The Woman in the Body: A Cultural Analysis of Reproduction* (Boston: Beacon, 1987), 27–53.

8. Vander, Sherman, and Luciano, 568.

9. Melvin Konner, "Childbearing and Age," *New York Times Magazine* (December 27, 1987), 22–23, esp. 22.

10. I have found but one exception to the opinion that the female is wasteful: "Smallpox being the nasty disease it is, one might expect nature to have designed antibody molecules with combining sites that specifically recognize the epitopes on smallpox virus. Nature differs from technology, however: it thinks nothing of wastefulness. (For example, rather than improving the chance that a spermatozoon will meet an egg cell, nature finds it easier to produce millions of spermatozoa.)" (Niels Kaj Jerne, "The Immune System," *Scientific American* 229, no. 1 [July 1973]: 53.) Thanks to a *Signs* reviewer for bringing this reference to my attention.

11. Bruce Alberts et al., *Molecular Biology of the Cell* (New York: Garland, 1983), 795.

12. In her essay "Have Only Men Evolved?" (in *Discovering Reality: Feminist Perspectives on Epistemology, Metaphysics, Methodology, and Philosophy of Science,* ed. Sandra Harding and Merrill B. Hintikka (Dordrecht: Reidel, 1983), 45–69, esp. 60–61). Ruth Hubbard points out that sociobiologists have said the female invests more energy than the male in the production of her large gametes, claiming that this explains why the female provides parental care. Hubbard questions whether it "really takes more 'energy' to generate the one or relatively few eggs than the large excess of sperms required to achieve fertilization." For further critique of how the greater size of eggs is interpreted in sociobiology, see Donna Haraway, "Investment Strategies for the Evolving Portfolio of Primate Females," in *Body/Politics,* ed. Mary Jacobus, Evelyn Fox Keller, and Sally Shuttleworth (New York: Routledge, 1990), 155–56.

13. The sources I used for this article provide compelling information on interactions among sperm. Lack of space prevents me from taking up this theme here, but the elements include competition, hierarchy, and sacrifice. For a newspaper report, see Malcolm W. Browne, "Some Thoughts on Self Sacrifice," *New York Times* (July 5, 1988), C6. For a literary rendition, see John Barth, "Night-Sea Journey," in his *Lost in the Funhouse* (Garden City, N.Y.: Doubleday, 1968), 3–13.

14. See Carol Delancy, "The Meaning of Paternity and the Virgin Birth Debate," *Man* 21, no. 3 (September 1986): 494–513. She discusses the difference between this scientific view that women contribute genetic material to the fetus and the claim of long-standing Western folk theories that the origin and identity of the fetus comes from the male, as in the metaphor of planting a seed in soil.

15. For a suggested direct link between human behavior and purportedly passive eggs and active sperm, see Erik H. Erikson, "Inner and Outer Space: Reflections on Womanhood," *Daedalus* 93, no. 2 (Spring 1964): 582–606, esp. 591.

16. Guyton (n. 3 above), 619; and Mountcastle (n. 5 above), 1609.

17. Jonathan Miller and David Pelham, *The Facts of Life* (New York: Viking Penguin, 1984), 5.

18. Alberts et al., 796.

19. Ibid., 796.

20. See, e.g., William F. Ganong, *Review of Medical Physiology,* 7th ed. (Los Altos, Calif.: Lange Medical Publications, 1975), 322.

21. Alberts et al. (n. 11 above), 796.

22. Guyton, 615.

23. Solomon (n. 6 above), 683.

24. Vander, Sherman, and Luciano (n. 4 above), 4th ed. (1985), 580.

25. Alberts et al., 796.

26. All biology texts quoted above use the word "penetrate."

27. Solomon, 700.

28. A. Beldecos et al., "The Importance of Feminist Critique for Contemporary Cell Biology," *Hypatia* 3, no. 1 (Spring 1988): 61–76.

29. Gerald Schatten and Helen Schatten, "The Energetic Egg," *Medical World News* 23 (January 23, 1984): 51–53, esp. 51.

30. Alberts et al., 796.

31. Guyton (n. 3 above), 613.

32. Miller and Pelham (n. 17 above), 7.

33. Alberts et al. (n. 11 above), 804.

34. Ibid., 801.

35. Ruth Herschberger, *Adam's Rib* (New York: Pelligrini & Cudaby, 1948), esp. 84. I am indebted to Ruth Hubbard for telling me about Herschberger's work, although at a point when this paper was already in draft form.

36. Bennett M. Shapiro, "The Existential Decision of a Sperm," *Cell* 49, no. 3 (May 1987): 293–94, esp. 293.

37. Lennart Nilsson, "A Portrait of the Sperm," in *The Functional Anatomy of the Spermatozoan,* ed. Bjorn A. Afzelius (New York: Pergamon, 1975), 79–82.

38. Ludwik Fleck, *Genesis and Development of a Scientific Fact,* ed. Thaddeus J. Trenn and Robert K. Merton (Chicago: University of Chicago Press, 1979), 38.

39. Jay M. Baltz carried out the research I describe when he was a graduate student in the Thomas C. Jenkins Department of Biophysics at Johns Hopkins University.

40. Far less is known about the physiology of sperm than comparable female substances, which some feminists claim is no accident. Greater scientific scrutiny of female reproduction has long enabled the burden of birth control to be placed on women. In this case, the researchers' discovery did not depend on development of any new technology. The experiments made use of glass pipettes, a manometer, and a simple microscope, all of which have been available for more than one hundred years.

41. Jay M. Baltz and Richard A. Cone, "What Force Is Needed to Tether a Sperm?" (abstract for Society for the Study of Reproduction, 1985), and "Flagellar Torque on the Head Determines the Force Needed to Tether a Sperm" (abstract for Biophysical Society, 1986).

42. Jay M. Baltz, David E. Katz, and Richard A. Cone, "The Mechanics of the Sperm-Egg Interaction at the Zona Pellucida," *Biophysical Journal* 54, no. 4 (October 1988): 643–54. Lab members were somewhat familiar with work on metaphors in the biology of female reproduction. Richard Cone, who runs the lab, is my husband, and he talked with them about my earlier research on the subject from time to time. Even though my current research focuses on biological imagery and I heard about the lab's work from my husband every day, I myself did not recognize the role of imagery in the sperm research until many weeks after the period of research and writing I describe. Therefore, I assume that any awareness the lab members may have had about how underlying metaphor might be guiding this particular research was fairly inchoate.

43. Ibid., 643, 650.

44. Schatten and Schatten (n. 29 above), 51.

45. Ibid., 52.

46. Surprisingly, in an article intended for a general audience, the authors do not point out that these are sea urchin sperm and note that human sperm do not shoot out filaments at all.

47. Schatten and Schatten, 53.

48. Paul M. Wassarman, "Fertilization in Mammals," *Scientific American* 259 no. 6 (December 1988): 78–84, esp. 78, 84.

49. Ibid., 78.

50. Ibid., 79.

51. Ibid., 78.

28 • *Siobhan Somerville*

SCIENTIFIC RACISM AND THE INVENTION OF THE HOMOSEXUAL BODY

DISCUSSION QUESTIONS

1. What was the role of comparative anatomy in the creation of classifications of racial and sexual differences?

2. Why does Somerville argue that in the beginning, sexology was related to and dependent on eugenics and antimiscegenation campaigns?

Originally published as the article: "Scientific Racism and the Invention of the Homosexual Body," by Siobhan Somerville, from *Journal of the History of Sexuality*, Volume 5, Issue 2, pp. 243–266.

3. How is medicine used to naturalize and legitimate dominant cultural myths?
4. Does this historical perspective offer any insight into understanding today's knowledge and debates around homosexuality and transgender identity?

One of the most important insights developed in the fields of lesbian and gay history and the history of sexuality is the notion that homosexuality and, by extension, heterosexuality are relatively recent inventions in Western culture, rather than transhistorical or "natural" categories. As Michel Foucault and other historians of sexuality have argued, sexual acts between two people of the same sex had been punishable through legal and religious sanctions well before the late nineteenth century, but they did not necessarily define individuals as homosexual per se.[1] Only in the late nineteenth century did a new understanding of sexuality emerge in which sexual acts and desires became constitutive of identity. Homosexuality as the condition, and therefore identity, of particular bodies is thus a production of that historical moment.

Medical literature, broadly defined to include the writings of physicians, sexologists, and psychiatrists, has been integral to this historical argument. Although medical discourse was by no means the only—nor necessarily the most powerful—site of the emergence of new sexual identities, it does nevertheless offer rich sources for at least partially understanding the complex development of these categories in the late nineteenth and early twentieth centuries. Medical and sexological literature not only became one of the few sites of explicit engagement with questions of sexuality during this period but also held substantial definitional power within a culture that sanctioned science to discover and tell the truth about bodies.

As historians and theorists of sexuality have refined a notion of the late nineteenth-century "invention" of the homosexual, their discussions have drawn primarily upon theories and histories of gender. George Chauncey, in particular, has provided an invaluable discussion of the ways in which paradigms of sexuality shifted according to changing ideologies of gender during this period.[2] He notes a gradual change in medical models of sexual deviance, from a notion of sexual inversion, understood as a reversal of one's sex role, to a model of homosexuality, defined as deviant sexual object choice. These categories and their transformations, argues Chauncey, reflected concurrent shifts in the cultural organization of sex/gender roles and participated in prescribing acceptable behavior, especially within a context of white middle-class gender ideologies.

While gender insubordination offers a powerful explanatory model for the "invention" of homosexuality, ideologies of gender also, of course, shaped and were shaped by dominant constructions of race. Indeed, although it has received little acknowledgment, it is striking that the "invention" of the homosexual occurred at roughly the same time that racial questions were being reformulated, particularly in the United States. This was the moment, for instance, of *Plessy v. Ferguson,* the 1896 U.S. Supreme Court ruling that insisted that "black" and "white" races were "separate but equal." Both a product of and a stimulus to a nationwide and brutal era of racial segregation, this ruling had profound and lasting effects in legitimating an apartheid structure that remained legally sanctioned for more than half of the twentieth century. The *Plessy* case distilled in legal form many fears about race and racial difference that were prevalent at the time. A deluge of "Jim Crow" and anti-miscegenation laws, combined with unprecedented levels of racial violence, most visibly manifested in widespread lynching, reflected an aggressive attempt to classify and separate bodies as either "black" or "white."

Is it merely a historical coincidence that the classification of bodies as either "homosexual" or "heterosexual" emerged at the same time that the United States was aggressively policing the imaginary boundary between "black" and "white" bodies? Although some historians of sexuality have included brief acknowledgments of nineteenth-century discourses of racial difference, the particular relationship and potentially mutual effects of discourses of homo-sexuality and race remain unexplored.[3] This silence around race may be due in part to the relative lack of explicit attention to race in medical and sexological literature of the period. These writers did not self-consciously interrogate race, nor were those whose gender insubordination and/or sexual transgression brought them under the medical gaze generally identified by race in these accounts.[4] Yet the lack of explicit attention to race in these texts does not mean that it was irrelevant to sexologists' endeavors. Given the upheavals surrounding racial definition during this period, it is reasonable to assume that these texts were as embedded within contemporary racial ideologies as they were within contemporary ideologies of gender.

Take, for instance, the words of Havelock Ellis, whose massive *Studies in the Psychology of Sex* was one of the most important texts of the late nineteenth-century medical and scientific discourse on sexuality. "I regard sex as the central problem of life," began the general preface to the first volume. Justifying such unprecedented boldness regarding the study of sex, Ellis said the following:

And now that the problem of religion has practically been settled, and that the problem of labour has at least been placed on a practical foundation, the ques-tion of sex—*with the racial questions that rest on it*—stands before the coming generations as the chief problem for solution.[5]

Despite Ellis's oddly breezy dismissal of the prob-lems of labor and religion, which were far from set-tled at the time, this passage points suggestively to a link between sexual and racial anxieties. Yet what exactly did Ellis mean by "racial questions"? More significantly, what was his sense of the relationship between racial questions and the "question of sex"? Although Ellis himself left these issues unresolved, his elliptical declaration nevertheless suggested that a discourse of race—however elusively—somehow hovered around or within the study of sexuality.

In this article, I offer speculations on how late nineteenth- and early twentieth-century discourses of race and sexuality might be, not merely juxtaposed,

but brought together in ways that illuminate both. I suggest that the concurrent bifurcations of catego-ries of race and sexuality were not only historically coincident but in fact structurally interdependent and perhaps mutually productive. My goal, however, is not to garner and display unequivocal evidence of the direct influence of racial categories on those who were developing scientific models of homosexuality. Nor am I interested in identifying whether or not individual writers and thinkers are racist. Rather, my focus here is on racial ideologies, the systems of repre-sentation and cultural assumptions about race through which individuals understood their relationships within the world.[6] My emphasis is on understanding the relationships between the medical/scientific dis-course around sexuality and the dominant scientific discourse around race during this period, that is, sci-entific racism.

My approach combines literary and historical methods of reading, particularly that which has been so crucial to lesbian, gay, and bisexual studies: the technique of reading to hear "the inexplicable pres-ence of the thing not named,"[7] of being attuned to the queer presences and implications in texts that do not otherwise name them. Without this collective and multidisciplinary project to see, hear, and con-firm queer inflections where others would deny their existence, it is arguable that the field of lesbian, gay, and bisexual studies itself, and particularly our knowledge and understanding of the histories, writ-ing, and cultures of lesbians, gay men, and bisexuals, would be impoverished, if not impossible. In a simi-lar way, I propose to use the techniques of queer reading, but to modulate my analysis from a focus on sexuality and gender to one alert to racial resonances as well.

My attention, then, is focused on the racial pressure points in exemplary texts from the late nineteenth-century discourse on sexuality, including those writ-ten by Ellis and other writers of the period who made explicit references to homosexuality. I suggest that the structures and methodologies that drove domi-nant ideologies of race also fueled the pursuit of sci-entific knowledge about the homosexual body: both sympathetic and hostile accounts of homosexuality were steeped in assumptions that had driven previous scientific studies of race.[8] My aim is not to replace a focus on gender and sexuality with one on race but rather to understand how discourses of race and gender buttressed one another, often competing, often overlapping, to shape emerging models of homosexuality.

I suggest three broadly defined ways in which discourses of sexuality seem to have been particularly engaged—sometimes overtly, but largely implicitly—with the discourse of scientific racism. All of these models pathologized to some degree both the non-white body and the non-heterosexual body. Although I discuss these models in separate sections here, they often coexisted, despite their contradictions. These models are speculative and are intended as a first step toward understanding the myriad and historically specific ways in which racial and sexual discourses shaped each other at the moment in which homosexuality entered scientific discourse.

VISIBLE DIFFERENCES: SEXOLOGY AND COMPARATIVE ANATOMY

Ellis's *Sexual Inversion,* the first volume of *Studies in the Psychology of Sex* to be published, became a definitive text in late nineteenth-century investigations of homosexuality.[9] Despite the series' titular focus on the psychology of sex, *Sexual Inversion* was a hybrid text, poised in methodology between the earlier field of comparative anatomy, with its procedures of bodily measurement, and the nascent techniques of psychology, with its focus on mental development.[10] In *Sexual Inversion,* Ellis hoped to provide scientific authority for the position that homosexuality should be considered not a crime but rather a congenital (and thus involuntary) physiological abnormality. Writing *Sexual Inversion* in the wake of England's 1885 Labouchère Amendment, which prohibited "any act of gross indecency" between men, Ellis intended in large part to defend homosexuality from "law and public opinion," which, in his view, combined "to place a heavy penal burden and a severe social stigma on the manifestations of an instinct which to those persons who possess it frequently appears

natural and normal."[11] In doing so, Ellis attempted to drape himself in the cultural authority of a naturalist, eager to exert his powers of observation in an attempt to classify and codify understandings of homosexuality.[12]

Like other sexologists, Ellis assumed that the "invert" might be visually distinguishable from the "normal" body through anatomical markers, just as the differences between the sexes had traditionally been mapped upon the body. Yet the study of sexual difference was not the only methodological precedent for the study of the homosexual body. In its assumptions about somatic differences, *Sexual Inversion,* I suggest, also drew upon and participated in a history of the scientific investigation of race.

Race, in fact, became an explicit, though ambiguous, structural element in Ellis's *Sexual Inversion.* In chapter 5, titled "The Nature of Sexual Inversion," Ellis attempted to collate the evidence from case studies, dividing his general conclusions into various analytic categories. Significantly, "Race" was the first category he listed, under which he wrote, "All my cases, 80 in number, are British and American, 20 living in the United States and the rest being British. Ancestry, from the point of view of race, was not made a matter of special investigation" (264). He then listed the ancestries of the individuals whose case studies he included, which he identified as "English . . . Scotch . . . Irish . . . German . . . French . . . Portuguese . . . [and] more or less Jewish" (264). He concluded that "except in the apparently frequent presence of the German element, there is nothing remarkable in this ancestry" (264). Ellis used the term "race" in this passage interchangeably with national origin, with the possible exception of Jewish ancestry. These national identities were perceived to be at least partially biological and certainly hereditary in Ellis's account, though subordinate to the categories "British" and "American." Although he dismissed "ancestry, from the point of view of race" as a significant category, its place as the first topic within the chapter suggested its importance to the structure of Ellis's analysis.[13]

Ellis's ambiguous use of the term "race" was not unusual for scientific discourse in this period, during which it might refer to groupings based variously on geography, religion, class, or color.[14] The use of the term to mean a division of people based on physical (rather than genealogical or national) differences had originated in the late eighteenth century, when Johann Friedrich Blumenbach first classified human beings into five distinct groups in *On the Natural Variety of Mankind*. This work in turn became a model for the nineteenth-century fascination with anthropometry, the measurement of the human body.[15] Behind these anatomical measurements lay the assumption that the body was a legible text, with various keys or languages available for reading its symbolic codes. In the logic of biological determinism, the surface and interior of the individual body, rather than its social characteristics, such as language, behavior, or clothing, became the primary sites of its meaning. "Every peculiarity of the body has probably some corresponding significance in the mind, and the cause of the former are the remoter causes of the latter," wrote Edward Drinker Cope, a well-known American paleontologist, summarizing the assumptions that fueled the science of comparative anatomy.[16] Although scientists debated which particular anatomical features carried racial meanings—skin, facial angle, pelvis, skull, brain mass, genitalia—the theory that anatomy predicted intelligence and behavior nevertheless remained remarkably constant. As Nancy Stepan and Sander Gilman have noted, "The concepts within racial science were so congruent with social and political life (with power relations, that is) as to be virtually uncontested from inside the mainstream of science."[17]

Supported by the cultural authority of an ostensibly objective scientific method, these readings of the body became a powerful instrument for those seeking to justify the economic and political disenfranchisement of various racial groups within systems of slavery and colonialism. As Barbara Fields has noted, however, "Try as they would, the scientific racists of the past failed to discover any objective criterion upon which to classify people; to their chagrin, every criterion they tried varied more within so-called races than between them."[18] Although the methods of science were considered to be outside the political

and economic realm, in fact, as we know, these anatomical investigations, however professedly innocent their intentions, were driven by racial ideologies already firmly in place.[19]

Ideologies of race, of course, shaped and reflected both popular and scientific understandings of gender. As Gilman has argued, "Any attempt to establish that the races were inherently different rested to no little extent on the sexual difference of the black."[20] Although popular racist mythology in the U.S. in the nineteenth century focused on the supposed difference between the size of African-American and white men's genitalia, the male body was not necessarily the primary site of medical inquiry into racial difference.[21] Instead, as a number of medical journals from this period demonstrate, comparative anatomists repeatedly located racial difference through the sexual characteristics of the female body.[22]

In exploring the influence of scientific studies of race on the emerging discourse of sexuality, it is useful to look closely at a study from the genre of comparative anatomy. In 1867, W. H. Flower and James Murie published their "Account of the Dissection of a Bushwoman," which carefully catalogued the "more perishable soft structures of the body" of a young Bushwoman.[23] They placed their study in a line of inquiry concerning the African woman's body that had begun at least a half-century earlier with French naturalist Georges Cuvier's description of the woman popularly known as the "Hottentot Venus," or Saartje Baartman, who was displayed to European audiences fascinated by her "steatopygia" (protruding buttocks).[24] Significantly, starting with Cuvier, this tradition of comparative anatomy located the boundaries of race through the sexual and reproductive anatomy of the African female body, ignoring altogether the problematic absence of male bodies from their studies.

Flower and Murie's account lingered on two specific sites of difference: the "protuberance of the buttocks, so peculiar to the Bushman race" and "the remarkable development of the labia minora," which were "sufficiently well marked to distinguish these parts from those of any ordinary varieties of the human species" (208). The racial difference of the

African body, implied Flower and Murie, was located in its literal excess, a specifically sexual excess that placed her body outside the boundaries of the "normal" female. To support their conclusion, Flower and Murie included corroborating "evidence" in the final part of their account. They quoted a second-hand report, "received from a scientific friend residing at the Cape of Good Hope," describing the anatomy of "two pure bred Hottentots, mother and daughter" (208). This account also focused on the women's genitalia, which they referred to as "appendages" (208). Although their account ostensibly foregrounded boundaries of race, their portrayal of the sexual characteristics of the Bushwoman betrayed Flower and Murie's anxieties about gender boundaries. The characteristics singled out as "peculiar" to this race, the (double) "appendages," fluttered between genders, at one moment masculine, at the next moment exaggeratedly feminine. Flower and Murie constructed the site of *racial* difference by marking the sexual and reproductive anatomy of the African woman as "peculiar." In their characterization, sexual ambiguity delineated the boundaries of race.

The techniques and logic of late nineteenth-century sexologists, who also routinely included physical examinations in their accounts, reproduced the methodologies employed by comparative anatomists like Flower and Murie. Many of the case histories in Krafft-Ebing's *Psychopathia Sexualis,* for instance, included a paragraph detailing any anatomical peculiarities of the body in question.[25] Although Krafft-Ebing could not draw any conclusions about somatic indicators of "abnormal" sexuality, physical examinations remained a staple of the genre. In Ellis's *Sexual Inversion,* case studies often focused more intensely on the bodies of female "inverts" than those of their male counterparts.[26] Although the specific sites of anatomical inspection (hymen, clitoris, labia, vagina) differed, the underlying theory remained constant: women's genitalia and reproductive anatomy held a valuable and presumably visual key to ranking bodies according to norms of sexuality.

Sexologists reproduced not only the methodologies of the comparative anatomy of races but also its iconography. One of the most consistent medical characterizations of the anatomy of both African-American women and lesbians was the myth of an unusually large clitoris.[27] As late as 1921, medical journals contained articles declaring that "a physical examination of [female homosexuals] will in practically every instance disclose an abnormally prominent clitoris." Significantly, this author added, "This is particularly so in colored women."[28] In an earlier account of racial differences between white and African-American women, one gynecologist had also focused on the size and visibility of the clitoris; in his examinations, he had perceived a distinction between the "free" clitoris of "negresses" and the "imprisonment" of the clitoris of the "Aryan American woman."[29] In constructing these oppositions, such characterizations literalized the sexual and racial ideologies of the nineteenth-century "Cult of True Womanhood," which explicitly privileged white women's sexual "purity," while implicitly suggesting African-American women's sexual accessibility.[30]

It is evident from the case histories in *Sexual Inversion* that Ellis gave much more attention to the presumed anatomical peculiarities of the women than to those of the men. "As regards the sexual organs it seems possible," Ellis wrote, "so far as my observations go, to speak more definitely of inverted women than of inverted men" (256). Ellis justified his greater scrutiny of women's bodies in part by invoking the ambiguity surrounding women's sexuality in general: "we are accustomed to a much greater familiarity and intimacy between women than between men, and we are less apt to suspect the existence of any abnormal passion" (204). To Ellis, the seemingly imperceptible differences between "normal" and "abnormal" intimacies between women called for closer scrutiny of the subtleties of their anatomy. He included the following detailed account as potential evidence for distinguishing the fine line between the lesbian and the "normal" woman:

Sexual Organs.—(a) Internal: Uterus and ovaries appear normal. (b) External: Small clitoris, with this irregularity, that the lower folds of the labia minora, instead of uniting one with the other and forming the frenum, are extended upward along the sides of the clitoris, while the upper folds are poorly developed, furnishing the clitoris with a scant hood. The labia majora depart from normal conformation in being fuller in their posterior half than in their anterior part, so that when the subject is in the supine position they sag, as it were, presenting a slight resemblance to fleshy sacs, but in substance and structure they feel normal (136).

This extraordinary taxonomy, performed for Ellis by an unnamed "obstetric physician of high standing," echoed earlier anatomical catalogues of African women. The exacting eye (and hand) of the investigating physician highlighted every possible detail as meaningful evidence. Through the triple repetition of "normal" and the use of evaluative language like "irregularity" and "poorly developed," the physician reinforced his position of judgment. Although he did not provide criteria for what constituted "normal" anatomy, the physician assumed abnormality and simply corroborated that assumption through sight and touch. Moreover, his characterization of what he perceived as abnormal echoed the anxious account by Flower and Murie. Although the description of the clitoris is a notable exception to the tendency to exaggerate its size, the account nevertheless scrutinized another site of genital excess. The "fleshy sacs" of this woman, like the "appendages" fetishized in the earlier account, invoked the anatomy of a phantom male body inhabiting the lesbian's anatomical features.[31]

Clearly, anxieties about gender shaped both Ellis's and Flower and Murie's taxonomies of the lesbian and the African woman. Yet their preoccupation with gender cannot be understood as separate from the larger context of scientific assumptions during this period, which one historian has characterized as "the full triumph of Darwinism in American thought."[32] Gender, in fact, was crucial to Darwinist ideas. One of the basic assumptions within the Darwinian model was the belief that, as organisms evolved through a process of natural selection, they also showed greater signs of differentiation between the (two) sexes. Following this logic, various writers used sexual characteristics as indicators of evolutionary progress toward civilization. In *Man and Woman,* for instance, Ellis himself cautiously suggested that since the "beginnings of industrialism," "more marked sexual differences in physical development seem (we cannot speak definitely) to have developed than are usually to be found in savage societies."[33] In this passage, Ellis drew from theories developed by biologists like Patrick Geddes and J. Arthur Thomson. In their important work *The Evolution of Sex,* which traced the role of sexual difference in evolution, Geddes and Thomson stated that "hermaphroditism is primitive; the unisexual state is a subsequent differentiation. The present cases of normal hermaphroditism imply either persistence or reversion."[34] In characterizing the bodies of lesbians or African-American women as less sexually differentiated than the norm (always posited as white heterosexual women's bodies), anatomists and sexologists drew upon notions of natural selection to dismiss these bodies as anomalous "throwbacks" within a scheme of cultural and anatomical progress.

THE MIXED BODY

The emergence of evolutionary theory in the late nineteenth century foregrounded a view of continuity between the "savage" and "civilized" races, in contrast to earlier scientific thinking about race, which had focused on debates about the origins of different racial groups. Proponents of monogeny argued that all races derived from a single origin. Those who argued for polygeny believed that each race descended from its own biological and geographical source, a view, not coincidentally, that supported segregationist impulses.[35] With Darwin's publication of *The Origin of Species* in 1859, the debate between polygeny and monogeny was superseded by evolutionary theory, which was appropriated as a powerful scientific model for understanding race. Its controversial innovation was its emphasis on the continuity between animals and human beings. Evolutionary theory held out the possibility that the physical, mental, and moral characteristics of human beings had evolved gradually over time from ape-like ancestors.[36] Although the idea of continuity depended logically on the blurring of boundaries within hierarchies, it did not necessarily invalidate the methods or assumptions of comparative anatomy. On the contrary, notions of visible differences and racial hierarchies were deployed to corroborate Darwinian theory.

The concept of continuity was harnessed to the growing attention to miscegenation, or "amalgamation," in social science writing in the first decades of the twentieth century. Edward Byron Reuter's *The Mulatto in the United States,* for instance, pursued an exhaustive quantitative and comparative study of the "mulatto" population and its achievements in relation to those of "pure" white or African ancestry. Reuter traced the presence of a distinct group of mixed-race people back to early American history: "Their physical appearance, though markedly different from that of the pure blooded race, was sufficiently marked to set them off as a peculiar people."[37] Reuter, of course, was willing to admit the viability of "mulattoes" only within a framework that emphasized the separation of races. Far from using the notion of the biracial body to refute the belief in discrete markers of racial difference, Reuter perpetuated the notion by focusing on the distinctiveness of this "peculiar people."

Miscegenation was, of course, not only a question of race, but also one of sex and sexuality. Ellis recognized this intersection implicitly, if not explicitly. His sense of the "racial questions" implicit in sex was surely informed by his involvement with eugenics, the movement in Europe and the United States that, to greater or lesser degrees, advocated selective reproduction and "race hygiene."[38] In the United States, eugenics was both a political and scientific response to the growth of a population beginning to challenge the dominance of white political interests. The widespread scientific and social interest in eugenics was fueled by anxieties expressed through the popular notion of (white) "race suicide." This phrase, invoked most notably by Theodore Roosevelt, summed up nativist fears about a perceived decline in reproduction among white Americans. The new field of eugenics worked hand in hand with growing anti-miscegenation sentiment and policy, provoked not only by the

attempts of African-Americans to gain political representation but also by the influx of large populations of immigrants.[39] As Mark Haller has pointed out, "Racists and [immigration] restrictionists... found in eugenics the scientific reassurances they needed that heredity shaped man's personality and that their assumptions rested on biological facts."[40] Ellis saw himself as an advocate for eugenics policies. As an active member of the British National Council for Public Morals, he wrote several essays on eugenics, including *The Problem of Race Regeneration,* a pamphlet advocating "voluntary" sterilization of the unfit as a policy in the best interest of "the race."[41] Further, in a letter to Francis Galton in 1907, Ellis wrote, "In the concluding volume of my Sex 'Studies' I shall do what I can to insinuate the eugenic attitude."[42]

The beginnings of sexology, then, were related to, and perhaps even dependent on, a pervasive climate of eugenic and anti-miscegenation sentiment and legislation. Even at the level of nomenclature, anxieties about miscegenation shaped sexologists' attempts to find an appropriate and scientific name for the newly visible object of their study. Introduced into English in 1892 through the translation of Krafft-Ebing's *Psychopathia Sexualis,* the term "homosexuality" itself stimulated a great deal of uneasiness. In 1915, Ellis reported that "most investigators have been much puzzled in coming to a conclusion as to the best, most exact, and at the same time most colorless names [for same-sex desire]."[43] Giving an account of the various names proposed, such as Karl Heinrich Ulrichs's "Uranian" and Carl von Westphal's "contrary sexual feeling," Ellis admitted that "homosexuality" was the most widely used term. Far from the ideal "colorless" term, however, "homosexuality" evoked Ellis's distaste because of its mixed origins: in a regretful aside, he noted that "it has, philologically, the awkward disadvantage of being a bastard term compounded of Greek and Latin elements" (2). In the first edition of *Sexual Inversion,* Ellis stated his alarm more directly: "'Homosexual' is a barbarously hybrid word."[44] A similar view was expressed by Edward Carpenter, an important socialist organizer in England and an outspoken advocate of homosexual and women's emancipation. Like Ellis,

Carpenter winced at the connotations of illegitimacy in the word: " '[H]omosexual,' generally used in scientific works, is of course a bastard word. 'Homogenic' has been suggested, as being from two roots, both Greek, i.e., 'homos,' same, and 'genos,' sex."[45] Carpenter's suggestion, "homogenic," of course, resonated both against and within the vocabularies of eugenics and miscegenation. Performing these etymological gyrations with almost comic literalism, Ellis and Carpenter expressed pervasive cultural anxieties around questions of racial origins and purity. Concerned above all else with legitimacy, they attempted to remove and rewrite the mixed origins of "homosexuality." Ironically, despite their suggestions for alternatives, the "bastard" term took hold among sexologists, thus yoking together, at least rhetorically, two kinds of mixed bodies: the racial "hybrid" and the invert.

Although Ellis exhibited anxieties about biracial bodies, for others who sought to naturalize and recuperate homosexuality, the evolutionary emphasis on continuity offered potentially useful analogies. Xavier Mayne, for example, one of the earliest American advocates of homosexual rights, wrote, "Between [the] whitest of men and the blackest negro stretches out a vast line of intermediary races as to their colours: brown, olive, red tawny, yellow."[46] He then invoked this model of race to envision a continuous spectrum of gender and sexuality: "Nature abhors the absolute, delights in the fractional. . . . Intersexes express the half-steps, the between-beings."[47] In this analogy, Mayne reversed dominant cultural hierarchies that privileged purity over mixture. Drawing upon irrefutable evidence of the "natural" existence of biracial people, Mayne posited a direct analogy to a similarly mixed body, the intersex, which he positioned as a necessary presence within the natural order.

Despite Carpenter's complaint about "bastard" terminology, he, like Mayne, also occasionally appropriated the scientific language of racial mixing in order to resist the association between homosexuality and degeneration. In *The Intermediate Sex,* he attempted to theorize homosexuality outside of the discourse of pathology or abnormality; he too

suggested a continuum of genders, with "intermediate types" occupying a place between the poles of exclusively heterosexual male and exclusively heterosexual female. In an appendix to *The Intermediate Sex,* Carpenter offered a series of quotations supporting his ideas, some of which drew upon racial analogies:

> Anatomically and mentally we find all shades existing from the pure genus man to the pure genus woman. Thus there has been constituted what is well named by an illustrious exponent of the science "The Third Sex". . . . As we are continually meeting in cities women who are one-quarter, or one-eighth, or so on, *male* . . . so there are in the Inner Self similar half-breeds, all adapting themselves to circumstances with perfect ease.[48]

Through notions of "shades" of gender and sexual "half-breeds," Carpenter appropriated dominant scientific models of race to construct and embody what he called the intermediate sex. These racial paradigms, along with models of gender, offered Carpenter a coherent vocabulary for understanding and expressing a new vision of sexual bodies.

SEXUAL "PERVERSION" AND RACIALIZED DESIRE

By the early twentieth century, medical models of sexuality had begun to shift in emphasis, moving away from a focus on the body and toward psychological theories of desire. It seems significant that this shift took place within a period that also saw a transformation of scientific notions about race. As historians have suggested, in the early twentieth century, scientific claims for exclusively biological models of racial difference were beginning to be undermined, although, of course, these models have persisted in popular understandings of race.[49]

In what ways were these shifts away from biologized notions of sexuality and race related in scientific literature? One area in which they overlapped and perhaps shaped one another was through models of interracial and homosexual desire. Specifically, two tabooed sexualities—miscegenation and homosexuality—became linked in sexological and psychological discourse through the model of "abnormal" sexual object choice.

The convergence of theories of "perverse" racial and sexual desire shaped the assumptions of psychologists like Margaret Otis, whose "A Perversion Not Commonly Noted" appeared in a medical journal in 1913. In all-girl institutions, including reform schools and boarding schools, Otis had observed widespread "love-making between the white and colored girls." [50] Both fascinated and alarmed, Otis remarked that this perversion was "well known in reform schools and institutions for delinquent girls," but that "this particular form of the homosexual relation has perhaps not been brought to the attention of scientists" (113). Performing her ostensible duty to science, Otis carefully described these rituals of interracial romance and the girls' "peculiar moral code." In particular, she noted that the girls incorporated racial difference into courtship rituals self-consciously patterned on traditional gender roles: "One white girl . . . admitted that the colored girl she loved seemed the man, and thought it was so in the case of the others" (114). In Otis's account, the actions of the girls clearly threatened the keepers of the institutions, who responded to the perceived danger with efforts to racially segregate their charges (who were, of course, already segregated by gender). Otis, however, did not specify the motivation for segregation: Did the girls' intimacy trouble the authorities because it was homosexual or because it was interracial? Otis avoided exploring this question and offered a succinct theory instead: "The difference in color, in this case, takes the place of difference in sex" (113).

Otis's explicit discussion of racial difference and homosexuality was extremely unusual in the burgeoning social science literature on sexuality in the early twentieth century. [51] Significantly, Otis characterized this phenomenon as a type of "the homosexual relation" and not as a particular form of interracial sexuality. Despite Otis's focus on desire rather than physiology, her characterization of the schoolgirls' "system" of romance drew upon stereotypes established by the earlier anatomical models. She used a simple analogy between race and gender in order to understand their desire: black was to white as masculine was to feminine.

Recent historical work on the lesbian subject at the turn of the century in the United States offers a useful context for considering the implications of Otis's account. In a compelling analysis of the highly publicized 1892 murder of Freda Ward by her lover, Alice Mitchell, Lisa Duggan has argued that what initially pushed the women's relationship beyond what their peers accepted as normal was Mitchell's decision to pass as a man. [52] Passing, according to Duggan, was "a strategy so rare among bourgeois white women that their plan was perceived as so radically inappropriate as to be insane." [53] Duggan characterizes passing as a kind of red flag that visually marked Mitchell and Ward's relationship. Suddenly, with the prospect of Mitchell's visible transformation from "woman" to "man," the sexual nature of their relationship also came into view—abnormal and dangerous to the eyes of their surveyors.

Following Duggan's line of analysis, I suggest that racial difference performed a similar function in Otis's account. In turn-of-the-century American culture, where Jim Crow segregation erected a structure of taboos against any kind of public (non-work-related) interracial relationship, racial difference visually marked the alliances between the schoolgirls as already suspicious. In a culture in which Ellis could remark that he was accustomed to women being on intimate terms, race became a visible marker for the sexual nature of that liaison. In effect, the institution of racial segregation and its cultural fiction of "black" and "white" produced the girls' interracial romances as "perverse." [54]

It is possible that the discourse of sexual pathology, in turn, began to inform scientific understandings of race. By 1903, a southern physician drew upon the language of sexology to legitimate a particularly racist fear: "A perversion from which most races are exempt, prompts the negro's inclinations towards the white woman, whereas other races incline toward the females of their own." [55] Using the medical language of perversion to naturalize and legitimate the dominant cultural myth of the black rapist, this account characterized interracial desire as a type of congenital abnormal sexual object choice. In the writer's terms, the desire of African-American men for white women (though not the desire of white men for African-American women) could be understood and pathologized by drawing upon emergent models of sexual orientation.[56]

DIVERGENCES IN RACIAL AND SEXUAL SCIENCE

The "invention" of homosexuality and heterosexuality was inextricable from the extraordinary pressures attached to racial definition at this particular historical moment in the late nineteenth century. Although sexologists' search for physical signs of sexual orientation mirrored the methods of comparative racial anatomists, the modern case study marked a significant departure from comparative anatomy by attaching a self-generated narrative to the body in question. As Jeffrey Weeks has written, Krafft-Ebing's *Psychopathia Sexualis* was a decisive moment in the "invention" of the homosexual because "it was the eruption into print of the speaking pervert, the individual marked, or marred, by his (or her) sexual impulses."[57]

The case study challenged the tendency of scientific writers to position the homosexual individual as a mute body whose surface was to be interpreted by those with professional authority. Whether to grant a voice, however limited, to the homosexual body was a heavily contested methodological question among sexologists. The increasingly central position of the case study in the literature on homosexuality elicited concern from contemporary professionals, who perceived an unbridgeable conflict between autobiography and scientific objectivity. Invested in maintaining authority in medical writing, Morton Prince, a psychologist who advocated searching for a "cure" to homosexuality, described in exasperation his basic distrust of the case history as a source of medical evidence, especially in the case of "perverts":

> Even in taking an ordinary medical history, we should hesitate to accept such testimony as final, and I think we should be even more cautious in our examination of autobiographies which attempt to give an analysis, founded on introspection, of the feelings, passions and tastes of degenerate individuals who attempt to explain their first beginnings in early childhood.[58]

For Prince, the "speaking pervert" was a challenge to the "truth" of medical examination and threatened to contradict the traditional source of medical evidence, the patient's mute physical body as interpreted by the physician. In Prince's view, the case history also blurred the boundaries between the legal and medical spheres:

> Very few of these autobiographies will stand analysis. Probably there is no class of people whose statements will less stand the test of a scorching cross-examination than the moral pervert. One cannot help feeling that if the pervert was thus examined by an independent observer, instead of being allowed to tell his own story without interruption, a different tale would be told, or great gaps would be found, which are now nicely bridged, or many asserted facts would be resolved into pure inferences.[59]

A "different tale" indeed. Prince's focus on "testimony" and "cross-examination" illustrated the overlapping interests and methods of the medical and the legal spheres. His tableau of litigation placed the homosexual individual within an already guilty body, one that defied the assumption that it was a readable text; its anatomical markers did not necessarily correspond to predictable sexual behaviors. The sure duplicity of this body demanded investigation by the prosecutor/physician, whose professional expertise somehow guaranteed his access to the truth.

Ellis, who sought legitimacy both for himself as a scientist and for the nascent field of sexology, also worried about the association between autobiographical accounts and fraud. In *Sexual Inversion,* he stated that "it may be proper, at this point, to say a few words as to the reliability of the statements furnished by homosexual persons. This has sometimes been called in{to} question" (89). Although he also associated the homosexual voice with duplicity, Ellis differed from Prince by placing this unreliability within a larger social context. He located the causes of insincerity not in the homosexual individual but in the legal system that barred homosexuality: "[W]e cannot be surprised at this [potential insincerity] so long as inversion is counted a crime. The most normal persons, under similar conditions, would be similarly insincere" (89).

With the movement toward the case study and psychoanalytic models of sexuality, sexologists relied less and less upon the methodologies of comparative anatomy and implicitly acknowledged that physical characteristics were inadequate evidence for the "truth" of the body in question. Yet the assumptions of comparative anatomy did not completely disappear. Although they seemed to contradict more psychological understandings of sexuality, notions of biological difference continued to shape cultural understandings of sexuality, particularly in popular representations of lesbians, gay men, and bisexuals.

TROUBLING SCIENCE

My efforts here have focused on the various ways in which late nineteenth- and early twentieth-century scientific discourses around race became available to sexologists and physicians as a way to articulate emerging models of homosexuality. Methodologies and iconographies of comparative anatomy attempted to locate discrete physiological markers of difference through which to classify and separate types of human beings. Sexologists drew upon these techniques to try to position the "homosexual" body as anatomically distinguishable from the "normal" body. Likewise, medical discourses around sexuality appear to have been steeped in pervasive cultural anxieties about "mixed" bodies, particularly the "mulatto," whose literal position as a mixture of black and white bodies acquires a symbolic position in scientific accounts. Sexologists and others writing about homosexuality borrowed the model of the mixed body as a way to make sense of the "invert." Finally, racial and sexual discourses converged in psychological models that understood "unnatural" desire as a marker of perversion: in these cases, interracial and same-sex sexuality became analogous.

Although scientific and medical models of both race and sexuality held enormous definitional power at the turn of the century, they were variously and complexly incorporated, revised, resisted, or ignored both by the individuals they sought to categorize and within the larger cultural imagination. My speculations are intended to raise questions and to point toward possibilities for further historical and theoretical work. How, for instance, were analogies between race and sexual orientation deployed or not within popular cultural discourses? In religious discourses? In legal discourses? What were the material effects of their convergence or divergence? How have these analogies been used to organize bodies in other historical moments, and, most urgently, in our own?

In the last few years alone, for example, there has been a proliferation of "speaking perverts" in a range of cultural contexts, including political demonstrations, television, magazines, courts, newspapers, and classrooms. Despite the unprecedented opportunities for lesbian, gay, bisexual, and queer speech, however, recent scientific research into sexuality has reflected a determination to discover a biological key to the origins of homosexuality. Highly publicized new studies have purported to locate indicators of sexual orientation in discrete niches of the human body, ranging from a particular gene on the X chromosome to the hypothalamus, a structure of the brain.[60] In an updated and more technologically sophisticated form, comparative anatomy is being granted a peculiar cultural authority in the study of sexuality.

These studies, of course, have not gone uncontested, arriving as they have within a moment characterized not only by the development of social constructionist theories of sexuality but also, in the face of AIDS, by a profound and aching skepticism about prevailing scientific methods and institutions. At the same time, some see political efficacy in these new scientific studies, arguing that lesbians, gay men, and bisexuals might gain access to greater rights if sexual orientation could be proven an immutable biological difference. Such arguments make an analogy, whether explicit or unspoken, to the previous understanding of race as immutable difference. Reverberating through these arguments are echoes of late nineteenth- and early twentieth-century medical models of sexuality and race, whose earlier interdependence suggests a need to understand the complex relationships between constructions of race and sexuality during our own very different historical moment. How does the current effort to re-biologize sexual orientation and to invoke the vocabulary of immutable difference reflect or influence existing cultural anxieties and desires about racialized bodies? To what extent does the political deployment of these new scientific "facts" about sexuality depend upon reinserting biologized racial categories? These questions, as I have tried to show for an earlier period, require a shift in the attention and practices of queer reading and lesbian, gay, and bisexual studies. We must begin to see questions of race as inextricable from the study of sexuality. To date, these connections have only been a part of our peripheral vision; we must make them a central focus.

NOTES

1. See, for example, Michel Foucault, *The History of Sexuality,* vol. 1, *An Introduction* (New York: Vintage, 1980); George Chauncey, "From Sexual Inversion to Homosexuality: Medicine and the Changing Conceptualization of Female Deviance," *Salmagundi,* nos. 58–59 (Fall 1982–Winter 1983): 114–46; Jeffrey Weeks, *Sex, Politics, and Society: The Regulation of Sexuality since* 1800 (New York: Longmans, 1981); and David Halperin, "Is There a History of Sexuality?" in *The Lesbian and Gay Studies Reader,* ed. Henry Abelove, Michèle Aina Barale, and David M. Halperin (New York: Routledge, 1993), 416–31. On the invention of the classification "heterosexual," see Jonathan Katz, "The Invention of Heterosexuality," *Socialist Review* 20 (1990): 17–34. For a related and intriguing argument that locates the earlier emergence of hierarchies of reproductive over non-reproductive sexual activity, see Henry Abelove, "Some Speculations on the History of 'Sexual Intercourse' during the 'Long Eighteenth Century' in England." *Genders* 6 (1989): 125–30.
2. Chauncey, "From Sexual Inversion to Homosexuality."
3. In "Homosexuality: A Cultural Construct," from his *One Hundred Years of Homosexuality; and Other Essays on Greek Love* (New York: Routledge, 1990), David Halperin has briefly and provocatively suggested that

all scientific inquiries into the aetiology of sexual orientation, after all, spring from a more or less implicit theory of sexual races, from the notion that there exist broad general divisions between types of human beings corresponding, respectively, to those who make a homosexual and those who make a heterosexual object-choice. When the sexual racism underlying such inquiries is more plainly exposed, their rationale will suffer proportionately— or so one may hope. (50)

In a recent article, Abdul R. JanMohamed offers a useful analysis and critique of Foucault's failure to examine the intersection of the discourses of sexuality and race. See his "Sexuality on/of the Racial Border: Foucault, Wright, and the Articulation of 'Racialized Sexuality,'" in *Discourses of Sexuality: From Aristotle to AIDS,* ed. Domna C. Stanton (Ann Arbor: University of Michigan Press, 1992), 94–116. I explore a different (though related) set of questions in this essay.
4. In *Disorders of Desire: Sex and Gender in Modern American Sexology* (Philadelphia: Temple University Press, 1990), Janice Irvine notes that, for example, "the invisibility of Black people in sexology as subjects or researchers has undermined our understanding of the sexuality of Black Americans and continues to be a major problem in modern sexology." She adds that Kinsey, the other major sexologist of the twentieth century, planned to include a significant proportion of African-American case histories in his *Sexual Behavior in the Human Male* (1948) and *Sexual Behavior in the Human Female* (1953) but failed to gather a sufficient number of them and so "unwittingly colluded in the racial exclusion so pervasive in sex research" (43).
5. Havelock Ellis, *Studies in the Psychology of Sex,* vol. 1, *Sexual Inversion* (1897; London, 1900), x, emphasis added.
6. My use of the concept of ideology draws upon Barbara Fields, "Slavery, Race, and Ideology in the United States of America," *New Left Review* 181 (1990): 95–118; Louis Althusser, "Ideology and Ideological State Apparatuses (Notes towards an Investigation)," in his *Lenin and Philosophy and Other Essays,* trans. Ben Brewster (New York: Monthly Review Press, 1971), 121–73; and Teresa de Lauretis, "The Technology of Gender," in her *Technologies of Gender: Essays on Theory, Film, and Fiction* (Bloomington: Indiana University Press, 1987), 1–30.
7. I borrow this phrase from Willa Cather's essay "The Novel Démeublé," in her *Not under Forty* (New York, 1922), 50.

8. I am not implying, however, that racial anxieties caused the invention of the homosexual, or that the invention of the homosexual caused increased racial anxieties. Both of these causal arguments seem simplistic and, further, depend upon separating the discourses of race and sexuality, whose convergence, in fact, I am eager to foreground.

9. Havelock Ellis, *Studies in the Psychology of Sex,* vol. 2, *Sexual Inversion,* 3d ed. (Philadelphia, 1915). Further references to this edition will be noted parenthetically unless otherwise stated. Although *Sexual Inversion* was published originally as volume 1, Ellis changed its position to volume 2 in the second and third editions, published in the United States in 1901 and 1915, respectively. In the later editions, volume 1 became *The Evolution of Modesty.*

   Ellis originally coauthored *Sexual Inversion* with John Addington Symonds. For a discussion of their collaboration and the eventual erasure of Symonds from the text, see Wayne Koestenbaum, *Double Talk: The Erotics of Male Literary Collaboration* (New York: Routledge, 1989), 43–67.

10. In "Sex and the Emergence of Sexuality," *Critical Inquiry* 14 (Autumn 1987): 16–48, Arnold I. Davidson characterizes Ellis's method as "psychiatric" (as opposed to "anatomical") reasoning. Arguing that "sexuality itself is a product of the psychiatric style of reasoning" (23), Davidson explains that "the iconographical representation of sex proceeds by depiction of the body, more specifically by depiction of the genitalia. The iconographical representation of sexuality is given by depiction of the personality, and it most usually takes the form of depiction of the face and its expressions" (27). The case studies in *Sexual Inversion,* and especially those of women, however, tend to contradict this broad characterization. My understanding of Ellis differs from that of Davidson, who readily places Ellis in a psychiatric model. Instead, Ellis might be characterized as a transitional figure, poised at the crossroads between the fields of comparative anatomy and psychiatry. To borrow Davidson's terms, anatomical reasoning does not disappear; it stays in place, supporting psychiatric reasoning.

11. Ellis, *Sexual Inversion* (1900), xi. Ironically, upon publication in 1897, *Sexual Inversion* was judged to be not a scientific work but "a certain lewd, wicked, bawdy, scandalous libel." Effectively banned in England, subsequent copies were published only in the United States. See Jeffrey Weeks, "Havelock Ellis and the Politics of Sex Reform," in *Socialism and the New Life: The Personal and Sexual Politics of Edward*

Carpenter and Havelock Ellis, ed. Sheila Rowbotham and Jeffrey Weeks (London: Pluto Press, 1977), 154; and Phyllis Grosskurth, *Havelock Ellis: A Biography* (New York: Knopf, 1980), 191–204.

12. For further discussion of Ellis's similarity to Charles Darwin as a naturalist and their mutual interest in "natural" modesty, see Ruth Bernard Yeazell, "Nature's Courtship Plot in Darwin and Ellis," *Yale Journal of Criticism* 2 (1989): 33–53.

13. Elsewhere in *Sexual Inversion,* Ellis entertained the idea that certain races or nationalities had a "special proclivity" to homosexuality (4), but he seemed to recognize the nationalistic impulse behind this argument and chided those who wielded it: "The people of every country have always been eager to associate sexual perversions with some other country than their own" (57–58).

14. Classic discussions of the term's history include Peter I. Rose, *The Subject Is Race: Traditional Ideologies and the Teaching of Race Relations* (New York: Oxford University Press, 1968), 30–43; and Thomas F. Gossett, *Race: The History of an Idea in America* (Dallas: Southern Methodist University Press, 1963). For a history of various forms and theories of biological determinism, see Stephen Jay Gould, *The Mismeasure of Man* (New York: Norton, 1981).

15. John S. Haller, Jr., *Outcasts from Evolution: Scientific Attitudes of Racial Inferiority, 1859–1900* (Urbana: University of Illinois Press, 1971), 4.

16. Ibid., 196. On Cope, see also Gould, *The Mismeasure of Man,* 115–18.

17. Nancy Leys Stepan and Sander Gilman, "Appropriating the Idioms of Science: The Rejection of Scientific Racism," in *The Bounds of Race: Perspectives on Hegemony and Resistance,* ed. Dominick LaCapra (Ithaca, NY: Cornell University Press, 1991), 74.

18. Fields, "Slavery, Race, and Ideology in the United States of America," 97, n. 3.

19. Haller, "Outcasts from Evolution," 48.

20. Sander Gilman, *Difference and Pathology: Stereotypes of Sexuality, Race, and Madness* (Ithaca, NY: Cornell University Press, 1985), 112.

21. According to Gilman, "When one turns to autopsies of black males from [the late nineteenth century], what is striking is the absence of any discussion of the male genitalia" (ibid., 89).

   The specific absence of male physiology as a focus of nineteenth-century scientific texts, however, should not minimize the central location of the African-American male body in popular cultural notions of racial difference, especially in the spectacle of lynching, which had far-reaching effects on both African-American and white attitudes toward the African-American male body. One might also consider the position of the racialized male body in one of the most popular forms of nineteenth-century entertainment, the minstrel show. See Eric Lott, *Love and Theft: Blackface Minstrelsy and the American Working Class* (New York: Oxford University Press, 1993).

22. The *American Journal of Obstetrics (AJO)* was a frequent forum for these debates. On the position of the hymen, for example, see C. H. Fort, "Some Corroborative Facts in Regard to the Anatomical Difference between the Negro and White Races," *AJO* 10 (1877): 258–59; H. Otis Hyatt, "Note on the Normal Anatomy of the Vulvo-Vaginal Orifice," *AJO* 10 (1877): 253–58; A. G. Smythe, "The Position of the Hymen in the Negro Race," *AJO* 10 (1877): 638–39; Edward Turnipseed, "Some Facts in Regard to the Anatomical Differences between the Negro and White Races," *AJO* 10 (1877): 32–33. On the birth canal, see Joseph Taber Johnson, "On Some of the Apparent Peculiarities of Parturition in the Negro Race, with Remarks on Race Pelves in General," *AJO* 8 (1875): 88–123.

This focus on women's bodies apparently differed from earlier studies. In her recent work on gender and natural history, Londa Schiebinger discusses how eighteenth-century comparative anatomists and anthropologists developed their theories by examining male bodies. See *Nature's Body: Gender in the Making of Modern Science* (Boston: Beacon, 1993), especially 143–83.

23. W. H. Flower and James Murie, "Account of the Dissection of a Bushwoman," *Journal of Anatomy and Physiology* 1 (1867): 208. Subsequent references will be noted parenthetically within the text.

Flower was the conservator of the Museum of the Royal College of Surgeons of England; Murie was prosector to the Zoological Society of London. For brief discussions of this account, see Gilman, *Difference and Pathology,* 88–89; and Anita Levy, *Other Women: The Writing of Class, Race, and Gender, 1832–1898* (Princeton, NJ: Princeton University Press, 1991), 70–72. Although she does not consider questions surrounding the lesbian body, Levy offers an astute reading of this case and its connection to scientific representations of the body of the prostitute.

24. Georges Cuvier, "Extraits d'observations faites sur le cadavre d'une femme connue à Paris et à Londres sous le nom de Vénus Hottentote," *Mémoires du Musée d'histoire naturelle* 3 (1817): 259–74. After her death in 1815 at the age of twenty-five, Baartman's genitalia

were preserved and re-displayed within the scientific space of the Musée de l'Homme in Paris.

On Baartman, see Schiebinger, *Nature's Body,* 160–72; and Stephen Jay Gould, *The Flamingo's Smile: Reflections in Natural History* (New York: Norton 1985), 291–305.

25. Richard von Krafft-Ebing, *Psychopathia Sexualis,* 12th ed., trans. Franklin S. Klaf (1902; reprint, New York: Putnam, 1965).

26. This practice continued well into the twentieth century. See, for example, Jennifer Terry's discussion of the anatomical measurement of lesbians by the Committee for the Study of Sex Variants in the 1930s, in "Lesbians under the Medical Gaze: Scientists Search for Remarkable Differences," *Journal of Sex Research* 27 (August 1990): 317–39; and "Theorizing Deviant Historiography," *differences* 3 (Summer 1991): 55–74.

27. In the first edition of *Sexual Inversion,* Ellis, who did search the lesbian body for masculine characteristics, nevertheless refuted this claim about the clitoris: "there is no connection, as was once supposed, between sexual inversion and an enlarged clitoris" (98).

28. Perry M. Lichtenstein, "The 'Fairy' and the Lady Lover," *Medical Review of Reviews* 27 (1921): 372. In "Lesbians under the Medical Gaze," Terry discusses sexologists' conjectures about the size of lesbians' genitalia in a report published in 1941. Researchers were somewhat uncertain whether perceived excesses were congenital or the result of particular sex practices. On the history of scientific claims about the sexual function of the clitoris, see Thomas Laqueur, *Making Sex: Body and Gender from the Greeks to Freud* (Cambridge: Harvard University Press, 1990), 233–37.

29. Morris, "Is Evolution Trying to Do Away with the Clitoris?" (paper presented at the meeting of the American Association of Obstetricians and Gynecologists, St. Louis, September 21, 1892), Yale University Medical Library, New Haven, CT.

30. See Hazel Carby, *Reconstructing Womanhood: The Emergence of the Afro-American Woman Novelist* (New York: Oxford University Press, 1987), 20–39; and Barbara Welter, "The Cult of True Womanhood, 1820–1860," in her *Dimity Convictions: The American Woman in the Nineteenth Century* (Columbus: Ohio University Press, 1976), 21–41.

31. Characterizing this passage as "punitively complete," Koestenbaum in *Double Talk* has suggested that Ellis also had personal motivations for focusing so intently on the lesbian body: "Ellis, by taking part in this over-description of a lesbian, studied and subjugated the

preference of his own wife; marrying a lesbian, choosing to discontinue sexual relations with her, writing *Sexual Inversion* with a homosexual [Symonds], Ellis might well have felt his own heterosexuality questioned" (54, 55).

32. George Fredrickson, *The Black Image in the White Mind: The Debate on Afro-American Character and Destiny, 1817–1914* (New York: Harper and Row, 1971), 246.

33. Havelock Ellis, *Man and Woman: A Study of Human Secondary Sexual Characters* (1894; New York, 1911), 13. Of course, the "beginnings of industrialism" coincided with the late eighteenth century, the period during which, as Schiebinger has shown, anatomists began looking for more subtle marks of differentiation. See Londa Schiebinger, *The Mind Has No Sex? Women in the Origins of Modern Science* (Cambridge: Harvard University Press, 1989), 189–212.

34. Patrick Geddes and J. Arthur Thomson, *The Evolution of Sex* (London, 1889; New York, 1890), 80. Ellis no doubt read this volume closely, for he had chosen it to inaugurate a series of popular scientific books (the Contemporary Science Series) that he edited for the Walter Scott Company. For more on this series, see Grosskurth, *Havelock Ellis,* 114–17.

35. For a full account of the debates concerning monogeny and polygeny, see Gould, *The Mismeasure of Man,* 30–72. Polygeny was a predominantly American theoretical development and was widely referred to as the "American school" of anthropology.

36. See Nancy Stepan, *The Idea of Race in Science: Great Britain, 1800–1960* (Hamden, CT: Archon Books, 1982), 53.

37. Edward Byron Reuter, *The Mulatto in the United States: Including a Study of the Role of Mixed-Blood Races throughout the World* (Boston, 1918), 338. Interestingly, in a paper delivered to the Eugenics Society of Britain in 1911, Edith Ellis (who had at least one long-term lesbian relationship while she was married to Havelock Ellis) had also used the phrase "peculiar people" to describe homosexual men and women. See Grosskurth, *Havelock Ellis,* 237–38.

38. Francis Galton (a cousin of Charles Darwin) introduced and defined the term "eugenics" in his *Inquiries into Human Faculty and Its Development* (1883; reprint, New York: AMS Press, 1973) as "the cultivation of the race" and "the science of improving stock, which . . . takes cognisance [*sic*] of all influences that tend in however remote a degree to give to the more suitable races or strains of blood a better chance of prevailing speedily over the less suitable than they otherwise would have had" (17).

39. For a discussion of Roosevelt's place within the racial ideology of the period, see Thomas G. Dyer, *Theodore Roosevelt and the Idea of Race* (Baton Rouge: Louisiana State University Press, 1980). See also John Higham, *Strangers in the Land: Patterns of American Nativism, 1860–1925* (New Brunswick, NJ: Rutgers University Press, 1955; reprint, New York: Atheneum, 1963), 146–57.

40. Mark H. Haller, *Eugenics: Hereditary Attitudes in American Thought* (New Brunswick, NJ: Rutgers University Press, 1963), 144.

41. Jeffrey Weeks, *Sexuality and Its Discontents: Meanings, Myths, and Modern Sexualities* (Boston: Routledge and Kegan Paul, 1985), 76; Grosskurth, *Havelock Ellis,* 410. See also Havelock Ellis, "The Sterilization of the Unfit," *Eugenics Review* (October 1909): 203–6.

42. Quoted by Grosskurth, *Havelock Ellis,* 410.

43. Ellis, *Sexual Inversion* (1915), 2.

44. Ellis, *Sexual Inversion* (1900), 1n.

45. Edward Carpenter, "The Homogenic Attachment," in his *The Intermediate Sex: A Study of Some Transitional Types of Men and Women,* 5th ed. (London, 1918), 40n.

46. Xavier Mayne [Edward Irenaeus Prime Stevenson], *The Intersexes: A History of Similisexualism as a Problem in Social Life* ([Naples?], ca. 1908); reprint, New York: Arno Press, 1975), 14.

47. Ibid., 15, 17.

48. Quoted in Carpenter, *The Intermediate Sex,* 133, 170. Carpenter gives the following citations for these quotations: Dr. James Burnet, *Medical Times and Hospital Gazette* 34, no. 1497 (November 10, 1906); and Charles G. Leland, "The Alternate Sex" (London, 1904), 41, 57.

49. In *New People: Miscegenation and Mulattoes in the United States* (New York: Free Press, 1980), Joel Williamson suggests that a similar psychologization of race was underway: "By about 1900 it was possible in the South for one who was biologically purely white to become behaviorally black. Blackness had become not a matter of visibility, not even, ironically, of the one-drop rule. It had passed on to become a matter of inner morality and outward behavior" (108). See also Elazar Barkan, *The Retreat of Scientific Racism: Changing Concepts of Race in Britain and the United States between the World Wars* (New York: Cambridge University Press, 1992).

Legal scholars have begun to explore the analogies between sodomy laws and anti-miscegenation statutes. See, for example, Andrew Koppelman, "The Miscegenation Analogy: Sodomy Law as Sex Discrimination," *Yale Law Journal* 98 (November 1988): 145–64. See also Janet Halley, "The Politics of the Closet: Towards Equal Protection for Gay, Lesbian, and Bisexual Identity," *UCLA Law Review* 36 (1989): 915–76. I am grateful to Julia Friedlander for bringing this legal scholarship to my attention.

50. Margaret Otis, "A Perversion Not Commonly Noted," *Journal of Abnormal Psychology* 8 (June–July 1913): 113–60. Subsequent references will be noted parenthetically within the text.

51. In "From Sexual Inversion to Homosexuality," Chauncey notes that "by the early teens the number of articles of abstracts concerning homosexuality regularly available to the American medical profession had grown enormously" (115, n. 3).

52. Lisa Duggan, "The Trials of Alice Mitchell: Sensationalism, Sexology, and the Lesbian Subject in Turn-of-the-Century America," *Signs: Journal of Women in Culture and Society* 18 (Summer 1993): 791–814.

53. Ibid., 798.

54. In a useful discussion of recent feminist analyses of identity, Lisa Walker suggests that a similar trope of visibility is prevalent in white critics' attempts to theorize race and sexuality. See her "How to Recognize a Lesbian: The Cultural Politics of Looking like What You Are," *Signs* 18 (Summer 1993): 866–90.

55. W. T. English, "The Negro Problem from the Physician's Point of View," *Atlanta Journal-Record of Medicine* 5 (October 1903): 468.

56. On the other hand, anti-lynching campaigns could also invoke the language of sexology. Although the analogy invoked sadism, rather than homosexuality, in 1935 a psychologist characterized lynching as a kind of "Dixie sex perversion . . . [m]uch that is commonly stigmatized as cruelty is a perversion of the sex instinct." Quoted in Phyllis Klotman, "'Tearing a Hole in History': Lynching as Theme and Motif," *Black American Literature Forum* 19 (1985): The original quote appeared in the *Baltimore Afro-American,* March 16, 1935.

57. Weeks, *Sexuality and Its Discontents.* Weeks points out that beginning with Krafft-Ebing's *Psychopathia Sexualis,* the case study became the standard in sexological writing. The dynamic between medical literature and a growing self-identified gay (male) subculture is exemplified by the growth of different editions of this single work. The first edition of *Psychopathia Sexualis,* published in 1886, contained 45 case histories and 110 pages; the twelfth edition, published in 1903, contained 238 case histories and 437 pages. Many of the subsequent case histories were supplied by readers who responded to the book with letters detailing their own sexual histories. This information suggests that, to at least some extent, an emerging gay male subculture was able to appropriate the space of "professional" medicolegal writing for its own uses, thus blurring the boundaries between professional medical and popular literature.

58. Morton Prince, "Sexual Perversion or Vice? A Pathological and Therapeutic Inquiry," *Journal of Nervous and Mental Disease* 25 (April 1898): 237–56; reprinted in *Psychotherapy and Multiple Personality: Selected Essays,* ed. Nathan G. Hale (Cambridge: Harvard University Press, 1975), 91.

59. Prince, *Psychotherapy and Multiple Personality,* 92.

60. Simon LeVay, *The Sexual Brain* (Cambridge: MIT Press, 1993); and Dean Hamer, *The Science of Desire: The Search for the Gay Gene and the Biology of Behavior* (New York: Simon and Schuster, 1994).

29 • *Sharon E. Preves, Ph.D.*

INTERSEX NARRATIVES
Gender, Medicine, and Identity

DISCUSSION QUESTIONS

1. Given the relatively common occurrence of intersex births, why do you think people are so much more knowledgeable and willing to talk about cystic fibrosis or Down syndrome, which occur with similar frequency?
2. Why do you think intersex children are treated medically? What are the consequences of medical treatment for these individuals? For society?
3. Imagine that you are intersexed. How would you have wanted your parents and/or the medical community to respond? What do you think would be the most difficult issues you would face?
4. If you became the parent of an intersex child, what, if anything, would you do? Would your response be any different after reading this chapter?

If doctors really want to do something for their intersexed patients, I would say the first thing is [to] put the intersex person in touch with other people who are intersexed. Number two is see number one. And number three is see number one. That's it. Doctors think that you're going to kill yourself if you find out the truth. People kill themselves because they feel alone and isolated and helpless; that's why they kill themselves. When doctors don't tell their patients the truth, certainly they're cutting them off then from the opportunity of incredible support.

(Excerpt from interview with Sherri)[1]

BEYOND PINK AND BLUE

I recently participated in a cultural diversity field trip with twenty-two second graders in St. Paul, Minnesota. When I arrived at their school, the kids were squirrelly with anticipation. They were a colorful and varied bunch—some were tall and thin, others short and stout. Moreover, they were from a variety of racial and ethnic backgrounds and spoke nearly half a dozen native languages. When it was time to begin our community walking tour, the teachers attempted to bring the busy group to order quickly. How did they go about doing so? They told the children to form two lines: one for girls and the other for boys. The children did so seamlessly, since they had been asked to line up in this manner countless numbers of times before. Within moments, the children were quiet and attentive. I was struck then, as I had been many times before, by how often and in the most basic ways societies are organized by a distinction between sexes. With children of every shape and color, the gender divide worked as a sure way to bring order to chaos. "Girls in one line, boys in the other." Sometimes the choice between the lines—and sexes—isn't so easy.

Which line would you join? Girls' or boys'? Think about it seriously for a minute. How do you even know whether to line up with the girls or the boys? For that matter, what sex or gender *are* you, and how did you *become* the gender you are? Moreover, how do you *know* what sex and gender you are? Who decides? These questions may seem ridiculous. You may be saying to yourself, "Of course, I know what gender I am; forget this article." But really stop to think about how you know what sex you are and how you acquired your gender. Most of us have been taught that sex is anatomical and gender is social. What's more, many of us have never had the occasion to explore our gender or sexual identities because neither has given us cause for reflection. Much like Caucasians who say they "have none" when asked to explore their racial identity, many women and men find it difficult to be reflective about how they know and "do" gender (West and Zimmerman, 1987).

This article explores what happens to people who, from the time of their birth or early adolescence, inhabit bodies that do not afford them an easy choice between the gender lines. Every day babies are born with bodies that are deemed sexually ambiguous, and with regularity they are surgically altered to reflect the sexual anatomy associated with "standard" female or male sex assignment. There are numerous ways to respond to this plurality of physical type, including no response at all. Because sex and gender operate as inflexible and central organizing principles of daily

existence in this culture, such indifference is rare if not nonexistent. Instead, interference with sex and gender norms is cast as a major disturbance to social order, and people go to remarkable lengths to eradicate threats to the norm, even though they occur with great regularity.

Recent estimates indicate that approximately one or two in every two thousand infants are born with anatomy that people regard as sexually ambiguous. Frequency estimates vary widely and are, at best, inconclusive. The estimates I provide here are based on a review of the recent medical literature (Blackless et al., 2000). This review suggests that approximately one or two per two thousand children are born with bodies that are considered appropriate for genital reconstruction surgery because they do not conform to socially accepted norms of sexual anatomy. Moreover, nearly 2 percent are born with chromosome, gonad, genital, or hormone features that could be considered "intersexed"; that is, children born with ambiguous genitalia, sexual organs, or sex chromosomes. Additional estimates report the frequency of this sexual variance as approximately 1 percent to 4 percent of all births (Edgerton, 1964; Fiedler, 1978; Money, 1989).

These estimates differ so much because definitions of sexual ambiguity vary tremendously (Dreger, 1998b; Kessler, 1998). This is largely because distinctions between female and male bodies are actually on more of a continuum than a dichotomy. The criteria for what counts as female or male, or sexually ambiguous for that matter, are human standards. That is, bodies that are considered normal or abnormal are not inherently that way. They are, rather, classified as aberrant or customary by social agreement (Hird, 2000). We have, as humans, created categories for bodies that fit the norm and those that do not, as well as a systematic method of surgically attempting to correct or erase sexual variation. That we have done so is evidence of the regularity with which sexual variation occurs.

Melanie Blackless and her colleagues (2000) suggested that the total frequency of nongenital sexual variation (cases of intersexed chromosomes or internal sexual organs) is much higher than one in two thousand.

They concluded that using a more inclusive definition of sexual ambiguity would yield frequency estimates closer to one or two per one hundred births, bringing us back to the 1 percent to 2 percent range.

To put these numbers in perspective, although its occurrence has only recently begun to be openly discussed, physical sexual ambiguity occurs about as often as the well-known conditions of cystic fibrosis and Down syndrome (see Desai, 1997; Dreger, 1998b; Roberts et al., 1998). Since approximately 4 million babies are born annually in the United States, a conservative estimate is that about two thousand to four thousand babies are born per year in this country with features of their anatomy that vary from the physical characteristics that are typically associated with females and males.[2] Some are born with genitalia that are difficult to characterize as clearly female or male. Others have sex chromosomes that are neither XX nor XY, but some other combination, such as X, XXY, or chromosomes that vary throughout the cells of their bodies, changing from XX to XY from cell to cell. Still others experience unexpected physical changes at puberty, when their bodies exhibit secondary sex characteristics that are surprisingly "opposite" their sex of assignment. Some forms of sexual ambiguity are inherited genetically, while others are brought on by hormonal activity during gestation or prescription medication that women take during pregnancy. Regardless of their particular manifestation or cause, most forms of physical sexual anatomy that vary from the norm are medically classified and treated as forms of intersexuality, or hermaphroditism.

INTERSEX IS A SOCIAL, NOT A MEDICAL, PROBLEM

While being born with indeterminate sexual organs indeed problematizes a binary understanding of sex and gender, several studies have shown—and there seems to be a general consensus (even among doctors who perform the "normalizing" operations)—that most children with an ambiguous sexual anatomy do not require medical intervention for their physiological health (Diamond and Sigmundson, 1997; Dreger,

1998a; Kessler, 1998). Nevertheless, the majority of sexually ambiguous infants are medically assigned a definitive sex, often undergoing repeated genital surgeries and ongoing hormone treatments to "correct" their variation from the norm.

I argue that medical treatments to create genitally *unambiguous* children are not performed entirely or even predominantly for the sake of preventing stigmatization and trauma to the children. Rather, these elaborate, expensive, and risky procedures are performed to maintain social order for the institutions and adults that surround these children. Newborns are oblivious to the rigid social conventions to which their families and caregivers adhere. Threats to the duality of sex and gender undermine inflexibly gendered occupational, education, and family structures, as well as heterosexuality itself. After all, if one's sex is in doubt, how would one's sexual orientation be identified, given that heterosexuality, homosexuality, and even bisexuality are all based on a sexual binary? So, when adults encounter a healthy baby with a body that is not easily "sexed," they may understandably be unable to imagine a happy and successful future for that child. They may wonder how the child will fit in at school and with its peers and will negotiate dating and sexuality, as well as family and a career. But most parents do not feel a real need to address these questions until years after a child's birth. Furthermore, I contend that parents and caregivers of intersexed children do not need to be so concerned about addressing the "personal troubles" of their children either. Rather, we should all turn our attention to the "public issues" and problems that are wrought by an unwavering, merciless adherence to sex and gender binarism (Mills, 1959:8).

Take Claire's experience as an example. Claire is a middle-class white woman and mother of two teenage daughters who works as a writer and editor. She was forty-four years old when she conveyed the following story to me during a four-hour interview that took place in her home. Claire underwent a clitorectomy when she was six years old at her parents' insistence, after clinicians agreed that her clitoris was just "too large" and they had to intervene. The size of her clitoris seemed to cause problems not for young Claire, but for the adults around her. Indeed, there was nothing ambiguous about Claire's sex before the surgery. She has XX chromosomes, has functioning female reproductive organs, and later in life went through a physically uneventful female puberty and pregnancies. Claire's experience illustrates that having a large clitoris is perceived as a physical trait that is dangerous to existing notions of gender and sexuality, despite the sexual pleasure it could have given Claire and her future sexual partners. In fact, doctors classify a larger clitoris as a medical condition referred to as "clitoral megaly" or "clitoral hypertrophy." Conversely, small penises for anatomical boys are classified as a medical problem called "micro-penis."

Reflecting on the reasons for the clitorectomy she underwent at age six, Claire said, "I don't feel that my sex was ambiguous at all. There was never that question. But I'm sure that [clitorectomies] have been done forever because parents just [do not] like big clitorises because they look too much like a penis." Even more alarming may be the physical and emotional outcomes of genital surgery that may be experienced by the patient. About the after effects of her surgery, Claire said:

> They just took the clitoris out and then whip stitched the hood together, so it's sort of an odd-looking thing. I don't know what they were hoping to preserve, although I remember my father thinking that if someone saw me, it would look normal because there's just a little skin poking out between my lips so it wouldn't look strange. I remember I was in the hospital for five days. And then it just got better and everything was forgotten, until I finally asked about it when I was twelve. [There was] total and complete silence. You know, it was never, never mentioned. I know you know what that does. I was just in agony trying to figure out who I was. And, you know, why... what sex I was. And feeling like a freak, which is a very common story. And then when I was twelve, I asked my father what had been done to me. And his answer was, "Don't be so self-examining." And that was it. I never asked again [until I was thirty-five].

During the course of my research, I spoke with many other adults across North America who had childhood experiences remarkably similar to Claire's. Their stories are laden with family and medical secrecy, shame, and social isolation, as well as perseverance, strength of spirit, and eventual pride in their unique bodies and perspectives.

RESEARCH METHODS

I was astonished to find that so little research had been conducted with former patients or families about the experience and outcome of medical "normalization" procedures. When I began this research more than ten years ago, some adult intersexuals began coming forward to tell their stories. From this point, they began to form intersex support and advocacy groups, spurring the beginning of a burgeoning intersex social movement. Because these events coincided with my own research on intersex, I became aware of the important opportunity to speak with intersexuals about their experiences and perspectives firsthand.

Initially, recruiting willing interviewees for my study was a challenge because sexual ambiguity is generally not visible, and members of this population typically do not self-identify to others as intersexed and therefore are generally not mobilized. During the course of my research, however, several intersex support and advocacy groups either emerged or came to my attention. Because they are a self-selected group, members of these organizations cannot be expected to represent the diversity of experience within the intersex population. In fact, given the difficulty of identifying members of this population, it is not possible to get a truly representative sample. Rather, these organizations served as a strategic and theoretically promising sampling base, given the social context of an emerging intersex social movement and my interest in the experience and process of social marginalization.

In the end, I interviewed thirty-seven intersexed adults from March of 1997 to September of 1998. The research participants ranged in age from twenty to sixty-five, with a mean age of forty, and lived in nineteen states and Canadian provinces. At the time of the interviews, 24 percent of the participants were living as a gender different from their sex of assignment and rearing; six were transitioning or had transitioned from female to male, and three from male to female. In 51 percent of the sample, intersexuality was apparent at birth or in infancy owing to genital ambiguity; for forty-nine percent, intersexuality was not apparent until puberty. I conducted the interviews in a private, face-to-face format, primarily in the participants' homes.

MEDICALIZATION, STIGMA, SECRECY, AND SHAME

The participants' experiences with medical attempts to "normalize" their bodies were amazingly consistent, despite the widespread variation of intersex diagnoses among those I interviewed. For example, intersexuals who underwent medical sex assignment in childhood experienced consistently negative and confusing messages about their bodies and their identities. In sum, the participants reported that they received the following three messages about themselves through medical sex assignment: (1) that they were objects of medical interest and treatment, (2) that they were not to know what was wrong with them or why they were receiving medical treatment, and (3) that such procedures were in their best interest and should remain uncontested and undisclosed. This model led the participants to lack information about their own bodies; open and honest communication within their familial, clinical, and friendship networks; and association with a potential peer group of intersexuals with whom to relate.

The objective of contemporary intersex medical treatment is to decrease social stigma and optimize the formation of clear and uncomplicated gender and sexual identities. The participants stated that because they were given false or incomplete information about their bodies and medical treatments and because they were encouraged to keep silent about their differences and surgical alterations, they experienced feelings of isolation, stigma, and shame—the very feelings that such procedures attempt to alleviate. The participants

spoke frequently of wanting autonomy over their bodies, of longing to talk with others who had a similar anatomy, and of wanting to participate in decision making related to medical intervention. Feelings of shame were most intense in those who had recurring medical examinations or treatments to impose clarity on ambiguous sexual anatomy. These individuals spoke of feeling "monstrous, Other, and freakish." In stark contrast, when the same people spoke of gaining accurate information about their bodies, telling others openly about their physical differences, and finding other intersexuals with whom to relate, they relayed feelings of "relief, acceptance, and pride" about their difference and their identities.

As a means of illustrating the extent to which medicine alienates and objectifies intersexuals in its effort to study and control intersex variation, I quote extensively from intersexuals' life histories in the following sections. Each of these individuals speaks directly about the procedures of medicalization, the consequences of receiving ongoing negative attention to their difference, and the process of coming to accept and cherish their intersexuality.

BEING AN OBJECT OF STUDY

If identity formation is interactive, as symbolic interactionist social psychologists suggest, then receiving repeated messages that one's own body is socially unacceptable leads to a lasting and damaging impact on one's concept of self (Becker, 1963; Cooley, 1964 [1902]; Davis, 1995; Goffman, 1963; Hewitt, 1989; Holstein and Gubrium, 2000; Jones et al., 1984; Mead, 1934; Plummer, 1975, 1995; Strauss and Corbin, 1991). Such is the case for intersexuals who undergo repeated group examinations and operations on their genitalia. Conversely, if individuals receive positive feedback about their health and adequacy from the reflection of self offered by others, they will develop a sense of self that reflects that input (Jones et al., 1984). Because children are less discerning about the world, they are more passive in the socialization process during their early years. As George Herbert Mead (1934), John Hewitt (1970), and others have argued, reflected appraisal of the self may carry considerably more weight in childhood than in other periods of the life course.

Symbolic interactionists see social realities as dependent upon a shared definition of the situation. In this sense, both deviance and stigma are social products that emerge from social encounters and negotiations (Plummer, 1975, 1995). In other words, no one is inherently "normal" or "deviant"; such characteristics do not lie objectively within a person; instead what is considered normal or abnormal is culturally variable and dependent on human reactions (Goffman, 1963; Jones et al., 1984). When characteristics central to one's core concept of self, such as sex/gender, race, age, or overall physical appearance, become stigmatized, it is difficult to deemphasize the importance of these characteristics. In these cases, damage to one's self-concept may be dramatic, leaving a mark or stigma associated with a predominant characteristic upon which the self-concept is based. Here, the stigmatized characteristic becomes so central to one's overall identity that a concept of self will be developed around it, leading to a pervasive self-stigmatization that is generalized and associated with other, seemingly unrelated, aspects of oneself. In this sense, the stigmatized characteristic may become a dominating aspect of self from which (all) other concepts of self take their meaning (Jones et al., 1984). For example, an intersexed child whose sexual anatomy is repeatedly assessed as problematic may come to view herself or himself as a misfit in other matters as well.

The contrast in self-concept between participants who did not undergo medical sex assignment and those who did is striking. Drew, who was thirty years old at the time of our interview, was one of only two people in my study who did not undergo surgical or hormonal sex assignment in childhood. Drew spoke of first encountering the notion that her body was somehow pathological when she went to see a gynecologist for a routine exam at the age of twenty:

> When I was twenty, I had my first medical experience as an intersexed person. [The gynecologist] said, "Has your clitoris always been this large? I'd like to do some tests 'cause I think maybe something's not normal." And she used the word "normal" specifically like something was not normal. It was the first negative association I'd had, and [I] started [having] this feeling that I wasn't normal.

Until this interaction, Drew had received feedback from other medical professionals, her family, and peers that she was healthy, adequate, and normal, and her obvious physical differences were without negative association until that point. The gynecologist's negative assessment of her clitoris, compounded by the authority of the doctor's medical position, led Drew to question her former concept of self in light of this new and contrary information (Fisher and Groce, 1985).

Similarly, Suegee was raised without medical attempts to diminish her/his sexual ambiguity. Despite identifying her/his own gender as intersexed, Suegee was raised as female and when we met was living as a man, legally married to a woman with a young child. Here thirty-five-year-old Suegee describes how she/he experienced positive reactions to her/his body:

> It was at some point in my youth when I was playing doctor with other kids, or playing take off your clothes and show and tell, and realizing that I was different from anybody else there. And I also remember it wasn't a big deal at all.
>
> Everybody was like, "Wow! That's cool. Hey, you look like this, I look like this. Oh, yeah cool, fine, whatever." And that wasn't really a big deal at all.

Similar to Drew, Suegee did not have negative associations with her/his genitalia until she/he went to see a gynecologist at the age of sixteen.

> When I was 16 and I went off to see a gynecologist for the first time, which I was so excited [about]; I was like, "Oh boy! I'll get a whole bunch of answers." And she could just stutter out that she could recommend a good surgeon. And that was about it. She decided to examine my genitals and she was way too interested in examining my genitals. She was like... got me up in the stirrups and she's going, "Wow. Wow, that's...that's big! That's, that's real big!" And she was totally insensitive and completely just mesmerized by what she found.

But unlike Suegee and Drew, 95 percent of the people I spoke with underwent repeated medical examinations and procedures to downplay their physiological differences. And because they received extensive and prolonged reflections of themselves as pathological, many internalized feelings of inadequacy and shame. The inability to deflect negative interpretations of self may be one of the most harmful and traumatizing aspects of being intersexed in a society that adheres to the medical "correction" of such variation. As a result, the attempt to develop a coherent and positive concept of self amid continuous attempts to "fix" or change one's sex may be a project doomed to failure. According to J8, who was a thirty-six-year-old graduate student when we spoke,[3]

> The primary challenge [of being born intersexed] is childhood; parents and doctors thinking they should fix you. That can be devastating not just from the perspective of having involuntary surgery, but it's even more devastating to people's ability to develop a sense of self. I have heard from people who are really shattered selves, they don't have a concept of who they are. The core of their being is shame in their very existence. And that's what's been done to them by people thinking that intersexuality is a shameful secret that needs to be fixed. So I think for most people the biggest challenge is not the genital mutilation, but the psychic mutilation.

According to Goffman, differences that become socially stigmatized are those that are easily seen, such as the differences found among wheelchair users, amputees, and people with obvious facial scarring. Because clothing typically covers genitalia, genital differences are not readily visible (Goffman, 1963). Thus, intersexuals' genitalia must be made visible in order to allow for stigmatization. Repeated genital exams are a part of the medical protocol for assessing intersex patients' physiological development. Often, these examinations are performed with several doctors present, for the purpose of teaching medical residents, interns, and other clinicians about sexual ambiguity firsthand. The participants spoke frequently of the shame associated with such public displays of their "private parts." As Goffman noted, lacking

control over others' access to one's body leaves individuals feeling threatened and out of control, as though "the stigmatized individual is a person who can be approached by strangers at will" (Goffman, 1963:16).

Several participants relayed stories about lacking autonomy during group medical examinations. Because these group examinations were a common element of their histories, several developed their own names for the alienating genital exam to express their feelings of being put on display. Some of these labels reflect the participants' feelings of being exhibited in a contemporary medical version of the freak show, such as "the dog and pony show" and "the parade." Carol, a thirty-eight-year-old social worker, wife, and mother, whose intersexuality was not apparent until her teenage years, was also the object of study at grand rounds when she was hospitalized for her upcoming orchiectomy, which is a procedure that removes abdominal testicles to ward off the possibility that they will become cancerous. At the time, Carol did not know that she was intersexed or that she had testicles or even the reason for her impending surgery. She spoke candidly of the shame and humiliation of one of the many "parades" to which she was subjected during her hospitalization at the age of nineteen:

> A few hours after I [checked in], the parade started. I stopped counting after one hundred. But I'm guessing about one hundred and twenty-five physicians, interns, [and] residents paraded by my bed over those five days that I was admitted to the hospital. I counted literally one hundred and then quit counting because I didn't want to know. They came in groups. They just stood around my bed in a semicircle and talked. The doctor would give a little bit of a case history. He just said things like, "One hundred twenty-four pounds . . . five foot eleven and three quarters" . . . and things like that. I got so numb to it that I was eating and a parade of about ten came in at once and I kept eating, and I just lifted my gown and kept eating. And they all touched, poked, looked, mumbled, and then left. And I don't even remember looking at them. [I] put [my gown] down [and] kept eating.

What makes Carol's experience with hospitalization at the age of nineteen even more alarming is that when she went to the hospital, she thought she was simply there for a checkup and had no idea that surgery to remove her abdominal testicles was impending. After she overheard the hospital staff discussing her surgery, she inquired as to its purpose and was given little to no information. In her words,

> [I said to the doctor] as he was leaving, "Excuse me, the nurse said I'm having surgery," and he said, "Yes it'll be first thing in the morning." And I said, "For what?" and he said, "Don't worry, everything will be fine." And I said, "Why? Fine from what? Why am I having surgery?" And he said, "Well, your condition has gonads that could have abnormal cell growth, and we must remove them before it gets out of hand." And I said, "I have cancer, don't I?" And he said, "Oh don't worry about it. Don't worry about it, you're just fine. No, no, no, don't be silly. No, you don't have cancer. Don't worry." I said, "Well, then, why do I have...." "Don't worry about it, you're just fine." And I thought, "He's lying. He is lying; I have cancer." 'Cause that was the best diagnosis I'd come up with yet.

FEARING THE UNKNOWN: "WHAT KIND OF MONSTER AM I?"

As was true of Carol's experience, one of the most common themes in intersexuals' stories centers on the lack of full disclosure by clinicians and family members regarding the true nature of their intersexed conditions. Withholding information from the individuals only compounds their feelings of confusion and shame because they are told that there is something wrong with them, but they cannot and should not know the specific details of their condition. For example, Sarah, a fifty-six-year-old retired community college professor and library cataloger, spoke of the silence and secrecy she experienced in her late twenties when trying to ascertain the details of her own anatomy from her physicians. As she put it:

> They wouldn't tell me anything. I knew that there was more to it than all this. I knew that I wasn't being

told the truth, but there was no way anybody was gonna tell me the truth. It was such a mess. There was so much lying and symboling going on that it's a wonder I ever figured it out. Mostly everybody figured it out for themselves.

In another case, Flora had the following experience with a genetic counselor when she was twenty-four:

> [The geneticist] said, "I'm obliged to tell you that certain details of your condition have not been divulged to you, but I cannot tell you what they are because they would upset you too much." So she's telling us we don't know everything, but she can't tell us what it is because it's too horrible.

Indeed, lacking peer contact with other intersexuals only served to further the participants' difficulty in formulating a coherent and stable self-concept because the participants had few, if any, accurate points of social comparison (Jones et al., 1984). Of this alienation, Tiger, who was subjected to sixteen failed genital surgeries in the hope that he would eventually be able to urinate from the tip of his penis, said, "The isolation is the *most* punishing aspect of this. You *really* do grow up with the internal sense of absolute freakishness." Having dealt with her difference in complete isolation all her life before finding a support group, Sherri, a thirty-nine-year-old lawyer said,

> The cruelest punishment we inflict on prisoners is solitary confinement. And intersex people have lived lives of solitary confinement. And I think that that is such a personal holocaust. Because to be completely separated from others, to not know that there are others, to only know it intellectually, but not know it viscerally is, without a doubt, solitary confinement.

In addition to experiencing their bodies as frightening and worthy of shame, many who had genital surgeries emphasized that the very operations that were intended to assuage their feelings of difference only served to deepen their sense of alienation. In reflecting upon the clitoral recession she underwent at age seven, Faye, a thirty-year-old scholar, spouse, and mother, said:

I looked back on it and thought, this must have been really necessary. And that sort of went with me through childhood. If they would do this to me, it must be that I'm unacceptable as I am. The point is the emotional damage you do by telling someone that "You're so fuckin' ugly that we couldn't send you home to your parents the way you were." I mean, give the parents some credit. Teach them. Help them to deal with their different child.

SEEDS OF CHANGE—SEEKING COMPREHENSIVE INFORMATION AND SIMILAR OTHERS

Regardless of how the quest for information was initiated, the participants invariably made a commitment to learning more about themselves, ultimately seeking additional information about their bodies. In doing so, they turned to medical professionals and their families for answers. Such efforts often proved to be irritating or fruitless when many medical professionals denied them access to accurate information about their diagnoses or medical histories. For this reason, the participants often found it necessary to be both cunning and assertive in their quest for information. Carol recalled one such attempt to acquire additional information from the surgeon who removed her abdominal testicles when she was nineteen years old. Here, she relays a conversation with this doctor when she was twenty-one years old, during which she chose to lie to elicit her true chromosomal makeup. Her method was successful in the end:

I said [to my doctor], "I have one more question for you. I would like to know what I have that necessitated that you removed my gonads." And he said, "Well, you're just fine, there's nothing wrong." I said, "Listen, for *years* I thought I had a debilitating condition. I thought I perhaps had a progressive disease. I really believed that I possibly could still have cancer, even though you removed the unusual cells. I need to know what I have." And he said, "You don't need to worry about it, *really.* It's not something that you need

to know." I said, "I need to know." And I thought, "He's not going to tell me. He's not gonna tell me. I *know* he's not going to tell me." And so I thought, "I've gotta either walk out and find somebody else [to tell me the truth] or I gotta nail this guy to the wall." And all of a sudden it hit me, I said, "Listen, I need to know because I am going into the Olympics this summer and I need to know if I'm going to test XY or XX." And he just froze. And he just looked totally panicked. And then he just dropped all pretense and he leaned over, he shook my hand with those great big long penetrating fingers, and he said, "Congratulations. You are such an intelligent woman. Congratulations for figuring it out." I said, "What did I figure it out? Do I have [androgen insensitivity syndrome]? And am I XY?" and he said, "Yes." And I said, "Well thanks for finally telling me the truth. Do I have cancer?" and he said, "No." And I said, "So, why did you remove them? Did my gonads have cancer? Were they cancerous?" He said, "There was some abnormal cell growth, but, no they weren't cancerous per se." "Where are my gonads?" I said. And he said, "Well, I sent them to the Clark Institute for inclusion in a research project." And I said, "And *what* did they learn about my gonads?!" and he said, "Um, ah, well, ah, I, I . . ." I said, "I would like to have copies of the research, please. Would you be able to get me copies of my research? I would like to find out *what* my gonads were all about, please." And he said, "Well I suppose I could," and I said, "I would also like to know if you have any more information on [androgen insensitivity syndrome] because I would like to read about it and learn more about it." He said, "If you insist."

Having successfully moved to a place of externalizing the dissatisfaction with their bodies and themselves and refocusing it on the source of that shame, as Carol conveyed, the participants were able to progress toward a greater acceptance and understanding of themselves. This development was easily notable in the participants' rejection of pathological references to the self. As Jana explained:

Intersexuality is not a disease. Nobody dies from Klinefelter's syndrome, for example. It's not a disease. I'm not even gonna say it's an abnormality. I simply say it's a variation. Now I like my body, and I think I would have liked my body when I didn't like my body if I had known *why* it was like it is. This is the way I am, and I can accept that now. And I think I could have accepted it then, had I known, but I didn't know.

Learning to demedicalize their identities and accept themselves as healthy human beings often left the participants with feelings of pride in their difference. As Robin said,

I feel special. My [intersex] has made me feel special, and it finally makes me understand why I am the way I am. It has made a big difference because I feel complete. I have found a part of myself that was lost.

Through this process of self-discovery, several participants became aware of other intersexuals' existence via electronic and print media, such as the Internet, television, and newspapers. While this initial association was certainly powerful, the connection remained incomplete for some until actual face-to-face meetings took place. The opportunity to meet other intersexuals signaled the end to a lifetime of seclusion. Melody, Claire, and Martha articulated the power of finding out they were not the only intersexuals after a lifetime of being sure that they would never encounter another human being with a body like theirs. In Melody's words, "You can't imagine what it was like! What a relief to find people and not to be alone! It was just incredible. It's like being green in a world of blue, and suddenly you find another green person. It was unbelievable. It was just really unbelievable." In Claire's account, "It's been incredibly freeing because there is that sense of not only finding someone like you, but finding a whole community where you belong. There's that wonderful sense of, 'Oh my god, I'm not alone.'" In a similar conversation, Martha added:

After having lived all my life in isolation with this, suddenly to hear another person speak the words that I have spoken in the past; share the thoughts that I've had. Well what it felt like was that I've been living on this alien planet, portraying myself, passing myself off as an earthling, and I've met someone from, one of my people, from this other planet. You know?

HERMAPHRODITES WITH ATTITUDE: EVIDENCE OF INTERSEX PRIDE

Having found others with whom to relate, many participants spoke directly to the importance of using social visibility as a strategy for destigmatization and empowerment. Here, Tiger speaks of his appearances on television talk shows in an effort to educate lay audiences about intersex and externalize his prior feelings of shame:

Becoming a person who is comfortable standing up in public, literally on television and saying, "No matter what you think of how I look or how I speak, no matter what I've done to fit into this world, I am not male or I am not female. And probably neither are you." To be in the position [of] making those kinds of statements and having all the signs and facts to back up my position, it's very exciting. This is a dramatic level of self-acceptance that I have fought with and been tortured by all my life. And to have come to a place where I realize that mine is a position of strength, *not* of disadvantageous exclusion, which is all it had ever been before... it's a good place to come to.

Similarly, in a rather gutsy and subversive move, the founding director of the Intersex Society of North America chose to embrace the alienating and shameful word *hermaphrodite* in the title of the group's newsletter. Speaking of her decision to do so, Cheryl said:

I was so tickled with the fact that we had made this incredibly traumatic thing into something with humor in it. And we came up with the name *Hermaphrodites with Attitude.* I thought of myself as incredibly subversive here. Here are all these little subversive messages winding their way out into the world. And [the newsletter] got *all* over the place. So many people told me, "I just saw the words *Hermaphrodites with Attitude,* and it changed my life in that moment. I was petrified and traumatized, that word had been so painful and yet, there it was out there. Just out there and then I picked up the newsletter, and it was my story on every page."

IMPLICATIONS

The implementation of radical, invasive, and life-changing medical sex-assignment procedures for children who are born with bodies whose sexual anatomy is labeled as different from the norm was standard practice until recently. However, the intersex patient advocacy and medical reform movement that began in the 1990s has gained tremendous legitimacy and ground in a short time. What's more, the patients' rights movement has upset this formerly unquestioned approach in medical education and practice and placed it into its current state of flux, controversy, crisis, and reform (Zucker, 2002).

One of the major lessons from these narratives is that sexual variation is nothing to be ashamed of and that it would not be experienced as shameful if it were recast as normal. Because sexual anatomy occurs on a continuum, diversity and variety are to be expected. Doctors, parents, and teachers have the ability and authority to reframe sexual variation in this way by responding to it with indifference. In addition to suspending unnecessary surgery on people with a sexual anatomy that is deemed ambiguous, these key socializing agents can truly destigmatize sexual variation by paying little attention to it.

Doctors, parents, and others have the ability to normalize sexual variation. In the meantime, they can help those who are labeled as intersexed by clearing the skeletons out of the closet and focusing on how best to love and support people who are cast as different. As the people in my study demonstrate, one of the most effective means of coping with difference is through relationships with others who are similarly alienated. Doctors and parents can easily assist those they care for by connecting them with the tremendous resources offered by intersex support and advocacy organizations. Doctors and parents can also engage in their own networking with the rapidly developing groups that are aimed at family and medical support, advocacy, and information exchange.

TO THE STORIES ONE LAST TIME

I opened this article with the words of one of the women I interviewed. I return to her words again, at the close, because she so eloquently conveyed the value of normalizing intersex through peer support, humor, and advocacy. Throughout her interview, Sherri spoke of feeling both grateful for and indebted to her support group for literally "saving her life." In closing, I turn to her resolution to carry her activism to her grave:

> I'll never repay, *ever,* in this lifetime I will never repay what I've been given. After I die, it all goes to the support group. My will is set up so that it all goes to the support group. My instructions in my will are to make my funeral as cheap as possible so that more money will go to the support group. That's where I want it to go. That's all I want it to go for. With the instruction that my headstone have the [support group's] web site address on it so that at least after I'm dead, people can still, I hope, pass by my gravestone and find information.

NOTES

1. Most research participants chose their own pseudonyms to be used in the presentation and publication of this research. Notably, 27 percent of those I interviewed chose to use their real names. I do not distinguish here or elsewhere between those who chose pseudonyms and those who did not.
2. National Center for Health Statistics (2001). Note that others have projected an annual birth rate of 1,500 to 2,000 intersexed children in the United States (Beh and Diamond, 2000).
3. This participant chose "J8" as her/his pseudonym. Rather than impose my own names on participants for the sake of legibility, I honored their choices in naming themselves.

REFERENCES

Becker, Howard. 1963. *The Outsiders.* New York: Free Press.
Beh, Glenn Hazel, and Milton Diamond. 2000. "An Emerging Ethical and Medical Dilemma: Should Physicians Perform Sex Assignment Surgery on Infants with Ambiguous Genitalia?" *Michigan Journal of Gender & Law* 7(1):1–63.
Blackless, Melanie, Anthony Charuvastra, Amanda Derryck, Anne Fausto-Sterling, Karl Lauzanne,

and Ellen Lee. 2000. "How Sexually Dimorphic Are We?" *American Journal of Human Biology* 12:151–166.

Cooley, Charles Horton. 1964 [1902]. *Human Nature and Social Order.* New York: Charles Scribner's Sons.

Davis, Lennard J. 1995. *Enforcing Normalcy: Disability, Deafness, and the Body.* New York: Verso.

Desai, Sindoor S. 1997. "Down Syndrome: A Review of the Literature." *Oral Surgery, Oral Medicine, Oral Pathology, Oral Radiology, and Endodontics* 84:279–285.

Diamond, Milton, and Keith Sigmundson. 1997. "Management of Intersexuality: Guidelines for Dealing with Persons with Ambiguous Genitalia." *Archives of Pediatric Adolescent Medicine* 151:1046–1050.

Dreger, Alice Domurat. 1998a. "'Ambiguous Sex'—or Ambivalent Medicine? Ethical Issues in the Treatment of Intersexuality." *Hastings Center Report* 28(3):24–36.

———. 1998b. *Hermaphrodites and the Medical Invention of Sex.* Cambridge, Mass.: Harvard University Press.

Edgerton, Robert. 1964. "Pokot Intersexuality: An East African Example of the Resolution of Sexual Incongruity." *American Anthropologist* 66:1288–1299.

Fiedler, Leslie. 1978. *Freaks: Myths and Images of the Secret Self.* New York: Anchor Books, Doubleday.

Fisher, Sue, and Stephen B. Groce. 1985. "Doctor-Patient Negotiation of Cultural Assumptions." *Sociology of Health & Illness* 7:342–374.

Goffman, Erving. 1963. *Stigma: Notes on the Management of Spoiled Identity.* Englewood Cliffs: Prentice-Hall.

Hewitt, John P. 1970. *Social Stratification and Deviant Behavior.* New York: Random House.

———. 1989. *Dilemmas of the American Self.* Philadelphia: Temple University Press.

Hird, Myra J. 2000. "Gender's Nature: Intersexuality, Transsexualism and the 'Sex'/'Gender' Binary." *Feminist Theory* 1:347–364.

Holstein, James A., and Jaber F. Gubrium. 2000. *The Self We Live By: Narrative Identity in a Postmodern World.* New York: Oxford University Press.

Jones, Edward E., Amerigo Farina, Albert H. Hastorf, Hazel Markus, Dale T. Miller, and Robert A. Scott. 1984. *Social Stigma: The Psychology of Marked Relationships.* New York: W. H. Freeman.

Kessler, Suzanne J. 1998. *Lessons from the Intersexed.* New Brunswick, N.J.: Rutgers University Press.

Mead, George Herbert. 1934. *Mind, Self and Society.* Chicago: University of Chicago Press.

Mills, C. Wright. 1959. *The Sociological Imagination.* New York: Oxford University Press.

Money, John. 1989 "Hermaphrodites: The Sexually Unfinished." *The Geraldo Rivera Show.* National Broadcasting Company, July 27.

National Center for Health Statistics. 2001. "Births: Preliminary Data for 2000." *National Vital Statistics Reports* 49(5). (PHS) 2001–1120. Washington, D.C.: U.S. Government Printing Office.

Plummer, Ken. 1975. *Sexual Stigma.* Boston: Routledge & Kegan Paul.

———. 1995. *Telling Sexual Stories: Power, Change and Social Worlds.* New York: Routledge.

Preves, Sharon E. 2003 *Intersex and Identity: The Contested Self.* New Brunswick, N.J.: Rutgers University Press.

Roberts, Helen E., Janet D. Cragan, Joanne Cono, Muin J. Khoury, Mark R. Weatherly, and Cynthia A. Moore. 1998. "Increased Frequency of Cystic Fibrosis Among Infants with Jejunoileal Atresia." *American Journal of Medical Genetics* 78:446–449.

Strauss, Anselm, and Juliet Corbin. 1991. "Experiencing Body Failure and a Disrupted Self-Image." In *Creating Sociological Awareness,* ed. Anselm Strauss, 341–359. New Brunswick, N.J.: Transaction Publishers.

West, Candace, and Don H. Zimmerman. 1987. "Doing Gender." *Gender and Society* 1:125–151.

Zucker, Kenneth J. 2002. "Intersexuality and Gender Identity Differentiation." *Journal of Pediatric Adolescence and Gynecology* 15:3–13.

AM I OBSESSED?

Gender Identity Disorder, Stress, and Obsession

DISCUSSION QUESTIONS

1. What are the consequences of pathologizing transgender people? For society more generally? What theoretical assumptions about sex, gender, and sexuality are embedded in this perspective?
2. How may other socially constructed categories, such as race or class, shape the experience and opportunities of transgender people?
3. What social institutions and structures are missing from the article that a transgender person must navigate? How can nontransgender people support gender-variant individuals within these social institutions?

I do my best not to speed when I am driving, and not for the sake of following the laws of the road. I try to schedule medical appointments with my life partner or, at least, with a supportive friend. I wait until the last possible moment to use a public restroom. I am always alert, constantly suspecting everyone as a potential perpetrator. I wear clothes that never even hint at my body's actual shape and size.

On the surface, it may seem that these are just idiosyncratic tendencies. However, upon further inspection, my actions are precise, deliberate, and carried out with such tenacity that they may even be considered *obsessive*. Yes, obsessive. I find I experience recurrent thoughts, images, and impulses that center on my gender and gender expression. Most of the time, obsession is considered a psychological disorder; however, my obsession has social foundations, and, I will argue, it is quite reasonable given the social context. Society is literally making me obsessed.

BRIEF HISTORY

Medical discourse on transgender identity began appearing in journals at the end of the nineteenth and early twentieth centuries. Historically, conceptions and explanations of gender variance focused on transsexuals. Today, the term *transgender* operates as an overarching umbrella to include multiple gender-variant identities, not just transsexuals; individuals who have moved further away from the so-called standard male and standard female identities.

Magnus Hirschfeld, a medical doctor from Germany, is credited with identifying "transsexualism." He advocated on behalf of transsexual people considering them "like homosexuals, to be one of innumerable types of 'sexual intermediaries' who existed on a spectrum from a hypothetical 'pure male' to 'pure female'" (Stryker and Whittle, 2006:28). Hirschfeld argued that transsexualism was too complex to reduce the understanding to some form of fetishism or psychopathology (Stryker and Whittle, 2006). Contrary to Hirschfeld, Richard von Krafft-Ebing, an influential professor of psychiatry in Vienna, can be partially credited with pathologizing nonprocreative sexual behavior because he thought that persons engaging in such behavior were "profoundly disturbed, and considered their desire for self-affirming transformation to be psychotic" (Stryker and Whittle, 2006:21). There was considerable emphasis on complete medical surgical changes during the early twentieth century in the initial development of transsexual "treatment." A real tension between medicine and psychology arose that affected the progress made in the United States.

If we fast-forward into the middle of the twentieth century, U.S. medical doctors were separately trying to identify an internal source of gender expression and conformity. A few private medical doctors, like Harry Benjamin,[1] advocated surgically altering the body. However, many doctors simply refused surgery as an option, basing their decisions on "moral and/or religious grounds," along with their "fear of a malpractice suit and reluctance to explain their actions to a local medical society" (Califia, 1997:65).

The increasing rejection of surgery as a legitimate option provided room for psychologists and psychoanalysts during the middle of the twentieth century to emerge as "experts." Developments among many psychologists and psychoanalysts understood gender and sexuality as separate from the body; thus, many saw gender "contradictions" as a psychological condition. In fact, Robert Stoller, an American psychoanalytic psychologist, in collaboration with his colleague Ralph Greenson (Meyerowitz, 2002), developed the three-part model of human psychosexual structures: "biological sex, social gender role, and subjective or psychological gender identity" (Stryker and Whittle, 2006:53). This theory of a psychological gender identity is still used today to understand a person's sense of herself or himself as a woman or man. Another influential contributor to the field of psychosexual understandings of gender variance is Richard Green, also an American psychiatrist. Green suggested that,

"Ultimately a comprehensive understanding, evaluation, and management of transsexualism will take into account the extensively rooted sources of this psychosexual phenomenon" because he realized the existence of cross-gender identified persons and the varied embodiments of gender expression among different cultures and across times (Califia, 1997:62).

Many psychologists who were concerned with cross-gender identification focused on prevention among young people (Meyerowitz, 2002). Several gender-identity clinics were established throughout the 1960s and 1970s that ultimately produced the needed medical terminology, meticulously describing gender nonconformity and prescribing "cures." Countless children were institutionalized in these psychiatric evaluation centers because their parents or guardians thought their gender behavior and expression contradicted their anatomically assigned sex category. Psychological rehabilitation seemed to be the mission of some of the most famous private and government-funded gender identity clinics housed at UCLA,[2] SUNY Stony Brook, the Roosevelt Institute in New York City, Fuller Theological Seminary, and the Logos Research Institute (Burke, 1996; Califia, 1997). Thus, "as funding for the study and treatment of gender nonconforming children increased, a need to create a specific psychiatric diagnosis for the condition" emerged (Burke, 1996:60).

While gay and lesbian activists successfully fought for the removal of homosexuality from the *Diagnostic and Statistical Manual of Mental Disorders* in 1973 (Piontek, 2006), both gender identity disorder (GID) in children and discrete psychiatric syndromes in adult transsexual and transvestite individuals were introduced seven years later in the third edition. As Eve Kosofsky Sedgwick (1991:21) explained, "The *de*pathologization of an atypical sexual object-choice can be yoked to the *new* pathologization of an atypical gender identification" [italics in original]. Despite inconclusive scientific evidence, many scientists continue this line of research with scholarly hopes of identifying hormones and genes that determine or, at least, influence an individual's gender expression and sexual desire.

GENDER IDENTITY (DIS)ORDER: A SOCIAL STIGMA

The construction of gender variance as a pathology and a "disorder" is extremely problematic. I am not psychologically disturbed, nor do I consider myself to have an illness, and many other transgender persons feel the same (see Finney Boylan, 2003; Green, 2004; Kailey, 2005). One outcome of the GID diagnosis is the development of social stigma. Erving Goffman (1963) described stigma as discrediting attributes that are considered failings, shortcomings, or handicaps. These psychological classifications enforce dichotomous social constructs of gender and define any deviation as a problem of individual character (Goffman, 1963). So, while some members of the transgender community embrace the "transgender" label, others resist it and see it as a form of "othering." [3] Rejecting the label is tricky, however. Accessing partial or complete insurance benefits to cover transgender-related procedures, which few insurance policies include, requires the GID diagnosis.

> The Harry Benjamin International Gender Dysphoria Association's Standards of Care for the Treatment of Gender Identity Disorders require that the transgender-specific medical interventions of hormone therapy and sex reassignment surgery be recommended by a mental health provider after a thorough psychological evaluation and, in most cases, a period of psychotherapy (Bockting et al., 2004:279).

Since the GID diagnosis is needed for hormones and/or surgery, many choose to embrace it strategically. Judith Butler (2006:280) questioned, however, "whether submitting to the diagnosis does not involve, more or less consciously, a certain subjection to the diagnosis such that one does end up internalizing some aspect of the diagnosis, conceiving of oneself as mentally ill or 'failing' in normality, or both, even as one seeks to take a purely instrumental attitude toward these terms."

I have been forced to ask myself, do I have GID? Have I internalized these medical and psychosexual constructions? Did I have this *mental disorder* as a child, or do I still have it as an adult? Did I ever try

urinating in a standing position? Did I think I might grow a penis? Did I ever believe I was born the wrong sex? Am I distressed because I am uncomfortable with my physical body? These questions highlight my obsession with gender expression and, even more important, the social origins of this obsession. It is the pathological construction of sex and gender variation that pushes anyone who does not conform to become obsessed.

MY OBSESSIONS

VIOLENCE

The first and most important issue is others' perceptions of me. One transgender murder per month [4] in the United States would make *you* obsessive about your gender appearance and acceptance, too. Transgender persons have an elevated risk of becoming victims of various types of transphobic [5] crimes. In the past few years, the media have shone a spotlight on the dangers of being transidentified. Films like *Boys Don't Cry* and *A Girl Like Me: The Gwen Araujo Story* have presented the true stories of transgender teenagers who were murdered. These violent crimes have a chilling effect on the transgender community nationwide.

"Gender based violence and discrimination results in an environment in which covert if not overt permission is given to society to 'punish' people for gender transgression" (Lombardi et al., 2001:91). As Califia (1997:82) wrote, "It is our fear and hatred of people who are differently-gendered that need to be cured, not their synthesis of the qualities we think of as maleness and femaleness, masculinity and femininity." If this fear and hatred continue, so will my obsession with how I appear to others.

Murder is just one form of violence that is perpetrated against transgender people. In fact, Lombardi et al. (2001) surveyed 402 transgender persons in 1997 and found that over half the participants had experienced verbal harassment at some point during their lifetime and 25 percent had experienced a violent incident. The same study indicated that being stalked was the second most common experience, and being assaulted without a weapon was the third most common event. Participants younger than age 18 were underrepresented (0.5 percent) in this study, leaving transgender youths' experiences of violence unrecorded.

Most transgender youths face significant prejudice and discrimination at school from their teachers, staff, and administrators, as well as from other students (Grossman and D'Augelli, 2006; Guiterrez, 2004). From abusive language to teachers' prejudice to unapproachable school counselors, school environments are unsafe for most lesbian, gay, bisexual, and transgender (LGBT) students (Price and Telljohann, 1991; Telljohann et al., 1995). "Nearly 70 percent of lesbian, gay, bisexual and transgendered youth report experiencing some form of harassment or violence in school, and they are three times more likely to attempt suicide than other youth, according to the National Mental Health Association" (Boykin, 2004).

Internalized homophobia and transphobia must also be examined. A San Francisco-based study of 515 transgender persons, conducted by Clements-Nolle, Marx, and Katz (2006), revealed that attempted suicide was higher for transgender persons younger than age twenty-five (47 percent) than transgender persons older than age twenty-five (30 percent). I am thankful to have passed the twenty-five year mark but am concerned that transgender youths have minimal space (literally and figuratively) to share experiences and gender "obsessions" with others in a safe environment.[6]

DRAMATIZING MY LIFE: THE MEDIA

The media provide viewers with exposure to gender specialists, gender therapists, psychotherapists, and psychologists, presenting authority figures who use medical and pathologizing language to establish a psychological framework. These trained professionals ultimately gain the audience's trust using highly specialized language that reinforces the medical paradigm and the "need" for gender transitions.

Television is a popular medium that spectacularizes gender variance through investigative lenses

of "unbelievable" transformations, capitalizing on before-and-after photographs. For instance, clips of transgender women applying makeup or practicing their voice lessons on *Oprah* (October 12, 2004) and dramatized presentations of their wives devastated over the loss of their once-heterosexual relationship and questions about the wives' own heterosexuality on *Grey's Anatomy* (November 9, 2006) have made these stories about real-life experiences voyeuristically engaging. Nancy Nangeroni, a transgender community activist, writer, and musician, began her own radio program after feeling poorly represented on numerous public television and radio shows (MacKenzie and Nangeroni, 2004). Aware of the media's goal to sensationalize transgender persons, I often feel obsessed with trying to offer an alternative analysis to these representations when I am aware of their showings.

I personally feel the effects of "TV knowledge" when people around me seek to understand my transgender identity with questions akin to, "So you're stuck inside a female body, but you really feel like a man?" because some transgender representatives who are portrayed in the media use these types of statements. Although they may not mean to, they simplify and maintain the gender binary of man and woman. This is not meant to discount those who feel trapped but, rather, to raise awareness of the complex realities of biological sex and gender expression and diversity within the transgender community. When I am asked this question, I explain that I am not "stuck" anywhere and that I do not think framing gender this way is useful. However, my own experience and expertise are often challenged as these people attempt to take on the "expert" role, and I become the pathologized one. This only reinforces my obsession with depathologizing gender variation.

The professional "transexperts" who are seen on television call upon the GID diagnosis and therefore supply their viewers with a psychological framework to comprehend transgender people. I have yet to witness one of these experts share the scientific evidence of the immense biological variation found within humans—that is, chromosomally, hormonally, and genitally. Nor do these experts invoke history to explain the ever-changing expression of gender in the United States that relies on hegemonic notions of white, Christian, middle-class, male, able-bodied heterosexuality. Perhaps the most interesting aspect of the authoritative psychological voice is the intentional exclusion of when or how GID became a diagnosable mental illness. This omission helps naturalize what is actually a constructed diagnosis. The limited perspective provided by the media leaves me in the position of having to refute this "knowledge" and provide alternative perspectives. Taking responsibility for challenging other people's understanding of sex, gender, and sexuality becomes extremely stressful.

MY BODY

My resistance to the sex and gender binaries, as well as GID, could potentially be misunderstood, since I have made "transitional" decisions. For instance, my determination to have "top surgery," otherwise known as a double mastectomy, and to receive testosterone injections (t-shots) may seem to reinforce dichotomous gender categories. However, masculinizing my chest is just one part of who I am, not my entire being. This surgery will free me from my obsession with how my chest appears and is perceived by others, but it will not erase my living and being addressed as a girl and woman for twenty-two years. The decision to take testosterone stems from my desire to have a deeper voice, not because I feel like a man in a woman's body. This wish does not negate my navigation through and appreciation of androgynous space and embodiment. I am not intentionally supporting the binary sex and gender systems but, rather, acting to limit my obsessions within these strictly controlled structures. My choices are constrained by the social context I must live in. These decisions led to new obsessions and stress, however. I became concerned about my family and how they would respond once they noticed the effects of t-shots, for example.

FAMILY: TAKING CONTROL

I have spent many hours thinking about my family's response and reaction to me as I safely become the person I am. How will my mother handle others seeing me as a man? Will she take responsibility for my identity, believing she has somehow failed me as a white, single, working mother of two? Will she succumb to the societal stereotypes that deviant and disturbed children come out of so-called broken families? Will my decisions push her over the edge? How is my homophobic brother going to respond? Will he use GID as a justification for keeping me away from his two-year-old daughter, my niece? Will I be allowed to watch her alone? Will he teach her to call me uncle? What is my distant father going to say? Will he blame my mother? Will he be willing to replace the old pictures of me with long hair, so my half-sisters can recognize me? What about my mother's parents, my only grandparents? Will Oma be just as emotionally devastated as she was when I came out to her as a lesbian? Will Opa stop talking to me because of his strongly committed Baptist beliefs? What about our longtime family friends? Will Oma and Opa still speak proudly about me to them? Will I still exist? Or will I disappear from their conversations altogether? Should I move to another city, so I do not have to confront my obsession and deal with the stress of explaining who I am?

It took many years to become confident with the idea that my life is my own, I can take control of it, and I am not responsible for anyone else. I told my mother I was starting testosterone almost a full year before I actually began. It was one of the hardest confessions I have ever had to make. I took a two-step approach: First, since I no longer lived at home, I wrote her a letter and left it on her bed to find when she arrived home. The final line read, *Please call me when you are finished reading this so I know you still love me.* The second step was meeting face to face to talk about my decision. My heart broke as I watched tears stream down her face that night. I devastated every dream she ever had for me. I was on the brink of changing the gender composition of her first-born child. And although I was to blame, I do not regret having that conversation with her. I knew I would never be able to mend her broken heart, but my decisions were important in order to live my life. I left my mother that night with swollen red eyes and tissues in hand.

The letter and conversation with my mother was the only premeditated session I had. Rather than obsessing and stressing over each conversation I would face, I decided it would be easier to inform my family and friends along the way as needed. Opportunities arose just a few short weeks after I started testosterone; some people noticed the subtle voice change immediately. On the one hand, I was thrilled to feel and hear an alteration in my voice, but in the midst of my excitement, I wondered what my brother and others thought when they heard my new tone—many never said a word. My plan to avoid stress was not entirely successful, however, as I spent hours stressing about what people thought, since their silence was indeed a response. Over time, my resolution to take the path of least resistance and not tell family members and friends about my decisions until needed began to disintegrate as I lost my courage to explain to my family *why* my voice was changing. Each time I spoke with my Oma on the phone, she would ask, *Are you sick? You sound sick. Are you sick?* My responses were like a broken record, constantly reassuring her that I was in good health. But I never had the nerve to tell her why my voice sounded the way it did. I had become so stressed about how my family was going to react that I literally stopped calling and became ultimately disconnected from the people I loved.

Isolation from my family took its toll, and for a time, my life at home did not fare any better, since the transition affected the intimacy I shared with my lover, my partner, my best friend. I was afraid that she, too, might resist my decisions and have difficulty with the changes it would bring to our relationship. Would her self-proclaimed identity as a lesbian deny our relationship if I no longer identified as such, or if strangers did not see us as a lesbian couple? How would she respond to my ever-changing body: the growth in body hair, the change in my sex drive, my skin shifting to a rougher texture, the modification in my pheromones, and the surgical procedure removing the breasts she had already redefined as masculine pecs? My fears that she only partially accepted

me emerged when we disagreed or spoke about future plans. I always assumed she was angry with me because of my choices. Her commitment, dedication, and, most importantly, love won out. She fought me long and hard, refusing to let me push her away. Instead, she transitioned with me. Through countless hours of encouragement and confirmation that her love is unconditional, she proved herself and, not surprisingly, became a part of the movement for transgender rights.

HEALTH CARE (MIS) TREATMENT

Most transgender persons have at least one horror story of institutional discrimination. I have one story of my own that has forcefully shaped each subsequent encounter I have had with the medical community. At age twenty-three, before I began testosterone, I was without health insurance. This should come as no surprise, considering that more than 43 million people younger than age sixty-five were uninsured in 2000 (Jillson, 2002). Unable to get rid of a powerful cold, I decided to visit the university student health center. I entered the office in what I considered "comfortable clothes" (e.g., a sweatshirt, sweatpants, T-shirt, and baseball cap), and, as with any first-time visit, I completed all the required paperwork. After my basic vitals were measured (blood pressure, fever, weight, height, and so forth), I patiently waited in a treatment room.

A male doctor and a female physician's assistant entered the room confidently and began to review my file while simultaneously asking me about my ailments and the reasons for my visit. Maybe the doctor's multitasking is what got him befuddled. He initially used male pronouns when speaking about me to his assistant but became confused when he looked at my intake form, which I had marked with the letter *F*. He did a sort of double-double-take: he looked at the chart, then back at me, then back at the chart, and right back at me. In a matter of seconds, something quite inappropriate transpired. To alleviate his confusion, he lifted the neckline of my shirt to look for the presence or absence of breasts to gauge my sex without permission or warning.

Not having any prior experience with this sort of abuse and invasion, I waited for the diagnosis and subsequent prescription and then left the clinic as fast as I could. This incident, which was out of my control, has produced more obsessive thoughts: am I going to be mistreated if, and when, I go to the doctor in the future? Will they humiliate me again? Will it be in the waiting room next time, in front of others? Will they tell me I am a "sick" person, yet refuse to treat my actual illness, as they did to transgender- and lesbian-identified Leslie Feinberg (1999) who had a temperature of 104 degrees but was refused treatment? Whenever I have to visit a medical or dental office, not to mention any other professional setting, I now experience high levels of stress.

Despite this stress, I am well aware that as a white middle-class person, my privilege mitigates this stress. As a consumer of health insurance, I have the privilege of seeking out transpositive health care providers. Besides having a comfortable and high-quality physician's visit, I am also ensured access to safe[7] prescription hormones and syringes. I do not have to rely on street hormones and shared needles like many young, poor, uninsured, urban, and transgender persons of color (Grossman and D'Augelli, 2006; Lombardi et al., 2001). One result of "black-market" hormones is the increased risk of HIV transmission from shared needles (Grossman and D'Augelli, 2006; Lombardi et al., 2001; Pettiway, 1996). I am free from this risk and stress, since I inject testosterone with clean needles in the comfort of my home. I have routine blood tests to measure the proper function of my liver and to monitor my cholesterol levels in case of increased hypertension. When it comes to health care, the most stress I have is finding a transpositive doctor.

EMPLOYMENT (MIS) FORTUNES

In 2005, I met an African American transwoman in Philadelphia, and we discussed some of our common stressors regarding employment. She had just obtained part-time employment working for a local community-based program designed by and for gender-variant persons. This program provides comprehensive HIV prevention and health education to many different clients.

At the time she was hired, her responsibilities included handing out information about safe-sex and safe-injection techniques to transgender persons working on the street. In what would be deemed an otherwise virtuous effort to discourage risky behaviors, she was extremely anxious about the work. Her stress resulted because of her shift: 10:00 p.m. to 2:00 a.m. Not only did she face the threat of physical assault, she was also at risk of harassment by the police. She explained, "I mean, I don't want to be arrested while I'm at work. I'll be scared to be doing my job. They'll [the police] think I'm selling or something and take me in." At that moment, I was reminded of just how pervasive gendered and racialized obsessions and stressors are in the transgender community.

She was, in fact, worried about being arrested or, at a minimum, being harassed by police officers who would be operating under the assumption that she was a sex worker. A simultaneous layer of complexity is the fact that whomever she talks to may become suspicious targets for the police as well. Her stress about the blatant presumption by the police force that transgender people who are out at night *must* be sex workers is a reality, especially in poverty-stricken urban areas. Our shared obsessions about physical safety—what to wear, how and with whom to communicate, what time our shifts are, and our geographic locations—are similar stressors. My relative privilege, however, provides a buffer, since I work at a university, and her responsibilities place her in a more vulnerable position.

Workplace obsession and stress seem to have two components. The first is being accepted and supported on the job. The second is the type of job a gender-variant person occupies. Discrimination claims are a little tricky, since there are currently no federal protections in place for gender-variant persons.[8] I am unaware of research that offers statistical data[9] on which professions value (e.g., invite and support) gender diversity and devalue (e.g., deny, demote, or fire) gender-variant persons; however, it is likely that there are systematic patterns adversely affecting transgender people by age, race, income, and ability. These struggles that directly affect living arrangements, the resources to pay for medical treatment, and the means to clothe and feed oneself (and others), are not shown on *Oprah* or *Grey's Anatomy*.

In fact, most of the stressors I face are not portrayed on the talk shows, docudramas made for television, or evening soap operas. Where is the portrayal of the real lives of transgender people in the United States? Who wants to know about the everyday violence perpetrated against transgender people? About the countless cases of employment discrimination? Or the transgender persons who are turned away from emergency rooms? The transgender parents who lose the rights to their biological children? Who shares these obsessions and stressors with us?

CONCLUSION

It is safe to say that both my mother and Oma obsess about my safety, too. They are fully aware of gender-based violence and do not want me added to the yearly statistics. My aunt always calls when she has watched a transgender-specific television show, mostly to share what she has learned and to ask for my perspective. My ever-increasingly tolerant brother has never invoked the constructed GID to deny a relationship with my niece, but instead playfully acknowledges my masculine appearance and my quasi-uncle status. A recent family vacation corroborated my mother's understanding of my (and other transgender people's) discomfort and the complications of sex-segregated facilities. We had to ask multiple park personnel if and where a family bathroom was located, walked fifteen minutes (one way) out of our intended direction, and made my overzealous cousins wait so I could visit the restroom *once* on our fifteen-hour-long outing.

I have found that sharing my obsessions and stressors with my family has since brought us together. I am no longer the only one worrying about my physical safety, experience with medical doctors, abuse by the authorities, and need for protection from my employers. The same family members I spent so much time worrying about have become a tremendous source of support. Just yesterday, my mother told me that one of her friend's grandchildren is expressing the desire to be a girl and said, "It's OK because the parents are very supportive." My obsessions and stress all have social, not psychological, foundations. They are a product of a social order that defines anyone who does not conform to our two-gender system as deviant and pathological. Because they are the result of social and cultural factors, they require social, not psychological, change. I have found it heartening in my own life to see this change begin in my own family.

AUTHOR'S NOTE

An update on my obsessions: I have recognized that my privilege (as a white, educated, able-bodied transman) substantially diminishes my life chances of being a victim of violence; my social statuses systematically offer financial and employment opportunities as well as access to places and spaces that others assume I belong in, or at least am not suspect when in them. The obsessions about my mother were all valid, and in three years I can proudly and admirably say that she has become an advocate. We have participated in our local PFLAG chapter to share our transition, together. She also, by herself, attended PFLAG specifically to support a mother as her child began the social and medical journey. And, I am just as proud of my brother as he has been the most cognizant and supportive of using *he, him,* and calling me his *brother.* We have never taught my niece about desired pronouns or my social role, as she has called me Uncle since the time she could speak the words. Recently she asked my aunt, *why is Uncle Tre wearing a girl's bathing suit?* referencing a picture as they surfed the album. My father, step mom, and two sisters have become much less distant and are transitioning too. The trans-advocate partner and I have taken different paths, and I know that her dedication and love are perfectly placed within the social justice projects that she has always fought for. In all of the relationships that I have committed to over the years, *I* still *exist.* They are still *proud of me.* And, they still *love me.*

APPENDIX: DIAGNOSTIC CRITERIA FOR GENDER IDENTITY DISORDER

A. *A strong persistent cross-gender identification* (not merely a desire for any perceived cultural advantages of being the other sex). In children, the disturbance is manifested by four (or more) of the following:

1. Repeatedly stated desire to be, or insistence that he or she is, the other sex.
2. In boys, preference for cross-dressing or simulating female attire; in girls, insistence on wearing only stereotypical masculine clothing.
3. Strong and persistent preferences for cross-sex roles in make believe play or persistent fantasies of being the other sex.
4. Intense desire to participate in the stereotypical games and pastimes of the other sex.
5. Strong preference for playmates of the other sex.

In adolescents and adults, the disturbance is manifested by symptoms such as a stated desire to be the other sex, frequent passing as the other sex, desire to live or be treated as the other sex, or the conviction that he or she has the typical feelings and reactions of the other sex.

B. *Persistent discomfort with his or her sex or sense of inappropriateness in the gender role of that sex.* In children, the disturbance is manifested by any of the following: In boys, assertion that his penis or testes are disgusting or will disappear or assertion that it would be better not to have a penis, or aversion toward rough-and-tumble play and rejection of male stereotypical toys, games, and activities. In girls, rejection of urinating in a sitting position, assertion that she has or will grow a penis, or assertion that she does not want to grow breasts or menstruate, or marked aversion toward normative feminine clothing.

In adolescents and adults, the disturbance is manifested by symptoms such as preoccupation with getting rid of primary and secondary sex characteristics (e.g., request for hormones, surgery, or other procedures to physically alter sexual characteristics to simulate the other sex) or belief that he or she was born the wrong sex.

C. *The disturbance is not concurrent with physical intersex condition.*

D. *The disturbance causes clinically significant distress or impairment in social, occupational, or other important areas of functioning.*

Code based on current age:

302.6 Gender Identity Disorder in Children
302.85 Gender Identity Disorder in Adolescents or Adults

Specify if (for sexually mature individuals):

Sexually Attracted to Males
Sexually Attracted to Females
Sexually Attracted to Both
Sexually Attracted to Neither

NOTES

1. Benjamin, a native German who immigrated to the United States before World War I, popularized the term *transsexual* through his advocacy on behalf of transgender persons. He did not support psychotherapy as a "cure." His relationship with Christine Jorgenson and his publication of *The Transsexual Phenomenon* in 1966 carved out a space for him to establish much of the medical practices that transgender persons go through today.
2. Stoller helped establish this clinic (Stryker and Whittle, 2006).
3. For example, Guiterrez (2004:72) shared the voice of a young self-identified woman, who said, "I don't consider myself transgendered, you know. I feel like me. We're women...it's a label that shouldn't be used."
4. *Remembering Our Dead,* a product of Gender Education & Advocacy, states that more than one antitransgender murder has been reported in the U.S. media every month since 1989, and many fatal assaults go unreported as gender-based violence, making this statistic low.
5. *Transphobic* is simply an adaptation of *homophobic* and expresses a phobia and hatred toward gender-nonconforming persons.
6. For more information on gender-based violence against youth, visit Gender Public Advocacy Coalition at www.gpac.org.
7. "Safe" is in quotes because no research that I am aware of has provided conclusive evidence of the safety of injecting androgens.
8. For more on transgender policies and issues in the workplace, visit Transgender Law and Policy Institute (www.transgenderlaw.org), National Center for Transgender Equality (www.nctequality.org), Sylvia Rivera Law Project (www.srlp.org), and Human Rights Campaign (www.hrc.org).
9. See Schilt (2006) for a qualitative project on transmen's experiences in the workplace and thus the visibility of gendered workplace disparities and disadvantages.

REFERENCES

Balagot, J. 2002. "In Memory of Gwen Araujo." Retrieved December 9, 2006, from http://www.transyouth.net/stories/gwen_araujo.html

Bockting, W., B. Robinson, A. Benner, and K. Scheltema. 2004. "Patient Satisfaction with Transgender Health Services." *Journal of Sex & Marital Therapy,* 30:277–294.

Boykin, K. 2004. "Sakia Gunn Remembered." Retrieved December 9, 2006, from http://www.keithboykin.com/arch/2004/05/11/sakia_gunn_reme

Burke, P. 1996. *Gender Shock: Exploding the Myths of Male and Female.* New York: Anchor Press.

Butler, J. 2006. "Undiagnosing Gender." In *Transgender Rights,* ed. P. Currah, R. M. Juang, and S. P. Minter, pp. 274–298. Minneapolis: University of Minnesota Press.

Califia, P. 1997. *Sex Changes: The Politics of Transgenderism.* San Francisco: Cleis Press.

Clements-Nolle, K., R. Marx, and M. Katz. 2006. "Attempted Suicide Among Transgender Persons: The Influence of Gender-based Discrimination and Victimization." *Journal of Homosexuality,* 51:53–69.

Feinberg, L. 1999. *TransLiberation: Beyond Pink or Blue.* Boston: Beacon Press.

Finney Boylan, J. 2003. *She's Not There: A Life in Two Genders.* New York: Broadway Books.

Fleener, P. E. n.d. "Diagnostic Criteria for Gender Identity Disorder." *Gender Identity Disorder Today.* Retrieved March 22, 2007, from http://www.mental-health-today.com/gender/dsm.htm#gid9

Goffman, E. 1963. *Stigma: Notes on the Management of Spoiled Identity.* New York: Simon & Schuster.

Green, J. 2004. *Becoming a Visible Man.* Nashville, Tenn.: Vanderbilt Press.

Grossman, A. H., &. A. R. D'Augelli. 2006. "Transgender Youth: Invisible and Vulnerable." *Journal of Homosexuality,* 51:111–128.

Guiterrez, N. 2004. "Resisting Fragmentation, Living Whole: Four Female Transgender Students of Color Speak About School." *Journal of Gay and Lesbian Social Services,* 16:69–79.

Hussey, W. 2006. "Slivers of the Journey: The Use of Photovoice and Storytelling to Examine Female to Male Transsexuals' Experience of Health Care Access." *Journal of Homosexuality,* 51:129–158.

Jillson, I. A. 2002. "Opening Closed Doors: Improving Access to Quality Health Services for LGBT Populations." *Clinical Research and Regulatory Affairs,* 19(2–3):153–190.

Kailey, M. 2005. *Just Add Hormones: An Insider's Guide to the Transsexual Experience.* Boston: Beacon Press.

Kenagy, G. P. 2005. "Transgender Health: Findings from Two Needs Assessment Studies in Philadelphia." *Health and Social Work,* 30:19–26.

Kosofsky Sedgwick, E. 1991. "How to Bring Your Kids Up Gay." *Social Text,* 29:18–27.

Lombardi, E., R. A. Wilchins, D. Priesing, and D. Malouf. 2001. "Gender Violence: Transgender Experiences with Violence and Discrimination." *Journal of Homosexuality,* 42:89–101.

Lucal, B. 1999. "What It Means to Be Gendered Me: Life on the Boundaries of a Dichotomous Gender System." *Gender and Society,* 13:781–797.

MacKenzie, G., and N. Nangeroni. 2004. "Gender Talk—Labor of Love." In *Pinned Down by Pronouns,* ed. M. Davies and T. Amato, pp. 109–112. Jamaica Plain, Mass.: Conviction Books.

Meyerowitz, J. 2002. *How Sex Changed: A History of Transsexuality in the United States.* Cambridge, Mass: Harvard University Press.

Pettiway, L. E. 1996. *Honey, Honey, Miss Thang: Being Black, Gay, and on the Streets.* Philadelphia: Temple University Press.

Piontek, T. 2006. *Queering Gay and Lesbian Studies.* Urbana: University of Illinois Press.

Price, J. H., and S. K. Telljohann. 1991. "School Counselors' Perceptions of Adolescent Homosexuals." *Journal of School Health,* 61:433–439.

Schilt, K. 2006. "Just One of the Guys?: How Transmen Make Gender Visible at Work." *Gender and Society,* 20:465–490.

Stryker, S., and S. Whittle. 2006. *The Transgender Studies Reader.* New York: Routledge.

Telljohann, S. K., J. H. Price, M. Poureslami, and A. Easton. 1995. "Teaching About Sexual Orientation by Secondary Health Teachers." *Journal of School Health,* 65:18–23.

Wise, T. 2001. "Why Whites Think Blacks Have No Problems." Retrieved April 5, 2005, from http://www.alternet.org/story/11192.

31 • *Elisabeth Sheff and Corie Hammers*

THE PRIVILEGE OF PERVERSITIES: RACE, CLASS AND EDUCATION AMONG POLYAMORISTS AND KINKSTERS

DISCUSSION QUESTIONS

1. According to the authors, what is the definition of kinky and poly? How does the label pervert operate in dominant discourse to shape meanings about people who identify as kinky or practice polyamory?
2. Why do elements of social stratification—such as race, education, and class—affect one's membership/visibility in kinky and poly communities?
3. How does this chapter help illustrate the ways that social structures, privilege, and power shape sexual identities and sexual practices?
4. What are some limitations of the research regarding the kink and poly sexual minority communities, and what do the authors suggest to improve future research?

INTRODUCTION

. . .

This article focuses on *kinksters*—people involved in 'kinky' or 'perverted' sexual acts and relationships frequently involving bondage/discipline, dominance/submission and/or sadism/masochism (BDSM, also referred to as sadomasochism), and *polyamorists*—people who engage in openly conducted, multiple partner, romantic and/or sexual relationships. Popular usage among polyamorists and kinksters indicates that people who identify themselves as kinky are more likely to accept and celebrate the pervert moniker, and polyamorists who do not identify themselves as kinky appear less likely to think of themselves as perverts. Conventional society, however, generally classifies as perverts people who have multiple and concurrent romantic and/or sexual relationships, engage in group sex and/or openly espouse non-monogamy. Polyamorists are thus defined as perverts by the popular imagination, even if they themselves do not identify as such.[1]

Being accused of being a pervert can have detrimental consequences such as alienation from family

Sheff, Elisabeth, and Corie Hammers. "The privilege of perversities: Race, class and education among polyamorists and kinksters." *Psychology & Sexuality* 2.3, (2011): 198–223. Reprinted by permission of the publisher Taylor & Francis Ltd., www.tandfonline.com

and friends (Barker, 2005a; Califia, 2000), harassment (Wright, 2006), loss of a job or custody of a child (Dalton, 2001; Hequembourg, 2007; Klein & Moser, 2006), physical attack (Keres, 1994), public excoriation and incarceration (Attias, 2004; White, 2006). Although everyone involved in 'perverted' sex risks social censure, people unprotected by social advantages are more vulnerable to the discriminatory impacts of this sexual stigma than are those shielded by racial and/or class privileges. This insulation provides greater social latitude to engage in and redefine sexual or relational 'deviance' than that available to those burdened by racism, poverty, inadequate education, limited job prospects and other forms of discrimination (Collins, 1996, 2005; Sanday, 2007; Steinbugler, 2005). Given the difficulty of simply surviving, members of disadvantaged populations might well be reluctant to invest scarce resources in relational forms that can threaten conventional family structures and have the potential to increase surveillance from authorities, be they mothers-in-law, employers or child protective services.

Scholars are increasingly emphasising the intersections of sexuality with other elements of social stratification (Collins, 1996, 2005; Schippers, 2000; Sharma & Nath, 2005). Disability, (trans)gender, sexual orientation, age—these elements and more— influence the ways in which people choose to, or are able to, express their sexual selves. In this article, we focus on race, education and class for three reasons. First, as white, middle-class sexuality researchers, we have attempted to address the implications of the overwhelmingly white populations who participated in our research. Second, race, education and class stand out as important constants in the field, indicating their significance for analysis. Finally, researchers have identified demographic characteristics, and especially race, as important factors impacting sexuality and specifically salient to research on polyamory and BDSM (Haritaworn, Lin, & Klesse, 2006; Langdridge & Barker, 2007). For instance, Willey (2006) and Noël (2006) examined poly discourse and highlighted the ways in which whiteness and class privilege are central to polyamory and those claims that seek to 'naturalise' the practice of

polyamory. As Willey noted, many feminist poly activists justify polyamory on the grounds that monogamy is unnatural and patriarchal because it works to quell our uncontainable sexual 'drives' while being deeply implicated in female subjugation. Yet, this same 'liberationist' rhetoric has historically been used to marginalise and stigmatise the poor and the people of colour for *their* 'uncontrollable' urges and *their* inability to conform to the monogamous, nuclear family (white) ideal. Noël and Willey also found troubling the depoliticising and atomising strain within poly discourse that typically focuses on individual experience and agency over and against institutional and coalitional challenges to the status quo, thus leaving unaddressed the intersections between poly practice and race, dis/ability, class and so on. Noël's (2006, p. 604) content analysis of 12 key texts on polyamory illuminated how polyamorists "offer a short-sighted, isolationist alternative that serves to further solidify privileges for a few rather than realize an improved reality for many." It is the manner in which these intersecting identities inform research and shape the interpretations of findings that we are most interested in exploring in this article.

. . .

This topic is influenced by our own experiences and social locations as (white, female) researchers of sexual minority communities. It is our strong belief that in studying only those who are most accessible and visible within poly and BDSM subcultures— those overwhelmingly white and middle class—we fail as researchers to understand alternative mappings of non-monogamous desire and BDSM practices. In other words, we fail to capture how even non-normative and sexually subversive communities depend on their own operations of white privilege and white ways of being. For instance, how might working-class individuals and/or people of colour 'do' polyamory or BDSM differently? Our objectives here are multi-fold, and we document the affiliation between polyamory and BDSM; demonstrate through a meta-analysis of extant literature the ways in which research on alternative sexual communities has often (unwittingly) reinforced and (re)constituted a homogenous image of these non-conformist subcultures;

support and augment this analysis with our own empirical data; and provide recommendations to improve research methods. By highlighting the race and class privileges that operate throughout these processes, we aim to foster dialogue about the ways in which we as sexuality researchers can mitigate this privilege and its potential impact on our collective research. In so doing, we first explain polyamorous and kinky people and their relationships and review relevant literatures. Second, we detail the aggregated results of 36 studies of polys and kinksters and discuss the factors that shape these two communities. These factors operate at the social and methodological levels, yielding samples that are overwhelmingly white, with relatively high socio-economic status. Third, we examine the ways in which researchers build samples and collect data, and suggest strategies to increase sample diversity. We conclude with an examination of the implications of these findings for the varied sexual and relational identities that comprise kinky and poly subcultures.

COMMUNITY CHARACTERISTICS

. . .

Neither academicians nor community members have achieved consensus on precise definitions of *kinkiness* or *polyamory*. In line with other researchers (Barker, 2005a, 2005b; Haritaworn et al., 2006; Weitzman, 2006, 2007), we define *polyamory* as a form of association in which people openly maintain multiple romantic, sexual and/or effective relationships. Polyamorists use the term *poly* as a noun (a person who is poly engages in polyamorous relationships), an adjective (to describe something that has polyamorous qualities) and an umbrella term that includes polyfidelity or relationships based in sexual and emotional fidelity among a group larger than a dyad.

With its emphasis on long-term, emotionally intimate relationships, polyamory differs from the form of swinging based on emotional exclusivity with one partner and sexual non-monogamy with multiple partners. Polyamory is also not adultery: the poly focuses on honesty and (ideally) full disclosure differs

markedly from the attempted secrecy definitional to adultery. Both men and women have access to multiple partners in polyamorous relationships, distinguishing them from those that are polygynous or polyandrous. Polyamorists routinely debate the definition of the term, the groups it includes and who is qualified to claim it as an identity.

Kinky people, relationships and communities share many characteristics with polyamorists, with a myriad of potential additional dimensions that can make kink even more complex. Kinksters are people who identify as kinky, frequently including (but not limited to) those who participate in BDSM; have multiple sexual and/or play partners; engage in role play and/or costuming as part of their sexual behaviour; have fetishes; blend gender characteristics; and/or modify their bodies in conjunction with or to augment their sexual practices. BDSM, the primary umbrella under which many of these identities are encompassed, stands for bondage and discipline; dominance and submission; and sadism and masochism, or sadomasochism. BDSM is the practice of consensual exchanges of personal power including (but not limited to) scripted 'scenes' involving some combination of corporal or psychic 'punishment,' intense physical stimulation (often pain), role playing and/or fantasy and/or varied sexual interactions (Langdridge & Barker, 2007; Moser & Kleinplatz, 2006a; Weinberg & Kamel, 1995). Among kinksters, definitions of who qualifies as a sexual partner and what counts as a sex act encompass far greater variety than those considered sex acts or partners among 'vanilla' (non-kinky) people. Typically, BDSM and poly communities cohere around a specific gender and sexual orientation. For instance, most public play parties are geared specifically towards gay men, lesbians or bisexual/heterosexual people. This is in part due to the origins of the BDSM subculture in the United States, which began as a gay male phenomena that later diverged to include lesbian, heterosexual and bi/pansexual communities (Ridinger, 2002). These various groups tend to self-segregate by sexual orientation and gender, although the growth of virtual and physical kink community has encouraged some amalgamation as well.

Poly and kinky research respondents emphasise negotiation, honesty, consent and personal growth as important components of successful relationships (Sheff, 2005a, 2005b, 2006, 2007, 2010; Barker & Ritchie, 2007; Weitzman, 2006, 2007). Similarly, many of them maintain multiple relationships with varied levels of emotional and sexual intimacy. Kinkiness appears to be a broader base for an identity than polyamory, encompassing a greater range of relationships and types of practices/identities. Many kinky people have multiple partner relationships but do not necessarily primarily identify as polyamorous—the number of people involved in their relationships is but one component among many aspects of kink identity, sexuality and relationships. For some, mostly non-kink poly people, the multiplicity of the relationships determines their status as poly. Those polys who engage in kinky sexual activities are more likely to view sexuality more broadly and numerosity as one, not necessarily the defining, element of their sexual identities. Additionally and more importantly, for the purposes of this article, the poly and kinky populations who have participated in research primarily comprise white, well-educated, middle-class professionals.

. . .

METHODS

The data for this article come from three sources: our own original research; others' studies of kinksters and polyamorists; and communication with other researchers online. In this section, we discuss our data sources, detail our methods and explain the limitations of this meta-analysis.

ORIGINAL RESEARCH

Sheff's longitudinal study of polyamorists has thus far produced two waves of data collected through participant observation, content analysis, Internet research and in-depth interviews. The first portion of the study (Gender, family, and sexuality: Exploring polyamorous communities 1996—2003) provided the base of 40 in-depth interviews with adults who identified as poly, and extensive participant observation data collected at a wide variety of poly events including co-ed and women's support groups, potlucks, community meetings and two national conferences. The second wave of data collection (Polymorous families study 2007—present) focuses on polyamorous families with children and includes 15 previous respondents[2] and has expanded the sample to incorporate an additional 41 people, for a current total sample of 81 across both studies. Race is the most homogeneous demographic characteristic, with 89% of the sample identifying as white. Socioeconomic status is high among these respondents, with 74% in professional jobs. Fully 88% report some college education, with 67% attaining bachelor's degrees and 21% completing graduate degrees.

Sheff also conducted a study of intersecting sexual identities (Overlapping identities study 2005) examining the overlap between polyamorists, swingers, people with fetishes and those who practice BDSM. Of the 64 respondents (31 men, 27 women and 6 others),[3] 31 were involved in BDSM, 19 in polyamory and 6 in swinging. The majority of respondents (58 or 90%) identified as white, with two African Americans, one Filipina, two people of multiracial heritage and one who identified himself simply as "other" also participating. Respondents were also highly educated, with all but three respondents (95%) having completed or currently enrolled in an undergraduate degree, and 48 (75%) of them completing at least some graduate school. All of the 26 respondents who reported fetishes were also involved in BDSM, and the two groups are so intricately involved that distinguishing between them did not provide any useful analysis. Swingers, however, stood out as socially distinct—if racially, economically and educationally similar to the other respondents. They neither identified themselves strongly with the other groups, nor were they identified as integral to a joint identity the way polys and kinksters identified each other. Although there are certainly intersections between polys and swingers (and to a lesser extent kinksters and swingers), these focus groups indicated a much stronger affiliation between polyamorists and kinksters than between either group and swingers.

In her ethnographic research on Canadian lesbian/queer bathhouses (*Bathhouse culture study* 2004), Hammers also found a largely white and well-educated population. Approximately 80% of the 33 interview respondents identified as white, with over half attaining either undergraduate or graduate degrees. Although highly educated, most of these women were only marginally middle class (Hammers, 2008). Hammers' current project, which explores the US lesbian/queer BDSM community (2007 to present), has found this population, like the bathhouse subculture, to be a relatively homogenous one. As with the bathhouse study, data for this BDSM project come from in-depth interviews with lesbian/queer BDSM practitioners/attendees and participant observation data derived from attendance at a variety of public lesbian/queer/women-only BDSM events in the United States. A total of 40 in-depth interviews with BDSM practitioners and self-identified kinksters have been conducted thus far. Of these, 36 individuals identify as white. Approximately 76% reported some university education, with 70% having attained a bachelor's degree.

Thus, a major interweaving theme that binds our studies and informs our views on race in the research setting, and the inadequate attention paid to race when it comes to alternative sexual subcultures, comes through at this juncture. We find that these alternative sex publics—which encompass such things as community meetings, national conferences, bathhouse events and public BDSM play parties—are predominantly white. It is this whiteness, we believe, that sexuality scholars must address.

OTHER STUDIES OF KINKSTERS AND POLYAMORISTS

To find pertinent studies, we searched in Google Scholar, as well as Sociological Abstracts and Sociological Collection in the Galileo search engine, using the search terms BDSM, sadomasochism, kink, SM and polyamor: To be eligible for inclusion, studies had to focus on polyamory and/or kinkiness and contain at least some demographic data relevant to the target populations. . . .

RESULTS OF STUDIES OF KINKSTERS AND POLYAMORISTS

The composite results from these 36 studies (20 of kinksters, 14 of polys and 2 of both) indicate a largely homogeneous universe populated with highly educated, white, middle- and upper-middle-class professionals, confirming numerous researchers' conclusions (Sheff, 2005a, 2005b; Sandnabba, Santtila, Alison, & Nordling, 2002; Spengler, 1977). These studies employed a variety of methods: six used surveys or e-interviews conducted entirely online; four 'offline' studies reported relying heavily on the Internet to recruit their samples and for some supplementary data collection; 12 used interviews; one combined interviews and a questionnaire; and 14 used questionnaires distributed in person or through magazines, at organisation/club meetings or at events. Twenty-one of the studies were conducted in the United States, five in Western Europe, two in Australia and one in China. There are three unpublished masters' theses and four unpublished dissertations. Sample sizes range from a low of six (Matthews, 2006; Mosher, Levitt, & Manley, 2006) to a high of 6997 (Brame, 2000) and span over time from Spengler's trailblazing 1977 study of male sadomasochists in Western Germany to Barker and Langdridge's (2010) volume that includes original research on polyamory. The percent of people of colour in the sample varies from a low of zero in four studies (Barker & Ritchie, 2007; Cook, 2005; Matthews, 2006; Mosher et al., 2006) to a high of 48 in Tomassilli, Golub, Bimbi, and Parsons's (2009) study of lesbians and bisexual women in New York City (Tables 31.1 and 31.2).

UNIQUE CASES

Some studies contribute to multiple areas or provide qualitative data unsuitable for tables. Taormino's (2008) study of 126 people in 'open relationships' includes data on polys and kinksters, with 62% identifying as polyamorous or polyfidelitous and 51% identifying as kinky. Of the entire sample of 126 people, 82% identified as white and 77% as

TABLE 31.1. Studies of Polyamorists

Author(s) and Location of Study	Sample Size	% Respondents of Colour	% College	% Graduate School	% Middle Class or Higher
Barker (2005b), online[a]	30	6[b]	[c]	[c]	[c]
Barker and Ritchie (2007), England[a]	8	0	[c]	[c]	87
Cook (2005)[a]	14	0	[c]	[c]	100
Ho (2006), Hong Kong	8	0 or 100, all ethnic Chinese in Hong Kong	50 college or above	10 PhD	"May be considered middle-class, but [that is] . . . complex" pg. 550
Keener (2004)	10	30	50 some college, 20 bachelors degree	10	40
Kirsten (1996)	142	15	96 some college	47 some graduate school	[c]
Klesse (2007), England	44	"Vast majority" White	[c]	[c]	"Vast majority" pg. 156
Ley (2006), online	102	[c]	74 some college, 27 bachelor's	31	71–83[d]
Loving More Survey 2001— Pallotta-Chiarolli (2006) and Weber (2002)	1010	2	25 some college, 70 completed at least undergrad	[c]	At least 75
Pallotta-Chiarolli (2010a, 2010b)[a], Australia	36	12	[c]	[c]	Over 90
Walston (2001)	430	16	64	22	[c]
Weitzman (2006, 2007) online	2169	14	[c]	[c]	[c]
Wolf (2003)[a]	229	6	27	40	[c]
Sheff (2005a, 2005b, 2006, 2007, 2010)	81 interview, 500 participant observation	10	67	21	97

Notes: Unless otherwise noted, the studies were conducted in the United States.
[a]Researchers provided the authors with data not included in their original publications.
[b]Respondents were asked to provide whatever information they deemed germane, and one identified as Chinese and British in one case and British of Indian parents in another. Other respondents may have also been persons of colour, but none so self-identified.
[c]These data were not collected or not available.
[d]Conservative lower range based on income less than $26,000 and upper range based on income, occupation, gender, age, number of children and education.

TABLE 31.2. Studies of Kinksters

Author(s) and Location of Study	Sample Size	% Respondents of Colour	% College	% Graduate School	% Middle Class or Higher
Bauer (2008), Western Europe and the United States[a]	54	3	50	[b]	64
Brame (2000), online[a]	6997	[b]	73 some college, 30 completed	20 completed	84
Breslow, Evans, and Langley (1985)	182	[b]	30 (male) and 35 (female) some college, 31 (male) and 20 (female) completed	22 (male) and 8 (female)	[b]
Connolly (2006)	132	7	58	17	67
Dancer, Kleinplatz, and Moser (2006)	146	6	[b]	[b]	[b]
Levitt, Moser, and Jamison (1994)	34 non–prostitute women	[b]	47 some college, 41 at least undergraduate degree	[b]	[b]
Matthews (2006)	6 women (queer/dyke/Lesbian)	0	33	66	100
Moser and Levitt (1987)	225	5	70 some college, 38 completed	[b]	[b]
Moser et al. (1993)	362	[b]	60	25	Majority "affluent" pg. 59
Mosher et al. (2006)	6	0	[b]	[b]	[b]
Newmahr (2006, 2008)[a]	18	"Relatively few but representative of the scene"	[b]	[b]	[b]
Sandnabba et al. (1999) Finland[a]	164 men	[b]	58	[b]	Majority had "comparatively high incomes"
Sandnabba et al. (2002) Finland[a]	184	[b]	"Highly educated (over a third had a university degree)" pg. 42	[b]	"Higher income level than the population in general" pg. 42
Sisson and Moser (2005)	31 women professional dominatrixes	26	96 some college, 35 completed	7	[b]
Spengler (1977), West Germany	245 men	[b]	15 some college, 25 completed	[b]	54
Tomassilli et al. (2009)[a]	347 lesbians and bisexual women	48	63 at least an undergraduate or graduate degree	[b]	[b]

(Continued)

TABLE 31.2. Studies of Kinksters (*Continued*)

Author(s) and Location of Study	Sample Size	% Respondents of Colour	% College	% Graduate School	% Middle Class or Higher
Weinberg et al. (1995)	262	11	69 at least an undergraduate or graduate degree	b	81
Yost (2006), online	212	11	30 some college, 22 completed	23	68
Hammers (2010)	40	10	6 some college, 70 completed	12	60

Notes: Unless otherwise noted, the studies were conducted in the United States.
[a]Researchers provided the authors with data not included in their original publications.
[b]These data were not collected or not available.

middle class or above. As previously discussed, Sheff's Overlapping identities study of polyamorists, swingers, kinksters and those with fetishes yielded similar results.

In the sole randomly selected sample of which we are aware, Richters, de Visser, Rissel, Grulich, and Smith (2008) surveyed a representative sample of 19,307 residents of Australia aged 16–59 years old and found that 1.8% of the sexually active respondents (2.2% of men and 1.3% of women) reported being involved in BDSM in the last year. Results also indicate that people involved in BDSM are more likely to have been "non-exclusive in a regular relationship (i.e. had sex with someone else besides their regular partner)" (Richters et al., 2008, p. 1663) in the last 12 months than are people with no involvement in BDSM, confirming the association between non-monogamy and BDSM. The study measured ethnicity through country of birth and language spoken at home, and only 1.3% of respondents spoke anything but English in their homes. Although respondents who engaged in BDSM also had higher levels of education, Richters (personal communication, 2009) cautioned that:

> My impression is that we cannot be certain whether the apparent high education levels and social class of BDSM people as anecdotally reported is an artefact of self-selection for study. It may be real, which would not be surprising given that BDSM is often highly verbal and symbolic. Nonetheless, our analysis clearly showed that demographic and psychological variables were swamped by the strong differences in sexual interest and breadth of experience/repertoire.

Although this most representative sample finds virtually the same racial, ethnic, class and educational characteristics of the other studies with less-randomly selected samples, the authors note that these select demographic characteristics are overshadowed by the sample's sexual characteristics.

REASONS FOR THESE RESULTS

Although it is quite unlikely that these samples are representative of the actual range of kink and poly people, they are certainly representative of the range of people involved in mainstream poly and kink communities. In addition to the possible selection effects that we discuss later in this article, there are several potential explanations for this consistency. As mentioned earlier, one plausible rationale is that poly and kinky people hold the same kind of racist views as do others of their social ilk. Living in the United States, Australia and/or Western Europe would make it virtually impossible for polys and kinksters to escape the pervasive racism and classism endemic in those societies and the accompanying white privilege (or lack thereof) that inflects their lives. In our experiences, poly and kink communities tend to eschew open racism and often support such liberal ideals as equality and celebration of diversity. White privilege, however, generally remains as invisible in these groups as is in more conventional society, thus becoming the dominant racial paradigm. In his study of 'dyke + BDSM spaces', Bauer (2008, p. 247) asserted that, rather than active racism, white privilege constructs a social environment in which:

> Gender and sexuality (and to a lesser extent age and class) are highly visible and consciously negotiated . . . while racialization of the white majority remains invisible and unexplored and functions as a nontransgressable . . . cultural taboo when it comes to interracial imaginary.

Although not generally ostensibly racist, these poly and kinky respondents live in worlds shaped by white privilege and its effects on their interactions, community networks and relational experiences. Thus, this privilege will in turn have an impact on the racial composition of public sexual spaces—in Bauer's case, BDSM public play parties.

INTERNET RECRUITMENT

Because the Internet serves as a primary tool for sexuality researchers to both engage and recruit target populations (Waskul, 2004), it is no surprise that numerous respondents in these kink and poly studies identify the Internet as a crucial element of their access to sexual non-conformist communities (Sheff, 2005a; Weber, 2002; Weitzman, 2006). The web has profoundly reshaped sexual minorities' communities, identities, networks and communications, and nine of the researchers cited in this article avail themselves of this expanded opportunity by examining poly and kink populations that would have previously been extremely difficult to find, or may in fact not exist, without the Internet. Although it is reasonable to recognise the Internet as an important site of community evolution, it is not sensible to rely so heavily on a single resource that will definitionally provide a limited sample.

Although the Internet has expanded sexual opportunity (for some) and created a virtual world wherein sexual minorities can find affirmation and community (Weinrich, 1997), this technological tool also reproduces (and possibly strengthens) pre-existing inequalities. Initial research indicated that the majority of Internet users were male, overwhelmingly white, middle class and well educated (Warf & Grimes, 1997), with an average income that was twice that of the national average (Kantor & Neubarth, 1996). Current research identifies lingering disparities in computer ownership (Ono & Zavodny, 2003) and use (Chakraborty & Bosman, 2005), which continue to disadvantage people of colour (Mossberger, Tolbert, & McNeal, 2008). Internet use and its impacts are complex, however, and measuring access alone is insufficient—researchers must also account for a variety of factors that shape the ways in which people use the Internet (Jackson, Ervin, Gardnera, & Schmitt, 2001; Roderick, 2008). Thus, depending on one's race and class location, the Internet can both enhance and hinder sexual opportunity and sense of belonging for members of unconventional sexual cultures, often reproducing predominately white and relatively affluent alternative sexual communities.

PROTECTIONS AFFORDED BY PRIVILEGES

Although they do not completely insulate people from the risks associated with deviance, race and class privileges can provide buffers to mitigate the myriad potential negative outcomes related to sexual and relational non-conformity. Like other sexual minorities, kinky and poly people have lost jobs, child custody and families' and friends' esteem. Indeed, Pallotta-Chiarolli (2006, p. 51) found that two indigenous Australian children in her study of poly families

> . . . kept to themselves in order to discourage any intimacy with other children that could lead to discovery and a further reason to harass them, as they were already experiencing ongoing racist harassment. They had also been warned by their parents not to let white teachers know or else they'd be taken away from their family, a theme that was all too real for this family

whose own childhoods had been mostly spent in mission homes after being removed from their families as part of Australia's racist and assimilationist policies.

Their family's experiences with racism sensitised them to the need to remain concealed to avoid further racialised persecution.

As groups comprised mainly white people with relatively high socio-economic statuses, mainstream polyamorists' and kinksters' privileges can buffer them from some of the negative impacts people risk when they eschew conventionally sanctioned roles. Respondents' levels of education and occupations indicate that they are generally skilled professionals with careers endowed with greater job security than low-skill, low-paying jobs, where employees are far more easily replaced and often subject to greater surveillance and less autonomy. Courts have repeatedly demonstrated their endorsement of conventional heterosexual families over those with sexual and/or gender non-conforming members (Klein & Moser, 2006; Polikoff, 1993). The intersections of these varied privileges bestow middleclass people with greater freedom to engage in behaviours and relationships that risk social approbation. Coupled with a relative lack of public awareness of polyamory and kinky relationships, these privileges allow some to pass as sexually or relationally conventional when they wish to do so, thus avoiding the consequences that can accompany detection. People in disadvantaged positions are often subject to levels of surveillance that make non-conformity riskier than it would be for others with greater resources. 'Perversity' then becomes another luxury more readily available to those who are already members of dominant groups.

DETERRENTS TO PARTICIPATION

. . .

Expense

Scarce funds can deter people with low incomes from participating in some kink and poly community events. Fetish wear, admission to public sex environments such as 'dungeons' and 'toys' such as floggers can be expensive, selecting-out entire categories of

people with little discretionary income. This is quite problematic, because 11 of the research samples to which we refer were drawn at least in part from those attending public 'play parties' and thus reflect only a portion of the population that is readily accessible—people with internet access and the privacy to use it, who are involved in groups or organisations and/or willing and able to afford to 'play' in public. It can be difficult to be a sexual minority in general, and to be one of the very few people of colour or with low socio-economic status in a group composed primarily of educated white people with professional jobs dressed in expensive fetish wear could exacerbate barriers that inhibit the assumption of poly or kinky identities.

Tokenism, Potential Discrimination and Community Rejection of Sexual Minorities

In her study of polyamorists in the Western United States, Sheff's respondents of colour cited a number of barriers to participation in poly community events. Yansa, a 29-year-old kink- and poly-identified African American health-care provider, reported acute discomfort when attending a poly pool party in the San Francisco Bay Area. She observed that:

> I was not sure if they wanted me there. Like I felt like maybe I had walked in on somebody else's thing and I wasn't invited . . . . [there were] 75, 80 naked people in this huge pool and I walked in and everybody just turned and looked . . . and I realized I am the only Black person here. I was the only person in a swimming suit so that could have been another issue, too, like maybe she's lost her way, what is she doing here?

Yansa's discomfort at being the sole Black person at the party was compounded by her unawareness of the community (un)dress code. Although the setting was 'clothing optional' in that people were neither compelled to nor barred from wearing clothing, the norm was universal nudity while in the swimming pool and various stages of undress to full clothing on the pool deck.

Though Yansa's initial discomfort eased as she socialised at that and other parties, she remained uneasy about the increased potential risks she faced for sexual non-conformity. She reported already feeling vulnerable at work because of her race and fearing that being a known polyamorist would mean termination. She described her employers as

> ... executives who went to Wharton and Harvard and were Republicans and assholes . . . very, very closed minded. And I got the impression that they were already not comfortable with me being a person of color. To throw in the other stuff that I did may confirm their stereotypes about Black people or they may have just thought she's the weirdest shit on the planet, I don't trust her . . . We don't want her on this job anymore, someone may find her out.

Yansa noted several reasons other African Americans had discussed with her for their lack of desire to attend poly or kink community events or identify as polyamorous or kinky. "I've heard from Black folk that they think it's a nasty white person thing to do. And they throw out the whole scenario of slavery you know they raped us and they took our women and impregnated them . . . that any respectable educated cultured Black person in their right mind wouldn't even think about doing something so disgusting." She similarly reported that:

> I've had Black people in the community tell me that they don't want to feel like the token Black . . . the novelty like the fat girl or the Asian girl. I don't want to feel like people are attracted to me and wanting to play with me or date me because they're trying to figure out something. Like I'm some Anthropological experiment or something.

It was not only their fear of objectification and denunciation of past abuses and negative stereotypes that deterred Yansa's compatriots of colour from joining the local poly community, but their active rejection of poly or kinky subcultures as white, foreign and potentially corrupt.

Victor, a poly-identified 36-year-old African American therapist, artist and college instructor, was more optimistic. He noted that the poly community in which he socialised was "monochromatic," though he was not sure if that was because of "issues of either privilege or even cultural interest." The whiteness of the setting did not bother him, in part because he had grown up in mostly white neighbourhoods and

was thus "acclimated" to white people, and in part because he felt that, "People who are interested in really relating with people and good whole truth telling are going to tend to be less racist . . . I've actually felt a lot of acceptance." Victor pointed out that his socio-economic status gave him access to a lifestyle that others did not have the freedom to enjoy. "It's sort of privilege related . . . if you're not worrying about certain things, then you have the privilege or the space to explore alternatives. . . . the freedom to explore polyamory sort of comes from a freedom either financially or just psychologically not having to [struggle to] survive in other ways." Even so, when thinking about mainstream African American communities' possible reactions to polyamory, he noted that, "I can imagine being in a room of Black people and them going that sounds like crazy white folks, that's some crazy shit."

Identity

People of colour, already labouring under stigma and racism, might be more reluctant to assume a potentially disadvantageous identity than white or ethnic majority people. Laksha, a 26-year-old African American graduate student and participant in Sheff's Overlapping identities study who identifies as bisexual, poly and "mostly vanilla," asserts that:

> I think African Americans are much less likely to go into a BDSM setting and think, ok, these are my people, this is my family, and take on that label. It is similar to feminism, in that many African American women have feminist principles and take feminist action and even participate in what some would consider feminist activism, but do not identify with the label. White people can more readily walk into the room and identify with the people, see them as their tribe, because race does not stand out to them, so kink can become their organizing identity. But it is not that easy for African Americans, race always stands out to us in a situation like that.

The disadvantage of a stigmatised identity, coupled with the added weight of racial strain that white or ethnic majorities do not experience, as well as feelings of discomfort or lack of belonging in the setting, can contribute to people of colour's reluctance to identify with kink and poly subcultures.

That many who might appear to be poly or kinky by others' definitions do not self-identify as such has important implications for the construction of identities. Although Victor asserted that mainstream African Americans would reject an organised poly identity, he hypothesised that there were ". . . communities of color where there are multipartner relationships going on I don't know whether they would call it poly or not. Probably not . . . . I think that populations tend to self select." Undoubtedly, there are people who openly maintain non-monogamous relationships or enjoy being spanked during sex, behaviours characteristic of (respectively) poly and kinky relationships, but nonetheless do not identify with those communities.

Equally certain is the existence of people who identify as poly or kinky but do not attend meetings or join groups. Again, it could be that those who feel marginalised or different from the more 'visible' members of the poly and kink community will remain outside the very organisations that purportedly represent their ilk. It is also possible that people of colour involved in unconventional sexual practices are just as active but more clandestine and maintain their own, more exclusive, list-serves, events and private sexual venues. Precisely how these more underground sexual networks and private play parties might differ from the more visible sexual subcultures requires additional research.

Finally, the (almost all white) researchers' race could deter people of colour from participating in research on kink and polyamory. Hammers' (2008) attempts to interview women of colour who chose to participate in lesbian/queer bathhouse culture certainly testify to this issue and the power that inheres within the researcher–interviewee relationship. This power differential is particularly salient when the focus is on sex and non-normative sexual practices. Many of the women of colour Hammers approached for her bathhouse study refused to speak to her precisely because she is white. Those people of colour who chose to participate in the study often linked the lack of participation by other people of colour to the perceived potential predation and appropriation of participants' experiences by the researcher. Only a few women of colour agreed to talk to Hammers about their experiences, several of whom expressed concern about other women of colour discovering their decision to do so.

RESEARCH STRATEGIES

. . .

PAST STRATEGIES

Researchers examining kinky and poly populations have dealt with issues of class and race in a variety of ways. Measuring race and class is quite complex even in a single society, and when the research is international it becomes very difficult to establish common meanings indeed. Ho (2006, p. 550) characterised class as difficult to quantify: "The participants in this study came from diverse social locations, even though many of them would be considered middle-class, but what constitutes 'middle-class' in Hong Kong is a complex question." Class status does not necessarily translate directly from income in a single nation, much less internationally: some have middle-class status with little disposable income, and others have money to spend but are not considered middle class. Although education and class can be strongly correlated, some poly or kinky people are highly educated but 'underemployed' or work in comparatively low-paid fields of counselling and academia and thus have less disposable income than their level of education might suggest.

Alternately, Bauer (2008, p. 238) questioned the stereotype of:

> BDSM people being overwhelmingly highly educated and of middle- to upperclass . . . [because] my sample is rather diverse in this regard. However, some interviewees put forth the idea that high-quality BDSM is only for those whom they perceive to be highly educated, "intelligent" or "classy" individuals, thus endorsing potentially excluding class-based criteria for membership in the community.

Bauer's (2008, p. 238) respondents report that the majority of the play parties they attend were populated primarily by white people and that "the race thing is partly class stuff and it's partly because most of the play parties that I've been to have been organized by white people."

Like class, measuring race presents a myriad of complexities, and researchers took a variety of approaches to this task. Of the reviewed studies, eight ignored the category of race altogether, rendering it virtually irrelevant in its invisibility (e.g. Sandnabba, Santtila, & Nordling, 1999, 2002). The fact that race was left unproblematised indicates that the populations were most likely white, as researchers and respondents alike would most likely have emphasised it as more highly salient had the samples included greater numbers of people of colour—a point to which we return. Others (14) collected data on race but refrained from addressing racial issues in their analysis. This lack of discussion indicates that many of these researchers were oblivious to, or actively chose to ignore, the impacts race can have on the construction of sexual identities. Still other researchers have attempted to over-sample people of colour (e.g. Sheff, 2005a, 2005b, 2006; see also Connolly, 2006; Klesse, 2007, p. 157). Sheff endeavoured to recruit as many respondents of colour as possible, interviewed all three people of colour in the Midwestern poly community and travelled to the California Bay Area with the explicit intent of increasing sample diversity. Even so, she found the demographic characteristics of the numerous mainstream poly communities in the Bay Area to closely mirror the Midwestern sample.

In an online open-ended questionnaire, Barker (2005b) asked respondents to provide whatever information about themselves they viewed as pertinent, providing an interesting snapshot of the relative importance of race and class to the respondents. None of the respondents identified class as important, though three mentioned working in the Information Technology industry, four listed masters' degrees and two additional respondents referred to attending a university but did not specify their degrees. Of those who indicated their racial, ethnic or national heritage, 12 identified as European or British, three specifically as white, one as British of Indian descent and one as mixed race Chinese and British. Six of the respondents identified themselves as American [*sic*] or by a

region of the United States but did not address their races directly. It is most likely that those who identify as citizens of a nation or denizens of a region are of the dominant racial, ethnic or social group; A striking difference, minority status or distinguishing characteristic that requires a modifier—*Chinese* British, *African* American—is most likely to stand out to respondents because it will impact their daily lives in a palpable manner. Majority social members labour under no such daily experience and are thus far less likely to see their race as salient. They are simply members of British or US society, unmodified by specific status. Conversely, Barker's respondents emphasised sexuality (especially bisexuality) far more so than race, thus casting it as more germane to their social identities. Such a blasé attitude towards race signals membership in the dominant category, with the comfort evidencing privilege. Similarly, in their study of 184 Finnish sadomasochists, Sandnabba et al. (2002) did not collect data on race or ethnicity. Finland is largely homogeneous (Statistics Finland, 2009), with very little racial or ethnic diversity, so it is sensible to assume that race or ethnicity would have little to no impact on respondents' experiences of sadomasochism.

Some researchers (E. Cook, personal communication, 2007; L. Wolf, personal communication, 2008) did not collect data on race because they perceived it as unrelated to their topic of study. Others intentionally avoided collecting data on race. G. Brame (personal communication, 2007) reported that:

> I did not set out or want to study what role if any race plays in SM. In part that is because, for economic and socio-political reasons, minorities are under-represented in the Scene. BDSM communities cut across all socio-economic, political lines; but while I suspect just as many minorities engage in kinky sex, IMX they do not tend to join sexual communities in number, the way mainstream white people do, so the population is very heavily skewed towards white. So we could measure the data and speculate about why their numbers are so low, but as data I think it asks far more questions than it answers. The whole issue of minorities in the SM/BDSM worlds really and truly deserves its own study. It's a vastly complicated issue.

. . .

The studies we review represent six different countries, and whereas most of them were conducted in the 'West,' one was completed in Hong Kong (Ho, 2006). Ho's study underlines the complexity of defining race, especially at an international level. As ethnic Chinese living in Hong Kong, Ho's respondents are either 0% people of colour or 100% people of colour, depending on the perspective used to judge. In their own social context, they are members of the social majority, and thus would not appropriately be considered people of colour (0%) in a numerical minority sense because the point of reference is the same racial and ethnic group. They would also evade the stigma, social pressures and disadvantage attached to being a 'minority' not only numerically, but with the attendant deprivation of social privileges. In the larger discussion in literature, however, Ho's respondents could be classified as 100% people of colour, because they are all Chinese. In that construction, they are people of colour in relationship to the external white measure, rather than their internal measure of majority status.

This begs the question 'People of color from whose perspective?' The term *people of colour* implies some neutral colourless other to which they are compared—the white perspective that underlies both mainstream poly and kink communities, as well as the research that seeks to understand them. M. Pallotta-Chiarolli (personal communication, 2008) highlighted this linguistic issue and clarified that:

> In Australia, the respectful term is 'indigenous Australians.' Indigenous Australians find the term 'people of color' offensive, as it doesn't differentiate between their experiences of colonialism, genocide, etc. and the experiences of Africans and others who are migrants and refugees.

Although in the United Kingdom some scholars use Black and Minority Ethnics to describe these populations, *people of colour* remains the standard language in the United States. We use it here not only because it is the standard scholarly rhetoric of our academic peers, but more importantly because it is the language our respondents use. Even so, the terminology is difficult and we acknowledge the problematic nature of the term. These issues are not idiosyncratic to research on polys and kinksters: the entire field of Sociology (and many others) is grappling with meanings of race and global social interactions.

RECOMMENDED STRATEGIES

. . . Sexual value systems and the meanings attached to particular sex acts and arrangements stem from Western, white heteropatriarchal standards of sex/gender normativity. Race is never not related to one's topic of study: race confounds the study of sexuality precisely because of its continued neglect.

Learning to deal with the complexities of measuring race is key to the success of inclusive research and requires a broader discussion of race, nationally and internationally. Scholars can use journals, conferences and online forums to discuss methodological issues and establish greater international communication. On an individual methodological level, researchers can ask respondents to self-identify racially and/or ethnically. When reporting their results, scholars should explain their terms and respondents' social locations to give readers the information necessary to understand respondents' racial and ethnic identities in the context of their own cultures.

Second, scholars studying this area must continue to oversample people of colour. This becomes complex, as who is 'of colour' is difficult to define. One strategy researchers can use is to approach people who appear to be of colour or are somehow a minority in the setting and request an interview, and ask the respondents (as with all other respondents) how they identify racially or ethnically. This process must be accomplished with sensitivity to avoid the mistakes of previous researchers who, in the process of getting to 'know and understand' certain groups, have been guilty of fetishizing 'the other' (Probyn, 1993).

Third, researchers in this area must shift their recruitment strategies to include a far broader range of options rather than relying so heavily on the Internet and homogeneous snowball samples (often coordinated through email or other Internet interactions as well). Although these sampling and recruitment methods remain useful, such complete dependence on them produces skewed and monochromatic samples. Instead, researchers could post flyers in coffee shops, laundromats, sex shops, libraries and on street posts and/or advertise in newspapers and local magazines that circulate among the general population and others that cater to target populations. Another approach would be to specifically target groups/facilities/businesses catering to people of colour and take care to place recruitment materials in places frequented by people of colour. For those examining practices and not identity, using more neutral language such as 'non-monogamous' or 'multi-partner,' rather than the more specific 'polyamory,' could significantly broaden samples. Once they have been able to establish initial contacts, researchers can use the popular method of snowball sampling to explore polys and kinksters of colours' social networks.

Fourth, increasing the number of researchers of colour examining these groups could significantly boost participation among kinksters and polyamorists of colour. Methodological literature indicates that disadvantaged groups such as people of colour (Collins, 1996), lesbians (England, 1994) and women (Gilbert, 1994) may be more open to participate in research conducted by those perceived as members of their own underprivileged group. The preponderance of white researchers studying this area could deter respondents of colour from participating in research. To increase the number and diversity of researchers studying unconventional sexualities, established scholars must actively support graduate students and colleagues who wish to study non-normative sexualities.

Fifth, it is important to understand the reasons why individuals do *not* identify with particular alternative sexual communities, despite participating in behaviours characteristic of those communities. Such an understanding will facilitate a broader examination of the full range of people having kinky sex or multiple partners and the ways in which people select the components of their identities. Furthermore, these studies can illuminate privileges that facilitate or hinder peoples' associations with particular identities, and the interlocking web of characteristics such as age, gender, race/ethnicity, ability, orientation, and experience that shape individuals' sexualities in idiosyncratic ways.

Sixth, researchers should study behaviour, as well as identity. Studies that include only people who identify as kinky or poly will miss these potential respondents whose behaviours may match the target population but whose self-identification precludes their participation in the study. This creates a double bind, because researchers must clearly define their sample populations to conduct a coherent analysis. On the one hand, relying on self-identification as a selection criteria has a long tradition in sexualities research (Berenson, 2002; Chung & Katayama, 1996; Golden, 1996; Rust, 2000) in part because it has proven problematic in the past when researchers assigned identities to behaviours and in part because it can be difficult to build a sample when investigating sexual minorities, and seeking people who self-identify and are willing to participate in research is one of the primary ways in which sexuality scholars have been able to conduct their research. On the other hand, relying on self-identification eliminates the category of persons who engage in the behaviour but do not classify it as an organising principle for self-identification, thus missing large sections of the population of practitioners (Savin-Williams, 2005; Vrangalova & Savin-Williams, 2010).

Most importantly, researchers must move beyond simple 'bean counting' to an examination of how race impacts the ways in which people 'do' sexuality. How does being Black and queer impact sexuality? Asian and gay affect sexual practices? Latina and poly shape identity formations? Native American and kinky affect participation in public organisations? To date, too many studies neglect to address these issues because they begin from a white frame, often fail to problematise race and thus assume a homogenous sample, all despite (potentially) statistically accounting for race.

CONCLUSION

. . .

Too frequently white researchers approach their studies from a white frame of reference and thus (usually unintentionally) exclude consideration of people of colour from the original research design. This initial exclusion then telescopes through the research project to shape the questions researchers ask and the populations they query. Research on poly and kinky populations remains impoverished to the degree that people of colour, as well as other social and numerical minorities such as people with disabilities and the aged, are absent from the analyses. There must be more sexuality research, particularly research that is mindful of privilege and intersections of oppression. A sophisticated analysis requires looking beyond the percentage of people of colour within study samples and moving towards a more holistic account of race and specifically the experiences of poly, kinksters and other sexual minorities of colour.

NOTES

1. The authors do not claim the right to define others' identities, but rather use the term *pervert* to describe polyamorists both because conventional society views them as such and for theoretical coherency.

2. Because the initial study was not designed to be a longitudinal research project and the Institutional Review Board (IRB) required that I destroy all identifying information, I was only able to locate those members of my original sample who retained enough contact with mainstream polyamorous communities to receive the calls for participation in the follow-up study. Thus, the current data cannot account for the perspective of those who left these poly communities. The initial study was also restricted to adults, and to date my sample of children is too small for analysis, so this discussion is similarly missing children's responses. Of the 17 previous respondents I was able to locate, 15 agreed to participate in the follow-up study. Only one of the previous respondents who consented to an interview no longer identified as polyamorous and had started seeking a monogamous relationship.

3. On the questionnaire, there was a line adjacent to the *other* category for self-identification. The responses were so varied that I aggregated them in to a single category of *other* for ease of discussion.

REFERENCES

Attias, B. (2004). Police free gay slaves: Consent, sexuality, and the law. *Left History, 10*(1), 55–83.

Barker, M. (2005a). On tops, bottoms and ethical sluts: The place of BDSM and polyamory in lesbian and gay psychology. *Lesbian & Gay Psychology Review, 6*(2), 124–129.

Barker, M. (2005b). This is my partner, and this is my . . . partner's partner: Constructing a polyamorous identity in a monogamous world. *Journal of Constructivist Psychology, 18,* 75–88.

Barker, M., & Langdridge, D. (2010). *Understanding non-monogamies.* London: Routledge.

Barker, M., & Ritchie, A. (2007). Hot bi babes and feminist families: Polyamorous women speak out. *Lesbian & Gay Psychology Review, 8*(2), 141–151.

Barnard, I. (1999). Queer race. *Social Semiotics, 9*(2), 199–212.

Bauer, R. (2008). Transgressive and transformative gendered sexual practices and white privilege: The case of the dyke/trans/BDSM communities. *Women's Studies Quarterly, 36*(3/4), 233–253.

Bauer, R. (2010). Non-monogamy in queer BDSM communities: Putting the sex back into alternative relationship practices and discourse. In M. Barker & D. Langdridge (Eds.), *Understanding non-monogamies.* London: Routledge.

Berenson, C. (2002). What's in a name? Bisexual women define their terms. *Journal of Bisexuality, 2*(2/3), 9–21.

Bettinger, M. (2005). Polyamory and gay men: A family systems approach. *Journal of GLBT Family Studies, 1*(1), 97–116.

Brame, G. (2000). *BDSM/Fetish demographic survey.* Retrieved from http://www.gloriabrame.com/therapy/bdsmsurveyresults.html

Breslow, N., Evans, L., & Langley, J. (1985). On the prevalence and roles of females in the sadomasochistic subculture: Report of an empirical study. *Archives of Sexual Behavior, 14,* 303–317.

Califia, P. (1979, December 12). A secret side of lesbian sexuality. *The Advocate, 287.*

Califia, P. (1981). Feminism and sadomasochism. *Heresies, 12,* 30–34.

Califia, P. (2000). *Public sex: The culture of radical sex.* San Francisco, CA: Cleis Press.

Chakraborty, J., & Bosman, M. (2005). Measuring the digital divide in the United States: Race, income, and personal computer ownership. *The Professional Geographer, 5*(3), 395–410.

Chancer, L. (2000). From pornography to sadomasochism: Reconciling feminist differences. *The Annals of the American Academy of Political and Social Science, 571,* 1.

Chung, Y., & Katayama, M. (1996). Assessment of sexual orientation in lesbian/gay/bisexual studies. *Journal of Homosexuality, 30*(4), 49–62.

Collins, P. (1996). *Black feminist thought.* New York, NY: Routledge.

Collins, P. (2005). *Black sexual politics: African Americans, gender, and the new racism.* New York, NY: Routledge.

Connolly, P. (2006). Psychological functioning of bondage/domination/sadomasochism (BDSM) practitioners. *Journal of Psychology & Human Sexuality, 18*(1), 79–120.

Cook, E. (2005). *Commitment in polyamorous relationships* (Unpublished Master of Arts in Liberal Studies (Psychology)). Regis University, Denver, CO. Retrieved from http://www.aphroweb.net/papers/thesis/chapter-4.htm

Dalton, S. (2001). Protecting our parent-child relationships: Understanding the strengths and weaknesses of second-parent adoption. In M. Bernstein & R. Reimann (Eds.), *Queer families, queer politics: Challenging culture and the state* (pp. 201–220). New York, NY: Columbia University Press.

Dancer, P., Kleinplatz, P., & Moser, C. (2006). 24/7 SM slavery. *Journal of Homosexuality, 50*(2), 81–101.

Dworkin, A. (1981). *Pornography: Men possessing women.* London: The Women's Press.

Easton, D., & Liszt, C. (1997). *The ethical slut.* San Francisco, CA: Greenery Press.

Ellis, H. (1903/1926). *Studies in the psychology of sex: Vol. III. Analysis of the sexual impulse, love and pain, the sexual impulse in women* (2nd ed.). Philadelphia, PA: F.A. Davis Company.

England, K. (1994). Getting personal: Reflexivity, positionality, and feminist research. *The Professional Geographer, 46*(1), 80–89.

Freud, S. (1938). *The basic writings of Sigmund Freud* (A.A. Brill, Ed. and Trans.). New York, NY: The Modern Library.

Gilbert, M. (1994). The politics of location: Doing feminist research at 'home'. *The Professional Geographer, 46*(1), 90–96.

Golden, C. (1996). What's in a name? Sexual self-identification among women. In R. Savin-Williams & K. Cohen (Eds.), *The lives of lesbians, gays, and bisexuals: Children to adults* (pp. 229–249). Fort Worth, TX: Harcourt Brace.

Hammers, C. (2008). Making space for an agentic sexuality?: The examination of a lesbian/queer bathhouse. *Sexualities, 11*(5), 547–572.

Hammers, C. (2010). Queer exclusions and corporeal silences: The promises and limitations of queer in public sexual spaces. In S. Hines & T. Sanger (Eds.), *Transgender Identities: Towards a social analysis of gender diversity.* London: Routledge.

Haritaworn, J., Lin, C., & Klesse, C. (2006). Poly/logue: A critical introduction to polyamory. *Sexualities, 9*(5), 515–529.

Hequembourg, A. (2007). *Lesbian motherhood: Stories of becoming.* New York, NY: Routledge.

Ho, P. (2006). The (charmed) circle game: Reflections on sexual hierarchy through multiple sexual relationships. *Sexualities, 9*(5), 547–564.

Hoople, T. (1996). Conflicting visions: SM, feminism, and the law. A problem of representation. *Canadian Journal of Law and Society, 11*(1), 177–220.

Jackson, L., Ervin, K., Gardnera, P., & Schmitt, N. (2001). The racial digital divide: Motivational, affective, and cognitive correlates of internet use. *Journal of Applied Social Psychology, 31*(10), 2019–2046.

Jay, K. (1995). *Dyke life: From growing up to growing old, a celebration of the lesbian experience.* New York, NY: Basic Books.

Jeffreys, S. (2003). *Unpacking queer politics: A lesbian feminist perspective.* New York, NY: Polity.

Kantor, A., & Neubarth, M. (1996). Off the charts: The internet. *Internet World, 7*(12), 44–51.

Keener, M. (2004). *A phenomenology of polyamorous persons* (Unpublished master's thesis). Department of Educational Psychology, The University of Utah, Salt Lake City, UT.

Keres, J. (1994). Violence against S/M women within the Lesbian community: A nationwide survey. *Female trouble.* National Coalition for Sexual Freedom. Retrieved from http://www.ncsfreedom.org/index.php?option=com_keyword&id=214

Kirsten, L. (1996). Intimate Relationships Inventory. *Loving More Magazine,* Winter.

Klein, M., & Moser, C. (2006). SM (sadomasochistic) interests in a child custody proceeding. *Journal of Homosexuality, 50,* 233–242.

Kleinplatz, P., & Moser, C. (2005). Is S/M pathological? *Lesbian & Gay Psychology Review, 6*(3), 255–260.

Klesse, C. (2007). *The specter of promiscuity: Gay male and bisexual non-monogamies and polyamories.* London: Ashgate Publishers.

Krafft-Ebing, R. (1898/1965). *The psychopathia sexualis: A medico-legal study.* Oxford: F.A. Davis Co.

Langdridge, D., & Barker, M. (2007). Situating sadomasochism. In L. Darren & B. Meg (Eds.), *Safe, sane and consensual.* New York, NY: Palgrave MacMillan.

Levitt, E., Moser, C., & Jamison, K. (1994). The prevalence and some attributes of females in the sadomasochistic subculture: A second report. *Archives of Sexual Behavior, 23*(4), 465–473.

Ley, D. (2006). *Demographics and psychosocial variables in polyamory: A preliminary survey* (Unpublished study). Licensed Clinical Psychologist, NM #834 Albuquerque, NM.

MacKinnon, C., & Dworkin, A. (Eds.) (1997). *In harm's way: The pornography civil rights hearings.* Cambridge, MA: Harvard University Press.

Matthews, M. (2006). *Lesbians who engage in public bondage, discipline, domination, submission, and sadomasochism (BDSM).* Ann Arbor, MI: ProQuest Company.

Meeks, C. (2001). Civil society and the sexual politics of difference. *Sociological Theory, 19*(3), 325–343.

Mint, P., & Robins, S. (2004). The power dynamics of cheating effects on polyamory and bisexuality. *Journal of Bisexuality, 4*(3/4), 55–76.

Moser, C. (2002). Are any of the paraphilias in the DSM mental disorders? *Archives of Sexual Behavior, 31*(6), 490–491.

Moser, C., & Kleinplatz, P. (2006a). Introduction: The state of our knowledge on SM. *Journal of Homosexuality, 50,* 2–3.

Moser, C., & Kleinplatz, P. (2006b). *Sadomasochism: Powerful pleasures.* New York, NY: Routledge.

Moser, C., Lee, J., & Christensen, P. (1993). Nipple piercing: An exploratory descriptive study. *Journal of Psychology & Human Sexuality, 6*(2), 51.

Moser, C., & Levitt, E. (1987). An exploratory-descriptive study of a sadomasochistically oriented sample. *The Journal of Sex Research, 23,* 322–337.

Mosher, C., Levitt, H., & Manley, E. (2006). Layers of leather. *Journal of Homosexuality, 51*(3), 93–123.

Mossberger, K., Tolbert, J., & McNeal, R. (2008). *Digital citizenship: The internet, society, and participation.* Cambridge, MA: MIT Press.

Munson, M. (1999). Safer sex and the polyamorous lesbian. *Journal of Lesbian Studies, 3*(1/2), 209.

Muscio, I., & Dodson, B. (2002). *Cunt: A declaration of independence.* New York, NY: Seal Press.

Newmahr, S. (2006). Experiences of power in SM: A challenge to power theory. *Berkeley Journal of Sociology, 50,* 37–60.

Newmahr, S. (2008). Becoming a sadomasochist: Integrating self and other in ethnographic analysis. *Journal of Contemporary Ethnography, 37*(5), 619–643.

Noël, M. (2006). Progressive polyamory: Considering issues of diversity. *Sexualities, 9*(5), 602–620.

Ono, H., & Zavodny, M. (2003). Race, Internet Usage and E-Commerce. *The Review of Black Political Economy, 30*(Winter), 7–22.

Pallotta-Chiarolli, M. (2006). Polyparents having children, raising children, schooling children. *Lesbian & Gay Psychology Review, 7*(1), 48–53.

Pallotta-Chiarolli, M. (2010a). To pass, border, or pollute: Polyfamilies go to school. In M. Barker & D. Langdridge (Eds.), *Understanding non-monogamies.* London: Routledge

Pallotta-Chiarolli, M. (2010b). *Border sexualities, border families in schools.* New York, NY: Rowman & Littlefield.

Polikoff, N. (1993). We will get what we ask for: Why legalizing gay and lesbian marriage will not dismantle the legal structure of gender in every marriage. *Virginia Law Review, 79*(7), 1535–1550.

Probyn, E. (1993). *Sexing the self: Gendered positions in cultural studies.* New York, NY: Routledge.

Richters, J., de Visser, R., Rissel, C., Grulich, A., & Smith, A. (2008). Demographic and psychosocial features of participants in bondage and discipline, 'sadomasochism', or dominance and submission (BDSM): Data from a national survey. *The Journal of Sexual Medicine, 5*(7), 1660–1668.

Ridinger, R. (2002). Things visible and invisible. The leather archives and museum. *Journal of Homosexuality, 43,* 1–9.

Riggs, D. (2010). Developing a 'responsible' foster care praxis: Poly as a framework for examining power and propriety in family contexts. In M. Barker & D. Langdridge (Eds.), *Understanding non-monogamies* (pp. 188–200). London: Routledge.

Roderick, G. (2008). The stylisation of internet life?: Predictors of internet leisure patterns using digital inequality and status group perspectives. *Sociological Research Online, 13,* 5.

Ross, M. (2007). Beyond the closet as raceless paradigm. In E.P. Johnson & M.G. Henderson (Eds.), *Black queer studies* (pp. 161–189). London: Duke University Press.

Rubin, G. (1982). The leather menace. In SAMOIS (Ed.), *Coming to power* (pp. 192–227). Boston, MA: Alyson.

Rubin, G. (1984). Thinking sex: Notes for a radical theory of the politics of sexuality. In C. Vance (Ed.), *Pleasure and danger* (pp. 267–319). New York, NY: Routledge.

Rust, P.C. (2000). Bisexuality: A contemporary paradox for women. *Journal of Social Issues, 56,* 205–221.

Rust, P.C. (2003). Monogamy and polyamory: Relationship issues for bisexuals. In L.D. Garnets & D.C. Kimmel (Eds.), *Psychological perspectives on lesbian, gay, and bisexual experiences* (2nd ed.) (pp. 475–496). New York, NY: Columbia University Press.

SAMOIS. (Ed.). (1982). *Coming to power.* Boston, MA: Alyson.

Sanday, P. (2007). *Fraternity gang rape: Sex, brotherhood and privilege on campus.* New York, NY: NYU Press.

Sandnabba, N., Santtila, P., Alison, L., & Nordling, N. (2002). Demographics, sexual behaviour, family background and abuse experiences of practitioners of sadomasochistic sex: A review of recent research. *Sexual and Relationship Therapy, 17*(1), 39–55.

Sandnabba, N., Santtila, P., & Nordling, N. (1999). Sexual behavior and social adaptation among sadomasochistically oriented males. *The Journal of Sex Research, 36*(3), 273.

Savage, D. (2005). *The commitment: Love, sex, marriage and my family.* New York, NY: Penguin Group.

Savin-Williams, R. (2005). *The new gay teenager.* Cambridge, MA: Harvard University Press.

Schippers, M. (2000). The social organization of sexuality and gender in alternative hard rock: An analysis of intersectionality. *Gender and Society, 14*(6), 747–764.

Seidman, S. (1996). *Queer theory sociology.* Cambridge, MA: Blackwell Press.

Sharma, J., & Nath, D. (2005). Through the prism of intersectionality: Same sex sexualities in India. In G. Misra & R. Chandiramani (Eds.), *Sexuality, gender, and rights: Exploring theory and practice in South and Southeast Asia.* New Delhi: Sage.

Sheff, E. (2005a). *Gender, family, and sexuality: Exploring polyamorous community* (Ph.D. dissertation). University of Colorado at Boulder, Colorado.

Sheff, E. (2005b). Polyamorous women, sexual subjectivity, and power. *Journal of Contemporary Ethnography, 34*(3), 251–283.

Sheff, E. (2006). Poly-hegemonic masculinities. *Sexualities, 9*(5), 621–642.

Sheff, E. (2007). The reluctant polyamorist: Auto-ethnographic research in a sexualized setting. In M. Stombler, D. Baunach, E. Burgess, D. Donnelly, & W. Simonds (Eds.), *Sex matters: The sexuality and society reader,* 2nd ed. (pp. 111–118). New York: Pearson, Allyn, and Bacon.

Sheff, E. (2010). Strategies in polyamorous parenting. In M. Barker & D. Langdridge (Eds.), *Understanding non-monogamies* (pp. 169–181). London: Routledge.

Sisson, K., & Moser, C. (2005). Women who engage in S/M interactions for money: A descriptive study. *Lesbian & Gay Psychology Review, 6*(3), 209–226.

Spengler, A. (1977). Manifest sadomasochism of males: Results of an empirical study. *Archives of Sexual Behavior, 6*(6), 441–456.

Sprinkle, A. (1998). Forty reasons why whores are my heroines. In J. Elias, V. Bullough, V. Elias, & G. Brewer (Eds.), *Prostitution: On whores, hustlers, and Johns* (pp. 114–115). Amherst, NY: Prometheus Books.

Statistics Finland. (2009, December). *Population.* Retrieved from http://www.stat.fi/tup/suoluk/suoluk_vaesto_en .html

Steinbugler, A. (2005). Visibility as privilege and danger: Heterosexual and same-sex interracial intimacy in the 21st century. *Sexualities, 8*(4), 425–443.

Taormino, T. (2008). *Opening up: A guide to creating and sustaining open relationships.* San Francisco, CA: Cleis Press.

Tomassilli, J., Golub, S., Bimbi, D., & Parsons, J. (2009). Behind closed doors: An exploration of kinky sexual behaviors in urban Lesbian and Bisexual women. *The Journal of Sex Research, 46*(5), 438–445.

Vrangalova, Z., & Savin-Williams, R. (2010). Correlates of same-sex sexuality in heterosexually identified young adults. *The Journal of Sex Research, 47*(1), 92–102.

Walston, J. (2001). *Polyamory: An exploratory study of responsible multi-partnering* (Unpublished master's thesis). Indiana University Southeast, New Albany, IN.

Warf, B., & Grimes, J. (1997). Counterhegemonic discourses and the internet. *Geographical Review, 87*(2), 259–274.

Warner, M. (1999). *The trouble with normal: Sex, politics, and the ethics of queer life.* New York, NY: The Free Press.

Waskul, D. (Ed.). (2004). *Net.seXXX: Readings on sex, pornography, and the internet.* New York, NY: Peter Lang.

Weber, A. (2002). Survey results: Who are we? And other interesting impressions. *Loving More Magazine, 30,* 4.

Weinberg, T., & Kamel, G. (1995). S&M: An introduction to the study of sadomasochism. In T. Weinberg (Ed.), *S&M: Studies in dominance & submission.* New York, NY: Prometheus Books.

Weinberg, M., Williams, C., & Calhan, C. (1995). 'If the shoe fits. . . '.: Exploring male homosexual foot fetishism. *The Journal of Sex Research, 32*(1), 17–27.

Weinrich, J.D. (1997). Strange bedfellows: Homosexuality, gay liberation and the internet. *Journal of Sex Education and Therapy, 22*(1), 58–66.

Weitzman, G. (2006). Therapy with clients who are bisexual and polyamorous. *Journal of Bisexuality, 6*(1/2), 137–164.

Weitzman, G. (2007). Counseling bisexuals in polyamorous relationships. In B. Firestein (Ed.), *Becoming visible: Counseling bisexuals across the lifespan* (pp. 312–335). New York, NY: Columbia University Press.

White, C. (2006). The spanner trials and changing laws on sadomasochism in the UK. In P. Kleinplatz & C. Moser (Eds.), *Sadomasochism: Powerful pleasures*. New York, NY: Hayworth Press.

Willey, A. (2006). Christian nations, polygamic races, and women's rights: Toward a genealogy of non/monogamy and whiteness. *Sexualities, 9*(5), 530–546.

Wolf, L. (2003). *Jealousy and transformation in polyamorous relationships* (Unpublished dissertation). The Institute for the Advanced Study of Human Sexuality. Retrieved from http://drleannawolfe.com/Dissertation.pdf

Wright, S. (2006). Discrimination of SM-identified individuals. *Journal of Homosexuality, 50*(2), 217–231.

Yost, M. (2006). *Consensual sexual sadomasochism and sexual aggression perpetration: Exploring the erotic value of power* (Unpublished dissertation). Department of Psychology, University of California, Santa Cruz, CA.

32 • Nadine Naber

ARAB AMERICAN FEMININITIES
Beyond Arab Virgin/American(ized) Whore

DISCUSSION QUESTIONS

1. How does Lulu's family's understanding of American culture and identity, Christianity, and Western feminism inform their conceptualization of her sexual identity?

2. How do the normative demands of middle-class American whiteness impact Lulu and her family?

3. What is Lulu's central marker of betrayal? Who maintains the cultural markers of her insider—outsider status?

4. What is the heterosexual imperative? How does this imperative reinforce the control over women's sexual and marriage practices in Arab and Western societies?

It was a typical weeknight at my parents' home. My father was asleep since he wakes up at 4:00 a.m. to open his convenience store in downtown San Francisco. I joined my mother on the couch and we searched for something interesting to watch on TV. My mother held the remote control, flipping through the stations. Station after station a similar picture of an Anglo American male and female holding one another in romantic or sexual ways appeared

Nadine Naber, "Arab American Femininities: Beyond Arab Virgin/American(ized) Whore." Reprinted by permission of the author.

on the screen. As she flipped the station, my mother remarked, "Sleep, Slept . . . Sleep, Slept . . . THAT is America!" She continued, "Al sex al hum, zay shurb al mai [Sex for them is as easy as drinking water]."

—Nadine Naber, journal entry, December 2, 1999

As I listened to my mother,[1] I recalled several experiences growing up within a bicultural Arab American familial and communal context. *Al Amenkan* (Americans) were often referred to in derogatory sexualized terms. It was the trash culture—degenerate, morally bankrupt, and not worth investing in. *Al Arab* (Arabs), on the other hand, were referred to positively and associated with Arab family values and hospitality. Similarly, throughout the period of my ethnographic research among middle-class Arab American family and community networks in San Francisco, California,[2] between January 1999 and August 2001, the theme of female sexuality circumscribed the ways my research participants imagined and contested culture, identity, and belonging. The theme of female sexuality tended to be utilized as part of some Arab immigrant families' selective assimilation strategy in which the preservation of Arab cultural identity and assimilation to American norms of "whiteness" were simultaneously desired. Within this strategy, the ideal of reproducing cultural identity was gendered and sexualized and disproportionately placed on daughters. A daughter's rejection of an idealized notion of Arab womanhood could signify cultural loss and thereby negate her potential as capital within this family strategy. In policing Arab American femininities, this family strategy deployed a cultural nationalist logic that represented the categories "Arab" and "American" in oppositional terms, such as "good Arab girls" vs. "bad American(ized) girls," or "Arab virgin" vs. "American(ized) whore." I coin the term Arab cultural re-authenticity to contextualize this process within Arab histories of transnational migration, assimilation, and racialization. Arab cultural re-authenticity, I suggest, is a localized, spoken, and unspoken figure of an imagined "true" Arab culture that emerges as a reaction or an alternative to the universalizing tendencies of hegemonic U.S. nationalism, the pressures of assimilation, and the gendered

racialization of Arab women and men. I use the term hegemonic (white) U.S. nationalism to refer to the official discourses of the U.S. state and corporate media and the notion of a universalized abstract American citizen that "at the same time systematically produces sexualized, gendered, and racialized bodies and particularistic claims for recognition and justice by minoritized groups."[3] . . .

It situates discussions on religious identity within the context of intersecting coordinates of power (race, class, nation, and so forth) and historical circumstances. Moreover, I do not present narratives as sites from which to universalize the experiences of all Arab American women, but to provide an opportunity to think beyond misperceptions and stereotypes. I locate myself in the context of multiple, contradictory loyalties, such as Arab daughter, sister, and cousin, anthropologist, researcher, community activist, and feminist. This location rendered me at once "insider" and "outsider," collaboratively and individually deconstructing, contesting, and often reinforcing the cultural logics that circumscribed my research participants' identities.

This article focuses on the tense and often conflictual location of Arab American femininities at the intersections of two contradictory discourses: Arab cultural re-authenticity and hegemonic U.S. nationalism. I explore the ways that the theme of sexuality permeated many Arab immigrant families' engagements with the pressures of assimilation vis-à-vis a series of racial and cultural discourses on Arabness and Americanness. I argue that although my research participants (and their parents) perceived their cultural location within a binary of Arabness and Americanness, when lived and performed, this binary constantly broke down, particularly along the lines of race, class, gender, sexuality, religion, and nation. Yet binary terms for expressing the themes of family, gender, and sexuality persisted throughout my field sites as a discursive mechanism for explaining more complex processes that implicate my research participants and their parents within a desire for a stereotypical "Americanization" that is predicated on "Arabness" as the crucial Other. A binary cultural logic of "us" and "them" that was gendered and sexualized was then a discursive reaction to the complex dichotomies of hegemonic U.S. nationalism that at once pressure racialized immigrants to assimilate into a whitened middle-class U.S. national identity while positioning them outside the boundaries of "Americanness." Both generations were mutually invested in expressing the two racial-ethnic-national categories (Arab and American) in dichotomous terms because it provided a discursive mechanism for engaging with the processes of immigration and assimilation in which Arabness and Americanness absolutely depend on each other to exist—as opposites and in unison. . . .

This article, then, is not an analysis of *all* second-generation Arab Americans, but of how locational conditions (especially when it comes to racialized, gendered, class, and religious identities) mediate and break down an imagined "Arab" identity in the context of the San Francisco Bay area of California. It is an exploration of how binary oppositions within Arab American discourses on gender and sexuality take on particular form among my research participants, a group of educated, middle-class, young women active in progressive Arab, Arab feminist, and/or queer Arab political movements whose parents are ethnic entrepreneurs and immigrated, or were displaced, to the San Francisco Bay area—a traditionally liberal, racially/ethnically diverse location. . . . I argue that the phenomena of intersectionality cannot be generalized as taking one singular form for all Arab Americans; that one must be cautious about using the terms "Arab American" or "Arab American women" in a U.S. national sense; and that feminist theory and practice vis-à-vis Arab American communities should take the specific ways that the coordinates of race, class, gender, sexuality, religion, and nation intersect in different contexts seriously. For example, perhaps part of the motivation behind the policing of an Arab daughter's behavior among middle-class business entrepreneurs invested in

economic mobility and the selective reproduction of patriarchal cultural ideals is that San Francisco is home to some of the most vibrant progressive Arab, queer Arab, Arab feminist, and Arab student movements alongside some of the most vibrant civil rights, racial justice, feminist, and queer movements in the nation. In the San Francisco Bay area, multiracial coalition building, transgressive sexual politics, and critiques of classism, capitalism, U.S.-led imperialism, and war heavily inspire young people, such as my research participants, who are either active in or loyal to progressive politics.

Among my research participants, the performativity of an idealized "true" Arab culture emerged in the context of "regulatory ideals" that they associated with "being Arab" and distinguished from the regulatory ideals of "being American," such as: knowing what is *abe* (shameful); knowing how to give *mujamalat* (flattery); knowing what you're supposed to do when someone greets you; drinking *shai* (tea) or coffee; talking about politics "sooo" much; getting up for an older person; respecting your elders; looking after your parents and taking care of them; judging people according to what family they are from; marrying through connections; gossiping and having a good reputation.[4]

Articulations of "selfhood" among my research participants were key sites where the oppositional logic of self/Other, us/them, Arab/American was reproduced among my research participants. Selfhood was often articulated in terms of a choice between "being an individual, being my own person, being an American," or "being connected, having family, and being 'Arab.'" Yet what ultimately distinguished "us" from "them," or *Al Arab* from *Al Amerikan*, among my research participants was a reiterated set of norms that were sexualized, gender specific, and performed in utterances such as *"banatna ma bitlaau fil lail"* (our girls don't stay out at night). Positioning the feminized subjectivities within my field sites in between the binary oppositions of good Arab daughter vs. bad American(ized) daughter, or Arab virgin vs. American(ized) whore, the discourse of Arab cultural re-authenticity reproduced a masculinist cultural nationalist assumption that if a daughter chooses to betray the regulatory demands of an idealized Arab womanhood, an imagined Arab community loses itself to the *Amerikan*. Jumana, recalling her parents' reinforcement of this distinction while she was growing up, explains,

> My parents thought that being American was spending the night at a friend's house, wearing shorts, the guy-girl thing, wearing make-up, reading teen magazines, having pictures of guys in my room. My parents used to tell me, "If you go to an American's house, they're smoking, drinking...they offer you this and that. But if you go to an Arab house, you don't see as much of that. *Bi hafzu 'ala al banat* [They watch over their daughters]."

My research participants generally agreed that virginity, followed by heterosexual (ethno-religious) endogamous marriage were the key demands of an idealized Arab womanhood that together, constituted the yardstick that policed female subjectivities in cultural nationalist terms. Here, discourses around Arab American femininities allow for a cultural, versus territorial, nationalist male Arab American perspective within the United States that emerges in opposition to hegemonic (white) U.S. nationalism and in the context of immigrant nostalgia. Here, an imagined notion of "Arab people" or an "Arab community" is inspired, in part, by a collective memory of immigrant displacement and romantic memories of "home" and "homeland culture." Among middle-class familial and communal networks in San Francisco, Arab American cultural nationalism was expressed in terms of an imagined Arab community or people that constituted "woman" as virgin or mother vis-à-vis an extended family context. Among Arab American cultural authorities in San Francisco, the ideal of marrying within one's kin group within the discourse of Arab cultural re-authenticity was refashioned in terms of marrying within the kin groups' religious group (Muslim or Christian); village of origin (Ramallah, Al Salt), economic class, national (Jordanian, Lebanese, Palestinian, or Syrian), or racialized/ethnic (Arab) group. These categories were hierarchical, as "religious affiliation" tended to supersede "national origin" and "national origin" superseded "racial/ethnicity identity" as the boundary to be protected through a

daughter's marriage. Although the regulatory demands of Arab womanhood were often framed as an alternative to assimilation and Americanization, the cultural discourses that controlled a daughter's marriagability simultaneously enabled a family strategy of assimilation to an appropriate American norm of whiteness that privileges heterosexual marriage—within particular boundaries of race and class—as capital.

The following...narrative emphasizes intersections of religion and sexuality....

THE HETEROSEXUAL IMPERATIVE

> Waiting for a friend at Café Macondo, in San Francisco's Mission district, graffiti reading QUEER ARABS EXIST caught my attention. Later, in conversations among Arab women activists, I learned that the graffiti artist was a Syrian American woman named Lulu. Lulu was also the coproducer of a special issue of *Bint Al Nas* on the theme of "sexuality." *Bint Al Nas* is a cyber magazine and network for queer Arab women and as part of this issue, Lulu designed the web art, "Virgin/Whore," where a collage representing herself as "virgin" (represented by drums, pita bread, camels, Allah, a Syrian flag, and a photograph of her family members wearing blindfolds) transforms into a second collage representing her as "whore" (represented by images of dildos next to her girlfriend's name written in Arabic, handcuffs, a blurred image of the picture that represents her parents, and a photo of Madonna). A few months later, Lulu and I made plans to meet at Café Flor, a queer hang out in the Castro district of San Francisco. I recognized Lulu from the tattoo of her girlfriend's name Amina in Arabic script on her arm and the Palestinian flag sewn onto her book bag. We talked about the collage and she explained, "What I am doing with the two images is showing how they are dichotomous, or at least they have felt that way, and how really, it has been an either/or situation. Also, I think it's how my mother would see my sexuality: dirty, sinful, dark. The reason for the roll over of images is to show that the two states can't coexist."

—Naber, journal entry, December 28, 2000

EXCERPTS FROM LULU'S ORAL HISTORY: *I grew up with this all the time: "Sex is an act of love in marriage. If you're not a virgin when you get married, you're in trouble." I fought that all the time. I would ask my mom about Syria. I would say, "If good Arab women are not having sex and Arab men can have sex, then who were the Arab men having sex with?" She would answer, "The Christian women." So the Christian women were the whores. That is very prevalent in my family, the Muslim virgin and the Christian whore. The whore is either American or Christian.*

My family is unique because we talked about sex. My sister was really vocal about having boyfriends and they were always black, which was even more of a problem. My parents are into the idea that Arabs are white. I think it's more of a Syrian—Lebanese thing. But I didn't have the same problems with my parents about boyfriends as my sister because I knew I was queer since I was thirteen or fourteen. It was when I came out when things erupted for me. It got to the point where they were asking, "Don't you want to have a boyfriend?"

My mom won't come visit me at my house because she doesn't want to see that I live with a woman. The bottom line is premarital sex. Lesbian sex doesn't happen because Arab girls don't have premarital sex. When I came out, it was like, "That's fine that you're gay—but don't act on it. We don't want you having sex." Everyday I heard, "Get married with a guy and..." suppress it basically. I said, "I can't do that." And I still get that... "We (Arabs) don't do that"... or "You're the only gay Arab in the world."

It became this thing that everyone was going to fix me. My uncles would come and take me out to lunch. They would say, "Let's talk. This doesn't happen in our culture. You've been brainwashed by Americans. You've taken too many feminist classes, you joined NOW, you hate men, you have a backlash against men...." It was like... "This is what this American society has done to our daughter."

When that was the reaction I received, I totally disassociated myself from Arabs. I felt I couldn't be gay and Arab. I felt that either I have to go home and be straight or be totally out and pass as white. But later, I got a lot of support from queer Arab networks.

One of the first people I met was Samah. She was doing some research and asked if she could interview me. I did it and we both cried. Then I went to a queer Arab women's gathering. I was the youngest one and everyone knew that I came out a week after I turned eighteen and was kicked out by my parents four months later. I was the baby. They all supported me. Over the years, they've become my family.

Now my mom tells me, "Just go have sex with a man—maybe you'll change," and I say, "Maybe you should try it with a woman." She keeps finding ways to say I'm too Americanized... and when I tell her, "You don't know how many queer Arabs I know." She says, "They're American, they're American born, they're not Arab..." or "They must be Christian" or "Their fathers must not be around because no father would accept his daughter being gay."

They blamed Western feminism and said I should go to a therapist. Then they changed their mind and said not to go because they don't want it on my hospital records that I am gay—because "You know," they would say, "After you change—someone might see on your hospital records that you were gay." Their idea was that they didn't want anyone finding out "after I change" and "once I get married," that I had this dark past. Then at the very end they did try to send me to a hospital. That was when the shit hit the fan, our big final fight. I was so strong in defending myself—and they thought that too was very American. So it became this thing of like—and they make it very clear—"You chose your sexuality over us. Sex is more important than your family." Which goes back to the tight-knit family Arab thing. It's all about group dynamics.

When Lulu's mother replaces the "American whore" with the "Christian Arab" she reveals the gaps and fissures within the idea of a unified Arab American nationalist identity and the ways that Arab cultural re-authenticity shifts depending on sociohistorical circumstances. Lulu's mother's association of the category "Syrian Christian" with the classification "Westernized Other" signifies the ways that the categories "Islam" and "Arabness" have often been conflated throughout Arab history and in several cases, juxtaposed against the notion of a Christian West.

According to her mother, the Syrian—Muslim self is to be protected from the corrupted, Westernized, Syrian—Christian Other.

Intersections between national origin and racial identification in Lulu's narrative further complicate Arab cultural identity in the United States. Lulu, in remembering why her parents did not accept her sister's black boyfriends, explains that identifying as white is "a Syrian—Lebanese thing." The Syrian—Lebanese distinction is common within hegemonic Arab American discourses in San Francisco. Many of my research participants agree that Syrian and Lebanese Arab Americans have had more access to the privileges of middle-class whiteness compared to other Arab Americans.[5] Steering Lulu's sister away from the racial Other, Lulu's mother, like Rime's father, secures a white middle-class positionality. Yet when it comes to Lulu's sexuality, the association of Syrians with whiteness is quickly disrupted as a sexualized, cultural, nationalist logic disassociates them as "Arabs" from the loose, sexually immoral American "feminist" Other in the name of controlling Lulu's sexuality. In Lulu's narrative, then, the *Al Arab/Al Amerikan* boundary is permeable and shifting. As Lulu explains, her parents uphold the normative demands of middle-class American whiteness to tame her sister's sexuality while they distinguish themselves from *Al Amerikan* when it comes to taming Lulu's behaviors.

Fissures in Arab cultural re-authenticity also emerge when Lulu's mother suggests that Lulu "try sex with a man." In the case of Lulu's queer identity, a heterosexual imperative becomes a more significant symbol of the Arab virgin/American whore boundary than the "virginity" ideal. Gloria Anzaldúa writes, "For the lesbian of color, the ultimate rebellion she can make against her native culture is through her sexual behavior. She goes against two moral prohibitions: sexuality and homosexuality."[6] Lulu's queerness, the central marker of her betrayal, underwrites her marginalization as traitor-outsider-American by cultural authorities such as her mother, her father, and her uncle. The extent to which she is seen as "unacceptable, faulty, damaged," culminate in her family's attempt to send her to a hospital to fix her so

that she might return "straight" home. Here, the stance of their conservativism is made possible by their inculcation and reproduction of white American middle-class norms, such as "therapy," within the discourse of Arab cultural re-authenticity. Lulu's parents thus reinforce a particular kind of assimilation constituted by the ways that Arabness and Americanness operate both as opposites and in unison in the policing of Arab American femininities throughout my field sites.

In overriding the virginity ideal with the heterosexual imperative, Lulu's mother reinforces the control over women's sexual and marriage practices that underlie the heterosexual conjugal ideal in Arab and Western societies. Yet beyond reinforcing a heterosexual imperative, Lulu's mother is also reinforcing family ideals critically inherited from Arab homelands that are not only conjugal, but include extended kin that are inscribed beyond household or nuclear terms. In attempting to reinstate Lulu's heterosexuality, Lulu's mother seeks to protect Lulu's father's honor as well as the family honor of her nuclear and her extended family. Moreover, the intervention of Lulu's uncle can be interpreted in terms of the re-fashioning of a patrilineal ideal in the diaspora, in which males and elders remain responsible for female lineage members (even after marriage) and men are responsible for providing for their families, which includes their current wives and underage children and may include aged parents, unmarried sisters, younger brothers, and the orphaned children of their brothers.[7]

As a form of political critique directed against patriarchy and patrilineality, Lulu's chosen family is a sign of her resistance. In the act of choosing her family, Lulu challenges Arab and Anglo-European ideologies that read blood and heterosexual marriage ties as the key foundation of kinship, demonstrating that all families are contextually defined. In undermining the association of kinship with biology, Lulu overtly performs the social, ideological, political, and historical constructedness of kinship. Yet when she meets Samah and joins queer Arab e-mail lists, Lulu finds an alternative to the Arab/American split in the coming together of what she understood to be her "queer" and her "Arab" identities. Lulu's insistence that QUEER ARABS EXIST is an act in resisting racism, homophobia, and patriarchy on multiple fronts: it undermines the Arab virgin/American (ized) whore that seeks to control women's sexuality by marking women who transgress the heterosexual imperative of Arab cultural authenticity as "American" and it disrupts the dualistic logic of hegemonic U.S. nationalist discourses that homogenize and subordinate Arab women as either veiled victims of misogynist terrorist Arab men or exotic erotic objects accessible to white/Western male heroes. Yet cultural identity, for Lulu, is more than "separate pieces merely coming together"—it is a site of tension, pain, and alienation that is constantly in motion.

Lulu's narrative signifies the critical inheritance of the polarization between Muslim and Christian Arabs from the homeland(s) to Arab San Francisco. It exemplifies the ways that this polarization took on local form among many bourgeois Arab American Muslims with whom I interacted. Throughout my field sites, hegemonic Arab Muslim discourses often privileged Arab Muslim women as the essence of cultural re-authenticity—as opposed to Arab Christian women who were often represented as promiscuous and therefore, "Americanized." Yet although cultural authorities often deployed religion as a framework for policing feminized subjectivities throughout my field sites, religious background alone did not determine the extent to which my research participants upheld, reconfigured, or transgressed the feminized imperatives of Arab cultural re-authenticity. My research participants who transgressed "good girl" behaviors through dating before marriage, interracial, and/or same-sex relationships were religiously diverse. In addition, religious affiliation alone did not determine the extent to which parents, aunts, or uncles circumscribed their daughters' behaviors and identities.

While Lulu explained that her mother deployed her Muslim identity to reinforce the normative demands of virginity, her parents' self-identification as "white" complexified their understanding of a "normative femininity." In addition, Lulu stated that her mother deployed a pan-ethnic "Arab" identity when

she asked her to suppress her lesbian identity. Thus, while the discourse of the "Muslim virgin" and the "Christian whore" policed Lulu's femininity, the "virgin/whore" dichotomy was also constituted by a series of intersecting and contradictory discourses such as white versus non-white, Arab versus American. The ways that these discourses operated to police femininities depended on the different ways that coordinates of race, class, gender, sexuality, religion, and nation intersected in each of my research participants' lives....

CONCLUSION

Walking down the street between one of San Francisco's largest populations of homeless women and men and the new dot-com yuppies, I did my usual skim of graffiti on Café Macondo's walls. The "FOR" in LESBIANS FOR BUSH had been crossed out and replaced with the word "EAT." As I turned to the wall behind me to find out whether QUEER ARABS still EXIST[ed], my eyes followed an arrow, drawn in thick black marker that pointed to the words QUEER ARABS and was connected to the words, ONE OF MANY PROBLEMS.

Looking closer, I noticed another message superimposed over QUEER ARABS EXIST in faint blue ink. A line was drawn between the words QUEER and ARABS and the letter "S" was added to the beginning of the word "EXIST." I re-read it several times before I finally understood that superimposed upon QUEER ARABS EXIST, the new message, in coupling the words ARABS and SEXIST, implied that ARABS are SEXIST. I thought about my research and the resemblance between the images on the wall and my research participants' everyday experiences. While Lulu's graffiti confronted the lumping of Arabs into the homogeneous categories "veiled victim" or "polygamous terrorist," the defacement of QUEER ARABS EXIST reinforced the binary construction of "the Arab" as Other. Similarly, while Rime, Lulu, and Nicole burst the boundaries of hegemonic Arab American and U.S. nationalisms on multiple fronts, they also rearticulate hegemonic nationalisms in binary terms as a coding for a more complex process in which the categories "Arab" and "American" are mutually constitutive and exist both as opposites and in unison, in the context of immigration, assimilation, and racialization.

As I took another glance at ARABS ARE SEXIST, superimposed over QUEER ARABS EXIST, I noticed another message, a much smaller message written in black letters in Spanish and English that framed the top right side of QUEER ARABS EXIST. It read ES ALGO BUENO. IT'S A GOOD THING.

—Naber, journal entry, June 2001

NOTES

I am grateful to Suad Joseph, Kent Ono, Ella Maria Ray, Martina Reiker, Minoo Moallem, Andrea Smith, Rabab Abdulhadi, and Evelyn Alsultany for providing me with invaluable feedback and support while I was developing this article. I would like to especially thank the editorial board members of *Feminist Studies* and the anonymous readers for their constructive suggestions and the immense time and effort they committed to seeing this article in publication. I am indebted to each and every person who participated in this project and I am grateful to Eman Desouky, Lilan Boctor, my mother, Firyal Naber, and my father, Suleiman Naber for their persistent support and encouragement throughout the period of my field research.

1. This is not a literal translation, but conveys the message of my mother's words. Throughout the rest of this article, I have edited my research participants' quotes into a readable form, maintaining the originality of the quote as much as possible. This process included cutting repetitive words and statements, rearranging the order of the narratives, and simplifying elaborate explanations. I have also altered names and places in order to protect my research participants' privacy.

2. These networks included local chapters of the American Arab Anti-Discrimination Committee, the Arab Women's Solidarity Association, the Muslim Students' Association, Students for Justice in Palestine, and the Arab Cultural Center.

3. Minoo Moallem and Ian Boal, "Multicultural Nationalism and the Poetics of Inauguration," in *Between Woman and Nation. Nationalisms. Transnational Feminism, and the State.* ed. Caren Kaplan, Norma Alarcon, and Minoo Moallem (Durham, N.C.: Duke University Press, 1999), 243–64.

4. Here, I use terms that were reiterated among my research participants to illustrate the ways that my research participants regularly associated "Americanness" with freedom and individualism and "Arabness" with family and connectivity.

5. Throughout my field sites, Palestinian and Jordanian Arab Americans tended to view Syrian and Lebanese Arab Americans as more "assimilated" than themselves. Several factors have produced this "difference." Historically, Syrian and Lebanese emigrated to the San Francisco Bay area in the early 1900s, before Palestinians and Jordanians, who first immigrated in the late 1950s.

6. Gloria Anzaldúa, *Borderlands: La Frontera* (San Francisco: Aunt Lute Books, 1987), 17.

7. Here, I build on Suad Joseph's definition of patrilineality in Arab families in "Gendering Citizenship in the Middle East," in *Gender and Citizenship in the Middle East,* ed. Suad Joseph (New York: Syracuse University Press, 2000), 3–32.

SECTION FIVE

Culture, Religion, and Technology

In prior editions of *Sex, Gender, and Sexuality*, we incorporated few pieces that dealt with religion/spirituality throughout the text where they seemed appropriate. However, for this edition, we chose to create a section that includes more chapters on faith while still including essential work on culture and technology. Our hope is to shed light on what has been considered a taboo realm of study and to illuminate the many ways that gender and sexuality intersect and interact with faith and spirituality and other powerful societal institutions.

This section begins with a poem by Nellie Wong which speaks to the internalization of racial oppression and the politics of 'whiteness as goodness,' detailing her struggle with longing for white skin as a child growing up in a white-dominated culture. Davis also discusses internalized oppression in terms of women's bodily/genital dissatisfaction in the age of pornography and the increasing popularity of 'labiaplasty.' Both of these authors speak in different ways to the power of various social institutions to define "good" and "bad" in terms of race, gender, sexuality, and so on.

This section also includes a new piece by Seth Goren that offers an interesting look at the complications of privilege. In "Gay and Jewish," he proposes that while being Jewish is typically considered societally oppressive, there are some Jewish traditions and institutions that are more accepting of his gay identity than some in the Christian faith. That is, while being Jewish may be overarchingly oppressive, his religion makes his identity as a gay man "easier" in some contexts than if he belonged to another religious institution. His text is a good reminder that privilege and oppression are never "black and white" but interconnected, complicated, and often mutually constitutive.

Next, Ayesha Kurshid furthers discussion on the complexities of privilege in "Islamic Traditions of Modernity: Gender, Class, and Islam in a Transnational Women's Education Project." She discusses the burgeoning movement to educate Muslim girls worldwide and specifically the *parlilikhi* (educated) classes of Muslim girls and women in Pakistan. Despite the misconceptions that abound in America regarding education and Islam, Kurshid argues that being *parlilikhi* makes Muslim girls and women *appear* middle class, or at least to embody middle-class values, which is generally seen as good for Islam writ large. That is, rather than viewing Muslim girls and women seeking education as somehow revolting against traditional Islamic values, the middle-class air that education affords them can be seen as making them better or stronger Muslims, regardless of gender.

Subsequently, Lynne Gerber and Jay Michaelson switch gears a bit and offer what might be seen as alternative or countercultural ideas regarding Christianity, the former regarding the complexities of masculinity and Christianity and the latter in terms of the possibilities of a Biblically based and gay-inclusive future of sexuality. Gerber discusses certain sectors of Christian culture, arguing that their Christian masculinities tend to rebuke rather than espouse some of the main tenets of hegemonic, violent masculinity. Godly masculinities, she suggests, discourage heterosexual conquest and promote emotionally intimate (while not sexual) relationships between men—all of which run counter to hegemonic masculine ideals. She ends by cautioning scholars in the field of gender, sexuality, and religion to avoid monolithic assumptions about men and masculinities.

Michaelson convinces us that gay, lesbian, bisexual, and transgender (GLBT) civil rights are, in fact, a religious issue, or at least *should* be if the movement hopes to succeed. First, citing bits of history and politics, he argues that "gay versus Christian" rhetoric is both stale and unproductive. Then, using a simple list of Biblical references, he demonstrates how Christianity and GLBT identities are anything but mutually exclusive and why those who identify as Christian need not feel as though they must defend an antihomosexuality stance based on religious doctrine.

Next, Rosalind Chou, Kristen Lee, and Simon Ho move us from the institutional discussion of religion to education. In "Love is (Color)Blind: Asian Americans and White Institutional Space at the Elite University," they detail qualitatively the experiences of Asian American students at an historically white college as they navigate sexuality and gender while simultaneously coping with common instances of racism. While most Asian women reported hearing comments regarding their "exoticism" or "submissiveness," many Asian men on the campus described often being asexualized or emasculated. In dealing with these racist and gendered incidences, Asian students employed a variety of strategies, including a form of "color-blindness" that would allow them to cope racially and otherwise while matriculating in an institutionally white space. The authors argue the pros and cons of employing such strategies.

Finally, both Brandon Andrew Robinson and C. J. Pascoe show us the ways in which continually evolving technologies serve to shape and redefine our sexual and affectional relationships with others. Robinson discusses the gay dating/hookup site Adam4Adam.com and the "preference" categories that effectively allow users to block those of certain races from gaining access to their profiles. Robinson argues specifically that in the context of Web dating, users can pass off as a simple matter of personal taste what, in other contexts, would likely be seen as blatantly racist, all the while never having to admit to racial bias. This serves as a good reminder for all of us to investigate where our biases might be lurking, despite lip service or well-intentioned action to the contrary.

Pascoe leaves us with hope for the future and the intersections of technology with sexuality. For her study she interviewed several youth who made use of Internet/chat/text technologies to navigate some of their first sexual relationships. Though most discourses surrounding teen sexuality and technology admonish against the multifarious dangers involved, such as pedophilia, predatory practices, and harassment, Pascoe's findings run contrary to these narratives. Most teens she interviewed expressed gratitude for the ways that technology has enhanced their emotional connections with others, and many said screen time eased some of their anxieties about sexuality. From her findings, Pascoe encourages a future where technology can be seen as an asset for sexual education of youth.

Overall, the chapters in this section remind us of the powerful ways societal institutions and cultural practices interact with and help to define our identities of gender, sexuality, class, and race. As you read them, think of the ways your participation within certain realms of society have shaped the way you view gender and sexuality. How might you see things differently, say, if you belonged to a different religion or institution? Or if tomorrow you woke up with a different gender identity? Questions like these are important in helping us to identify the ways in which society shapes who we are and how we might work together for a better future for all.

33 • *Nellie Wong*

WHEN I WAS GROWING UP

DISCUSSION QUESTIONS

1. What external social forces shape Wong's earlier desire to be white, and how are nationality and citizenship implicated?
2. How are gender and sexuality central to Wong's own sense of racial identity and how her racial identity is perceived by others?

I know now that once I longed to be white.
How? you ask.
Let me tell you the ways.

when I was growing up, people told me
I was dark and I believed my own darkness
in the mirror, in my soul, my own narrow vision

when I was growing up, my sisters
with fair skin got praised
for their beauty, and in the dark
I fell further, crushed between high walls

when I was growing up, I read magazines
and saw movies, blonde movie stars, white skin,
sensuous lips and to be elevated, to become
a woman, a desirable woman, I began to wear
imaginary pale skin

when I was growing up, I was proud
of my English, my grammar, my spelling
fitting into the group of smart children
smart Chinese children, fitting in,
belonging, getting in line

when I was growing up and went to high school,
I discovered the rich white girls, a few yellow girls,
their imported cotton dresses, their cashmere
sweaters,

their curly hair and I thought that I too should have
what these lucky girls had

when I was growing up, I hungered
for American food, American styles,
coded: white and even to me, a child
born of Chinese parents, being Chinese
was feeling foreign, was limiting,
was unAmerican

when I was growing up and a white man wanted
to take me out, I thought I was special,
an exotic gardenia, anxious to fit
the stereotype of an oriental chick

when I was growing up, I felt ashamed
of some yellow men, their small bones,
their frail bodies, their spitting
on the streets, their coughing,
their lying in sunless rooms,
shooting themselves in the arms

when I was growing up, people would ask
if I were Filipino, Polynesian, Portuguese.
They named all colors except white, the shell
of my soul, but not my dark, rough skin

when I was growing up, I felt
dirty. I thought that god

made white people clean
and no matter how much I bathed,
I could not change, I could not shed
my skin in the gray water

when I was growing up, I swore
I would run away to purple mountains,
houses by the sea with nothing over
my head, with space to breathe,

uncongested with yellow people in an area
called Chinatown, in an area I later learned
was a ghetto, one of many hearts
of Asian America

I know now that once I longed to be white.
How many more ways? you ask.
Haven't I told you enough?

34 • *Simone Weil Davis*

LOOSE LIPS SINK SHIPS

DISCUSSION QUESTIONS

1. Do you think women and men face the same expectations to possess aesthetically "appealing" genitalia? Why or why not?
2. Could this type of plastic surgery for women be compared to male circumcision? Why or why not?
3. Do you find similarities between the cosmetics and/or diet industries and this type of plastic surgery for women? What underlying ideas about women's bodies do they seem to share and promote?

> [They are] two excrescences of muscular flesh which hang, and in some women, fall outside the neck of the womb; lengthen and shorten as does the comb of a turkey, principally when they desire coitus....
> —Ambroise Paré (1579), quoted in Lisa Jean Moore and Adele E. Clarke,
> "Clitoral Conventions and Transgressions: Graphic Representations
> in Anatomy Texts, c1900–1991,"
> *Feminist Studies* 21 (Summer 1995)

DESIGNER VAGINAS

Perhaps you noticed some of the articles in women's magazines that came out in 1998; *Cosmopolitan, Marie Claire,* and *Harper's Bazaar* each carried one, as did *Salon* on-line, articles with titles like "Labia Envy," "Designer Vaginas," and "The New Sex Surgeries." More recently, *Jane* magazine covered the topic, and

Simone Weil Davis, "Loose Lips Sink Ships," from *Feminist Studies*, Vol. 28, No. 1 (Spring 2002). Reprinted by permission of *Feminist Studies*.

Dan Savage's nationally syndicated advice column, "Savage Love," stumbled explosively upon it as well. These pieces all discussed labiaplasty, a relatively recent plastic surgery procedure that involves trimming away labial tissue and sometimes injecting fat from another part of the body into labia that have been deemed excessively droopy. In contrast to the tightening operation known as "vaginal rejuvenation," labiaplasty is sheerly cosmetic in purpose and purports to have no impact on sensation (unless something were to go terribly awry).[1] Throughout coverage here and in Canada, the aptly named Doctors Alter, Stubbs, and Matlock shared much of the glory and the public relations. In the name of consumer choice, these articles provoke consumer anxiety. The *Los Angeles Times* quotes Dr. Matlock: "The woman is the designer...the doctor is just the instrument.... Honestly, if you look at *Playboy,* those women, on the outer vagina area, the vulva is very aesthetically appealing, the vulva is rounded. It's full, not flat.... Women are coming in saying, I want something different, I want to change things. They look at *Playboy,* the ideal woman per se, for the body and the shape and so on. You don't see women in there with excessively long labia minora."[2]

All the popular articles about the "new sex surgeries" that I've reviewed also include remarks from skeptical colleagues and from polled readers who feel okay about their labia. (In an unfortunate turn of phrase, one plastic surgeon describes Dr. Matlock as a bit too "cutting edge.") Despite this apparently balanced coverage, a brand-new worry is being planted, with the declaration in *Salon* that "many women had been troubled for years about the appearance of their labia minora," and with the use of words like "normal" and "abnormal" to describe non-pathological variations among genitalia. The November 1998 article in *Cosmopolitan* has an eye-catching blurb: "My labia were so long, they'd show through my clothes!" Having taken *that* in, the reader suddenly looks up at the accompanying photo with new eyes: the photograph is of a slim woman in fairly modest underwear; because of the picture's cropping, she is headless, but the posture is distinctive, awkward. She's somewhat hunched forward, her hands are both crotch-bound, and one finger slips beneath the edge

of her panties. Having read the caption, you think, "My God, she's tucking in her labia!"[3]

Ellen Frankfort's 1972 book, the women's liberationist *Vaginal Politics,* begins with the following scene.[4] Carol from the Los Angeles Self-Help Clinic "slips out of her dungarees and underpants," hops onto a long table in an old church basement and inserts a speculum into her vagina. The 50 other women present file up and look with a flashlight, and learn, too, how to self-examine with a speculum and a dimestore mirror. This self-exploration of what has often been referred to as "the dark continent" or just "down there" seemed the perfect symbol for the early claim of women's liberation that "the personal is political." How could a woman call for sexual autonomy without self-awareness? To reverse the phrasing of one of Second Wave feminism's most famous byproducts, how could we know "our selves" without knowing "our bodies" first?[5] This image of women using a well-placed mirror to demystify and reclaim their own bodies is rooted dimly in my teen-years memory. I found it eerily resurrected when the *Salon* piece by Louisa Kamps came up on my computer screen. Kamps starts off like this: "'Ladies, get out your hand mirrors,' begins a curious press release I find at my desk one Monday morning. 'Yes, it is true...the newest trend in surgically enhanced body beautification: Female Genital Cosmetic Surgery.'" The hand mirror this time is used to alert the would-be vagina shopper to any deficiencies "down below" that she may have been blithely ignoring. From 1970s' consciousness-raising groups and Judy Chicago's dinner plates, through Annie Sprinkle's speculum parties of the 1980s, and on to Eve Ensler's collaborative *Vagina Monologues,*[6] we came at the end of the 1990s to Dr. Alter and Dr. Stubbs. What's the trajectory from Second Wave feminist "self-discovery and celebration" to the current almost-craze for labiaplasty? And does the fact of this trajectory provide us with a warning?

THE CLEAN SLIT

The vagina. According to Freud, its first sighting is the first scandal. It is *the* secret, invariably broken, that, once seen, changes you forever, especially if "you" are a little boy in turn-of-the-century Vienna, stumbling in upon your mother *en déshabillé*. You discover, all at once, in a rude shock, that she lacks a penis. You tremble at the threat that her missing phallus implies to *your* little member: if it happened to her, it could happen to you (especially because you've got the gall to compete with your father for your mother's affections). For Freud, his followers, and even many of his feminist revisionists, the "scandal" of a woman's genitals is supposed to be due to what *isn't* there, not what is. This article is not about lack, however. It is about excess. And it is not (exactly) about what Jacques Lacan and Hélène Cixous celebrated as *jouissance*. It's about labia.

So the vagina betokens the horror of castration, we're told. Many have remarked that perhaps this scandal is more accurately defined as one of interiority. In a society that revolves around the visual, an orgasm that doesn't include ejaculation can seem maddeningly uncontrollable: you can't prove it (outside of a laboratory), and thus it can be faked.[7] Discussing hard-core cinematic pornography, Linda Williams claims that "[t]he woman's ability to fake the orgasm that the man can never fake...seems to be at the root of all the genre's attempts to solicit what it can never be sure of: the out-of-control confession of pleasure, a hard-core 'frenzy of the visible.' "[8]

In the Amero-European world of the late-eighteenth and the early-nineteenth centuries, an earlier notion of women's natural lustiness was transformed into the myth of feminine modesty.[9] This purported ladylike decorum has always been depicted as simultaneously innate for the female *and* a massively big job. For the same social world that generated the mythos of the delicate, proper lady has also continually spawned and recycled dirty jokes about "vagina dentata," fatal odors, and other horror-story imagery about female genitalia.[10] The off-color disgust has always been tied in a complex way to a vast, off-color desire, and these both have been concomitant with the prescription to stay dainty—no matter what—for at least three hundred years. The paradoxical welding of abhorrence and adoration is often "resolved" socially through a stereotyped decoupling of the two, although mythologies of the lurid and the pure female are in fact too interdependent ever to be truly

unbraided. Women have been branded good or bad, refined or fallen, on the basis of their race, their profession, their station in life, and so forth, with the judgments conveniently supporting the political, economic, and racial status quo (about which, more later). That being said, the paradox is also one that women negotiate individually, and this has been so for a remarkably long time. To see this conundrum's longevity, take a look at Jonathan Swift's eighteenth-century "dressing-room poems," animated by voyeuristic disgust for the female body, and compare them with "What Your Gynecologist Didn't Tell You about the Smell," a now-defunct joke web site that made fun of Dr. Matlock but did so via misogynist aversion—an aversion familiar to all women who feel compelled to contain this supposed foulness and to approximate the required delicacy.[11]

Although "feminine modesty" used to be the answer to this subtextual concern about vaginas, now the shameful zone needs to be brought into line for display, rather than hidden. The vulva is becoming a pioneer territory for cosmetic enhancement—surgical practitioners need above all to capitalize both on that preexisting shame and on the ever-greater need to provide a cyborgian spectacle of porno-gloss. The relative mainstreaming of the sex industry (think of Demi Moore in *Striptease,* for example) and the blurring of the lines between hard-core and advertising imagery (think Calvin Klein) have led to a perpetually increasing sense of pressure among many women, the pressure to develop and present a seamlessly sexualized, "airbrushed" body.[12] Drs. Alter, Stubbs, and Matlock want that sought-after body to include a specific labial look, one desirable enough to be worth "buying."

Before people will spend money on something as expensive and uncomfortable as cosmetic surgery, they need to be motivated not only by desire but by concern or self-doubt. Bringing the authoritative language of medical science to the aestheticization of the vagina is one key way to trigger such anxiety. Advertisers have frequently invoked and generated medicalized norms to sell products. Roland Marchand describes perhaps the classic example of this phenomenon: after the liquid known as Listerine proved a lackluster general antiseptic, it was decided to dramatize its function as a mouthwash. Foul tasting as it was, consumer incentive would be needed. The term "halitosis" was "exhumed from an old medical dictionary" by an advertising firm and became the driving force behind a subsequent, energetic scare campaign about the medical, social, and romantic risks of bad breath.[13] Advertisers have always been both matter-of-fact and explicit about delineating and then steadily working to create a sense of deficiency where once there was indifference or even, God forbid, enjoyment, working to incite new arenas of insecurity, new personal anxieties, so that more things can be marketed and sold.

Cosmetic surgery has worked with the same principles throughout its more than 100-year history, as detailed in histories of the profession by Kathy Davis, Elizabeth Haiken, and Sander Gilman.[14] For instance, in a particularly unnerving chapter on "micromastia" (the "disease" of flat-chestedness) and the surgeries developed to "correct" it, Haiken quotes a 1958 article by plastic surgeon Milton T. Edgerton and psychiatrist A. R. McClary, on "the psychiatry of breast augmentation": "Literally thousands of women in this country alone, are seriously disturbed by feelings of inadequacy in regard to concepts of the body image. Partly as a result of exposure to advertising propaganda and questionable publicity, many physically normal women develop an almost paralyzing self-consciousness focused on the feeling that they do not have the correct size bosom."[15] The rationale laid out here, which explains *but also helps create* "inferiority complexes," can be applied across the full topography of the human form, as borne out by the increasing prevalence of liposuction, face-lifts, buttock and tummy tucks. The latest realm to be scoured for "abnormalities" is the vagina, formerly spared from the scrutiny of the market because it was considered both too reviled and too quakingly desired to be addressed commercially.

These days, in part because of the video dissemination and the mainstreaming of pornography, women, regardless of gender preference, can see the vaginas of a lot of different other women. They may desire those vaginas, they may simultaneously identify with them,

but if they are rich enough or have great credit, they can definitely have them built.[16] A 1997 article in the Canadian magazine *See* interviews a patient of Dr. Stubbs in Toronto. Deborah "has had her eyes done and had breast implants and some liposuction. She says that she started thinking about her labia when her first husband brought home porn magazines and she started comparing herself. 'I saw some other ones that were cuter than mine' and I thought, 'Hey, I want that one,' she laughs."[17] Of course, the images we relish or bemoan in pornography are almost always tweaked technically. As Deborah did her "catalog shopping," the women she was admiring were perhaps themselves surgically "enhanced," but additionally, they were posed, muted with makeup and lighting, and the resultant photographic images were then edited with an airbrush or the digital modifications of Photoshop.

This is especially true of pornography that presents itself as "upscale," whether soft or hard core. As Laura Kipnis helps us realize, there's a crucial link between *Hustler*'s targeting of a working-class market and its being the first of the big three glossy "wank mags" to show what it called "the pink."[18] *Hustler*'s aggressive celebration of vulgarity informed its initial rejection of soft-core decorum about genitals; thus, its representations of vaginas were matter-of-fact, and often enough contextualized with very explicit, poorly lit Polaroid shots sent in by readers. When the vagina finally came to the pages of *Penthouse,* by contrast, it was as flaw-free and glossy as the rest of the models' figures. In "The Pussy Shot: An Interview with Andrew Blake," sex writer Susie Bright discusses the classed aesthetics of this pornographer, whose trademarks are his lavish sets (straight out of *Architectural Digest,* Bright remarks) and high-end production values: in this posh setting, it comes as no surprise that the star's labia are small and her "pussy is perfectly composed, with every hair in place."[19]

The evolution of a new strict standard of "beauty," rigid enough to induce surgery, does not occur in a vacuum. Among other factors, economics are in play—not just in the eagerness of a few cosmetic surgeons to up their patient load but in a far more intricate web of drives and desires intersecting with technological shifts and cultural and financial power plays. I will only nod here to the complexity of this phenomenon. A first example: in *Venus Envy: A History of Cosmetic Surgery,* Haiken points out that research catalyzed by World Wars I and II led to technological innovations that furthered the cosmetic surgery industry. Wars, which maim and disfigure people, increase the demand for and respectability of plastic surgery, allowing surgeons the grim opportunity to improve their skills and their public relations. Additionally, war means the invention and/or increased availability of new materials, like silicone and polyurethane, both of which were used for breast augmentation in the wake of World War II.[20] Could this new material on hand have *led* (in part) to the 1950s' notorious obsession with large breasts?

Here is a more recent example of the subtle interplay of cultural and economic forces that can help shape changes in beauty standards: Perhaps Rudolph Giuliani's New York City should be thought of as undergoing an urban labiaplasty. In this zoned, regulated era, newly comfortable for tourists if not for New Yorkers, the sex industry has been radically curtailed. This change has meant, tellingly enough, that almost all the sex clubs "connected" enough to remain open after 1998 favor "clone" women—Caucasian bodies, tidy tan lines, big blonde hair, collagen lips, surgically removed ribs, liposucked bottoms, and implanted breasts. With time, their labia may also be ubiquitously trimmed. Many women with bodies that diverge from the approved stereotype—biker chicks, Latina and Black dancers, plump or small-breasted women, the pierced girl with the monster tattoo—women who used to be able to dance erotically for an income, have been "sheered away," forced into unemployment, prostitution, or departure. These days in New York, only the clones can dance, and it is clone bodies alone that New York City strip club patrons now ogle.[21] The ripple effects such a change works, no doubt, multiply, and the Bloomberg era will see them continue.

In part because of the prevalence of just such a mainstreamed *Penthouse* and *Playboy* aesthetic, labias

in pornography are often literally tucked away (in the most low-tech variant of body modification).[22] If you review enough porn, however, especially lesbian porn or that which is unsqueamishly "déclassé" as in *Hustler,* you will see a wide variety in the female genitalia on display—wide enough to evoke the "snowflake uniqueness" analogy that is bandied around in popular coverage of the new cosmetic enhancement surgeries. And indeed the before-and-after shots available at some of the surgeons' web sites that I've found so far do reveal, unsurprisingly, that the single favored look for these "designer vaginas" is...the clean slit. Louisa Kamps of *Salon* magazine agrees: "What strikes me in the 'after' shots is the eerie similarity between the women...their genitalia are carbon copies of each other."

In a subtle but nontrivial way, this particular aesthetic and the surgery that manifests it cut back on women's experience of self-on-self contact, of tactility: Luce Irigaray celebrates the nonvisual, sensory experience women perpetually enjoy as their vaginal lips press and move against one another. She suggests that this physiological status makes women psychologically less invested in the myth of the monadic, self-reliant individual than are men. Irigaray's "two lips which are not one" would not touch each other much in a world of women "Altered."[23] What do the aesthetics of a streamlined vulva signify? The smooth groin of our favorite plastic android prototype, Barbie? A desire to approximate prepubescence? A fastidious minimization of marginal zones?[24]

Mary Russo writes of "the female grotesque" in terms that are relevant here: "The images of the grotesque body are precisely those which are abjected from the bodily canons of classical aesthetics. The classical body is transcendent and monumental, closed, static, self-contained, symmetrical, and sleek....The grotesque body is open, protruding, secreting, multiple and changing...."[25] Russo's contrasting of the grotesque with the classical is particularly resonant in this context, as plastic surgeons often invoke classical aesthetics and the metaphor of surgeon-as-sculptor; Stubbs even illustrates his site with photographs of classical statuary and presents his "before-and-after" shots in a "Surgical Art Gallery" captioned by Hippocrates: " 'Ars longa, vita brevis'— Art is long and life is short."[26] Elizabeth Haiken discusses "the classical context in which [early plastic surgeons] wished to place themselves; the term *plastic surgery* derives from the Greek *plastikos*, to shape or mold."[27] The asymmetries, protrusions, and changeability of Russo's grotesque are what the labiaplasty is meant to "shape or mold" and *cut* away.

Bodies do change with the passage of time, of course. If the living body is to approximate sculpture, change itself must be managed, *fixed*. Reading the following quote from Dr. Alter's web site, one is reminded of the Renaissance theory of the wandering womb, whereby female hysteria and misbehavior were deemed the results of a uterus that had dislodged and begun to storm about internally, wreaking havoc. A woman's "womb was like a hungry animal; when not amply fed by sexual intercourse or reproduction, it was likely to wander about her body, over-powering her speech and senses."[28] In Dr. Alter's prose, the older woman, "in dialogue with gravity,"[29] may find her previously pleasing vagina dangerously "on the move": "The aging female may dislike the descent of her pubic hair and labia and desire re-elevation to its previous location," Dr. Alter warns. So, it is woman's work to make sure her genitalia are snug, not wayward.

We are talking about vaginal aesthetics, and aesthetic judgments almost always evidence socially relevant metaphors at work on the material and visual planes. Ideas about feminine beauty are ever-changing: the classic example is a comparison of Rubens's fleshy beauties and the wraithlike super-model Kate Moss (who succeeded Twiggy). But, in a world where many women have never thought about judging the looks of their genitals, even if they care about their appearance more generally, we should ask what criteria make for a good-looking vagina, and who is assigned as arbiter. These (mutating) criteria should tell us something about the value system that generates them. To tease out some answers to these questions, this article goes on to put the labiaplasty phenomenon in a contextual frame with other vaginal modifications.

MODIFYING/CLASSIFYING

What representations of vulvas circulate in our society? And who, beyond Dr. Tight, is modifying the female genitalia, how and why? For one, among alternative youth (and the not-so-alternative, not-so-youthful, too) piercings are being sought to modify and decorate the labia, sometimes to extend them, and, ideally, to add to clitoral stimulation. What sensibilities mark these changes? Among body modifiers on the Web, conversation about body image, self-mutilation, and, contrarily, healing, is common, with an accepted understanding that many turn to piercing as a means of overcoming perceived past abuse. " 'Most folks use Bod-Mod to get back in touch with the parts of themselves that were hurt or misused by others.' 'BodMod has helped me undemonize pain....I was able to handle [childbirth] better, knowing that I'd survived...two ten-gauge labial piercings....' " Changing one's relationship to one's genitalia by becoming their "modifier" leads here to an aesthetic reassessment: " 'You know, I never liked to look at my puss until I got my rings. I have well-developed inner labia that always show, and I was always envious of those women who seemed to have nice neat little pussies with everything tucked inside. My puss looked like an old whore's cunt to me! So one reason I *know* I wasn't mutilating myself when I got my privates pierced was how much I liked to look at myself after the work was done. You might actually say I'm *glad* my labia are the way they are now.' "[30]

"Glad" is what the cosmetic surgeons do *not* want you to be about prominent labia minora. If you look at the opening paragraph of Ensler's *Vagina Monologues,* you begin to wonder if the unruliness now coming under the governance of the cosmetic surgeon isn't at least as symbolic as it is aesthetic. This is Ensler, introducing her project (interviews with real women, transcribed, performed onstage, and then collected in a book):

I was worried about vaginas. I was worried about what we think about vaginas, and even more worried that we don't think about them....So I decided to talk to women about their vaginas, to do vagina interviews, which became vagina monologues. I talked with over two hundred women. I talked to old women, young women, married women, single women, lesbians, college professors, actors, corporate professionals, sex workers, African American women, Hispanic women, Asian American women, Native American women, Caucasian women, Jewish women. At first women were reluctant to talk. They were a little shy. But once they got going, you couldn't stop them.[31]

Just as Ensler's own catalog of interviewees seems to burgeon and proliferate, so too the women with whom she spoke were "unstoppable." With a similar metaphoric expansion, in the cosmetic surgeons' promotional material, not only are women's *labia* depicted as in danger of distention, but one woman customer also described her *"hang-up"* about her pre-operative labia as "just growing and growing," until the doctor cut it short, that is. Loose lips sink ships.

I received a "free consultation" from one doctor who performs labiaplasties, and this doctor explained to me that the ideal look for labia minora was not only minimal and unextended but also symmetrical, "homogeneously pink," and "not wavy."[32] To the dangers and allures of what's hidden about the vagina, now is added the "too muchness" of labial tissue. In their heterogeneous dappling and their moist curves, labia mark the lack of tidy differentiation between inside and outside and that's just *too much.* One effect of this procedure is to reduce this sense of a "marginal" site between exterior and interior corporeality. Labia can be seen as "gateway" tissue, in other words, tissue that is somewhat indeterminate in texture and hue, yielding slowly from outer to inner and blurring the boundary between the fetishized gloss of the outer dermis and the wet, mushy darkness of the inside. This indeterminacy, actually a function of the labia's protective role, may be part of their association with excess.[33] In *Public Privates: Performing Gynecology from Both Ends of the Speculum,* Terry Kapsalis "reads" the images in a widely used medical text, *Danforth's Obstetrics and Gynecology.* She is struck by the lack of representations of healthy vaginas in *Danforth's* and argues that ultimately the

work's visual logic pathologizes female genitalia per se. Using language parallel to that which I have used here, she writes: "Perhaps it is not a lack that is threatening, but an excess. The fact is that even if no pathology exists, there *is* something there—namely, a vulva with labia, a clitoris, and so on, a marginal site occupying both the inside and the outside, an abject space (according to Julia Kristeva) that threatens to devour the penis (vagina dentata)."[34]

In the medical realm, much effort is expended to overcome the mysterious liminality of the vagina. Since the eras of the ancient anatomists Galen and Hippocrates and especially since the rise of gynecology in the nineteenth century, vaginas have been diagrammed and cataloged in medical textbooks. Running parallel, a variant of pornography has always picked up and parodied the objectifying eroticism of scientific conquest.[35] In this realm, large labia have often been associated with deviance—at least since the sixteenth century they have indicated to doctors the alleged presence of hypersexuality, onanism, and possible "tribadism" or lesbian tendencies. Jennifer Terry discusses a 1930s' study conducted in New York City, "under the auspices of the Committee for the Study of Sex Variants," in order "to identify, treat, and prevent homosexuality." A moderate-sized group of self-proclaimed lesbians were examined by a battery of experts, so that their "traits" could be characterized and profiled. These experts included gynecologists. The overseer of the project, one Dr. Dickinson, ultimately "identified ten characteristics which he argued set the sex variant [lesbian] apart from 'normal' women: (1) larger than average vulvas; (2) longer labia minora; (3) 'labia minora protrude between the labia majora and are wrinkled, thickened, or *brawny';* (4) 'the prepuce is large or wrinkled or in folds'; (5) the clitoris is 'notably erectile'...; (6) 'eroticism is clearly in evidence on examination, as shown by dusky flush of the parts, with free flow of clear, glairy mucus, and with definite clitoris erection....'" The study concludes that all "these findings can be the result of strong sex urge [presumably an innate or congenital condition], plus: (a) Vulvar and vulvovaginal self-friction; or (b) Homosexual digital or oral play; or (c) Heterosexual manual or coital techniques, singly or in any combination."[36] Terry rightly emphasizes the researchers' apparent fascination with the concept that homo/hypersexual desire (often conflated) could be strong enough that it could make the vulva a site of transformation. The prurience behind this possibility that perverted sex play could "rebuild" a vagina, seems great enough that it is allowed to overshadow the theory of a congenital distinction between heterosexual and homosexual anatomy.

Many American and British clitoridectomies and female castrations (the removal of healthy ovaries) were performed in the nineteenth century and as recently as the 1970s, as a response to just such indicators.[37] Isaac Baker Brown began to perform clitoridectomies in Britain in 1858, in order to reduce "hysteria" and other nervous ailments, but particularly to combat "excessive" masturbation. He was, by the 1860s, soundly critiqued in his own country and indeed expelled from Britain's Obstetrical Society in 1867; but his procedure (and its milder variant, circumcision of the clitoral hood) became popular in the United States by the late 1860s and was performed in this country for decades. Although experimentation in the development phases of sexual surgeries generally was exacted on the bodies of poor and disenfranchised women (mostly African American), the lady of leisure became the expressed target for these operations. Upper-middle-class and upper-class women had disposable incomes and time on their hands (to masturbate...or to recover from genital surgery). Robert Battey developed the practice of removing healthy ovaries to address a whole slew of complaints, from kleptomania to epilepsy, and this procedure was surprisingly widespread, particularly between 1880 and 1910. One 1893 proponent of female castration claimed that "the moral sense of the patient is elevated....She becomes tractable, orderly, industrious and cleanly." Although depleted misrule seems an unsurprising "benefit" of such operations, one would not expect *aesthetics* to spring up as a concern in this context, but Ben Barker-Benfield cites some clitoridectomy and castration patients who thought of the trend as a "fashionable fad" and found their scars "as pretty as the dimple on the cheek of sweet sixteen."[38]

In the 1970s and 1980s, James Burt, an Ohio gynecologist, gained notoriety—and eventually lost his license—performing what he called "the surgery of love" on more than 4,500 patients, apparently often without even garnering the pretense of informed consent, while they were anesthetized and "on the table" for another procedure. This procedure included a clitoral circumcision and a vaginal reconstruction that changed the angle of the vagina; he insisted before and after the malpractice suits that he had enhanced the sexual pleasure of 99 percent of the women upon whom he'd operated and that he was "correcting" the female anatomy, which he saw as God's mistake, by repositioning the genitalia. Women were left with loss of erotic sensation, enormous pain during intercourse, chronic bowel and urination problems requiring regular catheter use, and ongoing serious infections; the same set of medical sequelae have been reported among infibulated women.[39] In 1997, the Ohio Supreme Court ultimately awarded forty women compensation amounting to a total of $20 million. This award came after spectacular struggles in the courts over an eleven-year-period. The organization Patients-in-Arms, led by Carla Miller (who describes herself as "a victim of FGM" [female genital mutilation]), is devoted to helping women speak out about abuse and disfigurement at the hands of gynecologists. A review of the cases toward which Ms. Miller can direct one makes it excruciatingly clear both that this phenomenon is quite widespread and that it is made possible by the common and interlinked phenomenon of the "white wall of silence" that reduces the doctors' risk of being brought to task.[40]

In a related phenomenon that persists to this day, the erotic tissue of "intersexed" or ambiguously gendered babies and children is routinely, in fact just about ubiquitously, modified through surgery without the minor's consent, in what the medical profession calls a "psychosocial emergency." These modifications have been shown to leave behind serious psychological scarring; often enough, the surgeries profoundly compromise the sexual sensation of the people forced to undergo them. In a piece called "The Tyranny of the Aesthetic: Surgery's Most Intimate Violation,"

Martha Coventry explains that "girlhood is [almost always] the gender approximated through surgery in such circumstances." "It's easier to poke a hole than build a pole," as one surgeon remarks. Coventry quotes Suzanne Kessler, whose work represents an important contribution to the study of intersexed experience: "Genital ambiguity is corrected not because it is threatening to the infant's life, but because it is threatening to the infant's culture."[41]

The genitalia are cultural terrain that must conform to identificatory norms; this has been driven home by the historians of gynecological science. When mid-nineteenth-century physician Marion Sims developed the duck-billed speculum and an examination protocol that gave him a good view, he used the language of an imperial conquistador, beholding still uncharted territory: "I saw everything, as no man had seen before."[42] Much has been written, particularly by Irigaray, about the mythologization of female genitalia as "the dark continent," the "nothing to see," an Unknown supposedly waiting to be penetrated by pioneering masculine experts; Mary Ann Doane and Anne McClintock are among those who have etched out the linkage that such a metaphor immediately suggests between gender politics and racial imperialism.[43]

What if the "nothing," the furor about female absence, is in part a stand-in scandal for the *something* that is the vaginal bloom—just as the "vast wildernesses" of the Americas and Africa were an invader's myth that suppressed the inconvenient fact of inhabitation? It is exactly in the realms where gender and race intersect that we can see this being played out. Sander Gilman and Michele Wallace are among those who have discussed Saartjie (or Sara) Baartman, dubbed the Hottentot Venus. She and other African women were taken from their homes and put on show in the early nineteenth century; in this display, their labial "aprons" were rumored about and peeked at with as much eroticized condemnation as were their "steoptygic" buttocks, although the latter were more plainly in view.[44] When George Cuvier, Geoffrey St. Hilaire, and Henri de Blainville, eminent naturalists all, attempted to force a scientific examination of Baartman, de Blainville reported that

"she hid her apron carefully between her thighs—her movements were brusque and capricious like those of apes....It was only with great sorrow that she let drop her handkerchief for a moment."[45] The outrage of invasion so evident here is aggravated by the dehumanization of Baartman that drove the tragic endeavor. In the same commentary, Cuvier describes elements of her appearance as being "like an orangutan," "like an animal," and "like a dog."[46] Eager to inspect her labia, particularly as they were seeking a classificatory wedge that would distinguish the Hottentot from the European on the level of species, the scientists spent three days trying to convince Baartman to submit to the physical, even offering her money, which she refused. Alas, her early death afforded them ready access to her private parts, however, and Cuvier made a plaster cast of her body and had her brain and genitals preserved in jars. Although the skeleton remains at Paris's Musée de l'Homme, her body is due to be returned to South Africa for burial...and her brain and genitals have disappeared.[47]

It is no coincidence that the aforementioned Marion Sims, early American gynecologist, developed his surgery techniques only by repeated, public operations on the bodies of African American slaves and poor, white "washerwomen."[48] Doing symbolic work, nonwhite women in the Euro-American context have endured the exposure of their bodies only to have them decried and desired, first as heathenish, then as "abnormal." Meanwhile, the nonprostitute white woman's vagina was hidden, protected—shamed, too, but out of the limelight.

OUR VULVAS, OUR SELVES

Perhaps this context needs to be kept in mind when we consider another role played contemporarily by images of female genitals: among activists opposed to the circumcision of African females, even among those who are extremely sensitive to the liabilities of cultural bias, the documenting photo has a special, and somewhat problematic, status. In "Desiring the 'Mutilated' African Woman," Wacuka Mungai points out that there is a heated and eerily prurient interest expressed over the Web in accessing documentary photos of girls and women who have undergone clitero-dectomies, excisions, and infibulation.[49] Although photographs of excised and infibulated vaginas are available at "kinky" web sites alongside other images deemed freakish or gory, I agree with Mungai that, even beyond the overtly pornographic, their status as emblems of an "Othered" barbarity is also tinged with unacknowledged eroticism. As Mungai explains, these photos are typically taken with something like consent, but under circumstances when a girl would be hard pressed to withhold permission—in exchange for treatment, a foreign, light-skinned doctor who doesn't speak your language asks that you let her photograph you. You are not likely to refuse her, even though there may be trauma in the taking, and even though the photos then circulate the globe, representing only the wounded status of the African female. Like the gynecological diagram, like Baartman's genitals so long on formaldehyde display in Paris, like the "monster shot" in porn flicks, these images are partial, headless...vaginas emphatically dissevered from whole people, made creatures of their own—treated, perhaps, as the essence of the woman, the cut vagina the truest thing about her, a dangerous metonymy. Mungai points out that, by the same token, in media coverage of the debates over female circumcision among immigrants, the portraits of "cut" women's faces that accompany articles decrying the practice often serve to bring about the same delimiting reduction.

One North American woman with whom I spoke who had elected to have a labiaplasty laughed uproariously with me at the nerve of a European television news program that had approached her to ask if she'd like to do a segment on their show about her operation. The very *thought* of her face being linked to her imagined, modified vagina was preposterous to her, and she would certainly never have consented to being part of the show. Our laughter should continue to ring until it has turned livid, as we think about the many African girls and women who experience just this representational conflation.

[In keeping with the concerns voiced here about circulating images of "cut" female genitalia, I have decided not to present illustrations like those at the plastic surgeons' web sites mentioned here or those found in some anti-FGO (female genital operations) materials....]

CONFOUNDING THE BOUNDARIES

The U.S. Congress passed a measure criminalizing the circumcision of a minor female in 1996, and nine or ten states have passed anti-FGO acts since 1996 as well. In Illinois, Minnesota, Rhode Island, and Tennessee, this legislation felonizes operations performed on adults as well as on minors. But *which* operations? Anti-FGO laws that now exist in a number of U.S. states describe procedures that would definitely include those practiced by Drs. Alter and Matlock, but they use only language that addresses the "ritual" or custom and belief-based cutting of African immigrant bodies. Meanwhile, this legal language either elides or okays both the "corrective" cutting of the intersexed child and the surgery sought by the unsettled consumer who has been told by plastic surgeons that her labia are unappealing and aberrant. Thus American law marks out relations between the state and its citizen bodies that differ depending on birthplace, cultural context, and skin color.

In fact, however, it is a (prevalent) mistake to imagine a quantum distinction between Euro-American and African reshapings of women's bodies: far too often, they are measured with entirely different yardsticks, rather than on a continuum. Nahid Toubia, executive director of the advocacy group Rainbo, remarks that "[t]he thinking of an African woman who believes that 'FGM is the fashionable thing to do to become a real woman' is not so different from that of an American woman who has breast implants to appear more feminine."[50] In keeping with Toubia's remark, I propose here that a subtler and less culturally binaristic analysis of such phenomena will lead, not to political paralysis in the name of cultural relativism, but to deeper understanding of core issues like the nature of consent, of bodily aesthetics and social control, and of cross-cultural activist collaboration.[51]

Soraya Miré, Somali maker of the film *Fire Eyes*, remarks in Inga Muscio's (wo)manifesto, *Cunt: A Declaration of Independence*: "[Western women] come into conversations waving the American flag, forever projecting the idea that they are more intelligent than I am. I've learned that American women look at women like me to hide from their own pain.... In America, women pay *the money that is theirs and no one else's* to go to a doctor who cuts them up so they can create or sustain an image men want. Men are the mirror. Western women cut themselves up voluntarily."[52] Significantly, in Miré's construction, consent to genital surgery does *not* okay it so much as it marks the degrading depths of women's oppression. Although consent is at the heart of the issue of genital operations on children, a topic both urgent and not to be downplayed, we must also look at the social and cultural means whereby consent is manufactured, regardless of age, in the West as well as in African and other countries engaging in FGOs. In the North American popular imagination, the public address of advertising is not understood as infringing upon our power of consent. Indeed, the freedom to "pay the money that is [one's] own" is too often inscribed as the quintessential exemplar of life in a democracy. Perhaps due to that presumption, beauty rituals hatched on Madison Avenue or in Beverly Hills do not bear the onus of "barbarism" here, despite the social compulsions, psychological drives, and magical thinking that impel them.

By the same token, American oversimplifications suppress the fact that African women's relations to female genital operations are complex and variable, as are the operations themselves, of course. The operations can be roughly grouped into four sorts: circumcision, the removal of the clitoral hood or "female prepuce"; clitoridectomy, "the partial or total removal of the clitoris"; excision, "the removal of the clitoris and all or part of the labia minora"; and infibulation, "the removal of all external genitalia followed by the stitching together of most of the vaginal opening."[53] As will be discussed, motivations for any of these practices are highly variable across time and

between individuals as well as between cultures. Vicki Kirby points out the distortions that come with Western monolithizing: "What is 'other' for the West must thereby forfeit its own internal contradictions and diversities in this singular and homogenizing determination of alterity."[54]

Additionally, African vaginal aesthetics are not limited to such sheerings away of vulvular tissue. Although now it is predominantly the members of the royal family who still practice this technique (which is thus a sign of status), the Buganda people in Uganda have a tradition of stretching and massaging the labia and clitoris from childhood to extend them (for feminine beautification). As Londa Schiebinger describes, some say that the "Hottentot aprons," so fetishized by Europeans, were also the result of cosmetic manipulations, on the part of African women seeking beauty.[55]

If one considers all female circumcision practices in Africa to be analogous, as is too commonly the case in popular American analysis of the phenomenon, not only does one miss the dramatic differences between the different forms of FGO, but one also fails to understand the relevant differences between people who practice it as a part of their cultural life and those who experience it as a part of their religious life. Crucial issues of consent are blurred with such elisions. Western critics of African genital surgeries can also miss completely the role that it often plays in the symbolism of resistance and political struggle, both colonial and tribal.[56] In *Facing Mt. Kenya: The Tribal Life of the Kikuyu* (1953), Jomo Kenyatta remarks that "the overwhelming majority of [the local people] believe that it is the secret aim of those who attack this country's old customs to disintegrate their social order and thereby hasten their Europeanization."[57] An additional point: although female circumcision is not explicitly directed by any religious text, it is practiced as an expression of Muslim, Christian, and Jewish religious observance among various African populations. Overall, it should not be imagined as concomitant with Islam (which it regularly is, often in an anti-Arab conflation), or even as a primarily religious practice.

In most regions, female circumcision practices are determined more by cultural factors, and by ethnic, national, tribal, and postcolonial politics, than by religion. They are by no means solely or exotically "ritualistic" in a way that entirely distinguishes them from nonimmigrant American operations on vaginas. Female genital operations are understood, variously, as hygiene, as beautification, as a curb to female sexuality, as a clarification of the difference between the sexes, as an enhancement of male sexual pleasure, as conducive to fertility and/or monogamy, as disease prevention, and as a means of conforming with social norms and ensuring that one's daughter will be marriageable, that she will be able to take her place among her age set, and that the solidarity and social strength of older women's organizations will be able to flourish.[58]

SURGERY, SISTERLINESS, AND THE "RIGHT TO CHOOSE"

Among the key motivating factors raised by African women who favor female genital surgeries are beautification, transcendence of shame, and the desire to conform; these clearly matter to American women seeking cosmetic surgery on their labia, as well. Thus, the motivations that impel African-rooted FGOs and American labiaplasties should not be envisioned as radically distinct. Not only does such oversimplification lead to a dangerous reanimation of the un/civilized binary, but it also leaves the feminist with dull tools for analysis of either phenomenon. There are aesthetic parallels between the Western and the African procedures. The enthusiasm for the clean slit voiced so vigorously by the American plastic surgeon I consulted is echoed among a group of Egyptian mothers discussing female genital operations for their daughters in the 1990 documentary, *Hidden Faces*. Although several of the women laughingly nudge each other and say they wouldn't want the excisers to interfere much with "the front" (showing a clear zest for clitoral pleasure), one woman voices an aesthetic principle about which she feels strongly. Energetically, she decries the ugliness of dangling

labia, and explains to the filmmaker, with appropriate hand gestures, "Do you want her to be like a boy, with this floppy thing hanging down? Now, it should be straight Shhh. Smooth as silk." This aesthetic judgment is in keeping not only with the views of labiaplasters in the United States but also with the vocabulary of Mauritanian midwives: one such woman, who has argued to her colleagues for a milder version of circumcision in place of vigorous excision, "use[s] two words to refer to female circumcision, 'tizian,' which means to make more beautiful, and 'gaaad,' which means to cut off and make even."[59]

The group of women chatting on a rooftop in *Hidden Faces* invokes another continuum between African and American women's approaches to feminine beauty rituals and vaginal modifications. Simplistic depictions of a global patriarchy, wherein men curb, cow, cut, and dominate "their" women, may drive home the ubiquity of female subjugation, but they leave out an important factor at the same time: although both labiaplasties and African female circumcision should be (and are here) investigated through a feminist lens, that feminism should be informed by an awareness of women's agency. A knee-jerk celebration of that agency misleads, but its disavowal in the name of victimhood leads to dangerous blind spots. Across many different cultural contexts, female genital operations are contemplated and undergone by girls and women in a social and psychological framework shaped *in part* by other women.

The plastic surgeon whose office I visited provided me with two referrals, patients who had had the procedure done by him. As part of what seemed a well-worn sales pitch, he referred often to "self-help groups," a network of supportive, independent women helping each other find the professional care they wanted and deserved, in the face of an unfeeling, disbelieving medical profession. I was interested by what seemed an invocation of rather feminist sensibilities and wondered about this swelling, grassroots support group he seemed to be conjuring up for me. And, indeed, the image of the surgery consumer as a liberated woman and an independent self-fashioner did provide a crucial spin for the doctor, throughout his consultation. The consumer-feminist in support of other women he condoned; by contrast, he expressed an avowed disapproval of the women who came to him solely to please a domineering partner. He brought up this posited bad, weak, man-centric woman three times as we spoke, and each time his face clouded, he frowned, and his brow furrowed: he said that it was only this type of woman who complained of pain after the procedure, for instance, just to get the attention of her partner, whereas for most women, he insisted, the pain was minimal. He seemed to use these diverging models of female behavior to answer in advance any reservations the prospective client might have about a cosmetic operation on the genitalia (such as, "Should I really do something so drastic to my body just to please men?"). By insisting on his antipathy toward women who kowtowed to the male perspective, and celebrating the fearless vision of the pioneer consumer of "cutting edge" surgery, the doctor tried, I suspect, to ward off potential surges of feminist resistance to the procedure.

In the same spirit, one web site advertising the surgery fuels itself on a long-standing feminist call for a more responsive medical establishment by contrasting the surgeon being advertised with other doctors less sensitive to the needs of women. "Very few physicians are concerned with the appearance of the female external genitalia. A relative complacency exists that frustrates many women."[60] Rachel Bowlby has addressed the theoretical conflations between feminist freedom and the "freedom" to choose as a consumer.[61] The surgeon to whose sales pitch I listened and the creators of the web site noted here certainly understood that the feminist discourse of choice can be appropriated, funneled toward the managed choosing-under-duress of the consumer, becoming saturated along the way with commodity culture's directives.

One goal of this article is to raise the question of this ready appropriation. In *States of Injury: Power and Freedom in Late Modernity,* Wendy Brown examines some of the liabilities of the Left's reliance on the rhetoric of identity, injury, and redress, suggesting that it can result in a politics of state domination.[62] From Bakke on, we have certainly seen the language of affirmative action hauled into the arena of "reverse

racism." Perhaps by the same token, the language of choice, as central to the feminist project in this country as we could imagine, sprang up in a culture where the glories of consumer "choice" had already been mythologized. Revisiting and perhaps refiguring the conceptual framework behind "choice" in the face of manufactured consent, then, is to enable, not critique feminism. The hand mirror that allowed feminists of the 1960s and 1970s to get familiar with "our bodies, our selves" is positioned again so that we can see our vaginas. Only, it comes now with the injunction to look critically at what we see and to exert our selfhood through expenditure and remodeling of a body that is not "ourself" any longer but which is "ours," commodified and estranged, to rebuild.

Although the approach of the doctor I visited seemed agenda-driven and rather theatricalized, when I talked with the women to whom he referred me, I was struck by how very friendly and supportive they *did* seem. I had found the doctor likable but showy, like a much rehearsed salesman, but these women were engaged, candid, and genuinely warm. They were generous with their time (and with their permission to be cited anonymously in the present article), and they made it clear that they really did want to help other women with their "experience, strength, and hope." Perhaps these women were "incentivized" to speak well of the doctor (about whose care they raved): maybe they received discounted work in exchange for talking with prospective clients. Even with this possibility in mind they seemed sincerely ready to assume a common perspective, in fact an intimacy, between women discussing their bodies and body image. To overlook their candor, generosity, and *sisterliness* in order to critique the misogynist judgments that may have driven them to surgery would be to mischaracterize the phenomenon of gender display. We typically learn about and develop a gendered bodily performance, not in isolation, but as members of both real and imagined female "communities."[63] And in 2002, one senses the cultural shading that twentieth-century feminism has, ironically, brought to this community building: the rhetoric of choice making and of solidarity developed during the Second Wave ghosts through our conversations. It's a stereotypical joke that women *really* dress for each other—a deeper look at how this female-to-female hodgepodge of peer pressure and peer support really manifests itself is useful. And again, a look at the web of relations among women is helpful in understanding African female genital operations as well.

One on-line World Health Organization report discusses the impact of female circumcisions on girls' psychological health. Importantly, it mentions not only "experiences of suffering, devaluation and impotence" but also the "desirability of the ceremony for the child, with its social advantage of peer acceptance, personal pride and material gifts." Claire Robertson points out that among the functions of the circumcision ceremony in Central Kenya is the role female initiation plays in maintaining the social strength of organizations of older women.[64] The flip side of approving support, of course, is peer pressure. "When girls of my age were looking after the lambs, they would talk among themselves about their circumcision experiences and look at each other's genitals to see who had the smallest opening. If there was a girl in the group who was still uninfibulated, she would always feel ashamed since she had nothing to show the others."[65]

A reminiscent bodily shame lurks behind the support for labial modifications that my American patient contacts expressed. One (heterosexual) woman explained to me that although none of her boyfriends had ever remarked on her labia, "ever since I was fourteen, I felt like I had this abnormalcy; I felt uncomfortable changing in front of girlfriends." She went on to say that she felt she had to hide her vagina around other women and could never enjoy skinny-dipping because of her concerns about other women judging her appearance. Another labiaplasty patient reported a "120% shift" in her "mental attitude," and a "night-and-day" improvement in the looks of her genitalia, thanks to the surgery. "As sad as it is, it makes you feel inferior," she commented.[66] Her use of the second person (or the ethical dative, as it's known), so intimate in its extension of subjectivity, meant that her language included me....I too felt sad, I too felt inferior. And for a fee, the kind doctor was there to correct me.

NEW RITES

It is probably obvious from this piece that, even in the age where both informational and medical technology have led to bodies being reshaped, extended, reconfigured, and reconceptualized like never before, I believe that erotic tissue is far better enjoyed than removed.[67] In approaching the politics of female genital operations, however, I would argue that it is imperative that both consent issues and vaginal modifications themselves be considered *on a continuum* that is not determined along hemispheric, national, or racial lines. Instead, we peer at female genital operations with a prurient, bifurcating tunnel vision and pretend a clean break between the "primitive barbarism" of "ritual" cutting of African women, who are far too often represented as undifferentiated victims, and the aesthetic or medical "fixings" of those Amero-European women who are presented as either mildly deformed people in the wise hands of experts or consumer-designers of a cyborgian gender display.

In "Arrogant Perception, World-Traveling, and Multicultural Feminism: The Case of Female Genital Surgeries," Isabelle R. Gunning attempts to define and model a responsible approach to thinking about genital operations across cultures. She urges activists "to look at one's own culture anew and identify [...] practices that might prove 'culturally challenging' or negative to some other," and "to look in careful detail at the organic social environment of the 'other' which has produced the culturally challenging practice being explored."[68] I have tried, in this article, to meet her first criterion, and I hope that rendering American cosmetic surgery strange through a heedful look at this latest, not-yet-naturalized procedure can aid us in contextualizing and understanding genital surgeries born in other contexts as well.

Gunning examines some of the ramifications of legal "remedies" for African genital operations and concludes that criminalization of FGOs, whether on the grounds of violating human rights, women's rights, or children's rights, can seem to characterize African women and men as morally blighted, criminally bad parents, and blinded by a cultural tradition that would best be replaced with Western values.

Stan Meuwese and Annemieke Wolthuis of Defense for Children International remark that a "legal approach to the phenomenon...especially the use of criminal law, shows very clearly the limitations of the juridical system to combat historically and socially deeply-rooted behavior." One Somali woman points out that "if Somali women change, it will be a change done by us, among us. When they order us to stop, tell us what we must do, it is offensive to the black person or Muslim person who believes in circumcision. To advise is good, but not to order."[69]

Gunning, Robertson, and writers at Rainbo's web site are among those who advise that the socioeconomic dependency of women upon men is perhaps the key context for understanding and ultimately abandoning female genital surgeries.[70] They call for a two-pronged strategy: (1) work to improve women's socioeconomic autonomy, both globally and locally and (2) facilitate autonomous, community-generated cultural evolution rather than imposing punitive restrictions. These do seem fruitful emphases, as applicable in the American as in the African context. That they are realizable can be seen with the following story.

In 1997, Malik Stan Reaves reported in the *African News Service* about an alternative ritual that was replacing female circumcision in some rural sections of Kenya. I quote from his article:

A growing number of rural Kenyan families are turning to an alternative to the rite of female circumcision for their daughters. "Circumcision Through Words" grows out of collaborations between rural families and the Kenyan national women's group, Maendeleo ya Wanawake Organization (MYWO), which is committed to ending FGM in Kenya,...with the close cooperation of the Program for Appropriate Technology in Health (PATH), a nonprofit, nongovernmental, international organization which seeks to improve the health of women and children....

"People think of the traditions as themselves," said Leah Muuya of MYWO.[71] "They see themselves in their traditions. They see they are being themselves because they have been able to fulfill some of the initiations."...Circumcision Through Words brings the young candidates together for a week of seclusion

during which they learn traditional teachings about their coming roles as women, parents, and adults in the community, as well as more modern messages about personal health, reproductive issues, hygiene, communications skills, self-esteem, and dealing with peer pressure. The week is capped by a community celebration of song, dancing, and feasting which affirms the girls and their new place in the community.[72]

Willow Gerber, of PATH, confirms that as of December 2001, the Circumcision Through Words program is still ongoing and has been, over the last several years, expanded to other districts by a consortium of donors.[73] Considering this impressive endeavor, which has seen more than 1,900 girls grow to womanhood uncut, one is reminded of the words of Claire Robertson: "Central Kenyan women have been making increasingly successful efforts to stop FGM...[they show] strengths that U.S. women might well emulate in seeking to better their own status."[74]

How *might* we emulate "Circumcision Through Words"? Newly formed rituals in this country, at least those formally recognized as such, usually emerge in either New Age or evangelical settings and can grate the sensibilities of people beyond those spheres. Initiation of our girls into womanhood is often enough left to the devices of Madison Avenue and magazines like *YM, Teen People,* and *CosmoGirl.* And yet, for all the unconsciousness with which so many of us muddle through our life transitions in this country, nonetheless we too "feel that we have been ourselves" when we fulfill what we see as society's expectations for people at our stage of life. This is not an emotion to be belittled. (One Arabic term for the genital scar is *nafsi,* "my own self.")[75] Without the "years of research and discussion" that helped MYWO develop Circumcision Through Words, we would be hard pressed to generate new ways of bringing "our bodies, ourselves" into a symbolic relation with the social world that would prove both intelligible and affirmative. Just as analogies between genital cuttings are both important and exceedingly difficult to draw, so too is the conscious development of new, performative practices both worth emulating and only circuitously "applicable." Even in rural Kenya, the approach to "circumcision through words" varies dramatically from district to district.[76]

So I will not conclude this article with a glib, faux ritual for American women trained to hate the specificities of their bodies in the interest of capital accumulation. I will see, however, if I can leave you in a performative mode, offering a coda that I hope can "act" upon and through the reader as a textual "rite of antidote," speaking back to the cited language of abnormality, pathology, and sexual distrust with which this article began.

CODA

Dan Savage, syndicated sex advice columnist, responded to one reader concerned about the aesthetic effect of her long labia minora, by suggesting the work of Dr. Stubbs. He received many letters of protest, providing paeans to the appeal of prominent labia and/or suggesting that he advise self-admiration, not surgery. The enthusiastic adjectives these letter writers employed ("lavish," "luscious," "extravagant"), coupled with their emphasis on erotic pleasure, can remind us that perhaps "beauty" results from a harmony between form and function, and one key genital function is *pleasure*. I offer excerpts from some of these letters here.[77]

- ...You might have told Jagger Lips to toss her unappreciative lovers out of bed and find a boyfriend who sees the beauty of her as she exists....
- ...I have long inner labia and most of the women I've seen naked have inner labia that extend past the outer labia....If someone wants to see what vulvas really look like, they should put down *Penthouse* and start sleeping with lots of women.
- ...many men, myself included, don't find a thing wrong with longer labia minora. My girlfriend has one [*sic*] and I find it quite the enjoyable thing to suck on....
- Does female sexual pleasure mean anything to you? Not only do the labia minora engorge during sexual stimulation and have lots of nerve endings, they also increase friction....

- I am writing to Jagger Lips to discourage her from chopping off her labia minora. I prefer long labia. I find that they lend themselves more readily to being tugged, stretched, nibbled, etc....
- ...I remember a gorgeous actor, Savannah, who sadly committed suicide in the mid-1990s, who had a beautiful snatch with extravagant labia spilling (an inch and a half, easy) from her soft and salty cornucopia of love. She was rad, I hope she's resting in peace, and I'd recommend your reader try and rustle up a video....
- Our society tends not to be so pussy-positive, and most commercial pussy pictures are airbrushed on Planet Barbie, and shouldn't be considered reality. Labia (inner and outer) have lots of nerves and feel really good when they get stroked.
- ...Please tell the woman with the lavish labia not to have them removed....You were much too hasty to recommend clipping her butterfly wings!...

NOTES

1. Things certainly can happen. See Louisa Kamps, "Labia Envy," 16 Mar. 1998, <http://www. salon.com/mwt/feature/1998/03/16feature.html> (9 Dec. 2001).
2. *Los Angeles Times,* 5 Mar. 1998. See, too, the following Internet resources on labiaplasty: Dr. Alter: "Female Cosmetic and Reconstructive Genital Surgery," <http://www. altermd.com/female/index.html> (9 Dec. 2001); Julia Scheeres, "Vaginal Cosmetic Surgery," 16 Apr. 2001, <http://thriveonline.oxygen.com/sex/sexpressions/vaginal-cosmetic-surgery.html> (9 Dec. 2001); Dr. Stubbs, <http://psurg.com>; Laser Rejuvenation Center of LA, <http://www.drmatlock.com>; Dan Savage, "Long in the Labia," 16 Dec. 1999, <http://www.the stranger.com/1999-12-16/savage.html> (13 Dec. 2001); iVillage.com Archive Message Board, "Cosmetic Surgery," 7 Jan. 2000, <http://boards.allhealth.com/messages/get/bhcosmeticsx2.html> (13 Dec. 2001); Patients' chatboard, <http://boards.allhealth.com/messages/get/bhcosmeticsx2.html>.
3. See Kamps. Also, see Carrie Havranek, "The New Sex Surgeries," *Cosmopolitan,* November 1998, 146.
4. Ellen Frankfort, *Vaginal Politics* (New York: Quadrangle, 1972). See, too, Julia Scheeres, "Vulva Goldmine: How Cosmetic Surgeons Snatch Your Money," *Bitch* 11 (January 2000): 70–84.

5. Boston Women's Health Collective, *Our Bodies, Ourselves* (New York: Simon & Schuster, 1973). Updated editions have continued to be released. See Boston Women's Health Collective, *Our Bodies, Ourselves for the New Century: A Book by and for Women* (New York: Simon & Schuster, 1998).

6. See Amelia Jones, ed., *Sexual Politics: Judy Chicago's Dinner Party in Feminist Art History* (Berkeley: University of California Press, 1996); Shannon Bell, "Prostitute Performances: Sacred Carnival Theorists of the Female Body," from her *Reading, Writing, and Rewriting the Prostitute Body* (Bloomington: Indiana University Press, 1994), 137–84; and Eve Ensler, *The Vagina Monologues* (New York: Villard Press, 1998).

7. Although some women enjoy orgasmic ejaculation, it remains an exception to the rule.

8. Linda Williams's book is about pornographic films, especially those of the 1970s: *Hard Core: Power, Pleasure, and the "Frenzy of the Visible"* (Berkeley: University of California Press, 1989), 50.

9. See Michel Foucault, *The History of Sexuality,* vol. 1, *An Introduction* (New York: Random House, 1978).

10. See Gershon Legman, *Rationale of the Dirty Joke: An Analysis of Sexual Humor* (New York: Breaking Point Press, 1975), 547.

11. Jonathan Swift's "dressing room poems" include "To Betty the Grisette," "The Lady's Dressing Room," "A Beautiful Young Nymph Going to Bed," and "Strephon and Chloe." See Jonathan Swift, *The Complete Poems,* ed. Pat Rogers (New Haven: Yale University Press, 1983), 447–62. Also, see William Ian Miller, *The Anatomy of Disgust* (Cambridge: Harvard University Press, 1997).

12. In a mode that both ridicules and familiarizes the body modifications of plastic surgery, tabloids regularly feature articles about the "work" being done on celebrities, with a special emphasis on implant disasters. See, for instance, "Hollywood's Plastic Surgery Nightmares: When Breast Implants Go Bad," *National Enquirer,* 4 May 1999, 28–33. Kathy Davis discusses popular coverage of celebrity surgeries in *Reshaping the Female Body: The Dilemma of Cosmetic Surgery* (New York: Routledge, 1995), 18.

13. See the work of the late historian Roland Marchand, *Advertising the American Dream: Making Way for Modernity, 1920–1940* (Berkeley: University of California Press, 1985), 18–20.

14. Davis; Elizabeth Haiken, *Venus Envy: A History of Cosmetic Surgery* (Baltimore: Johns Hopkins University Press, 1997); Sander Gilman, *Making the Body Beautiful: A Cultural History of Aesthetic Surgery* (Princeton:

Princeton University Press, 1999). Also, see Claudia Springer, *Electronic Eros: Bodies and Desire in the Postindustrial Age* (Austin: University of Texas Press, 1996).

15. Milton T. Edgerton and H. R. McClary, quoted in Haiken, 244.

16. On the thin line between identification and desire, between wanting to be like someone and wanting to bed down with them (so exploited in consumer culture), see Diana Fuss, "Fashion and the Homo-spectatorial Look," in *On Fashion,* ed. Shari Benstock and Suzanne Ferriss (New Brunswick, N.J.: Rutgers University Press, 1994), 211–32; and Judith Butler, *Gender Trouble: Feminism and the Subversion of Identity* (New York: Routledge, 1990), esp. 57–72.

17. Josey Vogels, "My Messy Bedroom," *See,* 10 July 1997, <http://www.greatwest.ca/ SEE/ Issues/1997/970710/ josey.html> (13 Dec. 2001).

18. Laura Kipnis, *Bound and Gagged: Pornography and the Politics of Fantasy in America* (New York: Grove, 1996).

19. Susie Bright, "The Pussy Shot: An Interview with Andrew Blake," *Sexwise* (New York: Cleis Press, 1995), 82.

20. Haiken, 29–34, 136–45, 237, 246.

21. See Richard Goldstein, "Porn Free," *Village Voice,* 1 Sept. 1998, 28–34. My own research for a work-in-progress, "Choosing the Moves: Choreography in the Strip Club," also bears this out.

22. See Nedahl Stelio, "Do You Know What a Vagina Looks Like?" *Cosmopolitan,* August 2001, 126–28, on sex magazines' doctoring of vaginas and the increased prevalence of labiaplasty.

23. Luce Irigaray, *This Sex Which Is Not One,* trans. Catherine Porter (Ithaca: Cornell University Press, 1985), 209. Also see her *Speculum of the Other Woman* (Ithaca: Cornell University Press, 1986).

24. See Mary Douglas on a cross-cultural tendency to approach marginal zones, marginal people, and marginal periods with great apprehension, in *Purity and Danger: An Analysis of the Concepts of Pollution and Taboo* (1966; reprint, New York: Routledge, 1992).

25. Mary Russo, *The Female Grotesque: Risk, Excess, and Modernity* (New York: Routledge, 1994), 8.

26. See <http://www.psurg.com/gallery.html> (13 Dec. 2001).

27. Haiken, 5.

28. Natalie Zemon Davis, "Women on Top," in her *Society and Culture in Early Modern France* (Stanford: Stanford University Press, 1975), 124. See 124–31.

29. Denise Stoklos, remark made in Solo Performance Composition, her course offered by the Performance

Studies Department, New York University, Spring 2000. "Our primary dialogue is with gravity," Stoklos says.

30. See Ambient, Inc., "Body Modification: Is It Self-Mutilation—Even if Someone Else Does It for You?" 2 Feb. 1998, <http://www.ambient.on.ca/bodmod/mutilate.html> (13 Dec. 2001). Another web site dealing with body modification is <www.perforations.com> (13 Dec. 2001).

31. Ensler, 3–5.

32. This and all subsequent quotations from this plastic surgeon are from an office visit in a major American city—location to remain unspecified to ensure anonymity—in April 1999.

33. Elizabeth Grosz: "[W]omen's corporeality is inscribed as a mode of seepage." See her *Volatile Bodies: Toward a Corporeal Feminism* (Bloomington: Indiana University Press, 1994), 203.

34. Terri Kapsalis, *Public Privates: Performing Gynecology from Both Ends of the Speculum* (Durham: Duke University Press, 1997), 89. She references Julia Kristeva, *Powers of Horror: An Essay on Abjection* (New York: Columbia University Press, 1982). On the cultural and political implications of representations of genitalia in anatomical textbooks, see Lisa Jean Moore and Adele E. Clarke, "Clitoral Conventions and Transgressions: Graphic Representations in Anatomy Texts, c1900–1991," *Feminist Studies* 21 (Summer 1995): 255–301; and Susan C. Lawrence and Kae Bendixen, "His and Hers: Male and Female Anatomy in Anatomical Texts for U.S. Medical Students, 1890–1989," *Social Science and Medicine* 35 (October 1992): 925–36. Also, see Katharine Young, "Perceptual Modalities: Gynecology," in her *Presence in the Flesh* (Cambridge: Harvard University Press, 1997), 46–79.

35. Thomas Laqueur, *Making Sex: Body and Gender from the Greeks to Freud* (Cambridge: Harvard University Press, 1990). And see Lynn Hunt, *The Invention of Pornography* (New York: Zone, 1993).

36. Jennifer Terry, "Lesbians under the Medical Gaze: Scientists Search for Remarkable Differences," *Journal of Sex Research* 27 (August 1990): 317–39, 332 (emphasis added), 333.

37. See Ben Barker-Benfield, "Sexual Surgery in Late-Nineteenth-Century America," *International Journal of Health Services* 5, no. 2 (1975): 279–98; Andrew Scull and Diane Favreau, "The Clitoridectomy Craze," *Social Research* 53 (Summer 1986): 243; Barbara Ehrenreich and Deirdre English, *Complaints and Disorders: The Sexual Politics of Sickness* (New York: City University of New York Press, 1973); and Rachel P. Maines,

The Technology of Orgasm: "Hysteria," the Vibrator, and Women's Sexual Satisfaction (Baltimore: Johns Hopkins University Press, 1999).

38. Barker-Benfield, 287, 298.

39. See Daniel Gordon, "Female Circumcision and Genital Operations in Egypt and the Sudan: A Dilemma for Medical Anthropology," *Medical Anthropology Quarterly* 5 (March 1991): 7.

40. For more on this and similar cases, see Carla Miller's statement at <www.InMemoryoftheSufferingChild.com>. For coverage of the Burt case, see, for instance, Sandy Theis, "His Peers Waved Red Flags: Monitors' Concern Went beyond Love Surgery," *Dayton Daily News,* 4 Aug. 1991, 1A; Rob Modic, "Painful Testimony: Woman Testifies of Trust for Gynecologist Burt," *Dayton Daily News,* 1 June 1991, 1A; Judith Adler Hennessee, "The Love Surgeon," *Mademoiselle,* August 1989, 206; Gerry Harness and Judy Kelman, "A Mother's True Story: 'My Gynecologist Butchered Me!'" *Redbook,* July 1989, 22. Also see <http://www.nocirc.org> (13 Dec. 2001); <http://www.SexuallyMutilatedChild.org/index.html> (13 Dec. 2001).

41. See Suzanne Kessler, *Gender: An Ethnomethodological Approach* (1978; reprint, Chicago: University of Chicago Press, 1985), quoted by Martha Coventry in "The Tyranny of the Aesthetic: Surgery's Most Intimate Violation," <http://www.fgm.org/coventryarticle.html> (20 Dec. 2001).

42. Deborah Kuhn McGregor, *From Midwives to Medicine: The Birth of American Gynecology* (New Brunswick, N.J.: Rutgers University Press, 1998), 149. She is quoting Sims's autobiography. See also Kapsalis, chap. 2.

43. Mary Ann Doane, "Dark Continents: Epistemologies of Racial and Sexual Difference in Psychoanalysis and the Cinema," in her *Femmes Fatales: Feminism, Film Theory, Psychoanalysis* (New York: Routledge, 1991), 209–48; and Anne McClintock, *Imperial Leather: Race, Gender, and Sexuality in the Colonial Context* (New York: Routledge, 1995), esp. 1–4, and 21–31.

44. See Zola Maseko, director, *The Life and Times of Sara Baartman, "The Hottentot Venus,"* videorecording, London: Dominant 7, Mail and Guardian Television, France 3, and SABC 2, 1998.

45. Henri de Blainville, quoted in Maseko.

46. See Londa Schiebinger, *Nature's Body: Gender in the Making of Modern Science* (Boston: Beacon, 1995), chap. 5.

47. Maseko.

48. McGregor, 46–51.

49. Wacuka Mungai, "Desiring the 'Mutilated' African Woman," paper, 1999. Mungai is a doctoral student at

New York University and assistant program director at Rainbo, an organization devoted in large part to advocating for African women around the issue of female circumcision.

50. Nahid Toubia, *Female Genital Mutilation: A Call for Global Action,* 3d ed. (New York: Women, Ink, 1995), 35.

51. See Janice Boddy, "Body Politics: Continuing the Anticircumcision Crusade"; and Faye Ginsburg, "What Do Women Want? Feminist Anthropology Confronts Clitoridectomy," both in *Medical Anthropology Quarterly* 5 (March 1991): 15–19.

52. Inga Muscio, *Cunt: A Declaration of Independence* (Toronto: Seal Press, 1998), 134–35.

53. "Female Genital Mutilation: A Human Rights Information Pack" (London: Amnesty International, 1997).

54. Vicki Kirby, "On the Cutting Edge: Feminism and Clitoridectomy," *Australian Feminist Studies* 5 (Summer 1987): 35–56.

55. In New York City, March 1999, Wacuka Mungai shared one anecdote with me about a Buganda woman who took one trip to a gynecologist in North America: the doctor was flabbergasted and wanted to rush in a crowd of residents to stare at her. Of course, this reaction was not welcomed by the patient and she shied away from the entire profession afterward, rather than risk a reoccurrence of the circus atmosphere the doctor had created. See also, Lauran Neergard, "Doctors See More Female Circumcision," 17 Sept. 1999, posted at <http://www.worldafricannet.com/news/news7861.html>. And see this web site, that catalogs body modifications across cultures: <http://www.cadewalk.com/mods/modify.htm>. Also, see Schiebinger.

56. See Claire Robertson, "Grassroots in Kenya: Women, Genital Mutilation, and Collective Action, 1920–1990," *Signs* 21 (Spring 1996): 615–42, on some of the history of circumcision's changing meaning in Kenya over the course of the twentieth century. Mungai suggested that the *tribal* politics, in addition to the politics of colonial resistance, were perhaps more complex than Robertson's article describes. See also, Isabelle R. Gunning, "Arrogant Perception, World Traveling, and Multicultural Feminism: The Case of Female Genital Surgeries," *Columbia Human Rights Law Review* 23 (Summer 1992): 189–248.

57. Jomo Kenyatta, quoted in Gunning, 228.

58. See, for instance, Nadia Kamal Khalifa, "Reasons Behind Practicing Re-Circumcision among Educated Sudanese Women," *Ahfad Journal* 11, no. 2 (1994): 16–32; Anke van der Kwaake, "Female Circumcision

and Gender Identity: A Questionable Alliance?" *Social Science and Medicine* 35, no. 6 (1992): 777–87.

59. Claire Hunt and Kim Longinotto, with Safaa Fathay, *Hidden Faces,* videorecording (New York: Twentieth Century Vixen Production/Women Make Movies, 1990). And see Elizabeth Oram, introduction to Zainaba's "Lecture on Clitoridectomy to the Midwives of Touil, Mauritania" (1987), in *Opening the Gates: A Century of Arab Feminist Writing,* ed. Margot Badran and Miriam Cooke (Bloomington: Indiana University Press, 1990), 63–71.

60. See <http://www.altermd.com/female/index.html> (13 Dec. 2001).

61. See Rachel Bowlby, in *Shopping with Freud: Items on Consumerism, Feminism, and Psychoanalysis* (New York: Routledge, 1993), on theoretical conflations between feminist freedom and the "freedom" to choose as a consumer.

62. Wendy Brown, *States of Injury: Power and Freedom in Late Modernity* (Princeton: Princeton University Press, 1995).

63. Anonymous telephone interviews with two West Coast labiaplasty patients, August 1999. For an on-line example of this, see the fascinating archived chat between women about cosmetic surgery at iVillage, "Cosmetic Surgery Archive Board," 7 Jan. 2001, <http://boards.allhealth.com/messages/get/bhcosmeticsx2.html> (13 Dec. 2001).

64. See Robertson.

65. Anab's story, from "Social and Cultural Implications of Infibulation in Somalia," by Amina Wasame, in *Female Circumcision: Strategies to Bring about Change* (Somali Women's Democratic Organization), quoted in Toubia, 41.

66. Anonymous telephone interview with author, August 1999.

67. An important caveat: As the transgendered community has made clear, for some individuals, erotic enjoyment is enhanced via the genital modification that comes along with reassigning gender, even if that surgery has resulted in a reduction in nerve endings or sensation.

68. Gunning, 213.

69. See Frances A. Althaus, "Female Circumcision: Rite of Passage or Violation of Rites?" *International Family Planning Perspectives* 23 (September 1997), <http://www.agi-usa.org/pubs/journals/2313097.html#21> (20 Dec. 2001).

70. Alan Worsley, "Infibulation and Female Circumcision," *Journal of Obstetrics and Gynecology of the British Empire* 45, no. 4 (1938): 687.

71. For more information, see the web site for the Gender Learning Network, a partnership between twenty-three women-run NGOs, including MYWO, "working to promote women's rights and status in Kenya," <http://arcc.or.ke/gln/gln13sec.html> (13 Dec. 2001). And here are two relevant links to PATH's web site: (1) Anonymous, "Alternative rituals raise hope for eradication of Female Genital Mutilation," 20 Oct. 1997, <http://www.path.org/resources/press/19971020-FGM.html> (13 Dec. 2001), and (2) Anonymous, "Modern Rites of Passage," <http://www.path.org/resources/closerlooks/ f_modern_rites_of_passage.htm> (13 Dec. 2001).

72. PATH's Michelle Folsom heads a ten-year office in Kenya, and oversees the organization's collaboration on this and other projects with MYWO, and their work receives the support of the Kenyan government. See "Program for Appropriate Technology in Health," *Promoting a Healthy Alternative to FGM: A Tool for Program Implementers* (Washington, D.C.: PATH, 2001). See also, Davan Maharaj, "Kenya to Ban Female Genital Excision," *Los Angeles Times,* 15 Dec. 2001.

73. Robertson, 615. See also, Carolyn Sargent, "Confronting Patriarchy: The Potential for Advocacy in Medical Anthropology," *Medical Anthropology Quarterly* 5 (March 1991): 24–25.

74. Alan Worsley, 687.

75. See "Modern Rites of Passage," <http://www.path.org/closerlooks/f_modern_rites_of_passage.html> (13 Dec. 2001).

76. All letters quoted in Dan Savage, "Savage Love," *Village Voice,* 18 Jan. 2000, 126.

77. All letters quoted in Dan Savage, "Savage Love," *Village Voice,* 18 Jan. 2000, 126.

35 • Seth Goren

GAY AND JEWISH: THE ADVANTAGES OF INTERSECTIONALITY

DISCUSSION QUESTIONS

1. How does Goren's experience elucidate the complicated nature of intersectionality?
2. How does this chapter demonstrate the importance of an intersectional approach to privilege as well as oppression?

> Do I contradict myself?
> Very well then I contradict myself,
> (I am large, I contain multitudes.)
>
> —Walt Whitman, "Song of Myself"

Seth Goren, "Gay and Jewish: The Advantages of Intersectionality" (unpublished). Reprinted by permission of the author.

Over two decades ago, Peggy McIntosh's classic essay on White privilege captured the imagination of progressives worldwide and began serving as a foundational piece for diversity and inclusion education. Among the essay's most captivating portions is an inventory of how White privilege is manifested, providing specific examples of the ways in which White individuals reap privilege's benefits.

Following McIntosh's example, other lists have sprouted up surrounding a particular identity and the privilege it brings with it. By drawing attention to the privileges surrounding ability,[1] wealth,[2] sexual orientation,[3] class,[4] gender,[5] gender identity[6] and religion,[7] these enumerations have proven an efficient and effective way to educate readers with specific examples of how privilege operates.

At the same time that these privilege lists have proliferated, scholars have elaborated on privilege and pursued the ongoing development of privilege and related studies. Among these developments have been explorations of intersectionality, a term coined by Kimberlé Crenshaw referring to the ways in which a person's various identities interact and their combined impact on a person's experiences.[8] Much of the literature in this area has focused on the compounding negative impact of marginalized identities, with the experiences of Black women providing one such example.[9]

While the privilege inventories mentioned above provide excellent examples of privilege along a variety of single axes, few address intersectionality or more than one identity at a time.[10] This could be because much of the literature on intersectionality focuses on two or more marginalized identities and how those identities interact to magnify oppression. Regardless, as more privilege conversations include intersectionality as a vehicle for understanding and educating,[11] the classic McIntosh-style list format has the potential to be a helpful tool for individuals exploring their own intersecting identities and the intersectionalities around them.

. . . While I carry a number of privileged identities (*e.g.,* White, male), I also have (at least) two non-privileged identities: I identify religiously as Jewish, and I am openly gay. Individually, each of these independently marks me for exclusion in society as a whole, as numerous researchers have pointed out, and on a regular basis, I run into the ill effects of either straight privilege, religious privilege or both.

My experiences as an openly gay Jew generally affirm the negative synergies often associated with the intersectionality of two marginalized identities. Religious privilege flows through the LGBT community, just as it does the rest of society, making it more challenging, on the whole, to be Jewish than Christian (at least culturally Christian) in LGBT contexts. Similarly, Jewish settings are not immune from heteronormativity and sexual orientation privilege, and it is easier to be a straight Jew than an LGBT one. Several studies have highlighted the collision of these two identities and the difficulties faced by gay Jewish men in integrating these two aspects of who they are,[12] as well as the lower rates of practice and engagement for LGBT Jews when compared to the Jewish community as a whole.[13]

That said, the intersectional effect of being both gay and Jewish is, oddly enough, not entirely disadvantaging. Having had repeated conversations with gay non-Jews, I am struck by the way in which I enjoy certain unearned benefits that they do not based on my being Jewish. It is almost as if my Jewish identity, and the resources that flow from it, provide a queer-friendly (or at least a queer-friendlier) sanctuary from some of the heteronormativity and homophobia in the world at large.

For those more visually inclined among us, the following figure may be useful:

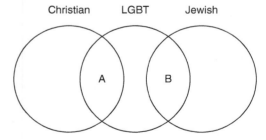

In essence, my experience as a resident of Area B is, in some ways, more advantaged than that of Area A dwellers. Because those in Area A carry religious privilege that I do not, this seems counterintuitive.

Nevertheless, examples of my Jewish identity giving me support unavailable to LGBT Christians are surprisingly numerous.

Increasingly mindful of these benefits and inspired like so many others by Peggy McIntosh, I have put together a list of some of the things that I, as a gay Jew, take for granted and that gay non-Jews are less likely to have. The items listed are not exclusively or universally Jewish; there are others who reap similar benefits, such as gay Unitarian-Universalists or LGBT individuals who affiliate with the Metropolitan Community Church, and the advantages I have included are uneven in their spread through the Jewish world, particularly pronounced in certain settings and absent in others.[14]

. . .

This list is not without caveats. Although I have done my best to isolate these two identities and how they interrelate, I am certain that other aspects of who I am have seeped in. Moreover, to be clear, this is not a "privilege list" along the lines of those enumerated elsewhere; it is difficult to see how a gay Jew could be "privileged" based on those identities in the way that men, straight people, White people or other holders of dominant identities are. This is, rather, an exploration of my own intersectionality, the gay-Jewish perks I often forget are not universal and the unexpected ways in which two salient, marginalized aspects of who I am interact.

With that introduction, the following is a list of benefits that I enjoy as a gay Jewish man that are largely unavailable to gay non-Jews:

1. Should I marry someone of the same gender, there is religious liturgy readily available for me to use, either verbatim or as a starting point for designing my own liturgy and there are clergy of my religion willing to officiate at same-gender wedding ceremonies.
2. Numerous institutions, agencies, places of worship and community organizations affiliated with my religion have workplace protections based on sexual orientation and gender expression or identity.[15]

3. Multiple denominations or movements of my religion have taken progressive stances on LGBT issues and historically have demonstrated support for marriage equality and legal protections for LGBT individuals.

. . .

5. Mainstream organizations and conferences for my religious group offer programs and sessions that present and have professionals who speak to LGBT issues in a positive way.

. . .

7. There are lesbian, gay, bisexual, transgender and allied clergy I can turn to for pastoral counseling, spiritual guidance and other forms of religious and spiritual support.
8. If I choose to become a clergyperson or lay leader in my religious community, I would have several options to select from in pursuing my goals, and being LGBT would not be an inherent obstacle to pursuing any of them.
9. Among the sacred texts of my religion are stories, narratives and directives that easily lend themselves to supporting LGBT perspectives and inclusive stances.
10. In public surveys, my religious community demonstrates comparatively strong support for issues of importance to the LGBT community.[16]
11. In filling out forms to join a religious organization, it is unlikely that I will have to modify the membership form to make it fit me and my family.
12. There are numerous organizations that focus on my religion specifically and its intersections with LGBT identities.[17]
13. When celebrating anniversaries and other relationship milestones. I can find a religious community that will honor them.

. . .

15. Dating websites that cater to people of my religion are likely to have searches for same-gender partners as an option.[17]
16. There are numerous books, websites, studies and other resources that respond to the intersectionality of my religion and LGBT identity in a positive way.

17. My experience with religious privilege, marginalization and oppression prepared me and gave me skills to respond to heteronormativity and straight privilege.

. . .

19. In looking nationally and internationally, I can see LGBT role models who share my religious identity in public life, including politics, academics and the arts.

. . .

21. People's general unfamiliarity with my religion makes it less likely that they will sense or point out any perceived conflict between me being religious and me being openly LGBT.

. . .

23. If my partner of the same gender passed away, my religion would accord me the appropriate respect due a mourner in my position.

. . .

More broadly, I am curious if this intersectional exercise would lead to similar contradictions for others based on who they are, especially in examining two overlapping marginalized identities. . . . How might this shape the way we approach privilege and intersectionality?

As we become increasingly aware of the benefits of an intersectionality-based approach to identity, power and privilege education, it would not surprise me if the contradictions multiply because surely, to paraphrase Walt Whitman, each of us carries contradictions and contains multitudes.

NOTES

1. http://www2.edc.org/WomensEquity/edequity/hypermail/1180.html
2. http://whatever.scalzi.com/2005/09/03/being-poor/
3. http://queersunited.blogspot.com/2008/10/heterosexual-privilege-checklist.html
4. http://www.thewtc.org/Invisibility_of_Class_Privilege.pdf
5. http://www.amptoons.com/blog/the-male-privilege-checklist/
6. http://www.amptoons.com/blog/2006/09/22/the-non-trans-privilege-checklist/
7. Lewis Z Schlosser, *Journal of Multicultural Counseling and Development*; Jan 2003; 31, 1.
8. Crenshaw, Kimberlé. "Demarginalizing the intersection of race and sex: A Black feminist critique of antidiscrimination doctrine, feminist theory and antiracist politics." *U. Chi. Legal F.* (1989): 139.
9. Crenshaw, Kimberlé. "Mapping the margins; Intersectionality, identity politics, and violence against women of color." *Stanford law review* (1991): 1241–1299. See also http://www.whiteprivilegeconference.com/pdf/intersectionality_primer.pdf.
10. The one example of an intersectional list I was about to find is "The Black Male Privileges Checklist," available at http://jewelwoods.com/node/9, which focuses on the privileges enjoyed by Black men over Black women.
11. Kimmel, Michael S. and Abby L. Ferber. *Privilege: A Reader.* 2016. Boulder, CO: Westview Press.
12. Coyle, Dr Adrian, and Deborah Rafalin. "Jewish Gay Men's Accounts of Negotiating Cultural, Religious, and Sexual Identity." *Journal of Psychology & Human Sexuality* 12, no. 4 (2001): 21–48; Schnoor, Randal F. "Being gay and Jewish: Negotiating intersecting identities." *Sociology of Religion* 67, no. 1 (2006): 43–60.
13. Cohen, Steven M., Caryn Aviv, and Ari Y. Kelman. "Gay, Jewish, or both: Sexual orientation and Jewish engagement." *Journal of Jewish Communal Service* 84, no. 1/2 (2009): 154–166.
14. Many of these benefits accrue in a most pronounced manner in larger metropolitan areas and in pluralistic Jewish or non-Orthodox Jewish organizations and places of worship. That said, I have often been surprised at the way in which these benefits accumulate even in less densely populated areas and in the Orthodox Jewish world.
15. http://www.hrc.org/joel
16. http://articles.washingtonpost.com/2013-03-06/politics/37500567_1_support-for-such-unions-jewish-voters-exit-polis
17. http://www.hrc.org/files/assets/resources/Workplace_ParticipatingOrganizations_JOEI_2012.pdf

36 • *Ayesha Khurshid*

ISLAMIC TRADITIONS OF MODERNITY
Gender, Class, and Islam in a Transnational Women's Education Project

DISCUSSION QUESTIONS

1. How does the author demonstrate the significance of context in understanding the construction and performance of gender?
2. How does an intersectional approach allow the author to challenge prevailing assumptions about binary constructs of modernity versus Islam?
3. What are the benefits of using a methodological approach that examines women's actual experiences to assess modernity projects?
4. How does the author examine, employ, and support the notion of embedded agency?

"You can tell just by looking at people if they are educated or not," Rehana commented as she instructed a group of young girls playing in the school courtyard to keep their voices low and behave like *parhay likhay* (educated) people. For Rehana, making sure that her kindergarteners learned "proper" manners was the most important part of her work. A 30-year-old woman with an energetic and warm personality, Rehana was a popular teacher at the girls' school in her low-income village where she had worked for five years. Her village was typical of the Pakistani rural landscape, with limited access to schools and low literacy rates, especially for women. Rehana was one of the first women in her village to complete a high school and college education. However, she did not consider her job or her academic credentials to be her most important marker of distinction. Instead, Rehana was proud that she had

learned to behave like an educated person. "People can tell that I am *parhi likhi*[1] even if they do not know about my educational background," she said.

Like Rehana, most of the women teachers I interviewed during my 16-month ethnography of girls' schools in Pakistan were among the first women in their rural and low-income communities to have received high school, college, and sometimes even graduate education. For these women, the primary purpose of education was to instill mannerisms associated with the middle class, such as polite and confident speech, conversing in English, dressing like city women, speaking confidently with strangers, establishing eye contact during interactions, and resolving conflicts without engaging in verbal or physical fights. On the one hand, the participants approached middle-class mannerisms as the distinctive feature of the *parhay likhay* people. On the other hand, they argued that acquiring

Khurshid, Ayesha, 2015. "Islamic Traditions of Modernity: Gender, Class, and Islam in a Transnational Women's Education Project." *Gender and Society* 29(1): 98–121. Copyright © 2015, © SAGE Publications.

education was an Islamic right and responsibility of all Muslims. In this narrative of women's education, the *parhi likhi* subjectivity instilled in women the mannerisms and values central to them becoming "good" Muslims as well as productive members of their families and communities. This *parhi likhi* subjectivity provides insights into a discourse where being educated, seen as synonymous with being a good Muslim, is validated through the performance of middle-class mannerisms. In a global context where education is seen as a universal tool to empower Muslim women, the experiences of *parhi likhi* teachers offer important insights into the intersections between education and gendered, class-based, and religious subjectivities among Muslim women from rural communities in Pakistan.

Women's education has been central to different discourses that have sought to modernize the developing and Muslim societies (Abu-Lughod 1998; Adely 2009; Chatterjee 1989; Cornwall 2007; Kandiyoti 2005; Najmabadi 1998). These multiple paradigms approach education as the process to *change* women: For example, international development agencies assume that education will equip Muslim women with tools to transform their "oppressive" culture, whereas religious militant groups such as the Taliban approach women's education as a tool of Western imperialism. Instead of mobilizing women's education as either an indicator of liberation or of oppression, this ethnographic article shows that although education presents new economic and social opportunities for women from marginalized communities, it also reinforces gendered and class-based norms and creates new restrictions on them. Second, it examines how education is experienced by the women participants of this study as having access to specific and limited forms of power that they used within, rather than against, the institutions of family, community, and Islam.

. . .

Global discourses on women's education are grounded in a modern versus traditional binary, where the West is seen as progressive, modern, and secular and Muslim societies are positioned as backward, traditional, and religious (Abu-Lughod 2009; Ahmed 1992; Asad 2003; Mahmood 2005; Scott 2007). In these international projects, women's education becomes an individualistic and market-oriented goal, whereas Islam is treated as a challenge that restricts women's access to schools, job markets, and political participation (Abu-Lughod 2009; Cornwall 2007; Kandiyoti 2005). There is no doubt that women's low literacy rates and limited access to educational facilities, especially in rural areas, are serious issues shaped by the lack of educational infrastructure, poverty, and—in some cases—cultural values that constrain women's mobility in public spaces. However, debates on women's education fail to capture how, despite these realities, the popular perception of women's education in Pakistan is overwhelmingly positive, connecting it to Islamic history rather than to Western values (Saigol 2012). . . .

"DOING EDUCATION": GENDER, CLASS, AND RELIGION

The discourse of Islamic modernity shapes how *parhi likhi* women participants negotiated and embodied a particular class-based Islamic morality. Feminist scholarship highlights how Muslim women create and recreate their gendered identities in complex ways, such as through attire, social relations, and a domestic/public division of labor (Huisman and Hondagneu-Sotelo 2005; Hutson 2001; Killian 2003; Marshall 2005; Predelli 2004; Read and Bartkowski 2000). For these women, Islam becomes a flexible resource (Predelli 2004) and a "dynamic tool kit" (Bartkowski and Read 2003) used to activate, reinforce, and subvert gendered boundaries. This context-specific engagement with Islam to define gender empowerment is captured in ethnographic accounts of Muslim women's participation in diverse Islamic movements (Mahmood 2005; Rinaldo 2013).

I employ the concept of "embedded agency," defined as a capacity to act in a particular context (Korteweg 2008). My approach is grounded in theories of gender as a social construction and a performance rather than a universal norm (Butler 1999; West and Fenstermaker 1995; West and Zimmerman 1987, 2009). This is a departure from more individualist notions often employed by the mainstream international development agencies that support women's education in countries like Pakistan (Adely 2009).

Specifically, I examine how context-specific structures of gender, class, Islam, and women's education enter into the gender performances of participants as they make claims to the *parhi likhi* subjectivity. This *parhi likhi* subject position provides insights into gender performance and gender empowerment as constitutive of multiple levels of contestations, contradictions, and tensions. For instance, Muslim women in countries like Pakistan have become the subject of global modernity projects, which present education as an avenue for entering into labor markets and escaping oppressive institutions of family, community, and Islam. Participants claimed modern womanhood through acquiring education: However, they also engaged in specific struggles regarding issues such as employment, mobility outside of the home, and participation in decision-making processes within, rather than against, their families, communities, and Islam. Embedded agency, in this context, involves participants claiming a subject position that has historically been reserved for Muslim men and middle-class women in colonial and postcolonial discourses. The use of choice and free will, in this case, may translate into *parhi likhi* women acquiring jobs but also in their reinforcing gendered norms about women's sexuality as well as reproducing hierarchies that distinguish them from the uneducated and un-Islamic women. We can recognize the meaning of such performances only by situating them in their local and global contexts, as this process of doing gender is legitimized through existing accountability structures (Messner 2000; Trautner 2005; Utrata 2011).

My context-specific analysis of *parhi likhi* subjectivity also approaches religion as a set of practices and discourses instead of solely a belief system (Asad 2003). For participants, being *parhi likhi* was synonymous with being good Muslims and productive members of their communities. Being Muslim, on the other hand, was less about bringing their lives into strict alignment with universal Quranic scriptures and more about performing context-specific configurations of Islam. . . .

This article emerged from a larger study that examined how a women-centered transnational development organization that I call the Institute for Education and Literacy (IEL) defined, developed, and implemented policies and practices to educate and empower women from marginalized communities in Pakistan. (I use pseudonyms for the organization and the research participants.) IEL is headquartered in the United States, with chapters in major cities across the United States, Canada, and the United Kingdom. . . . The organization manages more than 200 girls' schools with more than 16,000 students in low-income communities throughout Pakistan. It has recruited and trained more than 600 women from the same communities to work as teachers at its schools.

. . .

This approach to women's education reminded me of my own experiences growing up in a middle-class home in Pakistan where *parhay likhay* people were seen as wiser, modern, and good Muslims. As a graduate student living in the United States, I became curious to learn how these cultural perceptions interacted with the global preoccupation with women's education as the solution to all social and political ills. IEL and its girls' schools provided a productive site to examine the intersection of class, gender, and Islam in defining what being *parhi likhi* means in the rural villages of Pakistan.

This article focuses on the ethnographic data collected from the IEL women teachers to understand how they constructed and negotiated their identities as educated Muslim women. . . .

. . . Through my in-depth account of *parhi likhi* women, I show how *parhi likhi* subjectivity is constituted through dichotomous conceptions of middle vs. lower class, urban vs. rural, and authentic vs. un-Islamic characteristics of Muslim womanhood.

BECOMING *PARHI LIKHI* WOMEN: ISLAM, CLASS, AND GENDER

The importance of middle-class etiquette was a common theme in the research. The teachers, most of whom were the first women to receive education in their families, believed that as *parhi likhi* women, they were distinct from other women in their villages. They attributed this distinction to their dispositions, which they aimed to teach to their students. Interestingly, some of the women who were labeled *unparh* (uneducated) by interviewees had also attended school and some even had academic credentials. This became clear as Salma, the 28-year-old headmistress of an IEL school serving a low-income rural community, discussed the performance of women teachers at her schools:

> You should have seen my teachers when they started working at the school. They would come to school looking as if they had come to work in the fields and not to teach children. Their clothes would not be pressed, their hair would not be combed, their *dupatta* [scarf] would be hanging from their head, and they would be yelling at each other and at the students. They have their degrees, but can anyone call them educated? They are no different from other women in the village.

Salma felt that the teachers at her school did not qualify as *parhi likhi* because they neither looked nor behaved like educated women. They had attended schools but were unable to learn educated ways of being.

. . .

The IEL staff invited Salma to work at their school because there was an extreme shortage of educated women in her village. In Salma's narrative, being *parhay likhay* involved not only acquiring academic credentials but also learning the mannerisms of educated urbanites. Her ability to perform this identity qualified her as educated while excluding teachers who lacked the cultural styles of educated women. These cultural styles not only were significant within the space of the school but also shaped women's opportunities outside of school. For instance, Salma was the only woman to participate on village committees that worked with non-governmental organizations and state institutions to initiate development projects providing health care, roads, and clean drinking water to the community. In rural villages, participation in these decision-making processes is traditionally limited to male community elders and older men from families with kinship connections

and/or landholdings. The inclusion of Salma on the committees was partially a response to state and international agencies' emphasis on women's participation in development projects. However, the choice of Salma in particular, as compared to other village woman [*sic*] who possessed similar academic credentials, validated her status as the only true "educated woman."

This validation of Salma's educated status in the village is particularly pertinent because Salma, a confident and articulate woman, sometimes openly disagreed with male community elders during these meetings. However, the manners she cultivated allowed her to disagree in a way that community members viewed as respectable. Her father shared this perspective with me when I visited her family:

> People used to get upset when Salma disagreed with them in the meetings. But she was always polite and respectful and did not get into fights. Now, that's the difference between *parhi likhi* and *unparh* women, and people saw that. Today, people send their daughters to school because they want them to be like Salma.

. . .

Salma and other women participants often used Islam to convince their families to allow them to take up nontraditional roles. For example, women were to be accompanied by a close male relative in any public domain but especially while traveling outside of the village. However, Rafia, a 26-year-old teacher, convinced her father to allow her to attend IEL teacher training workshops in a nearby city by telling him how Islam asked Muslim men and women to seek knowledge at every cost. She described the argument she made to her father: "In our [Muslims'] history, women worked at schools, ran businesses, and even fought wars. Then why can't we have jobs [outside of home] or go for shopping on our own?" It was very common for participants to use Islamic teachings to justify new roles for *parhi likhi* women. Interestingly, for them, being *parhi likhi* also implied being a good Muslim who is aware of her rights and responsibilities.

The performance of politeness, hospitality, modesty, dressing well, and hygiene that qualified women participants as *parhi likhi* were seen as Islamic, rather than middle-class, virtues. Fatima, a 38-year-old teacher, explained this:

> I tell my girls to look at Fatima Jinnah [a woman leader who played a prominent role in the creation of Pakistan] to learn how to be a good Muslim. Women did not even get out of the house in her time [1930s–1960s], but she was so graceful and decent as she led the nation. After all, she was a *parhi likhi* woman.

In these narratives, the term *parhi likhi* was used not only as an indication of the ability of educated women to take up nontraditional roles but also as a reference to their qualifications as "good" Muslims who understood their rights and responsibilities.

Home was another site for shifting patterns of gendered participation as a result of access to education for women. This is reflected in the story of Noor, a 33-year-old teacher at an IEL elementary school. Noor lived with her elderly parents, her two brothers' wives, and their children, while her brothers lived in the city and worked government jobs. In Noor's low-income rural village, it was common for women to marry in their mid-twenties, but Noor's parents had not found a suitable match for her because Noor had a master's degree in a community where few men had studied beyond high school. Noor's refusal to marry a man who was less educated had troubled her family, but they eventually accepted her decision. Noor laughingly told me that her education had saved her from "serving a man" because her parents would not have honored her choices regarding marriage if she were not educated. . . .

WOMEN'S EDUCATION AND ISLAM: PUBLIC DISPLAYS OF DOMESTICITY

One of the main goals of the global project of women's education is to prepare Muslim women to participate in male-dominated public spaces. Such public mobility is meant to challenge oppressive institutions of family, community, and Islam. The participants in this study had become mobile in public spaces by seeking employment outside of the home

and, in some cases, participating in community-level decision-making processes. However, this mobility produced new economic and social opportunities as well as regulations for women. For example, at the age of 23, Noreen, an IEL teacher, took her first trip outside her village without a male relative escort. Although Noreen called it "traveling on my own," she was actually accompanied by a woman friend as she journeyed to visit the nearest doctor in a town 20 miles away. Noreen was filled with excitement as she described her "travel" to discuss her recurring cold with the doctor and described in detail how she and her friend waited for the public transport by the roadside, got off the bus at the right place, saw the doctor, bought medicine, and returned home. The success of this trip was a source of great pride for this young teacher at an IEL school serving low-income students in her village. She had accomplished something that most women were not allowed to do in her village: traveling without a close male relative. She was even more pleased when her father found out about this trip, which was made without his permission, but did not get upset. She explained, "My father did not get mad at me because he trusts me. He knows I am educated and will not do anything wrong." When I asked what she meant by doing anything "wrong," she smiled and looked at me as if the answer was self-evident before replying:

> This is not a city where women are smart enough to do everything on their own. Here, women can be so naïve. They are not educated to know the difference between right and wrong. I bet my cousins would not stop giggling on the bus if they were traveling on their own.

. . . In her opinion, only *parhi likhi* women could be trusted to navigate unfamiliar spaces because they were aware of their rights as well as their responsibilities as Muslim women.

Noreen's reluctance to trust *unparh* women with new freedoms was shared by most of my interviewees. These women spoke enthusiastically about women's education and Islamic rights for women as active and visible members of the community, but were apprehensive that *unparh* women lacked the awareness and self-control to work outside of the home, travel alone, and interact with men. They were less concerned with women's sexual morality than with their ability to comport themselves in a way that would display an Islamic and class-based respectability. . . .

> Young girls are like colorful butterflies who want to fly, have fun, see the world. But they can also be so easily lured too, right? I warn them to be careful if they want to live lives that are different from their mothers and grandmothers. If they want to become something, attend college, have a job, and have some say in their lives. But they have to prove that they can be trusted before they can have this freedom.

Rukhsana approached her young students' sexuality as something that had to be protected in order for them to have more opportunities than earlier generations of women. Her discussion of the possibility of young girls being lured into romantic or sexual relationships was not necessarily framed in terms of morality but referred to the expectations that educated women had to meet to be allowed certain kinds of freedoms as respectable Muslim women. Women suspected of having extramarital affairs before or after marriage were seen as bringing extreme dishonor to their families. Unlike men involved in such affairs, women's mobility would be strictly confined if they were caught, and they would not be allowed to attend school anymore. In extreme cases, especially when the partners in the affair belonged to different ethnic and caste groups, these acts lead to violence against those involved and/or long, drawn-out disputes between families. The wisdom of *parhi likhi* women, in this case, is to avoid actions that could potentially harm them and other women in their communities.

. . .

Participants' selective and strategic deployment of Islamic rights and local customs reflects how class, gender, and Islam intersect to construct *parhi likhi* Muslim women as agents of change. It also shows that family, community, and Islam are not merely rigid local structures against which women's education has to modernize, but rather are institutions in flux that shape the meaning of educated Muslim womanhood in different contexts. . . .

Salma, the participant discussed earlier, was strong and assertive but still agreed to an arranged marriage with a cousin despite having strong reservations about it. She believed that her refusal would have brought dishonor to her family and especially to her father who had supported her education against community wishes. Abiding by the wishes of her family won her the trust of her family and community and later helped her take a stand against her husband and in-laws to work as a teacher. Salma decided to stay in the marriage despite serious differences with her in-laws and physical abuse from her husband, because she wanted to keep her family intact. In a community where she was seen as a wise and respectable role model for girls, she did not consider divorce an option despite its being allowed in Islam and Pakistani law. In fact, she shared that her marriage remained intact primarily because she as a *parhi likhi* woman could see the potential consequences of divorce. It would not only bring dishonor to her family but also make it difficult for other girls in her community to pursue education, as people would view Salma's action as the outcome of her being educated. There were a number of cases in her village where women had separated from their husbands, but a *parhi likhi* woman was not expected to defy community norms. In other words, Salma saw her choice to stand up against her husband and in-laws as well as to enter into an arranged marriage and stay in the abusive relationship as a reflection of her making informed choices as a *parhi likhi* woman.

. . .

Ultimately, the lived experiences of participants complicate liberal notions of women's education as a tool to challenge patriarchal Islamic traditions. At the same time, they also highlight the tensions inherent in the subject position of *parhi likhi* women, who at times willingly embraced and reinforced structures of domination instead of opposing them in order to gain respectability equated with Islamic and middle-class morality. This analysis helps us understand how *parhi likhi* women actively participate as embedded agents, rather than passive objects of modernity discourses, by negotiating which cultural practices to transform and which ones to keep intact as they exercised the limited and specific forms of power available to them in day-to-day life. As discussed earlier, dominant structures sometimes benefited the participants by distinguishing them from "other" women in the community and enabling them to act in their own self-interest. Thus, embedded agency for the participants in this context meant deployment of education to claim empowerment within, rather than against, the institutions of family, community, and Islam. Second, whereas the Islamic modernity project provides a productive context for examining *parhi likhi* subjectivity, the analysis shows how Islam was one of multiple institutions that these women engaged with to define their status as modern educated Muslim women. This discussion helps us move away from the "oppressed Muslim woman" trope to better understand how Islam, gender, and class are simultaneously deployed in the making of *parhi likhi* subjectivity within a particular context.

CONCLUSION

. . .

This article makes a threefold contribution to gender theory. First, using ethnographic data, it challenges facile assumptions of women's education as an inherently beneficial project, and instead examines the ways in which education intersects with gender, class, and religion in the production of new subjectivities (*parhi likhi*) in Pakistan. These subjectivities open up new possibilities for gender equality while reinforcing other gender norms. These new subjectivities are complex as they respond to the global discourse of women's education and women's rights by mobilizing an indigenous understanding of women's education as an Islamic right and responsibility, instead of a Western import. The Islamic modernity project simultaneously constructs gender, class, and education by enabling educated Muslim women to step into male-dominated public spaces while prescribing the middle-class subjectivity necessary for women to become good Muslims and productive members of society. . . .

Second, this article speaks to the literature on Western imperialist modernity projects, particularly those involving Islamic states and communities (Abu-Lughod 1998; Adely 2009; Ahmed 1992; Chatterjee 1989; Kandiyoti 2005; Mahmood 2005). I employ Abu-Lughod's call for contextualized research by showing the complex configurations of religion, gender, and class among educated women in Pakistan. One of my major findings is that unlike the prevalent perception, Islam and modernity are not seen as oppositional, but rather are accessed simultaneously through notions of what constitutes the gendered subject. This is an important point for scholars to consider when examining gendered relations among religious communities: namely, to not assume that religion is constructed as "pre-modern" in these contexts, but to look more closely at how these dynamics are context-specific. . . .

Third, this article contributes to existing scholarship on "doing gender" (Butler 1999; West and Zimmerman 1987) and "embedded agency" (Korteweg 2008; Messner 2000; Trautner 2005; Utrata 2011) by showing their workings in a particular social and historical context. I unpack notions of gender performativity by examining how it is validated, facilitated, and constrained in a particular context by the institutions of family, community, and Islam. For example, certain forms of power became available to *parhi likhi* women only when they embraced other patriarchal structures. However, this embracing did not necessarily signal oppression but rather embedded agency as well as a perception of liberation that did not constitute challenging these structures. Instead of describing a linear narrative of women's access to labor markets, health care, rights, mobility, and leadership positions through academic knowledge and credentialing, this article uses lived experiences of the participants to highlight women's education as a contested terrain shaped by the intersections of local and global influences. This article thus shows how women teachers who enact a middle-class, modern Muslim subjectivity are not "victims" of their culture but active agents who stand in tension with as well as shape power hierarchies in their contexts.

AUTHOR'S NOTE

I am grateful to Myra Marx Ferree, whose mentorship and guidance was central to conceptualizing and developing this piece. I would also like to thank Mary Louise Gomez, Kirin Narayan, Katherin Pratt Ewing, Catherine Campton Lilly, and Carl Grant for their support to write this article. A very special thanks to Joya Misra and the three editors of the special issue as well as to the five reviewers whose comments were immensely helpful. This research was made possible with the help of grants from the Tashia Morgridge Fellowship Program and Mellon Foundation. I am deeply grateful to the IEL staff and policymakers as well as to the women teachers who made this project possible by generously sharing their experiences, reflections, and time.

NOTE

1. *Parhi likhi* is the Urdu term used to refer to educated women, whereas *parhay likhay* is often used as a gender-neutral term to refer to both educated men and women.

REFERENCES

Abu-Lughod, Lila. 1998. Introduction. In *Remaking women,* edited by Lila Abu-Lughod. Princeton, NJ: Princeton University Press.

Abu-Lughod, Lila. 2002. Do Muslim women really need saving? *American Anthropologist* 104:783–90.

Abu-Lughod, Lila. 2009. Dialectics of women's empowerment. *International Journal of Middle Eastern Studies* 41:83–103.

Adely, Fida. 2009. Educating women for development. *International Journal of Middle East Studies* 41:105–22.

Ahmed, Leila. 1992. *Women and gender in Islam.* New Haven, CT: Yale University Press.

Asad, Talal. 2003. *Formations of the secular: Christianity, Islam, modernity.* Stanford, CA: Stanford University Press.

Bartkowski, John P., and Jen'nan Ghazal Read. 2003. Veiled submission. *Qualitative Sociology* 26:71–92.

Bloul, Rachel. 1998. Engendering Muslim identities: Women living under Muslim law, December 20, 2012, http://www.wluml.org/english/pubsfulltxt.shtml?cmd%5B87%7%5D=i-87-2682.

Butler, Judith. 1999. *Gender trouble.* New York: Routledge.

Chakrabarty, Dipesh. 1997. The difference-deferral of a colonial modernity. In *Tensions of empire,* edited by Fredrick Cooper and Ann Laura Stoler. Berkeley: University of California Press.

Chatterjee, Partha. 1989. Colonialism, nationalism, and colonialized women. *American Ethnologist* 16:622–33.

Cornwall, Andrea. 2007. Myths to live by? *Development and Change* 38:149–68.

Giddens, Anthony. 1991. *Modernity and self-identity.* Stanford, CA: Stanford University Press.

Huisman, Kimberly, and Pierrette Hondagneu-Sotelo. 2005. Dress matters. *Gender & Society* 19:44–65.

Hutson, Alaine. 2001. Women, men, and patriarchal bargaining in an Islamic Sufi order. *Gender & Society* 15:734–65.

Kandiyoti, Deniz. 2005. The politics of gender and reconstruction in Afghanistan. Occasional Paper 4. Geneva: UNRISD.

Killian, Caitlin. 2003. The other side of the veil. *Gender & Society* 17:567–90.

Korteweg, Anna C. 2008. The Sharia debate in Ontario. *Gender & Society* 22:434–54.

MacLeod, Arlene Elowe. 1992. Hegemonic relations and gender resistance. *Signs* 17:533–57.

Mahmood, Saba. 2005. *Politics of piety.* Princeton, NJ: Princeton University Press.

Marshall, Gül Aldikacti. 2005. Ideology, progress, and dialogue. *Gender & Society* 19:104–20.

McClintock, Ann. 1997. No longer in a future heaven. In *Dangerous liaisons,* edited by Ann McClintock, Aamir Mufti, and Ella Sohat. Minneapolis: University of Minnesota Press.

Messner, Michael. 2000. Barbie girls versus sea monsters. *Gender & Society* 14:765–84.

Metcalf, Barbara. 1994. Remaking ourselves. In *Accounting for fundamentalisms,* edited by Martin E. Marty and Scott Appleby. Chicago: Chicago University Press.

Mian, Ali Altaf, and Nancy Nyquist Potter. 2009. Invoking Islamic Rights In British India. *The Muslim World* 99(2):312–34.

Minault, Gail. 1998. *Secluded Scholars.* New Delhi, India: Oxford University Press.

Mitchell, Timothy. 2000. Introduction. In *Questions of modernity,* edited by Timothy Mitchell. Minneapolis: University of Minnesota Press.

Najmabadi, Afsaneh. 1998. Crafting an educated housewife in Iran. In *Remaking women,* edited by Lila Abu-Lughod. Princeton, NJ: Princeton University Press.

Predelli, Line Nyhagen. 2004. Interpreting gender in Islam. *Gender & Society* 18:473–93.

Read, Jen'Nan Ghazal, and John P. Bartkowski. 2000. To veil or not to veil? *Gender & Society* 14:395–417.

Rinaldo, Rachel. 2013. *Mobilizing piety.* Oxford, UK: Oxford University Press.

Robinson, Francis. 2008. Islamic reform and modernities in South Asia. *Modern Asian Studies* 42:259–81.

Saigol, Rubina. 2012. The multiple self: Interfaces between Pashtun nationalism and religious conflict on the frontier. *South Asian History and Culture* 3:197–214.

Scott, Joan Wallach. 2007. *The politics of the veil.* Princeton, NJ: Princeton University Press.

Shakry, Omnia. 1998. Schooled mothers and structured play. In *Remaking women,* edited by Lila Abu-Lughod. Princeton, NJ: Princeton University Press.

Trautner, Mary Nell. 2005. Doing gender, doing class. *Gender & Society* 19:771–88.

Utrata, Jennifer. 2011. Youth privilege. *Gender & Society* 25:616–41.

West, Candace, and Sarah Fenstermaker. 1995. Doing difference. *Gender & Society* 9:8–37.

West, Candace, and Don H. Zimmerman. 1987. Doing gender. *Gender & Society* 1:125–51.

West, Candace, and Don H. Zimmerman. 2009. Accounting for doing gender. *Gender & Society* 23:112–22.

37 • *Lynne Gerber*

GRIT, GUTS, AND VANILLA BEANS
Godly Masculinity in the Ex-Gay Movement

DISCUSSION QUESTIONS

1. How does Gerber challenge and complicate the common association of Christian conservatism with hegemonic masculinity?
2. Do you agree that godly masculinity can be described as "queerish"? What are the implications of this?
3. What benefits might men find in embracing/employing the concept of godly masculinity?

Gender theory often conflates conservative religious masculinity with hegemonic masculinity (Flores and Hondagneu-Sotelo 2013; Robinson and Spivey 2007). Because conservative religious groups often support gender hierarchy with men dominant, the forms of masculinity they advocate are confused with the masculinity that actually dominates a social space and legitimizes the existing hierarchy. Conservative religious masculinities are read as hegemonic and conservatives themselves as hegemonic masculinity's supporters and defenders.

. . . I argue that such a conflation is often inaccurate and can obfuscate the specificity of conservative masculinities and the challenges they can pose to hegemonic

Gerber, Lynne, 2015. "Grit, Guts, and Vanilla Beans: Godly Masculinity in the Ex-Gay Movement." *Gender and Society* 29(1): 26–50. Copyright © 2014, © SAGE Publications.

masculinity. I use the ex-gay movement as one example of conservative religious masculinity that problematizes this fusion. Ex-gay ministries are conservative in their gender ideology and largely endorse gender hierarchy. They seek to secure male privilege for their male members by legitimizing their masculinity in the evangelical world and in the world at large. Yet they find many reigning cultural ideals of masculinity problematic. Rather than using hegemonic masculinity as the standard by which their members' masculinity is measured, they criticize it for falling short of divine intention. Instead, ex-gay leaders and members aspire to godly masculinity, an idealized maleness drawn from evangelical discourse that appropriates some aspects of hegemonic masculinity while criticizing others. While most believe that godly masculinity should be hegemonic, they recognize that it is not.

. . .

HEGEMONIC MASCULINITY AND GODLY MASCULINITY

Hegemonic masculinity, as developed by Connell (2005, 77), is the form of masculinity that dominates a given social space and provides the ideological and cultural ground for legitimizing male power and privilege. It exists within a field of multiple masculinities and dominates them all, along with all femininities and all women, by soliciting their complicity, subordinating them, or marginalizing them altogether. It is a structural position as well as a specific form of masculinity. It is generally presumed to be white, heterosexual, and upper class, but its content varies based on cultural context and geographic level of analysis (Connell and Messerschmidt 2005).

Although hegemonic masculinity has proven to be a generative concept, questions regarding its content and significance abound. One tension is between the characteristics of men who actually hold hegemonic power, but who may or may not personally behave in hegemonic ways, versus men who are symbols or exemplars of hegemonic masculinity, but may not themselves be holders of hegemonic power (Connell 2005, 77–78; Elias and Beasley 2009). A related

tension is between the models of idealized ma ity struggling for hegemonic power and thos actually have it. Movements focused on malenes masculinity offer competing visions of what kind of masculinity is best for men and/or society in general. While some are critical of male domination, others maintain that masculinity should be hegemonic yet have a range of opinions about what kind of masculinity should reign in that position. These competing ideals often contrast with the masculinity that actually holds that position, which is often so secure in its power that it need not thematize masculinity or gender at all (Connell 2005, 212; Donaldson 1993).

The content of hegemonic masculinity is also a problem. Reading the literature, it seems that, like pornography, it is hard to define, but we know it when we see it. Homophobia, the fear of women, and vigorous heterosexuality seem to be central to its construct (Donaldson 1993; Kimmel 1994), as do competition, aggression, and a certain social isolation between men. Bird (1996) argues that it includes emotional detachment, competitiveness, and the sexual objectification of women. Demetriou (2001) argues that the dominating masculinity should be thought of as a hegemonic bloc that maintains its power, in part, by appropriating aspects of dominated masculinities as is useful. Connell (2005) argues for "transnational business masculinity" as the emergent form of hegemonic masculinity in the era of globalization, one that is marked by its relationship to the neoliberal economic order and its decreasing allegiance to other institutions or sources of identity. Yet some are concerned that this is too vague a concept to pierce the dynamics of how power is generated and maintained, especially without the assistance of economic analysis (Donaldson 1993), or that it is conceived in too monolithic a way to account for the complexity of globalization (Elias and Beasley 2009). In this article, I do not argue for any specific model of hegemonic masculinity; rather, I demonstrate how one type of conservative, evangelical masculinity can challenge traits that are frequently evoked as emblematic of hegemonic masculinity by gender scholars.

Evangelical Christianity, a largely conservative form of Protestantism founded in Western Europe, developed in the United States, and global in presence, has a complicated relationship to both masculinity and hegemonic masculinity. Evangelicalism has its origins in eighteenth- and nineteenth-century revival movements noted for their blurring of racial and gendered social divisions (Brekus 1998; Hatch 1989). Although dominant in American religious life, by the mid–nineteenth century, American Protestantism had become feminized in participation and representation (Douglas 1977), leading to a cultural devaluation of religious identity in general that continued as secularism gained strength in the early twentieth century. A variety of cultural projects from both the liberal and conservative sides of the Protestant spectrum attempted to remedy this feminization of Protestantism by reconceiving it in masculine terms, for example, the YMCA and the Men and Religion Forward movement (Bederman 1989; Putney 2003). These projects can be read as attempts to claim religious masculinity as legitimately masculine while also demonstrating its compatibility with hegemonic masculinity, efforts that would theoretically be unnecessary if evangelical masculinity actually held a hegemonic position.

In the latter half of the twentieth century, evangelicalism was fused in the popular mind with traditional gender hierarchy and political opposition to feminism and gay rights. But recent research has suggested that evangelical thought and practice regarding gender and masculinity is more complex. Gallagher (2003) characterizes contemporary evangelical approaches to gender in marriage as a blend of "symbolic traditionalism and pragmatic egalitarianism." In his study of the Promise Keepers, a more recent evangelical gender project focused on cultivating Christian masculinity and known for its large gatherings of evangelical men in sports stadiums, Bartkowski (2004) found at least four masculine ideals in circulation, ranging in their affinity with hegemonic masculine ones. Whereas some aspects of hegemonic masculinity are abundantly evident in contemporary evangelical masculinity projects, for example, an emphasis on sports, others are challenged, for example, the pursuit of wealth and status at the expense of family.

"Godly masculinity" has been used by some scholars to designate masculinity in contemporary evangelicalism (Bartkowski 2004; Gallagher and Wood 2005). I use the term here to denote idealized forms of masculinity that evangelicals use to articulate subculturally specific gender ideals, criticize hegemonic forms of masculinity, and vie for their own hegemonic positioning in the culture at large. Like hegemonic masculinity, godly masculinity is rooted in a binary and hierarchical gender system and advocated by people who support the dominance of masculinity. But it operates by a different set of cultural rules and expectations, generating traits that can differ from those of hegemonic masculinity. It can also generate unintended outcomes that resemble the gender queerness evangelicals ostensibly reject.

The ex-gay movement is one example of an evangelical cultural project grappling with gender and arguing for godly masculinity. Made up of community-based ministries, regional and national organizations, therapists, pastoral counselors, congregations, and evangelical academics, it aims at changing sexual orientation through a mixture of therapeutic and devotional techniques. . . .

. . . Ex-gay ministries do appeal to a normative, idealized model of masculinity to which their charges aspire. But that ideal, grounded in evangelical models of godly masculinity and the lived experience of homosexually oriented members, looks quite different from hegemonic masculine ideals in contemporary American culture. In this article, I identify and analyze three aspects of godly masculinity that differ from hegemonic masculinity: de-emphasizing heterosexual conquest, inclusivity, and homo-intimacy. In analyzing these features of godly masculinity, I demonstrate that they allow expressions of masculinity and relationships between men that run counter to expectations regarding hegemonic masculinity, the ex-gay project, and opposition to homosexuality.

METHODS

My data include participant observation, interviews, and content analysis of ex-gay materials. . . .

I also conducted 35 in-depth, semi-structured interviews with then-current members of ex-gay ministries (28) and former (ex-)gays (7). . . .

Terminology in the ex-gay movement is freighted. Many in the movement dislike the term "ex-gay" because they feel it reduces their identity to sexual struggles. There is no agreed upon substitute. Movement opponents argue that the term should not be used because it is misleading, suggesting that changing sexual orientation is possible. When talking about individuals, I use "(ex-)gay" to indicate the population I am speaking of, using the most recognizable term while acknowledging the porous boundaries between gay and (ex-)gay. I use "ex-gay" to speak of ministries, leaders, and the movement itself. I use the movement's term "ever-straights" to refer to people with life-long heterosexual attraction and identity.

GODLY MASCULINITY IN THE EX-GAY MOVEMENT

In the ex-gay context, ideals of godly masculinity are developed in conversation with reparative therapy, the major discursive framework ministries use to understand homosexuality. In an effort to develop a more scientific-seeming position on homosexuality, movement leaders partnered with old school psychiatrists to develop a strand of psychological theory abandoned by the mental health mainstream (Bayer 1987). This theory claims that homosexuality is a disorder resulting from stunted gender development. In this view, men become gay when a disruption in the relationship with the father, either through the father's absence or neglect or the mother's over involvement, leads to so-called defensive detachment, alienation from men marked by active dissociation (Moberly 1983; Nicolosi 2004b). This relational block causes proto-homosexual men to wrongly identify with women, depriving them of male community within which "proper" masculine identification develops. . . .

This etiology frames homosexuality as a clinical issue, laying the groundwork for a measure of compassion and possible cure. The remedy lies in intensive social exposure to men and masculinity so that

identification develops. Sexual desire, the theory goes, is aimed at that which seems different from the self; thus, when a homosexually inclined man stops identifying with women and finds a home among men, desire should "naturally" turn toward his gender other. "The goal is not change as such," Moberly claims, "but fulfillment . . . that would in turn imply change" (1983, 31). This is effected through practices that appear like overt mimesis of hegemonic masculinity: sports activities, information sessions with ever-straights, and other male-male bonding opportunities. But it also works through a critique of hegemonic masculinity and the articulation of new norms.

. . . Godly masculinity is appealed to as a higher standard from which to evaluate the masculinity that is hegemonic in American culture. For example, in his book on achieving masculinity, ex-gay leader Alan Medinger writes that he will teach readers "what a man is, what the meaning of masculine [is], and what it is that men do—not just in the cultural sense, but what men do that reflects their universal God-designed manhood" (2000, xiii). In a workshop on masculinity, Andrew Comiskey critiques aspects of hegemonic masculinity, contrasting them to God's vision for men. He advises,

> It doesn't work. Whether it's climbing the corporate ladder, or whether it's prowling for prostitutes, same difference. We just say God, it doesn't work, it doesn't make me more manly, doesn't make anyone love me more. If anything it just brings destruction in its own way. I'm sick of it. So Lord I'm ready for your way. (n.d.)

In this account, sexual prowess and economic achievement, arguably two cornerstones of hegemonic masculinity, are explicitly rejected in favor of a more godly way. . . .

Despite the vagueness of godly masculinity, my research indicates three ways that its ideals differ from those of hegemonic masculinity: de-emphasizing heterosexual conquest, inclusive masculinity, and homo-intimacy. These both shape and reflect the compromises ex-gay ministries and their evangelical partners have made with contemporary homosexuality.

DE-EMPHASIZING HETEROSEXUAL CONQUEST

One distinction between secular and evangelical culture is in attitudes toward extramarital sexual activity. Evangelicals, like many conservative religious people, are deeply suspect of such activity and highly value sexual restraint. The ideal of limiting sexual activity to marriage puts evangelical masculinity at odds with hegemonic formulations prioritizing heterosexual conquest, a tension seen in many evangelical masculinity projects. In an essay on the Promise Keepers, for example, Stoltenberg (1999) notes that participants were urged to confess their sexual mistreatment of women and to recognize the instability of sexual conquest as a foundation for masculinity. E. Glenn Wagner, a Promise Keepers leader, told Stoltenberg:

> What we're trying to tell them is that masculinity, manhood, is not defined by how many people you've slept with, either male or female. And men are finally saying "Oh thank God!" Sexual prowess should have nothing to do with one's personhood or self-esteem, and yet our culture has made it that way. (1999, 97)

This rejection of heterosexual display as a standard for legitimized masculinity reflects the historic suspicion with which Christianity has treated sexuality (Krondorfer 1996). . . .

Like the Promise Keepers and other evangelical gender projects (Bartkowski 2004, 83; Cochran 2005; Ingersoll 2003), Exodus ministries ground their work on the rejection of same-sex sexuality. In conservative biblical hermeneutics, same-sex sexual practice is seen not only as a violation of biblical command, but a transgression against God's ideal for sexuality as presented in Genesis (Comiskey 1989, 37–41). . . .

This rejection of homosexual sex is unsurprising. What is less expected is how de-emphasizing heterosexual conquest as a sign of masculinity reconfigures the terms of the ex-gay project, making its goals more attainable while simultaneously funding a critique of hegemonic masculinity. One of the most tangible effects of this de-emphasis is a reduction in pressure for (ex-)gay men to demonstrate healing

through sex with women. Ex-gay ministries often cite the evangelical prohibition on sexual activity outside marriage to discourage (ex-)gay men from proving heterosexuality this way. It also relieves them from doing so. Participants are warned against rushing into heterosexual relationships as symbols of success (Davies and Rentzel 1993, 145; Nicolosi 2004b, 202–3), and even marriage is treated with reservation (Dallas 2003, 178). Ex-gay manuals issue cautions on dating and sexuality and try to ease the pressure to perform heterosexually, including on the wedding night (Davies and Rentzel 1993, 156). Medinger goes as far as suggesting that healing is achieved when heterosexual sex becomes merely possible, not actually realized:

> We are healed when we are ready to do well in assuming all obligations and privileges generally assigned to a man. Central to these is the ability to be an adequate husband and father. Note that I am using the word *ability*. We do not have to actually be living these roles at the present time, and many men will never marry. . . . But it is when we are capable of fulfilling these roles in a satisfactory way that we have reached full manhood and . . . recovery from homosexuality. (2000, 25–26)

This rejection of heterosexual conquest shifts the stakes of the ex-gay project. Building on an ethic suspicious of all forms of sexuality, it lowers the bar of heterosexual expectation.

This aspect of godly masculinity also allows ex-gay discourse to redeem (ex-)gay *hetero*sexuality, in sometimes exalted ways (Gerber, forthcoming). Divine release from heterosexual expectation supports a critique of the notion that healing should be measured by heterosexual desire. This is most evident in the common statement that the goal of ministry involvement is not heterosexuality at all. "The opposite of homosexuality," writes ex-gay leader Mike Haley, "is not heterosexuality—it's *holiness*" (2004, 134). And holiness, rather than heterosexuality, becomes the standard to which the (ex-)gay man should hold himself. The pursuit of holiness explains, and justifies, the absence of heterosexual desire in the recovering homosexual. . . .

(Ex-)gay sexuality is also redeemed by (ex-)gay heterosexuality's likeness to godly sexual norms. As heterosexual partner, (ex-)gay lovers can seem closer to godly ideals because their marital relationships are not contaminated by lust. These marriages are said to be based on personal knowledge, not sheer desire, giving them a more solid foundation. Sexual desires emerge from friendship rather than immediate visual attraction (Davies and Rentzel 1993, 162). For example, Comiskey writes of his marital relationship:

> In spite of glimmers of physical attraction, the catalyst for our relationship in its early stages was not erotic. That surprised me, as my homosexual experiences were fueled by "high octane" lust that burned out to reveal an emotional immaturity incapable of sustaining a long-term relationship. Annette and I took the reverse path. My erotic feelings for her arose out of a trust and an established emotional and spiritual complementarity. . . . Physical attraction was birthed out of our relationship; it wasn't its overblown starting point, charged with illusion and seductive posturing. (1989, 30–31)

His marriage endures, in this account, precisely because it is not marked by the heterosexual desire that hegemonic masculinity requires. . . .

(Ex-)gay heterosexual marriages are also considered immune to the threat of other women. Heterosexual desire in an (ex-)gay context is seen as specific to the individuals involved; even the most healed (ex-)gay men tend to fall in love with only one woman. Again, this reality can be interpreted as a sign of healing rather than evidence of its lack. For example, Craig, a West Coast ex-gay leader, told me, "I desire my wife sexually and I'm very glad that I don't have a problem with lust for other women or men. That my focus of my sexual expression can be on her. And her for me. I think that's a much healthier expression." The range of sexual sins that plague heterosexual men is also something that (ex-)gay heterosexual marriages are said to be relieved of:

> A high percentage of heterosexual men in good, loving Christian marriages struggle with attractions to disconnected, impersonal sex: to pornography or maybe to the body of a neighbor woman whom he doesn't even know. This almost never happens to male overcomers with respect to women. This is the reason why I believe that we are actually in a better place than most men. We are closer to God's original intent for our sexuality. (Medinger 2000, 204–5)

In this account, (ex-)gay men become even godlier than ever-straight men because they are not vulnerable to the heterosexual temptations that rend even upstanding Christian marriages. By bracketing the very issue that brings them to ex-gay ministries—homosexual desire—ex-gay discourse redeems (ex-)gay sexuality by depicting its heterosexual expression as exemplary of godly ideals for human relationships.

Thus, (ex-)gay men are transformed from grievous sinner to godly lover when they pursue healing. The critique that godly masculinity poses to hegemonic masculinity's emphasis on heterosexual conquest is especially pragmatic in this context. . . .

INCLUSIVE MASCULINITY

The ex-gay approach to gender flows directly from its approach to sexuality. The insistence on heterosexuality generates an ideological commitment to a binary system of distinct, opposing, and hierarchically ranked genders. Prohibiting homosexuality enables ex-gay ministries to maintain these key aspects of evangelicalism's conservative gender ideology. . . .

One effect of this approach to homosexuality is the feminization of gay men. A core assumption of reparative therapy is that (ex-)gay men feel alienated from their gender and identify with women. There is no recognition of gay men whose gender identity is masculine; that configuration is deemed impossible. But, in part because of evangelicalism's grappling with feminism, in part because of its feminized history, and in part because of its theology, feminization is not necessarily a bad thing. Some evangelical theology sees God as both masculine and feminine, something that ex-gay ministries emphasize, in part to validate feminized characteristics in men. For example, Medinger writes,

The problem in the homosexual man is not that he has too much of the feminine, but too little of the masculine. Can there also be too much of the feminine? Could we have too great a capacity to nurture, to communicate, to understand, too great an ability to respond and help? No, any man who has a surplus of these things is blessed and is likely to be a blessing to others. (2000, 90–91)

Evangelical theology also puts male believers in a feminized position of submission in relation to Christ, a feature of Christian thought that evangelical feminists use in arguing for gender equality (Cochran 2005, 132). Because they are feminized, (ex)gay men are discursively associated with the dominated gender and are, to some degree, dominated by association. But under the godly gender regime, this association need not be a death knell to claims to legitimate, if not hegemonic, masculinity. Feminization is not necessarily a reason to exclude (ex-)gay men from godly masculinity; indeed, it can serve as a means for establishing their common ground with it. Ministries use that potential to their advantage, carving out a masculine ideal in which their members can more comfortably fit, and thus more honestly claim.

(Ex-)gay men are also masculinized in ex-gay discourse. For example, at an Exodus workshop "Breaking the Myth of Masculinity," the (ex-)gay and ever-straight coleaders assured participants that they had a legitimate place in the masculine world. "If you read our description on the website," they told the audience,

we put a question in there and said do I have what it takes to be masculine? . . . We said if you come to our class that we would answer that question. And the answer to that question is absolutely yes. Because you know what? You were all born male. You were all born men. And everything that you need to be fully masculine is within you. (Goeke and Mayo 2008)

If masculinity is endowed entirely by biology, then men are automatically masculine by virtue of being born male; every person born male has a claim on its attributes and privileges. And because the category of masculinity must include all males, it needs to be inclusive enough for all men to find their place.

As a result, traits, preferences, and dispositions, or what Bridges (2014) terms "sexual aesthetics," can be integrated into godly masculinity that were once the very definition of non-masculinity. Ex-gay ministries work to resignify them as legitimately masculine rather than suspiciously feminine. This labor was evident in the "Breaking the Myth of Masculinity" workshop. There, the leaders talked about their various likes and dislikes. Mike Goeke, the (ex-)gay man, told the audience:

I love clothes, shopping, I really do, I'm proud of it . . . I like decorating, I do. Stephanie [his wife] and I love doing that stuff together and I have every bit of a strong opinion on it. I love architecture and art, things that are beautiful. . . . I love to write. . . . I love long dinners, talking about life. I love great conversation, any time where you can sit and talk about stuff, life, relationships.

Jay Mayo, the ever-straight, responded,

I love UFC [Ultimate Fighting Championship]. It's human cockfighting on . . . Jeeps. I also love love stories. I love chick flicks. I cry at every one. . . . I love to write. I love genuine conversation. I hate BSing. I hate walking into the context of guys and talking about nothing important. It's crap, but I did it most of my life. I love to hug. I love affection. I love candles. And my favorite flavor is vanilla bean. (Goeke and Mayo 2008)

This exchange served, in part, to put the stamp of legitimate masculinity on practices that are frequently used to delegitimize claims to masculinity and especially hegemonic masculinity. Hegemonic masculinity's power is based on the domination of women and has frequently involved the stigmatization of feminized traits in males, especially those who are homosexually oriented (Hennen 2008). But within an inclusive godly masculinity, some feminized traits are reconfigured as valid expressions of masculinity that can even be endorsed by ever-straights with UFC-loving credentials. When successful, these traits become part of a repertoire of legitimate masculinity that even those ever-straights can put into practice without shame (Bridges 2014).

. . . Going to therapy, attending support groups, and committing substantial time and energy to healing are reinscribed as masculine acts. Leaders take pains to show that this pursuit is imbued with the active spirit deemed essential to godly masculinity. "Reparative therapy is initiatory in nature," Nicolosi writes. "It requires not just a passive musing over insights into the self, but an active initiation of new behaviors" (2004a, 213). John Hinson (2007), leader of a "Fear of Men and Masculinity" workshop, painted the pursuit of healing as exemplary of masculine courage and endurance:

> I had a feeling about healing. [It's] not going to happen if you're passive. You need to be proactive and do whatever you need to get the kind of healing you want. You need to go do it. I've had four therapists, once when I was in Phoenix, he was in Los Angeles, went every other month and talked on the phone every week. Went to men's weekend in New York, in Florida. Did whatever to get the healing I wanted and needed. [It] takes grit, guts to do this work.

There are few other venues where seeing four different therapists and going to multiple men's weekends evidence the "grit" and "guts" of masculinity. But within godly masculinity, association with feminized activities need not threaten one's claim to male legitimacy; it may even enhance it.

. . .

HOMO-INTIMACY

A third distinction between godly masculine ideals and culturally hegemonic ones involves relations between men. . . .

According to reparative therapy, homosexual men become real men when they develop intimate relationships with other men, through mentoring relationships with (ex-)gay men further along in their healing or with ever-straights. These relationships are usually cultivated in church settings, men's groups, or the ministry itself. According to advocates of these relationships—and in contrast to hegemonic

assumptions about masculinity—men are happy to support (ex-)gays in their search for masculinity through positive, affirming, supportive processes, not through social trials that consolidate masculine identity by repudiating the abject "fag" (Pascoe 2007). Nicolosi (2005), for example, claims:

> [A] heterosexual man will work with a man who is trying to overcome his homosexuality and the reason why is because men cannot procreate the way women procreate, we cannot make babies. But men, we are wired to make boys into men. That's natural for us. And when we see a man come along who's struggling to find his masculinity, the manhood in you is prompted to mentor this guy and the fact that he's dealing with homosexuality is irrelevant.

. . .

Once established, these male-male relationships involve a level of emotional disclosure, intimacy, and closeness that also defy standards for hegemonic male-male relations. According to reparative therapy, men desire homosexual sex as a substitute for the deeper desire for identification and closeness with men. Sex, in this account, will never fill this purpose; only nonsexual male-male relationships can. Nicolosi writes, "The only way a man can absorb masculinity into his identity is through the challenge of nonsexual male friendships characterized by mutuality, intimacy, affirmation, and fellowship" (2004a, 100). These are notably not constitutive elements of hegemonic masculinity. In these relationships, men share the details of their lives, express their hopes and fears, and turn to other men for support, caring, and validation. Mark, for example, told me that his ministry participation allowed him to receive positive feedback from men for the first time. While he had received male praise before, in this group he was "able to share on a level that I had never been able to share." Because he knew these men so well, their positive feedback penetrated more deeply. "I was never really able to take in that [earlier] affirmation because they didn't know me. So once I was open and people [in the ministry] kept saying the same thing, then it began to sink in and mean something to help change me." Interpersonal knowledge, personal disclosure, and emotional receptivity are more likely to be derided as feminine than lauded as masculine under the hegemonic regime of masculinity; in the ex-gay context they become fundamental to the masculinization process itself (Medinger 2000, 111).

Physical, albeit nonsexual, intimacy also has a place in healing homosexuality. Ex-gay writer Chad Thompson writes about the touch deprivation he experienced, its role in developing his homosexuality, and healing it in the course of relationships with other Christian men (Thompson 2004). Alan Chambers (2005) told an audience at the Love Won Out conference about his experience of healing during a five-hour-long hug with men in his church:

> I had a struggle with my relationship with my dad growing up, and . . . in homosexual relationships I always wanted someone who would be that young, affirming, good-looking, wonderful father. Not for the purposes of sex, but I was craving what God intended for me to have, that intimacy and that connection. And I remember one night dealing, it was a couple of years into the process, dealing with this whole issue, praying through these issues and when it was over that night, after I had been hugged for about five hours by this man who was praying for me and another man from the church, I felt like God supernaturally healed my lifelong desire for that type of inappropriate relationship.

In the context of prayer and healing, touch, bodily contact, and the physical expression of closeness with other men become legitimate means of pursuing change rather than suspect expressions of homosexual desire. While this form of homosociality may well be pursued in order to consolidate the dominance of men over women (Sedgwick 1985), it looks strikingly different from the hegemonic form of masculinity that regards physical male-male closeness with suspicion.

. . .

. . . Indeed, under the guise of godly masculinity, (ex-)gays are allowed a wide range of emotional intimacies with people of the same gender that may be indistinguishable from, or indeed may be the heart of, homosexual desire.

CONCLUSION

Ethnographer Tanya Erzen has noted the queer quality of (ex-)gay men's sexual conversions (2006, 14). I would extend that observation to the realm of gender, suggesting that the inclusivity of godly masculinity generates a queerish masculinity, one that effects the kinds of gender blurring that queerness aspires to, without subscribing to the political priorities or critiques that fund more deliberately queer gender experimentation (Gerber 2008; Gerber, 2015). In its effort to include those who have been excluded on grounds of gender identity or performance, it runs the risk of including elements that undermine the very meaning of the category. An emphasis on male brokenness, the expression of feeling, and the legitimacy of a wide range of masculine expression would significantly change the terms of hegemonic masculinity and may even have the unintended potential of undermining it. Indeed, it may well have been a factor in Exodus's recent disavowal of sexual reorientation as a legitimate goal of Christian ministry and its dissolution as an organization. If highly feminized traits have a legitimate masculine home, for example, what does masculinity actually mean?

. . .

It also provides potential benefits for the evangelical world at large. Godly standards of masculinity, and the (ex-)gay men who remake those standards, can reduce "the costs of masculinity" (Messner 1997, 8). By broadening the repertoire of legitimate masculine expression and critiquing certain aspects of hegemonic masculinity, ex-gay gender experiments may increase the livable space for all evangelical men, regardless of sexual desire. At the same time, it gives the evangelical community the opportunity to maintain subcultural distinction through principled opposition to homosexual genital acts and political opposition to gay social movements (Smith 1998). They may also serve as ideological legitimization for the failure of conservative Christian men to live up to other standards of hegemonic masculinity.

These possibilities are just that: possibilities. . . . While ex-gay ministries have been successful in developing partnerships with powerful evangelical institutions, it is unclear whether that institutional legitimacy translates into lived legitimacy on the popular level or into theological innovation based on changing gender ideals. Taking (ex-)gay femininities into account, as well as female masculinities in the (ex-)gay context, would further develop our understanding of how godly masculinity works in relationship to hegemonic masculinity. And the specificities of this study in terms of race and nation raise problems for further research regarding the multiple masculinities at play in a globalized evangelicalism and how race and nation intersect with gender and religion and generate hegemony in these contexts. These important questions merit further research.

But looking at the discursive strategies within the ex-gay movement provides important reminders to scholars researching religion, sexuality, and gender. The most important, in my view, is the caution not to conflate conservative religious masculinity projects with hegemonic ones. Advocates for the hegemonic positioning of masculinity do not necessarily support the masculinity that is, in fact, hegemonic in a given social space, and there is no reason to think that they should. Godly masculinity is a contender in a field of multiple masculinities vying for hegemonic power. The fact that its advocates believe that gender relations should be hierarchical and that masculinity should be hegemonic does not keep them from advocating for a kind of masculinity that is more reflective of, and advantageous for, their particular position. Conflating the complex gender projects of the ex-gay movement, and evangelical Christianity more generally, with hegemonic masculinity makes it difficult to see the nuanced fault lines on which this project might stand or fall. . . .

AUTHOR'S NOTE

My deep thanks to Kent Brintnall, Sarah Quinn, Susan Stinson, Orit Avishai, Dawne Moon, and Elise Paradis for conversation, comments, and advice regarding this paper. Thanks, too, to the editors and reviewers at *Gender & Society*, for such engaged, useful feedback.

REFERENCES

Bartkowski, John P. 2004. *Promise Keepers: Servants, soldiers and godly men.* New Brunswick, NJ: Rutgers University Press.

Bayer, Ronald. 1987. *Homosexuality and American psychiatry: The politics of diagnosis.* Princeton, NJ: Princeton University Press.

Bederman, Gail. 1989. "The women have had charge of the church work long enough": The Men and Religion Forward movement of 1911–1912 and the masculinization of middle-class Protestantism. *American Quarterly* 41:432–65.

Bird, Sharon R. 1996. Welcome to the men's club: Homosociality and the maintenance of hegemonic masculinity. *Gender & Society* 10:120–32.

Brekus, Catherine A. 1998. *Strangers and pilgrims: Female preaching in America. 1740–1845.* Chapel Hill: University of North Carolina Press.

Bridges, Tristan. 2014. A very "gay" straight: Hybrid masculinities, sexual aesthetics, and the changing relationship between masculinity and homophobia. *Gender & Society* 28:58–82.

Chambers, Alan. 2005. Reaching the homosexual I: Teaching. Workshop given at Love Won Out, Seattle, Washington, June 25.

Cochran, Pamela D. H. 2005. *Evangelical feminism: A history.* New York: New York University Press.

Comiskey, Andrew. 1989. *Pursuing sexual wholeness: How Jesus heals the homosexual.* Lake Mary, FL: Charisma House.

Comiskey, Andrew. n.d. Masculinity [CD]. Grandview, MO: Desert Stream Ministries.

Connell, Raewyn. 2005. *Masculinities,* 2nd edition. Berkeley: University of California Press.

Connell, Raewyn, and James W. Messerschmidt. 2005. Hegemonic masculinity: Rethinking the concept. *Gender & Society* 19:829–59.

Dallas, Joe. 2003. *Desires in conflict: Hope for men who struggle with same sex identity,* revised edition. Eugene, OR: Harvest House.

Davies, Bob, and Lori Rentzel. 1993. *Coming out of homosexuality: New freedom for men and women.* Downers Grove, IL: InterVarsity Press.

Demetriou, Demetrakis Z. 2001. Connell's concept of hegemonic masculinity: A critique. *Theory and Society* 30:337–61.

Donaldson, Mike. 1993. What is hegemonic masculinity? *Theory and Society* 22:643–57.

Donovan, Brian. 1998. Political consequences of private authority: Promise Keepers and the transformation of hegemonic masculinity. *Theory and Society* 27:817–43.

Douglas, Ann. 1977. *The feminization of American culture.* New York: Knopf.

Elias, Juanita, and Christine Beasley. 2009. Hegemonic masculinity and globalization: "Transnational business masculinities" and beyond. *Globalizations* 6:281–96.

Erzen, Tanya. 2006. *Straight to Jesus: Sexual and Christian conversions in the ex-gay movement.* Berkeley: University of California Press.

Flores, Edward Orozco, and Pierrette Hondagneu-Sotelo. 2013. Chicano gang members in recovery: The public talk of negotiating Chicano masculinities. *Social Problems* 60:476–90.

Gallagher, Sally K. 2003. *Evangelical identity and gendered family life.* New Brunswick, NJ: Rutgers University Press.

Gallagher, Sally K., and Sabrina L. Wood. 2005. Godly manhood going wild? Transformations in conservative Protestant masculinity. *Sociology of Religion* 66:135–60.

Gerber, Lynne. 2008. The opposite of gay: Nature, creation, and queerish ex-gay experiments. *Nova Religio* 11:8–30.

Gerber, Lynne. 2011. *Seeking the straight and narrow: Weight loss and sexual reorientation in evangelical America.* Chicago: University of Chicago Press.

Gerber, Lynne. 2015. "Queerish" celibacy: Reorienting marriage in the ex-gay movement. In *Queer Christianities,* edited by Mark Larrimore, Michael Pettinger, and Kathleen Talvacchia. New York: New York University Press.

Goeke, Mike, and Jay Mayo. 2008. Breaking the myth of masculinity. Workshop presented at Exodus International Conference.

Gritz, Jennie Rothenberg. 2012. Sexual healing: Evangelicals update their message to gays. *The Atlantic,* June 20, 2012, http://www.theatlantic.com/national/archive/2012/06/sexual-healing-evangelicals-update-their-message-to-gays/258713.

Haley, Mike. 2004. *101 frequently asked questions about homosexuality.* Eugene, OR: Harvest House Publishers.

Hatch, Nathan O. 1989. *The democratization of American Christianity.* New Haven, CT: Yale University Press.

Heath, Melanie. 2003. Soft-boiled patriarchy: Renegotiating gender and racial ideologies in the Promise Keepers. *Gender & Society* 17:423–44.

Hennen, Peter. 2008. *Faeries, bears and leathermen: Men in community queering the masculine.* Chicago: University of Chicago Press.

Herman, Didi. 1997. *The antigay agenda: Orthodox vision and the Christian right.* Chicago: University of Chicago Press.

Hinson, John. 2007. Fear of men and masculinity. Workshop presented at Exodus International Conference.

Ingersoll, Julie. 2003. *Evangelical Christian women: War stories in the gender battles.* New York: New York University Press.

Kimmel, Michael S. 1994. Masculinity as homophobia: Fear, shame and silence in the construction of gender identity. In *Theorizing masculinities,* edited by Harry Brod and Michael Kaufman. Thousand Oaks, CA: Sage.

Krondorfer, Bjorn. 1996. Introduction. In *Men's bodies, men's gods: Male identities in a (post)-Christian culture,* edited by Bjorn Krondorfer. New York: New York University Press.

Medinger, Alan. 2000. *Growth into manhood: Resuming the journey.* New York: Shaw Press/Random House.

Messner, Michael. 1997. *Politics of masculinities: Men in movements.* Lanham, MD: AltaMira Press.

Moberly, Elizabeth. 1983. *Homosexuality: A new Christian ethic.* Cambridge, UK: James Clarke Ltd.

Nicolosi, Joseph. 2004a. *Healing homosexuality: Case stories of reparative therapy.* Lanham, MD: Rowman & Littlefield.

Nicolosi, Joseph. 2004b. *Reparative therapy of the male homosexual: A new clinical approach.* Lanham, MD: Rowman & Littlefield.

Nicolosi, Joseph. 2005. The condition of male homosexuality. Lecture given at Love Won Out, Seattle, Washington, June 25.

Pascoe, C. J. 2007. *Dude, you're a fag: Masculinity and sexuality in high school.* Berkeley: University of California Press.

Putney, Clifford. 2003. *Muscular Christianity: Manhood and Sports in Protestant America, 1880–1920.* Cambridge, MA: Harvard University Press.

Robinson, Christine M., and Sue E. Spivey. 2007. The politics of masculinity and the ex-gay movement. *Gender & Society* 21:650–75.

Rogers, Sy. 2005, *One of the boys remix: The Sy Rogers story* [DVD]. Fort Lauderdale, FL: Worthy Creations.

Sedgwick, Eve K. 1985. *Between men: English literature and male homosocial desire.* New York: Columbia University Press.

Smith, Christian. 1998. *Evangelicalism: Embattled and thriving.* Chicago: University of Chicago Press.

Stein, Arlene. 2005. Make room for daddy: Anxious masculinity and emergent homophobias in neopatriarchal politics. *Gender & Society* 19:601–20.

Stoltenberg, John. 1999. Christianity, feminism and the manhood crisis. In *Standing on the promises: The Promise Keepers and the revival of manhood,* edited by Dane S. Claussen. Cleveland: Pilgrim Press.

Thompson, Chad. 2004. *Loving homosexuals as Jesus would: A fresh Christian approach.* Grand Rapids: Brazos Press.

38 • *Jay Michaelson*

TEN REASONS WHY GAY RIGHTS IS A RELIGIOUS ISSUE

DISCUSSION QUESTIONS

1. What arguments does the author make to explain why gay rights is a religious issue? Are there other reasons you can identify?
2. How do your own views about religion or spirituality shape your feelings (perspectives) about Michaelson's arguments?
3. How does Michaelson, like Khurshid, complicate binary oppositions often employed in discussions of religion?

Civil rights movements that appeal to religion succeed. . . . As both pollsters and election results continually remind us, mainstream Americans do not respond to arguments about constitutional rights and equality: they respond to moral arguments, shared values, and religion—unsurprisingly, since over 90 percent of Americans profess a belief in God.

. . .

. . . Unless we activists engage with religion in a serious and convincing way, we will not prevail in our struggle. . . .

Nor will we speak for the millions of LGBT Americans who are religious themselves. For us, "God versus Gay" is bad spirituality, as well as bad political tactics. Doubtless, many gay activists have justifiably relegated religion to the same mental basement as other repressive ideas. But the basement is just another closet. By perpetuating "God versus Gay," secular gay rights activists perpetuate this psychological oppression of religious gays, this spiritual schizophrenia that continues to harm and distort.

Fortunately, gay rights is a religious issue. Religious people should not be for gay rights despite their religions' teachings; they should be for gay rights because of them. For too long, we have allowed far-rightist forces to distort our religious teachings. Politically and spiritually, this has been disastrous. And contrary to the cries of the fearful, while there are indeed some religious arguments against equality for LGBT people, there are more of them in favor of it. Here are ten of them.

1. IT IS NOT GOOD TO BE ALONE

Opponents of same-sex marriage remind us that in Genesis, "It's Adam and Eve, not Adam and Steve." But Adam and Eve is the solution to a problem, the existential crisis of aloneness. In fact, after the long series of good things God sees during the creation process, Adam's aloneness is the first thing that is not good (Gen. 2:18). It is the first natural condition which, the Bible tells us, is not to be left as is. Love, togetherness, mutual support—these are the essential qualities of the partnership God creates.

Religious and spiritual people, then, are faced with a fundamental religious imperative to heal loneliness where we find it and to insist on the importance of human relationship in so doing. . . . For millions of people around the world, to remedy this first, fundamental flaw of the human condition requires a same-sex relationship.

. . .

2. GOD LOVES US AND DOES NOT WANT US TO HARM OURSELVES

The suicide rate among gay teenagers is estimated to be six times that of straight ones. . . . What more do we need to know? Gay people exist, and some of them kill themselves because of the shame they feel.

Suicide is not, of course, the only form of harm gay people inflict upon themselves. The "closet" is another. As someone who lived in the closet for over a decade of my adult life, I can attest from personal experience that it is less a closet than a tomb. Constructed of lies, fear, and shame, it beats the soul down and alienates it not only from sexual expression but from all other forms of love as well, including authentic love of God. . . .

Of course, Christianity, Judaism, and other religions do ask us to curb our behavior, even behaviors we may really enjoy, such as wanton greed and selfishness (e.g., the kind evinced by some of our society's most famous celebrities). Sexuality, too is regulated by these religions traditions, in very different ways: Some permit all forms of sexual behavior within marriage; others do not. Some see celibacy as an ideal; others do not. But nowhere do we find individuals required to forego all sexual intimacy, sexual expression, or romantic love. God does not ask us to be Isaac on the *akedah* or Christ on the cross; we are asked to curb our impulses, but not to destroy ourselves. Were homosexuality merely a form of licentiousness

(as some suggest), then one could imagine it being prohibited by religious tradition. But homosexuality is not lust, it is a quality of the soul and a pathway to the most sacred forms of love.

Can a homosexual relationship be degraded? Yes. Can it be holy? Yes. Banning homosexuality because of its potential for "abuse" would be like banning heterosexuality because of prostitution. Religious people can and should debate how best the power of sexuality is to be understood according to their religious traditions, but to demand that an entire class of people completely repress, suppress, and mutilate their sexual drives is antithetical to the fundamental religious ideal that God loves us. A loving God could not want the closet.

3. COMPASSION IS HOLY

Spiritual progressives generally believe that, in the words of Richard Rorty, "cruelty is the worst thing we can do," and that, conversely, to alleviate suffering is a religious mandate. Thus, even apart from the theistic principle that God loves us and does not want us to crush our basic personalities, there is the ethical principal that cruelty is wrong and compassion is holy.

In this regard, gay rights—being compassionate rather than cruel to LGBT people—is simply a further widening of the sphere of ethical consideration that has extended concern to people from other religious/ethnic groups, people from other "racial" backgrounds, women, people with disabilities, and others. Once, the feelings and experiences of these "others" were deemed irrelevant to religious concern. Today, just as we have reexamined our religious ideas in the light of the experiences of these groups, so too is a reexamination of traditional religious approaches to homosexuality warranted by the experiences of gay and lesbian people.

. . .

4. JUSTICE IS HOLY

"Justice, justice, shalt thou pursue" (Deut. 16:20) has long been a watchword of spiritual progressives. Justice is holy; equality is holy; fairness is holy. These qualities, ethical monotheism tells us, matter to God. Discrimination is wrong. Fairness is right. There has been a tendency in contemporary political discourse to let the Right have God on their side, since we on the Left have liberalism, justice, and anti-discrimination on ours. This is outrageous. If the Bible is any guide at all, God is on the "side" of justice and fairness. It follows that denying same-sex couples the same benefits as opposite-sex couples is an offense to God.

. . .

5. BECAUSE THE HEBREW BIBLE DOESN'T SAY WHAT THE RIGHT SAYS IT DOES

Gay rights is also a religious issue because anti-gay forces are misrepresenting what the Hebrew Bible and the New Testament say, and thus distorting the word of God. . . . It is what Jews call a *chillul hashem,* a profanation of the Name, to twist scripture beyond its meaning to justify cruelty and fear. Thus to the extent that is taking place in the cases of Leviticus and Romans, it is of concern to all religious people even apart from the experiences of gays.

The most important aspect of these "problem texts" is that they are ambiguous. For this reason, when we turn to them, we do so bearing in mind the insights of the first four arguments. How we read these ambiguous verses depends on the fundamental values we bring to bear on interpreting them. Thus my claim is not (and need not be) that these readings are the only ones possible—just that they are the only ones consonant with our fundamental religious values.

This is not the place for a detailed reading of Leviticus 18:22, but briefly, we can note three aspects of it. First, the verse only discusses men. At the very least, 50 percent of gay people (i.e., lesbians) are completely untouched by it. To suggest that Leviticus prohibits lesbianism has no basis either in traditional Jewish law or in the plain meaning of the verse. Second, the verse only discusses, at most, anal sex. Again, both the plain meaning of the verse and the Jewish interpretive tradition (e.g., Rashi) make clear that "the lyings of woman" means, in the case of two men, penetrative

anal sex. Of course, there is a longstanding Jewish tradition to "build a fence around the Torah" and prohibit acts that, while themselves permissible, might lead to prohibited conduct. However, let's not pretend that's in the Torah; the verse itself prohibits, at most, anal sex. Third, whatever the prohibition is, it is of the same class—*toevah*—as remarriage (Deut. 24:4) and Egyptians eating with shepherds (Gen. 46:34). The only thing that is "abomination" about homosexuality is the word "abomination" itself, a total mistranslation that has no basis in Hebraic text.

6. BECAUSE THE NEW TESTAMENT DOESN'T SAY WHAT THE RIGHT SAYS IT DOES

New Testament texts are also quite different from how anti-gay forces present them. Homosexuality is scarcely mentioned in the New Testament (surprisingly, given its cultural context) and never by Jesus. As many scholars have observed, the condemnation in Romans 1:26-27 has almost nothing to do with contemporary understandings of homosexuality. Those verses read: "For this reason God gave them up to dishonourable passions. Their women exchanged natural relations for unnatural, and the men likewise gave up natural relations with women and were consumed with passion for one another, men committing shameless acts with men and receiving in their own persons the due penalty for their error." First, "their women exchanged natural relations for unnatural" was understood by Augustine, Clement of Alexandria, and all other early Church Fathers as referring to anal sex, not lesbianism. Second, "men committing unseemly acts with men" is about pederasty rather than homosexuality—the latter Greek term is *arsen,* which refers to young men, not *aner,* which refers to adults. Third, the clause "for this reason" explains that these sexual acts are the consequences, not the causes, of wrongdoing, which Romans 1:19-25 makes clear, is the veneration of images and idols. Fourth, the verses after 27 make clear that the real problem is not "homosexuality" (a nineteenth-century concept) but passing judgment when one is guilty oneself.

These introductory points are, of course, just that. But the central point is that these texts can be read as anti-gay only by extrapolating them from their historical and textual contexts, distorting the meanings of their plain words, and, of course, blowing them completely out of proportion to the other 23,212 verses in the Hebrew Bible and 7,957 verses in the New Testament. None of the contemporary arguments against homosexuality—"untrammeled homosexuality can take over and destroy a social system," according to the Family Research Council's Paul Cameron; homosexuality "is a sickness, and it needs to be treated" according to Pat Robertson; or it will lead to "a breakdown in social organizations," according to FRC's Robert Knight—are present in these texts.

If we value the Bible, we should not let bigots hijack and distort it to justify their fears to themselves and others (So too with the "sin of Sodom," which both Jewish and Christian sources long regarded as greed or inhospitality.). Whatever these problematic texts mean, they do not mean what the bigots say, and religious people should defend our sacred texts.

7. EVOLUTION OF RELIGIOUS DOCTRINE IS HEALTHY

Naturally, a pro-gay reading of scripture is not the only possible one: one may choose to read Leviticus broadly, Romans expansively, and 1 Corinthians selectively. Even the search for the "plain meaning" of the texts is an act of interpretation. Thus the question is not whether to interpret Scripture but *how* to do so. And when one reflects on two thousand years of biblical interpretation, it is clear that our readings of the Bible have indeed evolved as the human race has evolved. We have read slavery out of the Old and New Testaments. We have changed how we understand Eve being a "help-meet" to Adam. Our rabbis and church fathers have even read troubling texts virtually out of existence.

This is all part of healthy religious development. Do we really want as religionists, a hidebound faith that never changes? Is there a case in which fundamentalism and ultra-conservativism has led a religion to thrive? Movements of progression and regression, to be sure—but overall, religion evolves and that is why it remains vibrant. The plasticity of religious thought is as responsible for its durability as its commitment to core values is. For example, most of us no longer believe the world is 6,000 years old. If being religious depended upon such a view, we would be forced to abandon religion. Yet it does not. . . . For religion to endure, it needs both strong roots and expansive branches. Gay rights is the latest in a long line of moral questions to challenge religion and cause it to grow. This is a good thing.

8. CURBING BRUTISHNESS IS THE POINT

Building on point number seven, there is a specific kind of moral growth that gay rights brings about: a transcendence of traditional gender categories and primitive ideas about who men and women are. That these ideas are constructions of culture may be seen simply by traveling to places where men hold hands or women throw spears. But they are also particular kinds or constructions, which tend to reinforce a reductive view of brutish, mean men and delicate, wispy women dependent upon them.

Judaism and Christianity, in particular, have never held such primitive notions of gender in high regard. Goliath is not a Jewish hero; the lithe King David is. "Not by might, nor by power, but by my spirit, says the Lord." Christian saints submit to the will of God, submit even to the sword, just as Christ himself gave his life on the cross. . . .

Acceptance of sexual diversity is, particularly for many heterosexually identified men, not unlike feminism in this regard: it is one more way to query and perhaps curb culturally or instinctually prescribed notions of masculinity, in a morally significant way. In the Bible, God does not endorse brutishness, but rather our aspiration to be better, kinder, and more like angels than animals. The embrace of sexual diversity is a valuable step forward along this path.

9. BECAUSE THE SEPARATION OF CHURCH AND STATE HELPS THE CHURCH

One reason liberals avoid making religious arguments in the public sphere is their deeply held belief in the separation of church and state. Generally, this is framed in terms of the neutrality or secularism of the public square and in terms of protecting our government and institutions from incursions by religion.

Yet one of the most memorable metaphors for this system, "a wall of separation" between church and state, was coined by Roger Williams in 1644 not to protect the pristine sphere of politics from pollution by religion, but to protect pure religion from corruption by politics. Williams called for "a hedge or wall of separation between the garden of the church and the wilderness of the world." Indeed, for spiritual progressives, Williams's warning is all the more powerful today. Many of us have sat in pews and watched our spiritual leaders espouse deeply troubling political views. We have watched how money and power have distorted churches, synagogues, and mosques. And we have seen how religion is often employed not as a check on human selfishness but as an aggrandizement to it.

Gay rights is a religious issue because its use as a political wedge issue has distorted church teaching and politicized religion. . . .

10. SEXUAL DIVERSITY IS A BEAUTIFUL PART OF GOD'S CREATION

I learned in primary school that "God don't make no mistakes." Reflecting on the existence of homosexuality in over 1,500 animal species and in every human culture around the world then, one pauses to wonder and speculate as to the particular gifts of gayness. . . . Intellectually, we have every reason to expect that the liberation of sexual minorities will add as much to our cultural life as did the liberation of women—more perspectives, more questions, more complications, and thus more life.

. . .

These are but ten reasons—there are many more—why full equality for sexual minorities should be seen not as some accommodation of religion to a secular norm, but as a religious value itself. They are intended to be public reasons, that is, reasons that can be explored and discussed objectively regardless of our personal experience. But if there is an eleventh reason I would add, it would be of necessity a "private" one that every religious sinew in my body leans in the direction of liberation, love, and holiness. I have known life as a closeted gay man, and so I have the experience that many of my interlocutors do not. They presume, on television and online, to know me better than I do. They tell me that what I know of my soul is incorrect, that really I am making a wrong choice and turning astray.

But I, like other gay religious people, know that they have it exactly backwards. When my soul turns toward God, it turns toward more love, enduring bonds, and the fulfillment of human potential—and those are precisely the qualities engendered by loving and holy sexual expression, homo, bi, or hetero. . . .

I cannot extrapolate public norms from these subjective experiences. But insofar as the discerning mind and open heart can ever be relied upon, I know in which direction sanctity lies. Of love, there is no doubt.

39 • *Rosalind Chou, Kristen Lee, and Simon Ho*

LOVE IS (COLOR)BLIND: ASIAN AMERICANS AND WHITE INSTITUTIONAL SPACE AT THE ELITE UNIVERSITY

DISCUSSION QUESTIONS

1. How do gendered and sexual stereotypes of Asian men and women serve to reify White hegemonic masculinity?
2. What methods have Asian students at historically white colleges and universities employed to either cope with or challenge sexualized racism?
3. How do Chou, Lee, and Ho demonstrate, as other authors have in this section, the importance of studying gender and sexuality intersectionally?

In February 2013, more than 250 students gathered at Duke University to protest against an Asian-theme fraternity party that featured invitations with Team America Kim Jeong Il speaking in broken English and party-goers dressed as geishas and sumo wrestlers. The Kappa Sigma fraternity party, which seemed to have crossed the line between racial humor and raw insensitivity, received backlash from the university and gained national media attention. An outpouring of external support from Asian American organizations at other universities and celebrities bolstered the efforts of student activists. And yet, on campus the response was more varied. Within Duke's Asian American community, responses ranged from outrage to apathy. One student, Johnny Wei, wrote in the student newspaper:

As an Asian-American, I was naturally disappointed in Kappa Sigma's insensitive party theme. I was equally disappointed, however, in how Asian student organizations on campus chose to respond to this crisis. . . . As Duke's largest minority group, we Asians had the opportunity to take the high road and truly break new ground in eliminating these cultural insensitivities, a problem that seems to plague Duke perennially. (Wei 2013)

The Kappa Sigma party is a prime example of the racialized social landscape that undergraduates traverse, and the varied reactions that followed demonstrate the complexity of racial ideology. Asian Americans champion education as a pathway to success that transcends race (Chou and Feagin 2008). Asian Americans

Chou, Rosalind et al. "Love Is (Color)Blind: Asian Americans and White Institutional Space at the Elite University." *Sociology of Race and Ethnicity*, Vol. 1, No. 2 (2015): 302–316. Copyright © 2015, © SAGE Publications.

occupy a unique position within university structure; while they make up only 5% of the total U.S. population, they represent up to 30% of the student population in some elite universities (Clark 2009). Even as Asian Americans become a greater proportion of the university population, little effort has been given to understanding their university experiences. In the rare instance when they are included in racial discourse on higher education, "they have been reduced to a single, stubborn persistent narrative—as a 'model minority'" (Teranishi 2010:11). A few notable articles describe Asian American experiences with physical violence and verbal harassment in high school and college (Rosenbloom and Way 2004). Fewer studies still have examined the social context and romantic relationships of Asian Americans at universities.

Drawing on rich qualitative data, we place Asian American undergraduates in the driver's seat, exploring the language they use to cope, survive, and negotiate their social experience at a predominately white institution. The discourse Asian Americans use to make meaning of their racialized and sexualized relationships reveals the complicated positionality of Asian Americans as a "racial middle." On one hand, they are seen as "forever foreigners"; on the other hand, being stereotyped as a "model minority" or "honorary white" may encourage the use of color-blind racist discourse to explain their positions on campus and legitimize racist hierarchy (Tuan 1999). Stereotyping as either "forever foreign" or "model minorities" differentiates Asian Americans from white college students. To understand the meaning behind these practices, we interrogate the intersectionality of race, gender, and sexuality and the particular racialization of this group. We argue that elite campus culture, as white institutionalized space, leads Asian Americans socialized in this environment to both adopt and resist racialized messages.

THEORETICAL FRAMEWORK

WHITE INSTITUTIONAL SPACE, WHITE HABITUS

Historically white colleges and universities (HWCUs) have been used for centuries as institutions to enrich

students through their curriculum, providing them with the necessary knowledge and skills to be "productive members of society." It is also a place where students are socialized in each distinct campus climate. These institutions, formerly exclusively white, and many still overwhelmingly so, normalize a certain kind of personhood (Moore 2008). While these institutions were legally racially segregated, they became what Wendy Moore referred to as "white institutionalized spaces," where there is a process of learning that "whiteness is right." Eduardo Bonilla-Silva, Carla Goar, and David Embrick (2007) asserted that whiteness is normalized by "white habitus," which they defined as a "racialized uninterrupted socialization process that conditions and creates whites' racial tastes, perceptions, feelings, and emotions and their views on racial matters" (Bonilla-Silva 2003:104). . . . White power and privilege no longer rule through outright violence and intimidation. Instead, social practices enabled by institutional structure maintain racial hierarchy. . . . We argue that an elite campus can have the same effect on people of color by making them targets of racial stereotyping by their white peers as demonstrated through their use of color-blind discourse and the ways they describe their romantic tastes and interests.

Feagin's (2010) definition of "white racial framing" accounts for people of color who adopt these white normalized ideologies. Chou and Feagin (2008, 2014) contended that Asian Americans, at times, also see the world through a white racial frame and thus internalize racist messaging and negative stereotyping of other people of color. Gender and sexuality scholarship uses terms like "hegemonic masculinity" to discuss the powerful ideology of domination and how ideas become normalized (Connell and Messerschmidt 2005). Hegemonic masculinity is racialized, as men of color are "marginalized masculinities" and are stereotyped as less than ideal compared with white men (Connell and Messerschmidt 2005). While Bonilla-Silva and Embrick (2007:340) focused on the process that "creates and conditions [white] views, cognitions, and even sense of beauty" in segregated white spaces, we argue that "white habitus" permeates beyond the borders of those all-white spaces and is tacitly present throughout campuses in the United States.

The meanings derived from these spaces can be adopted by people of color, in this case Asian Americans. Here, we assert that Asian American students are socialized in the white habitus known as an elite university.

Wendy Moore (2008) specifically addressed campus climate at elite law schools, but white institutionalized space describes all HWCUs. Assumptions that Asian American students are largely high-achieving "model minorities" are inaccurate (Chou and Feagin 2008; Teranishi 2010). . . . Also mythologized is that the university, including elite universities, is a safe haven from ignorance and racial prejudice; however, Asian Americans are not free from racism on campus (Chou and Feagin 2008; Chou, Lee, and Ho 2012; Teranishi 2010; Tuan 1999). Our most prestigious universities are not outside of the existing racial structure in the United States. . . .

The components of white institutional space are (1) racist exclusion of people of color from access to power and from positions of power; (2) development of the white racial frame in the context that organizes institutional logic; (3) historical development of a curriculum based upon the white racial frame; and (4) assertion of curriculum as a neutral, impartial body of doctrine unconnected to power (Moore 2008). Through this process, students of all races are socialized into the racial order and, perhaps, fail to question the racial status quo.

TWENTY-FIRST CENTURY RACISM

The overt Jim Crow racism that ruled through segregation, derogatory language, and violence has in many ways been replaced by the subtleties of contemporary racism (Bonilla-Silva 2002). Today, racism still operates as a system based on an ideology of inferiority that allocates societal resources by racial hierarchy (Bonilla-Silva 1997). However, the "new" racism is more covert, more likely to dance around inferiority and inequality in the hidden language of "differences" (Bonilla-Silva 2002). Although the literature has chronicled various forms of this post–Civil Rights era racism, in the context of this article we focus on what Bonilla-Silva referred to as "color-blind

racism." A type of "racism without racists," color-blind racism is a racial ideology that allows whites to defend their racial interests while maintaining invisibility of whiteness and white privilege. Color-blindness refuses to examine racism within a social and historical context. It reduces race problems to matters of isolated individual prejudice and negates the existence of a larger socioeconomic racial structure with real economic, social, and political consequences for people of color (Prashad 2001). Common elements of color-blind racism are (1) discussing racial matters in the abstract, (2) attributing racially inferior standings in education and economy to cultural differences over biological explanations, (3) framing racial residential and school segregation as "natural," and (4) claiming that discrimination is a thing of the past (Bonilla-Silva 2002). . . . Through various denial strategies, color-blind racism obfuscates the problem of racial inequality, thus making it difficult to dismantle the white ruling class. We demonstrate that color-blind discourse is used by Asian Americans at HWCUs as well as by their white peers.

THE ROLE OF DISCOURSE IN COLOR-BLIND RACISM

Color-blind racism principally operates through the expression of conversations, media, and other forms of communication. There are numerous ways of communicating color-blind racism, but for the purpose of this paper we highlight three of its discursive practices: (1) the use of certain semantics to express racial views, (2) the almost complete incoherence when it comes to certain issues of race, and (3) the minimization of concerns about racial inequality (Bonilla-Silva 2002).

To adapt to the shift from Jim Crow racism to post–Civil Rights era realities where openly racist statements were no longer socially acceptable, color-blind discourse opted for specific language to express racial views. For example, one might couch a racist statement by emphasizing that it is not a racist comment. One might also use descriptors that are tacitly racialized, such as describing a neighborhood as a "ghetto" when one means to say that it is a minority community. . . . The minimization of concerns about racial inequality is fostered in color-blind racism by not only denying racial structure but also silencing those who raise the issue. For example, individuals might call Asian Americans outraged by racial discrimination "too sensitive" or "overreacting," in essence minimizing racism as an emotional problem. Embedded in the subtleties of talk, color-blind discourse may appear benign compared with the system of fear and violence that Jim Crow racism used. However, color-blind discourse could be more powerful for its tacit hegemony, moving through the minds of the majority and minority alike (van Dijk 2000).

Subordinated minorities are not immune to adopting and internalizing parts of color-blind racism. Claire Kim (1999) is one of the seminal critical race scholars to offer a structural framework to expand beyond black and white and consider the racial position of Asian Americans. She criticizes racial hierarchy for its one-dimensionality, which assigns status and privilege to whites at the top, blacks at the bottom, and other minorities like Asian Americans in the middle. Kim instead maps out white racial hierarchy on two axes: an axis of racial superiority–inferiority and an axis of insider–foreigner. In a position of "near whiteness," Asian Americans might be more likely to identify and promote white interests than other people of color. Effectively the racial triangulation of Asian Americans drives a wedge between themselves and other minorities. However, we argue that the two axes are not enough. . . . An analysis through an intersectional lens, including systems of gender, sexuality, and class complicates the simplified racial order that Kim outlined. Bonilla-Silva (2004) theorized a "tri-racial" model that includes class as a marker in determining racial superiority and inferiority but also fails to address the racial shuffling that occurs when including stereotypes of gender and sexuality. The common thread throughout these racial theories is that whiteness goes uninterrogated. Groups of color are compared against the standard of whiteness, and whiteness is not constructed as pathological. . . .

ASIAN AMERICAN SEXUAL POLITICS

Current Asian American racial formation and identity theories are inadequate. Racial analysis of Asian Americans is incomplete without consideration of gender and sexuality constructions. Connell and Messerschmidt (2005) coined the term "hegemonic masculinity" to describe the ideology of male dominance. White hegemonic masculinity constructs the white heterosexual male as the version of normalized manhood, whereas men of color are cast into weaker "subordinated masculinities." Subordinated masculinities are racially specific. For example, Asian American men face a particular placement on a gendered hierarchy and deal with battles against normalized constructions of masculinity that operate differently than those of their Latino or African American male counterparts (Chou 2012; Eng 2001). Racial stereotypes can and do change over time, but they continue to maintain the racial status quo. The stereotyping of early male Chinese immigrants was very similar to past and current constructions of African American men as hypersexual, aggressive, and dangerous (Takaki 2001). However, over time, stereotypes of Asian American men have changed, and now they are portrayed as hyposexual, impotent, and weak (Espiritu 2008). Hegemonic femininity works in similar fashion, promoting white women over women of color, although both are still subordinate to white men. . . .

We contend that Asian American sexuality is formed in ways that perpetuate white privilege, particularly for white men. Media and literature represent Asian and Asian American women in a dichotomous fashion, as either the mysterious "Dragon Lady" or a servile "Lotus Blossom" (Tong 1994). Both of these depictions erotize Asian and Asian American women, while Asian and Asian American men are simultaneously "castrated" or denied manhood. These representations exacerbate the "oriental fetishism" that Asian and Asian American women face (Prasso 2006). "Controlling images" of both Asian American men and women exist "to define the white man's virility and the white man's superiority" (Kim 1999:69). Again, at the core of these Asian portrayals is the strength of white hegemonic masculinity.

Defining white male virility and superiority through the demeaning representations of Asian Americans is essential to retain the existing racial structure. . . .

RACIALIZED LOVE

Higher education is a particular space where Asian Americans undergo racial identity management while exploring their romantic preferences (Chou 2012). Dating and romantic relationships are widely recognized as important parts of college life (Armstrong 2006). Asian American out-dating has been increasing rapidly while Asian American out-marriage is declining (Sassler and Joyner 2011). The racially exploratory nature of dating, especially in regard to Asian Americans, has been suggested as the reason behind this trend. This makes dating in an elite university, itself an exploratory space, an excellent setting to investigate the role of race in romantic interactions.

Patricia Hill Collins (2004:6) defined sexual politics as "a set of ideas and social practices shaped by gender, race, and sexuality that frame all men and women's treatment of one another, as well as how individual men and women are perceived and treated by others." . . . What we argue is that Asian Americans' social experiences and ideas at HWCUs are shaped by white habitus, the white racial frame, and white institutional space. The relationships between Asian Americans and their non–Asian American peers are shaped by the campus climate, which is part of the larger racialized society. . . .

Our research interrogates the intersectionality of race, gender, and sexuality and the unique position of Asian Americans at HWCUs. Although our data allude to a problematic white university culture in which whites engage in sexualized racism with little consequence, we find equally worrisome the emotional management that Asian Americans must perform to deal with such racism. We document how Asian Americans use language to negotiate the realities of sexualized racism and racialized romantic preferences. Finally, we detail the Asian American responses to racism, which range from resistance to racial resignation.

METHODS

Although there is much work to be done in understanding the experiences of all Asian Americans and Pacific Islanders, here we focus primarily on the experiences of East Asian American undergraduates. This project involved two qualitative research instruments rolled out in two phases from 2011 to 2012.

In the initial stage, semistructured face-to-face interviews were conducted with 14 Asian American undergraduates at an elite university hereafter referred to as Elite University. We recruited participants through purposive sampling in an attempt to gain a diverse demographic sampling and reflect a broad set of experiences (Denzin and Lincoln 2005). Our respondents self-identified as Chinese (1 female [F], 2 male [M]), Taiwanese (2F, 1M), Korean (2F, 3M), Indian (1F), Hapa ("Hapa" denotes half Japanese; this particular respondent self-identified as Hapa, a mix of Japanese and Irish descent) (1M), and Pacific Islander (1F). Thus, 7 were male and 7 were female. Geographical distribution was varied: West Coast ($n = 3$), Northeast ($n = 3$), Deep South ($n = 2$), South Atlantic ($n = 3$), Midwest ($n = 1$), Pacific West ($n = 1$), and 1 first-generation immigrant who self-identified as an international student. Of the interviewees, 13 were undergraduate students and 1 was a graduate student. Ages ranged from 18 to 24 years. Interviews consisted of a number of open-ended questions on family experiences; body image and media influences; hook-ups, dating, and marriage; the university social scene; and the presence of counter-narratives. On average, interviews lasted between one and two hours and were recorded and transcribed.

The second mode of inquiry used an open-ended, qualitative, online questionnaire based on the semi-structured interview questions to collect data from 47 additional Asian American undergraduates from Elite University. Survey participants were recruited via flyers, e-mail messages to Asian American organization e-mail lists, and the university's social science participant database. The survey collected demographic information on respondents' age, gender, sexuality, ethnicity, education level, number of relationships, and citizenship status. It also included a number of open-ended questions on familial expectations, social relationships, and racialized experiences while growing up and while attending university. Of the 47 respondents, 27 were female and 20 were male. Respondents self-identified as Chinese ($n = 22$), Asian ($n = 6$), Asian American ($n = 8$), Indian ($n = 2$), Korean ($n = 3$), Taiwanese ($n = 3$), mixed-Japanese ($n = 1$), and Vietnamese ($n = 2$). Respondents self-identified their sexuality as straight ($n = 40$), bisexual ($n = 3$), gay ($n = 1$), asexual ($n = 1$), and bi-curious ($n = 1$), with 1 nonrespondent. Ages ranged from 18 to 22 years. One of the 47 respondents identified as an international student. Respondents are identified in this paper via pseudonyms.

. . . As Asian American researchers, we also embraced reflexivity throughout the research process. This process allowed us to consider how our own experiences, assumptions, and context could influence the interpretation of participant narratives. As we gathered and analyzed our data systematically, we coded and recoded our field notes into categories emerging during the process. This also encouraged us to reflect critically on how we analyzed and assembled knowledge. Through this analysis, data in this article offer rare insight into racialized experiences of Asian American undergraduates.

RESULTS

At the university, a persistent stereotype of Asian Americans is that they are "quiet and content with the status quo" (Tatum 1997:161). In the *Myth of the Model Minority,* Chou and Feagin (2008) described individuals who have internalized this stereotype and deal with racism by ignoring it quietly. Our research documents Asian American undergraduates resorting to a color-blind discourse that prevents them from articulating the racialized nature of certain social experiences. The discursive strategy also at times leaves them unprepared to deal with and process racism. This ultimately creates a harmful positive feedback loop in which non–Asian Americans make racist remarks, Asian Americans in a color-blind

discursive do not actively resist or address racism, and non–Asian Americans continue to make racist comments without fear of backlash.

ASIAN AMERICAN FEMALES AS THE EROTICIZED OTHER

Racist comments that rely on so-called "good stereotypes" such as the model minority assumptions should not be prematurely dismissed as complimentary; their nature is far more complicated. Asian females can exploit racial sexualized stereotypes and racialized sexual desires to gain access to white privilege, but such a privilege can have associated costs of objectification and eroticized "othering." . . . Furthermore, when Asian Americans are faced with overt sexualized racism, a lack of a collective narrative on racism often prevents them from even identifying racist situations (Chou and Feagin 2008). For example, when asked about the transition to Elite University from a largely Asian American West Coast community, Jenny, a first-year Taiwanese American female, responded that the move had not been difficult but then followed up her answer by relating a story in which she was approached by a group of white and black males in her dormitory common room who made overtly racist and sexist comments to her:

> The football players approached me, "Oh little Asian girl I would definitely love to bang you." And I said Oh my god, where am I? [Uncomfortable laugh] It was very uncomfortable [it happened] in my dorm these boys were not drunk. It was 2 pm. I said, "I'm sorry I have a boyfriend" and left but I don't know what I don't know if they were just trying to like I don't know what they were doing because they're freshmen. It's O-Week I don't know how it is with upperclassmen but. . .

. . . Jenny experienced this clearly inappropriate comment in her dormitory. Thus, the male student's comment turned Jenny's home into a hostile racialized and sexualized space.

Instead of inserting a form of resistance in response, Jenny incorporated her answer within the frame of a color-blind discourse. Jenny was almost at a loss for words. She said, "I don't know" four times and, in line with color-blindness, offered two alternative reasons besides racism in trying to explain the racialized experience. Furthermore, note the language the male chose in his comments. Using the words "little" and "girl" infantilized Jenny. To him she was an objectified sexual object to be "banged." . . . The words "bang" and "little Asian girl" are reminiscent of Asian American female pornography titles like *Bang That Asian Pussy* and *Cute Asian Girl Getting F***ed* ("Asian Sex Movies" n.d.). In constructing Jenny as a subordinate sexual being, the male student reaffirmed his masculinity and sexuality, a key element to hegemonic masculinity and white racial framing. The situation described ended with Jenny apologizing ("I'm sorry I have a boyfriend") to the male who made an overtly hostile, racist sexual comment. It is quite possible the male will repeat his comments to another Asian woman, being no worse for the wear. . . .

When asked explicitly whether these racialized sexual incidents happen often, Jenny replied:

> Not since then since I do try to keep to myself most of the time with boys so because I've had bad experiences with them so far but um but no nothing has happened really but like Orientation Week I did go to [name of club] and I think people did kind of target me because I was Asian.

. . .

It is tempting to write off Jenny's experience as a singular case of extreme sexualized racism, but our survey data reveal other sexualized racist comments toward Asian American females. Mary, a Korean American female senior, said, "Just last week someone called me a 'Chinese bitch' and then told me to have a nice day because I was, in his words, 'sexy.'" Here, the juxtaposition of "Chinese bitch" against a commonplace pleasantry like "have a nice day" highlights how sexualized racism is delivered as if an everyday compliment. The male drew Mary into an eroticized image reminiscent of a "Dragon Lady" by calling her "sexy" and a "Chinese bitch" and in so doing enforced his own hegemonic masculinity by subordinating her. Some respondents took these comments as compliments. Charlotte, a Chinese American female senior,

said, "I guess in college when people say things like 'hot Asian chicks' it doesn't really bother me. I'm appreciative of compliments." These Asian American females' positive reaction or lack of reaction to sexualized racist comments probably did little to stop these men from continuing to make sexualized racist comments.

However, Jenny and other survey respondents described the emotional work they had to perform in order to deal with these comments. Lindsay, a Chinese American female first-year, said:

> People who say things like I'm a "sexy Asian" or something. I guess I am shallowly complimented, and then I get annoyed because there shouldn't be this discrepancy between "sexy" and "sexy Asian."

Lindsay raised the point that the "compliment" to her said something more specific about her race. For example, she is sexy *because* she is Asian or *in spite of* it. In this example, what may seem like "positive stereotyping" of an Asian American woman is another demarcation of racial difference. Susan, a Chinese American female senior, explained the psychological toll of sexualized racist comments: "It made me feel violated and that they are only looking at me from a sexual and very primitive point of view." Susan keyed into the way the male gaze has the power to control; using the adjective "violated" to describe how she felt in response to the male gaze, Susan suggested a trauma or almost an emotional violence. We argue that this sexualized and gendered trauma is racialized in the white institutional space of the elite university. Numerous universities across the country are making headlines because of their "rape tolerant" cultures (Heldman and Dirks 2014). This culture is a result of white institutional space being protective of white men, and we suggest that analysis of this campus culture includes race.

. . .

THE EXOTICIZED OTHER IN ROMANCE AND RELATIONSHIPS

Sexualized racism becomes more complicated in the context of relationships and romantic love. Our data document the ambivalence and emotional guesswork that our respondents negotiate in their interracial relationships, particularly in regard to "yellow fever." Yellow fever is a phenomenon in which white men prefer Asian or Asian American women because of preconceived notions about their exoticized sexuality, subservience, and submissiveness (Kim 2011). The constant negotiation of preconceived notions of Asian American exoticized sexuality in romantic relationships was particularly problematic in the respondents' partner selection. Mary, a survey respondent, said,

I feel fairly conflicted about the relationship between my race and my sexuality. At [Elite University], "yellow fever" is fairly prevalent and many people openly admit to this. The stereotypes applied to Asian women in particular are not necessarily positive— e.g., freaky girls who want to rebel against their traditional parents or girls who want to let loose after being repressed for so long. Although I'm fine with both my sexuality and my Asian identity, I'm always sensitive to the possible stereotypes that others might be applying to me. For example, if I get hit on at a bar and the person makes reference to my racial identity, I tend to be put on guard.

This respondent highlighted the frequency of yellow fever and the acceptability for "people to openly admit" to "yellow fever." Yet, she also spoke with a weariness of being targeted as an Asian female stereotype and a tendency to "be put on guard." . . .

When asked whether being called exotic bothered her, Kai, a Pacific Islander American female sophomore, said, "No, I like it. I eat it up." Throughout her interview, Kai asserted her pride in her Pacific Islander heritage. Her positive reaction to being called exotic could stem from her pride in her racial identity. However, Kai went on to make clear how being exoticized by her romantic partner led her to end the relationship:

I mean the fact that I was [a Pacific Islander] came up all the time . . . this one guy I was seeing I swear to God I mean this is kind of why I left him I swear to God he just loved me because I was the [Pacific Islander] chick and he could just tote me around as his. I tend to take it in stride. I'm like okay yeah maybe I am [Pacific Islander]. If that makes me oh so much

more desirable to you great for you but you would have to know me more than that. I don't know. I mean it's not. . . . Like you know like you know when guys go on vacation and they get to hook-up with that exotic girl and they talk about it all the time. I'm pretty sure he did that. I'm not positive but I have a pretty good idea that he did.

Kai ended her relationship with her partner because he treated her as an exoticized Pacific Islander and not as Kai, the person. Herein lies the problematic nature of yellow fever: The high sexual desirability placed on Asian American and Pacific Islander women may appear positive in terms of social position, but it also can give way to sexual objectification and racialized sexual desire. It facilitates relationships in which the Asian American females are drawn as sexual caricatures rather than people. Even the threat of yellow fever creates a shadow in interracial relationships. Janine, a Chinese American junior, said in regard to her white boyfriend, "I feel very like those 'Asian women are sexually something or whatever' I feel it makes me feel insecure about how people perceive me especially in relationships whether those thoughts ever enter my boyfriend's mind. So I don't want to be treated like an object and I don't want to be a victim of 'yellow fever' or anything like that." Janine spoke to the romantic questioning that she negotiated in response to yellow fever; she was on guard that she might be racially sought out even with her boyfriend, in her intimate partnership. Chou (2012:94) wrote, "There is no real test to accurately determine the motives that are not influenced by societal constructions." The exposure to yellow fever leaves Asian American females continuously wondering.

ASIAN AMERICAN MALE DOUBLE CONSCIOUSNESS

Continuous media and public discourse depicting Asian Americans in subordinate stereotypical roles may also contribute to the internalization and even belief in harmful stigmas associated with being Asian American. Asian American individuals who have internalized hegemonic masculinity begin to reflect negative feelings toward their minority group and oppress themselves through feelings of negative self-worth. This is extremely harmful, because it can lead to problems with double consciousness—perceiving Asian American characteristics as abnormal or inferior while also recognizing one's own Asian American identity (DuBois 1903). After being exposed to racialized mocking and stereotypical images of Asian American men on television, Daniel—a gay second-generation Taiwanese American senior—recounted his uncertainty and his dislike for his race:

> I tended to think that Asian guys are not really that attractive, to other people—to other guys. And, I think that Asian guys in media too, are portrayed as more effeminate unless, you look at martial arts or whatnot, in a lot of cases not in all cases, but in a lot of cases. So I struggled with that a lot, and I would say that I still struggle with that in terms of my own attractiveness to other people. And I think there's always been some kind of jokes, or stereotypes about Asian guys and cock size, things like that. But, I did struggle with that a little, because I did look kind of like the stereotype that was placed on us, and one that I thought would possibly be true, and not having a comparison, besides porn, where everyone had huge cocks, you know, you're not really sure.

Daniel's experiences are not uncommon compared with other responses given by Asian American men interviewed. All of the men interviewed mentioned that they were unsatisfied with the way Asian American men were portrayed in the media, and all mentioned that they had to negotiate the stereotype that Asian men have small genitalia. Although they tended to play down the impact of this stereotype, the fact that every single participant mentioned it makes it worthwhile to investigate, especially as sexualized insults are central to the making of contemporary adolescent masculinity (Pascoe 2007).

If there are widespread conceptions that Asian American men have small penises, and there is no easy mode of comparison of phallic size, these respondents may buy into problematic phallic-centric masculinity. Being surrounded by such controlling images and connecting the Asian American faces in the media to one's own can cause serious problems regarding

self-worth. Daniel mentioned that he had "struggled a lot" with the portrayals of Asian American men as "not attractive" and "effeminate" and that he still struggled with those internalizations. . . .

> I actually had a really hard time thinking about whether or not, I really had trouble or disliked being Asian at one point, and thought there was a lot of pressure associated with it and didn't really care for it. . . . I didn't think of my friends as—people I didn't necessarily know anyway because I just didn't have that much experience, and it was just kind of difficult in that sense to navigate socially what I was looking for in my friends.

The concept of racial self-hate, or rejection of Asian Americans by Asian Americans, is very apparent in Daniel's words. He made it clear that his feelings of negative self-worth were tied to his "dislike of being Asian." This can have far-reaching effects on other parts of life. For example, Daniel had a hard time navigating the social scene at his school and really questioned what he was looking for in his friends. Ted, a Chinese American sophomore male, also highlighted in his response how media messages inform our understanding of masculinity and beauty. When asked, "Do you feel Asian American bodies are attractive?" Ted responded,

> Compared to the mainstream culture here, no. I don't really know how to describe it, but if you compare a typical Asian American face, and what's considered to be a more attractive American face, the features are definitely sharper in the American. The bone structure is different. A lot of Asians, well this is really bad, but they have a nerdy look to them. You know what I mean.

It can be assumed that Ted meant "white" when he mentioned the "American" face. Images of white hegemonic masculinity deny the attractiveness and desirability of Asian American males on the basis of race. . . .

RACIAL ROMANTIC TASTES

All of the interviewed Asian Americans said they were interested in finding romantic partners in college but also seemed to recognize certain racial limitations and boundaries in their love lives. For Wade, a Chinese American male first-year, his internalization of these implicit regulations had gone so far that he had begun blaming himself for social pressures and racialized oppression out of his own control:

> Being that you are Asian, it definitely limits you to the number of social—the amount of different girls you can go for. If you are an Asian guy, girls you can pretty much go for are Asian girls. Going for other ethnicities is definitely much harder. Especially if you don't live in a large metropolitan area, then it's just difficult. It's just not widely accepted, and girls don't consider Asian guys. I think it's just self-imposed. I think I have, I'm going to be self-deprecating here but I think to some extent my standards are too high. Or I think the people I do want to go out with; I think there are obstacles too.

While Wade did not explicitly mention what criteria he meant by "amount of different girls," he later mentioned that Asian men can only be romantic with Asian women, much in the way black women found themselves limited to dating only black men (Hill Collins 2004). Although Wade started out suggesting that his problems were largely a consequence of social and geographic factors (interracial dating was not "widely accepted" for Asian men or was difficult outside of a metropolitan area), he then blamed himself for his standards.

. . . Being an Asian, and not on the top of the racial hierarchy, he felt that attempting to have a romantic relationship with someone above his racial tier would be too difficult and would present obstacles. We contend that this type of internalized messaging is a result of white habitus and white institutionalized space. This is extremely problematic, as following seemingly racialized perceptions of beauty and attractiveness leads to internalization of the racial hierarchy.

This racial hierarchy was articulated indirectly through our Asian female respondents' racial preferences. Diana, a Chinese American female senior, said this:

> I look for predominantly white males as partners, specifically those who are over 5'10" in height, with similar education level, and are career ambitious. I prefer white men because they are more independent and don't have a tendency to be as needy as Asian men in relationships. Also, my mom has somewhat encouraged me to seek white men because she believes they are more likely to take on equal child-rearing responsibilities. My mom has always complained about how my father did very little to raise me and my brothers. But in general, I prefer white men because they're more aggressive in all aspects of life, more independent, and are more readily seen as successful. I also feel more attractive when I'm dating someone white though it's hard to explain why. I guess in a way, I'm more proud to show off my white boyfriend than my Asian boyfriend. I just feel slightly more judged when I'm dating someone Asian and feel more prized when I'm dating someone white.

Diana used two frames to reason her preference for white males as romantic partners. The first frame of reasoning relies on seeming cultural differences; she described her mother's warning about the archetypal chauvinistic Asian male, unwilling to take responsibility for domestic and family responsibilities. The second frame stems from hegemonic masculinity. White men are "more aggressive" and "more independent," essentially more masculine, whereas Asian males are "needy" and subordinated.

. . .

While it is tempting to shrug off racial romantic preferences as natural or accidental, they are in fact guided by a larger racial hierarchy and are political in nature. When asked how her white family would react to her dating an African American male, Amy, an adopted Korean American sophomore, said the following:

> I feel like growing up in the South my mom's never been big on like Black Hispanic people Asian white whatever is okay. I think she'd be okay with anything but I guess she says like I don't see how they'd be attractive sometimes she's like, "I'm not attracted to them so I don't know whether you would be or not."

Although Amy described her partner preference based on the person and not the race, her white mother negatively describes African American and Hispanic males as unattractive and, in so doing, to some extent discourages her daughter from dating them.

. . . When Alex, a female Taiwanese American second-year, was asked what would happen if she brought home an African American male as her potential partner, she stated, "I don't think my family would be like 'oh no you can't do that,' but it would definitely be a source of discomfort." The source of discomfort she described would not be simply interracial dating but also her partner's specific race—African American.

RESISTANCE VS. RESIGNATION

Asian Americans in college seem to suffer from many racialized social experiences that shape how they live and navigate their daily lives. As elucidated above, these experiences often are intersectional, gendered, and raced. Many problems are complex and involve various social and personal pressures. Asian American students are faced with how to react to these problems on a daily basis. While there are many different ways Asian Americans have chosen to respond to these problems, navigating the white-dominated space of college universities requires significant emotional management on the part of its students of color, regardless of how they choose to react. To illustrate a dichotomy in responses, the way they deal with these problems has been grouped into two strands: resistance and resignation.

Resistance

White racial framing as part of white institutional space is not the only frame that people use (Chou 2012; Feagin 2010). To resist the white racial frame, whites and people of color use "counter frames" to resist the oppressive racial ideologies (Chou 2012; Feagin 2010). Many Asian Americans who came to Elite University from a more racially heterogeneous area were surprised to find that the university's social scenes were much divided along racial lines despite an undergraduate program full of intelligent students, of whom about 40 percent were people of color. The socialization process at college, which we argue is

"white habitus," informs students' romantic, social, and racialized life. Particularly the role that individuals play in the university culture is heavily dependent on their affiliation with the (historically white) Greek system. Tim, an Asian American junior, talked about his experience with the university's social scene:

> I can't really say it [the historically white Greek system] hasn't affected me because you go to the quad and you have white fraternities living there and they're the ones who have the parties, they're the ones who host things. So, it's really hard to not be affected by it on some level.

. . . Asian Americans who respond via resistance recognize the difficulties of being Asian American in a white-dominated space. Their responses are directed at creating space that is safe for them and acknowledging the Asian American identity as worthy.

Many Asian Americans interviewed said that they had close Asian American friends. Generally, Asian Americans chose other Asian Americans to befriend because they had lived through common racial experiences. Having Asian American friends appears important to coping with and resisting racialized experiences. . . . Common racialized experiences allow people of color to validate each other's struggles to deal with everyday racism rather than invalidate experiences through color-blindness. Janine, a Chinese American junior, also touched upon the struggle to combat colorblindness in her advice to those combating racism:

> Seek other people out. It is really comforting to hear other people affirm what you feel so like don't stop until you find someone who agrees with you and whatever you're feeling is right and then you can talk to that person about your troubles. It is really comforting to know that you are not crazy.

She advised those experiencing racism to find people who will affirm rather than dismiss racialized experiences. In color-blind racism, the racialized experience is negated and the person experiencing racism is meant to feel crazy, irrational, or paranoid and is less likely to speak out again. Her advice to have friends that affirm racism is a small but important step to building resistance against colorblind racism.

Moreover, respondents also spoke of Asian American undergraduate social organizations constructed in a way that resists stereotypical images by painting the opposite picture. Ted spoke of the counter-imaging in his Asian American fraternity:

> Our motto is, "to be leaders among men." But like not everyone tries to be a leader, that's just our motto. I guess our images [*sic*] is Asian guys who you know, who are sociable, who can throw down.

The Asian American fraternity is bound by a formal motto as well as a more common image that they "are sociable" and "can throw down." The desirable portrayal of Asian Americans as social leaders is a denial of stereotypical representations of Asian American males as quiet, socially awkward nerds who can't lead. The Asian Americans in this group attempt to redefine themselves and what it means to be Asian American.

Resignation

Resistance and resignation are not mutually exclusive responses to racism. Asian Americans responding via resignation direct their behavior and responses toward fitting into white space in an attempt to make it a safe space for them. Asian Americans using resignation affirm notions of Asian Americans as irregular and whites as normal. Ted grew up in the South, among a population with a majority of middle-class whites; here he talked about his perspectives on facing social problems as an Asian American:

> To an extent, I believe it's very overcomable [*sic*], if you're an Asian American with the right personality, the right character. I guess height always works in the business world. I would say that the generalizations always come from the fact that so many Asians falling under the stereotype. So we're obviously disadvantaged, but it's very overcomable [*sic*] if you're the right type of person.

. . . By mentioning being disadvantaged by "generalizations" stemming from other Asian Americans "falling under the stereotype," Ted shifted the blame for his difficulties fitting into a white society onto other Asian Americans.

With the creation of favorable racial social spaces, the strength of color-blindness elicits negative reactions from Asian Americans. When asked about how Asian Americans interact in social spaces, Kate, a Korean American female senior, said:

> So if someone takes [Asian American stereotypes] to heart, which they definitely can, it will make them less confident socially and more self-aware, more socially awkward, maybe less willing to engage with those different from them so maybe that would lead to them being more secluded and more self-segregated like hanging out with only Asians.

Kate, in using the term "self-segregation," internalized the language of white privilege and colorblindness. Use of the term "self-segregation" to accuse people of color of being exclusionary and to stigmatize minority social spaces is characteristic of colorblind discourse used by whites. . . .

Respondents also pointed to ignoring discrimination and racism as an effective way to deal with unwanted comments. When asked whether he had experienced any comments about his race, Richard, an Asian American male senior, said, "Yes, the common joke is that Asians have small penises. It obviously is very degrading and embarrassing, but I've never really paid attention to that type of bigotry." Moreover, when asked about advice for Asian Americans struggling with racism, Paul, an Asian American male first-year, said, "Even if they are being judged, they should ignore the discriminators and move on and/or have a third party intervene to reduce conflict." . . .

From the interview responses, it seems that Asian American undergraduates are divided between resistance and resignation as their principal strategies for coping with racism. In both resistance and resignation, Asian Americans must perform emotional work to cope with these racialized experiences at a HWCU.

Counternarratives

Another tool to combat hegemonic ideologies is the use of counter-narratives. The white racial frame is a concept that racial ideology is held consciously and unconsciously by most white Americans and many people of color. Elements of the frame include racial imagery, emotions, and narratives that shape their understanding of race and also shape their behavior (Feagin 2010). Creating a different racial perspective has been paramount for the development of African American support for racialized experiences. Asian Americans also have begun to develop a different "frame," through understanding how race shapes interactions in America from their perspective. This different frame, or counter-frame, aids people of color by helping them notice and make sense of their racialized experiences. Wade, a Chinese American first-year, described how his parents explained to him the merits of academic achievement. In his family, as in some other Asian American families, there is a fear that affirmative action works to the detriment of Asian Americans and unfairly rewards other people of color:

> [My parents] kept highlighting the fact that because you're Asian, it's more difficult for you to get into schools, so you need to do better. Also because my school was majority Asian, they were like, "you can already compare yourself with your peers, because your school is simply Asian, and because you're Asian yourself, you will be judged by higher standards, so you'll have to work harder."

This kind of conversation seems common among Asian American students, as affirmative action seems to be a racialized concept that is present in many middle-class Asian American homes. Noticing and recognizing that one will be treated differently based on race is an essential part of a successful counter-frame. It is unfortunate that the topic of affirmative action as part of the Asian American counter-frame may breed competition and seeds of distrust among the members of the Asian American community; however, it is still a valuable common perspective that brings the community somewhat closer together in terms of a collective racial conscious.

Another critically important aspect of a racial counter-frame is identifying the way in which society's structure favors whites and working against that structure as a person of color. In response to the question, "For Asian Americans struggling with racism and their identity, what advice would you give them?" Beth, a Chinese American female sophomore, said:

> Don't give a shit about what white people think you are supposed to do. Asians are not "supposed" to do anything. We operate with all the same rights, freedoms, desires, fears, sexual urges, despair, anger as white people—and, yes, even in dating and hooking up. You can have as much sex or as little sex or no sex with whomever you want. Asian women are just as beautiful as white women. Asian men are just as sexy as white men. Believe it, live it.

This respondent recognized and rejected Asian American racial boundaries that white ideology has created and attempted to remove expectations about sexualized racism and beauty. This counter-narrative attempts to free Asian Americans from subordination to whites by recognizing that Asian Americans' rights, emotions, and desires have value.

CONCLUSION

Contemporary discussion surrounding Asian Americans and college is fixated on admission rates. For Asian Americans themselves, the end goal may seem to be a ticket to an elite university (Yang 2011). Yet while Asian Americans may be ready to engage in the academic rigors of university, our data suggest that they are less prepared to navigate the white institutional social space of the ivory tower and the white racial framing that is entrenched in these HWCUs. Whether they choose to acknowledge it or not, the double consciousness of being Asian American and existing in a white-dominated space takes a psychological toll on the emotional well-being of Asian American students at a college or university. Through resistance, resignation, and counter-narratives, Asian Americans as individuals perform emotional work in either challenging or maintaining the white-dominated university spaces.

. . . In examining the words that Asian Americans use to describe these social settings, it is evident that color-blind discourse can provide opportunities to combat overt and covert everyday racism—which the racist commenter is confident that Asian American targets will not challenge. Even in the case of sexualized racism, in which white male preference for Asian women might seem to advantage Asian women, respondents described how sexualized comments were objectifying and traumatic. Although the club scene was noted as a place of racialized interaction, everyday racism in the dormitory also occurred. Overall, Asian Americans faced the emotional challenges of resisting and resigning to sexualized and everyday racism. We argue that the elite college campus is a white institutionalized space where Asian American females are confronted with a white masculine hegemonic structure through racialized dating preferences and where Asian American males internalize the hierarchy of racial preferences and experience psychological costs. . . . We demonstrated the intersectional nature of racism, particularly how it is sexualized and gendered. With this in mind, universities must move away from their complacency about Asian Americans and understand that the social culture is in want of reconstruction, beginning with the ways in which ideas, beliefs, and experiences are expressed.

REFERENCES

"Asian Sex Movies." *Redtube.* Retrieved May 5, 2011 (http://www.redtube.com/).

Armstrong, Elizabeth A. 2006. "Sexual Assault on Campus: A Multi-level Integrative Approach to Party Rape." *Social Problems* 53(4):483–99.

Bonilla-Silva, Eduardo. 1997. "Rethinking Racism: Toward a Structural Interpretation." *American Sociological Review* 62(3):465–80.

Bonilla-Silva, Eduardo. 2002. "The Linguistics of Color Blind Racism: How to Talk Nasty about Blacks without Sounding 'Racist.'" *Critical Sociology* 28(1):41–64.

Bonilla-Silva, Eduardo. 2003. *Racism without Racists: Color-blind Racism and the Persistence of Racial Inequality in the United States.* Lanham, MD: Rowman & Littlefield.

Bonilla-Silva, Eduardo. 2004. "From Bi-racial to Tri-racial: Towards a New System of Racial Stratification in the USA." *Ethnic and Racial Studies* 27(6):931–50.

Bonilla-Silva, Eduardo and David G. Embrick. 2007. "'Every Place Has a Ghetto ...': The Significance of Whites' Social and Residential Segregation." *Journal of Symbolic Interaction* 30(3):323–46.

Bonilla-Silva, Eduardo, Carla Goar, and David G. Embrick. 2007. "When Whites Flock Together: The Social Psychology of White Habitus." *Critical Sociology* 32(2–3):229–53.

Burawoy, Michael. 1998. "The Extended Case Method." Pp. 271–87 in *Ethnography Unbound,* edited by M. Burawoy, A. Burton, A. A. Ferguson, K. J. Fox, J. Gamson, N. Gartrell, L. Hurst, C. Kurzman, L. Salzinger, J. Schiffman, and S. Ui. Berkeley: University of California Press.

Chou, Rosalind S. 2012. *Asian American Sexual Politics: The Construction of Race, Gender, and Sexuality.* Lanham, MD: Rowman & Littlefield.

Chou, Rosalind S. and Joe R. Feagin. 2008. *The Myth of the Model Minority.* Boulder, CO: Paradigm.

Chou, Rosalind S. and Joe R. Feagin. 2014. *The Myth of the Model Minority.* 2nd ed. Boulder, CO: Paradigm.

Chou, Rosalind S., Kristen Lee, and Simon Ho. 2012. "The White Habitus and Hegemonic Masculinity at the Elite Southern University: Asian Americans and the Need for Intersectional Analysis." *Sociation Today* 10(2) (http://www.ncsociology.org/sociationtoday/v102/asian.htm).

Clark, Kim. 2009. "Do Elite Private Colleges Discriminate Against Asian Students?" *US News & World Report.* Retrieved July 8, 2013 (http://www.usnews.com/education/articles/2009/10/07/do-elite-private-colleges-discriminate-against-asian-students).

Connell, R. W. and James W. Messerschmidt. 2005. "Hegemonic Masculinity: Rethinking the Concept." *Gender & Society* 19(6):845–54.

Denzin, Norman K. and Yvonna S. Lincoln, eds. 2005. *The Sage Handbook of Qualitative Research.* 3rd ed. Thousand Oaks, CA: Sage Publications.

Du Bois, W. E. B. 1903. *The Souls of Black Folks.* Chicago: A. C. McClurg.

Eng, David. 2001. *Racial Castration: Managing Masculinity in Asian America.* Durham, NC: Duke University Press.

Espiritu, Yen Le. 2008. *Asian American Women and Men: Labor, Laws, and Love.* Lanham, MD: Rowman & Littlefield.

Feagin, Joe R. 2010. *White Racial Frame.* New York: Routledge.

Heldman, Caroline and Danielle Dirks. 2014. "Blowing the Whistle on Campus Rape." *Ms. Magazine,* February 18 (http://msmagazine.com/blog/2014/02/18/blowing-the-whistle-on-campus-rape).

Hill Collins, Patricia. 2004. *Black Sexual Politics.* New York: Routledge.

Kim, Bitna. 2011. "Asian Female and Caucasian Male Couples: Exploring the Attraction." *Pastoral Psychology* 60(2):233–44.

Kim, Claire J. 1999. "The Racial Triangulation of Asian Americans." *Politics and Society* 27(1):105–38.

Moore, Wendy L. 2008. *Reproducing Racism: White Space, Elite Law Schools, and Racial Inequality.* Lanham, MD: Rowman & Littlefield.

Pascoe, C. J. 2007. *Dude, You're a Fag: Masculinity and Sexuality in High School.* Los Angeles: University of California Press.

Prashad, Vijay. 2001. "Genteel Racism." *Ameriasia Journal* 26(3):21–33.

Prasso, Sheridan. 2006. *The Asian Mystique: Dragon Ladies, Geisha Girls & Our Fantasies of the Exotic Orient.* Cambridge, MA: Public Affairs Books.

Rosenbloom, Susan R. and Niobe Way. 2004. "Experiences of Discrimination among African American, Asian American, and Latino Adolescents in an Urban High School." *Youth and Society* 35(4):420–45.

Sassler, Sharon and Kara Joyner 2011. "Social Exchange and the Progression of Sexual Relationships in Emerging Adulthood." *Social Forces* 90(1):223–45.

Strauss, Anselm L. 1987. *Qualitative Analysis for Social Scientists.* New York: Cambridge University Press.

Takaki, Ronald. 2001. *Strangers from a Different Shore: A History of Asian Americans.* New York: Little, Brown.

Tatum, Beverly D. 1997. *"Why Are All the Black Kids Sitting Together in the Cafeteria?" and Other Conversations About Race.* New York: Basic Books.

Teranishi, Robert. 2010. *Asians in the Ivory Tower: Dilemmas of Racial Inequality in American Higher Education.* New York: Columbia University.

Tong, Benson. 1994. *Unsubmissive Women: Chinese Prostitutes in Nineteenth-Century San Francisco.* Norman: University of Oklahoma Press.

Tuan, Mia. 1999. *Forever Foreigners or Honorary Whites? The Asian Ethnic Experience.* New Brunswick, NJ: Rutgers University Press.

van Dijk, Teun. 2000. "New(s) Racism: A Discourse Analytical Approach." Pp. 33–49 in *Ethnic Minorities and the Media,* edited by S. Cottle. Milton Keynes, UK: Open University Press.

Wei, Johnny. 2013. An Asian American Response to the Backlash against Kappa Sigma. *Chronicle.* Retrieved July 1, 2013 (http://www.dukechronicle.com/articles/2013/02/07/asian-americans-response-backlash-against-kappa-sigma).

Yang, Lin. 2011. "The Hard Part Is Getting In: Asian Americans Navigate the Racially Charged Politics of the College Admissions Process." *Hyphen.* Retrieved July 7, 2013 (http://www.hyphenmagazine.com/magazine/issue-23-bittersweet/hard-part-getting).

40 • *Brandon Andrew Robinson*[1]

"PERSONAL PREFERENCE" AS THE NEW RACISM: GAY DESIRE AND RACIAL CLEANSING IN CYBERSPACE

DISCUSSION QUESTIONS

1. Do you think filters that allow for users to choose racial "preferences" should be allowed on dating sites such as those discussed in this article? Why or why not?
2. How do stereotypes pertaining to various racial/ethnic groups play into white users' "preferences" on Adam4Adam?
3. Why might it be that such racial "preferences" are tolerated in the realm of sexuality/online dating but may be construed as blatant racism in other facets of social life?
4. Can you think of other media relating to sexuality where the "new racism" is prevalent?

"Racially, it's generally white. Body type is usually athletic or muscular. Age range is between 25 and 35. . . . And that's it—that I can think of," exclaimed Koby, a 27-year-old Asian massage therapist when describing his sexual preferences on Adam4Adam.com. Later, when Koby and I were discussing how people could select individual physical preferences on Adam4Adam.com and other dating websites, he stated, "It's the beauty of online dating right? You can put in the parameters of what you want, and then, there you go." Koby's statement is telling: The search for gay male connections is changing in this digital age. Online spaces even install tools—such as filtering systems—into their interfaces for people to search for particular individuals online.

In this article, I uncover how the influence of race impacts online interactions on Adam4Adam.com—one of the most popular online gay personal websites in the United States (Dawley 2007). In 2008 and 2009, over 60 percent of gay and lesbian individuals met online, and it is the most common place for gay and lesbian populations to meet compared to any other space in the past (Rosenfeld and Thomas 2012). However, little is understood as to how race and racism are impacting these online encounters.

Racism has been well documented within (usually white) gay communities (Bérubé 2001; Caluya 2008). Gay men (and occasionally gay men of color) often racially stereotype and objectify queers of color, who in turn are pressured to conform to stereotypes in

Robinson, Brandon Andrew. ""Personal Preference" as the New Racism: Gay Desire and Racial Cleansing in Cyberspace." *Sociology of Race and Ethnicity*, Vol. 1, No. 2. (2015): 317–330.

order to be sexually viable online as well as offline (Caluya 2008; Paul, Ayala, and Choi 2010; Robinson 2008; Wilson et al. 2009). This objectification regularly takes place through the labeling of race as "just a preference" (Holland 2012), though the assumptions behind the discourse of "personal preference" usually remain masked. Therefore, I ask: How is the structure of Adam4Adam.com shaping people's racial preferences? And what larger cultural assumptions underlie this individualized discourse about racial desire?

By analyzing the structure of Adam4Adam.com, I posit that the filtering system on this website allows users to cleanse particular racial bodies from their viewing practices. Using Patricia Hill Collins's (2004) concept of the "new racism" and Sharon Holland's (2012) ideas around the everyday practices of racism within one's erotic life, I show how these social exclusionary practices toward gay men of color in cyberspace are seen as not racist practices. I also reveal the cultural assumptions behind this personal preference discourse in order to illustrate how larger racial structures influence interpersonal engagements on Adam4Adam.com. Ultimately, I turn to Roderick Ferguson's (2004) queer of color analysis to suggest that the structure of Adam4Adam.com and some gay users' practices lead to the remarginalization of all nonheterosexual individuals, though in qualitatively different ways. . . .

LITERATURE REVIEW

RACIALIZED SEXUALITIES

Social, economic, and political forces, which assign racial meaning to particular bodies, form the construction of race[1] (Omi and Winant 1994). Omi and Winant (1994) show that when European colonizers came into contact with people of a different phenotype, these colonizers, through extermination, the institution of slavery, and other coercive tactics, set out to establish themselves as different than and superior to indigenous and African people. This difference was established principally through biological racism, where different racial groups were categorized with

distinct, innate characteristics, with white people supposedly possessing superior characteristics (Omi and Winant 1994). Although disproven, this biological view of race still influences the knowledge circulated about racial groups, masking the historically constructed nature of racial meanings (McKittrick 2010). Nonetheless, race is socio-historical, and it varies over time and across cultures. The process of racialization gives race meaning through marking previously unclassified relationships and groups (Omi and Winant 1994). . . .

Racialization works in conjunction with sexualization. In *Conquest,* Andrea Smith (2005) argues that racialization within the United States began when the colonizer enacted genocide and (sexual) violence upon the Native Americans. Through this process, Native Americans were constructed as "dirty" pollutants and were seen as inferior to white men. Under slavery, white men commodified and objectified black women's bodies, and black women were viewed as property that could be bought, sold, and raped (Collins 2002). Similar to the racialization of Native Americans, black people were constructed as hypersexual rapists who were aggressive toward white women (Davis 2003). These notions of hypersexual black bodies live on today through the ideology of the jezebel and the buck that, respectively, construct black women as promiscuous and black men as aggressive criminals and rapists (Collins 2002, 2004).

Latino/as are often objectified in white tourists' imaginary as the exotic "other" (Cantú 2009; Padilla 2007). These ideologies of Latino/a sexualities and otherness abroad carry over into U.S. society, where Latinas are seen as hypersexual, dark women and Latinos as exotic and passionate (Brooks 2010; González-López 2006). Asian Americans, when first migrating to the United States, also were constructed as hypersexual (Chua and Fujino 1999). After gaining status through assimilation, Asian immigrants began to be emasculated because they often did "women's work" (e.g., domestic servants, launderers; Chong-suk 2006; Chua and Fujino 1999). As Asian Americans have become the "model" minority in the United States, notions of feminine Asian American men have re-emerged, but now Asian men are constructed as asexual and hence, still subordinate to white men (Chong-suk 2006; Chua and Fujino 1999).

RACIALIZED SEXUALITIES AND THE INTERNET

When Internet access was novel, many scholars believed online spaces would allow for a utopian democratic world without social inequalities or government regulations (for a critique of this view, see Lessig 2006). As such, individuals online could be free from constraining social structures of difference. However, Lessig (2006) argues that online codes that shape the architecture of cyberspaces actually affect and regulate what a cyberspace, like the Internet, offers. Such cyberspaces are products of power and culture, as Nakamura (2001, 2008) reveals that race, gender, and other social categories comprise the codes and structures of these spaces, making social differences salient, not erased.

Some recent quantitative sociological research has revealed that racial preference(s) is a part of online dating. In their study of heterosexual Internet dating profiles on Yahoo Personals, Feliciano, Robnett, and Komaie (2009) found that white men often exclude black women as possible dates, and white women often exclude Asian men as possible dates. In another study from the same data, Robnett and Feliciano (2011) showed that Latino/as are the most included minority group by whites, blacks, and Asians who are looking for dates online. Latino/as are also more likely to prefer to date whites than blacks; however, greater proximity to blacks promotes more acceptance of dating a black person (Feliciano, Lee, and Robnett 2011). In their study of initial contacts and responses on one of the largest online dating websites, Lin and Lundquist (2013) reveal that individuals often contact people of the same racial group but respond to those of equal or more dominant racial status. These quantitative studies have illuminated that racial mechanisms operate in online dating spaces; however, they focus on heterosexual populations and do not reveal *how* or *why* people are making these racial decisions—something I take as a central task in this study.

Accordingly, qualitative studies have begun analyzing racial preferences among online gay populations. For example, as part of people's online profiles and dating advertisements, race is objectified within gay cyberspaces in order to attract others (Paul et al. 2010). Sexual racism like race-specific sexual objectification and race-based sexual stereotyping occurs. Wilson and colleagues (2009:400), in a study of over 100 gay men who use the Internet to look for bareback sex, define race-based sexual stereotyping "as inferred beliefs and expectations about the attributes a sexual experience will take on based on the race of the partner involved in the experience." These race-based sexual stereotypes reflect historical ideologies about bodies of color, especially around sexual roles and behaviors, and erase heterogeneity among racial populations (Robinson 2008; Wilson et al. 2009). Black bodies are fetishized, objectified, and seen as being aggressive and having big penises; Asians are seen as sexually submissive and having small penises; and Latinos are seen as sensual and having uncut penises (Paul et al. 2010; Wilson et al. 2009). . . .

THEORETICAL FRAMEWORK

In her book *Black Sexual Politics,* Patricia Hill Collins (2004) defines the "new racism" as the reinvention of historical ideologies about black sexualities in new ideological forms, which people rely on to justify the discrimination and social exclusion of people of color. This new racism is transnational, based on patterns of corporate organization that created a global economy, and it is disseminated through mass media (Collins 2004). The Internet, as a form of mass media (that is globalized), also creates a space to further manipulate ideas around people of color, including but not limited to black sexualities.

One primary way these ideologies work is through neoliberal discourses around personal preference that normalize racism in cyberspace. *Neoliberalism* is the term used to describe the probusiness, anti-"big government" activism, beginning in the 1970s, where there was an upward redistribution of a range of resources (Duggan 2003). These economic policies influenced

everyday rhetoric, where discourses of individual responsibility began to veil the existence of structural
inequalities. People of color were seen as achieving
legal equality, and racism was constructed as not
existing (Holland 2012). Within the realm of the
erotic, acts like personal preference became seen as
life choices devoid of any racist beliefs. For Holland
(2012) though, racism is still operating, just not
mainly through overt prejudice but through affecting people's psychic lives, where people of different
racial groups are seen as not having the same consciousness. Individuals believe that people of different races have different histories, where the categories
of race keep people from belonging together and recognizing shared histories. These psychic effects limit
human desire as people of certain racial groups are
not even considered possible for an intimate engagement (Holland 2012).

Racialization, racism, and these psychic effects
cannot be understood as isolated social processes.
Sociologist Roderick Ferguson (2004:149) defines a
queer of color critique as an interrogation of "social
formations as the intersections of race, gender, sexuality, and class." These categories are not discrete social
formations, but rather they are bound up with one
another in and through the production of culture
(Ferguson 2004). . . .

In the following, I explore how race becomes constructed as a "personal preference" for the gay men in
this study. Using Holland's (2012) work on everyday
racism, intimacy, and desire, I suggest that this discourse of personal preference is disseminated through
the mass medium of the Internet, and it marks a form
of new racism (Collins 2004). I specifically show how
these neoliberal and homophilous discourses—the
tendency for people to form relationships with other
individuals based on similar statuses and/or values
(Lazarsfeld and Merton 1954)—lead to the objectification of and non-desire toward black and Asian individuals. Through illuminating how the structure
of Adam4Adam.com works in tandem with these
neoliberal and homophilous discourses, I show how
macro structures of racialization and micro interactions
of "personal choice" influence one another to further
an erotic new racism in the digital age. Accordingly,

through utilizing a critical queer of color analysis (Ferguson 2004), I highlight how social exclusionary practices toward certain people of color on Adam4Adam
.com materialize whiteness as the norm, which in
turn reifies heteronormativity.

METHODOLOGY

I present data obtained from 15 in-depth interviews
with self-identified gay, homosexual, and queer
men in an urban city in the Southwest who used
Adam4Adam.com for sexual purposes. I also present
data from a content analysis of 100 profiles in the
same city. All of the men interviewed were between
the ages of 22 to 28. Three men identified as white,
3 identified as white Hispanic,[2] 3 identified as Latino
or Hispanic, 2 identified as black, 1 identified as
black and Latino, 1 identified as Turkish and Greek,
1 identified as Asian, and 1 identified as white and
Indian. They also had a range of educational backgrounds and occupations. . . .

I followed a grounded theory approach to analyze
these texts and used coding (see Charmaz 2006),
where my codes were reflective of the data as closely
as possible, while also examining the action that was
emerging within this cyberspace. I would first examine the demographic characteristics provided by the
men themselves. From there, I would peruse what the
men wrote about themselves in their profiles, paying
particular attention to how they described their personal lives and hobbies as well as their sexual desires
and interests. Through inspecting profiles and interacting with the interface of the website, I became a
"participant-experiencer," where I strove to experience
the website similarly to how other users may experience
it (Garcia et al. 2009). As a participant-experiencer,
I was better informed to draft my interview guide
and engage in a more nuanced interview process with
the men I interviewed as I was more aware about the
particularities of Adam4Adam.com.

. . .

I conducted interviews in person between August
and December of 2012. There was no compensation for
participating in this study; all informants freely volunteered their time to be interviewed. The interviews

lasted around one hour, and they were semi-structured. I recorded the interviews, and later, I transcribed each interview. I then coded these transcriptions following a grounded theory approach. This method allowed my informants to speak for themselves, where I strove to not impose my own theoretical framework but rather, created new insights based on my participants' accounts (Charmaz 2006). . . .

One challenge I encountered with this method was the fact that locating gay men to interview can be difficult. Some people do not specifically identify with these identity categories, or they may be resistant toward scientific research for fear of being portrayed as deviants (Gamson 2000). Also, I was repeatedly flagged for spamming on this website, and I often had my accounts blocked. As Klein and colleagues (2010) suggested, I had other profiles already on hand to continue recruiting individuals when previous accounts were blocked. Eventually, the website barred my IP address, and I had to rely on colleagues to make accounts for me. Recruiting hard-to-reach populations who are using a website for purposes other than being recruited for research (i.e., dating and sex) could partly explain why this study took several months to recruit just 15 participants (for more information on similar issues, see Klein et al. 2010).

My racial identity—as a white person—potentially influenced my interviews. Many of my informants felt quite comfortable disclosing to me their desire for white men and their non-desire for people of color. I do not know if this candid disclosure about racialized desires would have been the same had I been a person of color. I was aware of these consequences and implications while conducting, transcribing, and analyzing the interviews as well as when I examined and wrote about each one of the findings.

FINDINGS

"I USUALLY JUST FILTER IT DOWN": CLEANSING CYBERSPACE

"Like since there is the filter thing that like lets you go by age, I usually just filter it down to like 18. I think I go up to 30, and then mainly just people

that I think are attractive," explained Raj, a 22-year-old self-identified half white and half Indian college student. Tanner, a 25-year-old white public relations worker, stated, "I would always set my filters to I think 20 to 32. I would look for white, Latino, or Middle Eastern men. And I don't remember if there were further fields. Oh, I wanted somebody who was nearby but not next-door; so I would set my search to the region that I was in." When a user makes his profile on Adam4Adam.com, he is required to fill out certain demographics to even inhabit the space. Salient characteristics such as ethnicity,[3] body size, age, height, and weight are *required* to be filled out from a drop-down menu, tacitly telling users that these demographics matter the most within this space if one wants to present their desirable self. Lessig (2006:83–84) describes users' behaviors and experiences online as "regulated" by codes and infrastructures of cyberspaces: "Regulated in the sense that bars on a prison regulate the movement of a prisoner, or regulated in the sense that stairs regulate the access of the disabled." The profile construction feature of Adam4Adam.com regulates how users must present themselves, limiting how people and desire are being constructed within this space. Accordingly, the website also places a further value judgment on certain demographics based upon its "quick search" feature. Through turning on this feature, users can choose to see only men within a certain age range and of a particular race or races, constructing these two social categories as the most important factors of desirability as they are the only two demographics that the space allows for one to filter.[4]

In his study of around 500 Los Angeles profiles on Adam4Adam.com and through interacting with other users with multiple profiles, Russell Robinson (2008) theorizes that race-based searching for online sexual partners may be impacting users' reification of white desirability. By showing how the gay men in this study are actually using this "quick search" feature, I empirically build off of Robinson's (2008) predictions about how these search engines may be affecting users' notions of desirability. Koby, Raj, and Tanner did not discuss hair color or one's attire as important to desirability; rather, they discussed the very same demographics that the website highlights the most—race and age. As Nakamura (2008) explains, racial identity is part of a user's self-representational online practices, especially in sites like Adam4Adam .com, which requires users to mark their own race to even inhabit the space. . . .

Tito, a 23-year-old self-identified white Hispanic who works in information technology, filters "from 18 to 39," and he selects to see "all races except black." Tito felt that this filter system on Adam4Adam.com set it apart from other gay dating applications like Grindr (which does not have a filter system) because it "allows you to just see your interests." Not only does race and age become visibly marked as the prime demographics of desirability with this space, but also the ability to filter out or to exclude certain races and ages when inhabiting Adam4Adam.com is viewed as a positive feature of the site.

Nonetheless, as Raj points out, "I've found people from all races attractive. I don't necessarily find like all black men attractive, but I've found some attractive at least. So you should be at least open to the possibility of that happening." Black men get named and marked as a group that is often not desirable for Raj; in stating that he finds *some* black men attractive, Raj marks this desire for black men as outside of his normative desires. However, Raj feels that people should be open to the possibility of finding certain people within a race as desirable, even if people do not generally find that race attractive.

People can choose to only search for white bodies within dating and hookup cyberspaces, never having to view a non-white body online (Robinson 2008). Russell Robinson (2008) argues that if white users were forced to see bodies of color in these spaces, they may find some of them desirable—something that Raj recognized as well. However, with this new cybernetic racial exclusion, Robinson (2008) ponders how whiteness can be left as the stable norm. Through the everyday practice of using the search feature on this site—a search feature that is premised on social inclusion and exclusion—users can erase and cleanse people of color through a simple click on the screen. As structures affect one's desires, website's designs

are impacting users' racial preferences (Robinson 2008; Wilson et al. 2009). . . .

"PEOPLE HAVE THEIR TURN-ONS AND TURN-OFFS": RACE AS A PERSONAL PREFERENCE

Before moving to the Southwest, Tanner went to college in New York City (NYC). His description of Adam4Adam.com and the people who use Adam4Adam.com in NYC reveals how racial stereotypes often operate in the gay imagination of desire:

TANNER: You had to cross the river to oftentimes visit the people on Adam4Adam. Manhunt [a paid subscription gay dating and hookup website] was more for the people in the city [Manhattan]. Manhunt was more lower-island—SoHo, Tribeca, the Villages, Chelsea. And Adam4Adam was really above 150th street; so like way up there or over in Brooklyn or even Queens. So it was just Manhunt was where you went for people in Manhattan who are white and not into weird kinky things—if that makes sense.

INTERVIEWER: And then Adam4adam was seen as . . . ?

TANNER: If you want to get fisted, you went on Adam4Adam, or if you had a Latino flair or something.

INTERVIEWER: There are more people of color on there?

TANNER: Yeah.

In Tanner's description of the different people who occupy different websites, one can understand how "personal preference" is shaped by and through race-based sexual stereotypes. Race-based sexual stereotypes erase people of color's individual traits (e.g., hobbies, sexual interests) that should be more important in whom one wants to date or have sex with. In NYC, Tanner preferred to pay for a subscription on Manhunt.net to connect with white people who were "not into weird kinky things." Bodies of color or white people who desire people of color (those who have "a Latino flair") get conflated with hypersexuality and kink (e.g., fisting). Whiteness gets associated with "proper" sexuality, where people of color and their admirers get relegated to being dirty, immoral, and perverse (Owens 2004). . . .

More specifically, Acar and Koby talked about not desiring black and Asian individuals, which also revealed the cultural associations and racialized sexual stereotypes that were operating underneath this personal preference discourse. "I can say that I have never had sex with Asian people and black people. It doesn't mean anything. It's just like, you know, people have their turn-ons and turn-offs," stated Acar, a 26-year-old Turkish-Greek graduate student. Koby held a similar view:

> I am open to all races, though I have a more—I don't want to say discriminate—but I do discriminate, I guess, against blacks. But not like discriminating in a bad way, it's just like, I don't have, I'm not attracted to black men. However, I have been attracted to like half-black and then all the other races are fine. I generally don't go toward Asians either.

Similar to Robnett and Feliciano's (2011) findings, social distancing through Internet dating is not just directed from white people toward black individuals, but it operates between and among people of color as well. Both Acar and Koby found Asian and black men to be undesirable. As previous research has shown, black and Asian men typically are abjected to the lowest realms of erotic racial preferences—black individuals for being seen as hypersexual and Asian men for being seen as asexual (Paul et al. 2010; Wilson et al. 2009). Acar and Koby do not see these racial desires as discrimination—"it doesn't mean anything." However, in not wanting to "go toward" black or Asian men, race becomes significant in these men's lives.

It is important to understand how race is marked as well as glossed over through the discourse of personal preference in order to uncover the cultural beliefs that are influencing these interpersonal and psychic desires. Directly before telling me his racial preferences, Acar told me that he only talks to people on Adam4Adam.com who seem "educated," "smart," "clean-cut," and "put together." The stereotype of being uneducated is often associated with dark skin (Maddox and Gray 2002), revealing how this

educational assumption may actually be driving Acar's "personal preference" to not talk to black men on Adam4Adam.com. Likewise, notions of "clean-cut" often get used to describe muscular, groomed, All-American men (Hokowhitu 2004; Malin 2003). Because of racialized sexual stereotypes, certain people of color are not part of this imaginary, as Asian men are typically not seen as being muscular, and black men are often not seen as being All-American—something often conflated with whiteness.

Likewise, Koby told me that he talks to people on Adam4Adam.com who "like the outdoors . . . kayaking . . . hiking . . . those are the ones that really draw me towards them." Asian bodies, as stereotypically emasculated, may not be associated with interests in these outdoor sporting activities. Likewise, black individuals are underrepresented in class-based sporting activities such as kayaking, where stereotypical assumptions about white people being more intelligent, and hence able to excel at certain sports, has been the dominant discourse (Hodge et al. 2008). Ideas about class, intelligence, bodies, and similar interests in hobbies are bound up within Koby's personal racial preferences. Also, right after telling me about his racial preferences, Koby also talked about how he is afraid of contracting HIV with men on the website. He told me that an individual has "to be careful with whom you are sleeping with" because people have "hidden agendas." Since Koby has only met up with white people from Adam4Adam.com, Koby appears to only trust that (at least some) white people are safe and do not have hidden agendas. Stereotypes of black men as hypersexual compounded with the disproportionate HIV infection rates among black men who have sex with men (Millett et al. 2006; even though these infection rates are not because black men engage in higher frequencies of "risky" sexual behaviors compared to other racial groups of men) may make black men seem unsafe to Koby.

Accordingly, Darryl, a 24-year-old African American underwriter, also used the word *discriminate* when describing how he interacts with black men on Adam4Adam.com: "I guess, hooking up–wise, I don't discriminate racially. I've only hooked up with one black person though. . . . I would date a black person before I would hook up with a black person. I don't know why, I just, something tells me to just stay away from skinny gay black boys that like to get fucked." This reference of staying away from "skinny gay black boys" may be linked to effeminacy as Darryl connects skinny to getting fucked or being penetrated during sex. This construction of effeminacy would make these men as not desirable [sic] for Darryl as he prefers "tall" men with "a good build," and he often sleeps with self-identified heterosexual, married men. This construction of the effeminate black man is outside the construction of the imaginary black "top," potentially making the effeminate black gay man even more abject than this other racialized sexual stereotype. Darryl also mostly engages in condomless anal sex, and he is adamant about only sleeping with people who he believes to be "clean." In this regard, like Koby, black men may be seen as unclean, so Darryl wants to date a black man to build trust, where Darryl already trusts that white men are telling the truth about being clean since he sleeps with them without having to date them.

Furthermore, Darryl talked about his experiences of black men messaging him on Adam4Adam.com: "The guys that pretty much hit me up are black—which is interesting. I don't know why I just said it was interesting. To me, it's interesting because [Darryl whispers] I don't really hook up with black people." Cisco, a 24-year-old Latino artist, also gave a detailed account of his thoughts on black men trying to talk to him on the website:

> Every so often it's the African Americans who hit me up, only because apparently I'm the Latino that they like. And I'm like, "I don't care; I really don't care. But you seem like a nice guy, I'll keep talking to you." And I keep mentioning that "I will not have fucking sex with you, just so you know." And they keep hinting and hinting, and I'm like "No dude, I'm not going to have sex with you."

Darryl, who is black, finds it "interesting" that black people contact him, as he is not interested in having sex with them, so it "never goes anywhere" because he is interested in white and Latino men. However, as Lin and Lundquist (2013) reveal, most

(heterosexual) online daters often contact people of the same race first. It is not surprising then that black people mainly contact Darryl, where Darryl even has to "initiate the first contact" with a white or Latino person whom he wants to hook up with. Nonetheless, Darryl does not like being contacted by black men, though they may only be contacting him because it is hard for black men, including Darryl himself, to make contact with non-black people on the website (Robinson 2008).

In Cisco's (who identifies as Latino) narrative, black people again get conflated with hypersexuality. Although Cisco, as well as all of the other men in this study except for Tanner, is looking for friendship on Adam4Adam.com, he describes his interactions with black individuals on the website solely in sexual terms. These black individuals get constructed as constantly pestering him about having sex, where Cisco has to constantly remind black men that he will talk to them, but he will not have sex with them. . . .

My informants saw black and Asian individuals as the least desirable. The larger structures and cultural assumptions of desirability that ideologically construct black men as hypersexual, uneducated, and unclean or Asian men as asexual and emasculated (Chong-suk 2006; Davis 2003; Smith 2005) demotes these individuals to a lower realm of desirability, though this interpersonal discrimination is glossed over by this personal preference discourse. Notably, Latino men, who are often seen as hypersexual and exotic (Brooks 2010; González-López 2006), were not treated in the same ways as black and Asian men. This explanation may be twofold. As Feliciano and colleagues (2011) found, when people were in greater proximity to black individuals, people accepted dating black individuals more. Likewise, this study took place in a city that is over 35 percent Latino/a; this greater proximity to Latino/as may be shaping some gay men's desire. Also, Latino/as have been the most included out-group for white online daters, where Latino/as may be seen as "honorary whites" (Feliciano et al. 2009; Robnett and Feliciano 2011). New ways of thinking about Latino/as, skin tone, proximity, and other social factors that may influence how Latino/a sexualities are racialized may be warranted.

"I'm So Aryan with My Sexual Preferences": Desiring Whiteness

"But it worried me that I was so into white-bread. Basically, I love white boys and blondes in particular. I'm so Aryan with my sexual preferences; it freaks me out a little bit," states Riley as he describes his taste for white men to me. Riley, who is a 24-year-old white college student, continues this talk by mentioning how he did have sex with many men of color: "So I really wanted to test that and just make myself get out of my comfort zone. And I basically did that while I was in college. And so I had sex with lots of different types of people and different types of men, and found that I was most comfortable where I started—with white boys." Riley's reflections on his erotic racial preference reveal two key things when it comes to race and sexuality: consumption and comfort.

. . .

Such a process of ending up where Riley started engenders notions of homophily, dating, and attraction. In their review of the literature on homophily, McPherson, Smith-Lovin, and Cook (2001) found that residential proximity is the number one predictor of homophily. Being around similar others actually shapes one's attraction to these similar others. Although there may be a breakdown of environmental constraints in online spaces, offline effects of homophily can still affect online choices with whom to contact and connect (Skopek, Schulz, and Blossfeld 2011). This finding is revealed in this study as well. The gay white men I interviewed, despite having access to meeting a variety of people on Adam4Adam.com, preferred to meet other white men.

. . .

Of the 100 profiles I analyzed for this research, 0 percent stated they were seeking explicitly a non-white race unless it was coupled with also seeking white men. On the contrary, a white preference was often mentioned within people's profiles as the desired race, regardless of the race of the user. As one profile explicates, he "usually only [hooks ups] with white guys." The text of this person's profile then goes on to talk more about himself and his hobbies right after defining himself through the people whom he desires. Another user is "into tall, lean, fit white

and Hispanic guys, in their late twenties to thirties"; he also enjoys traveling, cooking, and other activities. A racial preference becomes named and labeled alongside of activity preferences, where one should share a similar interest and race.

Several other examples include:

Mostly into white guys 21–40-sorry just a preference.

Into WHITE guys. Sorry just my preference. Like guys . . . close to my age. Not into fats or fems! Like real men!

INTO ALL KINDS OF MEN BUT MOSTLY LATINOS AND WHITES 18 TO 40

There are no stereotypes associated with these white men; rather, they represent the norm of beauty by which bodies of color are judged (Wilson et al. 2009). These users do not desire a particular whiteness (e.g., a white top) but just whiteness itself. One defines one's self as white (and/or as seeking whiteness), marking whiteness as the most desired racial category within this space.

Just as marking non-white races as undesirable is normalized through the discourse of personal preference, so too is whiteness marked as desirable within a similar neoliberal logic of "just a preference." Owens (2004) found in her study on race, sexual attractiveness, and Internet personals that when a user did not explicitly desire a particular race, then he or she would mention one's hobbies as a way to find similar others. On Adam4Adam.com, the story is different. People of color are defined through race-based stereotypes; on the contrary, white individuals can be seen as having hobbies. . . . This discourse around having similar activity and racial preferences masks the larger structures that shape one's desires, as it normalizes whiteness, linking it to attributes like cooking, which potentially increases one's desirability.

Some of my non-white informants explicitly discussed this naming and marking of whiteness. Tito, who lived in Miami before moving to the Southwest, stated that he now finds white men as the "most interesting" because they are "a novelty here" as he claims hardly any white men existed where he lived in Florida. Likewise, Cisco tersely stated, "Honestly, my attraction is mainly white men, so I usually click on white [men's profiles]." Darryl also said, "Yeah, so I prefer to date any race. Hooking up, pretty much white or Hispanic-Latinos."

White people, when compared to people of color, are far more likely to date within their own race (Robnett and Feliciano 2011). In fact, race is one of the main selection criteria white users look for on dating websites—more important than education or religious preferences (Feliciano et al. 2009). . . . Social distancing and the exclusion of black and Asian people from people's dating and sexual preferences happen by people of color as well (Robnett and Feliciano 2011). Both Tito and Cisco, as Latinos, and Darryl, as a black man, desire white men mostly. This desire for whiteness is not seen within a larger structure that values whiteness as the hegemonic beauty standard, but rather, it is again "just a preference." It masks its racial mechanics through neoliberal and homophilous discourses around "choice," "preference," and/or "my comfort zone." The Internet gives a space for this new racism to be expressed without any social repercussions because it is seen as a normal part of online dating.

DISCUSSION

Structures of inequality and cultural assumptions limit erotic desire. On Adam4Adam.com, which has a similar interface as most dating and hookup websites, these interactions take on new forms. . . . Racialization becomes a digital process (Nakamura 2008), where a person is read not by their skin tone (and the phenotype associated with it), but literally is read by the naming of race through the drop-down menu choice that appears in a user's profile. Users in this space further this racialization process when they only search for a particular race through the website's "quick search" feature. . . .

Aside from the structure of the website, users also use the neoliberal personal preference discourse to mask over how cultural assumptions affect their interpersonal and psychic desires. This personal preference is a form of new racism, where the Internet allows for a space to openly disclose these racist remarks but not

see them as racist. However, this choice is not independent of the larger structures that stereotype non-white sexuality as abnormal (Robinson 2008; Wilson et al. 2009). . . . This new racism works in tandem with the psychic erotic life of racism. As Holland (2012) theorized, race keeps people from belonging together because they feel each race has its own shared history, and therefore, people think that different races cannot relate. Empirically building on these claims, I revealed how cultural assumptions (often based on Collins's [2004] new racism but in conjunction with other stereotypes and potential shared histories) affected people's interpersonal and psychic desires. However, moving beyond Holland's claims, these desires, even among some people of color on Adam4Adam .com, were often directed toward whiteness, where whiteness may be revealed as the race to which people desire to belong. This desire for whiteness may affect how people of color are treated in this space. . . .

This erotic life of racism also does not allow my informants to see these racialized desires as potentially discriminatory, masking the larger white, hetero-patriarchal discourses that are influencing people's intimate lives. Utilizing a queer of color critique (Ferguson 2004), I suggest that these racial-specific sexual desires reconstruct larger heteronormative discourses about "proper" sexualities. Cultural assumptions and racialized sexual stereotypes of people of color being hypersexual and/or unclean are often heteronormative stereotypes used against gay men in general, regardless of race. Therefore, although discrimination based on racial characteristics organizes inequality within gay communities and selectively privileges some of their members, the racial exclusionary practices on Adam4Adam.com reify a larger structure—heteronormativity—and discourses that have traditionally marginalized those who are not heterosexual. . . . The ways in which white supremacy and heteronormativity work in tandem need to be exposed in order for all people to have the same potential in finding friends and partners online and for a queer politics to (re-)emerge for alliances to be built across all groups who are marginalized under white hetero-patriarchy (Cohen 1997; Ferguson 2004).

LIMITATIONS AND CONCLUSIONS

. . .

This study contributes to the literature on the Internet and race in gay men's lives. In combining Patricia Hill Collins's (2004) ideas around the new racism with Sharon Holland's (2012) conception of the quotidian aspects of racism and the erotic, this study has shown how racism has become digital and normalized in online gay dating spaces. As a pioneer empirical exploration of a website's filtering system, this piece suggests that the structure of a U.S.-based website may make cleansing racial bodies pedestrian and non-discriminatory. These new forms of racism are so ingrained in people's daily practices on these websites that the larger macro issues become effaced, reifying the hegemonic structures of inequality in society. . . . The racialized sexual stratification furthered through these discourses, as well as the structure of the website, need to be challenged in order for people of color to be seen as individuals and potential partners on dating and hookup websites. Seeing people of color as individuals will not only challenge white supremacy but also its complementary power structure heteronormativity.

NOTES

1. In line with Collins (2004), I do not put race or other social categories in quotation marks, as I take that all are socially constructed and none are necessarily more constructed than others.
2. I use the term *white Hispanic* only when referring to the three informants who directly stated this description as their racial identity. The use of the term *white Hispanic* is often traced to the U.S. Census, which creates racial and ethnic categories (Allen 1999). As Theodore Allen (1999) shows, the U.S. Census generated the categories "Hispanic" and "non-Hispanic" as an ethnic categorization separate from the race one could choose to identify with on the census. Latino/as have often contested this ethnic labeling, and many have self-identified as a racial group (Almaguer 2003). Identification of white Hispanic among my informants may point to the residual effects of this census classification that classified all Latino/as as an ethnic population (i.e., as Hispanics) who could have a

variation of phenotypes. Likewise, this identification with "whiteness" among three of my Latino informants also points to the diversity, discrimination, and tensions based on skin color within communities of color. Skin color still operates as a marker of access, treatment, and privilege, even among Latino/a populations (Vidal-Ortiz 2004); therefore, this identification as a white Hispanic may be a way to differentiate one's self from dark-skinned Latino/as or other people of color, in hopes of securing some rights in a racist society.

3. Adam4Adam.com labels racial categories as ethnicity.
4. On the Adam4Adam.com mobile application, age and ethnicity are still demographics that can be filtered, along with other nonrequired demographic information such as HIV status, looking for, practice, sexual role, scene, and dick size. Although this research project set out to examine the website Adam4Adam.com, many users also mentioned having the mobile application on their phone. However, of the demographics that all users are required to fill out, race and age are still the only two that can be filtered.

REFERENCES

Allen, Theodore W. 1999. "'Race' and Ethnicity': History of the 200 Census." *Cultural Logic: An Electronic Journal of Marxist Theory & Practice* 3(1). Retrieved August 1, 2014 (http://clogic.eserver.org/3-1%262/allen.html).

Almaguer, Tomás. 2003. "At the Crossroads of Race: Latino/a Studies and Race Making in the United States." Pp. 206–22 in *Critical Latin American and Latino Studies,* edited by J. Poblete. Minneapolis: University of Minnesota Press.

Bérubé, Allan. 2001. "How Gay Stays White and What Kind of White It Stays." Pp. 234–65 in *The Making and Unmaking of Whiteness,* edited by B. B. Rasmussen, E. Klinenberg, I. J. Nexica, and M. Wray. Durham, NC: Duke University Press.

Brooks, Siobhan. 2010. "Hypersexualization and the Dark Body: Race and Inequality among Black and Latina Women in the Exotic Dance Industry." *Sexuality Research & Social Policy* 7:70–80.

Caluya, Gilbert. 2008. "'The Rice Steamer': Race, Desire, and Affect in Sydney's Gay Scene." *Australian Geographer* 39(3):283–92.

Cantú, Jr., Lionel. 2009. *The Sexuality of Migration: Border Crossing and Mexican Immigrant Men.* Edited by N. A. Naples and S. Vidal-Ortiz. New York: NYU Press.

Charmaz, Kathy. 2006. *Constructing Grounded Theory: A Practical Guide through Qualitative Analysis.* Los Angeles: Sage.

Chong-suk, Han. 2006. "Being an Oriental, I Could Never Be Completely a Man: Gay Asian Men and the Intersection of Race, Gender, Sexuality, and Class." *Race, Gender & Class* 3/4:82–97.

Chua, Peter and Diana C. Fujino. 1999. "Negotiating Asian-American Masculinities: Attitudes and Gender Expectations." *The Journal of Men's Studies* 7(3):391–413.

Cohen, Cathy J. 1997. "Punk, Bulldaggers, and Welfare Queer: The Radical Potential of Queer Politics?" *GLQ* 3:437–65.

Collins, Patricia Hill. 2002. "The Sexual Politics of Black Womanhood." Pp. 193–206 in *Sexuality and Gender*, edited by C. Williams and A. Stein. Malden, MA: Blackwell Publishers.

Collins, Patricia Hill. 2004. *Black Sexual Politics: African Americans, Gender, and the New Racism.* New York: Routledge.

Davis, Angela. 2003. "Rape, Racism and the Myth of the Black Rapist." Pp. 575–82 in *Race, Gender, and Sexuality: Philosophical Issues of Identity and Justice*, edited by J. L. Anderson. Upper Saddle River, NJ: Prentice Hall.

Dawley, Heidi. 2007. "Among Gay Sites, All the Talk Is Global: It's a Race to Be the World's No. 1 Destination." *Media Life Magazine,* March 26. Retrieved June 26, 2013 (http://www.medialifemagazine.com/among-gay-sites-all-the-talk-is-global/).

Duggan, Lisa. 2003. *The Twilight of Equality? Neoliberalism, Cultural Politics, and the Attack on Democracy.* Boston: Beacon Press.

Feliciano, Cynthia, Rennie Lee, and Belinda Robnett. 2011. "Racial Boundaries among Latinos: Evidence from Internet Daters' Racial Preferences." *Social Problems* 58(2):189–212.

Feliciano, Cynthia, Belinda Robnett, and Golnaz Komaie. 2009. "Gendered Racial Exclusion among White Internet Daters." *Social Science Research* 38:39–54.

Ferguson, Roderick A. 2004. *Aberrations in Black: Toward a Queer of Color Critique.* Minneapolis: University of Minnesota Press.

Gamson, Joshua. 2000. "Sexualities, Queer Theory, and Qualitative Research." Pp. 347–65 in *The Landscape of Qualitative Research: Theories and Issues*, edited by Norman K. Denzin & Yvonna S. Lincoln. London: Sage.

Garcia, Angela Cora, Alecea I. Standlee, Jennifer Bechkoff, and Yan Cui. 2009. "Ethnographic Approaches to the Internet and Computer-mediated Communication." *Journal of Contemporary Ethnography* 38(1):52–84.

Gates, Gary J. 2012. *Same-sex Couples in Census 2010: Race and Ethnicity.* Los Angeles: Williams Institute, UCLA School of Law.

González-López, Gloria. 2006. "Heterosexual Fronteras: Immigrant Mexicanos, Sexual Vulnerabilities, and Survival." *Sexuality Research & Social Policy* 3(3):67–81.

Hodge, Samuel R., Louis Harrison, Jr., Joe W. Burden, Jr., and Adrienne D. Dixson. 2008. "Brown in Black and White—Then and Now: A Question of Educating or Sporting African American Males in America." *American Behavioral Scientist* 51(7):928–52.

Hokowhitu, Brendan. 2004. "Tackling Māori Masculinity: A Colonial Genealogy of Savagery and Sport." *The Contemporary Pacific* 16(2):259–84.

Holland, Sharon Patricia. 2012. *The Erotic Life of Racism.* Durham, NC: Duke University Press.

hooks, bell. 1992. "Eating the Other." Pp. 21–39 in *Black Looks: Race and Representation.* Boston: South End Press.

Klein, Hugh. 2009. "Differences in HIV Risk Practices Sought by Self-identified Gay and Bisexual Men Who Use Internet Websites to Identify Potential Sexual Partners." *Journal of Bisexuality* 9:125–40.

Klein, Hugh, Thomas P. Lambing, David A. Moskowitz, Thomas Alex Washington, and Lisa K. Gilbert. 2010. "Recommendations for Performing Internet-based Research on Sensitive Subject Matter with 'Hidden' or Difficult-to-reach Populations." *Journal of Gay & Lesbian Social Services* 22(4):371–98.

Kurdek, Lawrence A. 2003. "Differences between Gay and Lesbian Cohabiting Couples." *Journal of Social and Personal Relationships* 20(4):411–36.

Lazarsfeld, Paul F. and Robert K. Merton. 1954. "Friendship as a Social Process: A Substantive and Methodological Analysis." Pp. 18–66 in *Freedom and Control in Modern Society*, edited by M. Berger, T. Abel, and C. H. Page. New York: Van Nostrand.

Lessig, Lawerence. 2006. *Code: Version 2.0.* New York: Basic Books.

Lin, Ken-Hou and Jennifer Lundquist. 2013. "Mate Selection in Cyberspace: The Intersection of Race, Gender, and Education." *American Journal of Sociology* 119(1):183–215.

Lodge, Amy C. and Debra Umberson. 2013. "Age and Embodied Masculinities: Midlife Gay and Hetero-sexual Men Talk about Their Bodies." *Journal of Aging Studies* 27:225–32.

Maddox, Keith B. and Stephanie A. Gray. 2002. "Cognitive Representations of Black Americans: Reexploring the

Role of Skin Tone." *Personality and Social Psychology Bulletin* 28(2):250–59.

Malin, Brent. 2003. "Memorializing White Masculinity: The Late 1990s 'Crisis of Masculinity' and the 'Subversive Performance' of Man on the Moon." *Journal of Communication Inquiry* 27(3):239–55.

McKittrick, Katherine. 2010. "Science Quarrels Sculpture: The Politics of Reading Sarah Baartman." *Mosaic* 43(2):113–30.

McPherson, Miller, Lynn Smith-Lovin, and James M. Cook. 2001. "Birds of a Feather: Homophily in Social Networks." *Annual Review of Sociology* 27:415–44.

Millett, Gregorio A., John L. Peterson, Richard J. Wolitski, and Ron Stall. 2006. "Greater Risk for HIV Infection of Black Men Who Have Sex with Men: A Critical Literature Review." *American Journal of Public Health* 96(6):1007–19.

Nakamura, Lisa. 2001. "Head Hunting in Cyberspace." *The Women's Review of Books* 18(5):10–11.

Nakamura, Lisa. 2008. "Cyberrace." *Publications of the Modern Language Association of America* 123(5):1673–82.

Omi, Michael and Howard Winant. 1994. *Racial Formation in the United States: From the 1960s to the 1990s.* 2nd ed. New York: Routledge.

Owens, Erica. 2004. "Race, Sexual Attractiveness, and Internet Personal Advertisements." Pp. 217–34 in *Net. SeXXX: Readings on Sex, Pornography, and the Internet,* edited by D. Waskul. New York: Peter Lang.

Padilla, Mark. 2007. *Caribbean Pleasure Industry: Tourism, Sexuality, and AIDS in the Dominican Republic.* Chicago: The University of Chicago Press.

Paul, Jay P., George Ayala, and Kyung-Hee Choi. 2010. "Internet Sex Ads for MSM and Partner Selection Criteria: The Potency of Race/Ethnicity Online." *Journal of Sex Research* 47(6):528–38.

Rawlins, Claudia, Julie Indvik, and Pamela R. Johnson. 2008. "Understanding the New Generation: What the

Millennial Cohort Absolutely, Positively Must Have at Work." *Journal of Organizational Culture, Communications and Conflict* 12(2):1–8.

Robinson, Russell K. 2008. "Structural Dimensions of Romantic Preferences." *Fordham Law Review* 76:2787–819.

Robnett, Belinda and Cynthia Feliciano. 2011. "Patters of Racial-ethnic Exclusion by Internet Daters." *Social Forces* 89(3):807–28.

Rosenfeld, Michael J. and Rueben J. Thomas. 2012. "Searching for a Mate: The Rise of the Internet as a Social Intermediary." *American Sociological Review* 77(4):523–47.

Schwartz, Christine R. and Nikki L. Graf. 2009. "Assortative Matching among Same-sex and Different-sex Couples in the United States, 1990–2000." *Demographic Research* 21:843–78.

Skopek, Jan, Florian Schulz, and Hans-Peter Blossfeld. 2011. "Who Contacts Whom? Educational Homophily in Online Mate Selection." *European Sociological Review* 27(2):180–95.

Smith, Andrea. 2005. *Conquest: Sexual Violence and American Indian Genocide.* Cambridge, MA: South End Press.

Steinbugler, Amy C. 2012. *Beyond Loving: Intimate Racework in Lesbian, Gay, and Straight Interracial Relationships.* Oxford: Oxford University Press.

Vidal-Ortiz, Salvador. 2004. "On Being a White Person of Color: Using Autoethnography to Understand Puerto Ricans' Racialization." *Qualitative Sociology* 27(2):179–203.

Wilson, Patrick A., Pamela Valera, Ana Ventuneac, Ivan Balan, Matt Rowe, and Alex Carballo-Dieguez. 2009. "Race-based Sexual Stereotyping and Sexual Partnering among Men Who Use the Internet to Identify other Men for Bareback Sex." *Journal of Sex Research* 46(5):399–413.

41 • *C. J. Pascoe*

RESOURCE AND RISK: YOUTH SEXUALITY AND NEW MEDIA USE

DISCUSSION QUESTIONS

1. Despite societal fears often to the contrary, Pascoe's findings indicate that technology can be a very useful tool for teens navigating sexuality. Do you agree?
2. How do online media allow teens to forge deeper emotional connections than would not otherwise be possible?
3. Could social media be an integral/useful method for teaching sexual education for this generation?

Cautionary tales about young people's sexuality and their new media use permeate the daily news cycle. These stories feature teens meeting strangers online for sexual adventures, posting risqué pictures of themselves on their social network sites, and sending semi-nude self-portraits via their cell phones, inspiring parental fear about seemingly permanent digital footprints and social repercussions. The story of Jesse Logan emblemizes these cautionary tales. Jesse, a high school student from Cincinnati, Ohio sent nude photos of herself to her boyfriend via her cell phone. After they broke up, he forwarded the stored photos to other girls at their high school. These girls relentlessly harassed Jesse, and eventually she was so distraught she committed suicide (Celizic 2010). Stories like this one and countless others about teens meeting older adults for sexual liaisons, the presence of on-line sex predators, and accounts of cyberbullying reinforce messages directed at adults (and teens) that

adolescents are out of control, making poor decisions about their bodies, and that new media and teen sexuality are a combustible and dangerous mix.

During the 2 years I researched youth use of new media, I rarely heard stories from youth themselves that resembled these cautionary tales. Instead the young people with whom I spoke frequently shared stories like the following. Seventeen-year-old Josh said as soon as he gets out of the shower in the morning, he turns on his "PC, log[s] on to MSN,[1] and talk[s] to Alice," his girlfriend of 1 year. After logging off instant messaging, the couple frequently talk on their mobile phones as they commute to school. During the school day, they trade text messages such as "Im in da band room" about their whereabouts and plans. They use the phone to coordinate their activities and sometimes to arrange a private space away from adult supervision to "hook up." One text message interchange read as follows:

Pascoe, C. J. "Resource and Risk: Youth Sexuality and New Media Use." *Sexuality Research and Social Policy*, Vol. 8, No. 1 (Mar 2011): 5–17. Copyright © 2011, Springer Science + Business Media, LLC.

JOSH: I dunno if ne thing could happen my bro is going to be home.;_;

ALICE: I have a car. We can go somewhere.

JOSH: Sure.

ALICE: You choose destination. 123 not it!

JOSH: What time should I get there?

JOSH: I'm walking home now.

JOSH: Should I walk to ur house?

Several hours after he sent that final question, Josh wrote, referring to their meeting, "That was so good." After school Alice might join Josh at his house, completing her homework while he plays his favorite video game, Final Fantasy, or they might continue to communicate by sending messages such as "I'll be here for a while, go to sleep, I love you." While sexuality is part of their daily technology practices in that they seek out private spaces for physical intimacy, Josh and Alice's story sounds relatively tame compared to the ominous tales repeated by news outlets about teenagers, sexuality, and new media. Alice and Josh do text about sex (a practice some might consider "sexting"), but this sex takes place in the confines of a committed relationship. Both are highly concerned about safer sex practices. . . . This story and others like it provide a counterpoint to the parade of dangerous and irresponsible practices regularly featured in media releases about adolescence, sexuality, and new media use.

These stories represent two schools of thought regarding young people and new media. Policy makers, scholars, and pundits tend to cluster into two camps about youth technology use: boosters and detractors (Holloway and Valentine 2003; Thurlow and McKay 2003). Boosters tend to hype the educational (and economic) possibilities of increased media literacy, claiming that new media helps youth learn, makes them responsible citizens, and augments their social lives (Holloway and Valentine 2003; Livingstone 2002). Detractors are usually concerned about the same level of knowledge and use, arguing that new media

renders young people more vulnerable to predators, leads to social isolation, ruins concentration, and exposes youth to adult themes at early ages (Holloway and Valentine 2003; Livingstone 2002; Osgerby 2004; Thurlow and McKay 2003). Both factions highlight very real possibilities of new media. . . . As Thurlow and Bell (2009) argues [sic], "Whether young people are being lauded as 'wired whizzes' or pilloried as 'techno-slaves,' invariably overlooked is the situated, meaningful, and creative nature of their communicative practices." In other words, amidst the fervent claims, what is it that youth are actually doing in mediated environments and what role do these practices play in their daily social, romantic and sexual lives?

This paper address Thurlow's concern about the situatedness of youth new media practices. Looking at youth new media use in their social, romantic, and sexual lives indicates that new media technologies offer resources *and* pose risks for teens in their romance and sexuality practices. New media provide communication resources with which to seek out, build, and end intimate relationships. Online venues also provide important resources for information about issues of gender, sexuality, and relationships. That said, the online world is not without its dangers. Often these dangers are framed as issues of sexting or unwanted sexual attention from unfamiliar adults. However, this paper makes the case that it is necessary to pay attention to other, less sensational risks, in the ways that offline inequalities might be replicated in online environments. That is, inequalities in access and use might shape youth's sexual and social experiences as online venues and access to them might reflect offline inequalities in gender, sexuality, and class.

METHODS

The data in this paper are drawn from a multi-year, multi-site, collaborative ethnographic research project examining youth and new media use across a range of ages and locations. It comprised 28 researchers and research associates conducting 23 case studies. For a further description of the larger research project and approach, please see *Hanging Out, Messing Around and Geeking Out* (Ito et al. 2009).

This paper draws from interviews, diary studies, and ethnography with youth between the ages of 15 and 19 from across the USA. The research for this project included on- and off-line research. I conducted 40 interviews, 33 of which were performed in person and seven of which were conducted online. In these interviews, I asked respondents to discuss their regular new media use; examined their cell phones for calls, text messages, and pictures; visited their favorite web pages; and discussed their social network site profiles and other digital creations.

I also conducted nine diary studies with a subset of the interview subjects in which they were asked to keep track of their daily new media use. These diary studies consisted of youth taking pictures of technology every time they used it and then sending me an SMS message about what they were doing, who they were doing it with, and the length of time they engaged in that activity. They completed this diary study over the course of 48 hours. I then interviewed them about the contents of their diary. Because some new media use occurs when youth are alone, this approach helped to provide access to those more private realms of technological practice.

I recruited participants through online social networks, offline social circles, email lists, snowball sampling, and through classes at two northern California high schools. I also conducted 6 months of observation at the California Digital Arts School, often "hanging out" with respondents in non-school settings during this time, doing things like playing miniature golf and video games.

The research population was made up of teenagers from a range of socioeconomic backgrounds. Sixteen of them resided in suburban and 24 resided in urban settings. Eighteen of the respondents identified as female, 20 as male, one as gender neutral, and one as transgendered. Twenty-two of the respondents identified as white or Caucasian, six as Latino, five as Asian, two as of both Latino and white heritage, one of both Native American and white heritage, one of Asian and white descent, one of African-American

and white heritage, and one of Persian descent. One youth declined to state his racial ethnic heritage.

YOUTH NEW MEDIA USE

As American social life becomes increasingly wired, so too do contemporary youth cultures (Ito 2005; Montgomery 2000). Young people's daily activities and social worlds now orbit around new media such as cell phones and social network sites as well as new media practices such as instant messaging, and posting and watching online content (Miller et al. 2009; Rideout et al. 2005). By 2008, 93% of young people between the ages of 12 and 17 were online (Jones and Fox 2009). In fact, youth spend more time with media than any single other activity besides sleeping (Roberts and Foehr 2008). With the personalization of media as well as its miniaturization, youth can stay continually plugged in as computers, cell phones, and handheld devices become basic equipment (Roberts and Foehr 2008). Seventy-five percent of teenagers own cell phones (Lenhart et al. 2010). Seventy-three percent of wired teenagers are on social networking websites (Lenhart et al. 2010). In short, youth live in a mediated world. The ways in which their worlds are mediated depends upon the quality of their access to new media, a point I will address below. This generation of youth is more likely to engage with new media than are their parents, often integrating new media devices and practices into their social worlds in ways which are invisible to adults (Oksman and Turtainen 2004). . . .

For most young people, digital environments are not alternative worlds, virtual realities, or technological subcultures (Abbott 1998). Online communication is simply another way for them to connect with their friends and peers in a way that seems seamless with their offline life (Osgerby 2004). Social network sites play an important role in these social connections. Over half of those between the ages of 12 and 17 who go online have created profiles on these sites and prefer to communicate via these sites rather than email (something they see as a more formal communication mechanism) (Lenhart et al. 2007).[2]

While popular media outlets regularly air stories about youth logging on to these sites to meet strangers, young people typically use these sites to stay in contact with friends they already have and to make plans to hang out (Lampe et al. 2007; Lenhart and Madden 2007). These online practices augment youths' already existing social ties more than they extend them to unknown people. That said, digital technology provides the possibility of extending youths' domestic spaces and engenders a sense of freedom, much like the car used to do (Laegran 2002; Maczewski 2002). The online world has broadened young people's social horizons allowing youth to meet, stay in touch with, and make plans with others, both globally and locally (Holloway and Valentine 2003; Laegran 2002; Osgerby 2004). Thus, new media has the potential to reconfigure youths' social networks.

The quick incorporation of new media into youth culture has both alarmed and excited adults. Adults are profoundly anxious about what teens are doing online and these fears about the online world have dominated policy and popular culture discussions since the middle of the 1990s (Soderlund 2008). Like youth new media use, youth sexuality is often the focus of contemporary "moral panics" (Cohen 2002; Thompson 1998). These moral panics often establish a discourse about certain groups that ostensibly cause moral decline (Cohen 2002; Thompson 1998). Like youth internet use, youth sexuality is framed as a personal and social problem in need of social control (Russell 2005). . . .

RESOURCES

RELATIONSHIPS

The primary foci of youth culture are love, romance, and sexuality (Subrahmanyam and Greenfield 2008). Indeed teenagers report that their strongest emotion is that of being in love (Miller and Benson 1999). Thus, it is of little surprise that themes of dating and romance dominate young people's new media practices (Lenhart and Madden 2007; Oksman and Turtainen 2004). Youth meet others, flirt, maintain relationships, and break up in these "networked publics"

(Ito et al. 2009). These communication technologies mesh seamlessly with the fundamentally social nature of young people's romantic relationships (Brown 1999). Friends and social circles provide "opportunities to meet and interact with romantic partners, to initiate and recover from such relationships, and to learn from one's romantic experiences" (Collins and Sroufe 1999), activities that are even more viable with the explosion of online social networks and the possibility of continuous contact afforded by new media. New media technologies such as cell phones, instant messaging, text messaging, and social network sites allow youth to communicate with their friends (and sometimes strangers) out of the purview of their parents and other authority figures. Thus, these technologies provide a wider private sphere for youth dating practices, while also leaving digital footprints open to adult examination.

Contemporary youth romance culture is a primarily informal one (Bogle 2008; Modell 1989). This informality is reflected in young people's language, which frequently lacks a clear vocabulary to define relationship status or practices. Terms like "hanging out," "going out," and "talkin' to" have replaced terms like "courtship" or "dating" (Miller and Benson 1999). An informal culture, however, is not the same as an unstructured one. Youth have a, mostly, shared "media ideology" (Gershon 2010) about the role of technology in their relationships. They tend to meet people offline and then pursue the relationship online; a couple should proceed slowly as they correspond online using the appropriate communication tool; and when breaking up, they should do so in person, or at least over the phone (Ito et al. 2009).

In examining romantic breakups among college students, Ilana Gershon (2010) found that people's ideologies about media largely govern the role they think media should play in relationships, specifically their demise. She makes the case that people are still figuring out how to use new media in relationships. This process is a fundamentally social one as "people figure out together how to use different media and often agree on the appropriate social uses of technology by asking advice and sharing stories with each other" (Gershon 2010). People's media ideologies shape how they interpret the messages they receive. So rules about the relationship between intimacy and mediated practices are not necessarily about the message itself or the technology itself, but about the ideology. "Because these are new media, people haven't had time to develop a widespread consensus about how to use a medium, especially for relatively rare communicative tasks such as breaking up" (Gershon 2010). . . .

Liz and Grady exemplify the way in which some young people negotiate on and offline interactions when beginning a relationship. Grady shared with me that while he had known Liz since their freshman year he developed a crush on her only recently. They "didn't really talk" so flirting with her in person felt intimidating. Fortunately, Liz "had him on my Friend list from freshman year" on her MySpace page, though she only knew him casually through mutual friends. Grady took advantage of this casual "friendship" to initiate a relationship: "When I had a crush on her, I made sure I talked to her first in class before I sent her a comment on MySpace." Grady planned an offhand initial comment to introduce himself, writing, "Oh, wow, I didn't know we were Friends on MySpace," knowing of course that they were. Their process is paradigmatic of young people's contemporary meeting, flirting, and dating practices. Mediated venues play a central role in moving casual offline acquaintances to more intimate ones.

In the initial "getting to know you" part of a romantic relationship, the asynchronous nature of written communication (private messages and comments on social network sites and text messaging) allows for both continuous contact and the ability to save face (Goffman 1959) in potentially vulnerable situations. Alissa shared with me that "text messages" were "how I talked to Lisa (her girlfriend) a lot in the beginning." Alissa said that through text messages she could be "flirty in constant communication. [It was] easy to get messages across without having to phrase it perfectly." Boys seem particularly fond of using digital communications technologies for romance, meeting new girls and flirting (Lenhart and Madden 2007). As Grady said "really, that's the only reason to IM and stuff, girls, you know? I don't really talk to my guy friends that much. I just talk to

girls." He explained that it is "easier to talk to them (girls) there" than in person. The control over presentation of self afforded by new media helps to manage a profoundly unmasculine display of vulnerability by teenage boys often required by the process of flirting and getting to know someone. Indeed as Carter shared, "it's easier to message them than talk to them in the real world . . . because in the real world they're always with their friends or always in a group." This type of communication feels private, even if it may potentially be shared with exactly that group Carter finds so intimidating. Gershon (2010) notes that some of her respondents shared text messages with their friends in order to discuss intimate relationships.

Contrary to the implications of popular media stories, logging online to meet strangers for dating, romance or sexual liaisons is not a normative practice among the youth I studied. For the most part, these teens prefer to talk with people online that they or their friends know in an offline context. Teens often reported that meeting people only online was "weird," "unnatural," "geeky," or "scary." As Grady said, "I'm not going to start a conversation with a girl on MySpace or text messaging. I'm going to start in person first." In other words, Grady thought it was weird or geeky to start a conversation with a girl he liked online, rather than offline. . . .

Most youth in this study express hesitation about meeting people for the first time in an online environment, but this reluctance is not true of all youth. For marginalized young people, the internet allows them to meet other people like themselves who might not be immediately available in their local social circles (Holloway and Valentine 2003). This is true of racial minority and sexual minority youth, both of whom may face limited pools of potential dating partners in offline environments (Diamond et al. 1999). Best friends Gabbie and Cathy, both racial minorities (Chinese-American and Persian-American, respectively) in their primarily white high school, had used the internet for this purpose. Cathy had looked for Persian-American boyfriends on sites directed toward Persian-American communities. Similarly, Gabbie had logged onto Asian-town.net a social networking site directed at Asian-Americans to meet boys whom she could potentially date. Importantly, neither expressed hesitancy about meeting boys online before they met in person.

LGBT youth in this study (even those who lived in cities with large LGBT populations) also noted the relationship resources available in mediated environments. Mary Gray (2009b), for instance, elegantly notes the varied ways rural GLBTQ youth use new media to explore identities and practice coming out. Others use new media technologies to facilitate relationships. These communication technologies facilitate spaces where sexual minority teens can meet others for dating or for support and allows them to hide these relationships from their parents (Hillier and Harrison 2007). Jessica told me that one of her good gay male friends felt "very uncomfortable trying to pursue someone" at school so "he meets guys through MySpace because it's his opportunity." Robert, a gay teen, employed a similar strategy, having become frustrated about not finding other boys to date through his offline friendship circles. He wrote a Facebook "note" about his difficulties dating as a gay teen:

> Every time I have a crush or something, it doesn't work out (he's not gay, not enough time, etc.). I'm not a downer, but I'm just realizing that if a straight person's chance of compatibility is 1 in 100. AND only about 3 in 100 are gay, and the compatibility is still 2%, then my prospect is .03 in 100, or 3 in 10,000. That is not very encouraging!

Robert said that a friend set him up on a blind date as a direct result of the announcement he placed on Facebook. Unlike straight youth, he expressed little hesitancy about meeting someone to date online.

The independence digital communication affords allows youth to form romantic relationships which, in many ways, transcend adult control and geography. New media allows youth who are dating to maintain a digital co-presence, to be connected in a way that they cannot necessarily achieve in the physical world. These technologies also free youth from limiting their dating circles to those in their immediate vicinity. Multiple young people told me that they

were involved with someone who lived over an hour away. Aldo, in fact, met his girlfriend through a party at his cousin's house (located in a distant city) and now they keep in touch by cell phone about four times a week. They text, however, every day. Similarly, because they live over an hour apart, Missy told me that she is often on AIM with her boyfriend Dustin since they only see each other once a week or every 2 weeks.

. . .

This private sphere is especially important for youth whose parents have specific expectations of their dating partners. Indeed multiple young people (straight identified and LGBT) talked to me about how they carried on relationships outside of the purview of their parents. Lana and her girlfriend would talk multiple times a day, though, as Lana said, "my parents don't know about her." They had met at camp and started to date about a year later, maintaining a long distance relationship between Washington and New Hampshire. Outside of parental eyes, they were making plans to go to college together. Similarly, Missy's parents forbade her to have boyfriends, though that edict did not seem to significantly affect her relationship with her boyfriend, Dustin. Her parents frequently entered her room without knocking while she talked on the phone with Dustin. She would quickly tell Dustin "hold on, hold on" and place her phone under the pillow so that "Dustin can hear me and my mom talking." Missy also hid the online evidence of her relationship by listing her online status as "'single' because I keep him a secret. Well, not a secret. But I'm not allowed to have a boyfriend." . . .

Many of the youth I spoke with describe themselves as more tech savvy than their parents, so this sort of private sphere is fairly simple to maintain. Alice, whose immigrant parents forbade her from dating non-Chinese boys, told me that she set "all the administrator settings" on her family network. As such, according to her, her parents actually knew very little about her computer use. Given her secret relationship with Josh, this level of technological knowledge was actually quite important for her.

In addition to using new media to carve out these spheres of privacy, many youth also do the public performative work of a relationship through these technologies. Young people in relationships expect that these relationships will be publicly acknowledged through digital media. They expect significant others, for instance, to feature them in their MySpace "top eight."[3] Aldo, for instance, shared with me his surprise that he was not listed in his girlfriend's "top eight." "She used to have me in her top eight, but she took me off. I don't know why and I talked to her. I was like, 'how come I wasn't on?'" Similarly Josh and Alice bickered in front of me as Josh said, "Alice was not my original top one" on his MySpace site. Alice chimed in "I was like number 12 or something." Josh responded "Does it really matter? You know, does it really matter what your placement is really?" Alice answered, sarcastically, "Like he's not number one on my MySpace account." While this may seem like a relatively minor relationship imbalance, it illustrates the centrality of the importance of mediated performances of relationship [sic].

Youth also display tokens of affection on their social network pages. Aldo for instance, displayed a countdown to "me and my girlfriend's 1 year anniversary" which he said he put up there "so people will know" when it was. Youth in relationships also facilitate intimacy by sharing passwords. As Carissa told me when we logged on to her MySpace site, "She [her girlfriend] went into mine 'cause she knows my passwords and everything. And so she did all the colors and changed it." Alice and Josh also shared their passwords (though Josh cannot remember Alice's). Similarly, Carissa and her girlfriend share a LiveJournal on which they write back and forth and comment on each other's journal entries.

Not surprisingly, given the extent of the incorporation of new media in their relationships, youth also now experience mediated breakups. The media that some youth laud as a comfortable way to meet and get to know a romantic interest are viewed as a poor way to end a relationship with an intimate. Billy, for instance felt bad about encouraging a friend to break up with his girlfriend over text message as Billy and the friend spoke over IM. The friend took Billy's advice seriously and immediately broke up with his girlfriend via text message. Billy, who told me that

he had not actually been serious about this advice, "that was bad." Grady describes breaking up with someone on a social network site, the "lowest of the low" and Liz said "that's probably the worst one." Indeed, Grady said that most of his friends do not do this, though he had a friend who did. He:

> broke up with his girlfriend over a text message . . . He just sent her a text and was like . . . they hadn't talked in a while and they were fighting and everything. He called and she didn't answer, so he was just like, I'm going to end it now. I was over at his house and everything. He said I'm just going to end it. He sent her a text, 'we haven't talked in a while and it's not going well and I think we should just stop seeing each other.'

Grady said, however, "if you want to be respectful, you do it in person." In the same way that young people use the mitigation of vulnerability by new media to engage in flirtatious interchanges, it seems that they think that such vulnerability is appropriate in the end stages of a relationship. . . .

Sweeping up digital detritus of these relationships may have supplanted or at least now exists alongside time honored traditions of ridding one's room of relationship memorabilia. Gary, for instance, was left with a MySpace address that read "Sarah will always love Gary," after he broke up with his girlfriend, Sarah. He laughed sheepishly as he explained that he created the site with his now ex-girlfriend and could not change the title. Youth remove online pictures, make decisions about de-friending, and change shared passwords that had been indicative of their intimacy. Additionally, when youth break up, youth can keep closer tabs on each other than they could historically. Gabbie told me about her friend, Jason, who "had an ex who would check his MySpace and then Cathy would comment flirty comments, and then she [the ex] would be like—who is she? Why are you talking to him?" Some youth monitor those with whom they were previously intimate both for closure and for information about their current dating lives.

Mediated venues, as detailed in this section, serve as resources for youth to begin, maintain, and, less frequently, end intimate relationships. The same resources that make the internet attractive for forming relationships—privacy, lack of adults, protection from vulnerability, the ability to reach beyond geographic constraints, and the "always on" (Baron 2008) possibilities are also those facets that make the internet a uniquely suitable place for information about sexual health to be conveyed to young people.

Gender and Sexuality Information

While youth are busy using new media as resources for their practices of romance and sexuality, they are receiving less and less information from their schools about these same topics. As a culture, we have a difficult time treating sex as a normal, healthy part of adolescence (Schalet 2000). This view is reflected in sexual education curricula which have grown increasingly sex negative (Bay-Cheng 2005). In fact, only 14% of schools nationwide offer comprehensive sex education in which abstinence is taught as one option among other safer sex practices, a phenomenon that has in large part been encouraged by federal funding policies (Guttmacher Institute 2006).[4] The number of young people receiving comprehensive sex education is on the decline while those receiving information focused on abstinence has increased (Guttmacher Institute 2006; Kantor et al. 2008). As in other facets of adolescent life, LGBT youth are marginalized in sex education curricula that privilege heterosexuality and maintain raced, gendered, classed, and sexual inequalities (Connell 2009; Elia and Eliason 2010; Garcia 2009). This lack of education provides the backdrop for contemporary teen sexual practices in which sexually active teens in the USA are less likely to use safer sex methods than are their peers in other developed countries (Guttmacher Institute 2006). This lack of protection is important because US teens have shorter relationships and, consequently, more sexual partners over time (Guttmacher Institute 2006). Despite the decline of teenage pregnancy rates since 1990, the USA continues to have one of the highest teenage pregnancy rates in the developed world as well as high rates of sexually transmitted infections (Guttmacher Institute 2006).

Not surprisingly, given the lack of comprehensive sex education in schools and the intense use of new media in intimate relationships, the internet may be emerging as a prime resource for youth on issues of sexuality (Bay-Cheng 2005; Isaacson 2010; Levine 2003). The internet offers privacy, access to information, and has become a multifaceted source of sex education (Bay-Cheng 2005). Indeed information about sex and sexuality may be easier to obtain online than comprehensive formal sex education is in many schools. However, these online resources are not equally available to all youth, a topic that will be addressed in the next section.

. . . Youth often feel uncomfortable consulting physicians, peers, or other adults for information about sexuality because of concerns about confidentiality (Rideout et al. 2005; Suzuki and Calzo 2004). Bulletin boards, cell phones, social network sites, and static web sites are all venues through which youth can gather information about sexual health, puberty, sexual identity, and safer sex practices. Youth use the internet to find information on a range of health topics (Gray and Klein 2006). In fact, 25% of adolescents acquire some or a lot of sexual health information online (Tolani and Yen 2009). Some young people rely on new media to get information about intimate questions pertaining to gender, sexuality, and relationships. This reliance is especially true of youth who cannot get information elsewhere, such as school.

. . .

Some sex educators are looking to use new media to bypass school's control over the types of sex education available to young people. The BrdsNBz Text Message Warm Line[5] has marshaled the power of text messages to communicate with teens about sex and sexuality. Youth can text questions they have about sex and within 24 hours they can receive a response from the organization. Not surprisingly, social network sites also represent a fertile ground for sex education. Based on the knowledge that peers who have friends (either through social network sites or in "real life") who use condoms are more likely to use condoms themselves, two University of Southern California scholars, Eric Rice and Eve Tulbert, are designing an HIV prevention campaign using social network sites and viral video specifically aimed at homeless youth. Similarly, discussion venues on social network sites are important spaces for sexual minority young people to share their experiences (Crowley 2010; Dennis 2010).

Static sites which impart information can also be useful to teens. Informative sites include http://www.isis-inc.org, http://www.goaskalice.columbia.edu, http://www.youngwomenshealth.org, http://www.kidshealth.org/teen/, http://www.teenwire.com, http://www.sexetc.org, and http://www.gsanetwork.org. Alissa told me that some of the sites she visited daily contained information about sex and sexuality such as "dykestowatchoutfor.com, queerty.com and a handful of sexuality resources." Similarly, Devin visited a variety of sites when learning about being transgendered. He searched for "binders" online, where he also learned about testosterone access and dosages. Youth with whom I spoke relied on sites like these to build identity and culture, not just for information.

New media is a particularly salient resource because of the anonymity it affords, the confidentiality it promises, and the peer-to-peer nature of some of the bulletin boards and viral media. In other words, new media can be a fertile ground for both social and informational resources, connecting youth to communities and information that might not be available elsewhere. However, as Thurlow and Bell (2009) argues [sic], more work needs to be done to see what youth are actually doing with the resources on line [sic] and how youth are actually using them.

RISKS

While youth use new media in their sexual and romantic practices and they can find sexual resources online, none of this is to say that there are not risks online for which youth are both prepared and unprepared. Importantly, not all of the risks related to new media and youth sexuality are those around which contemporary moral panics revolve. Most of these risks are as much about gendered, classed, and raced inequalities as they are about online "predators." Thinking and policy making about these risks thus needs to include attention to young people's actual experiences of technology use and the replication of offline inequalities in online spaces. While new technologies provide a way for young people to come together and to create new cultures, their experiences of the internet and other new media also reflect the dominant ordering of power (Durham 2001). Gender, economic, race, and class inequality are implicated in who has access to and how people use technology. . . .

INFORMATION QUALITY AND ACCESSIBILITY

Though youth culture is quickly becoming digitized, not all are able to access technology or participate in digital culture to the same extent. Inequalities are reproduced through gradations in access to the digital world (DiMaggio et al. 2004). Variations in the technical means available to people to get online, the extent of autonomy people exercise in mediated spaces, the differing skill levels people bring to bear in media use, the social support upon which they can draw, and the purposes for which people use technology all shape and are shaped by people's social positionings (DiMaggio et al. 2004). In other words, one's ability to take advantage of opportunities posed by new media is shaped, much like other social and economic opportunities, by their family's socioeconomic status, their cohort, their education, income, gender, race, occupation, industry, region, and rural or urban home (DiMaggio et al. 2004).

One's economic positioning shapes one's experiences of and interactions with new media. The likelihood of a teen living in a house with a computer is strongly related to income (Eamon 2004; Lee 2008; Livingstone 2002; Roberts and Foehr 2008). Though families with children are more likely to have computers and internet access (Wang et al. 2005), poor youth are roughly two thirds less likely to own a home computer (Eamon 2004). Fewer than 60% of homes with incomes under 20,000 dollars a year have computers, as opposed to 90% of those earning 60,000 dollars a year or more (Roberts and Foehr 2008). Similarly, internet access only exists in 29% of homes with earnings under 15,000 dollars a year as opposed to 90% of those over 75,000 dollars a year (Roberts and Foehr 2008).

Of the 13% of American teenagers who do not use the internet, non-white youth are overrepresented: 87% of white teens go online, 89% of Latino teens do, while only 77% of African-American teens do (Lenhart et al. 2005). Similarly, 80% of all youth have access to the internet at home but only 61% of African-American youth do (Rideout et al. 2005). Ninety percent of white teens have personal computers, 80% of Latino teens do, and 78% of African-American teens do (Roberts and Foehr 2008). Cell phone use reflects a similar divide: 72% of white teens have cell phones, 71% of Latino teens do, and 65% of African-American teens have cell phones (Lenhart et al. 2008). This inequality of access affects youths' ability to participate in cultures of dating and romance as well as their information-gathering capabilities. This access also has much to do with rural versus urban access. Limited access and limited reliable access in rural communities compromises the availability of online information about sexuality (Gray 2009a).

. . .

While schools are increasingly wired, with 93% of schools reporting internet access (Roberts and Foehr 2008), class inequality still shapes access at these schools. Schools with the highest poverty concentrations have higher student-to-computer ratios (Roberts and Foehr 2008). In working class schools, internet access is more likely to be limited to structured class time, as opposed to middle class schools in which out of class technology access is more common (Lee 2008). This educational inequality is important because some young people might avoid searching for certain types of information at home, under fear of parental oversight, leaving schools and libraries as crucial access sites.

Some schools regularly censor the sort of information students can access by blocking sites they determine to be harmful (Subrahmanyam and Greenfield 2008). These schools might ban access to social network sites, instant messenger software, and sites containing "adult content" (which, at some schools, means websites or searches including words like *gay*, *lesbian*, or *breast*). Elena argued that "it's even hard to do a research paper, because if it's a disease that just has the word 'sexuality' in there or something it's blocked. We had to do a physio project about disease

and it was so hard." Eventually, Elena used her math teacher's computer to do the research because teachers' computers were not blocked. Multiple LGBT youth have reported to me that LGBT content is blocked at their school. The ACLU recently sued Knox County Schools and Metropolitan Nashville Schools in Tennessee for blocking access to this content. The schools, tellingly, did allow sites focusing on "reparative therapy" or "ex-gay" ministries (Kennedy 2009). Students from low income backgrounds who may not have regular internet access at homes [*sic*] may also find themselves in schools that have the least access as well.

Like the reparative therapy websites, the information that youth do access online is not necessarily accurate. This misinformation can build on myths about sexuality and reproduction that are widespread among adolescents (Tolani and Yen 2009). In general, online information about sexually transmitted infections is fairly accurate, but information about emergency conception [*sic*] (such as pharmacy availability), adolescent use of IUDs, and recommended age of first pap smear are often inaccurate (Tolani and Yen 2009). Thus, information about sexuality needs to be available and accurate, something that does not seem to be the case in the current distribution of new media resources and access.

SEXUALITY AND GENDER

Adults are profoundly concerned about the sexual victimization of children online. This concern is not an [*sic*] unfounded. Some youth in this study reported to me that they had received unwanted sexual attention online. However, what might get overlooked in the focus on unwanted sexual attention to youth online is the more mundane and pervasive way in which offline harassment around issues of gender and sexuality replicate themselves online, not in terms of sexual predators, but in terms of peer to peer interactions.

Several youth told me stories of being approached by strangers online, but they were by far in the minority of youth I interviewed. Elena said that the one time she went in a chat room the first question she was asked was "Where do you live? What's your phone number?" Elena and her friend Brett said that they had "heard a couple of things about sex predators being on MySpace" and in response, cancelled their accounts. Even though Elena only added people that she knew she said that she would occasionally receive "disgusting chat things" and "bad pictures" from people she did not know.

Some youth have a sophisticated sense of the "safety" of different online spaces. Many of the youth I spoke with said they could avoid undesired sexual content by making particular choices, such as avoiding chat rooms, only friending people they knew offline on social network sites, or choosing certain social network sites over others. For instance, Robert told me "MySpace vs. Facebook—stalker/creepy old men vs. your friends!" When crafting an online presence, some young people keep safety and privacy in mind and do not post an inordinate of [sic] personal information online (Hinduja and Patchin 2008). In fact, between 40% and 66% of youth who have a social network site have limited access to their profiles (Hinduja and Patchin 2008; Lenhart and Madden 2007; Patchin and Hinduja 2010).

Other young people also shared with me their strategies for avoiding unwanted content and contact. Aldo told me, if he did not know someone, "I won't add them and stuff. Like I'll just deny them as friends." Alice said that when "random guys" message on her Xanga blog saying "hey, you're cute," she responds with "yeah, I'm a stalker and I happen to be an ax murder [sic] too. Would you like to talk to me still?" Kevin exhibited perhaps the most concern about vulnerability resulting from his online participation. He claimed he was "super cyber-safe" and would not post his picture online, instead using an animal as an avatar. He told me "If you were approached by a cyberstalker, it's not because you were on the internet minding your own business, it's because you were adding friends that you didn't know that well, or because you were in public chat rooms. Why are you in a public chatroom and talking to people you don't know?" Kevin claimed that due to avoiding these practices "Nobody has ever approached me on MySpace. If somebody adds me and I don't

know them and I can tell that I have no clue who they are, I'm not going to add them."

There are several traits and activities that are more likely to put one in an uncomfortable online situation (Smith 2007). Those likely to be contacted by strangers about sexual topics are girls, those who have created a social network profile, and those who have posted pictures online (Smith 2007). Youth who receive sexual solicitations were also more likely to report experiencing offline physical abuse, sexual abuse, and alienation from their parents (Wells and Mitchell 2008). LGBT young people fit the profile of those more likely to receive unwanted sexual contact online as they are often marginalized, harassed, and isolated in high school settings (Pascoe 2007) and might not have the family support that non-sexual minority youth do.

Given that queer young people experience some of the risk factors that render them vulnerable to sexual contact by strangers, it is little surprise that I heard the following story from one of my respondents, Robert:

> So a couple times a week, after my parents went to bed, I visited some internet sites . . . , then after a while, I found a chat room web site, a gay teen chat room. I chatted with a lot of guys, eventually I started to talk to people outside of the chat room, on MSN messenger. There were people who wanted to do things with cameras and pictures, and for a while I went along with some of it, not really doing too much. Then one day, it wasn't a teenager who sent me their pic, but an old fat man, I was disgusted, beyond words. I smashed my computer camera, deleted my MSN, and barred any memory from those times out of existence until I recollect now. Today I have lots of friends, and am secure with my sexual identity, and don't ever go on chat rooms. *Anyways*, yeah, I am completely disgusted with myself that I ever did any of that, not that I ever did much, but that I had "IM sex," totally totally creepy.

To be fair, Robert willingly participated in an online environment where he seemed fine with some types of sexual contact. For space-deprived youth, new media might provide spaces where they can engage in some of the same sexual and emotional exploration other youth engage in offline. Like youth who explore offline, Robert seems to be exploring boundaries and figuring out what is pleasurable and what is not. However, online relationships often bear the taint of "creepiness" and inauthenticity. Thus, it is not that surprising that Robert expresses shame and disgust not only for his encounter with an older man he found unattractive (and who seems to have initially misrepresented his age) but with other age equal partners as well. Rather than reading this example as solely one about predatory behavior, it might be beneficial to see it as an example of the need for sexual and digital literacy skills which help youth, especially sexual minority youth, navigate the uncharted and unfamiliar waters of online intimacy so that they can practice sexual subjectivity both online and off. . . .

More frequently than stories of sexual solicitation, youth I spoke with shared stories about patterns of offline gender and sexual harassment moving online. In online environments, the types of policing gender and sexuality that typically occur offline can be executed not only with a larger audience but also with more lasting digital footprints. For instance, in offline environments, boys shore up masculine identities through teasing other boys for being too romantic, or letting their girlfriends control them (Pascoe 2007). New media technologies are now being put to use in those same gender practices. Trevor, for instance, told me the story of a friend of his, Brad, who he described as "pussy-whipped" with a MySpace page devoted to his girlfriend, which is entitled "Jenny is awesome." On their way to a concert as part of the school band, Brad showed Trevor a picture of him and his girlfriend at prom. On the back Trevor read the inscription, "I love you Pookie." Trevor explained that he and his friends took a picture of this inscription and sent "it to everyone Brad knows. And we all call him Pookie now. He gets so much flack for this. We were all laughing so hard." What might have once been a joke between friends about Brad's masculinity (or lack thereof) was spread across the school using the affordances of digital technology.

Additionally, the homophobic harassment that is so common offline among teenage boys (Pascoe 2007) has moved online. In one video Craig showed me, his friend Kevin sits at an IHOP, short money for dinner. Craig agrees to lend him money, but only on the following condition—that Kevin repeat a series of confessional phrases which Craig can videotape and place on YouTube. Kevin buries his head in his hands asking, "You're going to take a video of this and post it on YouTube aren't you?!" Craig ignores Kevin's plea saying, "Anyway, repeat after me. I Kevin James Wong."

KEVIN: I, Kevin James Wong.

CRAIG: 17 years old.

KEVIN (who at this point starts to giggle embarrassedly): 17 years old.

CRAIG: Senior at Valley High School.

KEVIN: Senior at Valley High School.

CRAIG: In Santa Clarita.

KEVIN: In Santa Clarita.

CRAIG: Am now confessing.

KEVIN: Am now confessing.

CRAIG: That I, Kevin Wong.

KEVIN: That I, Kevin Wong.

CRAIG: Am a homosexual male.

KEVIN: Am a homosexual male.

They devolved into laughter as their friend Jesse jumps into the frame behind Kevin. Craig posted the video on YouTube and eagerly showed it to me as I interviewed him in a local Starbucks. He and his friends giggled as they continued to show me other YouTube videos, one of which featured them imitating men engaging in anal intercourse and then bursting into fits of laugher. While there is little new about this type of homophobic harassment between boys (Kimmel 2001; Pascoe 2007), the ability to do it with so wide an audience and the attendant potential for widespread humiliation is.

This sort of harassment is not limited to boys. Gender practices framing girls as sexual objects also take place in online environments. Aldo's MySpace page, for instance, features a Mario brother cartoon in which Mario looks like he is having sex with the princess as she is bent over in front of him. . . . Other boys displayed to me proudly the "models" they had as friends. By featuring the "models," such as Tila Tequila, as friends on their MySpace or Facebook pages, boys engaged in a masculinizing discourse that promotes women as sexual objects.

While mediated environments may open avenues for learning about issues of gender and sexuality, they also pose risks. Mediated gender practices look a lot like non-mediated gender practices in the objectification of women and definitions of masculinity as homophobic and dominant. As well, online environments can pose risks of unwanted sexual attention for some young people.

CONCLUSION

This article looked to put into context stories like Jessie Logan's by exploring the relationships between young people's sexuality and new media use in their daily lives. These practices indicate that youth, in this study, are not necessarily meeting older adults for sexual liaisons, being traumatized by online predators, or experiencing cyberbullying that is quantifiably more common than the offline bullying they may experience. In fact, their online experiences are much more complex than that.

Youth have quickly put new media to use in their intimate relationships. The sexual practices in which young people engage take place in the context of these social relationships. The private, peer-oriented, and sometimes anonymous forums offered by new media help to manage the vulnerability inherent in such relationships. As such, new media are an ideal venue for conveying information about sensitive and potentially embarrassing topics like sex and sexuality.

Youth are eager to receive information about sexuality and relationships information and, statistically, are not likely receiving it elsewhere. They are turning to websites, discussion boards, and text messages to learn about their own sexuality, their bodies, and safer

sex practices. They are also turning to each other through mediated means. By publicizing these resources and ensuring the information is both available and accurate, health practitioners can circumvent some of the restrictions educators experience when it comes to the topic of sex and intimate relationships.

However, not all youth have equal access to new media, so when interventions are designed to bring information to young people about sexual health, we need to keep in mind the audience a given intervention might reach. Racial and class disparities still exist, both in terms of access and participation. Similarly, some sexual minority, homeless and other disenfranchised youth most in need of information about sexual health, may also experience online venues as riskier spaces to the extent they have access to them.

This article highlights the fact that the booster/detractor divide misses nuances in terms of the risks and resources afforded by new media, from the everyday love notes between Alice and Josh to the more problematic harassment of Jesse, to the myriad possibilities for informal learning outside of a formal institution (such as sex education outside of a school setting). In sum, new media provide a previously unavailable, direct line to many young people, a line of communication that might, for better or worse, evade adult monitoring and provide much needed information to youth about their bodies, their lives, and their sexual health.

ACKNOWLEDGMENTS

This research was funded by the Catherine T. and John D. MacArthur Foundation. The author acknowledges the generous assistance of Sara Diefendorf, Christo Sims, and two anonymous reviewers for their contribution to this manuscript.

NOTES

1. MSN is an instant messaging service.
2. Between 2004 and 2008, the percentage of teens who said they use email declined from 89% to 73% (Jones and Fox 2009).

3. While youth have largely moved to Facebook from MySpace, when youth were on MySpace, one's location in another's "top eight" friends signified the importance and seriousness of their friendship or romantic relationship.

4. These policies recently changed under the administration of Barack Obama. Government funding is no longer limited to those programs which promote abstinence (Rabin 2010).

5. The BrdsNBz Text Message Warm Line can be found here: http://appcnc.org/brdsnbz-text-message-warm-line.

REFERENCES

Abbott, C. (1998). Making connections: young people and the internet. In J. Sefton-Green (Ed.), *Digital diversions: youth culture in the age of multimedia* (pp. 84–105). London: UCL.

Baron, N. (2008). *Always on: language in an online and mobile world.* Oxford: Oxford University Press.

Bay-Cheng, L. (2005). Left to their own devices: disciplining youth discourse on sexuality education electronic bulletin boards. *Sexuality Research and Social Policy, 2*(1), 37–50.

Bogle, K. (2008). *Hooking up: sex, dating, and relationships on campus.* New York: New York University Press.

Brown, B. B. (1999). "You're going out with who?" Peer group influences on adolescent romantic relationships. In W. Furman, B. B. Brown, & C. Feiring (Eds.), *The development of romantic relationships in adolescence* (pp. 291–329). Cambridge: Cambridge University Press.

Celizic, M. (2010). *Teen 'sexting': youthful prank or sex crime?* Retrieved November 23, 2010, from http://today .msnbc.msn.com/id/29613192.

Cohen, S. (2002). *Folk devils and moral panics: the creation of the mods and rockers.* New York: Routledge.

Collins, W. A., & Sroufe, L. A. (1999). Capacity for intimate relationships: a developmental construction. In W. Furman, B. B. Brown, & C. Feiring (Eds.), *The development of romantic relationships in adolescence* (pp. 125–147). Cambridge: Cambridge University Press.

Connell, C. (2009). Beyond the birds and the bees: learning inequality through sexuality education. *American Journal of Sexuality Education, 4*(2), 83.

Crowley, M. S. (2010). How r u??? Lesbian and bi-identified youth on MySpace. *Journal of Lesbian Studies, 14*(1), 52–60.

Dennis, J. P. (2010). Drawing desire: male youth and homoerotic fan art. *Journal of LGBT Youth, 7*(1), 6–28.

Diamond, L. M., Savin-Williams, R., & Dube, E. M. (1999). Sex, dating, passionate friendships, and romance: intimate peer relations among lesbian, gay, and bisexual adolescents. In W. Furman, B. B. Brown, & C. Feiring (Eds.), *The development of romantic relationships in adolescence* (pp. 175–201). Cambridge: Cambridge University Press.

DiMaggio, P., Hargittai, E., Celeste, C., & Shafer, S. (2004). From unequal access to differential use: a literature review and agenda for research on digital inequality. In K. Neckerman (Ed.), *Social inequality* (pp. 355–400). New York: Sage.

Durham, M. G. (2001). Adolescents, the internet and the politics of gender: a feminist case analysis. *Race, Gender & Class, 8*(4), 20–41.

Eamon, M. K. (2004). Digital divide in computer access and use between poor and non-poor youth. *Journal of Sociology & Social Welfare, 31*(2), 91–113.

Elia, J. P., & Eliason, M. (2010). Discourses of exclusion: sexuality education's silencing of sexual others. *Journal of LGBT Youth, 7*(1), 29–48.

Garcia, L. (2009). "Now why do you want to know about that?": heteronormativity, sexism and racism in the sexual (mis)education of Latina youth. *Gender & Society, 23*, 520–541.

Gershon, I. (2010). *The breakup 2.0: disconnecting over new media.* Ithaca: Cornell University Press.

Goffman, E. (1959). *The presentation of self in everyday life.* New York: Anchor.

Gray, M. (2009a). *Out in the country: youth media and queer visibility in rural America.* New York: NYU Press.

Gray, M. L. (2009b). Negotiating identities/queering desires: coming out online and the remediation of the coming-out story. *Journal of Computer-Mediated Communication, 14*(4), 1162–1189.

Gray, N. J., & Klein, J. D. (2006). Adolescents and the internet: health and sexuality information. *Current Opinion in Obstetrics & Gynecology, 18*(5), 519–524.

Gray, N. J., Klein, J. D., Noyce, P. R., Sesselberg, T. S., & Cantrill, J. A. (2005). The internet: a window on adolescent health literacy. *The Journal of Adolescent Health, 37*(3), 243.

Guttmacher Institute. (2011). Facts on sex education in the United States. Retrieved March 7, 2011, from http:// www.guttmacher.org/pubs/FB-Teen-Sex-Ed.html.

Harvey, K., Churchill, D., Crawford, P., Brown, B., Mullany, L., Macfarlane, A., et al. (2008). Health communication and adolescents: what do their emails tell us? *Family Practice, 25*(4), 304–311.

Hillier, L., & Harrison, L. (2007). Building realities less limited than their own: young people practising same-sex attraction on the internet. *Sexualities, 10*(1), 82–100.

Hinduja, S., & Patchin, J. W. (2008). Personal information of adolescents on the internet: a quantitative content analysis of MySpace. *Journal of Adolescence, 31,* 125.

Holloway, S. L., & Valentine, G. (2003). *Cyberkids.* New York: RoutledgeFalmer.

Isaacson, R. B. (2010). "Teachable moments": the use of child-centered arguments in the same-sex marriage debate. *California Law Review, 98*(1), 121–157.

Ito, M. (2005). Technologies of the childhood imagination: Yugioh, media mixes, and everyday cultural production. In J. Karaganis & N. Jeremijenko (Eds.), *Structures of participation in digital culture.* Durham: Duke University Press.

Ito, M., Baumer, S., Bittanti, M., Boyd, D., Cody, R., Herr-Stephenson, B., et al. (2009). *Hanging out, messing around, and geeking out: kids living and learning with new media.* Cambridge: MIT Press.

Jones, S., & Fox, S. (2009). *Generations online in 2009.* Washington: Pew Internet & American Life Project.

Kantor, L. M., Santelli, J. S., Teitler, J., & Balmer, R. (2008). Abstinence only policies and programs: an overview. *Sexuality Research & Social Policy, 5*(3), 6–17.

Kennedy, R. (2009). *ACLU tackles Knox county schools' LGBT website block » metro pulse.* April 22. Retrieved December 3, 2010, from http://www.metropulse.com/news/2009/apr/22/aclu-tackles-knox-county-schools-lgbt-website-bloc/.

Kimmel, M. (2001). Masculinity as homophobia: fear, shame, and silence in the construction of gender identity. In S. Whitehead & F. Barrett (Eds.), *The masculinities reader* (pp. 266–287). Cambridge: Polity.

Laegran, A. S. (2002). The petrol station and the internet cafe: rural technospaces for youth. *Journal of Rural Studies, 18,* 157–168.

Lampe, C., Ellison, N., & Steinfield, C. (2007). *A familiar face(book): profile elements as signals in an online social network.* Conference on Human Factors in Computing Systems, San Jose, CA.

Lee, L. (2008). The impact of young people's internet use on class boundaries and life trajectories. *Sociology, 42*(1), 137–153.

Lenhart, A., & Madden, M. (2007). *Social networking websites and teens: an overview.* Washington: Pew Internet & American Life Project.

Lenhart, A., Madden, M., & Hitlin, P. (2005). *Teens and technology.* Washington: Pew Internet & American Life Project.

Lenhart, A., Madden, M., Rankin Macgill, A., & Smith, A. (2007). *Teens and social media.* Washington: Pew Internet & American Life Project.

Lenhart, A., Arafeh, S., Smith, A., & Macgill, A. R. (2008). *Writing, technology and teens.* Washington: Pew/Internet.

Lenhart, A., Purcell, K., Smith, A., & Zickuhr, K. (2010). *Social media & mobile internet use among teens and young adults.* Washington: Pew Internet & American Life Project.

Levine, J. (2003). *Harmful to minors: the perils of protecting children from sex.* New York: Thunder's Mouth.

Livingstone, S. (2002). *Young people and new media: childhood and the changing media environment.* London: Sage.

Maczewski, M. (2002). Exploring identities through the internet: youth experiences online. *Child & Youth Care Forum, 31*(2), 111–129.

Miller, B. C., & Benson, B. (1999). Romantic and sexual relationship development during adolescence. In W. Furman, B. B. Brown, & C. Feiring (Eds.), *The development of romantic relationships in adolescence* (pp. 99–121). Cambridge: Cambridge University Press.

Miller, N. C., Thompson, N. L., & Franz, D. P. (2009). Proactive strategies to safeguard young adolescents in the cyberage. *Middle School Journal, 41*(1), 28–34.

Modell, J. (1989). *Into one's own: from youth to adulthood in the United States, 1920–1975.* Berkeley: University of California Press.

Montgomery, K. (2000). Youth and digital media: a policy research agenda. *The Journal of Adolescent Health, 27S,* 61–68.

Oksman, V., & Turtainen, J. (2004). Mobile communication as a social stage. *New Media & Society, 6*(3), 319–339.

Osgerby, B. (2004). *Youth media.* New York: Routledge.

Pascoe, C. J. (2007). *"Dude, you're a fag": masculinity and sexuality in high school.* Berkeley: University of California Press.

Patchin, J. W., & Hinduja, S. (2010). Trends in online social networking: adolescent use of MySpace over time. *New Media & Society, 12*(2), 197–216.

Rabin, R. C. (2010). New spending for a wider range of sex education. *New York Times,* May 10.

Rideout, V., Roberts, D., & Foehr, U. (2005). *Generation M: media in the lives of 8–18 year-olds.* Menlo Park: The Henry J. Kaiser Family Foundation.

Roberts, D. F., & Foehr, U. G. (2008). Trends in media use. *Future of Children, 18*(1), 11–37.

Russell, S. T. (2005). Introduction to positive perspectives on adolescent sexuality. *Sexuality Research and Social Policy, 2*(4), 1–3.

Schalet, A. (2000). Raging hormones, regulated love: adolescent sexuality and the constitution of the modern individual in the United States and the Netherlands. *Body & Society, 6*(1), 75–105.

Smith, A. (2007). *Teen and online stranger contact.* Washington: Pew/Internet.

Soderlund, G. (2008). Journalist or panderer? Framing underage webcam sites. *Sexuality Research and Social Policy: Journal of NSRC, 5*(4), 62.

Subrahmanyam, K., & Greenfield, P. (2008). Online communication and adolescent relationships. *The Future of Children, 18*(1), 119.

Suzuki, L. K., & Calzo, J. P. (2004). The search for peer advice in cyberspace: an examination of online teen bulletin boards about health and sexuality. *Applied Developmental Psychology, 25,* 685–698.

Thompson, K. W. (1998). *Moral panics.* London: Routledge.

Thurlow, C., & Bell, K. (2009). Against technologization: young people's new media discourse as creative cultural practice. *Journal of Computer-Mediated Communication, 14*(4), 1038–1049.

Thurlow, C., & McKay, S. (2003). Profiling "new" communication technologies in adolescence. *Journal of Language and Social Psychology, 22*(94), 94.

Tolani, A. T., & Yen, S. (2009). *Many websites fail to dispel myths about IUDs, emergency contraception, birth control, and proper timing of pap smears.* Stanford: Lucile Packard Children's Hospital, Stanford University.

Wang, R., Bianchi, S., & Raley, S. (2005). Teenagers' internet use and family rules: a research note. *Journal of Marriage and the Family, 67,* 1249–1258.

Wells, M., & Mitchell, K. J. (2008). How do high-risk youth use the internet? Characteristics and implications for prevention. *Child Maltreatment, 13*(3), 227.

SECTION SIX

Politics and the State

Social constructions of sex, gender, and sexuality have had and continue to have material consequences and remain a feature of public and legal discourse. One of the most salient examples today is gay marriage. The Department of Justice confirmed that same-gender couples had access to the 1,100-plus federal rights, benefits, and privileges afforded to opposite-gender couples based on the historic *Obergefell v. Hodges* Supreme Court ruling on June 26, 2015. While this appears to be a civil rights milestone for lesbian, gay, bisexual, and transgender (LGBT) citizens, these people and others still face a number of basic inequalities along economic, social, medical, and legal lines, which grind exceedingly small.

There are other reasons to be hopeful about the public and legal progress in the matters of sex, gender, and sexuality. During his eight-year tenure, President Barack Obama signed an executive order that added gender identity as a category of protection in federal employment and that also prohibits federal contractors and subcontractors from discriminating against LGBT people; repealed the US military's "Don't ask, don't tell" policy regarding the right of gay people to serve openly in the armed forces; developed and implemented the United States' first comprehensive plan to respond to the domestic HIV epidemic; expanded access to health-care coverage so that insurers can no longer exclude LGBT on the basis of their sexuality or gender identity; extended federal benefits to the same-partners of federal employees, including members of the Foreign Service serving abroad; and took initial steps to reduce housing discrimination against LGBT people.

The chapters in Section Six discuss the power of the state to regulate our sexed, gendered, and sexualized bodies. For instance, both Eithne Luibhéid and Melanie Heath examine state control over marriage and the ways in which normative definitions of the "appropriate" American family are both reproduced and enforced. In doing so, they reveal the reliance of heterosexuality as an institution on specific gendered, racialized identities. While we hear often about the role of the state in allowing or prohibiting same-sex marriage, we often fail to realize the extent to which the state has historically regulated who can marry, which immigrants are permitted to bring their spouses and families with them to the United States, which families "appropriately" qualify for welfare, and so on. It was not until 1967, for example, that the Supreme Court struck down state laws prohibiting interracial marriage. We provide here two very different cases that exemplify the ways in which state control operates.

George Chauncey shows how he and other academics utilized the history of discrimination based on sexuality and sexual practices counter discursively to overturn antisodomy laws that targeted gay men in *Lawrence vs. Texas*. In the next chapter, Elias Virtulli examines the historical struggle to include transgender people in the Employment Non-Discrimination Act (ENDA). The dynamic political life of ENDA is as much about homonormativity and white privilege as it is about gender stereotypes. Another uniquely vulnerable population in the United States includes Latino migrant day laborers. In this chapter, Kurt Organista and colleagues deployed ethnography to better understand the sexual health of men in the San Francisco Bay Area and ultimately argue that the structural position of Latino migrant day laborers jeopardizes their sexual health and overall well-being. While transgender people and Latino migrant day laborers are fundamentally different, both are in vulnerable, political positions in the United States, which affect their overall well-being. Until we understand the interdependent structures of oppression, especially between groups that *are* different, inequality will continue and policies will reinforce it.

The final two chapters of this section move us away from the confines of US politics to global dynamics of sex, gender, and sexuality. Monica Sharma discusses the use of assisted reproductive technologies in cultures known to promote preferences for male children. In this case, Sharma points out the un/intended consequences that technological advancementcan have, chiefly gendercide, and additional social problems that result from unbalanced gender ratios. Lionel Cantu Jr. examines the double-sided coin of queer tourism in Mexico by first attending to the development of gay and lesbian tourism as an identity-based industry and then focusing on the effects that this niche market has on Mexican sexualities.

We hope that this section inspires you to intentionally seek out different histories than what is presented as the dominant narrative of history. We encourage you to get active and network with others about the issues that affect members in your local community. We want you to think about your day-to-day practices as they have multiple material impacts, positive and negative, both local and global.

A BLUEPRINT FOR EXCLUSION

The Page Law, Prostitution, and Discrimination against Chinese Women

DISCUSSION QUESTIONS

1. How does our regulation of immigration reinforce systems of race, gender/ sexuality, and class oppression?
2. How are gender, sexual, and race inequities reinforced in the construction of the U.S. nation and its citizens?
3. Why were Chinese prostitutes seen as a threat to white supremacy?
4. Why does Luibhéid argue that the categorization of prostitutes is a socially constructed designation?

The Page Law of 1875 established "the policy of direct federal regulation of immigration by prohibiting for the first time the entry of undesirable immigrants."[1] Immigrants designated as undesirable were those who could be classified as convicts, contract laborers, and Asian women coming to work in prostitution. The provisions regarding convicts and contract laborers had little effect at the time.[2] But the vigorously enforced bar on Asian women coming to work in prostitution had a noticeable effect on the ability of Chinese women to immigrate and served as a harbinger of multiple forms of sexuality based immigration exclusions.[3] The fact that the Page Law targeted Asian women, even when women of other nationalities were significantly involved in prostitution work too, highlights how the sexual monitoring of immigrants intersects with other systems of social hierarchy. . . .

To explain the origins of the Page Law and its profound effects on U.S. immigration control, this chapter first describes how fears about the future of white lives, cultural forms, and nation became channeled into concerns about prostitution among Chinese immigrants. It then maps out how such concerns became concretely incorporated into the immigration control process through the strategies that officials devised to try to identify and exclude Chinese prostitutes. Although these strategies remained incapable of generating reliable information about which Chinese women were prostitutes, they had important effects. The strategies transformed the immigration control apparatus into a system that constructed and regulated sexuality and, moreover, constituted Chinese women, individually and collectively, as subjectified in gender, racial, sexual, and class terms. These effects suggest that immigration

Eithne Luibhéid, "A Blueprint for Exclusion: The Page Law, Prostitution, and Discrimination against Chinese Women" from *Entry Denied: Controlling Sexuality at the Border* (University of Minnesota Press, 2002), pp. 31–54.

control reproduces inequalities not only through individual officials' prejudices but also through the routine monitoring strategies on which immigration control depends. These strategies, which were pioneered on Chinese women because of fears about their sexuality, gradually became extended to every immigrant who sought to enter America.

"COOLIE LABOR, IMMORAL AND DISEASED HEATHENS, AND UNASSIMILABLE ALIENS"

In order to understand the restrictions that were imposed on Chinese women by the Page Law, the law needs to be situated in relation to the larger, conflicted history of Chinese immigration to the United States. The first Chinese immigrants were overwhelmingly male, and San Francisco was the main port of entry. A majority came from the province of Guangdong and began arriving as part of the California gold rush of 1848. Like many other immigrants, they initially intended to make money and return to China. Thus, "although more than half of them were married, most did not bring their wives and families."[4] . . .

Among this predominantly male Chinese immigrant community, a prostitution industry developed. Chinese prostitution quickly emerged as a contentious issue in San Francisco. Yet prostitution was fairly common in the American West at that time:

> For the first few years of the 1850s, the arrival of Chinese female prostitutes accompanied that of European and Anglo-American *filles de joie*. The latter, and a few of the former, were primarily entrepreneurs or aspiring entrepreneurs who flocked to San Francisco to take advantage of the dramatic demand for their services. The temporary and migratory nature of the population, a critical shortage of women for companionship, and the lack of conjugal life stood out as the main features of this male-dominated society. . . . As a consequence, opportunities existed for prostitutes to move both upward in the profession and outward in the wider society.[5]

Despite the widespread existence of prostitution by many nationalities, Chinese prostitution attracted particular public attention, giving rise to negative images and discriminatory institutional structures. According to Judy Yung, "discrimination against Chinese prostitutes, as well as prostitutes from Latin American countries, was most apparent at the institutional level. Both groups of women were ghettoized and, in accordance with the racial prejudice of the day, consistently singled out for moral condemnation and legal suppression, even though white prostitution was more prevalent."[6] Laws explicitly directed at Chinese, rather than all, prostitutes began to develop. For instance, in 1854 municipal authorities in San Francisco passed an ordinance "To Suppress Houses of Ill-Fame Within City Limits" and enforced it mainly against Chinese and Mexican brothels. In 1865 municipal authorities passed an "Order to Remove Chinese Women of Ill Fame from Certain Limits in the City." A year later the state legislature passed "An Act for the Suppression of Chinese Houses of Ill-Fame," which resulted in the geographical confinement of Chinese prostitution, but not its elimination.[7] In 1867 "fourteen owners of houses of ill-fame were arrested—all of them Chinese. In 1869, there were twenty-nine arrests for importing prostitutes—all of them Chinese."[8] In March 1870 the state passed "An Act to Prevent the Kidnapping and Importation of Mongolian, Chinese, and Japanese Females for Criminal or Demoralizing Purposes." The Act stipulated that no Asian woman could land without proof that she had migrated voluntarily and was of good character. However, in 1874 the U.S. Circuit Court ruled that this Act was unconstitutional. The ruling judge added that while he was aware of anti-Chinese sentiment in California, "if their future immigration is to be stopped, recourse must be had to the federal government, where the sole power over this subject lies."[9]

Advocates for Chinese exclusion had already started looking to their representatives in Washington for assistance. They looked particularly to Horace Page, a Republican who "maintained his seat in the House for ten years, largely at the expense of the Chinese."[10] Although Page was initially unable to convince legislators of the need for full Chinese exclusion, he successfully argued for the passage of a bill that excluded Chinese women who were entering the United States for prostitution. This was the Page Law of 1875.

"AN INJURY AND A CURSE TO US"

Why target Chinese prostitution, in particular? Exclusionists' concerns centered not on the experiences and needs of poor Chinese girls and women who had been sold or tricked into prostitution, but on the fate of white men, white families, and a nation constructed as white. Transcripts of public hearings in San Francisco on Chinese immigration make this clear.[11] Mr. Pixley testified for the city that their concern was for white male laborers. "The true American hero is the man who takes his dinner out in his tin plate, works all day, six days in the week, and brings his wages home for his wife to expend in the maintenance and education of the family, in their clothing and their protection."[12] These American heroes were defined as coterminous with civilization and the U.S. nation in part because of their adherence to particular gender and sexual arrangements:

> Our white laborers are, as a rule, married, and fathers and heads of families, and according to our mode of civilization the poorest laborer with the poorest wife must occupy a room by himself for his bed and must have at least another room to cook and eat in. If he has a boy and a girl, growing to the ages of puberty, the boy must have a room for himself and the girl must have a room for herself, and both must be separate from the parents' bed. It is the ingrained decency of our civilization. It is as impossible to change it as to change us from the worship of the Christian God to the heathen tablet.[13]

Chinese immigrants were characterized not only as lacking these gender and sexual arrangements but also as threatening white families' ability to maintain them. For instance, Pixley related that Chinese men undercut white men's ability to earn, while Chinese women caused disease and immorality among white men. Testimony also attributed nine tenths of venereal disease in the city to Chinese prostitutes and accused prostitutes of spreading leprosy and incurable forms of syphilis. According to Dr. Charles C. O'Donnell, "the virus of the cooly [sic], in my opinion, is almost sure death to the white man. That is my opinion because I have seen it. There are cases of syphilis among the whites that originated from these Chinese prostitutes that are incurable."[14] Chinese women were also blamed for encouraging immorality, even among young boys:

> I am satisfied, from my experience, that nearly all the boys who have venereal disease contracted it in Chinatown. They have no difficulty there for the prices are so low that they can go whenever they please. The women do not care how old the boys are, whether five years old or more, so long as they have money.[15]

Even those who testified in support of Chinese prostitution were not concerned about the women involved but about how to ensure that Chinese men remained useful laborers who did not threaten white men, white families, and the white nation. Thus, Senator Sargent suggested that since many domestic servants were Chinese men, the fact they could have sex with Chinese prostitutes helped to "protect our own families."[16] On those grounds, "it would be better for the Chinamen if they had more of them."[17] Dr. Stout also believed that Chinese men should have access to more, not fewer, Chinese prostitutes:

> That physiological necessity of man must be satisfied or crime must ensue. It is amazing, it is astonishing that such a population of Chinese being in our country, and there being so few women to satisfy that necessity of nature, that so little crime results from it.... That number [of Chinese prostitutes in San Francisco] is too little. There should be more.... It is irrepressible; it is a necessity. If there is a certain supply of women of that character, the family is much more sacred and much more pure.[18]

Such views remained the minority, however. The majority consensus was that Chinese prostitutes represented a distinct threat to the lives of white families.

The association of Chinese prostitutes with danger to the life of white families had been constructed through multiple social and material processes. According to Stuart Creighton Miller, the writings and testimonies of missionaries, traders, and diplomats greatly shaped popular U.S. images of the Chinese. The growth of the popular press and the negative coverage of China during the Opium War "populariz[ed] the anti-Chinese themes developed and polished by diplomats, traders, and missionaries over several decades."[19] Domestic experiences with the Chinese further shaped perceptions. Chinese arrival coincided with debate among race theorists about the monogenetic versus polygenetic origin of humans and the increasing demarcation of racial hierarchies that stamped the Chinese as inferior. Some racial theorists also articulated the belief that biological racial differences could not be changed through exposure to the supposedly ameliorative effects of American institutions and ways of life; instead, racial differences corresponded to an inability to understand the very notion of democracy. Thus, the presence of the "racially distinct" Chinese presented a threat to democratic institutions.[20] . . .

The common perception that all Chinese women were likely to be enslaved prostitutes had direct connections to scientific racism, because some scientific racists held that the status of women within various groups mirrored larger racial hierarchies. Thus, H. Hotz, whose "copious historical notes" are included in Count A. de Gobineau's tract on *The Moral and Intellectual Diversity of the Races*,[21] argued that the varied treatment of women proves that different races exist and are unequal:

> It is said that all barbarians treat their women as slaves; but, as they progress in civilization, woman gradually rises to her legitimate rank. . . .
>
> But I totally disagree that all races, in their first state of development, treated women equally. There is not only no historical testimony to prove that *any* of the white races were ever in such a state of barbarity and moral debasement as most of the dark races are to this day, and have always been, but there is positive evidence to show that our barbarous ancestors

> assigned to woman the same position that we assign to her now: she was the companion, and not the slave of man. . . . it is possible to demonstrate not only that all races did not treat their women equally in their first stage of development, but also, that no race which assigned to woman in the beginning an inferior position ever raised her from it in any subsequent stage of development. *I select the Chinese for illustration.*[22]

Clearly, women in China were perceived to be treated particularly poorly, but rather than inspiring efforts on their behalf, the perception served mainly to support racist condemnation of all Chinese people. As Chandra Talpade Mohanty indicates, this perception served to erase any consideration of how racism and imperialism contributed to Chinese women's status, and to racially differentiate and elevate white women.[23]

Chinese arrival also coincided with the development of germ theory, which made North Americans conscious of the connection between germs and disease. Filtered through the lens of racism, germ theory suggested that different racial groups carried distinct germs to which they were immune but others were not. Commentators from the penny press to the American Medical Association (AMA) took seriously the notion that Chinese immigrants carried distinct germs to which they were immune, but from which whites would die if exposed. "The germ theory of disease provided an explanation of the manner in which an obviously inferior group might best a superior one, contrary to the natural law of the social Darwinists."[24] Many of the fears became concentrated in a particularly dense form around the bodies of Chinese women who worked in prostitution. The sexual labor of Chinese prostitutes was believed to be the nexus through which germs and disease could most easily be transmitted to white men (prompting the AMA to study whether Chinese prostitutes were poisoning the nation's bloodstream).[25] Sex with Chinese prostitutes seemed to be the vector through which white supremacy and the perpetuity of "the white race" was directly threatened. Havelock Ellis, one of the most prominent sexologists of the nineteenth century, captured the ways that sexual concerns were inevitably also racial, when he wrote that "the question of sex—with the racial questions that rest on it—stands before the coming generations as the chief problem for solution."[26]

Thus, the Page Law, which mandated the exclusion of Asian women coming to the United States to work as prostitutes, responded to a constellation of what were believed to be serious threats to "white" values, lives, and futures.

DIFFERENTIATING "REAL" WIVES FROM PROSTITUTES

By examining how the Page Law was implemented, we discover the microphysics of power through which sexuality entered U.S. immigration control. The task, as it was presented to officials, was to differentiate "real" wives from women posing as wives but bound for sex work. According to historians, officials found such a differentiation difficult to make and, driven by racism, they implemented the law so harshly that almost all Chinese women ended up being barred from the United States. Such analyses suggest that the problem with the Page Law was officials' racist manner of implementation—but not the law's demand to differentiate among women on the basis of sexuality.

I want to suggest an alternative formulation, which is that officials had difficulty differentiating "real" wives from women bound for sex work because there is no absolute differentiation that can be made....

...Scholarship suggests that distinctions between women who get labeled as prostitutes and other women derive not from any inherent characteristics within the women themselves but from social relations of power. In an article about the history of prostitution in the United States, Miller, Romenesko, and Wondolkowski suggest that there are a myriad of difficulties in trying to define who is a prostitute and "whether or not [women] are so labeled depends more on the political stance of the potential moral entrepreneur who would seek to label them than on the degree to which their actual behavior deviates from some norm of correct conduct."[27] Illustrating their argument, Judith Walkowitz has documented

that in Victorian England prostitutes emerged as a distinct social group, separate from regular working-class communities, not because of anything inherent in the women or distinctive about their behavior but because of strategies that officials used to enforce the Contagious Diseases Act, which aimed to control the spread of venereal disease.[28] Gayle Rubin described a similar process that occurred in the nineteenth-century United States. She explains, "prostitution began to change from a temporary job to a more permanent occupation [and distinct social group] as a result of 19th century agitation, legal reform, and police persecution. Prostitutes, who had been part of the general working class population, became increasingly isolated as members of an outcast group."[29]

Yet even as a class of marginalized women who were stigmatized as prostitutes took shape, not all women who sold or bartered sex were labeled as prostitutes. Deborah Rhode highlights the unevenness of the process whereby certain women get labeled and penalized as prostitutes:

> streetwalkers, who tend to come from the lowest socioeconomic group, account for 10 to 15 percent of all prostitutes, and 80 to 90 percent of all arrests. Women of color account for 40 percent of streetwalkers, 55 percent of those arrested, and 85 percent of those receiving jail sentences.[30]

Rhode's analysis makes clear how the label "prostitute" becomes attached to particular groups of women (but not others) through social relations that are racist, classist, and gendered rather than because of any distinguishing behavioral or moral traits of the women involved.

...The sex industry is multitiered and continually changing, but public crackdowns focus disproportionately on streetwalkers rather than on women in other tiers.[31] Thus, streetwalkers remain the paradigmatic image of "the prostitute," while other women are much less likely to be arrested, labeled, or stigmatized, even when they sell sex too.

Streetwalkers are particularly likely to become stigmatized and subjected to efforts at control in times of social transformation.... According to Ruth Rosen, discourses about prostitution in the United

States have provided a means for people to express concerns about "unrestricted immigration, the rate of venereal disease, the anonymity of the city, the evils of liquor, the growth of working class urban culture, and, most important of all, the changing role of women in society."[32] ...

... But which women become labeled and treated as "prostitutes" as a result depends greatly on what tier of the sex industry they work in, prevailing anxieties of the time, and how these anxieties become directed at some class and racial or ethnic groups but not others. The labels also reflect culture-specific beliefs about how sex and gender systems should operate. For instance, during hard times in China, women and girls were commonly sold into domestic service, concubinage, or prostitution, and one form of sale could lead to another.[33] Yet not all domestic servants, called *mui tsai*, were resold; some continued providing domestic service until freed through marriage. But the practice of selling women, and the difficulties of differentiating between various kinds of sales, led immigration officials to assume that all girls traveling in groups were surely prostitutes, rather than, for example, *mui tsai*.[34] A further source of confusion to officials was the fact that some Chinese men had concubines, in addition to first wives. Concubines, who were usually of lower social status and acquired through purchase, were legal members of the family, and their children were their fathers' legal heirs. But concubinage, which reflected a sex and gender system that was different from the dominant U.S. culture, contributed to officials' beliefs that virtually all immigrant Chinese women were enslaved prostitutes.[35]

The variety of sex/gender arrangements evident among Chinese immigrants actually underscores a more general point, which is that there is no necessary opposition between women who sell or trade sex while occupying various social statuses, and wives.[36] William Sanger's pioneering study of prostitution in New York City in the 1850s showed that among the 2,000 women he identified as prostitutes, 490 (or 25 percent) were also married, and 71 lived with their husbands while working in prostitution.[37] Historians of Chinese women in America have also documented that marriage was one of the routes through which sex workers left the industry. Based on census figures, Benson Tong estimates that "during the 1870s, a large number of Chinese prostitutes left the trade and very likely entered into matrimony."[38] Peggy Pascoe affirms that "the highly skewed sex ratio in immigrant Chinatowns ... and the absence of established in-laws, created unusual opportunities for immigrant prostitutes to marry and leave prostitution behind."[39] Indeed, Pascoe further suggests that many Chinese immigrant women "regarded prostitution as a means of finding a husband or making a financial start in the United States, an opportunity that would enable them to lead a better life or support a poverty-stricken family at home."[40] While marriage provided a way out of sex work for some early immigrant Chinese women, a small number of women were both married and engaged in sex work. Sucheng Chan notes that "the 1900 census manuscript showed that some brothels in San Francisco were run by couples, among whom a few wives were apparently continuing their profession [as prostitutes]."[41] Women in other racial and ethnic groups also combined marriage and sex work, too.

IMPLEMENTING THE PAGE LAW

... Racism and sexism ensured that "real" wives became labeled and treated administratively as prostitutes—because that category designates women who occupy positions of social vulnerability, rather than a distinct "type" of woman.

... During the first years after passage of the Page Law, the American Consul in Hong Kong played a pivotal role in its enforcement. Prior to emigration, each Chinese woman had to submit "an official declaration of purpose in emigration and personal morality" statement, accompanied by an application for clearance and a fee, to the American Consul.[42] The declaration was sent to an association of the most prominent businessmen in Hong Kong, the Tung Wah Hospital Committee, for investigation. A list of intending emigrants was also sent to the British colonial government in Hong Kong for investigation. The day before the ship sailed, each woman had to answer questions before the consul. These included such inquiries as:

> Have you entered into contract or agreement with any person or persons whomsoever, for a term of service within the United States for lewd and immoral purposes? Do you wish of your own free and voluntary will to go to the United States? Do you go to the United States for the purposes of prostitution? Are you married or single? What are you going to the United States for? What is to be your occupation there? Have you lived in a house of prostitution in Hong Kong, Macao, or China? Have you engaged in prostitution in either [*sic*] of the above places? Are you a virtuous woman? Do you intend to live a virtuous life in the United States? Do you know that you are at liberty now to go to the United States, or remain in your own country, and that you cannot be forced to go away from your home?[43]

On the day of sailing, each woman had to answer similar questions about morality and reasons for emigration, this time put by the Harbor Master. Once on board the ship, she was questioned again. Women who passed this rigorous series of interrogations were given a certificate of good moral character, which they had to present on arrival in San Francisco if they wanted to land. While the ship sailed, the Consul sent a photograph of each woman who had been approved, along with a letter testifying to her character, to the ship's destination. Sometimes he also sent a letter urging further investigation of a particular woman.[44]

Information about how women were processed on arrival in San Francisco after passage of the Page Law is somewhat sketchy. But transcripts of a habeas corpus hearing involving several Chinese women, held in San Francisco just prior to the passage of the Chinese Exclusion Act in 1882, provide some indication. According to testimony by Colonel Bee, the American Consul for the Chinese, he met all arriving ships from Hong Kong. Accompanied by his Vice Consul and interpreter and by the Deputy Surveyor of the Port of San Francisco, he boarded the ship, and "[got] access to the women before anyone else."[45] He gathered copies of their paperwork with the

photographs attached and, using the interpreter, he asked each woman the same questions that she had been asked in Hong Kong. The replies given in Hong Kong were included in each woman's paperwork, and these replies were cross-checked against what she said on arrival in San Francisco.[46] According to Bee's testimony, the questions asked of the women had changed somewhat since Consul Bailey's tenure. For the court, Bee listed the questions that women were asked:

> Native residence in Hong Kong; number of the storeys to the house; name of the people in the house; when and from what place I came to Hong Kong; person or persons with whom I came; name, country, and occupation of my father; name, country, and occupation of my husband; names and addresses of sureties; relatives or friends from whom inquiries can be made; the person or persons with whom I am going; the object of my going; the place to which I am going; the street and number of the house where I can be seen.[47]

If the women answered the questions with the same information that was included in their paperwork, and if they matched the photographs, "we have no authority whatever to detain them."[48] But if women did not answer the questions the same way, or did not match the photographs, or carried paperwork that was incompletely filled out, they were liable to be detained. George Peffer estimates that between 1875 and 1882 at least one hundred and perhaps several hundred women were sent back as a result of these procedures.

...In the case of Chinese women seeking to immigrate to the United States, biographical details were elicited only after they had been corralled into carefully controlled spaces. The first two interrogations were carried out in the Consul's and Harbor Master's offices, and on their terms. The third interrogation took place immediately before the ship sailed, in a manner designed to ensure that the woman who answered the officials' questions "correctly" was also the one who sailed for San Francisco (rather than a substitute being sent in her place). On arrival in San Francisco, the women were confined on the ship to ensure that Colonel Bee "[got] access to them before anyone else." Only after answering questions to Bee's satisfaction were the women permitted to join relatives and friends waiting on the dock. The strategic control of space that Chinese women endured was intended by officials to generate the "truth" of their sexual pasts and likely sexual futures. Spatial control was designed to minimize opportunities for the women to be "coached" about what to say to officials, to avoid substitutions, and most likely to provide women who had been kidnapped with an opportunity to speak openly outside the hearing of their procurers. Yet, as Benson Tong suggests, the likelihood of kidnapped women speaking openly to an unknown official was small (though it did sometimes happen).[49] Furthermore, the whole process was shaped by the larger, explicitly racist assumption that "a Chinaman prefers a lie to the truth" and that Chinese women were equally dishonest.[50] As Stuart Creighton Miller describes, a founding image among Western traders, diplomats, and missionaries was that the Chinese were dishonest, tricky, and sneaky, and this image led to the development of exhaustive regimes of questioning, conducted through strictly controlling space and minimizing contact with other Chinese people, which were believed to be the best way to elicit "truth" from Chinese immigrants.[51] Judy Yung underscores that this process was "different not only in degree but in kind" from that endured by other immigrants.[52] The process was not just racist but also racializing, in the sense of helping to literally construct the Chinese as a distinct and racialized group. After passage of the Page Law, Chinese women became subjected to an early form of this racializing process.[53]

The questioning to which Chinese women were subjected involved gender and class dimensions, too. For instance, although the women's individual histories mattered, their fathers' and husbands' mattered more. Officials assumed that women's likelihood of becoming sex workers in the United States depended on their family background and husbands' occupations. Therefore, they wanted to be sure that women came from "respectable" families and were joining husbands who were demonstrably able to support them. To some extent, the officials' approach was cognizant of the realities of limited economic possibilities for immigrant women of color in the U.S. economy at that time. It also took into account the fact that Chinese women did often enter the United States believing that they were joining husbands, only to find that they had been tricked and sold into prostitution. But rather than challenging these conditions, officials simply accepted that male intentions and actions were more likely to determine a woman's sexual future than her own actions and intentions, and processed her case accordingly. Thus, ironically, officials further institutionalized the structures of patriarchy for which they condemned Chinese men. Their processes also institutionalized a distinct class bias regarding Chinese women's possibilities for immigration.[54]

... Individual Chinese women's testimonies never enabled a reliable differentiation between "real" wives and prostitutes. But the testimonies' circulation structurally changed the organization of immigration control.

Biographical data, however, was made fully subjectifying only when it was attached to a photograph. Photographs provided one of the earliest methods for officially recording the body's distinctiveness and using the record to control an individual's mobility. This system was used on Chinese women before any other group of immigrants, because of the "threat" of their sexuality to the United States. A photograph was attached to each woman's consular clearance, and another photograph was sent in advance of the ship, so that when the ship arrived, officials already had in their possession photographs of the women who had been approved for migration. Women who arrived without photographs, or who did not match the photographs that had been sent in advance, were detained and returned to Hong Kong. Through these very simple techniques, officials tried to ensure that if a particular woman was cleared for immigration on the basis of biographical data provided, another woman was not sent in her place.[55]

By contrast, officials did not attempt to link together specific biographies and bodies in the case of Chinese men or anyone else who immigrated at the same time. In testimony before Congress in 1877, the collector of the port related that if one thousand

Chinese men were authorized to land and twelve hundred arrived, officials let any thousand land, without trying to determine exactly which thousand were cleared.[56] Some five years later, Colonel Bee testified in court that immigrating Chinese men were still treated less rigorously than women. "We go through the steerage and ask them if they are free laborers, if they come under contract to anybody or under bond to any one and if any one says he is not free we send him back."[57] Mr. Quint, the attorney representing several Chinese women who had been denied landing because they were suspected of coming to the United States for prostitution, asked, "are not each one of these [men] required to have papers the same as females?" But Bee affirmed, "No, I believe not, sir."[58] Men were also not required to carry photographs, nor to match photographs that had been sent in advance to San Francisco port authorities.

Thus, Chinese women were the first group of immigrants whose mobility was regulated by the exchange of photographs between officials. Photographs tied a specific body to biographical data that had been approved by officials for migration. Only as of the second decade of the twentieth century, according to John Torpey, would such a system become broadly implemented in the United States through passport controls.[59] Until then, racialized, gendered, and sexualized Others disproportionately bore the burden of such techniques, as the experience of Chinese women shows.

Other techniques also supplemented (and in some cases supplanted) the use of photography as a means to anchor a body to a specific biography in ways that ensured official control. For instance, Bertillionage, a system of taking nine measurements of different parts of the body and recording these measurements in file cards, was certainly used on Chinese immigrants by the turn of the century.[60] Immigrants who left and wanted to reenter had to submit to being remeasured; if their measurements matched those recorded in the file cards, they were let in. Fingerprinting also came to provide an unchangeable physical mark that officials used to tie individuals to specific biographies in ways that controlled them.[61] More recently, the INS has pioneered a biometric

data system called INPASS. As Daniel Sutherland describes:

> An INPASS is available to U.S. citizens and resident aliens who fly internationally on a regular basis. The [person] provided the INS with biographical data—home address, date of birth, office address, position in his company, and number of international trips he anticipates making—so the agency could verify that he is authorized by the government to travel. The INS then took an image of his hand geometry (a type of "biometric" data—physical characteristics that are unique to each person, such as a person's voice or retina pattern) and electronically recorded it on a plastic card. The agency also stored the biographical and biometric data in a central computer. Although INPASS is currently a voluntary program, it is designed to demonstrate the feasibility of including machine-readable biographical and biometric data on U.S. passports.[62]

The *New York Times* also reports that the INS has begun to rely on dental and bone X rays when trying to determine how to process people who arrive at airports without documents, or with questionable documents.[63] The X rays are intended to determine whether the person is under eighteen, because adults and minors are processed differently. At some large U.S. airports, arrivals with problematic or missing documents are brought directly to the airport dentist, where the dental drill and row of medicine bottles is their first glimpse of America, and where they are X-rayed. The use of X rays as a means to definitively determine age has been disputed, but nonetheless continues. Through these and other techniques, which were initially used against Chinese women after passage of the Page Law, official techniques for recording the body's distinctiveness and anchoring it to specific biographical data became the locus for new forms of subjection. . . .

I noted above that scientific racism and popular prejudice facilitated the assumption that bodies that "looked" Chinese were likely to be involved in prostitution. Of course, the idea that Chinese bodies "look" a particular way had to be constructed by scientific racism and then disseminated into popular wisdom.[64] At the risk of stating the obvious, these bodies also had to "look" female, in order to be presumed to be prostitutes. Little has been written about the significance of seeming to have a female, rather than a male, body when being processed for immigration, but there can be no doubt that gender appearance mattered.[65] The salience of gender is suggested by Lucie Cheng's description of how some Chinese tongs smuggled women into the United States for work in prostitution by dressing them as boys.[66] The strategy would be effective only if females and males were subjected to different regimes of processing, regardless of their common "Chineseness." Therefore, "looking" both Chinese and female was what triggered official suspicions that the immigrant was likely a prostitute.

Yet the conflation of Chinese women's bodies with prostitute bodies was never absolute, or officials would not have needed to try to differentiate prostitutes from "real" wives. Accordingly, other signs were also sought. A series of "scientific" discourses, which predated the Page Law, suggested that prostitute bodies carried distinct marks, in addition to features that we are accustomed to thinking of as racial or gendered, which set them apart. For instance, Dr. Alexandre Parent-Duchatelet published an 1836 book about Parisian prostitutes, describing his efforts to delineate a distinct prostitute physiognomy.[67] Subsequent work by the St. Petersburg physician Pauline Tarnowsky claimed that over the course of their lives, the faces of prostitutes looked more degenerate and more mannish, and their genitalia became visibly altered.[68] In 1893 Cesare Lombroso published a study that suggested that prostitutes had distinct genitalia and prehensile feet.[69] By the early twentieth century, eugenicists argued that prostitutes suffered from feeblemindedness and that this condition might be discerned from looking at the face, but could also be objectively diagnosed through use of the Binet intelligence test.[70] In these and other ways, prostitute bodies were believed to be visibly distinct, though no one could agree on what was a reliable differentiating mark.

But testimonies before Congress and reports in immigrant case files show that one of the physical marks that officials often seized upon when inspecting Chinese women was bound feet. At an 1877 hearing before the Joint Special Committee to Investigate Chinese Immigration, dissenting opinions were expressed about the extent to which bound feet were a reliable indicator of "respectability." But Judy Yung suggests that at least some inspectors relied heavily on bound feet when determining whether a Chinese woman was likely to be a prostitute:

> Only women such as my great grandmother who had bound feet and a modest demeanor were considered upper class women with "moral integrity." As one immigration officer wrote in his report, "There has never come to this port, I believe, a bound footed woman who was found to be of immoral character, this condition of affairs being due, it is stated, to the fact that such women, and especially those in the interior, are necessarily confined to their home and seldom frequent the city districts."[71]

This interpretation of the significance of bound feet was not necessarily accurate.[72] But for some officials, bound feet came to serve as a physical mark on which to rely when trying to differentiate prostitutes from "real" wives, as is evident from the extent to which immigration records regularly contain questions and notes about Chinese women's feet.

No doubt, questions of "prettiness," youth, demeanor, and how she walked, were among other bodily "clues" that shaped officials' responses to a Chinese woman seeking to immigrate. As Yung relates, the inspector who processed her great grandmother also wrote, "the present applicant No. 14418 is a very modest appearing woman whose evident sincerity, frankness of expression, and generally favorable demeanor is very convincing."[73]

Officials looked not only at the body but also at the woman's clothes when making judgments about her. Prostitutes have a history of dressing distinctively,[74] sometimes because they were required to, or as a means to advertise their services, display subcultural solidarity, or express class aspirations.[75] It is not entirely surprising, then, that immigration officials carefully examined the clothing of women seeking entry to the United States. At a hearing on Chinese immigration, one official asked, "I have heard there is a difference in the coloring of the lining of the sleeves of the gown [of prostitutes], and that they are distinguished by different costumes?"[76] Though differences in dress were not substantiated, dress remained another aspect of appearance that inspectors carefully examined.

In sum, the appearance of the body and clothing supposedly offered a range of possible clues about "inner character," on which some officials drew when trying to differentiate prostitutes from "real" wives. Though this approach, too, failed to yield any reliable differentiations, it ensured that the dominant philosophical paradigm of the time and the "scientific" studies it generated were centrally though informally incorporated into immigration control. The photographs that were employed to constrain Chinese women's mobility serve as traces of the incorporation of these other processes into immigration control....

The Page Law, which particularly targeted working-class Chinese immigrant women, required officials to differentiate "real" wives from women bound for sex work and to deny entry to the latter. It was an impossible task. The idea that such a differentiation could be made was, as Foucault puts it, a "ruse" that both marked and facilitated particular arrangements of power. But these arrangements were sanctioned because Chinese prostitutes had become popularly identified with multiple dangers to white lives, institutions, and nation. As a result, officials developed techniques for trying to differentiate "real" wives from prostitutes through the elicitation of biographical details, photography, and the creation of case files. Although these techniques never enabled officials to reliably differentiate among women, they had several important effects. For one, the techniques concretely introduced concerns about sexuality into U.S. immigration control processes. They compelled the production of discourses about sexuality and gave rise to varied circuits for exchanging and evaluating these discourses. The circuits linked together bureaucrats, experts, politicians, and the public in new ways, around preoccupations with sexuality, immigration, and nation. The techniques also enabled officials to constitute Chinese women as subjectified and disciplined in racial, gendered, class, and sexual terms.

Over time, the policing of immigrants around sexuality, which the Page Law inaugurated, became extended to all newcomers. It remains a central feature of immigration control today.

A focus on the problematic effects of techniques for trying to differentiate prostitutes from other women suggests the need to revise traditional analyses about how immigration control reproduces social inequalities. Certainly, discriminatory laws and officials' prejudices have substantially ensured that U.S. immigration control functioned to sustain racial, gender, sexual, and class hierarchies. But even if the laws were overturned and prejudiced officials let go, immigration control would still reproduce social hierarchies. This is because the techniques and systems of knowledge on which its daily operations depend are deeply rooted in histories of racism, sexism, imperialism, and exploitation, as the history of restrictions on Chinese immigrant women shows. To create real transformation, these techniques and systems of knowledge must also be analyzed and changed.

NOTES

1. U.S. Immigration and Naturalization Service, *Statistical Yearbook of the Immigration and Naturalization Service, 1991*, A1–2.
2. Three of the five provisions of the Page Law dealt with prostitution. E. P. Hutchinson summarizes, "The first section made it a duty of consular officials at any port from which subjects of China, Japan, or other Oriental nations were to depart for the United States to determine whether such travel was 'free and voluntary,' and to ascertain whether any such travelers were under contract or agreement to serve for 'lewd and immoral purposes' in the United States, and in the latter case, to refuse to grant the required permit for travel. The third section of the act forbade the importation of women for prostitution, outlawed all contracts and agreements for such importation, and made illegal importation a felony subject to imprisonment of up to five years and a fine of up to $5,000. The fifth section included 'women imported for the purposes of prostitution' as one of the excluded classes." See E. P. Hutchinson, *Legislative History*, 419–20. About the provisions for convicts and contract laborers, see Salyer, *Laws Harsh as Tigers*, 260 n. 76, and Peffer, *If They Don't Bring Their Women Here*, 8.

3. As chapter 1 shows, laws subsequently mandated the exclusion of prostitutes of every nationality, "immoral" women, single women who "arrived in a state of pregnancy," lesbians and gay men, polygamists, and other people considered undesirable as immigrants on sexual grounds.

4. Judy Yung, *Unbound Feet: A Social History of Chinese Women in San Francisco* (Berkeley: University of California Press, 1995), 18.

5. Benson Tong, *Unsubmissive Women: Chinese Prostitutes in Nineteenth-Century San Francisco* (Norman: University of Oklahoma Press, 1994), 4–5. Similarly, Judy Yung writes: "The scarcity of women in the American West, the suspension of social and moral restraints, and the easy access to wealth during the early years of the gold rush attracted women from different parts of the world. The first prostitutes to arrive were women from Mexico, Peru, and Chile; these were followed by women from France and other European countries, as well as women from American cities such as New York and New Orleans" (*Unbound Feet*, 26).

6. Yung, *Unbound Feet*, 31. Sucheng Chan corroborates this analysis, writing that "during the gold rush and for several decades thereafter, prostitutes of many nationalities lived and worked in San Francisco. Municipal authorities tried sporadically to suppress prostitution and they singled out Chinese women for special attention from the beginning" ("The Exclusion of Chinese Women," 97). See also Tomás Almaguer, *Racial Fault Lines* (Berkeley: University of California Press, 1994), 177–78.

7. Benson Tong notes that the city of San Francisco passed another anti-prostitution ordinance in 1869, this time directing that the doors of brothels should be kept shut (presumably so that passers-by could not see what was going on inside, and perhaps to also prevent women from advertising).

8. Jacqueline Barker Barnhardt, *The Fair but Frail: Prostitution in San Francisco 1849–1900* (Reno: University of Nevada Press, 1980), 49.

9. Quoted in Sucheng Chan, "Exclusion and Chinese Women," 103.

10. George Peffer, *If They Don't Bring Their Women Here*, 33.

11. *Chinese Immigration; Its Social, Moral and Political Effects*, Report to the California State Senate of its Special Committee on Chinese Immigration (Sacramento: State Printing Office, 1878), 272.

12. *Report of the Joint Special Commission to Investigate Chinese Immigration*, Rpt. 689, 44th Cong., 2d Sess., Senate (Washington, D.C.: USGPO, 1877), 19. (Hereafter *Report*.)

13. *Report*, 19.

14. *Report*, 1097.

15. *Report*, 14.

16. *Report*, 143.

17. *Report*, 143.

18. *Report*, 652.

19. Stuart Creighton Miller, *The Unwelcome Immigrant: The American Image of the Chinese* (Berkeley: University of California Press, 1966), 112.

20. Audrey Smedley, *Race in North America* (Boulder: Westview Press, 1993), 269.

21. De Gobineau was one of the preeminent scientific racists of the nineteenth century.

22. *The Moral* and Intellectual Diversity of the Races, from the French by Count A. De Gobineau, with an analytic introduction and copious historical notes by H. Hotz (Philadelphia: J.B. Lippincott and Co., 1865), 287, 385, 386. My emphasis.

23. Chandra Talpade Mohanty, "Under Western Eyes: Feminist Scholarship and Colonial Discourses" in Chandra Talpade Mohanty, Ann Russo, and Lourdes Torres, eds., *Third World Women and the Politics of Feminism* (Bloomington: Indiana University Press, 1991), 51–80.

24. Miller, *The Unwelcome Immigrant*, 166.

25. Ibid., 163.

26. Quoted in Siobhan Somerville, "Scientific Racism and the Emergence of the Homosexual Body," in *Journal of the History of Sexuality* 5, no. 2 (1994), 246.

27. Eleanor Miller, Kim Romenesko, and Lisa Wondolkowski, "The United States," in *Prostitution: An International Handbook of Trends, Problems, and Policies*, ed. Nanette J. Davis (Westport, Conn.: Greenwood Press, 1993), 309.

28. Judith Walkowitz, *Prostitution and Victorian Society: Women, Class, and the State* (Cambridge: Cambridge University Press, 1980).

29. Gayle S. Rubin, "Thinking Sex: Notes for a Radical Theory of the Politics of Sexuality," in *The Lesbian and Gay Studies Reader*, eds. Henry Abelove, Michele Aina Barale, and David M. Halperin (New York: Routledge, 1993), 17–18.

30. Deborah Rhode, *Justice and Gender: Sex Discrimination and the Law* (Cambridge: Harvard University Press, 1989), 261.

31. According to Priscilla Alexander, tiers in the sex industry include streetwalking, massage parlors, bar and café prostitution, brothels, and "call girl" or escort services. Priscilla Alexander, "Prostitution: A Difficult Issue for Feminists," in Frederique Delacoste and Priscilla Alexander, eds., *Sex Work: Writings by Women*

in the Sex Industry (Pittsburgh, PA: Cleis Press, 1987), 189–90. These tiers may have been modified since Alexander described them, with new tiers emerging.

32. Ruth Rosen, *The Lost Sisterhood: Prostitution in America, 1900–1918* (Baltimore: The Johns Hopkins University Press, 1982), xiii.

33. Alternatively, poor families might put their daughters up for adoption rather than sell them. Adoption took two forms: as a future daughter-in-law, which was considered a betrothal, or as a real daughter, in which case the girl became part of the family. See Sue Gronewold, *Beautiful Merchandise: Prostitution in China 1860–1936* (New York: Haworth Press, 1982), 39.

34. See Peffer, *If They Don't Bring Their Women Here*, 71.

35. For more information on the sex/gender system in nineteenth-century China, see Gronewold, *Beautiful Merchandise*; Kay Ann Johnson, *Women, the Family, and Peasant Revolution in China* (Chicago: University of Chicago Press, 1983); Olga Lang, *Chinese Family and Society* (New Haven: Yale University Press, 1946); Rubie S. Watson and Patricia Buckley Ebrey, eds., *Marriage and Inequality in Chinese Society* (Berkeley: University of California Press, 1991). On marriage resistance among women in Guangdong, which was the home of most early Chinese immigrants to California, see Janice Stockard, *Daughters of the Canton Delta* (Stanford: Stanford University Press, 1989). According to Gronewold (and contrary to dominant U.S. ideologies of the time), "the rite of marriage was almost universally regarded as a sad occasion" for Chinese women (p. 41).

36. Gail Hershatter puts the point more forcefully, arguing that both prostitution and marriage have to be situated on a shared continuum of claims to women's sexual services. See Gail Hershatter, "Prostitution and the Market in Women in Early 20th Century Shanghai," in Watson and Ebrey, eds., *Marriage and Inequality in Chinese Society*, 258. Hershatter's essay examines "similarities between marriage and prostitution in Shanghai, as well as the movement of individuals from one to the other" (259).

37. Sanger characterizes the existence of these 71 as "an announcement so disgraceful to humanity that . . . it would scarcely be credited." He also offers an analysis of why, in his view, married women might work as prostitutes: "Sufficient [*sic*] has been proved to show that in many cases, prostitution among married women is the result of circumstances which must have exercised a very powerful influence over them. The refusal of a husband to support his wife, his desertion of her, or an act of adultery with another woman, are

each occurrences which must operate injuriously upon the mind of any female, and, by the keen torture that such outrages inflict on the sensitiveness of her nature, must drive her into a course of dissipation. Many women thus circumstanced have actually confessed that they made the first false step while smarting from injuries inflicted by their natural protectors, with the idea of being revenged upon their brutal or faithless companions for their unkindness. Morality will argue, and very truly, that this is no excuse for crime; but much allowance must be made for the extreme nature of the provocation, and the fact that most of these women are uneducated, and have not sufficient mental or moral illumination to reason correctly upon the nature and consequences of their voluntary debauchery, or even to curb the violence of their passions." See William W. Sanger, *The History of Prostitution: Its Extent, Causes, and Effects Throughout the World* (New York: Eugenics Publishing Company Edition, 1937), 475–76.

38. Tong, *Unsubmissive Women*, 159.

39. Peggy Pascoe, *Relations of Rescue* (New York: Oxford University Press, 1990), 95.

40. Pascoe, *Relations of Rescue*, 96. Pascoe adds, "their employment as sexual 'slaves'—the fact that so troubled mission women—did not in itself lead them to request help; for the most part, they contacted missionaries only when they felt that their owners had treated them particularly badly."

41. Sucheng Chan, *This Bittersweet Soil: The Chinese in California Agriculture, 1860–1910* (Berkeley: University of California Press, 1986), 390. Chan also includes statistics on the small numbers of married Chinese women who worked as prostitutes, according to census data for the Sacramento Delta in 1880 and 1900. See 392–393.

42. George Peffer, "Forbidden Families: Emigration Experiences of Chinese Women under the Page Law, 1875–1882," *Journal of American Ethnic History* 6, no. 1 (fall 1986), 33.

43. Peffer, "Forbidden Families," 32. David Bailey, the American consul in Hong Kong between 1875 and 1877, asked these questions of women applicants who appeared at the consulate on the day that he got word of the Page Law's passage. Over time, he likely altered the questions somewhat, but this is one sample of what the questions covered.

44. Peffer, "Forbidden Families," 31–35; Tong, *Unsubmissive Women*, 34–77. According to Peffer, these procedures were developed by David Bailey. Peffer relates that Bailey's successor, Sheldon Loring, who served until 1879, was also reasonably diligent in following these

procedures, as was his successor, John Mosby, until 1881. After 1881 Mosby decided that he would no longer examine Chinese women departing on non-U.S. vessels, even if they were bound for the United States, and in June 1882 he declared that he had abolished the entire procedure established by his predecessors. However, Mosby's abolition of procedure "occurred too near the implementation of the [1882 Chinese] Exclusion Act to exert an impact on Chinese female immigration" (54). See Peffer, *If They Don't Bring Their Women Here,* 43–56.

45. Testimony of Col. F. A. Bee, in U.S. District Court, Northern California District, *In The Matter of Wah Ah Chin and Others for Their Discharge on Writ of Habeas Corpus,* No. 2495, March 1882, 19.

46. According to the ship's captain, Colonel Bee also had duplicates of the women's paperwork and photographs in his possession when he boarded the ship, which had presumably been sent to him from Hong Kong.

47. Testimony of Col. F. A. Bee, *In The Matter of Wah Ah Chin and Others,* 19–20.

48. Ibid., 20.

49. Tong suggests that most of the women "belonged to a different cultural and legal environment and had been brought up to believe that all 'foreign devils' were 'barbarians'—a belief reinforced by their agents during the voyage to America." This would have discouraged many of them from seeking assistance from U.S. officials. (*Unsubmissive Women,* 64.)

50. *Report,* 987.

51. Miller, *The Unwelcome Immigrant,* 14. Miller writes that "the allegedly universal dishonesty in China [was] mentioned by 37 [of 50] of the sample" of traders' accounts and echoed in books published by diplomats. See *The Unwelcome Immigrant,* 29–30.

52. Yung, *Unbound Feet,* 66.

53. In the years following the Page Law, control of space and detailed questioning were combined in acute forms to try to produce the "truth" of all Chinese immigrants' testimonies. For instance, "during his term as collector [of the port of San Francisco] between 1889 and 1893, Timothy Phelps devised a system of investigation which attempted to expose fraudulent testimony. The inspectors questioned the applicant and his [or her] witness separately and in great detail about their family and village in China. Inspectors would ask questions such as, How many steps were there out of the family's back door? How many houses were there in the village? Did the mother have bound feet? If discrepancies existed in the testimony, the inspectors assumed that the parties did not know each other and that the applicant's claim was false. Chinese immigrants dreaded the inspector's investigations. Over the years, the inspector's drilling became longer and more refined" (Salyer, *Laws Harsh as Tigers,* 59). These interrogations easily lasted weeks and even months, and while they were going on, immigrants were kept carefully separated from family and friends. They were detained either in the Pacific Mail steamship shed, or, after 1910, on Angel Island. In these locations, their movements were carefully circumscribed. For instance, exercise was barely permitted and sharply supervised so that immigrants could not talk to anyone else. Parcels and visitors were denied. Even food parcels were denied, because officials feared that information that coached immigrants in what to say to officials might be included in the food. Stories of ingenious Chinese methods for smuggling coaching information are legion; one story, related in an immigration report, sheds light on the reasons for the restrictions against outside food. According to the report, "the device adopted to deliver the coaching letter was this: the letter was written in small characters on a slip of tissue paper, which was rolled tightly and placed inside of a large peanut shell, the two halves of which were carefully glued together, and then placed in a bag and sent to the Chinaman." (See *Facts Concerning the Enforcement of Chinese Exclusion Laws,* House Document 847, U.S. House of Representatives, 59th Congress, 1st Sess., 25 May 1906 [Washington, D.C.: U.S. Government Printing Office], 10.) Contact with Chinese staff was also restricted to the greatest degree possible, for fear that staff had been paid to pass on coaching information. The authors of *Island* also relate that "a different interpreter was used for each session" of a case, to forestall collusion. See Him Mark Lai, Genny Lim, and Judy Yung, *Island: Poetry and History of Chinese Immigrants on Angel Island, 1910–1940* (San Francisco: HOCDOI, 1982), 22.

54. Under the Chinese Exclusion Act of 1882, this class bias would be extended to men.

55. As John Torpey expressed it, the principle involved is that "the person's body is used *against* him or her." *The Invention of the Passport,* 17.

56. See *Report,* 392–93.

57. Testimony of Col. F. A. Bee, *In The Matter of Wah Ah Chin and Others,* 24.

58. Ibid. Bee further told the court that "I have never sent any males back. We have sent females" (24).

59. Torpey, *The Invention of the Passport,* 117–18.

60. On the use of Bertillionage in the United States, see Donald C. Dilworth, ed., *Identification Wanted:*

Development of the American Criminal Identification System, 1893–1943 (Gaithersburg, Md.: International Association of Chiefs of Police, 1977); Alan Sekula, "The Body and the Archive," in Richard Bolton, ed., *The Contest of Meaning: Critical Histories of Photography* (Cambridge: MIT Press, 1989), 343–89; Shawn Michelle Smith, *American Archives* (Princeton: Princeton University Press, 1999), 68–93. I have found little information about the use of Bertillionage as a technique for immigration control. The one reference I found concerned using Bertillionage to control Chinese immigrants' entry, specifically between 1903 and 1906. See *Facts Concerning the Enforcement of Chinese Exclusion Laws*, 31.

61. According to Paul Rabinow, "the first practical use of fingerprints took place in Bengal. As Major Ferris of the India Staff Corps put it, 'the uniformity in the colour of the hair, eyes, and complexion of the Indian races renders identification far from easy.' The proverbial 'prevalence of unveracity' of the Oriental races provided another motivation for these gentlemen to perfect a reliable identification system, one whose basis lay in a marker beyond or below the cunning will of the native or criminal." (See Paul Rabinow, "Galton's Regret," in Rabinow, *Essays on the Anthropology of Reason* [Princeton: Princeton University Press, 1996], 113.) Although fingerprints are a mark of the body that cannot be altered and result in precise identitications, Rabinow relates that Galton's regret was precisely that fingerprints could not reveal anything about the "race" or "inner character" of the person.

62. Daniel W. Sutherland, "The High-Tech ID Menace," *The American Spectator* 32, no. 2 (February 1999), 60. Teeth X rays have been recently used as a means to determine the age of people seeking asylum who claim to be minors but are suspected of lying. See Chris Hedges, "Crucial INS Gatekeeper: The Airport Dentist," *New York Times*, 22 July 2000, A1.

63. See Chris Hedges, "Crucial I.N.S. Gatekeeper: The Airport Dentist," *New York Times*, 22 July 2000, A1, A14.

64. Robyn Wiegman refers to "the cultural training that quite literally teaches the eye not only how but what to see" (22), and she analyzes the role of visual regimes in "making race real" (21) in *American Anatomies: Theorizing Race and Gender* (Durham: Duke University Press, 1995). See especially "Economies of Visibility," 21–78.

65. Readers should keep in mind that beliefs that bodies can be divided unambiguously into male and female are culturally constructed, and, furthermore, there are differences between seeming to have a body that is culturally coded as male or female versus an individual's own bodily identifications.

66. Lucie Cheng Hirata, "Free, Indentured, Enslaved: Chinese Prostitutes in Nineteenth-Century America," in Lucie Cheng Hirata and Edna Bonacich, eds., *Labor Immigration under Capitalism: Asian Workers in the U.S. Before World War II* (Berkeley: University of California Press, 1984), 410.

67. Sander Gilman, *Difference and Pathology: Stereotypes of Sexuality, Race, and Madness* (Ithaca: Cornell University Press, 1985), 94.

68. Ibid., 95–96.

69. Gilman, *Difference and Pathology*, 98; Steven Jay Gould, *The Mismeasure of Man* (New York: Norton, 1981), 129.

70. According to Mark Haller, "The Massachusetts Commission for the Investigation of White Slave Traffic, in one of the most significant investigations of Vice, gave Binet tests to one hundred young prostitutes and two hundred experienced prostitutes. Not only did more than half test feebleminded, but the behavior of the prostitutes confirmed what the tests indicated: 'The general lack of moral insensibility, the boldness, egotism, and vanity, the love of notoriety, the lack of shame or remorse, the absence of even a pretense of affection for their own children or their parents, the desire for immediate pleasure without regard for consequences, the lack of forethought or anxiety about the future—all cardinal symptoms of feeblemindedness—were strikingly evident in every one of the 154 women.'" (See Mark H. Haller, *Eugenics: Hereditarian Attitudes in American Thought*, 103.) Eugenicists became directly involved in immigration administration. For instance, in 1912 Henry Goddard, a leading eugenicist, was invited to assist at Ellis Island in selecting immigrants who might be feeble-minded or mentally deficient and should be denied entry. See Alan M. Kraut, *Silent Travelers*, 74.

71. Yung, *Unbound Feet*, 24.

72. Gail Hershatter, for instance, has documented that courtesans in Shanghai sometimes had bound feet. See *Dangerous Pleasures*, 84. See also Wang Ping, *Aching for Beauty: Footbinding in China* (Minneapolis: University of Minnesota Press, 2000).

73. Yung, *Unbound Feet*, 24.

74. See Fernando Henriques, *Prostitution and Society*, 3 vols. (London: McGibbon and Kee, 1962, 1963, 1968), for a history of how prostitutes have used (or been required by authorities to use) clothing and other visual signs as a means to differentiate themselves.

75. See Walkowitz, *Prostitution and Victorian Society*, 26. See also Christine Stansell, *City of Women: Sex and Class in New York, 1789–1860* (New York: Knopf, 1986), 187, where she writes, "fancy dress signified a rejection of proper feminine behaviors and duties. For [working class] girls who donned fine clothes, dress was an emblem of an estimable erotic maturity, a way to carry about the full identity of an adult, and a sign of admission into heterosexual courting."

76. *Report*, 1146.

---

43 • *Melanie Heath*

STATE OF OUR UNIONS

Marriage Promotion and the Contested Power of Heterosexuality

DISCUSSION QUESTIONS

1. Why is there a "state interest" in heterosexual marriage? How has that interest manifested itself?
2. How has the state's interest reinforced race, class, gender, and sexual orientation inequality?
3. Heath examines the Oklahoma Marriage Initiative; can you identify other examples of state-sponsored marriage promotion?

STATE INTEREST IN HETEROSEXUAL MARRIAGE

Nation-building strategies tied to the white, nuclear family have a long history in the United States. Federal and state law has shaped marriage as a form of inclusion and exclusion by determining who can marry, the rights and obligations involved in marriage, and the conditions under which a marriage can end. Historian Nancy Cott (2000: 3) identifies how in the United States the government has promoted a particular model of marriage: "lifelong, faithful monogamy, formed by the mutual consent of a man and a woman, bearing the impress of the Christian religion and the English common law in its expectations for the husband to be the family head and economic provider." The ideal of the nuclear family in the United States evolved by separating "productive labor" from the home, creating a new social category: the "housewife" (Pascale 2001). Domesticity attributed to wealthy white women became the standard for all women, and the "Cult of True Womanhood" elevated the submissive housewife as morally superior (Brown 1990; Pascale 2001). In contrast, racial ethnic women have systematically been relegated to do the "dirty work" in domestic service and industry (Duffy 2007). Protecting the

---

family and nation has meant maintaining boundaries of racial and sexual purity. In building the nation, the federal and state government sought to "civilize" American Indians by instituting monogamous households, instilling a work ethic among men and domesticity among women (Cott 2000). Slaves were denied the right to marry, signifying their lack of civil rights that would entail the freedom to consent to marriage's obligations. Before and after slaves' emancipation, many states passed laws to ban marriage across the color line, as the specter of sexual relations between white women and African American men created moral panic. Concerns about race and morality also motivated the evolution of immigration law, which largely restricted the entry of Chinese and Japanese women.

Governmental intervention has changed over time in how it envisions protecting "the family," but the thread in this history can be traced to the need to safeguard the boundaries of the nation along the lines of race, class, gender, and sexuality (McClintock 1997). In recent years, federal and state concern has focused on "family breakdown." Sharp rises in female labor force participation, divorce, cohabitation, and single parenting have triggered a "deinstitutionalization" of marriage (Cherlin 2004). These changes, together with the growing movement to legalize same-sex marriage, call into question what constitutes "normal" family life in the United States (Stacey 1996). In the 1960s, President Lyndon Johnson drew on a report from a little-known senator, Daniel Patrick Moynihan, to address the problem of the "breakdown of the Negro family structure" (quoted in Blankenhorn 2007: 5). Controversy about the report ultimately led to a new consensus between conservative and liberal policy makers about what they viewed as the bad behavior of impoverished single mothers inherent in "welfare dependency" (Reese 2005). More recently, marriage advocate David Blankenhorn (2007: 5) has identified a united policy stance to address "the breakdown of *white* family structure" that he believes has followed the trends purportedly undermining Black families. These concerns now motivate federal and state policy to promote marriage. While race and class are visible in

these policies, below the surface are anxieties about changing gender relations and the challenge to heterosexuality presented by the increased visibility of lesbian and gay families. . . .

STUDYING MARRIAGE PROMOTION

To study marriage promotion, I conducted ethnographic research for 10 months in 2004 in Oklahoma. Oklahoma is home to the most extensive statewide marriage initiative in the nation, and consequently its policy "extends out" and is influenced by national marriage promotion politics (Burawoy 1998). In 1999, the governor employed the marriage promotion provisions of the Personal Responsibility and Work Opportunity Reconciliation Act to pioneer the Oklahoma Marriage Initiative at a time when few states opted to exercise this option. The Oklahoma Department of Human Services (OKDHS) committed $10 million from its federal TANF block grant and contracted with Public Strategies, Inc. (a private, for-profit firm) to develop and manage the initiative. The Oklahoma Marriage Initiative trains state employees, community leaders, and other volunteers to offer marriage education workshops throughout the state. The workshops use the Prevention and Relationship Enhancement Program (PREP), a research-based curriculum created by Howard Markman and Scott Stanley that teaches communication skills, conflict management, and problem solving. The initiative also trains volunteers to offer a Christian version of the PREP curriculum in settings that are not state funded. In exchange for receiving free workshop training, volunteers pledge to provide at least four free workshops in their communities.

In addition to its groundbreaking marriage initiative, Oklahoma is also well known for being a Bible Belt state. Nearly 60 percent of registered voters say they attend church regularly, compared to the national average of 40 percent (Campbell 2002). Oklahoma's high religiosity would appear to render it exceptional with respect to wide-ranging marriage promotion activities across the nation. Indeed,

Oklahoma's social and cultural environment is likely one reason that the marriage initiative was able to take root in the early years of welfare reform, as a Republican governor initiated it with little political resistance. While there are many unique aspects to the formation of the marriage initiative, Oklahoma has nevertheless served as a model for state and community marriage promotion programs across the nation. In recent years, Alabama, Georgia, North Carolina, New Mexico, New York, Ohio, Texas, and Utah have also designated portions of their TANF block grants for marriage promotion. Texas legislated $7.5 million a year.[1]

The Oklahoma Marriage Initiative blends two models of marriage promotion. On the one hand, it seeks to blanket the state with messages about marriage by providing free marriage workshops to as many Oklahomans as possible. On the other, it targets specific populations, including welfare recipients, low-income parents, high school students, the prison population, the military, and Native Americans. . . .

Fears about the declining significance of the nuclear family have spurred the Oklahoma Marriage Initiative to offer marriage education to the public as a mechanism to reinstitutionalize marriage. As one report puts it, the strategy of the marriage initiative is to provide marriage education services to all Oklahomans to effect "specific behavior change at the individual level" and to "restore support for the institution of marriage as a valued social good" (Dion 2006). When I interviewed the OKDHS director, he described being enlightened by reading Barbara Dafoe Whitehead's (1993: 84) *Atlantic Monthly* article "Dan Quayle Was Right," which explains "family breakup" as breeding behaviors that "damage the social ecology, threaten the public order, and impose new burdens on core institutions." Whitehead goes on to express concern that the once isolated breakup of Black families is now spreading to white ones. This implicit (and sometimes explicit) racial comparison is a common theme in the discourse of the marriage movement. Kay Hymowitz (2006: 78), the author of *Marriage and Caste in America*, argues that educating the young to be "self-reliant" members of a democratic society is "The Mission" of

white, middle-class families and that poor Black parents are not "simply middle-class parents *manqué;* they have their own culture of child-rearing, and—not to mince words—that culture is a recipe for more poverty." This philosophy harks back to nation-building principles that analogize marriage and the state as a necessary form of governance to produce worthy (white, middle-class) citizens (Cott 2000).

In the national discussion, the poor Black family remains an invisible standard of deviancy. As the focus of policy has turned to family breakdown, the mostly unspoken concern of marriage promotion leaders is the norm of the white, middle-class family and the harm caused to this norm. During our interview, the OKDHS director outlined the cost of "fractured families":

> Another piece of this, when you sit back and think about it, we spend $40 million in this state to run our child support enforcement division. Every one of those faces is a fractured relationship. So, we are spending $40 million in the state to do nothing but administer the transfer of cash from noncustodial parents to custodial parents who have experienced fractured relationships. You can see the high cost of having fractured relationships. It's worth the investment.

The director's words suggest that the "deviancy" of fractured families hurts middle-class families that consist of good citizens who pay taxes and embrace Hymowitz's (2006) "Mission."

The focus on fractured families reinforces a boundary around the normalcy of the white, middle-class, nuclear family. One of the top managers of the marriage initiative, a social worker who maintains a more critical stance, offered this evaluation:

> The way Governor Keating attached lowering the divorce rate through a poverty-funded program, who are we blaming for the divorce rate? I mean that kind of message is real strong in my mind. I've got an education so I was concerned about people living in poverty being blamed for the divorce rate and the state of families and that kind of thing.

Attaching marriage promotion to TANF shifts attention away from transformations taking place among white, middle-class families and places it on poor ones. Moreover, the welfare-to-work provisions in TANF, which enforce stringent work requirements and set time limits for receiving aid, help to ensure that poor "dependent" women (most often U.S.-born and immigrant women of color) are bound to low-wage jobs in the service industry.

Marriage promotion follows a long history in the United States of defending the ideal gendered family to preserve a bounded space of normalcy against "deviant" others, with attendant social consequences of race and class inequalities. While positioning fractured families as a social problem, the marriage initiative's practices on the ground predominantly focus on white, middle-class couples to promote a bounded heterosexual space to define the ideal family. In the marriage workshops, issues of race and class disappear, and the focus turns on the problematic of gender relations for heterosexual couples. Heterosexuality is the unexamined backdrop to teach about the "opposite sexes" within the ideal family.

TEACHING THE IMPORTANCE OF GENDER (AND HETEROSEXUALITY)

A dominant ideology of marriage promotion, and its historical presumption in the gendered behavior of the opposite sexes, view it as form[ing] the foundation of a cohesive and stable society. Crisis tendencies, in the form of growing marriage activism by gays and lesbians, are beneath the surface of this ideology, informing the need to strengthen heterosexual relationships. When I asked the OKDHS director, for example, about the goal of the marriage initiative, he confirmed the ideal of marital heterosexuality: "In terms of the marriage initiative, it's relationships between men and women which are committed preferably for life." His use of the words "relationships between men and women" announces the kind of relationships applicable—a declaration that would have been unnecessary 20 years ago—and suggests the prohibition of nonheterosexual love.

With heterosexuality as the unquestioned footing, the marriage workshops for the general population represent a forum to teach the mostly white, middle-class couples who attend about gender as *the* visible problem. The instruction encourages self-discipline and motivation to do gender in the manner compelled by the ideology of the "natural" family (Hay 2003). PREP, the secular version of the curriculum, engages communication and problem-solving skills. One of its main features is the speaker/listener technique, which instructs the speaker, who holds the "floor"— a tile that lists the rules of communication—to make brief "I" statements and the listener to paraphrase what he or she has heard. Despite the mostly gender-neutral curriculum, the 30 workshops I attended stressed gender relations in marriage.

The three-day, state-sponsored workshop leader training of PREP and its Christian version, taught by its creators—Howard Markman and Scott Stanley— and Vice President Natalie Jenkins, established the importance of gender to an implicit heterosexuality. Volunteers attending the training were predominantly white, many of them counselors and educators receiving continuing education units. Throughout, the three presenters focused on what men versus women do in relationships. Scott Stanley told the audience that he wanted to talk about gender differences and explained how researchers have found a pattern that involves women's pursuing an issue and men's withdrawing. He attributed this to men's tendency to be more physiologically reactive and women to be more emotionally aroused. Stanley acknowledged that these patterns of behavior are complex and that researchers have difficulty deciding what is physiological and what is not. Yet he suggested that the pattern seems to reflect a greater need for men not to argue with their mates. He conveyed that a central goal for teaching PREP is helping couples manage gender differences.

Stanley explained the impact of the decline of marriage on men and women. He argued that today, young people think that cohabiting is a good first step to test marriage but that in reality, practicing serial nonmonogamy hurts women because marriage is the only means to ensure a man's commitment. Citing research, Stanley told us that a young man who lives with his girlfriend tends to think she is not the "one," while a young woman thinks just the opposite. He explained, "We have talked young people out of thinking that marriage matters, particularly young women. Women get the worse deal if men don't marry them." Although it is not clear what he meant by the "worse deal," Stanley implied that women are naturally more committed to men, whereas men need the institution of marriage to become self-disciplined practitioners of lifelong monogamy. A dominant script of marital heterosexuality is that men know to settle down—that is, no longer act on their sexual urges—after they marry.

The curriculum includes a number of videos of real couples fighting. One shows a young African American couple who argue over the amount of time the man spends watching sports. During the young man's explanation for why his sport watching is not excessive, Howard Markman stopped the video to point out the way he lifts his hands up and "gazes towards heaven." Markman called this the "beam me up Scotty response." He explained, "This really is an appeal to God. We have a special message to the women in the room. If your partner, husband, son has this response, you might mistakenly think that he is withdrawing, but he is having a spiritual moment." I laughed along with the audience, but what makes this statement funny is the cultural assumption of an embattled masculinity. Markman implied that women cannot really understand the nature of men, which leads to the kind of exasperation shown in the video. Later, Scott Stanley told us that the young man is asking for his wife to accept this important part of him—the part that lives on sports. Statements like this place the onus on the wife to understand the "nature" of men.

Throughout the training, the presenters performed gender and made jokes that drew on the innate differences between men and women, providing a message about handling gender within heterosexual relationships (Butler [1990] 1999; West and Zimmerman 1987). These performances and dialogue subtly suggest a gender hierarchy compelling women to put up with men's idiosyncrasies since ultimately men are the stronger sex. At one point, Howard Markman told a joke about how many men it takes to change

the toilet paper. The punch line: There is no scientific answer because it has not happened. Underneath the humor is the suggestion that men have more important things to do than change toilet paper. Several moments later, he flipped the remote as if he were surfing television channels, distracting from Natalie Jenkins' presentation. She told him to "sit" and informed us that she forgot to take the batteries out of the men's toy. She quickly qualified that she "needed" these guys because she is not the most technologically advanced. As we watched a video of a couple fighting over the way the husband put the laundry soap in the washer, Jenkins asserted that the wife is "missing the miracle. He's doing the laundry!" Later, Jenkins discussed expectations and how, when she was first married, she wanted flowers because all her friends were getting them. She and her husband were having financial difficulties, so she found a 99-cent coupon for a dozen carnations. She put four quarters and the coupon on the fridge with a note saying, "Honey, if this coupon expires so will you."

All of this gender work solidifies the importance of the differences between men and women. Men play with toys (and are technologically advanced); women want flowers (and do laundry). The state's promotion of marriage makes visible the importance of these gendered practices, teaching men and women to monitor and accept the differences between men and women. At heart is a lesson about gender difference as the glue that keeps two people of the opposite sex together. The ideal for white, middle-class families is a configuration of gender hierarchy premised on institutionalized heterosexuality. Tying gender difference to understandings of bodies solidifies marital heterosexuality.

The union of gender differences and bodies together with institutionalized heterosexuality was even more pronounced in the breakout training session of the Christian version of PREP. Scott Stanley discussed how gender differences originate in the Genesis passage of the Bible. He explained,

> I think it is interesting that it says man [will leave his mother and father] and not man and woman. I have come to believe from science—and this is going to

sound sexist—why males are called to a higher level of commitment and sacrifice, biologically and scripturally. Women are inherently made more vulnerable than men because they have babies. Males need to protect. Unfortunately, in our culture, we have gutted that, and women bear the most burden by the lack of a sacrificial ethic.

His statement makes explicit the often implicit instruction on gender difference throughout the training—men are naturally less emotional and better equipped for certain responsibilities in marriage, namely, the need to protect their families. The interaction of gender and heterosexuality is important to position men and women hierarchically as part of a social order that rewards married, heterosexual (and mostly white, middle-class) men as husbands and often as the primary breadwinner.

Linking ideas of gender and heterosexuality directly to bodies, the instructor presented the definition of marriage as a union of male and female. According to Stanley,

> God meant something when he specified that there should be male and female and what to do with bodies. I don't just mean sex and physical union, but I mean oneness. They covered up where they are most obviously different. We don't cover up where we are similar. We fear rejection in relationships because of the possibility of difference. Difference symbolizes physical union, which is now apparent to them.

The heterosexual footing implied by the idea of the opposite sexes is also the ground for the performance of gender hierarchy. Through the state-sponsored instruction, potential instructors of PREP and the Christian version of PREP are taught to present ideas about gender and sexuality to encourage self-monitoring in relation to the ideal of the "natural," married family.

REHEARSING THE POWER OF HETEROSEXUALITY

...In the 30 marriage promotion workshops I attended, most included heterosexual married or engaged couples and sometimes a single woman or man. In two of the six-week workshops, however, there was one lesbian couple.[2] The first of these included 14 white heterosexual couples, one interracial heterosexual couple, and three female coaches, two white and one Black. Tammy and Chris, white lesbians in their fifties, had introduced themselves as "life partners" on the first day. They had a number of issues with communication. After hearing about the workshop on the radio, Tammy enrolled herself and "a friend." They told me they were relieved they were not asked to leave. The next workshop included Amanda and Jennifer, a white lesbian couple in their late twenties, among the 18 white couples, two white single men, and two female coaches, one white and one Black. Amanda and Jennifer were less talkative, but with their severe communication problems, by their own admission, they monopolized much of the coaches' energy during the practice exercises....

The focus on gender within the confines of marital heterosexuality ensured that the same-sex couples' presence remained invisible. This was true even in the case of Tammy and Chris, who were very vocal. The last class of the first six-week session on sensuality/sexuality offered one of the more poignant examples. David asked people to share how their families of origin had discussed sexuality with them when they were young. I was sitting at an end table with Tammy and Chris. David began at the table opposite us and stopped at the table next to ours to talk about his own upbringing, skipping Tammy, Chris, and myself. This omission did not deter the two from participating. When David asked about sensuality and touch, Tammy spoke up: "We assume that what we like, the other person likes." Her words drew attention to the fact that her partner is a woman and not a man. While it is probably true that heterosexuals and nonheterosexuals make this kind of assumption, her statement stood in bold relief to the dominant message of managing difference in heterosexual relationships. Comments such as this one challenge taken-for-granted assumptions of gender and sexuality.

All the participants I interviewed acknowledged awareness of the lesbian couples without my asking, and most admitted feeling a little uncomfortable due to either their disapproval of or their inexperience dealing with same-sex relationships. Tom, a white man in his mid-twenties who attended with Suzanne, said he was caught off guard by "the two girls who were there together. They were like lesbians. I was surprised, I guess." Becky, a white woman in her thirties who was married and had four children with Martin, an African American man in his early forties, answered my question about whether anything in the workshop made her uncomfortable:

> Mmm. I did feel uncomfortable with the fact that there were couples in there of the same sex, just because I feel strongly about family values and what the traditional family is. But I know it is something that is happening in the United States, and there is really nothing I can do about it. And, I mean, they are human. They have needs too. It doesn't mean that I agree with them.

Norm, a white man in his sixties who attended with his third wife, moved from talking about men's responsiveness to his disapproval of homosexuality. He said,

> At first, the unknown [was uncomfortable]. When you go around and there is more and more interaction, I felt like there was a quality of responses and information given by the men in that class that usually doesn't happen. [Pause] I do consider homosexuality a sin, but I'm not here to judge that. I have a lot of patients that are gay, and they have a lifestyle I do not approve of. But I thought even the gay couple had a lot of good information to toss out.

Some of the other participants expressed a subtle resentment about dealing with same-sex couples in the marriage workshop but admitted that these couples "have needs too." . . .

CONCLUSION

This research contributes to feminist theories of the state by problematizing the assumption of a male state with unidimensional control of its citizens or subjects. Instead, it reveals polycentric state practices that are structured as gendered and sexualized, and that uphold the dominance of the white, middle-class family and its importance to a cohesive national identity. In the case of marriage promotion, diverse state practices focus policy concerns on "deviant" (coded Black) single-mother families while resources are allocated to teach about gender hierarchy to predominantly white, middle-class couples. Putting feminist state theory and critical heterosexuality studies in dialogue demonstrates the importance of an unspoken heterosexuality to state control. State actors who seek to promote marriage rely on a particular, and conservative, interpretation of social scientific research on families as a noncontroversial way to focus policy concerns on the need to promote "healthy" (heterosexual) families. These policies demonstrate a perceived need on the part of the state to safeguard the health of the nation by strengthening the "mission" of white, middle-class (heterosexual) marriage. The race and class assumptions of this reasoning are largely made invisible as marriage promotion leaders use the rhetoric of health and social capital.

On the ground, marriage education becomes a tool to teach self-monitoring gendered practices within the confines of heterosexual marriage. In the workshops I attended, instruction on the "opposite" sexes signaled heterosexuality to reaffirm the sexual outsider status of same-sex couples as well as that of single-mother families. The on-the-ground practices of promoting heterosexual marriage mirror antigay countermovements, such as the ex-gay movement, which encourages individuals to police their behavior according to scripted gender and heterosexual norms (Robinson and Spivey 2007). This strategy provides states and social movements the ability to govern the behavior of citizens and members from a distance.

Marriage workshops rehearse dominant scripts on gender polarity to reinforce expectations of men's and women's "nature" to make marital heterosexuality appear instinctive and effortless. The decline of marriage and women's increased workforce participation during the past 40 years has challenged traditional norms that created social cohesion through gender hierarchy and implicit heterosexuality. Marriage workshops offer a forum to revisit ideas on hierarchical relationships between men and women. State training for workshop leaders teaches that managing gender differences is essential to a harmonious marriage. The trainers provide examples and offer gendered performances to focus on indisputable differences between men and women that cater to cultural ideas of men as rational (strong) and women as emotional (weak). These performances provide simple answers to complex negotiations that many families face as they juggle tight work schedules along with raising children and try to manage households that often bring children from previous marriages or relationships. The gendered performances teach that wives need to allow "men to be men" and that husbands need to cater to their wives' emotional needs.

NOTES

1. Many of these states, including Texas, have incorporated the "one percent solution," putting 1 percent of their Temporary Assistance to Needy Families money toward marriage promotion. From my calculations, Oklahoma designates roughly 5 percent of its Temporary Assistance to Needy Families block grant per year.

2. One of the initiative leaders told me that she knew of other same-sex couples attending marriage workshops. There was no way to find out how many actually did attend since the "All about You" forms that participants fill out at the beginning of the workshops do not ask about sexual orientation or same-sex relationships.

REFERENCES

Blankenhorn, David. 2007. *The future of marriage.* New York: Encounter Books.

Brown, Gillian. 1990. *Domestic individualism: Imagining self in nineteenth-century America.* Berkeley: University of California Press.

Burawoy, Michael. 1998. The extended case method. *Sociological Theory* 16:4–33.

Butler, Judith. [1990] 1999. *Gender trouble.* New York: Routledge.

Campbell, Kim. 2002. Can marriage be taught? *Christian Science Monitor*, July 18.

Cherlin, Andrew J. 2004. The deinstitutionalization of American marriage. *Journal of Marriage and Family* 66:848–61.

Cott, Nancy. 2000. *Public vows: A history of marriage and the nation.* Cambridge, MA: Harvard University Press.

Dion, Robin. 2006. *The Oklahoma Marriage Initiative: An overview of the longest-running statewide marriage initiative in the U.S.* ASPE research brief. Washington, DC: Office of the Assistant Secretary for Planning and Evaluation, U.S. Department of Health and Human Services.

Duffy, Mignon. 2007. Doing the dirty work: Gender, race, and reproductive labor in historical perspective. *Gender & Society* 21:313–36.

Hay, James. 2003. Unaided virtues: The (neo) liberalization of the domestic sphere and the new architecture of community. In *Foucault, cultural studies, and governmentality*, edited by Jack Z. Bratich, Jeremy Packer, and Cameron McCarthy. Albany: State University of New York Press.

Hymowitz, Kay S. 2006. *Marriage and caste in America: Separate and unequal families in a post-marital age.* Chicago: Ivan R. Dee.

McClintock, Ann. 1997. "No longer in a future heaven": Gender, race, and nationalism. In *Dangerous liaisons: Gender, nation, and postcolonial perspectives*, edited by Anne McClintock, Aamir Mufti, and Ella Shohat. Minneapolis: University of Minnesota Press.

Pascale, Celine-Marie. 2001. All in a day's work: A feminist analysis of class formation and social identity. *Race, Gender & Class* 8:34–59.

Reese, Ellen. 2005. *Backlash against welfare mothers.* Berkeley: University of California Press.

Robinson, Christine M., and Sue E. Spivey. 2007. The politics of masculinity and the ex-gay movement. *Gender & Society* 21:650–75.

Stacey, Judith. 1996. *In the name of the family: Rethinking family values in the postmodern age.* Boston: Beacon.

West, Candace, and Don Zimmerman. 1987. Doing gender. *Gender & Society* 1:125–51.

Whitehead, Barbara Dafoe. 1993. Dan Quayle was right. *Atlantic Monthly*, April, 47–84.

44 • George Chauncey

"WHAT GAY STUDIES TAUGHT THE COURT"

The Historians' Amicus Brief in *Lawrence v. Texas*

DISCUSSION QUESTIONS

1. How did the authors/contributors to the amicus brief use legal history to demonstrate how the word "sodomy" was usurped to specifically criminalize gay male sex?
2. How is the amicus brief an example of social justice via academic work? How might academics use their research to further social progress in other arenas?
3. In what other ways might we look to history to better understand our current constructions of sex, gender, and sexuality, as well as other identities?

INTRODUCTION

The historians' amicus brief reprinted here was submitted by a group of ten professors of history to the U.S. Supreme Court as it considered the constitutionality of Texas's "homosexual conduct law" in the case of *Lawrence v. Texas*. The Court cited the brief in the decision it issued on June 26, 2003, which overturned that law and the rest of the nation's sodomy laws. Although legal observers immediately began to debate the implications of the decision and the merits of its legal reasoning, there is no doubt that it constituted a major victory for the gay movement. Although the two plaintiffs in Texas were not the only ones to face such charges, few consenting adults had been prosecuted for sodomy even before the decision. But by criminalizing homosexual activity, the sodomy

laws had effectively criminalized all lesbians and gay men, and opponents of gay rights had regularly used this imputation of criminality in public debates and court decisions to justify everything from the exclusion of gays from the military to the removal of children from the homes of their lesbian mothers. Sodomy laws were an ideological cornerstone in the legal edifice of antigay discrimination.

In declaring those laws unconstitutional, the Court repudiated its decision in *Bowers v. Hardwick*, then only seventeen years old, which had upheld Georgia's sodomy statute. The Court is generally reluctant to reverse itself so quickly and therefore needed to offer an extensive explanation of why it had done so. To the surprise of the brief's authors, many commentators credited it and two other historically oriented amicus briefs (filed by the American Civil Liberties Union and the Cato Institute) with giving the *Lawrence* majority the scholarly grounds it needed. The press took notice. "What Gay Studies Taught the Court," ran the headline over the *Washington Post* article that provided the best analysis of how the historical briefs had influenced the Court's decision. "When Six Justices Changed the Law of the Land, They Turned to Its History," declared the *New York Times* when it published excerpts from our brief under the subheading "Educating the Court."[1]...

Ahistorical assumptions about the unchanging character both of homosexuality and of hostility to homosexuality had undergirded the *Bowers* decision. As many observers noted at the time, the majority in *Bowers* treated Georgia's sodomy law as if it applied only to homosexual conduct, when in fact it also prohibited oral or anal sex between men and women and between married as well as unmarried couples. This astonishing misreading of the statute under review was linked to the majority's misreading of the entire history of sodomy laws as distinctly antihomosexual measures, which Chief Justice Warren Burger, in a famous concurring opinion, claimed had the sanction of "millennia of moral teaching" against homosexual conduct.

His error was not unusual. In the common parlance of the 1980s (and of today), most people, not just the chief justice, assumed that sodomy laws referred only to homosexual conduct, even though most of them did not—and in fact could have been used to imprison millions of happily married heterosexuals.

Our brief sought to correct the historical errors used to bolster the majority's reasoning in *Bowers* by demonstrating the historical variability of sexual regulation and the historical specificity of the antigay hostility animating the Texas law (and, by extension, the *Bowers* decision itself). Part I of the brief shows that the medieval and colonial sodomy regulations alluded to by the Court did not provide evidence of a consistent preoccupation with the prohibition of homosexual conduct; they were concerned instead with a wide, inconsistent, and historically variable range of nonprocreative sexual practices, which typically included sexual acts between men and women or men and animals as well as between men and men, and

which typically did not include sexual acts between women. Although such laws often involved some of the behavior that would today be classified as "homosexual," sodomy as these statutes usually defined it was not the equivalent of homosexual conduct. Part II then argues that while sodomy laws had regulated various forms of sexual conduct, in which anyone (or at least any male person) could engage, it was only in the twentieth century that the state began to classify and discriminate against certain of its citizens on the basis of their status as homosexuals.

This argument laid the basis for our contention that the decision of Texas and several other states in the 1970s to enact new laws singling out "homosexual sodomy" for penalty at the very moment that they decriminalized "heterosexual sodomy" recast the historical purpose of sodomy laws by adding them to the distinctly twentieth-century array of discriminatory measures directed specifically at homosexuals....

The Court accepted this argument. As Associate Justice Anthony M. Kennedy wrote in his majority opinion, in a rebuke to the reasoning in *Bowers*, "[F]ar from possessing 'ancient roots,' American laws targeting same-sex couples did not develop until the last third of the twentieth century." He elaborated this premise in a historical survey that closely followed the outline of our brief, but he drew as well on supplemental research conducted by his own law clerks. He even cited John D'Emilio and Estelle B. Freedman's book *Intimate Matters* and Jonathan Ned Katz's *Invention of Heterosexuality* to acknowledge the claim that the category of the homosexual dated only from the nineteenth century....

...I found writing the brief a useful exercise, because it required the crafting of a single analytic narrative linking the regulation of sodomy to the rise and fall of antigay discrimination in the twentieth century. Doing so highlighted two historical phenomena with special force. First, it emphasized the degree to which the state's policy of systematically classifying and discriminating against certain people on the basis of their homosexual status was an invention of the twentieth century. We continue to live with the legacy of this discrimination, in the laws still on the books and in the hostility that such laws have expressed, legitimized, and perpetuated. But although we generally perceive such discrimination as both timeless and inevitable, in fact it is of remarkably recent origin and remarkably short duration. Most of the discriminatory laws and regulations that were put in place between the 1920s and the 1950s were dismantled between the 1960s and the 1990s. . . .

We reprint the brief here because it provides a short synthesis of historians' present understanding of the history of the regulation of sexual practices and identities. I hope that it will prove useful as such in courses and that it will encourage additional research and critical reflection on these questions. We print it also as a reminder that our scholarship matters and that it is both possible and incumbent on us to engage, as scholars, with the world beyond the academy. . . .

THE HISTORIANS' AMICUS BRIEF IN *LAWRENCE V. TEXAS*

. . .

INTRODUCTION AND SUMMARY OF ARGUMENT

Amici, as historians, do not propose to offer the Court legal doctrine to justify a holding that the Texas Homosexual Conduct Law violates the U.S. Constitution. Rather, *amici* believe they can best serve the Court by elaborating on two *historical* propositions important to the legal analysis: (1) no consistent historical practice singles out same-sex behavior as "sodomy" subject to proscription, and (2) the governmental policy of classifying and discriminating against certain citizens on the basis of their homosexual status is an unprecedented project of the twentieth century, which is already being dismantled. The Texas law at issue is an example of such irrational discrimination.

In colonial America, regulation of nonprocreative sexual practices—regulation that carried harsh penalties but was rarely enforced—stemmed from Christian religious teachings and reflected the need for procreative sex to increase the population. Colonial sexual regulation included such nonprocreative acts

as masturbation, and sodomy laws applied equally to male–male, male–female, and human–animal sexual activity. "Sodomy" was not the equivalent of "homosexual conduct." It was understood as a particular, discrete act, not as an indication of a person's sexuality or sexual orientation.

Not until the end of the nineteenth century did lawmakers and medical writing recognize sexual "inversion" or what we would today call homosexuality. The phrase "homosexual sodomy" would have been literally incomprehensible to the Framers of the Constitution, for the very concept of homosexuality as a discrete psychological condition and source of personal identity was not available until the late 1800s. The Court in *Bowers v. Hardwick* misapprehended this history.

Proscriptive laws designed to suppress all forms of nonprocreative and nonmarital sexual conduct existed through much of the last millennium. Widespread discrimination against a class of people on the basis of their homosexual status developed only in the twentieth century, however, and peaked from the 1930s to the 1960s. Gay men and women were labeled "deviants," "degenerates," and "sex criminals" by the medical profession, government officials, and the mass media. The federal government banned the employment of homosexuals and insisted that its private contractors ferret out and dismiss their gay employees, many state governments prohibited gay people from being served in bars and restaurants, Hollywood prohibited the discussion of gay issues or the appearance of gay or lesbian characters in its films, and many municipalities launched police campaigns to suppress gay life. The authorities worked together to create or reinforce the belief that gay people were an inferior class to be shunned by other Americans. Sodomy laws that exclusively targeted same-sex couples, such as the statute enacted in 1973 in Texas, were a development of the last third of the twentieth century and reflect this historically unprecedented concern to classify and penalize homosexuals as a subordinate class of citizens.[1]

Since the 1960s, however, and especially since the *Bowers* decision in 1986, official and popular attitudes toward homosexuals have changed, though vestiges of old attitudes—such as the law at issue here—remain. Among other changes, the medical profession no longer stigmatizes homosexuality as a disease, prohibitions on employment of homosexuals have given way to antidiscrimination protections, gay characters have become common in movies and on television, 86 percent of Americans support gay rights legislation, and family law has come to recognize gays and lesbians as part of nontraditional families worthy of recognition. These changes have not gone uncontested, but a large majority of Americans have come to oppose discrimination against lesbians and gay men.

In this case, the Court should construe the Equal Protection Clause and the Due Process Clause with a thorough and nuanced history of the subject in mind.

ARGUMENT

I. Bowers v. Hardwick *Rests on a Fundamental Misapprehension of the History of Sodomy Laws*

In *Bowers v. Hardwick*, this Court concluded, by a 5–4 vote, that the Constitution does not confer a fundamental right to engage in "homosexual sodomy." The majority's conclusion was based, in large measure, on the "ancient roots" of laws prohibiting homosexuals from engaging in acts of consensual sodomy.[2] The Court stated that in 1791 "sodomy" "was forbidden by the laws of the original thirteen States," that in 1868 "all but 5 of the 37 States in the Union had criminal sodomy laws," and that, "until 1961, all 50 States outlawed sodomy."[3] Accordingly, the Court reasoned, the right of homosexuals to engage consensually in the acts that have been labeled "sodomy" is not "deeply rooted in this Nation's history and tradition."[4] . . .

Recent historical scholarship demonstrates the flaws in the historical accounts endorsed by the Court and Chief Justice Burger. We concur with the accounts given of the history of sodomy laws and of their enforcement in colonial America and the United States by the American Civil Liberties Union and the Cato Institute in their amicus briefs. We will not endeavor to replicate their historical accounts here, but we do wish to stress two points about this history.

First, contrary to the Court's assumption in *Bowers*, sodomy prohibitions have varied enormously in the last millennium (and even since our own colonial era) in their definition of the offense and in their rationalization of its prohibition. The specification of "homosexual sodomy" as a criminal offense does not carry the pedigree of the ages but is almost exclusively an invention of the recent past.

Prohibitions against sodomy are rooted in the teachings of Western Christianity, but those teachings have always been strikingly inconsistent in their definition of the acts encompassed by the term. When the term "sodomy" was first emphasized by medieval Christian theologians in the eleventh century, they applied it inconsistently to a diverse group of nonprocreative sexual practices. In subsequent Latin theology, canon law, and confessional practice, the term was notoriously confused with "unnatural acts," which had a very different origin and ranged even more widely (to include, for example, procreative sexual acts in the wrong position or with contraceptive intent). "Unnatural acts" is the older category, because it comes directly from Paul in Romans 1, but Paul does not associate such acts with (or even mention) the story of Sodom (Genesis 19) and appears not to have considered that story to be concerned with same-sex activity.[5]

Later Christian authors did combine Romans 1 with Genesis 19, but they could not agree on what sexual practices were meant by either "unnatural acts" or "sodomy." For example, in Peter Damian, who around 1050 championed the term "sodomy" as an analogy to "blasphemy," the "sins of the Sodomites" include solitary masturbation. In Thomas Aquinas, about two centuries later, "unnatural acts" cover every genital contact intended to produce orgasm except penile–vaginal intercourse in an approved position.[6] Many later Christian writers denied that women could commit sodomy at all; others believed that the defining characteristic of unnatural or sodomitical sex was that it could not result in procreation, regardless of the genders involved.[7] In none of these authors does the term "sodomy" refer systematically and exclusively to same-sex conduct. Certainly it was not used consistently through the centuries to condemn that conduct. The restrictive use of the term in the Texas law at issue must itself be regarded as a historically recent innovation.

The English Reformation Parliament of 1533 turned the religious injunction against sodomy into the secular crime of buggery when it made "the detestable and abominable vice of buggery committed with mankind or beast" punishable by death. The English courts interpreted this to apply to sexual intercourse between a human and animal and anal intercourse between a man and woman as well as anal intercourse between two men.[8]

Colonial American statutes variously drew on the religious and secular traditions and shared their imprecision in the definition of the offense. Variously defining the crime as (the religious) sodomy or (the secular) buggery, they generally proscribed anal sex between men and men, men and women, and humans and animals, but their details and their rationale varied, and the New England colonies penalized a wider range of "carnall knowledge," including (but by no means limited to) "men lying with men." Puritan leaders in the New England colonies were especially vigorous in their denunciation of sodomitical sins as contrary to God's will, but their condemnation was also motivated by the pressing need to increase the population and to secure the stability of the family. Thus John Winthrop mused that the main offense of one man hanged in New Haven in 1646 for having engaged in masturbation with numerous youths—not, in other words, for "sodomy" as it is usually understood today—was his "frustratinge of the Ordinance of marriage & the hindringe the generation of mankinde."[9]

Another indication that the sodomy statutes were not the equivalent of a statute against "homosexual conduct" is that with one brief exception they applied exclusively to acts performed by men, whether with women, girls, men, boys, or animals, and not to acts committed by two women. Only the New Haven colony penalized "women lying with women," and this for only ten years. For the entire colonial period we have reports of only two cases involving two women engaged in acts with one another. As one historian notes, both cases "were treated as lewd and lascivious behavior, not as potential crimes against nature."[10] ...

It was only beginning in the 1970s that a handful of states, including Texas, passed legislation specifying homosexual sodomy while decriminalizing heterosexual sodomy. This legislation had no historical precedent, but resulted from a uniquely twentieth-century form of animus directed at homosexuals, which will be detailed in the next section of this brief.

Second, throughout American history, the authorities have rarely enforced statutes prohibiting sodomy, however defined. Even in periods when enforcement increased, it was rare for people to be prosecuted for consensual sexual relations conducted in private, even when the parties were of the same sex. Indeed, records of only about twenty prosecutions and four or five executions have surfaced for the entire colonial period. Even in the New England colonies, whose leaders denounced "sodomy" with far greater regularity and severity than did other colonial leaders and where the offense carried severe sanctions, it was rarely prosecuted....

The relative indifference of the public and the authorities to the crime of sodomy continued in the first century of independence. For instance, only twenty-two men were indicted for sodomy in New York City in the nearly eight decades from 1796 to 1873.[11] The number of sodomy prosecutions increased sharply in the last two decades of the nineteenth century and in the twentieth century. This was made possible by the decision of many states to criminalize oral intercourse for the first time. But it resulted in large measure from the pressure applied on district attorneys by privately organized and usually religiously inspired anti-vice societies, whose leaders feared that the growing size and complexity of cities had loosened the constraints on sexual conduct and increased the vulnerability of youth and the disadvantaged....

Thus, the majority in *Bowers* misinterpreted the historical record. Laws singling out sexual (or "sodomitical") conduct between partners of the same sex for proscription are an invention of our time, not the legacy of "millennia of moral teaching." And in practice, regulating sodomy has never been a major concern of the state or the public....

Furthermore, in its analysis of the Equal Protection Clause issue in this case, the Court should recognize what the foregoing history shows: sodomy laws have not only varied in content over time, but have also depended on the kinds of status-based distinctions and shifting justifications that are typical of irrational discrimination. Neither millennia of moral teaching nor the American experience teach *any* consistent message about which sexual practices between consenting adults should be condemned and why. . . .

II. Discrimination on the Basis of Homosexual Status Was an Unprecedented Development of the Twentieth Century

Over the generations, sodomy legislation proscribed a diverse and inconsistent set of sexual acts engaged in by various combinations of partners. Above all, it regulated *conduct* in which *anyone* (or, at certain times and in certain places, any male person) could engage. Only in the late nineteenth century did the idea of the homosexual as a distinct category of person emerge, and only in the twentieth century did the state begin to classify and penalize citizens on the basis of their identity or *status* as homosexuals. . . .

The unprecedented decision of Texas and several other states, primarily in the 1970s, to enact sodomy laws singling out "homosexual sodomy" for penalty, is best understood historically in the context of these discriminatory measures. The new sodomy laws essentially recast the historic purpose of such laws, which had been to regulate conduct generally, by adding them to the array of discriminatory measures directed specifically against homosexuals. Such discriminatory measures against homosexuals, although popularly imagined to be longstanding, are in fact not ancient but a unique and relatively short-lived product of the twentieth century.

It was only in the late nineteenth century that the very concept of the homosexual as a distinct category of person developed. The word "homosexual" appeared for the first time in a German pamphlet in 1868, and was introduced to the American lexicon only in 1892.[12] As Michel Foucault has famously described this evolution, "the sodomite had been a temporary aberration; the homosexual was now a species."[13]

The discriminatory measures we will describe responded to the growing visibility of gay and lesbian subcultures in American cities in the late nineteenth and early twentieth centuries. It should be noted, though, that many Americans responded to gay life with fascination and sympathy. Many people regarded the increasing visibility of gay life as simply one more sign of the growing complexity and freedom from tradition of a burgeoning metropolitan culture. Thousands of New Yorkers attended the drag balls organized by gay men in Harlem in the 1920s and 30s, for instance, and two of the most successful nightclubs in Times Square in 1931 featured openly gay entertainers.[14]

Others regarded the growing visibility of lesbian and gay life with dread. Hostility to homosexuals was sometimes motivated by an underlying uneasiness about the dramatic changes under way in gender roles at the turn of the last century. Conservative physicians initially argued that the homosexual (or "sexual invert") was characterized as much by his or her violation of conventional gender roles as by specifically sexual interests. . . .

Anti-vice societies organized in the late nineteenth century also opposed the growing visibility of homosexuality, which they regarded as an egregious sign of the loosening of social controls on sexual expression in the cities. They encouraged the police to step up harassment of gay life as simply one more part of their campaigns to shut down dance halls and movie theaters, prohibit the consumption of alcohol and the use of contraceptives, dissuade restaurants from serving an interracial mix of customers, and otherwise impose their vision of the proper social order and sexual morality. As a result of this pressure, the police began using misdemeanor charges, such as disorderly conduct, vagrancy, lewdness, loitering, and so forth to harass homosexuals. . . .

In some cases, state officials tailored these laws to strengthen the legal regulation of homosexuals. For example, in 1923 the New York State legislature specified for the first time one man's "frequent[ing] or loiter[ing] about any public place soliciting men

444 • POLITICS AND THE STATE

for the purpose of committing a crime against nature or other lewdness" as a form of disorderly conduct.[15] Many more men were arrested and prosecuted under this misdemeanor charge than for sodomy. Between 1923 and 1967, when Mayor John Lindsay ordered the police to stop using entrapment to secure arrests of gay men, more than 50,000 men had been arrested on this charge in New York City alone.[16] . . .

The persecution of gay men and lesbians dramatically increased at every level of government after the Second World War. In 1950, following Senator Joseph McCarthy's denunciation of the employment of gay persons in the State Department, the Senate conducted a special investigation into "the employment of homosexuals and other sex perverts in government."[17] The Senate Committee recommended excluding gay men and lesbians from all government service because homosexual acts violated the law.[18] The Committee also cited the general belief that "those who engage in overt acts of perversion lack the emotional stability of normal persons,"[19] and that homosexuals "constitute security risks."[20] . . .

. . . In 1953, President Eisenhower issued an executive order requiring the discharge of homosexual employees from federal employment, civilian or military.[21] Thousands of men and women were discharged or forced to resign from civilian and military positions because they were suspected of being gay or lesbian.[22]

In addition, President Eisenhower's executive order required defense contractors and other private corporations with federal contracts to ferret out and discharge their homosexual employees.[23] "Other private industries adopted the policies of the federal government . . . even though they had no direct federal contracts."[24] Furthermore, the FBI initiated a widespread system of surveillance to enforce the executive order. As one historian has noted, "The FBI sought out friendly vice squad officers who supplied arrest records on morals charges, regardless of whether convictions had ensued. Regional FBI officers gathered data on gay bars, compiled lists of other places frequented by homosexuals, and clipped press articles that provided information about the gay world. . . . Federal

investigators engaged in more than fact-finding; they also exhibited considerable zeal in using information they collected."[25] . . .

Lesbians, gay men, and their supporters challenged police harassment and state discrimination throughout this period, but with little success before the 1960s and 1970s. Through much of the twentieth century, gay men and lesbians suffered under the weight of medical theories that treated their desires as a disorder, penal laws that condemned their sexual behavior as a crime, and federal policies and state regulations that discriminated against them on the basis of their homosexual status. These state practices and ideological messages worked together to create or reinforce the belief that gay persons were an inferior class to be shunned by other Americans. Such forms of discrimination, harassment, and stigmatization were so pervasive and well established by the 1960s that it was widely imagined that they were the inevitable "residue of an age-old, unchanging social antipathy toward homosexuality."[26] But recent historical scholarship tells a different story. Discrimination on the basis of homosexual status was a powerful but unprecedented development of the twentieth century. Public conceptions and attitudes had changed, and they would change again.

III. Tolerance toward Homosexuals Has Increased, Resulting in Acceptance by Many, but Not All, Mainstream Institutions

Since the 1960s, official and popular attitudes toward homosexuals have changed significantly, with a dramatic attitudinal shift since *Bowers* was decided in 1986. Homosexuality remains a contentious moral and political issue and we still live with the legacy of the many discriminatory measures put in place between the 1930s and 1960s, but a significant number of those measures have been repealed in recent years as large segments of the American public have become more understanding and accepting of lesbians and gay men.

The widespread consensus in the first half of the twentieth century that homosexuality was pathological and dangerous has given way, with growing numbers of expert and ordinary Americans regarding it as a normal and benign variation of human sexuality. Major institutions that once helped legitimize antigay hysteria have changed their positions. Medical writers and mental health professionals whose stigmatization of homosexuality as a disease or disorder had been used to justify discrimination for decades—as discussed in Part II above—were among the first to change their views. In 1973, the American Psychiatric Association voted to remove homosexuality from its list of mental disorders.[27] The American Psychological Association and the American Medical Association soon followed suit.[28]

Religious attitudes toward homosexuals and homosexuality also began to change. The place of lesbians and gay men in religious life is still vigorously debated, but since the 1970s many mainline Protestant denominations have issued official statements condemning legal discrimination against homosexuals and affirming that homosexuals ought to enjoy equal protection under criminal and civil law. Several of these groups descended from the historically influential denominations whose religious authority had been invoked to justify colonial statutes against sodomy.[29] . . .

The federal government, which once prohibited the employment of homosexuals, now prohibits its agencies from discriminating against them in employment. The U.S. Civil Service Commission lifted its ban on the employment of gay men and lesbians in 1975.[30] President Clinton signed executive orders banning discrimination in the federal workplace on the basis of sexual orientation . . . and barring the use of sexual orientation as a criterion for determining security clearance. . . . Hundreds of companies have adopted similar measures. A survey of 319 of America's largest companies found that approximately "92 percent of the firms surveyed prohibit workplace discrimination against gays and lesbians."[31] . . .

Even those who are hostile to or made uneasy by homosexuality are against discrimination and intolerance. A 2002 Gallup Poll found that, while 44 percent of the people said homosexuality was unacceptable, 86 percent of those surveyed said

homosexuals should have equal rights in terms of job opportunities.[32] Only 56 percent of Americans supported gay rights legislation in 1977. The figure jumped to 83 percent in 1989, and increased to 86 percent in 2002.[33] . . .

Gay men and lesbians who parent together or as individuals have also become more numerous and visible. This has led to greater familiarity with and acceptance of gay parents. The experience of family courts that consider the best interests of individual children is revealing. Over the several decades in which courts have considered the rights of gay, lesbian, and bisexual parents, experience has led the vast majority of states to adopt custody standards that are neutral as to sexual orientation.[34] Acceptance has increased in part because research studies have led numerous influential medical and mental health groups, including the American Academy of Pediatrics, to endorse nondiscriminatory standards.[35] . . .

Additionally, laws permitting overt intolerance and discrimination against homosexuals, including same-sex sodomy laws in a handful of states, remain in force, with severe consequences for people's lives and livelihoods. For example, a review of twenty surveys conducted across America between 1980 and 1991 showed that between 16 and 44 percent of gay men and lesbians had experienced discrimination in employment.[36] Cheryl Summerville's separation notice from Cracker Barrel read: "This employee is being terminated due to violation of company policy. This employee is gay."[37] Labeling gay people criminals—as same-sex sodomy laws do—also leads to the imposition of many legal disabilities "because the law permits differential treatment of criminals."[38] Some—but by no means all—of the most important disabilities arise in parents' efforts to maintain relationships with their children.[39]

We ask the Court to consider the findings of recent historical scholarship on the history of sexual regulation, sodomy prohibitions, and antigay discrimination as it considers this case. In our judgment as historians, the lessons of this history are clear. The history of antigay discrimination is short, not millennial. In early American history, "sodomy" was indeed condemned, but the concept of "the homosexual" and the notion of singling out "homosexual sodomy" for condemnation were foreign. Through most of our Nation's history, sodomy laws prohibited some forms of same-sex conduct only as one aspect of a more general (and historically variable) prohibition.

It was only in the twentieth century that the government began to classify and discriminate against certain of its citizens on the basis of their homosexual status. An array of discriminatory laws and regulations targeting lesbians and gay men were put in place in a relatively short period of time. In recent years, a decisive majority of Americans have recognized such measures for what they are—discrimination that offends the principles of our Nation—yet a number of them remain in place. The 1973 Texas Homosexual Conduct Law at issue is an example of such discriminatory laws. They hold no legitimate place in our Nation's traditions.

CONCLUSION

The judgment of the court of appeals should be reversed.

Respectfully submitted,
ROY T. ENGLERT, JR.
Counsel of Record
ALAN UNTEREINER
SHERRI LYNN WOLSON
Robbins, Russell, Englert,
Orseck & Untereiner LLP
1801 K Street, N.W.
Suite 411
Washington, D.C. 20006
(202) 775–4500
Counsel for Amici Curiae
JANUARY 2003

NOTE TO INTRODUCTION

1. "What Gay Studies Taught the Court," *Washington Post*, July 13, 2003; "When Six Justices Changed the Law of the Land, They Turned to Its History," *New York Times*, July 20, 2003.

NOTES

1. Texas, *General Laws* (1973), c. 399, see. 1, 3.
2. Bowers v. Hardwick, 478 U.S. 186, 192 (1986).
3. Ibid., 192–93.
4. Ibid., 192–94.
5. Cf. *Ezekiel* 16:49–50, where the sin of Sodom is the arrogant and inhospitable refusal to share wealth and leisure.
6. Mark D. Jordan, *The Invention of Sodomy in Christian Theology* (Chicago: University of Chicago Press, 1997), 46, 144–45.
7. Mark D. Jordan, *The Silence of Sodom* (Chicago: University of Chicago Press, 2000), 62–71.
8. William Eskridge, Jr., "Law and the Construction of the Closet: American Regulation of Same Sex Intimacy, 1880–1946," *Iowa Law Review* 82 (1997): 1007, 1012; Ed Cohen, "Legislating the Norm: From Sodomy to Gross Indecency," *South Atlantic Quarterly* 88 (1989): 181, 185.
9. John Murrin, " 'Things Fearful to Name': Bestiality in Early America," in *American Sexual Histories*, ed. Elizabeth Reis (Malden, MA: Blackwell, 2001), 17; see also Robert F. Oaks, " 'Things Fearful to Name': Sodomy and Buggery in Seventeenth-Century New England," *Journal of Social History* 12 (1978): 268; Jonathan Ned Katz, "The Age of Sodomitical Sin, 1607–1740," in *Gay/Lesbian Almanac* (New York: Harper and Row, 1983), 23.
10. Murrin, 15; Katz, 29–30.
11. D'Emilio and Freedman, *Intimate Matters*, 123.
12. Jonathan Ned Katz, *The Invention of Heterosexuality*, with a foreword by Gore Vidal (New York: Dutton, 1995), 10. For a detailed philological explication, see David M. Halperin, *One Hundred Years of Homosexuality, and Other Essays on Greek Love* (New York: Routledge, 1990), 15 and n. 155.
13. Michel Foucault, *The History of Sexuality*, trans. Robert Hurley (New York: Pantheon Books, 1978), 43.
14. Chauncey, *Gay New York*, 258, 320.
15. Chauncey, *Gay New York*, 172.
16. George Chauncey, "A Gay World, Vibrant and Forgotten," *New York Times*, 26 June 1994, E17.
17. Congress, Senate, *Senate Report* 241, 81st Cong., 2d sess., 1950.
18. Ibid., 3.
19. Ibid., 4.
20. Ibid., 5. As historian David Johnson noted, however, the Senate Committee "could only uncover one example of a homosexual who was blackmailed into betraying his country, and for that, investigators had to reach

back to World War I and beyond America's shores, to a Captain Raedl, chief of the Australian Counterintelligence Service in 1912." David Johnson, "Homosexual Citizens: Washington's Gay Community Confronts the Civil Service," *Washington History* (Fall 1994/Winter 1995): 45, 48.

21. D'Emilio, *Sexual Politics, Sexual Communities: The Making of a Homosexual Minority in the United States, 1940–70* (Chicago: University of Chicago Press, 1983), 44.

22. Ibid.; Robert D. Dean, *Imperial Brotherhood: Gender and the Making of Cold War Foreign Policy* (Amherst: University of Massachusetts Press, 2001).

23. Johnson, 45, 53.

24. Ibid.

25. D'Emilio, *Sexual Politics*, 46–47.

26. Chauncey, *Gay New York*, 355.

27. Gary B. Melton, "Public Policy and Private Prejudice," *American Psychologist* 44 (1989): 933. See "Resolution of the American Psychiatric Association, Dec. 15, 1973," in Ibid., appendix A, 936.

28. "Resolution of the Council of Representatives of the American Psychological Association," *American Psychologist* 30 (1975): 633.

29. Statements in support of equal legal protection for homosexual persons were also adopted by the Central Conference of American Rabbis and the Union of American Hebrew Congregations as early as 1977. See Lutheran Church in America, "Social Statement: Sex, Marriage, and Family" (5th Biennial Convention, 1970); United Methodist Church, "Revision of 'Social Principles'" (General Conference, 1972), codified in Book of Discipline of the United Methodist Church, 162H (2000); United Church of Christ, "Pronouncement on Civil Liberties without Discrimination Related to Affectional or Sexual Preference" (10th General Synod, 1975); Protestant Episcopal Church (now Episcopal Church), "Resolution A-71: Support Right of Homo- sexual to Equal Protection of the Law" (65th General Convention, 1976), in Journal of the General Convention of the Episcopal Church (Minneapolis, 1976): C-109; Christian Church (Disciples of Christ), "Resolution

7747" (General Assembly, 1977); United Presbyterian Church in the U.S.A. (now Presbyterian Church [U.S.A.]), Minutes of the 190th General Assembly (1978), 265–66; American Lutheran Church, "Human Sexuality and Sexual Behavior" (10th General Convention, 1980), G(5); Central Conference of American Rabbis, "Resolution on Rights of Homosexuals" (88th Annual Conference, 1977); Union of American Hebrew Congregations, "Resolution on Human Rights of Homosexuals" (54th General Assembly, 1977).

30. D'Emilio and Freedman, *Intimate Matters*, 324.

31. Kirstin Downey Grimsley, "Rights Group Rates Gay-Friendly Firms," *Washington Post*, 14 August 2002.

32. Newport, "Homosexuality."

33. Ibid.

34. Stephanie R. Reiss, Meghan Wharton, and Joanne Romero, "Child Custody and Visitation," *Georgetown Journal of Gender and the Law* 1 (2000): 383, 392–97; see Jacoby v. Jacoby, 763 So. 2d 410 (Fla. Dist. Ct. App. 2000).

35. American Academy of Pediatrics, "Technical Report: Coparent or Second-Parent Adoption by Same-Sex Parents," *Pediatrics* 109 (2002): 341.

36. Statement of Anthony P. Carnevale, Chair, National Commission for Employment Policy, quoted in Congress, Senate, Committee on Labor and Human Resources, *Employment Discrimination on the Basis of Sexual Orientation: Hearings on S. 2238 before the Senate Committee on Labor and Human Resources*, 103d Cong., 2d sess., 1994, 70.

37. Ibid., 6.

38. Christopher R. Leslie, "Creating Criminals: The Injuries Inflicted by 'Unenforced' Sodomy Laws," *Harvard Civil Rights–Civil Liberties Law Review* 35 (2000): 103, 115.

39. See Bottoms v. Bottoms, 457 S.E. 2d (Va. 1995), 102, 108 (although "a lesbian mother is not *per se* an unfit parent [,] . . . [c]onduct inherent in lesbianism is punishable as a Class 6 felony in the Commonwealth . . . ; thus, that conduct is another important consideration in determining custody").

45 • *Elias Vitulli*

A DEFINING MOMENT IN CIVIL RIGHTS HISTORY? THE EMPLOYMENT NON-DISCRIMINATION ACT, TRANS-INCLUSION, AND HOMONORMATIVITY

DISCUSSION QUESTIONS

1. What does the concept of homonormativity mean, what is it based on, and who is represented by it? How does the notion of "queer" challenge homonormativity? Can you identify examples of homonormativity not mentioned in the article?
2. What is ENDA? Which sexual communities does ENDA privilege, and which does it stigmatize? What are the embedded assumptions in privileging and stigmatizing certain people and particular sexual practices?
3. What did you learn about the power of mainstream national advocacy organizations, their practices of representation and inclusion, as well as their investment in political processes?

INTRODUCTION

Congressional leaders' decision in 2007, supported by just a few gay and lesbian activists and organizations, to strip the Employment Non-Discrimination Act (ENDA) of its newly included gender identity protections sparked a loud, contentious, and very visible debate within the mainstream LG(BT) movement over the questions of trans-inclusion. This debate was by no means new to gay and lesbian political movements or communities. In fact, trans activists and supporters had been attempting to make ENDA trans-inclusive for over a decade and a half.

Hegemonic constructions of trans and gender nonconforming and gay and lesbian identities have been intertwined throughout their histories. For example, early constructions of homosexuality were understood through gender nonconformity, called gender "inversion" at the time, in which a man who was attracted to men was thought to be acting like or have the brain of a woman, and a woman who was attracted to women was thought to be acting like or have the

Vitulli, Elias. 2010. "A Defining Moment in Civil Rights History? The Employment Non-Discrimination Act, Trans-Inclusion, and Homonormativity." *Sexuality Research and Social Policy* 7:155–167. Copyright © 2010, Springer Science + Business Media, LLC.

brain of a man (Stryker 2008a). While the theory of inversion has been discredited, most dominant stereotypes of gays and lesbians still are based on gender nonconformity.

The development of gay and lesbian politics and movements also have been intertwined with and run parallel to the development of trans[1] politics and movements. Trans communities and gay and lesbian communities share similar histories and struggles. Throughout their histories, trans, gay and lesbian, and queer people have formed communities together, organized and resisted together, and understood their identities through or against each other. Many scholars have pointed out that trans and gender nonconforming people have been integral in gay rights movements from the beginning (see, for example, Denny 2006; Minter 2006; Stryker 2008a, 2008b).

The mainstream gay movement that emerged in the 1950s, 1960s, and 1970s and consolidated into a professionalized, politically reformist and assimilationist, homonormative establishment in the 1990s has long sought to separate itself from trans populations—along with other gender and sexual non-normative, racialized, immigrant, and low-income populations. The question of whether trans people are a part of this community and movement—and therefore deserve not only inclusion but also significant resource allocation—remains a contentious and ongoing debate. In this article, I show that the exclusion of gender identity protections from the 2007 ENDA is just the most recent event in the long history of the trans-inclusion debate and that it is inextricably linked to other aspects of homonormative strategies that have been employed in attempts to pass the bill and more generally to normalize gay and lesbian community and rights.

. . .

In this article, I focus on what I call the "mainstream LG(BT) movement,"[2] which refers to the gay and lesbian organizations and communities with the most political power and visibility in national politics and media. Organizations such as the Human Rights Campaign (HRC), the National Gay and Lesbian Task Force (the Task Force), and Parents, Family, and Friends of Lesbians and Gays (PFLAG) are central to this "community" and "movement." Therefore, the following brief history is only one of many different histories of gay, lesbian, queer, trans, and other gender and sexual minorities. I use "histories," instead of a singular "history," in this introduction not to indicate two separate and separable "gay" and "trans" histories but to point to the many different histories that these populations have. These histories are defined not only by gay and lesbian versus trans identities but by other gender, racial, class, national, and political identities. These histories are different but are also inextricably linked by dominant constructions of normative and deviant genders and sexualities, which are always contingent on race, class, citizenship status, ability, and other social categories. The movement and its history presented here should be understood as based in predominantly white, economically, and educationally privileged spaces. This whiteness and other privileges are an important part of the movement's homonormativity, as will be discussed in the first section.

Since the 1970s, the passage of federal antidiscrimination legislation that covers sexual orientation—and eventually gender identity—has been at the top of the national LG(BT) agenda. On May 14, 1974, Representative Bella Abzug introduced the Equality Act into the House of Representatives. The introduction of this bill marked the first time that a "gay rights" bill had been introduced on the federal level in the US ("Federal Gay Rights," 1974). Since then, some version of this bill has been introduced in every session but has only reached the floor of either house of Congress for a vote twice, in 1996 and 2007. This article focuses on the history of the work on and debate around trans-inclusion in this legislation through the development and recent institutionalization of homonormativity in the mainstream LG(BT) movement. . . .

THE LG(BT) MOVEMENT AND HOMONORMATIVITY

Within the last decade a small segment of the gay and lesbian population—predominantly white, middleclass and wealthy, and gender-normative—has gained increased visibility, acceptance, and political legitimacy in dominant US society. Increased visibility in entertainment and the media, the decriminalization of sodomy with the 2003 *Lawrence v. Texas* decision, and the growing acceptance and legalization of "gay marriage" have both contributed to and are a reflection of shifting boundaries of normative sexuality and familial structures. Scholars have described this as the emergence of homonormativity or the extension of heteronormative privilege to certain normative gays and lesbians (see, for example, Duggan 2003; Ferguson 2005; Puar 2007; Agathangelou, et al. 2008; Stryker 2008b). However, while homonormativity has facilitated (slightly) larger boundaries of what constitutes normative sexuality in the US, it ultimately re-entrenches interlocking systems of normative sexuality and gender and white supremacy.

Homonormativity, like heteronormativity, is defined in terms of whiteness, traditional and essentialized gender roles, property and wealth, monogamy and the nuclear family structure, able-bodiedness, and US citizenship. Both heteronormativity and homonormativity are interlocked with white supremacy and rely on constructions of normative whiteness. Their whiteness is seen in their normalization and naturalization of constructions of normative gender, sexuality, and family structures that are defined through whiteness, while racial difference operates as a sign of non-normativity and exclusion (Ferguson 2005). In other words, heteronormativity and homonormativity are defined in opposition to the sexuality of people of color. Homonormativity constructs gay identity as white and aligns gay politics with dominant constructions of knowledge and power that disqualify other (racialized and non-hetero/homonormative) modes of knowing that threaten dominant, normative space and authority (Stryker 2008b).

In the US, normative systems of gender and sexuality rely on constructions of normative bodies and stable, essentialized binary gender and sex, where "men" (who always have penises) are the opposite of "women" (who always have breasts and vaginas), which trans people challenge and threaten. Homonormativity similarly relies on and attempts to naturalize these normative constructions. Homonormative gay and lesbian identity assumes a stable, essentialized sexual object choice that is attached to normative "male" and "female" genitals corresponding to specific normative gender expressions. Queer or unstable sexual object choice and trans, gender non-conforming, and surgically altered bodies denaturalize and expose the performativity of these normative constructions of gender and sexuality and therefore remain outside homonormativity.

While heteronormativity is one of the most important, basic structures of the US state and dominant society, the emergence of homonormativity signals the reentrance of white, gender-normative gays and lesbians into the rights and privileges of US citizenship, allowing them to access racial and class privileges by conforming to gender and sexual norms. Homonormative gays and lesbians mimic (white) heteronormative gender, sexual, and family structures, strengthening both heteronormativity and white supremacy (Puar 2007).

The (white) mainstream LG(BT) movement relies on and has helped to construct and consolidate homonormativity. This movement has developed in the last decade or so into an institutionalized, professional nonprofit model that utilizes assimilationist, homonormative strategies. The model of "equality" that it espouses is one based on narrow, formal access to a few conservative institutions and hinges on a (homo)normative, domesticated, depoliticized right to privacy (Duggan 2003). This work has increasingly marginalized people of color, low-income people, and trans people as homonormative organizations work to integrate the most privileged sections of gay and lesbian populations into the US state.

This movement constructs issues mainly relevant to white, wealthy, and middle-class gender-normative gay men as generalized "gay issues," legitimizing this, in part, by framing itself as single issue and therefore universal to the "gay experience" while constructing issues that affect LGBT people of color, low-income people, trans people, and other queer people as special issues and thus outside the scope of sexuality. In other words, the homonormative subject's ability to (re)gain access to the state, citizenship, and white privilege is based on the reestablishment of racialized, sexualized, and gendered boundaries between "us" and "them" and the policing and reiterative performance of these boundaries. These strategies render power and identity differentials invisible within "the LGBT movement," thereby misrepresenting and naturalizing the unequal distribution of power within it (Cohen 1997).

In a recent article, Susan Stryker (2008b) identifies two different origins and usages of homonormativity. The more common usage, generally attributed to Lisa Duggan in *Twilight of Equality,* focuses on homonormativity as a product of neoliberal politics. Queer of color critique scholars have recently engaged with this usage to describe how normative, dominant homosexuality and gay politics are based on normative whiteness and white supremacy (see, for example, Ferguson 2005; Puar 2007; Agathangelou, et al. 2008). Stryker also identifies a different, earlier version of homonormativity that emerged out of trans communities and activisms and was articulated by Judith Halberstam in *Female Masculinity* that describes trans and gender non-conforming people's "double sense of marginalization and displacement" (p. 145) that arises out of their conflicts with gender-normative, assimilationist homosexuality, and gay politics. It is also a way to link the disparagement of gender non-normativity in gender-normative gay and lesbian contexts with similar disparagement in heteronormative ones.

I do not think that these two "versions" of homonormativity are in opposition or even in tension— nor do I think Stryker would say that they are—but that they focus on different aspects of homonormativity. Homonormativity, like heteronormativity, is based on interlocking systems of gender normativity, white supremacy, and neoliberalism—along with other systems of oppression like ableism and US xenophobia and nationalism. While some scholars have chosen to focus on particular aspects of homonormativity, all are vital parts of homonormative discourses and strategies. In this article, I hope to demonstrate how these different aspects work together to govern strategies around and work on ENDA.

. . .

The exclusion of trans people frequently is justified through their construction as freaks and deviant

and homonormative people's desire to separate themselves from this in order to construct themselves as normative. One important example of this is the discussion over "the shower issue," or the repeatedly expressed "concern" about pre- or non-operative transfeminine people showering in women's locker rooms with non-trans women. In fact, Rep. Barney Frank has repeatedly cited this as one of his greatest problems with gender identity protections.[3] This "concern" relies on understandings of transfeminine people as always inherently "men" and as freaks, sexual deviants, and sexual threats. As Frank cites this "concern," he draws a distinct line between the freakish, threatening trans women who seek to invade "real women's" space and normative (white) gay men like himself.

ENDA is an example of homonormative legislation in terms of both usages of homonormativity that Stryker identifies. The exclusion of gender identity from the bill is homonormative in the sense that gender non-normative people are excluded in favor of a vision of a completely gender-normative gay and lesbian "community." The bill in general is homonormative because it represents an attempt to assimilate gay and lesbian people into the "American dream" and the (white-washed, class-unconscious) normative discourse of individualism, hard work, and personal responsibility.

In addition, there have been important critiques of antidiscrimination laws that point out, for example, that they have been ineffective in eradicating discrimination, that most people do not have access to the legal resources to enforce these laws, and that they represent an investment in formal equality which ignores the situation of those who are most marginalized (Mananzala and Spade 2008). Matt Richardson (in Currah 2008a) points out that equal protection laws do not produce the same benefits for everyone because many people "are not recognized by the state as full citizens no matter what [their] passports say and whether or not [they] were born in the United States" (p. 100).

Anti-discrimination laws promote formal equality but do not address structural or systemic inequalities and have no redistributive power. This is in part because they are largely unenforced but more importantly because they focus on individual acts of discrimination and not larger institutional discrimination. Critical Race Theory scholars have critiqued civil rights laws and discourse and other anti-discrimination laws that largely focus on individual discrimination and do nothing to address institutional or systemic racism. By viewing racism and discrimination as aberrant, isolated acts by individuals, anti-discrimination and civil rights laws create structures of formal equality while simultaneously hiding and reinforcing the status quo of institutional racism (see for example, Crenshaw 1995; Freeman 1995; Gotanda 1995). By similarly refusing to address institutional power hierarchies and systems of oppression, such as heteronormativity, ENDA fails to address and cannot remedy structural heteronormativity. The understanding of inequality and oppression that anti-discrimination laws generally espouse is in line with homonormativity because they are ultimately depoliticized—they assume that discrimination is aberrant, individual acts and not normative in U.S. society and state—and are about inclusion in the U.S. state in a way that reinforces and legitimizes current structural inequalities.

Throughout the history of ENDA, numerous concessions and compromises have created a bill that privileges some sexual practices and identities while stigmatizing others. The legislation privileges monogamously coupled, procreative, unpromiscuous, noncommercial, non-kinky normative sexuality. Patrick McCreery (1999) argues that ENDA presumes the existence of normative sexual practices in which gays and lesbians engage and that "any presumption of 'normative sexuality' is a corollary of heteronormative culture" (p. 41). Homonormative discourses reinforce this by unlinking gay identity from sexuality, allowing ENDA to protect gay identity without actually protecting any expression of gay sexuality. Furthermore, by relying on the historically contingent categories heterosexual, homosexual, and bisexual, ENDA reinscribes heteronormative culture because these categories presume the existence of immutable binary gender and render any fluidity in sexuality unimaginable. It is also through these

stagnant categories that heterosexuality is constantly reinscribed as always normative. By relying on these categories, the legislation renders queer identity and trans and gender non-normative identities and relationships invisible and thus unprotectable. This invisibility and exclusion is necessary to sustain the homonormativity of the bill.

The history of the bill, in some ways, parallels the history of the mainstream LG(BT) movement. The bill was introduced in 1974 during the beginning of an assimilationist, reformist gay rights movement that was emerging out of the Gay Liberation Movement. It was a first effort at incorporation into the U.S. state and national politics. Throughout the 1970s, 1980s, and into the 1990s, the bill "refined" as a national gay and lesbian lobbying establishment emerged and consolidated. It was also an important vehicle and object for these developing lobbying efforts. The first two decades of the bill were mainly characterized by intensive, individual lobbying of Congress people to become supporters and cosponsors of the bill, which resulted in the slow but steady increase in cosponsors (Feldblum 2000b).[4] Over the next few decades, as this gay and lesbian political establishment developed, became more conservative and institutionalized, and as the new homonormativity developed, the bill reflected these changes, becoming less inclusive, less expansive, and continued to accommodate more and more exclusions and compromises. It is within this context of compromise that the decision to cut gender identity protections for the 2007 ENDA must be understood.

This strategy of compromise is inextricably intertwined with the view of trans people's place in the movement advocated by proponents of the split bills because it shows that they view trans and gender nonconforming people as expendable to the larger goals of the movement. Furthermore, the expendability of trans people is related to the expendability of other LGBTQ people, namely people of color, low-income people, immigrants, disabled people, and others. This expendability of the most marginalized queer people is an important element in the national mainstream LG(BT) movement's homonormative political strategy.

Legislative History

In 1974, Rep. Bella Abzug introduced the first federal "gay rights bill," the Equality Act, into the House of Representatives (H.R. 14752). The Act proposed to add the categories of sex, sexual orientation, and marital status to the Civil Rights Act of 1964. This anti-discrimination coverage would have included employment, housing, public accommodations, education, and federal programs ("Federal Gay Rights," 1974; H.R. 14752). In 1975, Abzug separated sexual orientation from sex and marital status, introducing the "Civil Rights Amendments of 1975," which proposed protections for "affectional or sexual preference" (H.R. 166; H.R. 5452). The Civil Rights Amendments were introduced with little change for the following eight Congressional sessions by Reps. Edward Koch and then Ted Weiss, attracting an increasing number of cosponsors, from none on the original bill in 1974 to 110 in 1991.

The analogous Senate bill had a slightly different history. In 1979, 5 years after Abzug introduced the Equality Act in the House, Senator Paul Tsongas introduced "A Bill to Prohibit Employment Discrimination on the Basis of Sexual Orientation" (S. 2081). Tsongas introduced a similar bill focusing on employment discrimination in the next two sessions of Congress (S. 1708 in 1981; S. 430 in 1983). The Senate bill did not extend beyond employment discrimination until Senator John Kerry introduced the Civil Rights Amendments Act of 1985 in the 99th session of the Senate (S. 1432), which was identical to the bill introduced in the House that year. Following 1985, the bills introduced in the Senate and the House were identical. Cosponsorship in the Senate rose steadily and slowly from three in 1979 to sixteen in 1991.[5]

In 1994, gay and lesbian activists and Congressional leaders chose to shift their strategy by whittling down the anti-discrimination bill to cover only employment discrimination. That year they introduced the Employment Non-Discrimination Act into both houses of Congress (H.R. 4636; S. 2238). . . .

This constriction of the gay rights bill was an important part in the effort to assimilate normative gays and lesbians into full US citizenship. The focus on equality in employment relies on white, heteronormative, middle-class, neoliberal constructions of "American values" of individualism, hard work, and personal responsibility that anybody who works hard can achieve the "American dream" of wealth, success, and full citizenship. . . . This homonormative strategy, while pulling certain gays and lesbians into normative citizenship, reinforces existing power structures and discourses that criminalize and exclude people of color, low-income people, and other queer people from normative citizenship by strengthening the link between full citizenship and "legitimate" employment.

The creation of ENDA, with the removal of other non-employment-related protections, was not the first and certainly would not be the last time that the bill was watered down and compromised to make it more "acceptable" and less threatening to its opponents. This willingness to repeatedly compromise often to the detriment of the purposes of the legislation is symptomatic of homonormative strategies. For example, prior to the creation of ENDA, the Civil Rights Amendments bill was rewritten not to amend the Civil Rights Act of 1964, thereby unlinking it from previous civil rights legislation and effectively ranking homophobia as something less than and separate from racism, sexism, and other covered oppressions (McCreery 1999).[6] This separation conforms to the homonormative, single-issue logic that separates "gay and lesbian issues" from "racial issues," "class issues," and others. It also assimilates itself to a legal system that cannot understand intersectionality and weakens the bill to help maintain the status quo.

Since the enormous compromise that created ENDA, the bill has been further rewritten almost every time it has been reintroduced to make it less "threatening" and consequentially weaker. Over the past decade and a half, numerous clauses have been written into the bill, including: broad exemptions for the military and religious organizations (exemptions that seem to get broader with each rewriting), a clause that explicitly forbids affirmative action aimed at gays and lesbians, and a clause that embeds into the bill Defense of Marriage Act's (DOMA) definition of marriage as between one man and one woman. Even the bill's definition of "sexual orientation" has been narrowed since 1994. While the original bill gave the broadest definition of sexual orientation, defining it as "lesbian, gay, bisexual, or heterosexual orientation, real or perceived, as manifested by identity, acts, statements, or associations," the following versions defined sexual orientation as "homosexuality, bisexuality, or heterosexuality, whether such orientation is real or perceived." Feldblum has explained that the "as manifested" language was removed in order to deny ENDA's critics a "hook" to begin talking about specific sexual practices that they could claim the bill endorsed (in McCreery 1999, p. 46). This ultimately separates these "identities" from actual sexual practices in order to reinforce the "normativity" of the gays and lesbians it is designed to protect.

. . .

MAKING ENDA TRANS-INCLUSIVE

The early 1990s saw a "tremendous burst of new transgender activism" (Stryker 2008a, p. 121). The emergence of this new trans activism is related to the formation of coherent trans identities and communities, the increased visibility of trans people in the media and entertainment industry, the emergence of trans studies in academia, and the loosening of the medical establishment's strict control over discourses on transsexuality and trans identity—mainly because of the ongoing activism of trans people over the previous four decades. A much more cohesive national trans movement and increased trans visibility and voice within established gay and lesbian organizations came out of this burst of activism. By the late 1990s and early 2000s, gay and lesbian organizations began to include trans people explicitly in their mission statements and their work and accepting trans people as integral parts of the gay and lesbian—reconceptualized as the LGBT—movement (Denny 2006). For example, the Task Force changed its mission statement in 1997 (NGLTF 2008), PFLAG in 1998 (PFLAG 2008), and HRC in 2001 (NTAC 2004). Despite this nominal progress, there has never been consensus among LGB people, or even trans people, that trans people belong in the gay and lesbian

community. Furthermore, while nearly all organizations have made these semantic changes to their names and mission statements, few resources have been allocated to "trans issues" and trans people remain extremely underrepresented in their staffs (Mananzala and Spade 2008).

Since the first drafting of ENDA, trans activists have fought to have gender identity protections included in the bill, with Congressional leaders and leading gay activists and organizations actively opposing this inclusion. Inclusion of gender identity threatens the homonormative construction of gays and lesbians by linking them with gender non-normativity. Gay and lesbian activists frequently fought—and still fight—against this linkage in order to be able to be incorporated into the normative state. As homonormative gays and lesbians constructed themselves as not threatening to the heteronormative state, they were able to gather more votes for ENDA. As Frank explained in 1993, the inclusion of gender identity protections would have caused "a very significant fall-off, especially among Republicans" (Brune 2004, paragraph 14), which he cited as the reason for their exclusion. While drafters of the 1994 bill very briefly considered including trans status, Feldblum (2000a) explains that this inclusion was decided against because it was believed that it would come at "significant political cost" (p. 627) and that this type of discrimination was covered under existing sex discrimination laws. More importantly, she explains that they "believed that discrimination based on transgender status was conceptually different from discrimination based on sexual orientation" (pp. 627–8) and that trans people were not integral parts of the community they serve. While a number of trans activists advocated for inclusion, they were "dismissed out of hand" (Keisling, personal communication, May 1, 2008).

The first public effort by trans activists to get gender identity included in ENDA was the attempt by Phyllis Frye and Karen Kerin to speak at the July 1994 Senate Hearings on ENDA (Keisling, personal communication, May 1, 2008). While they were not allowed to speak, they were able to talk to a number of members of Congress (Frye, personal communication, April 13, 2008). In March 1995, six trans activists, including Frye, Kerin, and Riki Ann Wilchins, lobbied Congress for an inclusive ENDA. Frye (2000) describes this event as the "first organized transgender lobbying event in our nation's capital" (p. 463). Frye and other activists also drafted an inclusive bill, which Jeffords had said he would introduce. Despite these efforts, on June 15, 1995, a non-inclusive ENDA was introduced in the Senate, angering trans activists who felt betrayed.

HRC, which helped push through the non-inclusive bill, was at the center of this "betrayal."[7] By September 1995, HRC agreed to meet with a number of trans activists, including Frye and Kerin. Following the meeting, HRC arranged to allow two trans activists to work with Feldman, the main author of the bill, on an amendment that would add gender identity protections. HRC agreed not to oppose this amendment if it were to be offered but did not agree to work for, support, or even recommend the introduction of such an amendment. This position was reaffirmed in a follow-up meeting between HRC and trans activists in 1996. Ultimately, this effort went nowhere (Frye, personal communication, April 13, 2008; Feldblum 2000a).

The reintroduction of a non-inclusive bill and the failed negotiations with HRC caused trans activists to change their strategy from focusing on Congressional leaders to focusing on HRC and other national organizations. Mottet (personal communication, April 23, 2008) explains that activists worked to get all the major gay and lesbian organizations to change their position on ENDA to supporting only an inclusive bill. While HRC continued its policy of non-inclusion, activists worked to isolate HRC and make them the "lone holdout."

Over the following years, most national gay rights organizations changed their positions on ENDA to actively supporting an inclusive bill. In January 1995, the National Lesbian and Gay Law Association became the first national gay and lesbian organization to pass a board resolution calling for trans-inclusion in ENDA. In 1998, PFLAG began advocating for an inclusive ENDA (Frye 2000). In 1999, The Task Force changed its position to supporting only an inclusive ENDA and became the first national gay and

lesbian organization to stop their work on the bill because of its lack of trans-inclusion (NGLTF 2008). Nearly every other major gay and lesbian organization quickly followed suit, except HRC (Mottet, personal communication, April 23, 2008).

In 1999, the Task Force officially requested to the staffs of Senators Jeffords and Kennedy that ENDA include gender identity protections. Both Senators rejected this request. However, Feldblum (2000b), who was involved with these requests, explains that they were able to have serious discussions with their staffs about inclusion and that both staffs believed that if there was a shift in the views of the "American public" on trans people, Congress would shift as well. As far as I know, this was the first official request by a mainstream LG(BT) organization to Congressional leaders that they make ENDA trans-inclusive.

During this time, trans activists continued to lobby Congress in order to increase their visibility. In October 1995, activists held another lobby day. Frye (2000) claims that in just 2 days, over 100 trans activists and supporters from 35 states lobbied 95% of Congress. Trans activists and supporters held lobby days in most of the ensuing years. Frye (personal communication, April 13, 2008) describes the responses of the members of Congress as mostly "very cordial" and that they would follow the lead of Kennedy and Frank.

By the early 2000s, trans activists had successfully positioned HRC as the lone holdout standing in the way of an inclusive bill. Organizations—including the Task Force, Pride At Work of the AFL-CIO, PFLAG, National Organization of Women, National Center for Transgender Equality (NCTE), and Gender Public Advocacy Coalition—together began to put pressure on HRC to change its position (see Ames et al. 2002). In August of 2004, a group of trans activists, including Keisling, Mottet, Minter, Jamison Green, Donna Rose, and others gave a presentation on trans-inclusion in ENDA to HRC's Board of Directors (Keisling, personal communication, May 1, 2008).[8] Keisling explains that they were probably allowed to give this presentation because the Board was "already almost there" in changing their official policy on trans-inclusion in ENDA and that the staff at the time was very supportive of an inclusive bill. Later that month, after nearly a decade of struggle, the Board of Directors voted not to support the proposed bill the following year unless it included gender identity protections, thereby officially changing the organization's policy and coming into line with the rest of the LG(BT) movement.

Following the victory with HRC and now possessing a united front, activists turned their full attention to convincing Frank, now the main Congressional leader on ENDA, to introduce a gender identity inclusive bill. It took nearly 2 years before Frank agreed to this change. While his decision to change was in part because activists could show him that they had more votes for an inclusive bill than ever before, it was due mainly to pressure from the LG(BT) movement. By 2006, it was very clear that the movement was unified behind an inclusive bill. Keisling (personal communication, May 1, 2008) explains that Frank agreed to introduce, but not necessarily to pass, an inclusive bill. He was willing to try to pass the inclusive bill but only with the understanding that if he needed to split the bill later, he would. By then, it was the end of the session of Congress, and Frank decided to wait for the next session to introduce the new bill.

THE EMPLOYMENT NON-DISCRIMINATION ACT OF 2007

On April 24, 2007, Frank introduced a new version of ENDA into the House (H.R. 2015). This bill marked the first time gender identity protections had been added to the sexual orientation protections. Activists with Lambda Legal, NCTE, the Task Force, the National Center for Lesbian Rights (NCLR), the American Civil Liberties Union, HRC, and Gay and Lesbian Advocates and Defenders (GLAD) had begun drafting the new bill in 2004 (Mottet, personal communication, April 23, 2008). The bill enjoyed wide support in 2007, attracting 174 co-sponsors (Chibbaro 2007a; Wendland 2007). It also had mainstream labor and corporate sponsorship, which further grounded the bill within the neoliberal economic and normative

U.S. state. At the time of its introduction, Frank and other House leaders were confident that the bill would pass the House.

On September 5, 2007, hearings were held on the inclusive bill. At this point, trans activists had no indication that there were significant problems with it. However, the mark-up meeting that was supposed to follow these hearings was postponed a number of times and activists began to hear rumors about trepidation over the bill's gender identity protections (Mottet, personal communication, April 23, 2008). Concerns among Democratic leadership started to arise over whether they had enough votes for an inclusive bill. Keisling (personal communication, May 1, 2008) contends that there was no real indication that they did not have the votes, that members of the House were just being "skittish," but pressure began to build on Democratic leadership.

As soon as they heard about a meeting between Reps. Frank, Tammy Baldwin and Speaker Nancy Pelosi to discuss stripping the bill of its gender identity protections, activists put together a statement reiterating their support for only a trans-inclusive ENDA. On September 27, nine national LGBT organizations—PFLAG, The Task Force, NCTE, NCLR, the National Stonewall Democrats, the National Coalition for LGBT Health, Pride At Work, the National Coalition of Anti-Violence Projects, and the Mautner Project of the National Lesbian Health Organization—issued a statement denouncing the stripping of gender identity protections from ENDA. It read, in part:

> Our organizations oppose the removal of protections for transgender people from ENDA. We would also oppose any employment nondiscrimination bill that did not protect transgender people. We are shocked and upset that. . .influential members of the House of Representatives have apparently made a decision to remove protections for transgender people from the bill. If true, this decision was made without consultation with leaders of the lesbian, gay, bisexual and transgender community (as quoted in Foreman 2007, ¶ 7).

This statement represented the inception of an unprecedented coalition of national and local LGBT organizations uniting to advocate for trans rights and trans-inclusion in the LG(BT) movement. HRC, however, did not sign the statement. The organization said it would not "assent" to stripping the bill of gender identity protections but did not indicate at this point how it would proceed (Eleveld 2007). This position not to outright oppose a non-inclusive bill angered many in the LG(BT) movement. It also represented a very quick reversal of HRC's stated policy regarding trans-inclusion. Less than a month earlier, Joe Solmonese, HRC's Executive Director, addressed the Southern Comfort conference, the largest trans conference in the country, stating: "We try to walk a thin line in terms of keeping everything in play and making sure that we move forward but always being clear that we *absolutely do not support and in fact oppose* any legislation that is not absolutely inclusive" ("Does HRC Support Transgender People?" 2008).

The 2007 ENDA controversy split the LG(BT) movement and brought the long standing disagreement over trans-inclusion to the forefront. As discussed in the introduction, over the past decade formal trans-inclusion has gained increasing acceptance within LG(BT) organizations and the movement as a whole. The formation of United ENDA and the overwhelming groundswell of support for inclusion of trans people in ENDA marked the first time that a large majority of LG(BT) organizations and their constituents came out to advocate for trans-inclusion and argue that trans people are integral parts of their communities. It also represented a deeper understanding of the connection between homosexuality, queer sexuality, trans-ness, and gender nonconformity. For example, some advocates argue that taking out gender identity stripped ENDA of any teeth it had. Lambda Legal (2007) called the bill "riddled with loopholes" because gays and lesbians are often discriminated against because of gender nonconformity and employers could claim that their conduct was based on gender expression not sexual orientation. This means that ENDA would protect soundly only white, middle-class, gender-normative gays and lesbians who need protection the least and allow discrimination against the most vulnerable LGBTQ people—trans

and gender non-conforming people, people of color, and low-income people.

The splitting of the movement around ENDA in the fall of 2007 was as much about strategy as it was about trans people's place in the LG(BT) movement. For those who came down on the side of a non-inclusive bill, namely Frank and HRC, expediency and the passage of any bill were most important. This stance is based in a homonormative strategy and history of not seeing the connection between gender transgression and sexual orientation. As an organization, HRC epitomizes the homonormative strategy (see Agathangelou et al. 2008). For example, HRC has acted to keep gender identity out of some gay rights legislation, most prominently ENDA and federal hate crimes legislation. Monica Roberts (2007), a trans activist and former Lobby Chair for the National Transgender Advocacy Coalition, claims that HRC has a history of "refusing to deal with trans people as equals not only in terms of civil rights legislation but even in hiring talented transgender people for their organization" (paragraph 39). In fact, HRC has been the subject of numerous protests by LGBTQ activists over the years. For example, in 2000, NTAC launched a campaign, called "Embarrass HRC," that encouraged activists across the country to protest HRC dinners and other events to call the organization out on its resistance to including trans people in ENDA (Roberts 2007). Given this history, it is not surprising that HRC was the lead organization supporting and possibly even advocating stripping the gender identity protections from ENDA.

On September 27, the day after nearly all the major national LG(BT) organizations issued the statement opposing taking gender identity protections out of the bill, Frank announced his plan to split ENDA into two bills (H.R. 3685 with sexual orientation; H.R. 3686 with gender identity). He planned to introduce two versions of ENDA in the House Education and Labor Committee, extending protections based on sexual orientation and the other based on gender identity ("A Civil Rights Law" 2007). The sexual orientation bill would immediately go to committee for mark-up and then proceed to the House floor for a vote. The gender identity bill would be put on a separate, slower track that would allow supportive legislators to hold hearings and better educate other legislators on employment discrimination based on gender identity (Eleveld 2007).

House Democratic leaders said they decided to drop gender identity from the bill following an internal Democratic head count that found that the bill would likely be defeated if it included gender identity (Chibbaro 2007a). Frank and other House leaders indicated that they were concerned that Republicans would introduce a motion to recommit, specifically to recommit promptly with instructions, which would force the bill back into committee where it would die. They believed that opponents would focus specifically on an aspect of trans-inclusion, such as trans daycare workers or teachers, that would make it very difficult for supportive Democrats to vote against the motion because of the fear of angering their constituents. Nearly everyone agreed that the original bill could pass; the concern was whether it could survive a motion to recommit. The controversy and decision to split the bill was never about overall passage (Mottet, personal communication, April 23, 2008).

Baldwin described the response from LGBT activists to the splitting of the bill as a "deluge of phone calls and email messages" sent to House members demanding that Democrats support a fully inclusive bill or no bill at all (Chibbaro 2008). Within 48 hours of the Congressional move to strip gender identity from ENDA, more than one hundred LGBT organizations from across the country mobilized to form the coalition United ENDA, whose purpose is to use grassroots mobilization to pass only the original, inclusive bill (Minter 2007). The United ENDA coalition quickly expanded to more than 200 organizations by early November (Chibbaro 2008).

HRC did not join United ENDA. On October 2, HRC's Board of Directors voted to "reaffirm [their] 2004 policy supporting a fully inclusive version" of ENDA, yet they took the position that they would not oppose the non-inclusive bill. They issued a statement that said, in part: "Since 2004, HRC has had in place a policy that supports only a fully inclusive version of ENDA and the Board of Directors voted to reaffirm that position . . . Therefore, we are not able to support, *nor will we encourage Members of Congress to vote against,* the newly introduced sexual orientation only bill" (HRC 2007, paragraph 3, emphasis added). This position represented a break with its earlier stated support for only an inclusive bill, as well as with nearly every other major national and local LG(BT) organization across the country, thereby positioning HRC in opposition to most of the LG(BT) movement. In the days and weeks before Frank announced the splitting of the bill, a time in which HRC was in close communication with Frank, HRC's position went from opposing a non-inclusive bill to being neutral to openly pushing the non-inclusive bill. In fact, they were quietly pushing for the non-inclusive bill before publicly taking that position (Mottet, personal communication, April 23, 2008).

Feldman (personal communication, June 15, 2009) explains that a very small group—consisting of Frank and other House leadership, HRC, and LCCR—made the decision that they did not have enough votes for the inclusive bill and to split them. No other groups were brought in. While the decision itself was not an unusual political decision, the decision not to consult the broader LG(BT) movement was extraordinary. It was especially strange that he did not consult with the Task Force or the ACLU, who are the other relevant organizations with lobbyists in DC. She explains that ultimately what caused the ensuing "train wreck" were the decision-makers' lack of community accountability and the leadership's "close-minded arrogance."

Despite little to no support from the LG(BT) movement, on October 18, 2007, the non-inclusive ENDA was voted out of committee by a vote of 27–21, with four Democrats voting against it because of its exclusion of gender identity,[9] and sent to the full House floor. Republicans proposed a number of amendments in committee that many claimed were aimed at gutting the bill. The Democratic-controlled committee voted down all these amendments; however, the House Rules Committee allowed three amendments to be considered, including one introduced by Rep. Mark Souder, who was actively trying to kill the bill (Chibbaro 2007b).

Souder's amendment struck a section of ENDA that prohibited employers from conditioning employment on a person being married or being eligible to be married (H.AMDT. 883). The second amendment, offered by Rep. George Miller, broadened and clarified the religious exemption to make it the same as Title VII's religious exemptions, stated that ENDA did not alter DOMA in any way and inserted language defining "married" in accordance with DOMA, and removed language referencing "a same-sex couple who are not married" in the Employee Benefits section (H.AMDT. 882).

The final amendment was offered by Baldwin and would reinsert the stripped gender identity protections (H.AMDT. 884). This amendment was Baldwin's last ditch effort to keep the bill inclusive; however, almost no one thought they had the votes to pass it. For a time, activists thought that if the vote was close, it could indicate that Pelosi and Frank had made a mistake in stripping the bill of its gender identity protections. However, as time went on, it became clear that the vote would not be close. Even supportive members were indicating that they would not vote for it because they feared it would kill the overall bill (Keisling, personal communication, May 1, 2008).

On November 7, 2007, ENDA was introduced on the House floor for a vote. After a few hours of debate, the House passed ENDA with a vote of 235 to 184. Seven Democrats voted against the bill because of its exclusion of gender identity.[10] The House also approved Souder and Miller's amendments by votes of 325 to 101 and 402 to 25, respectively. Baldwin introduced her amendment but then withdrew it immediately without seeking a vote. It was reported that Baldwin agreed to this after first-term House Democrats appealed to Pelosi not to have a separate vote on the trans-inclusion issue because it would hurt their reelection chances (Chibbaro 2007b). Ultimately, Baldwin introduced the amendment in order to be able to speak on the issue of gender identity, which without its introduction she could not have done (Keisling, personal communication, May 1, 2008). Reps. Souder and Buck McKeon attempted to use a parliamentary maneuver to prevent Baldwin from withdrawing her amendment in an attempt to kill the bill before the vote, but they were ruled out of order. A motion to recommit with instructions, which

called for adding language that would prevent courts from using ENDA to change the legal definition of marriage as being between one man and one woman, was also introduced by Rep. Randy Forbes. After a short debate, Forbes' motion to recommit was defeated 222 to 198 ("Employment Non-Discrimination Act of 2007," 2007).

CONCLUSION

. . .

On June 24, 2009, Frank reintroduced an inclusive ENDA into the House of Representatives (H.R. 3017). At the time of this writing, activists and Congressional leaders are planning a hearing in the House Committee on Education and Labor in September followed by a vote in the full House. Keisling (personal communication, July 30, 2009) explains that they are "extremely optimistic" that the bill will pass the House and believe that there is a "very good chance" that it will become law by the end of this Congressional session. This optimism is due in large part to the political and educational work on trans issues that happened in Congress in response to the events of 2007.

. . . Unfortunately, discussion over how trans-exclusion and homonormative strategies also silence the voices and ignore the needs of other marginalized queer people, particularly LGBTQ people of color and low-income LGBTQ people, has not been a significant part of the ENDA controversy (see Cohen 1997; Valentine 2007; Agathangelou et al. 2008; Currah 2008a; Mananzala and Spade 2008). There also has not been discussion about which trans people will remain excluded from the benefits of a trans-inclusive bill and from a more trans-inclusive LG(BT) movement, such as trans and gender nonconforming people of color and low-income people, because of their lack of racial and economic privileges. Instead of the current strategy of centering the most privileged LGBT people, I hope to see the creation of a movement that centers the most marginalized and oppressed, addressing the interplay of multiple oppressions and the lived realities of those who experience them.

. . .

ACKNOWLEDGMENTS

This article came out of research I did on ENDA while a Vaid Fellow at the Policy Institute at the National Gay and Lesbian Task Force. I want to thank Nick Ray and Jamie Grant for the opportunity and their support. I also would like to thank Carolyn Dinshaw, Jack Skelton, Lara Kelland, and the two blind reviewers provided by SRSP for comments and edits on various versions of this essay. Finally, thank you to Chai Feldblum, Phyllis Frye, Mara Keisling, and Lisa Mottet for lending me their time, memories, and knowledge.

REFERENCES

A Civil Rights Law; Employment Discrimination against Gays and Lesbians Should Be Outlawed. (2007). *The Washington Post,* p. A18.

Agathangelou, A. M., Bassichis, M. D., & Spira, T. L. (2008). Intimate investments: homonormativity, global lockdown, and the seductions of Empire. *Radical History Review, 100,* 120–143.

Ames, M., Bowman, C., Keisling, M., Mottet, L., Schlittler, R., Vives, O., et al. (2002). Letter to Winnie Stachelberg. On file with author.

Brune, A. (2004). HRC Vows No ENDA if No Trans Protection. *Washington Blade.* Retrieved March 28, 2008, from http://www.washingtonblade.com/2004/8-13/news/national/enda.cfm

Bull, C. (1997). No ENDA in Sight—Employment Non-Discrimination Act of 1996. *The Advocate.* Retrieved September 16, 2008, from http://findarticles.com/p/articles/mi_m1589/is_n733/ai_19736014

Chibbaro, Jr., L. (2007a). ENDA hits snag over transgender inclusion. *Washington Blade.* Retrieved September 16, 2008, from http://www.washblade.com/thelatest/thelatest.cfm?blog_id=14507

Chibbaro, Jr., L. (2007b). House passes ENDA in "Historic" vote. *Washington Blade.* Retrieved September 16, 2008, from http://www.washblade.com/thelatest/thelatest.cfm?blog_id=14845

Chibbaro, Jr., L. (2008). Activists seek reconciliation, renewed push for ENDA. *Washington Blade.* Retrieved September 16, 2008, from http://www.washblade.com/2008/2-22/news/national/12098.cfm

Cohen, C. J. (1997). Punks, bulldaggers, and welfare queens: the radical potential of queer politics? *GLQ, 3,* 437–465.

Crenshaw, K. (1995). Color-blind dreams and racial nightmares: reconfiguring racism in the post-civil rights era. In K. Crenshaw, N. Gotanda, G. Peller, & K. Thomas (Eds.), *Critical race theory: the key writings that formed the movement* (pp. 97–168). New York: New Press.

Currah, P. (2008a). Stepping back, looking outward: situating transgender activism and transgender studies—Kris Hayashi, Matt Richardson, and Susan Stryker Frame the movement. *Sexuality Research and Social Policy, 5*(1), 93–105.

Currah, P. (2008b). Expecting bodies, the pregnant man and transgender exclusion from the employment non-discrimination act. *Women's Studies Quarterly, 36*(3/4), 330–336.

Denny, D. (2006). Transgender communities of the United States in the late twentieth century. In P. Currah, R. M. Juang, & S. P. Minter (Eds.), *Transgender rights* (171–191). Minneapolis: University of Minnesota Press.

Devroy, A. (1995). Clinton backs ban on sexual orientation bias at work. *The Washington Post,* p. A07.

Does HRC Support Transgender People? (n.d.) Retrieved September 16, 2008, from the Youtube website: http://www.youtube.com/watch?v=v_GhTiBO8Cw

Duggan, L. (2003). *The twilight of equality? Neoliberalism, cultural politics, and the attack on democracy.* Boston: Beacon.

Eleveld, K. (2007). ENDA to be separated into two bills: sexual orientation and gender identity. *The Advocate.* Retrieved September 16, 2008, from http://www.advocate.com/news_detail_ektid49439.asp

Employment Non-Discrimination Act of 2007. (2007). *Congressional Record.* 110th Congress, 1st session, 2007.

Feldblum, C. (2000a). Gay people, trans people, women: is it all about gender. *New York Law School Journal of Human Rights, 17,* 623–702.

Feldblum, C. (2000b). The federal gay rights bill: from Bella to ENDA. In J. D'Emilio, W. B. Turner, & U. Vaid (Eds.), *Creating change: public policy, and civil rights* (pp. 150–187). St. Martin's Press.

Ferguson, R. A. (2005). Racing homonormativity: citizenship, sociology, and gay identity. In P. Johnson & M. G. Henderson (Eds.), *Black Queer studies: a critical anthology* (pp. 52–67). Durham: Duke University Press.

Foreman, M. (2007). A non-transgender-inclusive ENDA? No way! Retrieved April 18, 2008, from The Bilerico Project website: http://www.bilerico.com/2007/09/a_nontransgenderinclusive_enda_no_way.php

Freeman, A. D. (1995). Legitimizing racial discrimination through antidiscrimination law: a critical review of supreme court doctrine. In K. Crenshaw, N. Gotanda,

G. Peller, & K. Thomas (Eds.), *Critical race theory: the key writings that formed the movement* (pp. 29–45). New York: New Press.

Frye, P. (2000). Facing discrimination, organizing for freedom: the transgender community. In J. D'Emilio, W. B. Turner, & U. Vaid (Eds.), *Creating change: public policy, and civil rights* (pp. 451–468). St. Martin's Press.

Gotanda, N. (1995). A critique of "our constitution is color-blind." In K. Crenshaw, N. Gotanda, G. Peller, & K. Thomas (Eds.), *Critical race theory: the key writings that formed the movement* (pp. 257–275). New York: New Press.

Holmes, S. A. (1995). Clinton backs bill to protect homosexuals from job bias. *The New York Times*, p. 1.

Howlett, D. (1995). Senate bill protects gays in the workplace. *USA Today*, p. 2A.

Human Rights Campaign (HRC). (2007). Human rights campaign board of directors vote to reaffirm 2004 policy on ENDA supports ENDA legislation protecting the entire GLBT community. Retrieved May 4, 2008, from the HRC Back Story website: http://www.hrcbackstory.org/2007/10/human-rights-ca.html

Lambda Legal. (2007). Lambda legal's analysis of stripped down version of ENDA: gender identity protections gone and inadequate protections for lesbians, gay men and bisexuals. Retrieved May 6, 2008, from the Lambda Legal website: http://www.lambdalegal.org/news/pr/lambda-legals-analysisenda.html

Mananzala, R., & Spade, D. (2008). The nonprofit industrial complex and trans resistance. *Sexuality Research and Social Policy, 5*(1), 53–71.

McCreery, P. (1999). Beyond gay: "deviant" sex and the politics of the ENDA workplace. *Social Text, 61*(4), 40–58.

Minter, S. P. (2006). Do transsexuals dream of gay rights? getting real about transgender inclusion. In P. Currah, R. M. Juang, & S. P. Minter (Eds.), *Transgender rights* (pp. 141–170). Minneapolis: University of Minnesota Press.

Minter, S. P. (2007). Banding together. *The advocate.* Retrieved September 16, 2008, from http://www.advocate.com/exclusive_detail_ektid49796.asp

National Gay and Lesbian Task Force (NGLTF). (n.d.). Task Force's work to end discrimination against lesbian, gay, bisexual and transgender Americans. Retrieved April 18, 2008, from the National Gay and Lesbian Task Force website: http://www.thetaskforce.org/issues/nondiscrimination/timeline

National Transgender Advocacy Coalition (NTAC). (2004). Transsexual Menace, Others Protest HRC.

Retrieved April 24, 2008, from the Transgender Crossroads website: http://www.tgcrossroads.org/news/?aid=934

PFLAG: Parents, Family, and Friends of Lesbians and Gays. (n.d.). PFLAG's History. Retrieved April 24, 2008, from the PFLAG website: http://community.pflag.org/NETCOMMUNITY/Page.aspx?pid=267&srcid=191

Puar, J. K. (2007). *Terrorist assemblages: homonationalism in Queer Times.* Durham: Duke University Press.

Roberts, M. (2007). Why the transgender community hates HRC. Retrieved May 4, 2008, from the TransGriot website: http://transgriot.blogspot.com/2007/10/why-transgender-community-hates-hrc.html

Stevens-Miller, M. (n.d.). Miranda writes . . . Frankly, He doesn't give a damn. Retrieved May 4, 2008, from the Illinois Gender Advocates website: http://www.genderadvocates.org/Miranda%20Writes/M0008Frankly.html

Stryker, S. (2008a). *Transgender history.* Berkeley: Seal.

Stryker, S. (2008b). Transgender history, homonormativity, and disciplinarity. *Radical History Review, 100,* 145–157.

Sullivan, A. (2007). The LGBTQRSTZ "community." *The Daily Dish.* Retrieved April 24, 2008, from http://andrewsullivan.theatlantic.com/the_daily_dish/2007/11/the-lgbtqrstz-c.html

Valentine, D. (2007). *Imagining transgender: an ethnography of a category.* Durham, NC: Duke University Press.

Wendland, J. (2007). A new beginning for ENDA. *Political Affairs Magazine.* Retrieved September 16, 2008, from http://www.politicalaffairs.net/article/articleview/5099

Wetzstein, C. (1996). Senate debates bill to end gay job bias; vote set Tuesday on "marriage" ban. *The Washington Times*, p. A2.

NOTES

1. We currently lack language to adequately describe and name complex gender and sexual performances and identities. For example, some communities who are understood as trans by service providers and others outside the community internally identify as gay or as something else entirely. The language of "transsexuality" and "transgender" has been mostly constructed in the privileged, mainly white spaces of the medical-psychological establishment, academia, and certain kinds of activism and can exclude or render invisible gendered communities of color and low-income gendered communities (Valentine 2007). I have

chosen to use "trans" because it reflects the language used by mainstream LG(BT) organizations and because I believe it is the most inclusive language available at the moment. In this article, "trans" includes a wide range of gendered experiences, including everyone from transsexual people who have physically transitioned; to pre- or non-operative trans people; to genderqueer or other people who do not identify as one of the two socially recognized genders; to cross-dressers, drag kings, and drag queens; to masculine women and feminine men.

2. The parentheses signify the ongoing question of who actually is included in these different formulations of gay, lesbian, bisexual, transgender, and queer movements and communities. There are multiple conceptions of LGBT movements in the US, many of which are not always inclusive of the different kinds of LGBT identities. I have chosen to use "LG(BT)" in this essay both to reflect the most widely used label "LGBT" and to mark this movement's historical and ongoing exclusions of trans and bisexual people as well as its frequent privileging of (white) gay male interests.

3. I have found numerous accounts of Frank's transphobia around "the shower issue." For example, in a 1999 *Advocate* article, he claimed, "Transgendered people want a law that mandates a person with a penis be allowed to shower with women. They can't get that in ENDA" (quoted in Currah 2008b, p. 333). See also Miranda Stevens-Miller's (n.d.) description of an encounter she had with Frank.

4. Feldblum (2000b) explains that this work on the bill was backseated in 1983 because of AIDS and that serious efforts did not begin again until 1991. Throughout these 8 years, the national mainstream gay and lesbian political establishment matured a great deal and was integrated into the mainstream civil rights community.

5. See Feldblum (2000b) for an excellent, detailed history of the gay rights bill from 1974 to 1999.

6. It should be noted that Feldblum (personal communication, June 15, 2009) explains that this was done because any legislation that seeks to revise and expand existing civil rights laws also opens them up to revisions designed to repeal or weaken them. Therefore, the mainstream civil rights community will not support this type of legislation, which is one reason that the ADA is a free-standing bill. However, this points to the continued tenuous position of civil rights legislation, even though it has been law for over 40 years.

7. As the largest and most well resourced national LG(BT) organization and most influential on Capital Hill, many politicians see them as the representative of all LGBTQ people. Until recently, they were the only LGBT organization with professional federal lobbyists and still employ the most. They are the only LGBT organization with a Congressional scorecard on LGBT issues and the only one with a political action committee, which allows them to give money to politicians.

8. In her discussion of this presentation, Keisling (personal communication, May 1, 2008) emphasized that HRC made it clear that they were only talking about federal anti-discrimination legislation. Following this presentation and their change in policy on trans-inclusion in ENDA they continued to "weasel for years" about trans-inclusion in the federal hate crimes legislation they were trying to pass. She explained that a main reason for the differing policies on these legislations was that they believed that they had a chance of passing the hate crimes bill but not ENDA.

9. Reps. Dennis Kucinich from Ohio, Rush Holt from New Jersey, Linda Sanchez from California, and Yvette Clarke from New York ("Bill to Protect GLB Workers Advances Without the T," 2007).

10. Reps. Clarke, Jerrold Nadler, Edolphus Towns, Nydia Velasquez, and Anthony Weiner, all from New York City; Holt from New Jersey; and Michael Michaud from Maine.

46 • *Kurt C. Organista, Paula A. Worby, James Quesada, Sonya G. Arreola, Alex H. Kral, and Sahar Khoury*

SEXUAL HEALTH OF LATINO MIGRANT DAY LABOURERS UNDER CONDITIONS OF STRUCTURAL VULNERABILITY

DISCUSSION QUESTIONS

1. Why do the authors argue that Latino migrant day labourers are a structurally vulnerable population?
2. What major themes influence the participants' overall sexual health, according to the authors? How do core values, including gender ideology, shape their discourse about sexual desire and sexual practices?
3. How might you add to the suggested interventions at both the individual and structural level?

INTRODUCTION

Sexual health involves physical, emotional, mental and spiritual dimensions embedded in social, cultural and interpersonal relationship contexts. As such, optimal sexual health involves respectful and caring values, attitudes, beliefs and behaviours in sexual relationships that are relatively free of stigma and discrimination and, more specifically coercion, exploitation and violence. It also follows that optimal sexual health minimises the probability of negative outcomes such as HIV and STDs, unplanned pregnancies and so on and maximises the probability of sexual wellbeing within meaningful and satisfying relationships and lifestyles.

With the above definition in mind, we would assert that sexual health is inversely related to a population's degree of structural vulnerability or position in society, characterised by productions and reproductions of harsh living and working conditions that challenge sexual health by way of compromising health and wellbeing in general (Organista et al. 2012; Quesada, Hart, and Bourgois 2011). Such is the case for Latino migrant day labourers, a unique population of Latinos that experiences dislocation and discontinuity in their lives as a result of migrating to the USA in search of work to support families and interests back in Mexico and Central America.

While Latino migrant day labourers are hardly free of poverty and structural vulnerability in their

Organista, Kurt C., Paula Worby, James Quesada, Sonya G. Arreola, Alex Kral, Sahar Khoury. 2013. "Sexual Health of Latino Migrant Day Labourers Under Conditions of Structural Vulnerability." *Culture, Health and Sexuality* 15(1):58–72. Copyright © 2013 Taylor & Francis.

countries of origin, their unique experience in the USA, as a predominantly undocumented and stigmatised minority ethnic group, presents multiple challenges to sexual health and wellbeing and suggests risk-prevention and health-promotion strategies at the structural environmental level in order to mitigate their vulnerability. Only within the last decade have we begun to understand the background characteristics and experience of Latino migrant day labourers in the USA.

LATINO MIGRANT DAY LABOURERS

The informal day labour market is composed of mostly poor foreign-born Latino men who congregate in outdoor sites such as street corners to solicit temporary work (Valenzuela 2003). In California, some 40,000 day labourers are estimated to seek work on any given day (Gonzalez 2007), though this number excludes those who come in and out of the day labourer market seasonally (Nelson et al. 2012). In California, about 80% of day labourers are presumed undocumented, primarily from Mexico and secondarily from Central America (Gonzalez 2007). Harsher immigration policies have slowed migration over the Mexican border during the past decade but have also had the effect of 'trapping' undocumented persons in the USA in contrast to the circular migration patterns that previously allowed for frequent visits to country of origin (Passel and Cohn 2009). Different sources, including the 2004–2005 National Day Labour Survey (NDLS) that sampled sites across the continental USA (and the only effort to date of this magnitude), find about half of day labourers to be single, with the remainder having wives/partners and/or children back home (Valenzuela et al. 2006). The NDLS estimated the Latino migrant day labourer populations to be approximately 120,000, although this was eight years ago.

Research with day labourers in the past decade underscores their economic and socially marginal status and consequent stress. Valenzuela et al. (2006) estimated that annual incomes rarely exceed $15,000, keeping the vast majority near or below the federal poverty threshold, a problem exacerbated by the current economy (Bhimji 2010). The individual poverty threshold is currently an annual income of $11,170, a figure calculated by the Department of Health and Human Services to determine eligibility for federal aid, but only for citizens. In a study conducted with 219 day labourers in San Francisco in 2009, 65% reported that they did not get enough to eat and 54% reported having poor or only fair health (Nelson et al. 2012). When 102 day labourers were surveyed from two Northern California sites in 2008, high rates of stress were found for about 58%, related to instability, relationship and communication difficulties and alcohol/substance use (Duke, Bourdeau, and Hovey 2010). An earlier survey of day labourers in the same region of California yielded that unemployment and underemployment were the most highly endorsed concerns, followed by sadness and racism (Organista and Kubo 2005).

A pilot study among day labourers in the state of Washington documented a range of work-associated, economic and social stressors along with biologic measures associated with allostatic load in order to capture the so-called 'wear and tear' effect linking chronic stress to negative consequences for physical health (de Castro et al. 2010). While conclusions that would link more years in the US with worsening biological markers of stress were limited because of a small sample size, the study's findings suggest that Latino migrant day labourers are potentially at risk for high allostatic load because of the multiple psychosocial stressors prominent in their lives (de Castro et al. 2010).

Both quantitative survey and qualitative research that has focused exclusively on day labourers have highlighted lack of stable work and typically low-wage work that in turn create economic hardship leading to problems with housing, indebtedness and the inability to maintain relationships with partners left in a country of origin, or to establish such relationships in the USA (Duke, Bourdeau, and Hovey 2010; Negi 2011; Nelson et al. 2012; Ordoñez 2012; Quesada 2011; Walter, Bourgois, and Loinaz 2004). The social context that imposes isolation and vulnerability includes hostile attitudes by host communities, a lack of policies that would permit documentation or work authorisation and sometimes lack of key resources such as healthcare and adequate housing. All of these conditions constrain the ability to maintain adequate income, health and wellbeing (LeClere and Lopez 2011; Maney and Abraham 2008; Quesada, Hart, and Bourgois 2011; Walter et al. 2002).

. . .

HIV Risk

Day labourer research in the sexual-health-related area of HIV risk documents high use of sex workers (Galvan et al. 2008; 2009; Organista and Kubo 2005), occasional solicitation by men who have sex with men for paid sex (Galvan et al. 2008; Ordonez 2012), mixed attitudes towards condom use and HIV testing (Ehrlich, Organista, and Oman 2007; Organista and Ehrlich 2008; Ritieni et al. 2007; Solorio and Galvan 2009) and sexual activity mixed with drug and/or alcohol consumption (Galvan et al. 2009; Worby and Organista 2007). Despite these risk factors, relatively low HIV prevalence has been found (Wong et al. 2003), warranting research to better understand and maintain such levels, in addition to better prevalence studies on day labourers and other groups, such as farmworkers and Latino immigrants more generally. For example, research on migrants interviewed in the US-Mexico border region found similar low rates of HIV but higher sexual risk behaviours in migrants returning from the USA as compared to those travelling to the border from within Mexico (Martínez-Donate et al. 2005; Rangel et al. 2006). While the above research documents various sexual-risk factors, there continues to be a paucity of research delving into the complicated set of circumstances and challenges faced by, and coping strategies employed by, Latino migrant day labourers in terms of attaining sexual health.

Latino Migrant Day Labourers' Sexual Health and Structural Vulnerability

Latino migrant day labourers are a structurally vulnerable population, a term we use to describe the *positionality* of a population in society characterised by harsh living and working conditions produced and reproduced by particular sets of global economic, political, social and cultural factors (Organista et al. 2012; Quesada, Hart, and Bourgois 2011). As such, structural vulnerability is inversely related to

socioeconomic status and general wellbeing in which sexual health is embedded. Our current model of structural vulnerability for Latino migrant day labourers is adapted from the work of Gupta et al. (2008) that advocates conceptualising sexual risk, and HIV risk in particular, as a causal pathway stemming from distal structural and environmental factors to more proximal situational- and individual-level factors. More specifically, structural factors, such as severely restricted access to work authorisation for immigrants, create undocumented workers that inhabit environments marked by poverty and harsh, underpaid work, which jeopardises sexual health and wellbeing more generally. The lack of healthy sexual, relationship, social and interpersonal options for day labourers increases their participation in risky situations within which, for example, men resort to sex workers given the lack of healthier options, as well as problem drinking that often co-occurs with risky sexual partners (Organista and Kubo 2005). Such multi-level conceptualisations of sexual health and wellbeing not only better reflect the complexity of the world in which we live, but also suggest multiple points of intervention along the causal pathway beyond the individual level (e.g., scaling up community services and resources that mitigate harsh living and working conditions).

Against this background, the purpose of this study was to explore the sexual health and wellbeing of Latino migrant day labourers, with attention to conditions of structural vulnerability. The following research questions are addressed: (1) what are the goals and aspirations of Latino migrant day labourers related to sexual health, (2) what challenges to sexual health do Latino migrant day labourers face in the USA and (3) how do Latino migrant day labourers cope with challenges to their sexual health?

METHODS

. . .

Participants

Participants were 51 Latino migrant day labourers in the San Francisco Bay Area, 18 years of age or older, who perform day labour as their main source of income. Day labour eligibility was based on a functional definition of having worked three or more jobs with no one job lasting more than two months, in the last six months. Latino migrant day labourers speaking neither Spanish nor English, or inebriated when approached were excluded. Purposive sampling was used to recruit a sample resembling the basic demographics that characterise local Latino migrant day labourers (Singleton and Straits 1998). This was accomplished by continually updating a chart tracking current age, age at migration, number of years in the USA and nationality of each respondent. As such, charting was utilised to shape subsequent recruitment with the goal of obtaining diversity for all four of the above background characteristics. It was also decided to obtain two-thirds of the sample from San Francisco and a third from Berkeley, given the different magnitudes of day labourer populations in these two study sites. The sample size target was set at 50 in order to obtain both sufficient and information-rich data to learn about the key study variables and themes of the larger study from which this report comes (Patton 2002).

PROCEDURES

Latino migrant day labourers were recruited with the assistance of three non-profit agencies brought in to the project as subcontracted community partners. Each serves Latino immigrants in a variety of capacities. These agencies (two in San Francisco and one in Berkeley) provide a range of services, although each with a slightly different mix of shelter and work opportunities, health and social services (in some cases including counselling and rehabilitation) and brokering relations between Latino migrant day labourers, neighbours, police, employers and city services. Members of the research team also have longstanding relationships of trust with these community partners from past projects and mutually supportive activities.

The outreach workers from each of the three community partner agencies introduced research team members to the Latino migrant day labourers whom they serve and with whom they have established trusting relationships. To begin the ethnography, the outreach workers outlined the purpose of the study, explained that the project was a collaboration between the agencies and researchers and described how members of the research team would be in the vicinity observing and engaging the men in conversation, eventually followed by soliciting their voluntary, anonymous, confidential and compensated ($25) participation.

Gaining access to Latino migrant day labourers through the established and trusted networks of community partner agencies is highly advantageous given Latino migrant day labourer's understandable suspicions toward unknown people working in official capacities, prompted by fear of deportation and a history of immigration agents presenting themselves under false pretences (e.g., "US Officials Defend Ploys to Catch Immigrants," *The New York Times,* February 11, 2006). Another advantage of our community-based approach is that it provided us with the opportunity to meet frequently with our community partners, give them progress reports on our work and receive feedback that improved the ethnography. For example, agency partners were able to direct us to Latino migrant day labourers of varying background characteristics, including those with drinking problems attending a support group organised by one of the agencies.

Recruitment of Latino migrant day labourers for in-depth interviews took place at community agency sites, directly where they sought work in the streets and at nearby places where they congregate (e.g., parks and shelters), in all cases interviews were conducted privately. Interview solicitation was relatively easy with no refusals. All participants were provided informed consent, read to them in Spanish, to participate in a study about their experience as day labourers, including inquiry into sexual health and alcohol consumption. The requirement to sign informed consent was waived and informed consent also included an explanation of the Federal Certificate of Confidentiality obtained for this study (i.e., waives requirement of researchers to provide any identifying information about undocumented participants in the unlikely event of investigation by immigration authorities).

. . .

RESULTS

Participants were primarily from Mexico, secondarily from Central America and two-thirds were sampled in San Francisco with the remainder recruited in Berkeley (Table 46.1). One third was between 21 and 30 years of age, with the remainder fairly evenly divided across the subsequent three decades of age groupings. Of participants, 60% had been in the USA for less than 10 years.

. . . Three major themes emerged from the qualitative data analysis: (1) familism and masculinity as

TABLE 46.1. Background Characteristics of Latino Migrant Day Labourers in the San Francisco Bay area (*n* = 51).

Characteristic	%	Average
Nationality		
Mexican	53	
Guatemalan	27	
Honduran	8	
Salvadoran	6	
Nicaraguan	4	
Peruvian	2	
Age at interview		38
21–30	33	
31–40	22	
41–50	25	
51 and older (up to 62)	20	
Age at first migration (range: 13–49)		28
13–20	14	
21–30	53	
31–40	22	
41–50	12	
Years in USA (range < 1 –35 years)		10
< 1–4	27	
5–9	33	
10–19	25	
20 or more	14	
Day labourer site		
San Francisco	66	
Berkeley	34	

cultural context of sexual health, (2) frustration with limited options to meet life goals related to sexual health and (3) the challenge of coping with threats to sexual health in the USA.

CULTURAL CONTEXT OF SEXUAL HEALTH: FAMILISM AND MASCULINITY

When participants were asked why they had come to the USA, saturation was quickly found across interviews regarding their overarching goal of wanting to *progresar* [to progress] or work to earn enough money to support families in one's country of origin, alongside related aspirations to return and build a home, start a small business or buy a car. By saturation, we are referring to the reoccurrence of a theme so frequently across interviews that the learning value becomes exhausted as well as the need to pursue it further in subsequent interviews (Strauss and Corbin 1990).

With regard to the first research question, findings suggested that the goals and aspirations of Latino migrant day labourers related to sexual health were deeply embedded in the core value and practice of *familismo* or the centrality of the family in Latino life as the following example illustrates:

> [An ideal life] would be to have a family, if you have a lady, [to live] as a couple, that you have two children, that you have a little home . . . that you have a job where you work five days a week. And that there be love with your significant other. That's something ideal. (Jaime, Salvadoran, 55 years old, 8 years in USA)

Variations of the above theme were found repeatedly throughout interviews whenever men were asked their reason for migrating to the USA, underscoring the almost singular purpose in pursuing work in the USA as a way of compensating for the lack of work and ability to support families in country of origin. Further, adherence to *familismo* included a conception of Latino masculinity prescribing men as heads of family and providers. However, respondents described how this gendered central goal is undermined by prolonged physical absence from families and repeated failure to be adequate breadwinners given the unstable work in the day labour market.

This dilemma is articulated by two Guatemalans: 24-year-old Alejandro, with only two years in the USA and, 44-year-old Carlos, with 11 continuous years in the USA, respectively:

> If I told you [what is most important to me] it would be contradictory because it's important to be with family. But I don't have my family here so then for me only making money is left. Making money would be important.
>
> . . . Well, for me [not having seen my wife in 11 years is] difficult because she's the mother of my children and she's a good person because she's put up with a lot from me, the good and the bad. For example, right now it's been days since I haven't worked. I haven't sent her any money and, she's not questioning me: 'Why aren't you sending us money?' I tell you that when I talk to her, we speak normally. There's no arguing, nothing. . . . Well, I feel a little distant, let's say forgotten. Because I'm not with her, because my children, she's the one that you could say is struggling there with them, being both a mother and a father, right? And I'm apart from them.

FRUSTRATION WITH MEETING LIFE GOALS RELATED TO RELATIONSHIPS AND SEXUAL HEALTH

Latino migrant day labourers with prolonged time in the USA (e.g., greater than five years) evidenced greater frustration, disappointment and anxiety about not progressing as planned as compared to more recent arrivals. Latino migrant day labourers that had left partners back home also expressed more distress about the prolonged separations, including fear of losing partners and actual losses:

> My desperation is that even though I have nothing, I have to go back because the time goes on and what is going to end up happening is that I am going to lose my family . . . (Carlos, Salvadoran, 53 years old, 8 years in USA)
>
> I told my girlfriend that I was going away for some time. I told her that I loved her and wanted to marry her, but that I wanted to come to this country to do something like build a house, buy a car, have a fully

furnished house, you know, to have our children. Then, I told her that if she loved me that she would wait for me and that I was going to be here for three or four years until I could go back to Guatemala. She told me she really loved and adored me. . . . So I came over here, and within a year and a half she cheated on me and found another boyfriend. (Lobsang, Guatemalan, 27 years old, 6 years in USA)

Negative reactions to not achieving core economic, family and relationship-related goals provided answers to the second research question regarding challenges to sexual health aspirations. That is, goal frustration frequently resulted in the commonly cited problem of *caerse en vicio* [falling into vices] including sexual risk taking and problem drinking:

> Two months ago I had unprotected sex. There were three of us, other friends who are from over there, from Mexico. Well we were drinking, and then we got a bit drunk, I think, my friends [told] me to go over there walking, over here on 22nd [Street], around there. They told me they knew a girl and, 'Let's go visit her,' they told me. And we went. And no, we didn't find the girl but since it was late and on our way back, so we came back and we found a girl there on the road. We talked to her and got her in the car. And, well, obviously we gave her money. And yeah the girl wanted to, but we didn't have protection. No well. Well the girl wanted to. She didn't refuse anything. (Emiliano, Mexican, 25 years old, 3 years in USA)

Participants often gave themselves tacit permission to drink and satisfy pent-up sexual urges when their idealised romantic relationships proved unfeasible. Barriers to finding girlfriends in the USA, especially stemming from lack of economic stability, added to their frustration:

> I'm not even married, so I don't have anyone waiting on me, [or] children. . . . Another thing, at first here I didn't even want a girlfriend. For one thing I haven't had the luck, the other thing is girls here want a guy with money . . . you have to have a job, where to live and all that. (Kurtines, Mexican, 35 years old, 6 years in the USA)

DIFFICULTY COPING WITH CHALLENGES TO SEXUAL HEALTH

With respect to the third research question, regarding how Latino migrant day labourers cope with challenges to their sexual health, participants often reported condom use with sex workers given concerns about contracting diseases such as HIV and other STDs. Sex with sex workers emerged as the main sexual outlet for study participants and may be emblematic of the limited, less than satisfying and anxiety provoking sexual options available to Latino migrant day labourers in the USA. In contrast, sex without condoms was frequently mentioned in relation to intimate partners back home. Such challenges to sexual health and preferred sexual relations are illustrated below:

> I left [a girlfriend] in Mexico . . . [I did not use protection with her] because I know that person only has sex with me. And she knows, well, that when I have sex with others, I'm careful. (Esteban, Mexican, 28 years old, 1 year in USA)
>
> I think that I want to keep myself safe since I don't have my wife, it's that I want to keep myself abstaining from sex of whatever kind to see if God will give me a wife again. And if I go around having sex with some homosexual or with prostitutes and I get some diseases because there are diseases like syphilis, AIDS, gonorrhoea, and all that . . . because on more than two occasions, yes I paid for sex but with women. And only like that with a condom you know and I did it only to feel, you know, the, the, the thrill, you know to be there with a girl but no, this doesn't do it for me, doesn't do it for me. (Luis, Mexican, 45 years old, 19 years in the USA)

In terms of where sex partners were typically encountered, participants described finding casual or one-time sex partners on the street, in dance halls and drinking establishments or through fellow workers referring them to sex workers. Their narratives about such sexual encounters further reveal effort on the part of some of the men to use condoms as a strategy to reduce sexual risk and maintain their sexual health:

> I haven't had any, any encounter without protection here in the USA. I did have an encounter like, like a month ago. Eh, but I used protection the entire time, protection because, well because everyone knows there is so much spreading, so many problems with that, everything that it brings with it. (Seth, Mexican, 30 years old, first year in the USA)

Another strategy to try and avoid risky sexual partners was by limiting sexual encounters to women perceived as *limpia* or 'clean,' as exemplified by Rafael, a 42-year-old Mexican man with less than a year in the USA:

RAFAEL: So right now I don't [have sex] unless it's with a clean woman.

INTERVIEWER: How do you know if a woman is clean?

RAFAEL: If she's not a hooker. The only way to know would be to find a girlfriend, not a prostitute because they have diseases. Then, if you're too drunk, you don't analyse things well enough to have sex with a girl.

DISCUSSION

This study explored the sexual health of Latino migrant day labourers under conditions of structural vulnerability, and in particular challenges to sexual health and subsequent ways of coping. While literature on HIV risk in day labourers has begun to accrue (e.g. Galvan et al. 2009; Organista et al. 2012), this is one of the first explorations of sexual health with an emphasis on its structural-environmental and cultural context in this unique Latino population. As such, findings illustrate and provide insights into the immense challenge of cultivating culturally patterned Latino, family-oriented, romantic relationships while being frequently thwarted in adhering to the culturally patterned masculine role of being a present husband/father and provider. Rather than simply enumerating sexual-risk factors, this study describes aspirations related to sexual health found to be deeply embedded in the core value and practice of *familismo* or the centrality of the family in Latino life, manifested either in efforts to support one's wife/female partner and/or children back home or for single day labourers, pursuing the life goal of one day finding a wife and beginning a family.

Against the above contextual backdrop emerged the more immediate challenge of negotiating pent-up sexual desire, both physical/biological and romantic, often through sexual relations that the men settled for rather than preferred—sex with risky sexual partners such as sex workers, typically while drinking. Such sexual outlets, limited by the experience of day labourers in the USA, were generally experienced as dystonic deviations from the central life goal and value of having a wife and family, adequate work and income to live a modest and contented life. These challenges persisted for men whether they were struggling to support wives and families in country of origin, trying to develop romantic relationships while in the USA, and in some cases both. For example, one married man who was trying to find women to date on Craigslist (a classified advertisement website devoted to jobs, housing, personals, etc.) explained that this was his own private business while living and working in the USA.

With regard to study limitations, qualitative research trades off sample to population generalisability for a deeper understanding of topics that are new, theory-driven, underdeveloped or poorly understood in the literature (Miles and Huberman 1994). While the literature on Latino sexual health is growing, most of it does not focus on immigrants and extremely little includes day labourers. Nevertheless, purposive sampling was utilised in the current study to accrue a sample that resembled day labourers in two sites in the San Francisco Bay Area in terms of country of origin, years in the USA and age. As such, we believe the experiences of the men described, analysed and interpreted here capture commonalities among day labourers in San Francisco and Berkeley. For example, in Organista and Kubo's (2005) survey of 102 day labourers in Berkeley, participants were similarly two-thirds Mexican and a third Central American, and most worried about too little work and money to support selves and families back home. Further, a recent qualitative study by Ordoñez (2012) captured the anxiety frequently expressed among Berkeley

Latino migrant day labourers about losing their wives and money sent home to 'Sancho,' a humorous Mexican trope used to signify the lover that is likely replacing the migrant who is absent from wife, home and family (e.g., one man in this study joked that he hoped that Sancho would buy himself some nice new boots with the money he was sending home to his wife).

Regarding implications for improving the sexual health of Latino migrant day labourers, findings suggest several interventions at multiple levels consistent with a structural-environmental perspective. At the individual-level, condom promotion, prevention and treatment of problem drinking and stress reduction might benefit Latino migrant day labourers. For example, while one of the men quoted described unprotected sex with a sex worker under the influence of heavy drinking, another asserted always using protection in order to avoid diseases. How to promote the latter scenario and decrease the former could be explored with Latino migrant day labourers at community partner agencies where they congregate for various group discussions and activities. Hence, while structural vulnerability increases threats to the sexual health of day labourers, condom promotion represents one proximal behavioural strategy for coping with pent-up sexual urges and frustration frequently relieved with sex workers. Also, as previously mentioned, one of our community partner agencies provides support groups for Latino migrant day labourers experiencing drinking problems that warrant future evaluation research.

However, individual-level interventions are likely to have diminishing returns in the absence of larger structural environmental interventions to mitigate the ill health-engendering living and working condition of Latino migrant day labourers in the USA. Thus, implications from the current study also include the need to scale-up community and cultural resources and activities that improve the economic conditions of Latino migrant day labourers, as well as approximate more culturally familiar ways of socialising and establishing interpersonal relationships. For example, one of our community partners provides vocational English instruction to Latino migrant day labourers to help them better negotiate work and wages and to improve their work-related vocabulary (e.g., in housing construction work, landscaping, etc.). This community partner also organises weekly soccer games for Latino migrant day labourers in order to increase healthy recreational outlets believed to relieve stress and even curtail weekend binge drinking in response to not finding work at the end of the week. While the latter begins to approximate culturally familiar ways of recreating with fellow workers, finding ways to connect Latino migrant day labourers with local social networks in which the relationships they desire might be approximated need to be explored (e.g., local church groups or cultural celebrations uniting people from the same hometown or home country) and evaluated in future studies. While most participants indicated meeting women in bars, on the street and through friends familiar with local sex workers, a few indicated attending church to meet 'decent' women.

Finally, implications for structural interventions at the state and national level with the potential to mitigate the reproduction of the harsh living and working conditions that permeate the lives of Latino migrant day labourers should be considered. Such implications could include pragmatic ways of regulating migrant labour supply and demand to diminish the occurrence of undocumented worker status and dangerous border crossings and that promote regular work, fair wages and safe conditions beneficial to both Latino labour migrants and US employers. Such structural interventions also imply facile circular transnational migration allowing for regular visits home with wives/partners, families and friends, so essential to sexual health and general wellbeing.

. . .

ACKNOWLEDGEMENTS

This study was supported by a research grant from the National Institute of Alcohol Abuse and Alcoholism (1R01AA017592-01A2; Organista, PI).

REFERENCES

Agar, M. 1996. *The professional stranger: An informal introduction to ethnography.* Waltham, MA: Academic Press.

Bhimji, F. 2010. Undocumented Immigrant Day Laborers Coping with the Economic Meltdown in Los Angeles. *Cultural Dynamics* 22(3): 22.

Crabtree, B. F. and W. L. Miller. 1999. "Using Codes and Code Manuals: A Template Organizing Style of Interpretation." In *Doing Qualitative Research*, edited by B. F. Crabtree, and W.L. Miller, 163–78. Thousand Oaks, CA: Sage.

de Castro, A. B., J. G. Voss, A. Ruppin, C. F. Dominguez, and N. S. Seixas. 2010. Stressors among Latino Day Laborers. A Pilot Study Examining Allostatic Load. *American Association of Occupational Health Nurses Journal* 58(5): 185–96.

Duke, M. R., B. Bourdeau, and J. D. Hovey. 2010. Day Laborers and Occupational Stress: Testing the Migrant Stress Inventory with a Latino Day Laborer Population. *Cultural Diversity and Ethnic Minority Psychology* 16(2): 116–22.

Ehrlich, S. F., K. C. Organista, and D. Oman. 2007. Migrant Latino Day Laborers and Intentions to test for HIV. *Aids and Behavior* 11(5): 743–52.

Galvan, F. H., D. J. Ortiz, V. Martinez, and E. G. Bing. 2008. Sexual Solicitation of Latino Male Day Laborers by Other Men. *Salud Pública de México* 50(6): 439–46.

Galvan, F. H., D. J. Ortiz, V. Martinez, and E. G. Bing. 2009. The Use of Female Commercial Sex Workers' Services by Latino Day Laborers. *Hispanic Journal of Behavioral Sciences* 31(4): 553–75.

Gonzalez, A. 2007. Day Labor in the Golden State. *California Economic Policy* 3(3): 24.

Gupta, G. R., J. O. Parkhurst, J. A. Ogden, P. Aggleton, and A. Mahal. 2008. Structural Approaches to HIV Prevention. *Lancet* 372(9640): 764–75.

Leclere, O. A., and R. A. Lopez. 2011. The *Jornalero*: Perceptions of Health Care Resources of Immigrant Day Laborers. *Journal of Immigrant and Minority Health* 14(4): 691–7.

Lecompte, M. D., and J. J. Schensul. 2010. *Designing and Conducting Ethnographic Research: An Introduction.* Lanham, MD: AltaMira Press.

Maney, G. M., and M. Abraham. 2008. Whose Backyard? Boundary Making in NIMBY Opposition to Immigrant Services. *Social Justice* 35(6): 17.

Martínez-Donate, A. P., M. G. Rangel, M. F. Hovell, J. Santibáñez, C. L. Sipan, and J. A. Izazola. 2005. HIV Infection in Mobile Populations: The Case of Mexican Migrants to the United States. *Revista Panamericana de Salud Publica/Pan American Journal of Public Health* 17(1): 26–9.

Miles, M. B., and A. M. Huberman. 1994. *Qualitative Data Analysis: An Expanded Sourcebook.* 2nd ed. Thousand Oaks, CA: Sage.

Negi, N. J. 2011. Identifying Psychosocial Stressors of Well-Being and Factors Related to Substance Use among Latino Day Laborers. *Journal of Immigrant and Minority Health* 13(4): 748–55.

Nelson, R. W., G. Schmotzer, B. J. Burgel, R. Crothers, and M. C. White. 2012. Sociodemographic Characteristics, Health, and Success at Obtaining Work among Latino Urban Day Laborers. *Journal of Health Care for the Poor and Underserved* 23(2): 797–810.

Ordoñez, J. T. 2012. "Boots for my Sancho": Structural Vulnerability among Latin American Day Labourers in Berkeley, California. *Culture, Health & Sexuality* 14(6): 691–703.

Organista, K. C., and S. F. Ehrlich. 2008. Predictors of Condom Use in Latino Migrant Day Laborers. *Hispanic Journal of Behavioral Sciences* 30(3): 379–96.

Organista, K. C., and A. Kubo. 2005. Pilot Survey of HIV Risk and Contextual Problems and Issues in Mexican/Latino Migrant Day Laborers. *Journal of Immigrant Health* 7(4): 269–81.

Organista, K. C., P. Worby, J. Quesada, A. H. Kral, R. Diaz, T. Neilands, and S. G. Arreola. 2012. "The Urgent Need for Structural-Environmental Models of HIV Risk and Prevention in US Latino Populations." In *HIV Prevention with Latinos: Theory, Research, and Practice,* edited by K.C. Organista, 1–23. New York: Oxford University Press.

Passel, J. S., and D. V. Cohn. 2009. *Mexican Immigrants: How Many Come? How Many Leave?* Washington, DC: Pew Hispanic Center.

Patton, M. Q. 2002. *Qualitative Research and Evaluation Methods.* 3rd ed. Thousand Oaks, CA: Sage.

Quesada, J. 2011. No Soy Welferero: Undocumented Latino Immigration in the Crosshairs of Legitimation Maneuvers. *Medical Anthropology* 30(4): 12.

Quesada, J., L. Hart, and P. Bourgois. 2011. Structural Vulnerability and Health: Latino Migrant Laborers in the United States. *Medical Anthropology* 30(4): 23.

Rangel, M. G., A. P. Martínez-Donate, M. F. Hovell, J. Santibáñez, C. L. Sipan, and J. A. Izazola-Licea. 2006. Prevalence of Risk Factors for HIV Infection among Mexican Migrants and Immigrants: Probability Survey in the North Border of Mexico. *Salud Pública de México* 48(1): 3–12.

Rhodes, S. D., K. C. Hergenrather, D. M. Griffith, L. J. Yee, C. S. Zometa, J. Montano, and A. T. Vissman. 2009. Sexual and Alcohol Risk Behaviours of Immigrant Latino Men in the South-Eastern USA. *Culture Health & Sexuality* 11(1): 17–34.

Ritieni, A., J. Quesada, S. Gilbreath, and A. Kral. 2007. *HIV and Related Health Factors among Latino Migrant Day Laborers in San Francisco and Workers in the Agricultural Sector in Monterey County.* Sacramento, CA: California Department of Health Services, Office of AIDS.

Singer, M., and H. Baer. 2007. *Introducing Medical Anthropology: A Discipline in Action.* Lanham, MD: Alta Mira Press.

Singleton, R., Jr. and B. C. Straits. 1998. *Approaches to Social Research.* 3rd ed. New York: Oxford University Press.

Solorio, M. R., and F. H. Galvan. 2009. Self-Reported HIV Antibody Testing among Latino Urban Day Laborers. *Journal of the National Medical Association* 101(12): 1214–20.

Strauss, A. L., and J. M. Corbin. 1990. *Basics of Qualitative Research: Grounded Theory Procedures and Techniques.* Newbury Park, CA: Sage.

Valdez, A., A. Cepeda, N. J. Negi, and C. Kaplan. 2010. Fumando la Piedra: Emerging Patterns of Crack Use among Latino Immigrant Day Laborers in New Orleans. *Journal of Immigrant and Minority Health* 12(5): 737–42.

Valenzuela, A. 2003. Day Labor Work. *Annual Review of Sociology* 29: 303–33.

Valenzuela, A., N. Theodore, E. Meléndez, and A. L. Gonzalez. 2006. *On the Corner: Day Labor in the United States.* Los Angeles, CA: University of California, Los Angeles Center for the Study of Urban Poverty.

Walter, N., P. Bourgois, H. M. Loinaz, and D. Schillinger. 2002. Social Context of Work Injury among Undocumented Day Laborers in San Francisco. *Journal of General Internal Medicine* 17(3): 221–9.

Walter, N., P. Bourgois, and M. H. Loinaz. 2004. Masculinity and Undocumented Labor Migration: Injured Latino Day Laborers in San Francisco. *Social Science & Medicine* 59(6): 1159–68.

Winett, L., S. M. Harvey, M. Branch, A. Torres, and D. Hudson. 2011. Immigrant Latino Men in Rural Communities in the Northwest: Social Environment and HIV/STI Risk. *Culture Health & Sexuality* 13(6): 643–56.

Wong, W., J. A. Tambis, M. T. Hernandez, J. K. Chaw, and J. D. Klausner. 2003. Prevalence of Sexually Transmitted Diseases among Latino Immigrant Day Laborers in an Urban Setting–San Francisco. *Sexually Transmitted Diseases* 30(8): 661–3.

Worby, P. 2007. *Accounting for Context: Determinants of Mexican and Central American Im/Migrant Day Laborer Well-Being and Alcohol Use.* Doctoral Dissertation, University of California, Berkeley.

Worby, P., and K. C. Organista. 2007. Alcohol Use and Problem Drinking among Male Mexican and Central American Im/Migrant Laborers: A Review of the Literature. *Hispanic Journal of Behavioral Sciences* 29: 413–55.

47 • *Monica Sharma*[1]

TWENTY-FIRST CENTURY PINK OR BLUE

HOW SEX SELECTION TECHNOLOGY FACILITATES GENDERCIDE AND WHAT WE CAN DO ABOUT IT

DISCUSSION QUESTIONS

1. What does the acronym ART stand for? What are some benefits in the advancement and accessibility of ART, and what are some of its unintended consequences?
2. According to the author, what are the core motivations for engaging in sex determination and how do these differ based on nation-state? What are the suggested regulations to interrupt ART-inspired gendercide?
3. As a critical reader, what is needed to contextualize the culturally specific information offered in this chapter—meaning what are some popular stereotypes that exist about the nation-states and how do these influence your learning about sex determination through ART?

I. INTRODUCTION: SEX SELECTION IN THE 21ST CENTURY

When a son is born,
Let him sleep on the bed,
Clothe him with fine clothes,
And give him jade to play . . .
When a daughter is born,
Let her sleep on the ground,
Wrap her in common wrappings,
And give broken tiles for playthings.[2]

In the midst of a "genetic revolution in medicine,"[3] Assisted Reproductive Technology (ART) has become a well-established technique to help infertile women achieve pregnancy.[4] But many women are now turning to ART not just to circumvent infertility, but consciously to shape their families by determining the sex of their children.[5] ART now comprises a variety of techniques: gender selection kits containing special vitamins and hormones along with carefully tailored diets; innovations in spinning and sorting sperm; and a process of fertilizing a woman's ovum with either X or Y sperm, then implanting the fertilized ovum into the uterus.[6] Some sex-selection techniques are more drastic, including aborting the fetus and killing the child of the undesired sex.[7] Whatever the method, sex selection has led to a

Sharma, Monica. 2008. "Twenty-First Century Pink or Blue: How Sex Selection Technology Facilitates Gendercide and What We Can Do About It." *Family Court Review* 46(1):198–215. Copyright © 2007, John Wiley and Sons.

significant and growing gender imbalance in the world population.[8] In the United States, sex selection "is becoming a multimillion-dollar industry."[9]

Do these sex-selection techniques constitute a logical component of reproductive freedom, or do they serve to perpetuate gender discrimination, particularly in countries or cultural communities where there is deep-rooted bias against women? Developments in reproductive technology pose a serious ethical dilemma, with some medical ethicists concluding that sex-selection technology represents a new commodification of medicine.[10] This note explains how these new sex-selection technologies have contributed to gendercide, the killing of female fetuses solely based on their gender.[11] Indeed, the United Nations estimates that up to 200 million women and girls are demographically missing.[12] In order to prevent a worsening of an already dangerous sex imbalance, this note concludes with a proposal to implement regulations restricting the use of sex-selection technologies to cases of medical necessity.

. . .

II. REPRODUCTIVE TECHNOLOGY AND THE CORE MOTIVATIONS FOR ENGAGING IN SEX SELECTION

A. REPRODUCTIVE TECHNOLOGY IN GENDER SELECTION

Developments in reproductive technology have transformed fertility science and the opportunities for previously infertile women to bear children.[13] The term "sex selection" embraces a variety of practices including selecting embryos for transfer and implantation following in vitro fertilization (IVF), separating sperm, and selectively terminating a pregnancy.[14] A 2005 study examining the demand for sex selection found that 41 percent of infertility patients surveyed would use preimplantation sex selection if it were offered to them at no cost, and half of those women would still opt to choose the sex of their baby if they had to pay for the opportunity.[15]

Developed in the early 1990s, preimplantation genetic diagnosis (PGD) allows couples to prevent a pregnancy affected by a genetic condition or chromosomal disorder.[16] PGD is a technique used to identify genetic defects in embryos created through IVF prior to transferring them into the uterus.[17] The same technology has emerged as a reliable sex selection method.[18] MicroSort is the newest development in reproductive technology.[19] A technique available through the Genetics & IVF Institute, MicroSort "is used before conception to separate sperm into those that either primarily produce girls or those that primarily produce boys."[20] The sorted sperm sample is then combined with intrauterine insemination (IUI)[21] and, if necessary, IVF and intracytoplasmic sperm injection (ICSI)[22] to achieve pregnancy.[23] Using the MicroSort sperm separation process to increase the probability of conceiving a girl has resulted in 92% of the babies born female.[24] The success rate for male babies is 81%.[25]

B. THREE CORE MOTIVATIONS FOR ENGAGING IN SEX DETERMINATION

. . . Viewing gender preference from a global perspective, many countries have sought to ban sex selection, often in reaction to the dramatic gender imbalances found in India and China, which together account for nearly 40 percent of the world's population.[26]

In South Asia, millions of infant girls have been aborted or abandoned at birth or directly killed.[27] In large parts of Asia, "the sex ratio at birth has risen to unnatural and historically unprecedented levels over the past two decades—and in many spots this tendency appears to be continuing unabated, or even to be intensifying further."[28] The two most populous nations, India and China, "share a similar mix of patriarchal culture; family structure; agrarian histories; rapid economic, technological, and scientific development; and robust governmental initiatives for population control. *In toto,* this proves a fatal mix for potential females."[29] According to a recent report by the United Nations Children's Fund (UNICEF), 43 million girls and women are missing from India's population.[30] The Indian Census of 1991 found 945 girls born for every 1,000 boys born.[31] By the 2001 Census, the sex ratio had diminished, with only 927 girl babies for every 1,000 boy babies.[32] Economist Amartya Sen estimated that 50 million women are missing from China's population.[33] In sum, systematic gender discrimination in South Asia has substantially contributed to the worldwide gender gap of 200 million, largely attributable to sex-selective abortions and female infanticide.[34] In India, this potent gender preference has been abetted by the persistence of a dowry system, making girls far more expensive than boys.[35] One expert quoted Indian families who justify their decision by saying, "Better to pay $38 for an abortion now than $3,800 for a dowry later on."[36] In China, the strong bias against girls was exacerbated by the government's strict One Child Policy.[37] Chinese parents "who have more children can be fined, lose their jobs, or be forcibly sterilized."[38]

1. Cultural or Religious Bias in Favor of Male Offspring

"Grooming a girl is like watering a neighbor's garden."[39] This Indian proverb captures the strong and pervasive culture bias favoring sons over daughters. Certain Asian cultures, such as those in India, Pakistan, South Korea, and both Mainland China and Taiwan, have traditionally placed great value on producing a male heir.[40] The primacy of male children is woven into the cultural and religious structure.[41] A son is viewed as a permanent member of the family as opposed to a daughter who will eventually leave, go to the home of her husband, and take on the name and customs of her in-laws.[42] Sons are perceived as a critical source for family financial maintenance and parental social security and families thus demonstrate a richer emotional and material investment in sons than in daughters.[43] The continuity of patriarchal lineage is an essential part of Indian culture: the birth of a son, but not that of a daughter, elevates the family's social standing.[44]

2. Economic Bias Disfavoring Daughters

Male children are preferred because (i) they have a higher wage-earning capacity, especially in agrarian economies, (ii) they continue the family line, and (iii) they are generally the recipients of a family's inheritance.[45] Girls are often considered an economic burden because of the dowry system, and after marriage they typically become members of the husband's family, ceasing to have responsibility for their parents in illness and old age.[46] Son preference is manifested prenatally, through sex determination and sex-selective abortion, and postnatally through neglect and abandonment of female children, which leads to higher female mortality.[47]

3. Family Balancing: Gender Variation within the Family

MicroSort and many other IVF clinics have begun offering gender-selection methods to couples seeking to balance the sexual gender in their families.[48] Currently, although the United States does not regulate sex selection, professional organizations such as the American Society for Reproductive Medicine (ASRM) have established guidelines for their members.[49] To date, these private covenants are the only limitations on the practice and methods of sex-selection technology. Sex selection for social reasons has been banned in most industrialized countries.[50] Opponents have deemed the allowance of sex selection as the opening of a Pandora's box where choosing the gender for social reasons would open the door to selecting the hair color, eye color, or personal traits or, in short, picking the designer baby.[51] . . .

III. THE GLOBAL IMPACT OF SEX SELECTION

A. Abnormally High Sex Ratios

The majority of the more than 100 million women that demographically vanished from the world's population are missing from China and India.[52] The majority of the remainder are estimated to be missing from the populations of Afghanistan, Bangladesh, China, India, South Korea, Pakistan, Taiwan, and Iran.[53] This section will briefly examine three countries of particular interest: South Korea, India, and China. South Korea has succeeded in substantially reducing the differential sex ratio; India features marked has a unique One Child Policy which has regional differences in its sex ratios; and China led to an increased preference for males.

South Korea was the first country to report significant differential sex ratios at birth, suggesting a widespread practice of fetal sex selection.[54] The widespread use of sex-selective technology in South Korea preceded that of other Asian countries.[55] Beginning in the mid-1990s, the government advanced a public awareness campaign warning of the dangers of such distortions. Laws forbidding sex-selection technology were more strictly enforced, and there was a widespread and influential media campaign focusing on the anticipated shortage of brides. Together, these actions led to a decline in the male-to-female sex ratio from 116 in 1998 to 110 in 2004.[56] This sex ratio is still, however, dramatically skewed. The public awareness campaign launched in South Korea has so far reversed the population impact of prebirth sex selection and may have partially counterbalanced the cultural predisposition toward son preference.[57]

India "now has the distinction of being known as the nation that likes to ensure that girls are never born."[58] One egregious example is Punjab. Census data from 1991 reported that in Punjab all districts but one recorded a sex ratio of fewer than 900 girls to 1,000 boys.[59] More recent census data reveals, however, that most of the districts now record a ratio of 850 girls per 1,000 boys.[60] In fact, as many as 10 districts showed a sex ratio that is fewer than 800 girls for 1,000 boys.[61] The Chandigarh-based Institute for Development and Communication reported that, during 2002–2003, every ninth Punjabi household in the state acknowledged sex-selective abortion with the help of prenatal sex-determination tests.[62]

China has developed a low-fertility culture due in part to the unique One Child Policy introduced by the government in 1979.[63] Combined with a strong tradition of son preference, this national policy has led to the birth of approximately 1 million excess male births every year.[64] Daughters are lost through sex-selective abortion, excess female infant mortality, and neglect or mistreatment of girls up to age 3, in cities as well as rural areas.[65] There has been a steady increase in the reported sex ratio at birth from 106 in 1979, to 111 in 1990, and to 117 in 2001, increasing to as high as 130 in some rural counties.[66] By the third decade of the 21st century, one research report conservatively predicts 29–33 million young surplus males in China.[67]

Sex ratios vary widely throughout the world, evincing a global pattern of sex selection disfavoring females. Some examples of disparate sex ratios in selected nations. Table 47.1 illustrate the widespread nature of this phenomenon.

TABLE 47.1. Sex Ratios of Selected Jurisdictions (Males Born per 100 Females)[68]

Afghanistan	107
Andorra	107
Bahrain	134
Bangladesh	105
Bhutan	112
Brunei	107
Faeroe Islands	106
Guyana	108
Jordan	106
Kuwait	150
Libya	107
Oman	126
Pakistan	106
Palau	116
Pitcairn	108
Qatar	203
Samoa	108
Saudi Arabia	122
Solomon Islands	107
United Arab Emirates	210
Western Sahara	113
World	102

Nicholas Eberstadt, a researcher at the American Enterprise Institute for Public Policy Research, warns that "the global war against baby girls is expanding."[69] Widely disparate sex ratios are also in evidence in Europe and North America. European demographic analysis reveals problematic signs of male preference in Greece, Macedonia, and Yugoslavia.[70] In the United States, sex ratios at birth for the Chinese American population, the Japanese American population, and the Filipino American population, as well as for the Asian American population as a whole, are disturbingly high.[71] In Canada, "certain communities in British Columbia and Ontario, with large proportions of immigrants from India and China, are experiencing the same unusual sex ratios seen in those Asian countries."[72] In Coquitiam, British Columbia, where Chinese immigrants represent 12 percent of the population, the gender ratio in 2000 was 116 boys for every 100 girls born.[73] A similar trend may be seen in Brampton, Ontario, home to many Indian Sikh immigrants, which in 2001 reported 109 boys born for every 100 girls.[74]

These statistics suggest the prevalence of prebirth sex selection by Asian immigrant populations in North America. According to one report, the "old methods were a quick prayer before conception or a backroom abortion afterwards."[75] But now "well-to-do Indians are increasingly picking a new third option: making a six-day pilgrimage to an American fertility clinic, where the sex of their baby will be chosen using an $18,000 procedure called 'preimplantation genetic diagnosis.'"[76] One major sex-selection clinic which aggressively advertises for business from Indian parents is The Fertility Institutes, located in Los Angeles and Las Vegas.[77] The Fertility Institutes claims to run the largest sex-selection program in the world.[78] The medical director of its gender-selection program, Dr. Jeffrey Steinberg, stated that one-quarter of his Indian patients traveled from India to Los Angeles for the procedure, 90 percent of requests from Indian clients were for boys, and The Fertility Institute's Web page on sex selection generated 12,000 hits a month from India.[79]

B. NATIONS OF BACHELORS: DEVIANT BEHAVIORS ATTRIBUTABLE TO GENDER IMBALANCE

A markedly uneven gender distribution resulting in far more men than women is socially problematic and possibly devastating. Experts report that such a surplus of unmarried men will lead to increased violence including war, kidnapping, and rape.[80] A shortage of adult females increases the prevalence of child marriage and the selling of young girls into the sex trafficking underworld.[81] Moreover, the cultural norm disfavoring daughters makes a mockery of international norms on gender equality. One Chinese pediatrician's experience illustrates the dilemma: "If a baby boy gets sick, its parents will sell everything they own to save their son's life. If it's a girl, very often the parents . . . just stop the treatment and take the baby home."[82] Whether by preimplantation sex selection, gender-based abortion, or female infanticide, the resulting gendercide carries enormous implications for global stability.[83]

Gendercide also results in the creation of a large cohort of young men who will have difficulty finding wives and beginning their own families.[84] The Chinese term for such bachelors is "guang gun-er," or "bare branches."[85] They are "branches of the family tree that will never bear fruit, [because] [t]he girls who should have grown up to be their wives were instead disposed of."[86] China has already begun to witness an increase in kidnapping and selling of women to provide brides for those who can afford the price.[87] Another consequence is "fraternal polyandry," in which "one woman is forced to marry her husband's brothers, and is expected to produce sons for each of them."[88] Yet another result is the increase in the number of child brides, an ancient Indian custom made more prevalent by the paucity of women.[89]

By 2020, the Chinese and Indian "bare branches" will likely constitute 12 to 15 percent of the young adult male population.[90] Indian scholars have noted "a very strong relationship between sex ratios and violent crime rates in Indian states, which persists even after controlling for a variety of other possible variables."[91] Sociologically, the explanation is straightforward: "young adult men with no stake in society—of the lowest socioeconomic classes and with little chance of forming families of their own—are much more prone to attempt to improve their situation through violent and criminal behavior in a strategy of coalitional aggression with other bare branches."[92] Because China and India contain nearly 40 percent of the world's population, the diminished prospects for democracy, stability, and peace due to the extremely low status of women in those societies may well, in an interconnected world, spread far beyond Asia.[93]

Paradoxically, as women's relative numbers diminish, their value does not increase: "The problem is that the woman herself does not hold her value; it is actually the males around her that hold her value—her father, her husband, and then her in-laws."[94] In India, the growing scarcity of potential brides has not caused parents to start paying a "groom price;" instead, dowry prices have increased."[95] The connection between female value and gendercide is plain: "[U]nless that daughter in utero has value, she's not going to be born . . . and that's what's going to determine the ratio of young adults twenty years from now."[96]

IV. A CALL FOR REASONABLE REGULATION ALLOWING SEX SELECTION ONLY FOR MEDICAL NECESSITY

. . .

A. UNITED NATIONS INITIATIVES

The United Nations has in the past successfully brought global awareness to the plight of women and to the violations of serious human rights.[97] For example, many countries "have responded positively to the U.N. initiatives to stop female genital mutilation (FGM)."[98] Unfortunately, a similar effort at international cooperation on sex selection has not yet met with success. In 2007, the United States and South Korea jointly sponsored a resolution at the United Nations Commission on the Status of Women (CSW) calling for the elimination of infanticide and gender selection.[99] The resolution was withdrawn due to opposition from China, India, and several other countries.[100] China and India lobbied against this resolution, fearing that their country's failure to control these two epidemics would be highlighted in a global arena.[101] Another rationale for the reluctance of some nations to support the resolution is its perceived impact on abortion rights.[102] For example, the Abortion Rights Coalition of Canada has issued a position paper on sex selection, arguing that "we cannot restrict women's right to abortion just because some women might make decisions we disagree with."[103] There is clearly a legal and cultural tension between abortion rights and the CSW's theme for its 2007 session, "The elimination of all forms of discrimination and violence against the girl child."[104] The conflict between preserving reproductive autonomy and ending gendercide is, of course, quite problematic.[105] Resolution of the issue will require intensive effort and political acumen.

But the millions of missing girls are not only those unborn; many of them were born and then killed. A compromise pointing toward a diminution of sex-selection technology's capacity to engraft an increasingly harmful son preference upon the world population is imperative.[106] A budding consensus for such a compromise may be limned from the articulated views of many participants at the 2007 United Nations session who "agreed that the well-being of girls in society should be underpinned by a robust set of laws that safeguard the rights of all children and punished violators without exception."[107] But fair warning is in order: the ethical, legal, and cultural issues will only increase in difficulty, as medical ventures in baby making continue their rapid evolution and proliferation. Experiments in fertility-promoting measures, such as uterus transplants, artificial wombs, and cloning are underway, and have already provoked controversy.[108]

B. NATIONAL REGULATION

Regulation of issues related to gendercide has had a fitful start in India and China.[109] But both countries are implementing legal changes aimed at improving the lot of women and girls. India has "taken the life-cycle approach for the betterment of the girl child, focusing on improvements in sex-ratio, education, nutrition, health, and the elimination of violence and discrimination."[110] India has also established a commission "to oversee proper enforcement of children's rights and effective implementation of laws relating to children."[111] Indian law has since 1994 prohibited sex selection.[112] Specifically, that law made it a crime to "conduct or cause to be conducted any pre-natal diagnostic techniques including ultrasonography for the purpose of determining the sex of a foetus."[113] Prenatal diagnostics, including ultrasound, were to be used only when there is an independent medical need.[114] In 2003, the administrative rules implementing the 1994 Act were amended to regulate the sale of ultrasound machines.[115] These amendments prohibited the distribution of any ultrasound or other machine capable of "detecting the sex of the foetus" to any laboratory, clinic, or other person unless the recipient is registered under the Act.[116] Other measures taken by the Indian government include a plan to integrate child protection programs under one umbrella and an amendment to the Hindu Succession Act to allow daughters and widows equal rights to ancestral property.[117] Despite these legal and administrative efforts, India's efforts to prevent sex selection have not yet made much headway against the forces of tradition armed with modern medical technology. There is now "substantial data that reveals that private as well as government facilities are used for sex-selective abortions despite the law that prohibits it."[118] Over than 300 doctors have been prosecuted for violating the law, but few convictions have resulted, and the medical community has pressured the government not to prosecute doctors who reveal the sex of the fetus to the mother.[119] In a 2003 ruling on a lawsuit brought to demand more rigorous enforcement of the Pre-Natal Diagnostic Techniques legislation, the Indian Supreme Court acknowledged its poor implementation, but its ruling only called for local governments to enforce it more strictly.[120]

In China, the government has similarly criminalized sex-selective abortions and the use of ultrasound technology to ascertain the sex of the fetus.[121] In 2005,

a further amendment was submitted to the Standing Committee of the National People's Congress extending the ban to anyone who assists another with fetal sex selection and providing for substantial fines and a 3-year jail sentence for violators.[122] While it may be too soon to track the efficacy of these measures, one sign of broader acceptance is the decision by 29 provincial congresses to enforce regulations mandating "that all child gender selections without any medical necessity should be strictly prohibited."[123]

The Council of Europe's 1997 Convention on Human Rights and Biomedicine banned the use of medical technologies to choose a future child's sex, except where required to avoid a serious hereditary gender-linked disease.[124] In Great Britain, the use of PGD for sex selection in nontherapeutic cases is prohibited by the Human Fertilisation and Embryology Authority (HFEA).[125] In the United States, sex-selection technology is virtually unregulated.[126] The Fertility Clinic Success Rate and Certification Act of 1992 provided for the Department of Health and Human Services (HHS) to develop a model program for the certification of embryo laboratories.[127] In 1999, HHS promulgated a final notice proposing implementation of such a program, "to be carried out voluntarily by interested states."[128] Federal funds were not allocated to implement this law.[129] While the U.S. government has developed regulations involving many of the major aspects of ART practice and research, "direct federal regulation of these programs does not occur."[130] State regulation is quite limited.[131]

While the approaches taken in India, China, and Europe may not yet be described as successful, at least they have identified the critical problem and have sought to blend legal enforcement with campaigns to change harmful cultural and religious values.[132] Admittedly, cultures generally alter very slowly and do not always fall in line behind legal pronouncements. But, by contrast, the United States has been dubbed the "Wild West of reproductive technology."[133] The present unregulated state of American fertility clinics has rendered them a favorite destination for many globe-trotting sex-selection tourists.[134] The American insouciance about regulation has led to an exacerbation of the worldwide problem.

Several regulatory schemes may serve as appropriate models for American development. Great Britain's HFEA licenses all fertility clinics and oversees "safe and appropriate practice in fertility treatment and embryo research."[135] To carry out its mission, the HFEA performs four major functions: (1) creating and enforcing a Code of Practice to give "clear operational guidelines" to fertility clinics; (2) maintaining a register of patients and the results of treatments, including the details of any donor involved and any children born; (3) advising patients, donors, and clinics about the issues involved in fertility treatments; and (4) monitoring developments in the field of embryo and reproductive research.[136]

In the United States, Congress could enact legislation enabling the Centers for Disease Control and Prevention (CDCP)—or a separate agency—to carry out tasks similar to Great Britain's HFEA.[137] The U.S. President's Council on Bioethics met in 2003 to consider two working papers, one of which suggested that the widespread use of in vitro fertilization for infertile couples may need federal regulation.[138] Commissioners noted that no federal regulation or oversight now exists for a procedure that has produced millions of human embryos, most of which will die, either on their own or through scientific experimentation.[139] The Council's working papers complained of the lack of "oversight of how the new biotechnologies . . . affect the well being of the children conceived with their aid, egg donors, or gestational mothers," and that "there are no limits on what one can do to or with an embryo, so long as one is privately funded."[140] These documents also outlined four primary suggestions on how the U.S. government could regulate ART, including instituting a new regulatory agency, granting new authority to existing regulatory agencies, implementing specific legislative action, and/or utilizing government funding as a regulatory lever.[141]

Another consideration for American regulators should be the degree and scope of the regulations to be imposed. On these issues, the explicit terms of the Indian legal scheme serve as an exemplar of specific regulation focusing on medical necessity. India's Pre-Natal Diagnostic Techniques Act provides that "no pre-natal diagnostic techniques shall be conducted except for the purposes of detection" of a specific list of medical conditions.[142] The allowable conditions include chromosomal abnormalities, genetic metabolic diseases, haemoglobinopathies, sex-linked genetic diseases, congenital anomalies, and "any other abnormalities or diseases as may be specified by the Central Supervisory Board."[143] Moreover, no prenatal diagnostic techniques shall be conducted unless specific characteristics of the patient are established. The pregnant woman must be older than 35; she must have undergone two or more spontaneous abortions or fetal loss; she must have been exposed to potentially teratogenic agents such as drugs, radiation, infection, or chemicals; she must have a family history of mental retardation or physical deformities such as spasticity or any other genetic disease; or she must have some other threshold condition specified by the Central Supervisory Board.[144]

To the extent that a consensus is discernable in this rapidly changing area, one articulation of a possible common ground may be found in the European Council's decision to prohibit the "use of techniques of medically assisted procreation . . . for the purpose of choosing a future child's sex, except where serious hereditary sex-related disease is to be avoided."[145] Much debate remains, and the remaining issues will not be soon resolved. What are techniques of medically assisted procreation? What is a serious hereditary disease? But, at least the European Council's regulatory formulation suggests a way around the abortion dilemma, which—at least nominally—remains outside the scope of the regulation.[146] Whether the United States is ready to develop appropriate regulations limiting sex selection is a political unknown. But, given the history and growth of gendercide, the need could not be greater.

V. CONCLUSION: LEGAL AND CULTURAL RESPONSES TO GENDERCIDE

A Malthusian reaction to gendercide and the resulting widely disparate sex ratios might be to suggest that the emerging nations of bachelors will eventually either reverse sex selection or die off. But the adverse consequences of current population trends are already apparent, already worsening, and already spreading around the globe. Enforcing a ban on the use of medical technology for sex selection has been aptly described as "an immediate answer to a problem without an immediate solution."[147] Without cultural change, legal measures will continue to be undermined and ineffective. But the link between the technology and gendered abortions is so clear that nations must find the will and means decisively to implement such laws. At the same time, it is imperative that nations marshal the resources to reverse the culture of degrading women which sex-selection technology has exacerbated. The dream of a world of sons is a global nightmare with untold consequences. Neither nations nor cultures can afford to rest in the face of gendercide.

NOTES

1. L.L.M. in Family Law (with honors), Hofstra University (2001). My thanks to J. Herbie DiFonzo, my professor, confidant, and friend. He stimulated a new love of knowledge and provocative thought and for this I will always be grateful. I also thank my husband and two sons for being my inspiration and motivation to better myself every day. And, last, but not least, my parents, for always making every dream a reality despite whatever obstacles stood in my way.

2. Zou Hanru, *Unbalanced Ratio Caused by Rural Woes,* China Daily, Oct. 13, 2006, at http://www.chinadaily.com.cn/opinion/2006-10/13/content_707335.htm (quoting 3,000-year-old Chinese poem from "The Book of Songs").

3. GENETICS AND PUBLIC POLICY CENTER, REPRODUCTIVE GENETIC TESTING: WHAT AMERICA THINKS 1 (2004), at http://www.dnapolicy.org/images/reportpdfs/ReproGenTestAmericaThinks.pdf.

4. U.S. Dep't of Health and Human Services, Centers for Disease Control and Prevention [hereinafter CDCP], *Assisted Reproductive Technology: Home http://www.cdc.gov/ART/index.htm#Assisted.*

5. *See* CDCP, NATIONAL CENTER FOR HEALTH STATISTICS, 2004 ASSISTED REPRODUCTIVE TECHNOLOGY (ART) REPORT [hereinafter ART REPORT], http://ftp.cdc.gov/pub/Publications/

art/2004ART508.pdf (summarizing data provided by U.S. clinics that use ART to treat infertility).

6. *Choosing The Gender Of Your Baby,* http://www.genselect.com (discussing special diet, vitamins, and timing of intercourse to achieve baby of the desired sex); *see also* Center for Genetics and Society, *Preimplantation Genetic Diagnosis (PGD) and Screening,* http://www.genetics-and-society.org/technologies/other/pgd.html.

7. Indu Grewal and J. Kishore, *Female Foeticide in India,* International Humanist and Ethical Union, at www.iheu.org/node/1049 (2004). ("The killing of women exists in various forms in societies the world over. However, Indian society displays some unique and particularly brutal versions, such as dowry deaths and sati. . . . As a result of selective abortion, between 35 and 40 million girls and women are missing from the Indian population.")

8. G. Serour, *Ethical Guidelines on Sex Selection for Non-Medical Purposes: FIGO Committee for the Ethical Aspects of Human Reproduction and Women's Health,* 92 Int'l J. Gynecology & Obstetrics 329 (2006).

9. Osagie K. Obasogie, *Designing Your Own Baby,* Boston Globe, Aug., 8, 2005, at http://www.boston.com/news/globe/editorial_opinion/oped/articles/2005/08/08/designing_your_own_baby/

10. *See* Marcia Darnovsky, *Revisiting Sex Selection: The Growing Popularity of New Sex Selection Methods Revives an Old Debate,* GENE WATCH (Jan.–Feb. 2004), www.gene-watch.org/genewatch/articles/17-1darnovsky.html (arguing that allowing sex selection "would represent a significant shift towards treating children as commodities and the selection of a child's genetic make-up . . . to parental choice, exercised through paying a commercial company to provide this 'service.'")

11. Theodor H. Winkler, *Slaughtering Eve: The Hidden Gendercide,* IN WOMEN IN AN INSECURE WORLD: FACTS, FIGURES, AND ANALYSIS 1-2 MARIE VLACHOVD & LEA BIASON (eds.), (2005), at http://www.dcaf.ch/women/pb_women_ex_sum.pdf.

12. *Id.*

13. *See* ART REPORT, *supra* note 5, According to the National Center for Health Statistics, of the 60.2 million American women of reproductive age in 1995, 9.3 million had used some kind of infertility service (medical advice, tests, drugs, surgery, or other treatments), while 2.1 million married couples (representing 7.1 percent of all such couples) are infertile. U.S Dep't of Health and Human Services, Centers for Disease Control and Prevention, National Center for Health Statistics, VITAL AND HEALTH STATISTICS: FERTILITY, FAMILY PLANNING, AND WOMEN'S

HEALTH: NEW DATA FROM THE 1995 NATIONAL
SURVEY OF FAMILY GROWTH 7 (May 1997), at http://
www.cdc.gov/nchs/data/series/sr_23/sr23_019.pdf.

14. *See* World Health Organization, Genomic Resource
Centre, *Sex Selection and Discrimination* (2007), at http://
www.who.int/genomics/gender/en/index4.html.

15. *See Significant Number of Women Being Treated for
Infertility Would Choose the Sex of Their Next Child,*
News-Medical.Net, Mar. 14, 2005, at http://www
.news-medical.net/?id=8372. An identical result was
reached in an online poll conducted by BabyCenter
.com: 41 percent of 52, 816 respondents (as of
Sep. 2007) indicated that they desired to select the
sex of their baby. BabyCenter.com, *Would You Choose
Your Baby's Sex?,* at http://www.babycenter.com/
viewPollResults.htm?pollId=5099.

16. Reproductive Genetics Institute, *PGD,* at http://www
.reproductivegenetics.com/pgd.html.

17. J. J. Marik, *Preimplantation Genetic Diagnosis, E-Medicine*
(Apr. 13, 2005), at http://www.emedicine.com/med/
topic3520.htm.

18. *See* WORLD HEALTH ORGANIZATION, GENETIC
TECHNOLOGIES FOR SEX SELECTION (2007), at http://
www.who.int/genomics/gender/en/index4.html; Robin
Elise Weiss, *Girl or Boy? Sex Selection Techniques for
Everyone Before Pregnancy,* ABOUT.COM: PREGNANCY &
CHILDBIRTH, at http://pregnancy.about.com/od/
boyorgirl/p/girlorboy.htm (asserting that PGD is the
"most effective" technique in sex selection.); The Las
Vegas Fertility Institute, at http://www.lasvegasfertility
.net/index.html (claiming a 99.9% success rate in sex
selection using PGD). Of course, the process is not
without controversy. *See* Section III, *infra* at (discussing
criticisms of sex selection technologies).

19. Genetics and IVF Institute, MicroSort General
Information, at http://microsort.net. The process is
currently undergoing a Food and Drug Administration
clinical trial. *Id. See also* Obasogie, *supra* note 9.
("Businesses such as MicroSort, a sperm sorting service
that selects sex before pregnancy, are part of an ongoing
commercial effort to normalize sex selection. . . .").

20. Genetics & IVF Institute, MicroSort General
Information, *supra* note 20.

21. IUI is a medical procedure that involves placing sperm
into a woman's uterus to facilitate fertilization. *See* ART
REPORT, *supra* note 5, Appendix B, at http://www.cdc
.gov/ART/ART2004/appixb.htm#l.

22. Genetics & IVF Institute, MicroSort General
Information, *supra* note 20. ICSI is a procedure in
which a single sperm is injected directly into an egg.
ICSI is most commonly used to overcome male

infertility problems. See ART REPORT, *supra* note 5,
Appendix B.

23. MicroSort utilizes flow cytometric separation
technology to sort the X (female) or Y (male)
chromosome-bearing sperm, with the enriched fraction
of sorted sperm used to fertilize an embryo through
either IVF or IUI. The fertilized embryo is then
transferred into the uterus to achieve pregnancy. *See*
Genetics & IVF Institute, MicroSort Technology, at
http://www.microsort.net/technology.php. The
MicroSort method was developed by a U.S. Department
of Agriculture (USDA) animal physiologist in 1989
who was trying to improve reproductive efficiency in
livestock. In his work with pigs, rabbits and cattle, he
found he could separate sperm by staining them with a
fluorescent dye. Those carrying X chromosomes
absorbed more dye and glowed brightly, and the same
phenomenon may be observed in human sperm. By the
mid-1990s, the USDA technology had been adapted for
human sex selection. *Id.; see also* Genetics & IVF
Institute, MicroSort—Frequently Asked Questions, at
http://www.microsort.net/faqs.php.

24. Genetics & IVF Institute, MicroSort Current Results,
at http://www.microsort.net/results.php.

25. *Id.*

26. *See* Amartya Sen, *More Than 100 Million Women Are
Missing,* N.Y. REV. BOOKS, Dec. 20, 1990, at http://
ucatlas.ucsc.edu/gender/Sen100M.html.

27. *See* Adam Jones, *Case Study: Female Infanticide*
(1999–2000), Genercide Watch, at http://www
.gendercide/org/case_infantcide.html; *Rampant Female
Foeticide,* ReportingPeople.org (2004), at http://www
.reportingpeople.org/rpcat.
asp?a=children&catid=chl&sec=report.

28. Nicholas Eberstadt, *Power and Population in Asia:
Demogrpahics and the Strategic Balance,* Hoover Inst. Pol'y
Rev. (Feb.-Mar. 2004), at http://www.hoover.org/
publications/policyreview/3439671.html.

29. Ashley Bumgarner, *A Right to Choose?: Sex Selection in
the International Context,* 14 Duke J. Gender L. & Pol'y
1289, 1295 (2007).

30. *See India: The Missing Girls,* Frontline, PBS.org, Apr.
2004, at http://www.pbs.org/frontlineworld/
rough/2007/04/the_missing_girlinks.html.

31. *See India's Female Freefall,* CNN.com, June 19, 2001,
at http://edition.cnn.com/2001/WORLD/asiapcf/
south/06/19/india.ultrasound/index.html.

32. *Id.* In the Indian state of Punjab, the demographic fall
was even more precipitous, from 875 girls per 1,000
boys in the 1991 Census, to 793 girls per 1,000 boys in
the 2001 Census. *Id.*

33. Sen, *supra* note 29.
34. *See* Winkler, *supra* note 11.
35. *See India's Craving for Boy Babies Leads to Bride Shortage,* Telegraph.co.uk, July 3, 2003, at http://www.telegraph.co.uk/news/main.jhtml?xml=%2Fnews%2F2003%2F03%2F07%2Fwindia07.xml: Girls are considered a liability, because of the expensive dowries that have to be paid at their weddings. Even the poorest of peasants is under tremendous peer pressure to organise lavish weddings, often by taking out big loans. But boys are an asset. Even the most ineligible comes at a premium, commanding a dowry that can extend over years to a steady demand on the girl's family for money and other goods. Refusal to comply often leads to cases of "bride burning," a euphemism for murder, which remains rife.
36. Janice Shaw Crouse, *United States Resolution Shanghaied by China and India,* CONCERNED WOMEN FOR AMERICA, Mar. 9, 2007, at http://www.cwfa.org/articles/12532/BLI/reports/index.htm (quoting Indira Patel); *see* Joan Delaney, *Preference for Sons Causing Global Shortage of Women,* THE EPOCH TIMES, Mar. 16, 2007, at http://en.epochtimes.com/news/7-3-16/52898.html ("In India, where the cost of a dowry for a daughter can be prohibitive, financial pressure is often a reason for resorting to sex selective abortion or infanticide.")
37. See Bumgarner, *supra* note 32, at 1290 n.5 (noting that China's one-child policy was introduced in 1979 to slow population growth); *India: The Missing Girls, supra* note 33 ("In China, the One Child Policy created heavy financial penalties for couples who had more than one child and led to the murder of female infants.")
38. Bumgarner, *supra* note 32.
39. Quoted in Kimberly Downing, *A Feminist is a Person Who Answers "Yes" to the Question, "Are Women Human?": An Argument Against the Use of Preimplantation Genetic Diagnosis for Gender Selection,* 8 DePaul J. Health Care L. 431, 440 (2005).
40. *See* Judith Banister, *Son Preference in Asia—Report of a Symposium,* U.S. CENSUS BUREAU (1999), at http://www.census.gov/ipc/www/ebspr96a.html (analyzing the various levels of son preference in Asian nations); Doo-Sub Kim, *Missing Girls in South Korea: Trends, Levels and Regional Variations,* 59 POPULATION 865 (2004–2006), at http://www.cairn.info/article.php?ID_REVUE=POPE&ID_NUMPUBLIE=POPE_406&ID_ARTICLE=POPE_406_0865 ("There is little doubt that motivations for prenatal sex screening and sex-selective abortion stem from strong son preference along with gender discrimination against women.")
41. *See, e.g.,* ELIZABETH BUMILLER, MAY YOU BE BLESSED WITH A HUNDRED SONS (1986) (describing the clear cultural preference for sons).
42. Susan Seymour, *Family Structure, Marriage, Caste and Class, and Women's Education: Exploring the Linkages in an Indian Town,* 2 INDIAN J. GENDER STUD. 67 (1995).
43. *Id.*
44. *See* Elisabeth J. Croll, *Fertility Decline, Family Size and Female Discrimination: A Study of Reproductive Management in East and South Asia,* 17 ASIA-PACIFIC POPULATION J. 11, 21 (June 2002), at http://www.unescap.org/esid/psis/population/journal/articles/2002/v17n2a2.pdf ("blessings, status and good fortune are defined not in terms of daughters or children but of sons"); Vibhuti Patel, *A Cultural Deficit,* INDIA TOGETHER, Aug. 2003, at http://www.indiatogether.org/2003/aug/wom-sexratio.htm ("The birth of a son is perceived as an opportunity for upward mobility while the birth of a daughter is believed to result in downward economic mobility.")
45. Croll, *supra* note 47, at 22–26.
46. *See* Patel, *supra* note 47 (explaining the impact of the dowry system).
47. Banister, *supra* note 43.
48. *See, e.g.,* GenSelect.Com., Family Balancing, http://www.genselect.com/goodnews/FamilyBlancing ("The concept of family balancing is a measured approach to the use of preconception gender selection. Family balancing provides married couples having at least one child the opportunity to use various methods to increase the chance of having another child of the less represented sex in the family.")
49. *See* American Society for Reproductive Medicine, Guidelines, Statements and Opinions of the ASRM Practice Committee, at http://www.asrm.org/Media/Practice/practice.html; Darnovsky, *Revisiting Sex Selection: The Growing Popularity of New Sex Selection Method Revives an Old Debate, supra* note 10. ASRM concluded in a 2001 Report that if sex-selection methods are proven safe and effective, doctors should be free to offer them to couples who want "gender variety" if they are informed about the possibility of failure and agree to accept children of the wrong sex. *Id.*
50. Obasogie, *supra* note 9 ("at least 15 countries—including England, Australia, Canada, Germany, and France—proscribe sex selection"); Pacific News Service, *Indian Couples Seek out U.S. Sex Selection Clinics,* India West, June 30, 2006 at http://news.pacificnews.org/news/view_article.html?article_id=54a58cce914f335cb8fb6e722aa1028d. ("The United States is one of the few industrialized nations that

does not regulate the procedure, giving a few of the country's clinics a monopoly in this emerging market")

51. *See* Obasogie, *supra* note 9 (asserting that "there is a dubious relationship between embryonic sex identification and sex selection that leads one step closer to a new eugenics").

52. Sen, *supra* note 29.

53. *Id.*

54. Kim, *supra* note 43.

55. *Id.*

56. *Id.*

57. *Id.*

58. Kalpana Sharma, *No Girls, Please, We're Indian*, The Hindu, August 29, 2004, at http://www.hindu.com/mag/2004/08/29/stories/2004082900130100.htm. *See generally* Alison Wood Manhoff, *Banned and Enforced: The Immediate Answer to a Problem Without an Immediate Solution—How India Can Prevent Another Generation of "Missing Girls,"* 38 Vand. J Transnat'l L. 889, 892–99 (2005) (recounting the history of sex selection in India).

59. Sudha S. Rajan, *Sex Selective Abortions and Female Infantcide*, 30 Development and Change 585, 619–21 (2003).

60. *Id.*

61. *See* Sharma, *supra* note 61.

62. Iqbal Latif, *Selective Elimination of Female Fetuses in India*, GLOBAL POLITICIAN, Sep. 2, 2007, at http://www.globalpolitician.com/articledes .asp?ID=3374&cid=6&sid=20.

63. *See* Therese Hesketh & Zhu Wei Xing, *The Effect of China's One-Child Family Policy after 25 Years*, 353 NEW ENG. J. MED. 1171 (Sep. 15, 2005), at http://content .nejm.org/cgi/content/full/353/11/1171 (noting that the Chinese government "saw strict population containment as essential to economic reform and to an improvement in living standards").

64. Maureen J. Graham et al., *Son Preference in Anhui Province, China*, 24 INTERNATIONAL FAMILY PLANNING PERSPECTIVES 77 (June 1998), at http://www .guttmacher.org/pubs/journals/2407298.html.

65. Judith Banister, *Shortage of Girls in China Today*, JOURNAL OF POPULATION RESEARCH (May 2004), at http://findarticles.com/p/articles/mi_m0PCG/is_1_21/ai_n6155263. *See also* Arthur E. Dewey, *One-Child Policy in China*, TESTIMONY BEFORE THE HOUSE INTERNATIONAL RELATIONS COMMITTEE, DEC. 14, 2004, at http://www.state.gov/g/prm/rls/39823.htm ("the large fees and penalties for out-of-plan births assessed in implementing China's regulations are tantamount to coercion that leads to abortion").

66. Graham et al., *supra* note 67. The sex ratio for a stationary population (as determined by Western model life tables) is between 97.9 and 100.3 males per 100 females. Ansley Coale, *Excess Female Mortality and the Balance of the Sexes in the Population: An Estimate of the Number of "Missing Females,"* 17 POPULATION AND DEVELOPMENT REVIEW 518 (Sep. 1991).

67. Valerie M. Hudson & Andrea M. Den Boer, *A Surplus of Men, A Deficit of Peace: Security and Sex Ratios in Asia's Largest States*, 26 International Security 5, 11 (2002), at http://mitpress.mit/edu/journals/pdf/isec_26_04_5_0.pdf.

68. *See* GeoHive, *Total Population by Gender and Gender Ratio, by Country*, at http://www.xist.org/earth/pop_gender/aspx.

69. Nicholas Eberestadt, *The Global War Against Baby Girls*, American Enterprise Institute for Public Policy Research, www.aei.org/publications/filter.all .pubID25399/pub_detail.asp (Jan. 5, 2007).

70. Eberstadt, *supra* note 72.

71. *Id.*

72. Theresa Smyth, *Canadian Sex-Selection Abortions Exposed*, THE INTERIM, July 2006, at http://www.theinterim .com/2006/july/03canadian.html.

73. Andrea Mrozek, *Canada's Lost Daughters*, WESTERN STANDARD, June 5, 2006, at 34, available at http://www.ncln.ca/content/pdf/CanadaLostDaughters.pdf.

74. *Id.*

75. Ketaki Gokhale, *Indian Couples Seek Out U.S. Sex Selection Clinics*, INDIA WEST, June 30, 2006, at http://news.ncmonline.com/news/view_article.html?article_id=54a58cce914f335cb8fb6e722aa1028d.

76. *Id.*; *see also* Maxwell Pereira, *Sex Selection in India Dodges Existing Laws*, Indo-Asian News Service, Sep. 3, 2006, at http://news.newamericamedia.org/news/view_article .html?article_id=74832773372eba82348c055505376c87 (referring to the "increasing practice among Indian parents of accessing through the Internet facilities available in the US guaranteeing a male issue even at the pre-conception stage.")

77. Gokhale, *supra* note 78; *see also* Mandy Oaklander, *No Girls Please, We're Indian: Sex Selection Ads Land Ethnic Media in Hot Water*, New American Media, Sep. 10, 2007, at http://newamericamedia.org/news/view_article .html?article_id=3c7ed640212a030bc2f3163dfdcc8bcb

78. Oaklander, supra note 80.

79. *Id.*; Gokhale, *supra* note 78. The Fertility Institutes also caters to reproductive tourism from China. Its Web site features an image of the Chinese flag, and Dr. Steinberg reported that the site receives 140,000 hits a

month from China. *See* The Fertility Institutes, *supra* note 19; *Wealthy Go to US to Choose Baby's Sex*, China Daily, June 15, 2006, at http://chinadaily.com.cn/china/2006-06/15/content_617607.htm (describing global reproductive tourism).

80. *See* Valerie M. Hudson & Andrea M. Den Boer, *"Bare Branches" and Danger in Asia*, WASH. POST., July 4, 2004, at http://www.washingtonpost.com/wp-dyn/articles/A24761-2004Jul2.html; Janice Shaw Crouse, *The United Nations Abortion Dilemma*, TOWNHALL.COM, Mar. 2, 2007, at http://www.townhall.com/columnists/JaniceShawCrouse/2007/03/02/the_united_nations_abortion_dilemma; Andrea Mrozek, *When There Are Too Many Men*, WESTERN STANDARD, June 5, 2006, at 36, available at http://www.ncln.ca/content/pdf/CanadaLostDaughters.pdf.

81. Crouse, *supra* note 39.

82. Louise Lim, *China Fears Bachelor Future*, BBC.COM, Apr. 5, 2004, at http://news.bbc.co.uk/1/hi/world/asia-pacific/3601281.stm. Anecdotal accounts of the murder of daughters, placing a human face on demographic data, are quite common. *See, e.g.,* Mary Carmichael, *No Girls, Please: In Parts of Asia, Sexism is Ingrained and Gender Selection Often Means Murder*, NEWSWEEK, Jan. 26, 2007, at http://www.msnbc.msn.com/id/3990133/site/newsweek/ (reporting the story of an Indian midwife who, for a small fee, "will take a newborn girl, hold her upside down by the waist and "give a sharp jerk," snapping the spinal cord. She will then declare the infant stillborn."); Jones, *supra* note 30 (detailing the murder of an infant daughter by her mother, who refused to nurse the baby and then, to "silence the infant's famished cries," poisoned her).

83. Hudson & Den Boer, *supra* note 83. ("In societies where the status of women is so low that they are routinely culled from the population, even before birth, the prospects for peace and democracy are seriously diminished.")

84. *See* Sherry Karabin, *Infanticide, Abortion Responsible for 60 Million Girls Missing in Asia*, POPULATION RESEARCH INSTITUTE, June 13, 2007, at http://www.pop.org/main.cfm?id=310&r1=15.00&r2=2.00&r3=0.50&r4=0.00&level=3&eid=1096.

85. Hudson & Den Boer, *supra* note 83.

86. *Id.*

87. *Id.*

88. Manreet Sodhi Someshwar, *India's Women Battle the "Bad Luck" Label*, International Herald Tribune, Mar. 30, 2006, at http://www.iht.com/articles/2006/03/29/opinion/edmanreet.php; *see* also Pereira, *supra* note 79

(warning that the new sex selection technologies will lead to "further exploitation and abuse of women, violence against them, increased trafficking and sex trade, and re-emergence of practices like polyandry."); *Draupadi's Husbands: A Brief Study of Polyandry in Contemporary Himalayan Cultures,* at http://www.focusanthro.org/archive/2004-2005/polyandry9.pdf. (describing the practice of polyandry).

89. *See* Javier Delgado Rivera, *India: Child Brides to Child Mothers,* CafeBabel.com, Dec. 11, 2006, at http://www.cafebabel.com/en/article.asp?T=T&Id=8963; Nita Bhalla, *India's Underage Brides Wedded to Tradition,* Reuters, May 16, 2007, at http://www.alertnet.org/thenews/newsdesk/DEL11895.htm. Early marriages "contribute to high rates of maternal mortality—one woman dies every seven minutes from a pregnancy-related cause in India—with young bodies not mature enough for sex or pregnancy." Bhalla, *supra* note 92; *see also id.* (According to a recent report by the United Nations Children's Fund, girls under 15 are five times more likely to die during pregnancy and child birth than those in their twenties.)

90. Bhalla, *supra* note 92. Conservative estimates of the number of young adult "bare branches" to be found by 2020 are approximately 30 million in China, and 28 million in India. *Id.*

91. *Id.*

92. *Id.* More violent crime is committed worldwide by unmarried young adult men than by married young adult men. *Id. See also* Pereira, *supra* note 79 ("The increasing deficit of girls is also creating a social imbalance within society, with pockets in India where very few girls are born. Resulting in no brides for the burgeoning son population, with the prosepect of having to import girls from other regions. Resulting in social problems of purchasing young girls from poor regions, women treated as commodities, contributing to further fall in their status in society. This can only lead to further exploitation and abuse of women, violence against them, increased trafficking and sex trade, and re-emergence of practices like polyandry. Letting the cycle of discrimination and gender inequities to continue, fuelled now by newer and more accurate technologies for sex selection.")

93. Hudson and Den Boer, *"Bare Branches" and Danger in Asia, supra* note 83.

94. *See* Woodrow Wilson International Center for Scholars, Environmental Change and Security Program, *Is Our Security Threatened by Too Many Men,* July 19, 2004 (quoting Valerie Harper), at http://www.wilsoncenter.org/

index.cfm?fuseaction=topics.event_summary&topic_id=1413&event_id=86385.

95. *Id.* Moreover, the practice of dowry is now appearing even in Indian states which traditionally did not adhere to it. *Id.*

96. *Id.*

97. *See, e.g.,* UNICEF, *Child Protection from Violence, Exploitation and Abuse: Female Genital Mutilation/Cutting,* at http:///www.unicef.org/protection/index_genitalmutilation.html.

98. Canadian Children's Rights Council, Circumcision/Genital Mutilation, at http://wwwcanadiancrc.com/circumcision/circumcision.htm. In the United States, the federal government and 15 states have adopted legal measures targeting the practice of FGM. *See* Center for Reproductive Rights, *Legislation on Female Genital Mutilation in the United States* (2004), at http://www.reproductiverights.org/pdf/pub_bp_fgmlawsusa.pdf. The U.N. General Assembly adopted a resolution in 2002 on traditional or customary practices affecting the health of women and girls, which characterized female genital cutting "as a serious threat." Nirit Ben-Ari, *International Action Against FGM,* 17 Africa Recovery 4 (May 2003), at http://www.un.org/ecosocdev/geninfo/afrec/vol17no1/171wm1.htm. Various United Nations agencies have advocated for global awareness and reform by highlighting the serious health consequences associated with FGM. *See* UN Office for the Coordination of Humanitarian Affairs, *Razor's Edge—The Controversy of Female Genital Mutilation,* Oct. 3, 2007, at htpp://www.irinnews.org/IndepthMain.aspx?IndepthId=15&ReportId=62462; UNICEF, *Child Protection From Violence, Exploitation and Abuse: Female Genital Mutilation/Cutting, supra* note; UNFPA (United Nations Population Fund), *Ending Female Genital Mutilation/Cutting,* at http://www.unfpa.org/gender/practices1.htm.

99. Samantha Singson, *China, India and Canada Kill UN Resolution Against Selected Abortions,* LifeSite, Mar. 8, 2007, at http://www.lifesite.net/ldn/2007/mar/0703081.html; *UN Shelves Bid to Condemn Sex-Selection Abortion,* Mar. 9, 2007, at http://www.cwnews.com/news/viewstory.cfm?recnum=49762.

100. Singson, *supra* note 103; Catholic World News, *UN Shelves Bid to Condemn Sex-Selection Abortion, supra* note 103.

101. *See* Singson, *supra* note 103 ("It is likely that India and China objected because, even though the resolution focused on the global nature of the problem, they believed it would draw attention to the fact that theirs are the worst cases of female

infanticide and sex selected abortion."); Crouse, *United States Resolution Shanghaied by China and India, supra* note 39 (reporting that "two nations that are negatively affected by the practice (China and India) were leaders in pressuring the U.S. to withdraw its resolution.")

102. *See, e.g.,* Delaney, supra note 39 (reporting on the argument that support for abortion rights runs counter to support for ending gendercide).

103. *Id.*

104. REPORT OF THE SECRETARY GENERAL, THE ELIMINATION OF ALL FORMS OF DISCRIMINATION AND VIOLENCE AGAINST THE GIRL CHILD, "Elimination of Harmful Practices of Prenatal Sex Selection and Female Infanticide" (E/CN.6/2007/L.5), in UNITED NATIONS ECONOMIC AND SOCIAL COUNCIL, COMMISSION ON THE STATUS OF WOMEN, FIFTY-FIRST SESSION, FEB. 26–MAR. 9, 2007, at http://www.un.org/womenwatch/daw/csw/csw51/OfficialDocuments.html.

105. One extremely difficult issue is whether legislation barring sex selection will set an autonomy-limiting precedent in other areas of reproductive freedom. *See* Rachel Remaley, *"The Original Sexist Sin": Regulating Preconception Sex Selection Technology,* 10 Health Matrix 249, 254 (2000).

106. *Cf.* "Statement" submitted to the CSW by several international women's and other groups calling for "law enforcement" to have "adequate resources and training to respond to violence against the girl child," and for "legislation making religious and traditional practices which harm girls illegal, including female genital mutilation, underage marriages and forced abortion." *Statement Submitted by Centre for Women,* et al., in UNITED NATIONS ECONOMIC AND SOCIAL COUNCIL, COMMISSION ON THE STATUS OF WOMEN, FIFTY-FIRST SESSION, Feb. 26–Mar. 9, 2007, E/CN.6/2007/NGO/5, at http://www.un.org/womenwatch/daw/csw/csw51/OfficialDocuments.html.

107. *Well-Being of Girls Should Be Underpinned by Robust Set of Laws, Commission on Status of Women Told,* UNITED NATIONS ECONOMIC AND SOCIAL COUNCIL, COMMISSION ON THE STATUS OF WOMEN, FIFTY-FIRST SESSION, Feb. 26–Mar. 9, 2007, at http://www.un.org/News/Press/docs/2007/wom1612.doc.htm.

108. *See* Jacqueline Stenson, *The Future of Babymaking: Scientists Explore New Techniques for Tackling Infertility Problems,* MSNBC.com, July 22, 2003, at http://www.msnbc.msn.com/id/3076784/ (describing breakthroughs and prospects in transplanted or

artificial wombs and cloning.); Rob Stein, *First U.S. Uterus Transplant Planned: Some Experts Say Risk Isn't Justified,* Wash. Post, Jan. 15, 2007, at http://www.washingtonpost.com/wp-dyn/content/article/2007/01/14/AR2007011401091.html (noting that the operation "marks a confluence of two medical specialties—transplant surgery and reproductive medicine—that frequently spark controversy.").

109. *See, e.g.,* Hesketh and Xing, *supra* note 66 (discussing the ill effects of the legal regime regulating population in China); *No Girls, Please, We're Indian, supra* note 61 (describing government regulation in India as "inadequate and poorly implemented.").

110. *Well-Being of Girls Should Be Underpinned by Robust Set of Laws, Commission on Status of Women Told, supra* note 111 (quoting Manjula Krishnan, Indian Economic Adviser).

111. *Id.*

112. The Pre-Natal Diagnostic Techniques (Regulation And Prevention Of Misuse) Act, 1994, at http://www.medindia.net/Indian_Health_Act/PNDT/PNDT94_chap1.asp.

113. *Id.,* Sec. 6(b), at http://www.medindia.net/Indian_Health_Act/PNDT/PNDT94_chap3.asp.

114. *Id.,* Sec. 4.

115. The Pre-Natal Diagnostic Techniques (Regulation and Prevention of Misuse) Amendment Rules, 2003, at http://www.medindia.net/Indian_Health_Act/PNDT/PNDT2003.asp

116. *Id.,* No. 5 (setting forth new rule 3A, "Sale of ultrasound machines/imaging machines").

117. *Well-Being of Girls Should Be Underpinned by Robust Set of Laws, Commission on Status of Women Told, supra* note 111; *see also* Patel, *A Cultural Deficit, supra* note 47 (describing other legal measures implemented in India to counter sex selection).

118. Sharma, *supra* note 61.

119. Bumgarner, *supra* note 32, at 1303.

120. Ctr. for Enquiry into Health & Allied Themes v. Union of India, 4 I.L.R. 107 (S.C. 2003).

121. Gao Yan, *Sex-Selection Abortions Banned to End Population Imbalance: Mainland Doctors Performing Ultrasound Scans Will Not Be Able to Tell Parents the Gender of Their Babies Under a New Law,* South China Morning Post, Mar. 25, 2002, at http://www.laogai.org/news/newsdetail.php?id=1996. Under the law, ultrasound scans, abortions, and the issuance of morning after pills may legally only be done at government-approved centers, and three doctors must agree that a sex-identification test is medically indicated. *Id.*

122. *Lawmakers Call on* [sic] *Ban of Fetus Sex Selection,* China Daily, Feb. 27, 2005, http://www.chinadaily.com.cn/english/doc/2005-02/27/content_419843.htm; Liu Chang, *Jail for Those who Help Sex Selection,* China Daily, Dec. 26, 2005, at http://www.chinadaily.com.cn/english/doc/2005-12/26/content_506443.htm.

123. Chang, *supra* note 126.

124. Convention for the Protection of Human Rights and Dignity of the Human Being with regard to the Application of Biology and Medicine: Convention on Human Rights and Biomedicine, Oviedo, 4.IV.1997, Art. 14, at http://conventions.coe.int/treaty/en/treaties/html/164.htm.

125. Human Fertilisation and Embryology Authority (HFEA), at www.hfea.gov.uk; *see* BBC Health News, *Baby Gender Selection Ruled Out,* BBC News, Nov. 12, 2003, http://news.bbc.co.uk/1/hi/health/3257893.stm.

126. Rajani Bhatia et al., *Sex Selection: New Technologies, New Forms of Gender Discrimination,* CTR. GENETICS & SOC'Y (Oct. 2003), at http://genetics-and-society.org/resources/background/factsheet.html.

127. Fertility Clinic Success Rate and Certification Act of 1992, 42 U.S.C. 263a-1 *et seq.*

128. 64 Federal Register 39374 (July 21, 1999), at http://wwwn.cdc.gov/dls/pdf/art/fcsrca.pdf.

129. *Id.*

130. Assisted Reproductive Technology: A Systemwide Task Force Report and Recommendations to Strengthen Oversight and Improve Quality of Care, University Of California, Office of the President (Mar. 1996), App. C, at http://www.ucop.edu/healthaffairs/reports/art/.

131. *Id.* (describing state regulatory efforts.)

132. For example, India's religious leaders have condemned sex selective abortion as "shameful and inhuman," and have pledged to help their followers shun the practice. Sudha Ramachandran, New Technologies, *Old Prejudices Blamed For India's Vanishing Girls,* Panos Features, Sep. 15, 2001, at http://www.panos.org.uk/newsfeatures/featureprintable.asp?id=1036. Matching legal edicts have been forthcoming. In rejecting a claim by a couple that the ban on pre-conception gender selection violates the couple's liberty rights, the Mumbai High Court reasoned as follows:

> Sex selection is not only against the spirit of the Indian Constitution, it also insults and humiliates womanhood. It violates a woman's right to life. This is perhaps the greatest argument in favour of the ban on pre-natal sex-determination tests in India.

Gender Selection Akin to Murder, Says Mumbai Court Upholding Ban, InfoChangeIndia.org, Sep. 7, 2007, at http://www.infochangeindia.org/ChildrenItop .jsp?section_idv=4. *See also* Manhoff, *supra* note 61 (arguing that India should both vigorously enforce its proscription of sex selection and take measures to increase the value of women in society); Patel, supra note 47 (arguing that the shortage of girls in India is not merely a sociological phenomenon, but rather demands changing the mindset of doctors and patients to create a socio-cultural milieu conducive to the survival of Indian girls).

133. Suzanne Leigh, *Reproductive Tourism,* Health and Behavior USA TODAY May 2, 2005, www.usatoday .com/news/health/2005-05-02-reproductive-tourism_x .htm (quoting bioethicist Arthur Caplan).

134. *See, e.g., Shopping For The "Right" Gender: Wealthy Foreign Couples Are Traveling To The U.S. To Choose Their Child's Sex,* CBSNews.com, June 14, 2006, at http://www .cbsnews.com/stories/2006/06/14/health/main1711564 .shtml ("Well-off foreign couples are getting around laws banning sex selection in their home countries by coming to American soil, where it's legal, for medical procedures that can give them the boy, or girl, they want."); Peta Hellard, *$40,000 for their Designer Daughter,* Herald Sun (Australia) (Feb. 14, 2007) at http://biopoliticaltimes.org/article.php?id=3390 (reporting on an Australian couple who traveled to Los Angeles to have the sex selection process performed, a process illegal in Australia).

135. Human Fertilisation and Embryology Authority (HFEA), *supra* note 129. HFEA is a statutory body created in 1991 under the Human Fertilisation and Embryology Act (1990). *Id.*

136. *Id.* at http://www.hfea.gov.uk/en/390.html.

137. The Fertility Clinic Success Rate and Certification Act requires all clinics performing ART in the United States to annually report their success rate data to the CDCP, which publishes an annual report detailing the ART success rates for each of these clinics. This suggests a measure of agency expertise and prior Congressional confidence in the CDCP. *See* Fertility Clinic Success Rate and Certification Act of 1992 [FCSRCA], Section 2 [a] of P.L. 102-493 [42 U.S.C. 263 (a) -1]); ART report, *supra* note 5, at www.cdc.gov/ART/ART2004/faq .htm#3.

138. THE PRESIDENT'S COUNCIL ON BIOETHICS, U.S. PUBLIC POLICY AND THE BIOTECHNOLOGIES THAT TOUCH THE BEGINNINGS OF HUMAN LIFE: DRAFT RECOMMENDATIONS, Sep. 2003, at www.bioethics.gov/ background/bpprecommend.html.

139. *Id.*

140. *Id.*

141. *Id.*

142. Pre-Natal Diagnostic Techniques Act, *supra* note 116, at http://www.medindia.net/Indian_Health_Act/ PNDT/PNDT94_chap3.asp.

143. *Id.*

144. *Id.*

145. Convention on Human Rights and Biomedicine, *supra* note 128, Art. 14.

146. It is at least arguable that supporters of broad abortion rights will concede the inappropriateness of gender-linked abortion, and that opponents of abortion will concede the partial success of their efforts implicit in the same measure.

147. Manhoff, *supra* note 61, at 905.

DE AMBIENTE
Queer Tourism and Shifting Sexualities

DISCUSSION QUESTIONS

1. Why does Cantu argue that gay and lesbian tourism facilitates both sexual colonization *and* liberation?
2. Why does Cantu situate sexual tourism within an analysis of the political economy of the border? How does he link gay Mexican identity itself to transnational dynamics?
3. How do the dynamics of class and race delimit the experiences of gay Mexicans seeking the utopic "fantasy of gay life in the United States"?

> The coastal regions all around the country are noted for their sensual ambience. Perhaps it's the heat; but just about anywhere there's a beach and a city, there's action. Acapulco, Cancun, Vallarta, Mazatlan, and Veracruz are all hot, and so are the men.
>
> —Eduardo David, *Gay Mexico: The Men of Mexico*

"Do you know Mexico?" coyly poses the opening page of Mexico's official tourist web site.[1] Do you? Perhaps not. This is not a Mexico of social inequality, economic turmoil, indigenous uprisings, and mass emigration. No; this is a different Mexico—a sexy Mexico. Additional headers entice the reader to "Come Feel the Warmth of Mexico" where "...beaches are such as moods: bays that with happy smiles, beaches that spread in straight line, as to remind its steadiness, female beaches, smooth and with cadence, frisky beaches, that open and close, decline and go up [*sic*]." The sexual imagery of the web site leaves the reader (presumably heterosexual) with a sort of coquettish frustration and a desire for more than a "virtual tour" can provide. While it may seem otherwise, Mexico's flirtation with tourists is not limited to straight travelers.... The nation has become a major destination of gay and lesbian tourists, particularly Americans, in a growing global tourism industry. In turn, Mexico's *ambiente* (homosexual subculture...) is undergoing its own transformation, intimately linked to queer tourism.

The purpose of this chapter is to examine two sides of queer tourism "south of the border": (1) the

Lionel Cantu, Jr. "De Ambiente: Queer Tourism and Shifting Sexualities" from *The Sexuality of Migration: Border Crossings and Mexican Immigrant Men.* 2009. Edited by Nancy A. Naples and Salvador Vidal-Ortiz. Reprinted by permission of New York University Press.

development of gay and lesbian tourism in Mexico and (2) the effects of this industry on Mexican sexualities. As a point of clarification, I should also state up front that I refer to gay and lesbian tourism as an identity-based industry, and queer tourism as a larger market that encompasses a multitude of identities, including both native and foreign heterosexuals, bisexuals, and transgendered people. I argue that the relationship between gay and lesbian tourism and Mexican sexualities is a complex one in which dimensions of both sexual colonization and sexual liberation are at work. Furthermore, I assert that in order to understand Mexican sexualities we must move away from one-dimensional cultural models and instead examine them from a more complex and materialist perspective that recognizes that culture, social relations, and identities are embedded in global processes.

...I soon realized that tourism was not only an important factor in the lives of the men I interviewed but also a form of migration itself (in a broader sense of the word). While my ancestry is Mexican and I am fluent in Spanish, I am a Chicano—I am not Mexican. Thus, although my purpose in Mexico was entirely academic, I was a tourist. Despite the voyeuristic tendencies of both, there is a difference between my roles as ethnographer and as tourist that I think is relevant to this chapter and my analysis. My gaze as an ethnographer was armed at understanding the political economy of sexuality in Mexico as it differentially shapes the lives of men. I was not in Mexico on vacation; nonetheless, Mexicans often read me in the public spaces of the plazas, the bars, and the streets, not as a researcher but as a tourist. Thus, it is the intersection of my ethnographic and tourist roles that informs my analysis of queer tourism in Mexico....

...I address the following questions in this chapter: First, to what extent are Mexican sexualities and the dimensions that shape them "Mexican," and to what extent are they global? Furthermore, if tourism is to be understood as a modernist project built upon mediated representation and space, as Dean MacCannell (1999 [1976]) asserts, then how might these dimensions shape "native" identities and experiences? This chapter attempts to examine the complexities of Mexican sexualities from a political economic perspective, with a particular focus on queer tourism, in order to understand, in turn, how these dimensions are shaping the sexual identities of Mexican men.

ENCLACES/RUPTURAS FRONTERIZAS (BORDER LINKAGES/RUPTURES)

The border that delineates the nations of Mexico and the United States has been since its creation with the Treaty of Guadalupe in 1848 "an open wound." But as Anzaldua (1987) makes clear, la frontera is both real and imagined. It is a geopolitical boundary that links even as it separates the two nations, but it is also a metaphor for the spaces in which hybridity is created (in an often violent manner). In this section, my purpose is to highlight the political–economic linkages between the United States and Mexico that have given rise to the development of gay and lesbian tourism in Mexico. In addition, I highlight the border ruptures that are created through "tolerance zones"— a sexual "borderlands" in which Mexican male sexualities are fixed even as they are transformed.

Tourism has become an increasingly important sector of the Mexican economy. Beginning in the late 1960s Mexico created its own Ministry of Tourism (SECTUR), which is responsible for tourism as a whole, and FONATUR (in the early 1970s), which is responsible for infrastructure development projects in particular and has sponsored annual tourism trade fairs since 1996. In 1999, the World Trade Organization ranked Mexico seventh among the top ten destinations and tenth in foreign currency generated from tourism, and a majority of Mexican tourists continue to be from the United States (Guenette 2000). More precisely, more than 90 percent of Mexican tourists are from the United States (Arellano 1996). While it is impossible to know in any definitive way what proportions of Mexican tourists are gay, lesbian, or bisexual, there are factors that point to the development of queer tourism in the country.[2] These include the development and commodification of Mexican "gay" culture and space, and the rise of a Mexican gay and lesbian movement.

Gay bars in Mexico are a relatively new phenomenon, although they seem to be historically linked to urbanization and the development of *zonas de tolerancia* in the early part of the century.... *Zonas de tolerancia* (tolerance zones, or red light districts) developed after the revolution to control what were defined as forms of social deviance that included prostitution and homosexuality. The *zonas* were thus both gendered and sexualized spaces for those who transgressed gender norms and where men could satisfy their "licentious" desires. The spaces included areas where both male homosexual and transvestite bars were located and provided an escape from moral restraint for men who otherwise led more public heterosexual lives. Once established, the *zonas* became a legitimized space for "immoral activity" that attracted sexual tourism from north of the border where morality was more closely policed. For example, "Boys Town" brothels on the Mexican side of the border remain to this day rites of passage for young American men who cross the border looking for mostly heterosexual adventure. Thus, by the mid-twentieth century, the Mexican border towns were already firmly established as sites of sexual tourism for men on both sides of the border.[3]

Various scholars have mentioned the growing popularity of the term "gay" as an identity label in Mexico by both men and women (who also use the term "lesbian") (see Lumsden 1991; Murray 1995; Prieur 1998). While the label is sometimes written as "gai," it is clear that it refers to a sexual identity, culture, and movement and is thus similar in many ways to the term "gay" as used in the United States. Lumsden (1991) explains this shift in identity constructions as a consequence of several political factors. The combination of urbanization/industrialization, along with the creation of *zonas de tolerancia*, in all probability provided the social spaces whereby sexual minorities could establish social networks and, at least to some degree, create "community."

This spatial segregation resulted in queer zones or ghettoes in some cities like Guadalajara and Puerto Vallarta.[4] In Puerto Vallarta, the south side of the city has become the de facto "gay side" with bars, hotels, and other establishments that cater to a gay male—especially tourist—clientele. It should also be stated, however, that as is the case in the United States, an entire city has also become identified as a "gay space." ... The city of Guadalajara itself has over time become known as the San Francisco of Mexico due to its gay and lesbian population. As one middle-aged gay man told me, "in Guadalajara all the men are either *mariachis* or *maricones* [fags]." However, the development of a gay and lesbian community in Guadalajara, along with the movement for gay rights, has been hotly contested by conservative forces in the community.

Guadalajara and Acapulco were common vacation destinations for gay men from Mexico City in the 1980s and early 1990s (Sanchez-Crispin and Lopez-Lopez 1997).[5] However, since that time, Puerto Vallarta has developed into Mexico's premier gay resort town as a sort of satellite gay space for its big sister (Guadalajara), much as Fire Island is to New York and Palm Springs is to Los Angeles.[6]

Another factor that has contributed to the development of queer tourism in Mexico is the slow but steady rise of a Mexican gay and lesbian rights movement. Lumsden (1991) argues that the student movement in 1968 and the firing of a Sears department store employee can be understood as catalysts for challenging social oppression on the basis of sexual orientation in Mexico. Whether incidents like these were indeed the cause of the Mexican gay rights movement or not, what is clear is that the movement is not "new" to the Mexican political arena. Since the 1970s various gay and lesbian organizations have been created (and disbanded) throughout Mexico. Gay pride festivities are held in various Mexican cities and have become a tourist attraction in themselves. In fact, Cancun hosted the International Gay Pride Festival in 2001. These examples illustrate that a gay (and lesbian) identity exists in Mexico; and although it is not a clone of American constructions, there are many similarities.[7]

The rise of a gay identity is linked to the transnational ties of globalization between Mexico to the United States, in particular the gay United States.

My interviews with Mexican men in Guadalajara and migrants in the Los Angeles area were particularly useful in shedding light on this matter. These transnational links gave rise to a sexual identity label in the 1980s (still used to a certain degree)—*internacional*. Carrier reported use of the *internacional* (international) label by the then "hipper" and younger homosexual men during his field research.[8] The label, which referred to men who were versatile in their sexual repertoire, obviously has transborder connotations. Clearly, then, Mexican sexualities are being transformed through transnational processes and linkages, including that of tourism.

QUEER TOURISM IN MEXICO

> The reason why a million or more American visitors have traveled to Mexico in the course of recent years is that the average practical-minded person regards recreation travel from the angle of maximum returns at a minimum outlay of money and time. It is upon this purely practical consideration that Mexico makes its bid to the recreation-bent traveler.
>
> —Anonymous, "The Lure of Mexico"

While a growing body of literature has examined the impact of tourism and globalization on sexuality in the Pacific Rim (Truong 1990; Hall 1994a, 1994b), the way these phenomena are influencing Latin American countries has been largely ignored.[9] However, the fact that gay and lesbian tourism is a rapidly growing market in every part of the world—estimated at $17 billion (U.S.) dollars by the International Gay and Lesbian Travel Association (IGLTA)—demands greater attention.[10] With its proximity to the United States and the relatively low cost compared to other international sites, Mexico has become a desired destination for many gay and lesbian tourists. The recently created Tourist Promotion Board of Mexico plans to market "a number of product clubs featuring destinations and services *for certain types of people* like honeymooners, fishing buffs

or nature lovers" (Guenette 2000, 42). Although the gay and lesbian market niche is not mentioned specifically by the government organization, there are signs of strategic growth, including a growing number of gay and lesbian travel companies with travel programs in Mexico and publications that cater to the gay and lesbian tourist in Mexico.

Although Mexico has long been a favored site for vacationing among Americans, the growing popularity of Mexico as a *gay and lesbian* tourist destination is due in large measure to the marketing efforts of the gay and lesbian tourist industry. Founded in 1983, the IGLTA is an international organization with member organizations throughout the world and growing representation in Latin America,[11] including Mexico. The development of gay and lesbian cruise companies, such as Atlantis, RSVP, and Olivia, have also contributed to making Mexico a popular destination.[12] In addition, there are a number of travel magazines and web sites that cater to gay and lesbian patrons, as do a growing number of gay and lesbian travel agencies that offer packages throughout Mexico. *The Ferrari Guides Gay Mexico* (Black 1997) lists more than forty businesses that offer travel arrangements throughout Mexico aimed at gay and lesbian clientele; not surprisingly, nearly all of these are based in the United States (mostly, but not exclusively, in major urban centers) (Cordova 1999). Among the numerous international travel guides for gay and lesbian tourists—including comprehensive guides by Spartacus, Ferrari, Odysseus, and Damron—are several that focus on travel information for the queer tourist in Mexico. There are three queer tourist guide books that focus exclusively on Mexico and for the most part target a male audience: *Gay Mexico: The Men of Mexico* (David 1998), *The Ferrari Guides Gay Mexico: The Definitive Guide to Gay and Lesbian Mexico* (Black 1997),[13] and *A Man's Guide to Mexico and Central America* (Cordova 1999). Each of the guides gives both general information useful to any tourist (i.e., money exchange information and maps) and information specific to the queer tourist (e.g., bath house locations and helpful Spanish phrases for meeting men).

All three guides provide city-by-city information. Señor Cordova's *Man's Guide* lists fourteen cities,

Eduardo David's *Gay Mexico* has listings for twenty-five, and Richard Black's *Ferrari Guide* lists forty-three. While Mexico's urban centers (e.g., Mexico City, Guadalajara, and Monterey) and mainstream tourist destinations (i.e., Cancun, Acapulco, Los Cabos) are among the cities listed, the guides also list towns and cities that are more "off the beaten path," especially for the queer tourist. These include cities such as Leon in the state of Guanajuato (known as the shoe capital of the world) and the city of Oaxaca with its neighboring villages. The distinction between these sites and gay tourist sites is supposedly one of "authenticity." But while the travel guides forewarn gay tourists of the potential dangers of crossing into these native grounds, they are in reality tourist sites, too. Thus, "off the beaten path" does not necessarily mean that the sites are nontourist spaces but rather that they are more "mainstream," catering to a more "straight" clientele.

An examination of these guides and tourist services suggests that two "sides" of Mexico are most commonly represented: the "just like home" and the exotic. As Black (1997) explains in *The Ferrari Guides*, "For Americans, Mexico is close, yet foreign. For any traveler, it's different yet has many of the comforts of home. It offers something for everyone! You're in for a great time!" (14). While both the "just like home" and the exotic representations emphasize the homoerotic aspects of different sites in Mexico, one targets American tourists who want to vacation with all the gay comforts of home while the other seeks to attract those who seek an erotic adventure not to be found in any suburban American home life. Both speak to MacCannell's (1999 [1976]) insight that

[t]he frontiers of world tourism are the same as the expansion of the modern consciousness with terminal destinations for each found throughout the colonial, ex-colonial, and future colonial world where raw materials for industry and exotic flora, fauna, and peoples are found in conglomeration. The tourist world has also been established *beyond* the frontiers of existing society, or at least beyond the edges of the Third World. A *paradise* is a traditional type of tourist community, a kind of last resort, which has as its defining

characteristic its location not merely outside the physical borders of urban industrial society, but just beyond the border of the peasant and plantation society as well. (183)

Yet for queer tourism there also exists a "border" tension between the lure of an exotic "paradise" and the dangers of homophobia in foreign lands. Here, Mexico seems to represent a homosexual paradise free of the pressures of a modern "gay lifestyle"; where sexuality exists in its "raw" form yet where the dangers of an uncivilized heterosexual authority also threaten.

Gay and lesbian cruises seem to target those more inclined to a mediated adventure where one can enjoy prefabricated representations of the exotic and always return to one's "home away from home" either aboard ship or in a hotel. The cruise destinations tend to be located either in the "Mexican Caribbean" on the east coast or in the Baja area on the west. Take, for instance, Atlantis's description of its services:

Atlantis vacations are designed for the way we enjoy ourselves today. We created the concept of an all-gay resort vacation and are the leaders in all-gay charters of first class resorts and cruise ships. All at exotic locations, exclusively ours for these special weeks, with an emphasis on friendship and camaraderie. Places where you can always be yourself and always have fun. That's the way we play.

The "home-away-from-home" approach to gay travel thus allows for the "best of both worlds" where one can "play" on exotic beaches but under controlled conditions. A new *zona de tolerancia* is born—a queer space that protects inhabitants from the threat of cultural mismatch, including homophobia. Thus, in this queer borderland, the tourist can enjoy Mexico's pleasures under a controlled environment free from the less "civilized" world *del otro lado* (on the other side) of tourist boundaries.

In comparison to the vacation cruise advertisements, gay guide books are more apt to give stereotypical representations of Mexican men. Consider David's (1998) description:

Many Mexican men are often breathtaking in their beauty. They are sensual and often unabashedly sexual.

Proud to be male, aware of their physical nature, they are often ready to give of themselves and sometimes receive in return....

The adventurous visitor may want to go farther afield in search of the men for whom Mexico is particularly famed: the butch *hombres* who would never walk into a place known to be gay, but who are ready to spring to attention when they catch a man's eye. These are men who must be pursued. (27–28)

This excerpt exemplifies a *colonial desire* that Robert Young (1995) defines as the dialectic of attraction and repulsion, to conquer (and be conquered by) the hypermasculine and sexually charged racial Other. The colonial message is reinforced in the guide books by advice on "rewarding" Mexican men for their services with gifts or money, suggesting that financial compensation for homosexual sex is a cultural norm.

Such representations are reminiscent of what is commonly referred to as "Spanish fantasy heritage" (see McWilliams 1948). At the end of the nineteenth century and in the first half of the twentieth century, the prevailing image of Mexicans (both in the United States and Mexico) was of "gay *caballeros*" and "dark and lovely *señoritas*" lazily dancing the night away under Spanish tile roofs. These representations were utilized to sell a romantic and exotic image of California and Mexico to tourists in the early decades of the twentieth century. Contemporary gay tourist images seem to either play up the "Latin lover" image or place greater emphasis on a bit rougher and more "savage" version of the gay *caballero*, both of which abound in gay travel guides. Compare, for instance, the cover images of the three travel guides.

The images on the covers of both Black's guide (Figure 48.1) and Cordova's (Figure 48.2) represent the "Latin lover" look, a light-complected (though tanned) young man in romantic settings, at least partially clothed and waiting to give the queer male tourist a *bienvenida* (a welcoming). The image on the cover of David's guide (Figure 48.3) is a darker *mestizo* with facial hair in an ambiguous setting and framed suggestively (the reader is not sure of the

Figure 48.1

model's state of dress). Not surprisingly, it is David's book that contains more information for the traveler looking for experiences "off the beaten path." Beyond the stereotypes of Latino masculinity, these images represent contradictions of internalized homophobia and the quest for the elusive "real" man among gay tourist themselves.

One of the ironies of this search is that as more gay male toursits look for these exotic places—virgin territory, off the beaten path of mainstream gay tourist sites—the sites become, in effect, conquered territory—gay tourist spots. This type of "invasion" is complicated, of course, by the tensions between a certain level of sexual liberation versus sexual conquest. That is, as gay and lesbian tourists become more common to an area, there is a certain level of normalization that occurs through visibility. However, it is not clear to what extent the opening of

Figure 48.2

Figure 48.3

more legitimized queer space is a positive effect for Mexico's queer population and to what extent this space is framed as "American."

The expansion of the gay and lesbian tourism industry in Mexico is but one of the more visible manifestations of this queer manifest destiny.... Other signs of this development are the gay bars that now operate throughout Mexico, some with American-sounding names like Relax (Acapulco), Blue City (Cancun), MN'MS (Ciudad Juarez), and The Door (Mexico City). In each case, these Mexican gay bars are located in sites commonly visited by foreign gay tourists. While they are not technically or legally off-limits to queer Mexican nationals, only those of at

least a middle-class background and with more sophisticated tastes who might mix better with tourists are commonly found in such bars/discos. *Zonas de tolerancia*, yes, but within limits.

The question of how this tourism is influencing the lives and sexual identities of Mexican men and women remains to be researched, but Murray (1995; see also Black 1997) reports that the hospitality industry is a common employer of Mexican gays and lesbians.[14] In addition, male prostitution (as either an occupation or "part-time" activity) is obviously linked to gay male tourism (Carrier 1995). And more recently, epidemiologists have become more concerned with tourism and the spread of HIV in the country. In the following section I explore these questions more directly through the voices of Mexican men themselves.

GAY CABALLEROS AND PHALLIC DREAMS: LIFE IN THE SEXUAL BORDERLANDS

In…coordination of and responsibility for the diverse efforts of the nation, tourism has its place, a place that is characterized by its diversification, for it is indifferent to nothing and affects all, the local as much as the foreign.…And that does not refer only to foreign tourism, those visitors from afar who discover new realities, even as they offer them.

—Hector Manuel Romero, "Nada es indiferente al turismo"

Mexico's Gay *ambiente* has changed dramatically over the last decade. What was once an underground world of private parties in the homes of homosexual men has become a more public and therefore more visible phenomenon, as Santiago's observation (as noted in the previous chapter) that "anybody can be gay now" illustrates. The commodification of Mexican gay spaces presents a complex set of factors in the lives of queer Mexican men. The spaces created allowed for the development of an identity and community that served as the foundation of the gay and lesbian movement in Mexico. Queer tourists shape this space both through their contact with Mexicans and through the creation of new space to serve their needs. Contact provides an exchange of cultural and political information around issues of queerness that has an impact on men's lives.

Some men use this information as a rationale for migrating to the United States, which they construct as a more tolerant space/place. Armando is a 32-year-old man from Jalisco who lives in the Los Angeles area, where he works in HIV services. He is the oldest of eight children and moved to the United States in 1990. In 1995, he was living in Santa Ana after having moved from Los Angeles, where he had been living with his brother. At the time of the interview he was an undocumented immigrant. Armando learned about the United States through tourism, indirectly at first and later through his own

experiences. In Mexico, Armando was a seminarian studying to be a priest. In the seminary he heard stories of gay life in the United States from friends (including other seminarians) who had visited the "north," and later he himself visited the United States for missionary exchange programs. It was after he was advised by a priest to move to the north, where he could live more openly as a gay man, that Armando migrated.

Lalo, a 33-year-old gay-identified man from Guadalajara, is a similar case. The fifth of nine children, Lalo comes from what he describes as a "very poor" class background. Lalo explained that after being rejected by his family for being gay, he moved to Puerto Vallarta for a time, where he worked in hotels. He explained that many of his coworkers were also gay and that they helped him get by to the extent of giving him an apartment in which to live. He migrated to Southern California on the advice of his friends in 1983. He is now a legal resident and lives in Fountain Valley. He explained,

The people in the hotel would tell me "Go to the United States, it's beautiful, you make good money and there are a lot of homosexuals. You can hold [your lover's] hand and kiss in public and nothing happens." I thought it was an ideal world where homosexuals could be happy. [But I] learned that it wasn't true that homosexuals were free, that they can hold hands or that Americans liked Mexicans.

The reality that awaited Lalo was not a utopia but rather more of a nightmare. Soon after moving to the United States with the assistance of gay friends, he discovered not only that homophobia does exist in the United States but also that racism was a fact of life he would have to deal with, which is just one of the many tribulations and hardships that queer immigrants must face (see Luibheid 1998). The fantasy of gay life in the United States reported to Lalo is a common one. As mentioned, in my interview with Santiago he referred to it as the *sueizo falico*, or "phallic dream," in which queer men in Mexico envision the United States as a sexual utopia, an erotic land of milk and honey. The irony, of course, is that many

American gay tourists have a similar dream when they visit Mexico's gay resorts.

For those Mexican men who have the resources, travel to "gay-friendly" places is also an option, as in the case of Marcos discussed in the previous chapter. Another such case is that of Franco, who travels about once a year to the Los Angeles area to visit family. He and Angel, a gay cousin, always go to gay bars together and Franco admits to having a good time, but his real love is Cuba. With a grin he related, "The men in Cuba are fantastic. I always take some extra things like cologne and clothes. Cuban men will fuck you for a Nike baseball cap." Thus, like his American counterparts in Mexico who are tourists with expendable income, Franco seeks sexual conquest in exotic lands, in this case Cuba. The excerpt helps to highlight not only the diversity of Mexican male sexual experiences with tourism but also the importance of class in shaping the power relations of these experiences. Apparently, the phallic dream knows no borders.

But the road to the phallic dream that some Mexican men pursue is a two-way street, and the reality of racism in the United States is the slap that wakes them. Juan and Miguel, both in their midtwenties, are two Mexican men I met during my research in the Los Angeles area. They actually returned to Mexico in part because of the difficulty of living in the United States but also because of social and economic opportunities they felt existed in Mexico. Although Juan was a naturalized citizen of the United States, Miguel was an undocumented immigrant. On a return visit to the United States Juan explained,

> The situation for us here in the United States was just too difficult. The type of work that Miguel could find here, without papers, was very hard and did not pay well, and everything is so expensive too. We decided that it was better to go to Cancun and work with gay tourists there. I know English and I've learned a little French too. We have a very small apartment and it isn't always easy, but we are happy there.

Juan and Miguel chose to return to Mexico to pursue their dreams and a more comfortable life as gay men.

That is, with some of the social and economic capital (although it was limited) they acquired in the United States, Juan and Miguel were able to move to Cancun and begin anew in a better class position.

Some of the Mexican men whom I interviewed in the United States felt the same discomfort that Juan and Miguel expressed, but rather than return to Mexico to live, they vacation there. Julio, a Guadalajara native in his early forties, lives in Orange County, California. He migrated to the United States through a network of gay friends and soon after married a lesbian friend who is a U.S. citizen. Now a legal resident, he works as an accountant for most of the year and saves money so that he can return to Mexico for months at a time. Like his Mexican contemporaries, Julio also uses vacations and tourism as a strategy of escape, but from his American context.

> The men here are superficial and I haven't been able to meet someone that I can have a long-term relationship with. When I go to Mexico I visit my family and friends and I feel their warmth and love. I still have a lot of gay friends in Guadalajara and I always spend time in [Puerto] Vallarta too. I feel like I can be myself there and that people appreciate me for who I am.

The frustrations that Julio expressed to me were in reference to his experiences with American gay scenes in general, but he was also critical of gay Latino culture and norms in the United States. Julio feels that the affective connections and sense of community that he knows in Guadalajara are largely missing in the United States—even among gay Latinos. In addition, he feels that American gay culture, and American men in particular, are too superficial.

Mexican men's relationships with American men are not always contentious. Roberto is in his early forties and has resided in the United States since moving from Mexico City in 1996. The fourth of five children, he comes from a prestigious and well-to-do family in Nayarit, Mexico. Although never married, Roberto has a teenaged son who lives in Mexico with the son's mother. Roberto lives in Long Beach and works as an AIDS educator for a Latino community organization. Roberto explained to me that he was quite happy with his life in Mexico as a civil servant but that people had begun to gossip about his sexual orientation and he feared for his job security. Roberto had met a man from the United States who was vacationing in Mexico and had maintained a friendly relationship with the man. When the American suggested to Roberto that he move to the United States to live with him in the Los Angeles area, Roberto took advantage of the opportunity and moved to L.A. Although he is no longer in a relationship with the American, they continue to be friends.

My own experience researching issues of sexuality and migration has taught me that Roberto's experience is a common one. Many men become involved in "binational relationships" (i.e., relationships where partners are of different nationalities). Such relationships are not recognized by U.S. immigration policy, which therefore does not allow for the legal migration of same-sex spouses. Despite the "illegitimacy" of these relationships for immigration purposes, gays and lesbians do migrate from foreign countries any way they can to be with their partners.

Although he is not sure when and how he got infected, Roberto's story also speaks to the issue of HIV/AIDS and its connection to queer tourism (see Haour-Knipe and Rector 1996; Clift and Carter 2000). It is impossible to determine to what extent queer tourism is responsible for the spread of HIV in Mexico, but it would be foolish to suggest that there is no connection. However, queer tourism does play another important role related to HIV/AIDS. Condoms, lubricants, medications, and literature on safer sex that foreign tourists bring to Mexico are also shared with Mexican men. It should also be noted that the gay Mexico travel guides mentioned here even suggest that their readers assist Mexican men in such a manner (David 1998, 70). That is, travel guides recommend that gay American men take "plenty" of "lube and condoms" with them and leave any extras to Mexican "friends" they've met along the way.

As discussed previously, the image of the "gay *caballero*" marketed by gay travel guides is a fantasy that has very real implications for Mexican masculinities and sexualities. The frustration that many Mexican men feel over the racist macho stereotype that Americans have of them is a complaint that I heard time and again during my research. For instance, Javier is a bisexual man in his late twenties whom I met in Guadalajara. Javier is married and has two children but enjoys having sex with men. Javier bemoaned,

> I don't like to have sex with Americans. They always seem to want a sex machine. They want a big penis that screws them all night long. I don't have a big penis and I want someone who will hold me and kiss me. I don't want to be the *activo*. I just want a man to make love to me.

Throughout my interview with him, I was struck by the way in which Javier expressed his sexuality in a manner that was compatible with his masculine identity. Despite the fact that he admittedly enjoyed being *pasivo*, and contrary to much of the literature on the topic, he securely expressed a masculine non-homosexual identity. As a married bisexual man, Javier has social privileges that many other men who have sex with men do not. His sense of sexual repression is based not in Mexican norms but in American ones. In Javier's experience, American tourists come to Mexico seeking a stereotype of Mexican masculinity that Javier cannot meet and yet it is a gendered performance that is demanded time and again by gay American tourists' search for the macho.

CONCLUSION

. . . Mexico seems to represent a place fixed in time, where "real" men can be found. The stereotype of the Mexican macho is alive and well in the imagination of American tourists. However, far from being culturally stagnant, Mexico has undergone profound changes in the last several decades. These changes shape the everyday experiences of Mexican men and the meanings and identities of gender and sexuality. While anthropologists working in Mexico in the 1970s and 1980s asserted that "gay" identities did not exist as we understand them in an American context this is no longer the case in the twenty-first century. The boundaries of Mexican sexual identities are changing even as the spaces that produce them are remapped. The development of gay and lesbian tourism in the country is a key factor linked to these changes. The relationship between queer tourism and Mexican male sexualities is complex and multiply constituted, but in this chapter I have highlighted some of these dimensions, particularly as they are linked to a sexual political economy.

. . . My purpose in this chapter has been to point to some of the diversity of Mexican male sexualities that is shaped by a number of factors, including culture. By using a political–economic framework for understanding Mexican male sexualities, I assert that we might be able to better understand how Mexican men who have sex with men are differentially positioned in Mexico's *ambiente*. I have also argued that Mexico's *ambiente* is embedded not only in a nationalist development project but also in a global political economy. Although I have privileged the public sphere in my discussion, public and private spheres are neither clearly delineated nor mutually exclusive, especially in the realm of sexuality.

The geopolitical border that the United States and Mexico share is an often overlooked dimension in studies of Mexican and U.S. sexualities (epidemiological studies of HIV/AIDS being an exception). Historically, the Mexican border towns and "tolerance zones" have served as "safe spaces" wherein Americans could escape strict sexual mores and prying eyes in the United States. This early version of sexual tourism included space for homosexual activity that would gradually expand to other areas such as urban centers. These border zones and their linkages to a national development project are crucial to understanding the shifting boundaries of Mexican sexualities.

Mexico's modernization projects, including its industrialization and urbanization, have in part created the conditions for the development of commodified and more legitimized same-sex sexuality in urban centers. While space for same-sex sexuality is not necessarily "new," the greater visibility, legitimacy, and even identity basis of these spaces are. Queer communities such as those in Mexico City

have been instrumental in the creation of a Mexican gay and lesbian movement. Such changes helped to establish the conditions that would allow the establishment of a formal queer tourist industry. In addition, as part of its strategy for national development, the Mexican government prioritized tourism with aspirations for economic growth and controlled urbanization, and one of the "side effects" of this strategy is that it also contributed to the development of queer tourism.

As I discussed, gay and lesbian tourism in Mexico has resulted in an expansion of commodified space, which has had the dual effect of creating sites in the country that are both sexually liberating and exploitative. In some instances, segregated spaces are actually created for gay and lesbian tourists through specialized cruises and/or resorts. In other instances, gay and lesbian tourists are encouraged to "mix with the natives" and in so doing transform queer Mexican space. These spaces both reproduce and rupture the racialized politics of the U.S./Mexican border. While creating spaces by which identities and community may form, commodification also brings with it exclusionary norms and practices. "Gay Mexico" is marketed to mostly foreign tourists through organizations such as the IGLTA and venues such as travel guides and web sites. Part of the "sell" to this market relies upon stereotypes of Mexican men with racist undertones and images and the idea that Mexican men are "for the taking," particularly in those areas deemed to be more authentic than the controlled spaces of queer resorts.

The commodification of Mexican gay space presents a complex set of factors in the lives of Mexican men. While gay and lesbian tourist markets do not exclude Mexican nationals, socioeconomic constraints often do. Thus for many Mexican men, contact with gay tourists may occur more regularly not through leisure activities but through their labor as service workers. Such spaces, however, have their own boundaries or borders, whereby someone such as Lalo who worked in the industry had no "real" contact with Americans until he migrated to the United States. However, sometimes native/tourist contact brings with it information that serves as incentive for some Mexican men to emigrate to other countries and for some men to form binational relationships through tourist contacts, too.[15] Roberto is a case in point. However, the experiences that Lalo and Roberto had with American gay tourists should not be read as simply different. Class differences between the two men no doubt shaped these trajectories.

Gays and lesbians in Mexico have responded to social regulation and oppression in a number of ways depending upon their social locations. These responses range from the creation of a subculture and communities to social protest. While Mexico's gay and lesbian movement does have a long history (although this is not often acknowledged in the literature), gay and lesbian tourism is also a factor in the shifting boundaries of space and place for queer Mexicans. The growing visibility of the gay and lesbian tourist market (including events such as the IGLTA conference in Cancun) and the dependence of both local and national economies on tourism are important factors in the political environment for gays and lesbians in Mexico.

Tourism can also be a response to one's marginality. By traveling to other cities and countries some Mexican homosexual men are able to "escape" temporarily the constraints of their marginalized status. Again, social class is a key factor in determining the avenues by which the constraints of marginality might be maneuvered. Thus, while this chapter has focused on dimensions of American tourism to Mexico, the dynamics of Mexican queer tourism are not restricted to foreign tourists. Thus the tensions of sexual liberation/colonialism that arise with gay and lesbian tourism in Mexico are reproduced by Mexican upper-class men in other parts of the world as well.

Although the rise of gay and lesbian tourism in Mexico was not a planned outcome of the nation's tourist development project, it is an end result with important social and political reverberations. It is significant that those on the margins of Mexican society (los otros) and those on the margins of other nations, especially the United States (i.e., gays and lesbians) should come together under a nationalist project. However, as the border reminds us, and as I have argued here, life in these queer sexual borderlands has elements that are both liberating and oppressive. However, a central question remains: To what extent is the Mexican nationalist project willing to consciously embrace not only its gay and lesbian tourists but also, more importantly, its gay and lesbian citizens? The answer may ultimately lie not in the demands of Mexican gays and lesbians but rather in the demands of a queer market and the political economy of space.

NOTES

1. The web site has text in both English and Spanish. Interestingly, however, the messages are completely different. The text in English is extremely erotic; in Spanish, however, the discourse focuses on national treasures and seems to target tourism within Mexico (http://www.mexico-travel.com).
2. Although, to my knowledge, there are no statistics on the countries of origin of gay and lesbian Mexican tourists, one may assume (given the marketing tactics of the industry and Mexican tourism statistics) that their demographics reflect those of tourists in general, i.e., a majority are from the United States.
3. This phenomenon seems consistent with Chauncey's discussion of homosexuality in pre–World War II New York, where marginal (racially segregated) areas became havens for different types of "deviance," including homosexuality, and a sort of playground for the more well-to-do. However, it is not clear how prevalent the zonas were in areas other than border towns and the urban center of Mexico City.
4. To my knowledge, there does not exist any literature on the demographics of this community. However, traditional Mexican culture makes it easier for unmarried men (as opposed to women) to live apart from their families, and both economic conditions and the growing popularity of the area are also factors that affect the demographics of its residents.
5. Sanchez-Crispin and Lopez-Lopez (1997) also argue that the liberalization of Acapulco for gays and lesbians was due to its popularity among international gay and lesbian tourists.
6. The satellite space status of Puerto Vallarta is supported by the fact that many (if not all) bars in Guadalajara carry the Puerto Vallarta gay paper/flyer with all its ads and a map.

7. Even in the United States, the "gay" label fails to capture the numerous experiences and identities that are commonly grouped under it.

8. This terminology is reportedly also used by lesbians.

9. The Caribbean, particularly Cuba, is one area that is beginning to be studied. See, for instance, Davidson (1996) and Lumsden (1996).

10. International Gay and Lesbian Travel Association, 2000, http://www.iglta.com. Tourism Industry Intelligence estimated the global market at $10 billion (U.S.) dollars in 1994 (as reported in Holcomb and Luongo 1996), and an industry survey by Community Marketing (2008) estimates the American gay and lesbian market alone to be worth more than $64.5 billion.

11. The IGLTA is represented in Argentina, Brazil, Chile, Bolivia, Venezuela, Colombia, Ecuador, Panama, and Costa Rica as well.

12. While Atlantis and RSVP advertise as open to both men and women, their main market seems to be men, while Olivia targets a lesbian clientele.

13. While the *Ferrari Guide* does have some information for women, the guide is aimed mostly at men. This is due in part, no doubt, to the greater visibility of gay men as opposed to lesbians in Mexico.

14. Madsen Camacho (2000), who has conducted research on the Mexican tourist industry in Huatulco, Mexico, reports that businesses in the hospitality industry, particularly hotels, often desire gay men as workers due to their perceptions that gay men have a "higher" cultural aesthetic and more cultural capital, which serves the hospitality industry's needs (personal communication).

15. These dynamics are also transforming queer space in Los Angeles; thus my argument is not unilateral.

REFERENCES

Anzaldua, Gloria. 1987. *Borderlands/LaFrontera: The New Mestiza*. San Francisco: Aunt Lute.

Black, Richard. 1997. *The Ferrari Guides Gay Mexico: The Definitive Guide to Gay and Lesbian Mexico*. Phoenix, AZ: Ferrari Guides.

Clift, Stephen, and Simon Carter, eds. 2000. *Tourism and Sex: Culture, Commerce, and Coercion*. London: Pinter Press.

Cordova, Señor. 1999. *A Man's Guide to Mexico and Central America*. Beverly Hills, CA: Centurion Press.

David, Eduardo. 1998. *Gay Mexico: The Men of Mexico*. Oakland, CA: Floating Lotus Press.

Davidson, Julia. 1996. "Sex Tourism in Cuba." *Race and Class* 8(1): 39–49.

Guenette, Louise. 2000. "Touting Tourism." *Business Mexico* 10(3):42–47.

Hall, C. Michael. 1994a. "Gender and Economic Interests in Tourism Prostitution: The Nature, Development, and Implications of Sex Tourism in South-East Asia." Pp. 142–63 in *Tourism: A Gender Analysis*, edited by Vivian Kinnaird and Derek Hall. New York: Wiley.

Hall, C. Michael. 1994b. *Tourism in the Pacific Rim: Development, Impacts, and Markets*. New York: Halsted Press.

Haour-Knipe, Mary, and Richard Rector, eds. 1996. *Crossing Borders: Migration, Ethnicity, and AIDS*. London: Taylor & Francis.

Luibheid, Eithne. 1998. " 'Looking Like a Lesbian': The Organization of Sexual Monitoring at the United States-Mexican Border." *Journal of the History of Sexuality* 8(3):477–506.

Lumsden, Ian G. 1991. *Homosexuality, Society, and the State in Mexico*. Mexico: Solediciones, Colectivo Sol.

Lumsden, Ian. 1996. *Machos, Maricones, and Gays: Cuba and Homosexuality*. Philadelphia: Temple University Press.

MacCannell, Dean. 1999 [1976]. *The Tourist: A New Theory of the Leisure Class*. Berkeley: University of California Press.

Madsen Camacho, Michelle E. 2000. "The Politics of Progress: Constructing Paradise in Huatulco, Oaxaca." Ph.D. dissertation, University of California, Irvine.

McWilliams, Carey. 1948. *North from Mexico: The Spanish-Speaking People of the United States*. New York: Praeger.

Murray, Steven O. 1995. *Latin American Male Homosexualities*. Albuquerque: University of New Mexico Press.

Prieur, Annick. 1998. *Mema's House, Mexico City: On Transvestites, Queens, and Machos*. Chicago: University of Chicago Press.

Sanchez-Crispin, Alvaro, and Alvaro Lopez-Lopez. 1997. "Gay Male Places of Mexico City." Pp. 197–212 in *Queers in Space: Communities, Public Places, Sites of Resistance*, edited by Gordon Brent Ingram, Anne-Marie Bouthillette, and Yolanda Retter. Seattle: Bay Press.

Truong, Thanh-Dam. 1990. *Sex, Money, and Morality: Prostitution and Tourism in Southeast Asia*. Atlantic Highlands, NJ: Zed.

Young, Robert J.C. 1995. *Colonial Desire: Hybridity in Theory, Culture and Race*. New York: Routledge.

SECTION SEVEN

Future Forward

Previous sections have all provided examples of concrete social change that is occurring, often in specific local contexts. In this final, brief section we offer works that represent the kind of broad thinking about the future that is needed as well. These authors ask us to open our minds to thinking differently and creatively, to imagine new worlds and envision unthought-of futures.

Ryan A. Flores whets our imaginations first with his poem "Guess Who?" In it he beautifully describes how he is identified by different people and institutions according to context and other factors. He behooves the reader to delve into the multiple facets that make up a person's identity, ending with the question, "So who *am* I?" Is one definition even necessary? Such questions are of utmost importance to all of us involved in the work of social change.

Similarly, Judith Lorber asks the reader to envision a world without behavioral/ role and appearance expectations assigned according to sex. In a world so ubiquitously structured around masculinities and femininities, the idea of "degendering" culture is truly revolutionary. What might such a world look like? Rick Noack discusses one alternative: Sweden's intention to add a third gender pronoun (used both when someone's gender is unknown/irrelevant or for someone who does not identify with or through a gender binary) to the Swedish Academy's dictionary. The addition of "hen" reflects a cultural shift away from dichotomous thinking with regard to sex and gender and could serve as a progressive example for other nations.

Finally, Leslie Feinberg advocates for activists in various facets of the women's movement to move transfolks and transliberation from the margins to the center in order to liberate even cisgendered persons from the social constraints around sex and gender. She argues that our cultural myths and expectations surrounding what it means to be a "real" man or a "real" woman are all caricatures, effectively stymieing individual and creative self-expression. By placing gender-variant people at the center of a liberation movement, Feinberg asserts, we can begin to envision all of the beautiful and multifarious ways there are to be a human being.

The key feature of each chapter in Section Seven is its open-ended character. We must continue to ask questions and imagine different ways of organizing society around sexuality and gender in order to create a more equitable future for all. As Michel Foucault asks at the beginning of Lorber's piece, "But what is it that is impossible to think, and what kind of impossibility are we faced with here?" It is only by asking previously unthought-of questions that we can imagine new futures. The questions are as important as any answers we may conceive of.

49 • *Ryan A. Flores*

GUESS WHO?

DISCUSSION QUESTIONS

1. How does Flores demonstrate the importance/effects of other peoples' perceptions on our identities?
2. How can we begin to employ more fluid or multifaceted methods for embracing people in their entirety?

[an exercise in lateral thinking]

to my mother I am *son*
to my father I am *hijo*
to racist hillbillies of the Midwest
I am *wetback, spic*, and *beaner*
to cholos at Armijo I am *gringo*
to officials at the State Department
I need proof of *citizenship*
to la gente de México I am *güero*
in the Southwest I am *coyote*
at the university I am *Latino,*
Mexican-American, and *Chicano*
to the Census Bureau I am *Hispanic*
or "*more than one heritage*"
to mis abuelos I am *mezclado*

to those who hear me speak Spanish
I must be *Argentino* or *Español*
because of light skin and green eyes
because of maternal Bohemian ancestry
I muse as being *Chex-Mex* or *Czexican*
I could be the *United States* of existence
I could be *America*
I could be your neighbor
your boss, your teacher, your student
I could mow your lawn,
cook your food
I could be you

So, who *am* I?

Courtesy Ryan A. Flores.

50 • *Judith Lorber*

A WORLD WITHOUT GENDER
Making the Revolution

DISCUSSION QUESTIONS

1. Why does Lorber argue that there is "ambivalence" about contemporary gender divisions?
2. Do you agree with Lorber that we need to work toward a "gender-free" society? What do you find most appealing about this idea? What do you find most uncomfortable? What can you do in your own life to begin working toward abolishing gender?
3. Would a "degendering" of society lead to the erasure of differences among men and women?
4. How would degendering society change our conceptions of sexual identity?

> But what is it that is impossible to think, and what kind of impossibility are we faced with here?
>
> —Michel Foucault

With all the diversity and divisions of gender identities and gender practices, the ultimate paradox is that gender systems are still binary. Societies in developed and developing countries with vastly different cultures, complex economies, and a variety of family groupings organize their members into categories of people who have different statuses, roles, access to economic resources and skills training, and opportunities for leadership and political power. Gender is only one of those sorting mechanisms, but it is virtually universal. The ubiquity of gender as an organizing principle of social life leads to the belief that the man–woman division is a male–female division. It is not. Societies are not divided into "penises" and "vaginas" or "wombs" and "nonwombs" or "ovaries" and "testes." Nor are most modern societies divided into child bearers and non-child bearers. When gender as a social institution organizes a society, the divisions are "women" and "men"—social identities whose breaches are possible but often punishable. The comparative social categories for "woman" and "man" are not body types but social divisions like "slave" and "free man," "peasant" and "aristocrat," "Black" and "White." In societies that do not have third genders, you pass at great peril as a person of the gender category opposite the one you are legally assigned, but

Judith Lorber, excerpts from "A World Without Gender: Making the Revolution" from *Breaking the Bowls: Degendering and Feminist Change*. 2005.

it is done easily, especially when all it takes is a clothing change.

The insidiousness of such deeply embedded social categories is that they control our lives. They create differences between one group and its supposed opposite and designate the first group as primary, the norm, and the second as subordinate, the other. The differences are established through the contrast of socially created opposites. As Joan Wallach Scott notes, "Any unitary concept in fact contains repressed or negated material; it is established in explicit opposition to another term." Because the categorical opposites contain elements of the other, similarities must be suppressed; if the similarities were allowed to emerge, they would blur the boundaries between the two groups and undermine the distinction of one as dominant.

The distinctions between women and men and the dominance of men are hard to justify in modern Western societies, but they persist. Tracing the rise in women's status in the United States in the last 150 years, Robert Max Jackson argues that thanks to increasing bureaucratization and rationalization of many areas of modern life, women have substantial equality with men in jobs, legal rights, education, and voting power. Despite these marks of formal equality, what he calls residual inequalities are still to be tackled—the rarity of women in high political office and at the top levels of prestigious and lucrative professions, the widespread imbalance in domestic labor, greater costs to women in divorce and staying unpartnered, sexual harassment, rape, physical violence, and the persistent belief that women and men are inherently different.

Modern Western societies are comparatively less gender-divided and more gender-egalitarian than feudal, aristocratic, or eighteenth- and nineteenth-century bourgeois societies were. But the areas of inequality are stubbornly resistant to change. Most men living in households with adult women do not share equally in domestic work and child care, so most women have a double work shift, or they hire to do "their" work another woman from the supply of those disadvantaged by poor education or immigrant status. This unequal domestic division of labor diminishes women's worth in the paid workplace and cuts into opportunities to wield political power. Yet with modern technology, women and men can do much of the same work in home maintenance, child care, and the paid marketplace, and the presence of women at the top echelons of governments is becoming routine.

Nonetheless, the gender schema of male-female differences and men's dominance bubbles away beneath the public rhetoric of respect for individual differences and legal equality. The continued social endorsement of men's dominance over women spills out in sexual entitlement—harassment of subordinates for sexual favors, sly and overt groping, date rape, gang rape, rape as an instrument of war, prostitution. It is also manifest in population and abortion policies that give women little choice in when and whether to procreate. The continued belief in the biological origin of differences between women and men continues to justify the gender divisions of family and paid work and the resulting inequality of economic resources and political power.

The ambivalence over gender divisions and allocation of responsibilities for child care, household maintenance, and paid work characterizes a social order in transition. In many respects, women and men are so equal that the gender divisions seem unnecessary, and then, when they are ignored, major aspects of inequality thwart women's ambitions. The infamous glass ceiling that allows women to see the road to the top and then bump their heads on invisible barriers is a case of perennial gender inequality. Gender segregation in the workplace is another. Women and men more and more do similar work, but dominant men continue to monopolize the better jobs, and the work world continues to replicate occupational gender segregation even as women move into jobs formerly considered men's work. During the 1970s and 1980s, women who went into occupations where the employees were predominantly men soon found that their co-workers became predominantly women because the men left. The entry of women did not drive the men out; it was because the men were leaving increasingly unattractive work sectors that positions for women opened.

Similarly, women's and men's wages have become more equal because men's wages have declined, not because women's wages have increased; men still get the highest-paying jobs.

At the other end of the spectrum from the increase in formal equality in the Western world is the deepening of the gendered divisions of work in the global economy. Financed by capital from developed countries, work organizations around the world exploit the labor of poor, young, unmarried women under sweatshop-like conditions while reserving better-paid jobs and support for entrepreneurship for middle-class men. The policies of the International Monetary Fund and other financial restructuring agencies do not include gender desegregation or encouraging women's education and access to health resources, which would allow women to break into men's occupations. In many of these countries, violence and sexual exploitation, as well as the spread of AIDS heterosexually, seriously undermine efforts to upgrade the lives of women and girls. Population policies are embedded in gendered stratification systems. Feminist work here has all it can do to prevent women's lives from worsening and to influence the programs of development agencies to be attentive to the needs of women and girls.

The persistence of gender inequality makes it necessary to have a gendered perspective on how work and family are organized, how resources are awarded, and how power is distributed. However, I think that we also have to include in this perspective the other major social statuses intertwined with gender—at a minimum, social class, racial ethnic group, and sexual orientation. For many purposes, age, parental and relational status, physical ability, education, and religion have to be included as well. This multiple perspective fragments gender and breaks the hold of binary categorization. I think that for feminists in modern Western civilizations, going beyond gender is a needed step toward gender equality, with the immediate target for change the legal rigidity of gender statuses, their constant use in the allocation of family work and paid jobs, and the embedded notion of men's entitlement to women's services and sexuality.

FEMINISM AND SOCIAL CHANGE

Feminists have described the history and changing content of gender categories—the fluidity of "masculinity" and "femininity," the switches of tasks and jobs, the turnabouts of beliefs about what is "natural." Many feminists have intensively documented the practices that sustain the gendered social order in an effort to change the processes, expectations, and value systems that blight women's lives. But few feminists are now challenging the binary divisions themselves, perhaps because they, too, believe in their ultimate biological underpinnings. As Christine Delphy says, "Feminists seem to want to abolish hierarchy and even sex roles, but not difference itself." That is, while feminists want women and men to be equal, few talk now about doing away with gender divisions altogether. One who does is Sandra Lipsitz Bem, who advocates "a vision of utopia in which gender polarization . . . has been so completely dismantled that—except in narrowly biological contexts like reproduction—the distinction between male and female no longer organizes the culture and the psyche."

Eradicating the social division of women and men is hardly a new idea for feminists. In 1971, Shulamith Firestone said that "the end goal of feminist revolution must be . . . not just the elimination of male *privilege* but of the sex *distinction* itself: genital differences between human beings would no longer matter culturally." In 1972, Lois Gould's classic tale of childhood degendering, "X: A Fabulous Child's Story," was published in *Ms.* magazine. In 1980, Monique Wittig challenged lesbians and gay men to deny the divisive power of heterosexuality by refusing to think of themselves as women and men. In 1986, I said we needed to dismantle "Noah's ark"—lockstep binary thinking. Since 1990, postmodernists and queer theorists, following Judith Butler's lead in *Gender Trouble,* have questioned the twofold divisions of gender, sexuality, and even sex, undermining the solidity of a world built on men/women, heterosexuals/homosexuals, and male/female. Currently, in *Undoing Gender,* Butler argues that gender is a fluid, psychological, and sexual category but that collective social norms sustain gender divisions and the power intrinsic in gender hierarchies.

Yet feminism as a movement, in the fight for equal treatment within the present gender structure, has lost sight of the revolutionary goal of dismantling gender divisions. The present drive toward gender balance or mainstreaming gender continues the attempts to undo the effects of gender divisions, but it is these divisions that perpetuate gender inequality. The distinctions between women and men may be deceptive, as Cynthia Fuchs Epstein argues, but they are unlikely to wither away by themselves.

Part of the reason the dismantling of gender divisions was abandoned was that some feminists began to focus on women's bodily, sexual, and emotional differences from men and to valorize those differences, taking joy and pride in being a woman. Moving away from the goal of liberal feminists—to gain equality in the public world of work and politics—difference feminists insisted that what women gave men and children, and each other, in nurturance and emotional sustenance should not be relegated to secondary labor but should be rewarded as a primary contribution to society. In the debate over gender theory and politics, difference feminists and gender feminists became opposing factions.

GENDER, WOMEN, AND DIFFERENCE

Gender feminists argue for the value of the generality of the concept, contending that gender encompasses the social construction of masculinities as well as femininities, the interrelations of women and men, the division of labor in the economy and in the family, and the structural power imbalances of modern Western societies. Difference feminists argue that the concept of gender minimizes the body and sexuality, the significance of women's procreative and nurturing capacities, and the violent potentialities of men's control of women's bodies, sexuality, and emotions. Difference feminists, using psychoanalytic and linguistic analyses of bodies, sexualities, psyches, and cultural representations, have eschewed a concept of gender for a deconstruction of the symbolic social order as deeply divided between the dominant possessors of the phallus and oppressed others.

Standpoint feminism, a theoretical perspective that links the gendered division of labor in the work world and in the home to gendered consciousness, incorporates marxist and psychoanalytic theories of difference. Standpoint feminism locates the source of differences between women and men in the gendered structure of family work and paid work, as well as in bodies and sexualities. As physical and social reproducers of children, women use their bodies, emotions, thoughts, and physical labor, and so they are grounded in material reality in ways that men are not. Women are responsible for most of the everyday work, even if they are highly educated, while highly educated men concentrate on the abstract and the intellectual. Because women's lives connect them to their bodies and emotions, their unconscious, as well as their conscious, the view of the world is unitary and concrete. If women produced knowledge, what we know would be much more in touch with the everyday material world, with bodies, procreative rhythms, and the connectedness among people, because that is what women experience in the gendered social world.

Standpoint feminism privileges women's viewpoint; multicultural feminism asks, Which women? Multicultural and postcolonial feminists, addressing the national and international sources of women's oppression, claim that they are enmeshed in complex systems of class and racial ethnic dominance and subordination, in which some men are subordinate to other men and to some women as well. Feminist studies of men show that all men may have a "patriarchal dividend" of privilege and entitlement to women's labor, sexuality, and emotions, but some men additionally have the privileges of whiteness, education, prosperity, and prestige. These analyses see gender hierarchies as inextricable from the hierarchies of class and racial ethnic statuses.

In this sense, *difference* is expanded from men versus women to the multiplicities of sameness and difference among women and among men and within individuals as well. All these differences arise from different social locations or standpoints, and it is hard to justify privileging one over others. Joan Wallach Scott points out that within-gender differences are especially compatible with "an equality that rests on differences—differences that confound, disrupt, and render ambiguous the meaning of any fixed binary opposition." Working with these differences, feminist philosophers and political scientists have developed gendered theories of justice and have located gender in the matrix of complex inequality.

Feminist theories of justice contend that gender is a different form of inequality from social class or racial ethnic disadvantage because of women's responsibility for family work. Gendering family work produces inequality in the home because of the imbalance of the division of domestic labor. It also produces inequality in the workforce because women workers carry the extra baggage of care for husband, home, and children. Where they don't, there are other forms of inequality similar to those for men—in social class, racial ethnic categorization, sexual orientation, education, occupation, immigration. Thus, women as a group suffer from both public and private forms of injustice. As Leslie McCall says, "The discussion of inequality must therefore be expanded from one revolving around a unitary term—the new inequality—to one involving an open question about the overlapping and conflicting manifestations of gender, race, and class inequality."

DEGENDERING AND FEMINIST THEORIES

Many feminists have implicitly called for a gender-free society by urging the minimization of the effects of gender, to the point of gender's practical disappearance. I am arguing here for a gender-free society to be an *explicit and primary goal*. This goal is not incompatible with feminist theories of difference, standpoint feminism, psychoanalytic theories, or feminist theories of justice. In fact, in many ways it is the logical outcome of these theories.

Difference feminists argue that gender feminists neglect the valued qualities of women's lives that come from their bodies, sexualities, and intimate parenting—nurturance, interrelatedness, emotionality. The basis of standpoint feminism is that women live in a world in touch with bodies, children, and hands-on physical labor. Difference and standpoint feminists may argue that degendering will create a masculine world—objective, instrumental, and bureaucratic. However, men also do physical labor, for pay or as volunteers and do-it-yourselfers, so they are not all detached from the material world.

Men also do far more caring for others, including elderly parents and infants, than is recognized by gendered norms for masculine behavior. These norms expect men to look out for their buddies in times of war and danger, but men also care for elderly parents and sick spouses and partners. Degendering policies would encourage men to routinely care for children, the elderly, and each other and not leave emotional sustenance for family and friends to women. Thus, men as well as women would develop the valued qualities of nurturance, relatedness, and emotional expression.

Work relations in the modern world are both formal in organization and informal in practice, rule-based and relational, rational and emotional at the same time, and so are women and men workers. Organizational bureaucracies necessitate objectivity, rationality, and adherence to rules. The parallel informal organization of work creates circles of colleagues built on trust and loyalty and networks of sponsors, mentors, and novices, the "families" that make work life so attractive to men and women. Diminution of gender divisions as an organizing principle of workplaces would not turn warmhearted women into coldhearted men any more than it would turn warmhearted men into coldhearted women. It would, rather, degender the best—and the worst—qualities of people so that good and bad characteristics are no longer seen as "the way women are" or "the way men are."

Gender feminism has been accused of superficiality in that it does not attend to unconscious desires and deeply embedded personality patterns. In psychoanalytic theories of parenting, those are the outcome of women's primary parenting. These theories argue that women's openness to others and child-care capabilities are produced by continued identification of daughters with their mothers to the point of blurred ego boundaries. Men's repression of emotionality emerges from their need to separate from their mothers and from their hostility toward women, which in turn emerges from their fears that they, too, will lose their penises, just as their mothers must have. Sons develop the ego boundaries encouraged by identification with an emotionally distant father and demanded by the competitiveness of the world of men they enter as his heir. Castration fears are sublimated into control of emotions and dominating relationships with women.

Degendering parenting is a way of cutting into this loop of the reproduction of gendered children by gendered parents. Boys close to fathers who "mother" would not have to repress emotions to be masculine, and girls could identify with fathers and mothers. Misogynist views of women as castrated inferiors and potential castrators would also be diminished by boys' not having to reject everything womanly to be masculine. Degendering parenting would undercut distinct personality structures—objective and rational men, relational and emotional women—allowing boys and girls to develop the characteristics to compete and be authoritative, as well as to cooperate and befriend.

Feminist multicultural, social-class, and racial ethnic studies, as well as feminist studies of men, have long called for a perspective that locates gender in stratification systems of multiple domination or intersectionality. Degendering places gender within the matrix of complex inequality and calls for erasure of all invidious divisions and open access to economic resources, educational opportunities, and political power. These multiviewed perspectives have to be translated into praxis by seeking solutions to problems in ways that do not rely on conventional categories and conventional assumptions. As Carol Lee Bacchi warns, when we ask, what is the problem? we need to challenge "deeply held cultural assumptions, given specific historical, economic and cultural locations."

Gender balance—putting women's as well as men's needs and perspectives into public policies—perpetuates gender divisions and women's subordinate position, since women as a group are matched against dominant men. Since separate is never equal, we need gender "mainstreaming" policies built on the assumption that all groups are equally entitled to public resources but not in exactly the same way. The groups that are compensated in the fight for equality need to be carefully constructed to reflect multiple sources of disadvantage. Advantages only to women, just like a single-minded focus on the needs of disadvantaged racial ethnic or social-class groups, can too easily be undercut by protesters who invoke the needs of the other groups.

Iris Marion Young says that a just heterogeneous society would attend to the needs of different groups, not erase differences: "Justice in a group-differentiated society demands social equality of groups, and mutual recognition and affirmation of group differences." A policy of degendering would recognize people of different social classes, racial ethnic categories, ages, sexual orientations, parental and relational statuses, and so on, as shifting groups, cooperating and conflicting, depending on the situation and the policy question.

There is a testable equation in degendering. I am arguing that it is only by undercutting the gender system of legal statuses, bureaucratic categories, and official and private allocation of tasks and roles that gender equality can be permanently achieved. In the countries that are the most degendered in the sense of treating women and men the same, legally and bureaucratically, women and men have more equal statuses. They are more likely to be comparably educated, work in comparable occupations and professions, have comparable political power and economic resources, and have shared responsibility for the care of children.

Degendering is already common in many gender-equal societies, such as Sweden and Norway. The extent of degendering in those countries is in sharp contrast to the forcefulness of gendering in such countries as Saudi Arabia, where every aspect of women's and men's lives is controlled by gender, to women's marked disadvantage. The feminist task of gaining citizenship rights and economic equality for most of the world's women is undeniably of first priority, but a second task can be done where women are not so terribly unequal—challenging the binary structures just a little bit more by asking why they are necessary at all.

Degendering will not do away with wars and hunger and economic disparities. But I do think that degendering will undercut the patriarchal and oppressive structure of Western societies and social institutions and give all of us the space to use our energies to demilitarize, work for peaceable solutions to conflicts, grow and distribute food, and level the gaps between social classes.

A WORLD WITHOUT GENDER

In an essay about why war is futile, Jonathan Schell, recalling Marx's "all that was solid melted into air," begins:

> There are moments in history when a crack in time seems to open and swallow the known world: solid-seeming institutions, rotted from within, collapse or are discarded, settled beliefs are unsettled; old truths are discovered to be provisional; acts that were forbidden are permitted or even required; boundaries thought impassable are passed without comment; and outrageous and unreal events...flood in profusion from some portal of future that no one was guarding or even watching.

I think that in the not-too-far future, we will see this crumbling of gender divisions and statuses.

Throughout this book, I have suggested ways to think about families, work, political regimes, and political action from the perspective of multiple gendering. I have said that these multiplicities challenge the solidity of the binary gender order and provide examples of degendering practices. Now I would like to think beyond gender to the possibilities of a totally nongendered social order.

In *Paradoxes of Gender,* I described two thought experiments that render gender irrelevant. In the first, an imaginary society divided into two genders treats them strictly equally, with half of all jobs held by men and half by women, family work done half by women and half by men, men and women serving alternately as heads of governments, equal numbers of women and men in the officer corps and ranks of armed forces, on sports teams, in cultural productions, and so on throughout society. In the second imaginary society, all work is equally valued and recompensed, regardless of who does it, and families and work groups are structured for equality of control of resources and decisions. Either path would render gender irrelevant—strict parity by the interchangeability of women and men and strict equality by making no category of people more valuable than any other. Strict parity would make it pointless to construct and maintain gender differences; strict equality would contradict the purpose of gender divisions by undercutting the subordination of women by men. As Christine Delphy says:

> If we define men within a gender framework, they are first and foremost dominants with characteristics which enable them to remain dominants. To be like them would be also to be dominants, but this is a contradiction in terms....To be dominant one must have someone to dominate.

At the end of *Paradoxes of Gender,* I asked the reader to envisage a scrupulously gender-equal world. Here I am going further and trying to imagine a world without genders at all. Can we think the impossible and envisage societies where people come in all colors, shapes, and sizes and where body characteristics are not markers for status identification or for predetermined allocation to any kind of activity? Here is my vision of such a world:

Love and sexuality, friendships and intimacies revolve around people with a mutual attraction to each other's bodies, intellects, interests, and personalities. Males inseminate willing females through copulation or provide sperm for insemination. Females who want to, give birth to infants. These infants become part of families of different kinds of kinship groups and households composed of a variety of responsible adults. They are breast-fed by lactating females and cared for by competent child minders. They receive love and affection from the older children and adults in their circles of relationships. Their favorites and role models vary over time, but there is at least one legally responsible adult for every child.

Children are not sexed at birth—their genitalia are irrelevant in the choice of names, blankets, and clothing. "A child is born to...," the announcements read. In play groups and schools, children are organized by age, size, talents, skills, reading ability, math competence—whatever the needs of the group. Children's talents, skills, and interests shape their choices of further education and job training.

If we can assume nonassortment by other invidious categories, such as racial ethnic group, people are hired on the basis of their credentials, experience, interviewing skills, and connections. The salary scales and prestige value of occupations and professions depend on various kinds of social assessments, just as they do now, but the positions that pay best and are valued most are not monopolized by any one type of person. Science is done by scientists, teaching by teachers, cultural productions by writers, artists, musicians, dancers, singers, actors, and media producers. The beliefs and values and technologies of the time and place govern the content.

Positions of public authority in corporations, bureaucracies, and governments are attained by competition, sponsorship and patronage, networking, and other familiar forms of mobility. Charity, honesty, and competence are as evident as corruption, double-dealing, and shoddy work—people are people.

So there are still murders, wars, and other forms of violence although perhaps through an ethical evolution, societies might develop in which people are taught how to handle anger and conflict in positive ways. But rules are made to be broken, so there is still a need for police and soldiers, judges and prison guards.

Games and sports are played for fitness and fun. New games are devised that put less emphasis on body shapes and more on skill. In competitions, people of different levels of body functioning and abilities compete against one another in a variety of "Olympics."

In the major and minor religions, new liturgies and rituals are in use, but old ones are turned to for their historical cultural value, as are the old novels, plays, songs, and operas. Those who have the calling and the talent lead congregations and prayer services and speak for the god(s).

New language forms develop that do not mark or categorize the speaker or the spoken about. The old forms of language and literature are studied for their archaic beauty and what they tell us about the way people used to live and behave and think.

People group and identify themselves on the basis of all sorts of similarities and disdain others on the basis of all sorts of differences. Sometimes those who identify with each other wear similar clothing or hair styles or jewelry or cosmetics. Sometimes these displays become fashions for all who consider themselves chic. Group and individual ways of speaking, dressing, and behaving serve as cues for interaction and distancing.

There are no women or men, boys or girls—just parents and children, siblings and cousins and other newly named kin, and partners and lovers, friends and enemies, managers and workers, rulers and ruled, conformers and rebels. People form social groups and have statuses and positions and rights and responsibilities—and no gender. The world goes on quite familiarly but is radically changed—gender no longer determines an infant's upbringing, a child's education, an adult's occupation, a parent's care, an economy's distribution of wealth, a country's politicians, the world's power brokers.

To go back to the kabbalistic metaphor of broken bowls, a commentator on kabbalah said of Miriam the prophet, who led the women in dance at the shore of the Red Sea after the Israelites' safe passage, "By making a circle dance, she drew down the supernal light [from the source] where the categories of masculine and feminine do not exist." The goal of *tikkun olam*—repair of the world—is to gather the scattered points of light so all the world will be one. If we apply this metaphor of unification to degendering, at least one human division can be erased.

SWEDEN IS ABOUT TO ADD A GENDER-NEUTRAL PRONOUN TO ITS OFFICIAL DICTIONARY

DISCUSSION QUESTIONS

1. Though LGBTQ activists in the United States have employed similar third pronouns, the concept does not seem to have gained the popularity here that it has in Sweden. Why do you think that is?
2. Is a third pronoun option important for both cisgendered as well as genderqueer/agendered children? Why or why not?
3. How might adding a third pronoun (and the gendered concepts for doing so) contribute to changing public school classroom structures and policies in the United States?

In the Egalia, a preschool in Stockholm, there are no male or female students. Instead, all children are referred to as 'hen'—a gender-neutral pronoun that has become so established in Sweden that it will be recognized next month in the newest edition of the country's official dictionary.

The Swedish Academy's SAOL dictionary, which is updated every 10 years and will henceforth include 'hen' as an alternative to the male pronoun 'han' and the female 'hon.' The revised edition will also include thousands of other new words.

According to linguistic expert Sofia Malmgård, the gender-neutral term can be used in two ways. "First, if the gender is unknown or not relevant (as in: "If anyone needs to smoke, 'hen' may do so outside"). Second, it can be used as a pronoun for inter-gender people (as in: "Kim is neither boy nor girl, 'hen' is inter-gender")," she explained.

To many Swedes, the decision of the Swedish Academy reflects how quickly their society has embraced gender-neutral language. "Over the last few years, the word 'hen' has more and more found its way into the Swedish language," Malmgård told *The Washington Post*.

Five years ago, barely anyone in Sweden was aware of the word. The decision to now include 'hen' in the authoritative SAOL dictionary is expected to facilitate an even more frequent use of it in everyday conversations. Set up in 1785, the academy was established with the aim to adapt the Swedish languages to changing cultural and societal influences—a role the institution still feels committed to.

According to experts, the 'hen'-revolution in Sweden has two primary origins: LGBT groups have promoted the pronoun as a way to raise awareness for their cause. However, support for the idea has also come from a more unexpected side: Nurseries, kindergartens and preschools such as Egalia increasingly argue that the pronoun's usage allows children to grow up without feeling the impact of gender biases. "The public debate over the pronoun actually only started after the publication of the country's first gender-neutral children's book," Lann Hornscheidt, a professor of Scandinavian languages and gender studies at Berlin's Humboldt University explained.

Gender-neutral education in Sweden goes far beyond linguistics. As the BBC already observed in 2011, toys and games in some nurseries are placed deliberately next to each other, in the hope that children will feel free to choose the items they feel most comfortable spending their time with.

To Hornscheidt, the popularity of 'hen' has not come as a surprise. "The introduction of a pronoun which challenges binary gender norms has been an important step, following a more thorough debate over the construction of gender within the last 10 years," he said.

The Berlin-based researcher nevertheless cautions that simply introducing a gender-neutral pronoun in other countries may not be sufficient to fight sexism or gender-biases. Turkey, for instance, also has a gender-neutral pronoun. Nevertheless, the country was only ranked 125th in the 2014 gender equality report of the World Economic Forum. Sweden came fourth.[1]

NOTE

1. https://www.washingtonpost.com/news/worldviews/wp/2015/04/01/sweden-is-about-to-add-a-gender-neutral-pronoun-to-its-official-dictionary/

52 • *Leslie Feinberg*

WE ARE ALL WORKS IN PROGRESS

DISCUSSION QUESTIONS

1. Do you think that trans liberation should be a goal of the women's movement? Why or why not?
2. Why does the author argue that the struggles facing transgender people should be important to gender-normative people as well?
3. In your own life, how can you be involved in creating positive social change in the struggle against sex, gender, and sexual oppression?

Leslie Feinberg, "We Are All Works in Progress" from *Trans Liberation: Beyond Pink or Blue*. 1998. Reproduced by permission of Beacon Press.

The sight of pink-blue gender-coded infant outfits may grate on your nerves. Or you may be a woman or a man who feels at home in those categories. Trans liberation defends you both.

Each person should have the right to *choose* between pink or blue tinted gender categories, as well as all the other hues of the palette. At this moment in time, that right is denied to us. But together, we could make it a reality. . . .

I am a human being who would rather not be addressed as Ms. or Mr., ma'am or sir. I prefer to use gender-neutral pronouns like *sie* (pronounced like *"see"*) and *hir* (pronounced like *"here"*) to describe myself. I am a person who faces almost insurmountable difficulty when instructed to check off an "F" or an "M" box on identification papers.

I'm not at odds with the fact that I was born female-bodied. Nor do I identify as an intermediate sex. I simply do not fit the prevalent Western concepts of what a woman or man "should" look like. And that reality has dramatically directed the course of my life.

I'll give you a graphic example. From December 1995 to December 1996, I was dying of endocarditis—a bacterial infection that lodges and proliferates in the valves of the heart. A simple blood culture would have immediately exposed the root cause of my raging fevers. Eight weeks of round-the-clock intravenous antibiotic drips would have eradicated every last seedling of bacterium in the canals of my heart. Yet I experienced such hatred from some health practitioners that I very nearly died.

I remember late one night in December my lover and I arrived at a hospital emergency room during a snowstorm. My fever was 104 degrees and rising. My blood pressure was pounding dangerously high. The staff immediately hooked me up to monitors and worked to bring down my fever. The doctor in charge began physically examining me. When he determined that my anatomy was female, he flashed me a mean-spirited smirk. While keeping his eyes fixed on me, he approached one of the nurses, seated at a desk, and began rubbing her neck and shoulders. He talked to her about sex for a few minutes. After his pointed demonstration of "normal sexuality," he told

me to get dressed and then he stormed out of the room. Still delirious, I struggled to put on my clothes and make sense of what was happening.

The doctor returned after I was dressed. He ordered me to leave the hospital and never return. I refused. I told him I wouldn't leave until he could tell me why my fever was so high. He said, "You have a fever because you are a very troubled person."

This doctor's prejudices, directed at me during a moment of catastrophic illness, could have killed me. The death certificate would have read: Endocarditis. By all rights it should have read: Bigotry.

As my partner and I sat bundled up in a cold car outside the emergency room, still reverberating from the doctor's hatred, I thought about how many people have been turned away from medical care when they were desperately ill—some because an apartheid "whites only" sign hung over the emergency room entrance, or some because their visible Kaposi's sarcoma lesions kept personnel far from their beds. I remembered how a blemish that wouldn't heal drove my mother to visit her doctor repeatedly during the 1950s. I recalled the doctor finally wrote a prescription for Valium because he decided she was a hysterical woman. When my mother finally got to specialists, they told her the cancer had already reached her brain.

Bigotry exacts its toll in flesh and blood. And left unchecked and unchallenged, prejudices create a poisonous climate for us all. Each of us has a stake in the demand that every human being has a right to a job, to shelter, to health care, to dignity, to respect.

I am very grateful to have this chance to open up a conversation with you about why it is so vital to also defend the right of individuals to express and define their sex and gender, and to control their own bodies. For me, it's a life-and-death question. But I also believe that this discussion will have great meaning for you. All your life you've heard such dogma about what it means to be a "real" woman or a "real" man. And chances are you've choked on some of it. You've balked at the idea that being a woman means having to be thin as a rail, emotionally nurturing, and an airhead when it comes to balancing her checkbook. You know in your guts that being a man has nothing to do with rippling muscles, innate courage, or knowing how to handle a chain saw. These are really caricatures. Yet these images have been drilled into us through popular culture and education over the years. And subtler, equally insidious messages lurk in the interstices of these grosser concepts. These ideas of what a "real" woman or man should be straightjacket the freedom of individual self-expression. These gender messages play on and on in a continuous loop in our brains, like commercials that can't be muted.

But in my lifetime I've also seen social upheavals challenge this sex and gender doctrine. As a child who grew up during the McCarthyite, Father-Knows-Best 1950s, and who came of age during the second wave of women's liberation in the United States, I've seen transformations in the ways people think and talk about what it means to be a woman or a man.

Today the gains of the 1970s women's liberation movement are under siege by right-wing propagandists. But many today who are too young to remember what life was like before the women's movement need to know that this was a tremendously progressive development that won significant economic and social reforms. And this struggle by women and their allies swung human consciousness forward like a pendulum.

The movement replaced the common usage of vulgar and diminutive words to describe females with the word *woman* and infused that word with strength and pride. Women, many of them formerly isolated, were drawn together into consciousness-raising groups. Their discussions—about the root of women's oppression and how to eradicate it—resonated far beyond the rooms in which they took place. The women's liberation movement sparked a mass conversation about the systematic degradation, violence, and discrimination that women faced in this society. And this consciousness raising changed many of the ways women and men thought about themselves and their relation to each other. In retrospect, however, we must not forget that these widespread discussions were not just organized to *talk* about oppression. They were a giant dialogue about how to take action to fight institutionalized anti-woman attitudes, rape and battering, the illegality of abortion, employment and education discrimination, and other ways women were socially and economically devalued.

This was a big step forward for humanity. And even the period of political reaction that followed has not been able to overturn all the gains made by that important social movement.

Now another movement is sweeping onto the stage of history: Trans liberation. We are again raising questions about the societal treatment of people based on their sex and gender expression. This discussion will make new contributions to human consciousness. And trans communities, like the women's movement, are carrying out these mass conversations with the goal of creating a movement capable of fighting for justice—of righting the wrongs.

We are a movement of masculine females and feminine males, cross-dressers, transsexual men and women, intersexuals born on the anatomical sweep between female and male, gender-blenders, many other sex and gender-variant people, and our significant others. All told, we expand understanding of how many ways there are to be a human being.

Our lives are proof that sex and gender are much more complex than a delivery room doctor's glance at genitals can determine, more variegated than pink or blue birth caps. We are oppressed for not fitting those narrow social norms. We are fighting back.

Our struggle will also help expose some of the harmful myths about what it means to be a woman or a man that have compartmentalized and distorted your life, as well as mine. Trans liberation has meaning for you—no matter how you define or express your sex or your gender.

If you are a trans person, you face horrendous social punishments—from institutionalization to gang rape, from beatings to denial of child visitation. This oppression is faced, in varying degrees, by all who march under the banner of trans liberation. This brutalization and degradation strips us of what we could achieve with our individual lifetimes.

And if you do not identify as transgender or transsexual or intersexual, your life is diminished by our oppression as well. Your own choices as a man or a woman are sharply curtailed. Your individual journey to express yourself is shunted into one of two deeply carved ruts, and the social baggage you are handed is already packed.

So the defense of each individual's right to control their own body, and to explore the path of self-expression, enhances your own freedom to discover more about yourself and your potentialities. This movement will give you more room to breathe—to be yourself. To discover on a deeper level what it means to be your self.

Together, I believe we can forge a coalition that can fight on behalf of your oppression as well as mine. Together, we can raise each other's grievances and win the kind of significant change we all long for. But the foundation of unity is understanding. So let me begin by telling you a little bit about myself.

I am a human being who unnerves some people. As they look at me, they see a kaleidoscope of characteristics they associate with both males and females. I appear to be a tangled knot of gender contradictions. So they feverishly press the question on me: woman or man? Those are the only two words most people have as tools to shape their question.

"Which sex are you?" I understand their question. It sounds so simple. And I'd like to offer them a simple resolution. But merely answering woman or man will not bring relief to the questioner. As long as people try to bring me into focus using only those two lenses, I will always appear to be an enigma.

The truth is I'm no mystery. I'm a female who is more masculine than those prominently portrayed in mass culture. Millions of females and millions of males in this country do not fit the cramped compartments of gender that we have been taught are "natural" and "normal." For many of us, the words *woman* or *man, ma'am* or *sir, she* or *he*—in and of themselves—do not total up the sum of our identities or of our oppressions. Speaking for myself, my life only comes into focus when the word *transgender* is added to the equation.

Simply answering whether I was born female or male will not solve the conundrum. Before I can even begin to respond to the question of my own birth sex, I feel it's important to challenge the assumptions that the answer is always as simple as either-or. I believe we need to take a critical look at the assumption that

is built into the seemingly innocent question: "What a beautiful baby—is it a boy or a girl?"

The human anatomical spectrum can't be understood, let alone appreciated, as long as female or male are considered to be all that exists. "Is it a boy or a girl?" Those are the only two categories allowed on birth certificates.

But this either-or leaves no room for intersexual people, born between the poles of female and male. Human anatomy continues to burst the confines of the contemporary concept that nature delivers all babies on two unrelated conveyor belts. So are the birth certificates changed to reflect human anatomy? No, the U.S. medical establishment hormonally molds and shapes and surgically hacks away at the exquisite complexities of intersexual infants until they neatly fit one category or the other.

A surgeon decides whether a clitoris is "too large" or a penis is "too small." That's a highly subjective decision for anyone to make about another person's body. Especially when the person making the arbitrary decision is scrubbed up for surgery! And what is the criterion for a penis being "too small"? Too small for successful heterosexual intercourse. Intersexual infants are already being tailored for their sexuality, as well as their sex. The infants have no say over what happens to their bodies. Clearly the struggle against genital mutilation must begin here, within the borders of the United States.

But the question asked of all new parents: "Is it a boy or a girl?" is not such a simple question when transsexuality is taken into account, either. Legions of out-and-proud transsexual men and women demonstrate that individuals have a deep, developed, and valid sense of their own sex that does not always correspond to the cursory decision made by a delivery-room obstetrician. Nor is transsexuality a recent phenomenon. People have undergone social sex reassignment and surgical and hormonal sex changes throughout the breadth of oral and recorded human history.

Having offered this view of the complexities and limitations of birth classification, I have no hesitancy in saying I was born female. But that answer doesn't clear up the confusion that drives some people to ask me "Are you a man or a woman?" The problem is that they are trying to understand my gender expression by determining my sex—and therein lies the rub! Just as most of us grew up with only the concepts of *woman* and *man,* the terms *feminine* and *masculine* are the only two tools most people have to talk about the complexities of gender expression.

That pink-blue dogma assumes that biology steers our social destiny. We have been taught that being born female or male will determine how we will dress and walk, whether we will prefer our hair shortly cropped or long and flowing, whether we will be emotionally nurturing or repressed. According to this way of thinking, masculine females are trying to look "like men," and feminine males are trying to act "like women."

But those of us who transgress those gender assumptions also shatter their inflexibility.

So why do I sometimes describe myself as a masculine female? Isn't each of those concepts very limiting? Yes. But placing the two words together is incendiary, exploding the belief that gender expression is linked to birth sex like horse and carriage. It is the social contradiction missing from Dick-and-Jane textbook education.

I actually chafe at describing myself as masculine. For one thing, masculinity is such an expansive territory, encompassing boundaries of nationality, race, and class. Most importantly, individuals blaze their own trails across this landscape.

And it's hard for me to label the intricate matrix of my gender as simply masculine. To me, branding individual self-expression as simply feminine or masculine is like asking poets: Do you write in English or Spanish? The question leaves out the possibilities that the poetry is woven in Cantonese or Ladino, Swahili or Arabic. The question deals only with the system of language that the poet has been taught. It ignores the words each writer hauls up, hand over hand, from a common well. The music words make when finding themselves next to each other for the first time. The silences echoing in the space between ideas. The powerful winds of passion and belief that move the poet to write.

That is why I do not hold the view that gender is simply a social construct—one of two languages that we learn by rote from early age. To me, gender is the poetry each of us makes out of the language we are taught. When I walk through the anthology of the world, I see individuals express their gender in exquisitely complex and ever-changing ways, despite the laws of pentameter.

So how can gender expression be mandated by edict and enforced by law? Isn't that like trying to handcuff a pool of mercury? It's true that human self-expression is diverse and is often expressed in ambiguous or contradictory ways. And what degree of gender expression is considered "acceptable" can depend on your social situation, your race and nationality, your class, and whether you live in an urban or rural environment.

But no one can deny that rigid gender education begins early on in life—from pink and blue color coding of infant outfits to gender-labeling toys and games. And those who overstep these arbitrary borders are punished. Severely. When the steel handcuffs tighten, it is human bones that crack. No one knows how many trans lives have been lost to police brutality and street-corner bashing. The lives of trans people are so depreciated in this society that many murders go unreported. And those of us who have survived are deeply scarred by daily run-ins with hate, discrimination, and violence.

Trans people are still literally social outlaws. And that's why I am willing at times, publicly, to reduce the totality of my self-expression to descriptions like masculine female, butch, bulldagger, drag king, cross-dresser. These terms describe outlaw status. And I hold my head up proudly in that police lineup. The word *outlaw* is not hyperbolic. I have been locked up in jail by cops because I was wearing a suit and tie. Was my clothing really a crime? Is it a "man's" suit if I am wearing it? At what point—from field to rack—is fiber assigned a sex?

The reality of why I was arrested was as cold as the cell's cement floor: I am considered a masculine female. That's a *gender* violation. My feminine drag queen sisters were in nearby cells, busted for wearing "women's" clothing. The cells that we were thrown into had the same design of bars and concrete. But when we—gay drag kings and drag queens—were thrown into them, the cops referred to the cells as bull's tanks and queen's tanks. The cells were named after our crimes: gender transgression. Actual statutes against cross-dressing and cross-gendered behavior still exist in written laws today. But even where the laws are not written down, police, judges, and prison guards are empowered to carry out merciless punishment for sex and gender "difference."

I believe we need to sharpen our view of how repression by the police, courts, and prisons, as well as all forms of racism and bigotry, operates as gears in the machinery of the economic and social system that governs our lives. As all those who have the least to lose from changing this system get together and examine these social questions, we can separate the wheat of truths from the chaff of old lies. Historic tasks are revealed that beckon us to take a stand and to take action.

That moment is now. And so this conversation with you takes place with the momentum of struggle behind it.

What will it take to put a halt to "legal" and extralegal violence against trans people? How can we strike the unjust and absurd laws mandating dress and behavior for females and males from the books? How can we weed out all the forms of trans-phobic and gender-phobic discrimination?

Where does the struggle for sex and gender liberation fit in relation to other movements for economic and social equality? How can we reach a point where we appreciate each other's differences, not just tolerate them? How can we tear down the electrified barbed wire that has been placed between us to keep us separated, fearful and pitted against each other? How can we forge a movement that can bring about profound and lasting change—a movement capable of transforming society?

These questions can only be answered when we begin to organize together, ready to struggle on each other's behalf. Understanding each other will compel us as honest, caring people to fight each other's oppression as though it was our own.